Practical Real Estate Law

SECOND EDITION

New York Version

Practical Real Estate Law

SECOND EDITION

Daniel F. Hinkel

The National Center for Paralegal Training, Atlanta

New York Version
Prepared by Jane Kaplan

New York City Technical College

WEST PUBLISHING COMPANY

Minneapolis/St. Paul • New York • Los Angeles • San Francisco

Copyeditor: Barbara Hodgson
Text Design: Lois Stanfield, LightSource Images
Illustration: Alice B. Thiede, CartoGraphics
Cover Design: Roslyn Stendahl, Dapper Design
Cover Image: Donovan Reese / © Tony Stone Worldwide

WEST'S COMMITMENT TO THE ENVIRONMENT

In 1906, West Publishing Company began recycling materials left over from the production of books. This began a tradition of efficient and responsible use of resources. Today, up to 95% of our legal books and 70% of our college and school texts are printed on recycled, acid-free stock. West also recycles nearly 22 million pounds of scrap paper annually—the equivalent of 181,717 trees. Since the 1960s, West has devised ways to capture and recycle waste inks, solvents, oils, and vapors created in the printing process. We also recycle plastics of all kinds, wood, glass, corrugated cardboard, and batteries, and have eliminated the use of Styrofoam book packaging. We at West are proud of the longevity and the scope of our commitment to the environment.

Production, Prepress, Printing and Binding by West Publishing Company.

 TEXT IS PRINTED ON 10% POST CONSUMER RECYCLED PAPER

British Library Cataloguing-in-Publication Data. A catalogue
record for this book is available from the British Library.

COPYRIGHT © 1991 by   WEST PUBLISHING CO.
COPYRIGHT © 1995 by   WEST PUBLISHING CO.
                             610 Opperman Drive
                             P.O. Box 64526
                             St. Paul, MN 55164–0526

Library of Congress Cataloging-in-Publication Data

Hinkel, Daniel F.
    Practical real estate law / Daniel F. Hinkel. —2nd ed., New York version.
        p.   cm.
    Includes index.
    ISBN 0–314–04571–6 (hardbound)
    1. Vendors and purchasers—New York (State)   2. Real property—New York (State)
    3. Real estate business—Law and legislation—New York (State)   I. Title.
KFN5169.H56   1995
346.7304'3—dc20
[347.30643]   94–44140
                                                             CIP

To John Henry

Contents in Brief

Contents

Preface

As an instructor for The National Center for Paralegal Training, I have had the pleasure over the past two decades of teaching a real estate course to paralegal students. This textbook, a greatly expanded version of that course material, is directed toward the training and practice of legal assistants in the area of modern real estate transactions.

The book is designed to be used in two ways. It can be used as a classroom teaching source for the training of legal assistants. It also can be used as a reference work by legal assistants employed in a real estate legal practice. The book includes an explanation of legal principles, practical suggestions, and numerous forms. Using this text, the student, or practicing legal assistant, possesses in a single source a wealth of useful material.

The treatment of the subject assumes that the reader has no knowledge of real property law. The text introduces the reader to the basics of real property law and then proceeds step by step through all the areas of a modern real estate practice. A legal assistant cannot effectively assist a transactional real estate attorney unless the legal assistant is fully aware of all the substantive legal issues that are involved and has a good command of the various legal forms in use.

This text covers all the important issues that a real estate legal assistant will encounter in a modern real estate practice. I offer it to you with the sincere hope that you will find it useful.

TEXT ORGANIZATION

Based upon suggestions from various teachers, students, and reviewers of the first edition of this book, the format and content of the text has been revised. Chapter 1 introduces the student to the concept of property ownership, and the various types of ownership that can exist are discussed. Chapter 2 introduces the student to the situation in which real property is owned by more than one person and discusses all the forms of concurrent ownership. Chapter 3 is a new chapter and contains a discussion of condominiums, cooperatives, and time-shares. Chapter 4 is a discussion of the methods of describing real property and contains sample surveys and legal descriptions. Chapters 5 and 6 discuss the various encumbrances to the ownership of real property with a special emphasis on easements. Chapter 7 begins a discussion on contracts, and Chapter 8 is devoted to contract forms and the explanation of standard provisions found in real estate contracts. Chapter 9 is a discussion of deeds, complete with many examples and sample forms. Chapters 10, 11, and 12 discuss real estate finance. Chapter 10 discusses the business aspect of real estate lending and is designed to acquaint the student with the economic and practical needs of lender and borrower clients. Chapter 11 is a discussion of the substantive law of notes, mortgages, and foreclosures. Chapter 12 explains the various note and mortgage forms, as well as other documents used by lenders to document and secure residential and commercial loans. Chapter 13 and 14 are devoted to title examinations and title insurance. Chapters 15, 16, and 17 are devoted to the real estate closing. Chapter 15 is a full discussion of the substantive issues of real estate closings. Chapter 16 is a discussion of the government regulations that affect a residential real estate closing. Chapter 17 is devoted to forms and examples of closing documents, including a sample of a residential real estate closing transaction. Chapter 18 is a discussion of leases, complete with residential and commercial lease forms.

CHANGES TO THE SECOND EDITION

- **Forms**. Many of the forms in the first edition have been updated and new forms are included throughout the text.
- **Ethics**. The chapter on ethics, which was found in Chapter 18 of the first edition, has been replaced with an ethics comment in each chapter. Integrating the Ethical Considerations throughout the text allows for greater emphasis and comprehension.
- **Cases**. A number of teachers and students have requested that case decisions be added to the text. In the Second Edition, a number of edited cases have been introduced in many of the chapters to illustrate important points of law and to give students experience in reading and applying actual cases to chapter material.
- **State-Specific Editions**. State-specific editions of the text have been created for New York, Florida, Texas, and California. These versions contain margin annotations differentiating state specific material from the discussion in the main text. An appendix includes more extensive explanations and examples of state material.
- **Expanded Coverage**. Condominiums and Cooperatives is a new chapter (Chapter 3) including a brief history of the condominium/cooperative form of ownership, how a condominium is formed, the issues involved in representing a condominium unit purchaser or lender, the differences between condominiums and cooperatives, and time share ownership. A condominium declaration form, examples of various condominium statutes which regulate the formation and governance of a condominium, and copies of articles of incorporation and bylaws for condominium association are also included.

    Discussion of computer applications have been added to many skills sections throughout the text. For example, new software available to assist in the preparation of closing documents is covered in Chapter 17.

STUDENT LEARNING FEATURES

- **Chapter objectives** open each chapter to focus students' attention on the key concepts they will learn.
- **Checklists** are found in most chapters and include task-specific steps which students can apply to many aspects of a paralegal's work day. For example, Chapter 8 contains a Checklist for preparation and review of a commercial real estate contract and Chapter 17 includes a Checklist for a residential closing.

- **Terminology** is emphasized throughout each chapter. A glossary of new terms begins each chapter and provides brief definitions of the new legal terms which will be used in the chapter. Terms appear in boldface and are defined in context where they first appear. They are also listed at the end of each chapter for quick reference. Finally, a new comprehensive glossary ends the text.
- **A chapter-ending summary** provides an excellent review of the chapter's main points.
- **Review Questions, Case Problems, and Practical Assignments** at the end of each chapter have been updated, and in most chapters increased in number, providing your students with more exercises and opportunities to consider how they would handle specific tasks. For example, a practical assignment in Chapter 6 asks your students to draft an easement and a practical assignment in Chapter 11 asks your students to draft a note and a deed to secure debt based on hypothetical scenario.

EXTENSIVE TEACHING PACKAGE

- **Instructor's Manual and Test Bank** by the text author includes sample examinations, nutshell treatment of chapter material, sample homework, classroom assignments, and projects. The Test Bank includes approximately 30-40 true/false, multiple-choice, and essay questions.
- **Instructor's Manual and Test Bank on disk** The complete Instructor's Manual is available on disk for your convenience in testing and organizing.
- **Study Guide** by the text author includes review of chapter concepts, and additional application of concepts.
- *Strategies and Tips for Paralegal Educators* by Anita Tebbe of Johnson County Community College, provides teaching strategies specifically designed for the paralegal educator. It concentrates on how to teach and is organized in three parts of paralegal education: the Who—students and teachers, the What—goals and objectives; and the How—methods of instruction, evaluation, and other aspects of teaching. One copy of this pamphlet is available to qualified adopters.
- **WESTLAW** West's on-line computerized legal research system, offers students "hands-on" experience with a system commonly used in law offices. Qualified adopters can receive 10 free hours of WESTLAW. WESTLAW can be accessed with Macintosh and IBM PCs and compatibles. A modem is required.°
- **Paralegal Video Library**°: "The Drama of the Law II: Paralegal Issues" Videotape. This series of five separate dramatizations is intended to stimulate classroom discussion about various issues and problems faced by paralegals on the job today. Each dramatization is approximately five to seven minutes. Topics include intake interview, human error, strategic information, client confidentiality, and unauthorized practice. The scripts were written by John Osborne, author of *The Paper Chase* and are professionally produced.

"I Never Said I Was a Lawyer" Paralegal Ethics Videotape uses a variety of scenarios to inspire discussion and give students experience dealing with ethical dilem-

---

° Please ask your West representative about qualifications for these supplements.

mas. Topics explored include the unauthorized practice of law, identification of paralegals as non-lawyers, waiver of client's rights through breaches of confidentiality, and lack of attorney supervision. "Situation analysis," how to evaluate an ethical situation and decide on the proper course of action, is also covered. The tape was created by the Colorado Bar Association Committee on Legal Assistants but is non-state specific and will be useful in all paralegal programs.

"The Making of a Case" Videotape is narrated by Richard Dysart, star of *L.A. Law*. In this introduction to law library materials and legal research, a case is followed from the court system to the law library shelf. This gives a better understanding of what case law is, why it is important, and how cases are published.

"West's Legal Research" Videotapes teach the basis and rationale for legal research. The three types of legal research tools—Primary Tools, Secondary Tools, and Finding Tools—are covered. Topics like case law reporters, digests, computer assistance, statutes, special searches, and CD-ROM libraries are included. The nine segments are contained on two tapes.

ACKNOWLEDGMENTS

Acknowledgments are due Linda Selfridge who dedicated many hours to the typing of the manuscript and to the following individuals for their fine efforts in reviewing the manuscript.

REVIEWERS OF THE FIRST EDITION

David W. Arneson
Seattle University

Ann Hooper Hudson
Carteret CC

Rose M. Oramas
Dade Co. Regional Executive Office

Sally Jo Vasicko
Ball State University

David A. Dye
Missouri Western State College

George D. Schrader
Auburn University @ Montgomery

REVIEWERS OF THE SECOND EDITION

Sami S. Baghdady
Anna Maria College

Sumner Freedman
Fisher Junior College

Jay Hollowell
Commonwealth College

Mary Louis Kurr
University of Maine, Univ. College

David R. Mugridge
Fresno City College

Jim Rausch
Interstate Business College

Pamela Poole Weber
Seminole Community College

Table of Exhibits

Introduction to the Law of Real Property

For 'tis the only thing in the world that lasts. 'Tis the only thing worth working for, fighting for, dying for.

—Margaret Mitchell, Gone with the Wind

OBJECTIVES

After reading this chapter, you will be able to:

- Distinguish between real and personal property
- Understand the legal concept of property ownership
- Identify the modern estates of ownership for real property
- Understand and be able to explain the legal concept of adverse possession
- Identify various ways of becoming an owner of real property

GLOSSARY

Adverse possession Method of acquiring ownership to real property by possession for a statutory time period.

Appropriation In regard to water law, doctrine stating that water belongs to the person who first makes beneficial use of it.

Conveyance Act of transferring ownership from one person to another.

Devise Conveyance of real property by means of a last will and testament.

Estate at will Estate of real property the duration of which is for an indefinite period. An estate at will can be terminated at the will of the parties.

Estate for years Estate of real property the duration of which is for a definite period.

Fee simple absolute Estate of real property with infinite duration and no restrictions on use.

Fee simple determinable Estate of real property with potential infinite duration. The ownership of a fee simple determinable is subject to a condition the breach of which can result in termination of the estate. A fee simple determinable automatically expires on the nonoccurrence or occurrence of a condition.

Fee simple on condition subsequent Estate of real property with a potential infinite duration. The ownership of a fee simple on condition subsequent is subject to a condition the breach of which can result in termination of the estate. A fee simple on condition subsequent continues in existence until an action is brought to recover the property.

Fixture Item of personal property that becomes real property because of its attachment to the land or a building.

Inheritance Ability to acquire ownership to real property because of one's kinship to a deceased property owner.

GLOSSARY (cont'd)

Life estate   Estate of real property the duration of which is measured by the life or lives of one or more persons.

Possession   Occupation of land evidenced by visible acts such as an enclosure, cultivation, the construction of improvements, or the occupancy of existing improvements.

Riparian rights   Rights of the owners of lands adjoining streams, rivers, and lakes relating to the water and its use.

Tacking   Combination of possession periods by different adverse possessors.

Waste   Action or nonaction that causes a loss of value to real property.

Will   Legal document by which a person disposes of his property. A will takes effect on the death of the property owner.

New York:
Real estate is unique and valuable. Will Rogers said "buy land they ain't making any more of it." This is still true today.

The sentiments of Scarlett O'Hara's father about Tara are shared by millions of homeowners throughout the world. Home ownership ranks high on most people's wish list, and a home is considered the most valuable asset in many households. The real estate industry, with all its many facets, such as development, construction, sales, leasing, and finance, generates vast concentrations of wealth and creates millions of jobs. Real estate is a valuable commodity, and almost every aspect of its use, sale, and development is regulated by law. These laws are steeped in history and tempered with logic and practicality. Representation of real estate clients is a major area of practice for many law firms, and the opportunities for the trained real estate assistant are numerous. Preparation for this work begins with an introduction to the basic principles of real property law.

REAL PROPERTY LAW

What law governs real property transactions? The law of the United States comprises two separate systems of law: federal law and state law. Federal law applies uniformly throughout the country, whereas state law, because of differences in local history and conditions, varies from state to state. The law of real property in general is governed by state law and, therefore, is somewhat different in each of the various states. The law of the state in which the real property is located usually governs. For example, if a New York couple owns a beach house on Cape Cod, the laws of the Commonwealth of Massachusetts control the couple's ownership rights to the property and the form and content of the various legal documents and procedures involved in the sale, leasing, financing, inheritance, and so on of the property.

There are, however, basic legal principles that govern real estate transactions, and the approach of this text is to describe these principles and to mention the more important instances in which the states do not agree.

What is real property? The law recognizes two classifications of property: real and personal. Real property relates to land and those things that are more or less permanently attached to the land, such as homes, office buildings, and trees. Personal property refers to all other things, such as automobiles, furniture, stocks, and bonds. John E. Cribbet, former dean of the University of Illinois College of Law, in his treatise *Principles of the Law of Real Property*, points out that "the terminology makes no semantic sense because a car is just as 'real' as a farm and the family mansion is more 'personal' to the owner than shares of stock. The explanation lies not in the history of property, but in the history of procedure. In early common law a real action, so called because it led to the return of the thing itself, was used when land was wrongfully detained by another; a personal action, which gave only a money claim against the wrongdoer, was proper when things other than land were involved. Thus the thing took the name of the action, and we have, to this day, real property and personal property."

Real property is more than just earth and things that are attached to the earth. Real property includes everything beneath the surface of the earth and in the air space above. Early lawyers used the ancient maxim *"cujus est solum, ejus est usque ad coelum et ad infernos,"* which means that land, in its legal signification, extends from the surface downward to the center of the earth and upward indefinitely to the stars.

An owner of real property usually owns all the minerals beneath the surface of the land. These minerals, such as oil, gas, and coal, often are more valuable than the land's surface. The owner can sell the minerals separate from the surface or lease them to a company with the technology to extract the minerals, retaining a royalty or percentage of the profits from the minerals. Conversely, the surface of the land can be sold, and the owner can retain the rights to the minerals beneath the surface.

The owner of real property also owns the air space above the surface of the land. This air space can be quite valuable, such as in a crowded city like New York, where the air space can be used for building purposes. For example, a charitable organization in New York owned a four-story building that was located in the midst of multistory skyscrapers. The organization sold the air space above its building to a developer for several million dollars. The developer used the building as a foundation and constructed a skyscraper within the air space. Air space also can be valuable in less populous areas to preserve a scenic view of a mountain or a shoreline. The advent of solar energy has increased the value of air space, and most states provide for solar easements that create the right to purchase adjoining air space to permit the sun to shine on solar heating or cooling units of a building.

Trees, plants, and other things that grow in the soil may be considered real property. Trees, perennial bushes, grasses, and so on that do not require annual cultivation are considered real property. Annual crops produced by labor, such as wheat, corn, and soybeans, are considered personal property.

An owner of real property has certain ownership rights to use water that is located on the surface or beneath the surface of the land. The users of water are diverse, such as farmers, manufacturers, and consumers. Water pollution and changes in weather patterns that are responsible for below-average rainfall have combined to drastically reduce the amount of usable water available in many sections of the nation and have heightened competition among the users of water. Many states, in an effort to resolve this conflict, have enacted laws regulating the transfer, ownership, and use of water rights.

The source of water governs, to a great extent, a landowner's rights to own and use the water. The categories of water sources are (a) groundwater, such as an underground stream or spring; (b) surface water, which accumulates on the surface of the land from rain; and (c) water that accumulates in a river, stream, or natural lake.

Groundwater is water beneath the surface of the land. It is created by underground streams or by rain that soaks through the soil. A landowner's right to use an underground stream is governed by the same rules that govern rivers and streams on the surface of the land, which are hereinafter discussed. Groundwater that has been

New York:
NY EPTL 3–5.1 defines real property as "land or an estate in land, including leaseholds, fixtures and mortgages or other liens thereon." Personal property is defined as "any property other than real property, including tangible and intangible things."

New York:
While mineral rights are not too important in New York City (there have not been reports of any gold rushes or oil gushers lately) in the farmland areas of the state they have value. In New York air rights are very valuable and builders pay for these rights. The imposing building over Grand Central Station in New York City was built on air rights.

created by rain soaking through the soil is deemed to belong to the owner of the land on which the groundwater is found. The landowner has the right to use the groundwater in any way he or she chooses as long as the landowner does not use or divert the water in such a way as to intentionally harm an adjoining property owner.

A landowner can use *surface water* in any way he or she chooses as long as the use does not harm an adjoining property owner. The diversion of surface water by a landowner onto a neighbor's land may be a problem, especially when the terrain is hilly. For example, a property owner owns land that is at or near the bottom of a hill. Because of the natural flow of surface water, the property floods during rainy periods. The property owner decides to build a dam on the property to keep the surface water from flooding the land. The dam protects the property from flooding by diverting the water uphill onto a neighbor's property, causing the neighbor's property to flood. The flooding of the neighbor's property is unnatural because the flooding is caused by the artificial dam. The owner of the dam in this situation is liable to the neighbor for damages caused by the flooding because the dam altered the natural flow of the water. A property owner does not have the right to alter the natural flow of surface water.

Water located within a river, stream, or natural lake is owned by the state or federal government and not by the individual property owners whose properties adjoin the river, stream, or natural lake. Although an adjoining property owner to a river, stream, or natural lake does not have ownership rights of the water, in most states, the owner has a right to the beneficial use of the water. The right to the beneficial use of the water is governed by one of two areas of water law known as riparian rights and appropriation. *Riparian rights*, derived from the Latin word *ripa*, for river, are based on an ancient doctrine that all owners of riparian lands must share equally in the use of the water for domestic purposes. Riparian lands are those that border a stream, river, or natural lake. Under the riparian rights doctrine, an owner of riparian land has the right to use the water equally with other owners of riparian lands. This equal ownership means that a riparian owner does not have a right to interfere with the natural flow of the water in the river, stream, or lake. For example, an owner of riparian land could not create a dam across the river so that the water would cease to flow to other owners of riparian land. In addition, the riparian owner would not be able to channel the water from the river into a reservoir located on his or her property. Both the dam and the reservoir would alter the natural flow of the water and violate other owners' riparian rights to beneficial use of the water.

Appropriation, sometimes referred to as prior appropriation, is found in western states where water is scarce. This doctrine was developed in the nineteenth century to regulate the conflicts of water usage between settlers of the western states, predominantly miners, farmers, and ranchers. Under the appropriation or prior appropriation water rights doctrine, the right to use the water is given to the landowner who uses the water first. The date of appropriation determines the user's priority to use water, with the earliest user having the superior right. If the water is insufficient to meet all needs, those earlier in time or first in time obtain all the allotted water and those who appropriate later receive only some or none of the water. The first in time, or first-right appropriation, concept contrasts sharply with the riparian tradition of prorating the entitlement to water among all users during times of scarcity.

Under the appropriation theory of water rights, it is required that a landowner show valid appropriation. The elements of valid appropriation are (a) intent to apply water to a beneficial use, (b) an actual diversion of water from a natural source, and (c) application of the water to a beneficial use within a reasonable time.

A beneficial use that will support an appropriation must have a specific stated purpose. In general, water may be appropriated for any use the state deems beneficial.

All states that follow the appropriation theory of water rights usage have established administrative agencies to issue water permits in connection with water usage. The chief purpose of the administrative procedures is to provide an orderly method for appropriating water and regulating established water rights. Water rights under the appropriation theory are transferable from one property owner to another. It is possible to transfer water rights without a transfer of land and to transfer land without a transfer of water rights. Each state has its own regulatory system and requirements for the transfer of water rights.[1]

What are fixtures? It usually is easy to tell if an item is personal property or real property, but in some situations, the determination may be difficult. Take, for example, a stove and a refrigerator that are located in the kitchen of a house. Are these items real property or personal property? The answer to this question is governed by the law of fixtures.

A fixture is an article of personal property, such as an air conditioning unit or a dishwasher, that has been installed in or attached to land or a building and, on attachment, is regarded by the law as part of the real property. A number of judicial tests exist to determine if an article is a fixture. For example, some courts examine the manner in which the article is attached to the real property. The more permanent the attachment, the more likely the court will determine that the item is a fixture. Other courts examine the character of the article and its adaptation to the real property. If it is clear that the item has been specifically constructed or fitted with a view to its location and use in a particular building, such as a hot tub spa on the deck of a house, then the item is more likely to be a fixture. Other courts pay strict attention to the intention of the parties. If it is clear from the circumstances surrounding the attachment of the item to the building that the parties intended for it to be a fixture and part of the real property, this will be given weight by the court. In addition, if the parties have indicated in writing an intention that an item shall be a fixture or shall not be a fixture, a court will enforce this written intention.

The classification of an item as a fixture is important because if the item is a fixture, it is part of the real property and will be transferred with the real property unless there clearly is an intent for it not to be transferred. This means that if a person buys a building, he or she also obtains all the fixtures within the building. Classification also is important in a loan transaction because if a person pledges real property as security for a debt, not only will the real property be pledged, but also any items deemed to be fixtures located on the real property.

Failure to identify an item as a fixture may send a person to jail, as shown by the case of *Ex Parte Brown.*

New York:
In New York State, documents that relate to ownership in real property are filed in the County Clerk's Office of the county in which the property is located. These documents may include but are not limited to deeds, mortgages, releases, easements, satisfactions, and some leases.

---

[1] David H. Getches, Water Law in a Nutshell, 2nd Ed., St. Paul: West Publishing Company, 1990.

CASE

WRIGHT, Presiding Judge.

Ruby and Louis Brown were divorced by decree of the Lauderdale County Circuit Court in November 1983. As part of this decree, the husband was awarded the family home, "including all fixtures and realty appurtenant thereto." The wife was awarded all furniture in the home with the exception of the master bedroom suite, the dining room furniture, kitchen appliances and one-half of all silver, silverware and other kitchenware, which was awarded to the husband. The wife was to remove all of the furniture and personal property awarded to her prior to relinquishing possession of the home. In February 1984, the husband filed a petition with the circuit court asking that the wife be found to be in contempt for violating the property settlement provisions of the divorce decree. In May 1985, the court issued an order which specifically stated:

"The evidence shows that under the decree of divorce the Plaintiff [husband] was awarded certain items of personal property which the Defendant [wife] removed from the Plaintiff's home. A microwave of the value of $400.00 and a refrigerator of the value of $500.00. Further, the Plaintiff was awarded the family home and there was attached thereto a bookcase and china cabinets of the value of $2,000.00 which the Defendant removed from the home. Therefore, the Plaintiff was deprived of real and personal property of the value of $2,900.00 and the Defendant's action in removing these items is [a] violation of the decree and a contempt of the Court."

For her contempt, the court ordered the wife to serve ten days in the county jail, allowing, however, that she could purge herself of the contempt by making a payment of $2,900 to the Clerk of the Circuit Court of Lauderdale County. Thereafter, the wife filed this petition for certiorari asking that we review this finding of contempt.

﹡ ﹡ ﹡

We are perplexed by the wife's first argument for reversal. She admits that she acted in contempt of the court's order when she removed the microwave and refrigerator from the home, but argues that the bookcase and china cabinets were not fixtures appurtenant to the home and thus could be removed by her as furniture. She does not argue that the ten-day jail sentence was excessive, *see Williams v. Stumpe*, 439 So.2d 1297 (Ala.Civ.App.1983), nor that she is unable to pay the $2,900 necessary to purge herself of this contempt, *see Zeigler v. Butler*, 410 So.2d 93 (Ala.Civ.App.1982). Instead, the real issue she wishes this court to address is whether the $2,900 is an accurate assessment of the damage caused the husband by her contempt.

[1] It is settled that a trial court can assess damages in favor of an aggrieved party in civil contempt proceedings. *Lightsey v. Kensington Mortgage & Finance Corp.*, 294 Ala. 281, 315 So.2d 431 (1975); *Smith v. Smith*, 365 So.2d 88 (Ala.Civ.App.1978). It is also settled that "a party who has been found in contempt and who has been assessed compensatory damages should seek review of the finding of contempt by means of extraordinary writ (certiorari or habeas corpus), and should seek review of the question of the assessed amount of compensatory damages by appeal." *Smith, supra.* The wife has not appealed the $2,900 award. However, out of deference to the parties, we note that even if the wife had not admitted her contempt, there is ample evidence in the record to support the trial judge's determination that the bookcase and china cabinets were fixtures appurtenant to the house.

"A 'fixture' is an article that was once a chattel, but which, by being physically annexed or affixed to realty, has become assessory to it and 'part and parcel of it.' " *Milford v. Tennessee River Pulp and Paper Company*, 355 So.2d 687 (Ala.1978). Whether an article is a fixture is a determination that must be made on the particular circumstances of each case. *Id.* The supreme court has articulated the criteria to be used in making this determination as follows:

"(1) Actual annexation to the realty or to something appurtenant thereto; (2) Appropriateness to the use or purposes of that part of the realty with which it is connected; (3) The intention of the party making the annexation of making permanent attachment to the freehold. This intention of the party making the annexation is inferred; (a) From the nature of the articles annexed; (b) The relation of the party making the annexation; (c) The structure and mode of annexation; (d) The purposes and uses for which the annexation has been made."

Id. (quoting *Langston v. State*, 96 Ala. 44, 11 So. 334 (1891)).

In her own testimony, the wife revealed that the articles had all been custom-built for the express purpose of being used with the family house, not just to be used in any house. All of the articles were anchored to the walls, and the china cabinets were each set into a permanent base. Under our limited scope of review, we cannot say that this testimony does not support a finding that

the articles were intended to be fixtures, "part and parcel" of the house.

❋   ❋   ❋

We are of the opinion that the trial court has not committed error in finding that the wife acted in contempt of the divorce decree. Further, her sentence of ten days in jail, with the opportunity to purge her contempt by paying to the clerk $2,900, is not unconstitutional. The decision of the trial court is affirmed.

AFFIRMED.

BRADLEY and HOLMES, JJ., concur.

Ownership of Real Property

The legal profession, including legal assistants, spends time and clients' money worrying about the ownership of real property. The basic principle that only the owner of real property can sell or pledge it as security for a debt means that on any typical sale or loan transaction, title examinations and other efforts are made by legal counsel for the purchaser or lender to determine the extent of the seller's or borrower's ownership of the real property.

The chief legal rights accorded an owner of real property are possession, use, and power of disposition. An owner of real property has the right to possess the property. **Possession** is occupation of the land evidenced by visible acts such as an enclosure, cultivation, the construction of improvements, or the occupancy of existing improvements. Possession gives the property owner the right to exclude others from the land. Occupancy of land by someone without the permission of the owner is a trespass. The owner may evict the trespasser from the land and/or sue the trespasser for money damages or even have the trespasser arrested.

A landowner has the right to use the land for profit or pleasure. Absolute freedom to use land has never existed, and the modern owner is faced with a number of limitations on the use of land arising from public demands of health, safety, and public welfare as well as the rights of neighbors to the safety and enjoyment of their property. The law, however, does favor the free use of land, and doubts will be resolved in favor of the owner.

An owner of property has the right to dispose of that ownership. The power of disposition may take place at the owner's death by inheritance or will, or it may take place during the owner's lifetime by contract, deed, or lease. The law favors the free right to transfer ownership, and any restraint on this right will not be upheld unless the restraint supports some important public purpose or private right.

Private property rights are subject to the right of sovereignty exercised by federal, state, and local governments. Therefore, private ownership is subject to the powers to tax; to regulate the use of private property in the interest of public safety, health, and the general welfare; and to take private property for public use. A government's power to regulate, tax, and take private property for public use is discussed in Chapter 5.

METHODS OF ACQUIRING OWNERSHIP TO REAL PROPERTY

The main methods of acquiring ownership to real property are inheritance, devise, gift, sale, and adverse possession.

Inheritance and Devise

The first two methods, **inheritance** and **devise**, are ownership transfers that take place on the death of the previous owner. Inheritance, or descent, as it is also known, is the passage of title and ownership of real property from one who dies intestate (without a will) to people whom the law designates, because of blood or marriage, as the owner's heirs. Each state has its own descent statute, and the statutes vary slightly from state to state. The law of the state where the property is located decides who is to inherit.

An example of a schedule of kinship relation to a decedent based on typical descent statute is shown in Exhibit 1–1. The closest group of heirs to the deceased property owner will inherit all the property. For example, in Exhibit 1–1, if the deceased property owner is survived by a spouse and children, the spouse and children will inherit all the property. If the deceased property owner is not survived by a spouse or children, the deceased property owner's surviving parents and/or siblings, if any, will inherit the property.

The acquisition of ownership by **devise** is the passage of title of real property from one who dies *with* a will. A **will** is a legal document prepared during the property owner's lifetime that indicates where and how the owner's property is to be disposed of at the owner's death. The **conveyance** of real property in a will is referred to as a devise. The will must comply with the state law governing wills. Again, the state law where the real property is located will control.

Gift

Ownership to real property can be obtained by a gift. Once the gift is complete—and with real property this would be on the proper execution and delivery of a deed to the property—the gift is irrevocable. The promise to make a gift, however, usually is revocable. An exception to the revocation of gifts rule is in the event that the recipient of the gift has detrimentally relied on the belief that the gift would be made. The injured party may recover costs for the detrimental reliance. For example, you purchase insurance for a home based on someone's promise to give you that home. If the gift is not made, you would be able to recover the costs of the insurance.

Contract and Sale

Property ownership can be obtained by buying the property. This is the transaction that involves most real estate legal assistants and attorneys. A complete discussion of contracts and the sale of property is found in Chapters 7 and 8.

Adverse Possession

Possession of real property is given substantial legal protection. Even a party in unlawful possession of the real property has the right to exclude anyone else from possession except for the true owner. Possession, in and of itself, also engenders, through time, the inference that the possession began lawfully. The longer the continued possession, the stronger this inference. If possession is maintained long enough, it is possible that the person in possession becomes the owner through a process known as **adverse possession**. Adverse possession operates as a statute of limitations, in the sense that it precludes all others from contesting the title of the possessor.

The rules on adverse possession vary from state to state. Typically, the possessor must possessor the property for a period ranging from seven to twenty years. The possession also must be adverse, which means without the consent or permission of the true owner. In some states, it is necessary that an adverse possessor have knowledge that he is in adverse possession of the property. An example of how this works follows.

Assume that property owners Andy and Barbara are neighbors, and that Andy has built a fence on what Andy believes to be the property line, but in fact, the fence encroaches one foot onto Barbara's property. Andy is unaware of this encroachment and maintains the fence for twenty years. In a state that requires Andy to have knowl-

New York:
In New York, the doctrine of adverse possession exists. Property can be obtained by adverse possession, if there is open, notorious, hostile, and exclusive possession of that property for a period of ten years. One who has acquired property "adversely" for ten years may then acquire ownership of the property against all other persons. If the state is the owner, the period of adverse possession must be twenty years before title may be acquired. After that the possessor may go to court to obtain title, this lawsuit is called a suit to "quiet title."

EXHIBIT 1–1
Schedule of kinship relation to a decedent

edge that he is an adverse possessor, Andy, even though he has satisfied the statute of limitations for adverse possession, would not become the owner of this additional one foot of Barbara's property.

In addition to the possession being adverse, it must be public, continuous, peaceful, exclusive, and uninterrupted.

"**Tacking**" of possession is permitted if there is some contractual or blood relationship between the two adverse possessors. Tacking is the adding of possession periods by different adverse possessors. For example, adverse possessor Andy enters into possession of the property, keeps it for seven years, and then sells it to adverse possessor Barbara. Adverse possessor Barbara, in a state that requires twenty years of adverse possession, could tack or add onto adverse possessor Andy's period of possession because of the contractual relationship between the two. Then Barbara would have to stay in possession only thirteen years to obtain ownership.

The meaning of possession for purposes of adverse possession varies from state to state. Possession, in a strict sense, means occupancy and use of the property. Some states, however, require that the adverse possessor pay taxes on the real property during the period of possession.

Even though ownership to real property can be obtained through adverse possession, there is no written documentation or proof of this ownership. If the adverse possessor attempts to sell the real property, chances are he or she will have a difficult time establishing title. One means of establishing ownership through adverse possession is by bringing what is known as a "quiet title" action. In a quiet title action, the adverse possessor sues the entire world and challenges anyone to step forward and object to the adverse possessor's claim of ownership. In the suit, the adverse possessor would then bring proof through affidavits or witnesses as to the adverse possessor's necessary period of possession and the nature of that possession. If the court finds that the adverse possessor is now the owner, it will issue a judgment adjudicating the adverse possessor's ownership. This judgment could then be used to establish ownership for purposes of future sales.

HISTORY OF AMERICAN REAL PROPERTY LAW

The early settlers who came to America from Europe brought with them the laws of their native land, including the laws concerning land ownership. Except for Louisiana, Texas, and portions of the Southwest, where the civil laws of France and Spain have substantial influence, most modern real property law is the product of English feudal law, which developed into what is known as the common law.

Feudalism grew out of the chaos of the Dark Ages. Because of the collapse of all central law and order, people banded together for security and stability, with usually the strongest member of the group taking command. The stronger members became known as lords, and the weaker members became known as tenants or vassals of the lord. For the lord to keep the allegiance of the vassals, it became necessary to compensate them for their services. Because almost all the wealth of the lords at that time was in the form of land, the land was parceled out to the vassals for services. Tenures or rights to possession were created. The early tenures were of four main types: (1) *knight tenure*, land given in return for pledged armed services; (2) *serjeantry tenure*, land given in return for performance of ceremonial services for the lord (later this evolved into ordinary domestic services such as cook and butler); (3) *frankalmoin tenure*, land given for religious purposes to priests and other religious bodies; and (4) *socage tenure*, land given to farmers. These early field tenures

New York:
In feudal England title to all land was in the king and he granted lords "feuds," i.e. the the right to use the king's land. This was similar to a lease and the king was the lord of the land (landlord). These rights lasted for the lifetime of the lord. Later the lord was able to pass these rights on to his heirs and still later, lords (and individuals) were able to obtain title in their own name. This system of "feuds" was one of the reasons for the American Revolution. This system has changed dramatically and today, in the United States, we have the "allodial" system of ownership, i.e. property rights vest in the individual, with of course some limitations by government.

evolved into the concept of estates (derived from the latin word *status*), which became the primary basis of classification of interests in land. The word *estate* is still used today to express the degree, quantity, nature, duration, or extent of an owner's interest in real property.

Modern Day Estates in Real Property

There are six types of modern-day estates in real property: (1) fee simple or fee simple absolute, (2) fee simple determinable, (3) fee simple on condition subsequent, (4) life estate, (5) estate for years, and (6) estate at will.

Fee Simple or Fee Simple Absolute

Fee simple or **fee simple absolute** is the highest and best kind of estate an owner can have. It is one in which the owner is entitled to the entire estate, with unconditional powers of disposition during the owner's lifetime, and the power to transfer the property to heirs and legal representatives on the owner's death.

Fee simple or fee simple absolute is maximum legal ownership and of a potential infinite duration and unrestricted inheritability. In most states, no special language is needed to create a fee simple absolute. The presumption is that a fee simple estate is created at every conveyance unless a lesser estate is mentioned and limited in the conveyance. Most homes and commercial properties are owned in fee simple.

Fee Simple Determinable

A **fee simple determinable** is an ownership in real property limited to expire automatically on the happening or nonhappening of an event that is stated in the deed of conveyance or the will creating the estate. For example, Aaron conveys to Bill "to have to hold to Bill so long as the land is used for residential purposes. When the land is no longer used for residential purposes, it shall revert to Aaron." The use of the words *so long as* to preface the condition under ancient English common law created a fee simple determinable, and in modern times, most states recognize that the use of these words preceding the statement of a condition in a deed or will creates a fee simple determinable. The estate granted is a fee, and like the fee simple absolute, it can be inherited and may last forever so long as the condition is not broken. Yet it is a determinable fee because there is a condition. The estate will automatically expire on the nonoccurrence or occurrence of the event—for example, the use of the land for nonresidential purposes. The estate conveyed to Bill will automatically end if and when the land is used for nonresidential purposes, and Aaron will again own the estate in fee simple absolute. During the existence of Bill's ownership of the fee simple determinable, Aaron retains a future interest in the land called a possibility or right of reverter. Aaron's possibility of reverter can be passed on to Aaron's heirs at Aaron's death. Aaron's possibility of reverter also may be transferred to a third party at the time of the conveyance to Bill. For example, Aaron conveys to Bill to "have and to hold so long as the land is used for residential purposes and then to Carol. If the land is not used for residential purposes, it will go to Carol, Aaron's possibility of reverter having been transferred to Carol."

Fee Simple on Condition Subsequent

A **fee simple on condition subsequent** exists when a fee simple is subject to a power in the grantor (person who conveyed the fee) to recover the conveyed

New York:
In New York a conveyance of real property implies a fee simple ownership, unless a different intention is clearly stated. A fee simple is the highest, most complete form of ownership.

A fee on condition is created by using the words "if, condition, provided that, until, so long, or during."

estate on the happening of a specified event. "Aaron transfers to Bill on the express condition that the land shall not be used for nonresidential purposes, and if it is, Aaron shall have the right to reenter and possess the land." The use of the words *on the express condition that* under English common law created a fee simple on condition subsequent, and in modern times, most states recognize that the use of these words preceding the statement of a condition in a deed or will creates a fee simple on condition subsequent. Bill has a fee simple on condition subsequent, and Aaron has the right of entry or power of termination. On the happening of the stated event, the granted estate will continue in existence until Aaron effectively exercises the option to terminate by making entry or bringing an action to recover the property. A breach of the condition does not cause an automatic termination of the fee simple on condition subsequent estate. The basic difference, therefore, between the fee simple determinable and the fee simple on condition subsequent is that the former automatically expires on violation of the specified condition contained in the instrument creating the estate, whereas the latter continues until it is terminated by the exercise of the grantor's power to terminate. Aaron's right to reenter can be transferred to a third party in the same manner as the possibility of reverter in a fee simple determinable.

Creation of a fee simple determinable or fee simple on condition subsequent gives a property owner the means of controlling the use of the property after the transfer or after the property owner's death. This element of control may be important to the property owner for a number of reasons. For example, a farmer owns a farm that has been in the family for generations. The farmer has three children. Two of the children have left the farm and live in the city. The third child has expressed an interest in staying on the farm and taking it over on the farmer's retirement or death. The farmer may be able to satisfy his objectives by transferring the family farm to the child who desires to continue farming in fee simple on condition subsequent or fee simple determinable, on the condition that the land always be used as a farm.

Another example of when a conditional fee is used is in transfers of property to a charity. A property owner often is willing to transfer valuable land to a charity, provided it is used for specific charitable purposes. For example, a property owner is willing to convey land to her college, provided the land be used to expand the college's law school. The property owner could accomplish this by transferring a conditional fee to the college on the condition that the land be used for the expansion of the law school. The property owner may want to give the possibility of reverter or right of reentry to the property owner's family.

Fee simple determinable or fee simple on condition subsequent ownership, owing to the threat that ownership will terminate in the event the condition is breached, makes this form of ownership difficult to sell. In addition, most lending institutions who lend money on the security of real property will not make a loan or receive conditional fee title as security for a loan. These reasons have made the fee simple determinable and fee simple on condition subsequent somewhat uncommon forms of ownership.

Life Estate

A **life estate** has its duration measured by the life or lives of one or more persons.

An estate for life may be for either the life of the owner or the life of some other person or people ("measuring life"). Life estates may be created by deed, will, or an express agreement of the parties. For example, an elderly woman owns a duplex home. Her daughter, to provide her mother with money, wants to buy the duplex. The daughter is willing to give to the mother a life estate in the side of the duplex that the mother has been living in for the past several years. Therefore, the mother will continue living in her portion of the duplex during her lifetime, and on her death, the daughter would have full fee simple title to all the duplex.

At the time of the creation of a life estate, there also is retained or created a reversion or remainder interest. For example, Aaron transfers to Bill a life estate for the life of Bill. As part of this transfer, a reversion right to Aaron is implicitly created. This means that on Bill's death, the property will revert back to Aaron. Aaron's reversion right is not contingent on Aaron's surviving Bill, and Aaron's reversion right can be transferred by Aaron during Aaron's lifetime, or it may be inherited by Aaron's heirs at his death or transferred by Aaron's will. This reversion right also can be transferred by Aaron to a third party, and this transfer could take place at the time of the transfer of the life estate to Bill. For example, Aaron transfers to Bill a life estate for the life of Bill, then to Carol. This means that on Bill's death, the property will go to Carol. Carol has what is known as a vested remainder in fee simple. Carol's right to own the property in fee simple on Bill's death is not dependent on Carol's surviving Bill. If Carol dies before Bill, Carol's vested remainder in fee simple will pass to Carol's heirs or the devisees under her will. Carol's heirs or the devisees under the will will receive the property on Bill's death.

The owner of a life estate is entitled to the full use and enjoyment of the real property so long as the owner exercises ordinary care and prudence for the preservation and protection of the real property and commits no acts intending to cause permanent injury to the person entitled to own the real property after the termination of the life estate. If the life estate owner of the real property does not take care of the real property, the owner will be deemed to commit **waste** and the life estate will terminate, even though the measuring life is still alive. Failure to make needed repairs or improvements, the cutting of timber for sale, or the mining of minerals have all been held to be acts of waste. Because forfeiture of ownership is the penalty for waste, most courts are reluctant to find waste, and the decisions vary from state to state as to what acts of a life estate owner constitute waste.

As a general rule, the life estate owner is entitled to all income generated from the real property and is entitled to possession of the real property during the ownership of the life estate. Life estates are transferable, although the life estate owner can transfer only what he or she has, which is a life estate for the measuring life. A life estate owner usually has the obligation to pay taxes on the real property, keep the real property adequately insured, and pay debts secured by the real property. Because death terminates the life estate and death is so uncertain an event, a life estate ownership is difficult to sell or pledge as security for a loan.

Estate for Years

An **estate for years** is limited in its duration to a fixed period. For example, "Aaron to Bill for twenty years" would create an estate for years in Bill. The estate for years would continue until the period of ownership terminates. Next to the fee simple estate, the estate for years is the most common form of ownership. An estate for years may be a lease, but not all leases are estate for years. For a lease to be an estate for years, it must be clear that ownership to the real property is conveyed and not mere rights to possession.

A complete discussion on leases is contained in Chapter 18.

Estate at Will

An **estate at will** is an estate with no fixed term that is created by the express or implied agreements of the parties. An estate at will can automatically be terminated; however, under modern law, there may be some notice requirement (thirty- or sixty-day notice) before termination. An estate at will may be created by implication. For example, Aaron transfers to Bill an estate for years for twenty years. At the expiration of the twenty years, Bill remains in possession of the real property and continues to pay rental to Aaron, which Aaron accepts. Once the estate for years has expired (i.e., the twenty years), Bill is not in possession as an owner of an estate for years, so the law usually will imply that Bill now has an estate at will; that is, Bill is in possession with the consent of Aaron. Aaron can terminate Bill's possession and ownership rights immediately or on any statutory notice if required in the state where the real property is located.

ROLE OF LEGAL ASSISTANT IN REAL ESTATE LEGAL PRACTICE

Legal assistants participate in all aspects of a real estate practice. The skills used by legal assistants in a real estate practice include preparation of legal documents, examination and review of real property titles, preparation of land descriptions, preparation and review of leases, and fact-finding investigation required to represent purchasers, sellers, and lenders in connection with real estate transactions. Real estate legal assistants are employed in private law firms, corporate legal departments, and government agencies. Real estate is a "bread-and-butter" practice of many law firms, from sole practitioners to the largest national firms. Many corporations have as a major part of their business an involvement with real estate. These corporations include not only development and construction corporations, but also corporations that involve retail operations, such as Wal-Mart, K-Mart, and Gap. Banks and life insurance companies are major lenders of money for real estate projects, and many have in-house legal departments that supervise the company's real estate lending activities. Gas, telephone, and electric utility companies have corporate legal departments that deal with real estate. Government agencies, such as public housing authorities and rapid transportation authorities, are responsible for the regulation and development of real estate. Many of these law firms, corporations, banks, life insurance companies, utilities, and government agencies employ legal assistants. The opportunities for the real estate legal assistant are plentiful and diversified.

E T H I C S :   Introduction

Ethics, the service to others performed in a moral and honest manner, is the cornerstone of a professional practice. It is essential that the system for establishing and dispensing justice be developed and maintained in such a way that the public shall have absolute confidence in the integrity and impartiality of its administration. Such a system cannot exist unless the conduct and motives of the members of the legal profession merit the approval of all just and honest citizens. Not only is the future of this country and its justice system dependent on the ethical conduct of those who are licensed to administer justice, but the future of the legal profession depends on its members acting in an ethical manner. Lawyers are asked daily to deal with the most intimate and serious problems that affect clients. Only a profession made up of members with the highest ethical considerations can continue to deliver the service and confidence demanded by the public.

Attorneys are governed by two sets of ethical rules: the American Bar Association's Model Rules of Professional Conduct and Model Code of Professional Responsibility and the ethical codes and rules of professional responsibility promulgated by state bar associations. A violation of these rules can result in disciplinary action being brought against the errant attorney, including such drastic penalties as the loss of a license to practice law.

It is not clear that legal assistants are bound and covered by the various ethical codes and rules of professional conduct applicable to attorneys. Because legal assistants are not licensed, there is no removal of license sanction that could be imposed against a legal assistant for violation of ethical codes or rules of professional conduct. *Attorneys, however, who are responsible for and supervise the activities of the legal assistant can be sanctioned and disciplined for the actions of the legal assistant under the attorney's control and supervision.* It is in the best interest of the legal profession that legal assistants adhere to the ethical codes and rules of professional responsibility applicable to attorneys.

SUMMARY

Most legal assistants employed by law firms or corporations are used to assist in the transfer of ownership to real property, the development and leasing of real property, and the closing of loans secured by real property. At any sale, lease, or loan transaction, it is important to determine who owns the real property in question and what estate is held by the owner. It is important in each transaction that the estate owned be sufficient to satisfy all the parties' expectations to the transaction. A fee simple absolute estate usually would be satisfactory under all circumstances. The other estates may not be satisfactory, and a legal assistant must be conscious of the limitations that each of the lesser estates impose on the ownership and use of the real property.

Under many circumstances, the ownership of the real property is not vested in a single person. For example, it is common for husbands and wives to own homes together and for investment partners to collectively own commercial real property. A discussion of the legal issues involving co-ownership of real property follows in Chapter 2.

KEY TERMS

Adverse possession	Fee simple absolute	Life estate
Appropriation	Fee simple determinable	Possession
Conveyance	Fee simple on condition subse-	Riparian rights
Devise	quent	Tacking
Estate at will	Fixture	Waste
Estate for years	Inheritance	Will

REVIEW QUESTIONS

1. What is real property, and how does it differ from personal property?

2. What is the difference between riparian rights and appropriation?

3. What test does the court use to determine if an item is a fixture?

4. What are the chief legal rights accorded to an owner of real property?

5. How does a fee simple determinable differ from a fee simple on condition subsequent?

6. What is the concept of waste, and how is it applicable to a life estate?

7. Name the various ways a person can become an owner of real property.

8. What is the difference between inheritance and receiving property by devise?

9. What are the elements of adverse possession?

10. Why would anyone want to create a life estate?

CASE PROBLEMS

1. Oscar is the owner in fee simple of Black Acre, on which is located a weather-beaten old house. Adam has asked Oscar if he, Adam, might move into the house on Black Acre. Oscar grants the request and Adam moves in. Shortly thereafter, Oscar sells Black Acre to Barbara. The statute of limitations in the state where Black Acre is located is ten years for adverse possession. Adam knew nothing about Oscar's sale to Barbara and occupies the house for twelve years after such sale. Adam, during the whole period of occupancy, thinks he is occupying the property with Oscar's permission. Barbara discovers Adam's occupancy of the house and demands that Adam leave the house. Adam refuses to leave. Barbara sues Adam for trespass, and Adam defends that he is an adverse possessor and is now the owner of Black Acre. Who wins?

2. Aaron transfer to Bob a life estate in a house with the remainder to Carol. Carol dies before Bob. On Bob's death, will the property go to Aaron, or to Carol's heirs?

3. Aaron transfer a life estate to Bob for the life of Carol with the remainder to David. What interest does Carol have in the property? If Bob dies before Carol, who owns the property until Carol's death?

4. Aaron transfers property to Bill for the life of Carol then to David. Bill sells his life estate to Susan. Carol dies before Bill. Until Bill's death, who owns the property?

5. Adam has entered into a contract to sell his home to Barbara. The home contains a hot tub spa on its rear deck, a beautiful chandelier in the dining room, and a built-in home entertainment center in the den. These special features, among others, persuaded Barbara to enter into a contract to buy the home from Adam. The contract is not carefully written and does not expressly require Adam to sell these three items to Barbara. The contract only mentions that Adam will sell the home and all fixtures to Barbara. At the time the ownership of the home is to be transferred to Barbara, Adam takes the position that the spa, chandelier, and home entertainment center are not part of the sale. Can Barbara require Adam to sell these items to her pursuant to the contract? What are the main issues involved in such a determination?

PRACTICAL ASSIGNMENT

1. Obtain a copy of your state's statutes of inheritance or descent and compare them with the schedule of kinship shown as Exhibit 1–1.

2. What is required in your state for a person to obtain ownership to real property by adverse possession?

3. Research your state's law concerning waste by an owner of a life estate, and list three examples of things ruled to be waste by the courts of your state.

Concurrent Ownership

*Two live as one
One live as two
Two live as three
Under the bam
Under the boo
Under the bamboo tree*

—T.S. Eliot, Sweeney Agonistes

OBJECTIVES

After reading this chapter, you will be able to:

- Distinguish and explain the four types of concurrent ownership
- Identify the rights, duties, and liabilities of common owners
- Understand the difference between individual and community property
- Draft a cotenancy agreement

GLOSSARY

Community property law Rule of law in states following the civil law of Spain and France, which provides that real property acquired during marriage is owned equally by the husband and wife.

Contribution Right for a co-owner of real property to receive reimbursement from other co-owners for their share of expenses that are common to the real property.

Curtesy Interest in real property of the wife that the law in some states gives to the surviving husband at the time of the wife's death.

Dower Widow's interest in real property of her husband that provides a means of support after the husband's death.

Elective share Right given to a widow in many states to elect, at her husband's death, to receive either dower or some ownership (fee simple) share of her husband's real property.

Joint tenancy with right of survivorship Ownership of real property by two or more persons. Joint tenants with the right of survivorship hold equal interest in the real property, and on the death of any owner, the deceased owner's interest in the real property will pass to the surviving owner.

Partition Method by which co-owners of real property can divide the common property into separate ownerships. Partition may be by voluntary agreement of the co-owners or by court action.

Prenuptial agreement Agreement entered into by a married couple that, among other things, outlines an agreement between the couple regarding the division and ownership of property in the event of separation or divorce.

Real property may be owned by a single owner or by a group of owners. When a single owner owns real property, this is known as ownership in severalty. A single owner has all the attributes of ownership, that is, the sole exclusive right to possess and use the property, the right to transfer the property, and the responsibility for all expenses and other charges in connection with the property.

Real property often is owned by more than one person. The combinations are endless: married couples own homes together, family members inherit real property together, partners join together in commerical investment. Ownership of real property by more than one person provokes some interesting questions. Can one owner sell his or her interest without the consent of the other owners? Will the debts of an owner attach to the real property as a whole, thereby affecting the interests of the other owners? How are the expenses and income of the real property divided among the owners? What happens if an owner does not pay his or her share of the expenses? Can the owners terminate the group ownership and divide the real property among themselves? These and other questions are faced daily by attorneys and legal assistants when dealing with real property that is owned by more than one person.

To decide what rights group owners and third parties who deal with these owners have in the real property, it is necessary to determine how the concurrent ownership is held.

TYPES OF CONCURRENT OWNERSHIP

Four types of concurrent ownership exist: (1) joint tenancy with the right of survivorship, (2) tenancy in common, (3) tenancy by the entirety, and (4) community property. The law of the state in which the real property is located will determine how the concurrent ownership is held. For example, owners who reside in South Carolina but own property in California are bound by California concurrent ownership law.

The old common law term of "tenant" or "tenancy," which is synonymous with the modern use of the word "owner" or "ownership," is still used to describe some of the types of concurrent ownership.

Joint Tenancy with Right of Survivorship

A **joint tenancy with the right of survivorship** is recognized in most states. It can be created by a deed or a will. It usually occurs when real property is transferred to two or more persons with express language that they are to take the real property as "joint tenants with the right of survivorship," or similar language. Thus, when a joint tenancy is desired, most instruments use the following language: "to A and B as joint tenants with rights of survivorship, not as tenants in common."

New York:
In discussing concurrent "tenants" the word tenant does not mean someone who rents under a lease, but means the person who has ownership. New York recognizes three forms of co-ownership: tenancy in common, joint tenancy with rights of survivorship, and tenancy by the entirety.

New York:
To create a joint tenancy with right of survivorship, you must use specific language. It can only be created by a clear intention, e.g., words such as "To Walter and Jennifer as Joint Tenants with Right of Survivorship and not as Tenants in Common."

Under a joint tenancy with right of survivorship, each owner owns an equal and undivided interest in the whole of the real property. Each owner has the right to use and possess the entire real property; this right to use or possession is held in common with the other owners.

The existence of a single ownership as a unit rather than as separate interests in the individual units is the essence of joint tenancy with the right of survivorship. This emphasis on the estate as a unit led to the common law requirements that four items—interest, title, time, and possession—be present for the creation of a joint tenancy with the right of survivorship. In other words, each owner's interest must constitute an identical interest (e.g., fee simple or life estate), must accrue by the same conveyance (deed or will), must commence at the same time, and must be held in the same undivided possession. If any of the four items or "unities" is lacking in a conveyance, the estate is not a joint tenancy with right of survivorship but is instead a tenancy in common.

The outstanding feature of the joint tenancy with right of survivorship is the right of survivorship. The right of survivorship provides that if one of the joint owners dies, the real property is passed on to the surviving joint owners. This process will continue until the sole survivor of the joint owners owns all the real property. For example, Aaron, Bob, and Carl are joint tenants with right of survivorship. Aaron dies and wills his property to Donna. Donna will actually receive nothing. Bob and Carl will be joint owners with the right of survivorship, each owning one-half interest in the real property. Later, Bob dies and wills all the property to Ellen. Again, Ellen will receive nothing. At this point, Carl will be the sole owner of the property.

A severance of the joint tenancy means that the survivorship feature no longer takes effect. A joint tenancy with right of survivorship can easily be severed in most states. The sale of a joint tenant's interest in the real property will create a severance of the joint tenancy. In many states, a contract to sell or even the granting of a mortgage on the real property will sever the joint tenancy. An example of how this severance might work is as follows: Aaron, Bob, and Carl are joint tenants with the right of survivorship. Aaron, during the lifetime of Aaron, Bob, and Carl, conveys an undivided one-third interest to Donna. This conveyance will sever the joint tenancy as to the interest being conveyed to Donna, and Donna will be a tenant in common with Bob and Carl, who are still joint tenants with the right of survivorship. When Donna dies, Donna's interest will pass by will or by inheritance to Donna's heirs. When Bob dies, Bob's interest will pass to Carl. At such time, Donna (if living) and Carl would become tenants in common. Donna would own one-third and Carl two-thirds.

Under a joint tenancy with right of survivorship, each owner owns an equal and undivided interest in the whole of the real property. Each owner has the right to use and possess the entire real property; this right to use or possession is held in common with the other owners.

For example, Aaron and Bob own a twenty-acre farm as joint tenants with the right of survivorship. Aaron and Bob would each own an undivided 50 percent interest in the farm. Assume that a third party, Carl, wants to buy five acres of the farm. Neither Aaron nor Bob could sell the five acres to Carl, because each of them individually owns only an undivided 50 percent of the five acres. Carl, therefore, would have to purchase the five acres from both Aaron and Bob.

Tenancy in Common

Tenancy in common is a form of co-ownership in which two or more persons are each entitled to possession of the same real property. A tenancy in common may be created voluntarily by grant, lease, devise, or bequest or involuntarily by descent to heirs. Title does not have to arise at the same time or by the same instrument. Unlike a joint tenancy with right of survivorship, there is no right to survivorship in a tenancy in common. Each common owner's interest in the real property will pass by will or by inheritance on the common owner's death. In addition, under a tenancy in common, the owners may hold unequal shares, if so provided in the conveyance. For example, Aaron's deed conveys real property to Bob (an undivided one-quarter interest) and to Carl (an undivided three-quarters interest). Most states prefer a tenancy in common over a joint tenancy with right of survivorship. This means that if real property is conveyed to two or more persons and the deed or will does not indicate how the ownership is to be held, the ownership will be deemed a tenancy in common.

New York:
In New York, a deed to two people who aren't married to each other creates a tenancy in common, unless otherwise indicated.

Rights, Duties, and Liabilities of the Common Owners

Each common owner, whether it be a joint tenancy with right of survivorship or a tenancy in common, has a right to enter on the common real property and take possession of the whole property, subject only to the equal rights of the other common owners to do the same thing. Subject to the rights of the other common owners, a common owner of real property may use and enjoy the property as though he were the sole owner. A common owner may occupy and use every portion of the real property at all times and in all circumstances. The right to use and possess, however, is not exclusive, and each of the common owners has the same right. A common owner has been held to have a right to extract minerals, drill for oil, or cut timber from the common land. Any income produced from these activities that exceeds the common owner's proportionate share is to be distributed to the other common owners. A common owner is held to a standard of reasonable care and must take care of the real property as a prudent person would take care of his or her own property.

A common owner is entitled to his or her fractional proportionate share of rent or income produced from the real property. For example, a common owner with a 15 percent interest in the real property would be entitled to 15 percent of the income or rent from the real property. A common owner who has received money from a third party for the use of the common real property is a trustee of the amount collected for purposes of distribution to the other common owners for all sums over and above the common owner's share.

In a similar manner to rents and income, a common owner is responsible for expenses, such as taxes and repairs, in proportion to his or her respective interest in the real property. A common owner who pays more than his or her share of the common expenses is entitled to have the other common owners refund to him or her their proportionate shares of the amount paid. This right to reimbursement is known as the right of **contribution**. It is clear in most states (Alabama, Arkansas, California, Colorado, Delaware, Georgia, Idaho, Illinois, Indiana, Iowa, Kentucky, Maryland, Massachusetts, Michigan, Minnesota, Mississippi, Missouri, Nebraska, Nevada, New Hampshire, New Jersey, New York, North Carolina, Ohio, Oregon, Tennessee, Texas, Virginia, Washington, West Virginia, and Wisconsin) that payment of taxes or repairs made to preserve the property entitle a common owner to a right of contribution against the other common owners for their share of the taxes or repairs. It is not clear whether a co-owner is entitled to a contribution for the cost of an improvement if he or she has improved the real property without the consent of the other common owners. Some states (Illinois, Indiana, Kentucky, Michigan, Missouri, Texas, Virginia, and West Virginia) permit a common owner who improves real property in good faith to recover by contribution from the other common owners their share of the lesser of

(a) the cost of the improvement or (b) the increase in value to the common property by the improvement. For example, a common owner builds a garage onto a home that is held in equal shares by three common owners. The cost of the garage is $15,000, but the garage increases the value of the property only by $9,000. Therefore, the improving common owner can recover only $3,000 from each of the other common owners because the increase in value is less than the cost of the improvement.

Repairs usually are defined as expenditures for the purposes of keeping property in ordinary and efficient operating condition. Repairs do not add to the value of the property or appreciably prolong the property's life. Improvements, on the other hand, are defined as replacements, alterations, or additions to the property that prolong the life of the property, increase its value, or make it adaptable to a different use.

A common owner may enforce his or her right of contribution against other common owners by way of a lien on the other common owners' interests in the real property. This lien, if not voluntarily paid, can be enforced by a sale of the real property.

As to each common owner's undivided interest in the real property, he or she has a free right without the consent of the other common owners to sell, lease, or mortgage his or her undivided real property interest. A common owner, however, cannot convey a greater interest than he or she owns. A deed executed by a common owner will be treated as conveying only his or her undivided interest in the real property, even though the deed may, on its face, purport to convey the entire real property. A single common owner does not have the power to rent the common property, grant an easement across the property, sell the property, or mortgage the property without the consent of the other common owners. Common owners usually are not considered agents for one another, and one common owner cannot bind the other common owners to an agreement regarding the common property. The debts of a single common owner will bind his or her interest in the property but will not affect the common property. For example, a property is owned in common by Aaron, Bob, and Carol in equal shares. Aaron has substantial debts and judgments attached against him. Aaron's judgments will attach only to his undivided one-third interest in the property and will in no manner affect or attach to Bob's and Carol's interest in the common property. Common owners are, however, 100 percent responsible for injuries to a third person by reason of a dangerous condition on the common property.

Partition

The common owners may divide the common property into separate ownerships. This process is called **partition**. The partition may be by voluntary agreement of the common owners or by court action. The parties can voluntarily agree to a partition by executing an agreement allocating separate tracts to each owner or by exchanging deeds executed by all the common owners. A division by agreement or deed should be accompanied by a survey or plat showing the new agreed-on boundaries. No new consideration is necessary to support a written division.

If the common owners cannot agree on a voluntary division, the law in most states provides the judicial machinery for partitioning real property between common owners or selling it and dividing the proceeds. A suit to partition commonly owned real property can be brought by an owner of an undivided interest in the real property. Some states, however, do not permit a court-ordered partition for owners of a joint tenancy with survivorship. The defendants to the petition are each of the other people who own an interest in the real property. Holders of mortgages or other debt on the real property usually are joined in the partition. Notice of the partition normally is given personally to each owner.

The court usually divides the real property into parcels with a market value equivalent to each owner's undivided interest in the real property. For example, as tenants in common, Aaron owns 25 percent, Bob 25 percent, and Carol 50 percent. The court, on partition, will divide the property into parcels, of which Aaron's parcel will be equivalent to 25 percent of the value of all parcels, Bob's parcel will be equivalent to 25 percent of the value of all parcels, and Carol's parcel will be equivalent to 50 percent of the value of all parcels. The court usually has the authority to hire surveyors to describe the parcels and appraisers to establish values of each parcel. If the common owners do not want the real property divided or the real property is not capable of division, such as a single-family home, then the court will order the real property sold and the proceeds divided according to each owner's undivided interest in the real property.

Tenancy by the Entirety

A **tenancy by the entirety** is an estate held by husband and wife as a unit. Tenancy by the entirety is based on an old English common law view that a husband and wife are one person for the purpose of owning property. The married couple were treated as a single person, and the couple, both husband and wife, owned the property as a single unit. In this situation, neither the husband nor wife, so long as they were married, had an interest in the real property that could be sold, leased, or mortgaged. For example, the individual debt of a husband would not attach to the real property owned by the husband and wife as tenants by the entirety. Neither spouse could dispose of any interest in the tenancy by the entirety, and both spouses had to join in any sale, lease, or mortgage of the real property.

Several states recognize tenancy by the entirety (Arkansas, Delaware, Illinois, Indiana, Kentucky, Maryland, Massachusetts, New Hampshire, New Jersey, New York, North Carolina, Oregon, Pennsylvania, Tennessee, Vermont, Virginia, and Wisconsin). In a state that recognizes tenancy by the entirety, a conveyance to husband and wife automatically creates a tenancy by the entirety, unless the deed or will provides otherwise. A divorce will convert a tenancy by the entirety to a tenancy in common, with each party owning one-half interest in the real property.

A tenancy by the entirety contains a right of survivorship. On the death of one spouse, the surviving spouse owns the real property as a whole. Owners by the entirety have no individual interest that they can convey so as to break the unities of title and defeat survivorship. Thus, neither spouse can in any manner affect the right of survivorship with the other during their joint lives. For example, a husband and wife own a piece of property as tenancy by the entirety. The husband dies and wills all his property to his daughter by a first marriage. The daughter will not take an interest in the tenancy by the entirety property because the wife will, by the survival feature, own the entire interest in the real property.

Community Property

Tenancy by the entirety, joint tenancy with the right of survivorship, and tenancy in common are all English common law concepts. The rules of **community property**, however, are borrowed from the civil laws of Spain and France and currently are found in the states that were founded by the Spanish or French (Arizona, California,

New York:
A tenancy by the entirety applies to people who are legally married as husband and wife. The property automatically passes to the surviving spouse and there are no estate taxes. Divorce automatically terminates the tenancy by entirety and the parties become tenants in common. Either party can mortgage their interest and creditors can attach the property, but these creditors rights are all subject to the right of survivorship of the other tenant.

New York:
New York does not recognize community property laws.

Idaho, Louisiana, Nevada, New Mexico, Texas, and Washington). The system is entirely statutory and varies from state to state. A few general propositions will give some notion of the differences between the common law and the community property forms of ownership.

The community property system creates a form of common ownership of property by the husband and wife similar to that of a partnership. During marriage, all property individually or jointly acquired by the husband or wife, other than by gift, bequest, devise, or descent, is held by them as a community property. The property may consist of the earnings of both spouses, borrowings, land or buildings purchased by them, or the rents and profits received from these land and buildings.

States that follow community property law have a concept of separate property and community property. Property that is not part of the community property is termed separate property. It consists of all property owned by either spouse before marriage or acquired by one spouse during marriage by gift, inheritance, bequest, or devise. Income from separate property also is separate property in most states. Property acquired during marriage with funds derived from separate property usually will retain the separate property classification. If both community and separate funds are used, the property will be apportioned between the two spouses according to their respective contributions from each classification. For example, a husband and wife purchase a building during marriage. The husband contributes 50 percent of the purchase price from the sale of separate property. The other 50 percent is contributed through the joint earnings of husband and wife. The property will be deemed to be 50 percent separate property belonging to the husband and 50 percent community property, with the husband and wife each owning one-half interest. In other words, the husband will have a 75 percent interest in the new real property and the wife, 25 percent interest.

Property that is deemed to be community property is owned equally by both husband and wife, and neither can convey the whole without the other's consent. On divorce, the property typically is divided equally and is held to be owned by the husband and wife as tenants in common or the real property is partitioned, if partition is possible.

There are presumptions of law that exist in community property states. Property acquired during marriage and owned at the dissolution of marriage is presumed to be community property. When community property and separate property become so commingled as to make it impossible to identify the separate property, a presumption will render the property community property. It is important for husbands and wives in a community property state to keep accurate records of how the property was obtained to overcome presumptions of community property.[1]

One main difference between community property and the English forms of concurrent ownership (tenancy by the entirety, joint tenancy with right of survivorship, and tenancy in common) is that community property is created by operation of law and not by operation of conveyance. A conveyance in a community property state could be to an individual person. If the person is married and the property is community property, however, an unnamed spouse will be deemed to be a one-half owner of the property. For example, Harold and Maude are married. Phillip conveys community property to Harold. The deed from Phillip is to Harold only. Because the proper-

---

[1] Richard H. Chused, *A Modern Approach to Property* (New York: Matthew Bender & Co., 1985), 223, 225, 316–17, 330–36. Copyright 1985 by Matthew Bender & Co., Inc. Reprinted by permission of Matthew Bender & Co. and Richard H. Chused.

ty is community property, Maude will own one-half interest in the property, even though Maude is not mentioned in the deed.

Community Property and Prenuptial Agreements

Although not a romantic idea, some husbands and wives in both community property states and non–community property states may enter into agreements before marriage concerning the ownership of real property by the married couple or by the individual spouses. In community property states, the spouses may enter into an agreement that will set forth in detail what property is deemed to be separate property owned by the individual spouses and what property is deemed to be community property. This type of agreement resolves disputes of property ownership at the time of divorce or on sale of the property. A sample community separate property agreement is included at the end of this chapter (see Exhibit 2–1).

Some married couples in non–community property states may enter into **prenuptial agreements** regarding the division and ownership of property in the event of separation or divorce. It is common under these agreements for one spouse to renounce, waive, or give up claims to property owned by the other spouse. A form of prenuptial agreement is included at the end of this chapter (see Exhibit 2–2).

Dower and Curtesy

A **dower** is an interest in real property of the husband that the law in some states gives to the widow to provide the widow with a means of support after the husband's death. A dower interest is either a life estate or a fee simple interest and some undivided fraction (usually one-third or one-quarter) of the real property that the husband owned during the marriage. The requirements for a dower interest are (a) a valid marriage, (b) the husband owned the real property during the marriage, and (c) the husband dies before the wife.

Although the dower right does not become a present interest until the husband dies, it is created at the time of the marriage. It is necessary in a state that recognizes dower that all conveyances of property owned by the husband be consented to by the wife to release the dower interest in the conveyed property.

Many states provide to a husband a right similar to dower in the wife's property. This right is called **curtesy**. The requirements for a curtesy interest are (a) a valid marriage, (b) the wife owned real property during the marriage, and (c) the wife dies before the husband.

Dower and curtesy rights have been substantially altered or abolished in many states. It is necessary in dealing with dower or curtesy to check a particular state's law before proceeding.

Elective Share

Many states in which dower exists give to the widow at her husband's death the right to elect between her dower and some fee simple ownership share of property owned by her husband. Depending on the state, this fee simple ownership is either one-fourth or one-third interest in the property owned by the husband. The widow's share in some states (e.g., Alaska, Colorado, Connecticut, Georgia, Mississippi, New York, North Dakota, Oklahoma, Oregon, South Dakota, and Wyoming) may be limited to property that the husband owned at his death, which would mean that the widow would have no claim on property conveyed by the husband during his lifetime without her signature.

New York:
New York has abolished dower and curtesy for couples who were married after 9/1/30. Dower is a life estate that the surviving wife has in one-third of her husband's property and curtesy is the life estate a husband received in his wife's real estate. These are both abolished and instead a surviving spouse is given a "right of election" against the will of the deceased spouse.

New York:
In New York a child can be disinherited, but a spouse can not disinherit the other spouse. Since 1930 the spouse in New York has a right to "elect" against the will of their deceased spouse if they are domiciliaries of New York. Under NY EPTL sect. 5–1.1A the right of election is the greater of $50,000 or 1/3 of decedent's net estate.

In other states (e.g., Florida, Indiana, Iowa, Kansas, Maine, Maryland, Minnesota, Missouri, Nebraska, Pennsylvania, and Utah), the widow receives an ownership share in lieu of dower in all property owned during the lifetime of the husband. In these states, the wife's signature is necessary on any deed, mortgage, or contract of sale given by the husband.

Most states also provide for the husband a similar **elective share** in property owned by the wife.

Practice Note: Any time a transaction, such as a lease, sale, or loan, involves all the common real property, it will be necessary for each and every common owner of the property to sign all the legal documents involved. If the transaction involves property in a community property state or in a state that recognizes dower and curtesy, it is necessary for both the owner of the property and the owner's spouse to sign all deeds, leases, sales, mortgages, contracts, or other legal documents involving the property. The safest approach is to treat all real property owned by a married person in a community property state as community property and to require both the husband and the wife to execute all the legal documents. A table summarizing the various types of co-ownerships and the rights of each individual co-owner under each co-ownership is set forth as Exhibit 2–3 at the end of this chapter.

AGREEMENTS OF COTENANCY

Real property often is co-owned for investment or commercial purposes. Partners join together to build shopping centers, office buildings, and apartments. Groups of investors become co-owners of raw land for speculation or investment. When real property is co-owned for investment, the general rules of co-ownership discussed earlier in this chapter may not be totally appropriate for the investors' needs and purposes. Most states will permit the general rules to be altered and changed by contract among the co-owners. These agreements or contracts are called cotenancy or co-ownership agreements. The following checklist with examples and references to the discussions in this chapter may be used as a guide to the preparation of cotenancy agreements.

◗ CHECKLIST

Agreement of Cotenancy

❑ 1. *The names of addresses of the owners.* The names should be the same as they appear on the deed of ownership.

EXAMPLE 2–1

This Agreement of Cotenancy by and between John P. Ferris, an individual residing at 1616 Tupelo Avenue, Concord, Florida, Marie Bryant, an individual residing at 1340 Virginia Drive, Ellisville, Missouri, and Susan A. Roberts, an individual residing at 640 Clairmont Avenue, St. Petersburg, Florida (hereinafter referred to individually or collectively as "Cotenants").

❑ 2. *Recitals.* A brief history of the relationship of the cotenants may be stated to explain the agreement. Recitals usually are inserted at the beginning of the agreement. Recitals further serve to state the intent of the cotenancy and may explain some of the purposes and objectives of the cotenancy agreement.

EXAMPLE 2-2

WITNESSETH:

Whereas, each of the parties hereto owns an equal, undivided interest in and to certain real property (hereinafter called the "Property") located in Baker County, Florida, a description of which is attached hereto as Exhibit "A" and made a part hereof; and

Whereas, for the mutual convenience and protection of the parties it is desirable that they enter into an agreement setting forth the terms and conditions upon which they will hold, manage, and dispose of their undivided interest in the Property;

Now, Therefore, the parties hereto do hereby agree as follows:

❑ 3. *Term of the agreement*. A cotenancy agreement may be formed for a definite term and may be subject to termination by mutual agreement.

EXAMPLE 2-3

This Agreement shall be effective and shall continue in full force and effect until July 5, 2013, or until terminated by agreement of all the Cotenants hereto, whichever is sooner.

❑ 4. *Not a partnership*. Co-ownership of real property does not in and of itself make the owners partners for one another. Partners in a partnership are responsible for each of the partners' activities in connection with the partnership and may be fully responsible for all partnership liabilities and debts. Most co-owners of real property do not want to assume or create partnership liability on the part of each of the owners. Therefore, it is not unusual for a cotenancy agreement to clearly state that the intent of the agreement is not to create a partnership.

EXAMPLE 2-4

The Cotenants do not intend by this agreement to create a partnership or a joint venture, but merely to set forth the terms upon which each cotenant shall hold, manage, and dispose of his or her undivided interest in the Property. No cotenant hereto is authorized to act as agent for any other cotenant hereto, to act on behalf of any other cotenant hereto, to do any act which will be binding on any other cotenant hereto, or to incur any expenditures with respect to the Property, except as specifically set forth herein.

❑ 5. *Managing cotenant*. Co-ownership of real property usually requires that all the owners consent to any activity that affects the real property as a whole. This unanimous consent may not be practical in all circumstances, and it is not unusual for cotenancy agreements to appoint a managing owner who has the authority to act within limited parameters without the consent of the other owners. The consent of the other owners has been indirectly given by the appointment of the managing owner in the cotenancy agreement.

EXAMPLE 2–5

Marie Bryant hereby agrees to accept and discharge her responsibility as Property manager. At any time hereafter, Cotenants owning an interest in the Property totalling 50 percent or more of all interest in the Property shall have the right and authority to revoke such designation and designate a new Property manager.

Property manager is authorized to pay ad valorem taxes on the Property and to pay principal and interest on indebtedness encumbering the Property; she is authorized to incur only such other expenditures as may be approved from time to time by all the Cotenants.

The Property manager shall keep just and true books of account with respect to the Property. The books shall be maintained at the offices of the Property manager, or such other place as the Cotenants shall agree, and each Cotenant shall at all reasonable times have access to such books. The books shall be kept on the basis of a calendar year using the cash method of accounting and shall be closed and balanced at the end of each year. An accounting of all items, receipts, income, profits, costs, expenses, and losses arising out of or resulting from the ownership of the Property shall be made by the Property manager annually as of December 31 of each year, and also upon the death of any Cotenant hereto, and also upon termination of this agreement. A copy of each statement shall be delivered by the Property manager to each tenant hereto.

❑ 6. *Banking arrangements*. Bank accounts and other banking arrangements usually are stated in the agreement, including the people who are authorized to sign checks and to conduct banking transactions on behalf of the owners.

EXAMPLE 2–6

There shall be deposited in a checking account with First National Bank of Baker, Florida, all amounts deposited with the Property manager by the Cotenants hereto as hereinafter provided. All rentals and income from the Property and amounts deposited with the Property manager by the Cotenants hereto shall be received, held, and disbursed by the Property manager as a trust fund to be applied only for the purposes herein specified. Withdrawals of such trust funds shall be made in said account only for the purpose of making payments herein authorized and only by the Property manager.

❑ 7. *Owners' cash contributions and remedies for failure to make contributions*. Most cotenancies of property for investment require from time to time cash contributions from the various owners. A cotenancy agreement usually will outline the procedures and requirements for cash contributions of the various owners as well as the penalties for an owner's refusal or failure to make a required cash contribution.

EXAMPLE 2–7

(a) As monies are required from time to time to make payments as authorized herein, Property manager shall cause the monies to be withdrawn from said bank account and used to make such payments. In the event the trust fund shall be insufficient to make such payment, the Cotenants hereto shall, within thirty (30) days after written notice given by the Property manager, deposit with the Property manager in proportion to their respective interest in the Property, the funds required to make the payments.

(b) If any Cotenant should fail to so deposit his or her share of such funds with the Property manager within the time required, then any one or more of the other Cotenants hereto may advance such funds, and the amounts so advanced shall be a loan from the Cotenant or Cotenants advancing such funds to the Cotenant so defaulting in his or her obligation hereunder. Such loan shall bear interest at the rate of 10 percent per annum from the day so advanced until paid. If such loan, together with interest thereon, has not been paid within thirty (30) days from the date of such advancement, then the Cotenant or Cotenants so advancing said funds shall have the option to purchase from the defaulting Cotenant the interest of the defaulting Cotenant in the Property as follows:

(i) the purchase price of such interest in the Property shall be an amount equal to one-half (1/2) of the total of all amounts actually paid by such defaulting Cotenant for his or her interest in the Property, consisting of the initial payment made by such Cotenant at the time this agreement is executed, plus all amounts actually deposited with the Property manager under provisions of subparagraph (a) of this paragraph prior to the time such option is exercised; and

(ii) such purchase price shall be paid by cancelling the indebtedness of the defaulting Cotenant under subparagraph (b), with the balance, if any, payable in cash at closing. If such indebtedness exceeds the purchase price, the balance of such indebtedness shall be paid by the defaulting Cotenant at closing; and

(iii) said option to purchase may be exercised by giving notice in writing at any time within sixty (60) days after the date of said advancement, said notice stating that said option is hereby exercised, specifying the place, in the City of Baker, State of Florida, and a time when such purchase shall be closed. Said notice shall be signed by the Cotenant or Cotenants sending the same, shall be sent by United States registered or certified mail, postage prepaid, addressed to the last known address of such defaulting Cotenant. The date of such notice shall be the date that same is deposited in the mail. The closing of said purchase and sale shall be within thirty (30) days after the date of such notice at the time and place specified in the notice.

(c) Each Cotenant hereto hereby constitutes and appoints each other Cotenant hereto as his or her agent and attorney-in-fact for the purposes of executing and delivering any and all documents necessary to convey his or her interest in the Property pursuant to the provisions of this paragraph, and any conveyance so made shall fully divest the Cotenant whose interest is so conveyed of all right, title, or equity in or to the Property, and his or her interest therein. The power of attorney herein granted, being coupled with an interest, is irrevocable and shall not be revoked by the death or dissolution of any Cotenant. Each Cotenant hereto hereby releases the Cotenant who conveys any interest in the Property provided in this paragraph from any interest in the Property provided in this paragraph from any and all claims or liabilities for so conveying such interest.

(d) Time is of the essence with respect to this paragraph.

❏ 8. *Allocation of income and profits.* The cotenancy agreement will allocate the income and profits among the various owners.

EXAMPLE 2–8

All receipts and income arising out of or resulting from the ownership, leasing, and sale of the Property shall belong to the Cotenants hereto in proportion to his or her respective interest in the property.

❑ 9. *Sale of the Property as a whole.* Because all owners must consent to the sale of the co-owned Property as a whole, most cotenancy agreements establish a procedure for obtaining such consent.

EXAMPLE 2-9

The Cotenants hereto agree that they shall hold the Property for investment. The Property shall not be developed, or any improvements constructed thereon, except with the unanimous consent of the Cotenants. If Cotenants owning interests in the Property totalling 50 percent or more of all interests in the Property shall notify the Property manager in writing that they have received a written offer to purchase part or all of the Property and that they desire to accept the same, and shall enclose a copy of such offer to the Property manager with such notice, then all Cotenants shall be obligated to sell the Property (or the portion thereof covered by such offer) to the purchaser making such offer and for the price and on the terms and conditions set forth in the offer. Each Cotenant hereby specifically covenants that he or she will execute and deliver to the purchaser making such offer a general warranty deed conveying the interest of the Cotenant in the Property to the purchaser. Notwithstanding the foregoing, no Cotenant hereto shall be obligated to sell his or her interest in the Property pursuant to the provisions of this paragraph, unless such notice to the Property manager was signed by at least two Cotenants.

❑ 10. *Sale of an owner's undivided interest in the property.* A co-owner, as previously discussed, has a right to transfer his or her undivided interest in the property without the consent of the other owners. An unrestricted right to transfer an undivided interest in the common property often is an undesirable feature of co-ownership. Most people join together as co-owners because of a special relationship they have with one another. An owner usually trusts the other owners to do what is best for the entire group. The possibility of having one of these owners sell his or her undivided interest to a stranger is not welcomed. To protect against such an occurrence, most cotenancy agreements provide a procedure to prevent or at least make difficult the sale of an undivided interest in the property to a stranger.

EXAMPLE 2-10

No Cotenant shall have the right to assign, transfer, sell, or in any way dispose of any part of his or her interest in the Property except as herein provided:

(a) Any Cotenant may, at any time or from time to time, transfer all or any part of his or her interest in the Property to any other Cotenant.

(b) If any Cotenant should desire to sell or assign his or her interest in the Property, or any portion thereof, to any person other than another Cotenant, he or she shall first offer to sell such interest to the other Cotenants at a price not to exceed the price at which such Cotenant proposes to sell his or her interest to any prospective purchaser other than a Cotenant, and on the same terms and conditions offered or proposed to be offered to such prospective purchaser. The offeree shall have a period of thirty (30) days from the time such offer is received within which to accept the same. Each of the offeree Cotenants shall be entitled to purchase the interest in the Property so offered to them in the same proportion as his or her interest at the time of such offer bears to the total interest of the several offeree Cotenants; in the event any such offeree declines to purchase the interest which he or she is entitled to purchase, the remaining offerees shall have a period of ten (10) days after the expiration of the thirty (30)-day period specified above within which to accept the offer with respect to the interest so declined, but in no event will time for accepting the offer be extended beyond said ten (10)-day extension.

(c) In the event one or more of the offerees elects to buy the interest so offered for sale during the time specified above, such offeree shall, prior to the expiration of said time, pay to the offeror in cash 10 percent of the down payment required to be made under the terms of the proposed sale, said 10 percent to be earnest money that will be applied against the sales price at the closing or will be forfeited in the event the purchasing party fails to consummate the purchase hereinafter provided. The purchasing party shall thereafter have sixty (60) days from the date of making said 10 percent payment in which to close the purchase.

(d) If any Cotenant should desire to mortgage or pledge his or her interest in the Property, or otherwise to encumber such interest by using the same as security for borrowed funds, then he or she shall give the other Cotenants at least thirty (30) days time in which to provide, upon the same terms and conditions, the funds proposed to be obtained by so encumbering such interest.

(e) Any offer required to be made by this agreement shall be in writing, signed by the offerer, shall be sent by registered or certified mail to each Cotenant. Any acceptance to an offer made hereunder shall be in writing, signed by the offeree, shall be sent by registered or certified mail to the offerer.

(f) If any interest in the Property held by a Cotenant is offered for sale to the other Cotenants or is offered to be encumbered, as provided in the foregoing paragraph, and within the time provided the acceptances received from the offerees combined do not cover the entire amount of such offer, then none of such acceptances shall be valid and the offerer shall have a period of sixty (60) days after the expiration of the time within which an offer hereunder could have been accepted, within which to complete the sale or encumbrance, as the case may be, to any person not a party hereto, on the terms and conditions set forth in such offer. If such sale or encumbrance shall not be completed within said sixty (60)-days period, a new offer must be made to the parties hereto as required by the above paragraphs.

❑ 11. *Remedies for an owner's failure to perform.* A cotenancy agreement usually provides rights and remedies to enforce the performance of an owner's obligations under the agreement.

EXAMPLE 2–11

The Cotenants intend that their obligations under this agreement shall be enforceable by specific performance. The remedies of the Cotenants under this agreement are cumulative and shall not exclude any other remedies to which any Cotenant may be lawfully entitled. The failure of any Cotenant to insist upon strict performance of a covenant hereunder or of any obligation hereunder shall not be a waiver of such Cotenant's right to demand strict compliance therewith in the future.

❑ 12. *Partition.* The general law in most states permits a co-owner the right to have the common property divided or partitioned. Partition of common property owned for investment, however, can work a hardship on the other owners. For example, it is difficult to partition in kind a high-rise office building. Therefore, permitting a co-owner the right to partition would result in the office building being sold and the proceeds partitioned. The sale could have adverse tax consequences for all the co-owners as well as being a sale of a valuable asset against their wishes. The general law in most states permits the right of partition to be waived by co-owners, and most cotenancy agreements do limit or prohibit the right of partition.

EXAMPLE 2-12

The Cotenants hereby agree that no individual Cotenant, or any successor in interest to a Cotenant, shall have the right while this agreement remains in effect to have the Property partitioned, or to file a complaint or institute any procedure in law or in equity to have the Property partitioned, and each Cotenant, on behalf of himself or herself, his or her successors, representatives, heirs, and assigns hereby waives any such right.

☐ 13. *Successors and assigns.* Most cotenancy agreements are not personal to the original owners, but instead affect the co-ownership relationship of the property until termination. Therefore, all terms and provisions should be binding on the original owners and their successors and assigns.

EXAMPLE 2-13

This agreement, each and every provision hereof, shall be binding upon and shall inure to the benefit of the Cotenants, their successors, representatives, heirs, and assigns, and each Cotenant agrees on behalf of himself or herself, his or her successors, representatives, heirs, and assigns to execute any instruments that may be necessary or proper to carry out and execute the purposes and intentions of this agreement, and hereby authorizes and directs his or her successors, representatives, heirs, and assigns to execute any and all such instruments. Each and every successor in interest to any Cotenant, whether such successor acquired an interest in the Property by way of gift, devise, purchase, foreclosure, or by any other method, shall hold such interest subject to all the terms and provisions in this agreement.

☐ 14. *Counterparts.* It is not unusual for co-owners to reside in different parts of the country. It is cumbersome for the single agreement to have all the signatures appear on the same document. Most cotenancy agreements provide that the agreement can be executed in counterparts. Counterpart execution means that different copies of the same document are executed by the different parties. The original signatures of all the owners appear on different copies of the agreement, but all the copies are read as a single document and are enforceable.

EXAMPLE 2-14

This agreement can be executed in several counterparts, each which shall be considered an original, and shall be enforced according to the laws of the State of Florida.

☐ 15. *Signature and witnessing.* Cotenancy agreements are executed by all the owners. It also is common practice to have the signatures witnessed and notarized. The parties may even desire to record the agreement in the public records of the county wherein the property is located.

EXAMPLE 2-15

In Witness Whereof, the Cotenants have hereinto set their hands and seals, and set opposite their signature is the undivided interest in the Property owned by each, as of and effective this _____ day of _____.

Signed, sealed, and
delivered in the
presence of:

_____ (SEAL)
John P. Ferris, 33$^1/_3$ percent

_____
Witness

_____
Notary

Signed, sealed, and
delivered in the
presence of:

_____ (SEAL)
Marie Bryant, 33$^1/_3$ percent

_____
Witness

_____
Notary

Signed, sealed, and
delivered in the
presence of:

_____ (SEAL)
Susan A. Roberts, 33$^1/_3$ percent

_____
Witness

_____
Notary

 E T H I C S :   Unauthorized Practice of Law

You are a legal assistant with a law firm that represents a bank. Your main responsibility is to assist the attorneys of the firm in the closing of real estate loans. Through these activities, you have become good friends with a number of loan officers at the bank. These loan officers often call you directly with questions or comments on the various files you are working on. One afternoon, one of these loan officers calls to inform you that she and her husband are buying a home. They intend to buy the home as joint tenants with the right of survivorship because they heard on a radio talk show that this form of ownership does away with the necessity of having a will and avoids all probate proceedings. She asks that you advise her as to whether she and her husband need a will. You believe that you know the answer to her question and can advise her of the proper way to proceed. Do you give the advice, or do you refer her to one of the attorneys in the firm? What is the ethical consideration of your choice?

The practice of law is defined in many states to include conveyancing, preparing legal documents, rendering opinions as to the validity or invalidity of titles to real or personal property, and giving legal advice. Most ethical codes of conduct prohibit a lawyer from aiding a nonlawyer in the unauthorized practice of law. Because legal assistants are not licensed to practice law, the use of a legal assistant in the areas referenced above could result in a breach of ethics on the part of the attorney. A legal assistant, on the other hand, is actively involved in many aspects of the actions referenced above, which constitute the practice of law. This apparent conflict is resolved in most states by permitting the legal assistant to be involved in these activities, provided the lawyer maintains a direct relationship with the client involved, supervises and directs the work delegated to the legal assistant, and assumes complete and ultimate responsibility for the work product produced by the legal assistant. Supervision of the legal assistant's work by the attorney must be direct and constant to avoid any charges of aiding the unauthorized practice of law. Therefore, although it may be improper in many states for a legal assistant to actually close a real estate transaction without the assistance or supervision of an attorney, it is not improper for the legal assistant to prepare the closing documents and to arrange for other aspects of the closing, provided the legal assistant's work is closely supervised by the attorney.

The legal assistant in this example should refer the loan officer to an attorney at the firm for an answer to the question regarding the will. The answer involves the giving of legal advice which , if given by the legal assistant, would constitute an unauthorized practice of law.

SUMMARY

Real property may be owned by a single owner or by a group of owners. The ownership of real property by more than one owner creates a number of legal issues concerning the use, possession, and responsibility of the property among the co-owners as well as a number of legal issues involving the sale, mortgage, or lease of the real property to a person or party outside the ownership group. A legal assistant who is working on a transaction involving real property owned by more than one owner must be able to identify what form of co-ownership exists in regard to the property and must understand how that form of co-ownership will affect the transaction.

KEY TERMS

Community property
Contribution
Curtesy
Dower

Elective share
Joint tenancy with right of
   survivorship
Partition

Prenuptial agreement
Tenancy by the entirety
Tenancy in common

REVIEW QUESTIONS

1. What are the four unities required for a joint tenancy with right of survivorship?

2. What is the right of contribution, and why is it important to a co-owner of real property?

3. How is a tenancy in common different than a joint tenancy with right of survivorship?

4. What is the difference between a tenancy by the entirety and community property?

5. Explain the process of partition as it relates to the co-ownership of real property.

6. What property is considered to be separately owned property in a community property state?

7. What is an agreement of cotenancy, and when would it be used?

8. What is dower?

9. Explain the difference between the right of survivorship in a joint tenancy with right of survivorship and in a tenancy by the entirety.

10. What are the advantages of a prenuptial agreement and a community/separate property agreement?

CASE PROBLEMS

1. Aaron conveys by deed a parcel of real property to John, Jane, and Susan as joint tenants with right of survivorship. John, during the lifetime of all the joint owners, transfers his interest in the property to Carol. After John's transfer to Carol, Jane dies and wills her interest in the property to Barbara. After Jane's death, Susan dies and wills her interest in the property to Stewart. Who are the owners of the property, and in what proportion?

2. You are reviewing a deed. The deed indicates that the ownership of property has been transferred from Ajax Realty Company to David Farris, Mary Farris, and John Farris. What form of co-ownership do David, Mary, and John own in the real property?

3. You are a legal assistant working with a law firm that is representing a purchaser of a parcel of real property. The purchaser desires to purchase 100 percent of the property and has entered into a contract with Samuel Seller. The title examination of the property reveals that Samuel Seller owns the

property together with Susan Seller and Sarah Seller. What additional precautions or safeguards must you take to protect the purchaser in this transaction?

4. You are a legal assistant in a law firm that represents a creditor who has made a loan to Robert Black. You discover that Robert Black owns a parcel of real property together with his wife, Margo Black. Will the creditor be able to sell Robert Black's interest in the real property for purposes of satisfying the debt? What factors are important in answering this question?

5. You are a legal assistant in a law firm that represents a number of investors who are purchasing a shopping center. The investors intend to own the shopping center as tenants in common and have asked the firm to prepare an agreement of cotenancy. You have been asked to prepare the first draft of the agreement. What information are you going to need from the client to prepare it?

EXHIBIT 2–1
Community
Property Agreement

This community property agreement made _____ , 19_____ , between Henry Husband, of _____ [address], City of _____ , County of _____ , State of _____ , and Wendy Wife of _____ [address], City of _____ , County of _____ , State of _____

This agreement is made in consideration of the contemplated marriage of the parties.

Section One
Intent of Parties

(a) *Setting Forth Property Rights.* The parties have the intent and desire to define and set forth the respective rights of each in the property of the other after their marriage.

(b) *Separate Property.* The parties intend and desire that all property owned respectively by each of them at the time of their marriage, and all property that may be acquired by each of them from any source during their marriage, shall be respectively their separate property, except as otherwise provided in this agreement.

Section Two
Property of Parties

The parties to this agreement own property as follows:

(a) *Henry Husband's Personal Property.* Henry Husband owns personal property described as follows:

Description	Location	Value
_____	_____	$ _____
_____	_____	$ _____
_____	_____	$ _____

(b) *Henry Husband's Real Property.* Henry Husband owns the real property described as follows:

Legal Description	Location	Value
_____	_____	$ _____
_____	_____	$ _____
_____	_____	$ _____

(a) *Wendy Wife's Personal Property.* Wendy Wife owns personal property described as follows:

Description	Location	Value
_____	_____	$ _____
_____	_____	$ _____
_____	_____	$ _____

(b) *Wendy Wife's Real Property.* Wendy Wife owns the real property described as follows:

Legal Description	Location	Value
_____	_____	$ _____
_____	_____	$ _____
_____	_____	$ _____

EXHIBIT 2–1
Community
Property Agreement
(continued)

Section Three
Status of Separate and Community Property

All real and personal property owned by either of the parties at the time of their marriage, and all real and personal property that either may acquire from any source whatsoever during their marriage, shall be their respective separate property, except as otherwise provided, [or if property is to be community property:] All real and personal property, wherever located, now owned or possessed by either of the parties, and all real and personal property that either of them may hereafter acquire from whatever source, _____ (if appropriate, add: with the exception of damages recovered for personal injury) shall be their community property.

Section Four
Management of Community Property

If, at any time during the marriage of the parties, any community property that is subject to the sole management, control, and disposition of either of the parties is mixed or combined with community property that is subject to the sole management, control, and disposition of the other party, the combined property shall be subject to the sole management, control, and disposition of Wendy Wife.

Section Five
Liability for Debts

The debts contracted by each party prior to their marriage are to be paid by the party who shall have contracted the debts, and the property of the other party shall not in any respect be liable for their payments.

Section Six
Execution of Instruments

Each party shall cooperate fully in executing, acknowledging, and delivering any instruments required to accomplish the intent of and to effectuate this agreement.

Section Seven
Effective Date

This agreement shall take effect on the date the marriage contemplated by the parties has been solemnized under the laws of the State of _____.

In witness whereof, the parties have executed and sealed this agreement at the day and year first above written.

_____(SEAL)
Henry Husband
_____(SEAL)
Wendy Wife

EXHIBIT 2-2
Prenuptial Agreement

STATE OF GEORGIA
COUNTY OF FULTON

THIS AGREEMENT, made and entered into by and between _____ (hereinafter referred to as "_____"), presently residing at _____, Georgia, and _____ _____ (hereinafter referred to as "_____"), presently residing at _____, Georgia _____.

WITNESSETH

In anticipation of marriage the parties desire to fix and determine by this Agreement the rights and claims that will accrue to each of them in and to the income and property of the other and his or her estate which property is presently in existence or is hereafter acquired, by reason of their entering into a marital relationship or its subsequent dissolution by annulment, divorce, or death. (Here and hereinafter the term "property" shall include but not be limited to all real, personal, intangible, tangible, and intellectual property.)

The parties are intelligent adults attempting by this Agreement to deal with the realities of their several and joint financial situations before marriage, to define a relationship which preserves and promotes the individual identities of a man and a woman contracting to marry each other for mutual benefit and growth, and to eliminate possible areas of friction.

NOW, THEREFORE, in consideration of the love and affection between the parties, the promises, and of the mutual covenants and conditions herein contained and of the marriage and other good and available consideration, the parties agree as follows:

Dissolution upon Death

1.

In the event that either spouse to this marriage dies during the duration of the marriage, the rights and claims that will accrue to each of them in the estate and property of the other shall be exclusively governed by the terms of the Last Will and Testament of the deceased party. In the event that either spouse to this marriage does not have a valid Last Will and Testament at the time of his or her death, the surviving spouse agrees to take only as much of the estate and property of the deceased spouse as he or she would take under the laws of descent and distribution of the State of Georgia if the deceased spouse had died intestate.

2.

_____ hereby waives and releases unto _____ , her executors, administrators, or assigns, any and all rights to apply for year's support out of her estate (whether testate or intestate) under any statute, now or hereafter in force, of the State of Georgia or of any other state in which she may have property at the time of her death, or in which the parties or either of them may reside.

3.

_____ hereby waives and releases unto _____ , his executors, administrators or assigns, any and all rights to apply for year's support out of his estate (whether testate or intestate) under any statute, now or hereafter in force, of the State of Georgia or of any other state in which he may have property at the time of his death, or in which the parties or either of them may reside.

EXHIBIT 2-2
Prenuptial
Agreement
(continued)

Dissolution on Annulment or Divorce
or Separation of the Parties

4.

(a) Upon dissolution of the marriage by annulment or by a divorce and provided that at the time of such dissolution the parties have been married for a period of not less than five years, _____ agrees to pay _____ the lump sum of $_____ in cash.

The dollar amount of such lump sum payment shall also be adjusted upward or downward in accordance with any change from the date of this Agreement in the Consumer Price Index (the "All Items" index for Urban Consumers—(1967-100)—CPI-U) released by the Bureau of Labor Statistics for the Atlanta area by the Bureau of Labor Statistics, Southeastern Regional Office, Atlanta, Georgia in which _____ is residing.

The above-described lump sum payment shall be payable in monthly installments of $_____ per month on the filing of any divorce action by either party, and any balance shall be paid in full on the granting of the decree of divorce.

The parties agree that the above-described lump sum payment shall constitute full and final payment of any alimony, maintenance, support, property settlement, attorney's fees, or any other claim under the laws of the State of Georgia or any other state in which the parties or either of them may reside for the support or maintenance of _____, and in setting such amount, the parties have contemplated and provided for the effect that time and inflation and other economic factors may have on the value of said amount at the time of payment. In the event _____ does not comply with the provisions of this Agreement, nothing herein is intended to waive _____ right to seek attorneys' fees.

(b) In the event the marriage is dissolved by annulment or divorce within the first five years of marriage, and until the death or remarriage of _____, _____ agrees to pay to _____ the sum of $_____ per month from the date any such action is filed, said payments to continue until _____ obtains full-time employment but in any event for no more than _____ months after the separation of the parties.

(c) Except as provided herein, _____ agrees not tp make any claim and expressly waives her right to make any claim on the then existing or to be acquired estate or property of _____ for alimony, maintenance, support, property settlement, attorneys' fees, or any other claim under the laws of the State of Georgia or any other state in which the parties or either of them may reside for her maintenance and support, temporary or otherwise. In the event _____ does not comply with the provisions of this Agreement, nothing herein is intended to waive _____'s right to seek attorneys' fees.

(d) In the event the parties mutually agree in writing that _____ should give up her anticipated employment, the parties agree to negotiate the provisions of this Agreement. It is the intent of the parties that unless there is mutual agreement in writing that _____ should give up her employment, this Agreement will remain in full force and effect irrespective of whether _____ gives up her career unless the parties voluntarily renegotiate the Agreement.

5.

On dissolution of the marriage by annulment or by a divorce, and during any and all separations of the parties, _____ hereby agrees not to make any claim and expressly

EXHIBIT 2-2
Prenuptial
Agreement
(continued)

waives his right to make any claim on the then existing or to be acquired estate or property of _____ for alimony, maintenance, support, property settlement, attorneys' fees, or any other claim under the laws of the State of Georgia or any other state in which the parties or either of them may reside for his maintenance or support, temporary or otherwise.

6.

Having disclosed all properties and assets presently owned by each of them (a schedule of which is attached hereto as Exhibit A and incorporated by reference and made part of this Agreement) and the income derived therefrom and income from all other sources, the parties agree that during the marriage, in the event the marriage between the parties is dissolved at any time by annulment or by a divorce or in the event the parties become separated:

a. All property belonging to _____ at the commencement of the marriage shall remain the separate property of _____ .

b. All property belonging to _____ at the commencement of the marriage shall remain the separate property of _____ .

c. All property acquired individually by _____ during the marriage shall remain the separate property of _____ .

d. All property acquired individually by _____ during the marriage shall remain the separate property of _____ .

e. All property acquired by _____ individually out of the proceeds or income from property owned by _____ at the commencement of the marriage or acquired individually by _____ during the marriage, or attributable to appreciation in the value of said property, whether the enhancement is due to market conditions or to the services, skills, or efforts of its owner shall remain the separate property of

_____ .

f. All property acquired by _____ individually out of the proceeds or income from property owned by _____ at the commencement of the marriage or acquired individually by _____ during the marriage, or attributable to appreciation in value of said property, whether the enhancement is due to market conditions or to the services, skills, or efforts of its owner shall remain the separate property of

_____ .

g. All individual retirement accounts, HR-10 plans, employer-sponsored profit sharing, pension plans or retirement plans maintained by _____ shall remain the separate property of _____ .

h. All individual retirement accounts, HR-10 plans, employer sponsored profit sharing, pension plans, or retirement plans maintained by _____ shall remain the separate property of _____ .

i. All property hereafter acquired individually by _____ by gift, devise, bequest, or inheritance shall remain the separate property of _____ .

j. All property hereafter acquired individually by _____ by gift, devise, bequest, or inheritance shall remain the separate property of _____ .

7.

Property hereafter acquired jointly by the parties, upon marital dissolution by annulment or divorce or separation of the parties, shall be divided according to the pro rata share of the contribution of each of the parties.

EXHIBIT 2-2
Prenuptial
Agreement
(continued)

8.

In the event there is a dispute involving the reinvestment of the proceeds of the sale or the exchange of previously owned property, property acquired individually during the marriage, or property inherited or received by gift from third persons during the marriage, the challenging party shall have the burden of tracing such assets.

9.

In the event it is alleged that one party loaned the other party money to acquire property individually or jointly with the loaning party, such loan shall be deemed effective only if evidenced by a written instrument executed by both parties, otherwise such loan shall be deemed ineffective and the ownership of such property shall be determined as if no loan had been made.

10.

Notwithstanding any other provision of this Agreement, either party may transfer, convey, devise, or bequeath any property or gift to the other, or nominate the other as executor of his or her estate. In the event any party wishes to convey realty, such conveyance shall be deemed effective, complete, and binding only if accomplished by execution of appropriate written instrument, otherwise such transfer shall be deemed ineffective and the property shall remain the sole and separate property of the allegedly transferring party. Neither party intends by this Agreement to limit or restrict in any way the right to receive any such transfer, conveyance, devise, or bequest from the other, or to act as such executor if so nominated. The transferred property shall become the sole and separate property of the party receiving such property and shall remain in that party's separate estate, free and clear of any claim of the other.

11.

Each party shall be fully and solely responsible for protecting himself or herself from contingencies of disability, retirement, or prolonged illness, and each party shall take whatever steps he or she deems, necessary to protect himself or herself from the economic consequence of such contingencies irrespective of the actions of the other party.

12.

The parties agree to hold each other harmless from and against any and all claims, demands, losses, damages, or other payments, including reasonable attorneys' fees arising out of any existing or after acquired debt or obligation that he or she has or will incur, individually or jointly with any other or others, except that incurred jointly with each other.

13.

Each party shall hold the other party harmless from any and all assessments of any taxes imposed by all local, state, and federal governments on his or her individually owned property or income. The party responsible for any and all deficiencies that may be assessed in connection with any individual or joint income tax returns filed by the parties during the term of the marriage shall bear all costs of the assessment and indemnify the other party for all assessments, expenses, or losses of every kind, character, and description incurred in connection with such an assessment.

14.

If the marriage currently contemplated by the parties does not take place for any reason whatsoever, this Agreement shall be in all respects and for all purposes null and void.

EXHIBIT 2-2
Prenuptial
Agreement
(continued)

15.

Both parties hereby acknowledge that the other party has fully acquainted him or her with his or her means and resources; that he or she has informed him or her in detail of his or her net worth and income (see attached schedule); that they have ascertained and weighed all of the facts, conditions, and circumstances likely to influence their judgment herein; that all matters embodied herein as well as all questions pertinent hereto have been fully and satisfactorily explained to them; that they have given due consideration to such matters and questions; that they clearly understand and consent to all of the provisions hereof; that they have had the benefit of the advice of counsel of their own selection; and that they enter into this Agreement freely, voluntarily, and with full knowledge.

16.

This Agreement constitutes the entire understanding of the parties. There are no representations, warranties, promises, covenants, or undertakings, oral or otherwise, other than those expressly set forth herein.

17.

This Agreement shall inure to the benefit of and shall be binding upon the heirs, executors, and administrators of the parties.

18.

This Agreement shall be governed exclusively by the laws of the State of Georgia.

19.

Except as specifically provided for herein, no modification or waiver of any of the terms shall be valid unless in writing and signed by both of the parties. No waiver of any breach hereof or default hereunder shall be deemed a waiver of a subsequent breach of default of the same or a similar nature.

20.

In the event any of the provisions of this Agreement are deemed to be invalid or unenforceable, the same shall be deemed severable from the remainder of this Agreement and shall not cause the invalidity or unenforceability of the remainder of this Agreement. If such provision shall be deemed invalid due to its scope or breadth, such provision shall be deemed valid to the extent of the scope or breadth permitted by law.

21.

The parties recognize and agree that this Agreement makes no provision for any child or children who may be born to this marriage. Each party recognizes his or her individual responsibility for the support of any such child or children. This Agreement shall not affect the rights of any child or children of this marriage or of either party with respect to custody or other matters related to such child or children.

   IN WITNESS WHEREOF, the parties have hereunto set their hands and affixed their seals this _____ day of _____ , 199___.

Sworn to and subscribed before me this

_____ day of _____ , 19___.   _____ (SEAL)

_____

Witness

_____

Notary Public

Sworn to and subscribed before me this

_____ day of _____ , 19____.

_____

_____ (SEAL)

_____

Witness

_____

Notary Public

Attorney's Certification

The undersigned hereby certifies that she is an attorney at law, duly licensed to practice in the State of Georgia, that she has been employed by _____ , one of the parties to the foregoing Prenuptial Agreement, that she has advised and consulted with _____ with respect to his and _____ rights and has fully explained to him the legal significance of the foregoing Prenuptial Agreement and the effect that it has on his rights otherwise obtaining as a matter of law; that _____, after being fully advised by the undersigned, acknowledged to the undersigned that he fully understood the terms of the foregoing Prenuptial Agreement and the legal effect thereof, and that he had executed the same freely and voluntarily; and that the undersigned has no reason to believe that _____ did not fully understand such terms and effects or that he did not freely and voluntarily execute said Agreement, such execution being in the undersigned's presence.

Dated: _____

Attorney's Certification

The undersigned hereby certifies that he is an attorney at law, duly licensed to practice in the State of Georgia; that he has been employed by _____ , one of the parties to the foregoing Prenuptial Agreement; that he has advised and consulted with _____ with respect to her and _____ rights and has fully explained to her the legal significance of the foregoing Prenuptial Agreement and the effect that it has on her rights otherwise obtaining as a matter of law; that _____ , after being fully advised by the undersigned, acknowledged to the undersigned that she fully understood the terms of the foregoing Prenuptial Agreement and the legal effect thereof, and that she had executed the same freely and voluntarily; and that the undersigned has no reason to believe that _____ did not fully understand such terms and effects or that she did not freely and voluntarily execute said Agreement, such execution being in the undersigned's presence.

Dated: _____

EXHIBIT 2-2
Prenuptial
Agreement
(continued)

Exhibit 2–3   Co-ownership

FORM OF CO-OWNERSHIP	JOINT TENANCY WITH SURVIVORSHIP	TENANCY IN COMMON	TENANCY BY ENTIRETY	COMMUNITY PROPERTY
Creation	By conveyance • Deed • Will	By conveyance • Deed • Will	By conveyance • Deed • Will	Operation of law
Identity of owner	Two or more persons indentified in conveyance	Two or more persons identified in conveyance	Husband and wife identified in conveyance	Husband and wife by operation of law
Quantity of interest in property	Equal shares	Shares as set forth in conveyance may not be equal	Husband and wife as a unit own property, individuals own nothing	Equal shares
Nature of interest	Undivided	Undivided	Undivided	Undivided
Responsibility for expenses of ownership (taxes, mortgages, and insurance)	Equal responsibility	Responsibility according to percentage of ownership	Equal responsibility	Equal responsibility
Right of survivorship	Yes	No	Yes	No
Right of partition	Yes in some states; no in some states	Yes	No, except in event of divorce	No, except in event of divorce
Right to sell co-owner interest in common property	Yes	Yes	No	No
Debts of individual co-owner attach to co-owners interest in property	Yes	Yes	No	Yes
Debts of individual co-owner attach to common property as a whole	No	No	No	No

Condominiums and Cooperatives

Living together alone in our space.

—Anonymous

OBJECTIVES

After reading this chapter, you will be able to:

- Understand the condominium form of property ownership
- Understand the cooperative form of property ownership
- Understand the time-sharing form of property ownership
- Understand the difference between condominium and cooperative form of ownership
- Understand the requirements for condominium declarations and condominium plats
- Understand the content of the legal documents required to create a condominium

GLOSSARY

Assessment   Sum of money owed by a condominium owner for monthly upkeep of the common areas of the condominium.

Common areas   Common areas or common elements of a condominium is that portion of the condominium property that is owned in common by all the owners of units in the condominium.

Condominium   Form of property ownership in which the owner owns an individual unit in a multiunit building and is a tenant in common with other owners of units in the building in certain common areas.

Condominium association   Governing body of a condominium, the members of which are owners of condominium units. The condominium association usually is in the form of a nonprofit corporation.

Condominium declaration   Legal document required by state condominium acts to create a condominium.

Condominium plat   Plat of survey of condominium property required by state condominium acts. The plat must show in sufficient detail the location and dimensions of the real property, as well as all condominium units located on the real property.

Cooperative   Form of ownership of real property in which a corporation owns a multiunit building and leases living space in the building to the shareholders of the corporation.

Limited common area   Common area of a condominium that is limited in use to one or more condominium unit owners.

Rescission   Right to terminate a contract.

Time-share   Form of ownership of real property in which an owner owns the property for a short period, usually one or two weeks out of each year. Time-share ownership typically is used for vacation or recreational property.

New York:
For a discussion of Condominiums and Cooperatives in New York, see Appendix.

America's first 200 years of growth and settlement as a nation depended, to a large extent, on an abundance of cheap land. Early landowners were able to obtain individual tracts of land on which to construct homes and other improvements. Early development of the country was horizontal, across the surface of the land. Early cities consisted of rows of individually owned homes and businesses. Multifamily housing in the early cities was rental housing with a building being owned by a single landowner and the various apartments or living spaces being leased to tenants. During the late 19th century land, especially that in urban areas, became more expensive, and landowners, including residential landowners, began to build vertically, on the surface of the land. These early "high-rise" apartments were also under single ownership with the living spaces leased to tenants. As the wealth of the tenants grew and these high-rise apartments became more desirable, a new concept of ownership began to develop—the condominium or cooperative. Condominium and cooperative ownership have become popular, and condominiums and cooperatives exist in many states. Some are in high-rise or multistory buildings and some are in low-rise or cluster-detached housing. The condominium and cooperative concept extends beyond residential use. Condominium office buildings are commonplace in many areas.

It is essential, to assist in the representation of a client who is buying, selling, or making a loan on a condominium or cooperative, that a legal assistant understand the basic rules and concepts of condominium and cooperative property ownership.

CONDOMINIUM

New York:
A condominium owner receives a deed conveying a fee simple absolute for the unit. As a fee owner they have a right to mortgage the premises or leave it to their heirs. In addition the owner is bound by the bylaws of the homeowners association to which they must belong. The owner must pay common charges to cover the maintenance, management, and insurance for the common areas. The owners pay their own real estate taxes.

The word *condominium* is a combination of two Latin words: *con*, meaning one or more persons, and *dominium*, meaning control over an object or property. Similar to its name, the **condominium** concept of property ownership is a combination of individual and joint ownership. A condominium owner individually owns his or her unit, which usually is located in a multiunit building. In addition, together with the other individual condominium owners, he or she has joint ownership and control over the common property, sometimes referred to as the **common areas** or common elements of the condominium. The common areas usually consist of exterior walls of buildings, stairwells, elevators, walks, yards, roofs, entryways, and so on. In many residential condominiums, the common areas may include recreational areas, swimming pools, and, in some country club settings, even a golf course. The common areas are used by all the condominium owners and are jointly owned and maintained by the condominium owners.

The laws that govern and define condominium ownership are both statutory and contractual. All states have passed laws commonly referred to as condominium acts that set forth a comprehensive legal framework for the creation and governance of condominium ownership. In addition to the state regulation, condominium developers prepare a comprehensive set of contractual covenants, known as a **condominium declaration**, that will govern the ownership and control the governance of the condominium. The declaration is recorded, and each condominium owner is bound by its terms.

Birth of a Condominium

A developer can create a condominium either by purchasing an apartment building and converting it into a condominium or by developing and constructing a new condominium. In either situation, the developer is required by state law to prepare for each condominium a condominium declaration that sets forth the rules and regulations of the condominium, a **plat** that shows the location of all individual units as well as the common areas and to create a condominium homeowners' association that will govern the condominium property on final completion and sale of the units by the developer. The declaration, plat, and homeowners' association must be in place before the project can be considered a condominium and before individual units can be sold.

The declaration, sometimes called master deed or master lease, is the most important legal document in the creation of a condominium. It is prepared and signed by the condominium developer and recorded in the county where the condominium is located. The declaration describes and defines the boundaries of the units and the common areas or elements, creates or provides for the creation of the condominium government, and imposes restrictive covenants on the owners that regulate the use of the units and common areas. Most states' condominium acts require that the declaration contain certain express provisions for the condominium to be properly created. A unit owner may find it difficult to resell or obtain financing on a unit when the declaration is defective and does not comply with state law. An example of state condominium act requirements for the contents of a declaration is shown in Exhibit 3–1 at the end of this chapter.

In general, a condominium declaration contains the following information:

1. Name of the condominium, which in many states is required to contain the word *condominium* or to be followed by the words *a condominium*

2. Legal description of the entire property being submitted to the condominium form of ownership

3. Description or delineation of the boundaries of the individual condominium units, including horizontal, upper, lower, vertical, and lateral boundaries

4. Description or delineation of all common areas, including a designation of limited common areas. A **limited common area** is a common area that, by the declaration, is limited in use to one or more of the condominium owners. For example, an enclosed backyard or patio in a low-rise condominium project may be a limited common area assigned for use only to the property owner whose unit adjoins the patio or enclosed yard. Although the use of the limited common area is assigned only to a particular unit owner, the limited common areas are owned in common by all the owners in the condominium project

5. Creation of a governing body for the condominium or the requirement that one be created. The governing body usually is a nonprofit corporation in which each owner is entitled to one vote. These corporations often are referred to as the condominium association

6. Limitations or restrictions on the power of the condominium

7. Allocation of a share of liability for common area expenses to each condominium unit

8. Statement of all restrictive covenants in the general use of the units and common areas

9. Description of how the condominium can be expanded. It is not unusual for some developers to do phase condominiums. In a phase condominium, the developer may develop only a portion of the condominium to test the market. If the condominium sells, the developer will then add new units over a period of time. The declaration must spell out in detail how this phase of additional units will be accomplished

10. Statement of how the condominium form of ownership can be terminated

An example of a condominium declaration appears as Exhibit 3–2 at the end of this chapter.

A condominium developer, in addition to preparing and recording a declaration, must prepare and record a plat of the condominium improvements. The plat must show in sufficient detail the location and dimensions of the submitted property; the location and dimensions of all structural improvements located on any portion of the submitted property; the intended location and dimensions of all contemplated structural improvements committed to be provided by the declaration; and the location and dimensions of all easements appurtenant to the submitted property or otherwise submitted to the condominium form of ownership. An example of a state condominium act's requirements for a condominium plat appears as Exhibit 3–3 at the end of this chapter.

Articles and Bylaws of a Condominium Association

The internal operations of a condominium are governed by a homeowners' association or **condominium association**. The association takes the legal form of a nonprofit corporation, with each owner of a unit being entitled to a vote in the affairs of the association.

A condominium association, like any other corporation, is governed by two legal documents: the articles of incorporation and bylaws. The articles of incorporation form the basic corporate constitution or charter and are filed with the secretary of state's office in the state where the association is located. The articles of incorporation contain the following information:

- Name of the association
- Purpose of the association
- Period of the duration for the corporation
- Initial directors of the corporation
- Registered agent and registered office of the corporation. The registered agent is the person on whom service of process can be served for the corporation, and the registered office is the address for the registered agent
- Criteria for becoming an owner or member of the association and the name of the incorporator. The incorporator usually is the developer or an attorney for the developer

An example of articles of incorporation for a condominium association is shown as Exhibit 3–4 at the end of this chapter.

The bylaws of a condominium association are the rules and regulations by which the association is governed. Bylaws contain more detail about the association than do the articles of incorporation. The bylaws provide for the following:

- Selection of the board of directors
- How meetings are to be held and conducted
- How officers are to be appointed or elected
- How votes are to be counted and the governance of the corporation, whether resolutions must be passed by a simple majority or a three-fourths or two-thirds majority vote
- Regulation of the common elements
- Rights and responsibilities of unit owners
- Assessment and collection of monthly charges and other relevant matters

Bylaws usually are not required to be recorded or filed with a state agency. They must, however, be provided to a purchaser of a unit before the time of purchase. An example of condominium bylaws are set forth as Exhibit 3–5 at the end of this chapter.

A developer usually retains control of the condominium association until such time as either all the units have been sold to purchasers or a percentage of units have been sold. Most condominium associations that provide for this limited period of developer control have two levels of membership in the association: the owner's level of membership, with one vote for each unit owned, and the developer's voting rights, which usually consist of all the voting rights as long as the developer is a member. The developer usually turns over control to the unit owners on the sale of a set number of units, typically not less than 75 percent.

The costs and expenses of operating a condominium are borne by the condominium owners. Expenses include taxes on the individual units, taxes on the common elements, maintenance and repair of the common elements, and insurance.

Taxes on the individual units are paid by the individual unit owners. The units can be returned to the tax authorities for taxes the same as a single-family home or other property. Tax on the common elements, however, is an expense of the association and a joint obligation of all the owners. The repair and maintenance of the common area are also joint responsibilities and expenses of the owners. In addition, most condominium declarations and even some condominium acts require that the insurance on both the units and the common area be under one master policy and that such insurance be the expense of the condominium association and, indirectly, the joint expense of all the owners.

The joint responsibility for paying common area expenses such as taxes, maintenance, and insurance is handled by the use of an **assessment** against each owner's unit to cover that unit owner's share of the common area expenses.

The amount of the assessment is determined by the condominium association. The determination is made based on an operating budget for the year's expenses in regard to the common areas and allocation of this operating budget to the number of units in the association. If a condominium is composed of different sized units, the owner of a larger unit may be allocated a greater portion of the common area expense assessment than the owner of a smaller unit. The method for imposing assessments is determined both by state law and by condominium declaration.

If a common area assessment is not voluntarily paid by a unit owner, the association may have a lien against the unit for unpaid assessments. This lien, like any other lien, can be enforced by having the unit sold for the purpose of paying the lien. The association, in addition to imposing the lien, can sue an owner directly for nonpayment of delinquent assessments. It has been held in many states that an owner's obligation to pay is unconditional. This means that the owner is obligated to pay the assessment even if the association is not providing all the services required by the association. The policy behind this rule is explained in *Forest Villas Condominium Assoc. v. Camerio*, which follows.

CASE

Forest Villas Condominium Association, Inc. v. Camerio, et al.
422 S.E.2d 884 (Ga.App. 1992)

BEASLEY, Judge.

The central issue is the construction of OCGA § 44-3-80(d), part of the Georgia Condominium Act.

Forest Villas Condominium Association, Inc., sued Camerio and Elliot, owners of 23 out of the 94 units in the Association, to recover an arrearage of condominium fees. In addition to the accrued $28,060, the Association sought interest on the arrearage and the remaining assessments for the year.

Defendants denied the allegations of the complaint, alleged a number of affirmative defenses, and filed a counterclaim which asserted that the Association failed to honor its obligations to perform maintenance and make repairs on the units owned by defendants; the Association had discriminated against defendants and their units because they were rental units as opposed to owner-occupied; and the Association had mismanaged the funds paid to it by defendants. Defendants also alleged that due to the Association's failure to make certain repairs they had been forced to pay for those repairs themselves. They sought an accounting of the monies handled by the Association; a reimbursement by the Association for all expenses they incurred due to the association's breach of duty; a declaration that certain unspecified actions of the Association in contravention of Georgia law and the condominium declaration, bylaws, and rules be declared null and void; attorney fees; and the enjoining of the Association from expending its funds to install certain water meters.

The Association moved for summary judgment, contending that it was entitled to recover the fees because OCGA § 44-3-80(d) did not permit a unit owner any exemption from liability for assessments. It also urged that defendants' counterclaim sounded in equity and thus was beyond the authority of the state court. The Association also filed a motion in limine to preclude defendants from introducing any evidence relating to their counterclaim for the same reason.

The trial court denied the Association's motion for summary judgment altogether, concluding that there were genuine issues of material fact and that "the word 'exempt' found in OCGA § 44-3-80(d) does not mean that the Defendants in this case could never have any justification for withholding the assessments charged to them." The court denied the motion in limine, holding that the counterclaim defenses could be presented before it.

1. The first question is whether the court correctly construed OCGA § 44-3-80(d), contrary to the Association's contention that it misinterpreted plain and unambiguous language.

[1] The statutory subsection provides: "No unit owner other than the association shall be exempted from any liability for any assessment under this Code section or under any condominium instrument for any reason whatsoever, including, without limitation, abandonment, nonuse, or waiver of the use or enjoyment of his unit or any part of the common elements."

[2] The language is plain and susceptible of only one interpretation insofar as it relates to the defenses. See *Lunda Constr. Co. v. Clayton County*, 201 Ga.App. 106, 107, 410 S.E.2d 446 (1991). There is no legal justification for a condominium owner to fail to pay valid condominium assessments. This reflects a clear choice by the legislature that the owner's obligation to pay assessments be absolute and a condominium unit owner involved in a dispute with the condominium Association about its services and operations may not exert leverage in that controversy by withholding payment but must seek other remedy. The obligation to pay the assessment is independent of the Association's obligations to provide services. This is necessary because the communal business of the condominium Association for the benefit in common of all condominium owners continues unabated during the pendency of any such individual dispute. The public policy expressed in the statute assures that fulfillment of obligations and the functioning of a condominium Association as a whole not be jeopardized or compromised by individual disputes, which may or may not be meritorious. See *Rivers Edge Condo. Assn. v. Rere*, 390 Pa.Super. 196, 568 A.2d 261 (1990). See also *Newport West Condo. Assn. v. Veniar*, 134 Mich.App. 1, 350 N.W.2d 818 (1984).

The state court misinterpreted OCGA § 44-3-80(d) insofar as the defenses or "exemptions" urged by defendants are concerned. They do not assert, nor is there any evidence, that the condominium instruments were anything other than lawful, see OCGA § 44-3-76, or that the subject assessments were made other than in compliance with the condominium instruments and law. See OCGA §§ 44-3-71(5) and 44-3-76. Whether such would be a defense permitted under OCGA § 44-3-80(d) in a suit for unpaid fees is not before us. Cf. *San Antonio etc. Homeowners Assn. v. Miller*, 761 S.W.2d 460 (Tex.App.1988). Plaintiff Association was entitled to summary judgment on defendants' liability for unpaid assessments.

Unpaid assessments are also imposed on a purchaser of a unit if the assessments are unpaid at the time of purchase. It is prudent, when representing a condominium purchaser, to inquire of the association if assessments are unpaid on the unit being purchased. These unpaid assessments often are not in the form of a lien that is recorded, and therefore, the only method of determining if unpaid assessments exist is to inquire of the association.

Condominium owners also have a joint and several liability for damage or harm caused to person or property in connection with the common areas. This liability is covered by liability insurance that insures both the individual unit owners and the association. In some states, an owner's liability for injury or harm which takes place on the common areas may be limited to the owner's pro rata share of the common area. For example, if an owner has a 2 percent share of the common areas and there is liability caused by negligence, such as a slip and fall at the swimming pool, then this owner's liability for the harm would be limited to 2 percent.

Insurance covering casualty of the condominium improvements is a master policy that insures all unit owners and the condominium association. The insurance covers both the individual units and the common areas. State law and condominium declarations usually require that insurance money be used for restoration of the condominium improvements unless a specified number of homeowners—usually not less than 75 percent—agree not to restore. In the event restoration does not take place, the insurance proceeds would be paid to the owners according to their interest in the condominium. In the event insurance proceeds are insufficient to totally repair or restore the premises, it would be the joint obligation of the owners to contribute money necessary to complete the construction. This contribution could be imposed in the form of an assessment lien, the same as assessments for common area expenses and maintenance.

Representing the Condominium Unit Purchaser or Lender

A legal assistant's involvement with a condominium form of ownership usually takes the form of assisting a purchaser or lender who is buying or making a loan on a condominium unit. The legal assistant, to adequately assist in the representation of this client, must be knowledgeable of the condominium laws in the state where the condominium is located. In addition, the legal assistant should obtain copies of all the condominium documentation, such as the declaration, plat, articles of incorporation, and bylaws of the condominium association, and review them carefully.

The following is a checklist of issues and questions that need to be asked and answered when representing a condominium unit purchaser or lender.

New York:
Make sure the developer has sufficient financing. Check with owners of other units he has built to see if he keeps his word.

New York:
The developer retains control until not less than 75 percent of the units have been sold or by a certain time period such as 5 years.

New York:
Look at management contracts; sponsors often retain these at lucrative terms.

▥➡ C H E C K L I S T

Condominium Checklist

☐ 1. The reputation of the condominium developer or builder is related to the success of the developer's projects. A good reputation means that the builder builds good-quality condominium units that usually are trouble-free. The quality of construction in a condominium unit can greatly affect the cost of maintaining the unit and the resale value of the unit.

☐ 2. Does the condominium documentation comply with state law? A condominium declaration that is defective or does not comply with state law can affect the marketability and cloud the title of the condominium unit. Purchasers may not want to purchase property that is not technically in compliance with the state condominium laws, and lenders may decline to make loans on such property. It is possible in some states to obtain an endorsement from a title insurance company ensuring that the condominium has been properly formed and is in compliance with the state condominium act.

☐ 3. Carefully review the assessments while a developer is still in control of the condominium project. Not uncommonly, the developer, while in control, may subsidize the condominium budget and keep assessments artificially low during this period of ownership. It is important to obtain copies of the actual budget, if available, from the developer to determine what the assessments will be once the developer has sold the units and left the project.

☐ 4. Who controls the board of directors? During the development, it is not unusual for the developer to have control over the board of directors. The developer usually retains control until such time as a minimum number of units have been sold, usually not less than 75 percent of the units. Although it is not unusual for a developer to control the association during the period of development, the property owner needs to know when control will be turned over to the owners and to be aware that for a period of time, he or she may have little say in the internal affairs of the association.

☐ 5. Review the restrictions on use of the unit and common areas. A condominium contains restrictive covenants that affect the use of units and the common areas by the owners. These restrictive covenants are enforceable so long as they do not violate some public policy, such as racial discrimination. A potential condominium purchaser must be made aware that these covenants are enforceable and that there probably is someone in the condominium project who enforces them. If a condominium purchaser has trouble with any of the restrictive covenants, he or she needs to second-think the purchase.

☐ 6. Is there any control on the resale of the property? A few condominium declarations contain rights of first refusal restrictions on an owner's ability to resell his or her unit. The right of first refusal usually requires that the owner offer the unit first to the condominium association before it can be resold. The association seldom exercises these rights of first refusal, but this practice can affect an owner's ability to sell the unit or present problems at a closing in the event a notice of the sale was not sent to the association.

COOPERATIVE

The **cooperative** form of ownership, despite its popularity in Europe and other parts of the world, has had limited success in the United States. Cooperatives usually are found in urban areas along the East Coast. In the late 1960s and early 1970s they were used to provide publicly assisted housing. A limited number of these properties can still be found throughout the United States.

Cooperative ownership is quite different from condominium ownership. In a cooperative, a corporation owns the land, the building, and all common areas. A person who wants to become an owner purchases from the cooperative corporation shares of stock in the corporation. These shares of stock entitle the person to enter into a long-term lease for his or her cooperative unit with the corporation. A cooperative owner is, in essence, both a tenant under a long-term lease with the corporation and an owner because the person owns shares in the landlord cooperative corporation. The owner participates with other owners, who are also members of the corporation, in the governance of the corporation. The shares of stock and lease are transferable and, therefore, offer a cooperative owner, like a condominium owner, an opportunity to build value in his or her investment. Ownership in a cooperative usually is considered ownership of personal property rather than of real property.

Differences between Condominiums and Cooperatives

The main difference between a cooperative and a condominium is financing. With a condominium, each owner pays his or her own financing and pledges the unit as security for the loan. In cooperative financing, there is a blanket mortgage on all the cooperative property, including the living units and common areas. The cooperative purchaser agrees to pay his or her share of the blanket mortgage payments, which is based on the percentage of ownership of the total cooperative. At the time of purchase, a cooperative owner may also be required to make a substantial down payment, which typically is greater than a condominium down payment. A condominium owner usually can purchase a unit with a down payment of only 10 to 20 percent of the purchase price, whereas it is not unusual for a cooperative owner to have to pay as much as one-third of the purchase price as a down payment. The master financing of a cooperative versus individual financing of a condominium creates another set of problems for the cooperative owner. A cooperative owner could be making his or her payments each month to the cooperative corporation for his or her share of the common mortgage, but the other cooperative owners could be defaulting on their payment obligations. These collective defaults of other owners could cause the blanket mortgage to go into default and could threaten the foreclosure of the master mortgage on the cooperative owner's home.

Cooperative owners commonly have more restricted rights of resale than do condominium owners. Most condominium owners can resell their units without consent of the condominium association. Cooperative owners usually cannot sell their cooperative interests unless the board of directors of the cooperative corporation approves the new owners. This approval process is necessary because of the collective mortgage and the requirement that the cooperative owners work more closely together in a cooperative effort so that each cooperative owner can prosper and be protected in his or her ownership of a unit.

The financing difficulties and the restrictions on resale have caused the cooperative form of ownership to be less popular than the condominium form of ownership.

New York:
Cooperative ownership is usually found in New York City, it is much more prevalent there than elsewhere in the state (for further discussion, see Appendix).

New York:
Title to land and the building is held by a corporation and each purchaser gets stock in the corporation and a proprietary lease which gives her the right to occupy a certain space (the apartment being purchased). Real estate taxes are paid by the corporation and are included in the maintenance, along with management and insurance expenses.

New York:
Cooperative boards have been known to reject such celebrities as Richard Nixon, Barbara Streisand, and Gloria Vanderbilt.

TIME-SHARES

You like to ski, and each year you go to you favorite ski resort for a week. You enjoy the trip very much and think it might be a good idea to own property in the area of the ski resort. You are hesitant to buy a vacation condominium or home because you will only be using it one or two weeks out of the year. You are not certain if the unit can be rented the other fifty weeks to cover your costs and expenses of ownership. Wouldn't it be nice if you could just buy a condominium or home in the ski area for one or two weeks a year? It is this desire and demand that an industry known as time-sharing was created to satisfy. **Time-share**, or interval ownership, is a popular marketing device for resort developments in the United States. Under a time-sharing arrangement, a person purchases the right to use a home or condominium at a resort area for a limited period each year.

Time-share ownership comes in a number of legal forms. A time-share may be a cooperative in which the developer owns a corporation and each owner of the time-share purchases stock in the corporation. The amount of stock owned by the purchaser permits the owner to use units within the development during a certain period of the year. A time-share may be based on a form of interval ownership in which an owner of a time-share actually owns the unit for a certain time each year. A time-share may also be structured in such a way that the purchaser enters into a tenancy in common arrangement with other time-share owners for the entire resort development. This arrangement permits the owner to use a particular residential unit during a portion of the year.

Time-shares have been subject to abuse and fraud by developers and are heavily regulated by state law. The purchaser of a time-share is entitled to full disclosure concerning all operations of the time-share and is given a period of rescission after a contract to buy a time-share has been signed. During this period, usually five to seven days, the purchaser can change his or her mind and terminate the agreement.

ETHICS: Legal Assistant Correspondence

You are a closing legal assistant employed in a busy real estate department of a law firm. Your work requires a great deal of correspondence, and you share a secretary with your supervising attorney. Your secretary has taken a day's vacation and you are working with a temporary secretary. You have a number of letters that need to go out and you notice that the temporary has used firm letterhead for all your correspondence and has typed your name in such a way that it appears you are an attorney for the firm. It is late in the day, and it will take more than an hour to retype the letters. Do you send the letters, or have them retyped?

Many states provide that to the extent necessary to perform functions properly delegated to a legal assistant and to the extent that these functions do not fall within the definition of the practice of law, the legal assistant may correspond on the law firm letterhead in the legal assistant's own name. If a legal assistant in the employ of a member of the bar is permitted by the member to correspond on the law firm letterhead, the legal assistant must clearly identify his or her status by the use of an appropriate designation, such as "paralegal," "legal assistant," or "law clerk." Failure to do so might constitute a representation on the part of the law firm that the legal assistant is a member of the state bar and authorized to practice law within the state.

SUMMARY

The condominium and cooperative forms of property ownership combine individual and joint ownership. A condominium owner individually owns his or her unit and, together with other individual owners, has joint ownership and control over the common property. A cooperative owner has a lease on his or her living unit and owns stock in the cooperative corporation that owns the building in which the unit is located. A legal assistant who represents a purchaser, seller, or lender of condominium or cooperative property must be familiar with all the rules and regulations involving condominiums and cooperatives.

KEY TERMS

Assessment	Condominium declaration	Limited common area
Common areas	Condominium plat	Rescission
Condominium	Cooperative	Time-share
Condominium association		

REVIEW QUESTIONS

1. What is the difference between a common area and a limited common area in a condominium? Give an example of each.

2. What information is contained in a condominium declaration?

3. How are common area expenses paid for in a condominium?

4. What is a cooperative?

5. How does a cooperative differ from a condominium?

CASE PROBLEM

You are a legal assistant employed by a law firm who is representing a purchaser of a condominium unit. You have been asked to assist an attorney in the closing of the sale. What documentation in regard to the condominium would you request from the seller? What issues do you want answered from the seller or from a review of the condominium documentation?

PRACTICAL ASSIGNMENT

1. Research your own state's condominium act. How does your state's requirements for a condominium declaration differ from those contained in the condominium declaration statute shown as Exhibit 3–1 at the end of this chapter? How does your state's requirements for a condominium plat differ from those in the statute shown as Exhibit 3–3 at the end of this chapter?

2. Review the condominium declaration shown as Exhibit 3–2 at the end of this chapter in conjunction with your state's condominium act. Does the declaration satisfy all requirements of your state's condominium act? If not, list the areas in which the condominium declaration is deficient or areas that would need to be added to the condominium declaration.

EXHIBIT 3–1
State Condominium
Act Requirements
for Declaration

44-3-77. Contents of declaration.

(a) The declaration for every condominium shall contain the following:

(1) The name of the condominium, which name shall include the word "condominium" or be followed by the words "a condominium";

(2) The name of the county or counties in which the condominium is located;

(3) A legal description by metes and bounds of the submitted property, including any horizontal, upper and lower, boundaries as well as the vertical, lateral, boundaries;

(4) A description or delineation of the boundaries of the units, including any horizontal, upper and lower, boundaries as well as the vertical, lateral, boundaries;

(5) A description or delineation of any limited common elements showing or designating the unit or units to which each is assigned;

(6) A description or delineation of all common elements which may subsequently be assigned as limited common elements together with a statement that they may be so assigned and a description of the method whereby any such assignments shall be made;

(7) The allocation to each unit of an undivided interest in the common elements;

(8) The allocation to each unit of a number of votes in the association;

(9) The allocation to each unit of a share of the liability for common expenses;

(10) Any limitations or restrictions on the powers of the association and the board of directors;

(11) The name and address of the attorney or other person who prepared the declaration;

(12) A statement of any and all restrictions on the general use of the condominium or a statement that there are no such restrictions; and

(13) Such other matters not inconsistent with this article as the declarant deems appropriate.

(b) If the condominium is an expandable condominium, the declaration shall also contain the following:

(1) The explicit reservation of an option or options to expand the condominium;

(2) A time limit or date not exceeding seven years from the recording of the declaration upon which all options to expand the condominium shall expire together with a statement of any circumstances which will terminate any such option prior to the expiration of the time limit so specified; provided, however, that, if the condominium instruments so provide, the unit owners of units to which two-thirds of the votes in the association appertain, exclusive of any vote or votes appurtenant to any unit or units then owned by the declarant, may consent to the extension of any such option within one year prior to the date upon which the option would otherwise have expired;

(3) A statement of any other limitations on the option or options or a statement that there are no such limitations;

(4) A legal description by metes and bounds of the additional property, including any horizontal, upper and lower, boundaries as well as the vertical, lateral, boundaries;

(5) A statement as to whether portions of the additional property may be added to the condominium at different times, together with any limitations fixing the boundaries of those portions by legal descriptions setting forth the metes and bounds thereof or regulating the order in which they may be added to the condominium, or a statement that there are no such limitations;

(6) A statement of any limitations as to the location of any improvements that may be made on any portions of the additional property or a statement that there are no such limitations;

(7) A statement of the maximum number of units that may be created on the additional property. If portions of the additional property may be added to the condominium and the boundaries of those portions are fixed in accordance with paragraph (5) of this subsection, the declaration shall also state the maximum number of units that may be created on each such portion added to the condominium. If portions of the additional property may be added to the condominium and the boundaries of those portions are not fixed in accordance with paragraph (5) of this subsection, then the declaration shall also state the maximum average number of units per acre that may be created on any such portion added to the condominium;

(8) With regard to the additional property, a statement of whether any units may be created therein that may not be restricted exclusively to residential use and, if so, a statement of the maximum extent thereof or a limitation as to the extent of such nonresidential use;

(9) A statement of the extent to which any structures erected on any portion of the additional property added to the condominium will be compatible with structures on the submitted property in terms of quality of construction, the principal materials to be used, and architectural style or a statement that no assurances are made in those regards;

(10) A description of all other improvements that will be made on any portion of the additional property added to the condominium, or a statement of any limitations as to what other improvements may be made thereon, or a statement that no assurances are made in that regard;

(11) A statement that any units created on any portion of the additional property added to the condominium will be substantially identical to the units on the submitted property, or a statement of any limitations as to what types of units may be created thereon, or a statement that no assurances are made in that regard;

(12) A description of the declarant's reserved right, if any, to create limited common elements within any portion of the additional property or to designate common elements therein which may subsequently be assigned as limited common elements, in terms of the types, sizes, and maximum number of such limited common elements within each such portion, or a statement that no limitations are placed on that right; and

(13) A statement of a formula, ratio, or other method whereby, upon the expansion of any expandable condominium, there shall be reallocated among the units the undivided interests in the common elements, the votes in the association, and the liability for common expenses.

Plats or plans may be recorded with the declaration of any amendment thereto and identified therein to supplement or provide information required to be furnished pursuant to this subsection; and provided, further, that paragraph (8) of this subsection need not be complied with if none of the units on the submitted property are restricted exclusively to residential use.

(c) If the condominium contains any convertible space, the declaration shall also contain a statement of a formula, ratio, or other method whereby, upon the conversion of all or any portion of a convertible space, there shall be allocated among the units created therefrom such undivided interest in the common elements, such number of votes in the association, and such liability for common expenses as previously pertained to such convertible space.

(d) If the condominium is a leasehold condominium, with respect to any ground lease, other lease, or other instrument creating the estate for years, the expiration or termination of which may terminate or reduce the condominium, the declaration shall set forth the county or counties wherein the same are recorded and the deed book and page number where the first page of each such lease or other instrument is recorded. The declaration shall also contain the following:

(1) The date upon which such leasehold or estate for years is due to expire;

(2) A statement of whether any property will be owned by the unit owners in fee simple and, if so, a legal description by metes and bounds of any such property. With respect to any improvements owned by the unit owners in fee simple, the declaration shall contain a statement of any rights the unit owners shall have to remove the improvements after the expiration or termination of the leasehold or estate for years involved or a statement that they shall have no such rights;

(3) A statement of the name and address of the person or persons to whom payments of rent must be made by the unit owners unless such rent is collected from the unit owners as a part of the common expenses; and

(4) A statement of the share of liability for payments under any such lease or other instrument which are chargeable against each unit.

(e) Whenever this Code section requires a legal description by metes and bounds of submitted property or additional property, such requirement shall be deemed to include a requirement of a legally sufficient description of any easements that are submitted to this article or that may be added to the condominium, as the case may be. In the case of any such easement, the declaration shall contain the following:

(1) A description of the permitted use or uses;

(2) If the benefit of the easement does not inure to all units and their lawful occupants, a statement of the relevant restrictions and limitations on utilization; and

(3) If any person other than those entitled to occupy any unit may use the easement, a statement of the rights of others to such use.

Notwithstanding any other provision of this subsection, the foregoing requirements may be satisfied by attaching a true copy of any such easement to the declaration.

(f) Whenever this Code section requires a legal description by metes and bounds of submitted property or additional property, such requirement shall be deemed to include a separate legal description by metes and bounds of all property in which the unit owners collectively shall or may be tenants in common or joint tenants with any other persons. No units shall be situated on any such property, however, and the declaration shall describe the nature of the unit owners' estate therein. No such property shall be shown on the same plat or plats showing other portions of the condominium but shall be shown instead on separate plats unless such property is specifically shown and labeled as being owned subject to such a tenancy.

(g) Wherever this article requires a statement of a method for allocation or reallocation of undivided interests in the common elements, votes in the association, and the liability for common expenses, such method shall be so related to the physical characteristics of the units affected or otherwise so stated as to enable any person to determine the interest, vote, or share in such matters pertaining to any particular unit upon such allocation or reallocation. Certain spaces within the units, including, without limitation, attic, basement, and garage space, may but need not be omitted from such calculation or partially discounted by the use of a ratio so long as the same basis of calculation is employed for all units in the condominium. In the event that the declaration allocates or provides for the allocation to any unit of a different share of undivided interests in common elements than is allocated for liability for common expenses, such difference shall be based upon a good faith estimate of the declarant regarding the approximate relative maintenance or other costs occasioning such disparity, and the basis of such determination shall be stated in the declaration; provided, however, that no unit owner or other person may require any reallocation on account of any disparity between actual costs and the determination reflected in the declaration. Subject to the foregoing sentence of this subsection, nothing contained in this article shall be construed to require that the proportions of undivided interest in the common elements, of votes in the association, or of liability for common expenses assigned and allocated to each unit be equal, it being intended that such proportions may be independent. (Ga. L. 1975, p. 609, § 14; Ga. L. 1982, p. 3, § 44.)

EXHIBIT 3–1
State Condominium
Act Requirements
for Declaration
(continued)

STATE OF _____
COUNTY OF _____

DECLARATION OF CONDOMINIUM
FOR
CLAIREMONT OAKS, A CONDOMINIUM

THIS DECLARATION is made by The Farris Corporation (herein called the "Declarant").

WITNESSETH:

WHEREAS, Declarant is the fee simple owner of that certain tract or parcel of land lying and being in Land Lot 55 of the 6th District of Wayne County, _____(State)_____, as more particularly described in Exhibit "A" attached hereto and incorporated herein by reference, hereinafter called the "Property" subject to the matters set forth on Exhibit "B" attached hereto; and

WHEREAS, certain improvements have been constructed on the Property as shown on the Plat and the Plans which are referenced in Section 5.01(a) and (b) hereof and the matters attached hereto as Exhibit "C"; and

EXHIBIT 3–2
Condominium
Declaration

EXHIBIT 3-2
Condominium
Declaration
(continued)

WHEREAS, Declarant has duly incorporated Clairemont Oaks Condominium Association, Inc. as a nonprofit membership corporation under the laws of the State of _____, copies of the Articles of Incorporation, By-Laws and Organizational Meeting being attached hereto as Exhibits "D", "E" and "F"; and

WHEREAS, the Declarant desires to submit the Property to the condominium form of ownership pursuant to the provisions of the _____(State)_____ Condominium Act, as the same is in effect on the date hereof (as amended, hereinafter called the "Act"), the terms, conditions and provisions of which are incorporated herein by express reference, and the terms and conditions hereinafter set out.

NOW, THEREFORE, the Declarant does hereby make, declare and publish its intention and desire to submit, and does hereby submit, the Property to the condominium form of ownership pursuant to, subject to and in accordance with the provisions of the Act and the terms and conditions hereinafter set forth.

ARTICLE 1

Name

1.01 The name of the condominium shall be CLAIREMONT OAKS, A CONDOMINIUM (the "Condominium").

ARTICLE 2

Description of Submitted Property

2.01 The Property is located in Wayne County, _____(State)_____, in Land Lot 55 of the 6th District, and is more particularly described in Exhibit "A" attached hereto and incorporated herein by reference.

2.02 The Property is subject to the easements and other matters which are set forth on Exhibit "B" attached hereto and by reference made a part hereof.

ARTICLE 3

Definitions

3.01 The terms defined in Official Code of _____(State)_____, Section _____ shall have the meanings specified therein and wherever they appear in the condominium instruments unless the context otherwise requires.

ARTICLE 4

Convertible Space; Expandable Condominium

4.01 Convertible Space. The Condominium does not contain any convertible space.

4.02 Expansion of Condominium. This Condominium shall contain sixty (60) residential units, and is not expandable beyond that amount.

ARTICLE 5

Unit Information and Boundaries

5.01 The buildings and structures situated upon the property are:

(a) located thereon as shown on that certain plat of Clairemont Oaks, A Condominium, dated _____ , prepared by _____ , which plat has been

EXHIBIT 3–2
Condominium
Declaration
(continued)

prepared in accordance with Official Code of _____(State)_____ , Section _____ and has been filed contemporaneously herewith in Condominium Plat Book _____ , Page _____ , Wayne County, _____(State)_____ Records a copy of which is attached hereto as Exhibit "C" (hereinafter said condominium plat as recorded is referred to as the "Plat" or the "Condominium Plat");

(b) divided into sixty (60) residential units intended for independent ownership and use and as substantially shown upon those certain Plans for Clairemont Oaks, dated _____ , by _____ , and filed contemporaneously herewith in the Condominium Floor Plans Cabinet _____ , Folder _____ , _____ County, _____(State)_____ Records (hereinafter said plans are referred to as the "Plans" or the "Condominium Plans").

5.02 Unit Number. Each unit shall have the identifying number allocated to it in accordance with the Plat and the Plans.

5.03 Boundaries. The boundaries of the units are the floors, ceilings and walls delineated in the Plans.

5.04 Appurtenant Surfaces. If any chute, flue, duct, conduit, wire, bearing wall, bearing column or any other apparatus lies partially within and partially outside the designated boundaries of a unit, any portions thereof serving only that unit shall be deemed a part of that unit, and any portions thereof serving more than one unit or any portion of the common elements shall be deemed a part of the common elements.

5.05 Subdivision and Partition of Units; Relocation of Boundaries. The boundaries between adjoining units may be relocated from time to time, but no unit may be subdivided for the purpose of creating two or more units therefrom and no owner shall have the right of partition of a unit.

ARTICLE 6

Limited Common Elements

6.01 Generally. Any shutter, awning, window box, doorstep, porch, balcony, patio and any other apparatus designed to serve a single unit shall be deemed to be a limited common element appertaining to that unit exclusively.

ARTICLE 7

Allocation of Undivided Interest in the Common Elements

7.01 The undivided interest in the common elements allocated to each unit is set forth on Exhibit "G" attached hereto and incorporated herein by reference.

ARTICLE 8

Allocation of Votes in the Association

8.01 Generally. The number of votes in the Clairemont Oaks Condominium Association, Inc. for each unit shall be as designated on Exhibit "G" attached hereto.

8.02 Method of Voting. The persons entitled to exercise such votes at meetings of the Association, the method by which such votes may be exercised and the rights and obligations generally of members of the Association with regard to voting shall be in accordance with the By-Laws of the Association.

EXHIBIT 3–2
Condominium
Declaration
(continued)

ARTICLE 9

Allocation of Liabilities, Common Expenses and Utility Fees

9.01 Derivation of Amounts. The share of liability for each unit of the common expenses of the Association is shown on Exhibit "D" attached hereto and incorporated herein by reference.

9.02 Liability for Assessments. The owner of each unit shall, by acceptance of a deed from the Declarant or any direct or remote successor-in-interest to Declarant in any unit, be personally liable for and shall pay to the Association:

(a) any assessment with respect to all expenditures made or incurred by or on behalf of the Association in the operation, management and maintenance of the Property, including but not limited to: fees for management and supervision; printing, mailing, office equipment, all legal and accounting fees as required, secretarial and other expenses related to the conduct of the affairs of the Association and the Board of Directors; insurance; all utility charges in connection with the common elements, including gas, electric, water, sewerage and telephone charges; all expenses in connection with maintenance and repair of all common elements; security; and water, sewer, sanitary, gas and electric services and other similar charges for all units.

(b) any assessment, payable monthly or as otherwise billed, for utility fees chargeable to each unit for the providing of electricity, gas and such other utility service as may from time to time be provided to or for the unit.

(c) pursuant to the By-Laws of the Association, assessments may be made more often than annually, may be made for the purpose of defraying, in whole or in part, utilities, operating expenses, the cost of any construction or reconstruction, or unexpected repair or replacement of capital improvements in respect to the common elements.

The Declarant shall be liable for all common area and other assessments and utility fees on units owned by Declarant. The Declarant shall not be liable for any other assessments or expenses provided in this Article 9 of this Declaration prior to the date of the first unit sale.

9.03 Equitable Assessment for Limited Common Area Expenses. Any common expenses which:

(a) are incurred through or occasioned by the use or enjoyment of any common elements which benefits or is intended to benefit less than all the units, shall not be assessed against all the units pursuant to Section 9.01 hereof, but shall be specifically assessed equitably among those units which are so benefited or intended to be benefited; and

(b) are incurred by the conduct of less than all of those entitled to occupy all of the units or by the licensees or invitees of any such unit or units shall be especially assessed against the condominium unit or units, the conduct of any occupant, licensee or invitee of which occasioned any such common expenses.

9.04 Assessment for Exclusive Benefit of Particular Units. Any common expenses which relate to limited common elements assigned to any unit or units and reserved for the exclusive use of those entitled to the use of such unit or units shall be assessed against such unit or units only.

9.05 Lien Rights of Association. The Board of Directors shall have the authority to establish general rules applicable to all units providing that the lien for assessments shall include any one or more of the following: (i) a late or delinquency charge (not in excess of $10.00 or ten percent of the amount of each assessment or installment thereof not paid

EXHIBIT 3-2
Condominium
Declaration
(continued)

when due, whichever is greater), (ii) interest on each assessment or installment thereof, and any delinquency or late charge appertaining thereto, from the date the same was first due and payable, at a rate not in excess of ten percent per annum, (iii) the costs of collection, including court costs, the expenses of sale, any expenses required for the protection and preservation of the unit, and reasonable attorneys' fees actually incurred, and (iv) the fair rental value of the condominium unit from the time of the institution of suit until the sale of the condominium unit at foreclosure (or until the judgment rendered in such suit is otherwise satisfied).

ARTICLE 10

Association

10.01 Creation. The Declarant has caused the Clairemont Oaks Condominium Association, Inc., to be duly incorporated as a nonprofit membership corporation.

10.02 Powers Generally. The limitations and restrictions on the powers of the Association and on the Board of Directors of the Association are set out in the By-Laws of the Association.

10.03 Enforcement. The Association shall be empowered, in order to enforce compliance with the lawful provisions of the condominium instruments, including any rules or regulations contained in or promulgated in accordance with the By-Laws of the Association, to impose and assess fines and to suspend temporarily the right of use of certain of the common elements.

10.04 Restrictions on Powers. The Association shall have, except to the extent restricted herein, all those powers permitted by the provisions of Official Code of ____(State)____, Section _____, and except to the extent that it may not without the written consent of two-thirds of the unit owners (excluding Declarant) sell or transfer the common elements (excluding the grant of easements for public utilities or for any other public purposes consistent with the intended use of the common elements by the unit owners).

ARTICLE 11

Easements, Covenants and Use of the Condominium

11.01 Purposes. The Condominium is formed for residential purposes only and units shall be occupied and used by the owners thereof only as private residences for the owners and the families, tenants, invitees, and guests of such owners and for no other purposes whatsoever. Without derogating from the generality of the foregoing, no business shall be maintained or conducted in or from any unit.

11.02 Common Elements. All occupants of units and their guests shall have a nonexclusive right to use the common elements for the purposes for which they are intended, subject, however, to the following provisions:

(a) No such use shall enter or encroach upon the lawful rights of other persons; and

(b) The right of the Association to restrict the use and govern the operation of the common elements by promulgating reasonable rules and regulations with respect thereto, including, without limitation, the right to charge reasonable monthly fees for the use thereof by unit owners as the Association deems necessary or appropriate.

11.03 Strict Compliance. The owners of the units shall be entitled to all of the rights but shall be subject to all of the obligations provided for in the Act and all owners shall

EXHIBIT 3-2
Condominium
Declaration
(continued)

comply strictly with the provisions of the Condominium instruments including any restrictions, rules or regulations contained in or promulgated in accordance with the By-Laws of the Association.

11.04 Maintenance of Offices. The provisions of Section 10.01 hereof shall not affect the right of the Declarant and its duly authorized agents, representatives and employees to enjoy the easement provided for in Official Code of _____(State)_____ , Section _____ for the maintenance of sales and leasing offices and/or model units on the submitted property.

11.05 Construction Easement. The Property shall be subject to a nonexclusive easement in favor of Declarant and its officers, employees, agents, independent contractors and invitees for entry upon and passage over the Property for purposes of constructing the units and other improvements described herein.

11.06 Utility Easements. There shall be appurtenant to each unit a nonexclusive easement for use of all pipes, wire cables, conduits, utility lines, flues and ducts serving such unit and situated in any other unit. Each unit shall be subject to an easement in favor of other units for use of all pipes, wire, cables, conduits, utility lines, flues and ducts situated in such unit and serving such other units.

11.07 Encroachments. If any portion of the common elements now encroaches upon any unit, or if any unit now encroaches upon any other unit or upon any portion of the common element, or if any such encroachment shall occur hereafter as a result of (i) settling of a unit or units; (ii) repair, alteration or reconstruction of the common elements made by or with the consent of the Association; (iii) repair or reconstruction of a unit or units following damage by fire or other casualty; or (iv) condemnation or eminent domain proceedings, a valid easement shall exist for such encroachment and for the maintenance of the same so long as the Property remains subject to the Act.

11.08 Right of Access. The Association shall have the irrevocable right, to be exercised by the Board of Directors, to have access to each unit from time to time during reasonable hours as may be necessary for the maintenance, repair or replacement of any of the common elements therein or accessible therefrom, or for making emergency repairs therein necessary to prevent damage to the common elements or to another unit.

11.09 Maintenance of Common Elements. The necessary work of maintenance, repair and replacement of the common elements and the making of any additions or improvements thereto shall be carried out only as provided in the Act, this Declaration and the By-Laws.

11.10 Prohibited Work. No owner shall do any work which would jeopardize the soundness or safety of the Property, reduce the value thereof or impair any easement or hereditament without in every such case unanimous consent of all other owners being first obtained.

ARTICLE 12

Insurance and Casualty Losses

12.01 Insurance Coverage. The Association shall obtain and maintain in full force and effect, at all times, the following insurance coverages:

(a) Insurance covering all of the insurable improvements on the property (with the exception of improvements and betterments made by the respective unit owners or occupants) and all personal property as may be owned by the Association, against loss or dam-

EXHIBIT 3–2
Condominium
Declaration
(continued)

age by fire and other hazards covered by the standard extended coverage endorsement, and such other risk as from time to time shall be customarily covered with respect to buildings similar in construction, location and use as the units, including, but not limited to, vandalism and malicious mischief in an amount equal to the maximum insurable replacement value thereof (exclusive of excavation and foundations), as determined annually by the Association;

(b) Comprehensive public liability insurance covering all of the common elements and insuring against all damage or liability caused by the acts of the Association, its officers, directors, agents and employees, all unit owners and other persons entitled to occupy any unit or any other portion of the condominium, with liability limits in amounts authorized from time to time by the Association, but in no event less than the amounts required in the Act;

(c) Such other types and amounts of insurance as may from time to time be deemed necessary, desirable or proper, and be authorized by the Association by action of the Board of Directors or in its By-Laws.

12.02 Payment of Insurance Premiums. Premiums for all insurance carried by the Association shall be common expenses and shall be paid by the Association.

12.03 Policy Standards.

(a) All insurance coverage obtained by the Association shall be written in the name of the Association as trustee for, and for the use and benefit of, each of the unit owners and their mortgagees as their interest may appear, and their respective percentages of undivided interest in and to the common elements. Each such insurance policy shall be issued by an insurer authorized under the laws of the State of _____ to do business in ____(State)____ and to issue the coverage provided by the policy, and shall provide for the issuance of a certificate of insurance to each unit owner and its mortgagee, if any, which shall specify the proportionate amount of such insurance attributable to the particular unit owner's interest in the property.

(b) The Association shall use its best efforts to cause all of such insurance policies to contain: (i) a waiver of subrogation by the insurer as to any claims against the Association, any officer, director, agent or employee of the Association, the unit owners and their employees, agents, tenants and invitees, and a waiver of any defenses based on co-insurance or on invalidity arising from the acts of the insured; (ii) a waiver by the insurer of its right to repair and reconstruct instead of paying cash; (iii) a provision that the policy cannot be cancelled, invalidated or suspended on account of the conduct of any unit owner or any employee, agent, tenant or invitee of any unit owner, or any officer, director, agent or employee of the Association, without a prior demand in writing and delivered to the Association to cure the defect and the allowance of reasonable time thereafter within which the defect may be cured by the Association, any unit owner or any mortgagee; (iv) a provision that any "other insurance" clause in the policy shall exclude from its scope any policies of the individual unit owners; (v) a provision that the coverage may not be cancelled or substantially modified (including cancellation for nonpayment of premium) without at least thirty days written notice to any and all of the insured thereunder, including mortgagees; and (vi) a provision that the coverage will not be prejudiced by any act or neglect of the owners of the units when said act or neglect is not within the control of the Association, or any failure of the Association to comply with any warranty or condition regarding any portion of the property over which the Association has no control.

EXHIBIT 3-2
Condominium
Declaration
(continued)

12.04 Adjustment of Losses. Exclusive authority to adjust losses under insurance policies obtained by the Association shall be vested in the Association; provided, however, that no mortgagee shall be prohibited from participating in the settlement negotiations, if any, related thereto.

12.05 Individual Insurance by Unit Owners. It shall be the individual responsibility of each unit owner, at its sole cost and expense, to provide, as it sees fit any insurance coverage not required to be maintained by the Association. Any unit owner who obtains an individual insurance policy rejecting any risk as to which insurance is carried by the Association shall file a copy of such individual policy with the Association within thirty days after the purchase thereof.

12.06 Handling of Casualty Insurance Proceeds. All insurance policies purchased by and in the name of the Association shall provide that proceeds covered in casualty loss shall be paid to the Association. The Association shall receive such proceeds as are paid and delivered to it and hold the same in trust for the benefit of the unit owners and their mortgagees as follows:

(a) Proceeds on account of damage to the common elements not involving a unit shall be held to the extent of the undivided interest of each unit owner, for each unit owner, such interest to be equal to the undivided interest of each unit owner in and to the common elements.

(b) Proceeds on account of damage to units (or on account of damage to common elements involving a unit) shall be held for the owners of the damaged units in proportion to the cost of repairing the damage suffered by each unit owner, which cost shall be determined by the Board of Directors.

(c) In the event a mortgagee endorsement has been issued as to any unit under the policy under which such proceeds are paid, the share of that unit owner shall be held in trust for the unit owner and the mortgagee, as their interest may appear. Unless a determination is made not to repair or reconstruct pursuant to Section 12.07(b) hereof, and such proceeds, or such portion thereof as may be required for such purpose, shall be disbursed by the Association as payment of the cost and any expenses of repair or reconstruction, as hereinafter provided. Any proceeds remaining after payment of all cost and expenses of repair or reconstruction shall be common profits.

12.07 Damage and Destruction.

(a) Immediately after any damage or destruction by fire or other casualty to all or any portion of the property covered by insurance written in the name of the Association, the Association shall proceed with the filing and adjustment of all claims and losses arising under such insurance and obtain reliable and detailed estimates of the cost of repair or reconstruction of the damaged or destroyed property. Repair or reconstruction, as used in this paragraph, means repairing or restoring the property to substantially the same condition that existed prior to the fire or other casualty with each unit and the common elements having the same vertical and horizontal boundaries as before the casualty.

(b) Any damage or destruction shall be repaired or reconstructed unless: (i) the condominium is terminated pursuant to, subject to and in accordance with the provisions of the Act and this Declaration; (ii) the damaged or destroyed portion of the property is withdrawn from the condominium pursuant to, subject to and in accordance with the provisions of the Act; or (iii) the unit owners of the damaged or destroyed units, if any, and their mortgagees, together with the unit owners of other units to which two-thirds of the votes in the Association appertain and the mortgagees, exclusive of the votes appertaining

EXHIBIT 3-2
Condominium
Declaration
(continued)

to any damaged or destroyed units, agree not to repair or reconstruct such damage or destruction, pursuant to, subject to and in accordance with the provisions of the Act. Any such determination shall be conclusively made, if at all, not more than ninety days after the date of the casualty. Should a determination be made to terminate the condominium, as herein provided, then the insurance proceeds paid to the Association and held by it on account of such casualty shall be common profits, to be held and disbursed pursuant to, subject to and in accordance with Section 12.06 hereof. Should a determination be made to withdraw from the condominium the damaged portion of the property or not to repair or reconstruct the damage or destruction, as herein provided, then the insurance proceeds paid to the Association and held by it on account of such casualty shall be disbursed by the Association in accordance with the manner in which such proceeds are held by the Association, pursuant to Section 12.06 hereof. Any remittances with respect to units as to which mortgagee endorsements have been issued on the policies under which the proceeds were paid shall be payable to the unit owner and its mortgagee jointly, as their interest may appear.

(c) If the damage or destruction for which the insurance proceeds are paid is to be repaid and such proceeds are not sufficient to defray the cost thereof, the Association may levy an additional assessment against all unit owners in sufficient amounts to provide funds to pay such excess cost of repair or reconstruction. Further, additional assessments may be made in a like manner and any time during or following the completion of any repair or reconstruction. The proceeds from insurance and assessments, if any, received by the Association hereunder when the damage or destruction is to be repaired or reconstructed shall be disbursed as provided for in Section 12.06 hereof.

12.08 Non-Liability and Indemnity of Officers and Directors of the Association and Declarant. The officers and directors of the Association and Declarant shall not be personally liable to any unit owner for any mistake of judgment or for any other act or omission of any nature whatsoever in administering the Association, except for acts or omission which constitute gross negligence or willful misconduct. The Association shall indemnify and hold harmless each of the officers and directors of the Association and Declarant and their respective legal representatives, successors and assigns, from any liability, cost or expense arising out of any act or omission in administering the Association which is not deemed to be gross negligence or willful misconduct.

ARTICLE 13

Damage or Destruction

13.01 Obligation to Rebuild. In the event of damage to or destruction of the whole or any part of the building, the Association shall repair, rebuild or restore the building or such part as has been damaged or destroyed.

13.02 Compliance With Condominium Instruments. Such reparation, rebuilding or restoration shall be carried out in accordance with the provisions of the Act and the By-Laws of the Association.

ARTICLE 14

Sale or Leasing of Units

14.01 Notice Provisions. Any owner who sells or who leases his unit shall give notice in writing to the Board of Directors of such sale or of such lease stating the name and address of the purchaser or lessee and such other information as the Board may reason-

EXHIBIT 3–2
Condominium
Declaration
(continued)

ably require. The Board of Directors shall have authority to make and to enforce reasonable rules and regulations in order to enforce this provision, including the right to impose fines constituting a lien upon the unit sold or leased, pursuant to the Act; provided, however, no rule or regulation may create a right of first refusal in the Association or any other third party, this paragraph solely creating the obligation of an owner to give notice to sell or lease. Notice, as required herein, shall be given, in the case of a lease, not later than fifteen (15) days after commencement of the lease and, in the case of a sale, not later than the closing of the sale.

14.02 Leasing Provision. Units may be rented only in their entirety; no fraction or portion may be rented. There shall be no subleasing of units or assignment of leases. With the exception of a lender in possession of a condominium unit following a default in a first mortgage, a foreclosure proceeding, or any deed or other arrangement in lieu of foreclosure, no unit owner shall be permitted to lease his unit for transient or hotel purposes. All leases and lessees are subject to the provisions of the condominium units and rules and regulations adopted pursuant thereto. Any lease agreement shall be required to provide that the terms of a lease shall be subject in all respects to the provisions of the Declaration and By-Laws and that any failure by the lessee to comply with the terms of such documents shall be a default under the lease. All leases shall be in writing. Other than units owned by the Declarant and with the exception of a lender in possession of a condominium unit following a default in a first mortgage, a foreclosure proceeding, or any deed or other arrangement in lieu of foreclosure, all rentals must be for a term of no less than one year. The unit owner must make available to the tenant copies of the Declaration, By-Laws and Rules and Regulations.

14.03 Any unit owner or person having executed a lease or a contract for the purchase of a condominium unit requesting a recordable statement certifying to the receipt by the Association of the notice herein specified, or the waiver of the Association's rights to receive such notice shall be furnished such a statement. Any such statement shall be binding on the Association and every unit owner. Payment of a fee, not exceeding $25.00, may be required as a prerequisite to the issuance of such a statement.

ARTICLE 15

Eminent Domain

15.01 If any portion of the Condominium property is taken by eminent domain, the award shall be allocated as provided in Official Code of _____(State)_____ , Section _____ .

ARTICLE 16

Amendment of Condominium Instruments

16.01 By Owners. The Condominium instruments, including this Declaration, shall be amended only by the agreement of both the owners and mortgagees of units to which two-thirds (2/3) of the votes in the Association appertain, as provided in the By-Laws.

ARTICLE 17

Termination of the Condominium

17.01 Clairemont Oaks, a Condominium, shall be terminated only by the agreement of four-fifths (4/5) of the owners of the units and of all mortgagees of such units unless, in

EXHIBIT 3-2
Condominium
Declaration
(continued)

the case of the destruction of the entire development by fire or other casualty, following which the owners of the units decide not to rebuild, in which case the provisions of the By-Laws and the Declaration shall apply.

ARTICLE 18
Control by Declarant

18.01 Generally. The Declarant is hereby authorized in accordance with the By-Laws of the Association, incorporated herein by reference, to appoint and remove any member or members of the Board of Directors and any officer or officers of the Association with or without cause until the first of the following two occur:

(a) The third anniversary of the date of recording of this Declaration, or

(b) The date as of which units to which seventy percent (70%) of the undivided interests in the common elements have been conveyed by Declarant to unit owners other than a person or persons constituting Declarant, or

(c) The date as of which the Declarant surrenders the authority to appoint and remove all members of the Board of Directors by express amendment to the Declaration executed and recorded by the Declarant.

ARTICLE 19
Perpetuities

19.01 Should any of the provisions of this Declaration be unlawful, void or voidable for violation of the rule against perpetuities, then such provision shall continue only until twenty-one (21) years after the date that is ninety (90) years from and after the date of this Declaration.

ARTICLE 20
Miscellaneous

20.01 Notices. Notices provided for in the Act, this Declaration or the Articles or By-Laws shall be in writing, and shall be addressed to any unit owner at his/her or their unit at the condominium or at such other address as hereinafter provided. Notices to the Association shall be in writing and addressed to the President of the Association at his or her unit at the condominium, or to such other address as may hereafter be provided for and a written notice of such change of address furnished to all unit owners. Any unit owner may designate a different address for notices to him by giving written notice to the Association. Notices addressed as above shall be deemed delivered three business days after mailing by United States Registered or Certified Mail, or when delivered in person. Upon written request to the Association, the holder of any interest in any unit shall be given a copy of all notices to be given to the owner whose unit is subject to such interest.

20.02 Right to Notice, Attend Meetings and Inspection of Records. The owner of any interest in any unit, including any mortgagee, and any insurer or grantor of such mortgage, in addition to the rights set forth in the Act, shall have the right to inspect the books and records of the Association, including financial records, upon reasonable notice, and the right to attend and speak at any meeting of the Association, provided, however, no person other than a member as such shall have any voting rights. If the owner of any such interest files with the Association a written request, the Association shall have the right to notify such party of any violation by the owner of such unit, provided, however, that in no

EXHIBIT 3–2
Condominium
Declaration
(continued)

event shall the Association agree with any such party to furnish such notice unless such party agrees in writing that in no event shall the Association be liable for any claim or damages as a result of any failure to give such notice. Upon written request, any mortgagee shall have the right to receive a financial statement for the immediately preceding fiscal year.

20.03 Headings. The headings, sections and subsections in this Declaration and the Articles and By-Laws are for convenience or reference only and shall not in any way be deemed to limit or construe the intent of the parties or interpret the meaning of any document.

20.04 Number and Gender. As used in this Declaration, the singular shall include the plural, the masculine, feminine and neuter pronouns shall be fully interchangeable, where the context so requires.

20.05 Severability. If any provision of this Declaration or the Articles or By-Laws is held invalid, the validity of the remainder of this Declaration and the Articles and By-Laws shall not be affected thereby, and the remainder thereof shall be construed as if such invalid part was never included herein or therein.

20.06 Rights and Obligations. Each successor in title of the Declarant with respect to any part of the property, by the acceptance of a Deed of Conveyance, accepts the same subject to all restrictions, conditions, covenants, reservations, liens and charges created or reserved by this Declaration. All rights, benefits and privileges hereby imposed shall be deemed and taken to be covenants running with the land, and shall be binding inured to the benefit of any person having any interest or estate in the property, or any portion thereof.

ARTICLE 21

Author

21.01 This Declaration was prepared by _____ , with an office address of_____

_____.

IN WITNESS WHEREOF, the Declarant has executed this Declaration under seal on the _____ day of _____ , 19___.

DECLARANT:

Signed, sealed and delivered in the
presence of:

THE FARRIS CORPORATION

_____
Unofficial Witness

_____
Notary Public

By: _____
President

County of Appointment:
Expiration of Commission:
[Notary Seal]

Attest:_____
Secretary

[CORPORATE SEAL]

EXHIBIT 3–3
State Condominium
Code Requirements
for Condominium
Plat

44-3-83. Recording of plats and plans; contents; completion of structural improvements; certification by registered architect or engineer.

(a) Prior to the first conveyance of a condominium unit, there shall be recorded one or more plats of survey showing the location and dimensions of the submitted property; the location and dimensions of all structural improvements located on any portion of the submitted property; the intended location and dimensions of all contemplated structural improvements committed to be provided by the declaration on any portion of the submitted property; and, to the extent feasible, the location and dimensions of all easements appurtenant to the submitted property or otherwise submitted to this article as part of the common elements. With respect to all such structural improvements, the plats shall indicate which, if any, have not been begun by use of the phrase "Not Yet Begun." No structural improvement which contains or constitutes all or part of any unit or units and which is located on any portion of the submitted property shall be commenced on any portion of the submitted property after the recording of the plats. The declarant shall complete all structural improvements depicted on the plats, subject only to such limitations, if any, as may be expressly stated in the declaration with respect to those labeled "Not Yet Begun" on the plats, provided that, within six months after written notice from the association, the declarant shall be obligated to complete within a reasonable time every structural improvement actually commenced on the submitted property, notwithstanding any provision of the declaration, unless the declarant removes within a reasonable time all portions of any such structural improvement and restores the surface of the land affected thereby to substantially the same condition as that which existed prior to commencement of any such structural improvement; and provided, further, that nothing contained in this sentence shall exempt the declarant from any contractual liability to complete any such structural improvement. If the submitted property consists of noncontiguous parcels, the plats shall indicate the approximate distances between such parcels unless such information is disclosed in the declaration. If, with respect to any portion or portions, but less than all, of the submitted property, the unit owners are to own only a leasehold or estate for years, the plats shall show the location and dimensions of any such portion or portions and shall label each such portion by use of the phrase "Leased Land." To the extent feasible, the plats shall show all easements to which the submitted property or any portion thereof is subject. The plats shall also show all encroachments by or on any operation of the submitted property. In the case of any units which have vertical boundaries lying wholly or partially outside of structures for which plans pursuant to subsection (b) of this Code section are recorded, the plats shall show the location and dimensions of the vertical boundaries to the extent that they are not shown on the plans; and the units or portions thereof thus depicted shall bear their identifying numbers. Each plat shall be certified as to its accuracy and compliance with this subsection by a registered land surveyor. The specification within this subsection of items that shall be shown on the plats shall not be construed to mean that the plats shall not also show all other items customarily shown or required by law to be shown for land title surveys.

(b) There shall be recorded prior to the first conveyance of a condominium unit:

(1) Plans which have been prepared, signed, and sealed by a registered architect or registered engineer of every structure which contains or constitutes all or part of any unit or units located on or within any portion of the submitted property, which plans shall show:

(A) The location and dimensions of the exterior walls and roof of such structures;

EXHIBIT 3–3
State Condominium
Code Requirements
for Condominium
Plat
(continued)

(B) The walls, partitions, floors, and ceilings as constitute the horizontal boundaries, if any, and the vertical boundaries of each unit, including convertible space, to the extent that such boundaries lie within or coincide with the boundaries of such structures; and

(C) The identifying numbers of all units or portions thereof depicted on the plans; and

(2) A certification by such architect or engineer to the effect that he has visited the site and viewed the property and that, to the best of his knowledge, information, and belief:

(A) The exterior walls and roof of each structure are in place as shown on the plans; and

(B) Such walls, partitions, floors, and ceilings, to the extent shown on said plans, as constitute the horizontal boundaries, if any, and the vertical boundaries of each unit, including convertible space, have been sufficiently constructed so as to establish clearly the physical boundaries of such unit.

In addition, each convertible space depicted in the plans shall be labeled as such by use of the phrase "CONVERTIBLE SPACE." Unless the condominium instruments expressly provide otherwise, it shall be presumed that, in the case of any unit not wholly contained within or constituting one or more of the structures, the horizontal boundaries extend, in the case of each unit, at the same elevation with regard to any part of such unit lying outside of such structures, subject to the following exception: in the case of any unit which does not lie over any other unit other than basement units, it shall be presumed that the lower horizontal boundary, if any, of that unit lies at the level of the ground with regard to any part of that unit lying outside of the structures.

(b.1) There shall be recorded prior to the first conveyance of a condominium unit plans of every structure which contains or constitutes all or part of any unit or units located on or within any portion of the submitted property and a certification by a registered architect or registered engineer to the effect that he has visited the site and viewed the property and that, to the best of his knowledge, information, and belief:

(1) The foundation, structural members, exterior walls, and roof of each such structure are complete and in place as shown on the plans;

(2) The walls, partitions, floors, and ceilings, to the extent shown on the plans, as constituting or coinciding with the vertical and horizontal boundaries of each unit, including convertible space, within each such structure, are sufficiently complete and in place to establish clearly the physical boundaries of such unit and that such physical boundaries are as shown on the plans; and

(3) Each such structure, to the extent of its stage of completion at that time, is constructed substantially in accordance with such plans.

The plans shall show the location and dimensions of the horizontal boundaries, if any, and the vertical boundaries of each unit to the extent that such boundaries lie within or coincide with the boundaries of such structures, and the units, or portions thereof, thus depicted shall bear their identifying numbers. In addition, each convertible space depicted in the plans shall be labeled as such by use of the phrase "CONVERTIBLE SPACE." Unless the condominium instruments expressly provide otherwise, it shall be presumed that, in the case of any unit not wholly contained within or constituting one or more of the structures, the horizontal boundaries extend, in the case of each unit, at the same elevation with regard to any part of such unit lying outside of such structures, subject to the following exception: in the case of any unit which does not lie over any other unit other than basement units, if shall be presumed that the lower horizontal boundary, if any, of that unit lies at the level of the ground with regard to any part of that unit lying outside of the structures. This subsection shall apply to any condominium created prior to July 1, 1980, or to the expansion of any such condominium.

(c) Prior to the first conveyance of a condominium unit located on any portion of any additional property being or having been added to an expandable condominium, there shall be recorded new plats of survey conforming to the requirements of subsection (a) of this Code section and, with regard to any structures on the property being or having been added, plans conforming to the requirements of subsection (b) of this Code section or certifications, conforming to the certification requirements of subsection (b) of this Code section, of plans previously recorded.

(d) When converting all or any portion of any convertible space into one or more units or limited common elements, the declarant shall record, with regard to the structure or portion thereof constituting that convertible space, plans showing the location and dimensions of the horizontal boundaries, if any, and the vertical boundaries of each unit formed out of such space. The plans shall be certified by a registered architect or registered engineer in accordance with the certification requirements of subsection (b) of this Code section.

(e) When any portion of the submitted property is withdrawn, there shall be recorded a plat or plats showing the portion of the submitted property withdrawn and the remaining submitted property, which plat or plats shall be certified as provided in subsection (a) of this Code section.

EXHIBIT 3–3
State Condominium Code Requirements for Condominium Plat (continued)

EXHIBIT 3–4
Articles of Incorporation

ARTICLES OF INCORPORATION
OF
CLAIREMONT OAKS CONDOMINIUM ASSOCIATION, INC.

ARTICLE 1

The name of the corporation shall be:

CLAIREMONT OAKS CONDOMINIUM ASSOCIATION, INC.

ARTICLE 2

The corporation is organized pursuant to the provisions of the ___(State)___ Nonprofit Corporation Code.

ARTICLE 3

The corporation shall have perpetual duration.

ARTICLE 4

The corporation shall have no stock or stockholders; it is not organized and shall not operate for profit or pecuniary gain; and no part of the net earnings of the corporation

EXHIBIT 3-4
Articles of
Incorporation
(continued)

shall inure to the benefit of any member, director, officer of any private individual except that, pursuant to proper authorization, reasonable compensation may be paid for services rendered to or for the corporation affecting one or more of its purposes. No substantial part of the activities of the corporation shall be for carrying on of propaganda, or otherwise attempting to influence legislation, and the corporation shall not participate in or intervene in (including publishing or distributing statements) any political campaign on behalf of any candidate for public office.

ARTICLE 5

The purposes for which the corporation is organized are: to provide for the administration of a condominium to be known as Clairemont Oaks, A Condominium; to provide for the maintenance, repair, replacement and operation of portions of the condominium; to promote the health, safety and welfare of the owners and occupants of the condominium; to exercise all rights and privileges and perform all duties and obligations of the corporation as set forth in the _____(State)_____ Condominium Act and in the Declaration for Clairemont Oaks, A Condominium to be recorded in the Office of the Clerk of the Superior Court of Wayne County, _____(State)_____; and to perform such related functions as the board of directors of the corporation shall from time to time determine.

ARTICLE 6

In addition to, but not in limitation of, the general powers conferred by law, the corporation shall have the power to own, acquire, construct, operate and maintain property, buildings, structures and other facilities incident thereto; to supplement municipal or governmental services; to fix and collect assessments to be levied against and with respect to the condominium units and the owners thereof which assessments shall be a lien and permanent charge on said units as well as the personal obligation of said owners; to enforce any and all covenants, restrictions and agreements applicable to the condominium; to buy, hold, lease, sell, rent, manage and otherwise deal in property of every kind and description, whether real or personal; to borrow money, issue promissory notes and other obligations and evidences of indebtedness and to secure the same by mortgage, deed, security deed, pledge or otherwise; and, insofar as permitted by law, to do any other thing that, in the opinion of the board of directors, will promote, directly or indirectly, the health, safety, welfare, common benefit or enjoyment of the unit owners and occupants of said units; enhance, preserve or maintain property values within the condominium; enhance, preserve or maintain the appearance of the condominium and its surroundings; or be necessary, proper, useful or incidental to the carrying out of the functions for which the corporation is organized.

ARTICLE 7

The address of the initial registered office of the corporation shall be c/o _____ at _____, and the name of its original agent at such address is _____.

ARTICLE 8

The directors of the corporation shall be elected or appointed at the time and in the manner as provided in the By-Laws of the corporation as the same may from time to time be amended.

EXHIBIT 3-4
Articles of
Incorporation
(continued)

ARTICLE 9

The initial board of directors of the corporation shall number _____ (____) and the name and address of each person who is to serve as a member thereof is as follows:

Name   Address

_____   _____

                                                              _____

                                                              _____

_____   _____

                                                              _____

ARTICLE 10

The corporation shall have one class of members. Each owner of a condominium unit comprising a portion of Clairemont Oaks, A Condominium, shall automatically be a member of the corporation, which membership shall continue during the period of ownership by such unit owner Pursuant to the provisions of the _____(State)_____ Condominium Act, the number of votes in the corporation allocated to each condominium unit is set forth in the Declaration for Clairemont Oaks, A Condominium. Said votes shall be cast under such rules and procedures as may be prescribed in the By-Laws of the corporation, as amended from time to time, or by law.

ARTICLE 11

These Articles of Incorporation may be amended as by law provided pursuant to resolution duly adopted by the board of directors and by at least two-thirds of the votes which members present in person or by proxy at a duly called meeting are entitled to cast; provided, however, that no members shall be entitled to vote on amendments to these Articles of Incorporation for the sole purpose of complying with the requirements of any governmental or quasigovernmental entity authorized to fund or guarantee mortgages on individual condominium units, as such requirements may exist from time to time, which amendments may be adopted only at a meeting of the board of directors upon receiving the vote of a majority of the directors then in office.

ARTICLE 12

The corporation may be dissolved as by law provided pursuant to resolution duly adopted by the board of directors and by at least four-fifths of the votes of the members of the corporation.

ARTICLE 13

The name of the incorporator is _____, whose address is _____.

IN WITNESS WHEREOF, the incorporator has executed these Articles of Incorporation.

_____

CONSENT TO APPOINTMENT AS REGISTERED AGENT

To: Secretary of State
    Ex-Officio Corporation
    Commissioner
    State of _____

I, _____, do hereby consent to serve as registered agent for the corporation Clairemont Oaks Condominium Association, Inc.

This _____ day of _____, 19____.

_____

Address of Registered Agent:

_____

_____

_____

BY-LAWS OF
CLAIREMONT OAKS CONDOMINIUM ASSOCIATION, INC.

ARTICLE 1

Name and Location

Section 1. Name. The name of the association is Clairemont Oaks Condominium Association, Inc., a _____(State)_____ nonprofit membership corporation, hereinafter referred to as the "Association."

Section 2. Location. The principal office of the Condominium shall be located in Wayne County, _____(State)_____ . Meetings of members and directors may be held at such places within the State of _____, County of Wayne as may be designated from time to time by the Board of Directors.

EXHIBIT 3-5
Condominium
Association
By-Laws
(continued)

ARTICLE 2

Definitions

Section 1. General. The terms used in these By-Laws, unless otherwise specified or unless the context otherwise requires, shall have the meanings specified in Official Code of _____(State)_____ , Section _____ and the Declaration for Clairemont Oaks, A Condominium (hereinafter called the "Declaration"). Statutory references shall be construed as meaning the referenced statute of portion thereof as the same may exist from time to time.

ARTICLE 3

Membership and Voting Rights

Section 1. Membership. Each unit owner shall automatically be a member of the Association, which membership shall continue during the period of ownership by such unit owner.

Section 2. Voting Rights. The Association shall have one class of voting membership which shall consist of all unit owners. Such owners shall be entitled to exercise voting rights as provided in the _____(State)_____ Condominium Act, the Declaration and as prescribed herein. The number of votes allocated to each unit is as set forth in the Declaration. When a unit is owned by other than one or more natural persons, the person entitled to cast the vote for such unit shall be designated by a certificate signed by the record owner of such unit and filed with the Secretary. Each such certificate shall be valid until revoked, superseded by a subsequent certificate or a change occurs in the ownership of such unit. When a unit is owned by more than one natural person, they may, without being required to do so, designate the person entitled to cast the vote for such unit as provided above. In the event they do not designate such a person, the following provisions shall apply:

(a) If only one is present at a meeting, the person present shall be counted for purposes of a quorum and may cast the vote for the unit, just as though he owned it individually, and without establishing the concurrence of the absent person or persons.

(b) If more than one of such owners, whether or not all of them, are present at a meeting and concur, any one of the owners may cast the vote for the owners.

(c) If more than one of such owners, whether or not all of them, are present at a meeting and are unable to concur in their decision upon any subject requiring a vote, they shall lose their right to vote on that subject at that meeting.

The votes of the unit owners shall be cast under such rules and procedures as may be prescribed in the Declaration or in these By-Laws, as amended from time to time, or by law.

Section 3. Suspension of Voting Rights. During any period in which a unit owner shall be in default in payment of any assessment, the voting rights of such unit owner may be suspended by the Board of Directors until such assessment has been paid. Such rights of a unit owner may also be suspended, for a period not to exceed 30 days, for violation of any rules and regulations established by the Board of Directors.

ARTICLE 4

Meetings of Unit Owners

Section 1. Annual Meetings. The first annual meeting of the unit owners shall be called by the President upon request of the Declarant and shall be held within 12 months

EXHIBIT 3–5
Condominium
Association
By-Laws
(continued)

following the incorporation of the Association. Each subsequent regular annual meeting of the owners shall be held on the same day of the same month of each year thereafter unless otherwise provided by the unit owners at any previous meeting. If the day for the annual meeting of the unit owners is a legal holiday, the meeting will be held on the first day following which is not a legal holiday.

Section 2. Special Meetings. Special meetings of the unit owners may be called at any time by the President or by the Board of Directors, or upon written request of the unit owners who are entitled to vote at least _____ (____%) of the votes of the membership.

Section 3. Notice of Meetings. Written notice of each meeting of the unit owners shall be given by, or at the direction of, the Secretary or person authorized to call the meeting at least 21 days in advance of any annual or regularly scheduled meeting, and at least seven days in advance of any other meeting, stating the time, place and purpose of such meeting. Such notice shall be delivered personally or sent by United States mail, postage prepaid, to all unit owners of record at such address or addresses as any of them may have designated, or, of no other address has been so designated, at the address of their respective units. Such notice shall also be sent by United States mail, postage prepaid, to each institutional holder of a first mortgage on a unit having theretofore requested same in writing. Each such holder shall be permitted to designate a representative to attend each such meeting without voice or vote except pursuant to Section 5 of this Article 4.

Section 4. Quorum. The presence at the meeting of unit owners and/or proxies entitled to cast more than one-third of the votes of the membership shall constitute a quorum for any action except as otherwise expressly provided in the _____(State)_____ Condominium Act or in the Declaration. If, however, such quorum shall not be present or represented at any meeting, the unit owners and/or proxies entitled to cast a majority of the votes thereat shall have the power to adjourn the meeting from time to time, without notice other than announcement at the meeting, until a quorum as aforesaid shall be present or be represented.

Section 5. Proxies. Subject to the provisions of Article 3, Section 2, hereof, at all meetings of the unit owners, each unit owner may vote in person or by proxy. All proxies shall be in writing and filed with the Secretary. Each proxy shall be revocable, shall automatically cease upon conveyance by a unit owner of his unit and shall be effective only for the meeting specified therein and any adjournment thereof.

Section 6. Order of Business. The order of business at all annual meetings of the owners shall be as follows:

        (a) Roll call.
        (b) Proof of notice of meeting.
        (c) Reading of minutes of preceding meeting.
        (d) Reports of officers.
        (e) Report of Board of Directors.
        (f) Reports of committees.
        (g) Election of Directors.
        (h) Unfinished business.
        (i) New business.

Section 7. Decisions of Unit Owners. Unless otherwise expressly provided in the _____(State)_____ Condominium Act, the Declaration or these By-Laws, a majority of the votes cast on any particular issue shall be necessary to adopt decisions at any meeting of the unit owners. When the ____(State)____ Condominium Act, the Declaration or these By-Laws require the approval or consent of all or a specified percentage of mortgagees and/or other lien holders, no decision or resolution duly adopted by the unit owners shall be effective or valid until such approval or consent shall be obtained. During such time as the Declarant has the right to control the Association pursuant to the provisions of Official Code of ____(State)____, Section _____, no decision or resolution duly adopted by the unit owners shall be effective or valid until the Declarant's approval or consent shall have been obtained.

Section 8. Conduct of Meetings. The President shall preside over all meetings of the unit owners and the Secretary shall keep the minutes of the meetings and record in a minute book all resolutions duly adopted as well as a record of all transactions occurring at such meetings. The latest edition of Roberts Rules of Order shall govern the conduct of all meetings of the unit owners when not in conflict with the ____(State)____ Condominium Act, the Declaration or these By-Laws.

ARTICLE 5
Board of Directors

Section 1. Number and Qualifications. Following expiration of the period of the Declarant's right to control the Association pursuant to the provisions of Official Code of ____(State)____, Section _____, the Board of Directors of the Association shall be composed of three persons. With the exception of those persons appointed as directors by the Declarant pursuant to the provisions of Official Code of ____(State)____, Section _____, each such person shall be a member of the Association or the spouse of a member.

Section 2. Election and Term of Office. Upon the termination of the Declarant's right to control the Association pursuant to the provisions of Official Code of ____(State)____, Section _____, the Declarant shall give at least seven days' written notice to each member of a special meeting of the members, to be held not more than 30 days after the date of such termination, to elect a new board of directors. At such meeting, and at each annual meeting thereafter the unit owners shall elect three directors for a term of one year each. Except in the case of death, resignation or removal, each director elected by the members shall serve until the annual meeting at which his term expires and until his successor has been duly elected and qualified. Persons receiving the largest number of votes at any election of directors shall be elected whether or not such number constitutes a majority of the votes cast. Cumulative voting shall not be permitted.

Section 3. Removals; Vacancies. Following expiration of the period of the Declarant's right to control the Association pursuant to the provisions of Official Code of ____(State)____, Section _____, any director may be removed from the Board of Directors with or without cause, by a majority vote of the unit owners theretofore entitled to elect such director. In the event of death or resignation of a director, his successor shall be selected by the remaining members of the board. In the event of removal of a director, his successor shall be elected by the unit owners theretofore entitled to elect such director. Any such successor shall serve for the unexpired term of his predecessor.

Section 4. Annual Organization Meeting. The first meeting of the Board of Directors following each annual meeting of the unit owners shall be held within ten days thereafter, at such time and place as shall be fixed by the newly elected directors at such annual

EXHIBIT 3–5
Condominium
Association
By–Laws
(continued)

EXHIBIT 3-5
Condominium
Association
By-Laws
(continued)

meeting, and no notice shall be necessary in order legally to constitute such meeting.

Section 5. Regular Meetings. Regular meetings of the Board of Directors may be held at such time and place as shall be determined from time to time by the Board of Directors. Notice of the time and place of regular meetings shall be given to every director by mail or telephone at least three days prior to the date of such meeting.

Section 6. Special Meetings. Special meetings of the Board of Directors may be called by the President on two days notice to every director given by mail or telephone and stating the time, place and purpose of the meeting. Special meetings shall be called by the President or Secretary in like manner and on like notice on the written request of directors entitled to cast at least two votes at such meetings.

Section 7. Waiver of Notice; Action without Meeting. Whenever notice of a meeting of the Board of Directors is required to be given under any provision of these By-Laws, a written waiver thereof, executed by a director before or after the meeting and filed with the Secretary, shall be deemed equivalent to notice to the director executing the same. Attendance at a meeting by the director shall constitute a waiver of notice of such meeting by the director if such director attends the meeting without protesting prior thereto or at the meeting's commencement the lack of notice to him. Neither the business to be transacted at, nor the purpose of, any meeting of the Board of Directors need be specified in any written waiver of notice. Any action required or permitted to be taken at any meeting of the Board of Directors may be taken without a meeting provided that all directors consent to the action in writing and the written consents are filed with the records of the proceedings of the Board of Directors. Such consents shall be treated for all purposes as a vote at a meeting.

Section 8. Voting; Quorum of the Board; Adjournment of Meetings. At all meetings of the Board of Directors, each director shall be entitled to cast one vote. The presence in person of directors representing at least two-thirds of the votes of the Board of Directors shall be a quorum at any Board of Directors meeting and a majority of the votes present and voting shall bind the Board of Directors and the Association as to any matter within the powers and duties of the Board of Directors.

Section 9. Powers and Duties. The Board of Directors shall have the powers and duties necessary for administration of the affairs of the Association and may do all such acts and things except as by law or the Declaration may not be delegated to the Board of Directors by the unit owners. In exercising its powers and duties, the Board of Directors shall take as its standard the maintenance of the general character of the condominium as a residential community of the first class in the quality of its maintenance, use and occupancy. Such powers and duties of the Board of Directors shall be exercised in accordance with and subject to all provisions of the _____(State)_____ Condominium Act, the Declaration and these By-Laws and shall include without limitation powers and duties to:

(a) Operate, care for, maintain, repair and replace the common elements and employ personnel necessary or desirable therefor.

(b) Determine common expenses of the Association.

(c) Collect assessments from the unit owners.

(d) Adopt and amend rules and regulations covering the details of the operation and use of the condominium.

(e) Open bank accounts on behalf of the Association and designate the signatories required therefor.

(f) Manage, control, lease as lessor, and otherwise deal with the common elements, including power to make shut-offs of common services and other interruptions of the normal functioning of the buildings to facilitate performance of any maintenance or repair work or the making of additions, alterations or improvements by the Association or the unit owners pursuant to provisions of the Declaration. The Board of Directors shall use reasonable efforts to disrupt the unit owners and occupants as little as possible in exercising such authority to effect shut-offs and other interruptions.

(g) Purchase, lease or otherwise acquire units offered for sale or lease or surrendered by their unit owners to the Association.

(h) Own, sell, lease, encumber, and otherwise deal in, but not vote with respect to, units owned by the Association.

(i) Obtain and maintain insurance for the condominium pursuant to the provisions of the Declaration.

(j) (1) Make additions and improvements to and alterations of the common elements, and (2) make repairs to and restoration of the property after damage or destruction by fire or other casualty, or as a result of condemnation.

(k) Enforce by any legal or equitable remedies available all obligations of the unit owners or any of them to the Association. Such enforcement power shall include, without limitation, the power to levy, as assessments, fines against unit owners for default in the performance of said obligations in such amounts as from time to time the Board of Directors may deem proper in the circumstances, but not in excess of $_____ for any one violation, counting each day a violation continues after notice from the Board of Directors as a separate violation. If any owner fails to pay a fine within ten days after notification thereof, the Board of Directors may levy, as assessments, additional fines to enforce payment of the initial fine.

(1) Appoint auditors of the Association.

(m) Employ a manager or managing agent and delegate thereto any duties of the Board of Directors under subparagraphs (a), (c), (e), (i) and (o) of this Section 9.

(n) Conduct litigation and be subject to suit as to any cause of action involving the common elements or arising out of the enforcement of the provisions of the ___(State)___ Condominium Act, the Declaration or these By-Laws.

(o) Make contracts in connection with the exercise of any of the powers and duties of the Board of Directors.

(p) Take all other actions the Board of Directors deems necessary or proper for the sound management of the condominium and fulfillment of the terms and provisions of the ___(State)___ Condominium Act, the Declaration and these By-Laws.

In the case of those powers and duties specified in the foregoing clauses (d), (g), (h), (j), (l), and (m), the Board of Directors need exercise the same only to the extent, if any, it deems necessary or desirable or is required to do so by vote of the unit owners. The Board of Directors shall not be obligated to take any action or perform any duty imposed upon it requiring an expenditure of funds unless in its opinion it shall have funds of the Association sufficient therefor.

ARTICLE 6

Officers

Section 1. Designation. The Principal officers of the Association shall be the President, the Vice President, the Secretary and the Treasurer, all of whom shall be elected by the

EXHIBIT 3–5
Condominium
Association
By–Laws
(continued)

Board of Directors. One person may hold the office of Secretary and Treasurer simultaneously. The Board of Directors may appoint an assistant treasurer, an assistant secretary, and such other officers as in its judgment may be necessary. The Vice President may also hold the office of assistant secretary and perform the functions thereof in the absence of the Secretary. The President and Vice President shall be members of the Board of Directors. Any other officers may be, but shall not be required to be, members of the Board of Directors.

Section 2. Election of Officers. The officers of the Association shall be elected annually by the Board of Directors at the organization meeting of each new Board of Directors and shall hold office at the pleasure of the Board of Directors. Any vacancy in an office shall be filled by the Board of Directors at a regular meeting of the Board of Directors, or at any special meeting of the Board of Directors called for such purpose.

Section 3. Removal of Officers. Upon the affirmative vote of a majority of the votes of the Board of Directors, any officer may be removed, either with or without cause, and his successor may be elected at any regular meeting of the Board of Directors, or at any special meeting of the Board of Directors called for such purpose.

Section 4. Multiple Offices. The offices of Secretary and Treasurer may be held by the same person. No person shall simultaneously hold more than one of any of the other offices except in the case of special offices created pursuant to Section 1 of this Article 6.

Section 5. President. The President shall be the chief executive of the Association. He shall preside at all meetings of the unit owners and of the Board of Directors. He shall have all of the general powers and duties which are incident to the office of president of a corporation, including, but not limited to, the power to appoint committees from among the unit owners from time to time as he may, in his sole discretion, deem appropriate to assist in the conduct of the affairs of the Association.

Section 6. Vice President. The Vice President shall take the place of the President and perform his duties whenever the President shall be absent or unable to act. If neither the President nor the Vice President is able to act, the Board of Directors shall appoint some other member of the Board of Directors to act in the place of the President on an interim basis. The Vice President shall also perform such other duties as shall, from time to time, be imposed upon him by the Board of Directors or by the President.

Section 7. Secretary. The Secretary shall keep the minutes of all meetings of the unit owners and of the Board of Directors and shall have charge of such books and papers as the Board of Directors may direct. He shall, in general, perform all the duties incident to the office of secretary of a corporation and such other duties as shall, from time to time, be imposed upon him by the Board of Directors or by the President.

Section 8. Treasurer. The Treasurer shall have the responsibility for Association funds and securities and shall be responsible for keeping full and accurate financial records and books of account showing all receipts and disbursements, and for the preparation of all required financial data; he shall be responsible for the deposit of all monies and other valuable effects in the name of the Association, in such depositories as may from time to time be designated by the Board of Directors, and he shall, in general, perform all the duties incident to the office of treasurer of a corporation and such other duties as shall, from time to time, be imposed upon him by the Board of Directors or by the President.

Section 9. Compensation. Unless otherwise expressly provided by the Board of Directors, no officer shall receive compensation from the Association for acting as such, but shall be entitled to reimbursement from the Association as a common expense for rea-

CONDOMINIUMS AND COOPERATIVES

sonable out-of-pocket disbursements made by him in the performance of his duties. No officer shall be obligated to make any such disbursements.

ARTICLE 7
Officers and Directors: General Provisions

Section 1. Contracts with Interested Parties. No contract or transaction between the Association and one or more of its officers or directors, or between the Association and any other entity in which one or more of the association's officers or directors are officers, directors, partners or trustees, or have a financial interest, shall be void or voidable solely for this reason, or solely because the Association's officer or director is present at or participates in the meeting of the Board of Directors which authorizes the contract or transaction, or solely because his or their votes are counted for such purpose, if (a) the material facts as to his interest and as to the contract or transaction are disclosed or are known to the Board of Directors and the Board of Directors in good faith authorized the contract or transaction by a vote sufficient for such purpose without counting the vote or votes of the interested director or directors; or (b) the material facts as to his interest and as to the contract or transaction are disclosed or are known to the unit owners entitled to vote thereon, and the contract or transaction is specifically approved or ratified in good faith by vote of such unit owners; or (c) the contract or transaction is fair as to the Association as of the time it is authorized, approved or ratified by the Board of Directors or the unit owners. Interested directors may be counted in determining the presence of a quorum at a meeting of the Board of Directors which authorizes the contract or transaction.

Section 2. Indemnification. Pursuant to the provisions of Section 12.08 of the Declaration, the Association shall indemnify its officers and directors to the extent provided in and subject to the limitations of the Declaration.

ARTICLE 8
Books and Records

Section 1. Books and Records. The Association shall keep such books and records as by law provided and shall make same available for inspection by any unit owner, any institutional holder of a first mortgage on a unit, and their respective agents and attorneys, for any proper purpose at any reasonable time. In addition, an annual report of the receipts and expenditures of the Association, based upon an audit made by an independent public accountant, shall be rendered by the Board of Directors to all unit owners, and to each institutional holder of a first mortgage on a unit having theretofore requested same in writing, within three months after the end of each fiscal year.

ARTICLE 9
Amendments

Section 1. Amendments. These By-Laws may be amended only by the owners of the units to which two-thirds (2/3) of the votes in the Association cast their vote in person or by proxy at a meeting duly called for such purpose, written notice of which shall be delivered or sent to all unit owners not less than 21 days in advance of the meeting stating the time, place and purpose of such meeting and the subject matter of the proposed amendment or, in lieu of such vote, these By-Laws may be amended by an instrument duly executed by unit owners having at least two-thirds (2/3) of the entire voting interest of all unit owners. Amendments to these By-Laws for the sole purpose of complying with the

EXHIBIT 3–5
Condominium
Association
By-Laws
(continued)

EXHIBIT 3–5
Condominium
Association
By-Laws
(continued)

requirements of any governmental or quasi-governmental entity authorized to fund or guarantee mortgages on individual condominium units, as such requirements may exist from time to time, may be effected by an instrument duly executed by a majority of the directors of the Association. Each such amendment shall be effective when adopted or at such later date as may be specified therein.

ARTICLE 10
Miscellaneous

Section 1. Conflicts. In the event of any conflict between the Declaration and these By-Laws, the Declaration shall control.

Section 2. Association Seal. The Association shall have a seal in circular form having within its circumference the words: _____.

Section 3. Fiscal Year. The fiscal year of the Association shall begin on the first day of January and end on the 31st day of December of every year, except that the first fiscal year shall begin on the date on which the Association was incorporated under the laws of the State of _____.

Surveys and Land Descriptions

Halfway down a bystreet of one of our New England towns stands a rusty wooden house, with seven acutely peaked gables, facing towards various points of the compass, and a huge, clustered chimney in the midst.

—*Nathaniel Hawthorne*, The House of the Seven Gables

OBJECTIVES

After reading this chapter you will be able to:

- Read and understand three types of legal descriptions: government rectangular survey description, platted description, and metes and bounds description
- Review surveys
- Review a land survey for the accuracy of a legal description
- Prepare a legal description from a land survey

GLOSSARY

As–built survey Survey that locates all physical improvements on the land in relation to the boundary lines of the land.

Base line Imaginary east-west survey line used in the government survey system to establish township lines.

Call Course and distance describing a boundary line of land in a metes-and-bounds land description.

Chord Straight line drawn from the beginning point of an arc to the ending point of an arc.

Course In a metes-and-bounds legal description, it is the direction of a property boundary line.

Distance In a metes-and-bounds legal description, it is the length of a property boundary line, usually measured in feet and hundredths of a foot (example: 82.13 feet).

Legal description Description of real property by a government survey, metes and bounds, or lot numbers of a recorded plat, which description is complete enough that a particular parcel of land can be located and identified.

Plat Survey of real property that often is recorded.

Principal meridians Imaginary north and south lines used in a government survey system. Meridians intersect the base lines to form a starting point for the measurement of land under that system.

Range lines Division of a state in a government survey system being a six-mile-wide row of townships running north and south.

Section Division or parcel of land on a government survey comprising one square mile, or six hundred forty acres.

Survey Visual presentation of the physical boundaries of real property. The survey is used to describe real property.

In a scene from the classic film *Cocoanuts*, Groucho Marx explains real estate to Chico Marx. Groucho asks Chico if he knows what a lot is. Chico replies, "Yeah, too much." Groucho then says, "I don't mean a whole lot, just a little lot with nothing on it." Chico responds, with all of Chico's logic, "Anytime you gotta too much, you gotta whole lot. A whole lot is too much, too much is a whole lot; same thing."

New York:
In New York, the legal description may combine several methods, the most prevalent being a metes and bounds description. The metes are measurements and monuments, "bounds" are fixed objects as streets.

Regardless of whether you have a whole lot or a small lot with nothing on it, the lot has to be described. Real estate often is described casually, such as the "big white house on the corner of Wilton and Lullwater" or "the Harris farm at the end of the road." The competent practice of real estate law, however, demands that parcels of land be referred to more precisely. Every deed, mortgage, lease, easement, or other document that deals with land must state the exact size and location of the land according to an established system of land description. The purpose of the description is to fix the boundaries of the land and to distinguish the land in question from other land. A description that is too vague will render void any document in which it is incorporated. Therefore, a specific or correct description is called a **legal description** because it makes the document legal and enforceable. In many states, legal descriptions are prepared by registered land surveyors, and the real estate legal assistant only needs to proofread the description for mistakes. In other states, the preparation of a legal description is the task of an attorney or a legal assistant working under the supervision of an attorney. The land surveyor prepares a survey or drawing of the property showing the various boundaries, and it is the duty of the legal assistant to prepare a written legal description locating and identifying the property's boundaries as shown on the survey.

THE SURVEY

The word **survey** is derived from an old French word meaning "to look over." It refers to the evaluation of real property evidence to locate the physical limits of a particular parcel of land. The real property evidence considered by the surveyor typically consists of physical field evidence, written record evidence, and field measurements. The surveyor, having made an evaluation of the evidence, forms an opinion as to where the lines would be located

The surveyor then prepares a map, or plat of survey, to communicate his or her opinion to others. The map or plat is colloquially known as the survey.

New York:
For further discussion on surveys, see Appendix.

A survey may be a boundary survey, which locates the boundaries of the land in question and provides a description of the land. A surveyor may, however, be asked to prepare an **as-built survey**. An as-built survey locates all physical improvements on the land in relation to the boundary lines. On an as-built survey, the surveyor usually locates all fences, walls, driveways, pavements, building structures, and natural features such as streams and ponds. This information is necessary to determine both the presence of features that may limit the value or use of the land and the conformity with local ordinances regarding minimum building setbacks and other requirements. An example of an as-built survey is shown in Exhibit 4–1.

Note that the as-built survey reveals some interesting features of this property. For example, a thirty-six-inch concrete pipe runs underneath the corner of the house. In addition, a sanitary sewer line runs underneath the house. Both the concrete pipe

EXHIBIT 4–1   As–Built Survey

and the sewer line could cause substantial problems for the owner. These features may make it difficult for the owner to obtain a loan on the property as well as to sell the property. The utility companies that own rights to the concrete pipe and sanitary sewer line also could damage the house if they had to repair the pipe and line.

For purposes of land descriptions, a survey should provide the legal assistant with the following information: (a) the state, county, land district, and section in which the property surveyed is located; (b) an indication of which direction on the survey is north; (c) a point of beginning for a land description; (d) courses and distances for each property line; (e) the name of the surveyor; (f) a scale for distances not shown on the survey; and (g) a legend of abbreviations or symbols used.

LAND DESCRIPTIONS

Three types of land description are in use in the United States: (1) government rectangular survey description, (2) platted description, and (3) metes and bounds description.

Government Rectangular Survey Description

When the United States was first being established, a standard system of describing land was needed to make areas of land easy to locate and available for sale by federal land offices. Thomas Jefferson headed a committee that in 1785 devised a method of dividing land into a series of rectangles. The rectangular survey system is used in describing land in Alabama, Alaska, Arizona, Arkansas, California, Colorado, Florida, Idaho, Illinois, Indiana, Iowa, Kansas, Louisiana, Michigan, Minnesota, Mississippi, Missouri, Montana, Nebraska, Nevada, New Mexico, North Dakota, Ohio, Oklahoma, Oregon, South Dakota, Utah, Washington, Wisconsin, and Wyoming (see Exhibit 4–2).

The rectangular survey system is based on sets of two intersecting hypothetical lines: **principal meridians** and **base lines**. Principal meridians are vertical lines that run north and south. Base lines are horizontal lines that run east and west. Using the principal meridians and base lines, a state can be divided into land areas that are easily identified. Within these identifiable areas of land, any particular section or parcel of land can be located.

Principal Meridians

A principal meridian is a surveyor's line that runs due north and south through a particular area or state. Principal meridians are identifiable in terms of their distance in degrees, minutes, and seconds west of the Greenwich meridian. The United States contains thirty-five principal meridians, and each is assigned a name or number for identification purposes. For example, the principal meridians running north and south in the state of Louisiana are called the Louisiana meridian and the St. Helena meridian.

Base Lines

A base line is a surveyor's line that runs due east and west and is identified as being a certain number of degrees north of the equator. Only one base line will cross each principal meridian; therefore, a parcel of land can be described as being a certain dis-

New York:
Surveys are usually required when a mortgage is involved and you can either update the old one or, if it is several years old, the bank may require a new survey. Each bank has its own survey requirements. The survey must be certified to the buyer and the lending institution (or title company).

EXHIBIT 4–2
Methods of Land
Description in the
United States

tance east or west of a given principal meridian and a certain distance north or south of a given base line.

Township or Range Lines

Using only principal meridians and base lines, the areas of land are still large, and surveying a particular parcel within the areas would be difficult. To simplify the task of identifying a smaller parcel, township and range lines have been established. **Township lines** run east and west at six-mile intervals parallel with base lines and form strips of land or tiers called townships. Land on either side of the principal meridians is also divided into six-mile strips by north and south lines called **range lines**. Squares of land formed by the intersecting township lines and range lines make up a grid, with each square within the grid having about six miles on each side. These squares, called **townships**, make up the basic units of the rectangular survey system. In theory, each township is six miles square and contains thirty-six square miles; in reality, a slight overage or shortage may exist because of difficulties encountered during surveying.

Correction Lines and Guide Meridians

Because the earth is round, all range lines gradually approach one another to the point where they eventually meet at the north pole. Thus, an accurate survey of a township would show its north boundary line to be about fifty feet shorter than its south boundary line. In the case of the fourth township north of the base line, the difference is four times as great, or about 200 feet. The rectangular survey system uses *correction lines* to compensate for these resulting shortages. Each fourth township line (twenty-four miles) north and south of a base line is designated as a correction line. At each correction line, the east and west range lines are remeasured to the full distance of six miles apart. Each correction line serves as a new base line for townships that lie between it and the next correction line. *Guide meridians* are lines running due north and south at twenty-four-mile intervals (every fourth range line) on either side of the principal meridian. They begin at the base line and extend to the first correction line in either direction. Guide meridians are not parallel to the principal meridians or to one another. Combined with the correction lines, these guide meridians divide land territories into areas about twenty-four miles apart.

Township Squares

A *township square* is identified by using (a) the location of the township's strip in which the township is located; (b) the designation of the range strip, and (c) the name or number of the closest principal meridian. The first tier of squares immediately adjacent to and parallel with the base line is assigned Township 1, the second tier is assigned Township 2, and so on; therefore, each township in the first tier north of the base line is called Township 1 North of the base line; each in the second row is Township 2 North of the base line, and so on. Likewise, each township square in the first tier south of the base line is called Township 1 South; each township in the second tier is Township 2 South, and so on. Similarly, range numbers are assigned to each tier of township squares running parallel to a principal meridian, beginning with a row immediately adjacent to the principal meridian. Township squares in the first row east of the principal meridian are numbered Range 1 East of a particular principal meridian. Those in the second row east would be identified as Range 2 East, and so on. Similarly, townships located within range lines on the west side of the principal meridian would be identified as Range 1 West, Range 2 West, Range 3 West, and so on.

For example, in Exhibit 4–3, the township marked x is described as Township 5 North, Range 2 East of the Louisiana meridian. It is Township 5 North because the township is located within the fifth strip north of the base line. It is Range 2 East because the township is located within the second strip of land running north and south east of the Louisiana meridian. Finally, references are made to the Louisiana meridian because it is the closest principal meridian. The description can be abbreviated as T5 North, R2 East, Louisiana meridian.

Sections

The thirty-six mile township square is further subdivided into thirty-six sections, each section being one mile square and containing about 640 acres. The sections are numbered consecutively from 1 to 36, beginning in the northeast corner or upper right-hand corner of the township and proceeding west and east alternatively through the township, ending in the southeast corner with the number 36 (Exhibit 4–4).

Sections are subdivided into quarter sections and quarter sections can be further divided into halves or quarters. These halves of the quarter sections and quarter-quarter sections can be divided into smaller tracts. Exhibit 4–5 shows a section that has been subdivided. Note that in Exhibit 4–5, the SE 1/4 of the NE 1/4 of the section would be an area of land equal to forty acres. The S 1/2 of the SW 1/4 of the NE 1/4 would be an area of land equal to twenty acres.

Exhibits 4–5 and 4–6 are helpful in visualizing land descriptions and understanding the rectangular survey system.

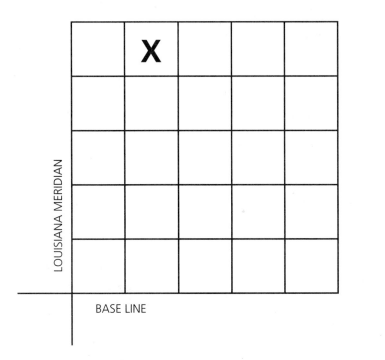

EXHIBIT 4–3
Principal Meridian and Base Line

EXHIBIT 4–4
Sections in a
Township

N

6	5	4	3	2	1
7	8	9	10	11	12
18	17	16	15	14	13
19	20	21	22	23	24
30	29	28	27	26	25
31	32	33	34	35	36

W   E

S

EXHIBIT 4–5
One Section of
Land

NW 1/4		NW 1/4 of NE 1/4	NE 1/4 of NE 1/4
		N 1/2 of SW 1/4 of NE 1/4	SE 1/4 of NE 1/4
		S 1/2 of SW 1/4 of NE 1/4	
W 1/2 of SW 1/4	E 1/2 of SW 1/4	N 1/2 of SE 1/4	
		S 1/2of SE 1/4	

EXHIBIT 4–6   A Section

A SECTION OF LAND	ACRES	LINEAR CHAINS (1 Chain= 66 feet)	LINEAR RODS (1 Rod = 16 1/2 feet)	LINEAR FEET	SQUARE MILE
ONE FULL SECTION	640	80	320	5,280	1
QUARTER SECTION	160	40	160	2,640	1/2
QUARTER QUARTER SECTION	40	20	80	1,320	1/4
QUARTER QUARTER QUARTER SECTION	10	10	40	660	1/8
QUARTER QUARTER QUARTER QUARTER SECTION	21/2	5	20	320	1/16
QUARTER QUARTER QUARTER QUARTER QUARTER SECTION	5/8	21/2	10	165	1/32

Practice Note in Reading Government Rectangular Survey Descriptions

A government rectangular survey description is read backward. That is, you read from the end of the description to the beginning to determine the location and size of the property. For example, consider the following description:

> The North 1/2 of the Northeast 1/4 of the Southeast 1/4 of Section 5, Township 3 North, Range 2 East of the Louisiana Principal Meridian.

To locate this tract of land from the description above, you read the description starting with the end. First search for the Louisiana principal meridian on the map of the United States. Then on a regional map, find the township in which the property is located by counting two range strips east to the Louisiana meridian and three townships north of its corresponding base line. After locating section 5 of the township on the map, divide the section into quarters, the southeast quarter into quarters, and then the northeast 1/4 of the southeast 1/4 into halves. The north half of the northeast 1/4 of the southeast 1/4 is the property in question. The property contains twenty acres. The description can be abbreviated as N 1/2, NE 1/4, SE 1/4 of Section 5, T 3N, R 2E, of the Louisiana principal meridian.

Platted Description

The platted, or short form, description describes a piece of land by reference to a recorded survey or plat. The first requirement for a platted legal description is that a land surveyor prepare a **plat** showing the dimensions and boundaries of the land. The plat is then recorded in the county records where the land is located. Platted descriptions commonly are used in single-family home subdivisions, condominiums, and industrial parks. The local custom in some areas also may dictate that almost all property be platted.

A legal assistant preparing a platted legal description need only make reference to the plat, indicating the book and page numbers where the plat has been recorded. The following is an example of a platted legal description:

EXAMPLE 3–1

ALL THAT TRACT or parcel of land lying and being in Land Lot 106 of the 18th district of DeKalb County, Georgia, and being Lot 3, Block A, Unit 1 of Farris Subdivision as shown on Plat of Subdivision recorded at Plat Book 10, Page 84, DeKalb County, Georgia Records.

Practice Note on Platted Description

The platted legal description refers to a certain lot being shown on a certain plat recorded in a certain plat book and page within the county. For the legal description to be correct, the land being described must in fact appear as designated in the brief reference. It is a good idea to obtain a copy of the recorded plat to make certain that the property is adequately and correctly described.

The requirements for a platted description are as follows:

- Land lot
- District
- County
- State
- Subdivision name and lot, block, and unit numbers
- Recorded reference to plat book and page numbers

Metes and Bounds Description

A metes and bounds description sets forth and completely describes the boundary lines of the land. Example 4–2 is an example of a metes and bounds description. The survey from which it was taken is shown in Exhibit 4–7.

Each boundary line, or "call," is described by a course and a distance. The **course** is the direction in which the boundary line travels, and the **distance** is the length of the boundary line. For example, the first call in Exhibit 4–7 measuring the eastern boundary of the property as it leaves Buckhead Avenue is north 00°52′00″ west 82.13 feet. The course of the call is northwest, and the distance of the call is 82.13 feet.

EXHIBIT 4–7 Metes and Bounds Survey

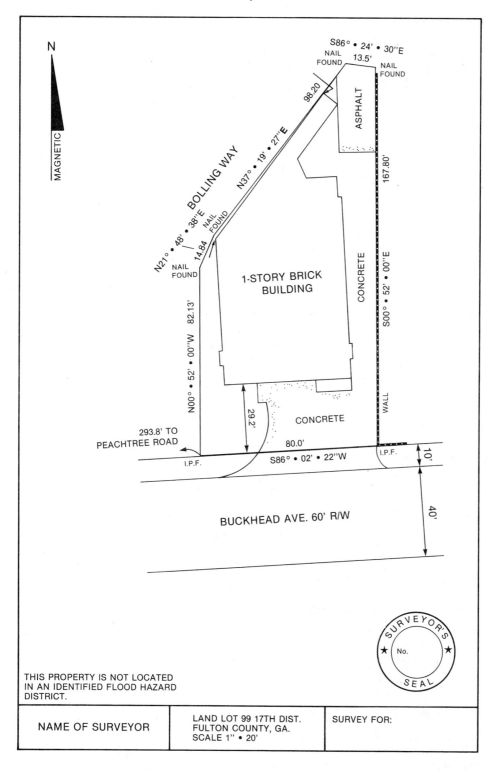

EXAMPLE 4-2

ALL THAT TRACT OR PARCEL OF LAND lying and being in Land Lot 99 of the 17th District of Fulton County, Georgia, and being more particularly described as follows:

TO FIND THE TRUE POINT OF BEGINNING, commence at a point formed by the intersection of the northerly side of Buckhead Avenue (a 60-foot right-of-way) and the easterly side of Peachtree Road; thence run east along the aforementioned right-of-way line of Buckhead Avenue a distance of 293.8 feet to an iron pin found and the TRUE POINT OF BEGINNING; thence running north 00 degrees 52 minutes 00 seconds west a distance of 82.13 feet to a nail found; thence north 21 degrees 48 minutes 38 seconds east a distance of 14.84 feet to a nail found on the southeasterly right-of-way line of Bolling Way; thence along the right-of-way line of Bolling Way north 37 degrees 19 minutes 27 seconds east a distance of 98.20 feet to a nail found; thence south 86 degrees 24 minutes 30 seconds east a distance of 13.5 feet to a nail found; thence south 00 degrees 52 minutes 00 seconds east a distance of 167.80 feet to an iron pin found on the northerly right-of-way line of Buckhead Avenue; thence south 86 degrees 02 minutes 22 seconds west along the northerly right-of-way line of Buckhead Avenue a distance of 80.0 feet to the TRUE POINT OF BEGINNING.

A metes and bounds description usually begins with an introduction that locates the land in a general part of the state. For example, the state of Georgia is subdivided into counties, and a county is further subdivided into land districts, and some districts are divided into sections. Within districts and sections are land lots that range from 40 to 490 acres. The boundaries of the counties, districts, sections, and land lots are all made definite by government survey. An example of an introduction to a metes and bounds description in Georgia is as follows:

EXAMPLE 4-3

All that tract or parcel of land lying and being in Land Lot 99 of the 17th District of Fulton County, Georgia and being more particularly described as follows:

Each metes and bounds description must begin somewhere, and that somewhere is called the point of beginning, or beginning point. The beginning point must be precise or the entire description will be incorrect; it must be a definitely ascertainable point and a point that can be located on the ground. Therefore, a beginning point must be either (a) at a known point (a monument, man-made or natural), such as a land lot corner, street corner, street intersection, intersection of the street with a railroad, or intersection of a street with a stream, or (b) a certain course and distance from a monument. The beginning point for the survey in Exhibit 4–7 and the legal description above is the intersection of two streets, Buckhead Avenue and Peachtree Road. The beginning point is described as follows:

EXAMPLE 4-4

TO FIND THE TRUE POINT OF BEGINNING, commence at a point formed by the intersection of the northerly side of Buckhead Avenue (60-foot right-of-way) and the easterly side of Peachtree Road; thence run East along the aforementioned right-of-way line of Buckhead Avenue a distance of 293.8 feet to an iron pin found and the TRUE POINT OF BEGINNING.

Review the other sample metes and bounds legal descriptions at the end of this chapter and see how each of the beginning points was obtained. It is incorrect to say as a beginning point, "Begin at an iron pin (found on a certain street)" or "Begin at a a point (on a certain street)" because there are an infinite number of iron pins or points along that street.

Once the beginning point has been fixed, the metes and bounds description proceeds along a series of calls, each **call** being a course and distance describing a boundary line of the land. Each of these calls is located on the survey by the land surveyor. A review of the legal description and the survey in Exhibit 4–7 as well as the sample legal descriptions and surveys at the end of this chapter show how the course and distances have been described. The course (the direction) of a boundary line usually is done by course bearings. These bearings are based on true north or true south compass readings, and each course is based on a north-south direction. The compass directions are based on a 360-degree radius, for which there are four 90-degree quadrants: northwest, northeast, southeast, and southwest (Exhibit 4–8).

EXHIBIT 4–8 Quadrants of Compass

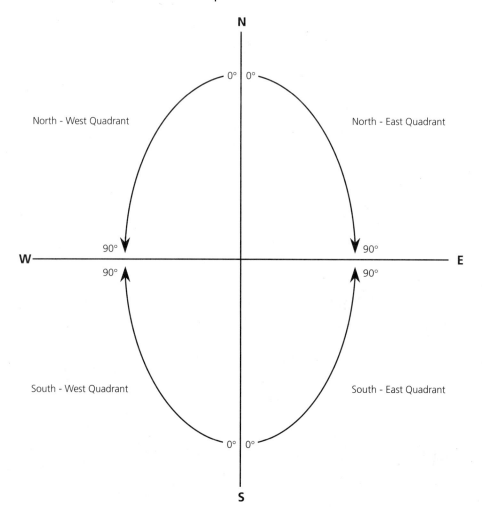

Each quadrant has 90 degrees; each degree has sixty minutes; and each minute has sixty seconds. For example, a line that is north 10°, 50′, 26″ west is a line that is 10° 50′ 26″ west of due north and is a line that would be found in the northwest quadrant of the compass.

The distance of a call usually is measured in feet or hundredths of feet. A call that is 56.8 feet is 56 and 80/100ths of a foot in length. In some parts of the country, especially in rural areas, the distances may be measured in rods and chains. A rod is 16.5 feet. A chain is 100 links, with each link being .66 feet; so the entire chain is 66 feet. It is rare for a distance to be given in yards.

Curved Property Lines

Not all property can be measured in straight lines, and many times a metes and bounds description involves a curved land boundary. Whenever a legal description involves a curve, the land surveyor should give the following information concerning each curve: (a) the arc distance of the curve; (b) the radius distance of the curve; (c) the chord course (**chord** being a straight line drawn from the beginning point of the arc to the ending point of the arc); and (d) the distance of the chord (Exhibit 4–9).

EXHIBIT 4–9   Elements of Curved Property Description

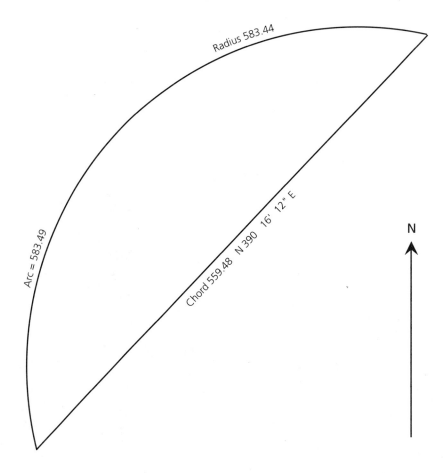

A legal assistant who has been given the arc distance, the radius distance of the curve, and the chord course and distance can prepare a land description involving a curved boundary. An example of a curved land description taken from Exhibit 4–9 is as follows:

EXAMPLE 4–5

THENCE, along the arc of a curve an arc distance of 583.49 feet to a point (said curve having a radius of 583.44 feet and being subtended by a chord bearing north 39° 16′ 12″ east, a chord distance of 559.48 feet).

Measurement of Courses by Angles

Sometimes surveyors use angles to measure the exact direction of a property line instead of or in addition to bearings.

A circle has 360 degrees (each degree has sixty minutes and each minute has sixty seconds), and this is the basis for angles used in legal descriptions. The only thing an angle has in common with the bearings is the use of the terms degrees, minutes, and seconds; a line running northeasterly at an interior angle of 60°14′30″ is not the same thing as a line running north 60°14′30″ east.

An angle runs from the last described course and is either interior (inside the property boundary) or exterior (outside the property boundary).

When reviewing a survey in which angles are used to describe courses, think of a property corner as an intersection of two lines. At the point of intersection, draw a circle, using that point as a center of the circle. The arc of the circle within the property boundary is the interior angle, and the arc outside the property boundary is the exterior angle.

At one corner of the example shown in Exhibit 4–10, there is an interior angle of 85 degrees and an exterior angle of 275 degrees; at another corner, there is an interior angle of 270 degrees and an exterior angle of 90 degrees. The calls would be any one of the following: thence north at an interior angle of 85 degrees (exterior angle of 275 degrees from the last described course); thence east at an interior angle of 85 degrees (exterior angle of 275 degrees from the last described course); thence south at an interior angle of 270 degrees (exterior angle 90 degrees) from the last described course; thence east at an interior angle of 270 degrees (exterior angle 90 degrees) from the last described course.

When angles are used, the interior-exterior angles are always the same, even though the property lines are described from different directions. Most surveyors locate only one interior-exterior angle at a corner, not necessarily both; but a circle always has 360 degrees, and the omitted angle can easily be computed if necessary.

Closure

A metes and bounds description must close. This means that the legal description starts at the beginning point, follows each boundary line by course and distance, and ends back at the beginning point. If the land description does not close, it is defective.

EXHIBIT 4–10
Measurement of
Courses by Angles

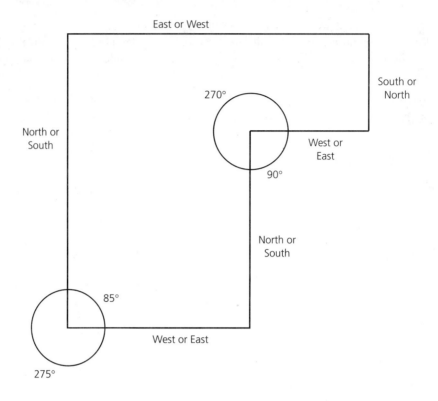

Practice Notes on Metes and Bounds Description

The basic requirements for a metes and bounds legal description are (a) identification of land lot, district, section, county, and state in which the property is located; (b) definite beginning point; (c) compass direction and distances from one point to the next; and (d) return to the beginning point.

New York:
After identifying the city, county, and state the description always begins "beginning at ..." and ends "to the place of beginning." Metes and bounds descriptions always make a full circle.

A metes and bounds legal description usually cannot be prepared without a survey. Most surveyors locate the beginning point on the survey and also give a course and distance for each property boundary line. The main problem in the metes and bounds description is carelessness: mistakes in reading the survey and omission of a boundary line description. It is a good practice to proofread a metes and bounds description with another person. The other person should read the legal description and the person responsible for the legal description should proof what is being read on the survey. Then roles should be swapped: the other person should read the survey and the person responsible for the description should proof the description.

E T H I C S :   Competency

You are a legal assistant with a small general practice firm that represents clients in a number of areas, including real estate. You are working with an attorney on a complicated real property transaction. The land description for the property is complicated. The attorney you work with remarks to you that she is not very good at drafting land descriptions. She mentions that because you received formal legal assistant training, you should be skilled in this area, and she requests that you do the land description. She does not know that you also have difficulty preparing land descriptions. You know that if you prepare the description, even though your supervising attorney will review it, it is questionable whether the attorney will be knowledgeable enough to catch any mistakes. Should you draft the land description and hope for the best?

The American Bar Association's Code of Professional Responsibility provides that a lawyer should represent a client competently. An attorney should strive to become and remain proficient in his or her practice and should accept employment only in matters in which he or she is or intends to become competent to handle. Although a legal assistant is not directly regulated by the American Bar Association's Code of Professional Responsibility, an ethical and professional legal assistant should act with competence and proper care in assisting attorneys in the representation of clients. When a legal assistant undertakes the duty of assisting an attorney in the representation of a client, the legal assistant should use proper care to safeguard the client's interest. If the legal assistant is working in an area beyond his or her competence but in which he or she is expected to become competent, it is the legal assistant's duty to diligently undertake the work and to study whatever is necessary to perform the work competently. Legal assistants should take pride in their professional endeavors. Their obligation to act competently requires a higher motivation to be a professional.

In this factual situation, the legal assistant should either decline to prepare the description and explain to the attorney his or her difficulty in preparing descriptions of this type or seek help from other members of the firm to see if someone else in the firm is competent in this area of practice. The legal assistant may also obtain help from title insurance companies, surveyors, or other professionals who may be willing to assist the legal assistant in gaining an understanding of the skills and tasks required to prepare the land description.

SUMMARY

It is important that the description of real property to be used in a contract, deed, lease, mortgage, or other document be accurate. A land survey is an important tool to assist in the preparation of a correct description of real property. Many land surveys not only describe the boundaries of the property, but also locate all improvements, easements, and other encumbrances situated on or affecting the real property.

KEY TERMS

As-built survey	Distance	Section
Baseline	Legal description	Survey
Call	Plat	Township
Chord	Principal meridians	Township lines
Course	Range	

REVIEW QUESTIONS

1. What information should a survey provide for the purpose of a land description?

2. Identify and describe the three types of land description.

3. What type of description commonly is used in a residential subdivision?

4. What is a base line, and what is its relation to a meridian line in a government rectangular survey?

5. How many acres are found in the north 1/2 of the northwest 1/4 of the southeast 1/4 of a section?

6. How many acres are found in the southeast 1/4 of the southwest 1/4 of the southeast 1/4 of a section?

7. What are the basic requirements for a platted description?

8. What information should a land surveyor give to prepare a legal description involving a curved land boundary?

9. What is required to have a correct point of beginning on a metes and bounds legal description?

10. In a metes and bounds legal description, each property boundary is described by a course and distance. What is a course, and what is a distance?

PRACTICAL ASSIGNMENTS

1. Prepare a metes and bounds legal description from the survey in Exhibit 4–14 at the end of this chapter.

2. Prepare a metes and bounds legal description from the survey in Exhibit 4–15 at the end of this chapter.

3. Prepare a metes and bounds legal description from the survey in Exhibit 4–16 at the end of this chapter.

4. The legal description for Exhibit 4–17 at the end of this chapter is incorrect. Please find the errors and prepare a correct legal description.

ADDENDUM OF SAMPLE SURVEYS AND LEGAL DESCRIPTIONS

Exhibit 4–11 Platted description survey
Exhibit 4–12 Metes and bounds description (including curves with descriptions)
Exhibit 4–13 Metes and bounds with use of interior angles
Exhibit 4–14 Metes and bounds survey—E. Ponce de Leon property
Exhibit 4–15 Metes and bounds survey—Mohawk Trail property
Exhibit 4–16 Metes and bounds survey—Dickey estate property
Exhibit 4–17 Metes and bounds survey with legal description—Willow Creek property

EXHIBIT 4-11
Platted Description Survey

ALL THAT TRACT or parcel of land lying and being in Land Lot 52 of the 18th District of DeKalb County, Georgia, being Lot 26, Block B, Emory Highlands, according to plat recorded in Plat Book 7 at page 87, in the office of the Clerk of the Superior Court of DeKalb County, Georgia.

EXHIBIT 4–12   Metes and Bounds Description

SURVEY FOR:

Land Lot: 57

District: 13th

County: Fulton

State: Georgia

SURVEYOR'S SEAL

ALL THAT TRACT or parcel of land lying and being in Land Lot 37 of the 13th District of Fulton County, Georgia, and being more particularly described as follows:

BEGIN at an iron pin at the intersection of the western right-of-way at Best Road (50-foot right-of-way) and the northeastern right-of-way of the Atlanta & West Point Railroad; thence, run north 58 degrees 12 minutes 18 seconds west 57.57 feet to an iron pin placed; thence, run in a northwesterly direction along the arc of a curve an arc distance of 583.49 feet to an iron pin (said curve having a radius of 583.44 feet and being subtended by a chord bearing north 28 degrees 18 minutes 21 seconds west, a chord distance of 559.48 feet); thence, north 00 degrees 20 minutes 40 seconds east 39.06 feet to an iron pin; thence, south 89 degrees 52 minutes 50 seconds east 318.77 feet to an iron pin located on the western right-of-way of Best Road; thence, run along the western right-of-way of Best Road south 00 degrees 29 minutes 17 seconds west 561.32 feet to the POINT OF BEGINNING.

EXHIBIT 4–13   Metes and Bounds with Use of Interior Angles

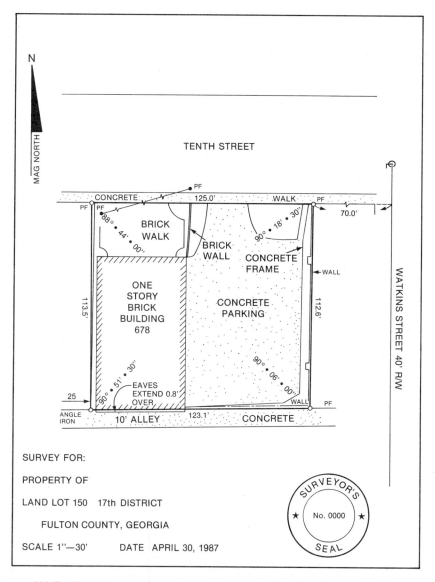

ALL THAT TRACT or parcel of land lying and being in Land Lot 150 of the 17th District of Fulton County, Georgia, and being more particularly described as follows:

BEGINNING at an iron pin found on the south side of 10th Street 70 feet west of the center line of Watkins Street (having a 40-foot right-of-way) as measured along the south side of 10th Street; thence south and forming an interior angle of 90 degrees 18 minutes 30 seconds from 10th Street 112.6 feet to a 3-inch steel fence post on the north side of an alley; thence, west along the north side of said alley and forming an interior angle of 90 degrees 06 minutes from the preceding call 123.1 feet to a 3-inch steel fence post; thence north and forming an interior angle of 90 degrees 51 minutes 30 seconds from the preceding call 113.5 feet to a 3-inch steel fence post on the south side of 10th Street; thence east along the south side of 10th Street and forming an interior angle of 88 degrees 44 minutes from the preceding call 125 feet to the point of BEGINNING; said property being known as 678 10th Street, N.W., according to the present system of numbering houses in the City of Atlanta, and being formerly known as Lots 4, 5, 6, 7 and 8, Block G of the Joe E. Brown Co. as per plat recorded in Plat Book 7, pages 86 and 87, Fulton County, Georgia Records; and being the same property shown on a plat of survey dated April 30, 1987.

TOGETHER WITH all of Grantor's right, title and interest, if any, in and to the ten (10) foot alley located along the rear line of the above-described property.

EXHIBIT 4–14 Metes and Bounds Survey

EXHIBIT 4-15   Metes and Bounds Survey

EXHIBIT 4–16   Metes and Bounds Survey

435.00' TO S.E. R/W
OF ARDEN ROAD
(IF EXIT)

N

63

N80° • 20' • 30"E ~ 220.70'

I.P.F.

WEST PINE VALLEY ROAD
(50' R/W)

I.P.F.

50' B

121.70

62

S08° • 47' • 28"E ~
109.80'

N20° • 27' • 14"E ~ 139.00'

ROCK WALL

WALL

ONE
STORY
FRAME

TILE
PORCH

CONC. DRIVE

ROCK
WALL

I.P.F.

ONE
STORY
FRAME

CONC.
WALL

22.17

ORIGINAL P L

I.P.F.

S74° • 23' • 15"W ~ 294.10'

I.P.F.

61

N00° • 54' • 14"E ~
20.40'

GEORGIA
REGISTERED
LAND SURVEYOR

3060 WEST PINE VALLEY ROAD
ATLANTA, GA

PROPERTY OF

LOT 62 & PART OF LOT 61
JAMES L. DICKEY
ESTATE PROPERTY
LAND LOT 142
DISTRICT: 17TH   SECTION:
COUNTY: FULTON
GEORGIA
DATE: 4/16/93   SCALE 1" = 50'

PB 18   PG 12

V.S.

EXHIBIT 4-17   Metes and Bounds Survey

ALL THAT TRACT or parcel of land lying and being in Land 65 of the 16th District, 2nd Section, Cobb County, Georgia, and being more particularly described as follows:

BEGIN at an iron pin found on the northeastern right-of-way of Willow Creek Drive (50-foot right-of-way), said iron pin being located 142.18 feet northwest of the intersection of the northeastern right-of-way of Willow Creek Drive with the northern right-of-way of Jamerson Road (100-foot right-of-way); run thence in a northwesterly direction along the northeasterly right-of-way of Willow Creek Drive 75.0 feet to a power box; run thence North 42°06'46" East 261.12 feet to an iron pin found; thence run South 87°29'00" West 110.25 feet to an iron pin found; thence run South 24°06'46" West 248.90 feet to an iron pin found; run thence South 59°17'03" West 35.0 feet to an iron pin found being the POINT OF BEGINNING.

Encumbrances

Taxes, of life's two certainties, the only one for which you can get an automatic extension.

—*White's Law Dictionary*

OBJECTIVES

After reading this chapter, you will be able to:

- Understand the public restrictions on the use of real property such as zoning, building codes, eminent domain, and subdivision restrictions
- Identify the various private encumbrances

GLOSSARY

Ad valorem taxes   Taxes assessed against real property usually measured by the value of the real property being taxed.

Building codes   Public laws that regulate methods and materials to be used in the construction of improvements.

Easement   Right granted to a nonowner of real property to use the real property for a specific purpose. For example, the right given to an electric utility company to locate an electric power line on a private user's real property.

Eminent domain   Power of government to take private property for public use.

Encumbrance   Claim, lien, charge, or liability attached to and binding real property that may exist in another person to the diminishment of the value of the real property or that interferes with the use of the real property by the owner.

Judgment   Money debt resulting from a lawsuit. Judgments are liens on real property owned by the judgment debtor.

Lien   Money debt attached to real property. The holder of the lien can sell the real property to pay the debt.

Mechanics' or materialmen's lien   Lien imposed by law on real property to secure payment for work performed or materials furnished for the construction, repair, or alteration of improvements on the real property.

Zoning   Legitimate police power of government to regulate the use of real property.

Ideally, a person who owns real property wants the use of the property to be unrestricted and the title to be debt-free. In real life, it is unusual for real property, especially urban real property, to be totally free of restrictions or debts. Most ownership to real property is burdened with encumbrances. An **encumbrance** is defined by *Black's Law Dictionary* as "any claim, lien, charge or liability attached to and binding real property which may exist in another person to the diminishment of the land's value or interfere with the unrestricted use of the land by the owner." Encumbrances usually include such things as zoning restrictions, restrictive covenants, money judgments against the owner, taxes, mortgages, and easements. Although some encumbrances, such as zoning restrictions, may have a positive effect on the ownership of the property, and encumbrance usually is viewed as an unwanted item. Encumbrances are discovered by title examinations, which are discussed later in this book, and it often is the legal assistant's responsibility to review encumbrances that pose problems for the client. The legal assistant normally works with an attorney to advise the client as to the acceptability of an encumbrance. This chapter is an overview of the types of public and private encumbrances that can affect real property. Many of the encumbrances are discussed in more detail in later chapters.

New York:
Although an individual has many rights in the land he owns, these are not absolute rights, they may be limited by governmental powers and private agreements.

PUBLIC ENCUMBRANCES

Federal, state, and local governments are vested with power to restrict or take private property for the purpose of promoting the health and welfare of the general public. This power to protect and promote the public welfare gives to governmental authorities the power to impose on private real property such things as zoning regulations, building codes, subdivision regulations, environmental protection laws, the power of eminent domain, and taxation.

Zoning

The power to regulate land use is within the legitimate power of a government, and it is not unusual for city and county governments to issue **zoning** regulations that restrict private land use. The main objective of zoning is to improve living and working conditions in congested areas by preventing the liberties of one property owner from interfering with the rights of another. For example, you can imagine how irate you would be as a property owner if you purchased a beautiful home in a quiet residential neighborhood and then discovered that your neighbor has sold his or her property to a company that intends to build a twenty-four-hour diner on the property.

Zoning is considered constitutional as long as the zoning regulation bears some reasonable relation to the public welfare. If a zoning regulation is unreasonable, it may amount to the "taking" of the real property, and the owner may be entitled to compensation or to having the zoning regulation voided.

Zoning consists of (a) dividing the city or county into districts; (b) prescribing within each district the types of structures and architectural designs for buildings to be located there; and (c) prescribing the uses for the buildings within each district.

For example, a city council may divide the city into four districts. One district may be reserved for single-family residential use; another district may be reserved for multifamily use, such as apartments, condominiums, and town houses; a third district may be retail commercial, in which there can be stores and offices; and the fourth district may be industrial, in which there could be manufacturing plants. Examples of

New York:
New York gives zoning powers to local government authorities. They determine the use to which a particular parcel can be put.

New York:
For discussion of New York zoning classifications, see Appendix.

a residential zoning ordinance and a commercial zoning ordinance are included at the end of this chapter (Exhibits 5–1 and 5–2).

Zoning is a political process; it usually is considered a legislative function of a governmental authority. Zoning requires procedural due process. This means that notice must be given and a hearing held before a zoning regulation can be passed. The notice usually is by means of a sign on the property or a notice in the newspaper. It is not required that landowners be given personal notice of an intention to change the zoning on their property. All zoning hearings are public. Landowners, with or without legal counsel, have an opportunity to speak at these hearings. The governmental authorities must present evidence to support the zoning classifications. A property owner does have a right to appeal a zoning decision or classification to a court of law. The court, however, in reviewing the zoning decision, will not overturn the governmental authorities' decision unless it finds that there is a clear case of abuse by the government.

Real property that has been used for a particular purpose but is later changed by the zoning regulations is deemed to be a preexisting or nonconforming use. These uses are permitted to continue, provided they are not expanded. Some zoning statutes provide a phase-out of nonconforming uses over a period of years. For example, you are the owner of a small neighborhood grocery in a residential neighborhood. The city decides to zone the entire neighborhood residential, making your retail grocery store a nonconforming use. You may continue to operate the grocery store as you have in the past under the nonconforming use protection. You would not, however, be able to change the grocery store into a restaurant or other use, nor would you be able to expand the existing facilities. *Shackford & Gooch v. The Town of Kennebunk*, 486 A.2d 102, illustrates the problems a property owner has in expanding or altering a nonconforming use.

Zoning is enforced through injunction by the public authorities. For example, a property owner decides to operate a business from her home. The property is zoned single-family residential, and the operation of the business is in violation of the zoning ordinance. The government could obtain an injunction that would order the property owner to stop operating the business. If the property owner continues to operate the business, she could be held in contempt of court and face both fines and imprisonment. The issuance of building permits is another way to enforce a zoning ordinance. A building permit will be refused unless the proposed improvement and its intended use comply with zoning.

New York:
If an area is zoned for single family residences there may be a reason to request a *variance,* i.e. right to improve property in a way not authorized by existing zoning. It may involve having a building closer to the building line than authorized or may require a change from commercial use to residential use. The zoning board would have a public hearing after giving notice to all neighboring property owners and the board would either decide to permit or deny the variance.

 CASE

Shackford & Gooch, Inc., et al.
v. The Town of Kennebunk, et al.
486 A.2d 102 (ME. 1984)

GLASSMAN, Justice.

Shackford & Gooch, Inc. *et al.*, opponents to the issuance of a building permit to B. & B. Coastal Enterprises, Inc., appeal from a judgment of the Superior Court, York County, ordering the Kennebunk Zoning Board of Appeals to issue a permit to B. & B. Coastal Enterprises to build and use a deck on the roof of its restaurant. B. & B. Coastal Enterprises cross-appeals, challenging that portion

of the judgment holding that the Zoning Board of Appeals was not estopped from enforcing its ordinance. We grant the appeal and deny the cross-appeal.

I.

B. & B. Coastal Enterprises, Inc., operates Bartley's Dockside Restaurant (Dockside) in a building that is nonconforming because its setbacks do not meet the requirements of the Kennebunk Zoning Ordinance. In March 1982, Dockside applied to the Kennebunk building inspector for a permit to build stairs on the outside of the restaurant. The inspector granted the permit, at the same time giving Dockside verbal authorization to build a deck on the flat roof of the restaurant, assuring Dockside that a building permit for the deck was not necessary. When Dockside began construction of the deck, Shackford & Gooch, Inc., owner of an abutting fish market, petitioned the building inspector to stop the work on the grounds that a building permit was necessary, and that the deck violated local zoning ordinances.

The controversy eventually came before the Kennebunk Zoning Board of Appeals (Board), which decided in June 1982 that, based on an estoppel theory, Dockside could retain and use the roof deck, subject to a restricted number of seats. On review of this decision, the Superior Court ruled that the Board's finding of estoppel was incorrect as a matter of law. The court vacated the decision of the Board and remanded the case for the Board to determine initially whether the deck met the requirements of the Kennebunk Zoning Ordinance and, if not, whether Dockside was entitled to a variance.

After hearing in September 1983, the Board found that Dockside's deck constituted an expansion of a nonconforming structure and did not comply with the setback requirements of the ordinance. The Board denied Dockside's request for the necessary variances. On review of the Board's decision, the Superior Court held as a matter of law that the deck as a vertical addition to the building did not extend the nonconforming horizontal setbacks of Dockside. The court further held the deck created no increase in Dockside's seating capacity that would necessitate a parking variance. Declining to reconsider the Superior Court's earlier ruling on estoppel, the court ordered the Board to issue a permit to Dockside to build and use its deck in accordance with the seating restriction established in the June 1982 hearing.

* * *

When the Superior Court acts as an appellate court reviewing an action of an administrative board, we directly examine the record developed before the board. *See Driscoll v. Gheewalla,* 441 A.2d 1023, 1026 (Me.1982); *see also Nancy W.*

Bayley, Inc. v. Maine Employment Security Commission, 472 A.2d 1374, 1377 (Me.1984). On review of an action taken by a zoning board of appeals, we may not make factual findings independent of those of the board, nor may we substitute our judgment for that of the board. *Mack v. Municipal Officers of the Town of Cape Elizabeth,* 463 A.2d 717, 719–20 (Me.1983); *Driscoll,* 441 A.2d at 1026. Our role is to determine whether the board abused its discretion, committed an error of law, or made findings not supported by substantial evidence in the record. *Mack,* 463 A.2d at 719; *Driscoll,* 441 A.2d at 1026.

The Board found in its remand hearing that Dockside's roof deck was not in compliance with the side yard, rear yard, or shoreland zoning setback requirements of the Kennebuck ordinance. The Board thus considered the deck to be an expansion of a nonconforming structure requiring a variance. The ordinance provides:

> No lawfully non-conforming use of buildings or land shall be changed, extended, or enlarged in any manner for any purpose not permitted under this Ordinance, except as may be permitted as a variance, not as an exception.

Kennebuck, Me., Zoning Ordinance § 1.4(B) (1963). The section on variance appeals provides:

> The Board may allow a relaxation, in a moderate degree, of the lot area, lot width, yard depth, or percentage of lot covered requirements of this Ordinance. Such a relaxation may be granted only when the Board determines that, by reason of physical consitions [sic] peculiar to the land or building under appeal (conditions virtually unique to that property and not arising or applying as to other land and building(s) adjoining or nearby within the same zoning district), unusual difficulty or particular hardship would be caused by literal application and rigorous enforcement of the terms of the Kennebuck Zoning Ordinance. The Board may also permit modest expansion of any lawfully non-conforming building or use of land, but only on land occupied by such use at the time the use became lawfully non-conforming and not onto any additional lot adjoining.

Id. at § 7.6(C)(2).

[4–6] We agree with the Board that the addition of a roof deck, or indeed, any significant alteration of a nonconforming structure is an extension or expansion. *See* 1 R. Anderson, *American Law of*

Zoning 2d § 6.43 at 455 (2d ed. 1976). Dockside argues that because the roof deck does not encroach any further into the nonconforming setbacks than do the lawfully nonconforming walls of the restaurant, it does not constitute an expansion of the nonconformity. To permit such an addition to a nonconforming structure without a variance, however, would offend the policy of zoning, which is to "gradually or eventually eliminate nonconforming uses as speedily as justice will permit." *See Keith v. Saco River Corridor Commission*, 464 A.2d 150, 154 (Me.1983). When an ordinance prohibits enlargement of a nonconforming building, a landowner cannot as a matter of right alter the structure, even if the alteration does not increase the nonconformity.

                     ❉ ❉ ❉

Judgment vacated;

Remanded for entry of judgment as follows: appeal denied; decision of Zoning Board of Appeals affirmed.

All concurring.

Building Codes

New York:
For a discussion of New York building codes, see Appendix.

Building code regulations also are a legitimate use of a city's or county's police power to protect the health and welfare of its citizens. For example, most cities have codes that regulate the electrical wiring and plumbing of homes and buildings. **Building codes** regulate methods and materials to be used in construction of improvements. Most cities and counties do not permit a building to be constructed and occupied without a permit and a final inspection by the building department.

Subdivision Regulations and Environmental Protection Laws

Most city and county governments can create and enforce subdivision laws. State and federal government can create and enforce environmental protection laws. Subdivision laws require that streets and sewers be approved in advance by the government. The streets and sewers are not accepted for public maintenance by the government without a satisfactory inspection.

New York:
In a 1969 amendment to the New York State Constitution, the legislators stated it shall be the policy of the state to "conserve and protect its natural resources."

The federal government regulates the environmental quality of real property. Groundwater pollution is regulated by the Federal Water Pollution Control Act (33 U.S.C. § 1251 et seq.); and hazardous waste, through the Federal Resource Conservation and Recovery Act (42 U.S.C. § 6901 et seq.) and the Comprehensive Environmental Response, Compensation and Liability Act (42 U.S.C. § 9601 et seq.).

The 1980 Comprehensive Environment Response, Compensation and Liability Act, often referred to as the Superfund, imposes liability on owners who own or operate real property that is contaminated with hazardous substances. Under the statute, current owners or operators as well as owners at the time of waste disposal are responsible for cleanup costs. Each party may be held liable for the full amount of cleanup costs, no matter how small his or her contribution has been in generating the hazardous substances. The liability is absolute, and lack of negligence or fault is no defense.

New York:
For a discussion of New York State's Environmental Conservation Law, see Appendix.

In addition to the federal laws that create liability for hazardous substances found on land, several states—for example, New Jersey and Massachusetts—have similar statutes.

Because an owner may be responsible for hazardous waste cleanup, even though the owner was not the creator of the hazardous waste, it is prudent for a purchaser of real property to inquire into the current and previous ownership and uses of the property and into the environmental compliance record of the prior property owners through a review of all available public or governmental records concerning compliance. It also is prudent for the purchaser to retain professional help to conduct an actual environmental inspection of the property. In addition, many purchasers ask for hazardous waste indemnities and representations from the seller at the time of sale.

Power of Eminent Domain

Federal, state, and local governments have the right known as **eminent domain** to take private property for public use. Thus, private ownership of all real property is held subject to a perpetual repurchase option in favor of the United States; the various states; the county, city, and other government agencies; and, in some cases, even privately owned public utilities. Because the taking of private property for public use can have a harsh and disastrous effect on the private owner, constitutional safeguards have been set up to protect the owner against arbitrary or unreasonable use of eminent domain power. The government cannot exercise its right of power of eminent domain without first establishing that the private property is needed for a public use and paying the private owner adequate compensation for the property.

A property owner is provided with a number of procedural safeguards with an exercise of the power of eminent domain. The property owner is entitled to due notice and a hearing before the time the private property can be taken. The property owner, at the hearing, has an opportunity to be represented by counsel and to prove that the taking is not necessary for public use or that the compensation being offered is unreasonable. The government has a wide range of public uses that support the exercise of the power of eminent domain, such as the taking of private property for the purpose of constructing public streets, sewer facilities, airports, government buildings, slum clearance or redevelopment projects, forest reserves, and even recreational areas, such as parks and wildlife preserves. Because of the wide range of public uses that support the exercise of the power of eminent domain, the main issue in most condemnation proceedings is that of compensation. A property owner is entitled to the fair market value of the property being taken.

Taxation

Governmental bodies have the right to tax real property that is located within their jurisdictional boundaries. It is not unusual to find real property taxed at both the city and the county levels. Sometimes real property taxes are called **ad valorem taxes**. This definition comes from the fact that the taxes are measured on the value of the real property being taxed.

The city or county tax authorities have the power not only to value the real property for purposes of taxation, but also to establish a millage rate for purposes of computing the tax. For example, if you have real property that had a tax assessment value of $51,900 and a millage rate of .0112500, you would multiply the millage rate by the assessed value, and the tax would be $583.87.

Most governmental bodies have a tax year, which may be the calendar year or some other period of time. The taxes become a lien or debt charged against the real property on the first day of the tax year. For example, if the tax year is the calendar year, then on January 1, the taxes for that year would become a lien, even though the taxes may not be due and payable until sometime later in the year. Tax liens have a super priority over a mortgage or other property interest in connection with the real property and must be paid before all other debts, liens, or claims. Tax liens can be enforced by foreclosure and sale of the real property by the public authority.

New York:
Once the government has determined that private property is needed for a public purpose, the property owner has no choice but to sell. It then becomes a matter of price. New York always allows the property owner to contest the amount of money offered. In New York, when part and not all of a parcel is taken, the owner can collect damages, not only for the value of the land taken, but also for any reduction in value of the remainder of the land.

New York:
Most state and local governments impose taxes on real estate and these pay for many local services such as police, fire, schools, and libraries.

New York:
For a discusion of full assessment, see Appendix.

New York:
Property taxes have first priority as liens. If a property owner fails to pay real estate taxes the taxing authority has the right to seize and sell the property at a tax sale and retain the proceeds to pay for the back taxes.

New York:
See Appendix for dis-
cussion of other liens.

Governmental authorities also have the right to levy special assessments against real property owners for the costs of such things as grading, curbing, paving, and establishing sewer and water lines or sidewalks, which benefit a person's real property. Special assessments are enforceable by foreclosure and public sale of the real property.

PRIVATE ENCUMBRANCES

Private encumbrances are voluntarily created by private parties who deal with the real property and consist of judgment liens, mechanics' and materialmen's liens, mortgages and trust deeds, easements, and restrictive covenants.

Judgment Liens

A **lien** is a money debt attached to real property. It is created when the property owner has been sued for a sum of money and a court has entered a judgment against the property owner. For example, a property owner is involved in an automobile accident. The property owner is sued for negligence and has assessed against him by a court of law a $50,000 judgment.

Judgment liens do not become liens on real property until they have been recorded in a special book, called the Judgment Book or General Execution Docket, in the county where the real property is located.

A judgment lien remains a lien on real property until it is has been paid or expires by passage of time. Most states have laws that limit the duration of a judgment lien. These laws provide that a judgment lien, if not paid, will expire within seven to fourteen years after becoming a lien on real property.

Mechanics' and Materialmen's Liens

New York:
For a discussion of
Mechanic's liens in New
York, see Appendix.

A **mechanics' or materialmen's lien** is imposed by law on real property to secure payment for work performed or materials furnished for the construction, repair, or alteration of improvements on the real property. Each state has its own laws for the creation of these liens. Claimants under most mechanics' or materialmen's lien statutes include contractors, laborers, subcontractors, material suppliers, lessors of equipment and machinery, architects, professional engineers, and land surveyors.

Most privately owned real property is subject to mechanics' or materialmen's liens. The lien attaches to all real property, including improvements, and all real property contiguous to the improved real property. Public real property is not subject to mechanics' or materialmen's liens.

Special Mechanics' and Materialmen's Lien Situations

Sometimes special situations exist that prompt the creation of mechanics' and materialmen's liens.

Landlord and Tenant. Work performed for a tenant of real property only attaches to the tenant's interest in the real property unless the landlord of the real property consents to the work and agrees to pay for the work.

Contract Seller and Purchaser. Work performed for a purchaser of real property before the contract closes only attaches to the purchaser's interest unless the seller has consented to the work.

Husband and Wife. Work performed at the request of one spouse is not a lien on the other spouse's real property interest unless the other spouse has consented or agreed to pay for the work.

Joint Tenants. A lien binds only the interest in the real property of the joint tenant who ordered the work. A joint tenant is not an agent for the other tenants, and unless the other tenants have consented or agreed to pay for the work, their interest in the real property is not liened.

Other Mechanics' and Materialmen's Lien Considerations

The amount of the lien depends on whether the state in which the construction takes place follows the New York or the Pennsylvania theory of lien claim. Under the New York theory, the amount of the mechanics' or materialmen's lien is limited to the contract price between the owner and the general contractor. Payment of the contract price by the owner is a defense to a mechanics' or materialmen's lien claim by a subcontractor or material supplier. Under the Pennsylvania theory, the original contract between the owner and the general contractor does not limit the amount of lien claims that can be filed by subcontractors and material suppliers. Payment of the contract price, under the Pennsylvania theory, is not a defense to subcontractor or material supplier lien claims.

For example, an owner of real property enters into a contract with a general contractor to build a home. The contract price for the construction is $100,000. A general contractor hires a number of subcontractors to build the home. The owner pays to the general contractor $80,000 of the $100,000 contract price. After having paid the $80,000, the owner discovers that a number of lien claims are filed against the home by subcontractors and material suppliers. The subcontractor and material supplier lien claims total $50,000. Under the New York theory, the owner would be responsible to the subcontractors and material suppliers only for $20,000 (the difference between the $100,000 contract price and the $80,000 previously paid to the general contractor). Under the Pennsylvania theory, the owner would be responsible to the subcontractors and material suppliers for the full amount of their claims, or $50,000.

The right to a mechanics' or materialmen's lien usually exists once the work is performed or the material is furnished. The lien right must be perfected by filing a notice or claim of lien in the public records where the real property is located. Most states require that this notice or claim of lien be recorded within a reasonable period of time after completion of the work (60 to 120 days). A claim or notice of lien requires the following information: (a) the amount of the claim, (b) the name of the lien claimant, (c) the name of the owner, (d) a description of real property to be liened, and (e) the notarized signature of the lien claimant.

The priority of a lien claim dates from the time the first work is performed or the material is furnished. It does not attach from the date the claim of lien is filed, except for architects, engineers, and land surveyors.

For example, a material supplier provides materials for the construction of a home on March 1. The material supplier is not paid and finally files a claim of lien on May 1 for the unpaid materials. The material supplier's lien claim dates from March 1, the date the materials were furnished. This also means that the material supplier is

New York:
A lot of time may pass between the start of a lawsuit and obtaining a judgment. During that period you may file a *lis pendens* which gives notice to anyone interested in the property that there is a "cloud" on title. In New York a *lis pendens* is also known as a notice of pendency.

A judgment may become a lien on real property owned by the debtor when it is filed with the county clerk. This is only for property located in the county in which the judgment is issued. You may get a transcript of judgment and file it in any other county where the debtor has property. This is good for ten years and can be renewed for another ten years. A judgment may be executed by forcing the sale of the debtor's property.

ahead in terms of priority and will be paid ahead of any other lien claims that date after March 1.

A mechanics' or materialmen's lien is enforced through a foreclosure suit or sale of the real property. States also impose time limits for filing the foreclosure suit. The most common time limit is one year from the date the claim is due.

A mechanics' or materialmen's lien can be waived and terminated by a written waiver or release of lien. Most states require that lien waivers or releases of lien be signed by the lien claimant and be witnessed or notarized.

Mortgages and Trust Deeds

Real property can be pledged as security to pay debts of the owner. Mortgages and trust deeds are fully discussed in Chapter 11.

Easements

The right to use real property for a special purpose, such as a roadway, can be given by the owner to a nonowner. A full discussion of **easements** can be found in Chapter 6.

Restrictive Covenants

New York:
Restrictive covenants are private agreements which limit the use of the property. Racial or ethnic restrictive covenants have been outlawed. In New York the County Clerk's office may not accept for recording any instrument which contains racial restrictions.

A subdivision builder may put in restrictive covenants that limit a subdivision owner to building a dwelling "not less than 3000 feet" or "each building lot may be 5 acres". These restrictions are generally valid.

It is possible for real property owners to restrict the use of the real property. These restrictive covenants may be in the form of restrictions or covenants found in deeds of conveyance to the real property or in restrictions that are recorded against the real property. It is not unusual for real property that has been subdivided, such as single-family home subdivisions, industrial parks, and condominiums, to have restrictions regarding the use of the property by future real property owners. Private restrictive covenants often perform the same function as public zoning regulations, but in many instances, they may be more restrictive than public zoning regulations. The private restrictions attempt to regulate the development of the real property in such a manner as to enhance the value of each individual owner's lot or share of the real property. For example, restrictive covenants found in residential subdivisions usually restrict the size of the homes that can be built on the lots, subject the homes to architectural review committees, regulate the height of the homes, and require that certain portions of the property be left vacant for purposes of creating front, rear, and side yards. All these restrictions are designed to create a nice residential environment that will enhance the value of each individual owner's home. An example of residential subdivision townhouse restrictions is included at the end of this chapter (Exhibit 5–3).

Restrictive covenants are enforced by injunction or suit for damages. Enforcement may be brought by any person who bought real property with notice of the restrictions and in reliance on the restrictions. Therefore, any homeowner in a single-family subdivision can enforce the restrictive covenants against other homeowners.

E T H I C S :   Abandonment of Work

A legal assistant works with a firm that represents real estate developers. She is working with an attorney representing a client who is purchasing vacant land for the purpose of developing the property into a warehouse club. The property is under contract with the closing only three weeks away. The legal assistant has been asked by the attorney to inquire into the zoning classification for the property and to obtain a copy of the zoning ordinance that affects the property. The assignment is given the afternoon before the legal assistant is scheduled to leave for a one-week vacation. On return from vacation, the legal assistant forgets about the request to obtain a zoning ordinance. On the day before the scheduled closing, the attorney is going over the closing checklist and requests at that time a copy of the zoning ordinance. The legal assistant mentions that she forgot to obtain the zoning ordinance and the attorney becomes quite upset and irritated. Is the supervisory attorney overreacting?

Professional ethics require that legal work be performed competently and to a timely completion. A legal assistant should not willfully abandon or willfully disregard any legal matter entrusted to him or her. When a legal assistant is given an assignment by an attorney, he or she should carry out the assignment to the end and not neglect or fail to perform the work at hand in a timely manner. The client's interest in having the transaction performed promptly is paramount. In this particular transaction, the zoning classification for the property is important and could affect the client's plans for the development of the property. Failure to obtain the zoning ordinance as requested is unprofessional and justifiable grounds for the attorney's irritation.

SUMMARY

An encumbrance is an unwanted item in connection with real property. Encumbrances are discovered by an examination of the record title or by physical inspection of the real property. The encumbrance may be a debt against the real property that must be paid by the owner to save the real property from being foreclosed or sold. The encumbrance may be a restrictive covenant that reduces or restricts the use an owner may make of the real property. An easement, although an encumbrance that may restrict an owner's use of real property, also may be a benefit to real property.

KEY TERMS

Ad valorem taxes	Eminent domain	Lien
Building codes	Encumbrance	Mechanics' or materialmen's lien
Easement	Judgment	Zoning

REVIEW QUESTIONS

1. List and briefly discuss various types of government regulation of private property.

2. What general methods does a government authority use to enforce its zoning regulations?

3. What is a real property owner's general responsibility for hazardous waste located on the real property?

4. What are the main legal issues involved in an eminent domain proceeding?

5. What is a judgment lien, and why should a real property owner be concerned about it?

6. Who is entitled to claim a mechanics' or materialmen's lien?

7. Briefly explain the New York theory and the Pennsylvania theory of lien claims and how each of these theories impact on the claims of a subcontractor or material supplier.

8. What is the general rule for the priority of a mechanics' or materialmen's lien claim, and why is this priority important?

9. What is required for a formal notice or claim of lien?

10. How are private restrictive covenants enforced?

PRACTICAL ASSIGNMENT

Research your state's mechanics' and materialmen's lien law. Prepare a memorandum outlining the following:

(a) List of claimants entitled to file a mechanics' or materialmen's lien claim

(b) Requirements for a claim of lien

(c) Requirements for foreclosing a mechanics' or materialmen's lien

---

EXHIBIT 5–1
R–4 Single-Family Residential District Regulations

Section 16-06.001   Scope of provisions.
Section 16-06.002   Statement of intent.
Section 16-06.003   Permitted principal uses and structures.
Section 16-06.004   Permitted accessory uses and structures.
Section 16-06.005   Special permits.
Section 16-06.006   Transitional uses, structures, requirements.
Section 16-06.007   Minimum lot requirements.
Section 16-06.008   Minimum yard requirements.
Section 16-06.009   Maximum height.
Section 16-06.010   Minimum off-street parking requirements.
Section 16-06.011   Limitations on signs.

Section 16–06.001   Scope of provisions.
The regulations set forth in this chapter or set forth elsewhere in this part when referred to in this chapter are the regulations in the R-4 Single-Family Residential District. (Ord. No. 1981-95A, Sec. 1, 12/19/80)

Section 16–06.002   Statement of intent.
The intent of this chapter in establishing the R-4 Single-Family Residential District is as follows:

(1) To provide for the protection of existing single-family communities and the development of new communities on lots of medium size at a density of not more than one (1) dwelling unit per 9,000 square feet.

(2) To provide for the development of recreational, educational and religious facilities as basic elements of a balanced community. (Ord. No. 1981-95A, Sec. 1, 12/19/80)

Section 16–06.003   Permitted principal uses and structures.
A building or premises shall be used only for the following principal purposes, and in no case shall there be more than one (1) main building and one (1) main use on a lot:

(1) Churches, synagogues, temples and other religious worship facilities, having a minimum lot area of five (5) acres and located on at least a four-lane collector street.

(2) Public schools through the secondary level operated by the City Board of Education, having no dwelling or lodging facilities except for caretakers.

(3) Single-family detached dwellings.

(4) Structures and uses required for operation of the Rapid Rail Transit System, but not including uses involving storage, train yards, warehousing, switching, or maintenance shops as the primary purpose. (Ord. No. 1981-95A, Sec. 1, 12/19/80)

Section 16-06.004   Permitted accessory uses and structures.

Uses and structures which are customarily incidental and subordinate to permitted principal uses and structures are permitted. These include but are not limited to the following, subject to limitations and requirements set forth herein or elsewhere in this part:

(1) Greenhouses, garden sheds, private garages and similar structures.

(2) Barns for keeping of horses, provided that no such barns shall be within 50 feet of any lot line.

(3) Guest houses, servant quarters, or lodging facilities for caretakers or watchmen.

(4) Swimming pools, tennis courts and similar facilities.

(5) Home occupation, subject to limitations set forth in section 16-29.001(17).

(6) Structures necessary for active construction projects.

(7) Devices for the generation of energy, such as solar panels, wind generators and similar devices.

Except in the case of home occupation, no accessory use shall be of a commercial nature.

No accessory building shall be constructed until construction of the principal building has actually begun, and no accessory building shall be used or occupied until the principal building is completed and in use. (Ord. No. 1981-95A, Sec. 1, 12/19/80)

Section 16-06.005   Special permits.

The following uses are permissible only by special permits of the kinds indicated, subject to limitations and requirements set forth herein or elsewhere in this part:

(1) *Special use permits:*

(a) Cemeteries, mausoleums and columbariums. (Ord. No. 1981-96, Sec. 5, 12/15/81)

(b) Child care nurseries, day care centers, pre-kindergartens, kindergartens, play and other special schools or day care facilities for young children.

(c) Churches, synagogues, temples and other religious worship facilities, where lot area is less than five (5) acres but more than one (1) acre.

(d) Civic, service, garden, neighborhood or private clubs.

(e) Colleges and universities, other than trade schools, business colleges and similar uses.

(f) Extraction or removal of sand, gravel, topsoil, clay, dirt, or other natural resources.

(g) Group homes.

(h) Landfills.

(i) Line-of-sight relay devices for telephonic, radio or television communication, including broadcasting equipment, but not including broadcasting studios.

(j) Nursing homes, convalescent homes, and similar care facilities.

(k) Parks, playgrounds, stadiums, baseball or football fields, golf courses, sports arenas, recreational centers, community centers, community service facilities, and the like, when not owned or operated by a governmental agency.

(l) Private schools.

(m) Rehabilitation centers.

(2) *Special administrative permits:* None.

(3) *Special exceptions:*

(a) Churches, synagogues, temples and other religious worship facilities, where lot

EXHIBIT 5-1
R-4 Single-Family
Residential District
Regulations
(continued)

area is one (1) acre or less.

(b) Structures and uses required for operation of a public utility, except uses involving storage, train yards, warehousing switching, or maintenance shops as the primary purpose. (Ord. No. 1981-95A, Sec. 1, 12/19/80)

Section 16-06.006   Transitional uses, structures, requirements.

None. (Ord. No. 1981-95A, Sec. 1, 12/19/80)

Section 16-06.007   Minimum lot requirements.

The following minimum lot requirements shall apply to all uses approved by special permits as well as permitted uses:

(1) *Churches, temples, synagogues, and similar religious facilities, except when authorized by a special permit:* Every lot shall have an area of not less than five (5) acres and a frontage of not less than 200 feet.

(2) *Single-family detached dwellings and all other uses:* Every lot shall have an area of not less than 9,000 square feet and a frontage of not less than 70 feet.

(3) If a lot has less area of width than herein required and was a lot of record on the effective date of this part, that lot shall be used only for a single-family dwelling. (Ord. No. 1981-95A, Sec. 1, 12/19/80; Ord. No. 1981-96, Sec. 8, 12/15/81)

Section 16-06.008   Minimum yard requirements.

The following minimum yard requirements shall apply to all uses approved by special permits as well as permitted uses:

(1) *Front yard:* There shall be a front yard having a depth of not less than 35 feet.

(2) *Side yard:* There shall be two (2) side yards, one (1) on each side of the main building, each having a width of not less than seven (7) feet. (Ord. No. 1983-32, Sec. 1, 5/4/83)

(3) *Rear yard:* There shall be a rear yard having a depth of not less than seven (7) feet.

(4) *Accessory structures:* Accessory structures other than fences, when permitted, shall be placed to the side or rear of the main structure within the buildable area of the lot so as not to project beyond the front of the main structure. For fences, see section 16-28.008(5). (Ord. No. 1981-95A, Sec. 1, 12/19/80)

Amendment Note: Ord. No. 1983-32, section 1, adopted 5/2/83, approved 5/4/83, amended subsection (2) to require 7-foot minimum side yards rather than combined yards of 15 feet, with no yard less than 7 feet.

Section 16-06.009   Maximum height.

The following height limitations shall apply to all uses approved by special permits as well as permitted uses: No building shall exceed 35 feet in height. See section 16-28.022 for excluded portions of structures. (Ord. No. 1981-95A, Sec. 1, 12/19/80)

Section 16-06.010   Minimum off-street parking requirements.

The following parking requirements shall apply to all uses approved by special permits as well as permitted uses (see section 16-28.014):

(1) *Single-family detached dwellings:* One (1) space per dwelling.

(2) *Schools, colleges, churches, recreational or community centers and other places of assembly:* One (1) space for each four (4) fixed seats (with 18 inches of bench length counted as one (1) seat, or one (1) space for each 35 square feet of enclosed floor area for the accommodation of movable seats in the largest assembly room, whichever is greater, plus the following:

(a) *Public or private elementary or middle school:* Two (2) spaces for each classroom.

(b) *High school:* Four (4) spaces for each classroom.

(c) *Colleges and universities:* Eight (8) spaces for each classroom.

(3) *Nursing homes, convalescent homes, and similar care facilities:* One (1) space per four (4) beds.

(4) *Child care centers, day care centers, pre-kindergartens, kindergartens, play and other special schools or day care centers for young children:* One (1) space per 600 square feet of floor area. In addition to providing off-street parking, such establishments shall provide safe and convenient facilities for loading and unloading children, as approved by the director, bureau of traffic and transportation.

(5) *Other uses:* One (1) space for each 300 square feet of floor area. (Ord. No. 1981-95A, Sec. 1, 12/19/80)

Section 16-06.011   Limitations on signs.

The following sign regulations shall apply to all uses approved by special permits as well as permitted uses (see section 16-28.017):

(1) No freestanding sign shall be higher than 10 feet above ground level.

(2) No sign shall have or consist of any rotating, revolving or otherwise moving part.

(3) No sign shall be internally illuminated, nor shall any sign be animated or changing.

(4) No general advertising signs shall be permitted.

(5) Signs shall be mounted flat to the wall of the building or not nearer than 30 feet to the street property line.

(6) For a residential use, one (1) permanent sign shall be permitted. Such sign shall not exceed two (2) square feet in sign area.

(7) For other approved uses, one (1) permanent sign per street frontage shall be permitted. Such signs shall not exceed 20 square feet in sign area.

(8) One (1) permanent sign per street frontage listing the name of a subdivision shall be permitted. Such sign shall not exceed 35 square feet in sign area. (Ord. No. 1981-95A, Sec. 1, 12/19/80)

EXHIBIT 5–2
C–1 Community
Business District
Regulations

Section 16-11.001   Scope of provisions.
Section 16-11.002   Statement of intent.
Section 16-11.003   Permitted principal uses and structures.
Section 16-11.004   Permitted accessory uses and structures.
Section 16-11.005   Special permits.
Section 16-11.006   Transitional uses, structures, requirements.
Section 16-11.007   Development controls.
Section 16-11.008   Minimum yard requirements.
Section 16-11.009   Maximum height limitations.
Section 16-11.010   Minimum off-street parking requirements.
Section 16-11.011   Limitations on signs.

Section 16-11.001   Scope of provisions.

The regulations set forth in this chapter, or set forth elsewhere in this part when referred to in this chapter, are the regulations in the C-1 Community Business District. (Ord. No. 1981-95A, Sec. 1, 12/19/80)

Section 16-11.002   Statement of intent.

The intent of this chapter in establishing C-1 Community Business District is as follows:

EXHIBIT 5-2
C-1 Community
Business District
Regulations
(continued)

(1) To provide for medium-intensity retail and service activities in areas already committed to development of this character, or consistent with areas so specified on the comprehensive development plan.

(2) To encourage residential use either as single or mixed use development. (Ord. No. 1981-95A, Sec. 1, 12/19/80)

Section 16-11.003   Permitted principal uses and structures.

A building or premises shall be used only for the following principal purposes:

(1) Banks, savings and loan associations, and similar financial institutions.

(2) Broadcasting towers, line-of-sight relay devices for telephonic, radio or television communication.

(3) Business or commercial schools.

(4) Child care centers, kindergartens and special schools.

(5) Churches, synagogues, temples and other religious worship facilities, on lots of one (1) acre or more.

(6) Clubs and lodges.

(7) Commercial greenhouses.

(8) Commercial recreation establishments, including bowling alleys, theaters, convention halls, places of assembly, and similar uses, with primary activities conducted within fully enclosed buildings. Pool halls, billiard parlors and amusement arcades are allowed only by special use permits. (Ord. No. 1981-96, Sec. 18, 12/15/81; Ord. No. 1982-11, Sec. 1, 4/13/82)

(9) Dormitories, fraternities and sororities.

(10) Eating and drinking establishments.

(11) General advertising signs, subject to limitations herein on number and area.

(12) Group homes, rehabilitation centers.

(13) Hospitals.

(14) Hotels and motels, rooming houses, boardinghouses.

(15) Institutions of higher learning , including colleges and universities.

(16) Laundry and dry cleaning, collection stations or plants, limited to no more than 5,000 square feet floor area, laundry and dry cleaning establishments where equipment is operated by customers.

(17) Multifamily dwellings, two-family dwellings and single-family dwellings. (Ord. No. 1981-96, Sec. 19, 12/15/81)

(18) Museums, galleries, auditoriums, libraries and similar cultural facilities.

(19) Nursing homes and convalescent centers.

(20) Offices, clinics (including veterinary if animals are kept within soundproof buildings), laboratories, studios, and similar uses, but not blood donor stations except at hospitals. (Ord. No. 1983-12, Sec. 1, 3/11/83)

(21) Parking structures and lots. (Ord. No. 1981-96, Sec. 20, 12/15/81)

(22) Professional or personal service establishments, but not hiring halls.

(23) Repair establishments for home appliances, bicycles, lawn mowers, shoes, clocks and similar articles.

(24) Retail establishments, including catering establishments, delicatessens and bakeries without wholesale operations.

(25) Sales and leasing agencies for new passenger automobiles, bicycles, mopeds, and commercial vehicles not exceeding one (1) ton in rated capacity, selling, servicing and repairing new vehicles and dealing in the disposal, servicing or repairing of used vehicles in connection therewith and all located on the same site.

(26) Security storage centers not exceeding 7500 square feet of floor area and having

EXHIBIT 5-2
C-1 Community
Business District
Regulations
(continued)

all pickup and delivery of items by passenger automobile or van.

(27) Service stations and car washes.

(28) Structures and uses required for operation of the Rapid Rail Transit System or a public utility but not including uses involving storage, train yards, warehousing, switching or maintenance shop as the primary purpose.

(29) Tailoring, custom dressmaking, millinery and similar establishments limited to not more than 5000 square feet in area.

(30) Adult businesses as defined in section 16-29.001(3). See also section 16-28.016. (Ord. No. 1981-96, Sec. 21,12/15/81)

Except for off-street parking, automobile sales lots, and necessary activities at commercial greenhouses and service stations, or as authorized by special permit, all commercial sales and service activities shall be conducted within completely enclosed buildings, and there shall be no uninclosed displays of merchandise. No wholesaling or jobbing shall be conducted from within the district. No use or manner of operation shall be permitted which is obnoxious or offensive by reason of odor, smoke, noise, glare, fumes, gas, vibration, unusual danger of fire or explosion, emission of particulate matter, or interference with radio or television reception, or for other reasons is incompatible with the character of the district and its relation to adjoining residential districts. (Ord. No. 1981-95A, Sec. 1, 12/19/80)

Amendment Note: Section 1 of Ord. No. 1983-12, adopted 3/10/83, approved 3/11/83, amended subsection (20) to allow veterinary clinics.

Section 16-11.004   Permitted accessory uses and structures.

Uses and structures which are customarily incidental and subordinate to permitted principal uses and structures, to include devices for generation of energy such as solar panels, wind generators and similar devices, except as otherwise herein provided, no merchandise shall be stored other than that to be sold at retail on the premises; and no storage for such merchandise shall occupy more than 25 percent of the total floor areas on the premises. No off-premises storage of such merchandise shall be permitted in the district as either a principal or accessory use. (Ord. No. 1981-95A, Sec. 1, 12/19/80)

Section 16-11.005   Special permits.

The following uses are permissible only by special permit of the kind indicated, subject to limitations and requirements set forth herein or elsewhere in this part:

(1) *Special use permits:*

(a) Helicopter landing facilities or pickup or delivery stations.

(b) Mortuaries, funeral homes.

(c) Outdoor amusement enterprises, exhibits, entertainments, meetings, displays or sales areas, or outdoor areas for religious ceremonies of 90 days' or more duration.

(d) Poolroom, billiard parlors, amusement arcades. (Ord. No. 1981-95A, Sec. 1, 12/19/80; Ord. No. 1981-96, Sec. 22, 12/15/81)

(2) *Special administrative permits:*

(a) Outdoor amusement enterprises, exhibits, entertainments, meetings, displays or sales areas, or outdoor areas for religious ceremonies of less than 90 days' duration.

(b) Zero-lot-line development (see section 16-28.001(6)).

(3) *Special exceptions:*

(a) Churches, synagogues, temples and other religious worship facilities, where lot area is less than one (1) acre.

(b) Off-street parking within 500 feet of primary use. (Ord. No. 1981-95A, Sec. 1, 12/19/80)

EXHIBIT 5-2
C-1 Community
Business District
Regulations
(continued)

Section 16-11.006   Transitional uses, structures, requirements.

(1) *Transitional Uses:* Where a lot in this district abuts a lot in any R-1 through R-G district at the side along the same street frontage, and without an intervening street, the first lot within this district, or the first 100 feet of such lot if it is wider than 100 feet, shall not be used for any drive-in facility, service station, mortuary or funeral home, sales lot for automobiles, or general advertising signs.

(2) *Transitional Height Planes:* Where this district adjoins a district in R-1 through R-G classification without an intervening street, height within the district shall be limited as follows: No portion of any structure shall protrude through a height limiting plane beginning thirty-five (35) feet above the buildable area boundary nearest to the common district boundary and extending inward over this district at an angle of forty-five (45) degrees.

(3) *Transitional Yards:*

(a) *Side yard:* Adjacent to an R District without an intervening street, 20 feet is required which shall not be used for the purpose of parking, paving, loading, servicing or storage activity and shall be planted and/or maintained in a natural state. (Ord. No. 1981-96, Sec. 26, 12/15/81)

(b) *Rear Yard:* There shall be a rear yard of 20 feet when adjacent to an R district that shall not be used for parking, or paving or for purpose of parking, loading or servicing.

(c) *Screening:* Where a lot in this district abuts a lot in an "R" district on the side or rear lot lines without an intervening street, opaque fencing or screening not less than six (6) feet in height shall be provided and maintained in a sightly condition. See Section 16-28.008(9). (Ord. No. 1981-95A, Sec 1, 12/19/80, as amended by Ord. No. 1982-54, Sec. 3, 7/26/82)

Amendment Note: Ord. No. 1982-54, Sec. 3, adopted 7/19/82, approved 7/26/82, deleted former subsection 16-11.006(3*c) and enacted a new subsection 16-11.006(3*c) in lieu thereof.

Section 16-11.007   Development controls.

(1) *Bulk Limitations:* For nonresidential uses and lodging uses, floor area shall not exceed an amount equal to 2.0 times net lot area. Multifamily dwellings shall be permitted up to the maximum ratios established for sector 3 shown on table I, section 16-08.007.

(2) *Minimum Lot Width, Area, All Uses:* No fixed minimum lot widths or areas are established for these districts, except as follows:

(a) *Churches, synagogues, temples and similar religious facilities:* Minimum net lot, one (1) acre except by special exception.

(b) *Single-family and two-family dwellings:* Minimum lot width of 50 feet; minimum net lot area of 5000 square feet.

(c) *Multifamily dwellings:* See section 11.007(1), "Bulk Limitations." (Ord. No. 1981-95A, Sec. 1, 12/19/80)

Section 16-11.008   Minimum yard requirements.

(a) *Front Yard:* 40 feet.

(b) *Side:* None, except if a building is not constructed to the lot line it shall be set back at least five (5) feet from the lot line and except as required in section 16-11.006.

(c) *Rear:* None, except as required in section 16-11.006. (Ord. No. 1981-95A, Sec. 1, 12/19/80)

(d) *Side Street Side:* On corner lots there shall be a setback along the side street of not less than half the required depth of the front yard. (Ord. No. 1981-96, Sec. 23, 12/15/81)

EXHIBIT 5-2
C-1 Community
Business District
Regulations
(continued)

Section 16-11.009   Maximum height limitations.

None, except as required in section 16-11.006. (Ord. No. 1981-95A, Sec. 1, 12/19/80)

Section 16-11.010   Minimum off-street parking requirements.

The following parking requirements shall apply to all uses approved by special permit as well as permitted uses (see section 16-28.104 and also section 16-28.015 for loading requirements):

(1) *Schools, colleges, churches, recreational or community centers and other places of assembly:* One (1) space for each four (4) fixed seats with 18 inches of bench length counted as one (1) seat, or one (1) space for each 35 square feet of enclosed floor area for the accommodation of movable seats in the largest assembly room, whichever is greater, plus the following:

(a) *Public or private elementary or middle school:* Two (2) spaces for each classroom.

(b) *High school:* Four (4) spaces for each classroom.

(c) *Colleges and universities:* Eight (8) spaces for each classroom.

(2) *Nursing homes, convalescent homes, and similar care facilities:* One (1) space per four (4) beds.

(3) *Child care centers, day care centers, pre-kindergartens, kindergartens, play and other special schools or day care centers for young children:* One (1) space per 600 square feet of floor area. In addition to providing off-street parking, such establishments shall provide safe and convenient facilities for loading and unloading children, as approved by the director, bureau of traffic and transportation.

(4) *Dwellings and lodgings:* See section 16-08.007, table I, for applicable ratios according to the appropriate floor area ratio.

(5) *Banks, savings and loan institutions, and the like:* One (1) space for each 200 square feet of floor area.

(6) *Business colleges, trade schools, conservatories, dancing schools, and the like:* One (1) space for each 200 square feet of floor area.

(7) *Drive-in establishments:* See section 16-28.021.

(8) *Fraternities, sororities, dormitories:* One (1) space for two (2) beds plus one (1) space for each 200 square feet of floor area designated or occupied other than for sleeping purposes.

(9) *Clubs, lodges:* One (1) space for each 200 square feet of floor area.

(10) *Retail establishments, including catering, delicatessen and bakeries, but not other uses as provided below:* One (1) space for each 200 square feet of floor area.

(11) *Eating and drinking establishments:* One (1) space for each 100 square feet of floor area.

(12) *Laundry and dry cleaning plants, collection stations, self-operated facilities:* One (1) space for each 200 square feet of floor area.

(13) *Tailoring, custom dressmaking, millinery and similar establishments:* One (1) space for each 400 square feet of floor area.

(14) *Repair establishments for home appliances, bicycles, lawn mowers, shoes, clocks and watches, and the like:* One (1) space for each 200 square feet of floor area.

(15) *Bowling alleys, poolrooms, billiard parlors and the like:* One (1) space for each 100 square feet of floor area.

(16) *Theaters:* One (1) space for each 100 square feet of floor area. (Ord. No. 1981-96, Sec. 24, 12/15/81)

(17) *Accessory uses:* All accessory uses cited in section 16-11.004 shall provide one (1) additional space per 300 square feet of floor area devoted to such space.

EXHIBIT 5-2
C-1 Community
Business District
Regulations
(continued)

(18) *Other uses:* One (1) space for each 300 square feet of floor area. (Ord. No. 1981-95A, Sec. 1, 2/19/80)

Section 16-11.011   Limitations on signs.

The following sign regulations shall apply to all uses approved by special permits as well as permitted uses (see section 16-28.017):

(1) Only three (3) business signs shall be permitted for each business establishment. Two (2) additional business signs shall be permitted for each additional street frontage.

(2) No animated or flashing signs shall be permitted.

(3) No sign, other than wall signs, shall extend over or project over the street property line.

(4) Only one (1) business sign, not exceeding 60 square feet in sign area, may encroach into the required front yard setback.

(5) A freestanding business sign shall not exceed 45 feet in height above ground level; provided, however, when the ground level is lower than the level of the adjoining street pavement, then a freestanding business sign may be raised so as to be not more than 25 feet above the level of the pavement.

(6) General advertising signs shall be permitted subject to the following restrictions:

(a) General advertising signs are prohibited within 100 feet of any residential district; provided, however, if the lot upon which the general advertising sign is to be located contains a depth of less than 200 feet, the general advertising sign shall be permitted within the buildable area of the lot at its furtherest possible distance from the residential district.

(b) All general advertising signs shall be restricted to the buildable area of the lot.

(c) A general advertising sign shall not be located within 200 feet of another general advertising sign on the same side of the street as measured point to point along the abutting right-of-way; provided, however, such a sign may be located within 200 feet of another sign when the signs are separated by buildings or other obstructions so that only one (1) sign facing located within the 200-foot zone is visible from the fronting street at any one (1) time. On streets which are a part of the interstate highway, limited-access freeway or expressway system within the city, no general advertising sign shall be located within 1000 feet of another general advertising sign on the same side of the highway as measured point to point along the abutting right-of-way; provided, however, such a sign may be located within 1000 feet of another sign when the signs are separated by buildings or other obstructions so that only one (1) sign facing located within 1000-foot zone is visible from the fronting highway at any one (1) time.

EXHIBIT 5-3
Townhouse
Restrictions

STATE OF
COUNTY OF

Declaration of Covenants
Conditions and Restrictions

THIS DECLARATION, made on the date hereinafter set forth by   , hereinafter collectively referred to as "Declarant".

Witnesseth:

WHEREAS,   is the owner of certain property on

in   County, State of   which is more particularly described in

EXHIBIT 5-3
Townhouse
Restrictions
(continued)

Exhibit "A", attached hereto and made a part hereof.

NOW THEREFORE, Declarant hereby declares that all of the properties described in Exhibit "A" shall be held, sold and conveyed subject to the following easements, restrictions, covenants and conditions, which are for the purpose of protecting the value and desirability of, and which shall run with the real property and be binding on all parties having any right, title or interest in the described properties or any part thereof, their heirs, administrators, successors and assigns, and shall inure to the benefit of each owner thereof.

Article I
Definitions

Section 1.

"Association": shall mean and refer to   , a   non-profit corporation, its successors and assigns.

Section 2.

"Owner" shall mean and refer to the record owner, whether one or more persons or entities, of a fee simple title to any lot which is a part of the Properties, but excluding those having such interest merely as a security for the performance of an obligation.

Section 3.

"Properties" shall mean and refer to that certain real property described in Exhibit "A" and such additions thereto as may hereafter be brought within the jurisdiction of the Association.

Section 4.

"Townhouse Lots" shall mean those lots on which townhouses shall be erected and which are described on Exhibit "B" attached hereto and made a part hereof by reference.

Section 5.

"Common Area" shall mean and refer to all that land owned by the Association and described in Exhibit "C" attached hereto and made a part hereof by reference. The said Common Area is also designated on the plat of

The Common Area shall be held for the common use and enjoyment of all of the owners, and shall be operated and maintained by the Association for the use and benefit of its members.

Section 6.

"Lot" shall mean and refer to any plot of land shown upon any recorded subdivision map of the Properties with the exception of the Common Area.

Section 7.

"Declarant" shall mean and refer to   as their interests may appear, their successors and assigns, if such successors or assigns should acquire more than one undeveloped lot from the Declarant for the purposes of development.

Section 8.

"Development Plan" shall mean preliminary plan or   prepared by   dated   and revised   .

EXHIBIT 5–3
Townhouse
Restrictions
(continued)

Article II
Property Rights

Section 1.   Owners' Easements of Enjoyment.

Every owner shall have a right and easement of enjoyment in and to the Common Area which shall be appurtenant to and shall pass with the title to every lot and every member of the Association shall have a right of enjoyment in the Common Area subject to the following provisions.

(a) The right of the Association to levy annual and special assessments and to charge reasonable admission and other fees for the use of any recreational facility situated upon the Common Area.

(b) The right of the Association to suspend the voting rights by a member for any period during which any assessment against his lot remains unpaid; and for a period not to exceed 60 days for any infraction of its published rules and regulations. Assessments shall continue during any suspension period.

(c) The right of the Association to dedicate or transfer all or any part of the Common Area to any public authority, agency, or utility for such purposes and subject to such conditions as may be agreed to by 2/3 members.

(d) The right of the Association to establish uniform rules and regulations pertaining to the use of the Common Area and the facilities thereon.

(e) The right of Declarant (and its sales agents and representatives) to the non-exclusive use of the Common Area for display and exhibit purposes, which right Declarant hereby reserves; provided, however, that such use shall not be for a period of more than 5 years after the conveyance of the Common Area to the Association, or the sale of all the residential lots within the Properties, whichever is the earlier; provided, further, that no such use by Declarant or its sales agents or representatives shall restrict the members in their use and enjoyment of the Common Area or facilities thereon.

Section 2.   Townhouse Owners Easements of Enjoyment.

Every owner of a townhouse lot shall have a right and easement of enjoyment in and to Common Area which shall be appurtenant to and shall pass with the title to every lot subject to the hereinbefore mentioned provisions of this Article II.

Section 3.   Delegation of Use.

Any owner may delegate, in accordance with the By-Laws, his right of enjoyment to the Common Area and facilities to the members of his family or tenants.

Section 4.   Title to Common Areas.

Title to the Common Area shall be conveyed to the Association free and clear of all liens and encumbrances, excluding (1) taxes for the current year which are not yet due and payable and (2) easements recorded, if any.

Section 5.   Parking Rights.

Ownership of each townhouse lot shall entitle the owner (or owners) thereof to the use of not more than two automobile parking spaces, which shall be as near and convenient to said lot as reasonably possible, together with the right of ingress and egress in and upon said parking area. If the Association deems it necessary it may, at its option, permanently assign one parking space for each lot.

EXHIBIT 5-3
Townhouse
Restrictions
(continued)

Article III
Membership and Voting Rights

Section 1. Members.

Every owner of a lot shall be a member of the Association as designated in Section 2 of this Article III. Membership shall be appurtenant to and may not be separated from ownership of any lot which is subject to assessment.

Section 2. Voting Rights.

Each owner shall be entitled to one vote for each such lot so owned. When more than one person holds an interest in any lot, all such persons shall be members. The vote for such lot shall be exercised as they among themselves determine, but in no event shall more than one vote be cast with respect to any lot.

Article IV
Covenant for Maintenance Assessments

Section 1. Creation of the Lien and Personal Obligation of Assessments.

The Declarant, for each lot owned within the Properties, hereby covenants, and each owner of any lot by acceptance of a deed therefore, whether or not it shall be so expressed in such deed, is deemed to covenant and agree to pay to the Association: (1) annual assessments or charges; and (2) special assessments for capital improvements, such assessments to be established and collected as hereinafter provided. If a delinquency occurs in the payment of annual and/or special assessments, the Association may have all rights and remedies against the owner which is permissible under   law at the time of said delinquency. Each such assessment, together with interest costs and reasonable attorney's fees, shall also be the personal obligation of the person who was the owner of such property at the time when the assessment fell due. The personal obligation for delinquent assessments shall not pass to his successors in title, unless expressly assumed by them by written agreement. Such annual or special assessments against the owner shall constitute a lien in favor of the association of the townhome or townhomes against which such assessment is levied and shall include (a) a late or delinquency charge, (b) interest on each assessment or installment thereof, in any delinquency or late charge appertaining thereto, from the date the same was first due and payable, (c) the cost of collection, including court cost, and reasonable attorney's fees actually incurred.

Section 2. Purpose of Assessments.

The assessments levied by the Association shall be used exclusively to promote the recreation, health, safety, and welfare of the residents of the Properties and for the improvement and maintenance of the Common Area. The Association shall pay any real and personal property taxes and other charges assessed against the Common Area.

The Association shall maintain a policy or policies of liability insurance insuring the Association and its agents, guest, permitees, and invitees and the Owners of the Lots against liability to the public or to said Owners, their guests, permitees or invitees incident to the ownership or use of the Common Properties, in an amount not less than Five Hundred Thousand Dollars ($500,000.00) for any one person injured, One Million Dollars ($1,000,000.00) for any one accident and One Hundred Thousand Dollars ($100,000.00) for property damage. Said limits shall be reviewed at intervals of not less than three (3) years

EXHIBIT 5-3
Townhouse
Restrictions
(continued)

and adjusted if necessary to provide such coverage and protection as the Association may deem prudent.

Section 3.   Maximum Annual Assessments.

Until January 1 of the year immediately following the conveyance of the first lot to an owner, the maximum annual assessment for any townhouse lot owned by the Declarant shall be 25% of the maximum annual assessment designated for owners of townhouse lots. The maximum annual assessment for any townhouse lot which is not owned by the Declarant shall be $ .00.

(a) From and after January 1 of the year immediately following the conveyance of the first lot to an owner, by vote of the Board of Directors, the maximum annual assessments may be increased each year above the maximum assessments for the previous year by not more than 20% without a vote of the membership.

(b) From and after January 1 of the year immediately following the conveyance of the first lot to an owner, the maximum annual assessments may be increased above 20% by a vote of two-thirds of each class of members who are voting in person or by proxy, at a meeting duly called for this purpose.

(c) The Board of Directors may fix the annual assessments at an amount not in excess of the maximum as hereinbefore set forth.

Section 4.   Special Assessments.

The association may levy, in any assessment year, a special assessment applicable to that year only for the purpose of defraying, in whole or in part, the cost of any construction, reconstruction, repair or replacement of a capital improvement upon any Common Area, including fixtures and personal property related thereto for the purpose of paying additional taxes, or for any other purpose which the association, in its sole discretion, may deem necessary. Provided, however, that any such assessment, including the due date of payments on account of such assessments, shall have the assent of two-thirds of the votes of the townhouse lot owners who are voting in person or by proxy at a meeting duly called for such purpose.

Section 5.   Notice and Quorum for any Action Authorized under Sections 3 and 4.

Written notice of any meeting called, in accordance with the By-Laws of the Association, for the purpose of taking any action authorized under Section 3 or 4 shall be sent to all members not less than 14 nor more than 60 days in advance of the meeting. At the first such meeting called, the initial presence of members or of proxies entitled to cast 50% of all the votes of each class of membership, shall constitute a quorum. If the required quorum is not present at the commencement of the meeting, another meeting may be called subject to the same notice requirements, and the required quorum at the subsequent meeting shall be 1/2 of the required quorum at the preceding meeting. No such subsequent meeting shall be held more than 30 days following the preceeding meeting. The members present at a duly organized meeting can continue to do business until adjournment, notwithstanding the withdrawal of the holders of enough shares to leave less than a quorum.

Section 6.   Uniform Rate of Assessment.

Both annual and special assessments must be fixed at a uniform rate and may be collected on a monthly, quarterly, or annual basis; provided, however, the amount of any assessment in any one year and from year to year may vary.

EXHIBIT 5-3
Townhouse
Restrictions
(continued)

Section 7. Date of Commencement of Annual Assessments: Due Dates.

The annual assessments provided for herein shall commence as to all members on the first day of the month following the conveyance of the Common Area. The first annual assessment shall be adjusted according to the number of months remaining in the calendar year.

The Board of Directors shall fix the amount of the annual assessment against each member at least 30 days in advance of each annual assessment period. Written notice of the annual assessment shall be sent to every owner subject thereto. The due dates shall be established by the Board of Directors. The Association shall, upon demand and for a reasonable charge, furnish a certificate signed by an officer of the Association setting forth that the assessments on a specified lot have been paid and any such properly executed certificate shall be binding upon the Association.

Section 8. Effect of Nonpayment of Assessments: Remedies of Association.

Any assessment not paid within 30 days after the due date shall bear interest from the due date at the rate of 8% per annum. The Association may bring an action at law against the owner personally obligated to pay the same; or the Association may seek any other remedy allowable under   law. No owner may waive or otherwise escape liability for the assessments provided for herein by non-use of the Common Area or abandonment of his townhouse.

Section 9. Subordination of the Lien to Mortgages.

The lien of the assessments provided for herein shall be subordinate to the lien of any first mortgage. Sale or transfer of any lot shall not affect the assessment lien. However, the sale or transfer of any lot pursuant to mortgage foreclosure or any proceeding in lieu thereof, shall extinguish the lien of such assessments as to payments which become due prior to such sale or transfer. No sale or transfer shall relieve such lot from liability for any assessments thereafter becoming due or from the lien thereof.

Article V
Architectural Control

No building, fence, wall or other structure shall be commenced, erected or maintained upon the Properties nor shall any exterior addition to or change or alteration therein be made until the plans and specifications showing the nature, kind, shape, height, materials, and location of the same shall have been submitted to and approved in writing as to harmony of external design and location in relation to surrounding structures and topography by the Architectural Control Committee composed of three members of the Board. In the event said Committee fails to approve or disapprove such design and location within 30 days after receipt of said plans and specifications, approval will not be required and this Article will be deemed to have been fully complied with. Nothing in this Article shall be construed to permit any review of architecture and/or building decision made by the Declarant with respect to any lot before its initial sale.

Article VI
Maintenance

Section 1. Common Areas.

The Association shall be responsible for the care and maintenance of the Common Areas, including both interiors and exteriors of the structures erected thereon; and shall

EXHIBIT 5–3
Townhouse
Restrictions
(continued)

also be responsible for the care and maintenance of property, including right-of-way, dedicated to an appropriate governmental or quasi governmental group or utility company where such group or company has not agreed to care for and maintain said property.

Section 2.   Individual Lots.

Except as otherwise provided herein, the owner of each lot shall be responsible for the care, maintenance and repair of his lot, the premises and all improvements situate thereon.

In the event that any owner shall fail to maintain any lot or the premises and the improvements situate thereon in a manner satisfactory to the Board, the Association, after approval by 2/3's vote of the Board of Directors, shall have the right, through its agents and employees, to enter upon said lot and to repair, maintain and/or restore the lot, the premises and any improvements erected thereon. Such right of entry and repair shall be exercisable only upon 15 days written notice given to the owner thereof, unless, in the discretion of the Board, a genuine emergency necessitates a shorter period of time. The costs of any such repairs, maintenance and/or restoration shall be added to and become part of the assessment to which such lot owner is subject. Enforcement of the right to recover these assessments may be had pursuant to Article IV, Section 8 herein.

Article VII
Party Walls

Section 1.   General Rules of Law to Apply.

Each wall which is built as a part of the original construction of the homes upon the properties and placed on the dividing line between the lots shall constitute a party wall, and, to the extent not inconsistent with provisions of this Article, the general rules of   law regarding party walls and liability for property damage due to negligence or willful acts or omissions shall apply thereto.

Section 2.   Sharing of Repair and Maintenance.

The cost of reasonable repair and maintenance of a party wall shall be shared by the owners who make use of the wall in proportion to such use.

Section 3.   Destruction by Fire or Other Casualty.

If a party wall is destroyed or damaged by fire or other casualty, any owner who has used the wall may restore it, and if the other owners thereafter make use of the wall they shall contribute to the cost of the restoration thereof in proportion to such use without prejudice, however, to the right of any such owners to call for a larger contribution from the others under any rule of law regarding liability for negligent or willful acts or omissions.

Section 4.   Weatherproofing.

Notwithstanding any other provisions of this Article, an owner who by his negligent or willful act causes the party wall to be exposed to the elements shall bear the whole cost of furnishing the necessary protection against such elements.

Section 5.   Right to Contribution Runs with Land.

The right of any owner to contribution from any other owner under this Article shall be appurtenant to the land and shall pass to such owner's successors in title.

EXHIBIT 5-3
Townhouse
Restrictions
(continued)

Section 6.   Arbitration.

In the event any dispute arising concerning a party wall, or under the provisions of this Article, such disputes shall be referred to arbitration. Each party shall choose one arbitrator, and such arbitrators shall choose one additional arbitrator, and the decision shall be by a majority of all the arbitrators, and shall be binding upon the parties. Pursuant to   law, judgment upon the award of the arbitrators may be maintained in any court of law with jurisdiction thereupon.

Article VIII
Use Restrictions

The following shall be restrictions on the use of the Properties which shall run with and bind the land, to-wit:

(A) None of the lots shall be used for any purpose other than for residential use. No business activities shall be conducted in or on any part of a lot or in any improvements thereon on the property; provided, however, that this use restriction does not apply to the Declarant to the extent mentioned in Article III(g).

(B) No noxious of offensive activity shall be carried on upon any lot nor shall anything be done thereupon which may become a nuisance to the neighbors.

(C) Unit owners shall not cause or permit anything to be hung or displayed on the outside of windows or placed on the outside walls or doors of any portion of their units, and no sign, awning, canopy, shutter or radio or television antenna (except for a master antenna system installed by the Developer in the place indicated on the Plat) shall be affixed to or placed upon the exterior walls or doors, roof, patios or balconies or any part hereof, or exposed on or at any window, without the prior written consent of the Board of Directors.

(D) No boats, boat trailers, trucks of a capacity of one ton or more or unlicensed vehicles may be parked in streets, driveways, front yards, or common parking areas for more than twenty-four hours.

(E) No temporary building, trailer, garage or building in the course of construction shall be used, temporarily or permanently, as a residence on any lot.

(F) No sign of any kind other than those of the Declarant, builder or their designated agent, shall be displayed to the public view of any lot except that one sign of not more than 2 square feet advertising that lot for sale or rent will be permitted.

(G) No trees, except during initial construction, shall be removed from any lot. The Board of Directors in its discretion, may adopt and promulgate rules and regulations regarding the preservation of trees and other natural resources and wild life upon the Properties. If it shall deem it appropriate, the Board may mark certain trees, regardless of size, as not removable without written authorization.

(H) Any fence to be constructed on any lot must conform to the same design, color and materials of the original fence provided by   , and shall enclose the entire rear yard. Fences shall not be permitted to be erected forward of the rear foundation wall of the house. The height of the fence must be the same as the original fence provided by   . The planting of trees, shrubs, or any other type of plantings that would afford privacy may be used in lieu of constructing additional fencing, provided, however, that they are maintained in accordance with the provisions set forth elsewhere in this Declaration.

(I) Storage sheds may be erected only if the roofing and siding materials to be used match that of the existing house.

(J) No animals, livestock, or poultry of any kind shall be raised, bred or kept on any lot, except that an ordinary number of dogs, cats or other household pets may be kept provid-

EXHIBIT 5–3
Townhouse
Restrictions
(continued)

ed they are kept in accordance with the duly adopted Rules and Regulations of the Association; and provided further, they are not kept, bred or maintained for any commercial purpose.

(K) No lumber, materials, bulk materials, refuse or trash shall be kept, stored, or allowed to accumulate on any lot except building materials during the course of construction, maintenance, or repair by the Declarant of any approved structure. Trash, garbage or other waste shall not be kept except in sanitary containers and such shall not be permitted to remain in public view except on days of trash collection. All containers or other equipment for the storage or disposal of such materials shall be kept in a clean and sanitary condition. If a central trash collection area is designated by the Association, then these areas will be under the control of the Association and all members will abide by the current regulations regarding the use of these trash enclosures.

(L) No water pipe, gas pipe, sewer pipe or drainage pipe shall be installed or maintained on any lot above the surface of the ground. Easements have been reserved for sewers, drainage and utility installations and maintenance for such purposes and uses as are shown on the Development Plan and/or any subdivision plat for the Properties. Within these easements no structure, planting or other material shall be placed or permitted to remain which may damage or interfere with the installation and maintenance of utilities, or which may change the direction or flow of drainage channels in the easements, or which may obstruct or retard the flow of water through drainage channels in the easements. The easement area of each lot and all improvements in it shall be maintained continuously by the owner of the lot, except for those improvements for which a public authority or utility company is responsible. The Declarant, its agents, successors and assigns, shall have the right to enter upon all parts of the easement area of each lot for any of the purposes for which said easements and rights-of-way are reserved. The Declarant shall also have the right at the time of, or after, grading any street, or any part thereof, to enter upon any abutting lot and grade the portion of such lot adjacent to such street, but there shall be no obligation on the Declarant to do such grading, unless otherwise properly required to do so by an appropriate governmental authority. The Declarant shall further have the right to establish a 5 foot drainage easement between any two adjacent lots if it is deemed necessary in the sole discretion of the Declarant. In addition, all Common Area is hereby deemed to be part of the drainage easement of the Properties.

(M) The rights and duties with respect to sanitary sewer and water, cable television, electricity, gas and telephone lines and facilities shall be governed by the following:

(i) Whenever water, sanitary sewer, electricity, gas, cable television or telephone connections, lines, cables or any portion thereof, are or have been installed within the Properties, the owner of any lot, or the Association shall have the right, and are hereby granted an easement to the extent necessary therefore, to enter upon or have a utility company enter upon any portion of the Properties in which said installations lie, to repair, replace and generally maintain said installations.

(ii) The right granted in Subparagraph (i) above shall be only to the extent necessary to entitle the owner or Association serviced by said installation to its full and reasonable use and enjoyment, and provide further that anyone exercising said right shall be responsible for restoring the surface of the easement area so used to its condition prior to such use.

(iii) In the event of a dispute between owners with respect to the repair or rebuilding of said connections, or with respect to the sharing of the cost thereof, upon written request of one of such owners addressed to the Association, the matter shall be submitted to its Board of Directors, who shall decide the dispute, and the decision of the Board shall be final and conclusive on the parties.

EXHIBIT 5-3
Townhouse
Restrictions
(continued)

(N) Easements over the Properties for the installation and maintenance of electric, telephone, cable television, water, gas, drainage, and sanitary sewer lines and facilities and the like are hereby reserved by Declarant, together with the right to grant and transfer the same during such time that Declarant is the owner of the property. Declarant also reserves the right to enter into the Common Area for the purpose of completing the improvements thereon, and on the lots, and for the further purpose of carrying out any obligations which it may have, or assume, with respect to the curing of any defects in workmanship or materials in the Properties or the improvements thereon.

(O) No clothing or any other household fabric shall be hung in the open on any lot unless the same is hung from a device which is removed from view when not actually in use.

(P) The Board of Directors shall have the right to enter upon any lot and trim or prune, at the expense of the owner, any hedge or other planting which in the opinion of the Board by reason of its location upon the lot or the height to which it is permitted to grow, is unreasonably detrimental to the adjoining property or obscures the view of street traffic or is unattractive in appearance; provided, however, that the owner shall be given 15 days prior written notice to correct the problem. The Association may bring an action at law against the owner personally obligated to pay same; or the Association may foreclose the lien against the property. No owner may waive or otherwise escape liability for the assessments provided for herein by nonuse of the Common Area of abandonment of his lot.

(Q) Nothing contained in this Article VIII shall be construed to limit in any way the rights and powers of the Board of Directors and the Architectural Control Committee to approve or disapprove of the erection of buildings, fences, walls, or other structures or of changes or alterations to the Properties as more fully provided in Article V hereof.

Article IX
Staged Developments

Additional land within the areas shown on the Development Plan may be annexed by the Declarant, its successors and assigns, without the consent of members within 7 years of the date of this instrument, provided that the Federal Housing Administration and/or the Veterans Administration determine the annexation is in accord with the Development Plan as previously approved by them. No lot will be sold to any individual homeowner in any section that has not been annexed. Said Development Plan shall not bind Declarant, its successors and assigns, to make the proposed additions or to adhere to the Development Plan in any subsequent development of the land shown thereon. The additions authorized hereunder shall be made by filing of record an Amendment to the Declaration of Covenants, Conditions and Restrictions with respect to the additional property which shall extend the scheme of the Covenants, Conditions and Restrictions of this Declaration to such Property. Upon the filing of any Amendment to the Declaration and the recordation of a plan of such addition, Owners of Lots situated on the annexed properties shall be immediately entitled to the number of votes as determined for members within the initial Properties subject to this Declaration.

Article X
General Provisions

Section 1.   Enforcement.

The Association, or any owner, shall have the right to enforce, by any proceeding at law or in equity, all restrictions, conditions, covenants, reservations, liens and charges now

EXHIBIT 5-3
Townhouse
Restrictions
(continued)

or hereafter imposed by the provisions of this Declaration. Failure by the Association or by any owner to enforce any covenant or restriction herein contained shall in no event be deemed a waiver of the right to do so thereafter.

Section 2.   Severability.

Invalidation of any one of these covenants or restrictions by judgment or court order shall in no way affect any other provision which shall remain in full force and effect.

Section 3.   Amendment.

The covenants and restrictions of the Declaration shall run with and bind the land, for a term of 20 years from the date this Declaration is recorded, after which time they shall be automatically extended for successive periods of 10 years. The Declaration may be amended during the first 20 years period by an instrument signed by not less than 75% of the townhouse owners, and thereafter by an instrument signed by not less than a majority of townhouse owners. Any such instrument shall become effective upon recordation.

Section 4.   Annexation.

Additional property and Common Area other than that referred to in Article IX may be annexed to the Properties by vote of 2/3's of the townhouse owners.

Section 5.   Conflicts.

In the case of any conflict between this Declaration and the By-Laws of the Association, the Declaration shall control.

Section 6.   Governmental Requirement.

Open area and buffer zone shall be maintained in accordance with County zoning regulations.

Article XI
Insurance

Section 1.   Coverage.

Each owner shall maintain fire insurance with extended coverage endorsement (or more extensive insurance) to insure full replacement value of the improvements on the lot owned by said owner. In the event the owner fails to have adequate insurance on his townhouse lot or the improvements located thereon, the association shall have the right to purchase adequate insurance on behalf of said owner and shall create a special assessment against said owner as provided in Article IV, Section 4 hereinabove. In addition, each owner shall make available to the association a certificate of insurance evidencing that he has obtained full replacement value on his townhouse.

Section 2.   Damage or Destruction of Townhouse.

It is hereby agreed by each owner that in the event of loss or destruction of his townhouse, he agrees to rebuild his townhouse as rapidly as possible and according to the original plans and specifications by which his townhouse was originally built. Notwithstanding, unless 80% of the owners vote in person or by proxy not to rebuild said townhouses, then the owner shall have the automatic duty and responsibility to rebuild same.

EXHIBIT 5-3
Townhouse
Restrictions
(continued)

Article XII
Exemption from Assessments

Notwithstanding anything else contained in this Declaration, the Declarant, and _____ shall be exempt from the payment of any assessments as set forth in Article IV hereof and shall not be liable for any assessments unless said townhouse shall be rented by, or occupied by an officer or an employee of either the Declarant and/or _____ .

IN WITNESS WHEREOF, the undersigned, being the Declarant herein, has hereunto caused the execution of these presents this _____ day of _____, 19_____.

Easements and Licenses

Trespass not on my heart; license is granted thee to dwell.

—Anonymous

OBJECTIVES

After reading this chapter you will be able to:

- Understand the uses of an easement
- Identify the various kinds of easements and their methods of creation and termination
- Explain the purpose of a license and distinguish it from an easement

GLOSSARY

Appurtenant easement Easement created to benefit a particular parcel of real property. The easement transfers automatically with a transfer of the ownership of the real property benefited by the easement.

Blanket easement Easement that covers real property without a specific location of the easement.

Dominant tenement Parcel of land benefited by an appurtenant easement.

Easement Right granted to a nonowner of real property to use the real property for a specific purpose; for example, a right given to an electric utility company to locate an electric line on real property.

Easement by necessity Easement for access to a public street that is necessary for the use and enjoyment of the property benefited by the easement.

Easement in gross Easement granting the owner of the easement the right to use real property for a particular purpose. The easement does not benefit a parcel of real property owned by the owner of the easement.

Implied easement Easement created by the conduct of the parties to the easement, not by written agreement.

License Authority or permission to do a particular act or series of acts on another person's land.

Prescriptive easement Easement created when a person uses real property for a period of time without the owner's permission.

Servient tenement Parcel of land on which an appurtenant easement is located.

As discussed in Chapter 5, real property can be encumbered by any number of things. An encumbrance is viewed by the property owner as an unwanted item. An easement, although an encumbrance, may be a benefit to real property. For example, Aaron and Carol each own neighboring lots of lakefront property. They are both constructing a vacation cottage on their respective lots. They discover during the construction process that it would be in their best interest to construct a driveway that would be located one-half on Aaron's property and one-half on Carol's property. Through the use of an easement, a joint driveway can be created for the benefit of Aaron and Carol. Aaron will give Carol an easement for the use of that portion of the driveway located on Aaron's property, and Carol will grant to Aaron an easement for the use of that portion of the driveway located on Carol's property. Aaron and Carol also could agree to share the costs of maintaining the driveway. Although the joint driveway easement restricts the use of both Aaron's and Carol's property, the restriction of use is minimal compared with the benefit that each owner receives through the use of the driveway.

Easements are common encumbrances. The legal assistant will encounter easements on almost all urban real property transactions and on many rural transactions. It is not uncommon for legal assistants to review easements and advise clients as to the restrictions and benefits of the easement. Legal assistants who are involved with the development of real property also prepare easements. This chapter discusses the general law regarding easements and provides some practical suggestions for the preparation of easements, including examples of easement forms.

EASEMENTS

An **easement** is a right to use the real property of another owner for a specific purpose. It is considered an encumbrance on the real property on which the easement is located. Some common examples of easements are utility easements and access easements. *Utility easements* are rights given to utility companies, such as the gas, electric, and telephone companies, that permit them to install transmission lines over real property. *Access easements* give a party the right to travel over or across real property to a public street. Samples of both an access easement and a utility easement appear at the end of this chapter (Exhibits 6–1 and 6–2).

Easements are divided into two categories: ***appurtenant easement*** and ***easement in gross***. An appurtenant easement is an easement created for the benefit of a particular tract of land. An example is shown in Exhibit 6–3.

An easement is created over Parcel A to provide access for Parcel B to the public street. Parcel B is know as the ***dominant tenement***, the parcel of land benefited by the easement, and Parcel A is known as the ***servient tenement***, the land on which the easement is located. This easement would be an encumbrance on Parcel A and a benefit to Parcel B.

Appurtenant easements are regarded as being so closely connected to the dominant tenement that on the sale of the dominant tenement, the easement passes automatically, even if the deed does not mention the easement. In other words, a sale of Parcel B, even with a deed that does not mention the easement over Parcel A, conveys Parcel B and the easement over Parcel A to the new owner.

An easement in gross does not benefit a particular parcel of land. Utility easements are easements in gross. For example, an electric power company acquires an easement to locate a high-tension electric power line across several owners' proper-

New York:

For a discussion on Easements in New York, see Appendix.

EXHIBIT 6–3
Appurtenant
Easement

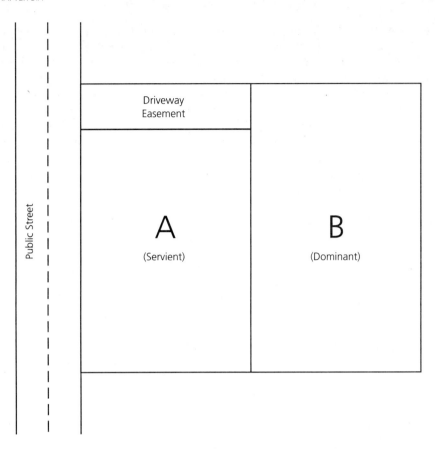

ties. The easement benefits the power company but does not benefit a particular parcel of real property owned by the power company.

Creation of Easements

An easement may be created by (a) express grant, (b) implication, (c) prescription, or (d) necessity.

Express Grant

An easement can be created by an express grant. The grant may be by a separate document or by a reservation of easement contained in a deed. The grant of an easement by a separate easement agreement is prepared with the same formality of requirements as a deed. The easement is in writing and describes the use of the easement and the real property on or over which the easement is located. It also is signed by the grantor (person giving the easement), witnessed, notarized, and delivered to the grantee (the recipient) of the easement.

The grantor of the easement must be the owner of the real property on which the easement is located. The grantor cannot convey an easement for any longer term than the grantor's ownership of the real property. For example, a grantor who owns a life estate in a parcel of real property can grant an easement only for the period of the life estate and no longer. A title examination of the grantor's real property is conducted to determine what rights the grantor of the easement has to the real property. In addition, encumbrances on the real property, such as a mortgage or a deed of trust, can create problems for the holder of the easement. A mortgage or a trust deed on the easement property that is recorded before the express grant of the easement has priority over the easement, and if the mortgage or the deed of trust goes into default and is foreclosed, the foreclosure terminates the easement. If an easement is granted over real property that is encumbered by a mortgage or a trust deed, the grantee of the easement may obtain the consent of the mortgagee or subordination of the mortgage or trust deed to the easement.

The grantee of an appurtenant easement is the owner of the real property being benefited by the easement. The grantee of an easement in gross is the party to whom the special use is being granted, such as a utility company. Easements in gross in some states are not assignable unless the express grant of easement provides so.

The following is a discussion of other issues that should be considered in the preparation of a formal grant of easement.

PREPARATION OF A FORMAL GRANT OF EASEMENT ____

1. *Consideration.* The rules in various states differ as to whether something of value, known as *consideration*, must be given in exchange for a valid express grant of easement. Nominal consideration ($10 and other good and valuable consideration) usually is sufficient in jurisdictions that require consideration. Therefore, it is a good idea, when preparing an express grant of easement, to include a recital of consideration. In addition, the grantor of an easement often will not grant the easement unless the grantor is being paid a sum of money. If money is being paid for the easement, the sum of money should be mentioned in the easement agreement.

New York:
New York requires some kind of consideration, although nominal, to be stated in the easement.

2. *Location.* The location of the easement should be described with specificity. A survey of the easement area should be prepared and a legal description taken from the survey. An easement that covers real property without a specific location is known as a **blanket easement**. Blanket easements commonly are found in utility company rights-of-way easements.

3. *Use.* All intended uses of an easement should be carefully described in the agreement. In cases where the use description is vague, ambiguous, or uncertain, all doubts are decided in favor of the grantor of the easement. For example, an easement for pedestrian traffic does not permit vehicular traffic. The owner of an access easement does not have the right to install pipes for water, gas, oil, or any other liquid unless the right is given in the easement.

4. *Term.* An easement may be made for any term or duration. Easements may be created for a term of years or months, for the life of the owner of the servient tenement or dominant tenement, or for perpetuity. When no limitation on the term is mentioned in the grant of easement, the easement is interpreted to be perpetual and last forever.

5. *Exclusive or nonexclusive.* An easement may be for the exclusive use of the owner of the easement, or it may be nonexclusive, wherein a number of people may use the easement, including the grantor of the easement. An easement that is silent as to exclusivity is interpreted to create a nonexclusive easement.

6. *Liability for easement area.* Access and utility easements create the possibility that someone may get hurt in the exercise of the use of the easement. For example, automobile accidents may take place on an access easement. Gas lines located within utility easements may rupture. Any dangerous conditions that exist on the easement area are the responsibility of the grantor. The grantor of the easement, however, usually relinquishes control and dominion over the easement area to the grantee of the easement. If that is the case, it is not unusual for the grantor of the easement to require the grantee of the easement to indemnify and hold the landowner harmless against any harm to person or property that may result directly or indirectly from the use of the easement. The grantor of an easement often requires, in addition to the indemnity, proof that the grantee of the easement has liability insurance to cover such claims. The grantor of the easement may ask to be made a named insured on the grantee's liability insurance.

7. *Repair and maintenance.* Many easements require the easement area to be repaired and maintained during the term of the easement. Absent an express obligation to repair and maintain, the law is unclear as to whether the grantor or the grantee is responsible for repair and maintenance. Most easement agreements allocate the responsibilities for repair and maintenance. If the easement areas are exclusively used by the grantee of the easement, then the obligation to repair and maintain usually is shifted entirely to the grantee. In the event of an easement in which the use is shared between the grantor and the grantee, such as a joint driveway easement, then the repair and maintenance responsibilities may be equally divided between the parties. Most easement agreements also provide that in the event a party responsible for repair and maintenance does not honor its obligations, the other party may perform the repair and maintenance responsibilities and assess the cost of doing so against the defaulting responsible party. For example, there is a driveway easement in which Aaron and Carol have each agreed to pay one-half the cost of maintenance and repair to the driveway. Aaron refuses to pay his share. Most easement agreements provide that Carol can pay Aaron's share and then assess the cost of doing so against Aaron. This assessment may be secured by a lien on Aaron's real property over which the easement travels. Easements also may provide that in the event Aaron does not pay his share of the repair and maintenance obligations, such failure will result in a termination of the easement.

The following checklist incorporates the previously discussed issues that are considered in the preparation or review of an easement.

||||➡ CHECKLIST

For Preparation of an Easement

❑ I. Parties
    ❑ A. Grantor—fee owner of easement area
        1. Conduct title examination to verify ownership
    ❑ B. Grantee—fee owner of property benefited by easement

❑ II. Description of Easement Area
    ❑ A. Blanket description of grantor's property with no specific location of actual area to be used

□ B. Specific location of easement area
    1. Boundary survey of easement area
□ C. Description of property to be benefited by easement. This is necessary for appurtenant easements, such as right-of-way or driveway easements

□ III. Purpose of Easement
□ A. General types of use
    1. Utility location (water, sewer, gas, electric)
    2. Access to and from public streets
    3. Parking
    4. Encroachment permission
□ B. Describe totally the intended use of the easement. Easements are enforced as written

□ IV. Purchase Price or Consideration
□ A. Mutual benefit, as in case of joint driveways
□ B. Nominal consideration ($10)
□ C. Negotiated purchase price

□ V. Term
□ A. Perpetual
□ B. Fixed terms (e.g., 1 year, 5 years)
□ C. Until the happening of some event, such as the dedication of a street or sanitary sewer line to public use

□ VI. Exclusive or Nonexclusive Use

□ VII. Maintenance Obligations
□ A. Joint maintenance where easement provides mutual benefit (joint driveway)
    1. Method of collection and enforcement of joint obligations to maintain
        a. Forfeiture of easement
        b. Suit and lien
□ B. Grantee of easement maintains
□ C. Grantor of easement maintains, but grantee of easement reimburses grantor for expenses of maintenance

□ VIII. Liability
□ A. Cross indemnities where easements provide mutual benefit (joint driveway)
□ B. Grantee of easement indemnifies grantor of easement
□ C. Requirement of liability insurance
    1. Both grantor and grantee of easement shown as named insureds

□ IX. Consent of Prior Mortgagees
□ A. Consent to the grant of easement by all prior mortgage holders or lien holders to prevent termination of easement in the event of foreclosure
□ B. Title examination of easement property to determine existence of prior mortgages or liens

□ X. Signatures
□ A. Signature of grantor
□ B. Signature of grantee if easement provides for grantee indemnities or other obligations such as maintenance
□ C. All signatures witnessed and notarized in a form to permit the easement to be recorded

□ XI. Recordation of Easement
□ A. Easement recorded to protect grantee against future purchasers, mortgagees, or lien holders of the easement property

Implied Easement

An easement may be created by implication. An **implied easement** can only be made in connection with a conveyance of the real property being served by the easement. Implied easements are based on a theory that when real property is conveyed, the conveyance contains whatever is necessary for the beneficial use and enjoyment of the real property or retains whatever is necessary for the beneficial use and enjoyment of real property retained by the grantor. In creating an implied easement, the law is attempting to arrive at the intent of the parties to the conveyance as shown by all the facts and circumstances under which the conveyance was made.

For example, Aaron received ownership to real property that is described as being bounded by a private street or right-of-way. Aaron receives an implied easement of access over the street. This easement is created provided that the seller of the real property owns the private street or road. In addition, a conveyance of real property by use of a platted description in which the plat describes certain rights-of-way and other easement rights benefiting the conveyed real property shall grant to the new owner an implied easement to these rights or other uses.

Another situation in which an implied easement is created is when the owner of two tracts of land sells one of the tracts without mention of an easement in the deed, and the result of the transaction is to cause the parcel sold to become landlocked. The courts in such a situation imply that there is an easement created over the remaining tract of land to benefit the land sold.

In the example shown in Exhibit 6–4, a single owner owns tracts A and B and sells tract B without reference to an easement. The law implies that there is an easement over tract A for the benefit of tract B to gain access to the public street.

EXHIBIT 6–4
Implied Easement

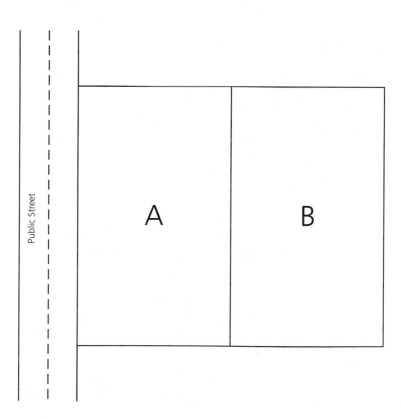

The reverse situation, however, does not always create a reserved right of implied easement. For example, a single owner owns tracts A and B and sells tract A without reference to a reservation of easement for the benefit of tract B. In this situation, the law is not uniform in granting the owner of tract B a reserved implied easement over tract A to benefit tract B. The law in some states grants the easement; the law in others denies the easement.

The court in *Russakoff v. Scruggs,* 400 S.E.2d 529, applied both of the previously discussed elements of an implied easement in holding that certain property owners held an implied easement for access to and use of a lake.

CASE

Russakoff v. Scruggs
400 S.E.2d 529 (Va. 1991)

LACY, Justice.

The issue we must decide on this appeal is whether lot owners established an easement for access to and use of a lake.

In the 1960s, Richmond Real Estate Developers, Inc., which was owned by E. Carlton Wilton and his two brothers as sole stockholders, began constructing Canterbury East subdivision, located in the Tuckahoe District of Henrico County. The subdivision included a man-made lake with a waterline at the contour line of about the 136´ elevation, as shown on the Canterbury East subdivision plat filed with the county. Richard L. and Diane Y. Russakoff, Edward E. Haddock, and Edwin M. Lohmann (collectively Russakoff), each own a lot in Canterbury East subdivision. Their rear lot lines abut the 140´ contour, thus leaving a strip of land approximately 20 feet wide, between the lots and the lake. This strip was reserved for flood plains, sewer lines, and water lines.

Richmond Real Estate Developers ceased paying taxes on the lake property, and it escheated to the Commonwealth. A tax sale was held on September 16, 1983, where Kerry I. and Doris J. Scruggs (collectively Scruggs) were the highest bidders. On May 25, 1984 the Commonwealth conveyed the lake property to Scruggs pursuant to the tax sale. Scruggs then posted "no trespassing" signs, erected a fence around the lake, and sent all homeowners surrounding the lake a letter offering them use of the lake by renting or purchasing shares. Further, Scruggs testified that, since the lake was in

"bad need of repair and hadn't had anything done to it for years," as of the date of trial he had spent $8,231.53 on improvements, which included approximately $3,000 in taxes and insurance.

By bill of complaint filed February 10, 1988, Russakoff alleged that the right to use the lake had been acquired under a number of legal theories, including adverse possession. The trial court sustained Scruggs' demurrer on the adverse possession claim, but overruled the demurrer as to the other theories. In an amended bill of complaint, Russakoff alleged a right to use the lake by virtue of prescriptive easement, oral agreement, license, easement by implication, and easement by necessity. After an *ore tenus* hearing, the trial court ruled that Russakoff was not entitled to any easement or other rights to use Canterbury Lake. The court dismissed the action, and Russakoff appeals.

In the amended bill of complaint, Russakoff advanced various theories in support of the right of access to and use of Canterbury Lake. The trial judge did not relate his factual findings to any theory Russakoff identified, but characterized the claims as ones based on easements, and stated in an opinion letter and final order that Russakoff was "not entitled to any easement rights" in Canterbury Lake or "to the use of" the lake. Therefore, we must review the record to determine whether Russakoff failed to establish an easement under any of the three easement theories he pled, which were an easement created by prescription, by implication, or by necessity.[*]

_____

[*] Scruggs argued to the trial court, and on appeal, that Russakoff sought an "implied easement (or easement by estoppel as it is sometimes called)." However, while any easement which is unwritten may be characterized as "implied," Russakoff neither pled nor sought a declaration that an easement was created by estoppel.

[1, 2] We begin by reviewing the applicable legal principles. Easements are not ownership interests in the servient tract but "the privilege to use the land of another in a particular manner and for a particular purpose." *Brown v. Haley*, 233 Va. 210, 216, 355 S.E.2d 563, 567–68 (1987). Easements are appurtenant to, and run with, the dominant tract if they benefit the owner in his use and enjoyment of that tract. *See Scott v. Moore*, 98 Va. 668, 675, 37 S.E. 342, 344 (1900).

[3] There are a number of ways an easement can be created. "Easements may be created by express grant or reservation, by implication, by estoppel or by prescription." *Bunn v. Offutt*, 216 Va. 681, 684, 222 S.E.2d 522, 525 (1976). In the case of easements over streets and roads, we have recognized the creation of an easement by reference in the deed to a plat showing the road, even if the street or road had not been created or was not being used at the time of conveyance. *Walters v. Smith*, 186 Va. 159, 169–70, 41 S.E.2d 617, 622 (1947). Within the category of easements created by implication, we have recognized easements created by necessity, *see, e.g., Middleton v. Johnston*, 221 Va. 797, 802, 273 S.E.2d 800, 803 (1981), and by pre-existing use (also referred to as quasi-easements), *see, e.g., Brown*, 233 Va. at 218, 355 S.E.2d at 569. *See also* 1 R. Minor, *The Law of Real Property* § 99 (F. Ribble 2d ed. 1928).

[4, 5] Russakoff claims, *inter alia*, an easement arising by implication. Such an easement is based on the legal principle that when one conveys land, he is presumed to transfer all that is necessary to the use and enjoyment of the land conveyed. *Brown*, 233 Va. at 218, 355 S.E.2d at 569. While one cannot have an easement on land he owns, if, before severance, one part of the land was used for the benefit of another part, a "quasi-easement" exists over the "quasi-servient" portion of the land. That easement is conveyed by implication when the dominant tract is severed; the grantee of the dominant tract obtains an easement over the servient tract, based on the previous use. *See generally Sanderlin v. Baxter*, 76 Va. 299 (1882); R. Minor, *supra*, § 99.

[6] While the extent of the easement right is determined by the circumstances surrounding the conveyance which divides the single ownership, the existence of the easement is established on a showing that (1) the dominant and servient tracts originated from a common grantor, (2) the use was in existence at the time of the severance, and that (3) the use is apparent, continuous, and reasonably necessary for the enjoyment of the dominant tract. *Brown*, 233 Va. at 219, 355 S.E.2d at 569; *Fones v. Fagan*, 214 Va. 87, 90–91, 196 S.E.2d 916, 919 (1973).

It is clear from the record before us that Russakoff's lots (dominant tracts), and the lake property (servient tract), were originally part of a single tract, thereby satisfying the first prong of the test. Next, the record is equally clear that, at the time Russakoff's predecessors in title took possession of the dominant tracts, the servient tract was a lake. Wilton testified as to the lake's existence, and the lake was reflected on the plat in the deeds conveying the dominant tracts to Russakoff's predecessors. The use of the servient tract as a lake, preexisting the severance, was established.

[7] Turning to the question of apparent and continuous use, the trial court identified Russakoff's use of a pump for lawn watering as the only use of the lake. This use, the trial court held, was not sufficient to establish an easement. Russakoff asserts that this holding is erroneous and that the record supports a finding that the use of the lake and strip of land to gain access to the lake was sufficient to establish an easement. We agree.

The record reflects that Russakoff and previous owners of the lots used the lake openly and continuously, through the construction of docks, piers, and sprinkler systems, and by using the lake for boating and ice skating. Mr. Lohmann, who purchased his lot in 1977, testified that he had a boat which his children used for fishing, frogging and "that type of thing," and when the lake was frozen in the winter they skated on the ice. Haddock testified that the lake was a "big consideration" in his purchase of his property in 1968. He "bought a boat along with the house so we could use it in the lake." The boat originally belonged to Mr. Sharp, Haddock's predecessor in title. Haddock testified that he used the lake for wading, built a pier (although it had disintegrated prior to Scruggs' purchase of the lake), and bought a canoe and used it on the lake. He also testified that his family as well as neighbors skated on the lake in the winter.

Dr. Stearns, Russakoff's predecessor in title, testified that he had used the lake since 1966. He constructed a pier, a lawn irrigation system, and a retaining wall. Additionally, he observed as many as 800 people ice skating on the lake in the winter. He had used the lake for almost 20 years before

Scruggs demanded that he pay $250 a year for access to and use of the lake.

Diane Russakoff testified that, in viewing the property prior to purchasing it from Stearns, she saw boats in Stearns' yard, as well as in the neighbors' yards. Mrs. Russakoff also observed that the grass was cut all the way to the water. Dr. Stearns informed her that he had made uninterrupted use of the lake since he had purchased the property. Additionally, Dr. Stearns showed the Russakoffs the sprinkler system from the lake to the lawn. Although the system was disconnected at the time of the purchase from Stearns, the Russakoffs reconnected the system and used it.

Our review of this record shows that the trial judge's finding that the only use of the lake was Russakoff's lawn sprinkler system, which he found to be insufficient to support an easement, is clearly erroneous. Rather, the record supports a contrary conclusion that use of the lake was continuous and apparent.

[8] The third prong of the test also requires that the easement be reasonably necessary to the use and enjoyment of the dominant tract. This determination requires a showing of need which, by definition, may be less than that required for establishing an easement by necessity, but must be something more than simple convenience. We have recognized that whether this element is established "generally will depend upon the circumstances of the particular case." *Jones v. Beavers,* 221 Va. 214, 221, 269 S.E.2d 775, 779 (1980).

[9] Here, we hold that a purchaser of a lot would have a legitimate expectation of the right to access and use the lake where a visual inspection and reference to the plat incorporated in the deed of conveyance showed the existence of a lake within 20 feet of one's lot line, and where investigation would disclose that the 20-foot strip between the lake and the lot line was retained solely for certain utility and flood plain uses. The Canterbury East developers contemplated enjoyment of the lake, as a lake, by purchasers of the lots surrounding the lake. Under these circumstances, the easement at issue was reasonably necessary to the use and enjoyment of the lakeside lots.

[10] An easement created by implication, which, as here, is appurtenant to the land, may be vitiated if, when the servient estate is purchased by another, the purchaser of the servient tract does not have notice of the easement or the use is not apparent. Under those circumstances, the purchaser takes the land free from such easement or use. *Ricks v. Scott,* 117 Va. 370, 384, 84 S.E. 676, 681 (1915). As discussed above, the evidence in this case supports a finding of a use which was apparent, continuous, and reasonably necessary to the enjoyment of the dominant tract. The record also clearly shows Scruggs' knowledge of the use. In addition to sending a letter indicating the lot owners could *no longer* use the lake without payment of a fee, Scruggs agreed that "numerous property owners were using the lake and had pumps in the water for getting water up on their lot[s]." Furthermore, Scruggs testified that shortly after purchasing the lake, he traversed the lake in a canoe and disconnected at least two of the existing sprinkler systems which used the lake water for lawn watering purposes, and Scruggs' actions show that the use of the lake by surrounding property owners was apparent, and that he was aware of the use.

At the time Scruggs purchased the lake, its use was apparent, continuous, and reasonably necessary to the enjoyment of property surrounding the lake. Therefore, we conclude that an easement by implication was established in favor of Russakoff for access to and use of Canterbury Lake.

In view of this holding, it is unnecessary to review Russakoff's claims to an easement created by prescription or by necessity.

Prescriptive Easement

An easement may be acquired by prescription. **Prescriptive easements** are created when a person uses property without the permission of the owner for a period of time. A prescriptive easement is similar to the concept of adverse possession discussed in Chapter 1. A person who acquires a prescriptive easement, however, does not exercise such dominion and control over the real property in question as to become an owner of the real property through adverse possession. Instead, the

New York:
In easement by prescription, similar to gaining title by adverse possession, claimants must have used the land for a "prescriptive period" of 10 years, openly and adverse, notorious and they obtain an easement.

owner of a prescriptive easement has used the real property only for a particular purpose and, therefore, acquires rights to continue to use the real property for that purpose. A prescriptive easement can be obtained over any private real property but cannot be acquired in real property belonging to the United States or any other governmental authority. A prescriptive easement requires that the prescriptive use take place for a period of time. This period of time varies from state to state, but periods of ten to twenty years are common.

An important element of a prescriptive easement is that the use made of the easement must be adverse and hostile to the owner of the real property over which the use is being made. Adverse use means without the owner's permission or consent. An owner's permission to the use before the time the prescriptive easement ripens (i.e., before the expiration of the term of years required to obtain a prescriptive easement) causes the prescriptive easement to terminate. Therefore, an owner can prevent prescriptive rights from being made to his or her real property by granting consent to the use. This consent can be given on conditions favorable to the owner of the real property. For example, a landowner notices that his neighbor is using a corner of his property as a right-of-way to a public street. The landowner grants the neighbor an express easement to use the corner of his property for a right-of-way. The express easement provides that the landowner can terminate the easement on thirty days' notice. The express grant of permission to the neighbor prevents the neighbor from obtaining perpetual prescriptive rights, and the landowner still maintains, with the thirty-day cancellation option, total control over his property.

In addition to the prescriptive use being adverse, the holder of the prescriptive easement must use and enjoy the easement on a continuous and uninterrupted basis. If at any time before the expiration of the term required to create a prescriptive easement the prescriptive use is interrupted by the owner of the land or is voluntarily abandoned by the party claiming the easement, the prescriptive easement is not created. The erection of gates and barriers as well as suits for trespass have all been held to be sufficient interruption by the landowner to defeat a claim of prescriptive use.

Prescriptive use also must be open, visible, and notorious. The use must be apparent enough to give the owner of the land knowledge or full opportunity to assert his or her rights to interrupt the prescriptive use.

In the example of prescriptive use shown in Exhibit 6–5, B does not have access to the public highway but starts driving across A's property. B drives across A's property for the necessary prescriptive period but without A's consent and without being interrupted by A. B will acquire the right to continue driving across A's property.

Prescriptive easements, once created, are perpetual. They also are appurtenant easements and are transferred with the dominant tenement. In the example shown in Exhibit 6–5, the sale of tract B will transfer the prescriptive easement over tract A.

Easement by Necessity

New York:

Easement by necessity arises when an owner sells part of his land so that there is no access to the street except over the other parcel of land. An example would be a driveway easement over one parcel so that the other parcel is not land locked.

Many states provide a landowner who does not have access to a public road or street the right to apply for the grant of a private way or an easement over adjacent lands to gain access. This is an **easement by necessity**. It grants to a landowner a quasi-private right to condemn an adjoining owner's land for purposes of acquiring an access easement to a public street or road. An easement by necessity requires that fair compensation be paid to the landowner of the condemned easement. Easements by necessity are created by statutory procedures. These statutes limit the width of the right-of-way as well as provide for a method to determine fair compensation. Because there are strict requirements concerning easements by necessity, it is important to check a particular state's requirements before proceeding.

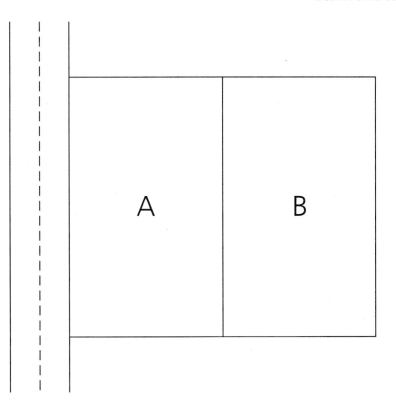

EXHIBIT 6-5
Prescriptive use

Termination of Easements

An easement, once granted, continues to exist until terminated by the operation of some rule of law or by the terms of the express grant. An easement may be terminated by (a) expiration of express term, (b) abandonment, (c) merger, (d) foreclosure of prior servient liens, or (e) express release or termination.

As previously mentioned, an easement by express grant can be made for any duration, or it can be terminated on the happening of a certain event. For example, a private road easement may be terminated on the dedication of the road to public use.

An easement may be terminated by abandonment. Abandonment is a matter of the intention of the grantee of the easement as evidenced by the acts of the grantee and surrounding circumstances. Abandonment is nonuse with the intent to never use again. Evidence of abandonment may be the permanent removal of physical installations, such as rails or bridges, that permit the use of the easement or actions that permit others to maintain obstructions to prevent the exercise of the easement. For example, a railroad has an easement for a spur/side track. After a number of years, the railroad stops using the spur/side tract and even removes the rails and ties. A strong argument could be made that the railroad has abandoned the easement and that the easement has terminated. Although easements usually cannot be lost by nonuse alone, nonuse is evidence of an intent to abandon.

An easement may be lost by the merger of the dominant and the servient tenement. For example, Aaron grants to Bob the right to cross over Aaron's property to the public road. The right-of-way over Aaron's property is an appurtenant easement to Bob's property. Later, Bob acquires the fee simple title to Aaron's property over which the easement travels. Bob now owns both the fee title and the easement over the former property of Aaron. This ownership of the dominant and servient tenements causes a merger, and the easement is terminated because Bob no longer needs the easement to travel over Bob's own property.

An easement also may be lost by the foreclosure of a mortgage or a deed of trust that was on the servient property before the time the easement was created. Easements in some states are terminated by a tax foreclosure sale of the servient estate.

An easement can be terminated by an express written release or termination given by the easement owner to the owner of the servient estate. Written releases of easements should be drafted with the same formality as the easement and be recorded in the public records of the county in which the easement is located.

LICENSES

Black's Law Dictionary defines a **license** as "the authority to do a particular act or series of acts upon another's land, without possession of any estate therein." For example, an owner of a farm that has a lake located on it gives a neighbor permission to fish in the lake. The permission to fish in the lake includes permission to walk across the farm fields to reach the lake. It is understood that the permission to fish in the lake can be terminated at any time by the farmer and that the neighbor acquires no rights in the farmer's land. A license is distinguished from an easement in that an easement is a property interest and a license is mere permission to perform a certain act.

A license can be created orally or in writing, or it can be implied from the conduct of the parties. An oral license without any consideration being paid for the license is revocable at the will of the person granting the license. On the other hand, a license in writing for which compensation and consideration have been paid usually is irrevocable. An implied license may come about from custom or from acts constituting an invitation, such as signs and advertisements. For example, the owner of a retail store extends a license to the customers of the store to enter on the land where the store is located, shop, buy merchandise, and so on. An implied license is revocable at any time, and once revoked, if the licensee does not leave the property, the licensee becomes a trespasser.

The terms of a license are strictly interpreted, and a licensee cannot extend or vary the terms. Third persons who interfere with the licensing or unlawful exercise of the license may be liable to the licensee in damages.

ETHICS: False Witness

Your supervising attorney has just had a difficult closing. The closing has lasted a day and has occupied a couple of conference rooms. It is near the end of the day, and the attorney brings you a stack of documents. The attorney asks you to witness a number of signatures on the documents. You indicate that you have not seen these people sign. The attorney apologizes but states that the people have already gone home and that the signatures must be witnessed. To avoid a confrontation, you witness the documents. Was this the proper thing to do?

It is unethical for an attorney or legal assistant to give false witness or commit perjury on behalf of a client. Few attorneys or legal assistants intentionally lie or misrepresent the facts involving a real estate transaction. These same honest attorneys and legal assistants, however, may routinely witness or notarize the unseen signature of parties to various legal documents.

Most legal documents, such as deed and mortgages, require a witness for the document to be recorded or be valid. They also require that the witness actually see the person sign the document. Witnessing a document in which the witness has not seen the party sign the document is a misrepresentation of fact and a breach of legal ethics. The notarization of a signature without having seen the party sign is even a more serious matter. When notarizing a signature, a notary is swearing under the notarial oath that she or he has seen the person sign the document. A notarization of the signature is, therefore, a witness under oath, and if the notary has not seen the person sign the document, the notary is committing perjury.

It is advisable that a legal assistant in the beginning of an employment situation confer with his or her supervising attorney concerning what procedures will be followed in the witness or notarization of legal documents. The legal assistant should strongly stress that he or she will not witness or notarize documents unless he or she has seen the signing of the documents.

SUMMARY

The use of easements and licenses is commonplace. Easements may be essential in the use and enjoyment of a parcel of real property. A legal assistant who is actively involved in real estate transactions will, with the supervision of an attorney, prepare easements and licenses.

KEY TERMS

Appurtenant easement	Easement by necessity	License
Blanket easement	Easement in gross	Prescriptive easement
Dominant tenement	Implied easement	Servient tenement
Easement		

REVIEW QUESTIONS

1. Explain the difference between an appurtenant easement and an easement in gross, and give an example of each.

2. What are the four ways an easement can be created?

3. The owner of parcel A gives to the owner of parcel B an easement to use a driveway located on parcel A. Which parcel is the dominant tenement and which parcel is the servient tenement?

4. What is a license, and how does it differ from an easement?

5. What is an easement by necessity, and how does it differ from a prescriptive easement?

6. Is there any written proof of a prescriptive or implied easement?

7. What is a blanket easement?

8. What are the requirements for an abandonment of an easement?

9. Explain how an easement can be lost by merger of the dominant and servient tenements.

10. Are prescriptive and implied easements appurtenant or easements in gross?

CASE PROBLEMS

1. You are a legal assistant in a law firm representing a property owner. The property owner is negotiating to purchase a driveway easement from a neighbor. You have been asked to prepare the easement agreement. What information do you need to prepare the easement?

2. You are a legal assistant in a law firm that represents a real estate developer. The developer has obtained a necessary driveway easement to her property. After the easement was obtained, it was discovered that the property over which the driveway is located had been earlier pledged as security for a debt to the First Bank and Trust. It also has been discovered that the First Bank and Trust debt is in default and that the First Bank and Trust is having a public auction of the property to pay the debt. Should the real estate developer be concerned? If so, what steps can be taken to protect the developer?

3. Aaron owns two lots of real property, lot 1 and lot 2. Lot 1 is located next to a public right-of-way, but lot 2 is landlocked from the public lot right-of-way by lot 1. Aaron conveys lot 2 to Bob with a deed, making no reference to any rights-of-way or any other kinds of easement benefiting lot 2. Bob then sells lot 2 to Carol. Carol claims against Aaron that she has a right-of-way easement over lot 1 for the purposes of providing access from the public street to lot 2. Does Carol have a valid claim?

4. David has a driveway easement over Carol's property. By the terms of the easement, the driveway easement expired six months ago. David continues to use the driveway easement. Can Carol sue David for trespass?

PRACTICAL ASSIGNMENTS

1. Research the law of your state regarding the requirements for an easement by necessity, and write a brief memorandum outlining the findings of your research.

2. Sea View Development Corporation is the owner of a certain parcel of property that fronts or joins onto the right-of-way of U.S. Highway 98. The property is more particularly described as follows: "A portion of Tract 7, Chase Heights No. 3 as recorded on Plat Book 14, Page 32, current Public Records, Walton County, Florida." Walton Construction Company owns a tract of land directly behind the property owned by Sea View Development Company. The property is described as follows: "Tract 6, Chase Heights No. 3 as recorded on Plat Book 14, Page 32, Public Records, Walton County, Florida." It is important to the development of the Walton Construction Company property that it obtain an easement for access about twenty feet in width over and across the property owned by Sea View Development Corporation. The location of the easement will be drawn by a specific survey and can be described on an exhibit to the easement agreement. Walton Construction Company intends to pay Sea View Development Corporation $1,000 for the easement. The easement will be perpetual and for the purpose of pedestrian and vehicular access from Highway 98 to the property owned by Walton Construction Company. The easement will be nonexclusive in that owners and tenants of tracts 6 and 7 may use the easement. Walton Construction Company intends to be fully responsible for the repair and maintenance of any road constructed on the easement area.

You are a legal assistant in the firm representing Walton Construction Company. You have been asked to prepare a first draft of an easement for the purposes set forth above. Prepare the first draft. You may want to use the easement set forth as Exhibit 6–1 as an example. Note that this assignment requires only an ingress and egress easement, so you will need to delete any references to the sanitary sewer easement set forth in Exhibit 6–1.

EXHIBIT 6-1
Sanitary Sewer
Easement and
Ingress and Egress
Easement

THIS SANITARY SEWER EASEMENT AND INGRESS AND EGRESS EASEMENT is made this 21st day of April, 19____, by and between
(herein with his heirs and assigns called "Grantor") and
(herein with their heirs and assigns called "Grantee").

WITNESSETH:

WHEREAS, Grantee has requested that Grantor convey to Grantee a non-exclusive twenty (20) foot permanent easement over real property described on Exhibit "A" (the "Sewer Easement Property") for the purpose of installing and maintaining a sanitary sewer line; and

WHEREAS, Grantor is willing to grant such a sewer easement upon all of the terms and conditions set forth in this Sanitary Sewer Easement and Ingress and Egress Easement; and

WHEREAS, Grantor desires to grant an ingress and egress easement over the property described on Exhibit "B" attached hereto; and

WHEREAS, Grantee desires to grant an ingress and egress easement over the property described on Exhibit "C" attached hereto; and

WHEREAS, Grantor and Grantee desires to grant such mutual ingress and egress easement on the terms and conditions set forth in this Sanitary Sewer Easement and Ingress and Egress Easement; and

WHEREAS, Grantor and Grantee desire to set forth herein and effectuate hereby their agreements in this regard;

NOW, THEREFORE, for and in consideration of the premises and other valuable consideration, the receipt and sufficiency of which is hereby acknowledged by each of the undersigned, Grantor and Grantee hereby agree as follows:

1. Upon all terms and conditions set forth in this Agreement, Grantor hereby grants and conveys to Grantee a twenty (20) foot permanent non-exclusive easement ("Sewer Easement") over, through and across the Sewer Easement Property, the Sewer Easement being designated "San. Sew. Esmt. 'A' " on that plat of survey for   and Acme Title Insurance Company prepared by Richard A. Scott, Georgia Registered Land Surveyor Number 1075 dated March 2, 19____, last revised April 15, 19____, for the purpose of installing, using, repairing, maintaining and replacing an underground sanitary sewer line. Grantor hereby retains the right to landscape the surface of the Sewer Easement and otherwise use said Sewer Easement in any manner whatsoever so long as such use shall not interfere with the use and maintenance of the easement granted herein. Without limitation to the foregoing, Grantor shall have the right to use the Sewer Easement to the fullest extent possible, including, without limitation: (a) paving the surface of the Sewer Easement for use as pedestrian and vehicular access ways, vehicle parking and sidewalks, (b) landscaping and installing irrigation systems on the Sewer Easement, (c) placing permanent structural supports in the Sewer Easement for walkways and construction of improvements in air space over the Sewer Easement, (d) installing, maintaining, repairing and replacing storm sanitary sewer lines and other utility lines and conduits in the Sewer Easement, (e) grading and adding fill to the surface of the Sewer Easement, (f) placing street lighting, fencing and signage in the Sewer Easement, (g) conveying to County, State or other governmental bodies for roads and streets and (h) placing a retention pond on the surface of the Sewer Easement.

2. After each entry by Grantee on the Sewer Easement for the purpose of repair, maintenance or replacement of said sanitary sewer line, Grantee shall, at the expense of Grantee, return the surface of the Sewer Easement within a reasonable time to the condi-

EXHIBIT 6–1
Sanitary Sewer
Easement and
Ingress and Egress
Easement
(continued)

tion in which such surface existed immediately prior to such installation or entry with proper compaction of the soil and proper ground cover to prevent erosion. All installations, repair, maintenance or replacements shall be conducted so as to minimize the interruption and interference of the Grantor's use of the Sewer Easement.

3. Grantor, his heirs and assigns, shall have the right to install one or more tap-ons to the sanitary sewer line constructed within the Sewer Easement, without payment of any fee or charge to Grantee, at any time chosen by Grantor, subject only to the following conditions:

(a) Each tap-on must comply with all applicable governmental regulations;

(b) The installation of the connection must be performed in a manner which does not substantially disrupt sanitary sewer service being provided by the sanitary sewer line within the Sewer Easement; and

(c) Grantor shall pay any and all costs related to such tap-ons. Grantor hereby indemnifies Grantee and agrees to hold Grantee harmless from and against any and all mechanic's and materialmen's liens and any other loss, damage or liability which Grantee may incur as a result of the exercise by Grantor of its rights under this Paragraph 3.

4. Grantee herby indemnifies Grantor and agrees to hold Grantor harmless from and against any and all mechanic's and materialmen's liens which may arise out of or in any way relate to the maintenance and repair of the sewer line by Grantee.

5. Grantee agrees not to dedicate the easement granted hereby to DeKalb County, Georgia, without the prior written approval by Grantor.

6. Grantor hereby reserves the right at any time and from time to time to relocate all or any portion of the sanitary sewer line contained in the Sewer Easement and to relocate at any time and from time to time the location of the Sewer Easement as Grantor may deem expedient and necessary or prudent with respect to the development of the property of the Grantor. Grantee hereby acknowledges and recognizes that Grantor reserves the right to develop the property of the Grantor in any manner that Grantor may deem prudent or expedient and, accordingly, Grantor reserves the right to relocate the Sewer Easement in any manner whatsoever so as to accommodate any development of the property of the Grantor. The Grantee shall not be responsible for any costs and expenses associated with relocation of the sanitary sewer line. Upon such relocation, Grantor shall deliver to Grantee an easement in recordable form for such relocated sewer line after which the sewer easement herein conveyed shall terminate. Any relocation shall be subject to the prior written approval of any first mortgagee having its deed to secure debt recorded in DeKalb County deed records.

7. This Sanitary Sewer Easement and Ingress and Egress Easement shall bind and inure to the benefit of the parties hereto and their respective heirs, executors, personal representatives, mortgagees, successors and assigns.

8. Grantor grants and conveys unto Grantee a perpetual non-exclusive easement for automobile and pedestrian ingress and egress over, upon and across the land described on Exhibit "B" hereto. Grantee grants and conveys unto Grantor a perpetual non-exclusive easement for automobile and pedestrian ingress and egress over, upon and across the land described on Exhibit "C" hereto. Included in the foregoing easements granted to Grantor is an easement for the construction and maintenance of a driveway. Grantor shall maintain the driveways so located thereon. The easements granted by this Paragraph 8 may be terminated by Grantor upon Grantor filing upon the deed records on the Courts of DeKalb County, a cancellation of this Easement. Upon such cancellation being filed the easements granted by this Paragraph 8 shall terminate. Any cancellation shall be subject to the prior written consent of any first mortgagee having a recorded deed to secure debt conveying the property described on Exhibit "A" hereto.

EXHIBIT 6–1
Sanitary Sewer
Easement and
Ingress and Egress
Easement
(continued)

This Sanitary Sewer Easement and Ingress and Egress Easement shall be interpreted and construed in accordance with the laws of the State of Georgia.

IN WITNESS WHEREOF, Grantor and Grantee have executed and sealed this Sanitary Sewer Easement and Ingress and Egress Easement the day and year first above written.

EXHIBIT "A"

ALL THAT TRACT or parcel of land lying and being in Land Lots 298 and 309 of the 18th District of DeKalb County, Georgia, and being a portion of Lots 18 and 19, Block "3" of the subdivision of Camp Gordon as shown on plat recorded in Plat Book 14, Page 51, DeKalb County, Georgia records, and being more particularly described as follows:

Starting at a point on the center line of New Peachtree Road and the intersection of the center line of West Hospital Avenue and running thence northeast along the centerline of New Peachtree Road, 440.35 feet to a point and the true point of beginning; running thence northeast along the center line of New Peachtree Road 445.0 feet to a point; thence southeast at an interior angle of 89 degrees 29 minutes 30 seconds from the center line of New Peachtree Road a distance of 563.9 feet to an iron pin; thence southwest at an interior angle of 90 degrees 30 minutes 30 seconds from the preceding course a distance of 416.00 feet to a point; thence northwest at an interior angle of 90 degrees from the last mentioned course a distance of 187.9 feet to a point; thence southwest at an interior angle of 270 degrees from the last mentioned course a distance of 24.0 feet to a point; thence northwest at an interior angle of 90 degrees from the last mentioned course a distance of 376.00 feet to the center line of New Peachtree Road and the point of beginning.

Excepted from the above described property is that portion lying within the right-of-way of New Peachtree Road and Brogdon Court.

EXHIBIT "B"

ALL THAT TRACT or parcel of land lying and being in Land Lots 298 and 309 of the 18th District of Dekalb County, Georgia, and being a portion of Lots 18 and 19, Block "3" of the subdivision of Camp Gordon as shown on plat recorded in Plat Book 14, Page 51, DeKalb County, Georgia records, and being more particularly described as follows:

Starting at a point on the center line of New Peachtree Road and the intersection of the center line of West Hospital Avenue and running thence northeast along the center line of New Peachtree Road, 440.35 feet to a point and the true point of beginning; running thence northeast along the center line of New Peachtree Road 6.0 feet to a point; thence southeast at an interior angle of 90 degrees from the center line of New Peachtree Road a distance of 376.0 feet to a point; thence southwest at an interior angle of 90 degrees from the preceding course a distance of 6.0 feet to a point; thence northwest at an interior angle of 90 degrees from the last mentioned course a distance of 376.0 feet to the center line of New Peachtree Road and the point of beginning.

Excepted from the above described property is that portion lying within the right-of-way of New Peachtree Road.

EXHIBIT "C"

ALL THAT TRACT or parcel of land lying and being in Land Lots 298 and 309 of the 18th District of DeKalb County, Georgia, and being a portion of Lots 18 and 19, Block "3" of the subdivision of Camp Gordon as shown on plat recorded in Plat Book 14, Page 51, DeKalb County, Georgia records, and being more particularly described as follows:

Starting at a point on the center line of New Peachtree Road and the intersection of the center line of West Hospital Avenue and running thence northeast along the centerline

EXHIBIT 6-1
Sanitary Sewer
Easement and
Ingress and Egress
Easement
(continued)

of New Peachtree Road, 440.35 feet to a point and the true point of beginning; thence southeast at an interior angle of 90 degrees from the center line of New Peachtree Road a distance of 376.0 feet to a point; thence southwest at an interior angle of 90 degrees from the preceding course a distance of 24.0 feet to a point; thence northwest at an interior angle of 90 degrees from the last mentioned course a distance of 376.0 feet to a point on the center line of New Peachtree Road; running thence northeast along the center line of New Peachtree Road 24.0 feet to the point of beginning.

Excepted from the above described property is that portion lying within the right-of-way of New Peachtree Road.

EXHIBIT 6-2
An Electric Power
Company Right-of-
Way Easement

STATE OF_____ , _____ COUNTY.

In consideration of the sum of _____ , ($_____) Dollars in hand paid by The American Power Company, hereinafter called the Company, the receipt and sufficiency whereof is hereby acknowledged, the undersigned, _____ , whose Post Office Address is _____ , _____ , does hereby grant and convey to said Company, its successors and assigns, the right, privilege and easement to go in, upon and along the tract of land owned by the undersigned to Land Lot _____ , of the _____ District of _____ County, known as No. _____ in or near the City or Town of _____ , _____ , together with the right to construct, operate and maintain upon said land its lines for transmitting electric current, erected on one line of poles, with wire and other necessary apparatus, fixtures and appliances; with the right to permit the attachment of the wires and appliances of any other company, or person, to said poles; together with the right at all times to enter upon said premises for the purpose of inspecting the lines, making repairs, removals, alterations and extensions thereon, thereto or therefrom; also the right to cut away or trim and keep clear of said lines all trees, limbs of trees and other obstructions that may interfere or be likely to interfere with the proper operation of said lines; also the right of ingress and egress over said lines to and from said lines.

The undersigned does not convey any land, but merely grants the hereinabove described rights, privileges and easements.

Said Company shall not be liable for, or bound by, any statement or agreement or understanding not herein expressed.

IN WITNESS WHEREOF, the said _____ , has hereinto set _____ hand_____ and seal_____ , this _____ day of _____ , 19_____ .

_____ (SEAL)
By: _____ (SEAL)
Title: _____ (SEAL)

Grantors
Signed, sealed and delivered in the presence of:

_____
Witness

_____
Notary Public
My Commission Expires:

_____

This document to be signed in the presence of two (2) witnesses, one of whom should be a Notary Public.

Contracts

But having passed his word, more or less, he stuck to it, and they went out behind the barn and made their bargain. Jabez Stone had to prick his finger to sign, and the stranger lent him a silver pen. The wound healed clean, but it left a little white scar.

—Stephen Vincent Benet, The Devil and Daniel Webster

OBJECTIVES

After reading this chapter you will be able to:

- Explain the requirements of a valid real estate contract
- Identify the remedies for default of a real estate contract
- Understand the role of a real estate agent in the procurement of a real estate contract
- Distinguish the three types of real estate agency listing agreements

GLOSSARY

Consideration   Something of value given to make the promises in a contract enforceable.

Contract   Agreement between two or more persons consisting of a promise, or mutual promises that the law will enforce or the performance of which the law recognizes as a duty.

Liquidated damages   Amount of money agreed on by the parties to a contract to be the damages in the event of a default of the contract.

Listing agreement   Agreement entered into between an owner and a real estate broker retaining the real estate broker to assist the owner in selling real property.

Power of attorney   Written document authorizing another person to act as one's agent.

Rescission   Remedy for default of a real estate contract wherein the contract is terminated and the defaulting party must reimburse the injured party for expenses incurred in connection with the contract.

Specific performance   Remedy for breach of real estate contract that requires a defaulting party to perform the promises under the contract.

New York:
For a discussion of Contract in New York, see Appendix.

O ne of the main areas of a legal assistant's involvement in real estate is the assistance in representing a purchaser or seller in the sale and purchase of real property. When ownership to real property is acquired through purchase and sale, the transaction requires the negotiation and preparation of a contract before the actual transfer of ownership to the real property. The contract sets forth the terms for the purchase and sale. A legal assistant who participates in a real estate contract transaction should be aware of the general legal rules governing the validity of a contract as well as the remedies available for an injured party in the event of a default under a contract. This chapter reviews the law regarding the validity of a real estate contract and the remedies for breach of a real estate contract. In addition, it briefly discusses the role of a real estate agent in procuring a real estate contract.

REQUIREMENTS OF A VALID CONTRACT

New York:
To enter into a binding contract for real estate in New York a person must be 18 years old and of sound mind. A married person, under 18, is considered an adult. Persons younger than 18 may enter into a valid contract, but it is voidable by the minor until a reasonable time after reaching the age of 18.

New York:
New York has a six year Statute of Limitations during which time the parties to a contract may sue to enforce their rights. Contracts for the sale of real property entered into on a Sunday, are enforceable. Another uniform requirement is that the agreement must be in "writing."

A **contract** is an agreement between two or more persons consisting of a promise or mutual promises that the law will enforce or the performance of which the law will in some way recognize as a duty. For a valid real estate contract to exist and the promises therein to be enforceable, a number of legal requirements exist. These requirements are (a) legal capacity of the parties, (b) mutual agreement, (c) consideration, (d) lawful purpose, and (e) written agreement. All the requirements must be present or the contract is invalid and the promises unenforceable.

Legal Capacity to Contract

The legal capacity means that the parties entering into the contract are responsible in such a way that the law will make them bound by their promises. In this section, we examine how this concept relates to minors, mental incompetents, corporations, partnerships, personal representatives, trustees, and agents.

Minors or Infants

The law protects a minor or infant from his or her contractual promises. A minor is deemed to be a person under a certain age (eighteen years in most states). A minor's contract is voidable at the election of the minor. The minor can void or fail to perform the contract if the minor so desires, but if the minor performs, the other party is bound. For example, an adult enters into a contract to purchase a car from a sixteen-year-old. If the sixteen-year-old decides not to sell the car, the adult has no legal recourse. On the other hand, if the adult decides not to buy the car, the sixteen-year-old can legally enforce the contract and require the adult to buy the car or pay damages.

Mental Incompetents

Mental incompetents do not understand the essence of the contract. They are protected from their promises in most states. They do not understand that they own property, the value of the property, or the value of what the purchaser is offering. A mental incompetent may be a person who does not understand that by signing the contract, he or she is obligated to perform some task, such as sell or purchase property. The test for mental incompetence is a high standard. The lack of knowledge or inability or failure to read a contract does not make one a mental incompetent. Illiteracy is not mental incompetence.

Corporations

A contract entered into by a corporation presents special legal capacity problems. A corporation is created by state statute and only has the power granted to it by state corporate law or its corporate charter. Most business corporations have the authority to buy and sell real property, and therefore, capacity is not a problem. Many nonprofit corporations, on the other hand, have limited powers. A nonprofit corporation's corporate charter should be examined to determine if the corporation has the legal authority to buy and sell real property.

Even though the corporation probably has the authority to enter into a contract, human representatives of the corporation negotiate and sign the contract. Do these representatives truly represent the corporation, and do they have the authority to make the contract binding on the corporation? These questions of authority and capacity should be carefully examined by the legal assistant. A corporate officer's authority is set forth in a resolution passed by the board of directors of the corporation. These board resolutions or corporate resolutions are obtained at the time the contract is signed. An example of a corporate resolution authorizing a contract as well as the representatives of the corporation to sign the contract is shown in Exhibit 7–1.

Partnerships

General partnerships and limited partnerships also create special authorization problems. A general partnership formed under the Uniform Partnership Act has the

New York:
A contract entered into by a corporation must be signed by the corporate officer as follows: XYZ Corp. by DJK, President. It is always best to get a copy of the corporate resolution authorizing the sale.

New York:
A general partner of a partnership in New York may enter into a contract for the partnership. It is not necessary for all the partners to join in.

EXHIBIT 7–1
Certification of Resolution and Written Action of the Executive Committee of First Arizona Savings, FSB September 9, 19___

I, Ardene J. Thompson, the duly elected Assistant Secretary for First Arizona Savings, FSB (the "Bank") do hereby certify that all the Members of the Executive Committee of the Bank adopted the following action by written consent in lieu of a meeting, pursuant to Article IV, Section 6 of the Bylaws of the Bank, which resolution has not been amended or revoked as of the date hereof.

"BE IT RESOLVED, that the Executive Committee hereby approves the sale of that certain property known as Paces Ferry Place, more particularly described in the attached Exhibit "A" (the "Property"), to Village Properties, an Arizona general partnership, for the sum of $2,200,000.00 pursuant to the terms of the Purchase Agreement dated June 6, 19____ ; and

BE IT FURTHER RESOLVED, that James J. Connor, Administrative Vice President, or Ruth K. McGuire, Executive Vice President, are each hereby authorized to execute on behalf of the Bank any and all documents as may be necessary and proper to contract for and to close on the sale of the Property."

IN WITNESS WHEREOF, I, Ardene J. Thompson, have duly set my hand and seal of the Bank.

September 9, 19____

_____
Assistant Secretary
[SEAL]

power to enter into contracts for the sale and purchase of real property. Unless the partnership agreement designates a managing partner, all partners must consent to any contracts entered into by the partnership. A review of the partnership agreement is necessary to determine what authority the partners have if less than all the partners are negotiating and signing the contract.

Limited partnerships formed under the Uniform Limited Partnership Act authorize the general partners to act on behalf of the partnership and to buy and sell partnership real property. The consent or agreement of the limited partners is not required. The powers of the general partners, however, can be limited by the partnership agreement, and a review of the agreement is necessary to determine what authority the general partners have to sign contracts binding on the limited partnership. In addition, general partners do not have the authority, without limited partners' consent, to sell all the assets of the limited partnership. A real property limited partnership may have only one asset, such as an apartment project or a shopping center. A careful examination of the affairs of the limited partnership as well as the agreement is necessary in these situations.

Personal Representatives

New York:
A fiduciary may be an executor or a trustee. The fiduciary's authority to act should be verified.

An executor or executrix of an estate has limited power to enter into contracts to buy and sell real property on behalf of the estate. An executor or executrix only has the power given by state law and under the will. An executor or executrix cannot act in violation of the will without a court order. Therefore, when reviewing contracts entered into with estates of deceased people, it is necessary to review not only state law regarding the executor's or executrix's powers, but also the actual will that appoints the executor or executrix.

An administrator of an intestate estate (one in which the deceased died without a will) has limited power to buy and sell property. In many states, an administrator cannot enter into a contract to sell estate property without a court order or without consent from all the heirs who would be entitled to inherit the property.

Trustees

Trustees of a trust have problems similar to those of executors or executrixes and administrators. A trustee only has the authority given by state law and by the actual trust instrument. A contract entered into with a trust requires that the trust document be carefully reviewed to see if the trustee has the authority to bind the trust to the contract.

Trustees also have a fiduciary responsibility to the beneficiaries of the trust. This means that the trustee cannot deal with trust property in such a way as to be detrimental to the beneficiaries. For example, a trustee could not enter into a contract to sell trust property to herself, her relatives, or any other entity in which the trustee has a financial interest. This would be self-dealing and a breach of the fiduciary duty. In addition, a trustee cannot enter into a contract to sell trust property if the trustee intends to use the proceeds for purposes other than to benefit the beneficiaries. In any situation where a trustee is breaching his or her fiduciary duty, the trustee does not have the authority to act and can act only if all the beneficiaries consent to the action. Beneficiaries who are under legal age cannot give their consent without the appointment of a guardian.

Agents

A person occasionally appoints an agent or an attorney-in-fact to sign contracts on his or her behalf. A person who appoints an agent is called a principal under the **power of attorney**. An attorney-in-fact only has the power granted to it by the express written agency appointment. These agency appointments are called powers of attorney. An example of a broad general power of attorney is set out in Exhibit 7–2.

EXHIBIT 7–2
Power of Attorney

KNOW ALL MEN BY THESE PRESENTS:

That I, ANDREW J. NELSON, resident of Clay County, Illinois, being desirous of arranging for the transaction of my business through an attorney-in-fact, have appointed, named and constituted, and by these presents do name, constitute and appoint SUSAN T. BRAXTON, a resident of Clay County, Illinois, as my true and lawful attorney-in-fact, and do authorize said attorney-in-fact, for me in my name, place and stead: to execute, and deliver, any and all sale documentation necessary in order to close a sale of my property known as the Clay County Office Park and being more particularly described on Exhibit "A" attached hereto and made a part hereof to BURTON INVESTMENTS COMPANY, INC. pursuant to a real estate contract by and between Andrew J. Nelson and Burton Investments Company, Inc. dated December 6, 19____, said sale documents to include but not be limited to, affidavits, general warranty deeds, assignment of warranties, assignment of leases and rents, and general warranty bill of sale.

I hereby further give and grant unto my said attorney-in-fact full power and authority to execute and deliver any and all other instruments and documents and to do and perform any and all other acts necessary and proper to be done in the exercise of any of the foregoing powers as largely, fully, and amply as I might or could do if I were personally present, with full power of substitution and revocation, and I hereby ratify and confirm all that my said attorney-in-fact shall lawfully do or cause to be done by virtue hereof.

It is my intent, and it is expressly understood, that the powers herein granted to my said attorney-in-fact shall not be terminated in the event that I become physically or mentally incompetent to manage my affairs. Said attorney-in-fact shall be authorized to exercise all powers herein granted notwithstanding said incompetency. Said attorney-in-fact shall not be required to seek the appointment of a guardian of my person or property, but may instead exercise all of the powers herein granted.

And I hereby declare that any act or thing lawfully done hereunder by my said attorney-in-fact shall be binding on myself, and my heirs, legal and personal representatives, and assigns, whether the same shall, have been done before or after my death or other revocation of this instrument, unless and until notice thereof shall have been received by my said attorney-in-fact. Unless any person has notice of the revocation of this power of attorney, any person relying on these presents shall presume that such power continues to be in full force and effect.

Any banks, bankers, trust companies, savings and loan associations, fiduciaries, depositories, or other institutions, persons, firms, or corporations may act in reliance hereon and shall be fully protected.

My attorney-in-fact herein named shall not be liable for any loss resulting from any action taken by said attorney-in-fact if done in good faith and in the absence of fraud.

Notwithstanding anything contained herein to the contrary, this power may be revoked, and notice of such revocation shall be deemed received by all the world, by writ-

New York:

New York has recently amended the rules governing powers of attorney in GOL 5–1501. The new law provides that the principal must initial each power that it wants the attorney in fact to exercise and the principal must initial a box that will make the power durable, i.e. survive disability or incapacity. This form can not be used to authorize health care decisions for the principal. The new law also expanded the notice provision. See Exhibit 7.1 in Appendix.

EXHIBIT 7–2
Power of Attorney
(continued)

ten instrument recorded in the Office of the Clerk of the Superior Court of Clay County, Illinois.

IN WITNESS WHEREOF the undersigned hereunto set his hand and seal, this _____ day of _____ , _____ .

Signed, sealed and delivered in the presence of:

_____
Witness

_____ (SEAL)
ANDREW J. NELSON

_____
Notary Public
My Commission Expires:

_____

[NOTARY SEAL]

In reviewing contracts signed by an attorney-in-fact, it is necessary to review the power of attorney carefully to make sure the attorney-in-fact is acting within the scope of authority. Powers of attorney cannot be expanded on, nor can any powers be implied. The language must be carefully drawn to provide the attorney with the power to act. For example, a power of attorney that gives the attorney the authority to sell property does not give the attorney the authority to purchase property.

When dealing with real property contracts, it is necessary that the agency appointment or power of attorney be written and have the same formality as the contract. For example, if the contract is under seal (usually designated by the word seal at the end of the signature lines), the power of attorney must likewise have the same formality and be under seal.

A power of attorney can be revoked at any time by the person appointing the agent. In addition, powers of attorney are automatically revoked by death or insanity of the principal or by the appointment of a new agent for the same purpose. It is essential to establish, as best one can, that the power of attorney has not been revoked at the time the agent signs the contract.

Mutual Agreement

A valid contract requires that an agreement and bargain be struck between the parties to the contract. The parties must agree on the same thing, on the same terms, and at the same time. This is referred to as "meeting of the minds." This mutual consent may be manifested by an offer on the part of one party and an acceptance of the offer on the part of the other party. The acceptance must be on the same terms as the offer. For example, Aaron offers to sell a house to Bill for $100,000. Bill responds with an offer to buy the house for $95,000. At this stage of negotiations, Aaron has offered to sell for $100,000 and Bill has offered to buy for $95,000. Bill's offer to buy for $95,000 is a counteroffer to Aaron's offer to sell for $100,000. Bill's counteroffer revokes Aaron's original offer. The only offer that can be accepted or rejected is Bill's offer to buy for $95,000. Until such time as Aaron and Bill agree on the same price, there is no mutual agreement and no contract.

Consideration

A contract must state the **consideration** flowing from one party to the other or from each to both. Consideration may be money, something of value, or, in many states, just a recital of the agreement of the parties to buy and sell.

Lawful Purpose

A contract must be for a lawful purpose to be enforceable. Contracts to commit crimes or contracts that are against public policy are unenforceable. Almost all real estate contracts are for a lawful purpose.

Written Agreements

Not every contract must be in writing to be enforceable; however, early in the development of contract law it was observed that oral agreements were subject to much abuse. Consequently, in 1677, the Statute of Frauds was enacted in England. Its purpose was to prevent any fraudulent practices as were commonly upheld by perjury in the law courts. The Statute of Frauds, which has been adopted in almost every state, basically provides that certain contracts are not enforceable unless there exists some written memorandum or agreement that is signed by the party to be charged with the obligation. The Statute of Frauds requires various categories of contracts to be in writing. These categories are (a) a contract to answer for the debt of another person (guaranty or surety contract); (b) an agreement made on consideration of marriage; (c) any agreement that is not to be performed within one year from the date thereof; and (d) any contract for the sale or transfer of land or any interest in land.

A written real estate contract should contain at least the following essential details: (a) names of the parties (seller and buyer); (b) stated agreement to buy and sell; (c) description of the real property to be bought and sold; (d) purchase price; (e) terms of payment; (f) amount and disposition of the earnest money paid by the purchaser; (g) date of closing (when the transfer of ownership is to take place); (h) statement that "time is of the essence"; (i) if the parties so desire, a list of conditions before the sale; and (j) signature of the parties. Chapter 8 contains a thorough discussion of contract provisions and sample forms of contracts.

REMEDIES FOR BREACH OF A REAL ESTATE CONTRACT

In the event one of the parties to a contract for the purchase and sale of real estate breaches the contract and fails to perform the obligations under the contract, the injured party is entitled to one of the following remedies: (a) specific performance, (b) money damages, (c) rescission, or (d) liquidated damages.

Specific Performance

The remedy of **specific performance** follows a theory that real property is unique; therefore, when a party defaults under a contract, that party should be required to perform the obligations under the contract. Under the remedy of specific performance, the party in default is ordered by the court to perform. For example, if a seller defaults on a contract, the court orders the seller to sell the real property to the purchaser pursuant to the terms of the contract. This is an ideal remedy for the purchaser because he or she receives what was originally bargained for—the real property at the agreed-to purchase price. Specific performance also can be awarded to a seller against a defaulting purchaser. In this case, the court orders the purchaser to pay the contract price to the seller and receive title to the real property.

One limitation on the use of specific performance is the ability of the defaulting party to perform. For example, a person who does not own a parcel of real property contracts to sell the real property to a purchaser. The seller then, because of lack of title, fails to perform. The court cannot order specific performance because performance is impossible; therefore, the injured party is left with money damages or rescission.

Money Damages

The theory for money damages is that the injured party is to be placed in the same situation he or she would be in if the contract had been performed, insofar as money can do it. The amount of money damage is the difference between the contract price and the market value of the real property at the time and place of default. For example, a seller can only recover damages for the purchaser's default if the fair market value of the real property is less than the contract price at the time of default. It is only in this circumstance that the seller has lost money as a result of the sale not closing. On the other hand, a purchaser can only recover from a seller for money damages if the fair market value of the real property is more than the purchase price at the time of the default. It is only under this circumstance that the purchaser has lost money as a result of the sale not going through. The determination of fair market value usually is done by expert witnesses such as appraisers.

Rescission

Rescission operates under a different theory than money damages or specific performance. Here, instead of trying to put the injured party in the position he or she would have been in had the contract been performed, the law attempts to place the injured party in the position he or she would have been in had the contract not been entered into. That is, restore the "status" to the time before entering into the contract. The remedy of rescission provides that the contract is to be terminated and the injured party reimbursed for expenses incurred in preparation for the performance of the contract. For example, the seller breaches the obligation to sell property to a purchaser. The purchaser, in preparation of performance of the contract, has hired an attorney to do a title examination and prepare the contract and a surveyor to survey the property. The purchaser has bills totalling $2,000. If the purchaser is awarded rescission, the contract is terminated and the seller is ordered to pay the purchaser $2,000 as reimbursement for expenses.

It is easy to see that money damages, specific performance, and rescission are inconsistent remedies. It is impossible to require a party to perform and collect money damages at the same time. A party cannot rescind or terminate the contract and also have the court order the performance under the contract. Because these remedies are inconsistent, the injured party is entitled to only one of the remedies. However, at the time of suit, to enforce the contract, the party need not "elect" a certain remedy but instead may ask the court to award in the alternative all three forms of relief. The courts then will decide, after all the evidence is presented, which remedy will be awarded. For example, if the seller does not own the real property or the real property has serious title defects that cannot be corrected, then performance is not granted. Instead, the purchaser is left with the remedy of either money damages or rescission. In the same example, if it turns out that the fair market value of the real property and the contract price are the same, then the purchaser cannot recover money damages but is left with rescission as the only remedy.

Liquidated Damages

Sometimes the parties do not want to rely on money damages, specific performance, or rescission as a remedy for breach of contract and instead agree within the contract that a certain sum of money is to be paid in the event of default. This agreed-upon sum, called **liquidated damages**, is enforceable, provided it does not result in a penalty. The amount agreed on must be reasonable, close to what actual money damages would be in the event of default. When liquidated damages are included within a contract, they typically are the exclusive remedy. The parties can only collect liquidated damages, unless for some reason the provision is not enforceable. It is not unusual for contracts to provide that the purchaser will forfeit earnest money as liquidated damages in the event of the purchaser's default.

A sample contract liquidated damages provision is shown in Example 7–1.

EXAMPLE 7–1

In the event the transaction contemplated hereby is not closed because of Purchaser's default, the Earnest Money Deposit shall be paid to Seller as full liquidated damages for such failure to close, the parties acknowledging the difficulty of ascertaining Seller's damages in such circumstances, whereupon neither party hereto shall have any further rights, claims, or liabilities under this Agreement except for the provisions that are made to survive the termination or cancellation of this Agreement. Said liquidated damages shall be Seller's sole and exclusive remedy, and Seller shall expressly not have the right to seek specific performance.

These contract provisions must be drafted carefully or the forfeiture may result in an unenforceable liquidated damage provision. This problem is illustrated in the case *Southeastern Land Fund, Inc. v. Real Estate World, Inc.*, 227 S.E.2d 340.

 CASE

**Southeastern Land Fund, Inc.
v. Real Estate World, Inc.**
227 S.E.2d 340 (Ga. 1976)

INGRAM, Justice.

Certiorari was granted in this case[1] for this court to consider whether a provision in a real estate sales contract, providing for the payment of earnest money, should be considered as a provision for liquidated damages. The Court of Appeals concluded this provision was a penalty and could not be enforced.

The litigation began when the seller filed suit against the buyer who defaulted under the contract. The buyer had paid $5,000 in cash as earnest money when the contract was signed. Thereafter, a promissory note for $45,000, representing additional earnest money, was executed and delivered by the buyer to the seller pursuant to the contract. The buyer defaulted at closing and the seller sued the

1. The decision of the Court of Appeals is reported in 137   Ga.App. 771, 224 S.E.2d 747 (1976).

buyer to collect the $45,000 note. The seller obtained a summary judgment in the trial court and the buyer's motion for summary judgment and counterclaim for return of the $5,000 earnest money were denied.

On appeal to the Court of Appeals, that court reversed in a 6–3 decision and held the earnest money provision of the contract amounted to a penalty. The Court of Appeals also ruled that the buyer's motion for summary judgment should have been granted by the trial court.

The contract provides: "In the event purchaser defaults hereunder after having paid the additional earnest money [$45,000] . . . seller shall be entitled to retain all original earnest money [$5,000] paid hereunder as partial liquidated damages occasioned by such default, to collect the proceeds of the indebtedness owed by purchaser as additional earnest money as further partial liquidated damages occasioned by such default, and to pursue any and all remedies available to him at law or equity including, but not limited to, an action for specific performance of this contract."

[1, 2] If, as the Court of Appeals found, this provision in the contract was a penalty, or is unenforceable as a liquidated damages provision, then the buyer can prevail in asserting a defense to the enforcement of the $45,000 note. If, on the other hand, this is a proper provision for liquidated damages, then the seller can prevail in enforcing the note. Of course, whether a provision represents liquidated damages or a penalty does not depend upon the label the parties place on the payment but rather depends on the effect it was intended to have and whether it was reasonable. See *Lytle v. Scottish American Mortgage Co.,* 122 Ga. 458, 50 S.E. 402 (1905). Where the parties do not undertake to estimate damages in advance of the breach and instead provide for both a forfeiture [penalty] plus actual damages, the amount, even though called liquidated damages, is instead an unenforceable penalty. See *Foote & Davies Co. v. Malony,* 115 Ga. 985, 42 S.E. 413 (1902).

[3] The seller argues that a seller who is not in default may *always* retain the earnest money paid

by the buyer and sue for actual damages above the amount of earnest money received under the contract. We do not agree with this argument and the seller cites no authority that supports it. While it is true that the earnest money feature of a real estate contract distinguishes it to some extent from a wholly executory contract, the same basic contract rules are used to determine available remedies for the breach of a real estate sales contract as for the breach of other contracts. The general contract law of remedies for a breach, as well as the intent of the parties in providing specific remedies in the contract, must be used in analyzing and deciding each particular case.

[4] Depending on the language used in the contract and the discernible intent of the parties, the existence of an earnest money provision in a real estate sales contract can have one of three effects in the case of a breach by the buyer. First, the money could be considered as partial payment of any actual damages which can be proven as the result of the buyer's breach.[2] Second, the money could be applied as part payment of the purchase price in the enforcement of the contract in a suit for specific performance by the seller. Third, the money could be liquidated damages for breach of the contract by the buyer. A provision for earnest money cannot, however, under Georgia law, be used for all three results as we shall see.

[5–7] Of course, if the real estate sales contract is silent on the remedy to be provided, the non-breaching seller is entitled to his proven actual damages. The ordinary measure of damages is the difference between the contract price and the market value of the property at the time of the buyer's breach. *Shives v. Young,* 81 Ga.App. 30, 57 S.E.2d 874 (1950). If the non-breaching seller sues for actual damages, the earnest money then becomes a fund out of which those damages are partially paid if the proven damages exceed the amount of the earnest money.[3]

[8] Even if the real estate contract is silent as to the remedy of specific performance, it is still available as a remedy unless it is specifically excluded as a remedy. In the cases in which rescission has

---

2. We do not decide in this case whether a breaching buyer may sue in the first instance for recovery of earnest money if the seller suffers no actual damages.

3. Apparently, in many instances where real estate sales contracts provide that earnest money will be retained by the seller to be applied toward seller's damages, as a result of the buyer's

default, no suit is brought by the seller to prove his actual damages and likewise the buyer does not contest whether the seller has actually suffered damages or the extent of them. In these circumstances, the earnest money is really treated by the parties as liquidated damages, after a breach by the buyer, even though the parties did not agree to liquidate the damages in their contract.

been used as a remedy the parties are put as nearly as is possible back to the status quo ante. See *Lightfoot v. Brower,* 133 Ga. 766, 66 S.E. 1094 (1909); *Walter Tally, Inc. v. Council,* 109 Ga.App. 100, 135 S.E.2d 515 (1964); *Woodruff v. Camp,* 101 Ga.App. 124, 112 S.E.2d 831 (1960). Cf. *Higgins v. Kenney,* 159 Ga. 736, 126 S.E. 827 (1924).

[9] Of course, Georgia law also recognizes that the parties may agree in their contract to a sum to liquidate their damages. Code Ann. § 20–1402 provides: "Damages are given as compensation for the injury sustained. If the parties agree in their contract what the damages for a breach shall be, they are said to be liquidated, and unless the agreement violates some principle of law, *the parties are bound thereby.*" (Emphasis supplied.) See also Code Ann. § 20–1403.

[10] In deciding whether a contract provision is enforceable as liquidated damages, the court makes a tripartite inquiry to determine if the following factors are present:

"First, the injury caused by the breach must be difficult or impossible of accurate estimation; second, the parties must intend to provide for damages rather than for a penalty; and third, the sum stipulated must be a reasonable pre-estimate of the probable loss." Calamari & Perillo, The Law of Contracts, 367 (1970). See *Tuten v. Morgan,* 160 Ga. 90, 92, 127 S.E. 143 (1924), and *Bernhardt v. Federal Terra Cotta Co.,* 24 Ga.App. 635, 101 S.E. 588 (1919). See also *Martin v. Lott,* 144 Ga. 660, 87 S.E. 902 (1915).

[11] Another feature implicit in the concept of liquidated damages in addition to the above factors is that both parties are bound by their agreement. See Code Ann. § 20–1402. See, e.g., *Jarro Building Industries Corp. v. Schwartz,* 54 Misc.2d 13, 281 N.Y.S.2d 420 (1967). A non-breaching party who has agreed to accept liquidated damages cannot elect after a breach to take actual damages should they prove greater than the sum specified. The breaching party cannot complain that the actual damages are less than those specified as liquidated damages. The liquidated damages become the "maximum as well as the minimum sum that can be collected." *Mayor etc. of Brunswick v. Aetna Indemnity Co.,* 4 Ga.App. 722, 727, 62 S.E. 475, 477 (1908).

The problem that this particular contract provision raises is whether the seller has tried to retain a right to elect to sue for actual damages rather than liquidated damages and in so doing has rendered the purported liquidated damages provision unenforceable. This particular paragraph in the contract provides for "partial" liquidated damages. This can be read that the parties intended for the two "partial" liquidated damages provisions to comprise the whole. However, it is also susceptible to the construction that these two partial liquidated damages were not intended to be the sole damages remedy for this particular breach of contract.

[12] The contract provision that included the retention of the right to elect specific performance as an alternative remedy to damages poses no problem in our analysis as it does not render a valid liquidated damages provision unenforceable. See, e.g., *Wells v. First National Exhibitor's Circuit, Inc.,* 149 Ga. 200, 99 S.E. 615 (1919). "The law is now well settled that a liquidated damages provision will not in and of itself be construed as barring the remedy of specific performance." *Rubinstein v. Rubinstein,* 23 N.Y.2d 293, 296 N.Y.S.2d 354, 244 N.E.2d 49 (1968). To bar specific performance there should be explicit language in the liquidated damages provision that it is to be the sole remedy. See also Restatement, Contracts, § 378. Thus the retention of the right to elect specific performance in this contract does not render the purported liquidated damages provision invalid. The answer must be found elsewhere in the construction of these contract provisions.

[13, 14] We think a correct resolution of this issue must be found in the doctrine that "in cases of doubt the courts favor the construction which holds the stipulated sum to be a penalty, and limits the recovery to the amount of damages actually shown, rather than a liquidation of the damages." *Mayor & Council of Brunswick v. Aetna Indemnity Co.,* supra, 4 Ga.App. p. 728, 62 S.E. p. 478. If the parties intended for the $5,000 and the $45,000 to represent the "maximum as well as the minimum sum that can be collected," from the buyer's breach, the contract should have made it clear that this was the effect intended by these provisions. It is the lingering ambiguity inherent in these provisions of the contract that persuades us to affirm the result reached by the Court of Appeals in construing the contract.

In summary, we hold that these contract provisions are not enforceable under Georgia law as proper liquidated damages provisions in this real estate sales contract. It follows that the trial court erred in granting summary judgment in favor of the seller and we affirm the Court of Appeals reversal of that portion of the trial court's order. However, the existence of the actual damages, if any, to be proven by the non-breaching seller precludes the grant of the buyer's motion for summary judgment. Therefore, that portion of the Court of Appeals opinion directing the grant of the buyer's motion for summary judgment must be reversed.

Judgment affirmed in part; reversed in part.

Real Estate Broker

Many real estate sale transactions are arranged by a real estate broker or agent, who earns a commission in matching the buyer and the seller.

Real estate brokers and agents are subject to license by various state agencies to protect the public from unscrupulous practices and to establish professional standards of conduct. Most licensing criteria require that the real estate broker or agent demonstrate a certain degree of competence in the area of real property law and that the broker or agent maintain continuing education credits. A broker or an agent who does not have a license or whose license has been suspended is not entitled to receive a real estate commission.

A broker or an agent earns a real estate commission if the broker or agent produces a person who is ready, willing, and able to purchase the real property at the price and on the terms required by the seller in the listing agreement. The broker or agent must be the procuring cause of the sale. This means that the broker or agent must find a purchaser within the time agreed in the listing, and the purchaser's offer must meet the terms of the listing unless modifications are agreed to by the real property owner. The term "able to buy" means that the purchaser has the financial ability as well as the legal and mental capacity to enter into an enforceable contract to purchase the real property. The broker or agent earns the commission once a purchaser who meets the terms of the seller's offer to sell the property is presented to the seller. The commission is earned even if the seller refuses the purchaser's offer, or if the seller and purchaser go to contract but the contract does not close.

Although the commission is earned at the time the purchaser and seller contract, it typically is not paid until the contract closes and the purchase money is received by the seller. The real estate commission typically is a percentage of the sales price and is paid by the seller. The real estate contract usually outlines the commission rights of a broker or agent, and the broker or agent is made a party to the contract for the purpose of enforcing the commission rights.

New York:

The Secretary of State of New York, through the Division of Licensing Services, has proscribed the laws for the employment of a broker. The manual issued by the Department of State states that a real estate broker's license does not give them the right to give legal advice or draw up legal documents.

Traditionally, brokers in upstate New York fill in contract forms but in New York City the seller's attorney usually prepares the contract. There are traditional "Blumberg" forms for real estate transactions, but one must have legal knowledge to fill in the blanks, to delete clauses, and to choose additional clauses.

LISTING AGREEMENTS

Owners hire brokers to sell real property with a **listing (agency) agreement**.

The main types of listing agreements are open, exclusive, and exclusive right to sell. Brokers' listing agreements usually provide that the real property is to be sold during a period of time (a listing period). These agreements also state that if the real property is introduced to a number of people during the listing period and sold to one of the people after the listing period, the agent is entitled to a commission. A seller should require that the agent submit to the seller a list of people to whom the real property has been shown before the expiration of the listing agreement. The agent also should agree that if the real property is sold to only these people within some reasonable period of time (e.g., 6 months) after the listing expiration, a commission will be due and payable.

Open Listing

Under an open listing, an owner of property hires an agent or a broker to sell the real property, but the owner still reserves the right to hire other agents or brokers and to sell the real property on his or her own efforts. The first agent or broker to bring a purchaser who is ready, willing, and able to purchase the real property at the price demanded by the seller earns the commission. Because open listings can result in a free-for-all, with a number of brokers and agents competing for the commission, most brokers or agents shy away from open listings. They would prefer to use energy and time on listings that increase their chances for a commission.

Exclusive Listing

Under an exclusive listing, an owner hires only one broker or agent to assist in the sale of the real property. The owner still reserves the right to sell the real property, and if the owner's efforts result in a sale, no commission is earned.

Exclusive Right-to-Sell Listing

Under an exclusive right-to-sell listing, an owner hires only one broker or agent to assist in selling the real property and the owner agrees that if the real property is sold, even through the owner's efforts, a commission is earned. Brokers and agents prefer this type of listing, which assures a commission if the real property is sold during the listing period.

Many brokers and agents participate in a multiple-listing service. A multiple-listing service is a cooperative of brokers who pool all their listings and make them available to all members of the service. By doing this, a seller's real property is made available to all brokers in the community and the chances for a quick sale are greatly enhanced.

New York:
There are three forms of listing in New York: 1) open listing; 2) exclusive agency listing (if you, the property owner, find a buyer, you will *not* have to pay a commission to the broker); and 3) exclusive right to sell (if you, the property owner, find a buyer for your house or if another broker finds a buyer, you *must* pay the agreed on commission to the broker).

New York:
New York does not allow the use of an automatic extension of a listing agreement.
    MLS Multiple Listing Service is not a listing but a group of brokers who agree to seek buyers for each others' listings.

New York:
For a discussion of binders, see Appendix.

 E T H I C S :   Commingling of Client Funds

A legal assistant is employed by a law firm. One of the firm's clients is purchasing a home. The attorney, with the legal assistant's help, has been requested to prepare the contract. The contract requires a down payment of $5,000 to be made at the time the contract is signed. The client signs the contract and gives to the legal assistant a check with the legal assistant shown as the payee for the down payment. The intent is that the check would be endorsed by the legal assistant into the firm's escrow account and that a check would be issued to the seller as an earnest money down payment. The legal assistant receives the check on Friday, noticing that it is made out to her. The legal assistant endorses the check and places it into her personal checking account, fully intending on Monday to write a check from the account to the firm's escrow account. Are the acceptance of the check made out to the legal assistant as payee and the depositing of the check into her personal account breaches of ethics?

One of the main ethical requirements for the practice of law is to separate client funds from personal funds. An attorney who commingles client funds with personal funds can face suspension or even loss of license to practice law. A legal assistant, likewise, should never, under any circumstances, commingle funds received by a client with his or her own funds. A legal assistant must always account for all monies or properties entrusted into his or her possession, and such money or property should be kept separate and apart from his or her own personal account. Acceptance of a check made payable to the legal assistant in this case is a breach of ethics. In addition, the deposit of the check into the legal assistant's own personal account, even though it may have been an innocent mistake on the legal assistant's part, is also a breach of ethics.

SUMMARY

The contract is an important legal document in the transfer of ownership to real property. It is the "legal glue" that binds seller and purchaser together. In addition to the agreements by the purchaser and seller as to the real property to be bought and sold and the purchase price, contracts address numerous other issues of importance to the purchaser and seller.

KEY TERMS

Consideration
Contract
Liquidated damages

Listing agreement
Power of attorney

Rescission
Specific performance

REVIEW QUESTIONS

1. What are the requirements of a valid real estate contract?

2. What is the Statute of Frauds, and what effect does it have on the validity of contracts?

3. Explain the difference between an exclusive listing and an exclusive right-to-sell listing.

4. Explain the three remedies available for the breach of a real estate contract.

5. Under what circumstances would a liquidated damage provision be unenforceable?

6. Why must contracts entered into with partnerships, executors, and trustees be carefully examined?

7. When is a real estate broker entitled to a commission?

8. Under what circumstances can a power of attorney be revoked?

9. Why is the contract of a mental incompetent unenforceable?

10. If a seller defaults on a contract, what is the most desirable remedy for the purchaser?

CASE PROBLEMS

1. Seller and purchaser enter into a contract for the sale and purchase of real property for a price of $90,000. The property has a value of $100,000. The purchaser fails to perform. What is the amount of money damages to be awarded to the seller? What is the amount of money damages owed to the purchaser if the seller fails to perform?

2. Susan Seller has contracted to sell her home to Bob Buyer. The sale is for $100,000 cash with no conditions except that title be marketable and the sale to close on July 20 at Susan's attorney's office. On July 18, Bob calls Susan and informs her that he had planned to buy the property by a "loan assumption" (i.e., he had assumed

that his rich uncle would lend him the money). The rich uncle, however, has refused and Bob does not have the cash to go ahead with the deal. Bob further mentions that he had owned some other real estate worth about $500,000 and perhaps he could sell or get a loan against this real estate and have enough cash to go ahead with the deal sometime in the future. Bob asks Susan if she will extend the closing for a month, until August 20. Susan says no and further informs Bob that she is ready, willing, and able to perform on July 20. On July 20, no closing takes place. On July 21, Susan sues Bob for breach of contract. Please answer the following questions with full discussion: (a) Has Bob breached the contract? (b) Does Susan have the right to sue Bob on July 21? (c) If Susan can sue Bob on July 21, what remedies are available to Susan for Bob's breach of contract?

3. You are a legal assistant with a law firm. One of the firm's clients, a corporation, has entered into a contract to purchase property from Dwight Sneed. The client, after entering into the contract, has discovered that Dwight Sneed is sixteen years old. The client is worried that Dwight Sneed's promises under the contract are unenforceable, and to avoid problems, the client wants to get out of the contract. Is the contract enforceable by Dwight Sneed against the corporate client?

4. You are assisting in the negotiation and preparation of a contract for the purchase and sale of real property. The seller of the property is a partnership composed of two partners. The partners are XYZ Realty Company, a Texas corporation, and ABC Realty Company, a Texas corporation. You have been asked to obtain proper documentation to demonstrate that the seller has the authority to

enter into the contract and will be bound by the terms of the contract. What documentation will you need?

5. Alice Skinflint has retained Honest Broker to assist her in selling her vacation home. Skinflint and Broker enter into a listing agreement wherein the property is to be offered for sale for $100,000 cash. The listing is to expire on May 1. On April 25, Honest Broker receives an offer to purchase Skinflint's vacation home from I. M. Rich. The offer is for $100,000 cash and Mr. Rich is a multimillionaire. Honest Broker calls Alice Skinflint and tells her that he has a purchaser for her vacation home and that he would like to meet with her before May 1 to have a contract signed. Alice Skinflint informs Honest Broker that she is going out of town for a vacation and will not be back until May 5 and that she cannot enter into a contract before the expiration of the listing on May 1. Alice Skinflint returns from her vacation on May 6, calls I. M. Rich, and signs a contract with I. M. Rich to sell the vacation home for $100,000. Honest Broker requests that Skinflint pay him a 6 percent commission on the sale. Skinflint refuses, saying that the property had not been sold before the expiration of the listing on May 1. What are the chances of Honest Broker recovering the commission from Skinflint?

6. Sam Seller offers to sell his home to Pat Purchaser for the sum of $75,000. Pat Purchaser responds that she will only purchase the home for $65,000. Sam Seller rejects Pat Purchaser's offer to purchase for $65,000. Pat Purchaser then offers $75,000 for Sam Seller's home. Is there a contract between Sam Seller and Pat Purchaser for the sale and purchase of the home at $75,000?

PRACTICAL ASSIGNMENT

1. Research your state's statute of frauds law and prepare a brief memorandum summarizing what contracts are required to be in writing in your state.

2. Research your state's laws concerning liquidated damages. What is required in your state for a liquidated dam-

age provision in a real estate contract to be enforceable? Prepare a brief memorandum regarding the conclusions of your research.

Preparation and Review of a Real Estate Contract

8

Contracts should always be in writing, as oral contracts aren't worth the paper they're printed on.

—White's Law Dictionary

OBJECTIVES

After reading this chapter you will be able to:

- Review a real estate contract for the sale and purchase of a home and understand its contents
- Prepare a real estate contract for the sale and purchase of a home
- Review a real estate contract for the sale and purchase of commercial real property and understand its contents
- Prepare a real estate contract for the sale and purchase of commercial real property

GLOSSARY

Cashier's check   Check issued by a bank, the payment of which is guaranteed by the full faith and credit of the bank.

Certified check   Personal check in which the bank certifies that the funds are in the account and that the check will be honored on presentment for payment.

Closing   Date set forth in a real estate contract on which the parties agree to perform all the promises of the contract. The date on which ownership of the real property is transferred from seller to purchaser and the purchaser pays the seller the purchase price for the real property.

Condition precedent   Condition in a contract that must be satisfied in accordance with the terms of the contract before one or both of the parties are required to perform their contractual obligations.

Earnest money   Money paid by the purchaser at the time the real estate contract is signed. The money may be used as a down payment on the purchase price or may be retained by the seller for damages in the event the purchaser defaults on the contract.

Estoppel letter   Sworn statement of fact.

Execution   Signature of a party to a legal document. The act of signing a legal document.

Option   A contract by which an owner of property, usually called the optionor, agrees with another person, usually called the optionee, that the optionee shall have the right to buy the owner's real property at a fixed price within a certain time on agreed terms and conditions.

Parol evidence rule   Rule of evidence that provides that a written agreement is the best and only evidence of the agreement between the parties and that the parties are not permitted to bring in oral testimony regarding other agreements concerning the transaction.

Time is of the essence   Provision contained in a contract that requires strict performance of the contract by the date or dates provided therein.

Legal assistants prepare real estate contracts for an attorney's final review or assist the attorney in a review of contracts prepared by other counsel or by real estate brokers. During the process of preparing or reviewing a contract, one should remember that the contract is the primary controlling document in a real estate sale transaction. It follows the negotiations of the parties and, it is hoped, captures their agreements in writing. It dictates the rights and responsibilities of the parties, and in most instances, its effect goes well beyond the consummation of the transaction it contemplates. Because of its vital importance to the transaction, a legal assistant must pay close attention to the contents of the real estate contract.

SYDNEY'S REAL ESTATE CONTRACT

It's Friday afternoon. The attorney you work for, Susan Barrister, has just received a call from Sydney Brownstreet, one of the firm's real estate developer clients. Susan has asked that you sit in on a telephone conversation with Sydney because she wants you to assist her in preparing whatever legal documents Sydney requires. When you enter her office, you hear Sydney's voice on the telephone speaker phone. "Listen, Susan, I need your help over the weekend. I've got a chance to buy a nice piece of property out on Delk Road that will be ideal for this new shopping center concept of mine. I need you to prepare a contract so that I will have it on Monday to present to the owner. The owner's name is Delk Road Development, Inc., and I want to offer $750,000 for the property. I can fax over to you a copy of the legal description. I also would like to close the deal by April 1. Is there anything else you need to know, Susan?"

Susan looks at you with a slight roll of her eyes toward the ceiling and then asks Sydney the following questions.

"Sydney, do you intend to buy the property in your name or in the name of your corporation, Brownstreet Shopping Centers, Inc.? Or are you going to form a new corporation or partnership to take title? Is the property vacant? Are there any easements that are necessary for your development of the property?

"How do you intend to pay for the property? Are you going to pay all cash at closing, or are the sellers going to take back a note? Do you need to line up financing for the purchase, and if so, should this be a condition to closing?

"Is there any debt existing on the property? If so, do you want to try and assume that debt?

"Are you satisfied with insurable title for the property? Do you want us to do a title examination? Do you want the seller to pay for it?

"Do you want to take possession of the property at closing? Before closing? Are taxes and all other expenses to be prorated as to the date of closing? Do you have any conditions that you want satisfied before closing? Are you satisfied with the zoning? Do you think that you can get a curb cut onto Delk Road? Do you need to do any soil tests to see if the soil will support your shopping center concept? Have you had the property examined for hazardous wastes? Is there sanitary sewer and other utilities to the property?

"Do you want a survey? Do you want the seller to pay for the survey? How much earnest money are you going to put down? Do you want to make it part of the purchase price? Are you willing to forfeit the earnest money if you don't go ahead and buy the property? Do you want the seller to hold the earnest money? Is there a real estate broker involved? Do you want the broker to hold the earnest money? Do

New York:

In New York, the essentials of a valid contract for the sale of real property are: 1) contract in writing and signed by the parties; 2) competent parties; 3) agreement to sell, offer, and acceptance, 4) consideration (price and terms of payment); and 5) legal description.

Custom dictates the use of different additional forms and different clauses in different areas of New York State. These forms can be obtained from a stationery store or title company. See Appendix for sample contract forms for a residential sale, condominium unit sale, commercial sale, and a cooperative sale. The usual forms and usual clauses are now on computer software programs. Most residential real estate contracts are not recorded.

you want to be able to assign the contract to some partnership that you are going to form in the future?"

As the conversation continues, it is easy to see that the preparation of a real estate contract requires the answers to more questions than just the identity of the seller and the purchaser, a description of the real property to be bought and sold, a purchase price, and a time for performance.

ELEMENTS IN A REAL ESTATE CONTRACT

The Parties

Obviously the contract will have a seller and a purchaser. Other parties may join in the execution of the contract, for example, a real estate broker or escrow agent. All parties signing the contract should be clearly and distinctly identified by name and capacity (i.e., seller, buyer, and agent). In addition, it is helpful to put the parties' addresses and telephone numbers on the contract. In the event that a party to a contract is not a natural person, such as a corporation or a partnership, the authority of the representative to sign should be revealed in the contract. For example, in a corporate contract, the corporation should be made a party to the contract, but the officer signing on behalf of the corporation should be identified as well as the office he or she holds with the corporation.

A seller should be identified in the contract exactly the way the seller holds title to the real property. Purchasers should be identified the way in which they desire to take title. The name of each person signing the contract should be typed underneath the signature line (Examples 8–1 and 8–20).

New York:
Indicate on the contract how the parties will hold title, e.g., tenants by entirety, tenants in common, etc.

EXAMPLE 8–1

THIS AGREEMENT OF PURCHASE AND SALE the "Agreement" is made and entered into as of the Effective Date, as hereinafter defined, by and between JOANNE SELLER, ALICE SELLER LONGWORTH, AND WARREN SELLER (hereinafter collectively "Seller"); and PURCHASER, INC., a Colorado corporation (hereinafter "Purchaser") and AMERICAN REALTY COMPANY, a Colorado corporation (hereinafter "Broker").

CONSIDERATION

A contract must state the consideration flowing from one party to the other or from each to both (Example 8–2). Consideration may be money or something of value. In many states, a recital of the agreement of the parties to buy and sell is sufficient.

EXAMPLE 8–2

That for and in consideration of the mutual promises and covenants herein contained and the mutual advantages accruing to Seller and Purchaser hereunder and the sum of $10.00 and other good and valuable considerations paid by Purchaser to Seller, receipt of which is hereby acknowledged by Seller, it is mutually covenanted and agreed by the parties hereto as follows:

The Agreement

At a minimum, a contract should contain statements whereby the seller agrees to sell and the buyer agrees to buy the property. Typically, the contract also contains other agreements between the parties, but without an agreement to buy and sell, the sales contract is not valid.

The Property

A contract should adequately describe the real property being bought and sold. A true and correct description of the real property prepared from a survey is preferable, but the minimum requirement in most states is that the real property be clearly and distinctively identified (Example 8–3). Does the description of the property point to a particular piece of identifiable property? If so, the description is adequate. If anything other than unimproved real property is the subject matter of a contract, it should so indicate. Any personal property to be included with the purchase should be accurately described. Although fixtures are included as part of the realty by operation of law, if there is any question as to whether an item is a fixture, the contract should cover the questioned item with certainty. It is better practice to clearly list all items included in the sale than to rely on items being included as fixtures by the operation of law. Likewise, if some items are to be excluded from the contract, they should be expressly excluded rather than relying on the operation of law to exclude them. If personal property items are to be excluded from the sale, the contract should discuss the method and time of removal and the means for repair to the real property if such repairs are required as a result of the removal of the excluded personal property.

New York:
The legal description will suffice to identify the real property. Any personal property should be described in detail, list items included such as drapes and microwaves and exclude items specifically excluded such as a crystal fixture in dining room. There may be a requirement to replace a fixture that is removed so that there are no loose hanging wires.

EXAMPLE 8-3

Property. Seller hereby agrees to sell and convey to Purchaser and Purchaser hereby agrees to purchase from Seller, subject to the terms and conditions hereinafter set forth, the property located in Land Lot 99, 17th District, Colorado Springs, Elk County, Colorado, described on *Exhibit A* attached hereto and made a part hereof containing approximately 2.544 acres (the "Land") as shown on that certain survey of the Land prepared by D.W. Transit, Colorado Registered Land Surveyor No. 1845, for JoAnne Seller et al., dated July 25, 19__, last revised December 17, 19__ (the "Existing Survey"), together with the following:

(a) *Improvements.* All improvements on the Land owned by Seller, including, without limitation, a two-story retail shopping center containing approximately 54,520 net rentable square feet more commonly known as the "Mountain Square" and together with drives, sidewalks, drainage, sewerage and utility facilities, and surface parking areas (collectively the "Improvements");

(b) *Tangible Personal Property.* All fixtures, equipment, machinery, building supplies, tools, furniture, and other personal property, if any, and all replacements thereof, located on or about the Land and Improvements and used exclusively in the operation and maintenance thereof (the "Tangible Personal Property"), but expressly excluding any and all property owned by tenants occupying the Improvements;

(c) *Intangible Property.* Any and all of the Seller's rights and interests in and to all intangible property pertaining to the Land, the Improvements or the Tangible Property or the use thereof, including without limitation, any trade names used in connection therewith, the landlord's interest in all leases regarding the Property to the extent assignable, and all other licenses, franchises, permits, tenant security deposits (unless Purchaser receives a credit for same), contract rights, agreements, transferable business licenses, tenant lists, correspondence with tenants and suppliers, booklets, manuals, advertising materials, transferable utility contracts, and transferable telephone exchange numbers (the "Intangible Property");

   (d) *Easements.* Any and all of Seller's rights in and to all easements, if any, benefiting the Land or the Improvements; and

   (e) *Rights and Appurtenances.* All rights and appurtenances pertaining to the foregoing, including any right, title, and interest of Seller in and to adjacent streets, alleys, or rights-of-way.

All of the property described in Subsections (a), (b), (c), (d), and (e) of this Section together with the Land, are hereinafter sometimes collectively referred to as the "Property."

The Price

A contract should state the purchase price of the real property or provide for an exact method by which the purchase price can be computed (Example 8–4). The easiest approach is to always have a fixed price for the real property, but that may not always be appropriate for the transaction. In dealing with commercial real property or undeveloped acreage, the price often is expressed in terms of dollars per acre, square foot, or feet of road frontage. If such is the case, the contract needs to speak to the following questions: (a) What method will be used to determine the area or frontage (a survey)? (b) Does either party have the right to question the accuracy of such a method? (c) Are all areas within the boundary of the survey to be used in the computation, or are certain areas (e.g., flood plains, easements, and public or private rights-of-way) excludable? (d) Is the seller warranting a minimum area or amount of frontage that is acceptable to the purchaser?

The Method of Payment

Closely related to the price is the way in which the price will be paid and received. A contract should provide for an exact method of payment and the medium (e.g., cash, certified funds, notes, or personal checks). The most common methods of payment are (a) cash; (b) the seller accepting a note, usually secured by the real property; (c) the purchaser assuming preexisting encumbrances or debts against the real property or taking title subject thereto; and (d) the seller accepting other property, either real or personal, in exchange for the real property that is the subject matter of the contract. Many transactions involve a combination of these methods (Example 8–4).

Cash

New York:
The most common method of payment is by certified or cashiers check at closing, made payable to seller. There is often a limit on how much cash will be allowed at closing (no one wants to walk around with $180,000 in dollar bills).

The simplest situation is one in which the purchaser is paying all cash for the real property. Although drafting and reviewing an all-cash contract requires less attention to the method of payment, there are some points that require thought. Do the parties in fact mean cash, or do they mean cash or its equivalent? It is unusual for purchasers to bring hundred-dollar bills to a closing. Cash equivalents often are the method of payment. Cash equivalents can be certified funds or a cashier's or treasurer's check. A **certified check** is a personal check in which the bank certifies that the funds are in the account and that the check will be honored on presentment for payment. A **cashier's** or **treasurer's check** is a check issued by a bank. Either mode of alternative payment usually is acceptable.

Seller Financing

The seller financing method of payment requires a great deal of skill and thought on the part of the legal assistant in drafting or reviewing the contract. It involves a continuation of rights and obligations between the parties subsequent to the closing of the purchase and sale. The contract should carefully detail each aspect of the financing instruments that will be executed at closing and, if possible, attach copies of these instruments as exhibits to the contract. At a minimum, a contract should touch on the following aspects of seller financing: (a) the security for the note (usually this is the real property being sold); (b) the priority of the lien created (is it a first mortgage lien or a junior lien?); (c) when installment payments are due under the note; (d) late penalties for payments not timely made; (e) prepayment penalties or privileges; (f) will the obligation be due on the subsequent sale by the purchaser of the property? (g) interest rates payable; (h) if the transaction so dictates, release provisions if the purchaser should desire to have a portion of the real property released from the lien before payment of the full loan; (i) maintenance of insurance on the real property for benefit of the seller; (j) personal liability to purchaser under the note and security instrument; and (k) the amount of the note and the exact method by which the amount of the note will be determined at closing.

Preexisting Obligations

The term *loan assumption* often is used to cover both the situation in which the purchaser is in fact assuming liability under some preexisting debt and the situation in which a purchaser is taking title to the property subject to a preexisting debt. The difference is one of liability for the purchaser. A purchaser who "assumes" a preexisting debt is personally obligated to pay the debt. A purchaser who takes "subject to" a preexisting debt is not personally responsible for payment. The maximum risk to a purchaser who takes "subject to" a preexisting obligation is the loss of the real property through foreclosure in the event the obligation is not paid. A thorough discussion of the differences between "assumption" and "subject to" appears in Chapter 11. A contract should clearly identify the preexisting obligation by giving the name of the holder thereof, the amounts and due dates of payments, the interest rates, the account or loan number (if any), and the loan balances as of a given date. Also, information concerning the assumability of the loan should be included in the contract. Certain representations concerning the preexisting obligation should be required from the seller, such as representation that the loan is not in default, that the seller will comply with all the terms and conditions of the financing documents in the normal course before closing, and of the existence or lack of any condition that the holder of such loan may impose on the purchaser.

Exchanges

An exchange of one parcel of real property for another parcel of real property is done for tax purposes to postpone the occurrence of a taxable event (e.g., the recognition of gain on the sale of appreciated real property). Contracts that contemplate a tax-free exchange should be carefully drafted and reviewed from both a tax and a real property law perspective. Legal assistants seldom are involved in the drafting or negotiation of tax-free exchange contracts.

New York:
If seller takes back a mortgage, it is called a purchase money mortgage. The contract should indicate who will pay for drawing up the mortgage papers (usually the purchaser).

If the purchaser is seeking FHA or VA financing, the contract must state that. If they are not seeking VA or FHA financing, the mortgage contingency will provide for a conventional loan.

EXAMPLE 8-4

(a) *Purchase Price.* The Purchase Price (the "Purchase Price") to be paid for the Property shall be Seven Million Three Hundred Thousand and No/100 Dollars ($7,300,000.00) to be paid in the following manner:

(i) Purchaser shall take subject to a first mortgage loan on the Property held by Wearever Life Assurance Company in the original Principal amount of Five Million Five Hundred Thousand Dollars ($5,500,000.00), which mortgage loan currently bears interest at the rate of ten percent per annum (10%) and is due and payable in full on January 1, 19___. Seller agrees to pay one-half of any and all transfer, assumption, or other fees assessed by the holder of the mortgage loan in connection with the transfer of the Property subject to the mortgage loan; and

(ii) Purchaser shall deliver to Seller a purchase money note ("Note") in the amount of Six Hundred Fifty-Four Thousand ($654,000.00). Said Note shall bear interest at ten percent per annum (10%) and shall be payable interest only quarterly with a final payment of all unpaid principal and accrued and unpaid interest being due and payable two years from the Closing Date (hereinafter defined). The Note shall provide that it can be prepaid in whole or in part at any time without premium or penalty. The Note shall provide that the holder of the Note shall give the Maker of the Note at least twenty (20) days written notice of default prior to any acceleration of the Note for default or exercise of any other remedies that the holder may have to collect the indebtedness evidenced by the Note; provided, however, the Note shall be cross-defaulted with the Wearever Life Assurance Company loan ("Wearever Loan") and defaults under the Wearever Loan are to be governed by the notice and cure periods provided for in the Wearever Loan. The Note shall be secured by a second priority Deed of Trust ("Deed") on the Property. The Deed shall provide that insurance and condemnation proceeds shall be used for restoration of the Property; shall provide for twenty (20) days written notice of default prior to any exercise of remedies thereunder; shall not provide for any tax or insurance escrows; shall not have any restrictions on the transfer of the Property or upon any further financing or encumbrancing of the Property. The Note and Deed shall be nonrecourse to Purchaser and shall contain no personal guaranty whatsoever. The Note shall be in the form of the Note attached hereto as Exhibit "___" and the Deed shall be in the form of the Deed of Trust attached hereto as Exhibit "___".

(iii) The balance of the Purchase Price in the approximate amount of One Million One Hundred Forty-Six Thousand Dollars ($1,146,000.00) shall be payable in cash or by bank check drawn on a Federal Reserve Bank of Denver or by wire transfer or good funds on the Closing Date (hereinafter defined). Upon request by Purchaser prior to closing. Seller shall designate the account of Seller into which the net proceeds of the sale are to be deposited.

Quality of Title

A contract should contain a description of the quality of title the seller is obligated to convey and the purchaser is obligated to accept at the time of closing (Example 8–5). The terms usually used in contracts are "marketable title" and "insurable title." A purchaser can agree to accept some lesser quality of title. In drafting or reviewing a contract, the inclusion of catch words such as marketable title and insurable title without a clear definition can create problems. Marketable title usually means title that a prudent purchaser with full knowledge of all the facts would accept. Insurable title means title that is insurable by a title insurance company as being marketable. Real property may be "marketable" for a particular purpose even though numerous liens and encumbrances exist against the title; and title to any property is insurable, provided the owner is willing to pay a sufficient premium or accept insurance that excepts to any and every defect in title. A complete discussion of title insurance is set forth in Chapter 14.

The contract should clearly set forth exceptions to title that the purchaser is willing to accept. All permitted exceptions should be specifically stated in the contract. Most purchasers are unwilling to accept title "subject to utility easements and other restrictions of record." Such a broad statement could include many title exceptions that are unacceptable or that would be detrimental to the real property. Be especially careful of standard permitted title exceptions, which often appear in preprinted forms. These preprinted form exceptions include (a) utility easements of record serving the real property, (b) zoning ordinances that affect the property, (c) subdivision restrictions of record, and (d) leases. The real property may be so heavily burdened by utility easements as to prevent any improvements from being constructed thereon. Zoning ordinances may preclude a purchaser from using the real property in the way he or she desires. Subdivision restrictions may place financial burdens on the purchaser or may require approval of owners' associations before the consummation of the transaction. Finally, agreeing to accept title subject to leases without first reviewing the leases can create serious problems.

A contract should require the purchaser to notify the seller of any unacceptable title exceptions disclosed as a result of an examination of the public records and afford the seller the opportunity to cure these defects. A contract should provide either a reasonable time to search title and reasonable time to cure defects, or a stated period of time for the purchaser to examine title and a stated period of time required for curative action by the seller. The contract should contain provisions dealing with the failure of the parties to meet their obligations with reference to the title.

A contract should provide that the seller shall not alter or encumber the title to the property after the date of the contract without the written consent of the purchaser.

EXAMPLE 8-5

(a) Seller shall sell, convey, and assign to Purchaser at Closing good and marketable fee simple title to the Property subject only to the Permitted Title Exceptions as defined and set forth on *Exhibit B* attached hereto.

(b) Within thirty (30) days after the effective date of this contract, Purchaser shall cause title to the Property to be examined and shall furnish Seller with a written statement of any and all title matters, other than the Permitted Title Exceptions to which Purchaser objects. Purchaser shall also have the right to examine, or cause to be examined, title to the Property at any time or times after such initial title examination and prior to Closing and to furnish Seller with a written statement or statements of any and all additional matters, other than the Permitted Title Exceptions that affect the title to the Property or the use thereof and that arise, or first appear on record from and after the date of the initial title examination hereunder and to which Purchaser objects. Seller shall cooperate with Purchaser after receipt of any such written statement to correct, cure, or remove all matters described in such statement, and covenants to exercise diligent and good faith efforts to do so. Notwithstanding the above or the terms of this Section, in the event that any such matter results from any affirmative action taken by Seller subsequent to the date hereof, Seller covenants to expend such money and to take such other actions as may be necessary to correct, cure, or remove same. The Closing Date shall be postponed automatically for thirty (30) days, if necessary, to permit Seller to cure. If Seller shall fail to correct, cure, or remove all such matters within the time allowed by this Section, then Purchaser, at its option exercised by written notice, may:

(i) decline to purchase the Property; or

(ii) waive such matter and proceed to close the purchase and sale of the Property without a reduction in the Purchase Price and allow Seller to convey title to the Property in accordance with the terms hereof; or

(iii) in the event the matter results from affirmative action of Seller subsequent to the effective date of this contract, require Seller by action of specific performance or otherwise to exercise diligent and good faith efforts to correct, cure, or remove such matters and convey the Property in accordance with the terms of this Agreement, in which case the Closing Date shall be postponed until such correction, cure, or removal by Seller has been completed (provided, however, that at any time during such period Purchaser may exercise its options as set forth in Section (b)(i) or Section (b)(ii) above).

Should Purchaser accept, by written waiver, its interest in the Property subject to matters in addition to the Permitted Title Exceptions, such acceptable matters shall be added to the list now set forth in *Exhibit B* and shall thereafter be deemed to be Permitted Title Exceptions except that, in the event any of such matters results from any affirmative action taken by Seller subsequent to the date hereof, such acceptance shall be without prejudice to Purchaser's thereafter seeking monetary damages from Seller for any such matter. If Purchaser shall decline to accept the Seller's interest in the Property subject to such matters, pursuant to Section (b) above, then Escrowee shall refund to Purchaser the Deposit and the parties hereto shall have no further rights, obligations, duties, or liabilities hereunder whatsoever, except for those rights, obligations, duties, and liabilities that, by the express terms hereof, survive any termination hereof and except for Purchaser's right to seek monetary damages from Seller for any matter which Seller shall have failed so to correct and which shall have resulted from any affirmative action taken by Seller after the date hereof.

(c) Purchaser may, at its expense, elect to obtain a standard ALTA Form 1990 owner's policy of title insurance pursuant to which fee simple title to the Property shall be insured. Seller covenants to Purchaser that title to the Property shall at Closing not only be good and marketable, but, in the event Purchaser elects so to purchase such an owner's policy of title insurance, shall be insurable by an ALTA title insurer or other title insurance company reasonably acceptable to Purchaser at its regular rates, without exceptions or reservations to coverage of any type or kind, other than the Permitted Title Exceptions.

Possession of the Property

New York:
If possession is delayed, the contract usually provides for escrow to make sure the premises are left in the condition called for in the contract.

A definite date and time for the purchaser to take possession of the property should be included in every contract. Ideally, the time of possession should follow immediately after the closing. In many situations, however, sellers may have legitimate business or personal reasons for remaining in possession for a few days after closing. For example, in a home sale, it is not unusual for the seller to remain in possession for a few days after the sale, to remove his or her personal effects from the property. If possession is delayed until after closing, the contract should address the issues of maintenance, insurance, loss through fire or other casualty, and rent for the period of the seller's possession after closing.

Closing or Settlement

The **closing** of a contract is the date on which the parties agree to perform all their promises under the contract. In some states, this date is referred to as settlement. It is the time when the purchaser is required to pay the purchase price and the seller is required to transfer title and ownership to the purchaser. The date, time, and, if possible, the place for the closing should be established in the contract (Example 8–6). If the closing date is omitted from the contract, the courts will impose on the parties a reasonable time and place to close the transaction.

EXAMPLE 8-6

Closing Date. Unless this Agreement is terminated by Purchaser pursuant to the terms of this Agreement, the Closing shall take place at the offices of Purchaser's attorneys, or such location as is mutually agreeable to Purchaser and Seller, beginning at 10:00 a.m. on a business day (in Colorado Springs, Colorado) selected by Purchaser on or before November 11, 19___. The date of Closing shall hereinafter be referred to as the "Closing Date." Purchaser shall give Seller notice of the Closing Date at least five (5) business days prior thereto; provided, however, if Purchaser gives Seller no such notice of the Closing Date, then the Closing Date shall be November 11, 19___.

Closing or Settlement Documents

A contract should list the documents that the parties will be expected to sign at closing (Example 8–7). Because, in most cases, a comprehensive list is not available before the closing itself, the parties should be obligated to execute such other documents as are reasonably necessary to carry out the purpose and intent of the contract. Closing documents usually include affidavits of title, settlement statements, deeds of conveyance, bills of sale, and assignments of warranty; notes, security instruments, and assignments of leases also may be included. A full discussion of closing documents appears in Chapter 17. Ideally, all closing forms would be identified and attached as exhibits to the contract; however, time and cost requirements and the fact that most of these documents have taken on a relative standard format have made that somewhat unnecessary. The contract should, however, identify the type of deed that will be executed at closing to convey title to the real property. The deed usually is a general warranty deed, wherein the seller warrants to the purchaser that the title to the real property is free from liens and claims by any parties other than those listed therein and the seller covenants to defend the title represented against any claims. If a contract is silent regarding the form of deed, a general warranty deed will be required. A lesser type of deed, however, can be contracted for. Deeds are discussed fully in Chapter 9.

New York:
New York City usually uses a Bargain & Sale Deed with Covenant against Grantor's Acts. In Upstate New York, the parties may want a Warranty deed. The type of deed to be delivered is indicated in the contract of sale.

EXAMPLE 8-7

Seller's Obligations. At Closing, Seller shall:

(a) Execute, acknowledge, and deliver to Purchaser a general warranty deed in recordable form, the form of which is attached hereto as *Exhibit* ___ conveying the Property to Purchaser subject only to (i) taxes for the years subsequent to the year of Closing; (ii) the zoning classification as of the Effective Date; and (iii) the Permitted Exceptions;

(b) Execute and deliver to Purchaser the following additional conveyance documents: (A) an Affidavit reciting Seller's non-foreign status within the meaning of Section 1445(f)(3) of the Internal Revenue Code of 1986; (B) an Assignment and Assumption of Leases assigning to Purchaser lessor's interest in the Leases, a form of which is attached hereto as *Exhibit* ___; and (C) an Assignment of Contracts, Other Rights, and Intangible Property assigning to Purchaser the Intangible Property, the form of which is attached hereto as *Exhibit* ___; and (D) Lender Estoppel Letter from the holder of the Mortgage Loan, a proposed form of which is attached hereto as *Exhibit* ___; (E) Subordination, Attornment, and Non-Disturbance Agreements satisfactory to Lender signed by tenants leasing at least eighty–five percent (85%) of the net rentable square footage of the Property, a proposed form of which is attached hereto as *Exhibit* ___;

(c) Execute and deliver to Purchaser a Closing Statement setting forth the adjustments and prorations to closing as well as the costs pursuant to this Agreement as elsewhere specifically provided herein (the "Closing Statement");

(d) Deliver to Purchaser a certified and updated rent roll reflecting all the tenants under Leases to the Property as of the Closing Date and indicating thereon any delinquencies with respect to rent due;

(e) Deliver to Purchaser all permits, certificates of occupancy, and licenses issued by Governmental Authorities or utility companies in connection with the occupancy and use of the Improvements as are in the possession of Seller;

(f) Deliver to Purchaser a form letter to all tenants under Leases stating that Purchaser has acquired the Property from Seller, that future rents should be paid as specified by Purchaser, and that Purchaser will be responsible for all tenants' security deposits, if any;

(g) A certificate of Seller stating (A) that Seller has no knowledge of any pending or threat-ened condemnation proceedings or any taking by any Governmental Authority that in any way affects the Property, (B) that there are no Leases (other than Leases approved by Purchaser), no Service Contracts (whether written or oral), no employees, no insurance policy endorsements or claims, no other notices from any Governmental Authority regarding any violations of any Requirements of Law affecting the Property except as heretofore provided to Purchaser as required elsewhere in this Agreement;

(h) The plans and specifications for the Improvements, including all amendments thereto, as are in the possession of Seller;

(i) The originals of all Leases, including all amendments thereto;

(j) All information and materials required for full compliance under the Foreign Investors in Real Property Tax Act;

(k) All keys to the Improvements in Seller's possession and a list of all other persons who, to the best of Seller's knowledge, are in possession of keys to the Improvements, other than keys to tenant space in the possession of tenants;

(l) Such other documents, instruments, and agreements as Purchaser may reasonably require to effect and complete the transactions contemplated herein and to obtain an owner's title insurance policy insuring the interest of Purchaser, as owner, in the amount of $7,300,000.00, free and clear of all exceptions except the Permitted Exceptions, for a premium calculated at standard rates, including, without limitation, a Seller's Affidavit of Title in the form attached hereto as *Exhibit* _____ and a Bill of Sale in the form attached hereto as *Exhibit* _____; and

Purchaser's Obligations at Closing. On the Closing Date, subject to the terms, conditions, and provisions hereof, Purchaser shall:

(a) Execute and deliver to Seller an assumption agreement whereby Purchaser assumes all liabilities and agrees to perform all obligations of Seller under all the Leases, the form of which is contained in *Exhibit* _____, and the Service Contracts and all employee contracts assumed by Purchaser pursuant hereto, the form of which is contained in *Exhibit* _____. Said assumption agreements shall contain an indemnification by Purchaser of Seller and an agreement to hold Seller harmless from and against any and all claims, debts, liabilities, and the like affecting or relating to the Property, or any part thereof, and the Leases after the Closing Date. Likewise, said assumption agreements shall contain an agreement to hold Purchaser harmless from and against any and all claims, debts, liabilities, and the like affecting or relating to the Property, or any part thereof, and the Leases prior to and including the Closing Date.

(b) Execute and deliver to Seller a copy of the Closing Statement.

Proration, Closing Costs, and Financial Adjustments

New York: Proration usually occurs as of midnight the day before closing, and in New York, the purchaser pays for the day of closing and for-ward. Usually prorated adjustments are for taxes, utilities, mort-gage (if it is being assumed), rents, or association fees.

Any item that will be prorated between the parties at the time of sale should be listed in the contract, along with the date of such proration (Example 8–8). These items usually include insurance premiums; property taxes for the current year; rents; inter-est on any loans against the real property that the purchaser is assuming; special assessments, such as sanitation fees, which are liens against the real property; utility charges; and mandatory owners' association fees. The contract should provide for the handling of any items that will be credits to either party and debits to the other, such as fees for utility deposits. Furthermore, a contract should designate which party will pay the costs involved in closing the transaction. These costs include document recording, taxes on transfer, title examination charges, legal fees for each party, survey, title insurance, intangible tax, assumption fees, and loan costs. Closing costs usually are negotiable, and the allocation of these costs will be whatever the parties agree to.

EXAMPLE 8-8

Closing Costs. In connection with Closing, Seller shall pay the Colorado real estate transfer tax and all costs relating to the satisfaction, cure, and removal of all title defects (except the Permitted Exceptions) undertaken by Seller as herein required and the payment of one-half ($^1/_2$) of all transfer, assumption, or other fees due the holder of the Mortgage Loan to obtain the consent to the transfer the Property to the Purchaser and the consent to the Note and Deed of Trust. Purchaser shall pay the costs of the premiums payable or costs incurred in connection with the issuance of the owner's title insurance commitment and the owner's title insurance policy in favor of Purchaser and all costs of recording the general warranty deed. The Purchaser shall be solely responsible for the new survey costs. Each party shall pay its own attorney's fees.

Prorations. The following items shall be apportioned and prorated (based on a 30-day month, unless otherwise indicated) between the Seller and the Purchaser as of the Closing Date so that credits and charges for all days prior to the Closing Date shall be allocated to the Seller and credits and charges for the Closing Date and for all days thereafter shall be allocated to the Purchaser:

(a) *Taxes.* At the Closing, all ad valorem property taxes, water and sewer charges and assessments of any kind on the Property for the year of the Closing shall be prorated between Purchaser and Seller as of 12:01 a.m. on the Closing Date. Such proration shall be based upon the latest ad valorem property tax, water, sewer charge, and assessment bills available. If, upon receipt of the actual ad valorem property tax, water, sewer, and assessment bills for the Property, such proration is incorrect, then either Purchaser or Seller shall be entitled, upon demand, to receive such amounts from the other as may be necessary to correct such malapportionment. This obligation so to correct such malapportionment shall survive the Closing and not be merged into any documents delivered pursuant to the Closing.

(b) *Rents.* Purchaser shall receive a credit for all amounts due under the Leases in effect at Closing, hereinafter referred to as the "Rent," collected by Seller prior to Closing and allocable in whole or in part to any period following the Closing Date. Seller shall deliver to Purchaser any Rent Received after Closing. Purchaser shall deliver to Seller any Rents Received after Closing that relate to periods prior to and through the Closing Date; provided, however, that any such Rents collected by Purchaser after the Closing shall be applied first toward Rents due which shall have accrued after the Closing Date and then toward Rents that accrued prior to the Closing Date. Purchaser shall use its best efforts (short of incurring legal fees and expenses or taking other action that would not be in its best interest as owner of the Property) to collect all such delinquent Rents.

In the event that Purchaser is unable to collect delinquent Rents due Seller within thirty (30) days after the Closing Date, then Seller may pursue collection of such delinquent Rents from the respective Tenants in accordance with its rights under Colorado law; provided, however, Seller shall have no right to collect Rents in any manner that would result in an interference with the Tenant's rights of possession under its lease or in any way interfere with the landlord/tenant relationship between Purchaser and the Tenant. (For example, Seller shall have no rights to dispossess Tenant in an effort to collect delinquent Rents.)

(c) *Other Expense Prorations.* All other reasonable expenses normal to the operation and maintenance of the Property that require payments either in advance or in arrears for periods that begin prior to the Closing Date and end thereafter. Without limiting the generality of the foregoing, such expenses shall include water; electric; telephone and all other utility and fuel charges; fuel on hand (at cost plus sales tax); any deposits with utility companies; employee wages, salaries, benefits and pension, health and welfare insurance, social security, and such other contributions; and charges under employee contracts and/or Service Contracts.

(d) *Security Deposits.* Purchaser shall receive a credit for the security deposits paid under the Leases in existence and in effect on the Closing Date.

(e) *Leasing Commissions.* Seller warrants and represents that there are no leasing commissions due and owing or to become due and owing under any of the Leases or any renewals and extensions thereof, as of the Closing Date. Seller agrees to hold harmless from and to indemnify and defend Purchaser from and against any and all such leasing commissions and all other fees, charges, and compensation whatsoever due any person or entity in connection with the procuring of any Lease together with all extensions and renewals thereof or otherwise relating to any Lease. This provision shall survive the Closing and the consummation of the transactions contemplated herein.

Condition of the Property and Risk of Loss

New York:
New York adopted the Uniform Vendor and Purchaser Risk Act, which provides that the seller (vendor) must bear any loss from a fire that occurs before title passes to the purchaser or the purchaser takes possession, whichever is earlier.

Most contracts provide that the real property will be in substantially the same condition at the time of closing as at the time of contract, natural wear and tear excepted. It is suggested this warranty be extended to the time of possession, if possession should occur after closing. In addition, contracts usually provide that heating, plumbing, and electrical systems will be in normal working order at the time of closing and further provide that the purchaser has the right and obligation to make inspection of these systems before closing. Many contracts provide the purchaser with a right of inspection or "walk through" before closing and require the seller to repair any items found in need of repair as a result of that inspection. Sellers often limit in the contract their responsibility to make repairs to the expenditure of a fixed sum of money, and the contract provides that if the repairs exceed the fixed sum of money, the purchaser does not have to purchase the real property.

A contract also should indicate which party bears the risk of loss by fire or other casualty to the real property during the contract period (Example 8–9). In most states, the purchaser bears the risk of loss unless the contract provides otherwise. Most purchasers are unaware of this rule, and many do not buy insurance until the day before closing. The contract should allocate the risk of loss during the contract period to the seller. The contract should indicate whether options are available to the purchaser if the real property should be partially damaged or totally destroyed before closing. These options might include consummating the transaction and receiving the proceeds of any insurance settlement resulting from the loss or requiring the seller to restore the real property with insurance proceeds or termination of the contract.

EXAMPLE 8-9

Risk of Loss. Risk of loss or damage to the Property or any part thereof by condemnation, eminent domain, or similar proceedings, or by deed in lieu or under threat thereof (collectively, a "Taking"), or by fire, flood, or other casualty from the effective date of the contract until delivery of the limited warranty deed will be on Seller and after the delivery of the limited warranty deed will be on Purchaser. In the event of any such loss or damage to all or to a material part of the Property or any part of the Improvements prior to the delivery of the general warranty deed, this Agreement may, at the option of Purchaser to be exercised by written notice to Seller, be declared null and void and Purchaser shall be returned the Deposit and both parties hereto shall be released from any further rights and duties hereunder, or this Agreement shall remain in full force and effect and Seller shall transfer to Purchaser on the Closing Date all insurance proceeds or condemnation awards received by Seller because of such casualty or Taking and all of Seller's rights, title, and interest in and to any recovery or claims under any insurance policies or condemnation awards relating to the Property.

Upon the happening of one of the events in the preceding paragraph, subsequent to the Inspection Deadline and prior to delivery of the general warranty deed, if the cost of repair or replacement or, in the event of a Taking, if the reduction in the value of the project is TWENTY-FIVE THOUSAND DOLLARS ($25,000.00) or less, Purchaser shall close and take the Property as diminished by such events and Seller shall transfer to Purchaser on the Closing Date all insurance proceeds or condemnation awards received by Seller because of such casualty or Taking and all of Seller's right, title, and interest in and to any recovery or claim under any insurance policies or condemnation awards relating to the Property together with a credit to Purchaser for the amount of any deductibles contained in any insurance policy.

Earnest Money

Earnest money is money paid by the purchaser at the time the contract is signed. It is not easy to describe what role in the contract the earnest money plays. Earnest money is not consideration for the contract unless the contract specifically provides so. Earnest money is not a partial payment of the purchase price unless so designated and delivered to the seller. Earnest money is not a prepaid penalty unless so provided in the contract. At best, earnest money seems to be a token deposit made to evidence the purchaser's intent to be bound by the terms of the contract (i.e., a showing of good faith). The contract should provide for the disposition of the earnest money in every possible situation (e.g., consummation of the transaction, default by seller, default by purchaser, failure of a contingency, exercise of an election to void the contract granted to either party, mutual termination of the contract) and for what purpose the earnest money deposit is to be used (Example 8–10). In addition, if real estate brokers are involved, a contract should take into account what claims, if any, the brokers may have on the earnest money deposit in all such events. Earnest money often is placed in a trust or an escrow interest-bearing account. Contracts should provide what quality of account it is to be invested in, for example, FDIC (Federal Deposit Insurance Corporation)-insured deposits. In addition, the contract should make it clear who is to get the interest. The party who is entitled to the interest should provide the holder of the escrow deposit with their federal tax identification number.

New York:
In New York the contract down payment is called down payment or deposit (it is called earnest money elsewhere). See Appendix for discussion.

EXAMPLE 8–10

Earnest Money Deposits. Purchaser shall deliver its earnest money deposit to Colorado Title Company (the "Escrowee") upon Purchaser's execution of this Agreement in the form of a cashier's check (drawn on a Colorado financial institution) in the sum of SEVENTY-FIVE THOUSAND DOLLARS ($75,000.00) (the "Earnest Money"), made payable to Escrowee in trust (said Earnest Money together with any interest earned thereon shall hereinafter be referred to as the "Deposit". The Deposit shall be held and disbursed by Escrowee as provided in this Agreement.

The Escrowee is directed to hold the Deposit as escrowed funds in an FDIC-insured, interest-bearing account, at The Second National Bank in Colorado Springs, Colorado. Purchaser represents that its U.S. federal tax identification number is 86–11314. Purchaser's tax identification number shall be credited with any interest earned on the Earnest Money prior to its being disbursed by Escrowee. Purchaser shall complete and execute a Payer's Request for Taxpayer

Identification Number (Form W-9). Seller and Purchaser hereby agree to hold Escrowee harmless from any loss of escrowed funds, including the Deposit, for any reason whatsoever except for Escrowee's fraud or gross negligence or for loss of interest caused by any delay in the deposit or early withdrawal of the Deposit, from the interest-bearing account. This Agreement shall serve as escrow instructions and an executed copy of this Agreement shall be deposited by Purchaser with Escrowee. At Closing, the Deposit shall be delivered to Seller and applied against the Purchase Price. In the event of a termination of this Agreement or a default under this Agreement, the Deposit shall be delivered or disbursed by the Escrowee as provided in this Agreement. If any dispute or difference arises between the Purchaser and Seller or if any conflicting demands be made upon the Escrowee, the Escrowee shall not be required to determine the same or to take any action thereon. Rather, the Escrowee may await settlement of the controversy or deposit the Deposit into the Registry of the Superior Court of Elk County, Colorado, in an interpleader action or otherwise for the purpose of having the respective rights of the parties adjudicated. Upon making such deposit or upon institution of such interpleader action or other actions, the Escrowee shall be fully relieved and discharged from all further obligations hereunder with respect to the sums so deposited.

Should any party terminate this Agreement, as permitted herein, or declare the other party in default of its obligations hereunder, and demand payment of the Deposit to it, then Escrowee shall pay to it the Deposit, provided that declaring party provides evidence of the other party's receiving its demand notice, and within seven (7) business days following the other party's receipt of same, the nondeclaring party has not delivered written objection to Escrowee's disbursing the Deposit. If any dispute arises that is not resolved within thirty (30) days after such written objection, Escrowee shall deposit the Deposit into the Registry of the Superior Court of Elk County, Colorado, whereupon Escrowee's obligations and liabilities hereunder shall cease and terminate.

Brokers

If a real estate broker is involved, the contract should provide for the rights of the broker to a commission and the obligations incumbent on the broker under the contract (Example 8–11). It is not unusual for contracts to provide that the commission will be payable only on the closing of the transaction and in accordance with the terms of the contract. In addition, if the seller should not receive full proceeds at closing, the payment of the commission might be tied to the subsequent receipt of such proceeds. This usually is done by requiring the broker to accept a note from the seller as part payment of the commission. The note requires a payment in the same ratio and at the same time the seller receives payment from the purchaser and conditions the seller's obligations to pay on purchaser's receipt of buyer's payments. For example, if the sales price is being paid in four equal annual installments, the contract may provide that the real estate commission will be paid by the seller to the broker in four equal annual installment payments at the same time the seller receives payment from the purchaser.

New York:
The contract should provide for a broker's commission and indicate there is a separate agreement giving the details. This commission agreement should be obtained prior to signing the contract.

Many preprinted contract forms used by realty or broker associations provide that the commission will be payable to the broker in full at closing. They also provide that a default of either purchaser or seller will enable the broker to enforce commission rights against the defaulting party, usually by application of the earnest money. In addition, the contract may include statements to the effect that neither party has relied on warranties or representations made by the broker, but rather only those made by the other parties; that the broker is acting for the accommodation of the parties in holding earnest money and is therefore indemnified by each against any claims in connection therewith; and that the broker is the procuring cause of the contract. A broker should be made a party of the contract to enforce commission rights.

If no broker is involved in the transaction, a contract should so indicate and have the parties mutually indemnify each other against the possible claims of brokers resulting from the actions of each.

EXAMPLE 8–11

Brokerage Commissions. Each party further represents to the other that except for American Realty Company ("Broker"), no broker has been involved in this transaction. Seller shall be solely responsible for paying any commission due to the Broker in connection with this transaction. Seller shall pay in cash or good funds at Closing brokerage commissions of one percent (1%) to Broker. No commission shall be due and owing Broker should the sale and purchase of the Property fail to close for any reason whatsoever, including, without limitation, the breach of this Agreement by Seller or Purchaser. Under no circumstances whatsoever shall Broker be entitled to retain any portion of the Deposit. In the event any other claims for brokerage commissions or fees are ever made against the Seller or the Purchaser in connection with this transaction, all such claims shall be handled and paid by the party whose actions or alleged commitments form the basis of such claim. Seller further agrees to indemnify and hold harmless the Purchaser from and against any and all such claims or demands with respect to any brokerage fees or agent's commissions or other compensation asserted by any person, firm, or corporation in connection with this Agreement or the transactions contemplated hereby arising from actions or alleged commitments of the Seller. Purchaser further agrees to indemnify and hold harmless the Seller from and against any and all such claims or demands with respect to any brokerage fees or agent's commission or other compensation asserted by any person, firm, or corporation in connection with this Agreement or the transaction contemplated hereby arising from actions or alleged commitments of the Purchaser. This provision shall survive Closing and the conveyance of the Property by Seller to Purchaser.

Survival

The law in many states provides that all the promises, conditions, and covenants contained in a contract are merged into the deed of conveyance at the time of closing and do not survive the closing of the sale. This rule can be circumvented by providing in the contract that all provisions shall survive closing or by having the parties sign at closing an agreement for the survival of warranties, representations, and obligations of the parties contained in the contract (Example 8–12).

EXAMPLE 8–12

Survival. The provisions of this Agreement shall survive Closing and the execution and delivery of the deed and instruments conveying the Property.

Assignment of Contract

The general rule is that contracts are freely assignable by the purchaser and seller unless assignment is prohibited in the contract. Most sellers do not agree to the unlimited assignability of the contract by the purchaser. This is particularly true when a unique relationship exists between the parties that is, at least in part, the reason the seller has entered into the contract, for example, when the seller is extending credit for a portion of the price and is relying on the financial strength of the purchaser, or when the seller is giving preferential price or terms to a friend or relative. It is, therefore, not uncommon for a contract to contain a provision requiring the seller's written consent before the assignment of the purchaser's interest. The giving of consent to assignment can be conditioned on, among other things, the proposed assignees' agreeing to assume all obligations binding on the assignor under the contract and being bound by all terms of the contract as if an original party. In addition, a seller may require the original purchaser to agree to remain liable for damages if the assignee should default under the contract. If, at the time of contracting, there exists a possibility that the purchaser may desire to close the sale in some name other than that in which the contract is executed—for example, a general or limited partnership or a corporation not yet in existence—the contract also should provide for the seller's consent (Example 8–13).

EXAMPLE 8–13

Assignability. Purchaser shall not have the right to assign this Agreement to any person(s), partnership, or corporation, including a partnership or corporation to be formed hereafter, without the consent of Seller. In the event of such assignment, the assignee shall assume the obligations of Purchaser under this Agreement, and Purchaser shall have no further obligation or liability under this Agreement. Seller may assign its rights but shall remain bound under the terms of this Agreement and the representations, warranties, and covenants contained herein.

Time Is of the Essence

New York:
Normally, the contract sets a closing date, which is interpreted to be "on or about" and the parties normally have a reasonable period, usually 30 days to close. Closings rarely take place on the date called for in the contract. If the contract states "time is of the essence," then the closing date is crucial and the contract must be performed on that date. Whoever does not close on that date is in default and is liable for damages. This type of clause could penalize either side and should be used with caution.

The general rule is that time limits set forth in a contract are not strictly enforceable unless **time is of the essence**. If time is not of the essence, then a date for performance is not an exact critical date. The courts will permit performance to take place within a reasonable period of time after the date specified in the contract. For example, if the closing date is August 15 and time is not of the essence, the courts will permit the parties to close within a reasonable period of time after August 15. Most sellers and purchasers do not want to operate within the nebulous realm of reasonable time and so desire that dates set forth in a contract be critical and strictly enforceable. Therefore, every contract should contain a provision that time is of the essence for the contract and for each and every obligation of the purchaser and seller (Example 8–14). The phrase most often used is simply "time is of the essence."

EXAMPLE 8–14

Time. Time is of the essence of this Agreement and of each of its provisions.

Warranties of the Parties

Any warranty, statements, or representations made by either the seller or the purchaser that were relied on by the other in deciding to enter the contract for purchase and sale of the property should be affirmatively set out in the contract (Example 8–15). Warranties commonly required of a seller include the following: (a) that the seller holds title to the real property of equal quality to that which the seller is required to convey; (b) that the seller will perform all duties and obligations of the contract; (c) that the seller has the right and full authority to enter into the contract;

(d) that no other party is expressing any claim to any portion of the real property and the seller will take no action before closing that would diminish the quality of title; (e) that the seller will make no change in the zoning of the real property; (f) that the seller is aware of no pending governmental action that will affect the real property or burden it with additional assessments; (g) that utilities are available to the real property; (h) that the real property is accessible by way of public roads; and (i) that the real property contains a minimum number of acres or square feet or has a minimum amount of frontage on a public street.

Warranties commonly asked for from a purchaser are (a) that the purchaser has the right and authority to enter into the agreement; (b) that the purchaser has financial resources to meet the financial obligations required under the contract; (c) that the purchaser will perform its duties in accordance with the agreement; and (d) that no parties have initiated or threatened any action that might affect the purchaser's ability to perform; and (e) that the purchaser will take no action that would diminish the quality of the seller's title before closing.

It is a good idea to have the parties reaffirm the warranties and representations at closing by separate instrument. The contract should provide that the parties will sign such a separate instrument at closing. Contracts also usually provide for the rights and obligations of the parties in the event that any warranty proves untrue. Specifically, the contract will provide that in the event a warranty proves untrue, a party can either terminate the contract or treat such failure as a default under the contract and exercise all its remedies for default.

EXAMPLE 8-15

(a) *Seller's Covenants and Representations.*

(i) Seller has obtained all consents, approvals, or authorizations necessary to execute this Agreement and to consummate the transaction contemplated hereby, and all documents referred to herein will be validly executed and delivered and binding upon Seller.

(ii) Seller has no knowledge of any material defect in the Improvements or any part thereof and has no knowledge of and has received no notice from any Governmental Authority (as defined below) of any violation of any Requirement of Law (as defined below) relating to the Property or any part thereof;

(iii) Seller has no knowledge of and has received no notice from any insurance company or board of fire underwriters or similar agency that there exists any condition or circumstances on the Property or any part thereof, which must be corrected in order to maintain the effectiveness, or as a condition precedent to the issuance of, any insurance policy affecting the Property or any part thereof or which is in violation of, any applicable fire code or similar rule, regulation, or order for such board of fire underwriters or similar agency;

(iv) Seller has no knowledge of and has received no notice of any litigation, claim, or suit that is pending or threatened that could adversely affect the Property or any part thereof or title thereto (exclusive of any litigation, claim, or suit brought against a tenant of the Property after the effective date of the contract wherein Seller is not named a defendant or a third party defendant and wherein no counterclaims are alleged against Seller, provided, however, that Seller will give Purchaser prompt notice of all such litigation, claims, and suits);

(v) Neither Seller nor, to the best of Seller's knowledge, any previous owner of the Property or any part thereof has used, generated, stored, or disposed of any Hazardous Materials (as defined below) in or on the Property or any part thereof; or has used or disposed of any Hazardous Materials in connection with the use, operation, construction, or repair of the Property or any part thereof. Seller shall hold Purchaser harmless and shall indemnify and defend Purchaser from and against any and all losses, damages, claims, and liabilities whatsoever in any way relating to or arising out of any breach of the foregoing representation. This provision shall survive Closing and the consummation of the transactions contemplated hereby;

(vi) Seller owns good and unencumbered title to the Tangible Personal Property and Intangible Personal Property, and Seller has done nothing to encumber same during Seller's ownership thereof other than those certain Loan Documents listed on *Exhibit* ____ attached hereto;

(vii) Seller has not operated the Property within the past five (5) years under any other name or trade name of which it has not notified Purchaser;

(viii) Seller shall not cause or permit to exist (A) any mortgage, deed to secure debt, security deed, security agreement, assignment, or other similar instrument or agreement or any lien or encumbrance whatsoever (other than the Permitted Exceptions or those listed on *Exhibit* ____) to attach to or affect title to the Property or any part thereof from and after the Effective Date except for the Leases approved by Purchaser; or (B) any matters not shown on the new survey;

(ix) Seller represents, to the best of its knowledge, that the mechanical, electrical, plumbing, HVAC, roofing, drainage, sanitary sewerage, and utility equipment facilities and systems servicing the Property and the improvements thereon are in operational order and shall be so maintained through and including the Closing Date. Seller represents that it is aware of no defects in any of said systems;

(x) Seller covenants that it shall not enter into any leases pertaining to the Property after the Effective Date without prior written approval of Purchaser. Purchaser shall approve leases containing reasonable business terms, including base rentals of at least $16.00 per square foot and $1.75 of C.A.M. Seller covenants and represents that it shall incur no brokerage commissions pertaining to leases entered into prior to the Closing Date on any leases negotiated in any respect by Seller prior to the Closing Date;

(xi) Seller represents that it has no notice of and is not aware of any violation of the Property and improvements of any applicable zoning laws, ordinances, or regulations including, without limitation, all parking requirements and building setback requirements (except as shown on the existing survey, which Purchaser has the right to consider during the inspection period);

(xii) Seller shall continue to operate, manage, and maintain the Property in good condition and in a good businesslike manner, such operation and maintenance to include the undertaking of any reasonably necessary capital improvements or repairs, through and including the Closing Date. Such continuous operation and maintenance shall also be a condition precedent to Closing; and

(b) *Purchaser's Covenants and Representations.* Purchaser hereby represents and warrants to Seller that Purchaser has obtained all consents, approvals, or authorizations necessary to execute this Agreement and to consummate the transaction contemplated hereby, and all documents referred to herein will be validly executed and delivered and binding upon Purchaser.

Contingencies

A **condition precedent** in a contract is a situation that must be resolved in accordance with the terms of the contract before one or both of the parties are required to perform their contractual obligations. These elements are called conditional clauses of the contract, or contingencies. A contract can be made conditional on virtually anything. Some of the more common contingencies include financing, rezoning, sale of other property, purchase of adjacent property, engineering reports, issuance of building or use permits, and review of documents affecting title to the property. In drafting conditional clauses, exact standards by which the parties can determine when and if the condition has been met must be provided. In addition, the contract should require the parties to use due diligence and good faith in attempting to meet

New York:
Contract clauses that are conditional, that is, conditioned on purchaser obtaining a mortgage commitment are truly "escape" clauses for the buyer. Sellers always wish to limit these. In New York many contracts are sold "subject" to a satisfactory engineer's report or termite report. These conditions normally must be satisfied within a short period, i.e. purchaser has two weeks to obtain an engineer's report and will notify seller if it is acceptable, etc.

the contingency. For example, a common contingency found in contracts is the financing contingency. This contingency means that the purchaser does not have an obligation to purchase the property unless the purchaser can obtain an acceptable loan for a large portion of the purchase price. Financing contingencies usually require that the contingency set forth the amount of the loan, the interest rate, and the repayment term of the loan that the purchaser is seeking to obtain. A financing contingency also requires the purchaser to make an application for a loan and to diligently try to obtain the loan. A failure to meet a condition precedent would make a contract unenforceable. Most contracts provide for repercussions in the event a contingency fails with regard not only to the contract as a whole, but to any earnest money as well. The contract also should indicate for whose benefit the condition applies and provide if either party has a right to waive the conditions.

Definitions

Although most terms and phrases used in a contract take on their ordinary meanings, many contracts include a definitions section that carefully and clearly defines key words and phrases. This is particularly important when the parties are not from the same geographical area and the possibility exists for misunderstanding as to the exact meaning of certain terms.

Default

A contract should provide the exact rights and obligations of the parties in the event that one party fails to perform in accordance with the terms of the contract. The contract also should list the events that constitute a default.

Notice

Because most contracts provide that parties need to notify each other of different events, such as title objections, date for closing, and results of inspection reports, there should be a paragraph that outlines when and how notices are to be given (Example 8–16). Most notice provisions deal with personal delivery and certified mail, although under modern practice, contracts should consider overnight express carriers as well as telephone facsimile transmissions. If one of the parties is a partnership or corporation, the contract should specify an individual to receive notice.

EXAMPLE 8-16

Notification. Any notice or demand under which the terms of this Agreement or under any statute must or may be given or made by the parties hereto shall be made in writing and shall be deemed to have been delivered when hand delivered; as of the date sent by an overnight courier; or as of the date of postmark affixed by the U.S. Postal Service, by mailing the same by certified mail return receipt requested addressed to the respective parties at the following addresses:

To Purchaser: Purchaser, Inc.
                                                535 East Paces Ferry Road
                                                Denver, Colorado
                                                Attn: George Purchaser

To Seller: c/o JoAnne Seller
                                                2970 Crabtree Road, N.W.

Suite 500

Colorado Springs, Colorado

Such addresses may be changed by the giving of written notice as provided in this paragraph; provided, however, that any mailed notice of changed address shall not be effective until the fifth (5th) day after the date of postmark by the U.S. Postal Service.

Entire Agreement

The **parol evidence rule** that is applicable in most states provides that a written agreement is the best and only evidence of the agreement between the parties and that the parties are not permitted to bring in oral testimony regarding other agreements concerning the transaction. The law in many states, however, requires that the contract contain a clause that indicates that it is the entire agreement and that no other written or oral agreements affecting the transaction exist (Example 8–17). Typically, the clause states that "the contract contains the entire agreement of the parties thereto concerning the subject matter thereof and that representations, inducements, promises, or agreements oral or otherwise not expressly set forth therein shall be of any force or effect."

In addition, the contract should provide that it cannot be amended or modified unless in writing and executed by all parties thereto.

EXAMPLE 8–17

Entire Agreement. No agreements, representations, or warranties unless expressly incorporated or set forth in this Agreement shall be binding upon any of the parties.

Applicable Law

The general rule in most states is that a contract for the sale and purchase of real property will be governed by the law of the state in which the real property is located. Despite this general rule, most contracts do specify the law of the state that will govern the construction and enforcement of the contract (Example 8–18).

EXAMPLE 8–18

This Agreement shall be construed and interpreted under the Laws of the State of Colorado.

Additional Provisions

It is not unusual, when using a preprinted form, to find additional provisions added to the contract by way of addendum or exhibit. It is important that there be a provision in the contract that provides that if conflict between the preprinted portion of the contract and the special stipulations contained in the addendum or exhibit should arise, the special stipulations will control.

Offer and Acceptance

Because most contracts are not signed at the same time by both seller and purchaser but are prepared by the seller or the purchaser and presented to the other party for consideration, it is important that the contract contain a clause that addresses the issue of when and how the offer is to be accepted and converted into a contract. This usually is done by a provision that indicates that the contract represents an offer that must be accepted by the signature of the other party to the contract on or before a certain date (Example 8–19).

In addition, it is preferable to make the date of the contract a certain date, especially if other dates, such as the date for doing a title examination or inspection of the property, are calculated from the date of the contract. For example, the purchaser must examine title and present objections to the seller not later than thirty days from the date of contract.

EXAMPLE 8-19

This instrument shall be regarded as an offer by the Purchaser or Seller who first signs to the other and is open for acceptance by the other until _____ o'clock _____.m., on this _____ day of _____, 19_____ by which time written acceptance of such offer must have been actually received.

The above offer is hereby accepted, _____ o'clock _____.m. on this _____ day of _____, 19_____.

Execution

The seller, purchaser, and other parties to a contract should **execute** the contract properly and in accordance with their authority (Example 8–20). It is not necessary for real estate contracts to be witnessed and notarized, and real estate contracts usually are not recorded. From the seller's perspective, recording of the contract is not advisable because if the contract is not closed, the record of the contract might represent a cloud on the property title, thus creating future problems for the seller.

EXAMPLE 8-20

IN WITNESS WHEREOF, the parties hereto have set their hands and seals as of the Effective Date.

PURCHASER:
PURCHASER, INC., a Colorado
corporation

By: _____ (SEAL)
    George W. Purchaser,
    President
Date Executed: _____

    SELLER:
_____ (SEAL)
    JoAnne Seller
_____ (SEAL)
    Alice Seller Longworth
_____ (SEAL)
    Warren Seller
    Date Executed: _____

> The undersigned as Escrowee hereby acknowledges receipt of a copy of this Agreement and of the initial Earnest Money deposit by check $_____ drawn on _____, subject to collection, and agrees to hold said funds pursuant to the terms of this Agreement.
>
> COLORADO TITLE COMPANY
>
> Dated: _____   By: _____
>
> Charles B. Jares, as
> Executive Vice President

The above is by no means an exhaustive list of all possible areas of concern in preparing or reviewing a real estate sales contract. The outline does touch on the major issues that a legal assistant can expect a real estate contract to address. A legal assistant should remember that each contract is unique and should reflect the agreement between the parties to that particular transaction. Drafting and reviewing a comprehensive sales contract requires time and careful attention to detail but should ultimately reduce the possibility of later misunderstanding between the parties.

SPECIAL COMMERCIAL CONTRACT ISSUES

The purchase and sale of a commercial investment property, such as a shopping center, office building, or apartment project, presents some special concerns for the purchaser and seller. The purpose of the following discussion is to itemize and briefly describe some of the provisions and issues that need to be addressed in the commercial real estate sale contract.

Description of the Property

The sale of a commercial real property includes more than just the real estate. Most apartment projects and office buildings contain a number of personal property items that are used in the maintenance and repair of the real property. These personal property items, such as snow removal equipment, irrigation systems, landscaping, and washing and dryer services, all need to be described and included within the description of the property being bought and sold. In addition, many times a parcel of commercial real property is being operated under a certain trade name, such as Brook Tree Apartments or Corporate Campus Office Center. The purchaser should obtain the rights to these trade names, and a provision for this assignment and transfer should be contained in the contract (see Example 8–3).

Representations, Warranties, and Covenants

In addition to the normal representations, warranties, and covenants made by a seller in a real estate contract, there are a number of additional representations, warranties, and covenants that normally are part of a commercial contract (see Example 8–15).

Warranties Regarding Leases

Most commercial properties are income-producing, which means that the real property has been leased to tenants. There usually is a warranty on the part of the seller that all the leases, agreements, rent rolls, and income and expense statements that had been previously delivered to the purchaser are true and correct. The seller also

usually agrees not to enter into any new leases during the contract period before closing without the purchaser's consent, or in the alternative, the contract will provide
certain rental guidelines, such as how much rent and term of the lease for the seller
to follow.

Service Contracts

Many commercial properties involve contracts for such services as janitorial, landscaping, and pest control. The seller should warrant that the copies of the service
contracts that have been provided to the purchaser are true and correct copies. The
seller also should warrant that it will not enter into any new service contracts before
closing or, in the alternative, will not enter into any service contracts that are not terminable within thirty days' notice.

No Litigation Affecting Seller or Property

The owners of commercial properties are more likely to have litigation filed against
them than the owners of homes. It is not unusual in large commercial projects for
there to be litigation between the owner and one or more of the tenants. There also
may be litigation against the seller in regard to accidents, such as a slip and fall in a
supermarket. Most commercial contracts require the seller to warrant that there is no
litigation either pending or threatened against the seller or the real property. If there
is litigation, the full disclosure of the litigation should be made in the contract. If litigation is threatened or pending, the purchaser usually wants indemnities from the
seller regarding the outcome of the litigation.

Purchaser's Inspection or "Free Look"

Most purchasers of commercial properties require that they be given a period of time
after the contract has been signed to inspect the real property. If during this inspection the property is found to be unacceptable, the purchaser can terminate the contract and receive a return of his earnest money. This inspection period is called a
"free look" because the purchaser has a period of time to decide whether or not to
buy the real property and can terminate during this period of time without any liability. Most inspections by purchasers of commercial properties go beyond just an
inspection of the physical condition of the real property. During the inspection period, the purchaser requires the seller to furnish copies of all leases, service contracts,
tenant correspondence files, tax notices, insurance premiums, operating and expense
reports, and any other documentation that in any way has an effect on the operation
or ownership of the real property.

Most contracts provide that the inspection period will not begin to run until the
items have been furnished by the seller to the purchaser. The contract usually provides that because this information regarding the real property is private and of a sen-
sitive nature, the purchaser agrees to keep such information confidential and will not
disseminate the information to anyone without the seller's permission. Practically
speaking, permission to provide the financial information concerning the property to
a lender usually is required because most purchasers require institutional lender
financing to purchase the commercial real property.

Closing Documents

The sale of a commercial real property requires several special closing documents in addition to the normal closing documents. Most purchasers require that the seller provide at closing a certified current rent roll and expense report. Purchasers also require that all leases be assigned, together with credits for all security deposits and prepaid rents (see Example 8–7). Purchasers also may require that each tenant sign an **estoppel letter** (Example 8–21). The average tenant estoppel letter has the tenant certify as to the accuracy of certain things regarding a lease, such as the date of the lease, date of amendments or modifications, term of the lease, renewal options, monthly rents, and security deposits. The estoppel letter also requires the tenant to swear that there are no defaults under the lease either by tenant or landlord and that the tenant has no claims, counterclaims, defenses, or setoffs against the landlord arising from the lease. A copy of the lease with all amendments is attached to the letter, and the tenant certifies that it is a true and correct copy of the lease. If the lease is guaranteed, the guarantor joins in the tenant estoppel letter.

EXAMPLE 8–21

Date: , 199___

Office Park Investments, Inc.
P.O. Box 510
Andersonville, Indiana

Re: *Farris Center Office Park*

Gentlemen:

It is our understanding that Office Park Investments, Inc. (hereinafter called "Purchaser") intends to purchase the above-captioned premises, and as a condition precedent, such Purchaser requires that this certification be made by the undersigned (hereinafter called "Tenant").

As an inducement to Purchaser to purchase the premises, and knowing that Purchaser will rely upon the information and agreements contained herein in making said purchase, Tenant hereby acknowledges, certifies, warrants, and covenants that:

1. Tenant presently leases approximately _____ square feet of space located on the above-referenced premises, pursuant to the terms and provisions of that certain Lease Agreement dated _____, 199___, by and between _____, as Landlord, and Tenant, as Lessee, a copy of said Lease being attached hereto and made a part hereof as Exhibit "A" (the "Lease").

2. Said Lease is in full force and effect and Tenant is primarily liable as Lessee thereunder, and the documents attached hereto as Exhibit "A" constitute a full, complete, and accurate copy of said Lease, and said Lease has not been modified, supplemented, or amended in any way, and there are no other promises, obligations, understandings, agreements, or commitments between Landlord and Tenant with respect to said premises other than as expressly set forth in said Lease.

3. All contingencies and conditions precedent to the commencement, effectiveness, validity, and enforceability of said Lease have been satisfied, and Tenant hereby ratifies said Lease. All duties of an inducement nature and all work required under said Lease to be performed by Landlord have been satisfactorily completed in accordance with the provisions of said Lease, and Tenant claims no offsets, rebates, concessions, abatements, recoupments, or defenses against or with respect to rent, additional rent, or other sums payable under the terms of said Lease, and there are no breaches or defaults under the terms of said Lease, and no event has occurred that, with the passage of time or the giving of notice, or both, shall constitute a default by Landlord or Tenant under the terms of said Lease.

4. The base monthly rental currently payable by Tenant under the terms of said Lease is _____ ($_____) Dollars per month, and no other rent

has been prepaid to Landlord or any other party, and there has been no security deposit paid to or currently held by Landlord with respect to said Lease.

5. The Lease Term pursuant to said Lease commenced on _____, 19___, and shall expire on _____, _____.

6. Tenant has no interest, rights, or claims with respect to said premises other than the interest, rights, or claims arising out of or with respect to said Lease.

7. Tenant is a corporation and is in good standing with the State of Indiana, and has full authority to execute the within document.

8. The undersigned officers of Tenant have full authority to execute and deliver this certificate as agents for and on behalf of Tenant.

9. Tenant is currently in actual, full, and complete physical occupancy and possession of said premises, and Tenant has accepted said premises as suitable for all uses and purposes contemplated or intended under said Lease.

10. Upon acquisition of said premises by Purchaser, Tenant shall attorn to Purchaser or any successor or assign of Purchaser's and recognize such party as Tenant's Lessor and Landlord pursuant to said Lease.

Very truly yours,

_____

By: _____
President

Lender's Estoppel

Many commercial real properties are sold subject to existing debt. The purchaser assumes or takes subject to the prior mortgage. Most commercial purchasers require that the prior mortgage holder sign an estoppel certificate and that the certificate be provided to the purchaser at closing (Example 8–22). A lender's estoppel usually requires the lender to attach a copy of the note and mortgage to the certificate and to certify that the attachments are true and correct copies and that there are no amendments or modifications to the note and mortgage. The estoppel also requires a certification as to the outstanding balance of the loan and a certification as to the balance of any escrows that may be held for taxes or insurance. The lender also certifies that the loan is not in default and that the sale of the real property to the purchaser shall not constitute a default. The lender acknowledges the purchaser's address for purposes of sending notices under the note and mortgage. An example of a lender estoppel letter is set forth below.

EXAMPLE 8–22

STATE OF _____
COUNTY OF _____

ESTOPPEL CERTIFICATE

The undersigned hereby certifies as of the date of execution hereof as follows:

(a) That the undersigned (the "Holder") is the holder of a certain Promissory Note dated May 11, 1991, from ACME DEVELOPMENT, INC., a California corporation, in the original principal amount of $3,560,000.00 (the "Note");

(b) That the Note is secured by a Deed of Trust from ACME DEVELOPMENT, INC. to Holder (the "Lender") dated May 11, 1991, and recorded in Deed Book 7244, Page 301, Oil County, California, records (the "Security Deed"), which encumbers certain property located in Oil County, California (the "Property"), more particularly described on Exhibit "A" attached hereto and made a part hereof;

(c) That true and correct copies of the Note and Security Deed are attached hereto as Exhibits "B" and "C";

(d) That the Note and Security Deed are in full force and effect and there have been no events of default in connection therewith;

(e) That all payments of interest and principal under the Note and Security Deed are current; that as of this date the outstanding principal balance due on the Note is $_____, that the last payment received on the Note was on the _____ day of _____, 19_____; and that the next payment on the Note is due on _____;

(f) Holder understands that HAMMOND CENTER, INC. is purchasing the property subject to the Security Deed; the purchase of the property is hereby consented to and approved and shall not constitute an event of default in connection with the Note or Security Deed;

(g) That there is no failure of compliance, breach, default, or event of default that has occurred in the Note or Security Deed as of this date;

(h) Holder agrees to provide to HAMMOND CENTER, INC., Suite 120, 450 Glenlake Parkway, San Diego, California, notice of any default under the Note or Security Deed and permit HAMMOND CENTER, INC. fifteen (15) days to cure any default under the Note or Security Deed, prior to Holder's acceleration of the Note. The undersigned acknowledges that Hammond Center, Inc. is relying on this Certificate in connection with its purchase of the property.

WITNESS my hand and seal this _____ day of _____, 19_____.

THE SECOND NATIONAL BANK

By _____ (SEAL)

[CORPORATE SEAL]

Signed, sealed, and delivered
in the presence of:

_____

Witness

Sworn to before me
this _____ day of
_____, 19_____.

_____

Notary Public
My Commission Expires:

_____

Rent Prorations

The proration between purchaser and seller of rent received from tenants occupying commercial real property is always contained in a commercial contract (Examples 8–23 through 8–25). Rent proration questions can be dealt with in a number of ways. The following issues, however, should be at least considered and addressed in any commercial rent proration provision: (a) Are rents to be prorated on the basis of rent paid or rent payable; that is, is the seller to receive credit at closing for rents that are delinquent or due but unpaid? (b) If the seller does not receive credit at closing for delinquent or due but unpaid rents, is the seller to be permitted to proceed against tenants of the project after closing to collect such rents allocable to periods before the closing date? The purchaser may object to permitting the seller to do this because it can unreasonably interfere with the purchaser's tenants at that time. (c) If the seller is not permitted to proceed against the tenants after closing to collect delinquent or due but unpaid rents, is the purchaser to have any obligation to the seller to make an effort with respect to this collection? In what order are funds received from tenants owing delinquent or due but unpaid rents to be applied? The following are sample provisions regarding prorations of rent.

EXAMPLE 8-23

All paid rents under the existing leases and the new leases shall be prorated as of the closing date. In the event that, at the time of closing, there are any past due or delinquent rents owing by any tenants of the project, Buyer shall have the exclusive right to collect such past due or delinquent rents and shall remit to Seller its pro rata share thereof, to the extent, and only to the extent, that the aggregate rents received by Buyer from each such tenant owing past due or delinquent rents exceeds the sum of (i) the aggregate rents and other sums payable by such tenant for periods from and after the closing date, (ii) any amounts expended by Buyer to collect such past due or delinquent rents. Buyer shall have no obligation to collect or enforce collection of any such past due or delinquent rents from or against a tenant.

EXAMPLE 8-24

Current rent paid under the existing leases and the new leases for the month in which the closing date occurs shall be prorated as of the closing date. The proration of such current rent paid shall be affected so that Seller shall be credited with all such rent accruing prior to but not including the closing date, and Buyer shall be credited with all such rent accruing thereafter. Buyer shall receive a credit in the amount of any prepaid rents paid to Seller as of the closing date. No proration shall be made for rents delinquent or due but unpaid as of the closing date; provided, however, that Seller shall deliver to Buyer on the closing date a schedule identifying the tenants who owe delinquent rents, and Buyer shall make reasonable efforts to collect for Seller such delinquent rents, and shall remit to Seller any rents for periods prior to the closing date actually paid to Buyer. All monies collected by Buyer from tenants owing delinquent rents shall be applied first to delinquent rents owed to Seller for the month during which the closing date occurs and the one preceding month, then to rent owed to Buyer for the period from and after the closing date to the date of collection and then to any other delinquent rents owed to Seller.

EXAMPLE 8-25

Rents under the existing leases and the new leases (and that of brokerage commissions) shall be prorated as of the closing date. Seller shall pay to Buyer that portion of the rent paid by the tenants under the existing leases and new leases applicable to periods subsequent to the closing date. No proration shall be made for rent delinquent or due but unpaid as of the closing date. All monies collected by Buyer from tenants owing delinquent or due but unpaid rents as of the closing date shall be applied first to current rents owing to Buyer by such tenants for periods from and after the closing date. From and after the closing date, Buyer shall use its best efforts to collect any delinquent or due but unpaid rents owing to Seller for periods prior to the closing date, and shall promptly remit to Seller any amounts collected by Buyer from tenants owing delinquent or due but unpaid rents, in excess of current rents owing to Buyer. Buyer shall have no obligation to incur any expense or to institute any litigation against any tenant, to collect any such delinquent or due but unpaid rent, but Seller shall have the right to exercise such rights and remedies as may be provided for or allowed by law or in equity to collect such rents other than the right to evict or dispossess such tenant.

Lease Commissions

It is quite common in commercial real estate transactions for the leases to involve commissions to brokers who obtained the leases for the seller. These brokerage commissions usually are a percentage of each month's rent for the remaining term of the lease and, in some cases, extensions or renewals of the lease. Broker commissions can be prorated between purchaser and seller in a number of ways. The purchaser can assume and pay all lease commissions earned and due in connection with the leases after the date of closing, whereas the seller is responsible to pay all lease commissions before the date of closing. The purchaser may want the seller to "cash out," or pay off, the lease commissions in full before the time of closing. Most brokers are quite willing to discount future lease commissions to a current value and receive a lump sum cash payment at the time of closing. If the lease commissions are to be cashed out by the seller at closing, it is prudent for the contract to provide that the seller will provide proof that such commissions have been paid. This proof can be in the form of a release from all the brokers of any claim for commissions under the leases that are assigned in connection with the sale of the property.

Security Deposits

Most tenants of commercial properties deliver to the landlord at the time the lease is signed a security deposit securing the tenant's performance under the lease. On expiration of the lease the security deposits are refundable to the tenant. Therefore, in most commercial contracts, the purchaser requires that it receive a credit for all security deposits that may be owed after the closing to the tenants (Example 8–26).

EXAMPLE 8-26

Buyer shall receive as a credit against the purchase price in the amount of all security deposits paid by tenants, and interest accrued thereon contingently payable to the tenant for his account there maintained, and Seller shall retain such funds free and clear of any and all claims on the part of the tenants. Buyer shall be responsible for maintaining a security deposit in the aggregate amounts so credited to Buyer in accordance with the provisions of the existing leases and the new leases relevant thereto.

Many states require that security deposits for tenants of apartment projects be placed in a special escrow account to assure their return on expiration of the lease. The provision shown in Example 8–27 may be found in an apartment project contract to handle the special escrow arrangement.

EXAMPLE 8-27

Seller shall deliver to Buyer a certified or cashier's check drawn upon or by a national bank having offices in the city where the property is located, payable to Buyer, in an amount equal to the total of all tenants security deposits held by Seller "as landlord" under the existing leases and the new leases, together with a schedule setting forth the name of each tenant for whose account a deposit is being held, the apartment unit with respect to which deposit is being held, and the amount of such deposit. Buyer shall promptly deposit the proceeds of such check into an escrow account, shall hold such deposits in trust for the benefit of the tenants of the project, and shall comply in all respects with the provisions of state law respecting security deposits. Buyer shall and hereby indemnify and hold Seller harmless from, against, and in respect of any and all liabilities, damages, losses, costs, expenses (including attorneys fees and expenses), causes of action, suits, judgments, claims, demands, and liens of any nature whatsoever arising in connection with such security deposit from and after the closing date.

Seller's Covenants Regarding Operation of Property

A critical issue regarding the operation of commercial property during the pendency of the contract is that of limitations on the seller's ability to enter into new leases with respect to the property and the requirement of the seller to maintain the status quo regarding insurance policies. The provision shown in Example 8–28 addresses these concerns.

EXAMPLE 8-28

Between the date hereof and the closing date, Seller: shall operate the project in an orderly course of business; shall maintain and repair the project so that, on the closing date, the project will be in the same condition as it now exists, natural wear and tear and loss by insured casualty alone excepted; shall comply with all obligations of the lessor or landlord under the existing leases and the new leases; shall continue to carry and maintain and enforce all existing policies of casualty and public liability insurance with respect to the property; shall not make or enter into any lease or other agreement for the use, occupancy, or possession of all or any part of the land or improvements except for leases that (1) are for a term including option renewal in terms that are no longer than three years; (2) provide for a rental rate not less than the rental rate being charged for some rent spaces in the project as of the date of Seller's execution of this agreement; and (3) are on standard form of lease used by Seller and approved by purchaser with respect to the project.

Hazardous Materials

The presence of hazardous waste materials on real property can create serious problems for the property owner. Federal and state law imposes on the owner of real property liability for all damage caused by hazardous waste as well as the cost of hazardous waste cleanup. An owner of real property may be responsible regardless of whether the owner created the hazardous waste material. Most purchasers will not purchase real property without having a hazardous waste inspection done by a professional inspection firm. In addition, most purchasers require that the contract contain certain representations, warranties, and indemnifications from the seller regarding hazardous waste materials. The provision shown as Example 8–29 addresses these concerns.

EXAMPLE 8-29

Hazardous Waste Indemnity. Purchaser's obligation to purchase the Property pursuant to this Contract is contingent upon there being no petroleum hydrocarbons or contaminants contained in the soil, surface or subterranean water which are in violation of local, state, or federal statutes and regulations and that there be no other existence of any hazardous substances or waste located upon the Property. For purposes of this Agreement, the term "hazardous substances or wastes" shall mean petroleum, including crude oil or any fraction thereof, flammable explosives, radioactive materials, asbestos, any material containing polychlorinated biphenyls, and any of the substances defined as "hazardous substances" or "toxic substances" in the Comprehensive Environmental Response, Compensation and Liability Act of 1980, as amended, 42 U.S.C. Section 9601 et seq., Hazardous Materials Transportation Act, 49 U.S.C. Section 1802 et seq., the Resource Conservation and Recovery Act, 42 U.S.C. Section 6901 et seq., and in the Toxic Substance Control Act of 1976, as amended, 15 U.S.C. Section 2601 et seq., or any other federal, state, local or other governmental legislation, statute, law, code, rule, regulation or ordinance identified by its terms as pertaining to the disposal, storage, generation or presence of hazardous substances or waste (the "Environmental Laws"). Purchaser shall at Seller's expense have the Property inspected for purposes of discovering if hazardous substances or wastes exist. Seller's share of the cost of the inspection shall not exceed $_____ (1) _____; if the inspection cost exceeds $_____ (2) _____, Seller shall pay $_____ (3) _____ and Purchaser shall pay the excess cost above $_____ (4) _____. If, upon inspection, hazardous wastes or substances are found to exist, Purchaser shall have the option of terminating this contract and receiving a refund of the earnest money down payment. In the alternative, Seller shall have the right at its own expense to remove all hazardous substances or wastes from the Property and to conclude the sale with Purchaser, or Seller may terminate this Contract without penalty.

Seller warrants, represents and agrees that (a) neither Seller nor any person has violated any of the applicable Environmental Laws as defined in the paragraph above relating to or affecting the Property; (b) the Property is presently in compliance with all Environmental Laws, and there are no facts or circumstances presently existing upon or under the Property or relating to the representations and warranties which violate any of the applicable Environmental Laws, and there is not now pending nor threatened any action, suit, investigation or proceeding against Seller or the Property (or against any other party related to the Property); (c) Seller or tenant has obtained all licenses, permits or other governmental regulatory approvals necessary to comply with Environmental Laws and Seller is in full compliance with the terms and provisions of all such licenses, permits or other governmental regulatory approvals; and (d) Seller has received no notice that any municipality or any governmental or quasi-governmental authorities are investigating or have determined that there are any violations of zoning, health, building, fire, pollution, environmental, or other statutes, ordinances, or regulations affecting the Property.

Indemnification

Most purchasers of commercial properties require indemnification from the seller with respect to liabilities pertaining to the property arising before the closing date. Most sellers likewise require an indemnification from the purchaser for such liabilities arising subsequent to the closing date. When drafting indemnification language, particular attention should be paid to the description of the liabilities covered and as to whether each party's indemnification is to be limited to the period of that party's actual ownership of the property, or to extend to all periods before the closing date (with respect to the seller's indemnification) and all periods subsequent to the closing date (with respect to the buyer's indemnification). An indemnity provision is shown in Example 8–30.

EXAMPLE 8-30

The Seller and Buyer shall and do each hereby indemnify, defend, and hold each other harmless from, against, and in respect to any and all liabilities, damages, losses, expenses (including counsel fees and expenses and disbursements of counsel), amounts of judgment, assessments, fines or penalties, and amounts paid in compromise or settlement, suffered, incurred, or sustained by the indemnified party on account, by reason, as a result of or in connection with any matter pertaining to the ownership, use, occupancy, management, maintenance, or operation of the property arising during the period of ownership of the property by the indemnifying party.

Seller's Disclaimer of Warranty

Although the purchaser tries to obtain as many warranties as possible from a seller, the seller often will only make warranties set forth in the contract and disclaim any and all other warranties. The provision shown in Example 8–31 is designed to allow the seller to achieve that result.

EXAMPLE 8–31

Except for the warranties of title to be included in Seller's instruments of conveyance to the project, Seller does not, by the execution and delivery of this agreement, and Seller shall not, by the execution and delivery of any document or instrument executed and delivered in connection with the closing, make any warranty, expressed or implied, of any kind or nature whatsoever, with respect to the project, and all such warranties are hereby disclaimed. Without limiting the generality of the foregoing, Seller makes, and shall make, no expressed or implied warranty of suitability or fitness of any of the property for any purpose, or as to the merchantability of title, value, quality, quantity, condition, or salability of any of the property, or that the use or sale of any of the property will not violate the copyright, trademark, or patent rights of any person. Sale of the property by Seller to Buyer hereunder shall be "as is" and "where is."

Real property usually is sold without any warranty concerning its physical condition unless the warranties are expressed in the contract or required by state law. The law in many states does require that certain warranties regarding the fitness and suitability of the improvement on the real property be given by the seller of a new residential home.

 CHECKLIST

For Preparation or Review of Commercial Real Estate Contract

The issues to be covered by a real estate contract are so numerous that without a checklist, it is easy to leave some issues out of the contract. A checklist for the preparation of a commercial contract follows.

❏ I. Parties to the Contract
    ❏ A. Seller should be the current owner of the property
    ❏ B. Purchaser should sign the contract in exactly the same form as he or she wants to obtain title. If the purchaser intends to have an entity such as a limited partnership or partnership to be formed to take title to the property, the contract should provide for the transfer and assignment of the contract to the new entity
    ❏ C. Brokers and agents usually are made a party to the contract to enforce commission rights

❏ II. Description of Property to Be Purchased
    ❏ A. Adequate description of real property and associated personal property
    ❏ B. Include easements appurtenant to the property
        1. Cross-easement agreements (shopping center)
        2. Off-site utility easements
        3. Access easements

❏ III. Purchase Price and Earnest Money
    ❏ A. Earnest money
        1. Specify amount and who holds the earnest money
        2. Additional earnest money payments for extensions of time to close

3. What happens to any interest on earnest money
4. Application of earnest money to purchase price
5. Application of earnest money in the event of default under contract
❏ B. Purchase price
   1. Calculation of purchase price
     a. Predetermined fixed amount
     b. Amount to be determined based on amount of acreage or square footage of property
       i. Establish method for determining acreage or square footage
       ii. Method of payment
         (a) All cash
         (b) Cash in excess of existing debt
           (i) Consider due on sale clause
           (ii) Which party bears expenses of transfer due holder of existing loan
         (c) Seller financing
           (i) All terms of seller financing, including amount, interest rate, and terms, should be identified
           (ii) Terms of the note and mortgage should be negotiated and copies attached as exhibits
         (d) New loan to be obtained by the purchaser
❏ IV. Title Examination
❏ A. Which party conducts examination
❏ B. Quality of title to be delivered by seller
   1. Marketable
   2. Insurable
   3. Free and clear of all matters of record
❏ C. Obligation of seller to correct title objections
   1. Defects curable by payment of money
   2. Other defects
     a. Defects existing before execution of contract
     b. Defects created after execution of contract
❏ V. Closing
❏ A. Which party establishes closing date
❏ B. Minimum or maximum periods to close
❏ C. Right to extend closing date
   1. Purchaser's right to extend closing by payment of money
   2. Seller's right to extend closing by reason of acts of purchaser
❏ D. Who bears closing cost
❏ E. Prorations
   1. Rent
     a. Fixed rent
     b. Overage or percentage rent
     c. Rent in arrears
   2. Interest on the existing debt
   3. Utilities and taxes
     a. Prorations when utilities and taxes are paid by landlord
     b. Prorations when utilities and taxes are paid by tenant
   4. Credits to purchaser for prepaid rents and security deposits
❏ F. Possession of property
   1. Normally delivered at closing
   2. When possession is delivered to purchaser before closing

        a. For limited purposes of installing fixtures

        b. For purpose of conducting business

           i. Specify what amounts are to be paid by purchaser for early occupancy

           ii. Specify risk of loss

    3. When possession is delivered to purchaser after closing

        a. For limited purpose of permitting seller to remove personal property from the premises

        b. Specify what amounts are to be paid by seller for continued possession

        c. Specify risks or losses due to possession by seller

❑ G. Documents to be delivered at closing

    1. Warranty deed

      a. General or limited

      b. Legal description to be based on new survey

    2. Assignment of leases

    3. Bill of sale to personal property

    4. Owner's affidavit

    5. General assignment of warranties

    6. Certified rent roll

    7. Termite bond

    8. Foreign person affidavit

    9. Escrow agreements for tenant work and tenant allowances

    10. Covenant not to compete

    11. Prior lender and tenant estoppel letters

    12. As-built survey

    13. Notice to tenants

    14. Copies of leases

    15. Evidence of payment of brokerage commission

      a. Brokerage commission arising out of purchase and sale

      b. Cash out of the leasing commissions

❑ VI. Covenants and Warranties of the Parties

  ❑ A. Purpose of warranties is to ensure accuracy of information on property

  ❑ B. Typical issues covered by warranties

    1. Seller's title to property

    2. Seller's authority to sign and carry out contract

    3. Removal of encumbrances

    4. Compliance of property with laws and ordinances

    5. No condemnation suit pending

    6. Right to possession

    7. True and correct copies of leases and agreements delivered to purchaser

    8. Accuracy of rent roll and expense statements

    9. Absence of mechanics' and materialmen's liens

    10. No litigation against seller or property

    11. Condition of property

    12. No encroachments

    13. No prior use from manufacture or storage of toxic or hazardous waste

  ❑ C. Limitations on warranties

    1. Best of knowledge

    2. Materiality

    3. Limited period of survival after closing

❑ VII. Conditions to Closing

❑　A. Purpose of conditions to closing
  1. Limitation on purchaser's obligation to close until seller completes certain items
  2. Substitute for complete warranties of seller
❑　B. Which parties have right to waive conditions
❑　C. Typical conditions
  1. Satisfactory inspection of property
  2. Satisfactory inspection of records involving the property
  3. Ability to obtain new loan
  4. Approval of board of directors of purchaser
  5. Receipt of estoppel certificates from lenders and tenants
  6. Truth and accuracy of seller's warranties on closing date
❑　VIII. Inspection by Purchaser
❑　A. Right to inspect physical condition of the property
  1. Time in which to exercise inspection
  2. Right to terminate after inspection
❑　B. Right to inspect seller's books and records related to property
  1. Place of inspection
  2. Right to copy records
  3. Permitted use of materials inspected
❑　C. Enforceability of free-look cancellation clauses
❑　IX. Casualty and Condemnation
❑　A. Purchaser's options on casualty or condemnation
  1. Materiality limitation on purchaser's right to terminate
  2. Time limits on exercise of option to terminate by purchaser
❑　B. Seller's obligations on casualty or condemnation
  1. Timely notice to purchaser of event of casualty or condemnation
  2. Is seller obligated to restore premises
❑　C. Should seller be required to carry insurance
❑　X. Remedies on Default
❑　A. Default by seller or purchaser
  1. Suit for damages or specific performance
  2. Liquidated damages
❑　XI. Brokerage
❑　A. Obtain warranties from each party as to brokers involved
❑　B. Specify which party pays brokerage commissions
❑　C. Cross-indemnity for brokerage claims
❑　XII. Confidentiality
❑　A. No recording the contract
❑　B. All information delivered to purchaser shall be kept confidential or delivered to other people only with seller's consent
❑　XIII. Miscellaneous Provisions
❑　A. Right to sign a contract
❑　B. Provisions for date and manner of delivering notices
❑　C. Time is of essence
❑　D. Survival of contract provisions
❑　E. Contract represents entire agreement between parties
❑　F. Severability of contract provisions
❑　G. Method of offer and acceptance
❑　H. Provide for approval and counterpart form

OPTIONS

Buyers and sellers of real property occasionally use an option initially instead of entering into a contract for the purchase and sale of the property. An option is a contract by which an owner of property, usually called the optionor, agrees with another person, usually called the optionee, that the optionee shall have the right to buy the owner's real property at a fixed price within a certain time on agreed terms and conditions. The effect of an option is to bind an owner of real property to an agreement to sell the property to the optionee in the event the optionee elects to purchase the property at the fixed price and on the terms set forth in the option. The decision to enter into the contract to purchase the property is entirely at the discretion of the optionee. An option usually is based on valuable consideration and is an irrevocable offer to sell by the owner of the real property. Option agreements must be in writing and be supported by something of value, usually money paid as an option price. An option form is shown as Exhibit 8–4 at the end of this chapter.

 E T H I C S :   Illegal or Fraudulent Activity

A legal assistant is employed with a law firm. A client of the firm is a real estate developer who builds and sells single-family homes. The developer is generally honest but is having trouble selling one of its homes. The developer finally has a purchaser who is willing to buy the home, but the purchaser does not have any money. The developer wants to prepare a contract that will show that the purchaser is making a down payment of 20 percent of the purchase price, which should enable the purchaser to go to a lending institution and get a loan for the other 80 percent. The developer, however, will not actually receive the 20 percent down payment. The developer instead will take a note from the purchaser for the 20 percent, which will be paid out over a period of time. This means that the purchaser actually will not have any money invested in the property at the time of the sale. This activity on the part of the developer and purchaser constitutes a fraud on the lending institution that will be making a loan to the purchaser.

The developer has explained all of this to an attorney who works at the firm. The attorney has decided that he will go ahead and prepare a contract that will show that a down payment of 20 percent has been made and received by the developer. The attorney has asked a legal assistant at the firm to assist in the preparation of the contract. Does the preparation of the contract, which shows that a down payment of 20 percent has been made when in fact it has not, constitute a breach of ethics on the part of the attorney as well as the legal assistant?

An attorney or a legal assistant should never assist a client in conduct that is illegal or fraudulent. Assisting a client to commit fraud can result in a loss of license to practice law on the part of the attorney and could subject both the attorney and the legal assistant to civil and criminal penalties. The participation by the attorney and legal assistant in the preparation of the contract to assist the developer in perpetrating a fraud on the lending institution is a serious breach of ethics.

SUMMARY

A purchaser and seller of real property each have a number of issues and concerns that must be addressed and agreed to in the contract for purchase and sale. A legal assistant who participates in the preparation and review of a real estate contract must not only be aware of the general issues and concerns of purchasers and sellers of real property, but also ask the client about any special issues or concerns. The contract is the agreement that outlines responsibilities and duties of the respective seller and purchaser, and is the blueprint that will be followed at the time of the closing of the sale and purchase. Careful thought and attention to detail must be given to the preparation and review of real estate contracts.

The real estate contract is the mutual promise of both purchaser and seller of the future transfer of ownership to real property. The contract does not transfer ownership, but merely promises to do so at some future date and time. At the time that ownership is to be transferred, the transfer is accomplished by a separate legal document known as a deed.

KEY TERMS

Cashier's check	Earnest money	Option
Certified check	Estoppel letter	Parol evidence rule
Closing	Execution	Time is of the essence
Condition precedent		

REVIEW QUESTIONS

1. Why is careful attention to detail required in the preparation of a real estate contract?

2. Briefly describe the various methods of payment for real property.

3. What does the "time is of the essence" phrase mean in a real estate contract?

4. What is a "free look," and in what circumstances would you expect to find a free-look provision in a real estate contract?

5. Explain the difference between marketable title and insurable title.

6. What items usually are prorated in a real estate contract?

7. If, under a real estate contract, the seller is to provide financing to the purchaser, what issues should be discussed concerning seller financing?

8. At what time do most real estate contracts provide that the purchaser will take possession of the property?

9. What is a closing, and why is its date important in a real estate contract?

10. What is earnest money, and what is its role in a real estate contract?

11. Why would a real estate broker want to be a party to a real estate contract?

12. What warranties commonly are required of a seller in a real estate contract?

13. What warranties commonly are required of a purchaser in a real estate contract?

14. What is a tenant estoppel letter, and when would one be required in a real estate contract?

CASE PROBLEMS

1. The following is a list of contract provisions. Do these provisions favor the seller or the purchaser?

    a. Seller is to convey insurable title to the real property at closing.

    b. Seller is to convey title to the real property subject to utility easements and other restrictions of record.

    c. Seller shall not alter or encumber the title to the real property after the date of the contract without the prior written consent of purchaser.

    d. The real estate contract is freely assignable.

    e. The contract is silent as to risk of loss between date of contract and date of closing.

2. Harold and Maude entered into negotiations with Sam to purchase Sam's home. The home was not new, and Harold and Maude had some concerns that the roof might leak. Sam verbally assured them that the roof did not leak. The written contract entered into between Sam and Harold and Maude, however, did not contain any written warranties concerning the roof. The contract also contained a provision that stated that no agreements, representations, or warranties, unless expressly incorporated or set forth in the contract, would be binding on any of the parties. After Harold and Maude purchased the home, they discovered that the roof leaked every time it rained. Harold and Maude have come to the law firm where you are a legal assistant and have asked for advice concerning their rights to sue Sam for his misrepresentation concerning the condition of the roof. You have been asked to research the issue and to report to your supervising attorney your conclusions concerning Harold and Maude's rights against Sam for the roof leak. What would your conclusion be?

PRACTICAL ASSIGNMENT

Review the contract for purchase and sale of a retail shopping center shown as Exhibit 8–3, and answer the following questions. Answer the questions with sufficient detail with reference to the contract paragraph number you used as authority for your answer.

1. How much is the brokerage commission in connection with this sale, and who is responsible for paying it?

2. Who is the holder of the real estate note and deed to secure debt that is going to be assumed by the purchaser in connection with this transaction?

3. What is the name of the property being sold?

4. What percentage of the tenant estoppels must the seller obtain?

5. Under what terms is the purchaser willing to consent to new leases on the property from the date of contract to the date of closing?

6. How many net rentable square feet are contained in the property being bought and sold?

7. Where is the closing to take place?

8. What amount of gross rental income from the property is guaranteed by the seller for the first year after closing date?

9. On what basis does the seller agree to pay the purchaser any income shortfall from the actual income generated from the property and the seller's guarantee of income?

10. Is Saturday considered a business day under the agreement?

11. What is the amount of the earnest money deposit?

12. When is the effective date as that term is defined under the contract?

13. What type of deed will be delivered to the purchaser at the time of the sale?

14. When will possession of the property be delivered to the purchaser pursuant to the agreement?

15. What is the seller's remedy for the purchaser's default?

16. Can the purchaser assign its rights under the contract to a partnership of which the purchaser is not a general partner?

17. If there is damage to the property before closing in the amount of $15,000, does this give the purchaser the right to terminate the agreement and not purchase the property?

18. Is the earnest money to be held in an interest-bearing or a non-interest-bearing account?

19. If the purchaser desires title insurance, who will pay for the title insurance?

20. What is the earliest date that the tenant estoppels required by seller can be dated?

21. Does the purchaser have a free look under this agreement, and when is the last date for fully exercising its free look?

22. If the holder of the existing mortgage loan charges an assumption fee, who will pay the assumption fee?

23. What is to happen to leasing brokerage agreements in connection with the property before closing?

24. Who has the risk of loss and damage to the property before closing?

25. How are security deposits paid under the leases to be prorated at time of closing?

ADDENDUM

1. Contract for purchase and sale of a home (Exhibit 8–1)
2. Contract for purchase and sale of large tract of vacant land (Exhibit 8–2)
3. Contract for purchase and sale of retail shopping center (Exhibit 8–3)
4. Option to purchase (Exhibit 8–4)
The exhibits referred to in the contracts are not included in the materials presented.

Note: This chapter contains excerpts from Donald E. Mize, *The Sales Contract: Real Estate Practice and Procedure Program Materials*, Institute of Continuing Legal Education, Athens, Georgia, 1985. Used by permission of the Institute of Continuing Legal Education.

EXHIBIT 8–1
Contract for
Purchase and Sale
of a Home*

PURCHASE AND SALE AGREEMENT

1994 Printing

Date _____, 19 _____

1. Purchase and Sale. As a result of the efforts of _____ a licensed Broker (hereinafter referred to as "Selling Broker") and _____, a licensed Broker (hereinafter referred to as "Listing Broker;" Listing Broker and Selling Broker being hereinafter sometimes collectively referred to as "Broker"), the undersigned Buyer agrees to buy, and the undersigned Seller agrees to sell all that tract or parcel of land, with such improvements as are located thereon, described as follows: All that tract of land lying and being in Land Lot _____ of the _____ District, _____ Section of _____ County, Georgia, and being known as Address _____, City _____ Zip Code _____, Multiple Listing # _____ according to the present system of numbering in and around this area, being more particularly described as Lot _____, Block _____, Unit _____, Phase/Section _____ of _____ subdivision, as recorded in Plat Book _____, Page _____, County, Georgia, records together with all lighting fixtures, all electrical ,mechanical, plumbing, air-conditioning, and any other systems or fixtures as are attached thereto; all plants, trees, and shrubbery now a part thereof, together with all the improvements thereon; and all appurtenances thereto, all being hereinafter collectively referred to as the "Property." The full legal description of said Property is the same as is recorded with the Clerk of the Superior Court of the county in which the Property is located and is made a part of this agreement by reference.

2. Purchase Price and Method of Payment. Buyer warrants and represents that at the time of closing Buyer will have sufficient cash (together with the loan or loans, if any, as described herein) to complete the purchase contemplated herein and that Buyer (according to his actual current

knowledge) | Buyer's Initial | **does** ("Sale of Buyer's Property Contingency Exhibit" attached) or | Buyer's Initial | **does not** have real property to sell or lease in order to complete the purchase contemplated herein. In the event of a "does not" selection above, Buyer further warrants that failure to sell the current residence or any other property will not be grounds for refund of earnest money in the event of loan denial. The purchase price of said Property shall be:

_____
to be paid as set forth in subparagraph A, B, or C [Select A, B, or C below. The others are not a part of this Agreement]:

☐ **A. All Cash At Closing:** At Closing, Buyer shall pay purchase price to Seller in cash, or its equivalent. Buyer's obligation to close shall not be contingent upon Buyer's ability to obtain financing. Buyer shall pay all usual and customary closing costs.

☐ **B. Where Loan Is To Be Assumed,** see Exhibit "_____" attached hereto and by reference made a part hereof.

☐ **C. Where New Loan Is To Be Obtained:** Buyer shall immediately disclose to Seller or its Broker, upon loan application, the name(s) of the lender(s) with which Buyer has applied.

(1) **Loan Terms:** This Agreement is made conditioned upon Buyer's "ability to obtain" (as hereinafter defined) a loan in the principal amount of _____ % of the purchase price or $_____, to be secured by a first lien security deed on the within described Property; said loan to be paid in consecutive monthly installments of principal and interest over a term of not less than _____ years. Initial monthly payments of principal and interest shall not be more than $_____. "Ability to obtain" as used herein means that Buyer is qualified to receive the loan described herein based upon lender's customary and standard underwriting criteria. Proceeds of said loan, together with any balance of such purchase price, shall be paid in cash or its equivalent by Buyer to Seller at closing. This loan shall be a [select (a), (b), (c), or (d) below. The others are not a part of this Agreement]:

(a) ☐ **Fixed Rate Mortgage Loan** with an interest rate of not more than _____ % per annum on the unpaid principal balance.

(b) ☐ **Adjustable Rate Mortgage ("ARM") Loan** with an initial interest rate of not more than_____ % per annum on the unpaid principal balance. The interest rate payable to lender by Buyer may increase or decrease according to the terms of said loan, and as a result, the monthly installments of principal and interest payable by Buyer may increase or decrease.

(c) ☐ **FHA or VA Loan** with an initial interest rate of not more than _____ % per annum on the unpaid principal balance, see Exhibit "_____," attached hereto and by reference made a part hereof.

(d) ☐ **Other Loan,** see Exhibit "_____," attached hereto and by reference made a part hereof.

(2) **Closing Costs:** _____ shall pay all usual and customary closing costs for said loan in a sum not to exceed _____ % of said loan amount. Buyer shall pay any usual and customary closing costs exceeding said sum. _____ shall pay the cost of any required survey.

(3) **Loan Discount:**_____ shall pay any Loan Discount payable in connection with said loan in a sum not to exceed _____% of said loan amount.

(4) **Private Mortgage Insurance:** The initial Private Mortgage Insurance Premium, if any, for said loan and any portion of private mortgage insurance premium, which is required by lender to be spread over subsequent monthly payments, shall be paid by Buyer.

(5) **Flood Insurance.** If flood insurance is desired by Buyer, or required by Buyer's lender, Buyer shall pay for said flood insurance.

(6) **Application and Escrow Deposits:** Buyer agrees to make application for said loan within _____ (_____) calendar days from Binding Agreement Date, to pursue said application diligently and in good faith, to execute all papers, to provide all documents, to perform all other actions necessary to obtain said loan and to accept such loan if approved by a lender. Should Buyer not apply for said loan in the time specified above, Seller may, upon written notification to Buyer, declare Buyer in default and Buyer thereafter shall have 5 calendar days to cure said default by providing Seller with written evidence of formal loan application. If required by lender, Buyer shall, in addition to the payment of principal and interest upon said loan, pay at closing the amount of money necessary to establish an escrow account and shall also pay, along with each monthly payment of principal and interest, one-twelfth of the annual ad valorem taxes and hazard insurance premiums for the Property, as estimated by lender. Buyer shall also pay each month the private mortgage insurance amount if required by lender.

(7) **Loan Options:** Buyer understands and acknowledges the possibility that many different loan programs, available from many different lenders, may well fit within the description of the loan set forth herein. No attempt has been made by Buyer to describe exactly all of the particular terms and conditions of said loan. The economics of this transaction, as bargained for by the parties, are such that Buyer agrees that a loan with terms consistent with those described herein shall be acceptable to Buyer and shall satisfy this loan contingency. Buyer, at his option and without voiding this agreement, may also apply for a loan with different terms and conditions and close the transaction provided (a) all other terms and conditions of this Agreement are fulfilled; and (b) the new loan does not increase the costs charged to the Seller. Buyer shall be obligated to close this transaction if Buyer has the ability to obtain a loan with terms as described herein and/or any other loan for which Buyer has applied and been approved.

(8) **Buyer's Loan Responsibility:** Buyer acknowledges and represents that he has not relied upon the advice or representations, if any, of Broker or Broker's Affiliated Licensees regarding the type of loan or the terms of any particular loan program to be obtained by Buyer. Buyer shall have the responsibility of independently investigating and choosing the lender, type of loan, and loan program to be applied for by Buyer in connection with Purchase Price and Method of Payment paragraph. Buyer agrees to hold harmless listing broker, selling broker and their affiliated licensees, from any claim or loss whatsoever arising out of Buyer's application and commitment for any loan, and with respect to the terms of the instruments evidencing or securing said loan.

F15 Purchase & Sale 12/01/93 Page 1 of 4

---

* Reprinted with permission of Georgia Association of REALTORS, Inc., Copyright 1994.

EXHIBIT 8-1
Contract for
Purchase and Sale
of a Home
(continued)

3. Earnest Money. Buyer has paid to the undersigned _____ Holder, Escrow Agent, $ _____ check, or $ _____ cash, receipt whereof is hereby acknowledged by Holder, as earnest money, which earnest money is to be deposited in Holder's escrow/trust account and is to be applied as part payment of the purchase price of said Property at time of closing. All parties to this Agreement agree that Holder may deposit the earnest money in an interest-bearing escrow/trust account and that Holder will retain the interest earned on said deposit. Buyer and Seller understand and agree that Holder shall deposit the earnest money in Holder's escrow/trust account within five (5) banking days following the Binding Agreement Date. In the event the Earnest Money check is returned for insufficient funds or otherwise not honored by the bank drawn upon and Buyer has not delivered good funds to Holder within three (3) days of bank's notice, then and in that event, the Seller in his sole discretion shall have the right to terminate this Agreement by giving written notice to the parties. The parties to this Agreement understand and acknowledge that disbursement of earnest monies held by Holder, escrow agent, can occur only as follows: at closing; upon written agreement signed by all parties having an interest in the funds; upon court order; upon failure of any contingency or failure of either party to fulfill his obligations contained in this Agreement; or as otherwise set out herein.

If any dispute arises between Buyer and Seller as to the final disposition of all or part of the earnest money, Holder may, at its option, notify Buyer and Seller in writing that Holder is unable to resolve such dispute and may, at its option, interplead all or any disputed part of the earnest money into court. Holder shall be entitled to be compensated by the party who does not prevail in the interpleader action for its costs and expenses, including reasonable attorney's fees incurred in filing said interpleader. If Holder decides not to interplead, Holder may make a disbursal of said earnest money upon a reasonable interpretation of this Agreement. If Holder decides to make a disbursal to which all parties to this Agreement do not expressly agree, Holder must give all parties fifteen (15) days notice in writing of Holder's intent to disburse. Such notice shall be delivered by Certified Mail to the parties' last known addresses and must recite to whom and when the disbursal will be made. After disbursement, Holder shall notify all parties by Certified Mail of such disbursement. In the event Holder interpleads the funds into court or makes a disbursal upon a reasonable interpretation of this Agreement, then and in either event, the parties thereafter shall make no claim against Holder or Broker for said disputed earnest money and shall not seek damages from Holder or Broker by reason thereof or by reason of any other matter arising out of this Agreement or the transaction contemplated hereunder.

4. Destruction of Property. Should the Property be destroyed or substantially damaged before time of closing, Seller is to notify immediately the Buyer or Broker. After which, Buyer may declare this Agreement void and receive refund of earnest money deposited. In the event Buyer elects not to void this Agreement at this time, then within five (5) calendar days after Seller receives notification of the amount of the insurance proceeds, if any, Seller shall notify Buyer of the amount of insurance proceeds and the Seller's intent to repair or not repair said damage. Within five (5) calendar days of Seller's notification, Buyer may declare this Agreement void and receive refund of earnest money deposited, or consummate this agreement and receive such insurance as is paid on claim of loss if Seller has elected not to repair said damage.

5. Condition of Property.

 A. Condition at Closing: Seller warrants that at time of closing the Property will be in the same condition as it was on the Binding Agreement Date, normal wear and tear excepted.

 B. Warranties Transfer: Seller agrees to transfer to Buyer, at closing, Seller's interest in any manufacturer's warranties, service contracts, termite bond or treatment guarantee, and/or other similar warranties which by their terms may be transferable to Buyer.

 C. Utility Services: Seller shall cause utility services, pool and spa to be operational so that Buyer may complete all inspections under this Agreement.

 D. Seller's Disclosure: [Buyer must initial either subparagraph (1) or (2) below; the uninitialled subparagraph is not part of this Agreement.] The Seller's Property Disclosure Statement:

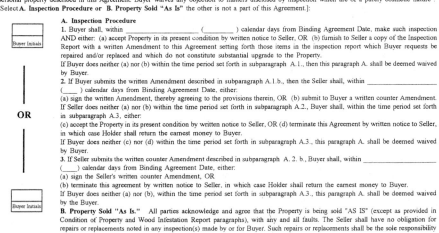

  (1) **Has not** been received by Buyer. Seller shall provide said Property Disclosure to Buyer no later than two (2) calendar days from the Binding Agreement Date. In the event Seller fails to provide said Property Disclosure in a timely manner or said Property Disclosure discloses conditions which are unacceptable to Buyer, may terminate this Agreement by giving Seller written notice thereof within four (4) calendar days from Binding Agreement Date, in which case Holder shall return the earnest money to Buyer. In the event Buyer fails to provide said written notice, Buyer waives the right to terminate this Agreement in accordance with this paragraph.

  OR

  (2) **Has** been received by Buyer.

6. Inspection. Buyer, his inspectors or representatives, at Buyer's expense and at reasonable times during normal business hours shall have the right and responsibility to enter upon the Property for the purpose of making a diligent, prudent and competent inspection (including conducting the final walk through), by examining, testing, and surveying the Property. Buyer agrees to assume all responsibility for the acts of himself, his inspectors, and representatives in exercising his rights under this paragraph and agrees to hold Seller, Broker and Broker's Affiliated Licensees harmless for any damages or injuries resulting therefrom. The inspection of the Property shall include, but is not limited to: all appliances remaining with the Property, heating and air conditioning systems; plumbing (including without limitation, sewer/septic and water/well systems, pool and spa); electrical systems; roof, gutters, structural components, foundation, fireplace and chimney; drainage conditions or evidence of excessive moisture adversely affecting the structure; excessive levels (as defined by the Environmental Protection Agency) of radon, toxic wastes, hazardous substances including, but not limited to: lead, asbestos and urea-formaldehyde, or other undesirable substances; any other condition or circumstance which may adversely affect the Property, and any personal property described in this Agreement. Buyer waives any objection to matters disclosed by inspection which are of a purely cosmetic nature . [Select **A. Inspection Procedure** or **B. Property Sold "As Is"** the other is not a part of this Agreement.]:

 A. Inspection Procedure

  1. Buyer shall, within _____ (_____) calendar days from Binding Agreement Date, make such inspection AND either: (a) accept Property in its present condition by written notice to Seller, OR (b) furnish to Seller a copy of the Inspection Report with a written Amendment to this Agreement setting forth those items in the inspection report which Buyer requests be repaired and/or replaced and which do not constitute substantial upgrade to the Property.

  If Buyer does neither (a) nor (b) within the time period set forth in subparagraph A.1., then this paragraph A. shall be deemed waived by Buyer.

  2. If Buyer submits the written Amendment described in subparagraph A.1.b., then the Seller shall, within _____ (____) calendar days from Binding Agreement Date, either:

  (a) sign the written Amendment, thereby agreeing to the provisions therein, OR (b) submit to Buyer a written counter Amendment. If Seller does neither (a) nor (b) within the time period set forth in subparagraph A.2., Buyer shall, within the time period set forth in subparagraph A.3, either:

  (c) accept the Property in its present condition by written notice to Seller, OR (d) terminate this Agreement by written notice to Seller, in which case Holder shall return the earnest money to Buyer.

  If Buyer does neither (c) nor (d) within the time period set forth in subparagraph A.3., this paragraph A. shall be deemed waived by Buyer.

  3. If Seller submits the written counter Amendment described in subparagraph A. 2. b., Buyer shall, within _____ (____) calendar days from Binding Agreement Date, either:

  (a) sign the Seller's written counter Amendment, OR

  (b) terminate this agreement by written notice to Seller, in which case Holder shall return the earnest money to Buyer.

  If Buyer does neither (a) nor (b), within the time period set forth in subparagraph A.3., this paragraph A. shall be deemed waived by the Buyer.

 B. Property Sold "As Is." All parties acknowledge and agree that the Property is being sold "AS IS" (except as provided in Condition of Property and Wood Infestation Report paragraphs), with any and all faults. The Seller shall have no obligation for repairs or replacements noted in any inspection(s) made by or for Buyer. Such repairs or replacements shall be the sole responsibility of Buyer.

 C. Property Acceptance. Notwithstanding anything contained herein to the contrary, Seller's responsibility in connection with the Property shall cease at closing, and closing shall constitute Buyer's acceptance of the Property unless provision is otherwise made in writing. Nothing contained in the Inspection paragraph shall amend, alter, or modify Seller's obligations under the Condition of Property Paragraph

EXHIBIT 8-1
Contract for
Purchase and Sale
of a Home
(continued)

7. Wood Infestation Report. No less than seven (7), but within thirty (30), days prior to the closing, the Seller shall cause to be made, at Seller's expense, an inspection of the main dwelling from a licensed pest control operator. If visible evidence of active or previous infestation is indicated, Seller agrees, prior to closing, to (A) treat said infestation and correct structural damages resulting from said infestation and provide documentation evidencing correction of same and/or (B) provide documentation, satisfactory to lender (if applicable), indicating that there is no structural damage resulting from any previous infestation. Seller, at closing, shall provide a letter on a standard form in accordance with the regulations of the Georgia Structural Pest Control Commission, stating that the main dwelling has been inspected and found to be free from visible evidence of active infestation caused by termite or other wood destroying organisms.

8. Sewer/Septic Tank And Public Water/Well. Any lender imposed inspection(s) of the septic tank or well systems shall be obtained and paid for by Buyer. Seller warrants that the main dwelling on the above described Property is served by:

A. Public Sewer _____ . _____ or Septic Tank _____ / _____ or Private Sewer _____ / _____

B. Public Water _____ _____ or Private Water _____ / _____ or Well _____ / _____
     (Buyer Initial)   (Seller Initial)   (Buyer Initial)   (Seller Initial)   (Buyer Initial)   (Seller Initial)

9. Home Warranty Program. Buyer acknowledges that a home warranty may be available for the main dwelling at an additional cost.

10. Title.
    A. Examination. Buyer shall have a reasonable time after the Binding Agreement Date to examine title and to furnish Seller with a written statement of objections affecting the marketability of said title. Seller shall have a reasonable time after receipt of such objections to satisfy all valid objections. If Seller fails to satisfy such valid objections within a reasonable time, then, at the option of Buyer evidenced by written notice to Seller, this Agreement shall be null and void. Marketable title as used herein shall mean title which a title insurance company licensed to do business in the State of Georgia will insure at its regular rates, subject only to standard exceptions unless otherwise specified herein. Buyer acknowledges that owner's title insurance may be purchased at closing, at Buyer's expense.
    B. Warranty. Seller warrants that he presently has title to said Property. At the time of closing, Seller agrees to convey good and marketable title to said Property by general warranty deed subject only to (1) zoning ordinances affecting said Property, (2) general utility, sewer, and drainage easements of record upon which the improvements do not encroach, (3) subdivision easements and restrictions of record, and (D) leases, other easements, other restrictions and encumbrances specified in this Agreement. In the event leases are specified in this Agreement, Buyer agrees to assume Seller's responsibilities thereunder to the tenant and to the broker who negotiated such leases.

11. Brokerage. In negotiating this Agreement, Broker has rendered a valuable service for which reason Broker is made a party to enable Broker to enforce his commission rights hereunder against the parties hereto on the following basis: Seller agrees to pay Broker the full commission when the sale is consummated. In the event the sale is not consummated because of Seller's inability, failure or refusal to perform any of Seller's covenants herein, then Seller shall pay the full commission to Broker immediately; and, Broker, at the option of Buyer, shall return the earnest money to Buyer. Buyer agrees that if Buyer fails or refuses to perform any of Buyer's covenants herein, Buyer shall forthwith pay Broker the full commission immediately; provided that Broker may first apply one-half of the earnest money toward payment of, but not to exceed, the full commission and may pay the balance thereof to Seller as liquidated damages to Seller, if Seller claims balance as Seller's liquidated damages in full settlement of any claim for damages, whereupon Broker shall be released from any and all liability for return of the earnest money to Buyer.
Commission to be paid in connection with this Agreement has been negotiated between Seller and Broker and shall be $_____ or _____ % of the Purchase Price, due and payable upon transfer of title (closing) or as otherwise provided herein. In the event this sale is made in cooperation with another Broker, Selling Broker shall receive _____ % and Listing Broker shall receive _____ % of the total real estate commission paid hereunder or as otherwise provided herein.

12. Agency Disclosure. In this transaction, the Listing Broker (if any) has acted for Seller and the Selling Broker's relationship with the parties to this Agreement is as specified in the attached Exhibit. (Either the "Agency Exhibit" or the "Transaction Broker Exhibit" is attached and made a part hereof by reference.)

13. Closing and Possession.
    A. Taxes: Real estate taxes on said Property for the calendar year in which the sale is closed shall be prorated as of the date of closing.
    B. Transfer Tax: Seller shall pay State of Georgia property transfer tax.
    C. Closing Date: This transaction shall be closed on or before _____, 19 _____, provided however, (1) that in the event the loan described in Purchase Price and Method of Payment Paragraph herein above is unable to be closed on or before said date, or (2) that Seller fails to satisfy valid title objections, either Buyer or Seller may, at his option, by written notice to the other party, extend this Agreement's closing date seven (7) calendar days from the above-stated closing date.
    D. Possession: Buyer agrees to allow Seller to retain possession of the Property until midnight _____ (_____) day(s) after closing. In the event that Seller retains possession of the Property beyond the day of closing, Seller does hereby guarantee that at the date of surrender of occupancy by the Seller, the Property shall be in the same condition as of the day of closing.
    E. Property Delivery Condition: Seller shall deliver Property clean and free of debris at time of possession.
    F. Prorations: Seller and Buyer agree to prorate between themselves, as of the date of closing or the day of surrender of the Property by the Seller (whichever is the later), association fees (if mandatory) and all utility bills rendered subsequent to closing which include service for any period of time the Property was owned/occupied by Seller or any prior owner/occupant.
    G. Closing Certifications: Buyer and Seller agree (1) to comply with and (2) to execute and deliver such certifications, affidavits, and statements as are required at the closing in order to meet the requirements of Internal Revenue Code Section 1445 .

14. Association/Assessment Fees. Unless otherwise stated in an Association/Assessment Fee Exhibit, there are no mandatory association fees nor any special assessments.

15. Other Provisions.
    A. Binding Effect. The terms, covenants and conditions of this Agreement shall inure to the benefit of, and be binding upon, the parties hereto, their heirs, successors, legal representatives and permitted assigns.
    B. Transfer or Assignment. This Agreement shall not be transferred or assigned without the written consent of all parties to this Agreement and any permitted assignee shall fulfill all the terms and conditions of this Agreement.
    C. Survival of Agreement. Any condition or stipulation not fulfilled at time of closing shall survive the closing, execution and delivery of the Warranty Deed until such time as said conditions or stipulations are fulfilled.
    D. Modification. This Agreement may not be modified, altered or amended except by written instrument executed by the parties hereto.
    E. Entire Agreement. This Agreement constitutes the sole and entire agreement between the parties hereto and no modification of this Agreement shall be binding unless signed by all parties to this Agreement. No representation, promise, or inducement not included in this Agreement shall be binding upon any party hereto.
    F. Governing Law. This Agreement is made and entered into as a contract for the purchase and sale of real property to be interpreted under and governed and enforced according to the laws of the State of Georgia.
    G. Terminology And Captions. All pronouns, singular, plural, masculine, feminine or neuter, shall mean and include the person, entity, firm or corporation to which they relate as the context may require. Wherever the context may require, the singular shall mean and include the plural and the plural shall mean and include the singular. The term "Agreement" as used herein, as well as the terms "herein," "hereof," "hereunder," "hereinafter," and the like mean this Agreement in its entirety and all exhibits, amendments and addenda attached hereto and made a part hereof. The captions and paragraph headings are for reference and convenience only and do not enter into or become a part of the context of this agreement.

EXHIBIT 8-1
Contract for
Purchase and Sale
of a Home
(continued)

16. Responsibility to Cooperate. All parties agree that such documentation as is reasonably necessary to carry out the responsibilities and obligations of this Agreement shall be produced, executed and/or delivered by said parties within time required to fulfill the terms and conditions of this Agreement.

17. Binding Arbitration Availability. All parties to this Agreement acknowledge that, in the event a dispute arises after execution of this Agreement, there are alternatives to litigation through alternate dispute resolution methods, such as mediation and binding arbitration, provided all parties agree in writing to employ such methods. In the event that the parties agree to resolve any disputes which may arise after execution of this Agreement through binding arbitration, they will enter into a separate Arbitration or Mediation Agreement.

18. Time is of the Essence. Time is of the essence of this Agreement.

19. Notices. Except as may otherwise be provided for in this Agreement, all notices or demands required or permitted hereunder shall be delivered either (A) in person; (B) by overnight delivery service prepaid; (C) by facsimile (FAX) transmission; or (D) by the United States Postal Service, postage prepaid, registered or certified, return receipt requested. Such notices shall be deemed to have been given as of the date and time the same are actually received by Broker or Broker's Affiliated Licensee or receiving party. In the event that any notice, demand, information or disclosure is required by the terms of this Agreement to be given by a party to "Broker," such Broker shall be deemed to be the Broker or Affiliated Licensee, if any, for the other party, and if none, then directly to the other party.

20. Disclaimer.
   A. Independent Expert Advice: Seller and Buyer acknowledge that they have not relied upon the advice or representations of Broker or Broker's Affiliated Licensees, including but not limited to: legal and tax consequences of this Agreement in the sale of the Property; the terms and conditions of financing; the purchase and ownership of the Property; the structural condition of the Property; the operating condition of the electrical, heating, air conditioning, plumbing, water heating systems, pool, spa and appliances in the Property; the availability of utilities to the Property; the investment potential or resale value of the Property; the availability and ownership of amenity package, if applicable; restrictive covenants and architectural controls; or any other system or condition enumerated in the "Inspection of Property" paragraph above or any other condition or circumstance which may adversely affect the Property. Seller and Buyer acknowledge that if such, or similar, matters have been of concern to them, they have sought and obtained independent advice relative thereto. Buyer acknowledges that closing shall constitute acceptance of the Property unless provision is otherwise made in writing.
   B. Property Conditions: Seller and Buyer acknowledge that various substances used in the construction of the improvements on the Property or otherwise located on the Property may now or in the future be determined to be toxic, hazardous or undesirable and may need to be specially treated, handled and/or removed from the Property. Persons who have an interest in the Property may be required by law to undertake the cleanup of such substances. Buyer and Seller acknowledge that: Brokers have no expertise with respect to toxic wastes, hazardous substances or undesirable substances; such substances can be extremely costly to correct and remove; Brokers have made no investigations or representations with respect to such substances; and Brokers shall have no liability to Seller or Buyer regarding the presence of said substances on the Property. Seller and Buyer release Broker and Broker's Affiliated Licensees from any claim, rights of action or suits relating to the presence of any hazardous substances, toxic wastes, or undesirable substances on the Property.

21. Instructions to Closing Attorney. Closing Attorney is instructed to: transfer "Survival of Agreement" paragraph to the closing statement; obtain and distribute to and from the appropriate parties such certifications, affidavits, and statements as are required in order to meet the requirements of Internal Revenue Code § 1445 (Foreign/Non-Foreign Sellers), or, in the alternative, to disburse and hold the sales proceeds in such a manner as may be required to comply with Internal Revenue Code § 1445; file with the Internal Revenue Service the IRS Form 1099B documenting this transaction, and comply with any other reporting requirements related thereto.

22. Exhibits And Addenda. In the event Personal Property shall remain with the property, the same shall be set out in a Bill of Sale attached hereto and made a part of this Agreement by reference thereto. The following Exhibits and/or Addenda are attached hereto and by reference made a part hereof:
_____"Agency Exhibit" or "Transaction Broker Exhibit"_____

SPECIAL STIPULATIONS: The following stipulations, if conflicting with any preceding paragraph, shall control:

☐   Special Stipulations Continued and made a part hereof.

Time Limit of Offer.
This instrument shall be open for acceptance until _____ o'clock _____M. on the _____ day of _____, 19 _____.

Acceptance Date
The above proposition is hereby accepted, _____ o'clock_____ M, on the _____ day of _____, 19 _____.

Binding Agreement Date
This instrument shall become a binding Agreement when written acceptance thereof, or a facsimile (FAX) transmission of the accepted instrument is actually received by Broker, Broker's Affiliated Licensees, or Offeror. Upon receipt of acceptance, the other party, Broker or Broker's Affiliated Licensee shall be notified immediately.

_____   (_____)   _____
Selling Broker   MLS Office Code   Buyer's Signature:
                                                                Print or Type Name:_____
By:_____
Broker or Broker's Affiliated Licensee
Print or Type Name: _____   _____
Bus. Phone: _____ FAX # _____   Buyer's Signature:
                                                           Print or Type Name:_____

_____   (_____)   _____
Listing Broker   MLS Office Code   Seller's Signature:
                                                                Print or Type Name:_____
By:_____
Broker or Broker's Affiliated Licensee
Print or Type Name: _____   _____
Bus. Phone: _____ FAX # _____   Seller's Signature:
                                                           Print or Type Name:_____

F15 Purchase & Sale 12/01/93 Page 4 of 4

STATE OF
COUNTY OF *BAKER*

CONTRACT FOR PURCHASE AND SALE

THIS IS A CONTRACT for the purchase and sale of certain real estate by and between JOHN J. JOHNS, a resident of Baker County, (hereinafter called "Seller"), THOMAS T. TOMS, a resident of Charlie County, (hereinafter called "Purchaser"), and **Community & Home Properties** (hereinafter called "Broker").

In consideration of the mutual covenants herein contained, and other good and valuable considerations, the receipt and sufficiency of which is hereby acknowledged, the parties hereby agree as follows:

1. Agreement to Buy and Sell

Seller hereby agrees to sell and Purchaser hereby agrees to buy all that tract or parcel of land described on Exhibit A attached hereto and made a part hereof lying and being in Land Lot 172 of the 14th District of Baker County, and being the same property conveyed to Seller by warranty deed dated January 4, 19   and recorded in Deed Book 140, Page 28, Baker County Records, which deed is incorporated herein by reference. The property which is the subject of this Contract (hereinafter called "the Property") includes the land, all crops, plants, trees and shrubbery thereon, all buildings thereon and all fixtures therein.

2. Survey

Prior to date of closing as hereinafter provided in Paragraph 7, Purchaser shall at Purchaser's expense cause an accurate survey to be made of the Property by a reputable surveyor registered under the laws of the State of   . The plat of such survey ("the plat") shall show the boundaries of the Property and the acreage therein computed to the nearest one-hundredth of an acre. Purchaser shall promptly furnish Seller with a copy of the plat and the plat shall conclusively determine as between Purchaser and Seller the acreage in the Property. Seller's conveyance to Purchaser shall be in accordance with said survey.*

3. Purchase Price

The purchase price for the Property shall be $5,000.00 per acre, and the total purchase price for the Property shall be determined by multiplying by said purchase price per acre the number of acres determined by the plat. Provided, however, that any portion of the Property lying within the rights-of-way of any road, street or easement, or below the high water mark of any streams and creeks, and all other areas to which Seller cannot convey title as provided herein, shall be excluded for purposes of determining the purchase price.

4. Payment

The purchase price of the Property shall be paid as follows:

(a) At the time of closing, Purchaser shall pay to Seller in cash or by Purchaser's [certified or cashier's] check an amount of money equal to *twenty-nine* percent (29%) of the purchase price, less a credit for all earnest money paid hereunder.

(b) The balance of the purchase price shall be paid by Purchaser's Promissory Note [in the form attached hereto as Exhibit B], which Note shall provide ten equal annual installments of principal, the first of which shall be due and payable on the fifth anniversary of

*If Purchaser or Seller have the right to review the plat of survey, see alternative provisions.

EXHIBIT 8-2
Contract for
Purchase and Sale
of Large Tract of
Vacant Land
(continued)

closing hereunder and subsequent installments shall be due on each anniversary there-after until paid in full.

(c) The Note shall bear interest on the unpaid balance of principal at the rate of eight percent (8%) per annum, which interest shall be payable on each anniversary of the closing hereunder.

(d) The Note shall provide that, after the last day of the calendar year in which closing hereunder takes place, the principal sum of said Note may be prepaid in whole or in part without penalty and without further interest on the amounts prepaid from the date of such prepayment. All partial prepayments shall be credited to installments of principal in the inverse order of maturity.

(e) The Note shall be secured by a Purchase Money Deed to Secure Debt conveying the Property to Seller as security. The form of said Deed to Secure Debt is attached hereto as Exhibit C and made a part hereof.

(f) The Note and Deed to Secure Debt shall provide that Seller shall not exercise any of Seller's remedies for Purchaser's default thereunder (including without limitation the right of acceleration of the balance of Purchaser's indebtedness thereunder) until the tenth day after written notice of said default (which written notice shall specify the nature of all such defaults and set out the method of cure of such defaults by Purchaser) is provided by Seller to Purchaser. If Purchaser has not cured all such defaults within ten days after receipt of such notice, Seller shall then be empowered to exercise all of Seller's remedies under the Note and Deed to Secure Debt.

(g) The Deed to Secure Debt shall provide for the release of the property described therein as set forth in Exhibit C attached hereto.

5. Warranties of Seller

Seller hereby warrants and represents that:

(a) Seller owns unencumbered fee simple title to the property, free and clear of all restrictions, liens and encumberances except as set forth on Exhibit A hereto and herein called "the Permitted Title Exceptions," that no assessments have been made against said property which are unpaid (except ad valorem taxes for the current year) whether or not they have become liens, that the Property is not subject to any other leases nor to the claims of any tenants in possession, and that so long as this Contract remains in force, Seller will not lease or convey any portion of the Property or any rights therein, nor enter into any agreements or amendments to agreements granting to any person or entity any rights with respect to the Property or any part thereof.

(b) The Property contains not less than 20 acres.

(c) The Property has not previously been used as a landfill or as a dump for garbage or refuse, and that no portion of the Property is subject to flood plain restrictions.

(d) That access to the streets and roads adjoining the Property is not limited or restricted except by applicable zoning laws.

(e) That all utilities, including but not limited to water, gas, sewer and electricity, are located within or at the boundary lines of the Property.

(f) That the Property is now zoned AG-1 under the present zoning laws of Baker County.

6. Title Objections

Purchaser shall have 30 calendar days from the date of this Agreement in which to examine Seller's title. If Purchaser finds any legal defects to title other than the Permitted Title Exceptions, Seller shall be furnished with a written statement thereof and shall have 30 calendar days in which to correct such defects, and Seller shall take all steps, including payment of money, necessary to correct said legal defects. If Seller shall fail to correct such legal defects within <u>30</u> days, then Purchaser shall have the choice of (a) accepting the Property with such legal defects after deduction from the purchase price otherwise payable hereunder the cost of correction of such legal defects which can be corrected by the payment of money; (b) postponing closing hereunder for not more than <u>ninety</u> calendar days until said defects are corrected or (c) declining to accept the Property with such legal defects, such choice to be exercised by written notice to Seller mailed within <u>10</u> calendar days following the end of the period provided above for the correction by Seller of such legal defects. Should Purchaser elect to postpone closing under (b) above and should, at the end of said ninety calendar day postponement period, said legal defects remain uncorrected, Purchaser shall have the further choice of options (a) and (c) set forth above in this paragraph, such choice to be exercised by written notice to Seller mailed within ten calendar days following the end of such postponement period. If Purchaser shall decline to so accept the Property subject to such legal defects, then this Contract shall, at Purchaser's option, be null and void and Purchaser's earnest money deposit shall be promptly refunded to Purchaser. Also, an amount of money equal to Purchaser's expenses in obtaining the title examination and the survey shall be paid by Seller to Purchaser.

7. Closing

(a) Unless extended as provided herein, Purchaser and Seller shall consummate and close the sale contemplated by this Agreement on or before the <u>120</u> calendar days following the date of this Agreement or the "final zoning" or defined in Paragraph <u>13</u> hereof, whichever is later, at such time, date and location as is designated by Purchaser in a written notice to Seller and Broker.

(b) At the closing each party shall execute and deliver all documents necessary to effect and complete the closing. The general warranty deed to be executed by Seller shall be on the form [attached hereto as Exhibit <u>D</u>] then generally used by <u>Security Mortgage Company</u> and shall convey to Buyer unencumbered fee simple title, free and clear of all liens, restrictions and encumberances except the Permitted Title Exceptions [and insurable as such by <u>Title Company</u> at standard rates on American Land Title Association Owner's Policy Standard Form <u>B–1987.</u>]. All blanks in all of the closing documents shall be filled in at the closing, and all documents shall otherwise be conformed to meet the requirements of the parties as expressed in this Contract.

(c) Seller shall pay the tax imposed on the warranty deed and shall pay the cost of recording and the Intangibles tax on the Deed to Secure Debt from Purchaser. Purchaser shall pay the cost of recording the warranty deed, the cost of examining and insuring title to the Property, and all other closing costs incurred by Purchaser.

(d) As of the date of closing, Purchaser and Seller shall prorate ad valorem taxes on the Property for the year in which the closing occurs, premiums, for hazard insurance on the Property, utility bills, soil bank payments and rents prepaid to Seller under any leases which are assigned to Purchaser. Seller shall assign and transfer to Buyer at the closing any leases or tenant contracts specified in the Permitted Title Exceptions and Purchaser shall assume Seller's obligations under such leases or contracts.

(e) At closing Seller shall execute a written statement of the warranties and representations contained herein.

8. Inspection

Commencing upon the date of this Agreement Purchaser shall have the right to go on the Property personally or through agents, employees and contractors for the purposes of making boundary line and topographical surveys of same, soil tests and such other

EXHIBIT 8–2
Contract for
Purchase and Sale
of Large Tract of
Vacant Land
(continued)

EXHIBIT 8-2
Contract for
Purchase and Sale
of Large Tract of
Vacant Land
(continued)

tests, analyses and investigations of the Property as Purchaser deems desirable. Purchaser shall pay all costs incurred in making such surveys, tests, analyses and investigations.

9. Condition and Possession of the Property

At closing Seller shall deliver to Purchaser possession of the Property in the same condition as on the date of this Contract. If all or any material portion of the Property shall be condemned, damaged or destroyed prior to the closing, Purchaser may elect to (i) terminate this Contract, or (ii) reduce the purchase price in the amount of the condemnation award or the decrease in value caused by the damage or destruction to the property, or (iii) receive such insurance proceeds or condemnation award as may be paid or payable with respect to such damage or destruction. Purchaser's election under this paragraph shall be exercised by written notice to Seller within 10 days after receipt of written notice from Seller of such taking, damage or destruction or of written notice of the amount of the insurance or condemnation award payable with respect to such taking, damage or destruction, whichever is later. If Purchaser elects to terminate this Contract under this paragraph, all earnest money paid hereunder shall be immediately refunded to Purchaser.

10. Default

If the sale contemplated by this Contract is not consummated through default of Seller, Purchaser's earnest money deposit shall be promptly refunded to Purchaser. If said sale is not consummated because of Purchaser's default, then Seller shall be entitled to retain Purchaser's earnest money deposit as full liquidated damages for such default of Purchaser. Nothing contained in this paragraph shall eliminate or limit Purchaser's right to sue for, and obtain, damages caused by Seller's default or specific performance of Seller's obligations hereunder. If Seller fails to consummate this sale for any reason other than Seller's inability to furnish to Purchaser marketable and insurable title to the Property as provided herein, Seller shall pay to Broker the real estate commission as provided in paragraph 11.

11. Commission

Seller shall at closing pay to Broker a real estate commission in the amount of ten percent of the purchase price. Purchaser and Seller hereby acknowledge that Broker has rendered a valuable service by negotiating this Contract, and Broker is therefore made a party to this Contract for the enforcement of Broker's rights to such commission. Purchaser shall have no obligations to pay any commissions.

12. Assignment

Purchaser shall have the right to assign this Contract in whole or in part only with the consent of Seller, which consent shall not be unreasonably withheld and the terms and provisions hereof shall be binding upon and shall inure to the benefit of the parties hereto, their successors, representatives, heirs and assigns. Upon the occurrence of an assignment of this entire Contract, Purchaser shall be relieved of Purchaser's obligations hereunder.

13. Zoning

(a) Commencing on the date hereof, Seller and Purchaser shall use their best efforts to obtain rezoning for all of the Property to the zoning classification of A-1 under the applicable Zoning Ordinances of Baker County,   so as to permit the development of the Property for apartment use in accordance with plans prepared by Purchaser at Purchaser's expense and submitted for use in connection with said rezoning. Purchaser [Seller] shall on or before 60 calendar days following the date hereof properly execute and

EXHIBIT 8–2
Contract for
Purchase and Sale
of Large Tract of
Vacant Land
(continued)

file at [Seller's] Purchaser's expense an Application for Rezoning of the Property with the proper officials of said County, attached to which shall be the plans prepared by the Purchaser. [Seller] Purchaser shall diligently and vigorously pursue said Application until a final decision has been made thereon by the governing body of said County and thereafter until all appeals and suits filed in connection with said rezoning have been finally disposed of. Seller and Purchaser shall cooperate in obtaining such rezoning and shall in no event either oppose or interfere with such rezoning.

(b) Said rezoning shall become "final zoning," as the term "final zoning" is used herein, on the date that such rezoning has been granted by the appropriate officials of said County pursuant to said Application of Purchaser [Seller], and any and all appeal periods as provided by law have expired without an appeal or suit having been filed, or, if filed, with such suit or appeal dismissed or resolved finally and conclusively in favor of such rezoning, and, at the expiration of such appeal periods, or at the conclusion of any such appeal or suit, the rezoning of the Property shall not have been further changed or withdrawn by the appropriate officials of said County.

(c) If said Application for Rezoning is not filed by Purchaser [Seller] within said 60 day period, then and in that event [Purchaser] Seller shall have the right to terminate this Contract by giving [Seller] Purchaser written notice of termination. Upon such termination, Purchaser's earnest money shall be promptly refunded in full to Purchaser.

(d) If Purchaser [Seller] complies with all of Purchaser's [Seller's] obligations as to rezoning set forth in this paragraph and if nevertheless said rezoning has been denied, or has neither been denied nor has become "final zoning" on or before 180 calendar days following the date hereof, then Purchaser shall have the right by written notice to Seller or Broker (i) to terminate this Contract and receive a prompt refund of Purchaser's earnest money or (ii) to postpone closing hereunder for not more than ninety calendar days thereafter until said "final zoning" is obtained or (iii) to terminate this Contract at the end of such postponement period if said "final zoning" remains unobtained and receive a prompt refund of Purchaser's earnest money or (iv) to waive the provisions of this paragraph and accept the Property without the "final zoning" described hereinabove.

14. Conditions to Closing

Unless waived by Purchaser, obligations of Purchaser under this Contract are expressly made subject to the following conditions:

(a) The truth and accuracy as of the date of this Contract and as of the date of closing of each and every warranty or representation herein made by Seller.

(b) The final rezoning of the Property as provided in Paragraph 13 hereof within the time specified, as such time may be extended.

(c) Purchaser's obtaining at or prior to the closing an easement for pedestrian and vehicular ingress and egress to and from the property across the adjoining property owned by Sam Smith, such easement to be in the form attached hereto as Exhibit E. Purchaser agrees to use Purchaser's best efforts to obtain such easement, to pay the cost of same (not to exceed $2,000.00), and to accept such easement if it is available.

15. Notice

Any notice required or permitted to be given hereunder shall be sufficient if in writing and sent by U.S. Certified Mail, postage prepaid, to the party being given such notice at the following addresses:

Seller: _____

_____

_____

survey, Purchaser shall mail a copy of said Plat to Seller in the manner hereinafter provided for giving notice, and, within ten calendar days after receipt of said copy, Seller shall notify Purchaser in writing if such plat is not acceptable to Seller. If Seller does not, within said ten day period, so notify Purchaser that such plat is not acceptable, said survey shall conclusively determine as between Purchaser and Seller the final acreage to be conveyed hereunder, and Seller's conveyance to Purchaser shall be in accordance with said survey.

If Seller does, within said ten day period, so notify Purchaser that such plat is not acceptable, Seller shall, simultaneously with the giving of such notification, cause at Seller's expense an accurate second survey of said Property to be made by a reputable surveyor registered under the laws of the State of   . The plat of such second survey shall show the boundaries of the Property and the acreage contained therein, computed to the nearest one-tenth of an acre. Within five calendar days after Seller's receipt of a plat of said second survey, Seller shall mail a copy thereof to Purchaser in the manner hereinafter provided for giving notice, and, within ten calendar days after receipt of such copy, Purchaser shall notify Seller in writing if such plat is not acceptable to Purchaser. If Purchaser does not, within said ten day period, so notify Seller that such plat is not acceptable, said second survey shall conclusively determine as between Purchaser and Seller the final acreage to be conveyed hereunder, and Seller's conveyance to Purchaser shall be in accordance with said second survey.

If Purchaser does, within said ten day period, so notify Seller that such plat is not acceptable, and if, within fourteen calendar days after receipt by Purchaser of such survey of Seller, Seller and Purchaser are unable to agree upon a survey, then both Seller and Purchaser shall cause their respective surveyors to name a third surveyor who shall be a reputable surveyor registered under the laws of the State of   . If said two surveyors have not named such third surveyor within seven calendar days following the last day of said fourteen day period, then said third surveyor shall be a reputable surveyor, registered under the laws of the State of   and named by the Superior Court Judge senior in point of service serving the county in which the Property (or the majority of said Property, if it lies in more than one county) lies.

Said third surveyor shall be promptly employed by Purchaser and Seller to make an accurate third survey of said Property, the cost of which third survey shall be borne equally by Purchaser and Seller. Said third surveyor shall furnish copies of the plat of said third survey to Purchaser and Seller upon completion of same; said plat shall show the boundaries of the Property and the acreage contained therein, computed to the nearest one-tenth of an acre. Said third survey shall conclusively determine as between Purchaser and Seller the final acreage to be conveyed hereunder, and Seller's conveyance to Purchaser shall be in accordance with said third survey.

The survey which, in accordance with provisions of this Paragraph 2, does in fact conclusively determine the final acreage to be conveyed hereunder shall be hereinafter referred to in this Agreement as "the survey."

EXHIBIT 8–2
Contract for
Purchase and Sale
of Large Tract of
Vacant Land
(continued)

AGREEMENT OF PURCHASE AND SALE

THIS AGREEMENT OF PURCHASE AND SALE (the "Agreement" is made and entered into as of the Effective Date, as hereafter defined, by and between _____

_____

_____ (hereinafter collectively "Seller"); and _____, a corporation (hereinafter "Purchaser").

WITNESSETH:

That for and in consideration of the mutual promises and covenants herein contained and the mutual advantages accruing to Seller and Purchaser hereunder and the sum of $10.00 and other good and valuable considerations paid by Purchaser to Seller, receipt of which is hereby acknowledged by Seller, it is mutually covenanted and agreed by the parties hereto as follows:

1. Property.

Seller hereby agrees to sell and convey to Purchaser and Purchaser hereby agrees to purchase from Seller, subject to the terms and conditions hereinafter set forth, the property located in Land Lot _____, _____ District, My Town, Great County, State described on *Exhibit A* attached hereto and made a part hereof containing approximately 2.544 acres (the "Land") as shown on that certain survey of the Land prepared by ___, Registered Land Surveyor No. 1845, for _____, dated July 25, 19___, last revised December 17, 19___ (the "Existing Survey"), together with the following:

(a) *Improvements.* All improvements on the Land owned by Seller, including, without limitation, a two-story retail shopping center containing approximately 54,520 net rentable square feet more commonly known as the "Village Square" and together with drives, sidewalks, drainage, sewerage and utility facilities and surface parking areas (collectively the "Improvements");

(b) *Tangible Personal Property.* All fixtures, equipment, machinery, building supplies, tools, furniture and other personal property, if any, and all replacements thereof, located on or about the Land and Improvements and used exclusively in the operation and maintenance thereof (the "Tangible Personal Property"), but expressly excluding any and all property owned by tenants occupying the Improvements;

(c) *Intangible Property.* Any and all of the Seller's rights and interests in and to all intangible property pertaining to the Land, the Improvements or the Tangible Property or the use thereof, including without limitation any trade names used in connection therewith, the Landlord's interest in all leases regarding the Property to the extent assignable, and all other licenses, franchises, permits, tenant security deposits (unless Purchaser, receives a credit for same), contract rights, agreements, transferable business licenses, tenant lists, correspondence with tenants and suppliers, booklets, manuals, advertising materials, transferable utility contracts, and transferable telephone exchange numbers (the "Intangible Property");

(d) *Easements.* Any and all of Seller's rights in and to all easements, if any, benefiting the Land or the Improvements; and

(e) *Rights and Appurtenances.* All rights and appurtenances pertaining to the foregoing, including any right, title and interest of Seller in and to adjacent streets, alleys or right-of-way.

EXHIBIT 8–3
Contract for
Purchase and Sale
of Retail Shopping
Center
(continued)

All of the property described in Subsections (a), (b), (c), (d), and (e) of this Section 1 together with the Land are hereinafter sometimes collectively referred to as the "Property."

2. Purchase Price and Earnest Money Deposits.

(a) *Purchase Price.* The Purchase Price (the "Purchase Price") to be paid for the Property shall be Seven Million Three Hundred Thousand and No/100 Dollars ($7,300,000.00) to be paid in the following manner:

(i) Purchaser shall take subject to a first mortgage loan on the Property held by Wearever Life Assurance Company in the original principal amount of Five Million Five Hundred Thousand Dollars ($5,500,000.00), which mortgage loan currently bears interest at the rate of ten percent per annum (10%) and is due and payable in full on January 1, 19___. Seller agrees to pay one-half of any and all transfer, assumption, or other fees assessed by the holder of the mortgage loan in connection with the transfer of the Property subject to the mortgage loan; and

(ii) Purchaser shall deliver to Seller a purchase money note ("Note") in the amount of Six Hundred Fifty Four Thousand Dollars ($654,000.00). Said Note shall bear interest at ten percent per annum (10%) and shall be payable interest only quarterly with a final payment of all unpaid principal and accrued and unpaid interest being due and payable two years from the Closing Date (hereinafter defined). The Note shall provide that it can be prepaid in whole or in part at any time without premium or penalty. The Note shall provide that the holder of the Note shall give the Maker of the Note at least twenty (20) days written notice of default prior to any acceleration of the Note for default or exercise of any other remedies which the holder may have to collect the indebtedness evidenced by the Note; provided, however, the Note shall be cross-defaulted with the Wearever Life Assurance Company loan ("WLA Loan") and defaults under the WLA Loan are to be governed by the notice and cure periods provided for in the WLA Loan. The Note shall be secured by a second priority Deed to Secure Debt ("Deed") on the Property. The Deed shall provide that insurance and condemnation proceeds shall be used for restoration of the property; shall provide for twenty (20) days written notice of default prior to any exercise of remedies thereunder; shall not provide for any tax or insurance escrows; shall not have any restrictions on the transfer of the Property or upon any further financing or encumbrancing of the Property. The Note and Deed shall be nonrecourse to Purchaser and shall contain no personal guaranty whatsoever. The Note shall be in the form of the Note attached hereto as Exhibit "L" and the Deed shall be in the form of the Deed to Secure Debt attached hereto as Exhibit "L-1".

(iii) The balance of the Purchase Price in the approximate amount of One Million One Hundred Forty-Six Thousand Dollars ($1,146,000.00) shall be payable in cash or by bank check drawn on a Federal Reserve Bank or by wire transfer or good funds on the Closing Date (hereinafter defined). Upon request by Purchaser prior to closing, Seller shall designate the account of Seller into which the net proceeds of the sale are to be deposited.

(b) *Earnest Money Deposits.* Purchaser shall deliver its earnest money deposit to Ajax Realty, Inc. (the "Escrowee") upon Purchaser's execution of this Agreement in the form of a cashier's check (drawn on a State financial institution) in the sum of SEVENTY FIVE THOUSAND DOLLARS ($75,000.00) (the "Earnest Money"), made payable to Escrowee in trust (said Earnest Money together with any interest earned thereon shall hereinafter be referred to as the "Deposit"). The Deposit shall be held and disbursed by escrowee as provided in this Agreement.

The Escrowee is directed to hold the Deposit as escrowed funds in an FDIC insured, interest-bearing account, at The Bank in My Town, State. Purchaser represents that his U.S. federal tax identification number is _____. Purchaser's tax identification

EXHIBIT 8-3
Contract for
Purchase and Sale
of Retail Shopping
Center
(continued)

number shall be credited with any interest earned on the Earnest Money prior to its being disbursed by Escrowee. Purchaser shall complete and execute a Payer's Request for Taxpayer Identification Number (Form W-9). Seller and Purchaser hereby agree to hold Escrowee harmless from any loss of escrowed funds, including the Deposit, for any reason whatsoever except for Escrowee's fraud or gross negligence or for loss of interest caused by any delay in the deposit or early withdrawal of the Deposit, from the interest-bearing account. This Agreement shall serve as escrow instructions and an executed copy of this Agreement shall be deposited by Purchaser with Escrowee. At Closing, the Deposit shall be delivered to Seller and applied against the Purchase Price. In the event of a termination of this Agreement or a default under this Agreement, the Deposit shall be delivered or disbursed by the Escrowee as provided in this Agreement. If any dispute or difference arises between the Purchaser and Seller or if any conflicting demands be made upon the Escrowee, the Escrowee shall not be required to determine the same or to take any action thereon. Rather, the Escrowee may await settlement of the controversy or deposit the Deposit into the Registry of the Superior Court of Great County, State, in an interpleader action or otherwise for the purpose of having the respective rights of the parties adjudicated. Upon making such deposit or upon institution of such interpleader action or other actions, the Escrowee shall be fully relieved and discharged from all further obligations hereunder with respect to the sums so deposited.

(c) Should any party terminate this Agreement, as permitted herein, or declare the other party in default of its obligations hereunder, and demand payment of the Deposit to it, then Escrowee shall pay to it the Deposit provided that declaring party provides evidence of the other party's receiving its demand notice, and within seven (7) business days following the other party's receipt of same, the nondeclaring party has not delivered written objection to Escrowee's disbursing the Deposit. If any dispute arises that is not resolved within thirty (30) days after such written objection, Escrowee shall deposit the Deposit into the Registry of the Superior Court of Great County, State, whereupon Escrowee's obligations and liabilities hereunder shall cease and terminate.

3. Inspection Period.

Purchaser shall have until 11:59 p.m. of August 26, 19____; (the "Final Inspection Date") within which to make an inspection of: the Property; all of Seller's operating financial records of the Property for the period of Seller's ownership of the Property (including the current year) pertaining to the Property and all items required to be delivered by Seller pursuant to this Agreement. All such records and items shall be made available to Purchaser at the office of the Seller in My Town, State. Purchaser shall have the right to enter upon the Property and make a complete inspection of the Property. Purchaser shall upon reasonable notice to Seller have the right to talk with all tenants, lenders' representatives (if any) and all service personnel involved with or connected with the Property. If for any reason the results of Purchaser's inspection are not deemed by Purchaser to be satisfactory for any reason whatsoever, in its sole discretion, then Purchaser may elect to terminate this Agreement by written notice of such election to Seller no later than the Final Inspection Date, in which event neither Purchaser nor Seller shall have any further rights or obligations hereunder, and Escrowee shall return to Purchaser the Deposit together with accrued interest and thereafter this Agreement shall be deemed terminated and of no further force or effect. If Purchaser fails to make such election to terminate this Agreement as aforesaid by the Final Inspection Date, then Purchaser shall be deemed to have waived its right to terminate this Agreement pursuant to this Section.

4. Title of the Property.

(a) Seller shall sell, convey and assign to Purchaser at Closing good and marketable fee simple title to the Property subject only to the Permitted Title Exceptions as defined and set forth on *Exhibit B* attached hereto.

(b) Within thirty (30) days following the Effective Date, Purchaser shall cause title to the Property to be examined and shall furnish Seller with a written statement of any and all title matters, other than the Permitted Title Exceptions to which Purchaser objects. Purchaser shall also have the right to examine, or cause to be examined, title to the Property at any time or times after such initial title examination and prior to Closing and to furnish Seller with a written statement or statements of any and all additional matters, other than the Permitted Title Exceptions which affect the title to the Property or the use thereof and which arise, or first appear of record from and after the date of the initial title examination hereunder and to which Purchaser objects. Seller shall cooperate with Purchaser after receipt of any such written statement to correct, cure or remove all matters described in such statement, and covenants to exercise diligent and good faith efforts to do so. Notwithstanding the above or the terms of this Section 4(b), in the event that any such matter results from any affirmative action taken by Seller subsequent to the date hereof, Seller covenants to expend such money and to take such other actions as may be necessary to correct, cure or remove same. The Closing Date shall be postponed automatically for thirty (30) days, if necessary, to permit Seller to cure. If Seller shall fail to correct, cure or remove all such matters within the time allowed by this Section 4(b), then Purchaser, at its option exercised by written notice may:

(i) decline to purchase the Property; or

(ii) waive such matter and proceed to close the purchase and sale of the Property without a reduction in the Purchase Price and allow Seller to convey title to the Property in accordance with the terms hereof; or

(iii) in the event the matter results from affirmative action of Seller subsequent to the Effective Date, require Seller by action of specific performance or otherwise to exercise diligent and good faith efforts to correct, cure or remove such matters and convey the Property in accordance with the terms of this Agreement in which case the Closing Date shall be postponed until such correction, cure or removal by Seller has been completed (provided, however, that at any time during such period Purchaser may exercise its options as set forth in Section 4(b)(i) or Section 4(b)(ii) above).

Should Purchaser accept, by written waiver, its interest in the Property subject to matters in addition to the Permitted Title Exceptions, such acceptable matters shall be added to the list now set forth in *Exhibit B* and shall thereafter be deemed to be Permitted Title Exceptions except that, in the event any of such matters results from any affirmative action taken by Seller subsequent to the date hereof, such acceptance shall be without prejudice to Purchaser's thereafter seeking monetary damages from Seller for any such matter. If Purchaser shall decline to accept the Seller's interest in the Property subject to such matters, pursuant to Section 4(b) above, then Escrowee shall refund to Purchaser the Deposit and the parties hereto shall have no further rights, obligations, duties or liabilities hereunder whatsoever, except for those rights, obligations, duties and liabilities which, that, by the express terms hereof, survive any termination hereof and except for Purchaser's right to seek monetary damages from Seller for any matter which Seller shall have failed so to correct and which shall have resulted from any affirmative action taken by Seller after the date hereof.

EXHIBIT 8–3
Contract for
Purchase and Sale
of Retail Shopping
Center
(continued)

EXHIBIT 8–3
Contract for
Purchase and Sale
of Retail Shopping
Center
(continued)

(c) Purchaser may, at its expense, elect to obtain a standard A.L.T.A. Form 1987–B owner's policy of title insurance pursuant to which fee simple title to the Property shall be insured. Seller covenants to Purchaser that title to the Property shall at Closing not only be good and marketable, but, in the event Purchaser elects so to purchase such an owner's policy of title insurance, shall be insurable by Ticor Title Insurance Company of California or by Chicago Title Insurance Company or other title insurance company reasonably acceptable to Purchaser at its regular rates, without exceptions or reservations to coverage of any type or kind, other than the Permitted Title Exceptions.

5. Survey.

(a) Purchaser shall have within thirty (30) days from the Effective Date the option to obtain a current accurate as-built survey of the Premises (the "New Survey") and such New Survey discloses any matter which is not set forth on the Existing Survey to which Purchaser objects (any such matter being herein referred to as "New Survey Objections"), then Purchaser shall give Seller notice of such New Survey Objections. Purchaser shall be entitled to make its best efforts to cure said New Survey Objections and Seller covenants that it shall cooperate with Purchaser to the extent necessary to effectuate said cures.

(b) If Seller shall have failed to correct, cure or remove all such New Survey Objections prior to time set for closing, then Purchaser, at its option, exercised by written notice, may:

(i) decline to purchase the Property; or

(ii) waive such matter and proceed to close the purchase and sale of the Property without a reduction in the Purchase Price and allow Seller to convey title to the Property in accordance with the terms hereof; or

(iii) or, if such New Survey Objection should arise by affirmative action of Seller after the Execution Date, require Seller by action of specific performance or otherwise to exercise diligent and good faith efforts to correct, cure or remove such New Survey Objections and convey the Property in accordance with the terms of this Agreement in which case the Closing Date shall be postponed until such correction, cure or removal by Seller has been completed (provided, however, that at any time during such period Purchaser may exercise its options as set forth in Section 5(b)(i) or Section 5(b)(ii) above).

Should Purchaser accept, by written waiver, its interest in the Property subject to New Survey Objections, such acceptable matters shall be added to the list now set forth in *Exhibit B* and shall thereafter be deemed to be Permitted Title Exceptions except that, in the event any of such matters results from any affirmative action taken by Seller subsequent to the date hereof, such acceptance shall be without prejudice to Purchaser's thereafter seeking monetary damages from Seller for any such matter. If Purchaser shall decline to accept the Seller's interest in the Property subject to such matters, pursuant to Section 5(b)(i) above, then Escrowee shall refund to Purchaser the Deposit and the parties hereto shall have no further rights, obligations, duties or liabilities hereunder whatsoever, except for those rights, obligations, duties and liabilities which, that, by the express terms hereof, survive any termination hereof and except for Purchaser's right to seek monetary damages from Seller for any matter which Seller shall have failed so to correct and which shall have resulted from any affirmative action taken by Seller after the date hereof.

6. Seller's Deliveries.

(a) Seller shall deliver to Purchaser or Purchaser's designee the following items, in possession of Seller or any entity related to Seller, as soon as reasonably possible after the Effective Date, but in any event within five (5) days after the Effective Date, unless another time period is otherwise indicated below:

(i) True, correct and complete copies of all leases of space on the Property together with any amendments thereto and all brokerage commission agreements relating thereto and together with all lease abstracts, tenant correspondence files, and other relevant information, all necessary information and documentation necessary to establish the base index, such as the consumer price index for the base year of such lease, for any escalation clause in any lease, and copies of all written correspondence to or received from any lessee regarding such additional rental charges or rental escalation provisions (all leases of space on the Property together with any amendments thereto and such brokerage commission agreements and other documents described hereinabove are hereinafter collectively referred to as the "Leases", and each lease of space on the Property together with any amendments thereto and such brokerage commission agreements is hereinafter individually referred to as a "Lease");

(ii) A true, correct and complete rent roll concerning all Leases as of the Effective Date or a more current date, indicating thereon any delinquencies with respect to rent due and owing and indicating all brokerage commissions and similar fees owing and relating to the Leases;

(iii) True, correct and complete copies of all contracts other than Leases, if any, pertaining to the Property (the "Service Contracts") in existence as of the Effective Date or a more current date, including but not limited to all management contracts, maintenance contracts, contracts or agreements relating to any unfinished improvements to the Property, service leases, and contracts for parking on a monthly or yearly basis, together with a list of those contracts which cannot be unilaterally terminated by Purchaser as of the Closing Date without further payment;

(iv) A true, correct and complete inventory of all the Tangible Personal Property as of the Effective Date or a more current date;

(v) [INTENTIONALLY DELETED]

(vi) True, correct and complete copies of the latest personal property and real estate tax bills for the Property and all tax bills, notices, assessments and communications relating to the Property, or any part thereof, promptly upon receipt of same by Seller;

(vii) True, correct and complete copies of the most recent title insurance policy relating to the Land, if any, in the possession of Seller; together with true, correct and complete copies of all exceptions listed on Schedule B thereof which are not inchoate liens or surveys exceptions;

(viii) True, correct and complete copies of all matters listed on *Exhibit B* attached hereto which are not inchoate liens or survey exceptions (to the extent that such copies are not furnished to Purchaser pursuant to Section 6(a)(vii) above);

(ix) True, correct and complete copies of all inspection reports and tests and studies relating to the Property, including, without limitation, engineering studies, environmental assessments or reports, and maintenance schedules;

(x) A true, correct and complete copy of any offering circular, private placement memorandum, registration statement or other similar information or materials relating to the Property, which is in the possession of the Seller;

(xi) True, correct and complete copies of all existing insurance policies relating to the Property (or if the Property is insured pursuant to a master policy, then true, correct and complete copies of all certificates (issued pursuant to such master policies) which evidence the insurance coverages relating to the Property) and true, correct and com-

EXHIBIT 8–3
Contract for
Purchase and Sale
of Retail Shopping
Center
(continued)

EXHIBIT 8–3
Contract for
Purchase and Sale
of Retail Shopping
Center
(continued)

plete copies of all records and communications concerning all claims, losses and demands made under any insurance policy relating to the Property since Seller acquired the Property and otherwise in possession of Seller, together with a listing of the names, addresses and account representatives of all insurance companies which issued policies relating to the Property since Seller acquired the Property and otherwise in the possession of Seller;

(xii) A memorandum, which Seller shall prepare if presently not in Seller's possession, describing all oral contracts and agreements pertaining to the Property, if any, which memorandum shall include, without limitation, the names, address and telephone numbers of all persons or entities which are parties to such contracts or agreements together with a detailed description of the terms, conditions and provisions of such contracts and agreements;

(xiii) True, complete and correct copies of all documents, including, but not limited to, plans, specifications, contracts, budgets, schedules, and certificates pertaining to the current construction, renovation, paving, and all other improvement to the Property;

(xiv) On or before November 1, 19____, tenant estoppel letters subsequentially in the form attached hereto as *Exhibit C* (the "Tenant Estoppels") each dated no earlier than October 1, 19____, duly executed by all tenants of the Property or in such form as required by Lender. Seller shall use its best efforts to obtain the Tenant Estoppels from all tenants. If Seller is unable to obtain Tenant Estoppels from tenants occupying at least eighty-five percent (85%) of the net rented square footage of the Improvements under leases existing as of October 1, 19____, as required above, then Purchaser may either (A) accept those Tenant Estoppels obtained by Seller and close the subject transaction otherwise in accordance with the terms of the Agreement; or (B) decline to purchase the Property. If Purchaser elects to close the subject transaction pursuant to its option set forth in Section 6(a)(xiv)(A) above, then with respect to all those Leases for which a tenant estoppel letter is not obtained and delivered to Purchaser at or before Closing, Seller shall deliver to Purchaser at Closing a certificate setting forth the status of each such Lease and providing the information set forth in the tenant estoppel letters;

(xv) True, correct and complete copies of all Permits (as defined below), certificates of occupancy and licenses issued by any Governmental Authority (as defined below) or utility company in connection with the occupancy and use of the Improvements as are in the possession of Seller;

(xvi) True, correct and complete copies, if any, of all notes and other unrecorded documents, agreements and instruments relating to indebtedness secured by the Property or any part thereof; and

(b) In the event any event of circumstances shall occur which renders any documents, materials or other information provided by Seller to Purchaser pursuant to Section 6(a) no longer true, correct and complete, Seller shall immediately deliver to Purchaser all documentation, material and information necessary to supplement the same so as to render such documents, material and information true, correct and complete. Purchaser shall have seven (7) business days in which to review such supplemental material and, in the event that such supplemental materials differ materially and adversely in Purchaser's sole opinion, from the information and materials previously furnished or made available to Purchaser and are not deemed by Purchaser to be satisfactory, then Purchaser may elect to terminate this Agreement by delivering written notice of such election to Seller no later than seven (7) business days after the receipt by Purchaser of such necessary material, to permit the running of such period of seven

EXHIBIT 8–3
Contract for
Purchase and Sale
of Retail Shopping
Center
(continued)

(7) business days. If, however, any such documents, materials or other information provided by Seller to Purchaser pursuant to Section 6(a) is untrue, incorrect or incomplete as of the date provided pursuant to Section 6(a), Seller shall be deemed to have breached this Agreement, and Purchaser shall be entitled to all remedies provided in Section 20 of this Agreement.

7. Legal Description.

In the event that the legal description of the Land as set forth in the New Survey differs from the legal description of the Land as set forth in the Existing Survey, Seller shall convey at Closing to Purchaser by quitclaim deed all Seller's right, title and interest in and to the Land as described in the New Survey, together with all Property relating thereto or existing therein; provided, however, that nothing in the preceding sentence shall limit Purchaser's right to deem any such material differences as a New Survey Objection, thereby entitling Purchaser to the rights and remedies set forth in Section 5 above. In any event, Seller must convey by a legal description for which Purchaser may obtain standard title insurance through Chicago Title Insurance Company, Ticor Title Insurance Company of California or Lawyers Title Insurance Company, at standard rates.

8. Purchaser's Access to the Property and Seller's Records.

At any time prior to Closing (unless this Agreement is terminated as herein provided), the Purchaser, its agents, employees and contractors, shall have the right to enter upon the Property after reasonable notice to Seller for purposes of surveying, inspecting and testing the Property; provided, however, that in the event this Agreement fails to close for any reason, Purchaser shall (on or before the scheduled Closing Date) restore the Property to its original condition and further provided that Purchaser shall use its best efforts not to disrupt the ordinary course of business of Seller or any of the tenants under Leases. Purchaser agrees to indemnify and hold Seller harmless against any property damage or personal injury or claim of lien against the Property resulting from the activities permitted by this Section (including, without limitation, reasonable attorneys fees and expenses paid or incurred by the Seller during litigation and appeals thereof, if any). All inspections, tests, investigations and other activities carried on by Purchaser pertaining to the Property, shall be at Purchaser's sole cost and expense. In addition to and not in limitation of Purchaser's rights elsewhere set forth herein. Purchaser shall have the right upon three (3) business days prior written notice to Seller to inspect all property, books, leases and records of Seller pertaining directly to the operation of the Property, for the period of Seller's ownership of the Property, provided that the cost of copying such items shall be borne by Purchaser and such items shall be made available to Purchaser by Seller at the Office of Seller in My Town, State or such other location in My Town, State where said items are normally stored.

9. Covenants and Representations.

(a) *Seller's Covenants and Representations.*

(i) Seller has obtained all consents, approvals or authorizations necessary to execute this Agreement and to consummate the transaction contemplated hereby, and all documents referred to herein will be validly executed and delivered and binding upon Seller;

(ii) Seller has no knowledge of any material defect in the Improvements or any part thereof and has no knowledge of and has received no notice from any Governmental Authority (as defined below) of any violation of any Requirement of Law (as defined below) relating to the Property or any part thereof;

EXHIBIT 8–3
Contract for
Purchase and Sale
of Retail Shopping
Center
(continued)

(iii) Seller has no knowledge of and has received no notice from any insurance company or board of fire underwriters or similar agency that there exists any condition or circumstances on the Property or any part thereof, which must be corrected in order to maintain the effectiveness, or as a condition precedent to the issuance of, any insurance policy affecting the Property or any part thereof or which is in violation of, any applicable fire code or similar rule, regulation or order for such board of fire underwriters or similar agency;

(iv) Seller has no knowledge of and has received no notice of any litigation, claim or suit which is pending or threatened which could adversely affect the Property or any part thereof or title thereto (exclusive of any litigation, claim or suit brought against a tenant of the Property after the Effective Date wherein Seller is not named a defendant or a third party defendant and wherein no counterclaims are alleged against Seller, provided, however, that Seller will give Purchaser prompt notice of all such litigation, claims and suits);

(v) Neither Seller, nor, to the best of Seller's knowledge, any previous owner of the Property or any part thereof has used, generated, stored or disposed of any Hazardous Materials (as defined below) in or on the Property or any part thereof; or has used or disposed of any Hazardous Materials in connection with the use, operation, construction or repair of the Property or any part thereof. Seller shall hold Purchaser harmless and shall indemnify and defend Purchaser from and against any and all losses, damages, claims and liabilities whatsoever in any way relating to or arising out of any breach of the foregoing representation. This provision shall survive Closing and the consummation of the transactions contemplated hereby;

(vi) Seller owns good and unencumbered title to the Tangible Personal Property and Intangible Personal Property, and Seller has done nothing to encumber same during Seller's ownership thereof other than those certain Loan Documents listed on *Exhibit K* attached hereto;

(vii) Seller has not operated the Property within the past five (5) years under any other name or trade name of which it has not notified Purchaser;

(viii) All documents, materials and information delivered to Purchaser pursuant to Section 6(a), as supplemented by such documents, materials and information delivered to Purchaser pursuant to Section 6(b), are true, correct and complete;

(ix) Seller shall not cause or permit to exist (A) any mortgage, deed to secure debt, security deed, security agreement, assignment or other similar instrument or agreement or any lien or encumbrance whatsoever (other than the Permitted Exceptions or those listed on *Exhibit K*) to attach to or affect title to the Property or any part thereof from and after the Effective Date except for the Leases approved by Purchaser; or (B) any matters not shown on the New Survey;

(x) Seller represents, to the best of its knowledge, that the mechanical, electrical, plumbing, HVAC, roofing, drainage, sanitary sewerage, and utility equipment facilities and systems servicing the Property and the improvements thereon are in operational order and shall be so maintained through and including the Closing Date. Seller represents that it is aware of no defects in any of said systems;

(xi) Seller covenants that it shall not enter into any leases pertaining to the Property after the Effective Date without prior written approval of Purchaser. Purchaser shall approve leases containing reasonable business terms, including base rentals of at least $16.00 per square foot and $1.75 of C.A.Ms. Seller covenants and represents that it shall incur no brokerage commissions pertaining to leases entered into prior to the Closing Date on any leases negotiated in any respect by Seller prior to the Closing Date;

(xii) Seller represents that it has no notice of and is not aware of any violation of the Property and improvements of any applicable zoning laws, ordinances or regulations including, without limitation, all parking requirements and building set back requirements (except as shown on the Existing Survey which Purchaser has the right to consider during the Inspection Period);

(xiii) [INTENTIONALLY DELETED]

(xiv) Seller shall continue to operate, manage, and maintain the Property in good condition and in a good business like manner, such operation and maintenance to include the undertaking of any reasonably necessary capital improvements or repairs, through and including the Closing Date. Such continuous operation and maintenance shall also be a condition precedent to Closing; and

(b) *Purchaser's Covenants and Representations.* Purchaser hereby represents and warrants to Seller that Purchaser has obtained all consents, approvals or authorizations necessary to execute this Agreement and to consummate the transaction contemplated hereby, and all documents referred to herein will be validly executed and delivered and binding upon Purchaser.

10. Additional Conditions Precedent.

(a) This Agreement is contingent upon Purchaser being able to Purchase the Property subject to the current mortgage loan in the original principal amount of FIVE MILLION FIVE HUNDRED THOUSAND AND NO/100 DOLLARS ($5,500,000.00) held by Wearever Life Assurance Company (the "Mortgage Loan") being evidenced by (a) certain Real Estate Note, dated December 17, 19____, from Seller to Wearever Life Assurance Company, (b) Deed to Secure Debt and Security Agreement by and between the same parties dated December 17, 19____, recorded at Deed Book 11234, Page 137, Great County, State Records, and (c) an Assignment of Leases and Rents by and between the same parties dated December 17, 19____, recorded at Deed Book 11234, Page 162, Great County, State Records (hereinafter referred to as the "Mortgage Loan Documents"). One-half ($^1/_2$) of all costs, assumption fees, transfer fees, paid to the holder of the Mortgage Loan to obtain permission to transfer the Property to Purchaser shall be paid by Seller and the other one-half ($^1/_2$) by Purchaser. The tax and insurance provisions contained in the Mortgage Loan Documents are to be waived upon the same terms and conditions they are presently being waived for Seller. The terms of the Mortgage Loan, including but not limited to, the rate of interest, the amount of the monthly installments, the Maturity Date, are to remain unchanged. Seller shall provide Purchaser with an Estoppel Agreement from the holder of the Mortgage Loan in substantially the same form as that attached hereto as *Exhibit "I".* Purchaser agrees to provide the holder of the Mortgage Loan with any financial information necessary to enable the holder of the Mortgage Loan to approve the transfer of the Property from Seller to Purchaser. This Agreement shall remain contingent upon the ability of Purchaser to obtain the Property subject to the Mortgage Loan and the consent by the holder of the Mortgage Loan to the Note and Deed.

If the Seller has not obtained the permission from the holder of the Mortgage Loan to transfer the Property to Purchaser subject to the Mortgage Loan and upon the terms set forth therein and the consent to the Note and Deed on or before September 26, 19___, then Purchaser may by written notice to Seller notify Seller of its election to terminate this Agreement, whereupon this Agreement shall terminate and the Deposit together with accrued interest thereon, shall be returned to Purchaser, and thereafter the parties hereto shall have no further rights, duties, obligations or liabilities hereunder.

EXHIBIT 8–3
Contract for
Purchase and Sale
of Retail Shopping
Center
(continued)

EXHIBIT 8–3
Contract for
Purchase and Sale
of Retail Shopping
Center
(continued)

(b) Seller shall continuously operate and maintain the Property in good condition and continue business like management through and including the Closing Date.

11. Closing Date.

Unless this Agreement is terminated by Purchaser pursuant to the terms of this Agreement, the Closing shall take place at the offices of Purchaser's attorneys, Winkom, Blinkholm and Nodd, 1400 Crabtree Place Tower, My Town, State, or such location as is mutually agreeable to Purchaser and Seller, beginning at 10:00 a.m. on a business day (in My Town, State) selected by Purchaser on or before November 11, 19___. The date of Closing shall hereinafter be referred to as the "Closing Date". Purchaser shall give Seller notice of the Closing Date at least five (5) business days prior thereto; provided, however, if Purchaser gives Seller no such notice of the Closing Date, then the Closing Date shall be November 11, 19___.

12. Seller's Obligations.

At Closing, Seller shall:

(a) Execute, acknowledge and deliver to Purchaser a limited warranty deed in recordable form, the form of which is attached hereto as *Exhibit D* conveying the Property to Purchaser subject only to: (i) taxes for the years subsequent to the year of Closing; (ii) the zoning classification as of the Effective Date; and (iii) the Permitted Exceptions;

(b) Execute and deliver to Purchaser the following additional conveyance documents: (A) an Affidavit reciting Seller's non-foreign status within the meaning of Section 1445(f)(3) of the Internal Revenue Code of 1986; (B) an Assignment and Assumption of Leases assigning to Purchaser lessor's interest in the Leases, a form of which is attached hereto as *Exhibit E*; and (C) an Assignment of Contracts, Other Rights and Intangible Property assigning to Purchaser the Intangible Property, the form of which is attached hereto as *Exhibit F*; and (D) Lender Estoppel Letter from the holder of the Mortgage Loan, a proposed form of which is attached hereto as *Exhibit "I"*; (E) Subordination, Attornment and Non-Disturbance Agreements satisfactory to Lender signed by tenants leasing at least eighty-five percent (85%) of the net rentable square footage of the Property, a proposed form of which is attached hereto as *Exhibit J*; and (F) a certificate that Seller knows of no defects in the system referred to in Sections 9(a)(x) and (xi) of this Agreement as of the Closing Date;

(c) Execute and deliver to Purchaser a Closing Statement setting forth the adjustments and prorations to closing as well as the costs pursuant to this Agreement as elsewhere specifically provided herein (the "Closing Statement");

(d) Deliver to Purchaser a certified and updated rent roll reflecting all the tenants under Leases to the Property as of the Closing Date and indicating thereon any delinquencies with respect to rent due;

(e) Deliver to Purchaser all Permits, certificates of occupancy and licenses issued by an Governmental Authorities or utility companies in connection with the occupancy and use of the Improvements as are in the possession of Seller;

(f) Deliver to Purchaser a form letter to all tenants under Leases stating that Purchaser has acquired the Property from Seller, that future rents should be paid as specified by Purchaser, and that Purchaser will be responsible for all tenants' security deposits, if any;

(g) A certificate of Seller stating (A) that Seller has no knowledge of any pending or threatened condemnation proceedings or any taking by any Governmental Authority which in any way affects the Property, (B) that there are no Leases (other than Leases approved by Purchaser), no Service Contracts (whether written or oral), no employees, no insurance policy endorsements or claims, no other notices from any Governmental Authority regarding any violations of any Requirements of Law affecting the Property except as heretofore provided to Purchaser as required under Section 6 above and elsewhere in this Agreement;

(h) The plans and specifications for the Improvements, including all amendments thereto, as are in the possession of Seller;

(i) The originals of all Leases including all amendments thereto;

(j) All information and materials required for full compliance under the Foreign Investors in Real Property Tax Act;

(k) All keys to the Improvements in Seller's possession and a list of all other persons which, to the best of Seller's knowledge are in possession of keys to the Improvements, other than keys to tenant space in the possession of tenants;

(l) Such other documents, instruments and agreements as Purchaser may reasonably require to effect and complete the transactions contemplated herein and to obtain an owner's title insurance policy insuring the interest of Purchaser, as owner, in the amount of $7,300,000.00, free and clear of all exceptions except the Permitted Exceptions, for a premium calculated at standard rates, including, without limitation, a Seller's Affidavit of Title in the form attached hereto as *Exhibit G* and a Bill of Sale in the form attached hereto as *Exhibit H*; and

(m) Seller's estoppel certificates to the extent required by Section 6(a)(xiv) above.

13. Purchaser's Obligations at Closing.

On the Closing Date, subject to the terms, conditions, and provisions hereof, Purchaser shall:

(a) Execute and deliver to Seller an assumption agreement whereby Purchaser assumes all liabilities and agrees to perform all obligations of Seller under all the Leases, the form of which is contained in *Exhibit E,* and the Service Contracts and all employee contracts assumed by Purchaser pursuant hereto, the form of which is contained in *Exhibit F.* Said assumption agreements shall contain an indemnification by Purchaser of Seller and an agreement to hold Seller harmless from and against any and all claims, debts, liabilities and the like affecting or relating to the Property, or any part thereof, and the Leases after the Closing Date. Likewise, said assumption agreements shall contain an agreement to hold Purchaser harmless from and against any and all claims, debts, liabilities and the like affecting or relating to the Property, or any part thereof, and the Leases prior to and including the Closing Date.

(b) Execute and deliver to Seller a copy of the Closing Statement.

(c) Deliver to Seller pursuant to the terms of Section 2 herein the Note and Deed and pursuant to Section 2 herein, the sums required to be paid hereinunder, and Purchaser shall execute such other documents, instruments, affidavits and agreements as may be required to close the transaction contemplated herein.

14. Closing Costs.

In connection with Closing, Seller shall pay the State real estate transfer tax and all costs relating to the satisfaction, cure and removal of all title defects (except the Permitted Exceptions) undertaken by Seller as herein required and the payment of one-half ($^1/_2$) all transfer, assumption or other fees due the holder of the Mortgage Loan to obtain the consent to the transfer the Property to the Purchaser and the consent to the Note and Deed. Purchaser shall pay the costs of the premiums payable or costs incurred in connection with the issuance of the owner's title insurance commitment and the owner's title insur-

EXHIBIT 8–3
Contract for
Purchase and Sale
of Retail Shopping
Center
(continued)

EXHIBIT 8–3
Contract for
Purchase and Sale
of Retail Shopping
Center
(continued)

ance policy in favor of Purchaser and all costs of recording the limited warranty deed. The Purchaser shall be solely responsible for the New Survey costs. Each party shall pay its own attorney's fees.

15. Prorations.

The following items shall be apportioned and prorated (based on a 30-day month, unless otherwise indicated) between the Seller and the Purchaser as of the Closing Date so that credits and charges for all days prior to the Closing Date shall be allocated to the Seller and credits and charges for the Closing Date and for all days thereafter shall be allocated to the Purchaser:

(a) *Taxes.* At the Closing, all ad valorem property taxes, water and sewer charges and assessments of any kind on the Property for the year of the Closing shall be prorated between Purchaser and Seller as of 12:01 a.m. on the Closing Date. Such proration shall be based upon the latest ad valorem property tax, water, sewer charge and assessment bills available. If, upon receipt of the actual ad valorem property tax, water, sewer and assessment bills for the Property, such proration is incorrect, then either Purchaser or Seller shall be entitled, upon demand, to receive such amounts from the other as may be necessary to correct such mal-apportionment. This obligation so to correct such mal-apportionment shall survive the Closing and not be merged into any documents delivered pursuant to the Closing.

(b) *Rents.* Purchaser shall receive a credit for all amounts due under the Leases in effect at Closing, hereinafter referred to as the "Rent", collected by Seller prior to Closing and allocable in whole or in part to any period following the Closing Date. Seller shall deliver to Purchaser any Rent received after Closing. Purchaser shall deliver to Seller any Rents received after Closing which relate to periods prior to and through the Closing Date; provided, however, that any such Rents collected by Purchaser after the Closing shall be applied first toward Rents due which shall have accrued after the Closing Date and then towards Rents which accrued prior to the Closing Date. Purchaser shall use its best efforts (short of incurring legal fees and expenses or taking other action which would not be in its best interest as owner of the Property) to collect all such delinquent Rents.

In the event that Purchaser is unable to collect delinquent Rents due Seller within thirty (30) days after the Closing Date, then Seller may pursue collection of such delinquent Rents from the respective Tenants in accordance with its rights under Georgia law; provided, however, Seller shall have no right to collect Rents in any manner which would result in an interference with the Tenant's rights of possession under its lease or in any way interfere with the landlord/tenant relationship between Purchaser and the Tenant (for example, Seller shall have no rights to dispossess Tenant in an effort to collect delinquent Rents.)

(c) *Other Expense Prorations.* All other reasonable expenses normal to the operation and maintenance of the Property that require payments either in advance or in arrears for periods which begin prior to the Closing Date and end thereafter. Without limiting the generality of the foregoing, such expenses shall include: water, electric; telephone and all other utility and fuel charges; fuel on hand (at cost plus sales tax) any deposits with utility companies; employee wages, salaries, benefits and pension, health and welfare insurance, social security and such other contributions; and charges under employee contracts and/or Service Contracts.

(d) *Security Deposits.* Purchaser shall receive a credit for the security deposits paid under the Leases in existence and in effect on the Closing Date.

(e) *Leasing Commissions.* Seller warrants and represents that there are no leasing commissions due and owing or to become due and owing under any of the Leases or any renewals and extensions thereof, as of the Closing Date. Seller agrees to hold harmless from and to indemnify and defend Purchaser from and against any and all such leasing commissions and all other fees, charges and compensation whatsoever due any person or entity in connection with the procuring of any Lease together with all extensions and renewals thereof or otherwise relating to any Lease. This provision shall survive the Closing and the consummation of the transactions contemplated herein.

16. Employees and Service Contracts.

Seller represents and warrants that there are no employees or employment contracts relating to the Property which cannot be terminated on or prior to Closing because of contractual terms or applicable law. From and after the Effective Date, Seller will not enter into or extend or renew any contracts relating to the Property which cannot by their express terms terminate with thirty (30) days notice, without the prior written approval of Purchaser. With respect to all other employees and contracts relating to the Property, Purchaser shall not be obligated to continue the employment of all such employees and to continue all such contracts and to assume all obligations therefor as of the Closing Date, unless Purchaser notifies Seller of its intention to continue the employment of employees under any or all of such employee agreements and/or contracts prior to Closing, in which event Seller shall be responsible for terminating the employment of such personnel and such contracts capable of being terminated and designated for termination by Purchaser's notice. With respect to any leasing brokerage agreements in connection with the Property, Seller shall terminate and obtain release of same prior to or on the Closing Date.

17. Brokerage Commissions.

Each party further represents to the other that except for_____

_____
(collectively "Brokers"), no broker has been involved in this transaction. Seller shall be solely responsible for paying any commission due to the Brokers in connection with this transaction. Seller shall pay in cash or good funds at Closing brokerage commissions of one percent (1%) to_____

_____ and one percent (1%) of the Purchase Price to_____. No commission shall be due and owing Brokers should the sale and purchase of the Property fail to close for any reason whatsoever, including, without limitation, the breach of this Agreement by Seller or Purchaser. Under no circumstances whatsoever shall Brokers be entitled to retain any portion of the Deposit. In the event any other claims for brokerage commissions or fees are ever made against the Seller or the Purchaser in connection with this transaction, all such claims shall be handled and paid by the party whose actions or alleged commitments form the basis of such claim. Seller further agrees to indemnify and hold harmless the Purchaser from and against any and all such claims or demands with respect to any brokerage fees or agent's commissions or other compensation asserted by any person, firm, or corporation in connection with this Agreement or the transactions contemplated hereby arising from actions or alleged commitments of the Seller. Purchaser further agrees to indemnify and hold harmless the Seller from and against any and all such claims or demands with respect to any brokerage fees or agent's commissions or other compensation asserted by any person, firm or corporation in connection with this Agreement or the transaction contemplated hereby arising from actions or alleged commitments of the

EXHIBIT 8–3
Contract for
Purchase and Sale
of Retail Shopping
Center
(continued)

EXHIBIT 8–3
Contract for
Purchase and Sale
of Retail Shopping
Center
(continued)

Purchaser. This provision shall survive Closing and the conveyance of the Property by Seller to Purchaser.

18. Risk of Loss.

Risk of loss or damage to the Property or any part thereof by condemnation, eminent domain, or similar proceedings, or by deed in lieu or under threat thereof (collectively, a "Taking"), or by fire, flood or other casualty from the Effective Date until delivery of the limited warranty deed will be on Seller and after the delivery of the limited warranty deed will be on Purchaser. In the event of any such loss or damage to all or to a material part of the Property or any part of the Improvements prior to the delivery of the limited warranty deed, this Agreement may, at the option of Purchaser to be exercised by written notice to Seller, be declared null and void and Purchaser shall be returned the Deposit and both parties hereto shall be released from any further rights and duties hereunder, or this Agreement shall remain in full force and effect and Seller shall transfer to Purchaser on the Closing Date all insurance proceeds or condemnation awards received by Seller because of such casualty or Taking and all of Seller's rights, title and interest in and to any recovery or claims under any insurance policies or condemnation awards relating to the Property.

Upon the happening of one of the events in the preceding paragraph, subsequent to the Inspection Deadline and prior to delivery of the limited warranty deed, if the cost of repair or replacement or, in the event of a Taking, if the reduction in the value of the project is TWENTY–FIVE THOUSAND DOLLARS ($25,000.00) or less, Purchaser shall close and take the Property as diminished by such events and Seller shall transfer to Purchaser on the Closing Date all insurance proceeds or condemnation awards received by Seller because of such casualty or Taking and all of Seller's right, title, and interest in and to any recovery or claim under any insurance policies or condemnation awards relating to the Property together with a credit to Purchaser for the amount of any deductibles contained in any insurance policy.

19. Purchaser's Default.

In the event the transaction contemplated hereby is not closed because of Purchaser's default, the Deposit shall be paid to Seller as full liquidated damages for such failure to close, the parties acknowledging the difficulty of ascertaining Seller's damages in such circumstances, whereupon neither party hereto shall have any further rights, claims or liabilities under this Agreement except for the provisions which are made to survive the termination or cancellation of this Agreement. Said liquidated damages shall be Seller's sole and exclusive remedy, and Seller shall expressly not have the right to seek specific performance.

20. Seller's Default.

If the Seller fails to perform any of the covenants of this Agreement, or if Seller otherwise defaults hereunder, the Purchaser shall have the right, in addition to all rights and remedies herein provided, to pursue any right or remedy it may have against Seller at law or in equity for such breach and/or default, including, without limitation, the right of specific performance of all provisions of this Agreement. Purchaser's monetary damages in the event of such breach and/or default by Seller shall be limited to $100,000.00. The parties hereto acknowledge the difficulty of ascertaining Purchaser's monetary damages in such event.

EXHIBIT 8−3
Contract for
Purchase and Sale
of Retail Shopping
Center
(continued)

21. Assignability.

Purchaser shall have the right to assign this Agreement to any person(s), partnership or corporation, including a partnership or corporation to be formed hereafter, with notice to but without the consent of Seller, and the transaction contemplated by this Agreement shall be consummated in the name of such assignee. In the event of such assignment, the assignee shall assume the obligations of Purchaser under this Agreement, and Purchaser shall have no further obligation or liability under this Agreement. Seller shall have the right to assign its interest in this Agreement, only with the written consent of Purchaser, except insofar as such assignment is made to effectuate a tax free exchange. In the latter instance, Seller may assign its rights but shall remain bound under the terms of this Agreement and the representations, warranties, and covenants contained herein.

Seller is entering into this contract with the intention of disposing of the Property through alike kind exchange of properties, pursuant to Section 1031 of the Internal Revenue Code of 1954, as amended. Purchaser agrees that, upon request of Seller, Purchaser will convey or cause to be conveyed to Seller at closing other like kind property acceptable to Seller in lieu of paying cash to Seller, or will pay the purchase price for the property to a third party, who will convey like kind property to Seller. At the election of Seller, Seller may convey the Property to a third party prior to closing as part of a like kind exchange of properties with such third party, provided that such third party agrees to be bound by all of the terms and provisions of this contract, and provided further that no such conveyance to any third party shall relieve Seller of any of its obligations hereunder. Anything contained herein to the contrary notwithstanding, Purchaser shall not be obligated to incur any additional liability or expense in connection with any exchange of properties by Seller. Furthermore, Seller shall indemnify Purchaser for any liability or expense incurred in any respect in connection with its cooperation with Seller in effectuating a tax-free exchange. Subject to the foregoing, this Agreement shall inure to the benefit of and shall be binding upon Seller and Purchaser and their respective successors and assigns.

22. Entire Agreement.

No agreements, representations, or warranties unless expressly incorporated or set forth in this Agreement shall be binding upon any of the parties.

23. Notification.

Any notice or demand under which the terms of this Agreement or under any statute must or may be given or made by the parties hereto shall be made in writing and shall be deemed to have been delivered when hand delivered; as of the date sent by an overnight courier; or as of the date of postmark affixed by the U.S. Postal Service, by mailing the same by certified mail return receipt requested addressed to the respective parties at the following addresses:

To Purchaser:

With Copies to:

To Seller:

With Copy to:

EXHIBIT 8-3
Contract for Purchase and Sale of Retail Shopping Center (continued)

Such addresses may be changed by the giving of written notice as provided in this paragraph; provided, however that any mailed notice of changed address shall be not be effective until the fifth (5th) day after the date of postmark by the U.S. Postal Service.

24. Time.

Time is of the essence of this Agreement and of each of its provisions.

25. Survival and Last Execution Date.

The provisions of this Agreement shall survive Closing and the execution and delivery of the deed and instruments conveying the Property. If this Agreement is not executed by all parties hereto on or before 5:00 P.M. on August 17, 19____, this Agreement shall be null and void.

26. Headings.

Descriptive headings are for convenience only and shall not control or affect the meaning or construction of any provision of this Agreement.

27. Binding Effect.

This Agreement shall be binding upon and shall inure to the benefit of the parties hereto and their successors and assigns subject to the provisions of Section 21 above.

28. Severability.

In case any one or more of the provisions contained in this Agreement shall for any reason be held to be invalid, illegal or unenforceable in any respect, such invalidity, illegality, or unenforceability shall not affect any other provision hereof, and this Agreement shall be construed as if such invalid, illegal, or unenforceable provision had never been contained herein.

29. Effective Date of this Agreement.

The Effective Date of this Agreement shall be the last date upon which either the Purchaser or Seller shall have executed this Agreement, as demonstrated by the date(s) below their respective signatures on the signature page to this Agreement.

30. Business Day.

If the Closing is to occur on a holiday or other non-business day, or if any period of time set forth in this Agreement expires on a holiday or other non-business day, then the Closing or the expiration date of such period shall be the next business day. For purposes of this Agreement, the term "business day" shall mean any day which is not a Saturday, Sunday or other day on which banks in My Town, State are not open for business during regular business hours.

31. Certain Definitions.

As used herein, the following terms are defined as follows:

(a) *Governmental Authority* means any nation or government, any state, municipal or other political subdivision thereof, and any entity exercising executive, legislative, judicial, regulatory or administrative functions of or pertaining to government.

(b) *Hazardous Materials* means all hazardous wastes, polychlorinated biphenyl (commonly known as "PCBs"), toxic substance and similar substances including, without limitation, substances defined as "hazardous substances" or "toxic substances" in the Comprehensive Environmental Response and Liability Act of 1980, as amended, 42 U.S.C. § 9601 et seq., the Hazardous Materials Transportation Act, and Recovery Act, as amended, 42 U.S.C. § 6901 et seq.

EXHIBIT 8–3
Contract for
Purchase and Sale
of Retail Shopping
Center
(continued)

(c) *Permits* means all consents, certificates, authorizations, licenses, approvals and permits required for the removal, alteration or demolition of any structure or improvement, or any part thereof, on the Land or for construction, completion, use, occupancy and operation of the Existing Improvements or the Improvements in accordance with all Requirements of Law affecting the Property, including, without limiting the generality of the foregoing, demolition permits, building permits, drainage permits, curb cut, access and traffic permits and approvals, sewerage, waste and drainage permits and environmental approvals and permits.

(d) *Requirements of Law* means any person or entity, the certificate of incorporation and by-laws or partnership agreement or limited partnership agreement or other organizational or governing documents of such person or entity, and any law, treaty, rule or regulation, or determination, judgment or order of an arbitrator or a court or other Governmental Authority, in each case applicable to or binding upon such person or entity or any of its property or to which such person or entity or any of its property is subject; and, as to the Real Property, any applicable environmental, zoning or building, land use laws, requirements, standards and regulations of the fire marshall and similar agencies, ordinances, rules or regulations of any governmental authority or agency, and any applicable covenants and restrictions.

32. Possession.

Seller shall deliver actual possession of the Property to Purchaser at Closing.

33. Seller's Guaranty of Income.

At closing, Seller will execute and deliver to Purchaser a Guaranty ("Guaranty") which guarantees the gross rental income from the Property as hereinafter set forth. For a period commencing with the Closing Date and ending one year from the Closing Date, Seller shall guarantee that the gross rental income from the Property shall not be less than Eight Hundred Fifty Thousand and No/100 Dollars ($850,000.00). Seller agrees to pay to Purchaser a sum equal to the difference of Eight Hundred Fifty Thousand Dollars ($850,000.00) and the actual gross rental income received from the Property during the one year period. Seller agrees to pay Purchaser the income shortfall on a quarterly basis. For example, during the first calendar quarter following the Closing Date if gross rental income from the Property does not equal $212,500.00, Seller shall pay to Purchaser on the last day of the quarter the difference between $212,500.00 and the gross rental income actually received during that period of time. The Seller's obligation to pay Purchaser for rental income shortfall pursuant to this paragraph shall not exceed $100,000.00 during the year succeeding the Closing Date. Purchaser shall provide Seller with a written itemized statement of all rentals received certified to be true and correct by Purchaser. Seller shall further agree that in the event that Seller does not pay Purchaser any rental deficit on a quarterly basis, Purchaser shall have the right to set off said amount due from Seller against the payments under the Note.

Commencing one year from the Closing Date and ending on the same day which is two years from the Closing Date, Seller guarantees that the gross rental income from the Property shall be Eight Hundred Seventy Five Thousand and No/100 Dollars ($875,000.00). Seller agrees to pay to Purchaser a sum equal to the difference between Eight Hundred Seventy Five Thousand Dollars ($875,000.00) and the actual gross rental income received from the Property during that period. Seller agrees to pay Purchaser the income shortfall on a quarterly basis. For example, during the first calendar quarter of the second year following the Closing Date if gross rental income from the Property does not equal $218,750.00, Seller shall pay to Purchaser on the last day of said quarter the difference

EXHIBIT 8-3
Contract for
Purchase and Sale
of Retail Shopping
Center
(continued)

between $218,750.00 and the gross rental income actually received during that period of time. The Seller's obligation to pay Purchaser for rental income shortfall pursuant to this paragraph shall not exceed $100,000.00 during the second year from Closing Date. Purchaser shall provide Seller with a written itemized statement of all rentals received certified to be true and correct by Purchaser. Seller shall further agree that in the event that Seller does not pay Purchaser any rental deficit on a quarterly basis, Purchaser shall have the right to set off said amount due from Seller against the payments under the Note.

Seller's obligation to pay Purchaser for the rental income shortfall shall be adjusted annually and in the event the rental income shortfall is less than the sum of the quarterly payments Purchaser has received from Seller, then Purchaser shall refund the difference between the annual rental income shortfall and the amount of rental guaranty payments received from Seller. The annual adjustment shall take place within thirty days from a date which is one year from Closing Date, and a second annual adjustment shall take place within thirty days from a date which is two years from Closing Date.

During the rental guaranty period as set forth herein, Purchaser shall make every effort to lease existing vacant spaces, including but not limited to, paying full commissions to outside brokers, market the Property in a quality manner and maintain the Property in a neat and professional manner. If Purchaser relocates any of the existing tenants in Village Square to another property owned by or affiliated with Purchaser, then the tenant's rental income based on the rental being paid by the tenant prior to relocation which would have been received by Purchaser had tenant not been relocated shall be credited against the annual gross rental income guaranteed by Seller (i.e. against the $850,000.00 during year one or the $875,000.00 during year two).

Any new space that is leased on the Property during the two year guaranty period will be created toward the income guaranty (i.e. toward the $850,000.00 during year one or the $875,000.00 during year two). Also, the credit will be the greater of $15.00 per square foot of annual gross rental or the actual gross rental amount received under the lease. Credit for new leases against Seller's income guaranty will commence the earlier of when rental payments begin or six months following occupancy by the tenant.

If Purchaser elects to terminate or not to renew any of the existing leases whereby the tenant wants to stay at the Property and is willing to pay the lesser of tenants present rent or fair market rent, then Seller shall receive a credit against the guaranteed income amounts of the amount of the lost rental. (i.e. against the $850,000.00 during year one or the $875,000.00 during year two).

34. Additional Provisions.

(a) In the event that Lender requires a form of Tenant Estoppel different from the form attached hereto as *Exhibit C* or in the event that Lender requires a form of Subordination, Attornment and Non-Disturbance Agreement difference from the form attached hereto as *Exhibit J*, then Purchaser shall deliver such different form(s) to Seller on or before October 1, 19____.

(b) In the event that the sale and purchase of the Property does not close for any reason other than Seller's default, Purchaser will provide Seller with copies of all surveys, reports, tests and other materials relating to the Property obtained by Purchaser pursuant to the terms of this Agreement.

35. Miscellaneous.

(a) This Agreement shall be construed and interpreted under the Laws of the State.

(b) No failure of Purchaser or Seller to exercise any power given either party hereunder or to insist upon strict compliance by either party of its obligations hereunder, and no custom or practice of the parties at variance with the terms hereof shall constitute a waiver of either party's right to demand exact compliance with the terms hereof. Any condition, contingency or right of termination or recision granted by this Agreement to either Purchaser or Seller may be waived in writing by the party for whose benefit such condition or right was granted.

(c) This Agreement may be signed in number of counterparts. Each counterpart shall be an original but all such counterparts shall constitute one agreement. It shall be fully executed when each party whose signature is required has signed at least one counterpart even though no one counterpart contains the signatures of all the parties.

IN WITNESS WHEREOF, the parties hereto have set their hands and seals as of the Effective Date.

PURCHASER:

Date Executed: _____

SELLER:

Date Executed: _____

The undersigned as Escrowee hereby acknowledges receipt of a copy of this Agreement and of the initial Earnest Money deposit by check $_____ drawn on _____, subject to collection, and agrees to hold said funds pursuant to the terms of this Agreement. The undersigned as Broker hereby agrees to the terms of Section 17 of this Agreement.

Dated: _____

EXHIBIT 8–3
Contract for
Purchase and Sale
of Retail Shopping
Center
(continued)

STATE OF _____)
) ss:
COUNTY OF _____)

OPTION TO PURCHASE

IN CONSIDERATION OF ONE HUNDRED AND NO/100 DOLLARS ($100.00) (herein called "Option Consideration") in hand paid, the receipt and sufficiency of which are hereby acknowledged, the undersigned FARRIS DEVELOPMENT CORPORATION, a _____ corporation (hereinafter referred to as "Optionor") hereby grants, conveys and extends to JAMES B. MILLER and ALICE C. MILLER (hereinafter collectively called "Optionee"), the exclusive right and option to purchase upon the terms and conditions set forth herein, all that tract or parcel of land lying and being in Land Lots 31 and 32 of the 13th District, _____ County, _____(state)_____ and being known as the Birch Hill Apartments, a 284 unit apartment complex, and being more particularly described on Exhibit "A" attached hereto and made a part hereof, together with all improvements situated thereon and appurtenances thereto (hereinafter called "Property").

1. Option Term. This Option shall begin on September 1, 19___ and terminate at 11:30 p.m. on December 15, 19___.

2. Exercise of Option. This Option may be exercised by Optionee any time prior to the expiration of the Option, by the execution and delivery to Optionor of that certain Real

EXHIBIT 8–4
Option to Purchase

EXHIBIT 8-4
Option to Purchase
(continued)

Estate Contract attached hereto as <u>Exhibit "B"</u> and made a part hereof. Upon the exercise of the Real Estate Contract by Optionee and submission to Optionor, Optionor shall sign the Agreement and it shall become a binding Agreement between the parties hereto. The executed Real Estate Contract is to be sent to Optionor at the following address:

604 Clairemont Avenue
_____(city)_____, _____(state)_____ 30060

3. <u>Purchase Price</u>. The Purchase Price for the sale of the Property shall be ONE MILLION FIVE HUNDRED THOUSAND AND NO/100 DOLLARS ($1,500,000.00) and shall be paid pursuant to the terms set forth in the Real Estate Contract attached hereto as <u>Exhibit "B"</u> and made a part hereof.

4. <u>No Assignment</u>. This Option is personal to the Optionee and is not assignable.

5. <u>Miscellaneous</u>. This agreement constitutes the entire agreement between the parties hereto and it is understood and agreed that all undertakings and agreements heretofore had between the parties have merged herein. No representation, promise, inducement not included herein shall be binding upon any party hereto.

IN WITNESS WHEREOF, the parties have hereunto set their hands and seals this _____ day of _____, 19___.

OPTIONOR:
FARRIS DEVELOPMENT CORPORATION
By: _____
David H. Farris, President
OPTIONEE:
_____ (SEAL)
JAMES B. MILLER
_____ (SEAL)
ALICE C. MILLER

Deeds

We were born on it, and we got killed on it, died on it. Even if it's no good, it's still ours. That's what makes it ours—being born on it, working it, dying on it. That makes ownership, not a paper with numbers on it.

—*John Steinbeck,* The Grapes of Wrath

OBJECTIVES

After reading this chapter you will be able to:
- Identify the type of deeds used in modern real estate practice
- Explain the basic requirements of a valid deed
- Prepare a deed

GLOSSARY

Caption   Portion of the deed that indicates the county and state in which the deed was signed by the grantor.

Consideration   Something of value given to make the promises of a contract enforceable. Consideration also is something of value given for a deed.

Conveyance   Transfer of title or ownership to real property from one person to another by deed. The terms may be used to include assignment, lease, mortgage, or encumbrance of real property.

Deed   Written document that transfers ownership of real property from one person to another.

General warranty deed   Deed containing full warranty of title.

Grantee   Person in whom real property has been transferred by deed.

Grantor   Transferor of real property by deed.

Habendum   Clause found in a deed that indicates what estate in real property is being transferred by the deed.

Limited or special warranty deed   Deed wherein the grantor covenants and warrants only against the lawful claims of people claiming by, through, or under the grantor.

Preamble   Portion of the deed that sets forth the parties to the deed and the date of the deed.

Quitclaim deed   Deed that contains no warranties of title. A quitclaim deed transfers only the interest that the grantor has in the land and not the land itself.

Testimonium   Portion of the deed that the grantor signs and the signature is witnessed or notarized.

Warranty or covenant   Promise that a fact is true or that an event will take place.

HISTORICAL DEVELOPMENT OF DEEDS _____

New York:
See Appendix for discussion of valid deeds in New York.

After the Norman conquest in 1066, English land titles were transferred by the actual physical delivery of land. Naturally, it was difficult to hand over a tract of land in the same way one hands over a horse, but the law encouraged the **conveyance** of land to be in the same manner as delivery of personal property. This required the actual delivery of vacant possession to the land. Typically, the seller and the purchaser would gather on the land in the presence of witnesses, and the seller would place or "seise" the purchaser with possession of the land.

As time passed, it became evident to landowners that documentary evidence was valuable to establish the terms of the land transfer. A document would be useful to identify the land, the names of the parties to the conveyance, the interest transferred (e.g., fee simple or life estate), and any warranties of title. The document could be signed and sealed by the grantor and a list of witnesses attached. Thus, it became the practice to prepare a deed or charter after the transfer of land. The early deeds were not necessary to transfer the ownership but were used as a chronicle or memorandum proving that the transfer had taken place.

The deed or charter became evidence of real property ownership, and the safety of the original document was a continuous source of worry to medieval landowners because both theft and forgery of deeds or charters were common. In one fifteenth-century case, a deed was kept in a chest too heavy to be brought into court. No doubt the chest was used to discourage theft of the deed. Other efforts were used to increase the safety of deeds. One effort was to pay royal clerks to record or transcribe a copy of the deed in the rolls where the office copies of royal communications were preserved. Another method was to execute duplicate deeds on the same piece of parchment, cutting the two copies apart with a ragged cut. Before the tear would be made, the word "chirographum" would be written across the line of the tear. If forgery was alleged, then it would be seen if the two documents fitted together. Such deeds or charters were called indentures, from the indented line of the cut.

The evolution of conveyancing continued, and the fine became the preferred method of conveyance. The fine was a written triparty indenture. Two of the parts would be sent to the parties to the fine, the grantor and the grantee, and the third part was reserved among the court records. The fine method continued to evolve until the present-day system of conveyancing, in which written **deeds**, recorded in the public land records of the county or parish in which the land is located, are used to convey title of land from one person to another. Deeds are important legal documents in a real estate transaction because they are the only written instrument that can transfer real property ownership during an owner's lifetime.

In most law firms, legal assistants prepare deeds. For this reason, this chapter discusses the general law involving deeds and offers practical suggestions for the preparation of deeds and samples of deed forms.

TYPES OF DEEDS _____

Three types of deeds commonly are used in the United States: (1) general warranty deed, (2) limited (special) warranty deed, and (3) quitclaim deed.

General Warranty Deed

Caveat emptor ("Let the buyer beware") applies to the law of real property transfers. In the absence of some express covenant for title, the full risk of title failure falls on the purchaser of real property. Therefore, the prudent purchaser will ask for and obtain certain covenants of title. These covenants usually are found in a deed known as a **general warranty deed**. The form of a general warranty deed varies from state to state. Some states require the warranties to be expressly set forth in the deed; in other states, the warranties may be included merely with the use of such words as "grant," "bargain and sell," or "warrant."

A general warranty deed contains six **covenants** or **warranties**: (1) covenant of seisin, (2) covenant of right to convey, (3) covenant against encumbrances, (4) covenant for further assurance, (5) covenant for quiet enjoyment, and (6) covenant for warranty. The covenants are made by the **grantor**, the person who is transferring ownership of the land to the **grantee**, the person who is receiving ownership of the land.

Covenant of Seisin

Seisin has its roots in the feudal law of England. There is a great deal of argument among legal scholars as to the exact meaning of seisin. Practically speaking, seisin means the right to possession of property. The grantor (the seller) under a general warranty deed will warrant that the grantor has possession of the land being transferred or has a right to the possession of the land. The covenant of seisin also warrants that the grantor has ownership or title to the land.

Covenant of Right to Convey

The covenant of the right to convey is a promise made on behalf of the grantor of the deed that the grantor owns the land and has the right to transfer ownership of the land. An interest in the land held by a person other than the grantor would cause a breach of this covenant.

Covenant against Encumbrances

The covenant against encumbrances is a promise or warranty by the grantor that the land is unencumbered; that is, the land is free and clear from mortgages, liens, taxes, leases, easements, or any other restrictions that might restrict the use of the land or be a debt on the land.

New York:
In the New York City area, the most commonly used deed is the Bargain & Sale with Covenant Against Grantor's Acts. See Appendix. The grantor promises he has not done anything to encumber the property while he owned it, i.e. to render title unmarketable. In upstate New York the full warranty deed is more common.

Covenant of Further Assurance

The covenant of further assurance is a promise by a grantor that in the future, the grantor will make any conveyance necessary to vest in the grantee of the deed the title intended to be conveyed. For example, if the grantor intends to convey fee simple absolute title by the deed but later discovers that he has only a conditional fee, through the covenant of further assurance, he agrees to satisfy or remove the conditions so the title to the land conveyed is fee simple absolute.

Covenants of Quiet Enjoyment and Warranty

The covenants of quiet enjoyment and warranty usually are the same and involve a warranty that the grantee of the deed will be able to quietly enjoy the land without fear of eviction and without fear of any third party assertions of adverse claims.

Present versus Future Covenants

The covenants of seisin, right to convey, and against encumbrances are called *present covenants* because if they are breached, it is at the time the deed is delivered. The immediate grantee (original purchaser or recipient of the land) is the only person who can sue for breach of a present covenant. Present covenants are not transferable when the land is subsequently sold.

The covenants of further assurance, quiet enjoyment, and warranty are called *future covenants* because they may be breached at sometime in the future. Future covenants are transferable and run with the land. Any owner of the land has standing to sue for breach of a future covenant contained in a general warranty deed.

The following example illustrates the distinction between present and future covenants. Aaron transfers land by general warranty deed to Bob. Bob transfers the same land by general warranty deed to Carol. Carol later transfers the same land again by general warranty deed to David. Each deed is a general warranty deed with all the six covenants. After the transfers have been made, David, the current owner of the land, discovers that there is a mortgage on the land that had been created by Aaron at the time Aaron owned the property. The mortgage, at the time of its discovery, is a breach of the covenant against encumbrances. Because the covenant against encumbrances is a present covenant, David can only recover losses as a result of the mortgage from Carol for the breach. If the holder of the mortgage attempts to foreclose and to evict David from possession of the land, the foreclosure and attempted eviction will become a breach of the covenant of quiet enjoyment (a future covenant). David, on breach of the future covenant, will have the right to recover from Carol, Bob, and Aaron because the covenant of quiet enjoyment is a future covenant that runs with the land and is transferable. A claim under a future covenant can be asserted by any owner of the land against any person who has given a general warranty deed in the chain of title.

A breach of a covenant in a warranty deed may be sued on by the grantee of the deed, even though the grantee was aware of, or should have been aware of, the defect at the time the grantee received the deed. This principle of law is illustrated in *Lunsford v. King*, 209 S.E.2d 27.

 C A S E

Lunsford v. King
209 S.E.2d 27 (Ga. 1974)

STOLZ, Judge.

Plaintiff Lunsford, vendee of a certain tract of land in Fulton County, Georgia, described in a contract of sale by metes and bounds, brought an action against Fulton County, Mrs. King (his vendor), and the vendor's predecessors in title, seeking to enjoin the county from taking or interfering with, without condemnation, the plaintiff's use of a strip of said tract which one of the defendant predecessors in title had dedicated to the defendant county for road-widening purposes, but which had been included in all of the legal descriptions in all of the subsequent warranty deeds, including the plaintiff's.

The complaint prayed alternatively, if it be judicially determined that the county could legally proceed under its right-of-way deed, for damages from the remaining defendants, his predecessors in title, jointly and severally, for breach of warranty in the amount of $2,475. The plaintiff appeals from the grant of the summary judgment in favor of the defendant vendor and defendant King-Williams Land Co., Inc., now King Williams Realty & Mortgage, Inc. (the vendor's immediate predecessor in title). The plaintiff's appeal from the trial court's judgment denying the injunctive relief against Fulton County, had been dismissed previously for lack of a certificate for immediate review. Lunsford v. Fulton County, 227 Ga. 547, 181 S.E.2d 865. *Held:*

"Where, as here, a certain tract of land is described in a contract of sale by definite boundaries, and it later appears that the vendor has no title to a portion of the tract contained within the described boundaries, this is a defect in the vendor's title as contemplated by Code § 29–202 rather than a deficiency in quantity as contemplated by Code § 29–201." Lawton v. Byck, 217 Ga. 676(2), 124 S.E.2d 369. The plaintiff's right to recovery of damages under Code § 29–202, is not defeated by his constructive knowledge of the prior recorded deed to the county. "A general warranty of title in a deed against the claims of all persons covers defects in the title though known to the purchaser at the time of taking the deed." Code § 29–304.

Accordingly, the plaintiff is entitled to prove his case before a jury, including the amount of the unliquidated damages for the "reduction of the price according to the relative value of the land so lost." Code § 29–202. Therefore, the trial judge erred in granting the summary judgment in favor of the defendant vendor, Mrs. King, and defendant King-Williams Land Co., Inc., now King Williams Realty & Mortgage, Inc.

Judgment reversed.

Limited (Special) Warranty Deed

A **limited** or **special warranty deed** is a warranty deed in which the grantor covenants only against the lawful claims of people claiming by, through, or under the grantor. For example, a grantor of a limited warranty deed would be liable only if the ownership of the land by the grantee of the deed is disturbed by some claim arising from some act of the grantor. For example, if the grantor has placed an easement on the property and warrants in the limited warranty deed an express covenant against encumbrances, then the grantor of the limited warranty deed would be responsible and could be sued for the easement. If the easement already existed on the land at the time the grantor of the limited warranty deed received title to the land and the easement was created by some person prior in title to the grantor, the grantor, by giving a limited warranty deed, would not be responsible for the easement. Remember that in this same example, if the grantor had given a general warranty deed, which is an absolute warranty against encumbrances, the grantor would have been responsible for the easement, regardless of whether the grantor was the cause or creation of the easement or the easement was created by a predecessor in title.

Quitclaim Deed

A **quitclaim deed** transfers only the interest the grantor has in the land and not the land itself. If the grantor of a quitclaim deed has complete ownership at the time of the execution of the deed, a quitclaim deed will pass complete ownership to the grantee. A quitclaim deed contains no covenants or warranties of title. If a grantor of a quitclaim deed conveys land that is encumbered or land not owned by the grantor, the grantee usually, absent some evidence of fraud, is without claim against the grantor. Quitclaim deeds often are found in other forms of deeds, such as foreclosure deeds (deeds received from foreclosures of property by mortgage or tax foreclosures), executor's deeds (deeds executed by the executor of an estate), administrator's deeds (deeds executed by an administrator of an intestate estate), and trustee's deeds (deeds executed by the trustee of a trust). A quitclaim deed in some states is referred to as a release deed or bargain and sale deed. Independent investigation of the title to the land is essential in a transaction that involves a quitclaim deed.

Generally speaking, purchasers of land will want the best kind of deed, the general warranty deed. The type of deed typically is negotiated within the contract for sale of the land, and every effort is made to obtain the best deed.

BASIC REQUIREMENTS OF A VALID DEED

The basic requirements of a valid deed are (a) written instrument, (b) competent grantor, (c) identity of the grantee, (d) words of conveyance, (e) adequate description of land, (f) consideration, (g) signature of grantor, (h) witnesses, and (i) delivery of the completed deed to the grantee.

Written Instrument

A deed must be in writing, but no generally prescribed form is essential to the validity of a deed. Even a letter in most states could constitute a valid deed, provided all the requirements are met.

Some states—for example, New York—by statute prescribe the form of a deed and the specific language that must be used for the deed to be valid. The law of the state in which the real property to be transferred is located will control as to the form required for the deed. Legal assistants should review the appropriate law before a deed is prepared.

Competent Grantor

The deed must be signed by a party who is competent. Deeds executed by minors (people under the age of eighteen years) are voidable, and deeds executed by mentally incompetent people usually are void. Partnership deeds should be executed by all the partners, and corporate deeds should have proper corporate authority from the board of directors. The grantor also must be the owner or have an ownership interest in the land conveyed by the deed.

Identity of the Grantee

A deed must identify with certainty the grantee. A deed to a nonexistent grantee is thought to be void. Every effort should be made to correctly identify the name of the grantee for both individual and corporate deeds. For corporations, the correct name is obtained from the corporate records' division of the secretary of state's office in the state of incorporation.

Words of Conveyance

A deed must contain words of conveyance that indicate the grantor's intent to make a present conveyance of the land by the instrument. No special words are needed, but words such as "grant, convey, assign, set over, transfer, and give" have all been held to express the intent to pass title and are sufficient to make an instrument a deed.

Description of the Property

The deed must describe the land being conveyed with specificity. A platted description, government rectangular survey description, or a metes and bounds description

New York:
New York requires the grantor to be of sound mind and over 18 years of age.

New York:
The deed must name the grantee so that she can be identifiable. In New York, both grantor and grantee must be identified by address if the deed is to be recorded.

New York:
Every deed must contain a lien covenant, i.e. that the seller holds the proceeds of sale in trust against unpaid improvements. New York has a "race-notice" jurisdiction so that the person who records the deed first has priority over a person who later records a deed to the same person.

New York:
The land being transferred must be identified with certainty.

based on a registered land surveyor's survey should be used. A deed conveys only the land described in the deed. The deed will convey all improvements, buildings, air rights, mineral rights, fixtures, and other appurtenances that belong to the owner of the land unless excluded by express reference.

Consideration

A deed must have **consideration** to be valid. Consideration is defined as something of value given for the deed. This value is the purchase price of the land being conveyed, although gift deeds for love and affection are recognized in all states. A recital of consideration is sufficient. A typical recital of consideration may be "for Ten Dollars and other good and valuable consideration."

Signed by the Grantor

The grantor is the only person required to sign the deed. Deeds are not signed by the grantee. Some states, however, require that the grantee sign if the grantee is assuming the payment of a mortgage on the land or is purchasing a condominium and intends to be bound by the covenants and restrictions of the condominium. Although a few states dictate where the deed must be signed, deeds typically are signed in the lower right-hand corner.

Witnessing of Deeds

The requirement for the witnessing, attestation, or acknowledgment of the grantor's signature to a deed varies from state to state. Some states require that deeds be witnessed only to permit the deed to be recorded. In these states, a deed is valid between the parties without recordation and, therefore, valid without witnessing. Other states require that the grantor's signature must be witnessed for the deed to be valid. Therefore, within these states, all deeds must be witnessed. Each state has its own witnessing requirements in terms of number and who may be a witness to a deed. A witness may be a notary public or other disinterested person. An interested witness, such as the grantee, cannot witness the grantor's signature to a deed. The usual number of required witnesses is two.

Delivery to Grantee

The deed does not transfer title to land until the deed is delivered to the grantee or someone on the grantee's behalf. A deed is delivered when the grantor places the deed in the possession of the grantee with the intention that the deed passes present title of the land to the grantee and the grantee accepts this delivery. There are many presumptions regarding the delivery or nondelivery of a deed. Possession of the deed by the grantee is a presumption of delivery. Possession of the deed by the grantor is presumption of nondelivery. Recordation of a deed in the public records is presumption of delivery. All these presumptions are rebuttable if facts can be shown to the contrary.

PREPARATION OF A VALID DEED

Real property law is local law, and the law of deeds is no exception. The law of the state in which the land to be conveyed by the deed is located controls the form as

New York:
New York does not require actual consideration to be stated in the deed. Generally, the deed states a nominal consideration as "Ten Dollars and other good and valuable consideration." If the property is being transferred by an executor/administrator it must state the actual consideration.

Even though the deed need only state a nominal consideration, in order to record a deed, New York state requires the payment of a real property transfer tax and the filing of a transfer tax report must accompany the deed.

New York:
In New York, the deed is valid if signed by the grantor. New York allows the signing of the deed by an attorney-in-fact who uses a power of attorney and this power of attorney is recorded with the deed.

New York:
The deed must be acknowledged (notarized) to be recorded.

well as the formal requirements of the deed. It is important to check local and state law before preparing a deed.

The preparation of a valid deed is a simple process. It is advisable to use the forms that are available from state bar associations, title companies, or law firms. Several examples of deed forms are included at the end of this chapter.

Most deed forms have the following formal parts: caption, premises or preamble, granting clause, description, **habendum**, warranty clause, and testimonium. The location of each of the formal parts of the deed is keyed by number on the sample deed form shown in Exhibit 9–1.

Caption

The **caption** or heading of a deed is designed to show the place of execution of the deed. The caption indicates the county and state in which the deed was signed by the grantor. The caption does *not* refer to the county and state in which the land is located.

Premises or Preamble

The premises or **preamble** to a deed is the section that sets forth the parties to the deed and the date of the deed. A deed is valid without a date, but most deeds are dated. The date should be the date of execution by the grantor. The parties to the deed are the grantor and grantee. Every effort should be made to use the correct name for both the grantor and the grantee. Titles such as Mr. and Mrs., and Ms. are seldom used.

Granting Clause

The granting clause contains the language indicating that the instrument is a deed and that the land is being granted or conveyed. Few states require any particular words, and therefore, any words indicating a present intent to transfer the land are sufficient. The granting clause in many deeds also contains a recital of consideration.

Description

The main portion of any deed is the description of the land to be conveyed. It is important to use the best description available, which usually is a description prepared by a registered land surveyor or a description prepared from a registered land survey.

Habendum Clause

The habendum clause indicates what estate is being transferred, such as life estate or fee simple.

Warranty Clause

The warranty clause usually contains words of warranty or, in the case of quitclaim deeds, a lack thereof of warranty words.

(1) caption, (2) premises or preamble, (3) granting clause, (4) description, (5) habendum, (6) warranty clause, and (7) testimonium.

EXHIBIT 9–1
Formal Parts of a
Deed

WARRANTY DEED

1

STATE OF   COUNTY OF

THIS INDENTURE, Made the   day of   , in the year
one thousand nine hundred   , between

2

of the County of   , and State of Georgia, as party or parties of the
first part, hereinafter called Grantor, and

as party or parties of the second part, hereinafter called Grantee (the words "Grantor" and
"Grantee" to include their respective heirs, successors and assigns where the context requires or
permits).

WITNESSETH that: Grantor, for and in consideration of the sum of
(   ) DOLLARS
in hand paid at and before the sealing and delivery of these presents, the receipt whereof is hereby
acknowledged, has granted, bargained, sold, aliened, conveyed and confirmed, and by these presents
does grant, bargain, sell, alien, convey and confirm unto the said Grantee,

3

4

TO HAVE AND TO HOLD the said tract or parcel of land, with all and singular the rights,
members and appurtenances thereof, to the same being, belonging, or in anywise appertaining, to the
only proper use, benefit and behoof of the said Grantee forever in FEE SIMPLE. **5**

AND THE SAID Grantor will warrant and forever defend the right and title to the above
described property unto the said Grantee against the claims of all persons whomsoever. **6**

IN WITNESS WHEREOF, the Grantor has signed and sealed this deed, the day and year above
written. **7**

Signed, sealed and delivered in presence of:

_____   _____ (Seal)

_____   _____ (Seal)

_____   _____ (Seal)

Testimonium

The **testimonium** is the execution portion of the deed. Most deeds are signed under hand and seal and are witnessed. A recital of this action is found in the testimonium.

Completing Sections of a Deed

The following are examples for completing the sections of a deed.

Preamble

The grantor and grantee designations, which appear in the preamble of a deed, may be completed as follows:

Grantor Designations

If the grantor is an individual, the preamble may read as follows:

> Joseph R. Snead, an individual

If the grantors are husband and wife, the preamble may read as follows:

> Joseph R. Snead and Mary T. Snead, husband and wife

If the grantor is an unmarried individual in a community property state, the preamble may read as follows:

> Joseph R. Snead, an unmarried individual

If the grantor is a corporation, the preamble may read as follows:

> The Farris Corporation, an Ohio corporation

If the grantor is a general partnership, the preamble may read as follows:

> Farris Associates, a North Carolina general partnership

If the grantor is a limited partnership, the preamble may read as follows:

> Farris Associates, Ltd., a North Carolina limited partnership

If the grantor is the trustee of a Trust, the preamble may read as follows:

> David H. Farris, Trustee of Trust created by Joseph R. Snead for the benefit of Mary T. Snead, pursuant to Trust Agreement dated July 26, 1992

If the grantor is the executor of an estate, the preamble may read as follows:

> David H. Farris, Executor under the Last Will and Testament of Joseph R. Snead, deceased of Richland County, Illinois

If the grantor is the administrator of the estate of a person who has died without a will, the preamble may read as follows:

> David H. Farris, Administrator of the intestate estate of Joseph R. Snead, deceased of Richland County, Illinois

Grantee Designations

If the grantee of a deed is an individual, married couple, corporation, partnership, trustee, executor, or administrator, the same language as that used above may be used to describe the grantee.

If the grantees of a deed are husband and wife and the property conveyed by the deed is located in a state that recognizes the tenancy by entirety form of ownership, the preamble for the grantee may read as follows:

Joseph R. Snead and Mary T. Snead, husband and wife and as tenants by the entirety

If the grantees of a deed want to hold title as joint tenants with the right of survivorship, the grantee preamble may read as follows:

Joseph R. Snead and Mary T. Snead, as joint tenants with the right of survivorship

If the grantees of a deed want to hold title as tenants in common, the grantee preamble may read as follows:

Joseph R. Snead and Mary T. Snead, as tenants in common

If the grantees of a deed are tenants in common and want to own unequal shares of the property, the grantee preamble may read as follows:

Joseph R. Snead (an undivided seventy-five percent) and Mary T. Snead (an undivided twenty-five percent), as tenants in common

Granting Clause

An example of a recital of nominal consideration in the granting clause is as follows:

Ten and No/100 Dollars ($10.00) and other good and valuable consideration

A deed of gift contains a recital of consideration such as the following:

For love and affection

Description

The legal description of the land conveyed by the deed should be described with full certainty on the face of the deed. If the description is too long to fit on the first page of the deed, it must be attached as an exhibit to the deed. A deed that uses an exhibit description should refer to the exhibit on the face of the deed. This reference can be as follows:

All that tract or parcel of land lying and being in Land Lot 75 of the 5th District of Hall County, Georgia, and being more particularly described on Exhibit "A" attached hereto and by reference incorporated herein

A general warranty deed warrants that the land is unencumbered. Often the land is encumbered, and exceptions to the warranty must be created. These exceptions often are stated in the description portion of the deed. The exceptions may be shown as follows:

This conveyance is subject to the following title exceptions:

(a) Taxes for the current year and subsequent years.

(b) Easement from The Farris Corporation to Alabama Power Company; dated August 12, 1990, and recorded August 18, 1990, at Deed Book 35, Page 749, Montgomery County, Alabama.

Title exceptions to a general warranty deed also may be shown on an exhibit to the deed.

This conveyance is subject to the title exceptions shown on Exhibit "A" attached hereto and by reference incorporated herein

It is the custom in some states to refer to title exceptions in general terms, such as:

This conveyance is subject to all easements, restrictions, and encumbrances of record

If the land conveyed in a deed is encumbered by a mortgage and the purchaser-grantee is willing to accept the land with the mortgage but not willing to assume personal responsibility for payment of the mortgage, the mortgage is described in the deed as follows:

This conveyance is subject to a Mortgage from The Farris Corporation to First Bank and Trust, dated April 12, 1992, recorded April 22, 1992, at Mortgage Book 632, Page 58, Carl County, North Dakota, securing the original principal indebtedness of $76,500.00.

If the purchaser-grantee is willing to assume personal responsibility for payment of the mortgage, the following language may be used in the deed:

This conveyance is subject to a Mortgage from The Farris Corporation to First Bank and Trust, dated April 12, 1992, recorded April 12, 1992, at Mortgage Book 632, Page 58, Carl County, North Dakota, securing the original principal indebtedness of $76,500.00 and the Grantee by the acceptance of this deed assumes and agrees to pay the outstanding indebtedness according to its terms and assumes and agrees to be bound by all other terms and covenants contained in the Mortgage.

Testimonium

If the grantor is an individual, the deed may be prepared for signature as follows:

_____(SEAL)

DAVID F. FARRIS

Deeds executed by partnerships are executed by all the partners.

D & F REALTY COMPANY, a
Georgia general partnership

By: _____(SEAL)
DAVID F. FARRIS
General Partner

By: _____(SEAL)
FRANCIS F. FARRIS
General Partner

A deed executed by a limited partnership is signed by all the general partners.

D & F Realty Company, Ltd., a New Jersey limited partnership by all the general partners:

By: _____(SEAL)
DAVID F. FARRIS
General Partner

By: _____(SEAL)
FRANCIS F. FARRIS
General Partner

Corporate deeds are executed by duly authorized officers on behalf of the corporation.

D & F REALTY COMPANY, INC., a
Georgia corporation

By: _____(SEAL)
DAVID F. FARRIS
President

Attest: _____(SEAL)
FRANCIS F. FARRIS
Secretary

[CORPORATE SEAL]

It is a good idea with corporate deeds to identify the names and titles of the officers who are signing the deeds and to affix the corporate seal to the deed.

A deed from a trust is executed by the trustee. The execution usually identifies the trustee and the trust instrument under which the trustee operates.

By: _____(SEAL)
DAVID F. FARRIS, Trustee under agreement with JANE FARRIS dated June 1, 1993, for the benefit of MARY S. FARRIS

Deeds executed by estates are done by the executor in the case of a testate estate and by the administrator in the case of an intestate estate. Again, the execution usually identifies the estate under which the deed is being signed.

(Testate estate)

_____(SEAL)
DAVID F. FARRIS, Executor under the Will of SUSAN F. FARRIS, Deceased, duly probated and recorded

(Intestate estate)

_____(SEAL)
DAVID F. FARRIS, Administrator of the Estate of SUSAN F. FARRIS, who died intestate under Letters of Administration issued August 15, 1993

Deeds executed by an attorney in fact pursuant to a power of attorney usually identify the principal, attorney in fact, and power of attorney by date and recording information, if the power of attorney is recorded.

_____
DAVID S. FARRIS, by his duly appointed attorney in fact, SUSAN F. FARRIS, pursuant to power of attorney dated September 25, 1994

Practical Exercises in Deed Preparation

Experience teaches competence in the preparation of deeds. It is helpful for a legal assistant who is first starting to prepare deeds to review deeds that have been used in other transaction.

In the deed shown in Exhibit 9–2 Alice Miller and David Miller are transferring ownership of their home to Susan Dickson and William Dickson. The home is encumbered by (a) an easement from Acme Land and Development Co. to Georgia Power and Light, dated June 8, 1978, recorded June 12, 1978, at Book 418, Page 292, Morris County, Georgia; and (b) unpaid real estate taxes for the current year. The land is described as follows:

> ALL THAT TRACT or parcel of land lying and being in Land Lot 341 of the 8th Land District of Morris County, Georgia, and being more particularly described as Lot 6, Block C of The Oaks Subdivision, as per plat recorded at Plat Book 6, Page 23, Morris County, Georgia Plat Records, which Plat is incorporated herein and made a part of this description by reference.

Exhibit 9–3 is an example of a deed to transfer ownership of land from the Knox Land Development Company, an Illinois corporation, to Carole S. Jackson. The land is encumbered by (a) unpaid real estate taxes for the current year and (b) a mortgage from Knox Land Development Company to First National Bank of Salem, dated October 14, 1986, recorded October 14, 1986, at Mortgage Book 21, Page 466, Knox County, Illinois. The mortgage secures an original principal indebtedness of $84,000. Carole Jackson is willing to assume the mortgage.

The land is described as property lying and being in the northeast quarter of Section 27, Township 24 South, Range 35 East, Knox County, Illinois. The description is too long to be included on the first page of the deed.

Using the deed shown in Exhibit 9–4 as a guide or a deed form from your state, practice preparing deeds for the following hypothetical transfer situations.

Practice Assignment No. 1

Hodges Development Co., Inc., a South Carolina corporation, is purchasing land from Mills Brothers Associates, a South Carolina general partnership, with Edward S. Mills and Thomas C. Mills as the general partners. The land is encumbered by (a) unpaid real estate taxes for the current year; (b) an easement from Harrison Maddox to South Carolina Power & Light, dated January 14, 1990, recorded January 26, 1990, at Book 253, Page 4, Spring County, South Carolina Records; and (c) restrictive covenants created by Declaration of Restrictive Covenants from Mills Brothers Associates, dated March 23, 1991, recorded at Book 261, Page 419, Spring County, South Carolina Records. The land is described as follows:

> ALL THAT TRACT or parcel of land lying and being in Land Lots 14, 15, and 16 of the 4th Land District of Spring County, South Carolina, and being more particularly described as Lots 21, 22, 23, and 24, Block C, Lots 15, 16, 19, and 22, Block D, and Lots 3, 4, 5, 8, 10, and 14, Block E, of The Mills Plantation Subdivision as per plat recorded at Plat Book 10, Page 103, Spring County, South Carolina Plat Records, which plat is incorporated herein and made a part of this description by reference.

Practice Assignment No. 2

Charles D. Hoover and Martha L. Hoover are transferring ownership of their home to James C. Brooks and Doris L. Brooks. James and Doris want to take the property

EXHIBIT 9-2
Miller–Dickson
Deed

WARRANTY DEED

STATE OF   COUNTY OF

THIS INDENTURE, Made the   day of   , in the year
one thousand nine hundred   , between

Alice Miller and David Miller

of the County of   , and State of Georgia, as party or parties of the
first part, hereinafter called Grantor, and

Susan Dickson and William Dickson

as party or parties of the second part, hereinafter called Grantee (the words "Grantor" and
"Grantee" to include their respective heirs, successors and assigns where the context requires or
permits).

WITNESSETH that: Grantor, for and in consideration of the sum of Ten Dollars
and other good and valuable consideration   ($10.00   ) DOLLARS
in hand paid at and before the sealing and delivery of these presents, the receipt whereof is hereby
acknowledged, has granted, bargained, sold, aliened, conveyed and confirmed, and by these presents
does grant, bargain, sell, alien, convey and confirm unto the said Grantee,

ALL THAT TRACT or parcel of land lying and being in Land Lot
341 of the 8th Land District of Morris County, Georgia being more
particularly described as Lot 6, Block C of The Oaks Subdivision
as per plat recorded at Plat Book 6, Page 23, Morris County, Georgia
Plat Records, which Plat is incorporated herein and made a part of
this description by reference.

THIS CONVEYANCE IS SUBJECT TO THE FOLLOWING TITLE EXCEPTIONS:

(a) Real estate taxes for the current year and subsequent years,
(b) An easement from ACME Land & Development Co., to Georgia
     Power and Light, dated June 8, 1978, recorded June 12, 1978
     at Deed Book 418, Page 292 Morris County, Georgia Records.

TO HAVE AND TO HOLD the said tract or parcel of land, with all and singular the rights,
members and appurtenances thereof, to the same being, belonging, or in anywise appertaining, to the
only proper use, benefit and behoof of the said Grantee forever in FEE SIMPLE.

AND THE SAID Grantor will warrant and forever defend the right and title to the above
described property unto the said Grantee against the claims of all persons whomsoever.

IN WITNESS WHEREOF, the Grantor has signed and sealed this deed, the day and year above
written.

Signed, sealed and delivered in presence of:

_____   _____   _____ (Seal)
Witness   Alice Miller
_____   _____   _____ (Seal)
Notary Public   David Miller
                  _____   _____ (Seal)
My Commission Expires:

    [NOTARIAL SEAL]

EXHIBIT 9-3
Knox–Jackson Deed

Associated – Champaign Office ● Chicago Title Insurance Company
201 North Neil – Champaign, Illinois 61820 – Phone 356-0501

DOCUMENT NO. _____

WARRANTY DEED

For Recorder's Certificate Only

THE GRANTOR__, _____
Knox Land Development Cormpany, an Illinois corporation

of the _____ of _____, in the County
of ___Knox_____, and State of ____Illinois_____,
for and in consideration of Ten Dollars ($10.00) and other good and
valuable consideration in hand paid, **CONVEY__** AND **WARRANT__** _to_
the **GRANTEE__**, _____
Carole S. Jackson

of the _____ of _____, County of ___Knox_____, and State
of ___Illinois_____, the following described real estate:

ALL THAT TRACT or parcel of land lying and being in the Northwest quarter
of Section 27, Township 24 South, Range 35 East, Knox County, Illinois and
being more particularly described on Exhibit "A" attached hereto and by
reference incorporated herein.

THIS CONVEYANCE IS SUBJECT TO THE FOLLOWING TITLE EXCEPTIONS:

(a)   Mortgage from Knox Land Development Company to First National Bank
       of Salem, dated October 14, 1986, recorded October 14, 1986 at
       Mortgage Book 21, Page 466, Knox County, Illinoix, securing the
       original principal indebtedness of $84,000.00. The Grantee by
       the acceptance of this deed assumes and agrees to pay the
       outstanding indebtedness according to its terms and assumes and
       agrees to be bound by all other terms and covenants contained in
       the Morrgage.

Subject to: (1) Real estate taxes for the year 19____ and subsequent years;
             (2) Covenants, conditions, restrictions and easements apparent or of record
             (3) All applicable zoning laws and ordinances;

Dated this _____ day of _____, 19____.

_____
                                              Knox Land Development Company, an
_____   Illinois corporation
                                              By: _____ (SEAL)
                                              Attest: _____, Its President
                                                                        , Its Secretary (SEAL)

STATE OF ILLINOIS }
                  } SS   I, the undersigned, a Notary Public in and for said County and State
CHAMPAIGN COUNTY }   aforesaid, **DO HEREBY CERTIFY,** that _____ [CORPORATE SEAL]

                              personally known to me to be the same person__ whose name__ _____
                              subscribed to the foregoing instrument, appeared before me this day in
                              person and acknowledged that __h____ signed, sealed and delivered the said
                              instrument as _____ free and voluntary act, for the uses and purposes
                              therein set forth, including the waiver of the right of homestead.

              (SEAL)   Given under my hand and Notarial Seal, this _____
                              day of _____, A.D. 19____.

                                                                              _____
                                                                                    Notary Public

Deed Prepared By: _____	Send Tax Bill To:
	__ _____
	_____
Exempt under provisions of Paragraph _____	Section 4, Real Estate Transfer Tax Act.
Date _____	Signature _____
	Buyer, Seller or Representative

EXHIBIT 9–4
Warranty Deed

WARRANTY DEED

STATE OF   COUNTY OF

THIS INDENTURE, Made the   day of   , in the year one thousand nine hundred   , between

of the County of   , and State of Georgia, as party or parties of the first part, hereinafter called Grantor, and

as party or parties of the second part, hereinafter called Grantee (the words "Grantor" and "Grantee" to include their respective heirs, successors and assigns where the context requires or permits).

WITNESSETH that: Grantor, for and in consideration of the sum of
( ) DOLLARS
in hand paid at and before the sealing and delivery of these presents, the receipt whereof is hereby acknowledged, has granted, bargained, sold, aliened, conveyed and confirmed, and by these presents does grant, bargain, sell, alien, convey and confirm unto the said Grantee,

TO HAVE AND TO HOLD the said tract or parcel of land, with all and singular the rights, members and appurtenances thereof, to the same being, belonging, or in anywise appertaining, to the only proper use, benefit and behoof of the said Grantee forever in FEE SIMPLE.

AND THE SAID Grantor will warrant and forever defend the right and title to the above described property unto the said Grantee against the claims of all persons whomsoever.

IN WITNESS WHEREOF, the Grantor has signed and sealed this deed, the day and year above written.

Signed, sealed and delivered in presence of:

_____   _____(Seal)

_____   _____(Seal)

_____   _____(Seal)

as joint tenants with the right of survivorship. The home is encumbered by (a) unpaid real estate taxes for the current year and (b) a mortgage from Charles D. Hoover and Martha L. Hoover to First Federal Savings and Loan Association securing the original principal indebtedness of $78,325, dated August 15, 1992, recorded August 16, 1992, at Mortgage Book 212, Page 82, Todd County, Wisconsin. The purchasers are willing to assume the mortgage. The land is described as follows:

> ALL THAT TRACT or parcel of land lying and being in the Southeast Quarter of Township 14 North, Section 3, Range 15 West, Todd County, Wisconsin, and being more particularly described as Lot 14, Block A, of The Blue Springs Subdivision as per Plat recorded at Plat Book 3, Page 47, Todd County, Wisconsin Plat Records, which Plat is incorporated herein and made a part of this description by reference.

CORRECTION OF DEEDS

Although every attempt should be made to avoid mistakes, mistakes do happen, and many times deeds must be corrected. The customary method of correcting an error in a deed is for the grantor to execute and deliver to the grantee a corrective deed. A corrective deed is valid without any additional consideration. Acceptance by the grantee is admission of the error found in the original deed.

Reformation and Cancellation of Deed

If a mutual mistake of fact is involved in the preparation, execution, and delivery of a deed, equity will reform the deed to its correct status. If there is some unilateral mistake of fact (only one party is mistaken) or fraud involved in the execution and delivery of a deed, the deed can be rescinded by the party who is mistaken or on whom the fraud was perpetrated.

Destruction of a deed does not return legal title to the grantor, nor does the return of a deed by the grantee to the grantor deliver title to the grantor. If it is desired for some reason that the grantee return the land to the grantor, the proper method is for the grantee to prepare, sign, and deliver a new deed to the grantor.

Practice Assignment No. 3

The deed shown in Exhibit 9–5 was prepared for the below described transaction and contains mistakes. Please review the deed, list all the mistakes, and prepare a corrective deed.

Pine Tree Development Company, Inc., is transferring title to Jacob Willson and Alice Willson. The property is unencumbered, and described as follows:

> ALL THAT TRACT or parcel of land lying and being in Land Lot 48 of the 14th District of Fulton County, Georgia and being more particularly described as follows:
>
> COMMENCING on the north side of Ponce de Leon Avenue 653.5 feet east from the northeast corner of Ponce de Leon Avenue and Bedford Place (formerly Fort Street), running east along the north side of Ponce de Leon Avenue, 90 feet; run thence north 365 feet; running thence west 89.5 feet; run thence south 381.9 feet to the POINT OF BEGINNING on Ponce de Leon Avenue and being improved property known as 638 Ponce de Leon Avenue, N.E., in the City of Atlanta, Georgia.

EXHIBIT 9-5
Deed Containing
Mistakes

WARRANTY DEED

STATE OF GEORGIA   COUNTY OF FULTON

THIS INDENTURE, Made the 11th   day of December   , in the year
one thousand nine hundred   , between

PINETREE DEVELOPMENT COMPANY, INC.

of the County of Fulton   , and State of Georgia, as party or parties of the
first part, hereinafter called Grantor, and

JACOB WILSON and ALICE WILSON

as party or parties of the second part, hereinafter called Grantee (the words "Grantor" and
"Grantee" to include their respective heirs, successors and assigns where the context requires or
permits).
WITNESSETH that: Grantor, for and in consideration of the sum of TEN AND NO/100
and other good and valuable consideration   ($10.00   ) DOLLARS
in hand paid at and before the sealing and delivery of these presents, the receipt whereof is hereby
acknowledged, has granted, bargained, sold, aliened, conveyed and confirmed, and by these presents
does grant, bargain, sell, alien, convey and confirm unto the said Grantee, all that tract
or parcel of land lying and being in Land Lot 48 of the 14th District
of Fulton County, Georgia, and being more particularly described as
follows:

COMMENCING on the north side of Ponce de Leon Avenue, 653.5 feet
east from the northeast corner of Ponce de Leon Avenue and Bedford
Place (formerly Fort Street), running thence east along the north
side of Ponce de Leon Avenue, 90 feet; running thence north 356
feet; running thence west 89.5 feet; running thence south 381.9
feet to the POINT OF BEGINNING on Ponce de Leon Avenue, and being
improved property known as 368 Ponce de Leon Avenue, N.E., in
the City of Atlanta, Georgia.

TO HAVE AND TO HOLD the said tract or parcel of land, with all and singular the rights,
members and appurtenances thereof, to the same being, belonging, or in anywise appertaining, to the
only proper use, benefit and behoof of the said Grantee forever in FEE SIMPLE.
AND THE SAID Grantor will warrant and forever defend the right and title to the above
described property unto the said Grantee against the claims of all persons whomsoever.

IN WITNESS WHEREOF, the Grantor has signed and sealed this deed, the day and year above
written.
PINETREE DEVELOPMENT CO., INC.

Signed, sealed and delivered in presence of:

By: _____ (Seal)
_____   Carol Tree, President
Unofficial Witness   _____ (Seal)

_____   Attest: _____ (Seal)
Notary Public   Susan Pine, Secretary

                                     (Corporate Seal)

E T H I C S :   Falsification of Documents

A legal assistant is helping an attorney represent a client in the transfer of ownership to real property. The transfer is taking place on October 2. During the closing of the transfer of ownership, the seller, a corporation, informs the attorney and legal assistant that its tax year ended on September 30 and that it had intended for this transfer of ownership to take place during its past tax year. The seller requested that the deed be backdated to September 30 so that the sale and transfer of ownership would appear to take place during the past tax year. Should the attorney and legal assistant backdate the deed?

The American Bar Association's Code of Professional Responsibility prohibits an attorney from falsifying a document for any reason. Likewise, a legal assistant should not, under any circumstances, falsify a document for a client. Changing the date of a deed to reflect a different time for transfer of ownership, especially one that may affect the taxable consequences of the transfer, would be a violation of ethics. The attorney and legal assistant in this situation should inform the client that they cannot falsify the document.

SUMMARY

Ownership to real property is transferred by deed. Legal assistants prepare and review deeds. A checklist to help in the preparation of a deed is included at the end of this chapter. Deed forms vary from state to state, and a legal assistant should be familiar with the forms used in the state in which he or she works. A number of forms from various states are included at the end of the chapter.

Every transaction that involves the sale and purchase of real property requires a deed. Most sales and purchases of real property also require that the purchaser borrow a portion of the purchase price. A number of financial institutions engage in the lending of funds for the purchase of real property. These financing sources are discussed in Chapter 10.

KEY TERMS

Caption
Consideration
Conveyance
Deed
General warranty deed

Grantee
Grantor
Habendum
Limited or special warranty deed

Preamble
Quitclaim deed
Testimonium
Warranty or covenant

REVIEW QUESTIONS

1. What six covenants or warranties are included in a general warranty deed?

2. What is the difference between a general warranty deed and limited warranty deed?

3. What are the basic requirements of a valid deed?

4. List and briefly describe the formal parts of a deed.

5. What is the difference between a present covenant and a future covenant contained in a general warranty deed?

6. What is a quitclaim deed, and what are some of its uses?

7. Which state's law will control the legal requirements for a deed?

8. When can a deed be rescinded?

9. Briefly list three presumptions regarding the delivery of a deed.

10. What is the importance of having a grantor's signature witnessed?

▦➡ C H E C K L I S T

For Preparing a Deed

❑ I. Research Before Preparation
  ❑ A. Review the contract or other agreement covering the transfer of ownership to the property.
  ❑ B. Review the title examination to make sure of the correct name of the title owner to the property.
  ❑ C. Confirm the correct spellings of all names of the grantor and grantee.
  ❑ D. Carefully review the title examination and determine what title exceptions should be identified in the deed.
  ❑ E. Confirm if prospective purchasers have any special requirements for taking title, such as joint tenancy with the right of survivorship and tenancy in common in a tenancy by entirety state or unequal shares.
  ❑ F. Review survey legal description with description in grantor's current deed to make sure no difference exists between the two descriptions.
❑ II. Preparing the Deed
  ❑ A. Draft the caption and preamble.
    1. Indicate the county and state in which the deed is signed.
    2. Date the deed with the date of execution and delivery.
    3. Indicate the correct name of the grantor, who should be the record titleholder of the property.
    4. Indicate the correct name of the grantee or grantees, indicating any special forms of ownership, such as joint tenancy, right of survivorship, and unequal shares.
  ❑ B. Draft the consideration. In most instances use a nominal recital of consideration.
  ❑ C. Draft the legal description.
    1. Use the correct legal description verified by survey and title examination.
    2. If the legal description is too long to be included on the face of the deed, use an exhibit and identify the exhibit on the face of the deed.
    3. List all title exceptions that are being transferred with the property.
  ❑ D. Draft signature blanks.
    1. The grantor is the only person who signs the deed.
    2. Correctly identify the grantor's name and confirm that it is the same as that shown in the preamble of the deed.
    3. Type all names underneath the signature lines.
    4. The deed must be signed and sealed.
    5. Make certain the deed contains the proper number of witnesses and the notary designation is correct.

CASE PROBLEMS

1. Samuel Adams is selling his Boston townhouse to Harrison Stone. Who is required to sign the deed in connection with the transfer of ownership?

2. Aaron owns a farm. Aaron has given to First Bank and Trust a mortgage on the farm. Aaron transfers ownership of the farm to Bob and gives Bob a general warranty deed. The general warranty deed to Bob warrants that there are no encumbrances on the farm and does not mention the mortgage to First Bank and Trust. Bob owns the farm only a short time and sells the farm by limited warranty deed to Carol. Carol decides that farm life is not for her, and sells the farm by general warranty deed to David. The general warranty deed does not mention the mortgage to First Bank and Trust. One week after David purchased the farm, First Bank and Trust notifies David of the mortgage. Is there a breach of any deed warranty or covenant and, if so, which covenant? At this stage can

David sue Carol? Can David sue Bob? Can David sue Aaron?

First Bank and Trust, after notifying David of its mortgage, commences foreclosure proceedings to sell David's farm to pay the debt. At this stage what deed covenant has been violated, if any? At this stage can David sue Carol for breach of covenant? Bob? Aaron?

3. You are a legal assistant involved in a closing of a purchase of real property. The real property is owned by Ruth White. Purchasers of the property are Albert Green and Linda Green. You have prepared the deed for Ruth White's signature, and you are in a state that requires two witnesses to Ruth White's signature. Can Timothy White, Ruth White's husband, witness her signature on the deed? Can Linda Green witness Ruth White's signature on the deed? Can you witness Ruth White's signature on the deed?

ADDENDUM

1. General Warranty Deed—North Carolina (Exhibit 9–6)
2. General Warranty Deed—Texas (Exhibit 9–7)
3. Warranty Deed (Joint Tenancy)—Illinois (Exhibit 9–8)
4. Limited Warranty Deed—Georgia (Exhibit 9–9)
5. Quitclaim Deed—Georgia (Exhibit 9–10)
6. Quitclaim Deed—California (Exhibit 9–11)
7. Executor's Deed—New York (Exhibit 9–12)
8. Administrator's Deed—Georgia (Exhibit 9–13)

267

EXHIBIT 9-6
General Warranty
Deed—North
Carolina

Excise Tax	Recording Time, Book and Page

Tax Lot No. .... Parcel Identifier No. ....

Verified by .... County on the .... day of ...., 19........

by ....

Mail after recording to ....

This instrument was prepared by ....

Brief description for the Index

NORTH CAROLINA GENERAL WARRANTY DEED

THIS DEED made this .... day of ...., 19........, by and between

GRANTOR	GRANTEE

Enter in appropriate block for each party: name, address, and, if appropriate, character of entity, e.q. corporation or partnership.

The designation Grantor and Grantee as used herein shall include said parties, their heirs, successors, and assigns, and shall include singular, plural, masculine, feminine or neuter as required by context.

WITNESSETH, that the Grantor, for a valuable consideration paid by the Grantee, the receipt of which is hereby acknowledged, has and by these presents does grant, bargain, sell and convey unto the Grantee in fee simple, all that

certain lot or parcel of land situated in the City of ...., ... Township,

.... County, North Carolina and more particularly described as follows:

EXHIBIT 9-6
General Warranty
Deed—North
Carolina
(continued)

The property hereinabove described was acquired by Grantor by instrument recorded in ....

....

A map showing the above described property is recorded in Plat Book .... page...................... .

TO HAVE AND TO HOLD the aforesaid lot or parcel of land and all privileges and appurtenances thereto belonging to the Grantee in fee simple.

And the Grantor covenants with the Grantee, that Grantor is seized of the premises in fee simple, has the right to convey the same in fee simple, that title is marketable and free and clear of all encumbrances, and that Grantor will warrant and defend the title against the lawful claims of all persons whomsoever except for the exceptions hereinafter stated.

Title to the property hereinabove described is subject to the following exceptions:

IN WITNESS WHEREOF, the Grantor has hereunto set his hand and seal, or if corporate, has caused this instrument to be signed in its corporate name by its duly authorized officers and its seal to be hereunto affixed by authority of its Board of Directors, the day and year first above written.

---   ---(SEAL)
        (Corporate Name)

By: ---   ---(SEAL)

------------------------------President   ---(SEAL)

ATTEST:

--   ---(SEAL)

----------------------------Secretary (Corporate Seal)

USE BLACK INK ONLY

SEAL-STAMP   NORTH CAROLINA, -----------------------------------County.

I, a Notary Public of the County and State aforesaid, certify that ---

-- Grantor,

personally appeared before me this day and acknowledged the execution of the foregoing instrument. Witness my

hand and official stamp or seal, this -------- day of ----------------------------------, 19------

My commission expires: -- Notary Public

SEAL-STAMP   NORTH CAROLINA, -----------------------------------County.

I, a Notary Public of the County and State aforesaid, certify that --,

personally came before me this day and acknowledged that ---- he is -------------------------- Secretary of

-- a North Carolina corporation, and that by authority duly

given and as the act of the corporation, the foregoing instrument was signed in its name by its ---------------

President, sealed with its corporate seal and attested by ----------- as its ---------------------------- Secretary.

Witness my hand and official stamp or seal, this -------day of ----------------------------, 19----------

My commission expires: -- Notary Public

The foregoing Certificate(s) of ---

----

is/are certified to be correct. This instrument and this certificate are duly registered at the date and time and in the Book and Page shown on the first page hereof.

---REGISTER OF DEEDS FOR---COUNTY

By --Deputy/Assistant - Register of Deeds

EXHIBIT 9–7
General Warranty
Deed—Texas

126—WARRANTY DEED   TEXAS STANDARD FORM

The State of Texas,
County of
{ # Know All Men by These Presents:

That

of the County of   State of   for and in consideration

of the sum of

DOLLARS

to   in hand paid by

as follows:

have Granted, Sold and Conveyed, and by these presents do Grant, Sell and Convey unto the said

of the County of   State of   all that certain

TO HAVE AND TO HOLD the above described premises, together with all and singular the

rights and appurtenances thereto in anywise belonging unto the said

heirs and assigns forever and   do hereby bind

heirs, executors and administrators, to Warrant and Forever Defend, all and singular the said premises

unto the said

heirs and assigns, against every person whomsoever lawfully claiming, or to claim the same, or any

part thereof.

WITNESS   hand   at

this   day of   19

Witnesses at Request of Grantor:

....

....

EXHIBIT 9-7
General Warranty
Deed—Texas
(continued)

Mailing address of grantee:

Name:
Address:
_____

(Acknowledgment)

STATE OF TEXAS
COUNTY OF

This instrument was acknowledged before me on the   day of   , 19   ,
by

My commission expires: _____

_____   Notary Public, State of Texas
                                           Notary's printed name:

(Acknowledgment)

STATE OF TEXAS
COUNTY OF

This instrument was acknowledged before me on the   day of   , 19   ,
by

My commission expires: _____

_____   Notary Public, State of Texas
                                           Notary's printed name:

(Acknowledgment)

STATE OF TEXAS
COUNTY OF

This instrument was acknowledged before me on the   day of   , 19   ,
by

My commission expires: _____

_____   Notary Public, State of Texas
                                           Notary's printed name:

126

Warranty Deed

FROM

TO

FILED FOR RECORD

This _____ day of _____ A.D. 19 ____

at _____ o'clock _____ M.

_____ County Clerk.

By _____ Deputy

RECORDED _____ A.D. 19 ____

In _____ County Records

In Book _____ on Page _____

_____ County Clerk.

By _____ Deputy

Recording Fee $ _____

This instrument should be filed immediately with the County Clerk for record.

WHEN RECORDED RETURN TO

The Odee Company, Dallas, TX 75238

EXHIBIT 9–8
Warranty Deed
(Joint Tenancy)—
Illinois

Associated – Champaign Office ● **Chicago** Title Insurance Company
201 North Neil – Champaign, Illinois 61820 – Phone 356-0501

WARRANTY DEED — Joint Tenancy

DOCUMENT NO._____

___ For Recorder's Certificate Only ___

THE GRANTOR__, _____

_____

_____

of the _____ of _____, in the County

of _____, and State of _____,

for and in consideration of Ten Dollars ($10.00) and other good and

valuable consideration in hand paid, **CONVEY__** and **WARRANT__** to

the **GRANTEES,** _____

_____,

of the _____ . of _____, County of _____, and State

of _____, not in **TENANCY IN COMMON**, but in **JOINT TENANCY**, the following described

real estate, to-wit:

Subject to: (1) Real estate taxes for the year 19____ and subsequent years;
(2) Covenants, conditions, restrictions and easements apparent or of record;
(3) All applicable zoning laws and ordinances;

hereby releasing and waiving all rights under and by virtue of the Homestead Exemption Laws of the State of Illinois.

To Have and to Hold, the above granted premises unto the said Grantees forever, not in **TENANCY IN COMMON**, but in **JOINT TENANCY**.

Dated this _____ day of _____, 19____.

_____   ____ _____

_____   _____

STATE OF ILLINOIS }
                             } SS
CHAMPAIGN COUNTY }

I, the undersigned, a Notary Public in and for said County and State aforesaid, **DO HEREBY CERTIFY**, that

personally known to me to be the same person__ whose name__ _____
subscribed to the foregoing instrument, appeared before me this day in person and acknowledged that __h____ signed, sealed and delivered the said instrument as _____ free and voluntary act, for the uses and purposes therein set forth, including the waiver of the right of homestead.

(SEAL)

Given under my hand and Notarial Seal, this _____
day of _____, A.D. 19____.

_____ Notary Public

Deed Prepared By: _____

Send Tax Bill To:

_____

_____

Exempt under provisions of Paragraph _____, Section 4, Real Estate Transfer Tax Act.

Date _____   Signature _____

Buyer, Seller or Representative

EXHIBIT 9–9
Limit Warranty
Deed—Georgia

STATE OF GEORGIA

COUNTY OF

LIMITED WARRANTY DEED

THIS INDENTURE made this   day of   197   , by and between

party or parties of the first part, hereinafter referred to as "Grantor", and

party or parties of the second part, hereinafter referred to as "Grantee", the words "Grantor" and "Grantee" to include the neuter, masculine and feminine genders, the singular and the plural;

WITNESSETH:

FOR AND IN CONSIDERATION of the sum of Ten Dollars ($10.00) in hand paid and other good and valuable consideration delivered to Grantor by Grantee at and before the execution, sealing and delivery hereof, the receipt and sufficiency of which is hereby acknowledged, the Grantor has and hereby does grant, bargain, sell and convey unto Grantee, and the heirs, legal representatives, successors and assigns of Grantee

TO HAVE AND TO HOLD said tract or parcel of land, together with any and all of the rights, members and appurtenances thereof to the same being, belonging or in anywise appertaining to the only proper use, benefit and behoof of the Grantee and the heirs, legal representatives, successors and assigns of Grantee, forever, in fee simple.

GRANTOR SHALL WARRANT and forever defend the right and title to said tract or parcel of land unto the Grantee and the heirs, legal representatives, successors and assigns of Grantee, against the claims of all persons whomsoever claiming by, through or under Grantor.

IN WITNESS WHEREOF, the Grantor has signed and sealed this deed the day and year first above written.

Signed, sealed and delivered in the presence of:

_____   _____ (SEAL)
(Unofficial Witness)

_____   _____ (SEAL)
(Notary Public)

3

EXHIBIT 9-10
Quitclaim Deed—
Georgia

QUITCLAIM DEED

STATE OF

COUNTY OF

THIS INDENTURE, made the   day of   in the year
one thousand nine hundred and sixty   , between

of the County of   , and State of   , as party
or parties of the first part, hereinafter called Grantor, and

of the County of   , and State of   , as party
or parties of the second part, hereinafter called Grantee (the words "Grantor" and "Grantee" to include their respective
heirs, successors and assigns where the context requires or permits).

WITNESSETH that: Grantor, for and in consideration of the sum of one dollar ($1.00) and other valuable
considerations in hand paid at and before the sealing and delivery of these presents, the receipt whereof is hereby
acknowledged, by these presents does hereby remise, convey and forever QUITCLAIM unto the said grantee

TO HAVE AND TO HOLD the said described premises to grantee, so that neither grantor nor any person or
persons claiming under grantor shall at any time, by any means or ways, have, claim or demand any right or title
to said premises or appurtenances, or any rights thereof.

IN WITNESS WHEREOF, Grantor has signed and sealed this deed, the day and year first above written.

Signed, sealed and delivered in the presence of:

_____(Seal)

_____   _____(Seal)
(Unofficial witness)

_____   _____(Seal)
(Notary Public)

EXHIBIT 9-11
Quitclaim Deed—
California

AND WHEN RECORDED MAIL TO

NAME

ADDRESS

CITY &
STATE

Title Order No. _____ Escrow No. _____

——————————————————— SPACE ABOVE THIS LINE FOR RECORDER'S USE———————

MAIL TAX STATEMENTS TO

NAME

STREET
ADDRESS

CITY &
STATE

Quitclaim Deed

THE UNDERSIGNED GRANTOR(s) DECLARE(s)
DOCUMENTARY TRANSFER TAX is $ _____
☐ _____ unicorporated area ☐ City of _____
Parcel No. _____
☐ computed on full value of property conveyed, or
☐ computed on full value less value of liens or encumbrances remaining at time of sale, and

FOR A VALUABLE CONSIDERATION, receipt of which is hereby acknowledged,

hereby REMISE, RELEASE AND FOREVER QUITCLAIM to

the following described real property in the

county of   , state of California:

Dated _____

STATE OF CALIFORNIA
COUNTY OF _____ } SS.
On this _____ day of _____, in the year
_____, before me, the undersigned, a Notary Public in
and for said County and State, personally appeared _____
_____
_____ ,
personally known to me (or proved to me on the basis of satisfactory
evidence) to be the person _____ whose name
_____ subscribed to the within instrument and
acknowledged that _____ executed the
same. "

Signature _____

_____
Name (Typed or Printed)
Notary Public in and for said County and State   (This area for official notarial seal)

MAIL TAX STATEMENT AS DIRECTED ABOVE 1-103 REV. 6/83 PRINTCO

EXHIBIT 9–12
Executor's Deed—
New York

Standard N.Y.B.T.U. Form 8005—10M   Executor's Deed—Individual or Corporation (single sheet)

CONSULT YOUR LAWYER BEFORE SIGNING THIS INSTRUMENT — THIS INSTRUMENT SHOULD BE USED BY LAWYERS ONLY

THIS INDENTURE, made the   day of   , nineteen hundred and

BETWEEN

as executor   of   the last will and testament of
                                                                    , late of
                                                                    , deceased,

party of the first part, and

party of the second part,

WITNESSETH, that the party of the first part, by virtue of the power and authority given in and by said last will and testament, and in consideration of

                                                                    dollars,
                    paid by the party of the second part, does hereby grant and release unto the party of the second part, the heirs or successors and assigns of the party of the second part forever,

ALL that certain plot, piece or parcel of land, with the buildings and improvements thereon erected, situate, lying and being in the

TOGETHER with all right, title and interest, if any, of the party of the first part in and to any streets and roads abutting the above described premises to the center lines thereof; TOGETHER with the appurtenances, and also all the estate which the said decedent had at the time of decedent's death in said premises, and also the estate therein, which the party of the first part has or has power to convey or dispose of, whether individually, or by virtue of said will or otherwise; TO HAVE AND TO HOLD the premises herein granted unto the party of the second part, the heirs or successors and assigns of the party of the second part forever.

AND the party of the first part covenants that the party of the first part has not done or suffered anything whereby the said premises have been incumbered in any way whatever, except as aforesaid.
AND the party of the first part, in compliance with Section 13 of the Lien Law, covenants that the party of the first part will receive the consideration for this conveyance and will hold the right to receive such consideration as a trust fund to be applied first for the purpose of paying the cost of the improvement and will apply the same first to the payment of the cost of the improvement before using any part of the total of the same for any other purpose.
The word "party" shall be construed as if it read "parties" whenever the sense of this indenture so requires.

IN WITNESS WHEREOF, the party of the first part has duly executed this deed the day and year first above written.

IN PRESENCE OF:

EXHIBIT 9–12
Executor's Deed—
New York
(continued)

STATE OF NEW YORK, COUNTY OF   SS:

On the   day of   19   , before me
personally came

to me known to be the individual   described in and who
executed the foregoing instrument, and acknowledged that
executed the same.

STATE OF NEW YORK, COUNTY OF   SS:

On the   day of   19   , before me
personally came

to me known to be the individual   described in and who
executed the foregoing instrument, and acknowledged that
executed the same.

STATE OF NEW YORK, COUNTY OF   SS:

On the   day of   19   , before me
personally came
to me known, who, being by me duly sworn, did depose and
say that   he resides at No.
                                                           ;
that   he is the
of
                        , the corporation described
in and which executed the foregoing instrument; that   he
knows the seal of said corporation; that the seal affixed
to said instrument is such corporate seal; that it was so
affixed by order of the board of directors of said corporation, and that   he signed h   name thereto by like order.

STATE OF NEW YORK, COUNTY OF   SS:

On the   day of   19   , before me
personally came
the subscribing witness to the foregoing instrument, with
whom I am personally acquainted, who, being by me duly
sworn, did depose and say that   he resides at No.
                                                           ;
that   he knows

                                to be the individual
described in and who executed the foregoing instrument;
that   he, said subscribing witness, was present and saw
                        execute the same; and that   he, said witness,
at the same time subscribed h   name as witness thereto.

Executor's Deed

TITLE NO.

                          TO

┌───┐
│ STANDARD FORM OF NEW YORK BOARD OF TITLE UNDERWRITERS │
│   Distributed by   │
│   CHICAGO TITLE   │
│   INSURANCE COMPANY   │
└───┘

SECTION

BLOCK

LOT

COUNTY OR TOWN

Recorded at Request of
CHICAGO TITLE INSURANCE COMPANY

Return by Mail to

┌───┐
│   │
│   │
│   │
│   Zip No.   │
└───┘

RESERVE THIS SPACE FOR USE OF RECORDING OFFICE

Form 10-11

Lawyers Title Insurance Corporation

ATLANTA BRANCH OFFICE

GEORGIA STATE OFFICE
TITLE BUILDING
ATLANTA 3, GEORGIA

ADMINISTRATOR'S DEED

STATE OF GEORGIA, COUNTY OF

THIS INDENTURE, Made the   day of   , in the year
one thousand nine hundred   , between

of the County of   , and State of Georgia, as administrat
of the estate of   deceased, hereinafter
called Grantor, and

hereinafter called Grantee (the words "Grantor" and "Grantee" to include their respective heirs, successors and assigns where the context requires or permits).

WITNESSETH that: Grantor, for and in consideration of the purchase price hereinafter set
forth in hand paid at and before the sealing and delivery of these presents, the receipt whereof is
hereby acknowledged, has granted, bargained, sold, aliened, conveyed and confirmed, and by these
presents does grant, bargain, sell, alien, convey and confirm unto the said Grantee,

EXHIBIT 9–13
Administrator's
Deed—Georgia

Said property is sold and conveyed by virtue of an order of the Court of Ordinary of
county entered after due notice of the application
thereof by publication as required by law; grantor having on the first Tuesday of the month and
year above set forth, within the legal hours of sale, at the place of public sales in said county, put
up and exposed said property to sale at public outcry to the highest bidder, after said sale had been
duly advertised by publication as required by law, and after all requirements of law had been fully
complied with; and said property having been bid off by the grantee at the price or sum of
dollars, grantee being
the highest and best bidder.

TO HAVE AND TO HOLD the said tract or parcel of land, with all and singular the rights,
members and appurtenances thereof, to the same being, belonging, or in anywise appertaining, to the
only proper use, benefit and behoof of the said Grantee forever in FEE SIMPLE.

IN WITNESS WHEREOF, the Grantor has signed and sealed this deed, the day and year above
written.

Signed, sealed and delivered
in the presence of the undersigned:

....(Seal)
(Unofficial Witness)   As administrat   aforesaid

....
(Notary Public)

EXHIBIT 9–13
Administrator's
Deed—Georgia
(continued)

Financing Sources in Real Estate Transactions

Creditors have better memories than debtors.

—Benjamin Franklin

OBJECTIVES

After reading this chapter you will be able to:

- Identify the various sources of mortgage loans
- Understand the difference between a conventional and an insured loan
- Explain the role of the FHA and VA in real estate financing
- Explain the purposes of FNMA, GNMA, and FHLMC
- Understand the difference between a permanent loan and a construction loan and their relation to each other
- Identify and understand the various forms of mortgage loan payment plans

GLOSSARY

Amortization   Reduction in a debt by periodic payments covering interest and part of the principal.

Balloon payment   Final payment of all unpaid principal and of accrued and unpaid interest on the loan which payment is greater than the periodic payments on the loan.

Bridge loan   Short-term loan with a maturity of one to two years that provides the borrower necessary financing to purchase real property. A bridge loan usually is refinanced by a long-term loan.

Construction loan   Mortgage loan made for the purpose of providing money to construct improvements on real property.

Conventional loan   Mortgage loan in which the risk of repayment of the debt rests solely on the ability of the borrower to pay and the value of the security provided by the mortgage.

Debt service   Payment of principal and interest on a loan.

Fannie Mae   Federal National Mortgage Association, a quasi-government agency organized for the purpose of investing in FHA and VA loans.

Freddie Mac   Federal Home Loan Mortgage Corporation, a corporation designed to purchase and invest in mortgages.

Fully amortized loan   Loan in which the partial payments of principal and accrued interest if paid for the stated period of time will result in the entire loan being paid at maturity.

Ginnie Mae   Government National Mortgage Association, a government corporation designed to administer special assistance programs and to work with the Federal National Mortgage Association to provide a market for mortgages.

GLOSSARY (cont'd)

Graduated payment mortgage   Mortgage loan that permits the borrower to pay lower monthly payments for the first few years and larger payments for the remainder of the term.

Insured loan   Mortgage loan in which the repayment of the loan is insured or guaranteed by either a government agency or a private insurance company.

Interest   Charge by a lender to a borrower for the use of money.

Loan-to-value ratio   Ratio of the amount of a mortgage loan to the value of the secured real property. For example, the amount of the loan is $80,000 and the market value of the real property pledged as security for the loan is $100,000, the loan-value ratio is 80 percent.

Mortgage loan   Loan secured by real property.

Negative amortization   Loan in which the payments are not sufficient to pay the interest costs of the loan. The unpaid interest is added to the principal of the loan, resulting in an increase in the principal amount of the loan during the term of repayment.

Permanent loan   Long-term loan that finances the acquisition of real property or refinances a construction loan on improvements.

Primary mortgage lender   Lender who makes mortgage loans directly to a borrower.

Private mortgage insurance   Insurance through private sources that a debtor will pay his or her loan.

Secondary mortgage market   Group of investors who purchase mortgage loans from primary mortgage lenders.

Servicing the loan   Collection of payments from the borrower of a mortgage loan.

Straight-line amortized loan   Mortgage loan in which the borrower will pay a different amount for each installment, with each payment consisting of a fixed amount credited toward principal and an additional amount for the interest due on the balance of the principal unpaid since the last payment.

Term loan   Loan in which the borrower makes periodic payments of interest with the principal being paid in one installment at the end of the loan term.

I t is unusual for real property to be purchased on an all-cash basis. The buyer in a real estate transaction usually borrows a major portion of the purchase price by pledging the real property involved as security for a loan. This is known as a **mortgage loan**. Mortgage loans on both residential and commercial properties usually are made by institutional lenders, such as savings and loan associations, commercial banks, mutual savings banks, life insurance companies, mortgage banking companies, mortgage brokers, and credit unions.

The closing of mortgage loans constitutes a major part of the practice of a real estate attorney or legal assistant. In this chapter, the business aspects of real estate finance are discussed.

SOURCES OF MORTGAGE LOANS

Most mortgage loans are granted by lending institutions, such as savings and loan associations, commercial banks, mutual savings banks, life insurance companies, credit unions, pension funds, and mortgage banking companies.

Savings and Loan Associations

Savings and loan associations were first formed in the early nineteenth century as organizations designed to lend only to their members and only to finance the pur-

New York:
In New York, most home loans were originated through savings and loan associations but today commercial banks are important sources for lending.

chases of homes for the members. To this day, savings and loan associations primarily specialize in long-term home mortgage loans. Savings and loan associations usually lend money secured by real property in the region close to their offices. Savings and loan associations also participate in the Federal Housing Administration (FHA)-insured and Veterans Administration (VA) guaranty loan programs.

Savings and loan associations are chartered either by the federal government or by the state in which they are located. Savings and loan associations are regulated on a national level by the Federal Home Loan Bank (FHLB) system. The FHLB sets up mandatory guidelines for its member associations and provides depositors with insurance for the safety of their deposits under the Federal Savings and Loan Insurance Corporation.

New York:
In New York State-chartered banks, it is mandatory to have FSLIC (Federal Savings Loan Insurance Corp.) in which the federal government guarantees all loans up to $100,000 for each account.

The savings and loan industry in the 1980s moved away from traditionally safe residential loans to more speculative high-yield construction loans, junk bonds, and commercial loans on shopping centers and office buildings. This entry into the high-yield/high-risk commercial lending market, especially in depressed areas of the economy, caused many savings and loan institutions to accumulate a large number of bad loans resulting in failures of the savings and loan institutions. The 1990s find the federal government involved in a multibillion-dollar rescue effort of the savings and loan industry.

Commercial Banks

Commercial banks usually are considered a main source of short-term (loans of less than three years' maturity) real estate financing. The short-term nature of bank lending is due to bank assets being tied up in demand deposits (checking accounts) rather than in long-term savings accounts. Commercial banks primarily make loans for construction of improvements and short-term bridge loans for the acquisition of property. A **bridge loan** for the acquisition of property with a maturity of one or two years enables the borrower to have the necessary financing to purchase real property. During the one- or two-year period, the borrower seeks out additional long-term financing to pay off the bridge loan. Commercial banks have also been active in second-mortgage home equity loans in which homeowners borrow money against the appreciated value of their homes. Commercial banks are chartered either by the federal government or by the state in which the bank is located. Depositors' accounts with commercial banks are insured by the Federal Deposit Insurance Corporation.

Mutual Savings Banks

New York:
Three-quarters of all assets of mutual savings banks are located in New York and Massachusetts.

The average price of a home in New York is over $150,000 and few people have that much cash to buy a home outright. They look to lenders to assist them in the purchase.

A mutual savings bank is owned by its depositors. All earnings are returned to them as savings account interest or dividends. Mutual savings banks are geographically concentrated in the capital surplus areas of the northeast and most of the savings banks are located in New York and Massachusetts. Mutual savings banks are active in the mortgage market, investing in loans secured by income property as well as residential real estate. Mutual savings banks also invest heavily in FHA-insured or VA-guaranteed loans.

Life Insurance Companies

Life insurance companies derive their funds from the premiums paid by their policy holders and investment income that remains after operating expenses, and policy claims are paid or provided for.

Although life insurance companies engage in a wide variety of lending activity, mortgage loans constitute a large percentage of their investment portfolio.

Most life insurance companies invest money in large long-term loans used to finance the acquisition or construction of commercial and industrial properties. Life insurance companies also invest in residential mortgage loans by purchasing large blocks of government-backed (FHA- and VA-guaranteed) loans from the Federal National Mortgage Association or other agencies that warehouse such loans for resale on the **secondary mortgage market**.

Many life insurance companies have also ventured into acquisitions in the projects they finance. Life insurance companies are active in joint ventures or partnership arrangements with the real estate developer. In this way, the life insurance company may make a loan to a developer in which the life insurance company is also a partner or joint venturer on the project. The life insurance company receives interest on the loan and earns a portion of any appreciation in value of the developed property through its partnership relationship.

Credit Unions

Credit unions are organizations associated with a large corporation or organization that permits employees of the corporation or members of the organization to deposit savings with the credit union. The credit union not only pays interest on these deposits, but also permits members of the credit union to borrow money from the credit union for personal use. Traditionally, credit unions have made only short-term consumer and home improvement loans, but credit unions have recently been active in making long-term first- and second-mortgage loans on residential property.

Pension Funds

Pension or retirement plans for large corporations and unions accumulate large sums of money for the retirement of plan participants. Like life insurance companies, pension funds retain some of their money to satisfy retirement benefits and to cover operating expenses and then invest the rest. Pension fund administrators are required by law to make only prudent and safe investments. Mortgage loans on both residential and commercial properties are considered prudent investments, and pension funds have been active in these areas.

New York:
In New York, the New York State Employee Pension Fund allows investments in individual mortgages.

Mortgage Banking Companies

Mortgage banking companies originate mortgage loans for insurance companies, commercial banks, pension funds, savings and loan institutions, and other investors throughout the country. Mortgage banking companies may originate these loans as a correspondent or agent on behalf of the permanent investor using the permanent investor's money to fund the loan. Some mortgage banking companies have sufficient funds of their own to make real estate loans that will later be sold to investors, with the mortgage company receiving a fee for servicing (collecting the money for) the loans. Mortgage banking companies are involved in all types of real estate loan activities.

Mortgage banking companies usually are organized as private corporations.

New York:
Mortgage brokers act as intermediaries between lenders and borrowers. The brokers get a fee from the banks where these loans are placed.

Mortgage brokers are increasing in popularity. They help bring the lender and purchaser together.

TYPES OF LOANS

A mortgage loan may be identified as either a **conventional loan** or an **insured** or guaranteed **loan**. With a conventional loan, the risk of payment of the debt depends solely on the borrower's ability to pay and the value of the security provided by the mortgage. The risk of repayment of an insured or guaranteed loan is additionally secured through insurance issued by a private mortgage insurance company or guarantees provided by the government through such agencies as the FHA or VA.

Conventional Loans

A lender who makes conventional loans will require the preparation of an appraisal of the value of the real property given as security for the loan. The lender will also review credit reports, financial statements, and other information concerning the prospective buyer's ability to repay the loan.

The ratio of the debt to the value of the secured real property is known as the **loan-to-value ratio**. A lender who makes conventional loans generally will require a lower loan-to-value ratio than it would otherwise require for an insured or guaranteed loan. Theoretically, the lender has less risk of repayment with a lower loan-to-value ratio. For example, a $60,000 loan secured by a home with an appraised value of $100,000 is a lower risk than a $90,000 loan secured by the same home.

Insured or Guaranteed Loans

In an insured or guaranteed loan, a third party, government agency, or private mortgage insurance company guarantees the lender a repayment of a portion of the loan. Government and private guaranties usually guarantee repayment from 60 percent to 90 percent of the loan, depending on the government program under which the guaranty is issued or the terms of the private mortgage insurance contract. A number of federal and state agencies offer guaranteed loans under certain terms and conditions, and a discussion of three large federal programs follows.

FHA-Insured Loans

Congress designed the FHA-insured mortgage loan in 1934. The FHA was created out of the National Housing Act of 1934 to ensure that quality housing would be made available to all U.S. citizens. The FHA operates under the Department of Housing and Urban Development (HUD). Despite popular belief, a person who wants to obtain an FHA loan does not borrow directly from the FHA, but instead, the borrower obtains financing from an approved lender who agrees to make the loan subject to an FHA commitment to insure the lender against losses caused by the loan default. An FHA loan is not made by the agency but is insured or guaranteed by it. The FHA insures loans made up to 97 percent of the loan-to-value ratio of the secured property. The FHA does have maximum dollar amounts for loans to be insured, which change from time to time, and sets standards for construction quality and neighborhood and credit requirements for borrowers.

VA-Guaranteed Loans

The Serviceman's Readjustment Act of 1944 authorized the VA to guarantee loans for the purpose of purchasing or constructing homes for eligible veterans. Similarly to the FHA, the VA does not lend money but guarantees loans made by private lending institutions approved by the agency. A VA loan is not made by the agency but is guaranteed by it. Although there is no VA limit on the amount of the loan the veteran can obtain, the VA does set a limit on the amount of the loan it will guarantee. This limit is 60 percent of the loan amount.

A veteran who is seeking a VA loan must apply for a Certificate of Eligibility. The Certificate of Eligibility does not mean that the veteran will receive a loan, but the certificate does set forth and guarantee the maximum amount of the loan the veteran is entitled to.

The VA also issues a Certificate of Reasonable Value for the property being purchased, stating its current market value based on the VA-approved appraisal. The certificate establishes the maximum amount of the VA loan allowed for the property. If the purchase price is greater than the amount set forth in the Certificate of Reasonable Value, the veteran must pay the difference in cash. The VA guarantees 60 percent of the amount of the loan up to a loan-to-value ratio of 100 percent, provided the loan amount does not exceed the amount on the Certificate of Reasonable Value.

Small Business Administration–Guaranteed Loans

The U.S. Small Business Administration (SBA) was formed to assist small businesses. One part of this assistance is a guaranty program that enables small business owners to obtain necessary capital to start or continue a small business. In some instances, the SBA lends the money directly to a small business, but in most cases, it does not lend the money but guarantees loans made by a private lending institution approved by the agency. An SBA guaranty usually is between 70 percent and 85 percent of the loan amount. The SBA sets maximum dollar amounts for loans to be insured and establishes strict criteria for a small business. SBA-guaranteed loans have become a major source of capital for small businesses.

Private Mortgage Insurance

A lender may also receive insurance through private sources that a debtor will pay his or her loan. These private sources or insurance companies will, for the payment of a fee, guarantee the mortgage lender that payment on a loan will be made. If the payments are not made, the mortgage insurance company buys the loan from the lender and enforces the debt against the debtor. With a privately insured lending program, home purchasers can obtain conventional mortgage loans for up to 95 percent of the appraised value at prevailing interest rates and reasonable mortgage insurance premium costs.

SECONDARY MARKET

There is both a primary and a secondary market for mortgage loans. The **primary market** consists of (a) lenders who, as an investment, supply funds to borrowers and (b) lenders who close or originate loans for the purposes of selling the loans to investors. Legal assistants usually are involved with closings in the primary market. Once a mortgage loan is closed in the primary market, the loan can be bought and sold in the **secondary market**.

Because a mortgage loan bears **interest**, it is viewed as an investment similar to a bond or a treasury bill. A number of investors, such as life insurance companies and pension plans, are willing to purchase mortgage loans to receive the interest. Likewise, a number of primary-mortgage lenders are willing to sell their inventory of mortgage loans. For example, a primary-mortgage lender, such as a savings and loan association, may want to sell a number of loans to raise money for the purpose of making new loans. Secondary-mortgage activities are a good source of new funds in the primary-mortgage market and are therefore beneficial when money is in short supply.

When a mortgage loan has been sold on a secondary market, the original lender may continue to collect the payments from the borrower. This arrangement is called **servicing the loan**. The servicing lender passes the payments to the investor who has purchased the loan and charges the investor a fee for servicing the loan.

A number of large warehousing agencies are active participants in the secondary-mortgage market. The warehouse agency purchases a number of mortgage loans and assembles them in one or more packages for resale to investors. The major warehousing agencies are the Federal National Mortgage Association (FNMA), the Government National Mortgage Association (GNMA), and The Federal Home Loan Mortgage Corporation (FHLMC).

Federal National Mortgage Association

The FNMA, often referred to as **Fannie Mae**, is a privately owned corporation organized to provide a secondary market for mortgage loans. FNMA primarily invests in FHA and VA loans. It raises money to purchase loans by selling government-guaranteed bonds at market interest rates. These bonds are secured by blocks or pools of mortgages acquired through FNMA programs.

Mortgage banking firms and other investors are actively involved in selling loans to FNMA while retaining the servicing (collection of payment) functions.

Government National Mortgage Association

The GNMA, or **Ginnie Mae** is a division of HUD. It is designed to administer special assistance programs and work with the FNMA in the secondary-mortgage market. FNMA and GNMA can in times of tight money and high interest rate join together through a tandem plan to improve the mortgage market. The tandem plan provides that FNMA can purchase high-risk/low-yield loans at full market rates with GNMA guaranteeing payment and absorbing the differences between the low-yield rate and the current market prices.

The Federal Home Loan Mortgage Corporation

New York:
SONYMA (State of New York Mortgage Agency) is an important source of money for New York home buyers. Their tax-exempt status allows mortgage money to be offered to New York State residents at a lower rate. This is usually available to first time home buyers.

The FHLMC, or **Freddie Mac**, provides a secondary market for conventional mortgage loans. Freddie Mac has the authority to purchase mortgages and to pool and sell bonds in the open market with mortgages as security.

The FNMA and FHLMC require standard loan document forms and issues loan guidelines for a lender to follow. Copies of the standardized FNMA–FHLMC forms are included in Chapters 11 and 12.

A legal assistant, when closing a residential loan, commonly uses the required loan document forms of FNMA or FHLMC.

PERMANENT AND CONSTRUCTION LOANS _____

A **permanent loan** is a long-term loan that finances the acquisition of real property or refinances a **construction loan** on improvements. The payments on a permanent loan are **amortized**, which means that the payment will pay both principal and interest on the loan. The loan will be paid in full at its maturity. A permanent lender's main concerns when underwriting a permanent loan are the market value of the real property given as security for the loan and the financial stability of the borrower. In addition, on commercial permanent loans, the lender considers the amount and reliability of income being produced from the real property and will not make the loan unless the income is sufficient to pay the expenses of management and maintenance of the real property as well as the payments on the loan. The payment of principal and interest on a loan is called **debt service**.

A construction loan is made for the purpose of constructing improvements on real property. Construction loans are short term with an average maturity of one year or less. The monthly payments of a construction loan are interest only with a total payment of all principal and interest due at maturity. The source of repaying the construction loan at maturity is the proceeds from a permanent loan. The borrower refinances a construction loan by obtaining a permanent loan. Many construction lenders will not make a construction loan unless the borrower has already obtained a commitment for a permanent loan. Because construction loans are for the purpose of building improvements, construction loans usually are disbursed in installments as the improvements are completed. Most construction lenders only disburse 90 percent of the cost of improvements during construction, retaining 10 percent to protect against cost overruns. The retainage is disbursed when construction is completed. The interest charged on construction loans is tied to the lender's source of funds: usual short-term rates, such as the prime lending rate, or the one-year treasury bill rate. Because construction loans are riskier than permanent loans, some construction lenders add a premium to the interest rates.

The underwriting concerns for a construction lender involve the construction lender's estimate of the cost of construction. Many construction lenders have staff engineers and contractors who can estimate the cost of building, or they hire professional architects or engineers to perform this service. Construction lenders inspect the real property each time money is requested to make sure the improvements have in fact been completed.

Interest

The sum of money charged for the use of money is called **interest**. Typically, interest is expressed in terms of a certain percentage of the principal that must be paid each year the debt is outstanding. For example, a lender may make a loan of $80,000 at 10 percent interest. The interest on the loan on an annual basis is 10 percent of the principal, or $8,000. The amount of interest due on any one of the installment payment days is calculated by computing the total yearly interest, based on the unpaid balance, dividing that figure by the number of payments made each year. For example, if the outstanding loan balance is $80,000 with interest at the rate of 10 percent per annum and the amount of monthly payments is $750, the interest and principal due on the next installment would be computed as follow: $80,000 times 10 percent equals $8,000 annual interest; $8,000 annual interest divided by 12 equals $666.67 monthly interest; $750 minus $666.67 equals $83.33 monthly principal. Interest may be due either at the end of each payment period (payment in arrears) or at the beginning of each payment period (payment in advance). Most mortgage loans are paid in arrears.

Payment Plans

Most mortgage loans are amortized loans. That is, regular payments are applied, first to the interest owed and then to the balance of the principal amount, over a term between twenty and thirty years. At the end of loan term, the full amount of principal and all interest due will be paid in full.

Most amortized mortgage loans are paid in monthly installments. Some, are paid quarterly or semiannually. Some examples of payment plans are as follows:

1. The most commonly used amortization plan is the **fully amortized loan**, which requires the borrower to pay a constant amount, usually monthly. The amount of each payment is first credited to the interest due and then the remainder is applied to reduce the principal of the loan. Because each payment is the same, the portion applied toward payment of principal will increase and the portion accredited toward interest will decrease as the unpaid balance of the loan is reduced.

2. A **straight-line amortized loan** is one in which the borrower pays a different amount for each installment, with each payment consisting of a fixed amount credited toward principal and an additional amount for the interest due on the balance of the principal outstanding since the last payment. The payments become smaller as the loan matures because the amount accredited to interest decreases as the principal amount of the loan decreases.

3. A *straight* or **term loan** is one in which the borrower may choose a straight payment plan that calls for periodic payments of interest with the principal being paid in full in one installment at the end of the loan term. Construction loans and interim bridge acquisition loans use this method of payment.

4. A **graduated payment mortgage** is one that permits the borrower to pay lower monthly payments for the first few years of the loan and larger payments for the remainder of the term. These loans typically are used to permit young, less affluent buyers to buy property or to permit buyers in times of high interest rates to purchase real estate on terms they can afford.

5. A borrower may make payments on a mortgage loan that will not fully amortize the amount of the loan by the time the final payment is due. The final payment then is a larger amount than the other payments. This payment is called a **balloon**, and this type of loan is called a **partially amortized loan**. For example, a loan is made for $80,000, 11.5 percent interest computed on a thirty-year amortization schedule but with the final balloon payment due at the end of the twentieth year. In this case, each monthly payment would be $792.24 (the amount taken from a thirty-year amortization schedule) with the final balloon payment of $56,340 (the amount of principal still owing after twenty years). The borrower at the time the balloon payment is due must either come up with the cash to pay the balloon payment or refinance the loan.

6. A borrower may make payment on a mortgage loan that will not even fully pay the interest that is due each month on the outstanding principal balance of the loan. This payment plan is known as a **negative amortization loan**. Because the interest is not being paid each month, the unpaid portion of the interest will be added to the principal. The principal balance of a negative amortized loan increases instead of decreases as the loan is being repaid. This can

result at maturity in the borrower having to pay a balloon payment that may be more than the original principal amount borrowed from the lender. A negative amortized loan is used only on a loan that provides for a variable interest rate, that is, an interest rate that will fluctuate with some index, such as the prime lending rate, or the rate on treasury securities. A negative amortization loan usually is used when interest rates are increasing to such a rate that the average borrower cannot afford additional payments to pay the interest in full. The negative amortization loan gives the borrower the benefit of reduced payments during the period when high interest payments are being made. The borrower's hope in repaying the loan is that the value of the real property serving as security for the loan will increase faster than the amount of the debt not being paid; therefore, the loan can be refinanced with a bigger loan at maturity. Because of the dangers inherent in negative amortization loans, they seldom are used.

 E T H I C S :   Overbilling

A legal assistant is employed with a law firm that represents a number of lending institutions. The state in which the law firm is located requires that an out-of-state lender be licensed by the state to make loans within the state. The set of rules that control this licensing is complex. The legal assistant was involved in a research project researching and outlining the requirements for licensing within the state by an out-of-state lender. The research project consumed more than forty hours of the legal assistant's time and the legal assistant was able to bill one of the firm's clients $65 per hour for each hour spent. The firm now has another out-of-state client that is requesting the same information. The legal assistant will spend about two hours reviewing and updating the research information from the last client's existing file. Had the legal assistant not performed the research for the previous client, it would take the legal assistant forty hours to perform the services required by the new client. Should the legal assistant bill the one or two hours of time necessary to review the existing information to the new client, or should the legal assistant bill the full forty hours?

It is unethical for an attorney or a legal assistant to overbill a client for services rendered to the client. If the client has agreed to pay for legal services based on time spent on the matter, it is unethical for the attorney or legal assistant to add phantom or additional hours that were not spent on the client's matter. It would be ethical for the law firm and the legal assistant in this case to bill the new client only for the additional time spent in revising and preparing the client's requested report or application for a license. It would be unethical to bill the new client for the forty hours of research performed for a previous client.

SUMMARY

A legal assistant may assist an attorney who represents one of the lending institutions mentioned in this chapter. The loans made by the lender may be construction or permanent loans and have different amortization payment plans. The legal assistant's chief duty is to make sure all requirements for the loan have been met and that all loan documents are properly prepared.

KEY TERMS

Amortization
Balloon payment
Bridge loan
Construction loan
Conventional loan
Debt service
Fannie Mae
Freddie Mac

Fully amortized loan
Ginnie Mae
Graduated payment mortgage
Insured loan
Interest
Loan-to-value ratio
Mortgage loan
Negative amortization

Permanent loan
Primary mortgage lender
Private mortgage insurance
Secondary mortgage market
Servicing the loan
Straight-line amortized loan
Term loan

REVIEW QUESTIONS

1. What is the difference between a conventional loan and an insured mortgage loan?

2. What is the loan-to-value ratio?

3. What role does the VA play in real estate financing?

4. What service does a private mortgage insurance company provide?

5. Who are the major investors in the secondary-mortgage market?

6. What is a construction loan, and how is the construction loan repaid?

7. What does it mean to pay a mortgage loan in arrears?

8. What is the difference between a fully amortized loan and a straight-line amortized loan?

9. What is a balloon payment?

10. What is a negative amortization loan?

CASE PROBLEMS

1. Assume a mortgage loan has an outstanding principal balance of $75,000 and the interest rate is 10.25 percent. Calculate what portion of a $710 monthly payment will be allocated to interest.

2. Assume a mortgage loan with a principal balance of $110,000 and an interest rate of 9.75 percent. The loan is to be repaid over twenty years and the monthly payment is to be $875.00. What type of amortization plan is this?

3. Assume a mortgage loan with an outstanding principal balance of $70,000 with an interest rate of 11 percent. The loan is to be repaid over twenty years. The monthly mortgage payment is $291.67 plus accrued interest. What type of amortization payment plan is this?

Legal Aspects of Real Estate Finance

Worm or beetle—drought or tempest—on a farmer's land may fall,
Each is loaded full o' ruin, but a mortgage beats 'em all.

—William McKendree [Will] Carleton, The Tramp's Story

OBJECTIVES

After reading this chapter you will be able to:

- Prepare a promissory note
- Prepare a guaranty
- Understand the basic provisions contained in a promissory note
- Understand the basic provisions contained in a guaranty
- List the legal requirements for a mortgage, deed of trust, or security deed
- Understand the risks inherent in a second mortgage
- Identify the various legal remedies available to both the borrower and the lender in the event of a default on a mortgage loan

GLOSSARY

Conversion Act of taking a person's property without a legal right to do so.

Deed of trust Legal document that conveys title to real property to a trustee who holds the title as security for a debt to a lender.

Deed to secure debt Legal document that conveys title to real property to a lender to secure a debt.

Due on sale clause Clause found in a mortgage that prohibits the sale of the real property described in the mortgage without the lender's consent. A sale in violation of this provision is a default of the mortgage.

Endorsement Method of transferring ownership of a promissory note.

Foreclosure Sale brought by a holder of a mortgage, deed of trust, or security deed of the real property conveyed in the instrument for the purposes of paying the debt secured by the real property.

Guarantor Person who signs a guaranty promising to pay the debt of another person.

Guaranty Legal document that obligates the maker of the document to pay the debt of another person.

Holder Person who is the owner of a promissory note.

Interpleader Judicial proceeding in which money is paid into the court and all parties who claim an interest in the money are allowed to process their claims to the money in the court proceeding.

Maker Party to a promissory note who promises to pay money.

R eal estate mortgage loans involve large sums of money and numerous risks for both the borrower and the lender. The borrower may be unable to pay the debt and may lose the real property pledged as security for the debt. The lender may not be repaid as promised and may resort to the real property security or other measures to collect on the debt. Over the years, a number of legal documents have been created to evidence and secure mortgage loan transactions. Legal assistants are actively involved in the preparation of these documents and need to be familiar with the different legal documents required to make a loan secured by real property. The main legal documents are a promissory note and a security instrument, which, depending on the location of the real property, may be a mortgage, a deed of trust, or a security deed. A promissory note is the written promise made by a property owner to repay the money borrowed from a lender or creditor; the security instrument (mortgage, deed of trust, or security deed) is the instrument conveying real property as security for the repayment of the money.

PROMISSORY NOTE

A **promissory note** is a promise by one party to pay money to another party. The parties on a promissory note are referred to as *payor*, or **maker** (the party who promises to pay), and **payee** (the party to whom the promise is made). A note may be negotiable or nonnegotiable. The term **negotiable** means that the note is capable of being transferred from the original payee to another person, referred to as a **holder**. A negotiable note can be transferred to a holder in due course. A holder in due course has a privileged status in the ability to collect payment on a note. A holder in due course of a promissory note usually defeats any defenses to payment that the maker of the note may have. For example, Ajax Realty Company sells a home to Mary Stewart. Ajax agrees, as part of the purchase price, to take a note from Mary Stewart in the amount of $50,000 payable over the next ten years. Ajax Realty Company also warrants to Mary Stewart that the roof of the house will not leak for ten years. After the sale of the home, the note from Mary Stewart to Ajax Realty Company is transferred to First Bank and Trust, a holder in due course. A year after the closing, the roof begins to leak, causing damage to Mary Stewart's personal possessions. Mary Stewart stops payment on the note. First Bank and Trust sues Mary Stewart for $50,000. Mary Stewart countersues, arguing the that roof is leaking and has damaged her possessions in the amount of $20,000. She argues that she should be entitled to pay only $30,000 on the note. If First Bank and Trust were not a holder in due course, Mary Stewart would be able to set off the $20,000 leaking-roof damages against the payment of the note. Because First Bank and Trust is a holder in due course, Mary Stewart is not able to set off the leaking-roof damages against the payment of the note. First Bank and Trust, as a holder in due course, can collect the full $50,000 from Mary Stewart.

A holder in due course defeats most defenses that a maker on a note would have to the payment of the note. Exceptions to this rule are (a) incapacity of the maker, (b) illegality of the purpose of the note, (c) duress of the maker in signing the note, (d) discharge of the maker in bankruptcy, (e) forgery of the maker's signature, and (f) fraud in factum. Fraud in factum is a situation in which a party signing the note did not have enough knowledge or reasonable opportunity to determine that a note was being signed. Except for these six defenses, a holder in due course is entitled to collect payment on a note from a maker.

It is in the best interest of investors and purchasers of promissory notes to be a holder in due course. For a holder in due course situation to exist, the note being held must be a **negotiable note** and the holder must have possession of the original note with all the necessary endorsements to establish title in the holder. The holder also must have purchased the note for value and in good faith without notice of any defenses or without notice that the note was overdue or dishonored.

Investors who purchase notes, such as the Federal National Mortgage Association (FNMA, Fannie Mae), the Government National Mortgage Association (Ginnie Mae), and other investors in the secondary-mortgage market, have a strong interest in being a holder in due course. This strong interest in being a holder in due course means that most notes that are prepared to secure a loan are negotiable. Lawyers and legal assistants, therefore, make every effort in the drafting of a note to make the note negotiable.

A **negotiable note**, by definition, is written, signed by the maker, and contains an unconditional promise to pay a sum certain of money on demand or at a definite time. If any part of this definition is missing, the note is not negotiable. For example, you have a written note in which the maker agrees to pay $10,000 on the completion of a contract. Because it is unknown when and if the contract will be completed the promise to pay is conditional and the note is not negotiable.

Negotiability should not be confused with enforceability. As discussed previously, a negotiable note can be transferred to a holder in due course. A nonnegotiable note may be enforceable; that is, a holder of a nonnegotiable note may be able to collect the money from the maker. A nonnegotiable note may be transferred, but it cannot be transferred to a holder in due course. Collection of a nonnegotiable note is subject to whatever defenses the maker may have toward the collection of the note.

Endorsement

Notes often are transferred by the payees. It is not uncommon in a real estate transaction for the original lender—for example a savings and loan institution—to sell the note to another investor, such as the FNMA. A note is transferred and sold by **endorsement**. An endorsement is simply a direction, usually printed on the back of the note or attached to the note, ordering that the money be paid to the order of the new owner of the note. Sample endorsements are shown in Example 11–1.

EXAMPLE 11–1

UNQUALIFIED ENDORSEMENT
FOR VALUE RECEIVED, pay to the order of:

_____
                                    By: _____ (SEAL)

QUALIFIED ENDORSEMENT NO. 1
FOR VALUE RECEIVED, without recourse, pay to the order of:

_____
                                    By: _____ (SEAL)

QUALIFIED ENDORSEMENT NO. 2
FOR VALUE RECEIVED, without recourse and warranty, pay to the order of:

_____
                                    By: _____ (SEAL)

An endorser who transfers a note by endorsement incurs certain contractual and warranty liabilities to the new owner of the note. The contractual liability is that the endorser will pay the note according to its terms in the event the maker does not. Contractual liability of an endorser to pay a note is secondary. The holder of the note must first present the note to the maker for payment and the maker must dishonor, or refuse or fail to pay, the note. Once the note has been presented to the maker and the maker has refused or failed to pay, a notice of dishonor must be sent to the endorser within three business days from the date of dishonor. If all these steps are performed by the holder of the note, an endorser is then responsible to pay the note. These three steps—presentment, dishonor, and notice of dishonor—can be waived by an endorser, and this waiver can be contained in the note that is endorsed. The purchaser of a note usually wants the waiver because the waiver will make it easier to collect the note from an endorser. An example of language contained in a note that waives presentment, dishonor, and notice of dishonor is shown in Example 11–2.

EXAMPLE 11–2

Waiver. Demand, presentment, notice, protest, and notice of dishonor are hereby waived by Borrower and by each and every co-maker, endorser, guarantor, surety, and other person or entity primarily or secondarily liable on this note.

In addition to a contractual obligation to pay the note, an endorser has warranty liabilities to the new owner of the note. An endorser who sells the note by endorsement warrants the following: (a) the endorser has good title to the note; (b) all signatures are genuine and authorized; (c) the note has not been materially altered; (d) there are no defenses to payment of the note; and (e) the endorser has no knowledge of any bankruptcy proceedings against the maker.

An endorser of a note may not want the obligation to pay the note. For example, a savings and loan institution closes a number of residential loans for the purpose of selling the loans to a life insurance company investor. The understanding between the savings and loan institution and the life insurance company is that the life insurance company will rely solely on the credit risks of the individual homeowners for repayment of the notes. There is no intent on the part of the life insurance company to look to the savings and loan institution for payment of the homeowners' notes.

An endorser can escape the contractual liability by giving a qualified endorsement. One type of qualified endorsement is the "without recourse" endorsement, shown as Qualified Endorsement No. 1 in Example 11–1. The "without recourse" endorsement negates contractual liability but still imposes warranty liability on the endorser, with the exception that in connection with the warranty of no defenses, the endorser who makes a "without recourse" endorsement warrants only that he or she has no knowledge of any defenses to the payment of the note.

An endorsement "without recourse and warranty" negates all contractual and warranty liabilities. This endorsement is shown as Qualified Endorsement No. 2 in Example 11–1. This type of endorsement is similar to a quitclaim deed in that it transfers whatever title the endorser has to the note but makes no warranties.

Few investors will purchase notes that contain a "without recourse and warranty" endorsement, and this endorsement seldom is used.

Payment

A maker's promise on a negotiable note is unconditional, and the maker is not released by the sale of the security securing the note. For example, a homeowner signs a note promising to pay $100,000 secured by her home. The homeowner later sells the home. The sale of the home does not release the homeowner from the promise to pay the $100,000 on the note.

In some situations, there are more than one maker on a note, such as in the case of a husband and wife signing a note for the purpose of purchasing a home. In such an event, each maker of the note, referred to as a comaker, is fully responsible for the payment of the note. The note can be collected from each of the comakers in full. This is known as joint and several liability. For example, Stanley White and Martha White purchase a home. As part of the purchase, they borrow $100,000 from First Bank and Trust and sign a note promising to pay the $100,000. The bank can collect the $100,000 in full from either Stanley White or Martha White.

The holder of a note is the only person entitled to payment, and a maker, when paying a note, should be careful to pay only the holder. Another risk in the payment of the note is to leave the note with the holder after it has been paid. What, other than honesty and integrity, is to prevent the holder from selling the note to a holder in due course after it has been paid? The holder in due course, if unaware that the note has been paid, is entitled by law to collect again from the maker. Therefore, to avoid multiple payments of the same note, it is not uncommon for makers of notes to demand that the original note be returned marked "paid" or "satisfied" at the time of payment.

Prepayment

A note cannot be prepaid before the date established in the note for payment. If the maker of the note wants the privilege to prepay, this privilege must be provided for in the note. It is not unusual for a lender to condition prepayment on the payment of an additional premium or penalty. Some lenders, such as life insurance companies that desire to have their loans outstanding without prepayment for a fixed period of time, may establish a prepayment privilege that is closed for a certain period of time and then is available with a penalty. An example of such a prepayment clause is shown in Example 11–3.

EXAMPLE 11-3

Prepayment Privilege. This note may not be prepaid in whole or in part except as herein specifically provided. No prepayment of the principal of this note shall be permitted or allowed prior to the end of the third (3rd) Loan Year, as hereinafter defined. After the end of the third (3rd) Loan Year, this note may be prepaid in whole, but not in part, upon any principal and interest payment date as provided herein, provided that (a) no later than sixty (60) days prior to the date of such prepayment, Borrower delivers written notice to Payee that Borrower intends to prepay the note in full on the date specified in the notice; and (b) Borrower pays to Payee at the time of such prepayment a percentage of the prepaid principal amount of the indebtedness as a prepayment premium. The amount of the prepayment premium shall be the product obtained by multiplying the prepaid principal amount of the indebtedness by the product of the following: (i) the amount obtained by subtracting the annualized yield on a United States Treasury Bill, Note, or Bond with a maturity date that occurs closest to the maturity date of this note, as such annualized yield is reported by *The Wall Street Journal,* on the business day preceding the date of prepayment, from 10.50% multiplied by (ii) the number of years and any fraction thereof remaining between the date of prepayment and the maturity date of this note.

Notwithstanding the foregoing, however, in the event of acceleration of this note at any time, including the period of time prior to the end of the third (3rd) Loan Year, and subsequent involuntary or voluntary prepayment, the prepayment premium as calculated above shall be payable, however, in no event shall it exceed an amount equal to the excess, if any, of (i) interest calculated at the highest applicable rate permitted by applicable law, as construed by courts having jurisdiction thereof, on the principal balance of the indebtedness evidenced by this note from time to time outstanding from the date hereof to the date of such acceleration; over (ii) interest theretofore paid and accrued on this note. Any prepaid amounts specified in any notice shall become due and payable at the time provided in such notice. Under no circumstances shall the prepayment premium ever be less than zero. The amount of prepayment shall never be less than the full amount of the then outstanding principal indebtedness and accrued interest thereon.

A Loan Year for the purposes of this note shall mean each successive twelve (12)-month period, beginning with the date of the first installment payment of principal and interest hereunder, provided, however, that the first (1st) Loan Year shall include the period from the date of this note to the date of such first installment payment of principal and interest.

Borrower further agrees to pay in addition to the above-described prepayment premium, a reinvestment fee of one-half of one percent ($^1/_2$%) of the outstanding prepaid principal indebtedness evidenced by this note to Payee. Borrower agrees that the reinvestment fee together with the prepayment premium shall be due and payable regardless of whether prepayment is made involuntarily or voluntarily.

The case of *Acord v. Jones* 440 S.E.2d 679 (Ga. 1994) is a good indication of the need for lenders such as life insurance companies to use a prepayment clause in the note.

CASE

Acord v. Jones
440 S.E.2d 679 (Ga. 1994)

TEXT: JOHNSON, Judge.

Acord appeals from the trial court's grant of Jones' motion for judgment on the pleadings.

Acord gave Jones two promissory notes which were secured by real property. The interest-bearing notes, which were payable in monthly installments and matured in five and ten years, were silent on the issue of prepayment. Acord attempted to pay them off prior to maturity by tendering the outstanding principal plus accrued interest. Jones refused the tender, maintaining that the notes did not allow prepayment and that, even if they did, the amount tendered did not cover the full indebtedness since it did not include unaccrued interest. Acord filed suit to force cancellation of the notes and security deeds since he had tendered what he considered to be the full amount due. Acord filed a motion for summary judgment and/or for judgment on the pleadings. Jones apparently filed a cross-motion for judgment on the pleadings. The trial court denied Acord's motion and granted judgment on the pleadings to Jones. Acord appeals. We reverse the trial court's decision.

In his sole enumeration of error, Acord contends that the trial court erred in holding that the terms of the contract did not allow prepayment. He argues that because the notes contain the phrase "[i]f not sooner paid,"[1] there is the implication that the notes may be paid prior to maturity. Neither party has cited, and our research has failed to uncover, any cases in which Georgia courts have been called upon to decide whether that language has the effect of allowing prepayment, and if so, whether the lender would be entitled to recover unearned interest.

"In construing contracts...the language used must be afforded its literal meaning and plain ordinary words given their usual significance." (Citations and punctuation omitted.) *Twin Oaks Assoc. v. DeKalb Venture*, 190 Ga.App. 854, 855(1) (380 SE2d 469) (1989). In its plain ordinary sense, the phrase "if not sooner paid" clearly contemplates

the possibility of early repayment. Further, the phrase would have to be construed against Jones as the drafter. *Roswell Properties v. Salle*, 208 Ga.App. 202, 206(3) (430 SE2d 404) (1993). Thus, we hold that Acord was entitled to prepay the indebtedness.

However, the issue of whether unaccrued interest can be required as part of the prepayment remains. In the absence of a contractual provision addressing the issue, we must apply existing law. See *State Farm Mutual Automobile Insurance Co. v. Hodges*, 111 Ga.App. 317, 321 (141 SE2d 586) (1965); *Jenkins v. Morgan*, 100 Ga.App. 561 (112 SE2d 23) (1959). The trial court and Jones rely upon *Cook v. Securities Investment Co.*, 184 Ga. 544 (192 SE 179) (1937), for the proposition that the payee of an installment note cannot be compelled to accept prepayment of the principal with interest to date only. Id. at 548. A careful reading of that case, however, reveals that it is not dispositive of the issues in the instant case. We note that what Jones refers to as the holding in *Cook* is merely dicta. There is nothing in the opinion in *Cook* which indicates that that case involved language comparable to the "if not sooner paid" phrase in the contracts which are the subject of the instant case. *Cook* involved the rights of a judgment creditor where legal title to the property of the debtor had been conveyed to a third party to secure a debt to the third party; accordingly, that case was decided pursuant to § 39-201 of the Code (now OCGA § 9-13-60), a section which is inapplicable here. Id. at 546-548.

Since *Cook* was decided 56 years ago, we have held that a contract which provides for the payment of purchase money notes "on or before maturity" does allow the maker to pay principal plus accrued interest at any time prior to maturity and relieves the maker of having to pay unearned interest. *Kuttner v. May Realty Co.*, 220 Ga. 163, 164 (137 SE2d 637) (1964). In addition, the legislature has enacted several statutes, such as the Motor Vehicle Sales Finance Act (OCGA § 10-1-30 et seq.), the

---

[1] The notes set forth the amount borrowed, interest rates, dates and amounts of installments and provide for payment of "a like amount on the same day of each succeeding month thereafter to be applied first to any interest due, then to principle [sic] until

the total of said indebtedness shall be paid in full. *If not sooner paid* the total balance due hereunder shall be paid at the expiration of Ten years from date."

Retail Installment and Home Solicitation Sales Act (OCGA § 10-1-1 et seq.), and the Industrial Loan Act (OCGA § 7-3-1), all of which, among other things, relieve consumers of the obligation to pay unearned interest when debts are paid off prior to maturity. While not applicable here, these statutes do show consistent recognition of a public policy in favor of allowing prepayment of loans without penalty. To require payment of unearned interest in this case would effectively impose a prepayment penalty where none has been contemplated by the terms of the contracts. The law does not favor penalties. See generally *Southern Guaranty Corp.*

v. Doyle, 256 Ga. 790, 792 (353 SE2d 510) (1987); *Wasser v. C & S Nat. Bank*, 170 Ga.App. 872, 873 (318 SE2d 518) (1984). We hold that, in the absence of an express contractual provision to the contrary, a maker may prepay principal plus accrued interest, without being required to tender unaccrued interest or pay any other penalty. Because Acord was entitled to prepay the debts and since he made a valid tender, Jones was required to accept the payment as satisfaction of the debts and cancel the security deeds.

Judgment reversed. McMurray, P.J., and Blackburn, J., concur

Usury

New York:

Usury is the charging of interest in excess of the legal rate. The rates vary as to who is giving the loan, the type of property, etc. Generally, GOL sect. 5–501(1) says the rate is 6%. Section 14–a(1) of the Banking Law says 16% is the legal rate. This is a complex area and many variables are involved.

Most states have statutes that establish a ceiling or maximum rate of interest to be charged on a loan. These statutes are called **usury** statutes. The penalty for usury varies from state to state. It usually is the loss of all interest on the loan, but it can be as extreme as the forfeiture of the entire loan amount. Lenders, therefore, are careful to establish an interest rate that does not violate the usury laws. Most notes contain what is known as a "usury savings clause." This is an attempt by the lender to credit any excess interest to either a reduction of principal or a refund to the borrower. An example of a usury savings clause appears in Example 11–4.

EXAMPLE 11-4

This note and all provisions hereof and of all documents securing this note conform in all respects to the laws of the State of Georgia so that no payment of interest or other sum construed to be interest or charges in the nature of interest shall exceed the highest lawful contract rate permissible under the laws of the State of Georgia as applicable to this transaction. Therefore, this note and all agreements between Borrower and Payee are limited so that in no contingency or event whatsoever, whether acceleration of maturity of the indebtedness or otherwise, shall the amount paid or agree to be paid to the Payee for the use, forbearance, or detention of the money advanced by or to be advanced hereunder exceed the highest lawful rate permissible under the laws of the State of Georgia as applicable to this transaction. In determining whether or not the rate of interest exceeds the highest lawful rate, the Borrower and Payee intend that all sums paid hereunder that are deemed interest for the purposes of determining usury be prorated, allocated, or spread in equal parts over the longest period of time permitted under the applicable laws of the State of Georgia. If, under any circumstances whatsoever, fulfillment of any provision hereof, or of any other instrument evidencing or securing this Indebtedness, at the time performance of such provision shall be due, shall involve the payment of interest in excess of that authorized by law, the obligation to be fulfilled shall be reduced to the limit so authorized by law, and if under any circumstances Payee shall ever receive as interest an amount that would exceed the highest lawful rate, the amount that would be excessive shall be either applied to the reduction of the unpaid principal balance of the Indebtedness, without payment of any prepayment fee (and not to the payment of interest), or refunded to the Borrower, and Payee shall not be subject to any penalty provided for the contracting for, charging, or receiving interest in excess of the maximum lawful rate regardless of when or the circumstances under which said refund or application was made.

Execution

A note is signed by the maker, but the signature is not witnessed or notarized. A note usually is not recorded, but in some states, such as Louisiana, a copy of the note is attached as an exhibit to the deed of trust and recorded.

New York:
For a discussion of New York Law, see Appendix.

Practice Suggestions

A note is an important legal document, and the original of the note is the best evidence of the note at the time of collection. Special care should be taken in preparing a note to make sure it correctly reflects the terms of the loan and the repayment of the money. Corrections on notes should be avoided. If an error on a note is corrected by whiting it out or using some other typing correction technique, the correction should be initialed by the maker. For notes that are more than one page long, the maker should initial each page of the note.

Three note forms are included at the end of this chapter: Exhibit 11–1, FNMA Residential Fixed Rate Note; Exhibit 11–2, FNMA Residential Adjustable Rate Note; and Exhibit 11–3, Commercial Loan Note. The following is a checklist to assist in the preparation of a note.

▉▶ C H E C K L I S T

Preparation of a Note

☐ I. Parties
   ☐   A. Maker (borrower)
   ☐   B. Payee or holder (lender)
☐ II. Amount of Note
☐ III. Interest Rate to be Charged on Note
   ☐   A. Fixed rate
   ☐   B. Adjustable rate
       (1) Identification of index to be used for adjustment (e.g., prime lending rate, three-year treasury security)
       (2) Intervals of adjustment (e.g., daily, monthly, annually)
       (3) Indication of any minimum or maximum interest rates
☐ IV. Payments
   ☐   A. Time and place of payments
   ☐   B. Amount of payments
☐ V. Maker's Right to Prepay
   ☐   A. May prepay in whole or in part at any time
   ☐   B. May prepay in whole at any time after reasonable notice
   ☐   C. No prepayment allowed
   ☐   D. No prepayment allowed for a certain period of time
   ☐   E. Prepayment allowed but on payment of prepayment fee
   ☐   F. No prepayment allowed for a certain period of time and after that period of time prepayment allowed only on payment of prepayment fee
☐ VI. Maker's Failure to Pay as Required

❑   A. Late charge for overdue payment
        (1) Time for late charge to commence (e.g., 10 days, 15 days after due date)
❑   B. Amount of late charge (e.g., 4 percent of late payment)
❑   C. Default for failure to pay
        (1) Grace period
        (2) Notice of default and period of time to cure default
        (3) Acceleration of loan on default
           a. optional acceleration
        (4) Payment of holder's cost and expenses for collection of note
           a. Attorney's fees
           b. Court costs and other reasonable expenses
        Default interest rate is higher during periods of default than normal note rate.
❑   VII. Identify Security Given for Note
❑   A. Mortgage or deed of trust
❑   B. Assignment of leases and rents
❑   C. Security agreement
❑   D. Other documents
❑   VIII. Usury Savings Clause
❑   IX. Choice of Applicable Law
❑   X. Waiver of Homestead Exemption or Other Debtor's Rights
❑   XI. Joint and Several Liability
❑   XII. Waiver of Notice of Default, Presentment of Notice of Dishonor
❑   XIII. Signatures
❑   A. Only maker signs note
        (1) Corporate maker
           a. Identify name of corporation
           b. Identify the officers of the corporation signing the note by name and by title
           c. Affix corporate seal
❑   B. Partnership maker
        (1) Identify partnership by name
        (2) Identify all partners signing the note by name
❑   C. Names of all people signing the note should be typed underneath the signature line
❑   D. Notes are not witnessed or notarized

GUARANTY

A mortgage lender may require a person other than the debtor to guarantee the payment of the debtor's note. For example, when making a loan to a corporate debtor, a mortgage lender may require the shareholders of the corporation to guarantee the loan. This **guaranty** gives the mortgage lender the right to sue the shareholders for payment of the note and, if necessary, the right to recover the debt from the personal assets of the shareholders.

A guaranty of a note must be written. The written guaranty form is closely interpreted by the courts, and the guarantor's liability is not extended by implication or interpretation. A guaranty may be a "payment guaranty" or a "collection guaranty." The **guarantor** who signs a payment guaranty unconditionally guarantees to pay the note when due without resort to any other party, including the maker of the note. The holder of a note may go directly to a payment guarantor for payment once the note becomes due and payable.

The guarantor who signs a collection guaranty promises to pay the note only after the holder of the note has sued the original maker of the note, has reduced the claim to a judgment, and has attempted to collect against the assets of the maker. A guarantor who signs a collection guaranty is required to pay the note only in the event the maker of the note is insolvent or otherwise lacks assets sufficient to pay the note.

Under the terms of both the payment guaranty and a collection guaranty, a change in the terms of the note being guaranteed without the guarantor's consent releases the guarantor. Therefore, anytime the note is modified or amended in any way, it is necessary that all guarantors consent to the modification and amendment.

A form of a payment guaranty is shown in Exhibit 11–4.

MORTGAGES, DEEDS OF TRUST, AND SECURITY DEEDS

The companion legal document to a promissory note secured by real estate is the security instrument. Depending on the state in which the real property is located, the security interest may be a mortgage, a deed of trust, or a security deed. Regardless of the form of security instrument being used, its main purpose is to convey real property as security for the repayment of the debt evidenced by the note.

The three basic types of security instruments are (1) **mortgage**, (2) **deed of trust**, and (3) **deed to secure debt**. Mortgage, deed of trust, and deed to secure debt forms are included at the end of this chapter Exhibit 11–5, Florida Mortgage; Exhibit 11–6, North Carolina Deed of Trust; Exhibit 11–7, FNMA Residential Deed to Secure Debt; and Exhibit 11–8, Georgia Commercial Deed to Secure Debt.

New York:
As a security interest, the lender gets a mortgage and a promise to repay the loan. In New York, the mortgage is a lien on property, security for the performance of the obligation of paying each month. The mortgagor retains title to the property. See Appendix.

Mortgage. Historically, the first real estate security instrument used was a mortgage. A mortgage created an encumbrance on the real property but left legal title to the property with the owner. Mortgages are still used in a number of states.

Deed of Trust. Several states use a deed of trust form for real estate loans. A deed of trust is a document wherein the owner of the real property conveys title to the real property to a third party, known as a trustee. The trustee then holds the title in trust for the benefit of the lender. If the debt being secured by the deed of trust is not paid, the trustee has the power to sell the title to the real property and to use the proceeds from the sale to pay the debt owed to the lender.

Deed to Secure Debt. A deed to secure debt is a security instrument wherein the owner of the real property conveys legal title directly to the lender as security for the repayment of the debt. The lender is given the power to sell the real property in the event the debt is not paid.

Regardless of which security instrument is used, the owner stays in possession of the real property and can use and enjoy the real property so long as the debt is being paid.

For simplicity of reference, all three security instruments are referred to as a mortgage throughout this chapter. Please keep in mind that, depending on the state in which the real property is located, the security instrument may be a mortgage, a deed of trust, or a deed to secure debt.

Requirements of a Mortgage

A mortgage must meet all the requirements of a deed, together with a description of the debt being secured. These requirements are (a) names of the parties, (b) words of conveyance or grant, (c) valid description of the property conveyed, (d) proper execution and attestation, and (e) effective delivery to the lender.

The mortgage may contain a power of sale as well as numerous other provisions designed to protect the lender in every conceivable situation.

Parties to a Mortgage

A mortgage is entered into by two parties, the **mortgagor** and the **mortgagee**. The mortgagor is the owner of the property (the debtor), or borrower, and the mortgagee is the lender, or creditor. A mortgage is given by the owner to the lender. In the case of a deed of trust, the instrument may be entered into by three parties, with the addition of the trustee.

Because it is a fundamental rule that only the owner of real property can pledge the real property as security for a loan, it is important that the title to the real property be examined to determine the correct owner and that the owner be made the mortgagor. If the mortgagor is a corporation, proper corporate authority must be presented not only to authorize the loan and the pledge of real property as security, but also to authorize the corporate officers to sign the mortgage. A mortgage signed by a partnership requires that all partners sign the mortgage or that a partner authorized by all the partners sign the mortgage. Mortgages given by co-owners of property require the signatures of all owners.

Secured Debt

A valid debt must exist to have a valid mortgage. A mortgage must describe in words and figures the debt secured. The date of the final maturity of the debt also is identified.

A mortgage may be given to secure any and all debt between the mortgagor and the mortgagee, including past debt, present debt, and even future debt incurred after the mortgage is in place. These mortgages are called **open-end** or **dragnet** because of the unlimited amount of debt that can be secured.

For example, on March 15, a borrower enters into a mortgage loan transaction with a lender wherein the borrower borrows $100,000 to buy a parcel of land. The mortgage given to the lender contains an open-end or dragnet provision that makes the mortgage secure any and all debts between the borrower and the lender. At the time the loan is entered on March 15, the borrower only owes $100,000 to the lender, and therefore, the mortgage only secures $100,000. On August 10 of the same year, the borrower goes to the lender and obtains another loan for an unrelated purpose in the amount of $25,000. The borrower signs a note to evidence the debt, but there is no discussion regarding the mortgage or any amendments to the mortgage. Despite the fact that the note does not refer to the mortgage and that there are no amendments to the mortgage, the dragnet or open-end effect of the mortgage causes the mortgage to secure the additional $25,000, for a total of $125,000. Furthermore, any future loans the borrower receives from the lender will be secured by the mortgage.

An open-end or dragnet mortgage can create a problem for the borrower because a default under any of the separate loans secured by the mortgage can give the lender the right to foreclose and have the real property sold. In addition, at the time the mortgage is to be paid and satisfied, the lender can require that all the debt between the borrower and the lender be paid in full before the mortgage is released.

Example 11–5 shows an open-end or dragnet clause.

EXAMPLE 11–5

This mortgage is made and intended to secure all indebtedness now or hereafter owing by Mortgagor to Mortgagee, however or whenever created, incurred, arising or evidenced, whether direct or indirect, joint or several, absolute or contingent, or due or to become due, and any and all renewal or renewals, extension or extensions, modification or modifications or any substitution or substitutions for said indebtedness, either in whole or in part.

Secured Property

Any land or interest in land that can be conveyed by ordinary deed may be conveyed by a mortgage. Real property in a mortgage is described with the same degree of accuracy as in a deed. The description usually is prepared from a land survey. Real property can be added to the mortgage by amendment or modification. The priority of the mortgage with respect to the added real property is determined as of the date of the addition and *not* as of the date of the original mortgage.

For example, a mortgage is given on Tract A on March 15. The priority of the mortgage as to Tract A is determined as of March 15. This means that the mortgage is subject to any outstanding property interests, such as other mortgages or easements, that occur before March 15, but it is superior and senior to any property interests created after March 15. On October 10, Tract B is added by amendment to the mortgage. Even though the mortgage is originally dated March 15, it only has priority, as to Tract B, from October 10. Any easements, mortgages, or other property interests that are created or exist against the Tract B project before October 10 have priority over the mortgage.

Assignment of Mortgage

Mortgages are freely assignable and often are. A person who buys a mortgage may exercise any and all powers contained in the mortgage. A transfer of mortgage conveys the real property and the secured debt, even though both may not be mentioned in the transfer. A transfer of the note usually includes a transfer of the mortgage, and a transfer of the mortgage includes a transfer of the note.

Most mortgages are assigned either by the inclusion of transfer or assignment language on the mortgage or by a separate assignment that is executed by the assigning lender and recorded. An example of an assignment is shown in Example 11–6.

EXAMPLE 11–6

TRANSFER AND ASSIGNMENT

FOR VALUE RECEIVED, the undersigned hereby transfers, assigns and conveys unto_____

all of its right, title, interest, powers and options in, to and under the within and foregoing Mortgage as well as the Premises described therein and the Indebtedness (without recourse) secured thereby.

IN WITNESS WHEREOF the undersigned has caused this transfer and assignment to be executed by its officer and its seal affixed hereto this _____ day of _____, 19___.

Signed, sealed and
delivered in the
presence of:

	By: _____
_____	Title: _____
Unofficial Witness	Attest: _____
_____	Title: _____
Notary Public	
	(Seal)

Transfer of Property Encumbered by a Mortgage

The fact that real property is mortgaged does not in itself prohibit the owner from selling the real property. However, close attention should be paid to the actual mortgage document. A provision known as **due on sale** commonly is found in mortgages. This provision prohibits the sale of real property without the mortgagee's consent. A sale in violation of this provision is a default of the mortgage and could result in a foreclosure of the real property.

Example 11–7 shows a mortgage due on sale provision.

EXAMPLE 11–7

If all or any part of the property or any interest in it is sold or transferred without mortgagee's prior written consent, mortgagee may, at its option, require immediate payment in full of all sums secured by this mortgage.

When the borrower is not a natural person, such as a corporation or a partnership, a lender may have a broadened definition of what constitutes a sale. An example of this type of mortgage due on sale provision is shown in Example 11–8.

EXAMPLE 11–8

Unless the written consent of mortgagee is first obtained, mortgagee shall have the right, at its option, to declare all sums secured hereby immediately due and payable if (a) mortgagor (by deed or contract of sale or otherwise) sells, conveys, transfers, or further encumbers the mortgaged property or any part thereof; or (b) mortgagor suffers its title or interest therein to be divested, whether voluntarily or involuntarily; or (c) mortgagor changes or permits to be changed the character or use of the mortgaged property; or (d) if mortgagor is a partnership and any of the general partner's interests are transferred or assigned, whether voluntarily or involuntarily to an entity that the general partner of the mortgagor is not also a general partner therein; or (e) if mortgagor is a corporation with fewer than 100 stockholders at the date of execution of this mortgage and more than 10% of the capital stock thereof is sold, transferred, or assigned during a twelve (12)-month period. If any of the events numerated in (a) through (e) above, inclusive, occurs, and if mortgagee consents to the same or fails to exercise its right to declare all sums secured hereby to be due and payable, such consent or failure shall not be deemed or construed as a waiver, and the consent of mortgagee shall be required on all successive occurrences.

Subject to Versus Assumption

Real property may be sold "subject to" or with an "assumption" of an existing mortgage. A purchaser who buys the real property "subject to" a mortgage does not have personal liability for payment of the debt. The new owner will make the loan payments to protect the real property from foreclosure, but the owner cannot be personally sued to recover on the debt. A lender in a "subject to" sale can foreclose and sell the real property in the event the debt is not paid, and the lender can sue the original mortgagor for payment of the debt because a sale of the real property does not release the original mortgagor.

A purchaser who buys real property and "assumes" the mortgage becomes personally liable for the debt. If the loan is in default, the lender can (a) foreclose on the real property, (b) sue the new owner of the real property who has assumed the debt, and (c) sue the original mortgagor. The express words used in the transfer from the original mortgagor to the new owner are determinative of whether the real property has been sold "subject to" or "assumption of" the mortgage. If the words "assume and agree to pay" appear in the deed or any other document that has been signed in connection with the deed, then there is an assumption and the new owner becomes personally liable.

The original mortgagor who sells the real property is not released from the obligation to pay the debt and will not be released unless a separate, written release from the mortgagee lender is obtained.

If the original mortgagor pays the mortgage in a "subject to" transaction, the mortgagor can recover only against the real property. The original mortgagor is substituted or subrogated in place of the lender and has the right to foreclose on the real property to recover on the debt. If the original mortgagor pays the lender in a "loan assumption" transaction, the original mortgagor can recover the payments by foreclosing against the real property, suing the current owner personally for recovery on the debt, or both, until payment is received in full.

Selling real property subject to a prior mortgage or with an assumption of a prior mortgage is a matter of negotiation between the purchaser and the seller. Purchasing real property subject to a mortgage is to the advantage of the purchaser, and purchasing property with a loan assumption is to the advantage of the seller. A lender benefits if the mortgage is assumed because an additional person is obligated on the debt. If the mortgage contains a due on sale provision and the lender's consent to the sale is necessary, it is not unusual for the lender to require that the purchaser assume the mortgage.

Cancellation or Satisfaction of Mortgage

A mortgage is automatically released by full payment of the debt. Full payment of the debt, however, does not release the mortgage of record, and the mortgagee has a duty to file a cancellation or satisfaction of mortgage in the deed records where the mortgage has been recorded. In many states, failure to satisfy or cancel the mortgage of record can impose a fine of money on the mortgagee lender. Example 11–9 shows mortgage cancellation or satisfaction.

EXAMPLE 11-9

Satisfaction

The indebtedness which this instrument was given to secure having been paid in full or other arrangements for payment of the indebtedness having been made to the satisfaction of mortgagee, this instrument is hereby cancelled and the clerk of the superior court of _____ county, _____ is hereby authorized and directed to mark it satisfied of record.

This _____ day of _____, 19____

By: _____

Title: _____

Second-Mortgage Loans

A borrower, unless prohibited by the express terms of the mortgage, can mortgage the real property more than once. In fact, a person can mortgage the real property as many times as a lender is willing to take the real property as security for a loan. Under the current economic environment, it is not unusual for home and commercial properties to have more than one mortgage.

A lender who makes a second-mortgage loan assumes some risk. The main risk is that the first mortgage (first in time on the real property and superior to the second mortgage) will be paid. If the first mortgage is not paid, goes into default, and is foreclosed, the second mortgage will be terminated at the foreclosure sale. It is, therefore, not unusual for second-mortgage lenders to receive estoppel certificates from the first-mortgage lender concerning the nature of the outstanding debt. The estoppel certificate provides that the first-mortgage lender will not foreclose the loan without first giving a notice of default to the second-mortgage lender and providing the second-mortgage lender with time to cure the default. A form of estoppel certificate is shown in Example 11–10.

EXAMPLE 11-10

STATE OF _____

COUNTY OF _____

ESTOPPEL CERTIFICATE

The undersigned hereby certifies as of the date of execution hereof as follows:

(a) That the undersigned (the "Lender") is the holder of a certain Promissory Note dated _____ from _____, in the original principal amount of $_____ (the "Note").

(b) The Note is secured by a Mortgage from _____ to Lender dated

_____ and recorded in Deed Book _____, Page _____, _____ County, _____ located in _____ County, _____ (the "Property") more particularly described on Exhibit "A" attached hereto and made a part hereof;

(c) True and correct copies of the Note and Mortgage are attached hereto as Exhibits "B" and "C";

(d) That the Note and Mortgage are in full force and effect and there have been no events of default in connection therewith;

(e) That all payments of interest and principal under the Note and Mortgage are current; that as of this date, the outstanding principal balance due on the Note is $_____, that the last payment received on the Note was on the _____ day of _____, 19____; and that the next payment is due on _____.

(f) Lender understands that _____ is pledging as security the Property to _____ to secure loans in the collective amount of $_____ (the

"Security Conveyance"). The Security Conveyance is hereby consented to and approved and shall not constitute an event of default in connection with the Note or the Mortgage;

(g) That there is no failure of compliance, breach, default or event of default that has occurred in the Note or the Mortgage as of this date;

(h) Lender agrees to provide to _____, notice of any default under the Note or the Mortgage and to permit _____ thirty (30) days to cure any default under the Note or Mortgage, prior to Lender's acceleration of the Note. _____ at its option, shall have the right to purchase the Note and Mortgage in the event the default cannot be cured.

The undersigned acknowledges that _____ is relying on this certificate.

WITNESS my hand and seal this _____ day of _____, 19____

_____ (Seal)

Signed, sealed and delivered
in the presence of: _____ (Seal)

_____
Witness

_____
Notary Public
Sworn to before me this _____
day of _____, 19____.
My Commission Expires:

_____

A second-mortgage lender also wants to provide in the mortgage that a default under any prior mortgage shall constitute an event of default under the second mortgage. The second-mortgage lender wants the right to cure any defaults under a prior mortgage and add the cost of curing the defaults to the debt secured by the second mortgage. The lender of a second mortgage takes the assignment of any excess proceeds that may be generated from the foreclosure and sale of a prior mortgage. An example of a mortgage provision providing these safeguards is shown in Example 11–11.

EXAMPLE 11–11

This Mortgage is subject to a prior mortgage held by _____ (hereinafter called the "Prior Mortgage"). Mortgagor covenants and agress that it will at all times fully perform and comply with all agreements, covenants, terms, and conditions imposed on the Mortgagor under the Prior Mortgage, and if Mortgagor fails to do so, Mortgagee may (but shall not be obligated to) declare such failure to be an event of default hereunder and or may take any action Mortgagee deems necessary or desirable to prevent or to cure any default by Mortgagor in the performance and compliance with any of Mortgagor's covenants or obligations under the Prior Mortgage. Any sums of money advanced by Mortgagee to cure Mortgagor's defaults under the Prior Mortgage shall be added to the Indebtedness secured hereby. Mortgagor shall immediately on receiving any knowledge or notice of any default under the Prior Mortgage give written notice to Mortgagee. Mortgagor assigns any proceeds that may belong to Mortgagor resulting from the foreclosure sale of the property by the holder of the Prior Mortgage.

New York:
For a discussion of
foreclosure in New
York, see Appendix.

FORECLOSURE AND OTHER MORTGAGEE REMEDIES ___

Mortgage documents would be unnecessary if all borrowers voluntarily paid debts on time. It is only in the situation where the borrower fails or is unable to pay the debt that the mortgage lender and its attorneys begin to carefully examine the mortgage documentation to see what rights and remedies the lender has. A holder of a mortgage on real property has a number of rights against the property and the borrower in the event the debt is not paid.

Foreclosure

Foreclosure is the big remedy that a mortgage holder has against the debtor property owner. Foreclosure is the legal means of requiring that the real property conveyed in the mortgage be sold and the sale proceeds used to pay the debt.

Grounds for Foreclosure

A holder of a mortgage does not have rights to foreclose or exercise other remedies unless the landowner (borrower) is in default under the mortgage. In addition to failure to pay the debt as it becomes due, most mortgages contain other provisions, the violation of which will result in default. These provisions include failure to pay taxes on the property, failure to insure the property, selling the property without the permission of the mortgagee, and failure to keep the property in good repair. The breach of any mortgage covenant gives the holder of the mortgage the right to foreclose or exercise its remedies.

Types of Foreclosure

Foreclosures take place either judicially or through a power of sale contained in the mortgage. Foreclosure procedures vary from state to state, and the state in which the real property is located will determine which type of foreclosure will be used. States that use mortgages generally require judicial foreclosure. States that use deeds of trust or deeds to secure a debt generally use the power of sale foreclosure.

Judicial Foreclosure. A judicial foreclosure is a lawsuit. The mortgage holder will file a complaint against the debtor alleging that a debt is owed; the debt is in default; and the debt is secured by real property given in a mortgage. The creditor will then ask the court to grant relief by ordering the real property sold to pay the debt. The debtor is given an opportunity to answer and a hearing is held on the merits to decide if foreclosure should occur. If the court agrees that the creditor has a right to foreclose, the court will then order the real property sold, usually by a public official such as a sheriff. The sale will be a public sale and will be held after proper notice has been given in the newspaper. Once a sale is held, it is then reported back to the court for approval and, on the court's approval, the sale is final.

A judicial foreclosure is time-consuming but does afford the debtor numerous opportunities to avoid foreclosure by refinancing and paying the debt or defending in the event the foreclosure is wrongfully filed.

Power of Sale Foreclosure. A power of sale foreclosure is a nonjudicial foreclosure right that is given to the mortgage holder in the mortgage. Under a power of sale procedure, the mortgage lender or its agent will conduct a nonjudicial but public sale of the real property. Generally, there are strict procedures in a state governing power of sale foreclosures. These procedures usually set forth the time of day the property can be sold in a public sale and perhaps even the day of the month. Also, it requires that a published notice of the sale be placed in a newspaper some three to six weeks before the sale. The lender, as well as the debtor, may purchase at the sale.

Effect of a Valid Foreclosure Sale

A valid foreclosure sale, whether judicial or nonjudicial, has the effect of extinguishing all ownership rights of the debtor in and to the real property. It also has the effect of divesting all junior encumbrances on the real property. Any encumbrance, mortgage, easements, or so on that have been created after the date of the mortgage that is being foreclosed will be terminated at the foreclosure sale. For example, a parcel of real property is encumbered by a mortgage dated December 10, 1992, to First Bank & Trust Company and a mortgage dated March 15, 1993, to Second Bank & Trust. A foreclosure sale of the mortgage held by First Bank & Trust will terminate the mortgage on the real property held by Second Bank & Trust.

In most states, the debtor's rights to pay off the debt and redeem the real property are terminated at foreclosure. Some states do provide for **redemption** after sale. The redemption price is the price the real property brought at the sale plus an interest or penalty charge. This redemption right may extend for one to two years from the sale date. This means that even though the real property has been sold, a debtor can, by paying the debt or the amount paid at the sale, whichever is greater, recover the real property. Post-sale redemptions do have the effect of interfering with the marketability of the real property, and only a few states recognize post-sale redemption.

A foreclosure sale does not automatically terminate a federal tax lien that is filed against the real property. Federal tax liens that are filed after the date of the mortgage being foreclosed are not terminated at the time of the foreclosure sale unless the Internal Revenue Service receives a written notice of the foreclosure sale twenty-five days before the date of the sale. If the required twenty-five days' notice is given to the Internal Revenue Service, then the tax lien is terminated at the time of sale. The Internal Revenue Service has a 120-day right of redemption to redeem the property after the date of the sale. The redemption price is the purchase price at the sale together with an interest penalty. Failure to give the required twenty-five days' notice permits the Internal Revenue Service tax lien to survive the foreclosure of the sale, and the purchaser at the sale takes the property subject to the tax lien.

New York:
In New York, there is no statutory right to redeem after sale. There is only the equitable right to redeem *prior* to the sale.

The purchaser at a foreclosure sale takes title clear of any claims of the parties to the foreclosure action.

If the sale results in less money than the judgment in foreclosure the mortgagee may get a deficiency judgment against the mortgagor. RPAPL 1371.

Distribution of Money in a Foreclosure Sale

The money received at a foreclosure sale commonly is used to pay the expenses of the sale and the debt. If there is excess money, this money belongs either to the debtor or to the holders of junior mortgages. Most mortgage lenders interplead the money into court to avoid liability. The **interpleader** proceeding is a means by which the money is paid into the court, and the debtor and all junior mortgage holders who may have an interest in the money are notified of the proceeding. The debtor and junior mortgage holders will then go into court and try to convince the court that they are worthy to receive the money. The interpleader has the effect of releasing the lender from any liability in making the decision as to where the excess money should go.

Remedies Other Than Foreclosure

A lender, on an event of default under a mortgage, may exercise certain remedies other than foreclosure. These remedies usually are taking possession of the mortgaged real property or having a receiver appointed to take possession of the property.

Mortgagee (Lender) in Possession. Most mortgages grant the mortgage holder the right to seize possession of the real property in the event of a default. This right to seize possession may become important if the real property is income-producing, such as an apartment project, because it gives the mortgage holder a chance to collect the rents from the tenants. A mortgagee in possession is an agent of the mortgagor, and income collected from the real property must be used to pay the debt. Mortgagees usually are permitted to deduct reasonable expenses of management and maintenance of the real property from income.

Appointment of a Receiver. A **receiver** is a third party appointed by a court to take possession of the real property in the event of a mortgage default. A receiver acts similar to a mortgagee in possession in that the receiver is responsible to take care of the real property, collect rents and income from the real property, and make sure this money is properly applied to the debt or to the expenses of the upkeep of the real property. Most mortgages give a mortgagee the right to have a receiver appointed. The appointment of a receiver is a court action, and the mortgagee will have to prove that the mortgage is in default and the mortgagee has a right under the mortgage for the appointment of a receiver.

Waiver of Default

If the mortgagee, on notice that there has been a default under the mortgage, does not act promptly to exercise its remedies or acts in such a manner as to indicate to the landowner that being in default is acceptable, the holder of the mortgage may, by these actions, waive the default and not be entitled to exercise its remedies. A good example of this is acceptance of late payments by the mortgage holder. Acceptance of late payments estops the mortgage lender from declaring a default unless ample notice is given to the landowner of the intention to require prompt payments in the future.

DEBTOR'S REMEDIES OR DEFENSE TO FORECLOSURE

The debtor's remedies or defense to foreclose include injunction, suit for conversion, and bankruptcy.

Injunction

If a debtor believes a foreclosure is not justified, the debtor has a right to seek an injunction to stop the sale. Grounds for injunctive relief are, for example, invalidity of debt, absence of default, payment of debt, and improperly conducted sale.

The debtor also may void a sale that has already been held on the same grounds as injunctive relief. In some states, a foreclosure sale can be voided if the property brought an inadequate price at the sale.

Suit for Conversion

Foreclosing on real property without the legal right to do so is the tort of **conversion**. A debtor can sue for conversion and recover not only actual damages, but also punitive damages from the foreclosing lender.

Bankruptcy

Bankruptcy is the debtor's main defense to a foreclosure because the filing of a bankruptcy petition has the effect of an automatic injunction stopping the foreclosure sale.

Bankruptcy law is federal law designed to protect debtors and to give debtors a fresh start. Bankruptcy petitions can be filed voluntarily or involuntarily. Once the bankruptcy petition is filed, the act of filing the petition operates as an automatic injunction of all litigation against the debtor and efforts to collect claims or enforce liens against the debtor's property, including foreclosure sales. This automatic injunction remains in force throughout the bankruptcy proceeding and is not terminated until the case is either closed or dismissed or the debtor's discharge is granted or denied. A creditor, such as a mortgage lender, who wants to seek relief from the automatic stay can bring an action in the bankruptcy court requesting that the court remove the injunction so that the mortgage lender can foreclose the real property. The grounds for lifting the automatic stay in a bankruptcy proceeding are as follows:

- The mortgage holder is not being "adequately protected" within the bankruptcy proceeding. Loosely defined, this term means that the mortgage security is declining in value in the bankruptcy proceeding. Adequate protection can be achieved by requiring the debtor to maintain the property or make payments on the mortgage loan, keep the property insured, and so on.
- The debtor has no equity interest in the real property (the value of the property is equal to or less than the amount of the debt).
- The real property is not necessary to an effective reorganization or liquidation of the debtor's estate.

The burden of proof is on the debtor to prove that the stay should remain in full force and effect. The issue of whether the debtor's real property is equal to or less than the value of the debt is an evidentiary burden of the creditor.

 E T H I C S :   Confidentiality of Client Information

The firm that employs you represents a high-profile real estate developer. The attorney you work for has just informed you that the developer has serious financial problems and has asked you to assist in the attempted restructure of a number of bank loans. That evening your spouse asks you if anything interesting happened at the office. Do you tell about the developer's financial problems, or do you discuss the upcoming firm's spring picnic?

The practice of law often involves the resolution of a client's most intimate personal problems. The client expects his or her attorney to be a trusted confidant. Without this trust, the client would be reluctant or unwilling to disclose to the attorney all the facts necessary for the attorney to evaluate the client's problem and give legal advice. Ethical considerations, therefore, require an attorney and a legal assistant to keep all client information and correspondence confidential. When working on a real estate transaction, the legal assistant should not discuss any aspects of the transaction with anyone except other members of the legal assistant's law firm.

Sometimes a legal assistant will be requested by another party in a real estate transaction to disclose confidential information received from a client. For example, a real estate developer client has had a parcel of property under contract for sale for a number of months. The contract has not closed, and the developer considers the contract to be null and void. The developer has applied for a loan on the property. An attorney or legal assistant representing the bank mentions to you that he has heard that the property is under contract for sale and that there may be a lawsuit concerning the contract. They ask you to confirm or deny this rumor. In a situation such as this, it is important to remember that only the client can give permission for the release or disclosure of confidential information. When a request for disclosure is made, the legal assistant should not make any disclosures until the matter has been discussed with the supervising attorney. It should be the responsibility of the supervising attorney to contact the client and respond to the request for confidential information.

The keeping of a client's confidence requires not only that the legal assistant not discuss confidential matters with third parties, but also that the legal assistant keep copies of all confidential letters and other documents out of the sight or view of third parties. It is not wise to bring files home from the office and leave them on tables and countertops in full view of neighbors, friends, and visitors.

SUMMARY

Although the legal concepts behind a note and security instrument to evidence and secure a mortgage loan are simple, the forms are complex and vary in format from state to state. Legal assistants prepare mortgage loan documents and assist in the mortgage loan closing process. It is important that the legal assistant be familiar with the different forms that are used in the state in which he or she practices and that he or she be aware of the many provisions that can be included in these forms.

KEY TERMS

Conversion	Guaranty	Negotiable note
Deed of trust	Holder	Open-end or dragnet clause
Deed to secure debt	Interpleader	Payee
Due on sale clause	Maker	Promissory note
Endorsement	Mortgage	Receiver
Foreclosure	Mortgagee	Redemption
Guarantor	Mortgagor	Usury

REVIEW QUESTIONS

1. Why is the negotiability of a promissory note important?

2. Explain the endorsement process, with its accompanying contractual and warranty liabilities.

3. What is an open-end or dragnet mortgage?

4. What is the importance of being a holder in due course?

5. What is the difference between purchasing real property subject to a mortgage and assuming a mortgage?

6. What risks are inherent in second-mortgage loans?

7. What is the difference between a promissory note and a guaranty?

8. What is the difference between a judicial and a nonjudicial power of sale foreclosure?

9. Why is bankruptcy a good debtor's defense to a foreclosure?

10. What remedies other than foreclosure are available to a real estate lender in the event of a default?

CASE PROBLEMS

1. Margo Maker executed and delivered a negotiable promissory note for $10,000 to Acme Bank and Trust. The note, while in Acme's possession, was altered from $10,000 to $100,000. Acme sold the altered note to Wherever Life Insurance Company for $95,000. The endorsement from Acme to Wherever is without recourse. Wherever Life Insurance Company then sells the note to Harrison Holder for $95,000. Wherever's endorsement to Harrison Holder is without recourse and warranty. At maturity, Harrison Holder presents the note to Margo Maker for payment. Can Harrison Holder recover $100,000 from Margo Maker? Does Harrison Holder have an action and recovery against Acme Bank and Trust? Does Harrison Holder have an action and recovery against Wherever Life Insurance Company?

2. You are a legal assistant assisting in the representation of a maker of a negotiable promissory note. The maker wants to pay the note in full and has asked you to obtain the original note marked paid and satisfied from the holder of the note. On contact with the holder of the note you learn that the holder cannot find the original note, claiming that it has been lost. Would you advise the maker of the note to pay the holder anyway?

3. You are assisting in the representation of a lending institution as the holder of a promissory note from the Good Earth Land Company. The note is personally guaranteed by the principal shareholder of Good Earth Land Company, Gooden Earth. The note is being modified to extend the final term for repayment for an additional five years. Is there documentation in regard to this extension of note that you should receive from Gooden Earth?

4. Ruth Thomas owns a home that has been pledged to First Bank and Trust to secure a mortgage debt of $60,000. Ruth Thomas sells her home to John Kendall, who purchases the home and assumes the mortgage held by First Bank and Trust. John Kendall subsequently sells the home to Mark Murphy, who purchases the home subject to the First Bank and Trust loan. The First Bank and Trust loan goes into default. Can First Bank and Trust Company foreclose on the home? Can First Bank and Trust Company sue Mark Murphy for the debt? Can First Bank and Trust Company sue John Kendall for the debt?

Can First Bank and Trust Company sue Ruth Thomas for the debt? In the event Ruth Thomas pays the bank in full, what remedies does she have against John Kendall or Mark Murphy or against the real property?

5. You are assisting a mortgage lender who specializes in making second-mortgage loans to homeowners. You have been requested to prepare an estoppel certificate to be signed by the first mortgagee on the home. What types of things would you include in the estoppel certificate to be signed by the first mortgagee?

6. You are a legal assistant working for a law firm that represents a lender who specializes in making second-mortgage loans. You have been asked to prepare some special stipulations to be contained in the lender's mortgages to protect them against possible problems caused by the first-mortgage holders on the secured properties. What types of provisions would you be including in the second-mortgage documents?

7. You are a legal assistant working for a law firm that represents a large shopping center developer. The developer has come to the firm with a problem with one of its major lenders. It appears that the lender is foreclosing on one of the shopping centers. The developer insists that the loan is not in default and that the foreclosure is being made because of some bad feelings between the developer and the lender. What types of actions can the developer take to stop the foreclosure sale?

8. You are working for a law firm that represents a lender who specializes in second-mortgage loans. It has come to your attention that the holder of a first mortgage on one of the properties securing this lender's loans has commenced foreclosure proceedings. Should the second-mortgage lender be concerned? If so, what steps could the second-mortgage lender take to protect its interest in the property?

9. You are a legal assistant in a law firm that handles foreclosures for mortgage lenders. You are attending a power of sale foreclosure. The bidder at the sale bids and buys the property for $100,000 more than the debt owed to the foreclosing lender. You are standing there with the $100,000 in hand and are approached by an individual. The individual tells you that he has a second mortgage on

the property in the amount of $50,000 and that he is entitled to that amount of the excess proceeds. Should you give this person the money? What should you do with the excess money?

PRACTICAL ASSIGNMENT

You are a legal assistant working for a law firm that represents the American Eagle Mortgage Company. American Eagle Mortgage Company is making a real estate mortgage loan to Constance Morton and Samuel Morton. The amount of the loan is $75,500 payable at an annual interest rate of 8 percent per annum over a period of thirty years. The monthly payment of $553.95 is due and payable on the first day of each month. The note is to be signed on February 23, 199__, with the first payment being due and payable on April 1, 199__. American Eagle Mortgage Company charges a late charge equivalent to 5 percent of the overdue payment if the payment is more than ten days late. American Eagle Mortgage Company's address is 1050 Cumberland Circle, Anytown, United States 27333.

The purpose of the loan is to enable the Mortons to purchase a home located at 1000 Riverview, Anytown, United States 27333. The legal description for the home is as follows:

> All that tract or parcel of land lying and being in Land Lot 6 of the 8th District of Madison County, Your State, and being more particularly described as Lot 3, Block A, Riverview Subdivision, as shown on plat of subdivision recorded at Plat Book 23, Page 19, Madison County, Your State Records.

Prepare a note and deed to secure debt for this loan transaction. You may either use Exhibits 11–1 and 11–7 found at the end of this chapter as forms or use the appropriate note and security instruments used in your state as the forms.

ADDENDUM

Exhibit 11–1. FNMA Residential Fixed Rate Note.
Exhibit 11–2. FNMA Residential Adjustable Rate Note.
Exhibit 11–3. Commercial Loan Note.
Exhibit 11–4. Payment Guaranty.
Exhibit 11–5. Florida Mortgage.
Exhibit 11–6. North Carolina Deed of Trust.
Exhibit 11–7. FNMA Residential Deed to Secure Debt.
Exhibit 11–8. Georgia Commercial Deed to Secure Debt.

EXHIBIT 11–1
FNMA Residential
Fixed Rate Note

NOTE

[Date]   [City]   [State]

[Property Address]

1. BORROWER'S PROMISE TO PAY

In return for a loan that I have received, I promise to pay U.S. $ (this amount is called "principal"), plus interest, to the order of the Lender. The Lender is   . I understand that the Lender may transfer this Note. The Lender or anyone who takes this Note by transfer and who is entitled to receive payments under this Note is called the "Note Holder."

EXHIBIT 11–1
FNMA Residential
Fixed Rate Note
(continued)

2. INTEREST

Interest will be charged on unpaid principal until the full amount of principal has been paid. I will pay interest at a yearly rate of   %.

The interest rate required by this Section 2 is the rate I will pay both before and after any default described in Section 6(B) of this Note.

3. PAYMENTS

(A) Time and Place of Payments

I will pay principal and interest by making payments every month.

I will make my monthly payments on the   day of each month beginning on   . I will make these payments every month until I have paid all the principal and interest and any other charges described below that I may owe under this Note. My monthly payments will be applied to interest before principal. If, on   , I still owe amounts under this Note, I will pay those amounts in full on that date, which is called the "Maturity Date."

I will make my monthly payments at   or at a different place if required by the Note Holder.

(B) Amount of Monthly Payments

My monthly payment will be in the amount of U.S. $

4. BORROWER'S RIGHT TO PREPAY

I have the right to make payments of principal at any time before they are due. A payment of principal only is known as a "prepayment." When I make a prepayment, I will tell the Note Holder in writing that I am doing so.

I may make a full prepayment or partial prepayments without paying any prepayment charge. The Note Holder will use all of my prepayments to reduce the amount of principal that I owe under this Note. If I make a partial prepayment, there will be no changes in the due date or in the amount of my monthly payment unless the Note Holder agrees in writing to those changes.

5. LOAN CHARGES

If a law, which applies to this loan and which sets maximum loan charges, is finally interpreted so that the interest or other loan charges collected or to be collected in connection with this loan exceed the permitted limits, then: (i) any such loan charge shall be reduced by the amount necessary to reduce the charge to the permitted limit; and (ii) any sums already collected from me which exceeded permitted limits will be refunded to me. The Note Holder may choose to make this refund by reducing the principal I owe under this Note or by making a direct payment to me. If a refund reduces principal, the reduction will be treated as a partial prepayment.

6. BORROWER'S FAILURE TO PAY AS REQUIRED

(A) Late Charge for Overdue Payments

If the Note Holder has not received the full amount of any monthly payment by the end of   calendar days after the date it is due, I will pay a late charge to the Note Holder. The amount of the charge will be   % of my overdue payment of principal and interest. I will pay this late charge promptly but only once on each late payment.

(B) Default

If I do not pay the full amount of each monthly payment on the date it is due, I will be in default.

(C) Notice of Default

If I am in default, the Note Holder may send me a written notice telling me that if I do not pay the overdue amount by a certain date, the Note Holder may require me to pay

EXHIBIT 11–1
FNMA Residential
Fixed Rate Note
(continued)

immediately the full amount of principal which has not been paid and all the interest that I owe on that amount. That date must be at least 30 days after the date on which the notice is delivered or mailed to me.

(D) No Waiver By Note Holder

Even if, at a time when I am in default, the Note Holder does not require me to pay immediately in full as described above, the Note Holder will still have the right to do so if I am in default at a later time.

(E) Payment of Note Holder's Costs and Expenses

If the Note Holder has required me to pay immediately in full as described above, the Note Holder will have the right to be paid back by me for all of its costs and expenses in enforcing this Note to the extent not prohibited by applicable law. Those expenses include, for example, reasonable attorneys' fees.

7. GIVING OF NOTICES

Unless applicable law requires a different method, any notice that must be given to me under this Note will be given by delivering it or by mailing it by first class mail to me at the Property Address above or at a different address if I give the Note Holder a notice of my different address.

Any notice that must be given to the Note Holder under this Note will be given by mailing it by first class mail to the Note Holder at the address stated in Section 3(A) above or at a different address if I am given a notice of that different address.

8. OBLIGATIONS OF PERSONS UNDER THIS NOTE

If more than one person signs this Note, each person is fully and personally obligated to keep all of the promises made in this Note, including the promise to pay the full amount owed. Any person who is a guarantor, surety or endorser of this Note is also obligated to do these things. Any person who takes over these obligations, including the obligations of a guarantor, surety or endorser of this Note, is also obligated to keep all of the promises made in this Note. The Note Holder may enforce its rights under this Note against each person individually or against all of us together. This means that any one of us may be required to pay all of the amounts owed under this Note.

9. WAIVERS

I and any other person who has obligations under this Note waive the rights of presentment and notice of dishonor. "Presentment" means the right to require the Note Holder to demand payment of amounts due. "Notice of dishonor" means the right to require the Note Holder to give notice to other persons that amounts due have not been paid.

10. UNIFORM SECURED NOTE

This Note is a uniform instrument with limited variations in some jurisdictions. In addition to the protections given to the Note Holder under this Note, a Mortgage, Deed of Trust or Security Deed (the "Security Instrument"), dated the same date as this Note, protects the Note Holder from possible losses which might result if I do not keep the promises which I make in this Note. That Security Instrument describes how and under what conditions I may be required to make immediate payment in full of all amounts I owe under this Note. Some of those conditions are described as follows:

Transfer of the Property of a Beneficial Interest in Borrower. If all or any part of the Property or any interest in it is sold or transferred (or if a beneficial interest in Borrower is sold or transferred and Borrower is not a natural person), without Lender's prior written consent, Lender may, at its option, require immediate payment in full of all sums secured by this Security Instrument. However, this option shall not be exercised by Lender if exercise is prohibited by federal law as of the date of this Security Instrument.

   If Lender exercises this option, Lender shall give Borrower notice of acceleration. The notice shall provide a period of not less than 30 days from the date the notice is delivered or mailed within which Borrower must pay all sums secured by this Security Instrument. If Borrower fails to pay these sums prior to the expiration of this period, Lender may invoke any remedies permitted by this Security Instrument without further notice or demand on Borrower.

WITNESS THE HAND(S) AND SEAL(S) OF THE UNDERSIGNED.

_____(Seal)   _____(Seal)
                         -Borrower   -Borrower
SSN: SSN:

_____(Seal)   _____(Seal)
                         -Borrower   -Borrower
SSN: SSN:

[Sign Original Only]

EXHIBIT 11–1
FNMA Residential
Fixed Rate Note
(continued)

EXHIBIT 11–2
FNMA Residential
Adjustable Rate
Note

ADJUSTABLE RATE NOTE
(1 Year Treasury Index—Rate Caps)

THIS NOTE CONTAINS PROVISIONS ALLOWING FOR CHANGES IN MY INTEREST RATE AND MY MONTHLY PAYMENT. THIS NOTE LIMITS THE AMOUNT MY INTEREST RATE CAN CHANGE AT ANY ONE TIME AND THE MAXIMUM RATE I MUST PAY.

..............................., 19.....   ...., ...
                                      [City]   [State]

....
[Property Address]

1. BORROWER'S PROMISE TO PAY

   In return for a loan that I have received, I promise to pay U.S. $ .... (this amount is called "principal"), plus interest, to the order of the Lender. The Lender is ....

....
I understand that the Lender may transfer this Note. The Lender or anyone who takes this Note by transfer and who is entitled to receive payments under this Note is called the "Note Holder."

2. INTEREST

   Interest will be charged on unpaid principal until the full amount of principal has been paid. I will pay interest at a yearly rate of ....%. The interest rate I will pay will change in accordance with Section 4 of this Note.

EXHIBIT 11–2
FNMA Residential
Adjustable Rate
Note
(continued)

The interest rate required by this Section 2 and Section 4 of this Note is the rate I will pay both before and after any default described in Section 7(B) of this Note.

3. PAYMENTS

(A) Time and Place of Payments

I will pay principal and interest by making payments every month.

I will make my monthly payments on the first day of each month beginning on ...., 19.......... I will make these payments every month until I have paid all of the principal and interest and any other charges described below that I may owe under this Note. My monthly payments will be applied to interest before principal. If, on ...., 20..........., I still owe amounts under this Note, I will pay those amounts in full on that date, which is called the "maturity date."

I will make my monthly payments at .... or at a different place if required by the Note Holder.

(B) Amount of My Initial Monthly Payments

Each of my initial monthly payments will be in the amount of U.S. $............................. This amount may change.

(C) Monthly Payment Changes

Changes in my monthly payment will reflect changes in the unpaid principal of my loan and in the interest rate that I must pay. The Note Holder will determine my new interest rate and the changed amount of my monthly payment in accordance with Section 4 of this Note.

4. INTEREST RATE AND MONTHLY PAYMENT CHANGES

(A) Change Dates

The interest rate I will pay may change on the first day of ...., 19........, and on that day every 12th month thereafter. Each date on which my interest rate could change is called a "Change Date."

(B) The Index

Beginning with the first Change Date, my interest rate will be based on an Index. The "Index" is the weekly average yield on United States Treasury securities adjusted to a constant maturity of 1 year, as made available by the Federal Reserve Board. The most recent Index figure available as of the date 45 days before each Change Date is called the "Current Index."

If the Index is no longer available, the Note Holder will choose a new index which is based upon comparable information. The Note Holder will give me notice of this choice.

(C) Calculation of Changes

Before each Change Date, the Note Holder will calculate my new interest rate by adding .... percentage points (..................%) to the Current Index. The Note Holder will then round the result of this addition to the nearest one-eighth of one percentage point (0.125%). Subject to the limits stated in Section 4(D) below, this rounded amount will be my new interest rate until the next Change Date.

The Note Holder will then determine the amount of the monthly payment that would be sufficient to repay the unpaid principal that I am expected to owe at the Change Date in full on the maturity date at my new interest rate in substantially equal payments. The result of this calculation will be the new amount of my monthly payment.

(D) Limits on Interest Rate Changes

The interest rate I am required to pay at the first Change Date will not be greater than ....% or less than ....%. Thereafter, my interest rate will never be increased or decreased on any single Change Date by more than two percentage points (2.0%) from the rate of interest I have been paying for the preceding twelve months. My interest rate will never be greater than ....%.

(E) Effective Date of Changes

My new interest rate will become effective on each Change Date. I will pay the amount of my new monthly payment beginning on the first monthly payment date after the Change Date until the amount of my monthly payment changes again.

(F) Notice of Changes

The Note Holder will deliver or mail to me a notice of any changes in my interest rate and the amount of my monthly payment before the effective date of any change. The notice will include information required by law to be given me and also the title and telephone number of a person who will answer any question I may have regarding the notice.

5. BORROWER'S RIGHT TO PREPAY

I have the right to make payments of principal at any time before they are due. A payment of principal only is known as a "prepayment." When I make a prepayment, I will tell the Note Holder in writing that I am doing so.

I may make a full prepayment or partial prepayments without paying any prepayment charge. The Note Holder will use all of my prepayments to reduce the amount of principal that I owe under this Note. If I make a partial prepayment, there will be no changes in the due dates of my monthly payments unless the Note Holder agrees in writing to those changes. My partial prepayment may reduce the amount of my monthly payments after the first Change Date following my partial prepayment. However, any reduction due to my partial prepayment may be offset by an interest rate increase.

6. LOAN CHARGES

If a law, which applies to this loan and which sets maximum loan charges, is finally interpreted so that the interest or other loan charges collected or to be collected in connection with this loan exceed the permitted limits, then: (i) any such loan charge shall be reduced by the amount necessary to reduce the charge to the permitted limit; and (ii) any sums already collected from me which exceeded permitted limits will be refunded to me. The Note Holder may choose to make this refund by reducing the principal I owe under this Note or by making a direct payment to me. If a refund reduces principal, the reduction will be treated as a partial prepayment.

7. BORROWER'S FAILURE TO PAY AS REQUIRED

(A) Late Charges for Overdue Payments

If the Note Holder has not received the full amount of any monthly payment by the end of .... calendar days after the date it is due, I will pay a late charge to the Note Holder. The amount of the charge will be ....% of my overdue payment of principal and interest. I will pay this late charge promptly but only once on each late payment.

(B) Default

If I do not pay the full amount of each monthly payment on the date it is due, I will be in default.

(C) Notice of Default

If I am in default, the Note Holder may send me a written notice telling me that if I do not pay the overdue amount by a certain date, the Note Holder may require me to pay immediately the full amount of principal which has not been paid and all the interest that I owe on that amount. That date must be at least 30 days after the date on which the notice is delivered or mailed to me.

EXHIBIT 11–2
FNMA Residential
Adjustable Rate
Note
(continued)

EXHIBIT 11–2
FNMA Residential
Adjustable Rate
Note
(continued)

(D) No Waiver By Note Holder

Even if, at a time when I am in default, the Note Holder does not require me to pay immediately in full as described above, the Note Holder will still have the right to do so if I am in default at a later time.

(E) Payment of Note Holder's Costs and Expenses

If the Note Holder has required me to pay immediately in full as described above, the Note Holder will have the right to be paid back by me for all of its costs and expenses in enforcing this Note to the extent not prohibited by applicable law. Those expenses include, for example, reasonable attorneys' fees.

8. GIVING OF NOTICES

Unless applicable law requires a different method, any notice that must be given to me under this Note will be given by delivering it or by mailing it by first class mail to me at the Property Address above or at a different address if I give the Note Holder a notice of my different address.

Any notice that must be given to the Note Holder under this Note will be given by mailing it by first class mail to the Note Holder at the address stated in Section 3(A) above or at a different address if I am given a notice of that different address.

9. OBLIGATIONS OF PERSONS UNDER THIS NOTE

If more than one person signs this Note, each person is fully and personally obligated to keep all of the promises made in this Note, including the promise to pay the full amount owed. Any person who is a guarantor, surety or endorser of this Note is also obligated to do these things. Any person who takes over these obligations, including the obligations of a guarantor, surety or endorser of this Note, is also obligated to keep all of the promises made in this Note. The Note Holder may enforce its rights under this Note against each person individually or against all of us together. This means that any one of us may be required to pay all of the amounts owed under this Note.

10. WAIVERS

I and any other person who has obligations under this Note waive the rights of presentment and notice of dishonor. "Presentment" means the right to require the Note Holder to demand payment of amounts due. "Notice of dishonor" means the right to require the Note Holder to give notice to other persons that amounts due have not been paid.

11. UNIFORM SECURED NOTE

This Note is a uniform instrument with limited variations in some jurisdictions. In addition to the protections given to the Note Holder under this Note, a Mortgage, Deed of Trust or Security Deed (the "Security Instrument"), dated the same date as this Note, protects the Note Holder from possible losses which might result if I do not keep the promises which I make in this Note. That Security Instrument describes how and under what conditions I may be required to make immediate payment in full of all amounts I owe under this Note. Some of those conditions are described as follows:

Transfer of the Property or a Beneficial Interest in Borrower. If all or any part of the Property or any interest in it is sold or transferred (or if a beneficial interest in Borrower is sold or transferred and Borrower is not a natural person) without Lender's prior written consent, Lender may, at its option, require immediate payment in full of all sums secured by this Security Instrument. However, this option shall not be exercised by Lender if exercise is prohibited by federal law as of the date of this Security Instrument. Lender also shall not exercise this option if: (a) Borrower causes to be submitted to Lender information required by Lender to evaluate the intended transferee as if a new loan were being made to the transferee; and (b) Lender reasonably determines that Lender's security will not be impaired by the loan assumption and that the risk of a breach of any covenant or agreement in this Security Instrument is acceptable to Lender.

To the extent permitted by applicable law, Lender may charge a reasonable fee as a condition to Lender's consent to the loan assumption. Lender may also require the transferee to sign an assumption agreement that is acceptable to Lender and that obligates the transferee to keep all the promises and agreements made in the Note and in this Security Instrument. Borrower will continue to be obligated under the Note and this Security Instrument unless Lender releases Borrower in writing .

If Lender exercises the option to require immediate payment in full, Lender shall give Borrower notice of acceleration. The notice shall provide a period of not less than 30 days from the date the notice is delivered or mailed within which Borrower must pay all sums secured by this Security Instrument. If Borrower fails to pay these sums prior to the expiration of this period, Lender may invoke any remedies permitted by this Security Instrument without further notice or demand on Borrower.

WITNESS THE HAND(S) AND SEAL(S) OF THE UNDERSIGNED.

.... (Seal)
-Borrower

.... (Seal)
-Borrower

.... (Seal)
-Borrower

[Sign Original Only]

EXHIBIT 11–2
FNMA Residential Adjustable Rate Note (continued)

$1,600,000.00   (City), (State)
                                             September 14, 19____

REAL ESTATE NOTE

FOR VALUE RECEIVED, the undersigned HARRIS OFFICE PARK LIMITED PARTNERSHIP, an Ohio limited partnership, hereinafter referred to as "Borrower", promises to pay to the order of WHEREVER INSURANCE COMPANY, an Ohio corporation, hereinafter referred to as "Payee", at the main office of Payee located at _____ _____, or at such other place as Payee shall designate in writing, in lawful money of the United States of America which shall at the time of payment be legal tender for payment of all debts, public and private, the principal sum of ONE MILLION SIX HUNDRED THOUSAND AND NO/100 DOLLARS ($1,600,000.00), together with interest thereon at the rate of ten and one-half percent (10.50%) per annum in two hundred seventy-six (276) consecutive monthly installments,

EXHIBIT 11–3
Commercial Loan Note

EXHIBIT 11–3
Commercial Loan
Note
(continued)

installments 1 to 275 both inclusive, being for the sum of FIFTEEN THOUSAND THREE HUNDRED EIGHTY NINE AND 88/100 DOLLARS ($15,389.88) each, and installment number 276 being for the balance of the principal and interest then owing.

Interest only on the outstanding principal balance of the indebtedness shall be due and payable on October 1, 19___ and the first of said monthly amortized installments of principal and interest shall be due and payable on November 1, 19___, and continue to be due and payable on the first day of each month thereafter, with the final installment of all unpaid principal and unpaid and accrued interest, unless sooner paid, being due and payable on the 1st day of October, 20 ____. Each such amortized installment of principal and interest, when paid, shall be applied first to the payment of interest accrued on the unpaid principal balance and the residue thereof shall be applied toward the payment of principal.

Notwithstanding anything contained in this note to the contrary, Payee shall have the right, at its sole option and discretion, to declare the entire outstanding principal balance of this note and all accrued and unpaid interest thereon to be due and payable in full at the end of the seventh (7th), twelfth (12th), seventeenth (17th), or twenty-second (22nd) Loan Years (hereinafter defined) and each date is hereinafter referred to as a ("Call Date"). Payee shall give notice of the exercise of such option to Borrower at least six (6) months in advance. In the event Payee shall elect to so declare this note due, then this note shall be and become due and payable in full on the due date of the eighty fourth (84th), one hundred forty forth (144th), two hundred fourth (204th), or two hundred sixty fourth (264th) installment of principal and interest due hereunder, depending upon whether or not Payee elects to declare this note due, and upon which Call Date Payee exercises the option to declare this Note due. No prepayment premium as hereinafter described shall be due and payable if this Note is prepaid because of Payee's exercise of its rights to declare the Note due pursuant to this paragraph.

Late Charge. Borrower shall pay a late charge of four percent (4%) of any payment of principal and interest which is not paid within fifteen (15) days of the due date thereof. The collection of any such late charge by Payee shall not be deemed a waiver by Payee of any of its rights hereunder or under any document or instrument given to secure this note. During the entire term of this note, Borrower shall pay all costs of collection, including reasonable attorney's fees not to exceed fifteen percent (15%) of the principal and interest due, if collected by or through an attorney-at-law.

Prepayment Privilege. This note may not be prepaid in whole or in part except as herein specifically provided. No prepayment of the principal of this note shall be permitted or allowed prior to the end of the third (3rd) Loan Year, as hereinafter defined. After the end of the third (3rd) Loan Year, this note may be prepaid in whole, but not in part, upon any principal and interest payment date as provided herein, provided that (a) no later than sixty (60) days prior to the date of such prepayment, Borrower delivers written notice to Payee, that Borrower intends to prepay the note in full on the date specified in the notice; and (b) Borrower pays to Payee at the time of such prepayment, a percentage of the prepaid principal amount of the indebtedness as a prepayment premium. The amount of the prepayment premium shall be the product obtained by multiplying the prepaid principal amount of the indebtedness by the product of the following: (i) the amount obtained by subtracting the annualized yield on a United States Treasury Bill, Note or Bond with a maturity date which occurs closest to the next applicable Call Date of this note, as such annualized yield is reported by *The Wall Street Journal,* on the business day preceding the date of prepayment, from 10.50% multiplied by: (ii) the number of years and any fraction thereof remaining between the date of prepayment and the next applicable Call Date of this note.

EXHIBIT 11–3
Commercial Loan
Note
(continued)

Notwithstanding the foregoing, however, in the event of acceleration of this note at any time, including the period of time prior to the end of the third (3rd) Loan Year, and subsequent involuntary or voluntary prepayment, the prepayment premium as calculated above shall be payable, however, in no event shall it exceed an amount equal to the excess, if any, of (i) interest calculated at the highest applicable rate permitted by applicable law, as construed by courts having jurisdiction thereof, on the principal balance of the indebtedness evidenced by this note from time to time outstanding from the date hereof to the date of such acceleration; over (ii) interest theretofore paid and accrued on this note. Any prepaid amounts specified in any notice shall become due and payable at the time provided in such notice. Under no circumstances shall the prepayment premium ever be less than zero. The amount of prepayment shall never be less than the full amount of the then outstanding principal indebtedness and accrued interest thereon.

A Loan Year for the purposes of this note shall mean each successive twelve (12) month period, beginning with the date of the first installment payment of principal and interest hereunder, provided, however, that the first (1st) Loan Year shall include the period from the date of this note to the date of such first installment payment of principal and interest.

Borrower further aggress to pay in addition to the above-described prepayment premium, a reinvestment fee of one-half of one (1/2%) percent of the outstanding prepaid principal indebtedness evidenced by this note to Payee. Borrower agrees that the reinvestment fee together with the prepayment premium shall be due and payable regardless of whether the prepayment is made involuntarily or voluntarily.

Collateral. This note is secured by, among other instruments, (i) a Deed of Trust of even date herewith executed by Borrower in favor of Payee (the "Security Deed"), conveying and covering certain real property lying and being in Land Lot 50 of the 17th District, of Simkin County, Ohio, as the same is more particularly described in the Security Deed (the "Premises"), (ii) Security Agreement of even date herewith executed by Borrower in favor of Payee (the "Security Agreement"), conveying a security interest in certain personal property as more particularly described in the Security Agreement, (iii) Assignment of Leases and Rents of even date herewith executed by Borrower in favor of Payee (the "Rent Assignment") covering the Premises.

Default. If Borrower fails to pay when due any amount payable under this note or if Borrower shall be in default under the Security Deed, Security Agreement or Rent Assignment, then Borrower shall be in default under this note. In the event Borrower shall be in default under this note, at the option of Payee and without further demand or further notice of any kind, the entire unpaid principal balance of this note together with accrued interest thereon, may be declared and thereupon immediately shall become due and payable, and the principal portion of such sum shall bear interest at the rate of two percent (2%) per annum in excess of the highest rate of interest then being charged under this note from the date of default until paid, and Payee, at the option of Payee and without demand or notice of any kind, may exercise any and all rights and remedies provided for or allowed by the Security Deed, Security Agreement, Rent Assignment or provided for or allowed by law or inequity. Any acceleration of payment of the indebtedness evidenced by this note pursuant to the terms hereof or pursuant to the terms of the Security Deed shall be considered prepayment of such indebtedness authorizing Payee, upon any such acceleration, and in addition to the balance of principal and interest accrued thereon and all other amounts due under this note and the Security Deed, to the extent permitted by applicable law, to recover any amount equal to the prepayment premium provided for hereinabove as if such indebtedness has been prepaid otherwise.

EXHIBIT 11–3
Commercial Loan
Note
(continued)

Time. Time is of the essence of this note.

Waiver. Demand, presentment, notice, protest, and notice of dishonor are hereby waived by Borrower and by each and every co-maker, endorser, guarantor, surety, and other person or entity primarily or secondarily liable on this note. Borrower and each and every co-maker, endorser, guarantor, surety, and other person or entity primarily or secondarily liable on this note: (i) severally waives, each for himself and family, any and all homestead and exemption rights by which any of them or the family of any of them may have under or by virtue of the Constitution or laws of the United States of America or of any state as against this note or any and all renewals, extensions, or modifications of, or substitutions for, this note; (ii) hereby transfers, conveys, and assigns to Payee a sufficient amount of such homestead or exemption as may be allowed, including such homestead or exemption as may be set apart in bankruptcy, to pay the indebtedness evidenced by this note in full, with all costs of collection; (iii) does hereby direct any trustee in bankruptcy having possession of such homestead or exemption to deliver to Payee a sufficient amount of property or money set apart as exempt to pay the indebtedness evidenced by this note, and any and all renewals, extensions, and modifications of, and substitutions for, this note, and (iv) does hereby appoint Payee attorney in-fact to claim any and all homestead exemptions allowed by law.

Third Party Liability. With the consent of Payee, this note may be extended or renewed, in whole or in part, without notice to or consent of any co-maker, endorser, guarantor, surety or other person or entity primarily or secondarily liable on this note and without affecting or lessening the liability of any such person or entity, and each such person or entity hereby waives any right to notice of or consent to such extensions and renewals. Failure of Payee to exercise any rights under this note shall not affect the liability of any co-maker, endorser, guarantor, surety or other person or entity primarily or secondarily liable on this note.

Forbearance. Payee shall not be deemed to waive any of Payee's rights or remedies under this note unless such waiver be express, in writing and signed by or on behalf of Payee. No delay, omission, or forbearance by Payee in exercising any of Payee's rights or remedies shall operate as a waiver of such rights or remedies. A waiver in writing on one occasion shall not be construed as a waiver of any right or remedy on any future occasion.

Governing Law and Severability. This note shall be governed by, construed under, and interpreted and enforced in accordance with the laws of the State of Ohio. Wherever possible, each provision of this note shall be interpreted in such manner as to be effective and valid under applicable law, but if any provision of this note shall be prohibited by or invalid under the applicable law, such provision shall be ineffective only to the extent of such prohibition or invalidity, without invalidating the remainder of such provision or the remaining provisions of this note.

This note and all provisions hereof and of all documents securing this note conform in all respects to the laws of the State of Ohio so that no payment of interest or other sum construed to be interest or charges in the nature of interest shall exceed the highest lawful contract rate permissible under the laws of the State of Ohio as applicable to this transaction. Therefore, this note and all agreements between Borrower and Payee are limited so that in no contingency or event whatsoever, whether acceleration of maturity of the indebtedness or otherwise, shall the amount paid or agree to be paid to the Payee of the use, forbearance, or detention of the money advanced by or to be advanced hereunder exceed the highest lawful rate permissible under the laws of the State of Ohio as applicable to this transaction. In determining whether or not the rate of interest exceeds the highest lawful rate, the Borrower and Payee intend that all sums paid hereunder which are

EXHIBIT 11–3
Commercial Loan
Note
(continued)

deemed interest for the purposes of determining usury be prorated, allocated, or spread in equal parts over the longest period of time permitted under the applicable laws of the State of Ohio. If, under any circumstances whatsoever, fulfillment of any provision hereof, or of any other instrument evidencing or securing this Indebtedness, at the time performance of such provisions shall be due, shall involve the payment of interest in excess of that authorized by law, the obligation to be fulfilled shall be reduced to the limit so authorized by law, and if under any circumstances Payee shall ever receive as interest an amount which would exceed the highest lawful rate, the amount which would be excessive shall be either applied to the reduction of the unpaid principal balance of the Indebtedness, without payment of any prepayment fee, (and not to the payment of interest) or refunded to the Borrower, and Payee shall not be subject to any penalty provided for the contracting for, charging, or receiving interest in excess of the maximum lawful rate regardless of when or the circumstances under which said refund or application was made.

Notices. All notices, requests, demands, and other communications of this note shall be in writing and shall be deemed to have been duly given if given in accordance with the provisions of the Security Deed.

Terms. The word "Borrower" as used herein shall include the legal representatives, successors, and assigns of Borrower as if so specified at length throughout this note, all of which shall be liable for all indebtedness and liabilities of Borrower. The word "Borrower" as used herein shall also include all makers of this note, and each of them, who shall be jointly and severally liable under this note, should more than one maker execute this note; and shall include all endorsers, guarantors, sureties, and other persons or entities primarily or secondarily liable on this note, and each of them; and shall include the masculine and feminine genders, regardless of the sex of Borrower or any of them; and shall include partnerships, corporations, and other legal entities, should such an entity be or become primarily or secondarily liable on this note. The word "Payee" as used herein shall include the transferees, legal representatives, successors, and assigns of Payee, as if so specified at length throughout this note, and all rights of Payee under this note shall inure to the successors and assigns of Payee.

IN WITNESS WHEREOF, Borrower by its duly authorized general partner has executed this note under seal and has delivered this note to Payee, this _____ day of September, 19____.

BORROWER:

HARRIS OFFICE PARK LIMITED
PARTNERSHIP, an Ohio limited
partnership

General Partner:

_____(SEAL)
Veronica F. Harris

EXHIBIT 11–4
Payment Guaranty

GUARANTY

_____ 19_____

_____
(City) _____ , (State) _____

FOR VALUE RECEIVED, the sufficiency of which is hereby acknowledged, and in consideration of any loan or other financial accommodation heretofore or hereafter at any time made or granted to _____ (hereinafter called the "Debtor") by _____ (hereinafter, together with its successors and assigns, called the "Bank"), the undersigned hereby unconditionally guarantee(s) the full and prompt payment when due, whether by declaration or otherwise, and at all times hereafter, of all obligations of the Debtor to the Bank, however and whenever incurred or evidenced, whether direct of indirect, absolute or contingent, or due or to become due (collectively called "Liabilities"), and the undersigned further agree(s) to pay the following (herein called "Expenses"): (a) all expenses paid or incurred by the Bank in endeavoring to collect the Liabilities or any part thereof from the Debtor, including attorney's fees of 15% of the total amount sought to be collected if the Bank endeavors to collect from the Debtor by law or through an attorney at law; and (b) all expenses paid or incurred by the Bank in collecting this guaranty, including attorney's fees of 15% of the total amount sought to be collected if this guaranty is collected by law or through an attorney at law. The right of recovery against the undersigned is, however, limited to _____ Dollars ($_____) of the principal amount of the Liabilities plus the interest on such amount and plus the Expenses as applicable thereto and as applicable to this guaranty.

Undersigned hereby represents that loans or other financial accommodations by the Bank to the Debtor will be to the direct interest and advantage of the undersigned.

Undersigned hereby transfers and conveys to the Bank any and all balances, credits, deposits, accounts, items and monies of the undersigned now or hereafter with the Bank, and the Bank is hereby given a lien upon security title to and a security interest in all property of the undersigned of every kind and description now or hereafter in the possession or control of the Bank for any reason, including all dividends and distributions on or other rights in connection therewith.

In the event of the death, incompetency, dissolution or insolvency (as defined by the Uniform Commercial Code as in effect at the time in Georgia) of the Debtor, or if a petition in bankruptcy be filed by or against the Debtor, of if a receiver be appointed for any part of the property or assets of the Debtor, or if any judgment be entered against the Debtor, or if the Bank shall feel insecure with respect to Liabilities and if any such event should occur at a time when any of the Liabilities may not then be due and payable, the undersigned agrees to pay to the Bank upon demand the full amount which would be payable hereunder by the undersigned if all Liabilities were then due and payable.

Bank may, without demand or notice of any kind, at any time when any amount shall be due and payable hereunder by any of the undersigned, appropriate and apply toward the payment of such amount, and in such order of application as the Bank may from time to time elect, any property, balances, credits, deposits, accounts, items or monies of such undersigned in the possession or control of the Bank for any purpose.

This guaranty shall be continuing, absolute and unconditional and shall remain in full force and effect as to the undersigned, subject to discontinuance of this guaranty as to any of the undersigned (including, without limitation, any undersigned who shall become deceased, incompetent or dissolved) only as follows: Any of the undersigned, and any per-

EXHIBIT 11–4
Payment Guaranty
(continued)

son duly authorized and acting on behalf of any of the undersigned, may given written notice to the Bank of discontinuance of this guaranty as to the undersigned by whom or on whose behalf such notice is given, but no such notice shall be effective in any respect until it is actually received by the Bank and no such notice shall affect or impair the obligations hereunder of the undersigned by whom or on whose behalf such notice is given with respect to any Liabilities existing at the date of receipt of such notice by the Bank, any interest thereon or any expenses paid or incurred by the Bank in endeavoring to collect such Liabilities, or any part thereof, and in enforcing this guaranty against such undersigned. Any such notice of discontinuance by or on behalf of any of the undersigned shall not affect or impair the obligations hereunder of any other of the undersigned.

The Bank may, from time to time, without notice to the undersigned (or any of them), (a) retain or obtain a security interest in any property to secure any of the Liabilities or any obligation hereunder, (b) retain or obtain the primary or secondary liability of any party or parties, in addition to the undersigned, with respect to any of the Liabilities, (c) extend or renew for any period (whether or not longer than the original period), alter or exchange any of the Liabilities, (d) release or compromise any liability of any of the undersigned hereunder or any liability of any other party or parties primarily or secondarily liable on any of the Liabilities, (e) release its security interest, if any, in all or any property securing any of the Liabilities or any obligation hereunder and permit any substitution or exchange for any such property, and (f) resort to the undersigned (or any of them) for payment of any of the Liabilities, whether or not the Bank shall have resorted to any property securing any of the Liabilities or any obligation hereunder or shall have proceeded against any other of the undersigned or any other party primarily or secondarily liable on any of the Liabilities.

Any amount received by the Bank from whatever source and applied by it toward the payment of the Liabilities shall be applied in such order of application as the Bank may from time to time elect.

The undersigned hereby expressly waive(s): (a) Notice of the acceptance of this guaranty, (b) notice of the existence or creation of all or any of the Liabilities, (c) presentment, demand, notice of dishonor, protest, and all other notices whatsoever, and (d) all diligence in collection or protection of or realization upon the Liabilities or any thereof, any obligation hereunder, or any security for any of the foregoing.

The creation or existence from time to time of Liabilities in excess of the amount to which the right of recovery under this guaranty is limited is hereby authorized, without notice to the undersigned (or any of them), and shall in no way affect or impair this guaranty.

The Bank may, without notice of any kind, sell, assign or transfer all or any of the Liabilities, and in such event each and every immediate and successive assignee, transferee, or holder of all or any of the Liabilities, shall have the right to enforce this guaranty, by suit or otherwise, for the benefit of such assignee, transferee or holder, as fully as if such assignee, transferee or holder were herein by name specifically given such rights, powers and benefits, but the Bank shall have an unimpaired right, prior and superior to that of any such assignee, transferee or holder, to enforce this guaranty for the benefit of the Bank, as to so much of the Liabilities as it has not sold, assigned or transferred.

No delay or failure on the part of the Bank in the exercise of any right or remedy shall operate as a waiver thereof, and no single or partial exercise by the Bank of any right or remedy shall preclude other or further exercise thereof or the exercise of any other right or remedy. No action of the Bank permitted hereunder shall in any way impair or affect this guaranty. For the purpose of this guaranty, Liabilities shall include all obligations of the

EXHIBIT 11-4
Payment Guaranty
(continued)

Debtor to the Bank, notwithstanding any right or power of the Debtor or anyone else to assert any claim or defense, as to the invalidity or unenforceability of any such obligation, and no such claim or defense shall impair or affect the obligations of the undersigned hereunder.

This guaranty is cumulative of and shall not effect, modify or limit any other guaranty executed by the undersigned with respect to any Liabilities.

This guaranty shall be binding upon the undersigned, and upon the heirs, legal representatives, successors and assigns of the undersigned. If more than one party shall execute this guaranty, the term "undersigned" shall mean all parties executing this guaranty, and all such parties shall be jointly and severally obligated hereunder.

This guaranty has been made and delivered in the State of Georgia, and shall be governed by the laws of that State. Wherever possible each provision of this guaranty shall be interpreted in such manner as to be effective and valid under applicable law, but if any provision of this guaranty shall be prohibited by or invalid under such law, such provision shall be ineffective to the extent of such prohibition or invalidity, without invalidating the remainder of such provision or the remaining provisions of this guaranty.

IN WITNESS WHEREOF the undersigned have hereunto set their hands and affix their seals the day and year above written.

_____ (SEAL)

_____ (SEAL)

_____ (SEAL)

EXHIBIT 11-5
Florida Mortgage

THIS INDENTURE, made this _____ day of _____ in the year of our Lord one thousand nine hundred and _____, by and between

_____

_____

of the _____, County of _____, and State of Florida, hereinafter called the Mortgagor; and _____; hereinafter called the Mortgagee:

Whereas the said Mortgagor is justly indebted to the said Mortgagee in the principal sum of _____

_____ Dollars, as evidenced by a certain promissory note of even date herewith, executed by

_____

_____ and payable to the order of the Mortgagee, with interest and upon terms as provided therein.

Said note provides that all instalments of principal and interest are payable in lawful money of the United States of America, which shall be legal tender for public and private debts at the time of payment, at the office of _____, or at such other place as the holder thereof may from time to time designate in writing. Said note also provides that the final instalment of principal and interest shall be due and payable on the _____ day of _____, 19_____.

EXHIBIT 11–5
Florida Mortgage
(continued)

Said note provides that each maker and endorser, jointly and severally, shall pay all costs of collection, including a reasonable attorney's fee, on failure to pay any principal and interest when due thereon, and that all principal due thereunder shall bear interest at the maximum permissible rate per annum from due date until paid.

Said note further provides that if any instalment of principal and/or interest shall not be paid when due, then the entire principal sum and accrued interest shall become due and payable at once, at the option of the holder thereof.

NOW THIS INDENTURE WITNESSETH, that the said Mortgagor, to secure said indebtedness and interest thereon, and also for and in consideration of the sum of One Dollar paid by Mortgagee, at or before the ensealing and delivery of these presents, the receipt whereof is hereby acknowledged, has granted, bargained, sold and conveyed and by these presents does grant, bargain, sell and convey unto the Mortgagee all that certain lot, parcel or piece of land lying and being in the County of _____ and State of Florida, more particularly described as _____

ALSO TOGETHER WITH all buildings and improvements thereon situate or which may hereafter be erected or placed thereon and all and singular the tenements, hereditaments, appurtenances and easements thereunto belonging or in anywise appertaining, and the rents, issues and profits thereof, and together with all heating, ventilating and air conditioning equipment, all plumbing apparatus, fixtures, hot water heaters, water and sprinkler systems and pumps, all lighting fixtures and all screens, awnings, venetian blinds, built-in equipment, and built-in furniture (whether or not affixed to land or building) now or hereafter located in or on said premises, including all renewals, replacements and additions thereto.

TO HAVE AND TO HOLD the above granted and described premises unto the said Mortgagee; its successors or assigns, forever.

And the said Mortgagor hereby covenants with the Mortgagee that the said Mortgagor is indefeasibly seized of said land in fee simple; that the said Mortgagor has full power and lawful right to convey the same in fee simple as aforesaid; that it shall be lawful for the Mortgagee at all times peaceably and quietly to enter upon, hold, occupy and enjoy said land and every part thereof; that the land is free from all encumbrances, except as aforesaid; that said Mortgagor will make such further assurances to prove the fee simple title to said land in said Mortgagee as may be reasonably required, and that said Mortgagor does hereby fully warrant the title to said land and every part thereof and will defend the same against the lawful claims of all persons whomsoever.

PROVIDED ALWAYS, and these presents are on this express condition, that if said Mortgagor shall well and truly pay said indebtedness unto the said Mortgagee, and any renewals or extensions thereof, and the interest thereon, together with all costs, charges and expenses, including a reasonable attorney's fee, which the said Mortgagee may incur or be put to in collecting the same by foreclosure, or otherwise, and shall perform and comply with all other terms, conditions and covenants contained in said promissory note and this mortgage, then these presents and the estate hereby granted shall cease, determine and be null and void.

And the said Mortgagor hereby jointly and severally covenants and agrees to and with the said Mortgagee as follows:

1. To pay all and singular the principal and interest and the various and sundry sums of money payable by virtue of said promissory note and this mortgage, each and every, promptly on the days respectively the same severally become due.

2. To pay all and singular the taxes, assessments, levies, liabilities, obligations and encumbrances of every nature and kind now on said described property, and/or that here-

EXHIBIT 11–5
Florida Mortgage
(continued)

after may be imposed, suffered, placed, levied or assessed thereupon and/or that hereafter may be levied or assessed upon this mortgage and/or the indebtedness secured hereby, each and every, before they become delinquent, and in so far as any thereof is of record the same shall be promptly satisfied and discharged of record and the original official document (such as, for instance, the tax receipt or the satisfaction paper officially endorsed or certified) shall be placed in the hands of said Mortgagee within ten days next after payment.

3. To keep the buildings now or hereafter situate on said land and all personal property used in the operation thereof continuously insured against loss by fire and such other hazards as may from time to time be requested by Mortgagee, in companies and in amounts in each company as may be approved by and acceptable to Mortgagee; and all insurance policies shall contain the usual standard mortgagee clause making the loss under said policies payable, without contribution, to said Mortgagee as its interest may appear, and each and every such policy shall be promptly delivered to and held by said Mortgagee; and, not less than ten (10) days in advance of the expiration of each policy, to deliver to said Mortgagee a renewal thereof, together with a receipt for the premium of such renewal. Any insurance proceeds, or any part thereof, may be applied by Mortgagee, at its option, either to the indebtedness hereby secured or to the restoration or repair of the property damaged.

4. To keep said land and the buildings and improvements now or hereafter situate thereon in good order and repair, and to permit, commit or suffer no waste, impairment or deterioration of said property or any part thereof.

5. To comply, as far as they affect the mortgaged property, with all statutes, laws, ordinances, decrees and orders of the United States, the State of Florida and of any political subdivision thereof.

6. In case Mortgagor shall fail to promptly discharge any obligation or covenant as provided herein, the Mortgagee shall have the option, but no obligation, to perform on behalf of the Mortgagor any act to be performed by Mortgagor in discharging such obligation or covenant, and any amount which Mortgagee may expend in performing such act, or in connection therewith, with interest thereon at the rate of ten (10) per cent per annum and together with all expenses, including reasonable attorney's fees, incurred by Mortgagee shall be immediately payable by Mortgagor and shall be secured by this mortgage; and Mortgagee shall be subrogated to any rights, equities and liens so discharged.

7. That if the principal or interest on the note herein described or any part of the indebtedness secured by this mortgage or interest thereon, be not paid within ten (10) days after they are due, or if default be made in the full and prompt performance of any covenant or agreement herein contained, or if any proceeding be instituted to abate any nuisance on the mortgaged property, or if any proceeding be instituted which might result to the detriment of the use and enjoyment of the said property or upon the rendering by any court of last resort of a decision that an undertaking by the Mortgagor as herein provided to pay any tax, assessment, levy, liability, obligation or encumbrance is legally inoperative or cannot be enforced, or in the event of the passage of any law changing in any way or respect the laws now in force for the taxation of mortgages or debts secured thereby for any purpose, or the manner of collection of any such tax, so as to affect this mortgage or the debt secured hereby; or if the Mortgagor shall make an assignment for the benefit of creditors, or if a receiver be appointed for the Mortgagor or any part of the mortgaged property, or if Mortgagor files a petition in bankruptcy, or is adjudicated a bankrupt or files any petition or institutes any proceedings under the National Bankruptcy Act, then on the happening of any one or more of these events, this conveyance shall

become absolute and the whole indebtedness secured hereby shall immediately become due and payable, at the option of the Mortgagee, and this mortgage may thereupon be foreclosed for the whole of said money, interest and costs; or Mortgagee may foreclose only as to the sum past due, without injury to this mortgage or the displacement or impairment of the remainder of the lien thereof, and at such foreclosure sale the property shall be sold subject to all remaining items of indebtedness; and Mortgagee may again foreclose, in the same manner, as often as there may be any sum past due.

8. Except during such period or periods as the Mortgagee may from time to time designate in writing, the Mortgagor will pay to the Mortgagee on the first day of each month throughout the existence of this mortgage a sum equal to the Mortgagee's estimate of the taxes and assessments next due on the mortgaged property and premiums next payable on or for policies of fire and other hazard insurance thereon, less any sums already paid the Mortgagee with respect thereto, divided by the number of months to elapse before one month prior to the date when such taxes, assessments and premiums become due and payable, such sums to be held by the Mortgagee, without interest, to pay such items. If at any time the estimated sum is insufficient to pay an item when due, the Mortgagor shall forthwith upon demand pay the deficiency to the Mortgagee. The arrangement provided for in this paragraph is solely for the added protection of the Mortgagee and entails no responsibility on the Mortgagee's part beyond the allowing of due credit, without interest, for sums actually received by it. Upon the occurrence of a default under this mortgage, the Mortgagee may apply all or any part of the accumulated funds then held, upon any obligation secured hereby. Upon assignment of this mortgage, any funds on hand shall be turned over to the assignee and any responsibility of the assignor with respect thereto shall terminate. Each transfer of the mortgaged property shall automatically transfer to the grantee all right of the grantor with respect to any funds accumulated hereunder.

9. That in case of default or the happening of any event which would enable the Mortgagee to declare the whole indebtedness secured hereby immediately due and payable, the Mortgagee shall be entitled to the appointment of a receiver of all the rents, issues and profits, regardless of the value of the mortgaged property and the solvency or insolvency of the Mortgagor and other persons liable to pay said indebtedness.

10. That the Mortgagee may collect a "late charge" not to exceed four cents (4¢) for each dollar of each payment due hereunder made more than fifteen (15) days in arrears to cover the extra expense involved in handling delinquent payments.

11. That the words "Mortgagor" and "Mortgagee" when used herein shall be taken to include singular and plural number and masculine, feminine or neuter gender, as may fit the case, and shall also include the heirs, administrators, executors, successors and assigns of the parties hereto. Each and all of the terms and provisions hereof shall extend to and be a part of any renewal or extension of this mortgage.

12. That this mortgage and the note secured hereby constitute a Florida contract and shall be construed according to the laws of that state.

IN WITNESS WHEREOF, the said Mortgagor has hereunto set his hand and seal the day and year first above written.

EXHIBIT 11-6
North Carolina
Deed of Trust

SATISFACTION: The debt secured by the within Deed of Trust together with the note(s) secured thereby has been satisfied in full.

This the .... day of ...., 19 ....

Signed: ....

....

....

Mail after recording to:

....

....

....

This instrument prepared by:

....

Recording: Time, Book and Page

NORTH CAROLINA DEED OF TRUST

THIS DEED of TRUST made this   day of   , 19   , by and between:

GRANTOR	TRUSTEE	BENEFICIARY
		SOUTHERN NATIONAL BANK OF NORTH CAROLINA, a national banking association

Enter in appropriate block for each party: name, address, and, if appropriate, character of entity, e.g. corporation or partnership.

The designation Grantor, Trustee, and Beneficiary as used herein shall include said parties, their heirs, successors, and assigns, and shall include singular, plural, masculine, feminine or neuter as required by context.

WITNESSETH: The Grantor is indebted to the Beneficiary in the sum of _____

_____ DOLLARS ($ ....)
(the "Debt") for money loaned, as evidenced by promissory Note(s) of even date herewith, the terms of which are incorporated herein by reference.

NOW, THEREFORE, as security for the Debt, together with interest thereon, and as security for all renewals, extensions, deferments, amortizations and re-amortizations thereof, in whole or in part, together with interest thereon whether at the same or different rates, and for a valuable consideration, receipt of which is hereby acknowledged, the Grantor has bargained, sold, granted and conveyed and does by these presents bargain, sell, grant and convey to the Trustee, his heirs, or

successors, and assigns, the real property situated in the City of _____, _____ Township, _____
County, State of North Carolina, particularly described as follows:

DESCRIPTION SET FORTH HEREINBELOW AND ON SCHEDULE "A", IF ANY, ATTACHED HERETO AND MADE A PART HEREOF

EXHIBIT 11—6
North Carolina
Deed of Trust
(continued)

TO HAVE AND TO HOLD said real property, including all buildings, improvements and fixtures now or hereafter located thereon, with all the rights, privileges and appurtenances thereunto belonging, to the Trustee, his heirs, or successors, and assigns forever, upon the trusts, terms and conditions, and for the uses hereinafter set forth.

If the Grantor shall pay the Debt secured hereby in accordance with the terms of the note(s) evidencing the same, and all renewals, extensions, deferments, amortizations and reamortizations thereof, in whole or in part, together with interest thereon, and shall comply with all the covenants, terms and conditions of the deed of trust, then this conveyance shall be null and void and may be cancelled of record at the request of the Grantor. If, however, there shall be any default in any of the covenants, terms, or conditions of the Note(s) secured hereby, or any failure or neglect to comply with the covenants, terms, or conditions contained in this deed of trust, then and in any of such events, if the default is not made good within (15) days, the Note(s) shall, at the option of the Beneficiary, at once become due and payable without notice, and it shall be lawful for and the duty of the Trustee, upon request of the Beneficiary, to sell the land herein conveyed at public auction for cash, after having first given such notice of hearing as to commencement of foreclosure proceedings and obtaining such findings or leave of court as may be then required by law and giving such notice and advertising the time and place of such sale in such manner as may be then provided by law, and upon such and any resales and upon compliance with the then law relating to foreclosure proceedings to convey title to the purchaser in fee simple.

The proceeds of the Sale shall, after the Trustee retains his commission, be applied to the costs of sale, the amount due on the Note(s) hereby secured and otherwise as required by the then existing law relating to foreclosures. The Trustee's commission shall be five per cent of the gross proceeds of the sale or the minimum sum of $ ...., whichever is greater, for a completed foreclosure. In the event foreclosure is commenced, but not completed, the Grantor shall pay all expenses incurred by Trustee and a partial commission computed on five per cent of the outstanding indebtedness or the above stated minimum sum, whichever is greater, in accordance with the following schedule, to wit: one-fourth thereof before the Trustee issues a notice of hearing on the right to foreclose; one-half thereof after issuance of said notice; three-fourths thereof after such hearing; and the greater of the full commission or minimum after the initial sale.

And the said Grantor does hereby covenant and agree with the Trustee and with the Beneficiary as follows:

1. INSURANCE. Grantor shall keep all improvements on said land, now or hereafter erected constantly insured for the benefit of the Beneficiary against loss by fire, windstorm and such other casualties and contingencies, in such manner and in such companies and for such amounts as may be satisfactory to or required by the Beneficiary. Grantor shall purchase such insurance, pay all premiums therefor, and shall deliver to Beneficiary such policies along with evidence of premium payment as long as the Note(s) secured hereby remains unpaid. If Grantor fails to purchase such insurance, pay the premiums therefor or deliver said policies with mortgagee clause satisfactory to Beneficiary attached thereto, along with evidence of payment of premiums thereon, then Beneficiary, at his option, may purchase such insurance. Such amounts paid by Beneficiary shall be added to the Note(s) secured by this Deed of Trust, and shall be due and payable upon demand by Grantor to Beneficiary.

2. TAXES, ASSESSMENTS, CHARGES. Grantor shall pay all taxes, assessments and charges as may be lawfully levied against said premises within thirty (30) days after the same shall become due. In the event that Grantor fails to so pay all taxes, assessments and charges as herein required, then Beneficiary, at his option, may pay the same and the amounts so paid shall be added to the Note(s), secured by this Deed of Trust, and shall be due and payable upon demand by Grantor to Beneficiary.

3. PARTIAL RELEASE. Grantor shall not be entitled to the partial release of any of the above described property unless a specific provision providing therefor is included in this Deed of Trust. In the event a partial release provision is included in this Deed of Trust, Grantor must strictly comply with the terms thereof. Notwithstanding anything herein contained, Grantor shall not be entitled to any release of property unless Grantor is not in default and is in full compliance with all of the terms and provisions of the Note(s), this Deed of Trust, and any other instrument that may be securing said Note(s).

4. WASTE. The Grantor covenants that he will keep the premises herein conveyed in as good order, repair and condition as they are now, reasonable wear and tear excepted, and that he will not commit or permit any waste.

5. WARRANTIES. Grantor covenants with Trustee and Beneficiary that he is seized of the premises in fee simple, has the right to convey the same in fee simple, that title is marketable and free and clear of all encumbrances, and that he will warrant and defend the title against the lawful claims of all persons whomsoever, except for the exceptions hereinafter stated. Title to the property hereinabove described is subject to the following exceptions:

6. CONVEYANCE; ACCELERATION: If Grantor sells, conveys, transfers, assigns or disposes of the hereinabove-described real property or any part thereof or interest therein, by any means or method, whether voluntary or involuntary, without the written consent of Beneficiary, then at the option of Beneficiary and without notice to Grantor, all sums of money secured hereby, both principal and interest, shall immediately become due and payable and in default, notwithstanding anything herein or in the Note(s) secured hereby to the contrary.

7. SUBSTITUTION OF TRUSTEE. Grantor and Trustee covenant and agree to and with Beneficiary that in case the said Trustee, or any successor trustee, shall die, become incapable of acting, renounce his trust, or for other similar or dissimilar reason become unacceptable to the holder of the Note(s), then the holder of the Note(s) may appoint, in writing, a trustee to take the place of the Trustee; and upon the probate and registration of the same, the trustee thus appointed shall succeed to all the rights, powers, and duties of the Trustee.

8. CIVIL ACTION. In the event that the Trustee is named as a party to any civil action as Trustee in this Deed of Trust, the Trustee shall be entitled to employ an attorney at law, including himself if he is a licensed attorney, to represent him in said action and the reasonable attorney's fees of the Trustee in such action shall be paid by Beneficiary and charged to the Note(s) and secured by this Deed of Trust.

9. PRIOR LIENS. Default under the terms of any instrument secured by a lien to which this deed of trust is subordinate shall consitute default hereunder.

IN WITNESS WHEREOF, the Grantor has hereunto set his hand and seal, or if corporate, has caused this instrument to be signed in its corporate name by its duly authorized officers and its seal to be hereunto affixed by authority of its Board of Directors, the day and year first above written.

(Corporate Name)

....　.. (SEAL)

By: ....

.... President　.. (SEAL)

ATTEST:　.. (SEAL)

....

.... Secretary (Corporate Seal)　.. (SEAL)

USE BLACK INK ONLY

SEAL-STAMP　STATE OF NORTH CAROLINA, COUNTY OF ....

Use Black Ink

I, ..., a notary public of said county do hereby certify that ....
.... Grantor, personally appeared before me this day and acknowledged the execution of the foregoing instrument. Witness my hand and official stamp or seal, this .... day of ...., 19 ....
My commission expires: 　.. Notary Public

SEAL-STAMP　STATE OF NORTH CAROLINA, COUNTY OF ....

Use Black Ink

I, ..., a Notary Public of the County and State aforesaid, certify that ...., personally came before me this day and acknowledged that .... he is .... Secretary of .... a North Carolina corporation, and that by authority duly given and as the act of the corporation, the foregoing instrument was signed in its name by its .... President, sealed with its corporate seal and attested by ....
.... as its .... Secretary.
Witness my hand and official stamp or seal, this .... day of ...., 19 ....
My commission expires: 　.. Notary Public

The foregoing Certificate (s) of ....
is/are certified to be correct. This instrument and this certificate are duly registered at the date and time and in the Book and Page shown on the first page hereof.
.... REGISTER OF DEEDS FOR .... COUNTY
By .... Deputy/Assistant - Register of Deeds

EXHIBIT 11—7
FNMA Residential
Deed to Secure
Debt

_____ [Space Above This Line For Recording Data] _____

SECURITY DEED

THIS SECURITY DEED ("Security Instrument") is given on ...., 19........ . The grantor is .... ("Borrower"). This Security Instrument is given to ...., which is organized and existing under the laws of ...., and whose address is .... ("Lender"). Borrower owes Lender the principal sum of ....Dollars (U.S. $ ....). This debt is evidenced by Borrower's note dated the same date as this Security Instrument ("Note"), which provides for monthly payments, with the full debt, if not paid earlier, due and payable on .... This Security Instrument secures to Lender: (a) the repayment of the debt evidenced by the Note, with interest, and all renewals, extensions and modifications of the Note; (b) the payment of all other sums, with interest, advanced under paragraph 7 to protect the security of this Security Instrument; and (c) the performance of Borrower's covenants and agreements under this Security Instrument and the Note. For this purpose, Borrower does hereby grant and convey to Lender and Lender's successors and assigns, with power of sale, the following described property located in .... County, Georgia:

which has the address of ...., ...,
_____[Street]_____[City]
Georgia .... ("Property Address");
_____[Zip Code]

   TO HAVE AND TO HOLD this property unto Lender and Lender's successors and assigns, forever, together with all the improvements now or hereafter erected on the property, and all easements, appurtenances, and fixtures now or hereafter a part of the property. All replacements and additions shall also be covered by this Security Instrument. All of the foregoing is referred to in this Security Instrument as the "Property."

   BORROWER COVENANTS that Borrower is lawfully seised of the estate hereby conveyed and has the right to grant and convey the Property and that the Property is unencumbered, except for encumbrances of record. Borrower warrants and will defend generally the title to the Property against all claims and demands, subject to any encumbrances of record.

   THIS SECURITY INSTRUMENT combines uniform covenants for national use and non-uniform covenants with limited variations by jurisdiction to constitute a uniform security instrument covering real property.

EXHIBIT 11-7
FNMA Residential
Deed to Secure
Debt
(continued)

UNIFORM COVENANTS. Borrower and Lender covenant and agree as follows:

1. Payment of Principal and Interest; Prepayment and Late Charges. Borrower shall promptly pay when due the principal of and interest on the debt evidenced by the Note and any prepayment and late charges due under the Note.

2. Funds for Taxes and Insurance. Subject to applicable law or to a written waiver by Lender, Borrower shall pay to Lender on the day monthly payments are due under the Note, until the Note is paid in full, a sum ("Funds") for: (a) yearly taxes and assessments which may attain priority over this Security Instrument as a lien on the Property; (b) yearly leasehold payments or ground rents on the Property, if any; (c) yearly hazard or property insurance premiums; (d) yearly flood insurance premiums, if any; (e) yearly mortgage insurance premiums, if any; and (f) any sums payable by Borrower to Lender, in accordance with the provisions of paragraph 8, in lieu of the payment of mortgage insurance premiums. These items are called "Escrow Items." Lender may, at any time, collect and hold Funds in an amount not to exceed the maximum amount a lender for a federally related mortgage loan may require for Borrower's escrow account under the federal Real Estate Settlement Procedures Act of 1974 as amended from time to time, 12 U.S.C. § 2601 *et seq.* ("RESPA"), unless another law that applies to the Funds sets a lesser amount. If so, Lender may, at any time, collect and hold Funds in an amount not to exceed the lesser amount. Lender may estimate the amount of Funds due on the basis of current data and reasonable estimates of expenditures of future Escrow Items or otherwise in accordance with applicable law.

The Funds shall be held in an institution whose deposits are insured by a federal agency, instrumentality, or entity (including Lender, if Lender is such an institution) or in any Federal Home Loan Bank. Lender shall apply the Funds to pay the Escrow Items. Lender may not charge Borrower for holding and applying the Funds, annually analyzing the escrow account, or verifying the Escrow Items, unless Lender pays Borrower interest on the Funds and applicable law permits Lender to make such a charge. However, Lender may require Borrower to pay a one-time charge for an independent real estate tax reporting service used by Lender in connection with this loan, unless applicable law provides otherwise. Unless an agreement is made or applicable law requires interest to be paid, Lender shall not be required to pay Borrower any interest or earnings on the Funds. Borrower and Lender may agree in writing, however, that interest shall be paid on the Funds. Lender shall give to Borrower, without charge, an annual accounting of the Funds, showing credits and debits to the Funds and the purpose for which each debit to the Funds was made. The Funds are pledged as additional security for all sums secured by this Security Instrument.

If the Funds held by Lender exceed the amounts permitted to be held by applicable law, Lender shall account to Borrower for the excess Funds in accordance with the requirements of applicable law. If the amount of the Funds held by Lender at any time is not sufficient to pay the Escrow Items when due, Lender may so notify Borrower in writing, and, in such case Borrower shall pay to Lender the amount necessary to make up the deficiency. Borrower shall make up the deficiency in no more than twelve monthly payments, at Lender's sole discretion.

Upon payment in full of all sums secured by this Security Instrument, Lender shall promptly refund to Borrower any Funds held by Lender. If, under paragraph 21, Lender shall acquire or sell the Property, Lender, prior to the acquisition or sale of the Property, shall apply any Funds held by Lender at the time of acquisition or sale as a credit against the sums secured by this Security Instrument.

3. Application of Payments. Unless applicable law provides otherwise, all payments received by Lender under paragraphs 1 and 2 shall be applied: first, to any prepayment

EXHIBIT 11–7
FNMA Residential
Deed to Secure
Debt
(continued)

charges due under the Note; second, to amounts payable under paragraph 2; third, to interest due; fourth, to principal due; and last, to any late charges due under the Note.

4. Charges; Liens. Borrower shall pay all taxes, assessments, charges, fines and impositions attributable to the Property which may attain priority over this Security Instrument, and leasehold payments or ground rents, if any. Borrower shall pay these obligations in the manner provided in paragraph 2, or if not paid in that manner, Borrower shall pay them on time directly to the person owed payment. Borrower shall promptly furnish to Lender all notices of amounts to be paid under this paragraph. If Borrower makes these payments directly, Borrower shall promptly furnish to Lender receipts evidencing the payments.

Borrower shall promptly discharge any lien which has priority over this Security Instrument unless Borrower: (a) agrees in writing to the payment of the obligation secured by the lien in manner acceptable to Lender; (b) contests in good faith the lien by, or defends against enforcement of the lien in, legal proceedings which in the Lender's opinion operate to prevent the enforcement of the lien; or (c) secures from the holder of the lien an agreement satisfactory to Lender subordinating the lien to this Security Instrument. If Lender determines that any part of the Property is subject to a lien which may attain priority over this Security Instrument, Lender may give Borrower a notice identifying the lien. Borrower shall satisfy the lien or take one or more of the actions set forth above within 10 days of the giving of notice.

5. Hazard or Property Insurance. Borrower shall keep the improvements now existing or hereafter erected on the Property insured against loss by fire, hazards included within the term "extended coverage" and any other hazards, including floods or flooding, for which Lender requires insurance. This insurance shall be maintained in the amounts and for the periods that Lender requires. The insurance carrier providing the insurance shall be chosen by Borrower subject to Lender's approval which shall not be unreasonably withheld. If Borrower fails to maintain coverage described above, Lender may, at Lender's option, obtain coverage to protect Lender's rights in the Property in accordance with paragraph 7.

All insurance policies and renewals shall be acceptable to Lender and shall include a standard mortgage clause. Lender shall have the right to hold the policies and renewals. If Lender requires, Borrower shall promptly give to Lender all receipts of paid premiums and renewal notices. In the event of loss, Borrower shall give prompt notice to the insurance carrier and Lender. Lender may make proof of loss if not made promptly by Borrower.

Unless Lender and Borrower otherwise agree in writing, insurance proceeds shall be applied to restoration or repair of the Property damaged, if the restoration or repair is economically feasible and Lender's security is not lessened. If the restoration or repair is not economically feasible or Lender's security would be lessened, the insurance proceeds shall be applied to the sums secured by this Security Instrument, whether or not then due, with any excess paid to Borrower. If Borrower abandons the Property, or does not answer within 30 days a notice from Lender that the insurance carrier has offered to settle a claim, then Lender may collect the insurance proceeds. Lender may use the proceeds to repair or restore the Property or to pay sums secured by this Security Instrument, whether or not then due. The 30-day period will begin when the notice is given.

Unless Lender and Borrower otherwise agree in writing, any application of proceeds to principal shall not extend or postpone the due date of the monthly payments referred to in paragraphs 1 and 2 or change the amount of the payments. If under paragraph 21 the Property is acquired by Lender, Borrower's right to any insurance policies and proceed resulting from damage to the Property prior to the acquisition shall pass to Lender to the extent of the sums secured by this Security Instrument immediately prior to the acquisition.

6. Occupancy, Preservation, Maintenance and Protection of the Property; Borrower's Loan Application; Leaseholds. Borrower shall occupy, establish, and use the Property as Borrower's principal residence within sixty days after the execution of this Security Instrument and shall continue to occupy the Property as Borrower's principal residence for at least one year after the date of occupancy, unless Lender otherwise agrees in writing, which consent shall not be unreasonably withheld, or unless extenuating circumstances exist which are beyond Borrower's control. Borrower shall not destroy, damage or impair the Property, allow the Property to deteriorate, or commit waste on the Property. Borrower shall be in default if any forfeiture action or proceeding, whether civil or criminal, is begun that in Lender's good faith judgment could result in forfeiture of the Property or otherwise materially impair the lien created by this Security Instrument or Lender's security interest. Borrower may cure such a default and reinstate, as provided in paragraph 18, by causing the action or proceeding to be dismissed with a ruling that, in Lender's good faith determination, precludes forfeiture of the Borrower's interest in the Property or other material impairment of the lien created by this Security Instrument or Lender's security interest. Borrower shall also be in default if Borrower, during the loan application process, gave materially false or inaccurate information or statements to Lender (or failed to provide Lender with any material information) in connection with the loan evidenced by the Note, including, but not limited to, representations concerning Borrower's occupancy of the Property as a principal residence. If this Security Instrument is on a leasehold, Borrower shall comply with all the provisions of the lease. If Borrower acquires fee title to the Property, the leasehold and the fee title shall not merge unless Lender agrees to the merger in writing.

7. Protection of Lender's Rights in the Property. If Borrower fails to perform the covenants and agreements contained in this Security Instrument, or there is a legal proceeding that may significantly affect Lender's rights in the Property (such as a proceeding in bankruptcy, probate, for condemnation or forfeiture or to enforce laws or regulations), then Lender may do and pay for whatever is necessary to protect the value of the Property and Lender's rights in the Property. Lender's actions may include paying any sums secured by a lien which has priority over this Security Instrument, appearing in court, paying reasonable attorneys' fees and entering on the Property to make repairs. Although Lender may take action under this paragraph 7, Lender does not have to do so.

Any amounts disbursed by Lender under this paragraph 7 shall become additional debt of Borrower secured by this Security Instrument. Unless Borrower and Lender agree to other terms of payment, these amounts shall bear interest from the date of disbursement at the Note rate and shall be payable, with interest, upon notice from Lender to Borrower requesting payment.

8. Mortgage Insurance. If Lender required mortgage insurance as a condition of making the loan secured by this Security Instrument, Borrower shall pay the premiums required to maintain the mortgage insurance insurance in effect. If, for any reason, the mortgage insurance coverage required by Lender lapses or ceases to be in effect, Borrower shall pay the premiums required to obtain coverage substantially equivalent to the mortgage insurance previously in effect, at a cost substantially equivalent to the cost to Borrower of the mortgage insurance previously in effect, from an alternate mortgage insurer approved by Lender. If substantially equivalent mortgage insurance coverage is not available, Borrower shall pay to Lender each month a sum equal to one-twelfth of the yearly mortgage insurance premium being paid by Borrower when the insurance coverage lapsed or ceased to be in effect. Lender will accept, use and retain these payments as a loss reserve in lieu of mortgage insurance. Loss reserve payments may no longer be required, at

EXHIBIT 11–7
FNMA Residential
Deed to Secure
Debt
(continued)

EXHIBIT 11–7
FNMA Residential
Deed to Secure
Debt
(continued)

the option of Lender, if mortgage insurance coverage (in the amount and for the period that Lender requires) provided by an insurer approved by Lender again becomes available and is obtained. Borrower shall pay the premiums required to maintain mortgage insurance in effect, or to provide a loss reserve, until the requirement for mortgage insurance ends in accordance with any written agreement between Borrower and Lender or applicable law.

9. Inspection. Lender or its agent may make reasonable entries upon and inspections of the Property. Lender shall give Borrower notice at the time of or prior to an inspection specifying reasonable cause for the inspection.

10. Condemnation. The proceeds of any award or claim for damages, direct or consequential, in connection with any condemnation or other taking of any part of the Property, or for conveyance in lieu of condemnation, are hereby assigned and shall be paid to Lender.

In the event of a total taking of the Property, the proceeds shall be applied to the sums secured by this Security Instrument, whether or not then due, with any excess paid to Borrower. In the event of a partial taking of the Property in which the fair market value of the Property immediately before the taking is equal to or greater than the amount of the sums secured by this Security Instrument immediately before the taking, unless Borrower and Lender otherwise agree in writing, the sums secured by this Security Instrument shall be reduced by the amount of the proceeds multiplied by the following fraction: (a) the total amount of the sums secured immediately before the taking, divided by (b) the fair market value of the Property immediately before the taking. Any balance shall be paid to Borrower. In the event of a partial taking of the Property in which the fair market value of the Property immediately before the taking is less than the amount of the sums secured immediately before the taking, unless Borrower and Lender otherwise agree in writing or unless applicable law otherwise provides, the proceeds shall be applied to the sums secured by this Security Instrument whether or not the sums are then due.

If the Property is abandoned by Borrower, or if, after notice by Lender to Borrower that the condemnor offers to make an award or settle a claim for damages, Borrower fails to respond to Lender within 30 days after the date the notice is given, Lender is authorized to collect and apply the proceeds, at its option, either to restoration or repair of the Property or to the sums secured by this Security Instrument, whether or not then due.

Unless Lender and Borrower otherwise agree in writing, any application of proceeds to principal shall not extend or postpone the due date of the monthly payments referred to in paragraphs 1 and 2 or change the amount of such payments.

11. Borrower Not Released; Forbearance By Lender Not a Waiver. Extension of the time for payment or modification of amortization of the sums secured by this Security Instrument granted by Lender to any successor in interest of Borrower shall not operate to release the liability of the original Borrower or Borrower's successors in interest. Lender shall not be required to commence proceedings against any successor in interest or refuse to extend time for payment or otherwise modify amortization of the sums secured by this Security Instrument by reason of any demand made by the original Borrower or Borrower's successors in interest. Any forbearance by Lender in exercising any right or remedy shall not be a waiver of or preclude the exercise of any right or remedy.

12. Successors and Assigns Bound; Joint and Several Liability; Co-signers. The covenants and agreements of this Security Instrument shall bind and benefit the successors and assigns of Lender and Borrower, subject to the provisions of paragraph 17. Borrower's covenants and agreements shall be joint and several. Any Borrower who co-signs this Security Instrument but does not execute the Note: (a) is co-signing this

EXHIBIT 11-7
FNMA Residential
Deed to Secure
Debt
(continued)

Security Instrument only to mortgage, grant and convey that Borrower's interest in the Property under the terms of this Security Instrument; (b) is not personally obligated to pay the sums secured by this Security Instrument; and (c) agrees that Lender and any other Borrower may agree to extend, modify, forbear or make any accommodations with regard to the terms of this Security Instrument or the Note without the Borrower's consent.

13. Loan Charges. If the loan secured by this Security Instrument is subject to a law which sets maximum loan charges, and that law is finally interpreted so that the interest or other loan charges collected or to be collected in connection with the loan exceed the permitted limits, then: (a) any such loan charge shall be reduced by the amount necessary to reduce the charge to the permitted limit; and (b) any sums already collected from Borrower which exceeded permitted limits will be refunded to Borrower. Lender may choose to make this refund by reducing the principal owed under the Note or by making a direct payment to Borrower. If a refund reduces principal, the reduction will be treated as a partial prepayment without any prepayment charge under the Note.

14. Notices. Any notice to Borrower provided for in this Security Instrument shall be given by delivering it or by mailing it by first class mail unless applicable law requires use of another method. The notice shall be directed to the Property Address or any other address Borrower designates by notice to Lender. Any notice to Lender shall be given by first class mail to Lender's address stated herein or any other address Lender designates by notice to Borrower. Any notice provided for in this Security Instrument shall be deemed to have been given to Borrower or Lender when given as provided in this paragraph.

15. Governing Law; Severability. This Security Instrument shall be governed by federal law and law of the jurisdiction in which the Property is located. In the event that any provision or clause of this Security Instrument or the Note conflicts with applicable law, such conflict shall not affect other provisions of this Security Instrument or the Note which can be given effect without the conflicting provision. To this end the provisions of this Security Instrument and the Note are declared to be severable.

16. Borrower's Copy. Borrower shall be given one conformed copy of the Note and of this Security Instrument.

17. Transfer of the Property or a Beneficial Interest in Borrower. If all or any part of the Property or any interest in it is sold or transferred (or if a beneficial interest in Borrower is sold or transferred and Borrower is not a natural person) without Lender's prior written consent, Lender may, at its option, require immediate payment in full of all sums secured by this Security Instrument. However, this option shall not be exercised by Lender if exercise is prohibited by federal law as of the date of this Security Instrument.

If Lender exercises this option, Lender shall give Borrower notice of acceleration. The notice shall provide a period of not less than 30 days from the date the notice is delivered or mailed within which Borrower must pay all sums secured by this Security Instrument. If Borrower fails to pay these sums prior to the expiration of this period, Lender may invoke any remedies permitted by this Security Instrument without further notice or demand on Borrower.

18. Borrower's Right to Reinstate. If Borrower meets certain conditions, Borrower shall have the right to have enforcement of this Security Instrument discontinued at any time prior to the earlier of: (a) 5 days (or such other period as applicable law may specify for reinstatement) before sale of the Property pursuant to any power of sale contained in this Security Instrument; or (b) entry of a judgment enforcing this Security Instrument. Those conditions are that Borrower: (a) pays Lender all sums which then would be due under this Security Instrument and the Note as if no acceleration had occurred; (b) cures any default of any other covenants or agreements; (c) pays all expenses incurred in

EXHIBIT 11–7
FNMA Residential
Deed to Secure
Debt
(continued)

enforcing this Security Instrument, including, but not limited to, reasonable attorneys' fees; and (d) takes such action as Lender may reasonably require to assure that the lien of this Security Instrument, Lender's rights in the Property and Borrower's obligation to pay the sums secured by this Security Instrument shall continue unchanged. Upon reinstatement by Borrower, this Security Instrument and the obligations secured hereby shall remain fully effective as if no acceleration had occurred. However, this right to reinstate shall not apply in the case of acceleration under paragraph 17.

19. **Sale of Note; Change of Loan Servicer**. The Note or a partial interest in the Note (together with this Security Instrument) may be sold one or more times without prior notice to Borrower. A sale may result in a change in the entity (known as the "Loan Servicer") that collects monthly payments due under the Note and this Security Instrument. There also may be one or more changes of the Loan Servicer unrelated to a sale of the Note. If there is a change of the Loan Servicer, Borrower will be given written notice of the change in accordance with paragraph 14 above and applicable law. The notice will state the name and address of the new Loan Servicer and the address to which payments should be made. The notice will also contain any other information required by applicable law.

20. **Hazardous Substances**. Borrower shall not cause or permit the presence, use, disposal, storage, or release of any Hazardous Substances on or in the Property. Borrower shall not do, nor allow anyone else to do, anything affecting the Property that is in violation of any Environmental Law. The preceding two sentences shall not apply to the presence, use, or storage on the Property of small quantities of Hazardous Substances that are generally recognized to be appropriate to normal residential uses and to maintenance of the Property.

Borrower shall promptly give Lender written notice of any investigation, claim, demand, lawsuit or other action by any governmental or regulatory agency or private party involving the Property and any Hazardous Substance or Environment Law of which Borrower has actual knowledge. If Borrower learns, or is notified by any governmental or regulatory authority, that any removal or other remediation of any Hazardous Substance affecting the Property is necessary, Borrower shall promptly take all necessary remedial actions in accordance with Environmental Law.

As used in this paragraph 20, "Hazardous Substances" are those substances defined as toxic or hazardous substances by Environmental Law and the following substances: gasoline, kerosene, other flammable or toxic petroleum products, toxic pesticides and herbicides, volatile solvents, materials containing asbestos or formaldehyde, and radioactive materials. As used in this paragraph 20, "Environmental Law" means federal laws and laws of the jurisdiction where the Property is located that relate to health, safety or environmental protection.

NON-UNIFORM COVENANTS. Borrower and Lender further covenant and agree as follows:

21. **Acceleration;** Remedies. Lender shall give notice to Borrower prior to acceleration following Borrower's breach of any covenant or agreement in this Security Instrument (but not prior to acceleration under paragraph 17 unless applicable law provides otherwise). The notice shall specify: (a) the default; (b) the action required to cure the default; (c) a date, not less than 30 days from the date the notice is given to Borrower, by which the default must be cured; and (d) that failure to cure the default on or before the date specified in the notice may result in acceleration of the sums secured by this Security

Instrument and sale of the Property. The notice shall further inform Borrower of the right to reinstate after acceleration and the right to bring a court action to assert the non-existence of a default or any other defense of Borrower to acceleration and sale. If the default is not cured on or before the date specified in the notice, Lender at its option may require immediate payment in full of all sums secured by this Security Instrument without further demand and may invoke the power of sale granted by Borrower and any other remedies permitted by applicable law. Borrower appoints Lender the agent and attorney-in-fact for Borrower to exercise the power of sale. Lender shall be entitled to collect all expenses incurred in pursuing the remedies provided in this paragraph 21, including, but not limited to, reasonable attorneys' fees and costs of title evidence.

If Lender invokes the power of sale, Lender shall give a copy of a notice of sale to Borrower in the manner provided in paragraph 14 and shall give notice of sale by public advertisement for the time and in the manner prescribed by applicable law. Lender, without further demand on Borrower, shall sell the Property at public auction to the highest bidder at the time and place and under the terms designated in the notice of sale in one or more parcels and in any order Lender determines. Lender or its designee may purchase the Property at any sale.

Lender shall convey to the purchaser indefeasible title to the Property, and Borrower hereby appoints Lender Borrower's agent and attorney-in-fact to make such conveyance. The recitals in the Lender's deed shall be prima facie evidence of the truth of the statements made therein. Borrower covenants and agrees that Lender shall apply the proceeds of the sale in the following order: (a) to all expenses of the sale, including, but not limited to, reasonable attorneys' fees; (b) to all sums secured by this Security Instrument; and (c) any excess to the person or persons legally entitled to it. The power and agency granted are coupled with an interest, are irrevocable by death or otherwise and are cumulative to the remedies for collection of debt as provided by law.

If the Property is sold pursuant to this paragraph 21, Borrower, or any person holding possession of the Property through Borrower, shall immediately surrender possession of the Property to the purchaser at the sale. If possession is not surrendered, Borrower or such person shall be a tenant holding over and may be dispossessed in accordance with applicable law.

22. Release. Upon payment of all sums secured by this Security Instrument, Lender shall cancel this Security Instrument without charge to Borrower. Borrower shall pay any recordation costs.

23. Waiver of Homestead. Borrower waives all rights of homestead exemption in the Property.

24. Assumption not a Novation. Lender's acceptance of an assumption of the obligations of this Security Instrument and the Note, and any release of Borrower in connection therewith, shall not constitute a novation.

25. Security Deed. This conveyance is to be construed under the existing laws of the State of Georgia as a deed passing title, and not as a mortgage, and is intended to secure the payment of all sums secured hereby.

26. Riders to this Security Instrument. If one or more riders are executed by Borrower and recorded together with this Security Instrument, the covenants and agreements of each such rider shall be incorporated into and shall amend and supplement the covenants and agreements of this Security Instrument as if the rider(s) were a part of this Security Instrument.

**EXHIBIT 11–7
FNMA Residential
Deed to Secure
Debt
(continued)**

EXHIBIT 11–7
FNMA Residential
Deed to Secure
Debt
(continued)

[Check applicable box(es)]

☐ Adjustable Rate Rider   ☐ Planned Unit Development Rider
☐ Graduated Payment Rider   ☐ Rate Improvement Rider
☐ Balloon Rider   ☐ 1–4 Family Rider
☐ Other(s) [specify]   ☐ Biweekly Payment Rider
☐ Condominium Rider   ☐ Second Home Rider

   BORROWER ACCEPTS AND AGREES to the terms and covenants contained in this Security Instrument and in any rider(s) executed by Borrower and recorded with it. IN WITNESS WHEREOF, Borrower has signed and sealed this Security Instrument.

Signed, sealed and delivered in the presence of:

....(Seal)
Unofficial Witness   –Borrower

                                         Social Security Number ....

....(Seal)
                                                                                            –Borrower

Notary Public, ... County   Social Security Number...

EXHIBIT 11-8
Georgia Commercial
Deed to Secure
Debt

STATE OF GEORGIA

COUNTY OF_____

SECURITY DEED AND AGREEMENT

THIS INDENTURE is made this _____ day of _____, by and between _____,
party of the first part, hereinafter referred to as "Grantor"; and _____
_____ party of the second part, hereinafter referred to as "Grantee";

WITNESSETH:

FOR AND IN CONSIDERATION of the financial accommodations to Grantor by Grantee resulting in the obligation which is hereinafter more particularly described, and in order to secure that obligation, Grantor hereby grants, bargains, conveys, transfers, assigns and sells unto Grantee the following described land:

TOGETHER WITH ANY AND ALL of the following: (i) all buildings, structures and other improvements now or hereafter located thereon or on any part or parcel thereof and all fixtures affixed or attached, actually or constructively, thereto; (ii) all and singular the tenements, hereditaments, easements and appurtenances belonging thereunto or in any wise appertaining thereto and the reversion and reversions, remainder or remainders thereof; (iii) all rents, issues, income, revenues and profits accruing therefrom, whether now or hereafter due; (iv) all accounts and contract rights now or hereafter arising in connection with any part or parcel thereof or any buildings, structures or improvements now or hereafter located thereon, including without limitation all accounts and contract rights in and to all leases or undertakings to lease now or hereafter affecting the land or any buildings, structures, or improvements thereon; (v) all minerals, flowers, crops, trees, timber, shrubbery and other emblements now or hereafter located thereon or thereunder or on or under any part or parcel thereof; (vi) all estates, rights, title and interest therein, or in any part or parcel thereof; (vii) all equipment, machinery, apparatus, fittings, fixtures whether actually or constructively attached thereto and including all trade, domestic and ornamental fixtures, furniture, furnishings and all personal property of every kind or description whatsoever now or hereafter located thereon, or in or on the buildings, structures and other improvements thereon, and used in connection with the operation and maintenance thereof, and all additions thereto and replacements thereof; and (viii) all building materials, supplies, goods and equipment delivered thereto and placed thereon for the purpose of being affixed to or installed or incorporated or otherwise used in the buildings, structures or other improvements now or hereafter located thereon or any part or parcel thereof. All of the foregoing are hereinafter sometimes referred to collectively as the "Premises."

TO HAVE AND TO HOLD the Premises to the only proper use, benefit and behoof of Grantee, forever, in fee simple.

GRANTOR WARRANTS that Grantor has good title to the Premises, that Grantor is lawfully seized and possessed of the Premises, that Grantor has the right to convey the Premises, that the Premises are unencumbered except as may be herein expressly provided and that Grantor shall forever warrant and defend the title to the Premises unto Grantee against the claims of all persons whomsoever.

THIS INSTRUMENT IS A DEED passing legal title pursuant to the laws of the State of Georgia governing deeds to secure debt and a security agreement granting a security interest pursuant to the Uniform Commercial Code of the State of Georgia, and it is not a mortgage. This deed and security agreement is made and intended to secure: (i) an obligation of Grantor to Grantee evidenced as follows:

(ii) any and all renewal or renewals, extension or extensions, modification or modifications thereof, and substitution or substitutions therefor, either in whole or in part; and (iii) all indebtedness now or hereafter owing by Grantor to Grantee, however or whenever created, incurred, arising or evidenced, whether direct or indirect, joint or several, absolute or contingent, or due or to become due, and any and all renewal or renewals, extension or extensions, modification or modifications of and substitution or substitutions for, said indebtedness, either in whole or in part. The obligations which this deed and security agreement is given to secure are hereinafter sometimes referred to collectively as the "Indebtedness." This deed and security agreement is hereinafter sometimes referred to as this "Security Deed."

GRANTOR COVENANTS AND AGREES: (1) *Junior Encumbrances:* Grantor shall not create or permit to exist any liens or encumbrances on the Premises which are junior and inferior in terms of priority to this Security Deed. (2) *Payments by Grantor:* Grantor shall pay, when due and payable: (i) the Indebtedness in accordance with the terms and conditions of the instruments evidencing the same; (ii) all taxes, all assessments, general or special, and all other charges levied on or assessed or placed or made against the Premises, this Security Deed, the Indebtedness or any interest of Grantee in the Premises, this Security Deed or the Indebtedness; (iii) premiums on policies of fire and casualty insurance covering the Premises, as required by this Security Deed; (iv) premiums on all life insurance policies now or hereafter pledged as collateral for the Indebtedness or any part thereof; (v) premiums for all liability, rental, mortgage and flood insurance policies required by this Security Deed or now or hereafter required by Grantee in connection with the Premises or the Indebtedness or any part of either; and (vi) all ground rents, lease rentals and other payments respecting the Premises payable by Grantor. Grantor shall promptly deliver to Grantee, upon request by Grantee, receipts showing payment in full of all the Indebtedness; provided, however, that Grantee shall not require a receipt showing payment in full of the Indebtedness. In the event any state, federal, municipal or other governmental law, order, rule or regulation becomes effective subsequent to the date hereof and in any manner changes or modifies the laws in force on the date hereof governing the taxation of the Indebtedness or the manner of collecting the taxes thereon so as to adversely affect Grantee by requiring that a payment or payments be made or other action be taken to protect Grantee's interest under this Security Deed or the Indebtedness, Grantor shall promptly pay any amounts required on or before the date the same are due or take any other action required on or before the date any such action must be taken. (3) *Grantee's Acts on Behalf of Grantor:* In the event Grantor shall either fail or refuse to pay or cause to be paid, as the same shall become due and payable, any item (including all items specified at Paragraph (2) immediately above) which Grantor is required to pay hereunder or which Grantor may pay to cure an event of default hereunder, or in the event Grantor shall either fail or refuse to do or perform any act which Grantor is obligated to do or perform hereunder or which Grantor may do or perform to cure an event of default hereunder, then Grantee, at Grantee's option, may make such payment or do or perform such act on behalf of Grantor. All such payments made by Grantee and all costs and expenses incurred by Grantee in doing or performing all such acts shall be and shall become part of the Indebtedness secured hereby and shall bear interest at the highest rate per annum then being charged with respect to any part of the Indebtedness secured hereby from the date paid or incurred by Grantee, and such interest thereon shall also be part of the Indebtedness secured hereby. (4) *Further Assurances:* Grantor shall, at any time and from time to time upon request by Grantee, make, execute and deliver, or cause to be made, executed and delivered, any and all other and further instruments, documents, certificates, agreements, letters, representations and other writings which may be necessary or desirable, in the opinion of Grantee, in order to effectuate, complete, correct, perfect or continue and preserve the obligations of Grantor under the Indebtedness and the lien and security interest of Grantee hereunder. Grantor shall upon request by Grantee certify in writing to Grantee, or to any proposed assignee of this Security Deed, the amount of principal and interest then owing on the Indebtedness and whether or not any set-offs or defenses exist against all or any part of the Indebtedness.

EXHIBIT 11-8
Georgia Commercial
Deed to Secure
Debt
(continued)

(5) *Rents and Leases:* Grantor hereby transfers, assigns and conveys unto Grantee all of Grantor's right, title and interest in and to all leases or undertakings to lease now or hereafter existing or made, and all other agreements for use or occupancy, with respect to the Premises or any part thereof, and grants to Grantee a security interest in all rents, issues, income, revenues, profits, accounts and contract rights due or to become due thereunder or otherwise deriving from the use and occupancy of the Premises. Grantor shall faithfully perform the covenants of Grantor as lessor under all present and future leases of all or any portion of the Premises and shall not do, neglect to do, or permit to be done, anything which may cause the termination of such leases, or any of them, or which may diminish or impair their value or the rents provided for therein or the interest of Grantor or Grantee therein or thereunder. Grantor, without first obtaining the written consent of Grantee, shall not further assign the rents, issues, income, revenues, profits, accounts or contract rights from the Premises or any part thereof, shall not consent to the cancellation or surrender of any lease of the Premises or any part thereof now existing or hereafter to be made, shall not modify any such lease so as to shorten the unexpired term thereof or so as to decrease the amount of the rent payable thereunder and shall not collect rents from the Premises or any part thereof for more than one month in advance. Grantor shall procure and deliver to Grantee upon request estoppel letters or certificates from each lessee, tenant, occupant in possession and other user of the Premises or any part thereof, as required by and in form and substance satisfactory to Grantee, and shall deliver to Grantee a recordable assignment of all of Grantor's interest in all leases now or hereafter existing or made with respect to the Premises or any part thereof, which assignment shall be in form and substance satisfactory to Grantee, together with proof of due service of a copy of such assignment on each lessee, tenant, occupant in possession or other user of the Premises or any part thereof. (6) *Maintenance and Repair:* Grantor shall maintain the Premises in good condition and repair, shall not commit or suffer any waste to the Premises, and shall comply with, or cause to be complied with, all statutes, ordinances, rules, regulations and directives of any governmental authority relating to the Premises or any part thereof or the use or occupancy of the Premises or any part thereof. No part of the Premises, including but not limited to any buildings, structures, parking lots, driveways or other improvements now or hereafter constructed on the land which is part of the Premises, shall be removed, demolished or materially altered without the prior written consent of Grantee. If at any time during the continuance of the Indebtedness any addition, alteration, change, repair, reconstruction or other work on the Premises of any nature, structural or otherwise, becomes necessary or desirable because of damage to or destruction of the Premises or any part thereof, the entire expense thereof, regardless of when the same shall be incurred or become due, shall be the sole obligation and responsibility of Grantor, and Grantor shall pay the entire expense thereof promptly when due. (7) *Hazard and Liability Insurance:* Grantor shall keep the Premises insured against loss or damage by fire and such other casualties and risks as the Grantee may require from time to time, with such companies, in such amounts and under such forms of policies as Grantee may approve. Such policies shall insure Grantee's interest in the Premises, name Grantee as an insured party thereunder, provide that losses thereunder shall be payable to Grantee pursuant to such forms of loss payable clauses as Grantee may approve and provide that no cancellation or reduction in coverage shall be effective unless the insuror first gives Grantee thirty (30) days prior written notice. Irrespective of the insurance required and approved by Grantee, Grantor shall assign and deliver to Grantee, as additional collateral for the payment of the Indebtedness, all policies of insurance which insure against loss or damage to the Premises, and Grantor hereby grants to Grantee a security interest in the proceeds from any and all such policies. Grantor shall also procure and maintain public liability insurance coverage with such companies, in such amounts and under such forms of policies as Grantee may approve, naming Grantee as an additional insured thereunder and providing that no cancellation or reduction in coverage thereunder shall be effective unless the insuror first gives Grantee thirty (30) days prior written notice. Forthwith upon the issuance of all such policies, Grantor shall deliver the same to Grantee together with evidence satisfactory to Grantee that the premiums therefor have been paid. Within fifteen (15) days prior to the expiration date of each such policy, Grantor shall deliver to Grantee a renewal policy together with evidence satisfactory to Grantee that the premium therefor has been paid. In the event of a foreclosure and sale by Grantee of the Premises, the purchaser of the Premises shall succeed to all rights of Grantor in and to such policies, including the right to the refund of unearned premiums and to dividends thereunder, and Grantee may, at Grantee's election, assign and deliver the policies to such purchaser without any warranty or representation, express or implied, and without recourse. In the event of damage to or destruction of the Premises or any part thereof, Grantee may adjust, settle or compromise claims under such policies, and the proceeds therefrom shall be paid to Grantee. Grantee, at Grantee's option and in Grantee's sole discretion, may either (i) apply the proceeds or any part thereof to the Indebtedness or (ii) require Grantor to repair, replace or reconstruct the Premises or any part thereof and disburse the proceeds to Grantor to be applied against the costs and expenses thereof as incurred or paid by Grantor. (8) *Flood Insurance:* Grantor represents and has certified to Grantee that no part of the Premises lies within a "special flood hazard area" as defined and specified by the United States Department of Housing and Urban Development pursuant to the Flood Disaster Protection Act of 1973. In the event Grantee determines that the rules or regulations of the Federal Reserve Board, the Comptroller of the Currency or any other governing agency licensing or regulating the operations of Grantee require that flood insurance coverage be obtained for the Premises or any part thereof in order for Grantee to comply with such rules or regulations or with the Flood Disaster Protection Act of 1973 as then in effect, then Grantor, upon receiving written notice from Grantee of such determination: (i) shall promptly purchase and pay the premiums for such flood insurance policies as Grantee deems required by such agency or agencies so that Grantee shall be deemed in compliance with the rules and regulations of such agency or agencies and with the Flood Disaster Protection Act of 1973 as then in effect; and (ii) shall deliver such policies to Grantee together with evidence satisfactory to Grantee that the premiums therefor have been paid. Such policies of flood insurance shall be in a form satisfactory to Grantee, shall name Grantee as an insured thereunder, shall provide that losses thereunder be payable to Grantee pursuant to such forms of loss payable clause as Grantee may approve, shall be for an amount at least equal to the Indebtedness or the maximum limit of coverage made available with respect to the Premises under the National Flood Insurance Act of 1968, as amended, whichever is less, and shall be noncancellable as to Grantee except upon thirty (30) days prior written notice given by the insuror to Grantee. Within ten (10) days prior to the expiration date of each such flood insurance policy, Grantor shall deliver to Grantee a renewal policy or endorsement together with evidence satisfactory to Grantee that the premium therefor has been paid. (9) *Condemnation:* To the extent of the Indebtedness, Grantor grants to Grantee a security interest in any and all payments, awards, judgments or settlements, including interest thereon, to which Grantor may be or may become entitled or which Grantee may receive by reason of injury or damage to, or loss of, the Premises or any part thereof as a result of the exercise of the right of eminent domain. Notwithstanding any injury or damage to, or loss of, the Premises or any part thereof as a result of the exercise of the right of eminent domain, Grantor shall continue to pay the Indebtedness. All sums paid or payable to Grantor by reason of any injury or damage to, or loss of, the Premises or any part thereof as a result of the exercise of the right of eminent domain shall be delivered to Grantee and Grantee, at Grantee's option and at Grantee's sole discretion, may either (i) apply the sum or any part thereof to the Indebtedness or (ii) require Grantor to repair, replace or reconstruct the Premises or any part thereof and disburse such sums to Grantor to be applied against the costs and expenses thereof as incurred or paid by Grantor. (10) *Inspection:* Grantor shall permit any person designated by Grantee to visit and inspect the Premises, to examine the books of account and other records of Grantor with respect to the Premises, and to discuss the affairs, finances and accounts of Grantor with and to be advised as to the same by Grantor or a knowledgeable and duly authorized representative of Grantor, all at such reasonable times and intervals as Grantee may desire. (11) *Restriction on Transfer:* Unless Grantee gives its written consent thereto and such consent is recorded in the public deed records of the Clerk of the Superior Court of the county in which this Security Deed is recorded, Grantor shall not grant, bargain, convey, transfer, assign, exchange or sell all or any portion of Grantor's interest in the Premises prior to the satisfaction and release by Grantee of this Security Deed.

EVENTS OF DEFAULT hereunder shall be the occurrence of any one or more of the following: (1) *Payment of Indebtedness:* Failure of Grantor to pay the Indebtedness or any part thereof when and as the same shall become due and payable, whether at the due date thereof or at a date fixed for prepayment or at a date fixed by reason of acceleration of the due date thereof or otherwise; (2) *Other Payments and Terms:* Failure of Grantor to make any payment (other than on the Indebtedness) required hereunder or to observe, perform, or comply with any of the covenants, terms or conditions set forth herein, or in any other instrument, document, agreement, letter or other writing heretofore, concurrently herewith or in the future executed by Grantor in favor of Grantee in connection with any transaction which resulted in the Indebtedness or any part thereof; (3) *False Statements:* If any certificate, representation, warranty, statement or other writing made herein or heretofore, now or hereafter furnished to Grantee by or on behalf of Grantor in connection with any transaction which resulted in the Indebtedness or any part thereof be false, untrue, incomplete or misleading in any respect as of the date made; (4) *Waste:* If the Premises or any part thereof should be subject to actual or threatened waste, or any part thereof be removed, demolished, or materially damaged or altered as a result of which the value of the Premises shall be diminished; (5) *Seizure or Levy:* If the Premises or any part thereof be seized or levied upon under legal process or a receiver be appointed for the Premises or any part thereof or for Grantor; (6) *Liens:* If any Federal tax lien or any claim of lien for labor, material or architectural or engineering services furnished or alleged to have been furnished in the improvement of or with respect to the Premises is filed of record against Grantor or the Premises and is not removed from record by payment or bond within thirty (30) days from the date of such filing; (7) *Priority Claim:* If any person shall assert any claim of priority over this Security Deed in any legal or equitable proceeding, and such claim shall not have been dismissed with prejudice within sixty (60) days after the filing thereof; (8) *Insolvency or Bankruptcy:* If Grantor shall become insolvent or make an assignment for benefit of creditors; or if Grantor should file a petition for bankruptcy or an arrangement pursuant to the Federal Bankruptcy Act or any similar statute, or if Grantor be adjudicated a bankrupt or an insolvent; or if any proceeding is instituted against or on behalf of Grantor alleging that Grantor is insolvent or unable to pay Grantor's debts as they mature; or if a petition for the bankruptcy or arrangement of Grantor, pursuant to the Federal Bankruptcy Act or any similar statute is filed; (9) *Receiver:* If there should be appointed a receiver, liquidator or trustee for Grantor or for any property of Grantor; (10) *Judgments:* If any judgment is rendered against Grantor which is not paid in full and satisfied or is not appealed from within the time allowed for appeals and paid in full and satisfied when it becomes final; (11) *Liquidation or Dissolution:* Should Grantor, if a corporation, be liquidated or dissolved or its articles of incorporation expire or be revoked, or, if a partnership or business association, be dissolved or partitioned, or, if a trust, be terminated or expire.

EXHIBIT 11-8
Georgia Commercial
Deed to Secure
Debt
(continued)

GRANTEE'S REMEDIES AND POWER OF SALE upon the occurrence of an event of default shall be that, at Grantee's option and election without notice to Grantor, Grantee may declare all or any portion of the Indebtedness to be immediately due and payable, whereupon the same shall be and shall become due and payable forthwith without presentment, demand, protest or notice of any kind, all of which are expressly waived by Grantor, and Grantee, at Grantee's option and election, may do any one or more of the following: (1) *Entry and Possession:* Grantee may enter upon the Premises or any part thereof and take possession thereof, excluding therefrom Grantor and all agents, employees and representatives of Grantor; employ a manager of the Premises or any part thereof; hold, store, use, operate, manage, control, maintain and lease the Premises or any part thereof; conduct business thereon; make all necessary and appropriate repairs, renewals, and replacements; keep the Premises insured; or carry out or enter into agreements of any kind with respect to the Premises. (2) *Collection of Rents:* Grantee may collect and receive all rents, issues, income, revenues, profits, accounts and contract rights from the Premises and apply the same to the Indebtedness, after deducting therefrom all costs, charges, and expenses of taking, holding, managing, and operating the Premises, including the fees and expenses of Grantee's attorneys, and agents. (3) *Payments:* Grantee may pay any sum or sums deemed necessary or appropriate by Grantee to protect the Premises or any part thereof or Grantee's interest therein. (4) *Other Remedies:* Grantee may exercise all rights and remedies contained in any other instrument, document, agreement or other writing, heretofore, concurrently herewith or in the future executed by Grantor in favor of Grantee in connection with the transactions resulting in the Indebtedness or any part thereof. (5) *Appointment of Receiver:* Grantee may make application to any court and shall be entitled to the appointment of a receiver to take charge of the Premises or any part thereof without alleging or proving, or having any consideration given to, the insolvency of Grantor, the value of the Premises as security for the Indebtedness or any other matter usually incident to the appointment of a receiver. (6) *U.C.C. Remedies:* With respect to the personal property in which a security interest is herein granted, Grantee may exercise any or all of the rights accruing to a secured party under this Security Deed, the Uniform Commercial Code (§§109A-9-101 *et. seq.* of the Ga. Code Annotated) and any other applicable law. Grantor shall, if Grantee requests, assemble all such personal property and make it available to Grantee at a place or places to be designated by Grantee, which shall be reasonably convenient to Grantor and Grantee. Any notice required to be given by Grantee of a public or private sale, lease or other disposition of the personal property or any other intended action by Grantee may be personally delivered to Grantor or may be deposited in the United States mail with postage prepaid duly addressed to Grantor at the address of Grantor last known to Grantee at least five (5) business days prior to such proposed action, and shall constitute reasonable and fair notice to Grantor of any such action. (7) *Power of Sale:* Grantee may sell the Premises, or any part thereof or any interest therein separately, at Grantee's discretion, with or without taking possession thereof, at public sale before the courthouse door of the county in which the Premises, or a part thereof, is located, to the highest bidder for cash, after first giving notice of the time, place and terms of such sale by advertisement published once a week for four weeks (without regard for the number of days) in a newspaper in which advertisements of sheriff's sales are published in such county. The advertisement so published shall be notice to Grantor, and Grantor hereby waives all other notices. Grantee may bid and purchase at any such sale, and the Grantee may execute and deliver to the purchaser or purchasers at any such sale a sufficient conveyance of the Premises, or the part thereof or interest therein sold. Grantee's conveyance may contain recitals as to the occurrence of any event of default under this Security Deed, which recitals shall be presumptive evidence that all preliminary acts prerequisite to such sale and conveyance were in all things duly complied with. The recitals made by Grantee shall be binding and conclusive upon Grantor, and the sale and conveyance shall divest Grantor of all right, title, interest and equity that Grantor may have had in, to and under the Premises, or the part thereof or interest therein sold, and shall vest the same in the purchaser or purchasers at such sale. Grantee may hold one or more sales hereunder until the Indebtedness has been satisfied in full. Grantor hereby constitutes and appoints Grantee as Grantor's agent and attorney-in-fact to make such sale, to execute and deliver such conveyance and to make such recitals, and Grantor hereby ratifies and confirms all of the acts and doings of Grantee as Grantor's agent and attorney-in-fact hereunder. Grantee's agency and power as attorney-in-fact hereunder are coupled with an interest, cannot be revoked by insolvency, incompetency, death or otherwise, and shall not be exhausted until the Indebtedness has been satisfied in full. The proceeds of each sale by Grantee hereunder shall be applied first to the costs and expenses of the sale and of all proceedings in connection therewith, including attorney's fees if applicable, then to the payment of the Indebtedness, and the remainder, if any, shall be paid to Grantor. If the proceeds of any sale are not sufficient to pay the Indebtedness in full, Grantee shall determine, at Grantee's option and in Grantee's discretion, the portions of the Indebtedness to which the proceeds (after deducting therefrom the costs and expenses of the sale and all proceedings in connection therewith) shall be applied and in what order the proceeds shall be so applied. Grantor covenants and agrees that, in the event of any sale pursuant to the agency and power herein granted, Grantor shall be and become a tenant holding over and shall deliver possession of the Premises, or the part thereof or interest therein sold, to the purchaser or purchasers at the sale or be summarily dispossessed in accordance with the provisions of law applicable to tenants holding over.

All rights and remedies set forth above are cumulative and in addition to any right or remedy provided for by statute, or now or hereafter existing at law or in equity, including without limitation the right of Grantee to collect or enforce the Indebtedness with or without taking any action with respect to the Premises. Grantee may, at Grantee's election and at Grantee's discretion, exercise each and every such right and remedy concurrently or separately.

ADDITIONAL PROVISIONS of this Security Deed, constituting additional covenants and agreements by Grantor, are as follows: (1) *Applicable Law:* This Security Deed shall be governed by and construed, interpreted and enforced in accordance with the laws of the State of Georgia. (2) *Forbearance:* Grantee shall not be deemed to waive any of Grantee's rights or remedies hereunder unless such waiver be in writing and signed by or on behalf of Grantee. No delay, omission or forbearance by Grantee in exercising any of Grantee's rights or remedies shall operate as a waiver of such rights or remedies, and a waiver in writing on one occasion shall not be construed as a consent to or a waiver of any right or any remedy on any future occasion. (3) *Time:* Time is and shall be of the essence of this Security Deed and the covenants and agreements by Grantor. (4) *Captions:* Any captions or heading preceding the text of separate sections, paragraphs and sub-paragraphs hereof are solely for reference purposes and shall not affect the meaning, construction, interpretation or effect of the text. (5) *Notices:* All notices, requests, demands and other communications hereunder shall be in writing and shall be deemed to have been duly given to Grantor if personally delivered or if mailed in the United States mail, by certified mail with a return receipt requested and with postage prepaid, to Grantor's last address known to Grantee. (6) *Severability:* In the event that any of the terms, provisions or covenants of this Security Deed are held to be partially or wholly invalid or unenforceable for any reason whatsoever, such holding shall not affect, alter, modify or impair in any manner whatsoever any of the other terms, provisions or covenants hereof not held to be partially or wholly invalid or unenforceable. (7) *Definitions:* The word "Grantor" as used herein shall include the plural should more than one Grantor execute this document; the masculine and feminine gender, regardless of the sex of Grantor or any of them; individuals, partnerships, joint ventures, corporations and other legal entities should such an entity execute this document; and the heirs, legal representatives, successors and assigns of Grantor. If more than one party shall execute this Security Deed, the word "Grantor" shall mean all parties signing, and each of them, and each and every agreement and obligation of Grantor shall be and mean the joint and several undertaking of each of them. The word "Grantee" as used herein shall include the transferees, successors, legal representatives and assigns of Grantee, and all rights of Grantee hereunder shall inure to the benefit of its transferees, successors, legal representatives and assigns. (8) *Other Provisions:* The terms and conditions set forth in Exhibit "B", if any, attached hereto are incorporated herein and made a part hereof by reference.

GRANTOR EXPRESSLY WAIVES the following: (1) *Notice and Hearing:* Any right Grantor may have under the Constitution of the State of Georgia or the Constitution of the United States of America to notice or to a judicial hearing prior to the exercise of any right or remedy provided to Grantee by this Security Deed, and Grantor waives Grantor's rights, if any, to set aside or invalidate any sale under power duly consummated in accordance with the provisions of this Security Deed on the ground (if such be the case) that the sale was consummated without prior notice or judicial hearing or both; and (2) all homestead exemption rights, if any, which Grantor or Grantor's family may have pursuant to the Constitution and laws of the United States, the State of Georgia or any other State of the United States, in and to the Premises as against the collection of the Indebtedness, or any part thereof. All waivers by Grantor in this paragraph have been made voluntarily, intelligently and knowingly by Grantor, after Grantor has been afforded an opportunity to be informed by counsel of Grantor's choice as to possible alternative rights. Grantor's execution of this Security Deed shall be conclusive evidence of the making of such waivers and that such waivers have been voluntarily, intelligently and knowingly made.

IN WITNESS WHEREOF, this Security Deed has been executed and sealed by Grantor the day and year first above written.

Signed, sealed and delivered
in the presence of:

_____(SEAL)

_____

Unofficial Witness   _____(SEAL)

_____

Notary Public   _____(SEAL)

Commercial Loan Department

Security Deed Form No. _____   _____(SEAL)

First Priority Lien Position

(Second Priority By Attaching Exhibit "B")

- 3 -

Mortgage Forms and Provisions

Mortgage. A thing about a house that gets the most interest.

—*Evan Esar,* Esar's Comic Dictionary

OBJECTIVES

After reading this chapter you will be able to:

- Understand the provisions contained in residential and commercial mortgages
- Understand the provisions contained in a construction loan agreement
- Understand the provisions contained in an assignment of leases and rents

GLOSSARY

Assigns   Persons who obtain the rights to a contract or other legal document by transfer from an original party to the contract or document.

Certificate of occupancy   Permit issued by an appropriate governmental authority granting occupancy to newly constructed improvements. The certificate usually is evidence that the improvements comply with all zoning, building codes, and health and fire regulations.

Exculpation   A real estate loan in which the borrower is not personally responsible for the repayment of the loan. If the loan is not repaid, the borrower will lose the real property pledged as security for the loan. The borrower will not be personally sued for payment of the loan.

Financing statement   Form that is recorded to give notice that there is a security interest in personal property owned by a debtor.

Habendum   Clause found in a deed or mortgage that indicates what estate in real property is being transferred by the deed or mortgage.

Homestead   Property that is exempt from creditors. A homestead cannot be seized by creditors and sold to satisfy debts.

Improvements   Permanent structures located on real property, such as a house or an office building.

Joint and several liability   Each borrower is fully responsible for the payment of the entire debt.

Novation   Substitution of parties to a contract to such an extent that the law declares that a new contract has been entered into. For example, A and B enter into a contract. A assigns its rights under the contract to C, who assumes all of A's obligations to perform under the contract. The law may declare that a novation has taken place; therefore, the old contract between A and B no longer exists and a new contract between B and C now exists.

Receiver   Third party appointed by a court to take possession of mortgaged property in the event of a mortgage default. The receiver's responsibilities are to collect the rents from the property and to maintain the property in good repair.

Retainage   Portion of the loan proceeds held by a construction lender until the construction is com-

Although the primary purpose of a mortgage is to convey real property to a lender to secure repayment of a debt, most mortgage documents address a wide range of issues of importance to the borrower and lender. For example, the lender wants assurance that property taxes will be paid on a current basis and that all buildings and improvements are insured with adequate insurance coverages during the term of the loan. A borrower may want the right to receive a notice of any default under the loan and an opportunity to cure the default before the mortgage is foreclosed. These and other matters are routinely covered in mortgage loan documents.

Mortgage loan documents are signed by a borrower each time a loan is secured by real property. These mortgage loan documents often are prepared by the legal assistant as part of the real estate closing process, which is discussed further in Chapters 15 through 17. It is, therefore, important for a legal assistant to be familiar with the contents of the various mortgage loan documents used in residential and commercial real estate loan transactions.

New York:
This chapter refers to the federal forms which are uniform throughout the state. The commercial clauses could also be applied in New York depending upon the situation.

RESIDENTIAL MORTGAGE PROVISIONS

The instrument set forth in Exhibit 12–1 is an FNMA/FHLMC uniform instrument. It is used to secure most residential loans throughout the nation. Brief explanations of the provisions contained in this mortgage follow.

Part A lists the date of the mortgage and the identity of the grantor, who will be the property owner. The grantor's identification should be shown exactly as it appears in the grantor's deed in the chain of title. The mortgagee, or lender, is the lending institution making the loan. The grantee's name should be identified as it officially appears on the lender's corporate records.

Part B describes the debt being secured by the mortgage. The debt typically is described as a debt evidenced by a note dated the same date of the mortgage and provided with a final maturity date. The statute of limitations enforcing a mortgage typically is twenty years from the date of the final maturity of the note. If the final maturity of the note is not revealed in the mortgage, it is twenty years from the date of the mortgage. Because many residential mortgage loans have a maturity greater than twenty years, it is important to show the final maturity date of the note in the mortgage.

Part C describes the real property being conveyed as security for the loan. The description must be complete. It should match any surveys for the real property as well as the description contained in the borrower's deed to the real property.

Part D is a **habendum** clause to a mortgage. It provides that in addition to the real property being conveyed as security, all easements, rights, appurtenances, rents, royalties, mineral and gas rights, and so on are conveyed. The intent is for the lender to receive everything the borrower owns in connection with the real property.

Part E is a warranty paragraph. The borrower sets out the same warranties that usually are found in a general warranty deed.

The uniform covenants include the following.

Covenant 1, Payment of Principal and Interest; Prepayment and Late Charges, is a reaffirmation of the promise to pay the debt when it is due, including any prepayment and late charges due under the note. Even though this promise is contained in the note being secured by the mortgage, most lenders have the promise repeated in the mortgage.

Covenant 2, Funds for Taxes and Insurance, is known as an escrow provision in a mortgage. The lender is concerned that taxes be paid on the real property and that the real property be insured against fire and other casualties. Because of the lender's concern about these two items, the lender requires the borrower to pay monthly, together with the monthly payment on the note, 1/12 of the annual taxes and 1/12 of the annual insurance premiums. These funds are escrowed by the lender and used to pay the taxes and insurance premiums when they become due. Typically, the funds are held by the lender interest-free and can be commingled with other funds of the lender.

Covenant 3, Application of Payments, provides that if a payment is made that is not sufficient to cover all the charges payable on the mortgage, the allocation of the partial payment will be applied first to late charges on the note, second to prepayment charges on the note, third to escrow deposits, fourth to interest, and fifth to the debt itself. The debt is reduced last, after all other charges have been paid.

In *Covenant 4, Charges; Liens*, the borrower promises to keep the real property lien-free and to pay any and all other charges and assessments that may be assessed against the real property.

Covenant 5, Hazard or Property Insurance, requires the borrower to purchase insurance, with the lender as mortgagee, under a standard loss payable mortgage clause. Because most of the value of the real property securing the loan will be in **improvements** that can be destroyed by fire and other casualty, the lender is careful to provide detailed descriptions of insurance requirements in the mortgage. The lender has the right to approve the insurance policy and is entitled to notice before the expiration of the insurance policy. The insurance proceeds usually are payable jointly to the lender and the borrower, and may be used either to restore the improvements or to repay the debt.

Covenant 6, Occupancy, Preservation, Maintenance and Protection of the Property; Borrower's Loan Application; Leaseholds. This paragraph contains a number of covenants on the part of the borrower. The borrower covenants that it will occupy and use the property as the borrower's principal residence within sixty days after the execution of the mortgage and will continue to use it as a principal residence for at least one year after the date of occupancy. The borrower agrees to maintain the real property and its improvements in good repair and not to commit any waste. The borrower agrees that it will be a default under the loan if it, in its loan application, gave any materially false or inaccurate information or statements to the lender.

Covenant 7, Protection of Lender's Rights in the Property, provides that if the borrower fails to perform any of the promises or covenants under the mortgage (e.g., pay taxes and insurance and keep the property in good repair), the lender may pay these charges and take whatever action is necessary to protect the property and its improvements. The cost of doing so is assessed against the borrower and is secured by the mortgage.

Covenant 8, Mortgage Insurance, provides that if the loan is insured by private mortgage insurance, the borrower will pay the premiums before they become due and delinquent. In the event that mortgage insurance becomes unavailable, the borrower agrees to pay a sum equal to 1/12 of the yearly mortgage insurance premium each month to the lender to be held as a loss reserve in lieu of mortgage insurance.

Covenant 9, Inspection, gives the lender the right to inspect the real property at reasonable times. Inspections of residential property are rare unless the real property has been abandoned. In commercial loans, it is not unusual for the lender to make an annual inspection of the real property.

EXHIBIT 12–1
Georgia FNMA/FHLMC Uniform Instrument

SECURITY DEED

A THIS SECURITY DEED ("Security Instrument") is given on .... , 19 .... The grantor is .... ("Borrower"). This Security Instrument is given to .... , which is organized and existing under the laws of .... , and whose address is .... ("Lender").

B Borrower owes Lender the principal sum of .... Dollars (U.S. $ ....). This debt is evidenced by Borrower's note dated the same date as this Security Instrument ("Note"), which provides for monthly payments, with the full debt, if not paid earlier, due and payable on .... This Security Instrument secures to Lender: (a) the repayment of the debt evidenced by the Note, with interest, and all renewals, extensions and modifications of the Note; (b) the payment of all other sums, with interest, advanced under paragraph 7 to protect the security of this Security Instrument; and (c) the performance of Borrower's covenants and agreements under this Security Instrument and the Note. For this purpose, Borrower does hereby grant and convey to Lender and Lender's successors and assigns, with power of sale, the following described property located in .... County, Georgia:

C

which has the address of .... , ... ,
[Street] [City]
Georgia .... ("Property Address");
[Zip Code]

D TO HAVE AND TO HOLD this property unto Lender and Lender's successors and assigns, forever, together with all the improvements now or hereafter erected on the property, and all easements, appurtenances, and fixtures now or hereafter a part of the property. All replacements and additions shall also be covered by this Security Instrument. All of the foregoing is referred to in this Security Instrument as the "Property."

E BORROWER COVENANTS that Borrower is lawfully seised of the estate hereby conveyed and has the right to grant and convey the Property and that the Property is unencumbered, except for encumbrances of record. Borrower warrants and will defend generally the title to the Property against all claims and demands, subject to any encumbrances of record.

EXHIBIT 12-1
Georgia FNMA/FHLMC Uniform Instrument
(continued)

THIS SECURITY INSTRUMENT combines uniform covenants for national use and non-uniform covenants with limited variations by jurisdiction to constitute a uniform security instrument covering real property.

UNIFORM COVENANTS. Borrower and Lender covenant and agree as follows:

1. Payment of Principal and Interest; Prepayment and Late Charges. Borrower shall promptly pay when due the principal of and interest on the debt evidenced by the Note and any prepayment and late charges due under the Note.

2. Funds for Taxes and Insurance. Subject to applicable law or to a written waiver by Lender, Borrower shall pay to Lender on the day monthly payments are due under the Note, until the Note is paid in full, a sum ("Funds") for: (a) yearly taxes and assessments which may attain priority over this Security Instrument as a lien on the Property; (b) yearly leasehold payments or ground rents on the Property, if any; (c) yearly hazard or property insurance premiums; (d) yearly flood insurance premiums, if any; (e) yearly mortgage insurance premiums, if any; and (f) any sums payable by Borrower to Lender, in accordance with the provisions of paragraph 8, in lieu of the payment of mortgage insurance premiums. These items are called "Escrow Items." Lender may, at any time, collect and hold Funds in an amount not to exceed the maximum amount a lender for a federally related mortgage loan may require for Borrower's escrow account under the federal Real Estate Settlement Procedures Act of 1974 as amended from time to time, 12 U.S.C. § 2601 *et seq.* ("RESPA"), unless another law that applies to the Funds sets a lesser amount. If so, Lender may, at any time, collect and hold Funds in an amount not to exceed the lesser amount. Lender may estimate the amount of Funds due on the basis of current data and reasonable estimates of expenditures of future Escrow Items or otherwise in accordance with applicable law.

The Funds shall be held in an institution whose deposits are insured by a federal agency, instrumentality, or entity (including Lender, if Lender is such an institution) or in any Federal Home Loan Bank. Lender shall apply the Funds to pay the Escrow Items. Lender may not charge Borrower for holding and applying the Funds, annually analyzing the escrow account, or verifying the Escrow Items, unless Lender pays Borrower interest on the Funds and applicable law permits Lender to make such a charge. However, Lender may require Borrower to pay a one-time charge for an independent real estate tax reporting service used by Lender in connection with this loan, unless applicable law provides otherwise. Unless an agreement is made or applicable law requires interest to be paid, Lender shall not be required to pay Borrower any interest or earnings on the Funds. Borrower and Lender may agree in writing, however, that interest shall be paid on the Funds. Lender shall give to Borrower, without charge, an annual accounting of the Funds, showing credits and debits to the Funds and the purpose for which each debit to the Funds was made. The Funds are pledged as additional security for all sums secured by this Security Instrument.

If the Funds held by Lender exceed the amounts permitted to be held by applicable law, Lender shall account to Borrower for the excess Funds in accordance with the requirements of applicable law. If the amount of the Funds held by Lender at any time is not sufficient to pay the Escrow Items when due, Lender may so notify Borrower in writing, and, in such case Borrower shall pay to Lender the amount necessary to make up the deficiency. Borrower shall make up the deficiency in no more than twelve monthly payments, at Lender's sole discretion.

Upon payment in full of all sums secured by this Security Instrument, Lender shall promptly refund to Borrower any Funds held by Lender. If, under paragraph 21, Lender shall acquire or sell the Property, Lender, prior to the acquisition or sale of the Property, shall apply any Funds held by Lender at the time of acquisition or sale as a credit against the sums secured by this Security Instrument.

3. Application of Payments. Unless applicable law provides otherwise, all payments received by Lender under paragraphs 1 and 2 shall be applied: first, to any prepayment charges due under the Note; second, to amounts payable under paragraph 2; third, to interest due; fourth, to principal due; and last, to any late charges due under the Note.

4. Charges; Liens. Borrower shall pay all taxes, assessments, charges, fines and impositions attributable to the Property which may attain priority over this Security Instrument, and leasehold payments or ground rents, if any. Borrower shall pay these obligations in the manner provided in paragraph 2, or if not paid in that manner, Borrower shall pay them on time directly to the person owed payment. Borrower shall promptly furnish to Lender all notices of amounts to be paid under this paragraph. If Borrower makes these payments directly, Borrower shall promptly furnish to Lender receipts evidencing the payments.

Borrower shall promptly discharge any lien which has priority over this Security Instrument unless Borrower: (a) agrees in writing to the payment of the obligation secured by the lien in a manner acceptable to Lender; (b) contests in good faith the lien by, or defends against enforcement of the lien in, legal proceedings which in the Lender's opinion operate to prevent the enforcement of the lien; or (c) secures from the holder of the lien an agreement satisfactory to Lender subordinating the lien to this Security Instrument. If Lender determines that any part of the Property is subject to a lien which may attain priority over this Security Instrument, Lender may give Borrower a notice identifying the lien. Borrower shall satisfy the lien or take one or more of the actions set forth above within 10 days of the giving of notice.

5. Hazard or Property Insurance. Borrower shall keep the improvements now existing or hereafter erected on the Property insured against loss by fire, hazards included within the term "extended coverage" and any other hazards, including floods or flooding, for which Lender requires insurance. This insurance shall be maintained in the amounts and

EXHIBIT 12-1
Georgia FNMA/FHLMC Uniform Instrument
(continued)

for the periods that Lender requires. The insurance carrier providing the insurance shall be chosen by Borrower subject to Lender's approval which shall not be unreasonably withheld. If Borrower fails to maintain coverage described above, Lender may, at Lender's option, obtain coverage to protect Lender's rights in the Property in accordance with paragraph 7.

All insurance policies and renewals shall be acceptable to Lender and shall include a standard mortgage clause. Lender shall have the right to hold the policies and renewals. If Lender requires, Borrower shall promptly give to Lender all receipts of paid premiums and renewal notices. In the event of loss, Borrower shall give prompt notice to the insurance carrier and Lender. Lender may make proof of loss if not made promptly by Borrower.

Unless Lender and Borrower otherwise agree in writing, insurance proceeds shall be applied to restoration or repair of the Property damaged, if the restoration or repair is economically feasible and Lender's security is not lessened. If the restoration or repair is not economically feasible or Lender's security would be lessened, the insurance proceeds shall be applied to the sums secured by this Security Instrument, whether or not then due, with any excess paid to Borrower. If Borrower abandons the Property, or does not answer within 30 days a notice from Lender that the insurance carrier has offered to settle a claim, then Lender may collect the insurance proceeds. Lender may use the proceeds to repair or restore the Property or to pay sums secured by this Security Instrument, whether or not then due. The 30-day period will begin when the notice is given.

Unless Lender and Borrower otherwise agree in writing, any application of proceeds to principal shall not extend or postpone the due date of the monthly payments referred to in paragraphs 1 and 2 or change the amount of the payments. If under paragraph 21 the Property is acquired by Lender, Borrower's right to any insurance policies and proceeds resulting from damage to the Property prior to the acquisition shall pass to Lender to the extent of the sums secured by this Security Instrument immediately prior to the acquisition.

   6. Occupancy, Preservation, Maintenance and Protection of the Property; Borrower's Loan Application; Leaseholds. Borrower shall occupy, establish, and use the Property as Borrower's principal residence within sixty days after the execution of this Security Instrument and shall continue to occupy the Property as Borrower's principal residence for at least one year after the date of occupancy, unless Lender otherwise agrees in writing, which consent shall not be unreasonably withheld, or unless extenuating circumstances exist which are beyond Borrower's control. Borrower shall not destroy, damage or impair the Property, allow the Property to deteriorate, or commit waste on the Property. Borrower shall be in default if any forfeiture action or proceeding, whether civil or criminal, is begun that in Lender's good faith judgment could result in forfeiture of the Property or otherwise materially impair the lien created by this Security Instrument or Lender's security interest. Borrower may cure such a default and reinstate, as provided in paragraph 18, by causing the action or proceeding to be dismissed with a ruling that, in Lender's good faith determination, precludes forfeiture of the Borrower's interest in the Property or other material impairment of the lien created by this Security Instrument or Lender's security interest. Borrower shall also be in default if Borrower, during the loan application process, gave materially false or inaccurate information or statements to Lender (or failed to provide Lender with any material information) in connection with the loan evidenced by the Note, including, but not limited to, representations concerning Borrower's occupancy of the Property as a principal residence. If this Security Instrument is on a leasehold, Borrower shall comply with all the provisions of the lease. If Borrower acquires fee title to the Property, the leasehold and the fee title shall not merge unless Lender agrees to the merger in writing.

   7. Protection of Lender's Rights in the Property. If Borrower fails to perform the covenants and agreements contained in this Security Instrument, or there is a legal proceeding that may significantly affect Lender's rights in the Property (such as a proceeding in bankruptcy, probate, for condemnation or forfeiture or to enforce laws or regulations), then Lender may do and pay for whatever is necessary to protect the value of the Property and Lender's rights in the Property. Lender's actions may include paying any sums secured by a lien which has priority over this Security Instrument, appearing in court, paying reasonable attorneys' fees and entering on the Property to make repairs. Although Lender may take action under this paragraph 7, Lender does not have to do so.

   Any amounts disbursed by Lender under this paragraph 7 shall become additional debt of Borrower secured by this Security Instrument. Unless Borrower and Lender agree to other terms of payment, these amounts shall bear interest from the date of disbursement at the Note rate and shall be payable, with interest, upon notice from Lender to Borrower requesting payment.

   8. Mortgage Insurance. If Lender required mortgage insurance as a condition of making the loan secured by this Security Instrument, Borrower shall pay the premiums required to maintain the mortgage insurance in effect. If, for any reason, the mortgage insurance coverage required by Lender lapses or ceases to be in effect, Borrower shall pay the premiums required to obtain coverage substantially equivalent to the mortgage insurance previously in effect, at a cost substantially equivalent to the cost to Borrower of the mortgage insurance previously in effect, from an alternate mortgage insurer approved by Lender. If substantially equivalent mortgage insurance coverage is not available, Borrower shall pay to Lender each month a sum equal to one-twelfth of the yearly mortgage insurance premium being paid by Borrower when the insurance coverage lapsed or ceased to be in effect. Lender will accept, use and retain these payments as a loss reserve in lieu of mortgage insurance. Loss reserve payments may no longer be required, at the option of Lender, if mortgage insurance coverage (in

EXHIBIT 12-1
Georgia FNMA/FHLMC Uniform Instrument
(continued)

the amount and for the period that Lender requires) provided by an insurer approved by Lender again becomes available and is obtained. Borrower shall pay the premiums required to maintain mortgage insurance in effect, or to provide a loss reserve, until the requirement for mortgage insurance ends in accordance with any written agreement between Borrower and Lender or applicable law.

9. Inspection. Lender or its agent may make reasonable entries upon and inspections of the Property. Lender shall give Borrower notice at the time of or prior to an inspection specifying reasonable cause for the inspection.

10. Condemnation. The proceeds of any award or claim for damages, direct or consequential, in connection with any condemnation or other taking of any part of the Property, or for conveyance in lieu of condemnation, are hereby assigned and shall be paid to Lender.

In the event of a total taking of the Property, the proceeds shall be applied to the sums secured by this Security Instrument, whether or not then due, with any excess paid to Borrower. In the event of a partial taking of the Property in which the fair market value of the Property immediately before the taking is equal to or greater than the amount of the sums secured by this Security Instrument immediately before the taking, unless Borrower and Lender otherwise agree in writing, the sums secured by this Security Instrument shall be reduced by the amount of the proceeds multiplied by the following fraction: (a) the total amount of the sums secured immediately before the taking, divided by (b) the fair market value of the Property immediately before the taking. Any balance shall be paid to Borrower. In the event of a partial taking of the Property in which the fair market value of the Property immediately before the taking is less than the amount of the sums secured immediately before the taking, unless Borrower and Lender otherwise agree in writing or unless applicable law otherwise provides, the proceeds shall be applied to the sums secured by this Security Instrument whether or not the sums are then due.

If the Property is abandoned by Borrower, or if, after notice by Lender to Borrower that the condemnor offers to make an award or settle a claim for damages, Borrower fails to respond to Lender within 30 days after the date the notice is given, Lender is authorized to collect and apply the proceeds, at its option, either to restoration or repair of the Property or to the sums secured by this Security Instrument, whether or not then due.

Unless Lender and Borrower otherwise agree in writing, any application of proceeds to principal shall not extend or postpone the due date of the monthly payments referred to in paragraphs 1 and 2 or change the amount of such payments.

11. Borrower Not Released; Forbearance By Lender Not a Waiver. Extension of the time for payment or modification of amortization of the sums secured by this Security Instrument granted by Lender to any successor in interest of Borrower shall not operate to release the liability of the original Borrower or Borrower's successors in interest. Lender shall not be required to commence proceedings against any successor in interest or refuse to extend time for payment or otherwise modify amortization of the sums secured by this Security Instrument by reason of any demand made by the original Borrower or Borrower's successors in interest. Any forbearance by Lender in exercising any right or remedy shall not be a waiver of or preclude the exercise of any right or remedy.

12. Successors and Assigns Bound; Joint and Several Liability; Co-signers. The covenants and agreements of this Security Instrument shall bind and benefit the successors and assigns of Lender and Borrower, subject to the provisions of paragraph 17. Borrower's covenants and agreements shall be joint and several. Any Borrower who co-signs this Security Instrument but does not execute the Note: (a) is co-signing this Security Instrument only to mortgage, grant and convey that Borrower's interest in the Property under the terms of this Security Instrument; (b) is not personally obligated to pay the sums secured by this Security Instrument; and (c) agrees that Lender and any other Borrower may agree to extend, modify, forbear or make any accommodations with regard to the terms of this Security Instrument or the Note without that Borrower's consent.

13. Loan Charges. If the loan secured by this Security Instrument is subject to a law which sets maximum loan charges, and that law is finally interpreted so that the interest or other loan charges collected or to be collected in connection with the loan exceed the permitted limits, then: (a) any such loan charge shall be reduced by the amount necessary to reduce the charge to the permitted limit; and (b) any sums already collected from Borrower which exceeded permitted limits will be refunded to Borrower. Lender may choose to make this refund by reducing the principal owed under the Note or by making a direct payment to Borrower. If a refund reduces principal, the reduction will be treated as a partial prepayment without any prepayment charge under the Note.

14. Notices. Any notice to Borrower provided for in this Security Instrument shall be given by delivering it or by mailing it by first class mail unless applicable law requires use of another method. The notice shall be directed to the Property Address or any other address Borrower designates by notice to Lender. Any notice to Lender shall be given by first class mail to Lender's address stated herein or any other address Lender designates by notice to Borrower. Any notice provided for in this Security Instrument shall be deemed to have been given to Borrower or Lender when given as provided in this paragraph.

15. Governing Law; Severability. This Security Instrument shall be governed by federal law and the law of the jurisdiction in which the Property is located. In the event that any provision or clause of this Security Instrument or the Note conflicts with applicable law, such conflict shall not affect other provisions of this Security Instrument or the Note which can be given effect without the conflicting provision. To this end the provisions of this Security Instrument and the Note are declared to be severable.

EXHIBIT 12-1
Georgia FNMA/FHLMC Uniform Instrument
(continued)

16. Borrower's Copy. Borrower shall be given one conformed copy of the Note and of this Security Instrument.

17. Transfer of the Property or a Beneficial Interest in Borrower. If all or any part of the Property or any interest in it is sold or transferred (or if a beneficial interest in Borrower is sold or transferred and Borrower is not a natural person) without Lender's prior written consent, Lender may, at its option, require immediate payment in full of all sums secured by this Security Instrument. However, this option shall not be exercised by Lender if exercise is prohibited by federal law as of the date of this Security Instrument.

If Lender exercises this option, Lender shall give Borrower notice of acceleration. The notice shall provide a period of not less than 30 days from the date the notice is delivered or mailed within which Borrower must pay all sums secured by this Security Instrument. If Borrower fails to pay these sums prior to the expiration of this period, Lender may invoke any remedies permitted by this Security Instrument without further notice or demand on Borrower.

18. Borrower's Right to Reinstate. If Borrower meets certain conditions, Borrower shall have the right to have enforcement of this Security Instrument discontinued at any time prior to the earlier of: (a) 5 days (or such other period as applicable law may specify for reinstatement) before sale of the Property pursuant to any power of sale contained in this Security Instrument; or (b) entry of a judgment enforcing this Security Instrument. Those conditions are that Borrower: (a) pays Lender all sums which then would be due under this Security Instrument and the Note as if no acceleration had occurred; (b) cures any default of any other covenants or agreements; (c) pays all expenses incurred in enforcing this Security Instrument, including, but not limited to, reasonable attorneys' fees; and (d) takes such action as Lender may reasonably require to assure that the lien of this Security Instrument, Lender's rights in the Property and Borrower's obligation to pay the sums secured by this Security Instrument shall continue unchanged. Upon reinstatement by Borrower, this Security Instrument and the obligations secured hereby shall remain fully effective as if no acceleration had occurred. However, this right to reinstate shall not apply in the case of acceleration under paragraph 17.

19. Sale of Note; Change of Loan Servicer. The Note or a partial interest in the Note (together with this Security Instrument) may be sold one or more times without prior notice to Borrower. A sale may result in a change in the entity (known as the "Loan Servicer") that collects monthly payments due under the Note and this Security Instrument. There also may be one or more changes of the Loan Servicer unrelated to a sale of the Note. If there is a change of the Loan Servicer, Borrower will be given written notice of the change in accordance with paragraph 14 above and applicable law. The notice will state the name and address of the new Loan Servicer and the address to which payments should be made. The notice will also contain any other information required by applicable law.

20. Hazardous Substances. Borrower shall not cause or permit the presence, use, disposal, storage, or release of any Hazardous Substances on or in the Property. Borrower shall not do, nor allow anyone else to do, anything affecting the Property that is in violation of any Environmental Law. The preceding two sentences shall not apply to the presence, use, or storage on the Property of small quantities of Hazardous Substances that are generally recognized to be appropriate to normal residential uses and to maintenance of the Property.

Borrower shall promptly give Lender written notice of any investigation, claim, demand, lawsuit or other action by any governmental or regulatory agency or private party involving the Property and any Hazardous Substance or Environmental Law of which Borrower has actual knowledge. If Borrower learns, or is notified by any governmental or regulatory authority, that any removal or other remediation of any Hazardous Substance affecting the Property is necessary, Borrower shall promptly take all necessary remedial actions in accordance with Environmental Law.

As used in this paragraph 20, "Hazardous Substances" are those substances defined as toxic or hazardous substances by Environmental Law and the following substances: gasoline, kerosene, other flammable or toxic petroleum products, toxic pesticides and herbicides, volatile solvents, materials containing asbestos or formaldehyde, and radioactive materials. As used in this paragraph 20, "Environmental Law" means federal laws and laws of the jurisdiction where the Property is located that relate to health, safety or environmental protection.

NON-UNIFORM COVENANTS. Borrower and Lender further covenant and agree as follows:

21. Acceleration; Remedies. Lender shall give notice to Borrower prior to acceleration following Borrower's breach of any covenant or agreement in this Security Instrument (but not prior to acceleration under paragraph 17 unless applicable law provides otherwise). The notice shall specify: (a) the default; (b) the action required to cure the default; (c) a date, not less than 30 days from the date the notice is given to Borrower, by which the default must be cured; and (d) that failure to cure the default on or before the date specified in the notice may result in acceleration of the sums secured by this Security Instrument and sale of the Property. The notice shall further inform Borrower of the right to reinstate after acceleration and the right to bring a court action to assert the non-existence of a default or any other defense of Borrower to acceleration and sale. If the default is not cured on or before the date specified in the notice, Lender at its option may require immediate payment in full of all sums secured by this Security Instrument without further demand and may invoke the power of sale granted by Borrower and any other remedies permitted by applicable law. Borrower appoints Lender the agent and attorney-in-fact for Borrower to exercise the power of sale. Lender shall be entitled to collect all expenses incurred in pursuing the remedies provided in this paragraph 21, including, but not limited to, reasonable attorneys' fees and costs of title evidence.

EXHIBIT 12–1
Georgia FNMA/FHLMC Uniform Instrument
(continued)

If Lender invokes the power of sale, Lender shall give a copy of a notice of sale to Borrower in the manner provided in paragraph 14 and shall give notice of sale by public advertisement for the time and in the manner prescribed by applicable law. Lender, without further demand on Borrower, shall sell the Property at public auction to the highest bidder at the time and place and under the terms designated in the notice of sale in one or more parcels and in any order Lender determines. Lender or its designee may purchase the Property at any sale.

Lender shall convey to the purchaser indefeasible title to the Property, and Borrower hereby appoints Lender Borrower's agent and attorney-in-fact to make such conveyance. The recitals in the Lender's deed shall be prima facie evidence of the truth of the statements made therein. Borrower covenants and agrees that Lender shall apply the proceeds of the sale in the following order: (a) to all expenses of the sale, including, but not limited to, reasonable attorneys' fees; (b) to all sums secured by this Security Instrument; and (c) any excess to the person or persons legally entitled to it. The power and agency granted are coupled with an interest, are irrevocable by death or otherwise and are cumulative to the remedies for collection of debt as provided by law.

If the Property is sold pursuant to this paragraph 21, Borrower, or any person holding possession of the Property through Borrower, shall immediately surrender possession of the Property to the purchaser at the sale. If possession is not surrendered, Borrower or such person shall be a tenant holding over and may be dispossessed in accordance with applicable law.

22. Release. Upon payment of all sums secured by this Security Instrument, Lender shall cancel this Security Instrument without charge to Borrower. Borrower shall pay any recordation costs.

23. Waiver of Homestead. Borrower waives all rights of homestead exemption in the Property.

24. Assumption not a Novation. Lender's acceptance of an assumption of the obligations of this Security Instrument and the Note, and any release of Borrower in connection therewith, shall not constitute a novation.

25. Security Deed. This conveyance is to be construed under the existing laws of the State of Georgia as a deed passing title, and not as a mortgage, and is intended to secure the payment of all sums secured hereby.

26. Riders to this Security Instrument. If one or more riders are executed by Borrower and recorded together with this Security Instrument, the covenants and agreements of each such rider shall be incorporated into and shall amend and supplement the covenants and agreements of this Security Instrument as if the rider(s) were a part of this Security Instrument. [Check applicable box(es)]

☐ Adjustable Rate Rider   ☐ Condominium Rider   ☐ 1–4 Family Rider

☐ Graduated Payment Rider   ☐ Planned Unit Development Rider   ☐ Biweekly Payment Rider

☐ Balloon Rider   ☐ Rate Improvement Rider   ☐ Second Home Rider

☐ Other(s) [specify]

BORROWER ACCEPTS AND AGREES to the terms and covenants contained in this Security Instrument and in any rider(s) executed by Borrower and recorded with it. IN WITNESS WHEREOF, Borrower has signed and sealed this Security Instrument.

Signed, sealed and delivered in the presence of: **F**

....(Seal)
Unofficial Witness   —Borrower

    Social Security Number...

....(Seal)
    —Borrower

Notary Public, ... County   Social Security Number...

Covenant 10, Condemnation, covers the application of condemnation proceeds in the event the real property is taken for some public purpose through eminent domain. Typically, the provisions state that the money will be paid jointly to the lender and the borrower and can be used either to restore the real property, if feasible, or to repay the debt. Note that this particular paragraph 10 in the FNMA/FHLMC mortgage contains an allocation of the moneys between the borrower and the lender in the event of a partial taking.

Covenant 11, Borrower Not Released; Forbearance By Lender Not a Waiver, provides that if the lender extends time for payment, this does not in any way release the borrower from its obligation to make payments. The lender will not waive any rights under the mortgage by delaying time in exercising rights.

Covenant 12, Successors and Assigns Bound; Joint and Several Liability; Cosigners, is a catchall paragraph. It basically states that all the covenants and provisions of the mortgage will bind the successors and **assigns** of the lender and the borrower and that the borrowers signing the note are jointly and severally liable. **Joint and several liability** means that each borrower is 100 percent responsible for the debt. This paragraph also provides that anyone who consigns a security instrument but does not execute the note is not personally obligated for the debt but can lose his or her real property through a foreclosure in the event the debt is not paid.

Covenant 13, Loan Charges, is a usury savings clause. It provides that if the interest on the loan should exceed the maximum interest permitted under law, the rate will be reduced to the permitted limit and all sums already collected will be refunded to the borrower or used to repay the debt.

Covenant 14, Notices, explains how notices are to be given under the mortgage.

Covenant 15, Governing Law; Severability, is a choice of law paragraph that explains which law will govern. It also provides that if any of the provisions should be unenforceable, those provisions will be deleted from the mortgage, leaving the remainder of the mortgage enforceable.

Covenant 16, Borrower's Copy, provides that the borrower is entitled to receive a copy of the note and mortgage.

Covenant 17, Transfer of the Property or a Beneficial Interest in Borrower, is a "due on sale" clause. It provides that the real property will not be sold without the lender's consent. The lender may condition its consent depending on the financial underwriting of the new owner, or require an increase in interest rates on the note or payments of other fees.

Covenant 18, Borrower's Right to Reinstate, provides that even though the borrower may be in default and the loan may be accelerated and due and payable in its entirety, if the borrower pays the amount of the delinquent payments plus all expenses, the loan will be reinstated. This particular paragraph is unusual and typically is found only in the FNMA/FHLMC uniform instrument.

Covenant 19, Sale of Note; Change of Loan Servicer, provides that the note or any partial interest in the note may be sold without prior notice to the borrower. It also provides that if there is a change in the place where monthly payments should be made, the borrower will receive notice of such change pursuant to the terms of the mortgage.

Covenant 20, Hazardous Substances, provides that the borrower will not cause or permit the presence, use, disposal, storage, or release of hazardous substances on the property. The borrower also agrees to promptly notify the lender of any investigation, claim, demand, lawsuit, or other action taken by any governmental or regulatory agent or private party involving the property and any hazardous substances in connection therewith.

The following are nonuniform covenants. Nonuniform covenants address matters that vary slightly from state to state. Nonuniform covenants of the FNMA/FHLMC mortgage are custom drafted for the state in which the mortgage is to be used. Exhibit 12–1 was designed for use in Georgia.

Covenant 21, Acceleration: Remedies, explains what remedies a lender has in the event of a default. The basic remedy is to foreclose and sell the real property at a public sale. The amount received from the sale will be used by the lender to pay the debt.

Covenant 22, Release, provides that on payment of the debt, the lender will release the mortgage.

Covenant 23, Waiver of Homestead, provides the borrower waives all rights of **homestead** exemption. Homestead is property that is exempt from creditors. Homestead, however, usually can be waived when homestead property is pledged to secure a debt.

Covenant 24, Assumption not a Novation, provides that in the event the property is sold and a new borrower becomes obligated on the debt, this will not create a **novation** and loss of priority. A novation, under law, can result in a loss of priority on the part of a mortgage lender.

Covenant 25, Security Deed, is unique to Georgia law. It provides that this conveyance is a security deed. This paragraph would not be found in mortgage documents used in other states.

Covenant 26, Riders to this Security Instrument, provides for additional **riders** or addendums to be attached to the mortgage.

Part F is the place for the signature of the borrower on the mortgage. Each borrower should sign, and the name should be typed beneath the line of the signatures. Mortgages typically are executed with the same formality as deeds and require witnesses and notarization. They are recorded in the public records of the county in which the real property is located.

COMMERCIAL MORTGAGE PROVISIONS

In addition to the standard provisions found in residential mortgages, mortgages on commercial properties contain a number of other provisions that reflect a lender's concerns regarding a commercial loan transaction. Examples of some of these provisions follow.

Assignment of Rents and Leases

Most commercial mortgages contain an assignment of all rental income and leases in connection with the real property. An example of such a provision is shown in Example 12–1.

EXAMPLE 12-1

Mortgagor hereby transfers, assigns, and conveys unto Mortgagee all of Mortgagor's right, title, and interest in and to all leases, now or hereafter existing or made, and all other agreements for use or occupancy, with respect to the premises or any part thereof and grants to Mortgagee a security interest in all rents, issues, income, revenue, profits, accounts, and contract rights due or to become due thereunder or otherwise deriving from the use and occupancy of the premises. Mortgagor shall faithfully perform the covenants of Mortgagor or lessor under all present or future leases on all or any portion of the premises and shall not do, neglect to do, or permit to be done anything that may cause the termination of such leases, or any of them, or that may diminish or impair the value of the rents provided for therein or the interest of the Mortgagor or Mortgagee therein or thereunder. Mortgagor, without first obtaining the written consent of Mortgagee, shall not further assign the rents, issues, income, revenue, profits, accounts, or contract rights from the premises or any part thereof, shall not consent to the cancellation or surrender of any lease of the premises or any part thereof now existing or hereafter made, shall not modify any such leases so as to shorten the unexpired term thereof or so as to increase the amount of the rent payable thereunder, shall not collect rents from the premises or any part thereof for more than one month in advance. Mortgagor shall procure and deliver to Mortgagee upon request estoppel letters or certificates from each lessee, tenant, occupant in possession, or other user of the premises or any part thereof as required by and in a form or substance satisfactory to Mortgagee and shall deliver to Mortgagee a recordable assignment of all the Mortgagor's interest in all leases now or hereafter existing or made with respect to the premises or any part thereof, which assignment shall be in a form and substance acceptable to Mortgagee, together with proof of due service of a copy of such assignment on each lessee, tenant, occupant in possession, or other user of the premises or any part thereof.

Security Agreement

As security for the loan, a mortgage grants to the lender all real property, including fixtures. Personal property is not covered by a mortgage but by a **security agreement**. A security agreement must be written, identify the debtor, describe the property being covered by the security agreement, and be signed by the debtor. Many lenders incorporate a security agreement within the mortgage to cover any personal property used in connection with the commercial real property. An example of such a provision is shown in Example 12–2.

EXAMPLE 12–2

Security Agreement. This Security Deed shall constitute a security agreement as defined in the Uniform Commercial Code ("Code") and shall create a security interest within the meaning of the Code in favor of Grantee on the Secured Personal Property and Rents, Leases, and Profits ("Collateral") comprising the Secured Premises. The remedies for any violation of the covenants, terms, and conditions of the agreement herein contained shall be (a) as prescribed herein, or (b) by general law, or (c) as to such part of the security that is also reflected in any financing statement by the specific statutory consequences now or hereafter enacted and specified in the Uniform Commercial Code, all at Grantee's sole election. Grantor and Grantee agree that the filing of such a financing statement and the records normally having to do with personal property shall never be construed as in any way derogating from or impairing this declaration and hereby stated intention of the parties hereto that everything used in connection with the production of income from the Secured Property and/or adapted for use therein is, and at all times and for all purposes and in all proceedings, both legal and equitable, shall be regarded as part of the real estate irrespective of whether (a) any such item is physically attached to the improvements, (b) serial numbers are used for the better identification of certain equipment items capable of being thus identified in a recital contained herein or in any list filed with the Grantee, or (c) any such item is referred to or reflected in any such financing statement so filed at any time.

The name of the record owner of said real estate is the Grantor. Information concerning the security interest created by this instrument may be obtained from the Grantee, as secured party as required by the code.

Rights Under Uniform Commercial Code. In addition to the rights available to a grantee of real property if an Event of Default shall occur, Grantee shall also have all the rights, remedies, and recourse available to a secured party under the Uniform Commercial Code, including the right to proceed under the provisions of the Uniform Commercial Code governing default as to any Secured Personal Property that may be included in the Secured Property or that may be deemed non-realty in a foreclosure of this Security Deed or to proceed as to such Personal property in accordance with the procedures and remedies available pursuant to a foreclosure of real estate.

Books, Records, and Financial Statements

A source of repayment for most commercial loans is the income generated from the commercial real property pledged as security for the loan. A lender requires current information concerning the financial condition of the commercial real property as well as the financial condition of the mortgagor. Typical mortgage provisions that require a mortgagor to provide annual financial information concerning the real property and mortgagor are shown in Example 12–3.

EXAMPLE 12-3

Mortgagor covenants and agrees to keep proper records and accounts with full, true, current, and correct entries of all its transactions with respect to the operation of the mortgaged property, in accordance with generally accepted accounting principals consistently applied with such other accounting method as Mortgagee may approve. Mortgagee shall have the right to inspect Mortgagor's books and records at any reasonable time after reasonable prior notice to Mortgagor.

Mortgagor covenants and agrees to furnish to mortgagee quarter annual operating statements showing all income and all expenditures relative to the mortgaged property. The term "income" shall mean all income, from whatever source, arising out of the operation of the mortgaged property and described in this mortgage given to secure the indebtedness, including without limitation, all rental income, vending machine rentals, and proceeds of the sale, lease, or other disposition of any personal property or fixtures located on or used in connection with the operation of the mortgaged property. These statements shall be due within thirty (30) days after the expiration of each calendar quarter and shall be prepared in accordance with generally accepted accounting principals and certified by a certified public accountant approved by Mortgagee. Mortgagee may with its prior written consent permit Mortgagor to verify the financial statements in lieu of a certified public accountant. If Mortgagor is a corporation or a partnership with a general partner who is a corporation, such verification by Mortgagor shall be by the principal officer of such corporation.

Hazardous Waste

Under federal law and the law of many states, a real property owner can be responsible for the removal of hazardous waste from that real property. In the event a mortgage loan goes into default, a lender can become an owner of the real property through foreclosure and may be responsible for the removal of hazardous waste. Many lenders seek an indemnity from the borrower concerning hazardous waste liability. An example of a commercial mortgage provision with a hazardous waste indemnity is set forth in Example 12–4.

EXAMPLE 12-4

(a) *Hazardous Waste.* Mortgagor will not, nor will Mortgagor permit or suffer any of its partners, officers, employees, agents, tenants, or any other licensee or invitee or trespasser to cause or to permit any hazardous waste, toxic substances, or related materials "hazardous materials" (as defined below) to be brought upon, kept, or used or disposed of on, under, in, or about the property.

(b) If Mortgagor breaches the representations, covenants, or obligations stated in this article, and because of such breach the presence of hazardous materials on, under, in, about, or near the property results in a contamination of the property or other properties by hazardous materials, then, in addition to other remedies available to Mortgagee, Mortgagor shall indemnify, defend, and hold Mortgagee and its officers, employees, agents, affiliates, and successors in interest harmless from any and all claims, judgments, damages, penalties, fines, costs, liabilities, and expenses, including actual attorneys' fees and the cost of any cleanup, and any losses that arise at any time as a result of such contamination, or allegation thereof by governmental agency, or the determination by any court or governmental agency, or by Mortgagee or its successor in interest, that the uses of the property must be limited or that the hazardous material should be removed and the damage to the property and its environs restored.

(c) The indemnification of Mortgagee and its officers, employees, agents, and successors in interest by Mortgagor contained in this article include, without limitation, costs incurred in connection with any investigation of site conditions, or any cleanup, remedial removal or restoration required by any federal, state, or local governmental agency or political subdivision, or by any insurance company, or by Mortgagee or its successor in interest in the exercise of its reasonable discretion, because of hazardous material present in the improvements, soil, ground, water, air, or otherwise in, on, under, about, or near the property.

(d) Without limiting the foregoing, if the presence of any hazardous material in, on, under, about, or near the property is caused or permitted by Mortgagor, its tenants, or either their successors in interest, officers, employees, agents, licensees or invitees, or by trespassers, and results in any contamination of the property or other properties, Mortgagor shall take all actions at its sole cost and expense that are necessary to return the property to the condition existing prior to the introduction of any such hazardous materials to the property; provided that Mortgagee's approval of such action shall be first obtained, which approval shall not be unreasonably withheld so long as such actions would not have an adverse long-term or short-term effect on the property.

(e) The foregoing cleanup and indemnification obligation shall survive the reconveyance or foreclosure of this mortgage.

(f) Mortgagor also agrees (i) to provide Mortgagee with copies of any communications between Mortgagor, or its tenants, or their officers, employees, agents, predecessors or successors in interest, licensees, or invitees and any third parties, including, but not limited to, governmental authorities relative to any hazardous material on, under, in, about, or near or affecting the property, and (ii) that Mortgagee is hereby granted the right (but not the obligation) to participate in any proceeding with any governmental agency or court relative to any hazardous materials on, in, under, about, near, or affecting the property.

(g) As used herein the term hazardous materials means any hazardous, toxic, infectious substance, material, gas, or waste that is or becomes regulated by any governmental authority, or the United States government, or any of their agencies, or that has been identified as a toxic, cancer-causing, or otherwise hazardous substance. The term hazardous materials including without limitation, any material or substance that is (a) petroleum, (b) polychlorinated biphenyls (pcb), (c) asbestos, (d) designated a hazardous substance pursuant to Section 307 of the Federal Water Pollution Control Act (3 U.S.C. § 1317), as currently existing or hereafter amended or designated as a hazardous substance pursuant to Section 311 of the Clean Water Act, 33 U.S.C. § 1251 et seq. (33 U.S.C. § 1321), (e) defined as a hazardous waste pursuant to Section 1004 of the Federal Resource Conservation Recovery Act, 42 U.S.C. § 6901 et seq. (42 U.S.C. § 6903), as currently existing or hereafter amended or (f) defined as a hazardous substance pursuant to Section 101 of the Comprehensive Environmental Response Compensation and Liability Act, 42 U.S.C. § 9601 et seq. (42 U.S.C. § 9601), as currently existing or hereafter amended.

In addition to presenting a potential liability to the lender, hazardous waste has a dramatic effect on the value of the real property. The presence of hazardous waste can cause the security for a loan to decline in value and the loan to become undercollateralized.

Non-Recourse or Exculpation Provisions

Many commercial mortgage loans are negotiated with the understanding that the lender will look only to the security of the mortgaged real property as recovery for the repayment of the loan. This means that in the event there is a default under the mortgage loan, the lender will only foreclose on the real property to recover on its debt and will not personally sue the borrower for payment of the debt or for any deficiency that might result from the sale of the mortgaged property. This type of mortgage loan is called a non-recourse or **exculpated** loan. A lender who agrees to an exculpated or non-recourse loan usually makes exceptions to this limitation of liability against the borrower in cases where the borrower has committed fraud, has intentionally injured the real property, or is responsible for hazardous waste cleanup. An example of a non-recourse or exculpated mortgage provision is set out in Example 12–5.

EXAMPLE 12-5

Mortgagee agrees by accepting this mortgage that it will look solely to the mortgaged property and the rents therefrom for the payment of the indebtedness, and all other amounts required to be paid out of the terms of this mortgage and the note and any other document executed in connection herewith and Mortgagee further agrees not to seek payment of the indebtedness from the Mortgagor. Mortgagee further agrees in connection with any action or foreclosure to enforce any provision of this mortgage or any other document executed in connection herewith, Mortgagee will not seek any deficiency judgment against Mortgagor; provided, however, (a) nothing in this paragraph shall be, or be deemed to be, a release or impairment of said indebtedness or the lien created hereby upon the mortgage property, or prohibit Mortgagee from suing upon the note and foreclosing this mortgage in case of any default or defaults hereunder, or from enforcing any of its rights, except as set out above. Notwithstanding the above, the Mortgagee shall not be precluded from seeking a judgment against Mortgagor to recover: (i) any rents received by or on behalf of Mortgagor from the obligors under the leases of the mortgaged property that have been collected either in violation of the loan documents executed in connection herewith or after the occurrence of any event of default of the loan documents executed in connection herewith; or (ii) any security deposits received by or on behalf of Mortgagor from the obligors under the leases of the mortgaged property; or (iii) any amounts representing intentional damage to or conversion of any part of the mortgaged property by Mortgagor or persons acting on Mortgagor's behalf; or (iv) all condemnation awards or insurance proceeds that are not utilized in accordance with the terms and conditions of this mortgage; or (v) any and all costs, expenses, damages, or liabilities incurred by Mortgagee, including, but not limited to, all reasonable attorneys' fees, directly or indirectly arising out of or attributable to the use, generation, storage, release, threatened release, discharge, disposal of, presence on, under, about the mortgaged property of any materials, wastes, or substances defined or classified as hazardous or toxic pursuant to federal, state, or local laws, regulations, including, without limitation, asbestos, lead, pcb, and herbicides.

MISCELLANEOUS COMMERCIAL LOAN DOCUMENTS

In addition to a mortgage, a lender on a commercial loan may require other loan documents in connection with the transaction. These loan documents usually consist of a Uniform Commercial Code (UCC) financing statement and an assignment of rents and leases. If the loan is a construction loan, a construction loan agreement and assignments of the construction contract and architectural contract are required.

Secured Transactions and Fixtures

A commercial real estate finance transaction may include personal property as security for the loan. Because a mortgage only creates a security interest in the real property and fixtures, a security interest in personal property must be created and perfected by additional documentation.

The method for securing a loan with personal property, including fixtures, is provided by Article 9 of the UCC (a standardized law that has been passed in all states except Louisiana). Under Article 9 of the UCC, a loan secured by personal property, including fixtures, is secured by having the debtor execute a security agreement and a UCC-1 **Financing Statement**. A security agreement is a written agreement conveying a security interest in personal property for purposes of securing a debt. Most mortgage forms also include additional language that makes the mortgage a security agreement. An example of that language is contained in Example 12–2.

The UCC-1 Financing Statement is a simple form (Exhibit 12–2). The financing statement is signed by the debtor and the secured party and filed in the public records where the real property is located if the personal property is a fixture. For personal property that is not deemed a fixture, the financing statement must be filed in the public records of the county in which the debtor resides. If the debtor is a corporation or partnership, the financing statement must be filed in the county in which the corporation or partnership has its principal place of business. Most states also require a central filing with the secretary of state's office.

The information required on a UCC-1 Financing Statement includes the debtor's name and address, secured party's (creditor) name and address, a description of the personal property, and a description of the real property on which the personal property is located. The personal property must be described with enough specificity that it can be identified. If the debtor resides in a county other than where the real property is located, a financing statement should be filed in both the county of the debtor's residence or principal place of business and the county in which the real property is located. This dual filing validly perfects the security interest in the personal property, regardless of its classification.

Assignment of Rents

In commercial loan transactions, it is common that, in addition to the assignment of leases and rents that may be contained in the mortgage, a separate assignment of rents and leases is executed and delivered by the borrower to the lender. A form of an assignment of rents and leases is included at the end of this chapter (Exhibit 12–3). A rent assignment essentially provides that all leases and rental income from the real property are assigned to the lender. In the event there is a default under the loan, the lender can take possession of the real property and collect the rent directly from the tenants. The assignment of rents and leases also requires the borrower not to collect in advance more than one or two months' rent from a tenant and prohibits the borrower from modifying, amending, or changing the leases in any way without the lender's prior written consent. The assignment of leases and rents is cross-defaulted with the mortgage and note; default under any of the documents shall constitute an event of default under all the documents.

An assignment of rents and leases is executed by the property owner, witnessed, notarized, and recorded along with the mortgage. It contains an exhibit that is a description of the property as well as a list of all leases being assigned. A description of the leases usually includes all current leases shown on the exhibit as well as all future leases.

EXHIBIT 12–2
UCC–1 Financing Statement

UCC-1 Financing Statement

STANDARD FORM

UNIFORM COMMERCIAL CODE – FINANCING STATEMENT – FORM UCC-1

JULIUS BLUMBERG, INC. NYC, 10013

INSTRUCTIONS:

1. PLEASE TYPE this form. Fold only along perforation for mailing.
2. Remove Secured Party and Debtor copies and send other 3 copies with interleaved carbon paper to the filing officer. Enclose filing fee.
3. If the space provided for any item(s) on the form is inadequate the item(s) should be continued on additional sheets, preferably 5" x 8" or 8" x 10". Only one copy of such additional sheets need be presented to the filing officer with a set of three copies of the financing statement. Long schedules of collateral, indentures, etc., may be on any size paper that is convenient for the secured party. Indicate the number of additional sheets attached.
4. If collateral is crops or goods which are or are to become fixtures, describe generally the real estate and give name of record owner.
5. When a copy of the security agreement is used as a financing statement, it is requested that it be accompanied by a completed but unsigned set of these forms, without extra fee.
6. At the time of original filing, filing officer should return third copy as an acknowledgement. At a later time, secured party may date and sign Termination Legend and use third copy as a Termination Statement.

This **FINANCING STATEMENT** is presented to a filing officer for filing pursuant to the Uniform Commercial Code:

3. Maturity date (if any):

1. Debtor(s) (Last Name First) and address(es)	2. Secured Party(ies) and address(es)	For Filing Officer (Date, Time, Number, and Filing Office)

4. This financing statement covers the following types (or items) of property:

5. Assignee(s) of Secured Party and Address(es)

This statement is filed without the debtor's signature to perfect a security interest in collateral. (check ☒ if so)

Filed with:

☐ already subject to a security interest in another jurisdiction when it was brought into this state.

☐ which is proceeds of the original collateral described above in which a security interest was perfected:

Check ☒ if covered: ☐ Proceeds of Collateral are also covered. ☐ Products of Collateral are also covered. No. of additional Sheets presented:

By:_____   By:_____
　　Signature(s) of Debtor(s)　　　　Title　　　　Signature(s) of Secured Party(ies)　　　　Title

(1) Filing Officer Copy-Alphabetical   **STANDARD FORM - FORM UCC-1.**   (For Use In Most States)

Construction Loan Agreement

A construction loan poses several risks for a lender. Money is advanced for the purpose of constructing improvements; therefore, the value of the security does not exist until the improvements are completed. The lenders must be careful in a construction loan to make sure the money is in fact used for the improvements and that the improvements are built according to plans and specifications previously approved by the lender. In addition, the lender must make sure that all the subcontractors, materials suppliers, and other people who may have potential mechanics' lien claims against the property are being paid during the progress of the construction. Because of these problems, many lenders who make construction loans require the borrowers to execute construction loan agreements. A form of construction loan agreement is included at the end of this chapter (Exhibit 12–4).

Generally, a construction loan agreement will contain a number of representations and warranties made by the borrower to the lender. These representations and warranties may contain recitals that (a) the borrower has good title to the real property; (b) the borrower has all necessary licenses and permits in connection with the proposed construction; (c) all construction will be in accordance with all private restrictive covenants as well as all zoning and building code requirements; (d) the borrower's contracts with the contractor, architect, engineer, and subcontractors are all valid and in full force and effect; (e) true and correct copies of these contracts have been provided to the lender; (f) there is no pending litigation affecting the borrower or the real property; (g) all utilities such as water, electric, and gas are available to the real property; (h) all roads necessary for full utilization of the improvements are available and have been dedicated for public use, or all necessary easements for private use have been obtained; and (i) all necessary insurance has been acquired to insure the construction of the improvements as well as liability for any accidents or other harm that may occur during the construction.

There may also be a requirement that in the event the loan proceeds prove to be insufficient to finish construction of the improvements, the lender may stop advancing money until the borrower has deposited the necessary funds with the lender to complete the construction.

A construction loan agreement will also set forth the requirements for the disbursement of loan proceeds during construction. The lender requires that all requests for proceeds be made on a form approved by the lender. The request explains in full detail how the funds will be spent. The lender retains an inspecting architect to inspect the work as it is completed. The lender may require that a title examination to the real property be updated to check for lien claims. Endorsements to the title insurance are issued insuring that each advance of the loan proceeds is free and clear of liens. The lender may require that a survey locating the foundation of the improvements be provided. This is important to determine if the improvements are located on the real property and comply with all necessary setback and building line restrictions. It also is not unusual for a lender to advance only a portion of the proceeds, for example 90 percent of the actual cost of construction. The ten percent holdback or retainage is held by the lender until the construction is completed. This retainage provides the lender with some security in the event there are cost overruns or unpaid bills.

The final advance under a construction loan agreement requires the same conditions as an interim advance and a few additional ones. Most lenders will not make the final advance under a construction loan agreement unless an architect's certificate of substantial completion has been issued. The lender also may require that a certificate of occupancy be issued by the appropriate governmental authority having jurisdiction over the improvements. This certificate of occupancy is evidence that the improvements do comply with all zoning and building codes and all health and fire regulations. A final advance usually is conditioned on an inspection made by the permanent lender and the receipt of a final survey showing all completed improvements to be located on the real property. A lender may require full and complete lien waivers from all people who have provided material or labor to the real property.

A construction loan agreement will describe those events that constitute default and identifies the remedies in case of defaults. Construction loan agreements typically are cross-defaulted with the note and mortgage, so that a default under any of the documents constitutes a default under all documents. General events of default are as follows:

- A violation by the borrower of any covenant or promise in the construction loan agreement
- The filing of any mechanics' liens for labor or materials or any liens for unpaid taxes
- Any litigation against the borrower or against the real property in connection with the construction
- Abandonment or stoppage of construction
- The use of improper materials, or not constructing the improvements in accordance with the plans or specifications

A construction loan agreement will provide remedies for the lender in the event of default. The lender has the right to accelerate the indebtedness and to foreclose on the real property. In addition, the lender has the right to take possession of the real property and complete construction. The lender has the right to advance retained loan proceeds toward completion of the construction. The lender also has the right to sue the borrower for any deficiencies required to complete the construction of the improvements.

A construction loan agreement will have general conditions. These general conditions usually include a statement to the effect that the construction loan agreement is personal between the borrower and the lender, and does not provide any third parties, such as contractors, subcontractors, laborers, or materials suppliers, with any benefits. This is necessary to prevent contractors or subcontractors from suing to obtain payment directly from the lender. A construction loan agreement provides that the lender is not an agent or representative of the borrower, and that the lender is not in any way responsible for the construction or for the payment of the cost of the construction. Other typical provisions found in the general conditions include no assignment by borrower, notices, amendments, governing law, and time is of the essence. Construction loan agreements are executed by both the borrower and the lender, witnessed, and notarized. Although construction loan agreements are in recordable form, they are seldom recorded in the public records where the real property is located.

A lender making a construction loan may take an assignment of all construction contracts and architects' and engineering contracts in connection with the real property. In the event there is a default or interruption in the construction, this assignment gives the lender the right to take over these contracts and complete the performance.

The assignment of architects, construction, and engineers' contracts also are consented to by the architect, contractor, and engineer.

 E T H I C S :   Misrepresentation

A legal assistant is employed by a law firm that represents lending institutions. One of the legal assistant's duties is to send copies of the note, mortgages, and other loan documents to the borrower for review before closing. The legal assistant receives a telephone call from a borrower who has received such a loan package. The borrower states that the documents are quite lengthy and asks if the documents contain a "due on sale" provision that would restrict the borrower's ability to sell the property in the future. The legal assistant is not totally familiar with the particular lending institution's documents and indicates to the borrower that she does not believe the documents contain a "due on sale" provision. After the telephone conversation with the borrower, the legal assistant discovers by reviewing the mortgage that it does contain a "due on sale" provision. Should the legal assistant call the borrower back and tell the borrower that she was mistaken and that the documents do contain a "due on sale" provision or remain silent, assuming that the borrower will discover the "due on sale" provision after he or she has fully read the documents so that no harm will be done in any event?

A legal assistant should never engage in professional misconduct, including dishonesty and willful misrepresentation. Although the statement to the borrower that the mortgage loan documents do not contain a "due on sale" provision was made in good faith at the time, the later discovery of the error needs to be corrected. Remaining silent after having given out false information concerning the content of a legal document constitutes dishonest and even willful misrepresentation. The ethical thing to do is for the legal assistant to call the borrower, explain that she was mistaken concerning the "due on sale" provision, and indicate to the borrower that there is such a provision and where it can be found in the loan documents.

SUMMARY

Mortgage loan documents attempt to address every conceivable issue and problem that could arise during the term of the mortgage loan. The terms of the mortgage loan documents are negotiated between the borrower and the lender. Familiarity with the provisions and their effect on either the borrower or the lender is essential to a legal assistant to effectively prepare or review mortgage loan documents and to participate in the loan closing process. Although most mortgage loan documents are prepared to protect the interest of the lender, a lender's safety in a mortgage loan does not end with the mortgage documents. A mortgage loan is only as secure as the borrower's title in the real property described in the mortgage.

KEY TERMS

Assigns	Homestead	Receiver
Certificate of occupancy	Improvements	Retainage
Exculpation	Joint and several liability	Rider
Financing statement	Novation	Security agreement
Habendum		

▐▐▐➡ CHECKLIST

Preparation of a Mortgage

- ❑ I. Parties
    - ❑ A. Mortgagor or grantor—record title owner of the property described in the mortgage
    - ❑ B. Mortgagee or grantee—creditor and holder of the note being secured by the mortgage

☐ II. Description of Property to be Conveyed
   ☐ A. Accurate description of real property and associated personal property
   ☐ B. Include easements appurtenant to the secured property
      1. Cross access easements
      2. Off-site utility easements
☐ III. Indebtedness
   ☐ A. Amount of indebtedness
   ☐ B. Final maturity date for payment of indebtedness
   ☐ C. Open-end or future advance provisions
☐ IV. Security Agreement
   ☐ A. To be included if personal property is part of the security
☐ V. Assignment of Leases and Rents
   ☐ A. To be included if property is a commercial investment or income-producing property
☐ VI. Miscellaneous Mortgage Covenants
   ☐ A. Payment of indebtedness
   ☐ B. Escrow for taxes and insurance
   ☐ C. Application of payments
   ☐ D. Hazard insurance
   ☐ E. Preservation and maintenance of property
   ☐ F. Lender's right to inspect
   ☐ G. Condemnation
   ☐ H. Lender's right to cure defaults
   ☐ I. Due on sale
   ☐ J. Prohibition on secondary financing
   ☐ K. Financial reporting
   ☐ L. Events of default
   ☐ M. Remedies on default
   ☐ N. Provision for giving notices
   ☐ O. Choice of law
   ☐ P. Forbearance not a waiver
   ☐ Q. Waiver of homestead and other debtor's rights
   ☐ R. Indemnity against hazardous waste
   ☐ S. Any other indemnities or provisions relative to the transaction
   ☐ T. Cross-default with other loan documents such as assignment of leases or construction loan agreements
☐ VII. Signature
   ☐ A. Mortgagor or grantor is only party to sign mortgage
      1. Corporate mortgagor or grantor
         a. Correctly identify name of corporation
         b. Correctly identify by name and title all officers signing on behalf of corporation
         c. Affix official corporate seal
      2. Partnership mortgagor or grantor
         a. Identify the partnership by name
         b. Identify by name all partners signing the mortgage
   ☐ B. Mortgagor or grantor's signature is witnessed and notarized with sufficient formality to permit the mortgage to be recorded
   ☐ C. Mortgage is recorded to protect mortgagee's priority against future purchasers or mortgagees.

REVIEW QUESTIONS

1. How can a lender protect itself against a borrower's failure to pay real estate taxes and to keep the secured buildings and improvements insured?

2. What is a security agreement?

3. What is the importance of filing a UCC Financing Statement?

4. Why do lenders who make construction loans require a borrower to sign a construction loan agreement?

5. What is a non-recourse loan, and who benefits from it?

6. What is the importance of an assignment of leases and rents to a lender?

7. What representations and warranties are required of a borrower in a construction loan agreement?

8. What is retainage in a construction loan, and why is it important?

9. What remedies does a lender have for a default under a construction loan agreement?

CASE PROBLEMS

1. You are assisting an attorney in the closing of a loan to be secured by an apartment project. Each apartment contains a refrigerator, an electric range, an oven, and a dishwasher. You have been asked to prepare a security agreement and to file a UCC Financing Statement to perfect the lender's security interest in those items. The apartment project is located in Calhoun County, but the borrower resides in Dobbins County. Where would you file the UCC Financing Statement?

2. The street in front of Sarah Baker's house is being widened from two lanes to four lanes. The widening will require the county to take approximately 10 feet of Sarah's front yard. The county has promised to pay Sarah $20,000 for the yard being taken. Sarah's home is secured by a loan to First Bank and Trust. You have been requested by the attorney who represents Sarah to review the First Bank and Trust mortgage papers to see if the lender has any claim to the proceeds. What would you look for in the mortgage loan documents, and what would you expect to find?

3. You have been asked to prepare a construction loan agreement for a lender client of the firm. The lender wants the maximum protection against problems as they disburse the loan proceeds. In drafting the construction loan agreement, what requirements would you add for the disbursement of the loan proceeds during construction?

4. You have been asked to prepare a mortgage to secure a real estate loan transaction. You have been asked to use the FNMA/FHLMC Uniform Mortgage. What information do you need to prepare the mortgage?

5. You have a mortgage on your home to First Bank and Trust. The mortgage is a FNMA/FHLMC Uniform Mortgage. You currently have the home under a contract for sale. You want to be able to sell the home and have the purchaser assume the mortgage to First Bank and Trust. Two days before the closing of the sale, you notify First Bank and Trust that you are selling the property and that the purchaser will assume the loan. First Bank and Trust responds that it will not consent to the sale unless you provide financial information concerning the purchaser and pay First Bank and Trust a fee of $1,000. First Bank and Trust also informs you that if you refuse to cooperate and sell the home without its consent, it will call the loan in default and foreclose. Can First Bank and Trust legally do this?

ADDENDUM

Exhibit 12–3 Assignment of Leases and Rents
Exhibit 12–4 Construction and/or Development Loan Agreement

EXHIBIT 12-3
Assignment of Leases and Rents

STATE OF_____

COUNTY OF _____

    THIS ASSIGNMENT is made and entered into this _____ day of September, 19____, by _____, a _____ (hereinafter referred to as "Assignor"), and it is delivered to _____, a _____ corporation (hereinafter called "Assignee").

WITNESSETH:

    WHEREAS, Assignor is justly indebted to Assignee, and said indebtedness is on the date hereof evidenced by Assignor's Real Estate Note of even date herewith, in the principal amount of _____ NO/100 DOL-LARS ($_____), hereinafter called the "Note";

    WHEREAS, the indebtedness evidenced by the Note and other indebtedness of Assignor to Assignee is secured by that certain Deed to Secure Debt and Security Agreement of even date herewith, from Assignor to Assignee, conveying the real property described on Exhibit "A", attached hereto and incorporated herein by reference, hereinafter called the "Property", which Deed to Secure Debt and Security Agreement is incorporated herein by reference and is hereinafter called the "Security Deed";

    WHEREAS, Assignee has required that Assignor assign to Assignee certain of Assignor's rights, title and interest with respect to the Property; and

    WHEREAS, Assignor has agreed to so assign such interests to Assignee and desires to make and deliver this assignment for that purpose.

    NOW, THEREFORE, in consideration of the foregoing premises, of the indebtedness of Assignor to Assignee and of other good and valuable consideration, all of which Assignor acknowledges constitutes sufficient consideration and value received by Assignor at the time of or before Assignor's execution hereof, Assignor hereby assigns and agrees as follows:

    1. *Assignment.* Subject to the terms and conditions hereinafter set forth, Assignor does hereby sell, transfer and assign unto Assignee the Leases and the Rents, as such terms are defined in the Security Deed, and does hereby ratify, affirm, confirm and reaffirm the sale, transfer and conveyance of the Leases and the Rents under and pursuant to the Security Deed. As used herein, the term "Leases" includes, but is not limited to, the lease agreements set forth on Exhibit "B" attached hereto and incorporated herein by reference and all future lease agreements involving the Property.

    2. *Purpose of Assignment.* This assignment is made and intended to secure the Indebtedness, as such term is defined in the Security Deed.

    3. *Power of Attorney.* Assignor does hereby authorize and empower Assignee, and does hereby irrevocably and duly constitute Assignee, as Assignor's attorney-in-fact, to receive any and all of the Rents, to collect any and all of the Rents by such means and taking such actions as Assignee shall deem necessary, and to act in all other ways with respect to the Rents and the Leases for Assignor and in Assignor's place and stead. Assignee shall have the right, as Assignor's attorney-in-fact, but not the obligation, to take any action hereby authorized in Assignor's name and to exercise any and all of Assignor's rights and remedies, whether available at law or in equity or otherwise, with respect to any of the Rents or the Leases. The foregoing appointment of Assignee as Assignor's attorney-in-fact is coupled with an interest, cannot be revoked by bankruptcy, insolvency, death, dissolution or otherwise and shall not terminate until the Indebtedness has been paid and satisfied in full.

    4. *Rents Payable to Assignee.* Assignor hereby directs, instructs and demands each and every person, partnership, corporation, association and other entity or organization now or hereafter owing any of the Rents to Assignor to pay any and all amounts so owed promptly and directly to Assignee upon demand therefor by Assignee. Assignor hereby represents and warrants that all payments so made shall have the same effect in satisfaction of obligations owed to Assignor as if made directly to Assignor, and Assignor shall not question or otherwise contest any tenant for any such payment authorized hereby. By accepting Assignor's delivery of this assignment, however, Assignee agrees that the Rents shall be payable to and collected by Assignor until such time as Assignee may demand payment thereof

EXHIBIT 12–3
Assignment of Leases and Rents
(continued)

directly to Assignee and that Assignee shall not demand such payment until after a default occurs under this assign-ment; provided, however, that Assignee's agreement and Assignor's privilege to continue collecting the Rents shall automatically terminate if Assignor collects any installment of rent or any other payment (by cash, note or otherwise) which is part of the Rents more than one (1) month in advance of the date such rent or other payment is due.

5. *Notification of Obligations.* Promptly upon request by Assignee: (i) Assignor shall deliver to Assignee a copy of any of the Leases which are written; (ii) Assignor shall notify the other party or parties to any of the Leases, whether written or oral, and whether now or hereafter made or executed, of the content and existence of this assignment and of the agreements and obligations of Assignor with respect to payment of the Rents as set forth in paragraphs 3 and 4 hereof; and (iii) Assignor shall obtain and deliver to Assignee a written consent from, and agreement by, any and all such parties, and any and all parties owing any Rents to Assignor, to pay any and all Rents so owed directly to Assignee, and not to Assignor, as provided for by this assignment. Any and all notices, consents and agreements required hereunder shall be in such form and substance as Assignee may prepare.

6. *Default.* If: (i) Assignor should fail to perform its duties and obligations under, or should violate or breach or fail to observe, satisfy or comply with any of the terms, covenants, conditions, agreements, requirements, restrictions or provisions set forth in, this assignment or (ii) any representation or warranty made herein should be false, untrue, incomplete or misleading in any material respect when made; or (iii) Assignor shall otherwise be in default under the Note or the Security Deed then, in any of such events, Assignor shall be in default under this assignment.

7. *Rights on Default.* If Assignor shall be in default under this assignment, Assignee may, at its option and elec-tion and without notice to Assignor, do any one or more of the following: (i) exercise any or all of assignee's rights and remedies under this assignment, the Note or the Security Deed, or any other instrument evidencing or securing all or any part of the Indebtedness; (ii) take possession of the Leases; (iii) take such measures or actions as Assignee deems appropriate or necessary to enforce the payment of all Rents; (iv) contest, litigate and compromise any claim for rebate, setoff, loss, demand, abatement or reduction in connection with the Leases or the Rents; or (v) lease or rent any of the Property and employ and pay a rental agent or a broker a commission to facilitate such leasing or renting, such commission to be added to the Indebtedness. Assignor shall pay all of the costs and expenses incurred by Assignee in exercising or enforcing assignee's rights hereunder. Assignee may use and apply the Rents collected by Assignee under this assignment toward the following purposes, in such order as Assignee shall determine: (i) real property ad valorem taxes, sanitary taxes and charges, and personal property ad valorem taxes, with respect to the Property; (ii) premiums for insurance policies required under the Security Deed; (iii) the costs and expenses of repair-ing and maintaining the Property in such a manner as Assignee may reasonably determine consistent with prior usage and practice; (iv) the costs and expenses to perform completely Assignor's duties, obligations, responsibilities and liabilities under any of the Leases, and in connection with or with respect to any of the Rents; (v) any and all other costs and expenses incurred by Assignee in connection with the Property, including without limitation any and all costs and expenses incurred by reason of assignee's exercise of its rights under this assignment or the Security Deed or both; (vi) interest and default interest accrued on the Indebtedness; and (vii) the outstanding principal bal-ance of the Indebtedness. All of Assignee's rights and remedies in the event of a default hereunder are cumulative of and in addition to, and not restrictive of or in lieu of, the rights and remedies of Assignee under the Note and the Security Deed, or as may be provided or allowed by law or in equity or otherwise, and Assignee may elect one or more or all of the rights and remedies available under this assignment or otherwise.

8. *Assignor's Covenants.* Assignor covenants that: (i) Assignor will fully and faithfully perform all of the duties and obligations of the lessor, landlord or owner of the Property under the Leases, and observe, satisfy and comply with all of the terms, covenants, conditions, agreements, requirements, restrictions and provisions of the Leases, and do all acts otherwise necessary to maintain and preserve the Rents and prevent any diminishment or impairment of the value of the Leases or the Rents or the interest of Assignor or Assignee therein or thereunder, it being expressly understood and agreed that Assignee neither undertakes nor assumes any of Assignor's liabilities, responsibilities, duties or obligations in connection with the Leases or the Rents; (ii) Assignor will enforce the full and faithful perfor-

EXHIBIT 12-3
Assignment of Leases and Rents
(continued)

mance of all of the duties and obligations of each of the tenants and lessees under the Leases, and the observance, satisfaction and compliance with all of the terms, covenants, conditions, agreements, requirements, restrictions and provisions of the Leases required to be observed, satisfied or complied with by the tenants and lessees thereunder; (iii) Assignor will appear in and prosecute and defend, as shall be necessary, any action or proceeding arising under, out of, with respect to or in connection with any of the Leases, and, upon request by Assignee, do so in the name of and on behalf of Assignee, and pay all costs and expenses, including attorney's fees, incurred by Assignee in connection therewith; (iv) Assignor will not further assign the Leases or the Rents, shall not terminate, alter, modify or amend in any respect, or accept the surrender of, any of the Leases without the prior written consent of Assignee; (v) Assignor shall be the lessor or landlord under all of the Leases; *provided, however,* that Assignor may appoint a leasing agent to act on its behalf upon prior written notice to Assignee of the identity and mailing address of such leasing agent; (vi) Assignor, shall not permit, consent to or acquiesce in any subleasing, assignment, renewal or extension, in whole or in part, of or under any of the Leases without the prior written consent of Assignee; (vii) Assignor will not relocate or consent to or acquiesce in the relocation of any lessee, tenant or other user or occupant of all or any part of the Property without the prior written consent of Assignee; (viii) Assignor will not collect Rents for more than one (1) month in advance and will not accept any security deposit, damage deposit or similar funds under or in connection with any of the Leases for an amount in excess of one (1) month's rent without the prior written consent of Assignee; (ix) Assignor will keep the Leases and the Rents free from any and all liens, encumbrances and security interests whatsoever, other than the security interest created by this assignment and the Security Deed; and (x) Assignor will promptly pay and discharge all taxes assessed against the Leases or the Rents and all liens which may attach to the Leases or the Rents. The foregoing covenants are cumulative of and in addition to those now or hereafter imposed by law.

9. *Liability of Assignee.* Assignee shall not be liable to Assignor for a failure to collect any part or all of the Rents, and Assignee may be required to account for only such sums as Assignee actually collects.

10. *Forbearance.* Assignee shall not be deemed to waive any of Assignee's rights or remedies under this assignment unless such waiver is express, in writing and signed by or on behalf of Assignee. No delay, omission or forbearance by Assignee in exercising any of Assignee's rights or remedies under this assignment shall operate as a waiver of such rights or remedies. A waiver in writing on one occasion shall not be construed as a waiver of any right or remedy on any future occasion. Neither the existence of this Assignment nor the exercise by Assignee of Assignee's right to collect any of the Rents shall be construed as a waiver by Assignee of any of Assignee's rights to enforce payment of the Indebtedness in strict accordance with the terms and provisions of the Note and the Security Deed.

11. *Term of Assignment.* The term of this assignment shall be until the Indebtedness has been paid in full and the Security Deed has been cancelled and satisfied of record. The cancellation and satisfaction of record of the Security Deed shall automatically constitute a satisfaction, cancellation and release by Assignee of Assignor's obligations and Assignee's rights under this assignment.

12. *Applicable Law.* This assignment shall be governed by, construed under and interpreted and enforced in accordance with the laws of the State of _____.

13. *Time.* Time is and shall be of the essence of this assignment and of each covenant and agreement by Assignor.

14. *Captions.* All captions or headings preceding the text of separate sections, paragraphs and subparagraphs of this assignment are solely for reference purposes and shall not affect the meaning, construction, interpretation or effect of the text.

15. *Not Additional Security.* This assignment shall not be deemed or construed to be merely additional security or collateral for the Indebtedness but rather primary and unconditional security. Assignee may exercise all rights granted hereunder without regard to the existence, value or adequacy of any other collateral or security for the Indebtedness held by Assignee. All collateral and security for the Indebtedness is primary and unconditional collateral

EXHIBIT 12–3
Assignment of Leases and Rents (continued)

and security. Assignor hereby authorizes, directs and instructs any trustee or receiver in bankruptcy having possession of the Leases or the Rents or any of them to deliver the same to Assignee in the event of a default by Assignor and the exercise by Assignee of its rights hereunder.

16. *Notices.* All notices, requests, demands and other communications under this assignment shall be in writing and shall be deemed to have been duly given if given in accordance with the provisions of the Security Deed.

17. *Definitions.* The word "Assignor" as used herein shall include the legal representatives, successors, and assigns of Assignor as if so specified at length throughout this assignment, and all covenants, agreements, duties, obligations, liabilities and responsibilities of Assignor shall be binding upon and enforceable against the legal representatives, successors and assigns of Assignor. The word "Assignee" as used herein shall include the transferees, successors, legal representatives and assigns of Assignee as if so specified at length through this assignment, and all rights of Assignee under this assignment shall inure to the benefit of the transferees, successors, legal representatives and assigns of Assignee. The words "Assignor" and "Assignee" shall include the neuter, masculine and feminine genders, and the singular and the plural.

IN WITNESS WHEREOF, Assignor, by its duly authorized representatives, has executed this assignment under seal and Assignor has delivered this assignment to Assignee, all the day and year first written above.

Signed, sealed and delivered this _____   ASSIGNOR:

day of _____, 19____, in the

presence of:

_____

Unofficial Witness

_____

Notary Public
My Commission Expires:

_____

[Notarial Seal]

EXHIBIT 12–4
Construction and/or Development Loan Agreement

AGREEMENT made by and between the undersigned (hereinafter "Borrower") and _____ Bank, _____ (address).

WITNESSETH:

WHEREAS, Borrower is the owner of certain real property described in a Deed to Secure Debt of even date (the "Deed") given this day in favor of Lender to secure a Construction Loan Note of even date in the original principal amount of $_____ (the "Note"); and

WHEREAS, Borrower intends to fully develop and/or construct improvements upon said real property in accordance with certain "plans and specifications" heretofore delivered by Borrower to the Lender; and

WHEREAS, Borrower has obtained a commitment from the Lender to make Borrower loans and advances, evidenced by the Note, for such development and/or construction on terms and conditions therein contained, which commitment is incorporated herein by reference;

EXHIBIT 12-4
Construction and/or Development Loan Agreement (continued)

NOW, THEREFORE, in consideration of the premises and the making of the loan to Borrower, the Borrower herein agrees as follows:

1. (a)   Unless waived by the Lender, no materials shall have been placed upon the real estate prior to the date hereof, and development and/or construction shall not commence sooner than 24 hours, plus any intervening Saturday, Sunday, or holiday, after date hereof.

   (b)   Unless otherwise approved in writing by the Lender, development and/or construction shall commence not later than expiration of the applicable commencement period specified below.

2. (a)   All development and/or construction shall be fully completed in strict accordance with the plans and specifications heretofore delivered by Borrower to the Lender.

   (b)   All development and/or construction shall be fully completed within the applicable completion dates set forth below.

3. Lender will from time to time make advances to Borrower pursuant to inspection or certification of progress of construction or development in place, up to the total principal amount of the Note set forth below, provided that:

   (a)   At the time of the first advance, Borrower shall have complied fully with the provisions of paragraphs 1(a) and 1(b) above.

   (b)   Borrower has delivered, in form and content satisfactory to the Lender, a Promissory Note duly executed by Borrower.

   (c)   Borrower has delivered to Lender a Deed to Secure Debt, in form and content satisfactory to the Lender.

   (d)   Borrower has conveyed to the Lender by Security Agreement, in form and content satisfactory to the Lender (including the execution of a U.C.C. financing statement), a security interest in all personal property of Borrower used in connection with or intended as part of the development and/or construction contemplated herein.

   (e)   No lien or other interest shall have been permitted to attach to the real estate or other property superior to the legal title of the Lender under the Deed to Secure Debt or Security Agreement.

   (f)   No event of default, as herein defined, shall have occurred.

   (g)   Borrower has performed each obligation herein contained or made in the commitment or any other instrument given pursuant hereto or thereto.

   (h)   All construction up to the date of the advance has been in strict accordance with the plans and specifications heretofore delivered to the Lender, and satisfactory evidence thereof has been furnished to the Lender, and all change orders which have been agreed to between Borrower and Contractor have been approved in writing by the Lender.

   (i)   At the time of each advance, the Lender is fully satisfied with the timeliness, progress, and quality of development and/or construction, and, in the sole opinion of the Lender, the estimated cost of development and/or construction in accordance with the plans and specifications does not exceed the balance of the loan to be advanced.

4. Borrower herein represents as follows:

   (a)   All prior funds advanced shall have been spent only in the development and/or construction of the project or agreed-to soft costs, and satisfactory evidence thereof shall be furnished to the Lender as may be requested from time to time.

   (b)   The real estate and other property is free and clear of all liens and encumbrances except for the security instruments of the Lender and except for the lien for real estate taxes not yet due and payable.

   (c)   All evidence, statements, and other writings delivered to the Lender by Borrower in connection with this loan are true and correct and omit no material fact, the omission of which would make such statements and other writings misleading.

EXHIBIT 12-4
Construction and/or Development Loan Agreement (continued)

(d)　All bills for labor, materials, and fixtures used, or on hand to be used, in development and/or construction of the project have been paid in accordance with the terms hereof, and no one is asserting a lien against the real estate or other property with respect thereto.

(e)　All terms of the commitment have been complied with in full, insofar as the same are required to be complied with at the time of each advance.

(f)　That he will furnish the Lender, upon Lender's request, with satisfactory evidence (certificates or affidavits of architects, contractors, subcontractors, or attorneys) showing:

(1)　the value of the development and/or construction then existing;

(2)　that all outstanding claims for labor, materials, and fixtures have been paid in accordance with the terms thereof;

(3)　that no liens (other than the inchoate lien for real estate taxes not yet due) are outstanding or unpaid superior to the security title of the Lender;

(4)　that Borrower has complied with all of the terms hereof, the commitment, the Note, the Deed to Secure Debt, and the other loan documents; and

(5)　that all construction has been performed in strict accordance with the plans and specifications.

5. (a)　If required by the Lender's commitment, Borrower will immediately deposit all funds advanced by the Lender into a separate account maintained at _____ Bank; and if not required by Lender then in a commercial banking institution or a savings and loan association, the deposits of which are insured by the Federal Deposit Insurance Corporation, to be known as the "Development and/or Construction Account," to be withdrawn and used solely for the payment of bills for labor, materials, and fixtures used in connection with the development and/or construction contemplated hereby, and to furnish the Lender with satisfactory evidence of the establishment of the account specified above and with verified copies of all deposit and withdrawal transactions applicable thereto.

(b)　Borrower shall advise Lender of all requests for change orders all of which must be approved in advance by Lender. Borrower shall furnish Lender with copies of all change orders immediately upon their origination.

6. (a)　Lender shall have no obligation to make any advance if:

(1)　any claim of lien is filed against the real estate or other property;

(2)　Borrower breaches or fails to perform, observe, or meet any covenant or condition made herein or made in any instrument or document executed by Borrower pursuant hereto;

(3)　any warranty or representation of Borrower made, or agreed to be made, or contained in any instrument or document executed by Borrower pursuant hereto, shall be false or materially misleading;

(4)　a levy is made under service of process on, or a receiver is appointed for, the real estate or any other property of Borrower (including Borrower's personal property unconnected with this transaction);

(5)　any proceedings for relief under Federal or State bankruptcy laws or other laws designed for debtor relief are brought by or against Borrower;

(6)　Borrower commits any act of bankruptcy;

(7)　Borrower is alleged to be insolvent or unable to pay his debts as they become due in any legal proceeding;

(8)　Borrower commits, or omits to do, any act, or any event occurs, as a result of which any obligations of Borrower may be declared immediately due and payable to the holder thereof; or

(9)　Borrower fails to pay any other debt on the contractually required due date.

(b)　Each of the events recited in provision 6(a) above shall be regarded as, and shall be known as (for purposes of this agreement and all other instruments or documents executed by Borrower pursuant hereto), "events of default," and upon the occurrence of any of them, the Lender may, at its discretion, declare immediately due and payable all evidences of debt given by Borrower to the Lender.

EXHIBIT 12-4
Construction and/or Development Loan Agreement (continued)

7. (a) Lender may, at its option, collect interest on the sum of advances outstanding from time to time by deducting from the Borrower's loan-in-process account the interest that may become due under the Note.

(b) Interest during the construction and/or development period shall be calculated as and from the day funds are advanced and is due and payable monthly in accordance with the Note terms.

(c) No building shall be occupied by anyone before completion of construction and a final inspection by the Lender without the prior written consent of the Lender, and no building shall be occupied by anyone after completion of construction and a final inspection by the Lender without the prior written consent of the Lender.

(d) No oral or written lease or rental agreement shall be offered or executed by Borrower concerning the real estate or other property without the prior written consent of the Lender.

(e) Progress inspections shall be made by the Lender or by a duly qualified and licensed architect or engineer selected by the Lender in its sole discretion. All inspections, reviews, and certifications shall be performed solely for the benefit of the Lender, and all costs and expenses incurred in connection therewith shall be promptly paid by Borrower.

(f) If at any time during development and/or construction of the project, it is determined by the Lender, in its sole discretion, that the balance of the funds remaining unadvanced from the loan are insufficient to pay for completion of the project in accordance with the plans and specifications, then no further advances shall be required to be made by the Lender until Borrower shall have deposited with the Lender sums sufficient to fully complete the project in accordance with the plans and specifications.

(g) Borrower, upon request by Lender, shall pay various subcontractors and materialmen only ninety percent (90%) of the total contract amount due them for work completed or material furnished at the time of Borrower's request for an advance; the balance of funds due such subcontractors and materialmen shall be retained by the Lender until satisfactory completion of the project.

(h) In the event a mechanic's lien or materialman's lien is filed, or legal proceedings instituted, which lien or proceedings are not satisfied or removed, as the case may be, by Borrower within ten (10) days of written notice thereof from the Lender, Lender may apply the balance remaining in Borrower's loan-in-process account to the payment thereof.

(i) Lender and its agents, at all times during development and/or construction, shall have the full right of entry and free access to the real estate and all improvements erected thereon and the right to inspect all work done, labor performed, and material delivered to and furnished in and about the project and the right to inspect and make copies of all books, ledgers, statements, writings, invoices, and other documents and records of the Borrower pertaining thereto.

(j) Borrower will not store or permit others to store any building materials, equipment, supplies, or fixtures of any kind whatsoever on the real estate described in the Deed which are not intended to be used in, for, or in connection with the project.

(k) Borrower will not enter into any agreement with any other person, firm, or entity concerning or pertaining to the real estate which involves easements, cross-easements, rights-of-way, dedications of facilities, streets, or which in any way diminishes the size or limits the use or other rights in the real estate, without the prior written consent of the Lender.

8. (a) Development and/or construction shall be performed strictly in accordance with all applicable ordinances and statutes (both Federal and State) and in accordance with the requirements of all regulatory authorities having jurisdiction over the project.

(b) Upon Lender's request, Borrower will provide the Lender, at Borrower's expense, with appropriate evidence of compliance with all statutory and regulatory requirements of the appropriate governmental authorities, including, by way of illustration, but not limited to, preliminary reports, certifications, surveys, filings, drawings, plans, specifications, final reports, tests, data, announcements, publications, instruments, or agreements filed with,

EXHIBIT 12–4
Construction and/or Development Loan Agreement (continued)

approved by or proposed to be used in compliance with local health regulations, zoning ordinances, or licensing or permit regulations required by local building authorities, the Federal Interstate Land Sales Act, the Georgia Land Sales Act, the Georgia Condominium Act, or Department of Housing and Urban Development regulations. If requested by the Lender, all statutory or regulatory permits, certificates, licenses, etc., shall be obtained by the Borrower in such form that they are fully transferable to the Lender.

(c) (1) All development and/or construction will be performed in accordance with the standards of good workmanship and will be of "first class quality," and all work will be performed on, and the improvements erected upon, only that real estate described in the Deed; and

(2) Development and/or construction will not encroach upon or overhang any easement or right-of-way or upon the land of others; all improvements erected will be within applicable building restriction lines, however established, and will not violate applicable use or other restrictions contained in prior conveyances, recorded plats, ordinances, or regulations.

(d) Borrower will furnish the Lender from time to time, upon Lender's request, with a current survey, signed, sealed, dated, and certified to the Borrower, and also to the Lender as mortgagee, by a registered land surveyor, showing that all development and/or construction is entirely upon the real estate described in the Deed, is in accordance with the plans and specifications, and that no violation of the provisions of (c) (2) above have occurred; Borrower will, in any event, provide the Lender with a proper survey showing the location of each building foundation upon the lot prior to the first advance of funds after the closing, and upon request by Lender, with a final survey, upon completion of all improvements, showing the location of all streets, sidewalks, walkways, driveways, patios, and other permanent improvements, prior to a request for a final advance.

(e) Borrower will maintain at all times during the term of this Agreement and until construction is fully completed and the Deed in favor of Lender has been satisfied Builder's Risk and such other insurance, including fire, theft, vandalism and extended coverage, as required by Lender. Such insurance shall be in an amount and with a company acceptable to Lender with Lender being named as loss payee. Borrower shall provide to Lender evidence of such insurance prior to the first advance of funds being made to Borrower after the closing.

(f) Borrower represents that it has worker's compensation insurance in place as required by law and that it will maintain such insurance at all times during construction, and further that all of its subcontractors also have such insurance as required by law in place while they are working on the project.

(g) Borrower will provide to Lender on or before the first advance of funds after closing a building permit from the proper governmental authority authorizing Borrower to begin construction and/or development of the project.

9. Lender shall be entitled to collect from Borrower a fee for each inspection of $_____ per inspection.

10. Lender has had no control over, will have no control over, has not supervised, and will not supervise the construction of improvements on the property. Lender has not, does not, and will not make any representations, warranties, guarantees, or promises concerning the construction, workmanship, materials, or design employed in, to be used in, or constituting the improvements on the property. Lender's relationship to the construction and/or improvements on the property is solely that of a mortgage lender, and all periodic inspections and any appraisals made by the Lender are for the sole purpose of protecting Lender's security interest in the real estate and determining that progress has been made for the disbursement of construction loan funds as work has been completed.

11. In the event that the Lender advances funds for the payment of taxes, insurance, or other expenses related to the protection of the Lender's interest in the property, the Lender may charge a reasonable fee for such service. In the event that a check written by the Borrower is returned for insufficient funds, the Lender may impose a reasonable charge for collecting the amount due from Borrower.

EXHIBIT 12–4
Construction and/or Development Loan Agreement (continued)

---

12. (a)   If at any time prior to completion of the project, Borrower abandons the project, or if work ceases thereon for a period of more than ten (10) days without the prior written approval of the Lender, the Lender may, without notice to Borrower, declare all sums theretofore advanced immediately due and payable.

(b)   In the event of default and at the request of the Lender, Borrower shall transfer and assign, or cause to be transferred and assigned, all permits, registrations, vendor's warranties or guarantees used or obtained in connection with the project, in favor of the Lender or its nominee.

13. Provided Borrower is not in default hereunder, Lender shall release certain portions of the real estate, provided it is in accordance with the release provisions set forth in Lender's commitment letter.

Commencement of work must occur by _____ and be completed by _____.

The maximum amount to be advanced under the Lender's Note is $_____.

IN WITNESS WHEREOF, the undersigned has hereunto set its hand(s) and seal(s).

Date: _____

_____
Borrower

_____
Borrower

LENDER: _____

By: _____

GUARANTEE

The undersigned, being the Contractor for the Borrower named herein, for and in consideration of One Dollar ($1.00) and as an inducement to the Lender named herein to make the loan, hereby guarantees completion of all improvements in full accordance with the plans and specifications heretofore submitted to Lender, and hereby guarantees performance by Borrower in accordance with the terms and conditions of the foregoing agreement. The undersigned further guarantees that all bills, invoices, and other charges incurred by the undersigned for labor and material used and to be used in the construction of improvements on the property will be paid in full.

Date: _____

_____
Contractor

EXHIBIT 12-4
Construction and/or Development Loan Agreement (continued)

DISBURSEMENT AUTHORIZATION

Borrower hereby directs Lender to make all advances under the foregoing agreement directly to the Contractor named below. Borrower further hereby authorizes _____, as the agent of the Contractor named below, to apply for and receive all advances under the foregoing agreement for the purpose of paying all bills for labor and materials employed in the construction and/or development which is the subject of the foregoing agreement.

Date:

_____ Borrower

_____ Contractor _____ Borrower

AUTHORIZATION FOR DIRECT DEPOSIT TO CHECKING ACCOUNT
Construction Loan Department

The undersigned Borrower hereby authorizes the Construction Loan Department of _____ Bank to make direct deposits/advances from Borrower's construction loan funds to Borrower's _____ Bank Checking Account.

Borrower understands and agrees to the following terms and conditions:

(1)   No deposits or advances will be made if the loan account is delinquent on or before the date of the requested deposit.

(2)   No deposits or advances will be made unless all conditions precedent as set forth in the Construction and/or Development Loan Agreement have been satisfied.

(3)   _____ Bank shall not be responsible for any insufficient funds, charges or dishonored items in connection with the above checking account, and Borrower hereby releases Lender from any and all liabilities for such charges. Borrower agrees to assume all liability and responsibility for maintenance of said checking account and for compliance with _____ Bank's stated requirements before any deposits are made.

(4)   This authorization will remain in effect for the term of the loan until rescinded by Borrower in writing.

(5)   (a)   All Available Funds

All available funds will be transferred automatically to the account named below following each requested construction inspection, and in an amount calculated in accordance with the draw schedule adopted by the Construction Loan Department of _____ Bank, based on the progress of construction. _____ Bank will make deposits or advances only if all of the above requirements are met and Borrower is in full compliance with all terms of the Construction and/or Development Loan Agreement, Deed to Secure Debt, and Promissory Note in favor of Lender;

or

EXHIBIT 12–4
Construction and/or Development Loan Agreement
(continued)

(b)   Amount Requested Only

Funds will be transferred to the account named below, following each requested construction inspection, in an amount requested by the Borrower. The amount transferred, however, shall not be greater than the maximum amount available as calculated in accordance with _____ Bank's draw schedule based on progress of construction in place at each inspection. In no event will funds be transferred until an inspection is made by _____ Bank's Construction Inspector. _____ Bank will make deposits or advances only upon request of the undersigned Borrower, and only if all of the above requirements are met, and Borrower is in full compliance with all terms of the Construction and/or Development Loan Agreement, Deed to Secure Debt, and Promissory Note in favor of Lender.

CHECKING ACCOUNT INFORMATION

Title: _____

Number: _____

Borrower's Name: _____

Loan Number: _____   Date: _____

_____   _____
          Borrower   Borrower

Title Examinations

Titles are shadows.

—Daniel Defoe

OBJECTIVES

After reading this chapter you will be able to:

- Recognize the importance of title examinations
- Explain the three types of recording statutes
- Understand the process and procedures involved in conducting a title examination
- Review a title examination report
- Identify potential title problems and know how to solve them

GLOSSARY

Actual notice Title matters that a purchaser has direct knowledge or information about.

Bona fide purchaser for value Person who purchases real property in good faith for valuable consideration without notice of any claim to or interest in the real property by any other party.

Chain of title Historical sequence of all owners to a particular tract of real property beginning with the original owner and all successive owners who have derived their title from the original owner.

Constructive notice A presumption of law that charges a person with notice of all title matters that can be discovered from an inspection of the real property or an examination of public real property records.

Grantee index Alphabetical index of the public real property records that lists the last name of all people who are grantees of real property interest during a given year within the county.

Grantor index Alphabetical index of the public real property records that lists the last name of all people who are grantors of real property interest during a given year within the county.

Lis pendens Notice recorded in the real property records that informs that a lawsuit affecting title to real property described in the notice has been filed and is pending.

Plat index Index of all plats that have been recorded within the county within a given year.

Quiet title action Judicial proceeding to establish the ownership of real property.

Recording statutes State statutes that regulate the recordation of real property documents.

Record title holder Owner of real property as shown on the deed records from a title examination of the property.

Title examination Examination of the real property records to determine the ownership to a particular tract of real property.

One of the main responsibilities of a real estate attorney or legal assistant is to make certain that a client has good title of ownership to real property. A real estate attorney representing a purchaser will insist that the seller produce satisfactory evidence of good title before the purchase. A real estate attorney representing a lender will insist that the borrower produce satisfactory evidence of good title before the loan is made. Typically, this evidence of good title of ownership is provided by a title examination of the public real property records and the issuance of title insurance.

The role of the legal assistant in title examinations varies from state to state and even among law firms within a given state. In some law firms, a legal assistant conducts the title examination. A real estate closing legal assistant usually does not conduct the examination but is responsible for ordering the title examination, reviewing it, and converting it into a title insurance commitment, as discussed in Chapter 14. Regardless of whether the legal assistant is performing, ordering, or reviewing the title examination, an understanding of the process and procedures involved is essential for the legal assistant to carry out his or her responsibilities.

BONA FIDE PURCHASER FOR VALUE RULE

Why examine the public records of real property to obtain proof of ownership of property? Why record real estate documents? Warranty deeds, contracts, leases, mortgages, and easements are all enforceable without recording. Real estate attorneys and legal assistants, however, spend substantial time preparing these documents and having them executed with the formality required to place the documents on public record. Why? The answer is the common law **bona fide purchaser for value rule**. This rule states that anyone who purchases property in good faith for valuable consideration and without notice of any claim to or interest in the property by any other party is a bona fide purchaser and takes the property free and clear of any claims to or interests in the property by other parties.

For example, Sam Owner has pledged his farm to secure a debt owed to Aunt Owner. Sam Owner has executed and delivered to Aunt Owner a mortgage on the farm, but the mortgage was not recorded. Sam Owner sells the farm to Catherine Purchaser. At the time of the sale, Catherine Purchaser is unaware of the unrecorded mortgage to Aunt Owner. Catherine Purchaser is a bona fide purchaser for value and purchases the farm free and clear of Aunt Owner's mortgage. Aunt Owner's mortgage is unenforceable against the farm after the sale to Catherine Purchaser.

A bona fide purchaser must pay something of value for the property, although the consideration paid need not be equal to the market value of the property. The person taking title to property by inheritance or as a recipient of a gift has not given valuable consideration and, therefore, is not protected as a bona fide purchaser. This means that a person who has inherited real property takes the real property subject to all valid claims against the real property, regardless of whether the person had notice of the claims or whether the claims were recorded.

The bona fide purchaser status provides special protection not only to the bona fide purchaser but also to anyone purchasing from the bona fide purchaser. The protection is extended to the subsequent purchaser whether or not the subsequent purchaser has notice of any prior adverse claim or interest to the property. The rationale for the extended protection is to permit the bona fide purchaser to sell the property for full value.

A bona fide purchaser for value receives ownership to real property subject to any and all claims of which the bona fide purchaser has actual or constructive notice of at the time the property is acquired. **Actual notice** occurs when the purchaser has direct knowledge or information about title matters. Actual notice includes any facts that the purchaser can see with his or her own eyes, any facts that the purchaser learns about the property, and any information the circumstances of which should put the purchaser on duty to conduct an investigation that would lead to the finding of certain facts in regard to the property.

Constructive notice is a presumption of law that charges a purchaser with the responsibility of learning about all title matters that would result from an inspection of the property or an examination of the public real property records. Possession of land is notice to the world of the possessor's rights therein. For possession to constitute notice, it must be open, notorious, and exclusive. For example, a purchaser of a supposedly vacant lot of real property visits the lot and finds an inhabited mobile home on the lot. The purchaser is placed on notice to inquire about the mobile home inhabitant's rights to the property. If the mobile home inhabitants have a fifty-year unrecorded lease of the property, the prospective purchaser would purchase the property subject to the fifty-year lease, and the inhabitants of the mobile home would be permitted to remain on the property until the lease terminated. A purchaser of real property has a duty to inquire as to a party in possession's rights to the property. If no inquiries are made, the purchaser takes the property subject to any rights the possessor may have. A prudent purchaser will satisfy the constructive notice requirements of inspection by either inspecting the property or obtaining a full survey of the property by a registered land surveyor, or both.

The second form of constructive notice is in regard to matters that an inspection of the public real property records would reveal. All states maintain public real property records for the purpose of recording real estate documents and establishing ownership to real property. A prudent purchaser will satisfy the constructive notice requirements by examining the public records in which the documents are recorded.

Constructive notice is imparted to the purchaser only to the extent that recorded instruments are in the **chain of title**. A chain of title is the sequence of subsequent owners to a particular parcel of property, beginning with the original owner and moving through all successive grantors and grantees to the current owner. The chain of title concept limits the number of records imparting constructive notice and the number of records that must be examined. Courts in the states of Massachusetts and New York have pronounced views on the definition of chain of title. The laws in other states follow either the Massachusetts or the New York definition. Under the Massachusetts definition of chain of title, a purchaser need only examine conveyances from the point at which each owner received the property and until that owner conveyed the property to another owner. All other transactions are considered to be outside the chain of title and are held not to provide constructive notice to a purchaser. Under the New York definition of chain of title, the purchaser must examine all instruments made by successive owners and not merely the instruments made during the ownership.

New York:
In the New York chain of title, all instruments issued by successive owners must be checked.

Constructive notice also is imparted to unrecorded instruments that are referred to in a recorded instrument. For example, a recorded deed may make reference to an unrecorded mortgage. The purchaser must exercise reasonable diligence and prudence to ascertain the contents of the unrecorded mortgage because he or she may be responsible to pay the debt secured by the mortgage.

In summary, if a person obtains an interest in property by way of being a purchaser, a lender of a security deed or mortgage, the holder of an easement, or so on, the only way this property interest can be protected against subsequent purchasers is to record the deed, easement, mortgage, or instrument in the proper records. The act of recording the instrument in its proper place will place future purchasers on constructive notice. These future purchasers will purchase the property subject to the rights of the holder of the recorded instrument.

Recording an instrument is essential to impart constructive notice. The time and location for such recording normally are expressed in what is known as a state's recording statute. It is not always clear when an instrument is deemed recorded so as to impart constructive notice. Some courts have held that merely depositing the instrument in the office of the recorder is sufficient to impart constructive notice. Other courts have held that to impart constructive notice, the instrument must actually be transcribed in a permanent record book.

There also is a split of authority as to notice when an error has occurred in transcribing the instrument into the permanent record book. Some courts have imposed a duty on the person recording the instrument to make sure that it is correctly recorded, and such person shall bear full risk of the failure of the registrar of deeds to correctly record the instrument. An examination of the title records after the instrument has been recorded is necessary to discharge the duty. The examination is for the purpose of confirming that the recorded document has been correctly recorded and is in the chain of title. Under this view, the registrar of deeds is deemed to be the agent of the recording party. According to this view, an incorrectly recorded instrument does not impart constructive notice.[1]

Other courts have held that when an instrument is filed, constructive notice is given, regardless of whether the instrument was correctly indexed or recorded, provided that the party recording the instrument has complied with the state's recording statute and that the mistake was made by the clerk's or registrar's office.

RECORDING STATUTES

New York:
For a discussion of Recording Statutes in New York, see Appendix.

New York:
New York recognizes a race statute. Priority is established by the date of recording, not the date on the deed or document.

The common law bona fide purchaser for value rule has been modified in many states by **recording statutes**. Recording statutes (a) give the community notice of the changes in ownership of the property; (b) protect subsequent purchasers and encumbrancers of property from the same common grantor by giving them notice of information contained in the recorded documents; and (c) determine priority among conflicting claims to real property.

There are three types of recording statutes: race, notice, and race-notice. The first type is used by the least number of states. Under the race statute, priority between successive grantees of the same land from a common grantor is determined by who wins the race to the recording office. No notice is imparted to a subsequent purchaser or encumbrancers until the instrument is recorded in the prescribed manner. The first to record an instrument has priority of title, irrespective of whether he or she was a prior or subsequent purchaser. Moreover, a purchaser with actual knowledge of a prior but unrecorded instrument from a common grantor of the same property will have priority if such subsequent purchaser is the first to record his or her instrument. For example, Alice Owner conveys her home to Aaron Purchaser by deed dated March 1. Aaron Purchaser does not record the deed until March 4. Alice

---

[1] Robert S. Maxwell and David B. Summers, "Recording Statutes: Their Operation and Effect," *Washburn Law Journal* 17 (1978): pp. 615–637.

Owner on March 2 conveys the same home to Bob Purchaser. Bob receives the deed to the home on March 2 with full knowledge that a deed had been given by Alice Owner on the previous day to Aaron Purchaser. Bob Purchaser records the deed to the home on March 3. Under a race recording statute, Bob Purchaser would be the owner to the property because Bob Purchaser recorded the deed to the property before the recording of the deed by Aaron Purchaser.

The notice type of recording statute relies on the notice given by the recording of the instrument or on the notice obtained through means other than recording. Under the notice statute, the grantee of a deed is not required to record the deed to obtain the priority in title over some subsequent purchaser of the same property. The notice statute provides that an unrecorded instrument is valid to a subsequent purchaser if the purchaser paid value with notice of the unrecorded instrument and is invalid if the subsequent purchaser paid value without notice of the unrecorded instrument. Therefore, actual knowledge by a subsequent purchaser of the existence of a prior unrecorded document serves as notice in the same manner as the proper recording of the document. For example, Aaron Owner conveys his property to Robert Purchaser by deed dated January 1. Robert Purchaser neglects to record the deed promptly. On February 1, Aaron conveys the same property to Cindy Buyer, who has full knowledge of the deed to Robert. Cindy's deed is recorded on February 2. Thereafter, Robert on March 1 records the deed from Aaron dated January 1. Robert has priority of title even though Robert has the later recorded deed. This is so because Cindy had actual knowledge of the conveyance from Aaron to Robert at the time Cindy received Aaron's deed from Aaron.

The race-notice recording statute is the most common type. It combines the theory and recording requirements of both the race recording statute and the notice recording statute. The race-notice statute combines the theory that knowledge of a prior unrecorded instrument serves as notice in the same manner as the proper recording of the instrument with the recording principle that the first party to record an instrument has priority of title, regardless of whether that person was a prior or subsequent purchaser. Thus, under a race-notice statute, a subsequent purchaser has priority over the holder of a prior but unrecorded instrument if such subsequent purchaser makes the purchase without notice of the prior unrecorded instrument and records the instrument before the recording of the prior instrument. This type of recording statute operates as a pure notice statute until a subsequent purchaser takes title from the common grantor as a bona fide purchaser without notice of the prior recorded instrument. On that occurrence, the race-notice statute operates as a pure race statute in determining priority solely on the basis of which party records first.

The following is an example of the effect of the various recording statutes on the same factual course of events: Alice Owner conveys her home to Ajax Purchaser on March 1. Ajax Purchaser does not record the deed until March 3. On March 2, Alice Owner conveys the same home to Beth Purchaser, who purchases the home on March 2 with no knowledge of the March 1 deed from Alice Owner to Ajax Purchaser. Beth Purchaser does not record her deed until March 4. Under a race-notice statute, Ajax would have priority of title and would be the owner of the home because Ajax purchased the home without notice of any other claims and was the first to record the deed to the home. Under a notice statute, Beth would have priority of title and would be the owner of the home because Beth was a purchaser without notice of the prior unrecorded deed to Ajax, and the subsequent recording by Ajax does not divest the title and ownership existing in Beth. Under a race statute, Ajax would have priority and be the owner of the home because Ajax was the first to record a deed.

City of Richland Hills v. Bertelsen discusses both the concept of bona fide purchaser for value and the policy issues behind recording statutes.

 C A S E

City of Richland Hills v. Bertelsen
724 S.W. 2d 428 (Texas 1987)

OPINION

BURDOCK, Justice.

Appellant, the City of Richland Hills, appeals the trial court's denial of its motion for summary judgment and entry of partial summary judgment for appellee. The summary judgment motions arose from appellee, Keith Bertelsen's action for a declaratory judgment seeking to invalidate the city's claim to property owned by him.

We affirm as modified.

Appellee purchased the real property described below from Frank C. Campbell, for $30,000 cash:

> Lots A–L inclusive, Block 53, and Lots A–K inclusive, Block 44, Long Addition to the City of Richland Hills, Tarrant County, Texas, according to the revised Plat recorded in Volume 388–68, Page 29, Deed Records of Tarrant County, Texas.

Subsequently, appellee requested that the recorded plat of the land be vacated by the city's Planning and Zoning Commission. Later the city informed appellee it claimed a public park and easement on Lots K and L in Block 53, and Lot K in Block 44 of the property, pursuant to an antecedent unrecorded plat given the city by appellee's grantor.

Appellant, the city, filed a motion for summary judgment, claiming as a matter of law there was a dedicated public park and drainage easement on the property. Appellee filed a motion for partial summary judgment and severance, solely contending that appellant had no valid claim to a public park on the property. The trial court granted appellee's motion for partial summary judgment and severance, removing the cloud placed on the property by appellant's claim to a public park.

In three of its points of error, appellant alleges the trial court erred in finding appellee was a bona fide purchaser of the property for value, and in failing to find Campbell, appellee's grantor, had dedicated the lots as a public park.

* * *

[1] Before considering any rights appellee may have in the land in dispute, we must first determine whether or not he was a bona fide purchaser. A person qualifies as a bona fide purchaser for value if he purchases property in good faith for valuable consideration without notice. *Neal v. Holt*, 69 S.W.2d 603, 609 (Tex.Civ.App.—Texarkana 1934, writ ref'd). Since appellant does not allege appellee failed to pay valuable consideration or exhibited bad faith, we must only decide if appellee had notice of the city's claim.

It is elementary doctrine that, independent of valuable consideration and good faith, notice will destroy the character of a bona fide purchaser and defeat the protection otherwise given to him. *Id.* at 609.

Texas law has long favored the purpose of recording acts, which make land title information available to interested persons. *Leonard v. Benford Lumber Co.*, 110 Tex. 83, 216 S.W. 382, 383 (1919); *Hancock v. Tram Lumber Co.*, 65 Tex. 225, 232 (1885). In *Anderson v. Barnwell*, 52 S.W.2d 96, 101 (Tex.Civ.App.—Texarkana 1932), *affirmed*, 126 Tex. 182, 86 S.W.2d 41 (1935), the court stated:

> The intention of the recording acts is to compel every person receiving conveyances of real property to place such an instrument of record, not only that he may thereby protect his own rights, but also those of all others who may afterwards seek to acquire an interest in the same property.

Anderson, 52 S.W.2d at 101.

To be effectively recorded, an instrument relating to real property must be recorded in the public records in the county in which a part of the property is located. TEX.PROP.CODE ANN. sec. 11.001(a) (Vernon 1984). In addition, any conveyance of real property or an interest in real property is void as to a subsequent purchaser for valuable consideration without notice, unless the instrument has been acknowledged and filed for record as required by law. *See* TEX.PROP.CODE ANN. sec. 13.001(a) (Vernon 1984).

[2–4] Constructive notice is described as that notice one is charged with which is given by instruments of record, irrespective of any actual knowledge. 5 Lange, *Texas Land Titles*, sec. 811 (1961). Actual notice, on the other hand, exists when a person actually knows the facts charged to him, or should have known them if he had inquired about them, after learning of facts which put him on inquiry. *West v. Jennings*, 119 S.W.2d 685, 686 (Tex.Civ.App.—San Antonio 1938, no writ); 5 Lange, at sec. 811. We find appellee purchased the property in good faith and for valuable consideration and without constructive notice of appellant's claim.

An examination of the pleadings here shows the only plat on file with the county clerk was a properly acknowledged plat, signed by appellee's grantor. The subsequent unsigned plat which the city relies on was incapable of being recorded, and would only be discovered if appellee had reason to search the city records. Appellee had a right to rely on the records properly recorded in the office of the Tarrant County Clerk. *See Lesley v. City of Rule*, 255 S.W.2d 312, 314 (Tex.Civ.App.—Eastland 1953, writ ref'd n.r.e.).

If the plat held by the city had been recorded, it would have been in appellee's chain of tile and sufficiently put appellee on inquiry to inspect the city records. However, since nothing had been filed in the county records which constructively notified appellee of the existence of a dedicated park, we find he had no duty to search the city records. Without actual notice of the existence of a dedicated park, appellee takes the land free of the burden of a dedication to the city. *Pokorny v. Yudin*, 188 S.W.2d 185, 193 (Tex.Civ.App.—El Paso 1945, no writ).

In its third point of error, the city alleges the trial court erred in granting appellee's motion for summary judgment because appellant raised numerous fact issues. Most of appellant's complaints under this third point have already been discussed and overruled in our treatment of the first two points of error.

However, appellant raises one critical issue with its allegation that a fact issue existed regarding appellee's actual notice of the property's status as a city park. Ordinarily, actual notice is a fact question for the jury. *Goodwin v. Abilene State Bank*, 294 S.W. 883, 889 (Tex.Civ.App.—Eastland 1927, writ ref'd).

In support of its third point of error, the city relies in part on certain requests for admissions and their answers. A review of the record reveals that the city's requests for admissions and Bertelsen's answers are not included in the record on appeal pursuant to TEX.R.APP.P. 51, 52. Therefore, they are not before the court.

Even if the requests and answers were properly before the court, appellant's third point of error could not be sustained. In response to appellant's requests for admissions, appellee denied he had either actual or constructive knowledge of the city's claim of a park at the time he purchased the property from Campbell. The pleadings and affidavits filed by appellant do not indicate appellee knew or should have known the property was a park.

* * *

Affirmed.

ORDERING A TITLE EXAMINATION _____

The primary purposes of a **title examination**, as discussed previously, are to ensure that a seller has the ability to convey good title to the purchaser at the time of the closing or that a borrower has good title to the property being pledged as security for a loan. The purchaser's or lender's attorney or legal assistant usually orders or conducts the title examination. It is best to have the examination performed as early as possible to allow time for dealing with unexpected complications. In addition, a title "check down" or update usually is done immediately before the closing of the sale or loan. This update ensures that no adverse interest had been recorded against the property between the date of the preliminary title examination and the closing of the transaction for which the examination was made.

New York:
While it is best to order a title examination as soon as possible, this is usually not done until the client has a mortgage commitment. At the closing, the title closer calls in to make sure there are no changes in the quality of title. New York title companies insure the gap between the closing and the recording of the instruments.

Information Needed to Do an Examination

A title examiner should have as much accurate information as possible to perform the examination. The minimum information required is (a) a legal description of the property to be examined, (b) the name of the current owner, and (c) copies of all deeds, surveys, or any prior title examinations or title insurance policies that affect the property. If the examination is being prepared in connection with a sale, the sale's contract will have a description of the property to be purchased and the seller of the property should be the current owner. If the examination is being prepared in connection with a mortgage loan, the loan application usually contains a description of the property, and the loan applicant, it is hoped, is the current owner of the property. The property owner should be contacted to see if he or she has information, such as prior title examinations, surveys, or deeds, concerning the property. It is a good idea to use a title order form on which pertinent information may be written. An example of title order form is shown in Exhibit 13–1.

EXHIBIT 13–1
Abstract Order

Our File Number: _____ Date Ordered: _____ Need By: _____

Ordered by: _____ Date of Closing: _____

Present Owner/Seller: _____

Name of Purchaser: _____

RE Broker: _____

Brief Legal: _____

_____

Street Address: _____

Length of Search: _____

MISCELLANEOUS INFORMATION KNOWN:

Plat Information: _____

Back Title Policy: ( ) Yes ( ) No   Back Title Notes: ( ) Yes ( ) No

With Who: _____   _____

_____   _____

_____   _____

PLEASE PROVIDE US WITH ANY BANKRUPTCY INFORMATION: ( ) yes ( ) no

Other Information:

_____

_____

_____

_____

_____

_____

In Addition, please provide the following:

( ) Copies of applicable Restrictive Covenants of record

( ) Copies of applicable easements of record

( ) Copies of any liens, executions, fi fa, etc. of record

( ) City, State and County Mileage Rates (latest figures available)

( ) _____

( ) _____

( ) _____

EXAMINING TITLE TO REAL PROPERTY _____

Place to Search

Title examinations usually are conducted in the courthouse of the county in which the property is located. If the property is located in more than one county, it may be necessary to conduct the examination in each county to have a full title examination. The public official who is responsible for keeping real property records varies from state to state, but he or she usually is the clerk of the court or a registrar of deeds. The real property records typically are kept in a record room located within the county courthouse.

New York:
In New York a search usually goes back 60 years. If a problem is discovered it may go back further. The search will begin in either the grantor/grantee index or the lot and block index depending in the county being searched.

Period of Examination

A title examination searches the owner's chain of title by starting at the present time and working backward to some predetermined point. The examination establishes a source of title for each owner in the chain. Title examinations are classified as either full or limited searches. The length of time for a full search differs from state to state but usually requires that an owner's chain of title be established for fifty or sixty years. Most potential defects in title, both recorded and unrecorded, will have no effect on the current ownership of the property after fifty or sixty years.

A limited search title examination is for a period less than that required for a full search. Limited searches often are performed for loan assumptions and second-mortgage closings. The theory supporting a limited search in these situations is an assumption that a full search was performed for the first security mortgage holder and that all defects and objections were cured at that time. A title examination beginning from the recording date of the first mortgage should be sufficient to protect the interest of the parties. A limited search may be possible when the property is covered by a title insurance policy for which the full search was performed, or when the examiner can obtain a copy of a previous full title examination. Most title insurance companies issue title insurance based on a limited search from the date of an earlier title insurance policy. The client must be informed of the extent of the title examination in the title examiner's title opinion letter. The client also should be made aware that a limited search does not qualify as a full legal search and does not protect against title matters created before the starting date of the limited search.

What to Search

A title examination involves searching through a grantee index of the owner's chain of title backward in time to some predetermined point to establish a source of title for each owner in the chain. Then, for each grantor in the chain of title, the examiner searches the grantor's index from the date the grantor acquired title to the next grantor in the chain. Finally, the examiner searches other indices to determined whether there are any other recorded claims against the property, such as judgment liens, mechanic's liens, and tax liens.

Grantee and Grantor Indices

Most real property record rooms are indexed by the names of the grantees and the grantors of real property and the interest recorded therein. Each entry referenced in the grantee or grantor index usually provides the following information:

- Name of grantor
- Name of grantee
- Date of instrument
- Date of recording of instrument
- Nature of the instrument (e.g., deed, mortgage, easement)
- Brief description of the property covered
- Place where the instrument can be found so that it can be examined and read (record book and page reference)

Grantee index. The **grantee index** is an alphabetical index by last name of all people who are grantees of any property interest during a given year within the county. The index is maintained on a year-by-year basis from the beginning of time that the county maintained records. The grantee's property interest consists of purchasers, holders of mortgages and security deeds, easement holders, tenants, holders of liens, and so on.

The grantee index enables an examiner to build a chain of title from the present to the past. The first link in the chain of title is the conveyance to the current owner of the property. To find this first link, the examiner begins in the current year's grantee index and looks for the name of the current owner of the property. The examiner continues to search in each year's grantee index until the examiner finds the name of the current owner. Once this name is located, it is matched to the property in question. The examiner then looks to see who gave the property to the current owner (i.e., who was the grantor of the deed to the current owner); this person then becomes the next link in the chain of the title. The examiner searches the grantee index until this person's name is found. This process continues for fifty or sixty years in the grantee index, at which time the examiner should have a list of successive owners of the property, the dates they acquired ownership, and the dates they transferred ownership away for the fifty- or sixty-year history. Once this is done, the examiner uses the grantor index.

Grantor index. A **grantor index** is an annual alphabetical index by last name of all people who are grantors of a real property interest within the county. Grantors of property are sellers, borrowers, mortgagors, grantors of easements, and so on. The examiner begins with the grantor index from the past and follows it to the present. The examiner starts with the last grantee that was found in the grantee index and then examines the grantor index until this person's name is found and there is a transfer of the property from them. For example, if the examiner, at the conclusion of the grantee index search, finds that in 1944 (fifty-year search beginning in 1994) Mary T. Sneed was the owner of the property, the examiner begins the grantor index searching for the name of Mary T. Sneed. He or she will begin in the 1944 index. The examiner continues the search in 1944, 1945, 1946, and so on until Mary T. Sneed's name is located as the grantor of a deed transferring ownership of the property. At this juncture, the examiner searches for the name of the grantee of the deed from Mary T. Sneed, and this person becomes the next grantor to be located. The examiner stays with this person until they have conveyed away the property by deed. By reviewing the grantor index, the examiner can discover any easements, mortgages, or other title exceptions to the property.

Plat Index

Most counties maintain a **plat index or tract index**, and copies of all plats that have been recorded within the county. The index to the plats usually is based on one of the following criteria: (a) land lot and district (location designation), (b) name of owner

New York:
New York City has established the lot and block system for indexing and this is used instead of the grantor/grantee index. The entire city is mapped and divided into lots and blocks. To search a title you must look at all the transactions involving that lot and block. It is like finding a post office box—once you find the box usually all your mail is in there.

designation, or (c) subdivision designation. For example, title is being examined to property in the Pine Tree Subdivision, which was developed by the Acme Realty Company and was located in Land Lot 100 of the 17th District of Salem County, Virginia. An index to a plat reference (a book and a page where a plat is recorded) for the subdivision can be found in one of three ways. First, there may be an entry under Land Lot 100 of the 17th District for Pine Tree. Second, there may be in the owner index a listing for Acme Realty Company and a list of all plats filed by Acme Realty Company, with a book and a page where the plats are located. Third, there may be a listing in the subdivision index for Pine Tree Subdivision. Once the plat has been found, it should be carefully examined. The plat contains a legal description of the property, and it should match the description being used for the examination. Any discrepancies in the description should be noted. Plats often have restrictive covenants printed on them that are binding on an owner of the property. Plats also show building setback lines, easements, and other matters. Most courthouses have photocopy equipment to enable the examiner to make a copy of the plat, and it is advisable to request that a copy be made for the legal assistant and the client.

Reviewing the Various Instruments in the Chain of Title

A title examiner carefully examines each instrument's property description to make certain that it is the same as the property that is being examined. Title examiners should note any errors or discrepancies in the legal description. The legal description may change over the course of time because a current parcel of property may have been included within larger tracts in the past history of the property. For example, a title examiner is examining record title to a residential subdivision lot. The lot is described by a plat book and page reference. The residential subdivision lot in its past history was part of a farm that was described by a metes and bounds legal description.

The examiner maps out each property conveyance, including the property conveyed and the property excluded from the conveyance, to determine that the property in question is being transferred each time and that the current legal description is a true description of the property vested in the current record owner. Subtle differences in property description that go undetected early can seriously impair the validity of the title examination.

When reviewing deeds, easements, or mortgages, an examiner usually does the following:

- Notes the identity of the parties to the instrument, the date the instrument was signed, and the date it was filed
- Examines the signature and witnessing requirements
- Makes a notation of what estate was being conveyed (e.g., fee simple, life estate)
- Pays particular attention to any covenants or other requirements that may be set out in the instruments

Most title examiners make copies of all instruments in the chain of title that currently affect the property and attach the copies as exhibits to the title examination report.

Other Things to Examine

In addition to searching the grantee and grantor indices and reviewing various documents contained therein, there are other potential title problems an examiner must look for. These items may change slightly from state to state but usually include the following:

Judgments

New York:
Judgments against real estate in New York are good for ten years and may be renewed for another ten years. Unpaid traffic tickets are also considered judgments aginst the owners in New York City. Unpaid bail bond is also a lien against property as are claims filed by the Welfare Department, and sidewalk repair violations.

Title company does an update of the title search up to the time that title closes to make sure no last minute judgments have been filed.

A money debt resulting from a lawsuit is called a judgment. A judgment may have been entered against an owner in the chain of title. Once a judgment has been recorded in the public records, it becomes a lien on all property of the judgment debtor. A docket or index for judgments can be found in the real property record room. The docket lists in alphabetical order the names of all people within the county within a given year against whom a judgment has been recorded. The index also refers to a book and page of a judgment book in which a copy of the judgment can be found. The index does not indicate the amount of the judgment or whether the judgment has been paid and satisfied. An examination of a copy of the judgment in the judgment book reveals the amount as well as whether or not the judgment has been satisfied. Most clerks print the word "Paid" or "Satisfied" on a judgment when it has been paid. Judgments in most states have only a seven-year lifetime, but they can be renewed for an additional seven years. Because judgments attach at the time of recordation to all property then owned by the judgment debtor or to any property thereafter acquired by the judgment debtor, it is necessary for the examiner to examine the judgment index for the names of all people who have owned the property during the lifetime of a judgment (seven years). For example, Bryan Thompson, Martha Farris, and the Winston Company, Inc., have by the grantee-grantor search been found to be owners at one time or another of the property during the past seven years. All these names should be searched in the judgment index.

Federal and State Tax Liens

The federal and state governments have the right to file a lien against the property of any delinquent taxpayer. A federal tax lien, once filed, becomes a lien on all property owned by the taxpayer at the time of filing as well as all future property acquired by the taxpayer until the lien has been paid in full. Most record rooms maintain a separate index for federal tax liens and a separate book in which the federal tax liens can be examined. The same considerations and procedures for examining judgments apply to federal and state tax liens, except that a federal or state tax lien usually does not have a limited lifetime and remains in full force and effect until it has been paid or satisfied.

Delinquent Taxes

New York:
When searching a cooperative title, always look in the county where the property is located for UCC financing statements. For other searches check the state capital, in Albany, for filings.

All property is taxed by county or city governments and may be separately assessed for sanitary, sewer, or other services. These tax liabilities and other assessments are liens on the property. Liens for assessments may be found in a tax assessor's or tax collector's office, which may be separate and apart from the real property record room. In many localities, there are specialized tax services that examine tax and assessment records for a reasonable price. Most title examiners and law firms use these services where they are available to determine the tax obligations of a particular piece of property.

Uniform Commercial Code

Many real estate transactions involve both real and personal property. When personal property is involved, it is necessary for the examiner to search the Uniform

Commercial Code (UCC) financing statement index to determine if any of the personal property has been pledged as security for a loan. This index is an alphabetical listing of the last name of all debtors who have pledged personal property as security for a loan. In states that also have central filing of UCC financing statements with the secretary of state's office, a state search must be conducted as well as a local search.

Lis Pendens

A lawsuit affecting title to real estate that has not been resolved and is still pending is not a cloud on the title to the property unless a **lis pendens** is filed in the real property records. A lis pendens charges third parties with notice that an action is pending against certain property and that if they purchase the property or acquire a loan on the property, they will be bound by the subsequent judgment in the lawsuit. Both real and personal property are subject to a lis pendens. A lis pendens is inapplicable in a suit for a personal or money judgment. Lis pendens is applicable only in an action that directly affects title to property. For example, a lis pendens would be applicable to any suit that challenges the current ownership of the property. In addition, a lis pendens would be applicable in a suit for breach of contract against a current owner if the suit is asking for specific performance of the contract. An action for divorce does not ordinarily invoke a lis pendens, except when specific property is sought for either alimony purpose or a property settlement.

A lis pendens usually is a simple document that gives notice that a lawsuit has been filed as well as information concerning the lawsuit, such as the court in which the lawsuit was filed, the parties involved, a civil action file number, and a brief description of the nature of the lawsuit. If a lis pendens is filed, the property in the lis pendens is subject to the outcome of the lawsuit, and a lis pendens is considered to be a cloud on the title. Most counties maintain separate record for the lis pendens. The record index is maintained alphabetically in the name of the property owner.

Civil Suits

Technically, a pending civil suit, regardless of its nature, does not have any effect on title to real property unless a lis pendens notice has been recorded. Many title examiners, however, examine the civil dockets for informational purposes. For example, if a client is in the process of purchasing property from a seller and the examiner finds on the civil docket a number of lawsuits against the seller for breach of contract, the client should be advised to be cautious.

Probate Court Records

Property may pass through probate and estate proceedings because of the death of one of the owners. It may be necessary for the examiner to examine the probate court records to make sure that the will is properly probated and that the property has been distributed to the devisees under the will or the heirs at law, in the case of an intestate estate. In addition, if property has been sold by the executor of an estate, the title examiner searches the probate or estate records to ascertain if the proper authority for the sale had been obtained by the executor.

New York:
Probate Court is called Surrogate's Court in New York. It may also be necessary to do a "kinship affidavit" to determine who the heirs to property are.

Mechanics' Liens

A mechanics' lien or lien given to a contractor, laborer, or material supplier who has contributed to the construction of improvements on real property may be found in the grantor index or in a separate index.

Preliminary Title Report

Once a title examination is completed, the examiner reports in writing the conclusion of the examination. If title insurance is being obtained, the examiner certifies title to the title insurance company and an insurance commitment or binder is issued before the closing. At a minimum, the title report should reveal the following: (a) the name of the current record title holder; (b) legal description of captioned property; (c) existing unpaid loans or mortgages; (d) other lien holders; (e) status of taxes; (f) listing of all easements, covenants, and other restrictions; (g) any objections to marketability; (h) other matters that affect title; and (i) requirements for vesting marketable title in the purchaser.

The title examination should be reviewed as soon as it is received. Defects that may take time to cure should be addressed promptly to avoid a delay in closing.

Title Examination Example

An example of a title examination is shown in Example 13–1.

EXAMPLE 13–1 TITLE EXAMINATION

Property

ALL THAT TRACT or parcel of land lying and being in Land Lot 50 of the 3rd District, Fulton County, Georgia, Lot 3, Block A, Pines Subdivision, per plat recorded at Plat Book 10, page 64, Fulton County, Georgia Records.

Situation

Your firm represents a purchaser of the above-referenced property who has a contract with John Samson. You have been asked to examine title to the property to determine the title of John Samson. You have in your possession a title policy insuring title to the property under the name of the ABC Company, dated with an effective date of November 4, 1974. You have been asked to do a limited title examination from November 4, 1974, through the current date. The 1974 title policy revealed no exceptions to title.

The following is an example of the title notes taken from this limited title examination:

Grantee Index: (FIRST ENTRY): 3-1-92, Samson, John—Sarah T. Davis—3-1-92—WD—Lot 3, Block A, Pines Subdivision—DB 604, Page 91.

(SECOND ENTRY): 6-9-87—Davis, Sarah T.—George Farris—6-9-87—WD—Lot 3, Block A, Pines Subdivision—DB 496, Page 831.

(THIRD ENTRY): 2-7-78—Farris, George—ABC Co.—2-7-78—WD—Lot 3, Block A, Pines Subdivision—DB 291, Page 204.

(FOURTH ENTRY): 11-4-74—ABC Co.—Fred Smith—11-4-74—WD—20 Acres—Pines Subdivision—DB 283, Page 61.

Grantor Index: (FIRST ENTRY): 11-4-74—Smith, Fred—ABC Co.—11-4-74—WD—20 Acres—Pines Subdivision—DB 283, Page 61.

(SECOND ENTRY): 11-4-74—ABC Co.—First Bank—11-4-74—DSD—20 Acres—Pines Subdivision—DB 283, Page 63.

(THIRD ENTRY): 7-9-77—ABC Co.—Georgia Power—7-9-77—EASE—Pines Subdivision—DB 289, Page 150.

(FOURTH ENTRY): 2-7-78—ABC Co.—George Farris—2-7-78—WD—Lot 3, Block A, Pines Subdivision—DB 291, Page 204.

(FIFTH ENTRY): 2-7-78—Farris, George—S.L. of Tucker—2-7-78—DSD—Lot 3, Block A, Pines Subdivision—DB 291, Page 205.

(SIXTH ENTRY): 6-9-87—Farris, George—Sarah T. Davis—6-9-87—WD—Lot 3, Block A, Pines Subdivision—DB 496, Page 831.

(SEVENTH ENTRY): 3-1-92—Davis, Sarah T.—John Samson—3-1-92—WD—Lot 3, Block A, Pines Subdivision—DB 604, Page 91.

(EIGHTH ENTRY): 5-10-94—Samson, John—Acme Finance—5-10-94—DSD—Lot 3, Block A, Pines Subdivision—DB 608, Page 200.

Explanation of Title Notes

To prepare the title notes in Example 13–1, the title examination would have proceeded as follows:

Step 1. Armed with a description of the property and the current owner's name, John Samson, the examiner goes to the Fulton County Courthouse.

Step 2. The examiner first examines the subdivision plat of Pines Subdivision. It is not necessary to use a plat index to locate the plat because a plat book and page number for the plat are part of the legal description. If the plat book or page number for the plat were not provided, it could have been obtained by looking in the subdivision name index under the Pines Subdivision.

Step 3. The plat shows the dimensions of Lot 3. The examiner notes any restrictive covenants, easements, or setback lines that affect Lot 3. The examiner makes a copy of the plat and attaches it to the title report.

Step 4. The examiner is now ready to start in the grantee index. The examiner looks in the current year's index under the "S's" for John Samson. Because John Samson may be a common name in the county, the examiner may find many entries for John Samson, but the examiner is only interested in the entry for John Samson that affects Lot 3, Block A, Pines Subdivision. According to the title notes, the examiner does not find any entries in the current year or any year until 1992. In the 1992 book, the examiner finds an entry dated March 1, 1992, from John Samson—Sarah T. Davis, a warranty deed affecting the property and recorded at Deed Book 604, Page 91. The examiner at this stage stops indexing and goes to Deed Book 604, Page 91, and looks at the deed to make sure that it is in fact the same parcel of property being examined. Once assured that it is the same parcel of property, the examiner returns to the grantee index for further indexing.

Step 5. The next person the examiner looks for in the grantee index is Sarah T. Davis. The examiner looks in the 1992 book for Davis because she may have acquired the property the day before she sold it to Brown. The examiner does not find Davis in the 1992 book and looks in the 1991, 1990, 1989, 1988, and 1987 books. In the 1987 book, the examiner finds an entry to Sarah T. Davis from George Farris, a warranty deed for the same property. Once this deed has been discovered, George Farris becomes the next person to look for in the grantee index. The examiner stays in the same period, 1987, and searches the "F's" for George Farris. The examiner then does the indices for 1986, 1985, 1984, 1983, 1982, 1981, 1980, 1979, and 1978. In the 1978 grantee index, the examiner finds an entry to George Farris from the ABC Co. for this property. ABC Co. then becomes the next grantee, and the examiner indexes ABC Co. all the way back to 1974, where the examiner finds an entry to ABC Co. from Fred Smith.

Step 6. Because the search is limited, this is the end of the grantee indexing. The grantee search gives the following information: ABC Co. owned the property from 11-4-74 to 2-7-78; George Farris owned the property from 2-7-78 to 6-9-87; Sarah T.

Davis owned the property from 6-9-87 to 3-1-92; and John Samson bought the property on 3-1-92 from Sarah T. Davis. The examiner does not know if John Samson is still the owner of the property. This information cannot be determined except for a needle-in-the-haystack type of search from the grantee index. This information is more readily available in the grantor index.

Step 7. The examiner starts searching in the grantor index from the past to the present. The examiner starts in the grantor index for 1974 with the name Fred Smith and finds an entry from Fred Smith to ABC Co. on 11-4-74. The next grantor, then, is ABC Co., and the examiner stays with the name in the 1974 book. The examiner finds an entry on the same day to the First Bank. It is a DSD, which is an abbreviation for deed to secure debt. The examiner stays with ABC Co. They have not transferred property but have only pledged the property as security for a loan to First Bank. The examiner runs the 1974, 1975, 1976, and 1977 books for ABC Co. In the 1977 grantor index, the examiner finds an entry from ABC Co. to Georgia Power, something called an EASE. This is an abbreviation for easement. (Many counties abbreviate all the identification of the instruments, and it may take a few days to learn all the abbreviations.) This entry to Georgia Power still does not divest ABC Co. of title to the property, and ABC Co. remains grantor. The examiner searches the 1978 index for ABC Co. and finds an entry of a warranty deed to George Farris. This entry does divest ABC Co. of title, and George Farris then becomes the next grantor. The examiner then switches to the 1978 index under the "F's" and finds an entry from George Farris to the S&L of Tucker. It is another deed to secure debt, which means that George Farris has pledged the property as security for a loan. The examiner stays with George Farris and looks in the 1978, 1979, 1980, 1981, 1982, 1983, 1984, 1985, 1986, and 1987 grantor index books for George Farris. In the 1989 grantor index, the examiner finds an entry from George Farris to Sarah T. Davis. It is a warranty deed entry, and Sarah T. Davis now becomes the next grantor. The examiner searches Davis for 1987, 1988, 1989, 1990, 1991, and 1992. In the 1992 book, there is an entry from Davis to John Samson, a warranty deed. John Samson now becomes the next grantor. The examiner searches Samson for 1992, 1993, and 1994, and in 1994 there is an entry from John Samson to Acme Finance, another deed to secure debt. The property has been pledged another time as security for a loan. The examiner continues to search John Samson forward to the most current date of the examination. Every attempt should be made to examine up to the date of the examination; however, some record rooms may be behind in indexing, and the search can only go as far as the record day. Most clerks post each day the "record date" of the system.

Once both the grantee and the grantor search are finished, the examiner can determine from the title notes the following: (a) John Samson owns the property and (b) the property is subject to a (i) deed to secure debt from ABC Co. to First Bank; (ii) an easement from ABC Co. to Georgia Power; (iii) a deed to secure debt from George Farris to S&L of Tucker; and (iv) a deed to secure debt from John Samson to Acme Finance.

It is now necessary for the examiner to review each and every document, including every deed in the chain of title. These documents are found by going to the deed book and pages that were discovered during the indexing. Satisfactions of deeds to secure debts or mortgages often are stamped in the book and are difficult to find through the indexing process.

Once all the deeds, security deeds, easements, and so on have been examined, the examiner does the other searches regarding judgments, tax liens, lis pendens, and so on.

TITLE DEFECTS AND PROBLEMS _____

A real estate legal assistant should be familiar with common title defects and basic procedures for curing them. Space does not permit more than a short summary of title objections that can arise from a title examination. The exact procedure to be followed in resolving these objections varies from state to state. The course of corrective action also depends on the nature and severity of the defect and the purpose for which the property is being purchased.

A sale or loan closing cannot be completed until title defects and objection have been removed.

Record Title Holder

The owner of the real property as shown in the deed records is known as the **record title holder**. In most cases, the seller named in the sales contract or the borrower who is applying for the loan is the holder of the record title. If the title examination reveals that someone else is the record title holder, there is a problem. Sometimes the problem is simple, as when a husband signs the sales contract but record title is in the wife's name. The closing legal assistant can easily verify with the real estate agent if the wife is the real seller. At other times, the problem is not so simple, as when an heir signs the sales contract but the record title holder is the deceased. In this case, an estate probate proceeding may be necessary.

Another situation arises when the seller is not the record title holder but has been in possession of the captioned property for more than the statutory adverse possession period. The closing should not take place until a judicial proceeding, a suit to **quiet title**, is brought to establish the seller as the record title holder. Another solution is to obtain quitclaim deeds from all parties with a possible interest in the property.

Breaks in the Chain of Title

A chain of title is composed of consecutive links of the grantors and grantees of the captioned property: A to B, B to C, C to D, with D holding current record title. Occasionally there is a missing link: A to B, D to E. The record title does not reveal how B was divested of title or how D acquired title. A break in the chain of title can be caused by any number of factors, such as an unrecorded deed, a name change, an unadministered estate, or a foreign divorce decree. Unless the missing link can be reconstructed by verifiable sources outside the record, the defect is a serious cloud on the title.

The link must be established before it can be determined what is necessary to protect the record. Often all that can be done is to advise the parties of the problem and require them to establish the missing link. If the current owner and the predecessors in title have satisfied the statutory requirements for adverse possession, a quiet title action brought by D against B and his heirs would resolve the problem, assuming that B or his heirs do not have a valid defense.

Under a contract to purchase, the purchaser cannot force the current owner to prosecute a suit to quiet title. Legally, the purchaser can only reject title until the defect is corrected or seek damages in a suit for breach of contract.

Errors in Prior Recorded Deeds

Errors in a prior recorded deed in the chain of title, such as an erroneous legal description, misspelled name, or improper execution, must be cured before title is acceptable. When possible, such errors may be cured by a corrective deed from the grantor to the grantee of the defective deed. A corrective deed has the same format as the original deed, with the error corrected and a clause inserted:

> This deed is given to correct [describe error] contained in a prior deed between the parties dated _____, 19___, recorded _____, 19___, in the Clerk's Office, Circuit Court of _____ County, Virginia, at Deed Book _____, Page _____.

The corrective deed must be recorded. A corrective deed may not be used to change a greater estate to a lesser estate (i.e., fee simple to life estate); nor can it be used to change the identity of a grantor altogether, although it may correct misspellings. It is the responsibility of the current owner to locate the parties and obtain the corrective deed.

An error in a prior recorded mortgage or deed of trust is of no consequence so long as the mortgage or deed of trust is paid and released before closing.

Name Variances

Name variances, as distinguished from a simple misspelling, is a variation between the name by which a record title holder acquired title to the property and a name by which the holder conveyed the title. If variances in the name of a previous record title holder exist, the current owner should be asked to provide an affidavit from the prior owner that the person whose name appears in the two documents are one and the same person. If the variances are in the name of the current owner, a clause in the deed explaining the variance is sufficient. For example:

> Grantor named herein is one and the same person as John D. Adams, the Grantee named in a prior deed dated _____ day, 19___, and recorded _____ day, 19___, in the Clerk's Office, Circuit Court of _____ County, Colorado, in Deed Book _____, Page _____;

Corporations and partnerships can present a similar problem. In the case of the corporation, a certified copy of an amendment changing the corporate name should be obtained from the Clerk of the State Corporation Commission. In the case of a general partnership, affidavits from each partner may be required to verify a name change, merger, or death of a partner. When one general partner has power of attorney to act on behalf of the others, a single affidavit may be sufficient. Similarly, in the case of a limited partnership, a single affidavit from the general partner normally is sufficient.

Improper and Missing Power of Attorney

When a deed in the owner's chain of title was signed for the owner by an attorney-in-fact, a properly executed power of attorney should have been recorded with the deed. If it was not, the effect is the same as if the deed itself was not signed. The defect may be cured by having the current owner obtain and record a correction deed or quitclaim deed signed by the prior owner.

Sales Contracts, Options, and Leases

If the title examination reveals that the property is subject to a contract or an option to sell or lease, the owner should provide proof by affidavit or other means that the contract or option has expired. If the contract or option has not expired, the seller should be required to obtain a quitclaim deed from the purchaser or optionee named in the contract. The quitclaim deed should be recorded if the contract or option was recorded.

If the property is subject to a lease or if a lease is discovered during the title examination, all parties should be advised to make inquiry as to possession. Depending on the purchaser's purpose in acquiring the property, the lease may or may not constitute a defect. A lender also should be advised of the outstanding possessory rights of any person other than a purchaser or borrower.

Because leases often are unrecorded or not in writing, the purchaser or lender should always be advised to physically inspect the property well in advance of closing. A discovery that the premises are occupied by someone other than or in addition to the current owner indicates a possible possessory interest in a third party.

Unsatisfied or Unreleased Mortgages

If an existing mortgage or deed of trust is to be assumed by the purchaser, it will be necessary to obtain an assumption package from the lender. If the debt is to be satisfied at closing, it is necessary to obtain a payoff amount from the lender and make certain that the debt is in fact satisfied from the sale proceeds. Sometimes a mortgage or deed of trust in the owner's chain of title will have been satisfied but never released of record. In this situation, the owner should obtain a release from the lender or an affidavit of repayment.

Mortgages and deeds of trust commonly are satisfied by one of two forms of release: (a) a marginal release entered in the margin of the deed book in which the mortgage or deed of trust is recorded, or (b) a certificate of satisfaction from the lender to the record title holder recorded in the office in which the mortgage or deed of trust is recorded. Mortgages also may be partially released when more than one parcel of property is secured by a single mortgage or deed of trust. When dealing with a series of parcel releases, it is important to make sure that they constitute a complete release of record of the property in question.

New York: If an unsatisfied mortgage is found, and seller claims he satisfied it, the title company usually escrows at least twice the amount of the mortgage until the satisfaction is found.

Notice of Lis Pendens

A notice of lis pendens is a recorded notice that there is a pending suit or lien of attachment that may affect the title to the property. Such a notice must be released of record before the property can be sold or pledged as security for a loan. This usually requires that the suit itself for which the lis pendens serves as notice be settled or dismissed with prejudice.

Easements

An easement may be created in property by grant, prescription, implication, or necessity. A full discussion of easements is set forth in Chapter 6. Many title examiners routinely object to all recorded easements as defects in the title. As a practical matter, only those easements that in some way restrict the use of the property by the owner are of any consequence. It is important to note that all easements that may restrict the owner's use may not be recorded. Easements that are not recorded include prescriptive easements, easements of necessity, and implied easements.

Nonrestrictive easements, such as those routinely granted to utility companies to allow a reasonable ingress and egress for the purpose of maintaining utility service, usually do not require further action. When a utility easement has been granted a general description (blanket easement), it is wise to ascertain the manner in which the easement has been exercised in the past to make sure that the exercise will not interfere with the owner's use. It is possible to obtain from many utility companies a containment agreement in which the utility company agrees that its easement rights are limited to the actual location of its lines and an area reasonably surrounding such location to provide for maintenance access to the lines. Easements that do restrict the owner's use in a serious manner or that would prevent certain additions or improvements from being made on the property are serious title defects that do need to be resolved before the closing of the sale or loan.

Restrictive Covenants and Conditions

All unexpired restrictive covenants and conditions should be reported to the parties. These normally are of little significance unless restrictions interfere with the owner's use of the property or unless the covenant contains a reversion or forfeiture clause. A reversion or forfeiture clause provides that on violation of the condition, title reverts to the grantor or is otherwise forfeited by the violation. If such a clause is found, the seller should provide proof by affidavit or other means that there has been no violation. Minor violations of covenants or conditions not subject to reversion or forfeiture may be released or waived by the owners of the property benefited by the restrictions. For example, if the house on the property is shown as violating a private building line, it is possible to obtain a waiver from all other owners in the subdivision that such building line violation is acceptable.

Recorded restrictions may be found in the individual deeds of conveyance, or they may be noted on the recorded subdivision plat, or both. Subdivision restrictions or regulations may not be recorded on every deed; however, restrictions may attach by implication to each parcel conveyed from a common developer if there is evidence of a general plan or scheme of development. This general plan or scheme operates as constructive notice of the possible existence of restrictions on use.

Restrictive covenants and conditions often are limited in duration by their terms. Subdivision regulations also may be limited in duration but may be renewed by the action or lack of action of a majority of the affected landowners. When restrictions are not limited in duration, changing conditions over the years may make them unreasonable and, therefore, unenforceable. It also is possible to have restrictions on use waived by the owners of the benefited property before any violation, thereby removing an objection that might otherwise be a serious title defect.

Mechanics' and Materialmen's Liens

Recorded mechanics' and materialmen's liens must be treated as adverse claims against the property. A full discussion of mechanics' and materialmen's liens is set forth in Chapter 5. The owner of the property should be required to pay the liens and satisfy them of record or discharge them by filing a proper bond before or at the sale or loan of the property. If the liens are to be satisfied at the closing of a sale, contact must be made with the holders of the lien to obtain the amount of the lien and to arrange for payment. If the owner objects to paying the lien, the owner should be required to post a bond that, in most states, will release the property from the lien.

Unperfected liens also are of concern to the purchaser because the purchaser will take property subject to all mechanics' and materialmen's liens for work or material furnished within the past 60 to 100 days, regardless of whether or not a claim of lien has been filed. For this reason, a seller should be required to provide an affidavit that no improvements have been made or materials supplied within the necessary statutory period before the date of the sale or loan on the property.

UCC Financing Statements

If an examination of the UCC index reveals a financing statement describing personal property or fixtures that are considered part of the realty being transferred or pledged as security for the loan, the owner should be required to terminate the security interest.

Judgment Liens

Final judgments for money damages constitute liens against all real property that the defendant owns or subsequently acquires. A title examiner will report such judgments as objections when there is a possibility that the current owner is the named defendant.

When the judgment is known to be or is admitted to be against the current owner, the owner must be required to satisfy the lien before or at closing. The judgment lien holder should be contacted to obtain the amount of balance due, and care should be taken to make sure the judgment is in fact satisfied from the sale or loan proceeds.

If it is not certain that the judgment is against the owner and the owner denies that he is the defendant named in the judgment, an affidavit to this effect may be sufficient to protect the title to the property. An example of the language used in the affidavit is as follows:

> Affiant does state under oath that he is not one and the same person as John D. Adams named as defendant in the judgment dated _____, 19___, recorded _____, 19___ in the Clerk's Office, Circuit Court of _____ County, Indiana, in Judgment Docket _____, Page _____ for _____ dollars in favor of Acme Loan Company, plaintiff.

A judgment against prior owners of the captioned property may remain as valid liens against the property despite the fact that the property has been subsequently conveyed. If judgments are found against the prior owners that do affect the property, the current seller is required to satisfy these judgments of record.

Tax Liens

Unpaid county or city property taxes should be paid before or at closing, except for the current year's taxes that are not yet due and payable. It is necessary to obtain pay-off figures from the appropriate tax officials and to supervise that the taxes are in fact paid from the sale or loan proceeds.

Federal tax liens and state income tax liens of many states, when recorded, are liens against all the real property owned or subsequently acquired by the delinquent taxpayer. Tax liens should be handled in the same manner as judgments, except that payoff figures are obtained from the Internal Revenue Service or the state's Revenue Commission. The Internal Revenue Service will provide a certificate of release or discharge when the lien has been satisfied or may, in certain circumstances, provide a partial release as to the parcel of property being sold or pledged for a loan. In situations where the owner of the property has a name similar to that of a delinquent tax-

New York:
A UCC–1 statement is used to file the security interest and a UCC–3 statement must be used to terminate the security interest. The UCC financing statements are filed in the county where the property is located, and the state. The UCC–3's will also be filed in the county and or state, the same places the UCC–1 is filed.

New York allows a "quiet title action" to resolve any title disputes.

payer and it can be verified that the owner is not the same person as the delinquent taxpayer, the Internal Revenue Service will issue certificates of nonattachment that release the owner's property from the effect of the tax lien.

Title Through Estates

The title examination may reveal that the property has been conveyed by the heirs or representatives of a deceased record title holder. In this situation, the fee title may now be unified in a single record title holder, or it may be fragmented into separate shares owned by the grantees of the various heirs or representatives. To be certain that the current owners in fact hold title in fee simple to the property in question, it may be necessary to account for all possible fragments of interest. In most cases, a list of heirs recorded in the county clerk's office or a probate office allows the title examiner to follow and document these conveyances. If, for some reason, no list of heirs has been filed, it may be necessary to obtain an affidavit of descent from a person with personal knowledge of the decedent and his or her family. An example of an affidavit of descent is shown in Example 13–2.[2]

EXAMPLE 13–2

Affidavit of Descent

STATE OF _____   Re: PROPERTY OF _____

COUNTY OF _____   Deed Book _____,

Page _____,

_____ County Records

The undersigned Deponent, being duly sworn, deposes and says on oath that (s)he was personally acquainted with _____, deceased, over a period of _____ years; that Deponent is (not) related to said decedent (as a _____); that said decedent died (in)testate, a resident of the City of _____, County of _____, State of _____, on the _____ day of _____, 19___, and all debts of the estate have been fully paid; that said decedent was married _____ time(s) as follows:

Name of each Husband or Wife	Age and Address, if living Date of death, if deceased
_____	_____
_____	_____

Deponent further says on oath that the following are the children ever born to or adopted by said decedent:

Name of each Child	Age and Address, if living Date of death, if deceased
_____	_____
_____	_____
_____	_____
_____	_____
_____	_____
_____	_____

Deponent further says on oath that the following are all the children of the above children who died before the decedent:

---

[2] Wade W. Berryhill, "Title Examination in Virginia," *University of Richmond Law Review* 17, no. 2 (1983): pp. 229–255. By permission of *University of Richmond Law Review*.

Name of each Child	Name of Deceased Parents	Age and Address, if living; Date of death, if deceased
_____	_____	_____
_____	_____	_____
_____	_____	_____
_____	_____	_____

Deponent says on oath that the living persons above named constitute all the heirs at law of said decedent, and that all of said heirs are of age and sound mind, except:

_____

Deponent's attention has been directed to the fact that the within affidavit will be relied upon by prospective purchasers or lenders dealing with the heirs herein named.

Sworn to and subscribed before me this
_____ day of _____, 19___.

_____
Notary Public

_____
Deponent
Address: _____

 E T H I C S :   Document Falsification

A legal assistant works with a law firm in the real estate department. One of his duties is to receive title notes from the firm's title examiner and transcribe the notes into a title examination report that is then sent to the client. The legal assistant is overloaded with work and receives an extensive set of title notes from a title examiner. The supervisory attorney requests that a written title examination report be sent to the client by the end of the day. While the legal assistant is reviewing the title notes, he notices there are about eight utility easements affecting the property. A quick review of these easements leads him to believe that they do not materially affect the property. The legal assistant decides that to transcribe the notes into a written report to be sent to the client by the end of the day, he will delete four of the easements from the title examination report. Is this decision a correct one?

A legal assistant should never be involved in falsifying a document for any reason. Failure to list all the utility easements in the title examination report makes the report misrepresent record title to the property. It could be considered falsifying a title examination report. Even though the legal assistant believes the omitted easements do not materially affect the property, it is improper to omit the easements from the title examination report. An overload of work or time pressures to complete an assignment are not justifiable excuses for preparing a legal document that is false or incomplete.

SUMMARY

This chapter has explained the importance of recording a deed, mortgage, easement, or other document conveying an interest in real property and has introduced the student to the process of examining the public deed records to determine the ownership of real property. The procedures for examining the real property is detailed, and a number of title problems can be discovered from the examination. Although title examinations are mandatory on almost any type of real estate transaction that involves a transfer of ownership or a pledge of real property as security for a loan, the efforts by the legal profession to protect and ensure quality of title do not end with the title examination. Most transactions involve the issuance of title insurance.

KEY TERMS

Actual notice
Bona fide purchaser for value
Chain of title
Constructive notice

Grantee index
Grantor index
Lis pendens
Plat index

Quiet title action
Recording statutes
Record title holder
Title examination

▥➡ CHECKLIST

Ordering or Performing a Title Examination

❑ I. Purpose of Examination
   ❑ A. Purchase and sale of property
   ❑ B. Mortgage loan transaction
   ❑ C. Acquisition of easement
   ❑ D. Lease transaction
❑ II. Items Required for Examination
   ❑ A. Current owner's name
       1. The seller in the contract for sale
       2. The borrower in the application for a loan
       3. The landlord of a lease
   ❑ B. Legal description of property to be examined
   ❑ C. Plats or survey of property to be examined
   ❑ D. Prior title insurance policies on property to be examined
   ❑ E. Prior title examinations or abstracts on property to be examined
❑ III. Period of Examination
   ❑ A. Full examination (50–60 years)
   ❑ B. Limited examination
       1. From date of prior title policy
       2. Date of prior mortgage
       3. From date of prior title examination
❑ IV. Indices to be Checked
   ❑ A. Plat index
   ❑ B. Grantee index
   ❑ C. Grantor index
❑ V. Other Records to Be Searched
   ❑ A. Judgment index and records

   ❑ B. Federal and state tax lien index and records
   ❑ C. Lis Pendens
   ❑ D. UCC financing index
   ❑ E. Tax records
   ❑ F. Special assessments (sanitary and water)
   ❑ G. Probate records
   ❑ H. Civil docket
❑ VI. Preliminary Title Examination
   ❑ A. Certification to title company if title insurance is involved
   ❑ B. Copies of all title exceptions
❑ VII. Title Defects or Problems
   ❑ A. Breaks in chain of title
   ❑ B. Errors from prior recorded deeds
   ❑ C. Name variances
   ❑ D. Improper or missing power of attorney
   ❑ E. Sale contracts, options, and leases
   ❑ F. Unsatisfied or unreleased mortgages or deeds of trust
   ❑ G. Notices of lis pendens
   ❑ H. Easements
   ❑ I. Restrictive covenants and conditions
   ❑ J. Mechanics' or materialmen's liens
   ❑ K. Tax liens
   ❑ L. Unpaid real estate taxes or assessments
   ❑ M. UCC financing statements
   ❑ N. Title through estates
   ❑ O. Judgment liens

REVIEW QUESTIONS

1. Why is it important to have a title examination performed?

2. What is the difference between actual and constructive notice?

3. What are the three types of recording statutes, and how do they differ?

4. Identify at least five potential title problems, and explain how to solve them.

5. Explain the bona fide purchaser for value rule.

6. What is the difference between a grantor and a grantee index?

7. What information is required to perform a title examination?

8. What information usually is given in an index entry for a grantor or grantee index?

9. What is a lis pendens? Explain its use.

10. What should a title examiner look for when reviewing the recorded documents in a chain of title?

CASE PROBLEMS

1. John has been using a road over his neighbor Sam's property for the past twenty years. In the state where John and Sam live, the use by John of the road for twenty years gives John a prescriptive easement. There are no written documents evidencing the easement. The road is plainly visible from an inspection of the property. Sam sells his property to Alice. Does Alice have a right to stop John from using the road?

2. Mary owns a small apartment complex. At the time Mary purchased the apartment complex from Sam, she gave Sam a mortgage securing a debt for $100,000. The mortgage was mentioned in the deed from Sam to Mary for the apartment complex, but the mortgage was not recorded. Mary sells the apartment complex to John. Mary does not tell John about the unrecorded mortgage to Sam. After the sale of the apartment complex from Mary to John, is the mortgage held by Sam enforceable against the apartment complex?

3. Would it be easier to find a recorded mortgage from Alice Owner to Sam Seller by looking under Alice Owner's name in the grantor index or by looking under Sam Seller's name in the grantee index?

4. You are assisting an attorney in the closing of a real estate sale transaction. You have in your possession a copy of the contract for the purchase and sale of the property. The contract contains the names of both the purchaser and the seller and a complete legal description of the property being bought and sold, and it has attached as an exhibit a survey of the property. You have been asked to order a title examination on behalf of your client. What information do you need to give to the title examiner?

5. The purchaser and seller have entered into a contract for the sale of real property. Before closing, the seller has refused to honor the contract and decides to sell the property to a third party. The purchaser files suit against the seller for breach of contract. What else should the purchaser do to protect the purchaser's rights against the seller and in the property?

6. You are assisting an attorney in the closing of a real estate transaction. The seller of the property under the contract is known as David F. Farris. The title examination reveals that the title is currently owned by a D. Frank Farris. What measures should you take to assure that David F. Farris and D. Frank Farris are one in the same person?

Title Insurance

We shall make good our title. It is in the hands of my solicitor. My solicitor will be here presently to protect the property. Transportation or the gallows for anybody who shall touch the property!

—Charles Dickens, Bleak House

OBJECTIVES

After reading this chapter you will be able to:

- Recognize the importance of title insurance
- Understand the coverage provided by the American Land Title Association owner's and mortgagee's title insurance policies
- Prepare a title insurance commitment
- Review a title insurance commitment and title insurance policy
- Identify title problems that are not insured by a title insurance policy
- Learn how to delete standard title insurance exceptions

GLOSSARY

Affidavit   Sworn statement of fact.

Marketable title   Title to real property that is free from doubt and enables the owner to hold the real property in peace; free from the hazard of litigation or adverse claims.

Mortgagee or loan policy   Policy of title insurance that insures the interest of a mortgagee or lender to the title of real property.

Owner policy   Policy of title insurance that insures an owner's title to real property.

Pending disbursement clause   Clause found in a construction loan title insurance policy that provides

that the insurance coverage under the policy will be in the amount of the loan as it is disbursed to the borrower up to and not to exceed the face amount of the policy.

Title endorsement   Amendment to a title insurance policy that generally modifies existing coverage or adds special coverage to the policy.

Title insurance   Contract to indemnify the insured against loss through defects in the title to real property.

Title insurance commitment   Commitment or contract by a title insurance company to issue a title insurance policy.

One of the main responsibilities of a real estate attorney or legal assistant is to make certain that the client has good title to real property. This title assurance comes about by the use of three safeguards: (1) general warranty deed of conveyance to the property, (2) title examination before conveyance, and (3) title insurance.

General warranty deeds and title examinations are discussed in Chapters 9 and 13, respectively. Both of these methods for title assurance are highly recommended, and it would be imprudent to proceed without them; however, these methods do have certain limitations.

For example, liability on a warranty deed is difficult to enforce and collect. The grantor of the deed may have died or disappeared or be insolvent. Even if the grantor is present and solvent, in most states, liability under a warranty deed is limited to the original purchase price of the property and does not extend to the value of improvements that were erected on the property or the appreciated value of the property. In many states, attorney's fees and other costs of enforcing a warranty deed are unrecoverable.

A title examination is only as good as the skill and solvency of the examiner. The title examiner may not have the financial ability to pay for errors or mistakes in the examination. Although most title examiners carry malpractice insurance, the limits of this insurance may not be sufficient. In addition, some "remote risks" are not covered by a competent title examination and, thus, not recoverable from the examiner in a malpractice action. Some of these remote risks are as follows:

- Impersonation of the real owner
- Forged signatures on deeds or releases
- Documents executed under a false power of attorney or a power of attorney that has expired
- Deeds delivered after the death of the grantor or without the consent of the grantor
- Undisclosed or missing heirs
- Wills that have not been probated
- Deeds, mortgages, or easements executed by minors or incompetents
- Mistakes made in the indexing of legal documents (documents are lost in records room)
- Falsification of public records
- Confusion arising from similarity of names
- Titles passing by improperly conducted foreclosure sales

Because of these limitations, American ingenuity came up with a product to fill the gap. The product is **title insurance**, and the main function of title insurance is to eliminate all risks and prevent any loss caused by defects in title to the property.

Title insurance is a contract to indemnify the insured against loss through defects in the insured title or against liens or encumbrances that may affect the insured title at the time the policy is issued.

The main economic justifications of title insurance are to cover the remote risks of title examinations and to add financial substance to the title examination and to the deed warranties. Most title companies have deep pockets of money reserves that are annually audited by state authorities. It is rare that a valid claim is not paid by a title company because the title company lacks the money to pay for the claim.

Title insurance, unlike other forms of insurance, such as life, health, and fire insurance, does not assume risk. The main role for title insurance is risk elimination. A title insurance company will not issue a policy of title insurance unless it has performed an extensive title search and believes that there are no problems to the title. Some practitioners joke that if a title insurance company is willing to issue title insurance, then you probably don't need it because the title is risk-free. Title insurance, therefore, is issued only after a title examination has been conducted. The payment for title insurance is a one-time premium and can range from $1 to $3 per each $1,000 of coverage.

There are many title insurance companies across the country; most of them belong to the American Land Title Association (ALTA), a private trade association of title insurance companies. The ALTA has prepared over the years a number of standard form title insurance policies that they request and, in some cases, require the member companies to use. These forms are referred to as ALTA Owner's Policy Form No. B or ALTA Mortgagee-Loan Form No. B. The standard forms enable lawyers to transact a real estate practice on a national basis with a title company that belongs to the ALTA. Because most title insurance is issued on ALTA forms, the remainder of this chapter is a discussion of the basic provisions of the ALTA forms.

OWNER'S POLICY

The most commonly used **owner's title insurance** form is the ALTA Owner's Policy Form B. A copy of this form of policy is included at the end of this chapter (Exhibit 14–1). The ALTA owner's form contains many standard printed provisions concerning—for example, notice of loss and claim provisions—and two basic parts known as Schedule A and Schedule B. Schedule A is an identification schedule that sets forth the date of the policy (which usually is the date the deed or other instrument that is insured is filed for record), the amount of insurance covered by the policy, the identity of the insured, the estate or interest covered (whether it is a fee simple, life estate, and so on), the identity of the parties in whom title is vested as shown by the deed records, and a full description of the property insured.

Schedule B of the policy contains a list of exceptions to coverage. Any item shown on Schedule B is not insured against in the insurance policy. Schedule B typically contains some standard exceptions, such as matters of survey, implied easements, building line restrictions, and rights of persons in possession. These standard exceptions can be deleted by the use of proper **affidavits** and a survey. The title company, when issuing its Schedule B, lists all title exceptions found in the title examination of the property. Because Schedule B items are not insured against, it is important that in reviewing title insurance policies, copies of all the documents that represent Schedule B exceptions are obtained and carefully reviewed.

Insuring Provisions of an ALTA Owner's Policy

There are four basic insuring provisions of an ALTA owner's policy, and it is against loss or damage incurred as a result of these four covered risks that the policy insures. The covered risks are (1) insurance that title to the estate or interest described in Schedule A is vested in the insured; (2) insurance against any defect, lien, or encumbrance on such title; (3) insurance that the property has access to public road; and (4) insurance that the title is **marketable**. The ALTA Form "A" policy used in some states does not insure marketability.

Vesting of Title

This provision is straightforward insurance that the insured owns the real property set forth in the policy. This coverage is the basic undertaking in the policy and the undertaking from which other title insurance protections spring.

New York:

All title insurers in New York are members of the New York Board of Title Underwriters and are subject to supervision by the New York Insurance Department. All title insurers in New York issue policies at uniform rates and all title companies use the standard form of the ALTA Owners Policy.

New York:

For a discussion of the Torrens system of land registration, see Appendix.

Defects, Liens, or Encumbrances on Title

Title insurance protects against loss or damage incurred by reason of any defect in or lien or encumbrance on the title to the insured property. This language is concise in its application to title defects, liens, or encumbrances that have attached to title as of date of the issuance of a policy of title insurance. Coverage is provided against three separate kinds of title flaws—defects, liens, or encumbrances—each being somewhat distinct from the other. A title defect is the want or absence of something necessary for completeness or perfection of title or a lapse or absence of something essential to completeness of title. For example, the adjudicated incompetency of a prior grantor before the execution of a deed in a chain of title renders the title defective.

A lien is not an imperfection in the passage of title, but a claim or charge on the property as security for the payment of a debt or the fulfillment of an obligation. The broader term "encumbrance" includes liens but extends to every right or interest in property existing in third parties that diminishes the value of the real property but is consistent with the passing of a fee title such as restrictive covenants, or easements.

Access to and from the Property

An owner's policy insures against loss incurred by the insured for reason of the lack of a right of access to and from the land. This extension of coverage recognizes the obvious, that landlocked property is of little use or value. It is through the operation of this clause that the insured is protected against loss resulting from the nonexistence of a legal enforceable right to get to and from the property. There is, however, no insurance that the access will be the most convenient or appropriate way to and from the property, that the access will be by way of the route expected by the insured, or that the legal enforceable access way will be one that can be easily used or is physically passable. Stated affirmatively, the right-of-access coverage means the right to go between the property and the public right-of-way without unreasonable restrictions. Title insurance coverage protects against record title defects in the the right of access but not against the physical difficulties that may be associated with getting to and from the property.

This concept that title insurance insures only against title defects and not the defects of the physical condition of the land is illustrated in *Title & Trust Company of Florida v. Barrows*.

 C A S E

**Title & Trust Company of Florida
v. Barrows**
381 So. 2d 1088

McCORD, Acting Chief Judge.

This appeal is from a final judgment awarding money damages to appellees for breach of title insurance policy. We reverse.

Through a realtor, appellees purchased, for $12,500, a lot surrounded on three sides by land owned by others, all of which is a part of a beach subdivision. The fourth side of appellee's lot borders on a platted street called Viejo Street, the right-of-way for which has been dedicated to and accepted by St. Johns County. The right-of-way line opposite appellees' lot abuts a Corps of Engineers' right-of-way in which there is a stone breakwater. The intracoastal waterway flows on the other side of the breakwater.

The realtor who sold the lot to appellees represented to them that the county would build a road in the right-of-way along Viejo Street when appellees began plans for building on their lot. There have been no street improvements in the

dedicated right-of-way, and St. Johns County has no present plans for making any improvements. The "road" is merely a continuation of a sandy beach.

A year after purchasing the land appellees procured a survey which disclosed that the elevation of their lot is approximately one to three feet above the mean high water mark. They later discovered that their lot, along with the Viejo Street right-of-way abutting it, is covered by high tide water during the spring and fall of each year.

At the time appellees purchased their lot, they obtained title insurance coverage from appellant. The title policy covered:

"Any defect in or lien or encumbrance on the title to the estate or title covered hereby ... or a lack of a right of access to and from the land; ...."

Appellees' complaint of lack of right of access was founded on the impassable condition of the platted street. After trial without a jury, the trial court entered final judgment finding that appellees did not have access to their property and, therefore, were entitled to recover $12,500 from appellant—the face amount of the policy.

[1–3] Appellant and Florida Land Title Association, appearing as amicus curiae, argue that appellant cannot be held liable on grounds of "lack of right of access to and from the land" since there is no defect shown by the public record as to their right of access; that the public record shows a dedicated and accepted public right-of-way abutting the lot. They contend that title insurance does not insure against defects in the physical condition of the land or against infirmities in legal right of access not shown by the public record. See *Pierson v. Bill*, 138 Fla. 104, 189 So. 679 (1939). They argue that defects in the physical condition of the land such as are involved here are not covered by title insurance. We agree. Title insurance only insures against title defects.

The Supreme Court of North Carolina in *Marriott Financial Services, Inc. v. Capitol Funds, Inc.*, 288 N.C. 122, 217 S.E.2d 551 (1975), construed "right of access" to mean the right to go to and from the public right-of-way without unreason-able restrictions. Compare *Hocking v. Title Insurance & Trust Company*, 37 Cal.2d 644, 234 P.2d 625 (1951), where, in ruling that the plaintiff failed to state a cause of action in a suit brought under her title policy, the court said:

"She appears to possess fee simple title to the property for whatever it may be worth; if she has been damaged by false representations in respect to the condition and value of the land her remedy would seem to be against others than the insurers of the title she acquired."

In *Mafetone, et al., v. Forest Manor Homes, Inc., et al.*, 34 A.D.2d 566, 310 N.Y.S.2d 17 (N.Y.1970), the plaintiff brought an action against a title insurance company for damages allegedly flowing from a change in the grade of a street. There the court said:

"The title company is not responsible to plaintiffs for the damages incurred by reason of the change in elevating the abutting street to its legal grade, since the provisions of the standard title insurance policy here in question are concerned with matters affecting *title* to property and do not concern themselves with physical conditions of the abutting property *absent* a specific request by the person ordering a title report and policy..." (Emphasis supplied.)

In *McDaniel v. Lawyers' Title Guaranty Fund*, 327 So.2d 852 (Fla. 2 D.C.A.1976), our sister court of the Second District said:

"The man on the street buys a title insurance policy to insure against defects in the record title. The title insurance company is in the business of guaranteeing the insured's title to the extent it is affected by the public records."

In the case here before us, there is no dispute that the public record shows a legal right of access to appellant's property via the platted Viejo Street. The title insurance policy only insured against record title defects and not against physical infirmities of the platted street.

REVERSED.

If any particular form of access is required by the insured for the full enjoyment of the property, the insured would be well advised to have that access specifically insured by the title insurance policy. This can be accomplished by having additional easement parcels included in the legal description on Schedule A or by endorsing the policy to expressly insure access to the property by way of a described route.

Unmarketability of Title

The concept of marketability of title is legal in nature, rather than economic. A **marketable title** is title free from doubt that enables the owner to hold the land in peace, free from the hazard of litigation or adverse claims. Through this coverage, title insurance usually provides protection for those matters that would render the title unmarketable. Once again, the focus is on marketability of title as a legal concept and not sale marketability. The ability to sell the property is an economic concept. Defects that merely diminish the value of the property do not render the title unmarketable within the meaning of the title insurance coverage.

Exclusions from Coverage

The ALTA Owner's Policy contains several exclusions from coverage. These exclusions are not negotiable and cannot be deleted from the policy. The exclusions are (a) zoning and other governmental police power rights; (b) rights of eminent domain; (c) matters created, suffered, assumed, or agreed to by the insured; (d) title defects not known to the insurance company and not shown by public records, but known to the insured, either at the date of the policy or when the insured acquired the estate or interest, and not disclosed in writing to the insurance company before the date he became an insured; (e) matters resulting in no loss or damage to the insured; (f) title defects that are first attached or created after the effective date of the policy; and (g) matters resulting in a loss or damage that would not have been sustained if the insured had paid value for the estate or interest insured. The ALTA forms also exclude environmental protection matters.

Zoning and Other Governmental Regulations

This exclusion is primarily designed to indicate that matters of zoning are not insured against by the title policy. Beyond that, the exclusion also relates to building and other use restrictions as well as restrictions concerning the right of occupancy and any government regulations concerning further subdivision of the property. This exclusion reflects the fact that all ownership of property ultimately is subject to control and regulation by the government. It is important that zoning information be independently obtained and reviewed to see if it unreasonably interferes with the proposed use of the real property. It is possible in some states to obtain a zoning **endorsement** from the title insurance company that insures against loss if the zoning classification is other than stated in the endorsement. Another endorsement that is available in some situations protects an insured against loss if the land as currently improved violates zoning or other governmental regulations. A title insurance company will not insure against future changes of government regulations.

Eminent Domain and Police Power

This exclusion recognizes that ownership for private property is subject not only to government control but also to a government taking of the property by eminent domain or regulation under police power. If a notice of the exercise of such rights appears in the public records as of the effective date of the policy, as, for example, would be the case in a condemnation action, then the title insurance must disclose that fact to the insured or insure against any loss for failure to disclose.

Matters Created, Suffered, Assumed, or Agreed to by the Insured

This policy language excludes from coverage defects, liens, encumbrances, adverse claims, or other matters created, suffered, assumed, or agreed to by the insured

New York:
Marketability means it is reasonable for the buyer to take title even though it is not an absolutely perfect title. Marketability is not a precise concept and is subject to reasonability.

claimant. This clause has the effect of limiting the title company's liability when the insured has expressly or implicitly assumed or agreed to various defects, liens, or encumbrances in the course of dealing with the property or when the defect, lien, or encumbrance resulted from the insured's misconduct or inequitable dealings. For example, Pat Purchaser is purchasing real property from Sam Seller. As part of the transaction, Pat Purchaser is to give a mortgage to Sam Seller to secure part of the purchase price that will be paid to Sam Seller over a period of time. The mortgage would be an encumbrance on the property purchased by Pat Purchaser, but it is an encumbrance created by Pat Purchaser and, therefore, not insured by Pat Purchaser's title insurance policy.

On the other hand, the clause will not operate to limit the insurance company's liability for title defects, liens, or encumbrances resulting from the insured's negligence. The theory is that the title problem must result from the insured's knowing or intentional affirmative act or the insured's intentional failure to prevent the attachment of the adverse item. The courts usually apply this exclusion to protect the insurance company from liability for a loss resulting from the insured's wrongful conduct.

Title Defects Not Known to the Insurance Company

This exclusion, known as the "secret defect" exclusion, covers title matters that are not recorded but that the insured claimant knew about and failed to tell the title insurance company at the time of the transaction. The insured claimant must give written disclosure of all "off record" matters that affect the insured property. This exclusion does not apply to record matters even if the insured knows of their existence. The insured claimant must know about the adverse matter for the exclusion to apply. Knowledge usually means actual knowledge, not constructive knowledge, or notice that may be imputed to an insured by reason of any public records.

If a matter fits into the requirements of this exclusion, the only prudent way for the insured to obtain title insurance protection over the item is to make written disclosure of the item to the title insurance company and cause the title company to provide affirmative insurance against the item.

Matters Resulting in No Loss or Damage to the Insured Claimant

This provision fits into the concept that title insurance is a contract of indemnity. Simply put, if there is no loss, there is nothing for the indemnification aspects of the insurance obligation to operate on.

Title Defects That Are First Attached or Created After the Effective Date of the Policy

Title insurance is a rather unique insurance product. For a single premium, the insured obtains protection for so long as an interest in the insured property is retained. In general, however, title insurance covers only those risks that exist in the title at the time the insured interest is taken. The exclusion for defects, liens, encumbrances, adverse claims, or other matters attaching or created subsequent to the date of the policy makes it clear that the title insurance policy is not prospective in operation and provides no protection for agreements, liens, or problems arising after the policy is issued. The insurance covers only the losses attributable to matters in existence on the date of the policy. Title insurance policies contain an effective date, which usually is the date of the recording of the deed or, in the event of a loan policy, the date of the recording of the mortgage.

Matters Resulting in a Loss or Damage That Would Not Have Been Sustained If the Insured Had Paid Value for the Estate or Interest Insured

This exclusion is an example of how title insurance provisions reflect the protection afforded by the various state recording laws. If the recording laws of a state do not protect a party who takes real property for no consideration against a prior interest in the same property, the title policy will not protect the insured as well. For example, if you are representing someone who is receiving property as a gift, it is necessary to obtain an endorsement to the title policy to delete this exclusion.

Schedule A

Schedule A is an identification schedule that localizes or customizes the title insurance to the transaction. A form of Schedule A is shown in Exhibit 14–2.

New York:
Schedule A includes the legal description, metes and bounds and/or lot and block.

Policy Date

The date of the policy is important because of the nature of title insurance. Unlike other insurance that covers the future occurrence of risk, title insurance, with some limited exceptions, insures against risks that have already occurred but that have not manifested themselves. The date of the policy is the cutoff for coverage. The policy date is the date the transaction documents, such as the deed or mortgage, are recorded.

Amount of Insurance

The dollar amount of insurance coverage is the maximum loss the title insurer will bear in the event of an occurrence of a covered risk. It also is the prime factor in

OFFICE FILE NUMBER	POLICY NUMBER	DATE OF POLICY	AMOUNT OF INSURANCE
1	2	3	4 $

1. Name of Insured:

2. The estate or interest in the land which is covered by this Policy is:

   Fee Simple

3. Title to the estate or interest in the land is vested in the Insured.

4. The land herein described is encumbered by the following mortgage or trust deed, and assignments:

   and the mortgages or trust deeds, if any, shown in Schedule B hereof.

5. The land referred to in this Policy is described as follows:

EXHIBIT 14–2
Schedule A of Owner's Policy

determining the amount of policy premium. The insured must balance the need to obtain adequate insurance coverage against the cost of the coverage. The amount of title insurance usually is the purchase price of the insured property for an owner's policy and the amount of the loan secured by the insured property for a loan policy.

Occasionally, however, to save premiums, the insured may deliberately underinsure. The title insurance company is aware that the property is being underinsured and that the insured has self-insured a portion of the risk. This situation brings a coinsurance clause into account. Through this clause, the insurer limits its liability to that proportion of the loss, damage, or defense cost that the policy amount bears to the market value of the insured property at the time of the loss. For example, a purchaser buys a $100,000 parcel of property but only insures for $60,000. Under the coinsurance rules, if there is a loss in the amount of $30,000 under the title policy, the title insurance company will only pay 60 percent of the loss ($60,000 versus $100,000), or $18,000.

On the other hand, an insured may want more coverage than would be indicated by the amount of the transaction. An owner may anticipate an increase in the property value caused by natural market forces or because the property will be improved. A lender may want more insurance than the original amount of a loan in situations where negative amortization will occur.

Most title insurance companies are willing to sell additional coverage on the demonstration of a reasonable basis for the requested coverage.

Even after a policy is issued, the insured may approach the insurance company to increase the policy amount. This can be done by an endorsement that either changes or does not change the effective date of the policy.

Some insureds do not want to leave the availability of this coverage to chance. Although they seek adequate insurance at the outset (i.e., insurance in the amount of the purchase price of the property), they want to save the payment of the premium for more insurance until the additional value is added to the property. Although the insurer may be willing to agree to give this insurance, the insurer wants the insured's agreement to purchase the insurance. This is accomplished through an endorsement that contains the insured's agreement to purchase more insurance and the title company's undertaking to increase the policy amount and change the effective date of the policy, subject, however, to exception of matters created, recorded, attaching, or coming to the insured's attention subsequent to the original policy's effective date.

An owner may seek additional coverage to protect against the effects of inflation. This is done through inflation protection increases in the policy amount over time. This inflation protection can easily be built into Schedule A of a policy of insurance insuring residential property so that the insured amount will automatically increase by 10 percent on each of the first five policy anniversary dates.

Inflation protection also can be obtained on commercial policies. This coverage is given by endorsement that raises the policy amount by some index rate, such as the consumer price index. In both residential and commercial policies, the inflated policy amount will not exceed 150 percent of the original amount of insurance.

The Insured

The insured should be correctly identified. It should be noticed that, by definition, the insured extends not only to the name insured but also to those who succeed to the interest of the insured by operation of law, as distinguished from purchase, including but not limited to heirs, distributees, devises, survivors, personal representatives, next of kin, or a corporate and fiduciary successor.

A successor insured is subject to the same rights or defenses that the title company had against a named insured.

Because title insurance policies are issued for a one-time premium, it is of economic necessity to the title insurance company that the insurance undertaking be definitionally limited to not extend to those who take by purchase. In other words, an owner's title insurance policy is not transferable to someone who purchases the property from the owner. If the purchaser desires insurance, the purchaser will need to purchase a new policy.

A loan policy of insurance, however, extends the insurance by defining the named insured as the owner of the indebtedness secured by the insured mortgage, each successor in ownership of the indebtedness, and any governmental agency or instrumentality that insures or guarantees the indebtedness. The title insurance industry is aware that mortgage loans often are transferred from one lender to another and to accommodate this industry practice with a minimum of cost has provided that the holder of the insured mortgage will be the named insured under the loan policy.

Insured Property

The policy definition of real property is the real property expressly described in Schedule A and the improvements affixed to the real property. Title to personal property is not included in the coverage of a title insurance policy.

It is of primary importance that the legal description contained in Schedule A be the same real property that the insured is purchasing or using to secure a loan.

The insured property often is made up of several parcels or tracts of land. It is important that the policy description set forth a full description of the parcels that are insured. If these parcels are being consolidated into one parcel, the insured should request that the title insurance company issue an endorsement insuring that the tracts or parcels are contiguous to one another and that no gaps exist between the parcels. In addition, if the insured property involves a fee parcel and an easement for access to the fee parcel, the insured should request the contiguity endorsement. This endorsement insures that the land described in both parcels is contiguous and the areas can be served with no intervening adverse interest.

Schedule B

Schedule B of an owner's policy contains exceptions to the insurance coverage. These exceptions are divided into two categories: (1) standard exceptions and (2) exceptions found in the title examination of the insured property. An example of a Schedule B to an owner's policy is shown in Exhibit 14–3.

The standard exceptions to an owner's policy are (a) rights or claims of parties in possession not shown by public records; (b) encroachments, overlaps, boundary line disputes, and any other matters that would be disclosed by an accurate survey and inspection of the premises; (c) easements or claims of easement not shown by the public records; (d) any lien, or right to a lien, for services, labor, or material heretofore or hereafter furnished, imposed by law, and not shown by the public records; (e) taxes or special assessments not shown as existing liens by the public records.

Rights of Parties in Possession

The first of the general exceptions provides that the policy does not insure against loss or damage incurred by reason of the rights or claims of parties in possession not

EXHIBIT 14-3
Schedule B of
Owner's Policy

SCHEDULE B

Policy Number: _____
                         Owners

EXCEPTIONS FROM COVERAGE

This policy does not insure against loss or damage (and the Company will not pay costs, attorneys' fees or expenses) which arise by reason of:

General Exceptions:

(1) Rights or claims of parties in possession not shown by the public records.

(2) Encroachments, overlaps, boundary line disputes, or other matters which would be disclosed by an accurate survey and inspection of the premises.

(3) Easements, or claims of easements, not shown by the public records.

(4) Any lien, or right to a lien, for services, labor, or material heretofore or hereafter furnished, imposed by law and not shown by the public records.

(5) Taxes or special assessments which are not shown as existing liens by the public records.

Special Exceptions: The mortgage, if any, referred to in Item 4 of Schedule A.

Countersigned

_____
      Authorized Signatory

shown by the public records. Through this exception, the insurance company is relieved of liability when the defect is caused by a claim of a party in possession. For example, a small retail shopping center is leased to a number of tenants. The tenants' leases are not recorded. The tenants are in possession of the property and are parties in possession. A purchaser purchases the shopping center for $500,000. The purchaser receives a title insurance policy that contains an exception for the rights of parties in possession. It is later discovered that one of the tenants has an option to purchase the shopping center for $400,000. The title insurance company does not insure the purchaser against any loss that it might suffer if the tenant should exercise its option to purchase the property.

There is a rational basis for the presence of this exception. Constructive notice of rights in real property comes from many sources. Two such sources are the property itself and the public records. A title insurance company makes its underwriting determination based on a review of the public records and does not usually visit the property to determine what can be learned by viewing it and talking to the parties in possession. The purchaser, on the other hand, inspects the property, perhaps several times, in making the purchase determination. The purchaser thus has the ability to uncover the rights that can be determined from this inspection by seeking information of the parties in possession. Therefore, under this exception, a title insurance company does not insure against anyone who claims title to the property by way of adverse possession, any person who is a tenant with an unrecorded lease, or any person who exercises unrecorded easement rights over the property.

This exception can be deleted from a title policy by obtaining a title affidavit from the owner of the property. In this affidavit, the owner swears under oath that no other parties are in possession of the property except for the owner. A form of title affidavit is included at the end of this chapter (Exhibit 14–4).

Survey Exception

The second general exception precludes title insurance liability for encroachments, overlaps, boundary line disputes, and other matters that would be disclosed by an accurate survey or inspection of the premises. Through the use of this exception, the title insurance company protects itself against liability for matters that are primarily shown by the view of the land itself, through either the untrained eye of the insured or the trained eye and technical expertise of the surveyor.

A simple example of the application of this exception can be found in a situation where the insured purchased property and began to erect an industrial building. The building was placed on the site so as to afford adequate clearance for trucks using the building's loading docks. The owner of the adjoining property erected a fence along the property line at a point some three feet inside the place that the insured believed the line to be, thus blocking the effective use of the loading docks. A lawsuit resulted. It developed that the adjoining owner's survey was right about the location of the property line and the insured's survey was incorrect. A court held in this situation that the survey exception protected the title insurance company from liability over this boundary line dispute.

A general survey exception can be removed by preparing a survey in compliance with title insurance standards and by providing the title insurance company with the survey. On the receipt of a survey prepared according to title standards, a title insurance company usually will remove the standard survey exception but will add special exceptions for matters that appear on the survey.

Unrecorded Easement Exception

Another general exception states that the policy does not insure against loss incurred by the insured by reason of easements or claims of easements not shown by the public records. These easements include implied or prescription easements, as discussed in Chapter 6. This exception primarily applies to unrecorded easements or rights-of-way that can only be discovered by a physical inspection of the land.

For example, John is a neighbor of Sam. John has been using a road on Sam's property for access to and from John's property for more than twenty years. In the state where John and Sam live, John has a prescriptive easement to use the road on Sam's property. John's prescriptive easement would be an easement or claim of easement not shown by the public records.

A legal assistant should pay close attention to such features as footpaths, driveways, water and power lines, and other like matters that appear on the survey of the insured property because all these features could be evidence of implied or prescriptive easement rights.

The standard unrecorded easement exception can be removed from the policy by providing the title company with a survey showing no easements prepared according to title standards and an affidavit from the owner swearing that no implied or prescriptive easements affect the insured property.

Mechanics' Lien Exception

An owner's policy does not insure against loss by reason of a lien or right to a lien for services, labor, or materials heretofore or hereafter furnished imposed by law and not shown by the public records. Once again, the title insurance policy reflects the insurance of record matters but not nonrecord matters. If a claim of lien has been filed in the public records, it will, as a general rule, be excepted as a special exception under Schedule B or covered by the policy's protection. If it is not reflected of record as of the date of policy, it is, by operation of this general exception, excluded from liability, regardless if the lien relates to work or materials furnished before or after the effective date of the policy.

The mechanics' lien exception may be removed from the title insurance policy. The title insurance company may require, as a condition precedent to the deletion, lien waivers from all contractors, materialmen, and laborers supplying labor or materials to the property, an affidavit that all bills have been paid, or an affidavit that no work has been performed within the period of time required for the filing of a lien.

Taxes and Special Assessments

This general exception states that the policy does not insure against loss or damage incurred by reason of "taxes or special assessments which are not shown as existing liens by the public records." This exception focuses on the public records on the day the policy is issued and covers real estate tax and special assessment laws within the jurisdiction where the real property is located. A title insurance company's liability will preclude liability for special assessments for real estate tax liens that become liens after the effective date of the policy.

Schedule B Special Exceptions

In addition to the standard exceptions, Schedule B contains all defects, encumbrances, liens, covenants, restrictions, or other matters that affect the insured property that were revealed by the title examination to the property.

MORGAGE OR LOAN POLICIES

A title insurance policy also can be obtained to insure the interest of the mortgagee or lender who has a mortgage loan secured by real property. A form of ALTA **loan policy** is included at the end of this chapter (Exhibit 14–5). The ALTA loan policy contains a Schedule A; Schedule B, Part I; and Schedule B, Part II.

Schedule A of a loan policy contains much of the same information as Schedule A of an owner's policy: (a) the effective date of the policy; (b) the amount of coverage; (c) the named insured; (d) the fee simple owner of the property; (e) a description of the mortgage or loan deed being insured; and (f) a description of the real property conveyed in the mortgage or loan deed. An example of a Schedule A to a loan title insurance policy is shown in Exhibit 14–6.

Schedule B, Part I, of a loan policy contains both standard exceptions and special exceptions resulting from a title examination of the insured property. The standard exceptions are the same as the exceptions in an owner's policy and can be deleted from a loan policy in the same manner, that is, by the use of surveys and title affidavits. The special exceptions are the title matters reported in the title examination.

The Schedule B, Part II, items are exceptions to the title with a priority junior and inferior to the insured loan. An example of a Schedule B, Part II, exception would be tenants of a commercial property with leases that are expressly subordinate to any mortgage or loan deed on the property.

Insurance Provisions

The first four insurance provisions of a loan policy are the same as those of an owner's policy, to wit: (1) title is vested in the borrower or maker of the mortgage or loan deed; (2) the property is free and clear of title defects, liens, and encumbrances, except those shown in Schedule B; (3) the property has access to a public road; and

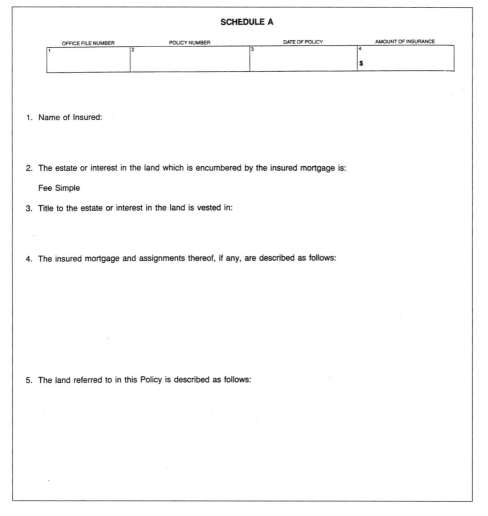

EXHIBIT 14–6
Schedule A of Loan Policy

(4) borrower's title to the property is marketable. In addition to these four items, the following insurance provisions are provided in the loan policy: (a) the mortgage is valid and enforceable, and the lender shall have the right to foreclosure in the event the debt is not paid; (b) the priority of the mortgage; (c) the mortgage is insured against any claims that may be asserted by mechanics' or materialmen's liens; and (d) the policy insures the validity and enforceability of any assignment of the mortgage or loan deed.

Validity or Enforceability of the Lien

The ALTA loan policy insures against loss resulting from the invalidity or unenforceability of the lien of the insured mortgage on said estate or interest. This is the most basic form of protection to a lender, insuring that the lien in the mortgage or deed of trust is a valid and enforceable lien on the property described therein.

There are two exceptions that the title insurance company does not insure. Title insurance does not insure against the invalidity or unenforceability of the mortgage lien that arises out of the transaction evidenced by the insured mortgage and is based on (a) a claim of usury or (b) any consumer credit protection or truth in lending claim.

Priority

The next area of lender's coverage is the natural complement to insurance of the validity and enforceability of the lien: insurance against priority of any lien or encumbrance over the lien of the insured mortgage. Thus, through these two insurance clauses, the lender obtains coverage for the validity, enforceability, and priority of the insured mortgage. This insurance provision is important because most lenders are concerned that the lien be of a required priority to satisfy regulatory and contractual requirements, and that on foreclosure, the full value of the secured property is made available to the lender.

Mechanic's Liens

Although mechanics' liens usually appear as a special exception to coverage in an owner's policy, they are expressly insured against in a loan policy.

Validity or Enforceability of an Assignment

The last insurance clause is written in the context of an increasingly active secondary-mortgage market. It insures against loss caused by the invalidity or unenforceability of any assignment shown in Schedule A of the insured mortgage and the failure of said assignment to vest title to the insured mortgage in the named assignee free and clear of all liens. This insurance clause is written to anticipate the assignment of the mortgage into the secondary-mortgage market simultaneous with the mortgage origination. If the mortgage and assignment documents are recorded, Schedule A of the policy, when issued, will show the record identification of the insured mortgage and the insured assignment. If the assignment is not recorded at the time of the issuance of the loan policy, it will not be described in Schedule A and will not be insured under the insuring clause. Insurance of the assignment must then be obtained by way of endorsement.

A loan policy has the same exclusions to coverage as an owner's policy, with the addition of an exclusion against any unenforceability of the insured mortgage because of the lender's not being qualified to do business within the state in which the property is located.

Miscellaneous Provisions

A loan policy is transferable, and the owner of the mortgage or loan deed being insured will be the insured under the policy. A loan policy usually is for the amount of the loan and decreases as the loan is repaid. This rule can create problems in transactions in which the insured mortgage secures a revolving line of credit loan, such as a home equity loan, or a business line of credit loan, which contemplates that monies secured by the mortgage will be borrowed and repaid, reborrowed and repaid, and so on. A revolving line of credit mortgage requires an endorsement to the title insurance policy providing that the amount of insurance will always be the outstanding balance of the loan, despite the fact that monies have been borrowed and repaid numerous times under the loan.

Construction Title Insurance

If the loan being insured under a loan policy is a loan to finance the construction of improvements, the title insurance policy will contain a **pending disbursement clause** (Example 14–1). This clause provides that the insurance coverage being provided under the policy will be in the amount of the loan as it is disbursed to the borrower up to and not to exceed the face amount of the policy. The clause also provides that as funds are disbursed to the borrower, the loan deed will be insured free and clear of mechanics' liens and claims, provided no claims and liens are filed of record and the lender has no knowledge of any claims or liens that have been asserted against the property. Many pending disbursement clauses require an endorsement to the policy as the construction advances are made to the borrower. Each endorsement requires a title update from the effective date of the policy and the date of the endorsement to ensure that no lien claims have been filed.

EXAMPLE 14–1 PENDING DISBURSEMENT CLAUSE

Pending disbursement of the full proceeds of the loan secured by the mortgage insured, this policy insures only to the extent of the amount actually disbursed without knowledge of any intervening lien or interest, but increases as each disbursement is made, up to the face amount of the policy. At the time of each disbursement of the proceeds of the loan, the title must be continued down to such time for possible liens, including mechanics' liens, and other objections, intervening between the date hereof and the date of such disbursement.

CLAIMS PROCEDURES UNDER TITLE INSURANCE POLICIES

Both an owner's and a lender's policy protect the insured against title defects that are not excluded or excepted from the coverage of the policy and that are created or attached before the effective date of the policy. The company settles these title defects or pays in the form of reimbursement to the insured sums of money lost as a result of the title defect up to the amount of the total insurance provided under the policy. A title company also has the obligation to defend, at its own expense, title defects that are insured against. The insured has an obligation to immediately notify the title company once the title defects are discovered and to provide the title company with full information concerning the title defects.

COMMITMENTS FOR TITLE INSURANCE _____

New York:
After the commitment but no later than the closing, the title company runs a "continuation" search to make sure there are no new judgments or liens entered after the commitment was issued.

An owner's title insurance policy cannot be issued until the owner in fact owns the property. That is, the title insurance is a postclosing item that comes after the transaction and sale have been completed. The same is true with a loan policy: a lender cannot be insured until it in fact becomes a lender, which means that the insurance follows the funding and closing of a loan. Because title insurance is essentially a postclosing item, it is necessary that before the closing, the attorney or legal assistant representing the proposed insured obtain a pro forma copy of the insurance. This is accomplished by means of the title company issuing a **title commitment** or title binder, a contract to issue insurance once the transaction is closed. (An example of a title commitment appears at the end of the chapter as Exhibit 14–7.) The commitment is, for the most part, an example of how the actual policy will appear once the transaction is closed. The commitment shows all title exceptions and exclusions that will appear in the policy and contains information concerning the insurance provisions of the policy. The main purpose of the commitment is to assure the proposed purchaser or lender that if it complies with the terms of the commitment, closes the transaction, and pays the necessary insurance premium, the proposed insured will have a title insurance policy subject only to the exceptions that appear in the commitment unless defects, liens, encumbrances, or other matters intervene between the date of the commitment and the date of the policy. It is important that the date of the title commitment be as close as possible to the date of the actual closing of the transaction. In many cases, a marked binder or marked commitment that brings the effective date down to the exact minute the deed or mortgage is recorded is used at closing.

A commitment for title insurance consists of three basic parts: Schedule A, Schedule B-1, and Schedule B-2. Schedule A shows the effective date of the title commitment (which, in most cases, is the date of the title examination of the property), sets forth the amount of coverage and the type of policy (either a loan or an owner's policy) that will be issued, reflects the current record owner of the property and the type of interest he owns (e.g., fee simple, life estate), and fully describes the property to be covered by the policy.

Schedule B, Section 1, of the commitment sets forth the requirements that must be met before the transaction closes for the title insurance to be issued.

Schedule B, Section 2, is a list of exceptions that will appear in Schedule B of the policy and that will not be insured against.

Preparation and Review

New York:
In New York, the legal assistant reviews the title report and makes sure all the exceptions can be satisfied prior to or at closing. Law firms do not generally act as title agents in New York.

Depending on local custom, a real estate legal assistant either reviews title commitments for clients or prepares title commitments from title examinations of the property. In some states, law firms are title agents and issue title insurance commitments and policies.

A title insurance commitment cannot be issued until a title examination has been completed. A common practice is for the examining attorney or legal assistant to certify the examination to the title insurance company and to include copies of all title exceptions that were found. A legal assistant with this information can then prepare a title commitment.

Preparation of Schedule A proceeds as follows:

Step 1.   The effective date of the title commitment is the date of the examination by the examining attorney or legal assistant. The examining attorney or legal assistant gives this information as part of the examination.

Step 2.   The type of policy—either an owner's policy or a loan policy—is dictated by the client. The name of the insured is the name of the purchaser or the name of the lending institution. The amount of the insurance coverage is either the purchase price of the property, which can be obtained from the contract, or the amount of the loan, which can be found in the loan commitment. When issuing commitments without full information, it is permissible to identify the proposed insured as "to be determined" and to show the amounts to be the "purchase price" or the "amount of loan." Once this information is obtained, the commitment can be endorsed or amended to provide the exact information.

Step 3.   The name and the estate or interest of the current owner are set out in the commitment. This information is obtained from the title examination. In most instances, the current owner is the seller of the property under the contract or the borrower under a loan transaction.

Step 4.   A description of the property, provided by the title examination, is included.

Step 5.   Schedule B, Section 1, is an important part of the commitment because it identifies conditions or requirements that must be met for the title insurance to be issued. A legal assistant, when reviewing the commitment, should make certain that all these conditions are satisfied before or at closing. A legal assistant preparing a title commitment should become familiar with the Schedule B, Section 1, conditions. Standard Schedule B, Section 1, conditions (which often are printed on the commitment form) are as follows:

- *Execution, delivery, and recordation of the instruments necessary to vest title in the named insured.* In the case of the owner's policy, this would be a warranty deed from the current owner of the property to the proposed insured. In the case of a loan policy, this would be the execution of a mortgage or trust deed from the owner of the property to the proposed insured lender. In some transactions, the closings are simultaneous sales and loan closings, in which case both a warranty deed from the current owner of the property to the proposed new owner of the property and a mortgage or loan deed from the new owner of the property to the lender are required.
- *Payment of consideration of the transfer.* Transfers of title or loans are not valid unless consideration has been paid. The title company requires proof of payment of consideration.
- *Payment of all taxes and assessments.*
- *Title affidavit.* Many title companies require this affidavit, which permits them to remove mechanics' or materialman's liens.

Additional requirements can be obtained from the title examination. For example, if a commitment is being issued to insure a particular lender a first-priority mortgage on the property and the title examination reveals a judgment tax lien and a prior mortgage on the property, it will be necessary to provide in Schedule B, Section 1, of the commitment that the prior tax lien and prior mortgage will be satisfied and cancelled of record before the insurance is issued. The satisfaction and cancellation of these items may take place at closing, and many times, funds are paid out of the closing proceeds to satisfy these items.

Step 6.   Schedule B, Section 2, of the commitment includes all the title exceptions that will appear in Schedule B to the policy and that will not be insured against. These are the exceptions that will survive closing. It is a good idea to have copies of these exceptions, so that when the commitment is forwarded to the client, copies of the exceptions can be forwarded as well. The legal assistant who reviews a title commitment should pay particular attention to all Schedule B, Section 2, title exceptions. These exceptions should be carefully reviewed to see how they will affect the client, since title insurance coverage will not be provided for these exceptions.

An example of a title commitment that has been prepared from a title examination appears at the end of this chapter (Exhibit 14–8). The title commitment is being prepared for the Second Federal Savings and Loan Association. The Second Federal Savings and Loan Association is making a $250,000 first-priority mortgage loan to Tall Oaks, Inc., a Maryland corporation.

 E T H I C S :   Personal Conflict of Interest

The responsibilities of a legal assistant working for a title insurance agency are to review title examinations and prepare title insurance commitments and title insurance policies. While working on a title insurance policy for a real estate sale transaction, the legal assistant discovers that a judgment lien is outstanding against the owner/seller of the property. Pursuant to the laws of the state in which the transaction is taking place, the judgment, unless it is levied on or paid, will expire in six months. The seller of the property has requested that the title insurance company insure over the judgment rather than pay the judgment. The title insurance company has agreed to the request but has asked that an amount of money equal to the amount of the judgment plus interest and other costs be deposited with the title insurance company until such time as the judgment expires. The legal assistant is personal friends with someone who works for the company that is the judgment creditor. After the transaction has closed, the legal assistant calls the friend at the creditor company and informs her that a sum of money is being held by the title insurance company to pay the judgment. Was this an ethical thing for the legal assistant to do?

Professional ethics mandate that an attorney or a paralegal shall avoid conflicts of interest that may arise from family relationships or personal or business interests. The legal assistant in this particular transaction is working for a title agency whose customer was the owner/seller of the property. This customer/client had requested the title insurance company to not pay the judgment but instead to insure over it and to escrow money in the event the judgment holder should come forth and demand payment. The legal assistant's conflict of interest through his or her friendship with an employee of the judgment creditor and the telephone call informing the judgment creditor of the escrowed money is a conflict of interest and a breach of ethics. The legal assistant had a duty of loyalty and responsibility to the customer, which is a greater duty than the friendship with the employee of the judgment creditor.

SUMMARY

Title insurance is useful in protecting a purchaser or lender from economic loss resulting from defects in the title to real property. It does not, however, give complete protection to the purchaser or lender. It is important in any real estate transaction to completely understand what title defects are not covered by the title insurance. It is equally important to understand what coverages are available from title insurance and how the standard title exceptions can be removed from the insurance policy. Complete familiarity with title insurance is important for a legal assistant who assists in the real estate closing process.

KEY TERMS

Affidavit	Owner policy	Title insurance
Marketable title	Pending disbursement clause	Title insurance commitment
Mortgagee or loan policy	Title endorsement	

▐▐▐▶ CHECKLIST

Preparation of a Title Insurance Policy

❑ I. Purpose of Policy
  ❑ A. Owner's policy
  ❑ B. Loan policy
❑ II. Conditions Precedent to Issuance of Title Insurance
  ❑ A. Title examination
  ❑ B. Title examiner's certification to title company
  ❑ C. Title commitment
  ❑ D. Survey
  ❑ E. Title affidavits
❑ III. Owner's Policy, Schedule A Information
  ❑ A. Effective date of title policy
  ❑ B. Name of insured
  ❑ C. Amount of insurance
  ❑ D. Description of property
❑ IV. Loan Policy, Schedule A Information
  ❑ A. Effective date of policy—date mortgage was recorded
  ❑ B. Name of insured
  ❑ C. Name of record title owner to property—borrower

❑ D. Amount of insurance—loan amount
❑ E. Description of insured property
❑ V. Procedures for Deletion of Standard Schedule B Exceptions
  ❑ A. Survey of property according to title insurance company standards
  ❑ B. Title affidavit
❑ VI. Schedule B, Section 2, Exceptions
  ❑ A. Receive copies of all exceptions
  ❑ B. Review exceptions to see if acceptable
  ❑ C. Delete as many exceptions as possible
❑ VII. Special Endorsements
  ❑ A. Zoning
  ❑ B. Contiguous parcels
  ❑ C. Pending disbursement
  ❑ D. Revolving line of credit endorsement
  ❑ E. Condominium endorsement
  ❑ F. Planned unit development endorsement
  ❑ G. Adjustable rate endorsement

REVIEW QUESTIONS

1. Identify and discuss the three safeguards that assure a good title.

2. What risks are covered by an ALTA owner's policy?

3. How does an ALTA loan policy differ from an ALTA owner's policy?

4. How are exclusions from coverage on a title insurance policy different from exceptions to title?

5. Why is a review of Schedule B to a title policy so important?

6. What is a title commitment, and why is it important in a real estate transaction?

7. What is the effective date of a title insurance policy, and why is it important?

8. What are the requirements of a title insurance company to pay or defend a claim made under a title insurance policy?

9. What are the standard exceptions to an ALTA title insurance policy?

10. What risks are insured by an ALTA loan policy?

CASE PROBLEMS

1. Kim Buyer is purchasing a home. The purchase price for the home is $125,000. Kim is obtaining a loan from Acme Loan Company for $105,000. What is the amount of title insurance that Kim can purchase? What is the amount of title insurance that Acme Loan Company can purchase?

2. T. Sawyer has purchased a home. T. Sawyer obtained an owner's title insurance policy that insured the home to be free and clear of any liens and encumbrances. T. Sawyer, after purchasing the home, sells the home to B. Thatcher. B. Thatcher does not buy title insurance. Later it is discovered that there is a mortgage on the property held by H. Finn that dates before the effective date of T. Sawyer's title insurance policy. Does B. Thatcher have any claim against the title insurance purchased by T. Sawyer? Would the result be different if B. Thatcher had inherited the property from T. Sawyer on T. Sawyer's death?

3. You are reviewing a title commitment that contains a standard exception for parties in possession. Your client does not want the standard exception to be included in the title insurance policy. What steps can you take to have the title insurance company delete the "parties in possession" exception?

4. You are assisting in a real estate sale transaction. The title examination to the property reveals that there is a mortgage on the property from Sam Owner to Acme Loan Company in the amount of $50,000 and a mortgage on the property from Sam Owner to First Bank and Trust in the amount of $100,000. The contract for the sale of the property indicates that the purchaser is going to assume the $50,000 mortgage from Sam Owner to Acme Loan Company. You have been asked to prepare a title commitment in connection with the transaction. Would the mortgage from Sam Owner to Acme Loan Company appear on Schedule B-1 or Schedule B-2 of the title commitment? Would the mortgage from Sam Owner to First Bank and Trust appear on Schedule B-1 or Schedule B-2 of the title commitment?

5. You are involved in a real estate sale transaction. The sale took place on December 26, but the deed was not recorded until January 5. When you receive the owner's title insurance policy, you note that the effective date of the policy is December 26. Is this the correct effective date?

6. You are assisting in a real estate transaction. After the transaction has closed, you are reviewing the owner's title insurance policy. You note that the legal description to the property as described in the policy contains a number of typographical errors. Should you be concerned?

ACKNOWLEDGMENT

Portions of this chapter have been excerpted from *The Basics of Title Insurance* by Raymond J. Werner, Title Insurance: The Lawyer's Expanding Role, pages 3–67 (1985) American Bar Association all rights reserved; reprinted by permission of the American Bar Association.

PRACTICAL ASSIGNMENT

Big Bank, N.A., is making a first-priority loan to Jason and Marie Phillips in the amount of $100,000. The loan is to provide Jason and Marie Phillips with money to purchase a home from Arnold Development, Inc., for $125,000. A copy of the title examination that has been completed on the property to be insured is included as Exhibit 14–9 at the end of this chapter. Review the title examination carefully, and prepare a title commitment from the information contained in the examination for both an owner's policy insuring Jason Phillips and Marie Phillips and a loan policy insuring Big Bank, N.A. Blank Schedule A; Schedule B, Section I; and Schedule B, Section II title commitment forms are included as Exhibit 14–10 at the end of this chapter. These forms may be used to complete this practical assignment.

ADDENDUM

Exhibit 14–1 Owner's Policy—ALTA
Exhibit 14–4 Owner's Affidavit
Exhibit 14–5 Loan Policy
Exhibit 14–7 Title Commitment
Exhibit 14–8 Title Opinion
Exhibit 14–9 Title Examination Form for Practical Assignment
Exhibit 14–10 Title Commitment Forms for Practical Assignment

EXHIBIT 14-1   Owner's Policy—ALTA

AMERICAN LAND TITLE ASSOCIATION
OWNER'S POLICY
(4-6-90)

SUBJECT TO THE EXCLUSIONS FROM COVERAGE, THE EXCEPTIONS FROM COVERAGE CONTAINED IN SCHEDULE B AND THE CONDITIONS AND STIPULATIONS,
, herein called the Company, insures, as of Date of Policy shown in Schedule A, against loss or damage, not exceeding the Amount of Insurance stated in Schedule A, sustained or incurred by the insured by reason of:

1. Title to the estate or interest described in Schedule A being vested other than as stated therein;
2. Any defect in or lien or encumbrance on the title;
3. Unmarketability of the title;
4. Lack of a right of access to and from the land.

The Company will also pay the costs, attorneys' fees and expenses incurred in defense of the title, as insured, but only to the extent provided in the Conditions and Stipulations.

In Witness Whereof, :   has caused this policy to be signed and sealed as of Date of Policy shown in Schedule A, the policy to become valid when countersigned by an authorized signatory.

EXHIBIT 14-1   Owner's Policy—ALTA (continued)

EXCLUSIONS FROM COVERAGE

The following matters are expressly excluded from the coverage of this policy and the Company will not pay loss or damage, costs, attorneys' fees or expenses which arise by reason of:

1. (a) Any law, ordinance or governmental regulation (including but not limited to building and zoning laws, ordinances, or regulations) restricting, regulating, prohibiting or relating to (i) the occupancy, use, or enjoyment of the land; (ii) the character, dimensions or location of any improvement now or hereafter erected on the land; (iii) a separation in ownership or a change in the dimensions or area of the land or any parcel of which the land is or was a part; or (iv) environmental protection, or the effect of any violation of these laws, ordinances or governmental regulations, except to the extent that a notice of the enforcement thereof or a notice of a defect, lien or encumbrance resulting from a violation or alleged violation affecting the land has been recorded in the public records at Date of Policy.

    (b) Any governmental police power not excluded by (a) above, except to the extent that a notice of the exercise thereof or a notice of a defect, lien or encumbrance resulting from a violation or alleged violation affecting the land has been recorded in the public records at Date of Policy.

2. Rights of eminent domain unless notice of the exercise thereof has been recorded in the public records at Date of Policy, but not excluding from coverage any taking which has occurred prior to Date of Policy which would be binding on the rights of a purchaser for value without knowledge.

3. Defects, liens, encumbrances, adverse claims or other matters:

    (a) created, suffered, assumed or agreed to by the insured claimant;

    (b) not known to the Company, not recorded in the public records at Date of Policy, but known to the insured claimant and not disclosed in writing to the Company by the insured claimant prior to the date the insured claimant became an insured under this policy;

    (c) resulting in no loss or damage to the insured claimant;

    (d) attaching or created subsequent to Date of Policy; or

    (e) resulting in loss or damage which would not have been sustained if the insured claimant had paid value for the estate or interest insured by this policy.

4. Any claim, which arises out of the transaction vesting in the insured the estate or interest insured by this policy, by reason of the operation of federal bankruptcy, state insolvency, or similar creditors' rights laws.

EXHIBIT 14-1   Owner's Policy—ALTA (continued)

SCHEDULE A

OFFICE FILE NUMBER	POLICY NUMBER	DATE OF POLICY	AMOUNT OF INSURANCE
1	2	3	4 $

1. Name of Insured:

2. The estate or interest in the land which is covered by this Policy is:

   Fee Simple

3. Title to the estate or interest in the land is vested in the Insured.

4. The land herein described is encumbered by the following mortgage or trust deed, and assignments:

   and the mortgages or trust deeds, if any, shown in Schedule B hereof.

5. The land referred to in this Policy is described as follows:

This Policy valid only if Schedule B is attached.

EXHIBIT 14-1   Owner's Policy—ALTA (continued)

SCHEDULE B

Policy Number: _____
                              Owners

EXCEPTIONS FROM COVERAGE

This policy does not insure against loss or damage (and the Company will not pay costs, attorneys' fees or expenses) which arise by reason of:

General Exceptions:

(1)   Rights or claims of parties in possession not shown by the public records.

(2)   Encroachments, overlaps, boundary line disputes, or other matters which would be disclosed by an accurate survey and inspection of the premises.

(3)   Easements, or claims of easements, not shown by the public records.

(4)   Any lien, or right to a lien, for services, labor, or material heretofore or hereafter furnished, imposed by law and not shown by the public records.

(5)   Taxes or special assessments which are not shown as existing liens by the public records.

Special Exceptions: The mortgage, if any, referred to in Item 4 of Schedule A.

Countersigned

_____
        Authorized Signatory

Schedule B of this Policy consists of   pages.

EXHIBIT 14-1   Owner's Policy—ALTA (continued)

CONDITIONS AND STIPULATIONS

1. DEFINITION OF TERMS

The following terms when used in this policy mean:

(a) "insured": the insured named in Schedule A, and, subject to any rights or defenses the Company would have had against the named insured, those who succeed to the interest of the named insured by operation of law as distinguished from purchase including, but not limited to, heirs, distributees, devisees, survivors, personal representatives, next of kin, or corporate or fiduciary successors.

(b) "insured claimant": an insured claiming loss or damage.

(c) "knowledge" or "known": actual knowledge, not constructive knowledge or notice which may be imputed to an insured by reason of the public records as defined in this policy or any other records which impart constructive notice of matters affecting the land.

(d) "land": the land described or referred to in Schedule A, and improvements affixed thereto which by law constitute real property. The term "land" does not include any property beyond the lines of the area described or referred to in Schedule A, nor any right, title, interest, estate or easement in abutting streets, roads, avenues, alleys, lanes, ways or waterways, but nothing herein shall modify or limit the extent to which a right of access to and from the land is insured by this policy.

(e) "mortgage": mortgage, deed of trust, trust deed, or other security instrument.

(f) "public records": records established under state statutes at Date of Policy for the purpose of imparting constructive notice of matters relating to real property to purchasers for value and without knowledge. With respect to Section 1(a)(iv) of the Exclusions From Coverage, "public records" shall also include environmental protection liens filed in the records of the clerk of the United States district court for the district in which the land is located.

(g) "unmarketability of the title": an alleged or apparent matter affecting the title to the land, not excluded or excepted from coverage, which would entitle a purchaser of the estate or interest described in Schedule A to be released from the obligation to purchase by virtue of a contractual condition requiring the delivery of marketable title.

2. CONTINUATION OF INSURANCE AFTER CONVEYANCE OF TITLE

The coverage of this policy shall continue in force as of Date of Policy in favor of an insured only so long as the insured retains an estate or interest in the land, or holds an indebtedness secured by a purchase money mortgage given by a purchaser from the insured, or only so long as the insured shall have liability by reason of covenants of warranty made by the insured in any transfer or conveyance of the estate or interest. This policy shall not continue in force in favor of any purchaser from the insured of either (i) an estate or interest in the land, or (ii) an indebtedness secured by a purchase money mortgage given to the insured.

3. NOTICE OF CLAIM TO BE GIVEN BY INSURED CLAIMANT

The insured shall notify the Company promptly in writing (i) in case of any litigation as set forth in Section 4(a) below, (ii) in case knowledge shall come to an insured hereunder of any claim of title or interest which is adverse to the title to the estate or interest, as insured, and which might cause loss or damage for which the Company may be liable by virtue of this policy, or (iii) if title to the estate or interest, as insured, is rejected as unmarketable. If prompt notice shall not be given to the Company, then as to the insured all liability of the Company shall terminate with regard to the matter or matters for which prompt notice is required; provided, however, that failure to notify the Company shall in no case prejudice the rights of any insured under this policy unless the Company shall be prejudiced by the failure and then only to the extent of the prejudice.

4. DEFENSE AND PROSECUTION OF ACTIONS; DUTY OF INSURED CLAIMANT TO COOPERATE

(a) Upon written request by the insured and subject to the options contained in Section 6 of these Conditions and Stipulations, the Company, at its own cost and without unreasonable delay, shall provide for the defense of an insured in litigation in which any third party asserts a claim adverse to the title or interest as insured, but only as to those stated causes of action alleging a defect, lien or encumbrance or other matter insured against by this policy. The Company shall have the right to select counsel of its choice (subject to the right of the insured to object for reasonable cause) to represent the insured as to those stated causes of action and shall not be liable for and will not pay the fees of any other counsel. The Company will not pay any fees, costs or expenses incurred by the insured in the defense of those causes of action which allege matters not insured against by this policy.

(b) The Company shall have the right, at its own cost, to institute and prosecute any action or proceeding or to do any other act which in its opinion may be necessary or desirable to establish the title to the estate or interest, as insured, or to prevent or reduce loss or damage to the insured. The Company may take any appropriate action under the terms of this policy, whether or not it shall be liable hereunder, and shall not thereby concede liability or waive any provision of this policy. If the Company shall exercise its rights under this paragraph. it shall do so diligently.

(c) Whenever the Company shall have brought an action or interposed a defense as required or permitted by the provisions of this policy, the Company may pursue any litigation to final determination by a court of competent jurisdiction and expressly reserves the right, in its sole discretion, to appeal from any adverse judgment or order.

(d) In all cases where this policy permits or requires the Company to prosecute or provide for the defense of any action or proceeding, the insured shall secure to the Company the right to so prosecute or provide defense in the action or proceeding, and all appeals therein, and permit the Company to use, at its option, the name of the insured for this purpose. Whenever requested by the Company, the insured, at the Company's expense, shall give the Company all reasonable aid (i) in any action or proceeding, securing evidence, obtaining witnesses, prosecuting or defending the action or proceeding, or effecting settlement, and (ii) in any other lawful act which in the opinion of the Company may be necessary or desirable to establish the title to the estate or interest as insured. If the Company is prejudiced by the failure of the insured to furnish the required cooperation, the Company's obligations to the insured under the policy shall terminate, including any liability or obligation to defend, prosecute, or continue any litigation, with regard to the matter or matters requiring such cooperation.

5. PROOF OF LOSS OR DAMAGE

In addition to and after the notices required under Section 3 of these Conditions and Stipulations have been provided the Company, a proof of loss or damage signed and sworn to by the insured claimant shall be furnished to the Company within 90 days after the insured claimant shall ascertain the facts giving rise to the loss or damage. The proof of loss or damage shall describe the defect in, or lien or encumbrance on the title, or other matter insured against by this policy which constitutes the basis of loss or damage and shall state, to the extent possible, the basis of calculating the amount of the loss or damage. If the Company is prejudiced by the failure of the insured claimant to provide the required proof of loss or damage, the Company's obligations to the insured under the policy shall terminate, including any liability or obligation to defend, prosecute, or continue any litigation, with regard to the matter or matters requiring such proof of loss or damage.

In addition, the insured claimant may reasonably be required to submit to examination under oath by any authorized representative of the Company and shall produce for examination, inspection and copying, at such reasonable times and places as may be designated by any authorized representative of the Company, all records, books, ledgers, checks, correspondence and memoranda, whether bearing a date before or after Date of Policy, which reasonably pertain to the loss or damage. Further, if requested by any authorized representative of the Company, the insured claimant shall grant its permission, in writing, for any authorized representative of the Company to examine, inspect and copy all records, books, ledgers, checks, correspondence and memoranda in the custody or control of a third party, which reasonably pertain to the loss or damage. All information designated as confidential by the insured claimant provided to the Company pursuant to this Section shall not be disclosed to others unless, in the reasonable judgment of the Company, it is necessary in the administration of the claim. Failure of the insured claimant to submit for examination under oath, produce other reasonably requested information or grant permission to secure reasonably necessary information from third parties as required in this paragraph shall terminate any liability of the Company under this policy as to that claim.

6. OPTIONS TO PAY OR OTHERWISE SETTLE CLAIMS; TERMINATION OF LIABILITY

In case of a claim under this policy, the Company shall have the following additional options:

(a) To Pay or Tender Payment of the Amount of Insurance.

To pay or tender payment of the amount of insurance under this policy together with any costs, attorneys' fees and expenses incurred by the insured claimant, which were authorized by the Company, up to the time of payment or tender of payment and which the Company is obligated to pay.

Upon the exercise by the Company of this option, all liability and obligations to the insured under this policy, other than to make the payment required, shall terminate, including any liability or obligation to defend, prosecute, or continue any litigation, and the policy shall be surrendered to the Company for cancellation.

(b) To Pay or Otherwise Settle With Parties Other than the Insured or With the Insured Claimant.

(i) to pay or otherwise settle with other parties for or in the name of an insured claimant any claim insured against under this policy, together with any costs, attorneys' fees and expenses incurred by the insured claimant which were authorized by the Company up to the time of payment and which the Company is obligated to pay; or

(ii) to pay or otherwise settle with the insured claimant the loss or damage provided for under this policy, together with any costs, attorneys' fees and expenses incurred by the insured claimant which were authorized by the Company up to the time of payment and which the Company is obligated to pay.

EXHIBIT 14-1   Owner's Policy—ALTA (continued)

Upon the exercise by the Company of either of the options provided for in paragraphs (b)(i) or (ii), the Company's obligations to the insured under this policy for the claimed loss or damage, other than the payments required to be made, shall terminate, including any liability or obligation to defend, prosecute or continue any litigation.

7. DETERMINATION, EXTENT OF LIABILITY AND COINSURANCE

This policy is a contract of indemnity against actual monetary loss or damage sustained or incurred by the insured claimant who has suffered loss or damage by reason of matters insured against by this policy and only to the extent herein described.

(a) The liability of the Company under this policy shall not exceed the least of:

(i) the Amount of Insurance stated in Schedule A; or,

(ii) the difference between the value of the insured estate or interest as insured and the value of the insured estate or interest subject to the defect, lien or encumbrance insured against by this policy.

(b) In the event the Amount of Insurance stated in Schedule A at the Date of Policy is less than 80 percent of the value of the insured estate or interest or the full consideration paid for the land, whichever is less, or if subsequent to the Date of Policy an improvement is erected on the land which increases the value of the insured estate or interest by at least 20 percent over the Amount of Insurance stated in Schedule A, then this Policy is subject to the following:

(i) where no subsequent improvement has been made, as to any partial loss, the Company shall only pay the loss pro rata in the proportion that the amount of insurance at Date of Policy bears to the total value of the insured estate or interest at Date of Policy; or

(ii) where a subsequent improvement has been made, as to any partial loss, the Company shall only pay the loss pro rata in the proportion that 120 percent of the Amount of Insurance stated in Schedule A bears to the sum of the Amount of Insurance stated in Schedule A and the amount expended for the improvement.

The provisions of this paragraph shall not apply to costs, attorneys' fees and expenses for which the Company is liable under this policy, and shall only apply to that portion of any loss which exceeds, in the aggregate, 10 percent of the Amount of Insurance stated in Schedule A.

(c) The Company will pay only those costs, attorneys' fees and expenses incurred in accordance with Section 4 of these Conditions and Stipulations.

8. APPORTIONMENT

If the land described in Schedule A consists of two or more parcels which are not used as a single site, and a loss is established affecting one or more of the parcels but not all, the loss shall be computed and settled on a pro rata basis as if the amount of insurance under this policy was divided pro rata as to the value on Date of Policy of each separate parcel to the whole, exclusive of any improvements made subsequent to Date of Policy, unless a liability or value has otherwise been agreed upon as to each parcel by the Company and the insured at the time of the issuance of this policy and shown by an express statement or by an endorsement attached to this policy.

9. LIMITATION OF LIABILITY

(a) If the Company establishes the title, or removes the alleged defect, lien or encumbrance, or cures the lack of a right of access to or from the land, or cures the claim of unmarketability of title, all as insured, in a reasonably diligent manner by any method, including litigation and the completion of any appeals therefrom, it shall have fully performed its obligations with respect to that matter and shall not be liable for any loss or damage caused thereby.

(b) In the event of any litigation, including litigation by the Company or with the Company's consent, the Company shall have no liability for loss or damage until there has been a final determination by a court of competent jurisdiction, and disposition of all appeals therefrom, adverse to the title as insured.

(c) The Company shall not be liable for loss or damage to any insured for liability voluntarily assumed by the insured in settling any claim or suit without the prior written consent of the Company.

10. REDUCTION OF INSURANCE; REDUCTION OR TERMINATION OF LIABILITY

All payments under this policy, except payments made for costs, attorneys' fees and expenses, shall reduce the amount of the insurance pro tanto.

11. LIABILITY NONCUMULATIVE

It is expressly understood that the amount of insurance under this policy shall be reduced by any amount the Company may pay under any policy insuring a mortgage to which exception is taken in Schedule B or to which the insured has agreed, assumed, or taken subject, or which is hereafter executed by an insured and which is a charge or lien on the estate or interest described or referred to in Schedule A, and the amount so paid shall be deemed a payment under this policy to the insured owner.

12. PAYMENT OF LOSS

(a) No payment shall be made without producing this policy for endorsement of the payment unless the policy has been lost or destroyed, in which case proof of loss or destruction shall be furnished to the satisfaction of the Company.

(b) When liability and the extent of loss or damage has been definitely fixed in accordance with these Conditions and Stipulations, the loss or damage shall be payable within 30 days thereafter.

13. SUBROGATION UPON PAYMENT OR SETTLEMENT

(a) The Company's Right of Subrogation.

Whenever the Company shall have settled and paid a claim under this policy, all right of subrogation shall vest in the Company unaffected by any act of the insured claimant.

The Company shall be subrogated to and be entitled to all rights and remedies which the insured claimant would have had against any person or property in respect to the claim had this policy not been issued. If requested by the Company, the insured claimant shall transfer to the Company all rights and remedies against any person or property necessary in order to perfect this right of subrogation. The insured claimant shall permit the Company to sue, compromise or settle in the name of the insured claimant and to use the name of the insured claimant in any transaction or litigation involving these rights or remedies.

If a payment on account of a claim does not fully cover the loss of the insured claimant, the Company shall be subrogated to these rights and remedies in the proportion which the Company's payment bears to the whole amount of the loss.

If loss should result from any act of the insured claimant, as stated above, that act shall not void this policy, but the Company, in that event, shall be required to pay only that part of any losses insured against by this policy which shall exceed the amount, if any, lost to the Company by reason of the impairment by the insured claimant of the Company's right of subrogation.

(b) The Company's Rights Against Non-insured Obligors.

The Company's right of subrogation against non-insured obligors shall exist and shall include, without limitation, the rights of the insured to indemnities, guaranties, other policies of insurance or bonds, notwithstanding any terms or conditions contained in those instruments which provide for subrogation rights by reason of this policy.

14. ARBITRATION

Unless prohibited by applicable law, either the Company or the insured may demand arbitration pursuant to the Title Insurance Arbitration Rules of the American Arbitration Association. Arbitrable matters may include, but are not limited to, any controversy or claim between the Company and the insured arising out of or relating to this policy, any service of the Company in connection with its issuance or the breach of a policy provision or other obligation. All arbitrable matters when the Amount of Insurance is $1,000,000 or less shall be arbitrated at the option of either the Company or the insured. All arbitrable matters when the Amount of Insurance is in excess of $1,000,000 shall be arbitrated only when agreed to by both the Company and the insured. Arbitration pursuant to this policy and under the Rules in effect on the date the demand for arbitration is made or, at the option of the insured, the Rules in effect at Date of Policy shall be binding upon the parties. The award may include attorneys' fees only if the laws of the state in which the land is located permit a court to award attorneys' fees to a prevailing party. Judgment upon the award rendered by the Arbitrator(s) may be entered in any court having jurisdiction thereof.

The law of the situs of the land shall apply to an arbitration under the Title Insurance Arbitration Rules.

A copy of the Rules may be obtained from the Company upon request.

15. LIABILITY LIMITED TO THIS POLICY; POLICY ENTIRE CONTRACT

(a) This policy together with all endorsements, if any, attached hereto by the Company is the entire policy and contract between the insured and the Company. In interpreting any provision of this policy, this policy shall be construed as a whole.

(b) Any claim of loss or damage, whether or not based on negligence, and which arises out of the status of the title to the estate or interest covered hereby or by any action asserting such claim, shall be restricted to this policy.

(c) No amendment of or endorsement to this policy can be made except by a writing endorsed hereon or attached hereto signed by either the President, a Vice President, the Secretary, an Assistant Secretary, or validating officer or authorized signatory of the Company.

16. SEVERABILITY

In the event any provision of the policy is held invalid or unenforceable under applicable law, the policy shall be deemed not to include that provision and all other provisions shall remain in full force and effect.

17. NOTICES, WHERE SENT

All notices required to be given the Company and any statement in writing required to be furnished the Company shall include the number of this policy and shall be addressed to the Company at the issuing office or to:

EXHIBIT 14–4
Owner's Affidavit

STATE OF GEORGIA   )
)   ss:

COUNTY OF FULTON   )

The undersigned, being duly sworn, states:

That the undersigned is the President of MARKAM INDUSTRIES, INC., a Georgia corporation (the "Company"), and is duly authorized to execute this affidavit in his capacity on behalf of the Company as well as in his individual capacity;

That the principal place of business, principal office and chief executive office of the Company is located in Gwinnett County, Georgia and has been located in said County at all times since the formation of the Company;

That the Company is the fee simple title owner of the real property described on Exhibit "A" attached hereto and incorporated herein by reference (the "Property").

That the lines and corners of the Property are clearly marked and there are no disputes concerning the location of said lines and corners;

That no improvements or repairs have been made or contracted for by the Company on the Property during the three (3) months immediately preceding the date of this affidavit, for which there are outstanding bills for labor or services performed or rendered, or for material supplied or furnished, or incurred in connection with improvements or repairs on the Property, or for the services of architects, surveyors or engineers in connection with improvements or repairs on the Property;

That, except for the matters set forth on Exhibit "B" attached hereto and incorporated herein by reference, the Property is free and clear of all claims, liens and encumbrances, and there is no outstanding indebtedness for or liens against any equipment or fixtures attached to, installed on, incorporated in or located on, or otherwise used in connection with the operation or maintenance of, the Property or the improvements thereon;

That there are no persons or other parties in possession of the Property who have a right or claim to possession extending beyond the date hereof;

That there are no suits, proceedings, judgments, bankruptcies, liens, or executions against the Company which affect title to the Property, the improvements thereon or the fixtures attached thereto;

That the undersigned is making this affidavit with the knowledge that it will be relied upon by lenders, attorneys, and title insurance companies interested in the title to the Property.

Sworn to and subscribed before me this
_____ day of _____, 19___.

_____   _____

Notary Public   JIM BAXTER

My Commission Expires:

_____

[Notarial Seal]

EXHIBIT 14–5   Loan Policy

AMERICAN LAND TITLE ASSOCIATION
LOAN POLICY
(4-6-90)

SUBJECT TO THE EXCLUSIONS FROM COVERAGE, THE EXCEPTIONS FROM COVERAGE CONTAINED IN SCHEDULE B AND THE CONDITIONS AND STIPULATIONS, herein called the Company, insures, as of Date of Policy shown in Schedule A, against loss or damage, not exceeding the Amount of Insurance stated in Schedule A, sustained or incurred by the insured by reason of:

1. Title to the estate or interest described in Schedule A being vested other than as stated therein;
2. Any defect in or lien or encumbrance on the title;
3. Unmarketability of the title;
4. Lack of a right of access to and from the land;
5. The invalidity or unenforceability of the lien of the insured mortgage upon the title;
6. The priority of any lien or encumbrance over the lien of the insured mortgage;
7. Lack of priority of the lien of the insured mortgage over any statutory lien for services, labor or material:
   (a) arising from an improvement or work related to the land which is contracted for or commenced prior to Date of Policy; or
   (b) arising from an improvement or work related to the land which is contracted for or commenced subsequent to Date of Policy and which is financed in whole or in part by proceeds of the indebtedness secured by the insured mortgage which at Date of Policy the insured has advanced or is obligated to advance;
8. The invalidity or unenforceability of any assignment of the insured mortgage, provided the assignment is shown in Schedule A, or the failure of the assignment shown in Schedule A to vest title to the insured mortgage in the named insured assignee free and clear of all liens.

The Company will also pay the costs, attorneys' fees and expenses incurred in defense of the title or the lien of the insured mortgage, as insured, but only to the extent provided in the Conditions and Stipulations.

In Witness Whereof, ·   has caused this policy to be signed and sealed as of Date of Policy shown in Schedule A, the policy to become valid when countersigned by an authorized signatory.

EXHIBIT 14-5   Loan Policy (continued)

EXCLUSIONS FROM COVERAGE

The following matters are expressly excluded from the coverage of this policy and the Company will not pay loss or damage, costs, attorneys' fees or expenses which arise by reason of:

1. (a) Any law, ordinance or governmental regulation (including but not limited to building and zoning laws, ordinances, or regulations) restricting, regulating, prohibiting or relating to (i) the occupancy, use, or enjoyment of the land; (ii) the character, dimensions or location of any improvement now or hereafter erected on the land; (iii) a separation in ownership or a change in the dimensions or area of the land or any parcel of which the land is or was a part; or (iv) environmental protection, or the effect of any violation of these laws, ordinances or governmental regulations, except to the extent that a notice of the enforcement thereof or a notice of a defect, lien or encumbrance resulting from a violation or alleged violation affecting the land has been recorded in the public records at Date of Policy.

   (b) Any governmental police power not excluded by (a) above, except to the extent that a notice of the exercise thereof or a notice of a defect, lien or encumbrance resulting from a violation or alleged violation affecting the land has been recorded in the public records at Date of Policy.

2. Rights of eminent domain unless notice of the exercise thereof has been recorded in the public records at Date of Policy, but not excluding from coverage any taking which has occurred prior to Date of Policy which would be binding on the rights of a purchaser for value without knowledge.

3. Defects, liens, encumbrances, adverse claims or other matters:

   (a) created, suffered, assumed or agreed to by the insured claimant;

   (b) not known to the Company, not recorded in the public records at Date of Policy, but known to the insured claimant and not disclosed in writing to the Company by the insured claimant prior to the date the insured claimant became an insured under this policy;

   (c) resulting in no loss or damage to the insured claimant;

   (d) attaching or created subsequent to Date of Policy (except to the extent that this policy insures the priority of the lien of the insured mortgage over any statutory lien for services, labor or material); or

   (e) resulting in loss or damage which would not have been sustained if the insured claimant had paid value for the insured mortgage.

4. Unenforceability of the lien of the insured mortgage because of the inability or failure of the insured at Date of Policy, or the inability or failure of any subsequent owner of the indebtedness, to comply with applicable doing business laws of the state in which the land is situated.

5. Invalidity or unenforceability of the lien of the insured mortgage, or claim thereof, which arises out of the transaction evidenced by the insured mortgage and is based upon usury or any consumer credit protection or truth in lending law.

6. Any statutory lien for services, labor or materials (or the claim of priority of any statutory lien for services, labor or materials over the lien of the insured mortgage) arising from an improvement or work related to the land which is contracted for and commenced subsequent to Date of Policy and is not financed in whole or in part by proceeds of the indebtedness secured by the insured mortgage which at Date of Policy the insured has advanced or is obligated to advance.

7. Any claim, which arises out of the transaction creating the interest of the mortgagee insured by this policy, by reason of the operation of federal bankruptcy, state insolvency, or similar creditors' rights laws.

CONDITIONS AND STIPULATIONS

1. DEFINITION OF TERMS

The following terms when used in this policy mean:

(a) "insured": the insured named in Schedule A. The term "insured" also includes

(i) the owner of the indebtedness secured by the insured mortgage and each successor in ownership of the indebtedness except a successor who is an obligor under the provisions of Section 12(c) of these Conditions and Stipulations (reserving, however, all rights and defenses as to any successor that the Company would have had against any predecessor insured, unless the successor acquired the indebtedness as a purchaser for value without knowledge of the asserted defect, lien, encumbrance, adverse claim or other matter insured against by this policy as affecting title to the estate or interest in the land);

(ii) any governmental agency or governmental instrumentality which is an insurer or guarantor under an insurance contract or guaranty insuring or guaranteeing the indebtedness secured by the insured mortgage, or any part thereof, whether named as an insured herein or not;

(iii) the parties designated in Section 2(a) of these Conditions and Stipulations.

(b) "insured claimant": an insured claiming loss or damage.

(c) "knowledge" or "known": actual knowledge, not constructive knowledge or notice which may be imputed to an insured by reason of the public records as defined in this policy or any other records which impart constructive notice of matters affecting the land.

(d) "land": the land described or referred to in Schedule A, and improvements affixed thereto which by law constitute real property. The term "land" does not include any property beyond the lines of the area described or referred to in Schedule A, nor any right, title, interest, estate or easement in abutting streets, roads, avenues, alleys, lanes, ways or waterways, but nothing herein shall modify or limit the extent to which a right of access to and from the land is insured by this policy.

(e) "mortgage": mortgage, deed of trust, trust deed, or other security instrument.

(f) "public records": records established under state statutes at Date of Policy for the purpose of imparting constructive notice of matters relating to real property to purchasers for value and without knowledge. With respect to Section 1(a)(iv) of the Exclusions From Coverage, "public records" shall also include environmental protection liens filed in the records of the clerk of the United States district court for the district in which the land is located.

(g) "unmarketability of the title": an alleged or apparent matter affecting the title to the land, not excluded or excepted from coverage, which would entitle a purchaser of the estate or interest described in Schedule A or the insured mortgage to be released from the obligation to purchase by virtue of a contractual condition requiring the delivery of marketable title.

2. CONTINUATION OF INSURANCE

(a) **After Acquisition of Title.** The coverage of this policy shall continue in force as of Date of Policy in favor of (i) an insured who acquires all or any part of the estate or interest in the land by foreclosure, trustee's sale, conveyance in lieu of foreclosure, or other legal manner which discharges the lien of the insured mortgage; (ii) a transferee of the estate or interest so acquired from an insured corporation, provided the transferee is the parent or wholly-owned subsidiary of the insured corporation, and their corporate successors by operation of law and not by purchase, subject to any rights or defenses the Company may have against any predecessor insureds; and (iii) any governmental agency or governmental instrumentality which acquires all or any part of the estate or interest pursuant to a contract of insurance or guaranty insuring or guaranteeing the indebtedness secured by the insured mortgage.

(b) **After Conveyance of Title.** The coverage of this policy shall continue in force as of Date of Policy in favor of an insured only so long as the insured retains an estate or interest in the land, or holds an indebtedness secured by a purchase money mortgage given by a purchaser from the insured, or only so long as the insured shall have liability by reason of covenants of warranty made by the insured in any transfer or conveyance of the estate or interest. This policy shall not continue in force in favor of any purchaser from the insured of either (i) an estate or interest in the land, or (ii) an indebtedness secured by a purchase money mortgage given to the insured.

EXHIBIT 14-5   Loan Policy (continued)

SCHEDULE A

OFFICE FILE NUMBER	POLICY NUMBER	DATE OF POLICY	AMOUNT OF INSURANCE
1	2	3	4
			$

1. Name of Insured:

2. The estate or interest in the land which is encumbered by the insured mortgage is:

   Fee Simple

3. Title to the estate or interest in the land is vested in:

4. The insured mortgage and assignments thereof, if any, are described as follows:

5. The land referred to in this Policy is described as follows:

This Policy valid only if Schedule B is attached.

EXHIBIT 14–5   Loan Policy (continued)

SCHEDULE B

Policy Number: _____
                            Loan

EXCEPTIONS FROM COVERAGE

This policy does not insure against loss or damage (and the Company will not pay costs, attorneys' fees or expenses) which arise by reason of:

Special Exceptions:

Countersigned

_____
      Authorized Signatory

Schedule B of this Policy consists of   pages.

EXHIBIT 14-5 Loan Policy (continued)

(c) Amount of Insurance. The amount of insurance after the acquisition or after the conveyance shall in neither event exceed the least of:

(i) the Amount of Insurance stated in Schedule A;

(ii) the amount of the principal of the indebtedness secured by the insured mortgage as of Date of Policy, interest thereon, expenses of foreclosure, amounts advanced pursuant to the insured mortgage to assure compliance with laws or to protect the lien of the insured mortgage prior to the time of acquisition of the estate or interest in the land and secured thereby and reasonable amounts expended to prevent deterioration of improvements, but reduced by the amount of all payments made; or

(iii) the amount paid by any governmental agency or governmental instrumentality, if the agency or instrumentality is the insured claimant, in the acquisition of the estate or interest in satisfaction of its insurance contract or guaranty.

3. NOTICE OF CLAIM TO BE GIVEN BY INSURED CLAIMANT

The insured shall notify the Company promptly in writing (i) in case of any litigation as set forth in Section 4(a) below, (ii) in case knowledge shall come to an insured hereunder of any claim of title or interest which is adverse to the title to the estate or interest or the lien of the insured mortgage, as insured, and which might cause loss or damage for which the Company may be liable by virtue of this policy, or (iii) if title to the estate or interest or the lien of the insured mortgage, as insured, is rejected as unmarketable. If prompt notice shall not be given to the Company, then as to the insured all liability of the Company shall terminate with regard to the matter or matters for which prompt notice is required; provided, however, that failure to notify the Company shall in no case prejudice the rights of any insured under this policy unless the Company shall be prejudiced by the failure and then only to the extent of the prejudice.

4. DEFENSE AND PROSECUTION OF ACTIONS; DUTY OF INSURED CLAIMANT TO COOPERATE

(a) Upon written request by the insured and subject to the options contained in Section 6 of these Conditions and Stipulations, the Company, at its own cost and without unreasonable delay, shall provide for the defense of an insured in litigation in which any third party asserts a claim adverse to the title or interest as insured, but only as to those stated causes of action alleging a defect, lien or encumbrance or other matter insured against by this policy. The Company shall have the right to select counsel of its choice (subject to the right of the insured to object for reasonable cause) to represent the insured as to those stated causes of action and shall not be liable for and will not pay the fees of any other counsel. The Company will not pay any fees, costs or expenses incurred by the insured in the defense of those causes of action which allege matters not insured against by this policy.

(b) The Company shall have the right, at its own cost, to institute and prosecute any action or proceeding or to do any other act which in its opinion may be necessary or desirable to establish the title to the estate or interest or the lien of the insured mortgage, as insured, or to prevent or reduce loss or damage to the insured. The Company may take any appropriate action under the terms of this policy, whether or not it shall be liable hereunder, and shall not thereby concede liability or waive any provision of this policy. If the Company shall exercise its rights under this paragraph, it shall do so diligently.

(c) Whenever the Company shall have brought an action or interposed a defense as required or permitted by the provisions of this policy, the Company may pursue any litigation to final determination by a court of competent jurisdiction and expressly reserves the right, in its sole discretion, to appeal from any adverse judgment or order.

(d) In all cases where this policy permits or requires the Company to prosecute or provide for the defense of any action or proceeding, the insured shall secure to the Company the right to so prosecute or provide defense in the action or proceeding, and all appeals therein, and permit the Company to use, at its option, the name of the insured for this purpose. Whenever requested by the Company, the insured, at the Company's expense, shall give the Company all reasonable aid (i) in any action or proceeding, securing evidence, obtaining witnesses, prosecuting or defending the action or proceeding, or effecting settlement, and (ii) in any other lawful act which in the opinion of the Company may be necessary or desirable to establish the title to the estate or interest or the lien of the insured mortgage, as insured. If the Company is prejudiced by the failure of the insured to furnish the required cooperation, the Company's obligations to the insured under the policy shall terminate, including any liability or obligation to defend, prosecute, or continue any litigation, with regard to the matter or matters requiring such cooperation.

5. PROOF OF LOSS OR DAMAGE

In addition to and after the notices required under Section 3 of these Conditions and Stipulations have been provided the Company, a proof of loss or damage signed and sworn to by the insured claimant shall be furnished to the Company within 90 days after the insured claimant shall ascertain the facts giving rise to the loss or damage. The proof of loss or damage shall describe the defect in, or lien or encumbrance on the title, or other matter insured against by this policy which constitutes the basis of loss or damage and shall state, to the extent possible, the basis of calculating the amount of the loss or damage. If the Company is prejudiced by the failure of the insured claimant to

provide the required proof of loss or damage, the Company's obligations to the insured under the policy shall terminate, including any liability or obligation to defend, prosecute, or continue any litigation, with regard to the matter or matters requiring such proof of loss or damage.

In addition, the insured claimant may reasonably be required to submit to examination under oath by any authorized representative of the Company and shall produce for examination, inspection and copying, at such reasonable times and places as may be designated by any authorized representative of the Company, all records, books, ledgers, checks, correspondence and memoranda, whether bearing a date before or after Date of Policy, which reasonably pertain to the loss or damage. Further, if requested by any authorized representative of the Company, the insured claimant shall grant its permission, in writing, for any authorized representative of the Company to examine, inspect and copy all records, books, ledgers, checks, correspondence and memoranda in the custody or control of a third party, which reasonably pertain to the loss or damage. All information designated as confidential by the insured claimant provided to the Company pursuant to this Section shall not be disclosed to others unless, in the reasonable judgment of the Company, it is necessary in the administration of the claim. Failure of the insured claimant to submit for examination under oath, produce other reasonably requested information or grant permission to secure reasonably necessary information from third parties as required in this paragraph, unless prohibited by law or governmental regulation, shall terminate any liability of the Company under this policy as to that claim.

6. OPTIONS TO PAY OR OTHERWISE SETTLE CLAIMS; TERMINATION OF LIABILITY

In case of a claim under this policy, the Company shall have the following additional options:

(a) To Pay or Tender Payment of the Amount of Insurance or to Purchase the Indebtedness.

(i) to pay or tender payment of the amount of insurance under this policy together with any costs, attorneys' fees and expenses incurred by the insured claimant, which were authorized by the Company, up to the time of payment or tender of payment and which the Company is obligated to pay; or

(ii) to purchase the indebtedness secured by the insured mortgage for the amount owing thereon together with any costs, attorneys' fees and expenses incurred by the insured claimant which were authorized by the Company up to the time of purchase and which the Company is obligated to pay.

If the Company offers to purchase the indebtedness as herein provided, the owner of the indebtedness shall transfer, assign, and convey the indebtedness and the insured mortgage, together with any collateral security, to the Company upon payment therefor.

Upon the exercise by the Company of either of the options provided for in paragraphs a(i) or (ii), all liability and obligations to the insured under this policy, other than to make the payment required in those paragraphs, shall terminate, including any liability or obligation to defend, prosecute, or continue any litigation, and the policy shall be surrendered to the Company for cancellation.

(b) To Pay or Otherwise Settle With Parties Other than the Insured or With the Insured Claimant.

(i) to pay or otherwise settle with other parties for or in the name of an insured claimant any claim insured against under this policy, together with any costs, attorneys' fees and expenses incurred by the insured claimant which were authorized by the Company up to the time of payment and which the Company is obligated to pay; or

(ii) to pay or otherwise settle with the insured claimant the loss or damage provided for under this policy, together with any costs, attorneys' fees and expenses incurred by the insured claimant which were authorized by the Company up to the time of payment and which the Company is obligated to pay.

Upon the exercise by the Company of either of the options provided for in paragraphs (b)(i) or (ii), the Company's obligations to the insured under this policy for the claimed loss or damage, other than the payments required to be made, shall terminate, including any liability or obligation to defend, prosecute or continue any litigation.

7. DETERMINATION AND EXTENT OF LIABILITY

This policy is a contract of indemnity against actual monetary loss or damage sustained or incurred by the insured claimant who has suffered loss or damage by reason of matters insured against by this policy and only to the extent herein described.

(a) The liability of the Company under this policy shall not exceed the least of:

(i) the Amount of Insurance stated in Schedule A, or, if applicable, the amount of insurance as defined in Section 2 (c) of these Conditions and Stipulations;

(ii) the amount of the unpaid principal indebtedness secured by the insured mortgage as limited or provided under Section 8 of these Conditions and Stipulations or as reduced under Section 9 of these Conditions and Stipulations, at the time the loss or damage insured against by this policy occurs, together with interest thereon; or

EXHIBIT 14-5   Loan Policy (continued)

(iii) the difference between the value of the insured estate or interest as insured and the value of the insured estate or interest subject to the defect, lien or encumbrance insured against by this policy.

(b) In the event the insured has acquired the estate or interest in the manner described in Section 2(a) of these Conditions and Stipulations or has conveyed the title, then the liability of the Company shall continue as set forth in Section 7(a) of these Conditions and Stipulations.

(c) The Company will pay only those costs, attorneys' fees and expenses incurred in accordance with Section 4 of these Conditions and Stipulations.

8. LIMITATION OF LIABILITY

(a) If the Company establishes the title, or removes the alleged defect, lien or encumbrance, or cures the lack of a right of access to or from the land, or cures the claim of unmarketability of title, or otherwise establishes the lien of the insured mortgage, all as insured, in a reasonably diligent manner by any method, including litigation and the completion of any appeals therefrom, it shall have fully performed its obligations with respect to that matter and shall not be liable for any loss or damage caused thereby.

(b) In the event of any litigation, including litigation by the Company or with the Company's consent, the Company shall have no liability for loss or damage until there has been a final determination by a court of competent jurisdiction, and disposition of all appeals therefrom, adverse to the title or to the lien of the insured mortgage, as insured.

(c) The Company shall not be liable for loss or damage to any insured for liability voluntarily assumed by the insured in settling any claim or suit without the prior written consent of the Company.

(d) The Company shall not be liable for: (i) any indebtedness created subsequent to Date of Policy except for advances made to protect the lien of the insured mortgage and secured thereby and reasonable amounts expended to prevent deterioration of improvements; or (ii) construction loan advances made subsequent to Date of Policy, except construction loan advances made subsequent to Date of Policy for the purpose of financing in whole or in part the construction of an improvement to the land which at Date of Policy were secured by the insured mortgage and which the insured was and continued to be obligated to advance at and after Date of Policy.

9. REDUCTION OF INSURANCE; REDUCTION OR TERMINATION OF LIABILITY

(a) All payments under this policy, except payments made for costs, attorneys' fees and expenses, shall reduce the amount of the insurance pro tanto. However, any payments made prior to the acquisition of title to the estate or interest as provided in Section 2(a) of these Conditions and Stipulations shall not reduce pro tanto the amount of the insurance afforded under this policy except to the extent that the payments reduce the amount of the indebtedness secured by the insured mortgage.

(b) Payment in part by any person of the principal of the indebtedness, or any other obligation secured by the insured mortgage, or any voluntary partial satisfaction or release of the insured mortgage, to the extent of the payment, satisfaction or release, shall reduce the amount of insurance pro tanto. The amount of insurance may thereafter be increased by accruing interest and advances made to protect the lien of the insured mortgage and secured thereby, with interest thereon, provided in no event shall the amount of insurance be greater than the Amount of Insurance stated in Schedule A.

(c) Payment in full by any person or the voluntary satisfaction or release of the insured mortgage shall terminate all liability of the Company except as provided in Section 2(a) of these Conditions and Stipulations.

10. LIABILITY NONCUMULATIVE

If the insured acquires title to the estate or interest in satisfaction of the indebtedness secured by the insured mortgage, or any part thereof, it is expressly understood that the amount of insurance under this policy shall be reduced by any amount the Company may pay under any policy insuring a mortgage to which exception is taken in Schedule B or to which the insured has agreed, assumed, or taken subject, or which is hereafter executed by an insured and which is a charge or lien on the estate or interest described or referred to in Schedule A, and the amount so paid shall be deemed a payment under this policy.

11. PAYMENT OF LOSS

(a) No payment shall be made without producing this policy for endorsement of the payment unless the policy has been lost or destroyed, in which case proof of loss or destruction shall be furnished to the satisfaction of the Company.

(b) When liability and the extent of loss or damage has been definitely fixed in accordance with these Conditions and Stipulations, the loss or damage shall be payable within 30 days thereafter.

12. SUBROGATION UPON PAYMENT OR SETTLEMENT

(a) The Company's Right of Subrogation.

Whenever the Company shall have settled and paid a claim under this policy, all right of subrogation shall vest in the Company unaffected by any act of the insured claimant.

The Company shall be subrogated to and be entitled to all rights and remedies which the insured claimant would have had against any person or property in respect to the claim had this policy not been issued. If requested by the Company, the insured claimant shall transfer to the Company all rights

and remedies against any person or property necessary in order to perfect this right of subrogation. The insured claimant shall permit the Company to sue, compromise or settle in the name of the insured claimant and to use the name of the insured claimant in any transaction or litigation involving these rights or remedies.

If a payment on account of a claim does not fully cover the loss of the insured claimant, the Company shall be subrogated to all rights and remedies of the insured claimant after the insured claimant shall have recovered its principal, interest, and costs of collection.

(b) The Insured's Rights and Limitations.

Notwithstanding the foregoing, the owner of the indebtedness secured by the insured mortgage, provided the priority of the lien of the insured mortgage or its enforceability is not affected, may release or substitute the personal liability of any debtor or guarantor, or extend or otherwise modify the terms of payment, or release a portion of the estate or interest from the lien of the insured mortgage, or release any collateral security for the indebtedness.

When the permitted acts of the insured claimant occur and the insured has knowledge of any claim of title or interest adverse to the title to the estate or interest or the priority or enforceability of the lien of the insured mortgage, as insured, the Company shall be required to pay only that part of any losses insured against by this policy which shall exceed the amount, if any, lost to the Company by reason of the impairment by the insured claimant of the Company's right of subrogation.

(c) The Company's Rights Against Non-insured Obligors.

The Company's right of subrogation against non-insured obligors shall exist and shall include, without limitation, the rights of the insured to indemnities, guaranties, other policies of insurance or bonds, notwithstanding any terms or conditions contained in those instruments which provide for subrogation rights by reason of this policy.

The Company's right of subrogation shall not be avoided by acquisition of the insured mortgage by an obligor (except an obligor described in Section 1(a)(ii) of these Conditions and Stipulations) who acquires the insured mortgage as a result of an indemnity, guarantee, other policy of insurance, or bond and the obligor will not be an insured under this policy, notwithstanding Section 1(a)(i) of these Conditions and Stipulations.

13. ARBITRATION

Unless prohibited by applicable law, either the Company or the insured may demand arbitration pursuant to the Title Insurance Arbitration Rules of the American Arbitration Association. Arbitrable matters may include, but are not limited to, any controversy or claim between the Company and the insured arising out of or relating to this policy, any service of the Company in connection with its issuance or the breach of a policy provision or other obligation. All arbitrable matters when the Amount of Insurance is $1,000,000 or less shall be arbitrated at the option of either the Company or the insured. All arbitrable matters when the Amount of Insurance is in excess of $1,000,000 shall be arbitrated only when agreed to by both the Company and the insured. Arbitration pursuant to this policy and under the Rules in effect on the date the demand for arbitration is made or, at the option of the insured, the Rules in effect at Date of Policy shall be binding upon the parties. The award may include attorneys' fees only if the laws of the state in which the land is located permit a court to award attorneys' fees to a prevailing party. Judgment upon the award rendered by the Arbitrator(s) may be entered in any court having jurisdiction thereof.

The law of the situs of the land shall apply to an arbitration under the Title Insurance Arbitration Rules.

A copy of the Rules may be obtained from the Company upon request.

14. LIABILITY LIMITED TO THIS POLICY; POLICY ENTIRE CONTRACT

(a) This policy together with all endorsements, if any, attached hereto by the Company is the entire policy and contract between the insured and the Company. In interpreting any provision of this policy, this policy shall be construed as a whole.

(b) Any claim of loss or damage, whether or not based on negligence, and which arises out of the status of the lien of the insured mortgage or of the title to the estate or interest covered hereby or by any action asserting such claim, shall be restricted to this policy.

(c) No amendment of or endorsement to this policy can be made except by a writing endorsed hereon or attached hereto signed by either the President, a Vice President, the Secretary, an Assistant Secretary, or validating officer or authorized signatory of the Company.

15. SEVERABILITY

In the event any provision of this policy is held invalid or unenforceable under applicable law, the policy shall be deemed not to include that provision and all other provisions shall remain in full force and effect.

16. NOTICES, WHERE SENT

All notices required to be given the Company and any statement in writing required to be furnished the Company shall include the number of this policy and shall be addressed to the Company at the issuing office or to:

EXHIBIT 14-7   Title Commitment

AMERICAN LAND TITLE ASSOCIATION COMMITMENT — 1966

COMMITMENT FOR TITLE INSURANCE

, herein called the Company, for a valuable consideration, hereby commits to issue its policy or policies of title insurance, as identified in Schedule A, in favor of the proposed Insured named in Schedule A, as owner or mortgagee of the estate or interest covered hereby in the land described or referred to in Schedule A, upon payment of the premiums and charges therefor; all subject to the provisions of Schedules A and B and to the Conditions and Stipulations hereof.

This Commitment shall be effective only when the identity of the proposed Insured and the amount of the policy or policies committed for have been inserted in Schedule A hereof by the Company, either at the time of the issuance of this Commitment or by subsequent endorsement.

This Commitment is preliminary to the issuance of such policy or policies of title insurance and all liability and obligations hereunder shall cease and terminate six months after the effective date hereof or when the policy or policies committed for shall issue, whichever first occurs, provided that the failure to issue such policy or policies is not the fault of the Company.

IN WITNESS WHEREOF, (:aused this Commitment to be signed and sealed as of the effective date of Commitment shown in Schedule A, the Commitment to become valid when countersigned by an authorized signatory.

By:

Issued by:

ATTEST: President.

                                     Secretary.

_____
Authorized Signatory

EXHIBIT 14–7   Title Commitment (continued)

COMMITMENT

SCHEDULE A

¹ OFFICE FILE NUMBER	

² COMMITMENT NUMBER	³ EFFECTIVE DATE	⁴ LOAN AMOUNT
		OWNERS AMOUNT

1. Policy or Policies to be issued:
   ALTA LOAN POLICY.
   Proposed Insured:

   ALTA OWNER'S POLICY, Form
   Proposed Insured:

2. The estate or interest in the land described or referred to in this Commitment and covered herein is a fee simple, and title thereto is at the effective date hereof vested in:

3. The Land is described as follows:

Note: This Commitment consists of insert pages labeled in Schedule A, Schedule B-Section 1, and Schedule B-Section 2. This Commitment is of no force and effect unless all schedules are included, along with any Rider pages incorporated by reference in the insert pages.

EXHIBIT 14–7   Title Commitment (continued)

COMMITMENT

SCHEDULE B — Section 1

Commitment Number

Requirements

The following are the requirements to be complied with:

1. Instrument(s) creating the estate or interest to be insured must be approved, executed and filed for record, to wit:

2. Payment of the full consideration to, or for the account of, the grantors or mortgagors.

3. Payment of all taxes, charges, assessments, levied and assessed against subject premises, which are due and payable.

4. Satisfactory evidence should be had that improvements and/or repairs or alterations thereto are completed; that contractor, subcontractors, labor and materialmen are all paid.

EXHIBIT 14–7   Title Commitment (continued)

COMMITMENT

SCHEDULE B—Section 2

Commitment Number

Exceptions

Schedule B of the policy or policies to be issued will contain exceptions to the following matters unless the same are disposed of to the satisfaction of the Company.

1. Defects, liens, encumbrances, adverse claims or other matters, if any, created, first appearing in the public records or attaching subsequent to the effective date hereof but prior to the date the proposed Insured acquires for value of record the estate or interest or mortgage thereon covered by this Commitment.

2. Any owner's policy issued pursuant hereto will contain under Schedule B the standard exceptions set forth on the inside cover. Any loan policy will also contain under Schedule B thereof, the standard exceptions set forth on the inside cover of this commitment relating to the owner's policy.

3. Standard Exceptions 2 and 3 may be removed from the policy when a satisfactory survey and inspection of the premises is made.

4. Taxes and assessments for the year   and subsequent years.

Note: On loan policies, junior and subordinate matters, if any, will not be reflected in Schedule B.

EXHIBIT 14-7   Title Commitment (continued)

STANDARD EXCEPTIONS FOR OWNER'S POLICY

The owner's policy will be subject to the mortgage, if any, noted under item one of Section 1 of Schedule B hereof and to the following exceptions: (1) rights or claims of parties in possession not shown by the public records; (2) encroachments, overlaps, boundary line disputes, and any matters which would be disclosed by an accurate survey and inspection of the premises; (3) easements, or claims of easements, not shown by the public records; (4) any lien, or right to a lien, for services, labor, or material heretofore or hereafter furnished, imposed by law and not shown by the public records; (5) taxes or special assessments which are not shown as existing liens by the public records.

CONDITIONS AND STIPULATIONS

1. The term "mortgage," when used herein, shall include deed of trust, trust deed, or other security instrument.

2. If the proposed Insured has or acquires actual knowledge of any defect, lien, encumbrance, adverse claim or other matter affecting the estate or interest or mortgage thereon covered by this Commitment other than those shown in Schedule B hereof, and shall fail to disclose such knowledge to the Company in writing, the Company shall be relieved from liability for any loss or damage resulting from any act of reliance hereon to the extent the Company is prejudiced by failure to so disclose such knowledge. If the proposed Insured shall disclose such knowledge to the Company, or if the Company otherwise acquires actual knowledge of any such defect, lien, encumbrance, adverse claim or other matter, the Company at its option may amend Schedule B of this Commitment accordingly, but such amendment shall not relieve the Company from liability previously incurred pursuant to paragraph 3 of these Conditions and Stipulations.

3. Liability of the Company under this Commitment shall be only to the named proposed Insured and such parties included under the definition of Insured in the form of policy or policies committed for and only for actual loss incurred in reliance hereon in undertaking in good faith (a) to comply with the requirements hereof, or (b) to eliminate exceptions shown in Schedule B, or (c) to acquire or create the estate or interest or mortgage thereon covered by this Commitment. In no event shall such liability exceed the amount stated in Schedule A for the policy or policies committed for and such liability is subject to the insuring provisions, the Exclusions from Coverage and the Conditions and Stipulations of the form of policy or policies committed for in favor of the proposed Insured which are hereby incorporated by reference and are made a part of this Commitment except as expressly modified herein.

4. Any action or actions or rights of action that the proposed Insured may have or may bring against the Company arising out of the status of the title to the estate or interest or the status of the mortgage thereon covered by this Commitment must be based on and are subject to the provisions of this Commitment.

EXHIBIT 14-8
Title Opinion

TO: ___LAW FIRM_____   RE: ___TALL OAKS, INC._____
_____   ___825 Collins Hill Road____
_____   ___Gwinnett County, Maryland___
_____   _____
_____   _____

     A search of the record of title to the real estate described in Exhibit "A" as of an effective date of ___December 19, 1994___ reveals title to be vested in ___TALL OAKS, INC., a Maryland corporation_____

_____, subject to the exceptions and objections set out on page two herein.
     All questions with reference to the following are expressly excepted from this opinion:
     (a)   All matters of record subsequent to the date of this opinion;
     (b)   Matters affecting the title which are not of record, or which, if of record, are not indexed in a proper manner;
     (c)   Such state of facts as would be disclosed by a competent civil engineer's accurate survey of the property; (A timely survey is preferred so as to determine the existence of encroachments, overhangs, overlaps, that the improvements are within

EXHIBIT 14-8
Title Opinion
(continued)

the boundaries of subject property, and that the lines and corners of the property are clearly and properly marked.)

(d) Encroachments, except such as in this Attorney's opinion do not materially affect the value of the property;

(e) Title to that portion of the property within the bounds of any public road;

(f) Riparian rights of abutting owners on any stream running through property;

(g) Adverse claims of tenants in possession;

(h) All zoning laws, ordinances or regulations, municipal or county, and all Governmental regulations of the use and occupancy of the property described including the regulations or condemnation of the land or any building or structure thereon;

(i) Taxes due the appropriate County and city authority;

(j) Unrecorded claims of lien for labor or material furnished for the improvement of said property;

(k) Street improvement liens which have not been properly placed of record;

(l) Unpaid and/or past due water bills and sanitation assessments;

(m) Any fee or cost associated with water or sewer systems to the property.

(n) All matters prior to the date of the basis of this opinion.

The following indices were reviewed for a seven year period (ten years for Federal Tax Liens): General Execution Docket; Lis Pendens Docket; Suit Docket; Federal Tax Lien Docket; Uniform Commercial Code Docket; and OTHER: _____.

The Following names were run on the above-named indices:

 Tall Oaks, Inc., a Maryland corporation _____

_____

_____

This is a ____60____ year search.

EXHIBIT "A"

ALL THAT TRACT or parcel of land lying and being in Land Lot 11 of the 7th District of Gwinnett County, Maryland, containing 5.00 acres, same being more particularly described as follows:

BEGINNING at an iron pin found on the easterly Right-of-Way Line of Collins Road (Eighty (80') foot Right-of-Way), which iron pin found is located northwesterly a distance of 62.54 feet along said Right-of-Way Line from a Right-of-Way monument which marks the intersection of the easterly Right-of-Way Line of said Collins Road with the northerly Right-of-Way Line of Maryland Highway No. 316 (Three hundred forty (340') foot Right-of-Way); thence traveling along the easterly Right-of-Way Line of said Collins Road north 34 degrees 31 minutes 28 seconds west a distance of 709.55 feet to an iron pin found on said Right-of-Way Line; thence leaving said Right-of-Way Line and traveling north 55 degrees 40 minutes 26 seconds east a distance of 320.59 feet to an iron pin set; thence traveling south 30 degrees 00 minutes 08 seconds east a distance of 789.15 feet to an iron pin found; thence traveling south 72 degrees 19 minutes 34 seconds west a distance of 269.96 feet to an iron pin found on the easterly Right-of-Way Line of said Collins Road, which iron pin found is the TRUE POINT OF BEGINNING .

Note: RTV means Tall Oaks, Inc.

EXCEPTIONS and OBJECTIONS

1. Mortgage from Tall Oaks, Inc. to J. H. Patton, dated 12-16-90 recorded 12-16-90 at Deed Book 3985, page 22 in the orig. princ. amt. of $490,000.00.

2. Right of Way Easement-RTV to Jackson Electric Membership Corporation, dated 4-13-92, recorded 5-10-92 at Deed Book 4886, page 17.

EXHIBIT 14-8
Title Opinion
(continued)

3. Septic Sewer Easement-RTV to the Academy, Inc. dated 3-15-92, recorded 3-17-92 at Deed Book 4801, page 301.
4. Easement for Right of Way from J. H. Patton to Universal Power Company, dated 2-20-68, recorded 3-6-68 at Deed Book 291, page 591.
5. Right of Way Deed From J. H. Patton to Gwinnett County Dept. of Transportation, dated 5-2-78, recorded 5-5-78 at Deed Book 1465, page 220.

This the 27th day of December, 1994.

Sincerely,

TITLE EXAMINER

This is a search coming out of an Owners Policy of Title Insurance from _____ Title Insurance Company, Policy # _____, dated _____.

This is a limited search coming forward from the latest priority Purchase Money Security Deed, being at Deed Book _____, page _____.

Title Commitment Progress Form
Schedule A

Number 100   Effective Date
                               December 19, 1994

1. Policy or Policies to be issued:
    OWNER'S: $
    Proposed Insured:
LOAN: $250,000.00
Proposed Insured:
    Second Federal Savings and Loan Association
2. The estate or interest in the land described or referred to in this Commitment and covered herein is a fee simple, and title thereto is at the effective date hereof vested in:
    Tall Oaks, Inc.
3. The land referred to in the Commitment is described in Schedule C.

Schedule B—Section 1

The following are the requirements to be complied with:
1. Instrument(s) creating the estate or interest to be insured must be approved, executed and filed for record, to wit:
    (a) Corporate Resolution from Tall Oaks, Inc. authorizing the loan.
    (b) Mortgage from Tall Oaks, Inc. to Second Federal Savings and Loan Association.
2. Payment of the full consideration to, or for the account of, the grantors or mortgagors.
3. Payment of all taxes, charges, assessments, levied and assessed against subject premises, which are due and payable.
4. Satisfactory evidence should be had that improvements and/or repairs or alterations thereto are completed; that contractor, subcontractors, labor and materialmen are all paid.
5. Payment and satisfaction of record of mortgage from Tall Oaks, Inc. to J. H. Patton, dated 12-16-90 recorded at Deed Book 3985, page 22, Gwinnett County, Maryland Records.

Schedule B—Section 2

Schedule B of the policy or policies to be issued will contain exceptions to the following matters unless the same are disposed of to the satisfaction of the Company.
1. Defects, liens, encumbrances, adverse claims or other matters, if any, created, first appearing in the public records or attaching subsequent to the effective date hereof

but prior to the date the proposed Insured acquires for value of record the estate or interest or mortgage thereon covered by this Commitment.

2. Any owner's policy issued pursuant hereto will contain under Schedule B the standard exceptions set forth at the inside cover hereof. Any loan policy will contain under Schedule B standard Exceptions 1, 2 and 3 unless a satisfactory survey and inspection of the premises is made.

3. Right of Way Easement—Tall Oaks, Inc. to Jackson Electric Membership Corporation, dated 4-13-92, recorded 5-10-92 at Deed Book 4886, page 17.

4. Septic Sewer Easement—Tall Oaks, Inc., to Academy, Inc. dated 3-15-92, recorded 3-17-92 at Deed Book 4801, page 301.

5. Easement for Right of Way from J. H. Patton to Universal Power Company, dated 2-20-68, recorded 3-6-68 at Deed Book 291, page 591.

6. Right of Way Deed from J. H. Patton to Gwinnett County Dept. of Transportation, dated 5-2-78, recorded 5-5-78 at Deed Book 1465, page 220.

Schedule C

The land referred to in this Commitment is described as follows:

ALL THAT TRACT or parcel of land lying and being in Land Lot 11 of the 7th District of Gwinnett County, Maryland, containing 5.00 acres, same being more particularly described as follows:

BEGINNING at an iron pin found on the easterly Right-of-Way Line of Collins Road (Eighty (80') foot Right-of-Way), which iron pin found is located northwesterly a distance of 62.54 feet along said Right-of-Way Line from a Right-of-Way monument which marks the intersection of the easterly Right-of-Way Line of said Collins Road with the northerly Right-of-Way Line of Maryland Highway No. 316 (Three hundred forty (340') foot Right-of-Way); thence traveling along the easterly Right-of-Way Line of said Collins Road north 34 degrees 31 minutes 28 seconds west a distance of 709.55 feet to an iron pin found on said Right-of-Way Line; thence leaving said Right-of-Way Line and traveling north 55 degrees 40 minutes 26 seconds east a distance of 320.59 feet to an iron pin set; thence traveling south 30 degrees 00 minutes 08 seconds east a distance of 789.15 feet to an iron pin found; thence traveling south 72 degrees 19 minutes 34 seconds west a distance of 269.96 feet to an iron pin found on the easterly Right-of-Way Line of said Collins Road, which iron pin found is the TRUE POINT OF BEGINNING.

EXHIBIT 14–8
Title Opinion
(continued)

EXHIBIT 14–9
Title Examination Form for Practical Assignment

Certificate of Title

TO:

RE: Arnold Development Inc.
Gwinnett County
File No. 4094

Gentlemen:

This to certify that we have examined the record of title to the real estate described in Exhibit A attached to this Certificate and incorporated herein by this reference and made a part hereof, and we find the fee simple title to said

EXHIBIT 14-9
Title Examination Form for Practical Assignment   (continued)

property to be vested in   Arnold Development, Inc. by virtue of a Warranty Deed from Trust company Bank of Gwinnett County successor in title to Gwinnett Commercial Bank, dated March 23, 1989, filed March 28, 1989, 3:00 p.m., recorded in Deed Book 2749, page 313, Gwinnett County Records   subject to those objections and exceptions set out in Exhibit B attached to this Certificate and incorporated herein by this reference and made a part hereof.

All questions with reference to the following are expressly excepted from this Certificate, and this opinion is limited to the names of married women as they appear in the chain of title and as furnished to examining counsel:

(a)   All matters of record subsequent to the date of this Certificate.

(b)   Matters affecting the title which are not of record, or which, if they are of record, are not indexed in such a manner that a reasonably prudent search would have revealed them to the examiner.

(c)   Such state of facts as would be disclosed from a competent civil engineers accurate survey of said property. (It is always advisable that survey be made in order to determine if there are encroachments, over-hangs, over-laps, that the improvements are within the boundaries of caption, and the lines and corners of caption are clearly marked.)

(d)   Encroachments, except such as in our opinion do not materially affect the value of the property.

(e)   Title to that portion of the premises with in the bounds of any public road.

(f)   The riparian rights of abutting owners on any stream running through the premises.

(g)   Adverse claims of tenants in possession.

(h)   All zoning laws, ordinances or regulations, municipal or county, and all Governmental regulations of the use and occupancy of premises described, including the regulations or condemnation of the land or any building or structure thereon.

(i)   Taxes not due and payable at the date of this Certificate, and taxes coming due and payable for all future times.

(j)   Unrecorded claims of liens for labor or material furnished for the improvements of said property.

(k)   Street improvement liens which have not been properly placed of record.

(l)   Past due water bills, which, while not technically liens, will deter the municipal authority form transferring water meters until the bills have been paid.

(m)   Pay-as-you-enter water or sewer lines, which, while not technically liens, will be payable upon connection with such lines.

The effective date of this Certificate of Title is October 12, 1994, at 5:00 o'clock p.m.

EXHIBIT "A"

All that tract or parcel of land lying and being in Land Lot 81 of the 5th District of Gwinnett County, Michigan being Lot 45, Block B, Summerville Subdivision, Unit IV, according to a plat of survey recorded at Plat Book 25, page 11, Gwinnett County Records, which plat is incorporated herein by reference thereto.

EXHIBIT "B"

1.   1994 State and County taxes are paid in the amount of $1046.50 on 65.78 acres.

2.   Recorded plat at Plat Book 25, page 11, reveals the following:

a)   35 foot building setback line;

b)   Protective covenants;

c)   5 foot drainage easement;

d)   20 foot drainage easement along rear property line;

e)   Fence along rear property line;

f)   10 foot side line.

3.   Mortgage from Arnold Development, Inc. to Trust Company Bank of Gwinnett County, dated March 23, 1989, filed March 28, 1989, 3:00 p.m., recorded in Deed Book 2749, page 338, Gwinnett County Records, in the amount of $52,000.00 being due March 23, 1989.

EXHIBIT 14-10
Title Commitment Forms for Practical Assignment

COMMITMENT

SCHEDULE A

1 OFFICE FILE NUMBER		
2 COMMITMENT NUMBER	3 EFFECTIVE DATE	4 LOAN AMOUNT
		OWNERS AMOUNT

1. Policy or Policies to be issued:
   ALTA LOAN POLICY.
   Proposed Insured:

   ALTA OWNER'S POLICY, Form
   Proposed Insured:

2. The estate or interest in the land described or referred to in this Commitment and covered herein is a fee simple, and title thereto is at the effective date hereof vested in:

3. The Land is described as follows:

Note: This Commitment consists of insert pages labeled in Schedule A, Schedule B-Section 1, and Schedule B-Section 2. This Commitment is of no force and effect unless all schedules are included, along with any Rider pages incorporated by reference in the insert pages.

EXHIBIT 14-10
Title Commitment Forms for Practical Assignment　(continued)

COMMITMENT

SCHEDULE B — Section 1

Commitment Number

Requirements

The following are the requirements to be complied with:

1. Instrument(s) creating the estate or interest to be insured must be approved, executed and filed for record, to wit:

2. Payment of the full consideration to, or for the account of, the grantors or mortgagors.

3. Payment of all taxes, charges, assessments, levied and assessed against subject premises, which are due and payable.

4. Satisfactory evidence should be had that improvements and/or repairs or alterations thereto are completed; that contractor, subcontractors, labor and materialmen are all paid.

EXHIBIT 14-10
Title Commitment Forms for Practical Assignment   (continued)

COMMITMENT

SCHEDULE B—Section 2

Commitment Number

Exceptions

Schedule B of the policy or policies to be issued will contain exceptions to the following matters unless the same are disposed of to the satisfaction of the Company.

1. Defects, liens, encumbrances, adverse claims or other matters, if any, created, first appearing in the public records or attaching subsequent to the effective date hereof but prior to the date the proposed Insured acquires for value of record the estate or interest or mortgage thereon covered by this Commitment.

2. Any owner's policy issued pursuant hereto will contain under Schedule B the standard exceptions set forth on the inside cover. Any loan policy will also contain under Schedule B thereof, the standard exceptions set forth on the inside cover of this commitment relating to the owner's policy.

3. Standard Exceptions 2 and 3 may be removed from the policy when a satisfactory survey and inspection of the premises is made.

4. Taxes and assessments for the year   and subsequent years.

Note: On loan policies, junior and subordinate matters, if any, will not be reflected in Schedule B.

Real Estate Closings

Just know your lines and don't bump into the furniture.

—Spencer Tracy

OBJECTIVES

After reading this chapter you will be able to:

- Review a real estate contract and prepare a closing checklist for both the purchaser and the seller
- Review a mortgage loan commitment and prepare a closing checklist for the borrower
- Understand the legal procedures required for the closing of a sale of real property
- Understand the legal procedures required for the closing of a mortgage loan

GLOSSARY

Closing   Consummation of a real estate purchase and sale transaction

Escrow   Agreement that requires the deposit of a document or money into the possession of a third party to be held by that party until certain conditions are fulfilled

Loan closing   Consummation of a loan secured by real property

Loan commitment   Contract between a borrower and a lender to make and accept a mortgage loan secured by real property. The loan commitment sets forth the terms, requirements, and conditions for the mortgage loan

Mortgagee loss payable clause   Endorsement to a policy of fire and hazard insurance whereby the owner of the insured property and the insurance company agree that any and all proceeds payable under the policy are to be paid directly to the lender who has a mortgage on the insured property

Y ou enter a large room. Windows dominate one side of the room, offering the occupants a beautiful view of a downtown skyline. Framed English hunting prints adorn the other three walls. The focal point of the room is a large Queen Anne conference table ringed with a dozen chairs. Two couples are seated across from each other at one end of the table. One couple appears nervous. They look at each other and smile. Although the other couple appears sophisticated and blasé to the events that are taking place, they, too, look uneasy. A middle-aged well-dressed person seated in the corner of the conference room is talking on the telephone. The telephone caller has an appointment book and appears to be transacting business, oblivious to the other occupants of the room. At the other end of the conference table there is a large stack of manila folders and papers, a yellow legal pad, and some kind of metal seal or stamp.

As you enter the room, everyone except the telephone caller in the corner, who is still in phone oblivion, immediately looks in your direction. You have just entered that phenomenon known as the Real Estate Closing Zone.

The consummation of a real estate transaction is called a **closing**. Closings may be simple, as in the purchase and sale of a home, or complicated, as in the closing of a purchase and sale of a major resort hotel. The consummation of a loan secured by a mortgage is also called a closing, or **loan closing**. Many transactions involve a simultaneous sale and loan closing.

The real estate legal assistant is actively involved in helping the attorney in a real estate closing. Although ethical considerations in many states prohibit a legal assistant from actually conducting the closing, all states permit the legal assistant to assist the attorney in all phases and aspects of the closing.

New York:
Closing, settlement, transfer of title—all these refer to the day the buyer pays the entire purchase price and gets a deed. All the promises made in the contract must be completed. The deed is exchanged for money. Usually the mortgage loan closes at the same time as the transfer of title.

THE ENVIRONMENT

Residential real estate transactions do not close in a perfect, stress-free environment. Months have passed since the contract has been signed; frustrations and delays have been encountered at every turn. Credit reports have been lost; appraisals have been difficult to schedule or have turned out to be insufficient and have had to be rescheduled. The sellers desperately need the proceeds check because they have purchased another home and cannot afford two mortgage payments. The purchasers' dream house that looked so pretty two months ago has been slightly tarnished over the passage of time. The rooms appear smaller. There are cracks in the plaster. Everyone is concerned about the rubber raft tied to the third step of the basement. The real estate brokers have spent their commission and desperately need the check to pay creditors. The loan officer is being paid a base salary plus a percentage of all loans closed and is behind on her quota. Residential loan closings are not a high-fee item for law firms and can only be profitable from a high volume. The real estate attorney often juggles more loan closings than the Karuchi Brothers juggle knives. Everything is done at hyper speed. It is not unusual for people to arrive in the reception area before the loan package arrives from the lender. The U.S. Postal Service is passed over for more efficient means of delivery, such as courier and telephone facsimile. Everything resembles the trading floor of a commodities exchange. In this environment, the professional real estate legal assistant must maintain order and composure and produce a quality, error-free package. This requires training, discipline, organization, and a good sense of humor.

Closing a commercial transaction is similar to and yet very different from closing a residential transaction. Commercial transactions are easier because the people involved are not strangers to the transaction. They know what they want and what to expect, and they are not under the pressures of having a moving van full of household belongings circle the block waiting for the closing to be completed.

Although commercial closings involve more sophisticated parties, they also involve larger sums of money and larger risks. The legal techniques used for commercial closings are more sophisticated, and translating these techniques into documents that properly set forth in plain, concise language what everyone has agreed to and understands can be difficult. Until you have it right, patient communication is necessary.

Unlike residential transactions, in which most of the documentations are preprinted forms, commercial loan transactions use more negotiated and tailored documentation. Lenders usually start with the basic form, but the form will be negotiated over the course of the loan closing transaction or will be tailored to each particular transaction. Unlike most residential closings, in which purchaser and seller are not represented by counsel and do no more than quickly review the documentation, all parties to commercial transactions usually are represented by competent counsel and the documents are reviewed many times, negotiated, debated, and changed before or at closing.

Commercial closings offer the luxury of higher fees for a law firm, and therefore, more time can be spent on a single file. This does not mean that commercial loan closings are easier than residential, but it does mean that the legal assistant's attention does not have to be divided among ten or fifteen files at the same time but can concentrate on perhaps two or three.

One of the advantages in closing commercial loans is the opportunity to work with skilled counsel and other skilled legal assistants. It is easier to close a transaction if all the participants have a high level of knowledge with regard to real estate law.

Both residential and commercial closings have advantages and disadvantages, and most legal assistants specialize in one or the other.

In some states, residential and even commercial closings may be handled by title insurance companies. Unless a legal assistant is employed by the title insurance company, he or she may not be directly involved in the closing but only involved in the review of closing documents on behalf of a client. This chapter is based on the assumption that the legal assistant is employed by a law firm, corporate legal department, or title insurance company and is directly involved in the preparation for and closing of a real estate transaction.

ANATOMY OF A REAL ESTATE CLOSING

The difference between success and failure in a real estate closing is determined by the amount of preparation that was done before the closing. A real estate closing can be broken down into six areas: (1) file creation; (2) information gathering; (3) document preparation; (4) the closing; (5) disbursement, recording, and transmittal of the closing package; and (6) final close out.

File Creation

The first step in a real estate closing is the organization of the file. Most law firms that specialize in real estate have as clients lending institutions, such as savings and loan associations, banks, and life insurance companies, that make loans secured by residential and commercial properties. The case is referred to the firm for closing by

New York:
Customarily, closings take place at the lending institution or the sellers' attorney, but it can be anywhere the parties agree.
Attendees include the bank representative, a representative from the sellers' bank, broker(s), title company agent, buyer, and seller (in New York, the buyer and seller are each usually represented by an attorney).

The buyer should check the premises prior to closing, for a thorough "walkthrough."

way of a transmittal package from one of the loan officers at the lending institution or, if there is a rush to close, by telephone call. An initial closing package typically includes a copy of the sales contract and a copy of the lender's loan commitment. It is common practice in some areas of the country for the lender to send an entire package of loan documents to the law firm.

Once the case is referred and the package is received, the law firm opens a file for purposes of billing in the name of the client and cross references the other parties involved, such as the seller, purchaser, and any brokers. The firm monitors and reviews all the names involved in the closing to check for conflicts of interest. If a firm already has as a client one of the other parties, the potential exists for ethical problems or conflicts of interest. If a conflict of interest exists, the firm either declines representation of all parties in connection with the closing or obtains written consent from all parties after full disclosure of the conflict.

Assuming that no conflicts of interest exist, the file is logged onto the firm's computer system for billing and a file is opened. The file may consist of nothing more than a manila folder with a label indicating the names of the parties and a file number for purposes of billing and reference.

It is advisable for a legal assistant to maintain his or her own filing system separate and apart from the firm's own internal file keeping. The separate file provides a convenient source of information to verify what the legal assistant has done in respect to a particular transaction.

Information Gathering

Most law firms use legal assistants to gather information required to prepare the sale and loan documents and to close the transaction.

A starting point for gathering information is the closing package received by the firm, which usually contains a real estate sales contract and a lender's commitment letter. These two basic documents provide most of the clues for the type of information needed to close the transaction. It is advisable to review the contract and loan commitment promptly on receipt of the file and to prepare a checklist of the items required for the sale and the loan closing. File folders should be prepared for each item shown on the checklist. As the items are received or prepared, they can be placed in their own folders and easily reviewed or recalled when needed.

Reviewing the Real Estate Contract

The real estate contract sets forth the obligations of the purchaser and seller in regard to the sale transaction. It is the main document to review to prepare a sale closing checklist. The contract sets forth the names of the parties (seller, purchaser, broker), the legal description of the property, the purchase price of the property, the amount of the earnest money, the date for closing, and what documents the respective seller and purchaser must furnish to each other at the closing.

The names of the seller, purchaser, and broker should be contained in the real estate contract, along with their addresses and telephone numbers. If telephone numbers are not included in the contract, they should be obtained because there will be numerous contacts with each party before closing. It is necessary to verify the correct spelling of each of the names because the seller's and purchaser's names will appear in most of the closing documents.

It is important when reviewing a real estate contract to determine the anticipated date of closing. Most contracts provide a closing date; however, the parties may

New York:
The legal assistant must juggle all the parties and arrange for the bank attorney, the parties and their attorneys and title company all to be present at the same time for the closing.

want to close earlier or the closing date may have been extended by an amendment. Early verification of the closing date is essential to prioritize activity. For example, if the closing is two weeks away, then the closing does not become a high-priority item, and the information can be gathered in a regular, orderly manner. Title examination orders, survey orders, payoff letters, and other routine correspondence can be handled by mail, thereby obviating the need for courier or facsimile transmittals. On the other hand, if the closing is scheduled for the day after tomorrow, then the gathering of the information becomes a high-priority item and must be done in the quickest manner available. The closing date also needs to be verified with the lender's expiration date on its loan commitment. Because of the fluctuation of interest rates, loan commitments have short durations. Although the closing on the contract may not be for a couple of weeks, the loan commitment may be effective only for a week. Therefore, to close under the current terms of the loan, the sale needs to close early. Another problem encountered in residential and commercial transactions is the availability and convenience of the parties. The parties often have a conflict with the date of closing set forth in the contract, and therefore a different closing date must be scheduled. Although it is not rational, parties to a real estate contract may place other, personal events ahead of the closing. It is not unusual for real estate closings to be scheduled around vacation plans or work schedules. It is recommended that legal assistants obtain large calendars or appointment books to schedule all the closing activities for a given month.

The contract should contain a legal description of the property. The legal description is important, as it will be used on all the sale and loan closing documents as well as to order title examinations and surveys.

The real estate contract will probably describe in some detail the documents required by the seller and purchaser at the time of closing. These requirements need to be carefully reviewed, understood, and added to any checklist being prepared. It is not unusual for preprinted broker's contracts, often used on residential transactions, to be sketchy in regard to the documents required at closing. These contracts may refer only to the deed of the seller to the purchaser. On any real estate sale transaction, the seller is required to furnish, at minimum, the following documentation: (a) owner's or title affidavit; (b) corporate resolution, if the seller is a corporation; (c) warranty deed; (d) bill of sale for any personal property included in the transaction; (e) an assignment of all appliance or other manufacturer's warranties in connection with the property, such as roof warranty and furnace warranty; (f) foreign person affidavit; and (g) Form 1099–B. The Internal Revenue Service requires that on all real estate transactions that involve a foreign person, a percentage of the sales proceeds be withheld from the closing and remitted to the Internal Revenue Service. It is the purchaser's responsibility to withhold the funds and to remit them to the government. The purchaser can be relieved of this responsibility by obtaining an affidavit from the seller that the seller is not a foreign person. The purchaser is entitled to rely on the sworn affidavit. A copy of the foreign person affidavit is included in Chapter 16.

New York:
The person "responsible for the closing" must prepare the 1099B and file it. The Tax Reform Act of 1986 requires every real estate sale to be reported to the Internal Revenue Service by the person "responsible for the closing." The report is made on the IRS Form 1099–S and must be filed before February of the following year.

The Internal Revenue Service also requires that the closing agent, usually the law firm, report all sales of one- to four-family residences to the Internal Revenue Service. This report usually is done by preparing Form 1099–B with all the necessary sale information and having it signed by the seller. A copy of Form 1099–B is included in Chapter 16.

In addition to the above minimum requirements, a seller also may be required to provide such things as (a) termite clearance letters, (b) keys, (c) warranties, (d) assignment of leases and security deposits, (e) assignments of service contracts, and (f) estoppel letters from prior lenders and tenants.

A purchaser under a contract is required to provide money and proof of insurance at closing. The purchaser's checklist may be extended if the contract provides for seller financing, as the purchaser will provide a note and mortgage to the seller at the time of closing.

The following is a closing checklist prepared from the sample contract that follows the checklist (Form 14–1).

IIII▶ C H E C K L I S T

Closing

1. Title examination
2. Title commitment/policy
3. Survey
4. Hazard insurance
5. Foreign person affidavit
6. Form 1099–B
7. Title affidavit
8. Hazardous waste affidavit
9. Warranty deed
10. Bill of sale
11. Assignment of warranties
12. Broker indemnity
13. Settlement statement

**EXHIBIT 15–1
Real Estate Sales
Contract**

This Contract is entered into this _____ day of January, 19_____ by and between ACME, INC., as ("Purchaser"), I.M. SELLER ("Seller") and BROKER & ASSOCIATES, as ("Broker").

FOR VALUABLE CONSIDERATION RECEIVED, the receipt and sufficiency of which are hereby acknowledged, the parties hereby agree as follows:

1. Purchaser agrees to buy and Seller agrees to sell subject to the terms and conditions of this Contract as set forth herein ALL THAT TRACT OF PARCEL OF LAND with such improvements as are located thereon lying and being in Land Lot 1135, 2nd District, 2nd Section of _____ County, _____ and being more particularly described on Exhibit "A" attached hereto and made a part hereof (hereinafter referred to as the "Property").

2. **Purchase Price.** The purchase price for the Property shall be SIX HUNDRED FIFTY THOUSAND AND NO/100 DOLLARS ($650,000.00) which shall be paid as follows: Purchaser shall pay to the Seller the sum of $650,000.00 in cash at closing.

3. **Earnest Money.** Purchaser has paid to Broker & Associates, a licensed broker acting on behalf of the Seller, FIVE THOUSAND AND NO/100 DOLLARS ($5,000.00) in the form of a check, the receipt whereof is hereby acknowledged by Broker & Associates as earnest money ("Earnest Money"), which Earnest Money shall be applied as part payment of the purchase price of said Property at the time the sale is consummated or paid to Seller or returned to Purchaser as otherwise provided herein.

4. **Warranties of Title.** Seller warrants that Seller presently has title to said Property and at the time the sale is consummated, agrees to convey good and marketable title to said Property to Purchaser by a general warranty deed subject only to such title exceptions as Purchaser shall agree to.

5. **Title.** Purchaser shall move promptly and in good faith after acceptance of this Contract by Seller to examine the title to said Property and to furnish Seller with a written statement of objections affecting the marketability of said title.

EXHIBIT 15-1
Real Estate Sales
Contract
(continued)

Seller shall have a reasonable time after receipt of said such objections to satisfy all valid objections specified by Purchaser and if Seller fails to satisfy such valid objections within a reasonable time, then Purchaser at Purchaser's option may cancel this Contract by giving Seller written notice of such cancellation and this Contract shall become null and void and Purchaser shall be entitled to a return of the Earnest Money. Marketability of title as used herein shall mean the quality of title which a title insurance Company licensed to do business in the State of _____ and a member of the American Land Title Association would insure at its regular rate without exception.

6. **Hazardous Waste Indemnity.** Purchaser's obligation to purchase the Property pursuant to this Contract is contingent upon there being no petroleum hydro carbons or contaminants contained in the soil, surface or subterranean water which are in violation of local, state, or federal statutes and regulations and that there be no other existence of any hazardous substances or waste located upon the Property. For purposes of this Agreement, the term "hazardous substances or wastes" shall mean petroleum, including crude oil or any fraction thereof, flammable explosives, radioactive materials, asbestos, any material containing polychlorinated biphenyls, and any of the substances defined as "hazardous substances" or "toxic substances" in the Comprehensive Environmental Response, Compensation and Liability Act of 1980, as amended, 42 U.S.C. Section 9601 *et seq.*, Hazardous Materials Transportation Act, 49 U.S.C. Section 1802 *et seq.*, the Resource Conservation and Recovery Act, 42 U.S.C. Section 6901 *et seq.*, and in the Toxic Substance Control Act of 1976, as amended, 15 U.S.C. Section 2601 *et seq.*, or any other federal, state, local or other governmental legislation, statute, law, code, rule, regulation or ordinance identified by its terms as pertaining to the disposal, storage, generation or presence of hazardous substances or waste (the "Environmental Laws"). Purchaser shall at Seller's expense have the Property inspected for purposes of discovering if hazardous substances or wastes exist. If upon inspection, hazardous wastes or substances do exist, Purchaser shall have the option of terminating his contract and receiving a refund of his $5,000.00 earnest money down payment. In the alternative, Seller shall have the right at its own expense to remove all hazardous substance or waste from the Property and to conclude the sale with Purchaser.

Seller warrants, represents and agrees that (a) neither Seller nor any person has violated any of the applicable Environmental Laws as defined in the paragraph above relating to or affecting the Property; (b) the Property is presently in compliance with all Environmental Laws, and there are no facts or circumstances presently existing upon or under the Property or relating to the representations and warranties, which violate any of the applicable Environmental Laws, and there is not now pending nor threatened any action, suit, investigation or proceeding against Seller or the Property (or against any other party related to the Property); (c) Seller has obtained all licenses, permits or other governmental regulatory approvals necessary to comply with Environmental Laws and Seller is in full compliance with the terms and provisions of all such licenses, permits or other governmental regulatory approvals; and (d) Seller has received no notice that any municipality or any governmental or quasi-governmental authorities are investigating or has determined that there are any violations of zoning, health, building, fire, pollution, environmental, or other statutes, ordinances, regulations affecting the Property.

7. **Inspection.** Purchaser, its agents and representatives, at Purchaser's expense and at reasonable times during normal business hours, shall have the right to enter upon the Property for purpose of inspection, examining, testing, surveying the Property. Purchaser assumes all responsibility for acts of itself, its agents, representatives, in exercising its rights under this paragraph and agrees to hold Seller harmless for any damages resulting therefrom.

8. **Condition of Improvements.** Seller warrants until the sale is consummated, that the Improvements located on the Property will be in the same condition as they are on the date this Contract is signed by the Seller, natural wear and tear excepted. Should the Improvements located on the Property be destroyed or substantially damaged before the Contract is consummated, then at the election of the Purchaser, (a) the Contract may be cancelled and Earnest Money refunded to Purchaser or (b) Purchaser may consummate the Contract and receive all insurance proceeds paid or due on the claim of loss.

This election is to be exercised within ten (10) days after the Purchaser has been notified in writing by Seller of the amount of the insurance proceeds, if any, Seller shall receive on the claim of loss; if Purchaser has not been notified within forty-five (45) days, subsequent to the occurrence of such damage or destruction, Purchaser may at its option cancel this Contract and receive a refund of its Earnest Money.

9. **Possession.** Seller shall deliver title and possession of the Property to Purchaser at closing free and clear of the claims of any and all tenants and all leases existing on the Property shall be cancelled and terminated by Seller at Seller's expense prior to closing.

10. **Closing.** Closing shall be held at the offices of attorney of Purchaser, _____, 1400 Peachtree Place Tower, 999 Peachtree Street, N.E., _____, _____, or at such location as is agreeable to Purchaser and Seller, on a day selected by Purchaser not later than Sixty (60) days from the date Seller can deliver title and possession of the Property free and clear of any and all leases or other rights of tenants in regard to the Property and a date not later than _____, 19____. Purchaser shall give Seller notice of the closing date at least five days prior thereto; provided, if Purchaser gives Seller no such notice of the closing date, then the closing date shall be _____, 19_____.

11. **Execution of Documents.** Seller shall execute and deliver to Purchaser a general warranty deed in recordable form conveying the Property to Purchaser as provided herein and shall execute and deliver to Purchaser all necessary affidavits in order for Purchaser to obtain a title insurance policy without exception and an affidavit indicating Seller's non-foreign status within the meaning of Section 1445(f)(3) of the Internal Revenue Code of 1986 and any and all other documents which may be required by Purchaser to carry out the terms of this Contract.

12. **Closing Costs.** In connection with the closing, Seller shall pay the real estate Transfer Tax and all costs for the satisfaction, cure and removal of all title exceptions undertaken by the Seller as herein required. All other closing costs incurred by Purchaser in connection with the sale shall be paid by Purchaser. Each party shall pay its own attorney's fees.

13. **Prorations.** At the closing all ad valorem property taxes, water and sewer charges and assessments of any kind on the Property for the year of the closing shall be prorated between Purchaser and Seller as of 12:01 a.m. on the closing date. Such proration shall be based upon the latest ad valorem property tax, water, sewer charge and assessment bills available. If, upon receipt of the actual ad valorem property tax, water, sewer and assessment bills for the Property, such proration is incorrect, then either Purchaser or Seller shall be entitled, upon demand, to receive such amounts from the other as may be necessary to correct such malapportionment. This obligation to correct such malapportionment shall survive the closing and not be merged into any documents delivered pursuant to the closing.

14. **Brokerage Commissions.** Upon consummation of the closing of the sale contemplated herein, a sales commission shall be paid by the Seller to Broker & Associates, Inc., Broker, which commission has been negotiated between Broker and Seller. Purchaser shall

EXHIBIT 15–1
Real Estate Sales
Contract
(continued)

have no obligation whatsoever to Broker & Associates, Inc. for any real estate commission. Seller further agrees to indemnify and hold harmless the Purchaser from and by any and all claims or demands with respect to any brokerage fees or agent's commissions or other compensation asserted against any person, firm, or corporation in connection with this Contract or sale or the transactions contemplated hereby arising from actions or alleged commitments of the Seller. This provision shall survive closing and the conveyance of the Property by Seller to Purchaser.

15. **Purchaser Default.** In the event the transaction contemplated hereby is not closed because of Purchaser's default, the Earnest Money shall be paid to Seller as full liquidated damages for such failure to close, the parties acknowledging the difficulty of ascertaining Seller's damages in such circumstances, whereupon neither party hereto shall have any further rights, claims, or liabilities under this Agreement except for the provisions which were made to survive the termination or cancellation of this Agreement. Said liquidated damages shall be Seller's sole and exclusive remedy and Seller shall expressly not have the right to seek specific performance or other damages.

16. **Sellers Default.** If Seller shall be unable to deliver title in accordance with this Agreement, Seller's liability shall be limited to the return of the Earnest Money paid hereunder. In the event Seller fails to perform other covenants of this Agreement or if Seller otherwise defaults hereunder, the Purchaser shall have the right to, in addition to all rights and remedies herein provided, to pursue any right or remedy it may have against Seller at law or in equity for such breach and/or default, including without limitation, the right of specific performance of all provisions of this Agreement. Purchaser's monetary damages in the event of such breach and/or default shall be limited to $25,000.00. The parties hereby acknowledge the difficulty of ascertaining Purchaser's monetary damages in such event.

17. **Assignability.** Purchaser shall have the right to assign this Agreement to any corporation or partnership of which Purchaser is a shareholder or partner without notice to and without consent of Seller, and the transaction contemplated by this Agreement shall be consummated in the name of such assignee. Purchaser shall not have the right to assign the Contract to any other party except as mentioned above without the prior written consent of Seller.

18. **Notification.** Any notice or demand under which the terms of this Agreement or under any statute must or may be given or made by the parties hereto shall be made in writing and shall be deemed to have been delivered when hand delivered; as of the date sent by an overnight courier; or as of the date of postmark affixed by the U.S. Postal Service, by mail of same by certified mail, return receipt requested, addressed to the respective parties at the following addresses:

TO PURCHASER:

TO SELLER:

TO BROKER:

19. **Time is of the Essence.** Time is of the essence of this Agreement and of each of its provisions.

This instrument shall be regarded as an offer by the Purchaser or Seller who shall first sign this Contract to the other party and is open for acceptance by the other party until _____ : _____ __.m. on the _____ day of _____, 19_____.

The above proposition is hereby accepted this _____ day of _____, 19____.

```
        IN WITNESS WHEREOF, the undersigned parties hereinto set their hand and seal to
    this Contract.
                                        PURCHASER:
                                        _____ (SEAL)

                                        SELLER:
                                        _____ (SEAL)

                                        _____ (SEAL)

                                        BROKER
                                        By: _____
```

EXHIBIT 15–1
**Real Estate Sales
Contract
(continued)**

CONTACT WITH SELLER, PURCHASER, AND BROKER ____

One of the first things the legal assistant needs to do is verify the correctness of the names that appear in the contract. The seller should be requested to provide any title information or surveys that the seller may have regarding the real property. If the seller is a corporation, copies of the articles of incorporation, bylaws, and a certificate of good standing with the secretary of state's office should be requested. A corporation should provide a corporate resolution with the names and titles of the people who will be signing on behalf of the corporation. The corporate seller should bring the corporate seal to closing. All the items above are required to ensure that the corporation has the authority to sell the real property.

If the seller is a partnership, a request should be made for copies of the partnership agreement and the names of all the partners who intend to be present at the closing to sign the closing documents. In the situation of a partnership, all partners must sign the documents unless the partnership agreement authorizes an individual partner or group of partners to sign. If less than all the partners intend to sign the closing documents, a partnership resolution should be obtained from all the partners giving their consent and authorizing the signature partners to consummate and close the transaction.

The seller should be questioned about loan numbers of any outstanding loans on the subject property. These computer loan numbers are necessary to obtain payoff information. Also discuss with the seller the approximate date of closing and any special instructions you might need to know in regard to the closing.

The purchaser should be contacted to verify the names that are to appear on the warranty deed and the name of their insurance agent and to inquire about any special instructions. The purchaser should receive an explanation of the steps in a closing and assurance that closing money figures will be available at least on the day before the closing to give the purchaser adequate time to obtain the necessary funds.

After the purchaser and seller are contacted, the real estate agents should be contacted to notify them of the approximate date of closing and to verify the amount of the real estate commissions due the agents.

Ordering the Title Examination

It is unusual for a closing legal assistant to examine the title to the property. Most title examinations are prepared by other members of the firm or by specialized firms that

New York:
In New York, once the parties know the deal is firm, i.e. the mortgage commitment has been obtained, the purchasers' attorney orders the title search. At the date of closing, the title company does a "continuation search" to make sure nothing new has appeared on the title search.

have a retainer relationship with the closing law firm. Title examinations may be handled by title insurance companies in some states. A title examination should be ordered quickly even though the closing may be several weeks away. The earlier the examination is received, the more time there will be to correct defects that may be revealed by the examination. The title examiner needs, at a minimum, the following information to conduct the examination: (a) the name of the current owner, which usually is the seller under the sale contract; (b) the legal description of the real property; and (c) any title information or surveys available.

The title examiner should be informed of the name of the title company issuing the title insurance so that the title examiner's certification can be prepared and sent to the title company. The title examiner should be instructed to make copies of all exceptions to title. These copies should be provided to both the legal assistant and the title insurance company. The title examiner should establish a firm date for completion of the examination. This date should be recorded on a calendar or appointment book. It is a good idea to call the title examiner the day before the scheduled date of completion. This telephone call should be made not for the purpose of trying to obtain the title examination a day early but to confirm that the title examination will be available on the date scheduled for completion. The title examiner's response to this preemptive telephone call may be that the title examination has already been completed and can be picked up on the day of the call, which means that the examination is delivered one day early. Or the preemptive telephone call may remind the title examiner of the date set for completion and will act as a further reminder to provide the title examination on time.

Ideally, a title examination order is given in writing by using a title examination form. A copy of such form is shown in Exhibit 15–2. Because of the fast-track nature of most residential closings, title examinations typically are ordered by telephone. Even if a telephone request is made, it is a good idea to complete the written title examination form before making the call. This requires collecting the necessary information for the title examination and increases the efficiency of the telephone call. Ordering a title examination without completing the form could result in the examiner's receiving incomplete information. This will cause the title examination to be incomplete or necessitate a second call to the examiner.

**EXHIBIT 15–2
Title Examination
Form**

Abstract Order

Our File Number: _____ Date Ordered: _____ Need By: _____
Ordered by: _____ Date of Closing: _____
Present Owner/Seller: _____
Name of Purchaser: _____
RE Broker: _____
Brief Legal: _____
_____
Street Address: _____
Length of Search: _____

MISCELLANEOUS INFORMATION KNOWN:
Plat Information: _____
Back Title Policy: ( ) Yes ( ) No   Back Title Notes: ( ) Yes ( ) No

With Who: _____   _____

_____   _____

_____   _____

PLEASE PROVIDE US WITH ANY BANKRUPTCY INFORMATION: ( ) yes   ( ) no
Other Information:

_____

_____

_____

_____

_____

_____

_____

_____

_____

In addition, please provide the following:
( )   Copies of applicable Restrictive Covenants of record
( )   Copies of applicable easements of record
( )   Copies of any liens, executions, judgments, etc. of record
( )   City, State and County Millage Rates (latest figures available)
( )   _____
( )   _____
( )   _____

EXHIBIT 15–2
Title Examination
Form
(continued)

Ordering the Survey

Most law firms have a relationship with a surveying and engineering firm that can prepare surveys to satisfy title insurance company and lender client requirements. The names and telephone numbers of these surveyors will be provided to the legal assistant. Most surveys are ordered by telephone, and a surveyor will need, at minimum, the following information: (a) legal description of the property to be surveyed, (b) information regarding previous surveys, (c) the correct names of the purchasers as they appear on the survey, (d) the correct name of the lending institution as it appears on the survey, and (e) special lender requirements for a survey.

The surveyor will prepare an as-built survey locating the improvements and all easements, setback lines, and so on on the survey. The surveyor will indicate if the property is located in a flood hazard zone. In some states, the surveyor may prepare a title insurance company inspection report form. If so, the surveyor will need to know which title insurance company is issuing the insurance so that the company's form can be used. At least six prints of the survey should be received, and the surveyor should be reminded to enclose a bill with the survey so that it can be paid at closing.

A firm date for the completion of the survey should be obtained from the surveyor. If possible, a survey should be received at least five business days before closing. The date for completion should be recorded on a calendar or appointment book and a preemptive call made the day before the due date.

New York:
Surveyor must know the name of title company, so that they can be named as insured. If there already is a survey on the property, the purchaser may be satisfied with an updated survey.

Ordering Hazard and Fire Insurance

Insurance against fire and other casualties is a requirement on all real estate closings that involve improved property. Often the insurance will be obtained by the purchaser or by one of the real estate agents in connection with the sale. An insurance company must receive the following information: (a) the name of the purchaser; (b) the correct address of the property; (c) the amount of the loan because most lenders require that, at minimum, the insurance be for the amount of the loan; and (d) the name and address of the lender because the lender will appear as a mortgagee on the insurance policy. This **mortgagee endorsement** contains both the name of the mortgagee and its address. If flood insurance is necessary, the agent should be given the finished flood elevation, which can be obtained from the surveyor. The insurance company should be given a date for delivery of the insurance.

Most lenders require the insurance premium to be paid one year in advance from date of closing and the proof of such payment to be provided at closing. The insurance agent will provide a paid receipt for the insurance.

Most residential lenders require that the original policy be available at the time of closing. On commercial transactions, commercial insurance policies are more difficult to obtain, and many lenders are willing to close on a binder or certificate of insurance. The policy will be provided after closing.

In the event the purchaser or real estate agent undertakes the task of obtaining the fire and casualty insurance, it is a good idea to receive from them the name of the agent and to verify with the agent all the necessary information that must appear in the policy. This direct communication with the insurance agent often reduces the number of mistakes in the final policy. Although most mistakes, such as misspelled names and incorrect property addresses, are not serious and usually will not hold up a closing, they do require corrective work after the closing.

Obtaining the Termite Clearance Letter or Bond

In many areas of the United States, termites present special problems for real estate closings. It is not unusual in residential and even in commercial transactions that a termite clearance letter be required within the terms of the contract. These clearance letters or bonds are prepared by licensed pest control companies. The certificate reports that the pest control company has inspected the property in question and has either found no termites, powder-post beetles, or other wood-boring insects or found such insects and treated the property. In addition, termite clearance letters report either that no damage was observed from past infestation of termites, powder-post beetles, or other wood-boring insects or that past damage has been repaired.

Because of the serious nature of termite infestation, it is advisable that termite clearance letters be obtained before the date of closing. By obtaining the termite letter early, any termite infestation problem identified can be corrected by the closing date. Experience shows that a number of closings have been adjourned because termite letters that were delivered at the closing stated that the property had been damaged by infestation of termites. Receiving such a letter at the closing gives the closing attorney little time to react, and the termite inspector who issued the report often is not available to answer questions during the closing. The result is that the closing must be adjourned until more information can be received. Such adjournment wastes time, creates a major inconvenience, and potentially increases the interest rates and charges that the purchaser must pay if the loan commitment expires.

Reviewing the Title Examination

Once the title examination has been received, it should be carefully reviewed for objections to title. All prior loans or debts on the property need to be paid at closing.

It will be necessary to obtain from each lender or creditor a payment or satisfaction letter.

Satisfaction of Loans and Liens

Most lenders assign a computer number to each loan, and this number is needed to obtain a satisfaction amount for the loan. Some lenders will not give out information concerning any loan over the telephone or even by letter without the customer's consent and permission. It is a good idea to anticipate such problems and request the seller to contact their lender to obtain loan information or at least approve the legal assistant's obtaining such loan information. When requesting a payoff amount, it is necessary to give the lender a closing date and request a per diem interest charge if the sale does not close on the scheduled date. Ideally, loan payoffs should be verified by written communication with the lender; however, because of the fast-track nature of residential loans, many loan payoffs are handled by telephone.

A sample loan payment request is shown in Exhibit 15–3. This form should be used even with a telephone request. It is advisable when receiving a telephone satisfaction amount that the name and telephone number of the person giving the information be obtained. A letter can then be sent from the firm to the lender verifying the telephone conversation and requesting to be notified immediately if the information contained in the letter is incorrect. A similar letter indicating that the check is being sent as payment in full pursuant to a telephone conversation of a certain date should be sent to the lender after closing. If a payoff letter was received, a copy of that letter should be enclosed with the letter accompanying the check.

The amount of unpaid taxes can be obtained by calling the tax collector's office. Most delinquent taxes accrue penalties and interest; thus, a satisfaction amount as of the date of closing with a per diem charge is required.

The satisfaction of judgment liens or mechanics' liens requires a telephone call to the attorney representing the judgment creditor or lienor. The attorney's name and address usually appear somewhere on the recorded judgment or lien. It is advisable in obtaining satisfaction of liens and judgments that written information be provided. This is handled by making telephone contact and requiring the attorney representing the judgment creditor or lienor to provide a letter setting forth the amount needed for satisfaction. Arrangements also need to be made with judgment creditors and lienors to obtain a written satisfaction of the judgment or lien. This may require the attorney for the creditor or lien holder to attend the closing and tender the written satisfaction of lien or judgment in return for the payment check.

Satisfaction information for federal and state tax liens can be obtained through the Internal Revenue Service for federal tax liens and the state department of revenue for state tax liens. When speaking with the government authorities, full information concerning the lien, such as the date of the lien, the name of the taxpayer, and the place where the lien was filed and recorded, should be given. In addition, the closing date and a per diem interest charge should be provided.

REVIEWING THE MORTGAGE LOAN COMMITMENT

The mortgage **loan commitment** provides a legal assistant with clues about what information and documents are required to close the transaction. A mortgage loan commitment is addressed to the borrower. It indicates the mortgage lender's approval of the borrower's loan application and the lender's commitment to loan the

New York:
It is a good idea to get the mortgagee's name and the number of the mortgage so that you can request a "payoff" letter.

New York:
If there are unpaid taxes, the title company can pick these fees up at closing.

New York:
If there are judgments of record, check to see if they are against your client, as they may just be judgments against a party by the same name, i.e. there are many Sarah Smith's in an area. If they are not against your client, the title company will take an affidavit to that effect. If they are against your client, they must be satisfied and paid, prior to or at the closing.

EXHIBIT 15-3
Loan Payment
Request

File #_____   Purchaser:
                                Phone: (H)   (W)

● ●

( )R.E. AGENTS: Seller: (%)   Phone:
       (%)   Buyer: (%)   Phone:

( )ABSTRACT: Date Ordered: From:
                                                       ()collect at closing
                    Date Received: Cost:$ ()included in fee

( )SURVEY: Date Ordered: From:
                                                       ()collect at closing
                    Date Received: Cost:$ ()poc

( )TERMITE   Date Ordered: From:
   LETTER   ()collect at closing
                    Date Received: Cost:$ ()poc
                    ( )to be mailed   ( )to be delivered at closing
----
( )HAZARD INS: Date Ordered: Date Received:
                    From: Phone:
                    Address: Agent:

                    Amt. of Coverage: $ Eff. Date:
                                                       ()collect at closing
         ()new   * Yearly Premium: $ ()poc
         ()exist.   ()collect at closing
         ()trans. * Additional Prem: $ ()poc

( ) FLOOD INS: Date Ordered: Date Received:
                    From: Phone:
                    Address: Agent:

                    Amt. of Coverage: $ Eff. Date:
                                                       ()collect at closing
         ()new   * Yearly Premium: $ ()poc
         ()exist.   ()collect at closing
         ()tran. * Additional Prem: $ ()poc

( ) PAYOFFS: Date Ordered: Date Received: Ordered by:

         ()1st: To: Deed Book:
                    Address: Phone:
                                                          Loan No.:
                                                          Attention:
                  * Payoff is: $ as of: Per Diem:$

         ()2nd: To: Deed Book:
                    Address: Phone:
                                                          Loan No.:
                                                          Attention:
                  * Payoff is: $ as of: Per Diem:$

         ()3rd: To: Deed Book:
                    Address: Phone:
                                                          Loan No.:
                                                          Attention:
                  * Payoff is: $ as of: Per Diem:$

( ) OTHER CHARGES: Paid by:

                    () Attorneys Fees $ Buyer   Seller
      (P/A/C/LT)   () Title Insurance $ Buyer   Seller
                    () Toll Charges $ Buyer   Seller
      ()Loan   () Assignments $ Buyer   Seller
      ()Owners   () Power of Attorney $ Buyer   Seller
      ()S.1.   () Photo Copies $ Buyer   Seller
      ()Const.   () Federal Express $ Buyer   Seller
                    () $ Buyer   Seller
                    () $ Buyer   Seller

amount requested, provided the borrower agrees to comply with all the conditions listed in the commitment. It is the responsibility of the legal assistant to make certain that all the lender's requirements set forth in the loan commitment have been satisfied before or at the time of closing. The commitment is a binding legal agreement and will govern all future disputes between the borrower and the lender and the drafting of the formal loan documents.

The following is a discussion of the conditions and terms that can be found in a mortgage loan commitment. Some of these items can be found in any loan commitment and others apply only to commercial loan transactions.

New York:
Check the commitment to make sure the mortgage amount, interest rate, and terms are the same as what the client applied for. Check to see if there are any conditions that must be satisfied prior to closing on the loan.

Parties

The parties to a loan commitment are the prospective borrower and the lender.

Loan Amount

The amount of the loan should be clearly indicated in every loan commitment. This amount is used throughout in the preparation of all the necessary loan documents, such as notes, mortgages, and assignment of rents and leases.

Interest Rate

The commitment should clearly specify the annual interest rate for the loan. The interest rate will be either fixed or a floating rate that adjusts pursuant to some index.

Term of Loan

The commitment should specify the exact number of years over which the loan must be repaid. The term should commence on the loan closing date or such other date as the loan funds are disbursed to the borrower.

Repayment Terms

The commitment should specify how the loan is to be repaid. It is customary to provide for monthly payments, but payments on any other basis may be agreed on.

Prepayment Terms

The loan commitment should indicate whether the loan can be prepaid before maturity. Most residential loans are prepayable in full or in part, provided the prepayments are made on a date otherwise scheduled for a regular payment of principal and interest. For example, if payments are made on the first day of each month, a prepayment must be made on the first day of each month as well.

Most institutional commercial lenders do not allow a voluntary prepayment of the loan in whole or in part during the first few years of the loan term. Thereafter, it is customary to provide for prepayment subject to the payment of a premium.

Security

A mortgage loan commitment indicates what security is required by the lender for the loan. As a general rule, the lender requires a valid and enforceable first lien on the real property being offered by the borrower, which, in most situations, is the real property being purchased with the proceeds of the loan. The lender typically requires that it receive fee simple title to the real property. Occasionally a commercial lender may make a loan based on an estate for years or leasehold interest. The commitment letter indicates what quality of title the lender is requiring as security for the loan.

Appraisal

Most loan commitments require that before closing, the lender be provided with a formal written appraisal of the value of the proposed real property security. This appraisal of value ensures that the lender is not lending more money than the real property security is worth or more money than a percentage of the total fair market value of such real property security versus loan amount.

Insurance

A mortgage loan commitment requires that at or before closing, the borrower deliver to the lender insurance policies indicating that the real property security is covered by the following types of coverages: (a) fire, with extended and additional extended insurance; (b) vandalism and malicious mischief; (c) sprinkler; (d) war (if available); (e) rent or business interruption; (f) public liability; (g) plate glass liability; (h) boiler liability; and (i) flood. The insurance company and the dollar limits of such coverage also are subject to the approval of the lender. With respect to the amount of fire coverage, the general rule is that the policy must be for at least the original amount of the loan or the full amount of the replacement value of the improvements on the real property as determined at regular intervals, whichever is less.

New York:
At the closing, the mortgagor must show an insurance policy with a paid receipt for the first year.

All policies must have a proper mortgagee clause or endorsement attached thereto insuring the lender as the first mortgagee. A lender also may require a carrier to provide that it will not cancel the policy for any reason without prior written notice to the lender. Thirty days is the time period often required for such notice.

With respect to the payment of insurance proceeds, most lenders require a standard **mortgagee loss payable** endorsement to a policy whereby the insured and carrier agree that any and all proceeds payable under the policy are to be paid by the carrier directly to the lender or to a mutually agreed on third party. Thereafter, the loan documents allow the lender to use such proceeds either as an offset of the borrower's outstanding indebtedness or for restoration of the real property security.

Escrow

A commitment may require that at closing, the borrower establishes with the lender an escrow account to assure the lender that all real estate taxes, special assessments, and insurance premiums relating to the security will be paid when due. The borrower is required to make monthly deposits to such account in the amount of one-twelfth of the annual taxes, assessments, and hazard insurance premiums as estimated by the lender. Thereafter, all tax, assessment, and insurance premium payments are made by the lender, and a failure to make the requisite monthly deposits may be deemed a loan default by the borrower. No interest is paid on such deposits, and they are not held in trust but may be commingled with the general assets of the lender.

Title Insurance

Most loan commitments require that the borrower obtain a mortgagee (loan) title insurance policy insuring that the proposed mortgage or deed of trust creates a valid first lien on the title to the real property security.

Survey

Most mortgage loan commitments require that an as-built survey of the real property be prepared. An as-built survey shows not only the perimeter lines of the subject property and all improvements located thereon but also the location and path of any and all easements of record or those evident from an inspection of the property.

Compliance with Law

Most loan commitments require that the lender be provided with proof that all improvements on the real property (and their uses) comply fully with any and all applicable zoning and building laws, ordinances, and regulations and all other applicable federal, state, and municipal laws, rules, and regulations.

Financial Documents

Most loan commitments require that all financial information submitted by the borrower to the lender in connection with the mortgage loan application be recertified by the borrower at the time of closing. This typically is done by an affidavit of no adverse change wherein the borrower swears that all financial information previously submitted to the lender is true and correct and that there has been no adverse material change in its financial condition since the application.

Documents

The commitment specifies what loan documents are needed to close the loan. These documents include a note, a mortgage or deed of trust, and, in the case of a commercial loan, an assignment of leases and rents, a security agreement, and a Uniform Commercial Code (UCC) Financing Statement. Construction mortgage loan commitments also may require a construction loan agreement and assignments of the construction contract and the architects' and engineers' contracts.

Defaults and Late Charges

A loan commitment provides that the loan documents include default provisions. Most default provisions are subject to reasonable notice and grace periods to cure before the various remedies available to the lender can be invoked. With respect to monetary defaults, such as failure to pay the debt or pay taxes or pay insurance premiums, a five- or ten-day right to cure is common. In the case of nonmonetary defaults, the borrower may be given twenty to thirty days to cure such default.

A loan commitment may specify a late fee for note payments not made on time. This fee reimburses the lender the cost of processing late payments. In addition to a late fee, the loan commitment may require that a default rate of interest be applied to the unamortized portion of the loan at the date of default. Default rates are substantially higher than the interest rate applicable to the loan when the borrower is not in default.

Commitment Fee

Most loan commitments require the borrower to deliver to the lender before closing a specified sum of money as consideration for the issuance of the commitment. This fee may be called a commitment fee deposit, standby fee, earnest money, or a similar name.

Loan Expenses

The commitment provides that all expenses, fees, and costs incurred with respect to the loan, including but not limited to lender's attorney fees, title insurance fees, survey costs, recording and filing fees, mortgage taxes or other taxes on the note and mortgage, cost of appraisals, and personal inspections, be paid by the borrower.

Closing and Commitment Expiration Date

A loan commitment indicates the date on which the loan closing is to be held and the lender is to disburse the loan proceeds. The closing is conditioned on the borrower's having complied with all conditions of the commitment to the satisfaction of the lender and its counsel.

In addition to the loan closing date, a commitment may set forth a commitment expiration date, which may or may not coincide with the closing date.

Disbursement of Loan Proceeds

A loan commitment specifies how the proceeds of the loan are to be disbursed on closing to the borrower, whether by cash, lender's check, check on federal funds, bank wire, or wire of federal funds. The lender may place good funds in the closing attorney's escrow account, and the closing attorney will disburse all checks from that account.

Acceptance of a Loan Commitment

A loan commitment is not effective or binding until it has been accepted by the borrower.

Assignability

A loan commitment is personal to the borrower and cannot be assigned without the lender's consent.

A review of the loan commitment provides the legal assistant with a checklist of items needed to close and fund the loan. A checklist of closing requirements compiled from an example of a loan commitment for a residential loan (Exhibit 15–4) follows.

American Eagle Mortgage Company
March 7, 19 ___

EXHIBIT 15–4
Loan Commitment
for Residential Loan

Ms. Helen Davis
849 Mentelle Drive, N.E.
Atlanta, Georgia 30308

Re: Mortgage Loan Commitment—$38,000.00 at 11% for thirty (30) years

Dear Ms. Davis:

American Eagle Mortgage Company (the "Company") is pleased to inform you that it has acted upon your application and has approved a loan to you, subject to all terms and conditions of this letter. The loan will be in the principal sum of $38,000.00 at an annual rate of 11%, to be repaid as follows:

In equal consecutive monthly installments of $361.89 per month for thirty (30) years. Each installment, when paid, shall be applied first to the payment of accrued interest and then to the unpaid principal balance.

The holder may collect a "late charge" not to exceed an amount equal to four percent (4%) of any installment which is not paid within fifteen (15) days of the due date thereof, to cover the extra expenses involved in handling delinquent payments.

The loan proceeds shall be used for the acquisition of improved real estate (the "Property") located at 5167 Tilly Mill Road, Atlanta, Georgia.

The loan shall be secured by a first priority lien on the Property and on all improvements now or hereafter existing thereon. The Company's agreement to make the loan to you is subject to satisfaction of the following conditions, all at your sole cost and expense and in a manner acceptable to the Company.

1. The Company shall procure a standard form ALTA mortgagee's policy of title insurance insuring the loan as a first priority lien against the Property, showing there is to be no other encumbrances against the Property which render it unmarketable.

2. You shall provide the Company prior to closing with a recent plat of survey of the Property, together with a surveyor's certificate in form satisfactory to the Company's title insuror, depicting and certifying all improvements on the Property to be completely within the boundary lines of the Property and to be in compliance with all applicable building or set-back line restrictions.

3. You shall provide the Company prior to closing with fire, lightning and extended coverage insurance issued by a company or companies and upon terms acceptable to the Company in at least the sum of $38,000.00. Premiums for such insurance shall be paid by you for not less than one year in advance. All policies shall be issued with a mortgagee clause in favor of and acceptable to the Company and shall be non-cancellable without at least ten (10) days prior written notice to the Company.

4. The Company shall select an attorney to close the loan and to prepare all documents deemed necessary or appropriate by the Company to evidence the loan and to establish the Company's first priority lien against the Property and the Policy. All such loan documents will be in form and substance satisfactory to the Company's closing attorney.

5. All actual fees or expenses (including, without limitation, such closing attorney's fees, title insurance premiums, cost of title examination, abstract of title fee, document preparation fee, cost of survey, appraisal fee, recording fees and intangibles or other taxes) incurred in connection with reviewing your loan application, or with closing, servicing, collecting or cancelling the loan, shall be paid by you.

EXHIBIT 15–4
Loan Commitment
for Residential Loan
(continued)

6. The loan may be assumed by a transferee of the Property, provided the Company gives prior written consent thereto; but any transfer of title to all or any part of the Property whatsoever, or any further encumbrance or other lien imposed against the Property without the Company's prior written consent, will authorize the Company to declare the loan immediately due and payable. Any such assumption, transfer or encumbrance to which the Company shall consent shall be upon such terms and conditions as the Company shall determine and approve.

7. You shall pay a non-refundable commitment fee of $100.00 to the Company upon your acceptance of this commitment letter.

8. You shall provide the Company with photographs of all buildings or other structural improvements on the Property prior to closing.

9. You shall pay an appraisal fee to the Company in the amount of $150.00.

10. The loan is to be escrowed for taxes and insurance premiums.

Very truly yours,
AMERICAN EAGLE MORTGAGE COMPANY

By: _____

J. Perry Drake
Treasurer

▐▐▐➡ CHECKLIST

Loan Commitment for a Residential Loan

1. Title commitment/insurance
2. Survey
3. Hazard insurance
4. Truth-in-lending statement
5. Borrower's affidavit
6. Note
7. Mortgage
8. Settlement statement

EXHIBIT 15–5
Commercial Loan
Commitment Letter

RE: First Mortgage Loan—$1,150,000
    Acme, Inc.   , Mortgagor
    $10^3/_4$% 25 year amortization
    Call options in year 10, 15, 20

Dear Mr.

We are pleased to advise that our Investment Review Committee has approved the above captioned first mortgage loan. The loan will be in the amount of $1,150,000 at an interest rate of $10^3/_4$% per annum, and is to be amortized over a period of twenty-five (25) years by equal monthly installments of $11,068.75, including interest. Lender reserves the right to declare the entire amount of outstanding principal and all unpaid accrued interest thereon to be immediately due and payable on any one of the following dates: ten (10), fifteen (15), or twenty (20) years from the first installment of principal and interest. Such

EXHIBIT 15-5
Commercial Loan
Commitment Letter
(continued)

right shall be exercised by lender by giving written notice to borrower at least six (6) months prior to date on which said payment of all principal and interest shall be due and payable.

An interest bearing escrow account is to be established in the amount of $300,000 with an escrow agent acceptable to lender, with all interest accruing in the name of the borrower. Said escrow will be held until such time that 23,089 square feet is leased at an average of $12.50 per square foot, net of free rent or other rental concessions, producing a gross income of at least $288,613 annually. Said leases are to be for a minimum term of one year and shall be acceptable to lender. If the above requirements have not been met prior to January 31, 199__ the $300,000 shall be applied to reduce the principal balance of the loan without penalty and in inverse order to the normal monthly payments owing.

This commitment is issued subject to the following conditions:

1. The loan is to be secured by a valid first lien on the fee simple title to the following described property, together with the improvements thereon, located in the city limits of _____. Said property is a rectangle that contains approximately 2.11 acres with 248 feet of frontage on Carpenter Drive. The physical address is 275 Carpenter Drive.

We are to be provided with a complete and accurate legal description subject to our approval prior to closing of this loan.

2. All loan documents, agreements or other instruments used in connection with this transaction shall first have the approval of our Legal Department and must be prepared by an attorney designated by our Legal Department.

3. All legal fees and other expenses in connection with the closing of this loan are to be paid by the mortgagor. It is further understood that the mortgagor will pay any expenses incident to this transaction should for any reason the loan not be closed after said expenses have been incurred.

4. Fire and extended coverage insurance policies are to be furnished in an amount at least equal to the amount of the loan and not less than the full insurable value of the improvements, issued by a company or companies satisfactory to us. If the policy carries a co-insurance clause or other clause limiting the amount of coverage under certain conditions the insurance must be in such an amount as to give full coverage under all conditions. All insurable buildings and personal property or easily removable real estate items or fixtures included in the security instrument must be covered by such insurance.

5. The loan documents shall contain the following items or provisions:

a. No prepayment of the principal of this note shall be allowed prior to the fifth anniversary of the date hereof. After the fifth anniversary of the date hereof, the principal of this note may be prepaid in whole but not in part, on any interest payment date herein, provided that: (1) not later than sixty (60) days prior to such prepayment, Applicant delivers written notice to Holder, and that Applicant intends to prepay the note in full on the date specified in such notice; and (2) Applicant pays to Holder at the time of such prepayment, a percentage of the prepaid principal amount as a prepayment premium. Such percentage shall be the product obtained by multiplying the prepaid principal amount by the product of the following:

(i) the amount obtained by subtracting the annualized yield on a United States Treasury Bill, Note or Bond with maturity date which occurs closest to the next applicable call date of this Note, as such annualized yield is reported by *The Wall Street Journal* on the business day preceding the date of prepayment from $10^3/_4\%$ multiplied by:

(ii) the number of years and fraction thereof remaining between the date of prepayment and the next applicable call date of this note.

EXHIBIT 15–5
Commercial Loan
Commitment Letter
(continued)

Notwithstanding the foregoing, however, in the event of acceleration of the Note at any time and subsequent involuntary or voluntary prepayment, the Prepayment Premium shall be payable, however in no event shall it exceed an amount equal to the excess, if any, of (i) interest calculated at the highest applicable rate permitted by applicable law, as construed by courts having jurisdiction thereof, on the principal balance of the Note from time to time outstanding from the date hereof to the date of such acceleration, over (ii) interest theretofore paid and accrued on the Note. Any prepaid amounts specified in such notice shall become due and payable at the time provided in such notice. A "Loan Year" for the purposes of this Note shall mean each successive twelve (12) month period beginning with the date of the first installment payment of interest hereunder provided however, that the first Loan Year shall include the period from the date of this Note to the date of such first installment payment of interest. Under no circumstances shall the prepayment premium ever be less than zero. The amount of prepayment shall never be less than the full amount of the then outstanding principal and interest.

In addition to the above described prepayment penalty, a reinvestment fee of $\frac{1}{2}$ of 1% of the outstanding loan balance will be due in the event of prepayment prior to the maturity of this loan.

b. An assignment of rents in a form satisfactory to our Legal Department.

c. The holder may collect a "late charge" not to exceed an amount equal to four percent (4%) of any installment which is not paid within fifteen (15) days of the due date thereof, to cover the extra expense involved in handling delinquent payments, provided that collection of said late charge shall not be deemed a waiver by the holder of any of its other rights under this note.

d. The Lender is to be furnished with a certified, itemized statement of annual income and expenses on the property covered by this loan within 90 days following the end of each fiscal or calendar year.

e. The usual covenant requiring monthly escrow deposits for annual payment of ad valorem taxes and hazard insurance premiums.

f. It shall be a default under the mortgage if, without the Lender's prior written consent, the real property security for this loan or any part thereof is sold, transferred, conveyed or encumbered in any way. Notwithstanding the above, Lender hereby agrees to allow a one time transfer of ownership and assumption of this loan by a qualified borrower acceptable to Lender. As consideration for this transfer and assumption, the Lender will receive a non-refundable 1% fee based on the then outstanding balance, payable at the time of transfer.

g. Installments shall be due and payable on the first day of each month.

h. The Promissory Note taken in this transaction will include a provision which reads "Subject to the terms of the next succeeding paragraph and notwithstanding anything to the contrary otherwise contained in this Note, it is agreed that the promise of Maker to pay the principal indebtedness and the interest on this Note shall be for the sole purpose of establishing the existence of an indebtedness; Holder's source of satisfaction of said indebtedness and of Maker's other obligations hereunder and under the Loan Documents is limited solely to (a) the property described in the Mortgage, (b) Holder's receipt of the rents, issues and profits from the property described in the Mortgage and (c) any separate agreements guaranteeing the payment of the amounts due hereunder and under the Loan Documents and Makers' performance hereunder and under the Loan Documents; Holder shall not seek to procure payment out of any other assets of Maker, or to procure any judgment against Maker for any amount which is or may be payable under this Note, the Mortgage or any of the other Loan Documents or for any deficiency

EXHIBIT 15–5
Commercial Loan
Commitment Letter
(continued)

remaining after foreclosure of the Mortgage; provided, however, that nothing herein contained shall be deemed to be a release or impairment of said indebtedness or the security therefor intended by the Mortgage, or be deemed to preclude Holder from foreclosing the Mortgage or from enforcing any of Holder's rights thereunder, or in any way or manner affecting Holder's rights and privileges under any of the Loan Documents or any separate agreements guaranteeing Maker's payment and performance hereunder and under the Loan Documents.

Notwithstanding the foregoing limitation of liability provision, it is expressly understood and agreed that Maker shall be personally liable for the payment to the Holder of:

(a) all security deposits of tenants, any rents that are collected more than one (1) month in advance, and all income, rents, issues, profits and revenues derived from the property described in the Mortgage which are not promptly applied to payment of the indebtedness evidenced by the Note and/or to the costs of normal maintenance and operation of such property;

(b) any loss due to fraud or misrepresentations to Holder by Maker (or by any of its general partners, by any of the general partners of any of its general partners or by any of its or their agents, if applicable);

(c) the misapplication of (i) proceeds paid under any insurance policies by reason of damage, loss or destruction to any portion of the property described in the Mortgage to the full extent of such misapplied proceeds, or (ii) proceeds of awards resulting from the condemnation or other taking in lieu of condemnation of any portion of such property, to the full extent of such misapplied proceeds or awards;

(d) any loss due to waste of the property described in the Mortgage or any portion thereof, and all costs, including reasonable attorneys' fees, incurred by Holder to protect such property and any other security for the indebtedness evidenced by this Note or to enforce such Note, the Mortgage and any of the other Loan Documents; and

(e) any taxes, assessments and insurance premiums for which Maker is liable under this Note, the Mortgage or any of the other Loan Documents and which are paid by Holder; and

(f) arising under the hazardous substance indemnification and hold harmless agreement and the borrower's hazardous substances covenant's warranties and representations provisions contained in the attached as Exhibits "A & B".

6. Prior to closing, the Borrower must furnish to the Lender, at the Borrower's sole cost and expense, the original of an environmental audit and certification addressed to Lender and Lender's successors and assigns, with form acceptable to Lender, and prepared by a licensed engineer and geotechnical consultant ("Engineer") or either including field reconnaissance, site history records survey, tenant use history record survey, and an examination of the Compensation and Liability Systems Record in the State in which the property is located, to establish that a thorough investigation of those records and an inspection of the property site and improvements reveal no evidence of any pollutant or other toxic or hazardous substance, as defined under the Comprehensive Environmental Response, Compensation, and Liability Act ("CERCLA"), 42 U.S.C. 9601 *et seq.*, as amended, or any other federal, state or local law ("Hazardous Substance"). In the event the Engineer determines in his or her professional judgment that an examination of the sub-surface soils is necessary, then the parties contemplate that Borrower will require that the Engineer provide the Borrower with an estimate of the additional charges which will be incurred in such examination. In the event that Borrower provides Lender with written notice, received by Lender within five (5) days of the Borrower's receipt of the estimate, that Borrower has determined that the additional charges are not acceptable, then Borrower may simultane-

EXHIBIT 15–5
Commercial Loan
Commitment Letter
(continued)

ously provide Lender with Borrower's written election to cancel this Commitment Letter in which event the commitment fee will be refunded to Borrower and neither Borrower nor Lender will thereafter have any liability to the other under this Commitment Letter. In the event that Borrower either: (i) fails to provide Lender with receipt of written notice within the said five (5) days of receiving said estimate, or, (ii) determines that the additional charges are acceptable, then the Borrower will be deemed to have elected to close without regard to such additional charges and said audit and certificate must be provided to Lender by Borrower and must include a sub-surface soils examination or any other examination deemed necessary and the cost thereof will be paid by Borrower. In any event, the charges for the environmental audit and certification will be paid in full by Borrower.

With respect to any Hazardous Substance found on the property, the environmental audit must indicate the nature of the substance, the statutory control over the removal process, the time and costs of removal, and the assessment of risk.

The loan documents will contain the Borrower's covenants, representations, warranties and indemnities, in the identical form of the wording attached hereto as Exhibit "A & B".

The Borrower must, at the Borrower's sole cost and expense, obtain and provide to Lender at or before closing the original of a letter addressed to Lender from the Regional Office of the Environmental Protection Agency establishing whether the property or property in the vicinity of the property has been the location of a hazardous waste site.

In the event that the environmental audit or the letter from the Environmental Protection Agency reveals that the property has or has had any Hazardous Substance located on or in the property or the improvements located on the property, or any other condition which Lender determines to be objectionable, then Lender, may at its option elect not to close this loan. If Lender, after reviewing any item required of Borrower under this provision, determines not to close this loan, then this Commitment Letter will be canceled and the commitment fee will be refunded to Borrower and neither Borrower nor Lender will thereafter have any liability to the other under this Commitment Letter.

7. The financing statement covering the fixtures and equipment will be properly executed and recorded, and the properly executed security agreement delivered to us.

8. We are to be furnished with an engineer's survey, certified to by a registered surveyor, dated within 90 days prior to closing, showing no encroachments other than those approved by us and showing the improvements to be within lot and building lines.

9. We are to be furnished with a mortgagee title insurance policy issued by a company approved by us, or an endorsement to a previously issued title policy, which will insure that the Lender has a first lien without exceptions, other than those specifically approved by us.

10. Any outstanding unpaid taxes and assessments are to be paid prior to our disbursement of the loan proceeds.

11. We will require loss of rent insurance in an amount not less than nine (9) months gross rental.

12. In order to comply with IRS Regulation TD 8047, we are to be furnished with the social security number, in the case of an individual mortgagor, or the tax identification number for all other mortgagors. We must be provided with this number prior to the closing of this loan.

13. We are to be furnished a current written opinion of counsel for the Borrower, satisfactory to Lender, to the effect that the subject loan is not usurious or otherwise illegal under applicable law and that all loan documents are valid and binding upon Borrower and are enforceable in accordance with their terms.

EXHIBIT 15–5
Commercial Loan
Commitment Letter
(continued)

14. We have tentatively scheduled this loan for closing sometime during the month of January, 199__, and this commitment shall expire January 31, 199__.

15. Provided this commitment is acceptable, you are to forward your check, within ten (10) business days from the date hereof, in the amount of $34,500. This amount plus $11,500 previously received from you will be held by us in a non-interest bearing account as a commitment fee. If and when this loan is closed under the terms and conditions of this commitment letter, $43,500 of the above $46,000 commitment fee will be refunded. However, if this loan is not closed, it is agreed and understood that upon expiration or cancellation of this commitment this fee will be retained by Lender as consideration for this commitment. If Borrower should elect to do so, Lender will accept $23,000 of the above fee in the form of a Letter of Credit. The Letter of Credit must be drawn on an institution and be in a form acceptable to Lender with an expiration date no earlier than March 31, 19__.

16. Lender reserves the right to cancel this commitment and terminate its obligations hereunder at any time upon the happening of any of the following events:

a. Borrower's failure to comply with any of the applicable conditions of this commitment within the time specified.

b. Non-payment of any of the fees or expenses to be paid by the Borrower in connection with this commitment.

c. Any infirmity in Borrower's title to the real estate, filed by or against Borrower any petition in bankruptcy or insolvency or for the reorganization of Borrower or appointment of a receiver or trustee or the making of an assignment for the benefit of creditors.

17. This agreement is made for the sole protection of the Borrower and the Lender, its successors and assigns and no other person or persons shall have any right of action thereon, and this commitment is not assignable or transferable by Borrower.

Lender reserves the absolute right to partially or totally assign this commitment to a third party lending institution for the purpose of facilitating a participation loan. By acceptance of this commitment letter, Borrower acknowledges and agrees that this loan may be a loan in which an additional lender may act as a participating lender at the time of funding.

We appreciate your offering us the opportunity to make this loan and trust that it will be handled to your entire satisfaction.

Sincerely,

The following is a checklist of closing requirements compiled from Exhibit 15–5.

CHECKLIST

Loan Commitment for a Commercial Loan

1. Title examination and title commitment
2. Survey and surveyor's inspection report
3. Fire insurance
4. Borrower's attorney's opinion
5. Copy of personal property
6. Copy of leases
7. Tenant estoppel letters for all leases
8. Subordination and nondisturbance attornment agreement for all leases

9. Certificate of occupancy for all leases	**18.** Letter from regional office of Environmental Protection Agency
10. Certified articles of incorporation and bylaws—Acme, Inc.	**19.** Borrower's affidavit
11. Certificate of good standing—Acme, Inc.	**20.** Promissory note
12. Corporate resolution—Acme, Inc.	**21.** Deed to secure debt
13. Environmental audit	**22.** Assignment of rents and leases
14. Photograph of improvements	**23.** Security agreement
15. Federal tax ID number	**24.** UCC financing statement
16. Zoning letter	**25.** Rental achievement escrow
17. Utility letters	**26.** Loan closing statement

SPECIAL PROVISIONS IN A CONSTRUCTION LOAN COMMITMENT

A commitment for a construction loan may contain special provisions in addition to the regular provisions found in other loan commitments.

A lender in a construction loan wants the right to (a) review and approve all preliminary and final plans or specifications; (b) be consulted on and approve any and all changes in such plans of specification; (c) establish minimum standards for construction; (d) establish a time schedule for the various stages of construction from commencement to completion; (e) receive periodic progress reports; (f) undertake periodic inspections of the construction; (g) be supplied with a certificate of the architect as to the satisfactory completion of the work in accordance with the plans and specification; (h) be supplied with a certificate of borrower as to the total construction costs required for the project; (i) be supplied with a certificate of borrower stating that all utility lines (electricity, gas, water, and sanitary sewers) are completed, connected, and adequate; and (j) be supplied with pictures of the project as construction progresses.

These additional construction requirements may necessitate submission of the following items to the lender before closing: (a) a copy of the construction contract; (b) a copy of all major subcontracts; (c) a copy of the building permit; (d) utility letters; (e) final plans and specifications; (f) the architect's contract; (g) the engineer's contract; (h) a cost breakdown of all construction components; and (i) the retention of a construction supervisor or inspector.

In addition, construction loans require other forms of documentation. For example, a construction loan agreement and an assignment of all major contracts are required. Copies of these forms are included in Chapter 12. The title insurance policy contains a pending disbursement clause and may require periodic title change checkdowns and endorsements to insure the loan in full as construction progresses. The fire and casualty insurance is in the form of builder's risk insurance. Builder's risk insurance insures the risk of a building during the stages of construction. Liability insurance and workman's compensation insurance are required on construction projects.

Most construction loans are paid from a refinancing of the construction loan with a permanent loan. Therefore, a construction loan commitment provides that the permanent commitment must be in existence before the funding of the construction loan. A construction lender may require an assignment of the permanent commitment along with the permanent lender's consent to the assignment. This permits the construction lender, in the event there is a default during construction, to take over the project, finish it, and deliver the permanent loan, thereby receiving the proceeds from the permanent loan.

Hazardous Waste

Most loan commitments provide that the borrower will indemnify the lender against damage or liability caused by hazardous waste located in or on the property. These indemnities are carried over and included in the loan documents.

Leasehold Loans

If the loan commitment contemplates taking as security a leasehold interest, it will contain several additional provisions. The commitment requires an assignment of the borrower's interest as tenant under the lease as well as an assignment of borrower's interest in any underlying subleases, licenses, or other agreements. The loan commitment requires the borrower to supply the lender at closing with a certificate from the landlord of the ground lease stating (a) the ground lease is in full force and effect; (b) it has not been modified, supplemented, or amended except as set forth in such certificate; (c) the rent payments are current and have not been paid in advance except as required by such lease; (d) the tenant is not in default under any of the terms or provisions of such lease; or (e) if tenant is in default, the nature of such default is explained.

The loan commitment requires that the unexpired term of the lease being offered for security be of sufficient duration to cover the term of the loan.

With respect to a ground lease taken as security, the lender requires its counsel to review such lease. In some instances, the lender requests that the ground lessor subordinate its interest to the mortgage loan by signing the mortgage documents. This permits the lender, in the event of default, to foreclose on the leasehold as well as the fee and to obtain fee simple title at foreclosure.

A leasehold loan commitment may require the borrower, as a condition of closing, to give to the lender a document providing that the ground lessor will give written notice of any default by tenant or borrower under the lease to lender and allow lender adequate time to cure any such default. A lender may require that in the event the ground lease terminates, the landlord will enter into a new lease with the lender for the unexpired term of the ground lease on the same terms and conditions as the ground lease.

THE CLOSING AND AFTERMATH ⎯⎯⎯⎯⎯⎯⎯⎯⎯⎯⎯

By the time the closing day arrives, it is hoped that most of the requirements and all the loan and sale documents have been prepared. All the parties (seller, purchaser, and brokers) have been notified of the date, time, and place of the closing. The purchaser knows the exact amount of money to bring to the closing and has been instructed to bring good funds in the form of a certified or cashier's check.

Most closing proceeds are disbursed through the law firm's escrow account. The purchaser, therefore, should be instructed to bring funds in the form of a cashier's check made payable to the law firm.

Closings usually take place in a conference room of the law firm handling the closing or at the office of the title insurance company. After the introduction of the parties to one another, the closing usually commences with the closing attorney

New York:

The title closer, in addition to insuring good title, verifies the payoff figure for the sellers' mortgage. Photo identification is necessary for both the buyer and seller.

See Appendix for further discussion of closing in New York.

explaining the sale documents to the seller and the purchaser. Ideally, the seller and purchaser have received copies of all documents and have already reviewed and approved them. In many residential transactions, this ideal is not met, and the parties may be seeing the documents for the first time at the closing table. Additional copies of each document should be prepared so that each party will have its own copy to review while the documents are being explained. The item of prime interest is the closing statement, in which all the closing disbursements and costs have been outlined. The seller is interested in making certain that all payoffs and satisfaction of prior liens are correct according to his or her records and that brokerage commissions and other expenses he or she are required to pay are in the correct amounts. The agents are interested in determining that commission amounts are true and correct. It is not unusual for closing adjustments to be made at the time of closing. Unpaid charges, such as cleanup bills or other expenses that need to be reimbursed between the parties, may not be brought to the closing attorney's attention until the date of closing. Sums of money allocated to pay for termite protection, hazard insurance, and surveys may have already been paid and need to be deleted from the closing statement. Most seasoned closing attorneys review the closing statement first; if changes are to be made, they are taken care of while the closing is progressing. This results in a new and corrected closing statement at the end of the closing, which can then be signed.

The usual sequence of events for most closings is to handle the sale aspects first, with the seller signing all the transfer documents. Then the loan transaction takes place, with the purchaser signing all the loan documents. It may be desirable and prudent on some commercial transactions for the loan closing to take place before the sale. Many commercial borrowers do not want the seller to know what terms were arranged for financing the property. If this is desired by the parties, then two closings will be scheduled: first the loan closing and then the sale closing.

After all the documents have been signed, witnessed, and notarized, good funds have been verified from the purchaser and the lender, and all checks have been cut and disbursements made to those parties present at closing, the closing is finished. On many residential transactions, the seller delivers keys to the purchaser, and the date for vacating and occupying the property are clearly understood between the parties. Purchaser and seller should receive copies of all closing documents signed by the seller and purchaser in connection with the closing. Most brokers require that only a copy of the closing statement be given to them.

Representatives of the lenders on residential closings seldom attend the closing. Representatives of the lender on a commercial closing may be present at the closing. This is important because last-minute details in the loan often are negotiated at the closing table. Documents that are changed at closing should be either retyped or altered at the table. All alterations should be initialed by all parties affected by the alterations.

Disbursing, Recording, and Transmittal of Final Documents

After the purchaser, seller, and agent have gone home, the closing legal assistant still has much to do before the job is done. Checks have already been disbursed to the seller and real estate agents at closing. The next checks to disburse immediately after closing are the checks to pay off all prior mortgages, liens, or encumbrances against the real property. Before disbursing any monies, the legal assistant should be satisfied that the check received from the purchaser will be honored by the bank on which it is drawn and satisfied that the check provided by the lender will be honored when it is presented. Because most firms disburse all monies through their escrow accounts and all checks paid from closing will be firm checks, it is required that lenders, purchasers, or anyone supplying funds for the closing provide either cashier's or certified checks drawn on a federal reserve bank. If funds are to be wired into the firm's escrow account, they should be sent by federal wire. It is important when issuing checks that a ledger card be used to balance the funds received against the funds paid out.

The custom in some states is to record all the documents before disbursements are made. If the legal assistant is closing in a state that has this custom, he or she would then record the documents before making any disbursements to the parties in connection with the transaction.

All closing documents that are to be recorded should be recorded immediately after closing. This usually includes the deed of conveyance from seller to purchaser and the mortgage from purchaser or borrower to the lender. It also may include assignments for rents and leases, UCC financing statements, satisfaction of liens, or other matters that may be recorded in connection with a particular transaction. Most firms use couriers to deliver the recorded documents to the clerk's office. In some parts of the country, rush recording is available for an additional fee. With rush recording, the clerk's office can index, record, and copy the documents and return the originals the same day.

All monies to pay off liens or satisfactions should be sent by transmittal letter. The transmittal letter should include a statement that the money being sent constitutes payment in full of the debt and that the check is being cashed based on that assumption. It is a good idea to request that all satisfactions and releases of mortgages or liens be returned to the legal assistant. The legal assistant should provide a self-addressed, stamped envelope for the return. It also is advisable to call the person to whom satisfaction money has been sent to make sure that he or she has received it and that the sum is sufficient to pay off the debt.

Most lenders require that a loan document package consisting of all the original documents except those documents that have been sent to record be delivered to them the day after the closing. The transmittal package to the lender is important because it reveals the quality of the firm's work. There should be no errors, and all the lender's instructions should be followed to the letter. Making errors or not following instructions could lead to the law firm's being removed from the lender's approved list and could seriously affect the firm's economic viability.[1]

Final Close Out

After all deeds, mortgages, and other loan documents have been recorded and returned from the clerk's office and all cancellations and other satisfactions have been returned and recorded, it is time to close out the file. Original recorded documents need to be sent to the parties entitled to receive them. The purchaser is entitled to receive the warranty deed, and the lender, the recorded mortgage, assignment of rents, UCC financing statements, and so on.

Another aspect of the close out is the issuance of the final title insurance policies. A final title examination is necessary to verify that the deed and loan documents have in fact been recorded and do properly appear in the index of the record room. A final title examination also searches for the recorded satisfactions on all prior liens and security deeds.

Most lenders will not accept title policies unless the general standard exceptions for parties in possession, matters of survey, unrecorded easements, and mechanics' liens are deleted. In addition, if any restrictive covenants are set forth in Schedule B, most lenders require the inclusion of an affirmative provision in the policy stating that said restrictive covenants have not been violated to date and that any future violation will not result in the forfeiture or reversion of title.

The title policy should follow the commitment exactly. The effective date of the owner's policy is the date of the recording of the deed, and the effective date of the loan policy is the date of the recording of the mortgage.

After the title policies have been prepared and sent to the lender with the recorded mortgage and to the purchaser with the recorded warranty deed, the file should be rechecked to make sure that everything has been taken care of and that all checks have been disbursed, ledger cards balanced, all documents recorded and delivered to the proper parties, and all liens and other debts satisfied and cancelled. The entire transaction is now completed and the file can be sent to storage.

It is not unusual for four to six weeks to elapse between the closing and the final completion of the file.

A real estate closing is a complicated procedure, and it is essential that the legal assistant be organized and pay attention to detail. The best method to achieve organization and attention to detail is to prepare a checklist for all the items required in a real estate closing. As previously discussed, each real estate closing is unique and has its own checklist. The checklists that appear earlier in the chapter are examples of the types of things one would expect to find in a real estate closing. The following checklist is a general outline of all the aspects of a real estate closing.

▐▐▐▶ CHECKLIST

Real Estate Closing

❑ I. File Creation
   ❑ A. Open file
      1. Client name
      2. Client number
      3. Billing information
      4. Cross reference and conflict check
❑ II. Information Gathering
   ❑ A. Review real estate contract
      1. Name of seller
      2. Name of purchaser
      3. Name of broker
      4. Description of real property
      5. Date of closing
      6. Requirements of seller
      7. Requirements of purchaser
   ❑ B. Prepare closing checklist from review of real estate contract
   ❑ C. Review loan commitment
      1. Name of lender
      2. Name of borrower
      3. Amount of loan
      4. Commitment expiration date
      5. Loan closing requirements

❑ D. Prepare a loan closing checklist
❑ E. Order title examination and title policy
      1. Description of real property
      2. Date when examination is required
      3. Name of title company
      4. Name of insured
      5. Insured amount
❑ F. Order survey
      1. Legal description of property
      2. Information regarding previous survey
      3. Name of purchaser and other names to appear on survey
      4. Name of lending institution to appear on survey
      5. Flood hazard certification
      6. Other special requirements for survey
      7. Date of completion for survey
❑ G. Order hazard and fire insurance
      1. Name of insured
      2. Proper address of property
      3. Amount of insurance
      4. Proof insurance premium has been paid one year in advance

     5. Name of lender for mortgagee clause
     6. Date for delivery of insurance policy
❏ III. Preclosing Procedures
   ❏ A. Review title examination and title policy
   ❏ B. Obtain copies of all title exceptions
   ❏ C. Request satisfaction amounts from any mortgages, liens, or encumbrances to be paid at closing
   ❏ D. Review survey
     1. Do improvements encroach over property line?
     2. Is survey in compliance with purchaser and lender requirements?
   ❏ E. Verify that all sale obligations have been met by both purchaser and seller
   ❏ F. Verify that all mortgage loan commitment requirements have been satisfied
❏ IV. Document Preparation
   ❏ A. Preparation of all purchase and sale documents
   ❏ B. Preparation of all loan documents
❏ V. Closing
   ❏ A. Inform all parties (purchaser, seller, broker, lender representatives) of the date, time, and place of closing
   ❏ B. Inform purchaser of proper amount of proceeds needed for closing and instruct purchaser to bring good funds
   ❏ C. Verify that lender has deposited loan proceeds with firm
   ❏ D. Reserve conference room

   ❏ E. Prepare closing packet of documents for purchaser and seller
❏ VI. Disbursing, Recording, and Transmittal of Final Documents
   ❏ A. Transmit deed, mortgage, and other documents to be recorded to courthouse for recording
   ❏ B. Transmit money necessary to pay prior liens, mortgages, and encumbrances to proper parties
   ❏ C. Prepare final package for purchaser and seller
   ❏ D. Prepare final loan package for lender
❏ VII. Final Closeout
   ❏ A. Obtain all deeds, mortgages, and other documents recorded from courthouse
   ❏ B. Obtain all satisfactions and cancellations for prior mortgages, liens, and encumbrances
   ❏ C. Order final title examination and verify proper recording and indexing of deed, mortgage, and other recorded documents
   ❏ D. Obtain and review title insurance policy
   ❏ E. Transmit recorded deed and title insurance policy to purchaser
   ❏ F. Transmit recorded mortgage and other loan documents and title insurance policy to lender
   ❏ G. Final review of file to verify that all closing procedures have been completed
   ❏ H. Close file and send to storage

 E T H I C S : Conflicts of Interest

You are a legal assistant with a firm that represents a bank. The bank makes a number of consumer home loans. You have received a new loan and have just contacted the purchasers for the purpose of going over the closing checklist. During your conversation, you realize that the purchasers think you represent them in the transaction. Should you keep quiet, or quickly inform the purchasers that you represent the bank and advise the purchasers to obtain their own legal representation?

Attorneys cannot accept employment in those situations in which the attorney's own interest might impair his or her independent professional judgment. This means that an attorney cannot represent a client in which the attorney has a financial interest or represent two clients in the same transaction. The residential real estate attorney daily faces these conflicts of interest. In many transactions that involve residential real estate, the attorney represents the lender but is the only attorney involved in the transaction. The seller and purchaser often look to this attorney for advice and even believe that the attorney is representing their interests in the transaction. It is necessary for the attorney and the legal assistant to be aware of this potential conflict of interest. Law firms and bar associations have different ways of resolving the conflict. Some law firms resolve the conflict by informing the parties early in the transaction as to the firm's representation. For example, a firm that represents the lender would notify, at the beginning of the transaction, both the seller and the purchaser that the attorney is representing the lender's interest. The attorney would invite both the seller and the purchaser to seek their own counsel in connection with the transaction. This early disclosure can help to resolve the conflicts of interest problem.

SUMMARY

The real estate closing is the main fee-generating transaction for most real estate attorneys. A real estate closing is the real-life event that requires the practical use of all a real estate attorney's or real estate legal assistant's knowledge about title examinations, surveys, deeds, mortgages, and general real estate law. Although an accumulated knowledge of all areas of real estate law is required to accomplish a successful real estate closing, the closing process has its own identity with its own set of rules and procedures.

KEY TERMS

Closing   Loan closing   Mortgagee loss payable clause
Escrow   Loan commitment

REVIEW QUESTIONS

1. Explain some of the general differences between residential and commercial real estate closings.

2. What helpful information with respect to a real estate closing can a legal assistant obtain from reviewing the real estate contract?

3. What helpful information with respect to a real estate loan closing can a legal assistant obtain from reviewing the loan commitment?

4. What is the minimum documentation that a seller must furnish at a real estate closing?

5. What minimum documentation does the purchaser need to provide at the real estate closing?

6. What information does the surveyor need to prepare a survey?

7. What is the importance of hazard and fire insurance, and what is a mortgagee loss payable clause?

8. Why is it important for a legal assistant to prepare a checklist of documents and procedures to be followed in a real estate closing?

9. What special requirements are found in a construction loan commitment?

10. What is a prepayment fee or premium, and how is it different from a late charge?

PRACTICAL ASSIGNMENT

1. You are a legal assistant representing a firm responsible for the closing of a real property sale transaction. You have been provided with a copy of a contract for closing between Daniel B. Farris as purchaser and Acme, Inc., as seller, said contract being shown as Exhibit 15–6 at the end of this chapter. Review the contract carefully, and

prepare a closing checklist of all documents or other items that will be required from both purchaser and seller to close the sale.

2. You are a legal assistant involved in the closing of a mortgage loan. You have been provided with a copy of the

mortgage loan commitment shown as Exhibit 15–7 at the end of this chapter. Review the commitment carefully, and prepare a closing checklist of all documents and other items that will be required to close the mortgage loan.

ACKNOWLEDGMENTS

Portions of this chapter have been excerpted from *The Residential Real Estate Closing* by Daniel J. Falligant, *Real Estate Practices and Procedures Program Materials* (pp. 5a. 1-5a.11: Institute of Continuing Legal Education of Georgia, 1985, Athens, Georgia). Used by permission of the publisher.

Portions of this chapter have been excerpted from "A Practical Guide to Mortgage Loan Commitments" by George J. Walsh, III, *Real Estate Law Journal 8* (1980): pp. 195-229. Used by permission of Warren, Gorham & Lamont, Inc.

ADDENDUM

EXHIBIT 15–6
Sample Contract for
Closing Checklist

Real Estate Sales Contract

This Contract is entered into this _____ day of January, 19____ by and between DANIEL B. FARRIS, as ("Purchaser"), ACME, INC., a Delaware corporation (collectively "Seller") and BROKER & ASSOCIATES, as ("Broker").

FOR VALUABLE CONSIDERATION RECEIVED, the receipt and sufficiency of which are hereby acknowledged, the parties hereby agree as follows:

1. Purchaser agrees to buy and Seller agrees to sell subject to the terms and conditions of this contract as set forth herein ALL THAT TRACT OF PARCEL OF LAND with such improvements as are located thereon lying and being in Land Lot 1135, 2nd District, 2nd Section of _____ County, _____ and being more particularly described on Exhibit "A" attached hereto and made a part hereof (hereinafter referred to as the "Property").

2. **Purchase Price.** The purchase price for the Property shall be SIX HUNDRED FIFTY THOUSAND AND NO/100 DOLLARS ($650,000.00) which shall be paid as follows: (a) Purchaser shall pay to the Seller the sum of $150,000.00 in cash at closing; and (b) the balance of $500,000.00 shall be paid over a period of thirty (30) years with interest at the rate of ten percent (10%) per annum represented by a purchase money note and deed to secure debt encumbering the Property as security for payment thereof. The purchase money note shall bear interest at the rate of ten percent (10%) per annum and principal and interest shall be payable semi-annually over a period of thirty (30) years. The semi-annual payments shall begin six (6) months after closing, with each payment being applied first to interest on the unpaid principal and the balance to the principal. The note shall be an exculpated, nonrecourse note to Purchaser. The note shall contain a notice of default and fifteen (15) day right to cure default for monetary default and a notice of default and thirty (30) day right to cure for nonmonetary defaults. The note is to contain provisions that it can be prepaid at any time in whole or in part without penalty or premium. The note shall be in a form substantially similar to that note attached hereto as Exhibit "B".

The note shall be secured by a first lien purchase money deed to secure debt encumbering the Property in a form substantially similar to the form attached hereto as Exhibit

EXHIBIT 15-6
Sample Contract for
Closing Checklist
(continued)

"C". The purchase money deed to secure debt shall also contain provisions as follows: (a) if all or any part of the Property or any interest in it is sold or transferred without prior written consent of Grantee, Grantee may at it's option, require immediate payment in full of all sums secured by the purchase money deed to secure debt. Notwithstanding the above, the purchase money deed to secure debt shall provide that the Property may be transferred by Purchaser ("Grantor") to a corporation or partnership of which Purchaser is a shareholder or partner and there shall be no prohibition or restrictions on Purchaser's right to place junior deeds to secure debt on the Property to secure other debts. The Purchaser shall have the right to alter or improve the improvements located on the Property, including grading of the site on the Property without Seller's prior written consent, so long as such alteration, improvements or grading shall not in any way cause a decline in value to the Property as security for the note.

3. **Earnest Money.** Purchaser has paid to Broker & Associates, a licensed broker acting on behalf of the Seller, FIVE THOUSAND AND NO/100 DOLLARS ($5,000.00) in the form of a check, the receipt whereof is hereby acknowledged by Broker & Associates as earnest money ("Earnest Money"), which Earnest Money shall be applied as part payment of the purchase price of said Property at the time the sale is consummated or paid to Seller or returned to Purchaser as otherwise provided herein.

4. **Warranties of Title**. Seller warrants that Seller presently has title to said Property and at the time the sale is consummated, agrees to convey good and marketable title to said Property to Purchaser by a general warranty deed subject only to such title exceptions as Purchaser shall agree to.

5. **Title.** Purchaser shall move promptly and in good faith after acceptance of this Contract by Seller to examine the title to said Property and to furnish Seller with a written statement of objections affecting the marketablility of said title.

Seller shall have a reasonable time after receipt of said such objections to satisfy all valid objections specified by Purchaser and if Seller fails to satisfy such valid objections within a reasonable time, then Purchaser at Purchaser's option may cancel this Contract by giving Seller written notice of such cancellation and this Contract shall become null and void and Purchaser shall be entitled to a return of the Earnest Money. Marketability of title as used herein shall mean the quality of title which a title insurance company licensed to do business in the State of _____ and a member of the American Land Title Association would insure at its regular rate without exception.

6. **Hazardous Waste Indemnity.** Purchaser's obligation to purchase the Property pursuant to this Contract is contingent upon there being no petroleum hydro carbons or contaminants contained in the soil, surface or subterranean water which are in violation of local, state, or federal statutes and regulations and that there be no other existence of any hazardous substances or waste located upon the Property. For purposes of this Agreement, the term "hazardous substances or wastes" shall mean petroleum, including crude oil or any fraction thereof, flammable explosives, radioactive materials, asbestos, any material containing polychlorinated biphenyls, and any of the substances defined as "hazardous substances" or "toxic substances" in the Comprehensive Environmental Response, Compensation and Liability Act of 1980, as amended, 42 U.S.C. Section 9601 *et seq.*, Hazardous Materials Transportation Act, 49 U.S.C. Section 1802 *et seq.*, the Resource Conservation and Recovery Act, 42 U.S.C. Section 6901 *et seq.*, and in the Toxic Substance Control Act of 1976, as amended, 15 U.S.C. Section 2601 *et seq.*, or any other federal, state, local or other governmental legislation, statute, law, code, rule, regulation or ordinance identified by its terms as pertaining to the disposal, storage, generation or presence of hazardous substances or waste (the "Environmental Laws"). Purchaser shall at Seller's

EXHIBIT 15–6
Sample Contract for
Closing Checklist
(continued)

expense have the Property inspected for purposes of discovering if hazardous substances or wastes exist. If upon inspection, hazardous wastes or substances do exist, Purchaser shall have the option of terminating his contract and receiving a refund of his $5,000.00 earnest money down payment. In the alternative, Seller shall have the right at its own expense to remove all hazardous substance or waste from the Property and to conclude the sale with Purchaser.

Seller warrants, represents and agrees that (a) neither Seller nor any person has violated any of the applicable Environmental Laws as defined in the paragraph above relating to or affecting the Property; (b) the Property is presently in compliance with all Environmental Laws, and there are no facts or circumstances presently existing upon or under the Property or relating to the representations and warranties, which violate any of the applicable Environmental Laws, and there is not now pending nor threatened any action, suit, investigation or proceeding against Seller or the Property (or against any other party related to the Property); (c) Seller has obtained all licenses, permits or other governmental regulatory approvals necessary to comply with Environmental Laws and Seller is in full compliance with the terms and provisions of all such licenses, permits or other governmental regulatory approvals; and (d) Seller has received no notice that any municipality or any governmental or quasi-governmental authorities are investigating or has determined that there are any violations of zoning, health, building, fire, pollution, environmental, or other statutes, ordinances, regulations affecting the Property.

7. **Inspection.** Purchaser, its agents and representatives, at Purchaser's expense and at reasonable times during normal business hours, shall have the right to enter upon the Property for purpose of inspection, examining, testing, surveying the Property. Purchaser assumes all responsibility for acts of itself, its agents, representatives, in exercising its rights under this paragraph and agrees to hold Seller harmless for any damages resulting therefrom.

8. **Condition of Improvements.** Seller warrants until the sale is consummated, that the Improvements located on the Property will be in the same condition as they are on the date this Contract is signed by the Seller, natural wear and tear excepted. Should the Improvements located on the Property be destroyed or substantially damaged before the Contract is consummated, then at the election of the Purchaser, (a) the Contract may be cancelled and Earnest Money refunded to Purchaser or (b) Purchaser may consummate the Contract and receive all insurance proceeds paid or due on the claim of loss.

This election is to be exercised within ten (10) days after the Purchaser has been notified in writing by Seller of the amount of the insurance proceeds, if any, Seller shall receive on the claim of loss; if Purchaser has not been notified within forty five (45) days, subsequent to the occurance of such damage or destruction, Purchaser may at its option cancel this Contract and receive a refund of its Earnest Money.

9. **Possession.** Seller shall deliver title and possession of the Property to Purchaser at closing free and clear of the claims of any and all tenants and all leases existing on the Property shall be cancelled and terminated by Seller at Seller's expense prior to closing.

10. **Closing.** Closing shall be held at the offices of attorney of Purchaser,

_____

_____, or at such location as is agreeable to Purchaser and Seller, on a day selected by Purchaser not later than sixty (60) days from the date Seller can deliver title and possession of the Property free and clear of any and all leases or other rights of tenants in regard to the Property and a date not later than _____, 19___.
Purchaser shall give Seller notice of the closing date at least five days prior thereto; pro-

EXHIBIT 15–6
Sample Contract for
Closing Checklist
(continued)

vided, if Purchaser gives Seller no such notice of the closing date, then the closing date shall be _____, 19___.

11. **Execution of Documents.** Seller shall execute and deliver to Purchaser a general warranty deed in recordable form conveying the Property to Purchaser as provided herein and shall execute and deliver to Purchaser all necessary affidavits in order for Purchaser to obtain a title insurance policy without exception and an affidavit indicating Seller's non-foreign status within the meaning of Section 1445(f)(3) of the Internal Revenue Code of 1986 and any and all other documents which may be required by Purchaser to carry out the terms of this Contract.

12. **Closing Costs.** In connection with the closing, Seller shall pay the _____ real estate Transfer Tax and all costs for the satisfaction, cure and removal of all title exceptions undertaken by the Seller as herein required. Seller shall pay the Intangibles Tax on the purchase money note and deed to secure debt. All other closing costs incurred by Purchaser in connection with the sale shall be paid by Purchaser. Each party shall pay its own attorney's fees.

13. **Prorations.** At the closing all ad valorem property taxes, water and sewer charges and assessments of any kind on the Property for the year of the closing shall be prorated between Purchaser and Seller as of 12:01 a.m. on the closing date. Such proration shall be based upon the latest ad valorem property tax, water, sewer charge and assessment bills if available. If, upon receipt of the actual ad valorem property tax, water, sewer and assessment bills for the Property, such proration is incorrect, then either Purchaser or Seller shall be entitled, upon demand, to receive such amounts from the other as may be necessary to correct such malapportionment. This obligation to correct such malapportionment shall survive the closing and not be merged into any documents delivered pursuant to the closing.

14. **Brokerage Commissions.** Upon consummation of the closing of the sale contemplated herein, a sales commission shall be paid by the Seller to Broker & Associates, Inc., Broker, which commission has been negotiated between Broker and Seller. Purchaser shall have no obligation whatsoever to Broker & Associates, Inc. for any real estate commission. Seller further agrees to indemnify and hold harmless the Purchaser from and by any and all claims or demands with respect to any brokerage fees or agent's commissions or other compensation asserted against any person, firm, or corporation in connection with this Contract or sale or the transactions contemplated hereby arising from actions or alleged commitments of the Seller. This provision shall survive closing and the conveyance of the Property by Seller to Purchaser.

15. **Purchaser Default.** In the event the transaction contemplated hereby is not closed because of Purchaser's default, the Earnest Money shall be paid to Seller as full liquidated damages for such failure to close, the parties acknowledging the difficulty of ascertaining Seller's damages in such circumstances, whereupon neither party hereto shall have any further rights, claims, or liabilities under this Agreement except for the provisions which were made to survive the termination or cancellation of this Agreement. Said liquidated damages shall be Seller's sole and exclusive remedy and Seller shall expressly not have the right to seek specific performance or other damages.

16. **Sellers Default.** If Seller shall be unable to deliver title in accordance with this Agreement, Seller's liability shall be limited to the return of the Earnest Money paid here-

EXHIBIT 15–6
Sample Contract for
Closing Checklist
(continued)

under. In the event Seller fails to perform other covenants of this Agreement or if Seller otherwise defaults hereunder, the Purchaser shall have the right to, in addition to all rights and remedies herein provided, to pursue any right or remedy it may have against Seller at law or in equity for such breach and/or default, including without limitation, the right of specific performance of all provisions of this Agreement. Purchaser's monetary damages in the event of such breach and/or default shall be limited to $25,000.00. The parties hereby acknowledge the difficulty of ascertaining Purchaser's monetary damages in such event.

17. **Assignability.** Purchaser shall have the right to assign this Agreement to any corporation or partnership of which Purchaser if a shareholder or partner without notice to and without consent of Seller, and the transaction contemplated by this Agreement shall be consummated in the name of such assignee. Purchaser shall not have the right to assign the Contract to any other party except as mentioned above without the prior written consent of Seller.

18. **Notification.** Any notice or demand under which the terms of this Agreement or under any statute must or may be given or made by the parties hereto shall be made in writing and shall be deemed to have been delivered when hand delivered; as of the date sent by an over night courier; or as of the date of postmark affixed by the U.S. Postal Service, by mail of same by certified mail; return receipt requested, addressed to the respective parties at the following addresses:

TO PURCHASER:

TO SELLER:

TO BROKER:

19. **Time is of the Essence.** Time is of the essence of this Agreement and of each of it's provisions.

This instrument shall be regarded as an offer by the Purchaser or Seller who shall first sign this Contract to the other party and is open for acceptance by the other party until _____ : _____ __.m. on the _____ day of _____, 19___.

The above proposition is hereby accepted this _____ day of _____, 19___.

IN WITNESS WHEREOF, the undersigned parties hereinto set their hand and seal to this Contract.

PURCHASER:

_____(SEAL)

SELLER:

_____(SEAL)
_____(SEAL)

BROKER:

By: _____

EXHIBIT 15–7
Mortgage Loan
Commitment

RE: First Mortgage Loan—$1,600,000
          Mortgagor—Acme, Inc.

          Property—

          Rate—10.5%
               Term—23 years, callable by
               lender 7th, 12th, 17th, and
               22nd loan years

Dear Mr.

We are pleased to advise that our Investment Review Committee has approved the above captioned first mortgage loan. The loan will be in the amount of $1,600,000 at an interest rate of 10.5% per annum, and is to be amortized over a period of 23 years by equal monthly installments of $15,389.88, including interest. Lender receives the right to declare the entire amount of outstanding principal and all unpaid accrued interest thereon to be immediately due and payable on any one of the following dates: seven (7), twelve (12), seventeen (17), and twenty two (22) years from the first installment of principal and interest. Such right shall be exercised by Lender by giving written notice to Borrower at least six (6) months prior to date on which said payment of all principal and interest shall be due and payable.

This commitment is issued subject to the following conditions:

1. The loan is to be secured by a valid first lien on the fee simple title to the following described property, together with the improvements thereon, located in the city limits of _____. The property is located at _____. The site is irregular in shape with approximately 200 feet of frontage on _____, a 25 foot wide easement from the property to _____ roughly 580 feet of depth, and with a total land area of 3.11 acres. The site contains five (5) office buildings containing a total of approximately 54,500 gross square feet or 47,400 net square feet.

We are to be provided with a complete and accurate legal description subject to our approval prior to closing of this loan.

2. All loan documents, agreements or other instruments used in connection with this transaction shall first have the approval of our Legal Department and must be prepared by an attorney designated by our Legal Department.

3. All legal fees and other expenses in connection with the closing of this loan are to be paid by the mortgagor. It is further understood that the mortgagor will pay any expenses incident to this transaction should for any reason the loan not be closed after said expenses have been incurred.

4. Fire and extended coverage insurance policies are to be furnished in an amount at least equal to the amount of the loan and not less than the full insurable value of the improvements, issued by a company or companies satisfactory to us. Such policies are to be obtained and held by you. If the policy carries a co-insurance clause or other clause limiting the amount of coverage under certain conditions the insurance must be in such amount as to give full coverage under all conditions. All insurable buildings and personal property or easily removable real estate items or fixtures included in the security instrument must be covered by such insurance.

5. The loan documents shall contain the following items or provisions:

     a. No prepayment of the principal of this note shall be allowed prior to the third (3rd) anniversary of the date hereof. After the third (3rd) anniversary of the date hereof, the principal of this note may be prepaid in whole but not in part, on any interest payment

EXHIBIT 15-7
Mortgage Loan
Commitment
(continued)

date herein, provided that: (1) not later than sixty (60) days prior to such prepayment, Applicant delivers written notice to Holder, and that Applicant intends to prepay the note in full on the date specified in such notice; and (2) Applicant pays to holder at the time of such prepayment, a percentage of the prepaid principal amount as a prepayment premium. Such percentage shall be the product obtained by multiplying the prepaid principal amount by the product of the following:

(i) the amount obtained by subtracting the annualized yield on a United States Treasury Bill, Note or Bond with maturity date which occurs closest to the next call option date of this Note, as such annualized yield is reported by *The Wall Street Journal* on the business day preceding the date of prepayment, from 10.5% multiplied by:

(ii) the number of years and fraction thereof remaining between the date of prepayment and the next call option date of this note.

Notwithstanding the foregoing, however, in the event of acceleration of the Note at any time and subsequent involuntary or voluntary prepayment, the Prepayment Premium shall be payable, however in no event shall it exceed an amount equal to the excess, if any, of (i) interest calculated at the highest applicable rate permitted by applicable law, as construed by courts having jurisdiction thereof, on the principal balance of the Note from time to time outstanding from the date hereof to the date of such acceleration, over (ii) interest theretofore paid and accrued on the Note. Any prepaid amounts specified in such notice shall become due and payable at the time provided in such notice. A "Loan Year" for the purposes of this Note shall mean each successive twelve (12) month period beginning with the date of the first installment payment of interest hereunder provided, however, that the first Loan Year shall include the period from the date of this Note to the date of such first installment payment of interest. Under no circumstances shall the prepayment premium ever be less than zero. The amount of prepayment shall never be less that the full amount of the then outstanding principal and interest.

In addition to the above described prepayment penalty, a reinvestment fee of $1/_2$ of 1% of the outstanding loan balance will be due in the event of prepayment prior to the maturity of this loan.

b. An assignment of rents in a form satisfactory to our Legal Department.

c. The holder may collect a "late charge" not to exceed an amount equal to four percent (4%) of any installment which is not paid within fifteen (15) days of the due date thereof, to cover the extra expense involved in handling delinquent payments, provided that collection of said late charge shall not be deemed a waiver by the holder of any of its other rights under this note.

d. The Lender is to be furnished with a certified, itemized statement of annual income and expenses on the property covered by this loan within 90 days following the end of each fiscal or calender year.

e. The usual covenant requiring monthly escrow deposits for annual payment of ad valorem taxes and hazard insurance premiums.

f. It shall be a default under the mortgage if, without the Lender's prior written consent, the real property security for this loan or any part thereof is sold, transferred, conveyed or encumbered in any way. Notwithstanding the above, Lender, hereby agrees to allow the transfer of ownership and assumption of this loan by a qualified borrower of equal or greater financial strength, credit standing and management expertise. As consideration for this transfer and assumption, the Lender will receive a non-refundable

EXHIBIT 15–7
Mortgage Loan
Commitment
(continued)

one percent (1%) fee based on the then outstanding balance, payable at the time of transfer.

g. Installments shall be due and payable on the first day of each month.

h. The Promissory Note taken in this transaction will include a provision which reads "Subject to the terms of the next succeeding paragraph and notwithstanding anything to the contrary otherwise contained in this Note, it is agreed that the promise of Maker to pay the principal indebtedness and the interest on this Note shall be for the sole purpose of establishing the existence of an indebtedness; Holder's source of satisfaction of said indebtedness and of Grantors' other obligations hereunder and under the Loan Documents is limited solely to (a) the property described in the Mortgage, (b) Holder's receipt of the rents, issues and profits from the property described in the Mortgage and (c) any separate agreements guaranteeing the payment of the amounts due hereunder and under the Loan Documents and Makers' performance hereunder and under the Loan Documents; Holder shall not seek to procure payment out of any other assets of Maker, or to procure any judgment against Maker for any amount which is or may be payable under this Note, the Mortgage or any of the other Loan Documents or for any deficiency remaining after foreclosure of the Mortgage; provided, however, that nothing herein contained shall be deemed to be a release or impairment of said indebtedness or the security therefor intended by the Mortgage, or be deemed to preclude Holder from foreclosing the Mortgage or from enforcing any of Holder's rights thereunder, or in any way or manner affecting Holder's rights and privileges under any of the Loan Documents or any separate agreements guaranteeing Maker's payment and performance hereunder and under the Loan Documents.

Notwithstanding the foregoing the limitation of liability provision, it is expressly understood and agreed that Maker shall be personally liable for the payment to the Holder of:

(a) all security deposits of tenants, any rents that are collected more than one (1) month in advance, and all income, rents, issues, profits and revenues derived from the property described in the Mortgage which are not promptly applied to payment of the indebtedness evidenced by the Note and/or to the costs of normal maintenance and operation of such property;

(b) any loss due to fraud or misrepresentations to Holder by Maker (or by any of its general partners, by any of the general partners of any of its general partners or by any of its or their agents, if applicable);

(c) the misapplication of (i) proceeds paid under any insurance policies by reason of damage, loss or destruction to any portion of the property described in the Mortgage to the full extent of such misapplied proceeds, or (ii) proceeds of awards resulting from the condemnation or other taking in lieu of condemnation of any portion of such property, to the full extent of such misapplied proceeds or awards;

(d) any loss due to waste of the property described in the Mortgage or any portion thereof, and all costs, including reasonable attorneys' fees, incurred by Holder to protect such property and any other security for the indebtedness evidenced by this Note or to enforce such Note, the Mortgage and any of the other Loan Documents; and

(e) any taxes, assessments and insurance premiums for which Maker is liable under this Note, the Mortgage or any of the other Loan Documents and which are paid by Holder; and

(f) arising under the hazardous substance indemnification and hold harmless agreement and the borrower's hazardous substances covenant's warranties and representations provisions contained in the Loan Documents.

EXHIBIT 15–7
Mortgage Loan
Commitment
(continued)

6. Prior to closing, the Borrower must furnish to the Lender, at the Borrower's sole cost and expense, the original of an environmental audit and certification addressed to Lender and Lender's successors and assigns, with form acceptable to Lender, and prepared by a licensed engineer and geotechnical consultant ('Engineer') or either including field reconnaissance, site history records survey, tenant use history record survey, and an examination of the Compensation and Liability Systems Record in the State in which the Property is located, to establish that a thorough investigation of those records and an inspection of the Property site and improvements reveal no evidence of any pollutant or other toxic or hazardous substance, as defined under the Comprehensive Environmental Response, Compensation, and Liability Act ("CERCLA"), 42 U.S.C. 9601 *et seq.*, as amended, or any other federal, state or local law ("Hazardous Substance"). In the event the Engineer determines in his or her professional judgment that an examination of the subsurface soils is necessary, then the parties contemplate that Borrower will require that the Engineer provide the Borrower with an estimate of the additional charges which will be incurred in such examination. In the event that Borrower provides Lender with written notice, received by Lender within five (5) days of the Borrower's receipt of the estimate, that Borrower has determined that the additional charges are not acceptable, then Borrower may simultaneously provide Lender with Borrower's written election to cancel this Commitment Letter in which event the commitment fee will be refunded to Borrower and neither Borrower nor Lender will thereafter have any liability to the other under this Commitment Letter. In the event that Borrower either: (i) fails to provide Lender with receipt of written notice within the said five (5) days of receiving said estimate, or, (ii) determines that the additional charges are acceptable, then the Borrower will be deemed to have elected to close without regard to such additional charges and said audit and certificate must be provided to Lender by Borrower and must include a subsurface soils examination or any other examination deemed necessary, and the cost thereof will be paid by Borrower. In any event, the charges for the environmental audit and certification will be paid in full by Borrower.

With respect to any Hazardous Substance found on the Property, the environmental audit must indicate the nature of the substance, the statutory control over the removal process, the time and costs of removal, and the assessment of risk.

The loan documents will contain the Borrower's covenants, representations, warranties and indemnities, in the identical form of the wording attached hereto as Exhibit "A's".

The Borrower must, at the Borrower's sole cost and expense, obtain and provide to Lender at or before closing the original of a letter addressed to Lender from the Regional Office of the Environmental Protection Agency establishing whether the Property or property in the vicinity of the Property has been the location of a hazardous waste site.

In the event that the environmental audit or the letter from the Environmental Protection Agency reveals that the Property has or has had any Hazardous Substance located on or in the Property or the improvements located on the Property, or any other condition which Lender determines to be objectionable, then Lender, may at its option elect not to close this loan. If Lender, after reviewing any item required of Borrower under this provision, determines not to close this loan, then this Commitment Letter will be canceled and the commitment fee will be refunded to Borrower and neither Borrower nor Lender will thereafter have any liability to the other under this Commitment Letter.

7. We are to be furnished with an engineer's survey, certified to by a registered surveyor, dated within 90 days prior to closing, showing no encroachments other than those approved by us and showing the improvements to be within lot and building lines.

EXHIBIT 15-7
Mortgage Loan
Commitment
(continued)

8. We are to be furnished with a mortgagee title insurance policy issued by a company approved by us, or an endorsement to a previously issued title policy, which will insure that the Lender has a first lien without exceptions, other than those specifically approved by us.

9. Any outstanding unpaid taxes and assessments are to be paid prior to our disbursement of the loan proceeds.

10. The financing statement covering the fixtures and equipment will be properly executed and recorded, and the properly executed security agreement delivered to us.

11. We will require that all the lessees be advised in writing of the existence of the assignment of said leases. We specifically agree, however, not to exercise any such assignments until such time as a default exists in the terms of the mortgage.

12. We will require an Estoppel and Subordination Letter from each tenant. The form of these letters must be approved by our Legal Department.

13. We will require loss of rent insurance in an amount not less than nine (9) months gross rental.

14. In order to comply with IRS Regulation TD 8047, we are to be furnished with the social security number, in the case of an individual mortgagor, or the tax identification number for all other mortgagors. We must be provided with this number prior to the closing of this loan.

15. We are to be furnished a current written opinion of counsel for the Borrower, satisfactory to Lender, to the effect that the subject loan is not usurious or otherwise illegal under applicable law and that all loan documents are valid and binding upon Borrower and are enforceable in accordance with their terms.

16. The property site is to be inspected and approved by a duly authorized agent of Lender.

17. Lender requires that the site and improvements be inspected by an engineer or other qualified party to determine if there is deferred maintenance on the property and to determine the cost to cure the identified deferred maintenance. The inspecting party(s) must be approved by the lender. The Borrower is responsible for the cost of this inspection and is to pay the bills directly.

18. If the inspection report identified in item #17 above identifies deferred maintenance, then lender will require an escrow account be established for the amount identified. The borrower will have six (6) months to complete all identified items and if all work is not done at that point then lender will apply the escrowed funds to the loan balance without penalty and in reverse order to payments owing. If all identified work is completed within six (6) months, then the borrower may obtain all the escrowed funds at the point of completing the work. Borrower must provide the lender with sufficient information to prove that bills in conjunction with this work are paid and that no liens have been filed against the property, prior to receiving the escrowed funds.

19. We have tentatively scheduled this loan for closing sometime during the month of August, 199__, and this commitment shall expire August 31, 19____.

20. Lender will retain and has earned a loan processing fee of $4,000 or $1/_4$% of the loan amount. Lender acknowledges receipt of $4,250 for the loan processing fee. Lender will apply the balance ($250) to the below referenced refundable commitment fee.

21. Provided this commitment is acceptable, you are to forward your check, within ten (10) business days from the date hereof, in the amount of $46,750. This amount plus $17,250 previously received from you will be held by us in a non-interest bearing account as a commitment fee. If and when this loan is closed under the terms and conditions of this commitment letter, the above $64,000 commitment fee will be refunded. However, if

EXHIBIT 15–7
Mortgage Loan
Commitment
(continued)

this loan is not closed, it is agreed and understood that upon expiration or cancellation of this commitment this fee will be retained by Lender as consideration for this commitment. If Borrower should elect to do so, Lender will accept $32,000 of the above fee in the form of a Letter of Credit. The unconditional irrevocable Letter of Credit must be drawn on an institution and be in a form acceptable to Lender, with an expiration date no earlier than October 31, 199___.

22. Lender reserves the right to cancel this commitment and terminate its obligations hereunder at any time upon the happening of any of the following events:

a. Borrower's failure to comply with any of the applicable conditions of this commitment within the time specified.

b. Non-payment of any of the fees or expenses to be paid by the Borrower in connection with this commitment.

c. Any infirmity in Borrower's title to the real estate, filed by or against Borrower any petition in bankruptcy or insolvency or for the reorganization of Borrower or appointment of a receiver or trustee or the making of an assignment for the benefit of creditors.

This agreement is made for the sole protection of the Borrower and the Lender, its successors and assigns and no other person or persons shall have any right of action thereon, and this commitment is not assignable or transferable by Borrower. Lender reserves the absolute right to partially or totally assign this commitment to a third party lending institution for the purpose of facilitating a participation loan. By acceptance of this commitment letter, Borrower acknowledges and agrees that this loan may be a loan in which an additional lender may act as a participating lender at the time of funding.

We appreciate your offering us the opportunity to make this loan and trust that it will be handled to your entire satisfaction.

Sincerely,

Government Regulation of Real Estate Closings

*Society in every state is a blessing, but Government, even in its best state, is but a necessary evil;
in its worst state, an intolerable one.*

—*Thomas Paine,* Common Sense

OBJECTIVES

After reading this chapter you will be able to:

- Understand the purposes of the Real Estate Settlement Procedures Act, the Truth-in-Lending Act, and the Adjustable Rate Mortgage Disclosure Requirements
- Identify real estate loans that require a right of rescission
- Prepare right of rescission notice forms
- Prepare adjustable rate disclosure forms

GLOSSARY

Consumer   Term used in the Truth-in-Lending Act to mean a natural person to whom a loan for personal, family, or household purposes is offered.

Consumer credit   Term used in the Truth-in-Lending Act to mean a loan offered or extended primarily for personal, family, or household purposes.

Consummation   Term used in the Truth-in-Lending Act to mean the time a consumer becomes contractually obligated under state law to make payments under a loan.

Finance charge   Term used in the Truth-in-Lending Act to mean any charge or fee payable directly or indirectly by the consumer to obtain a consumer loan.

HUD–1   Uniform settlement statement required by the Real Estate Settlement Procedures Act for all real estate transactions that involve a federally related mortgage loan.

Kickback   Payment of money or something of value to a person for the purpose of obtaining business from that person.

Rescission   Act of repealing or voiding something or some action.

RESPA   Real Estate Settlement Procedures Act, a federal law designed to reform the real estate settlement process and to ensure that consumers receive more information about real estate settlement costs.

Settlement costs   All costs involved in the settlement or closing of a real estate transaction. Such items include but are not limited to attorney's fees, surveyor's fees, title insurance premiums, recording fees, and appraisal fees.

Truth–in–Lending Act   Federal law designed to provide consumers with information for an informed use of credit. The Truth-in-Lending Act requires creditors to disclose to consumers the true costs of a consumer loan.

Real property closings have become increasingly controlled by federal regulation. Most federal regulations focus on lenders, and many have a direct impact on the real property closing. Regulatory bodies such as the Federal Reserve Bank, the Federal Home Loan Bank Board, the Office of the Controller of the Currency, the Federal Deposit Insurance Corporation, the Federal Savings and Loan Insurance Corporation, and Housing and Urban Development (HUD) have promulgated and enforced such regulations as Truth-in-Lending Act, Real Estate Settlement Procedures Act, Regulation B Equal Credit Opportunity Act, National Flood Insurance Act, Fair Credit Reporting Act, Fair Debt Collection Practices Act, Fair Housing Act, Community Reinvestment Act, Home Mortgage Disclosure Act, and Right to Financial Privacy Act. All these regulations affect how real estate closings take place.

The area has become so inundated with regulations that real estate attorneys and real estate legal assistants must work hard to keep abreast of the changes. This discussion does not provide an in-depth review of all the regulations. Rather, it is a cursory overview of three regulations that must be complied with when lenders make residential real estate loans.

New York:
The government regulations referred to in Chapter 16 are the same throughout the country, but each state and each locality has its own customs.

REAL ESTATE SETTLEMENT PROCEDURES ACT

RESPA, passed in 1974, was designed to reform the real estate closing or settlement process to ensure that consumers receive more information about the settlement and to protect consumers from unnecessarily high settlement costs. RESPA requires advance disclosure of **settlement costs**, eliminates kickbacks and referral fees, and mandates the maximum amount that may be required to be placed in escrow accounts for payment of recurring charges or assessments that affect the lender's real property security.

Transactions Subject to RESPA

A real estate transaction that involves a federally related mortgage loan secured by a first lien on residential real property (defined as real property improved with a one- to four-family dwelling) is subject to RESPA. The term "federally related mortgage loan" is broadly defined. It includes loans that are
(a) made by a lender regulated by a federal agency or whose deposits are insured by a federal agency (such as a federal bank with deposits insured by the Federal Deposit Insurance Corporation, or a federal savings and loan association with deposits insured by the Federal Savings and Loan Insurance Corporation);
(b) made, insured, guaranteed, supplemented, or assisted by a federal agency. Loans that would fall within this category are loans guaranteed by the Veterans Administration or by the Federal Housing Administration;
(c) intended to be sold to the Federal National Mortgage Association, Government National Mortgage Association, or Federal Home Loan Mortgage Corporation; or
(d) made by a creditor who makes or invests more than $1 million per year in residential real estate loans.

New York:
Each party will receive a copy of the Uniform Settlement Statement by HUD, but it will not make as much sense as the closing statement each attorney prepares for their client. The closing statement will include what transpired at closing, who was there, and a financial summary of the transaction.

Exemptions from RESPA

The following are federally regulated mortgage loans that are exempted from RESPA coverage:

- A loan to finance the purchase or transfer of twenty-five or more acres
- Home improvement loan, refinance loan, or other loan that does not involve a legal transfer of title
- Vacant lot loan in which no proceeds are used for construction of a one- to four-family structure
- Assumption transactions, except the conversion of a construction loan to a permanent loan to finance the purchase of a home by a first user
- Construction loans, except when the construction loan is used or converted to a permanent loan to finance the purchase by a first user

Required Disclosures and Prohibitions of RESPA

RESPA provides for the following disclosures and prohibitions.

Special Information Booklet

A special information booklet written by HUD is to be distributed by lenders to each loan applicant within three business days after the application for credit. The booklet explains to consumers the costs related to real estate settlements.

Good Faith Estimates

Lenders are required to give the loan applicant an estimate of the amounts and types of costs the applicant can expect to incur to consummate the loan and close the purchase. The estimated costs must bear a reasonable relation to the actual charges. Also, the applicant must be informed that additional costs may be charged. The estimate must be given to the applicant within three business days after the application for credit.

Uniform Settlement Statement

RESPA requires the use of a uniform settlement statement (**HUD–1**) for all transactions that involve a federally related mortgage loan (see Exhibit 16-1 at the end of this chapter). All charges imposed on borrowers and sellers must be conspicuously and clearly itemized. HUD has prescribed regulations that contain line-by-line instructions for the correct completion of the forms.

One-Day Advance Inspection

On request of the borrower, the settlement agent (attorney) shall permit the borrower to inspect those settlement cost items known to the settlement agent during the business day immediately preceding the closing date. The settlement agent must provide the settlement form in as complete a condition as possible.

Escrow Limitation

RESPA permits a lender to establish an advance deposit escrow account to ensure the payment of recurring charges or assessments that affect the lender's security. Typical escrow items include various taxes, insurance, and assessments. The lender may escrow an amount sufficient for the lender to pay the charges as they become due, plus a cushion of one-sixth (two months) the estimated annual total charges. The lender is permitted to collect one-twelfth the estimated annual total charges for escrow items with each monthly mortgage installment. For example, a mortgage loan closes on April 15 and the current year's tax bills are due on October 1. The first payment under which the lender will receive one-twelfth of the tax amount will be made on June 1. At closing, the lender then can collect ten months of the current year's tax bill. How is this calculated? By indicating that twelve months are due on October 1, the lender will receive one-twelfth on June 1, one-twelfth on July 1, one-twelfth on August 1, and one-twelfth September 1, or four-twelfths in total. The lender needs twelve-twelfths on October 1, so the lender will be eight months short. Because RESPA permits a lender to accumulate two additional months, the lender can collect ten months' tax escrow at closing (see Example 16-1).

EXAMPLE 16–1

Loan Closes: April 15
Taxes Due: October 1
First Payment
Due on Loan: June 1
Tax Bill: $1,200
$1,200 amount of tax bill divided by 12 = $100/mo. escrow
$100 paid June 1, July 1, August 1, September 1 ($400 total)
$1,200 due October 1 minus $400 = $800 needed
$800 + $200 (two months' additional escrow permitted under RESPA) $1,000 collected at closing

---

Title Insurance

A seller, as a condition of sale, shall not require title insurance from any particular company. A violation of this regulation results in a seller's being liable for three times the title insurance charge paid by the purchaser.

Kickbacks

RESPA provides that no person shall give and no person shall accept any fee, **kickback**, or thing of value pursuant to any agreement or understanding, oral or otherwise, that involves the referral of business incident to or part of a real estate settlement involving a federally related loan. For example, (a) a lender cannot pay a real estate broker or another originating party a kickback to obtain business; (b) a real estate broker cannot pay a lender a kickback to obtain a loan for the client; (c) a title company cannot pay an attorney, an abstractor, a real estate broker, or a lender a kickback to obtain business; (d) an attorney cannot pay a kickback to a lender, a real estate broker, a title company, an abstractor, or others to obtain business; and (e) an insurance agent, surveyor, or termite inspector cannot pay a kickback to any party to obtain business.

Unearned Fees

RESPA provides that no person shall give and no person shall accept any portion, split, or percentage of any charge made or received for the rendering of a real estate settlement service in connection with a transaction that involves a federally related mortgage loan other than for services actually performed. A split payment for services actually performed is permitted by RESPA.

Penalties

The civil and criminal penalties for violation of RESPA are severe. The violator may be fined $10,000 and could be sentenced to one year imprisonment. In addition, violators are liable for civil penalties in an amount equal to three times the amount of the fees wrongfully charged plus court costs and reasonable attorneys' fees.

A legal assistant's main exposure to RESPA is in the preparation of the uniform settlement statement at the time of closing. Instructions for completing the uniform settlement statement appear in Chapter 17.

TRUTH-IN-LENDING ACT

The **Truth-in-Lending Act** was passed by the U.S. Congress on July 1, 1969. It was aimed at economically stabilizing and strengthening the competition among financial institutions by providing a means for the informed use of credit. The purpose of the act also was to protect consumers against inaccurate and unfair billing practices and to facilitate the informed use of credit by requiring the disclosure of credit terms in such a manner that consumers could readily compare the various terms available from different lenders.

The Truth-in-Lending Act was substantially simplified and shortened in 1981 and continues to undergo periodic amendments.

Disclosures for Closed-End Real Property Transactions

Who Must Make Disclosures?

The regulation requires that a creditor must make the disclosures. For purposes of closed-end credit (the lender makes a one-time advance), the regulations define "creditor" as a person to whom an obligation is payable and who regularly extends consumer credit that is subject to a **finance charge** or is payable by written agreement in more than four installments. For purposes of transactions secured by a home, a person "regularly extends consumer credit" only if credit has been extended more than four times in the preceding or current calendar year. **Consumer credit** is credit offered or extended primarily for personal, family, or household purposes.

Who Must Receive the Disclosure?

The disclosure must be made to the consumer or borrower. The regulations define **consumer** as a natural person to whom consumer credit is offered.

When Must Disclosures Be Made?

In residential mortgage transactions subject to RESPA, the creditor must make a good faith estimate of the disclosure no later than three business days after receiving the consumer's written application for credit. For real estate transactions not subject to RESPA, the disclosures must be made before the consummation of the transaction. The creditor should redisclose before consummation if early disclosures become inaccurate. **Consummation** is narrowly defined by the regulations to mean the time when a consumer becomes contractually obligated under state law to make payments under a credit transaction. In most real estate loan transactions, this would be at the time the promissory note is signed by the consumer or borrower.

What Format Must Be Used for Disclosure?

The disclosures must be made clearly and conspicuously in writing and in a form that the consumer may keep. The disclosures must be segregated from all nondisclosure information. To comply with this requirement, the disclosure should be made on a separate sheet of paper or must be circumscribed from other information with a bold print dividing line. The Federal Reserve Board has provided a series of standard disclosure forms to be used by lenders to comply with the regulations. A copy of a disclosure form is shown in Exhibit 16–2 at the end of this chapter.

What Must Be Disclosed?

Disclosure must be based on the terms of the legal obligation between the borrower and the lender. The note and mortgage establish the legal obligation. Disclosures that are not relevant to the transaction may be omitted.

The law allows the following items to be disclosed at the option of the lender: the date of the transaction, the consumer's name and address, the consumer's account number, and an acknowledgment of receipt of the disclosure.

The following disclosures *must* be made.

Creditor.   The creditor must be identified by name. The creditor's address and telephone number must be included.

Amount Financed.   The amount financed is the amount of credit provided to the customer. The amount financed usually is the loan amount less the prepaid finance charges. Prepaid finance charges are discussed below.

Finance Charge.   Finance charge is the cost of credit as a dollar amount. Subject to certain exceptions, the finance charge includes any charge or fee payable directly or indirectly by the consumer and imposed directly or indirectly by the creditor as an incident to or condition of an extension of credit. The finance charge must be disclosed more conspicuously than other disclosure items. The finance charge on most residential real estate loans is the total of all monthly payments made under the loan together with any loan discount or loan origination fees charged by the lender to make the loan.

Annual Percentage Rate

The annual percentage rate is the cost of credit as a yearly rate. A calculation of the annual percentage rate is a technical computation. Most law firms use calculators that have special programs designed to compute the annual percentage rate. The tolerance for inaccurate disclosure is one-eighth of one percentage point above or below the correct annual percentage rate.

Prepaid Finance Charge

The following items are prepaid finance charges that must be subtracted from the loan amount to arrive at the *amount financed* and added to the total payments made under the loan to arrive at the *finance charge*: (a) interest on the loan, (b) loan discount points, (c) service or carrying charges, (d) loan fees, (e) appraiser's fees or credit reporting costs, and (f) the cost of guaranty of insurance to protect the creditor against consumer defaults, such as credit life insurance or private mortgage insurance.

Variable Rate Disclosure

When the annual percentage rate may increase after consummation of the transaction, such as would happen under an interest rate that varies according to some index such as three-year treasury bills, the creditor must disclose the circumstances under which the rate may increase, any limitation on the increase, the effect of an increase, and an example of the payment terms that would result from an increase. No variable rate disclosure needs to be made if the payment schedule is known and fixed before consummation.

Payment Schedule

The creditor must disclose the number, amount, and timing of the payment schedule to repay the obligation. The payment schedule should include not only the repayment of principal but also all elements of any finance charges imposed.

Total of Payments

The total of payments is the total amount the consumer will have paid if all scheduled payments are made.

Demand Feature

If the obligation has a demand feature—that is, it becomes due before its normal amortization—such demand feature must be disclosed.

Prepayment Provisions

The creditor is required to disclose whether or not a penalty will be assessed against a consumer if the obligation is prepaid in full before its normal maturity. Also, the creditor must state whether the consumer will be entitled to a refund of part of a precomputed finance charge in the event of early prepayment.

Late Payment Charges

The creditor must disclose any charges that may be imposed for individual late payments before the maturity of the loan.

Security Interest

The creditor must describe any security interest taken as part of the transaction. If the security interest is in property being purchased with the proceeds of the transaction, disclosure need only provide a general identification. If the security interest is taken in property in a nonpurchase money transaction, the property in which the security interest is taken must be identified by item or type.

Insurance Charges

If the contractual relationship between the creditor and the borrower requires property insurance coverage, that fact must be disclosed. Also, a written disclosure is required of credit-related insurance, such as credit life or credit disability insurance, to exempt the cost of such insurance from the calculation of the finance charge.

Exempt Transactions from Truth-in-Lending

Truth-in-lending applies only to consumer transactions. If the loan or extension of credit is made to an entity other than a natural person, such as a corporation, a partnership, or a joint venture, truth-in-lending does not apply. If the purpose of the loan is for business, commercial, or agricultural purposes, truth-in-lending does not apply. The primary purpose of a transaction must be ascertained by reviewing the transaction as a whole.

Right of Rescission

In addition to the disclosure of credit terms, truth-in-lending provides the consumer homeowner with a right of **rescission**. The right of rescission gives the consumer, whose principal dwelling may be encumbered to secure a real estate loan, a three-business-day cooling-off period to think over the transaction and to cancel it for any reason without penalty. *Loans created or retained to finance the acquisition or initial construction of a dwelling are exempt from the rescission rights.*

New York:
A bank can not release mortgage funds until after the three day "right to rescind" has expired. Refinances and home equity loans are covered under this.

Who Has the Right to Rescind?

Any natural person with an ownership interest in a dwelling who uses it as a principal residence has the right to rescind if that ownership is or may be encumbered in connection with the real estate loan transaction. Any person who has the right to rescind may rescind a transaction on behalf of others with the right with or without the consent of the other parties. For example, a husband and wife own a home; either the husband or the wife may rescind the transaction without the other's permission.

Notice of the Right to Rescind

The creditor must give two copies of the notice of the right to rescind to each consumer who is entitled to rescind the transaction. The notice must be on a separate document that identifies the transaction. The transaction may be identified by simply giving its date. The notice also must disclose the following information: (a) the retention or acquisition of a security interest in the consumer's principal dwelling, (b) the consumer's right to rescind, (c) how the right of rescission may be exercised, (d) the effects of rescission, and (e) the date at midnight when the three-business-day rescission period expires.

The Federal Reserve Board provides sample notices of the right to rescind for use in transactions (see Exhibit 16–3 at the end of this chapter). It also is a good practice to obtain an affidavit from the consumers indicating that they have not rescinded at the expiration of the three-day period (see Exhibit 16–4 at the end of this chapter).

How a Consumer Rescinds

A consumer may rescind a transaction by notifying the creditor in writing during the rescission period. The rescission is effective on mailing of the notice, not on receipt.

Effect of Rescission

If the rescission is effective, the security interest giving rise to the right of rescission becomes void as of the time of rescission. The creditor has twenty days to terminate the security interest and return any money or property that has been given to any person in connection with the transaction.

Waiver of the Right to Rescind

The consumer may waive the right to rescind to permit performance during the rescission period. The consumer must inform the creditor in writing that the extension of credit is needed to meet a bona fide personal financial emergency period. This waiver, which cannot be on a preprinted form, must describe the emergency and must be signed and dated by all consumers who have a right to rescind.

The Federal Reserve Board has asserted that it believes that the waiver of the right to rescind should not be a routine matter. Creditors are not insulated from liability for failing to provide a rescission right because they rely on a borrower's waiver. Creditors must make a reasonable investigation to make sure that the waiver is bona fide.

Disbursement of Money Before Expiration of Rescission Period

A creditor's obligation does not end with the providing of the notice of the right to rescind. A creditor must be reasonably satisfied that any consumer with the right to rescind has not rescinded before any money or property is delivered or any services are performed under the transaction. A creditor will not disburse the loan proceeds until the rescission period has expired and the statement of nonrescission (see Exhibit 16–4) has been received.

ADJUSTABLE INTEREST RATE DISCLOSURES

The past ten years ushered in an unprecedented era of interest rate volatility. Real estate lenders have seen the costs of funds fluctuate wildly over a short period of time. The same lenders, however, have made long-term real estate loans based on a fixed rate of interest. This imbalance between the cost of funds and the return on real estate investments is partially responsible for the savings and loan crisis that began in the early 1980s. Mortgage lenders quickly learned to match investment return with cost of funds by making adjustable-rate mortgage (ARM) loans. The rate of interest would adjust to an index, such as treasury bills or prime rate, that was closely tied to the lender's cost of funds. A long-term mortgage loan, however, with an adjustable interest rate can create problems for the borrower. During periods of increasing interest rates, a borrower can experience serious increases in the mortgage payment. The U.S. Congress, believing that a borrower should be made aware of the risks and problems inherent in an adjustable interest rate loan, enacted laws that require mortgage lenders to disclose the terms of an adjustable interest rate loan.

Types of Loans Covered by ARM Disclosure Requirements

The new disclosure requirements apply to ARMs that are secured by the consumer's principal one- to four-family residence and that have a term of more than one year. The loan must be extended primarily for personal, family, or household purposes.

When Must ARM Disclosures Be Made?

ARM disclosures are required at the time an application form is provided to a consumer or before the consumer pays a nonrefundable fee for the loan, whichever is earlier.

Content of the Disclosure

A consumer or borrower entering into an ARM loan is entitled to a copy of the *Consumer Handbook on Adjustable Rate Mortgages*, which is issued by the Federal Reserve Board. The borrower also is entitled to receive the following information: (a) the fact that the interest rate, payment, or term of the loan may change; (b) the index or formula used in making adjustments and a source of information about the index or formula; (c) an explanation of how the interest rate and payment will be determined, including an explanation of how the index is adjusted; (d) a statement that the consumer should ask about the current margin value or current interest rate; (e) if applicable, the fact that the interest rate will be discounted and a statement that the consumer should ask about the amount of the interest rate discount; (f) the frequency of interest rate and payment changes; (g) any rules relating to changes in the index, interest rate, payment amount, and outstanding loan balance, including, for example, an explanation of interest rate or payment limitations, any negative amortization, or interest rate carryover permitted; (h) an historical example based on a $10,000 loan amount that illustrates how payments and the loan balances would have been affected by interest rate changes implemented according to the terms of the loan program, based on index values beginning in 1977 and updated annually to reflect the most recent fifteen years of index values, including all significant loan program terms that would have been affected by the index movement during the period; (i) an explanation of how the consumer may calculate the payments for the loan amount based on the most recent payments shown on the historical example; (j) the maximum interest rate and payment for a $10,000 loan originated at the most recent interest rate shown on the historical sample and assuming the maximum periodic increases in rates and payments under the program, including the initial interest rate and payment for that loan; (k) the fact that the loan program contains a demand feature, if it does; and (l) the type of information that will be provided and notices of adjustments and the timing of such notices.

Exhibits 16–5 and 16–6, located at the end of this chapter, are examples of ARM loan program disclosures.

Subsequent Disclosures

The lender periodically must send to the consumer an adjustment notice. An adjustment notice must be sent at least once each year during which an interest rate adjustment is made without an accompanying payment change. If any payment change accompanies the interest rate adjustment, the lender must send an adjustment notice at least 25 calendar days but not more than 120 calender days before a payment at the new level is due. An adjustment notice must contain the following information: (a) the current and prior interest rates; (b) the index values on which the current and prior interest rates are based; (c) the extent to which the creditor has forgone any increase in the interest rate; (d) the contractual effects of the adjustment, including the payment due after the adjustment is made and the statement of the loan balance; and (e) if the payment is different from that referred to in subsection (d), the monthly amount required to fully amortize the loan at the new interest over the remainder of the loan term.

Exhibit 16–7, located at the end of this chapter, is an example of a subsequent ARM Disclosure.

Index Requirements

The ARM disclosure law also regulates the type of index that can be used for the adjustment in the interest rate. The requirements provide that the loan documents must specify an index to which the changes in the interest rate will be linked. The index must be readily available to and verifiable by the consumer and must be beyond the control of the lender. For example, a bank could not use its own prime lending rate as an index. A bank would have to use another bank's prime lending rate or the rate on treasury bills.

Interest Rate Cap

The Competitive Equality Banking Act of 1987 requires that any ARM loan secured by a lien on a one- to four-family dwelling originated by a national bank must include a lifetime cap on the interest rate.

Since October 1, 1988, the maximum interest rate to be charged must be included in the initial ARM disclosure and in the loan documents. The interest cap must be stated in a manner that allows the consumer to easily ascertain what the rate ceiling will be over the term of the loan. For example:

The maximum rate will not exceed _____%.

The interest rate will never be higher than _____ percentage points above the initial rate of _____ percent.

⮕ CHECKLIST

Disclosure Forms

The disclosures listed in the following checklist are to be given to a borrower at the time the borrower obtains a consumer loan secured by the borrower's residence.

- ❑ I. Real Estate Settlement Procedures Act
  - ❑ A. Special Information Booklet. This booklet is given by the lender to the consumer or borrower within three business days after the consumer's application for the loan.
  - ❑ B. Good Faith Estimate. This estimate must be provided by the lender to the consumer or borrower within three days after the borrower's application for the loan.
  - ❑ C. Uniform Settlement Statement (HUD-1). This uniform settlement statement must be used at the closing of all residential loan transactions that involve a federally related mortgage loan. The HUD-1 must be made available to the borrower for inspection at least one day before closing.
- ❑ II. Truth-In-Lending Act
  - ❑ A. Truth-In-Lending Disclosure Statement. A truth-in-lending disclosure statement must be given to the borrower before the time the borrower signs the promissory note.
  - ❑ B. Right of Rescission Notice. The right of rescission notice must be given to a consumer/borrower before the time the borrower signs a note. The right of rescission notice is given only on loans secured by the borrower's residence and the loan is being made not for the purpose of purchasing or constructing the residence. The borrower has three business days from receiving the right of rescission to rescind.
  - ❑ C. Affidavit of No Rescission. This form should be obtained from a consumer/borrower who has received a notice of rescission after the three-business-day period has expired. This form should be received before the disbursement of any loan proceeds to the borrower.
- ❑ III. ARM Disclosure Requirements
  - 1. Consumer Handbook on Adjustable Rate Mortgages. This booklet should be given by the lender to the borrower at the time the borrower applies for an ARM loan.
  - 2. ARM Loan Program Disclosure Form. This form should be given to a borrower on an ARM loan before the time the borrower signs the note. When interest rates on an ARM change, the lender is required to give an adjustment notice.

E T H I C S :   Communication with Parties Represented by an Attorney

A legal assistant works for a law firm assisting attorneys in the closing of residential loans. The legal assistant is responsible for preparing the documents and obtaining necessary information to close the loans. This work involves contact between the legal assistant and the borrowers. Many borrowers are not represented by attorneys and frequently call the legal assistant to ask for information and nonlegal advice. On one transaction, the legal assistant is aware that the borrowers are represented by an attorney. The attorney has requested that all documents be forwarded to her for review before closing and has had other telephone and written communication with the legal assistant. The legal assistant, in the process of closing the loan, has a number of questions that need answers from the borrowers. The legal assistant, rather than requesting this information from the attorney representing the borrowers, calls the borrowers directly to obtain the information. Did the legal assistant act ethically in this respect?

Professional ethics require that attorneys and legal assistants shall not communicate or cause another to communicate with a party the attorney or legal assistant knows to be represented by a lawyer in a pending matter without the prior consent of the lawyer representing such party. This ethical restriction is necessary to protect the confidential relationship between a client and an attorney and to protect a party from having opposing counsel attempt to obtain information, exert undue influence, or take some advantage of the party. The legal assistant in this situation is fully aware that the parties are represented by an attorney and did act unethically in contacting the parties directly to obtain information. The legal assistant should have spoken with the attorney first to see if direct contact with the client was permissible or request the information through the attorney.

SUMMARY

A legal assistant involved in the closing of a residential real estate loan transaction must be aware of the various federal laws that regulate the transaction. Most law firms have the necessary forms to comply with the federal laws, and a legal assistant need only make certain that the forms are properly completed and the necessary disclosures are made to the consumer or borrower at the appropriate times.

KEY TERMS

Consumer	HUD-1	RESPA
Consumer credit	Kickback	Settlement costs
Consummation	Rescission	Truth-in-Lending Act
Finance charge		

REVIEW QUESTIONS

1. What is the purpose of the RESPA?

2. What transactions are subject to RESPA? Which transactions are exempt?

3. Why are kickbacks prohibited under RESPA?

4. What is the purpose of the Truth-in-Lending Act?

5. What real estate transactions are subject to the Truth-in-Lending Act?

6. Which transactions are exempt from the Truth-in-Lending Act?

7. What disclosures does the Truth-in-Lending Act require before the closing of a residential real estate loan transaction?

8. What is the purpose of the right of rescission under the Truth-in-Lending Act?

9. What disclosures must be made under the adjustable interest rate disclosure requirements?

10. What residential loans are exempt from the right of rescission under the Truth-in-Lending Act?

CASE PROBLEMS

1. You are assisting an attorney in the closing of a loan made by a federally insured savings and loan association to facilitate the purchase of a home. The loan is closing on October 15. The first payment under the loan will be due December 1. The real estate taxes on the home for the current year were due and payable on September 1, and they have been paid in the amount of $1,800. If the lender requests that you escrow taxes under its loan, how much money do you need to collect for the escrow at the closing on October 15?

2. The firm you work with closes a number of real estate loans with a Federal Deposit Insurance Company–insured bank. The firm does not do its own title examination work but instead retains an independent title examiner to do the title examinations. The firm at closing charges a title examination fee of which 75 percent of the fee goes to the title examiner and 25 percent of the fee is retained by the firm to compensate the firm for reviewing the title examination and typing the title examination from the title examiner's notes. Is this practice legal under RESPA?

3. How many copies of the right to rescind must be given in a loan transaction secured by a vacation home owned by a husband and wife?

4. You are assisting in a real estate closing that closes on July 2. The closing is subject to the truth-in-lending right of rescission. On what day does the right of rescission expire?

NOTE

1. Part of the material contained in this chapter is from Robert R. Stubbs, *Lending in a Changing Environment: Real Estate Practices and Procedures*. Program Materials (1985); Institute of Continuing Legal Education in Georgia. Used by permission.

ADDENDUM

Exhibit 16–1 HUD-1 Settlement
Exhibit 16–2 Truth-in-Lending Disclosure Statement
Exhibit 16–3 Notice of Right to Rescission
Exhibit 16–4 Non-Rescind Statement
Exhibit 16–5 Initial ARM Disclosure Format—H–4(C) Variable-Rate Model Clauses
Exhibit 16–6 Initial ARM Disclosure Format—H–14 Variable-Rate Mortgage Sample

EXHIBIT 16-1   Hud-1 Settlement Statement

A. SETTLEMENT STATEMENT   U.S. Department of Housing and Urban Development

OMB No. 2502-0265

B. Type of Loan

1. __ FHA 2. __ FmHA 3. __ Conv. Unins.	6. File Number	7. Loan Number	8. Mortgage Insurance Case No.
4. __ VA 5. __ Conv. Ins.			

C. NOTE: This form is furnished to give you a statement of actual settlement costs. Amounts paid to and by the settlement agent are shown. Items marked (P.O.C.) were paid outside the closing; they are shown here for information purposes and are not included in the totals.

D. Name and Address of Borrower	E. Name and Address of Seller	F. Name and Address of Lender

G. Property Location	H. Settlement Agent	
	Place of Settlement	I. Settlement Date

J. SUMMARY OF BORROWER'S TRANSACTION:		K. SUMMARY OF SELLER'S TRANSACTION:	
100. Gross Amount Due From Borrower		**400. Gross Amount Due To Seller**	
101. Contract sales price		401. Contract sales price	
102. Personal property		402. Personal property	
103. Settlement charges to borrower (line 1400)		403.	
104.		404.	
105.		405.	
Adjustments for items paid by seller in advance		**Adjustments for items paid by seller in advance**	
106. City/town taxes to		406. City/town taxes to	
107. County taxes to		407. County taxes to	
108. Assessments to		408. Assessments to	
109.		409.	
110.		410.	
111.		411.	
112.		412.	
120. GROSS AMOUNT DUE FROM BORROWER		**420. GROSS AMOUNT DUE TO SELLER**	
200. Amounts Paid By or In Behalf of Borrower		**500. Reductions In Amount Due To Seller**	
201. Deposit or earnest money		501. Excess Deposit (see instructions)	
202. Principal amount of new loan(s)		502. Settlement charges to seller (line 1400)	
203. Existing loan(s) taken subject to		503. Existing loan(s) taken subject to	
204.		504. Payoff of first mortgage loan	
205.		505. Payoff of second mortgage loan	
206.		506.	
207.		507.	
208.		508.	
209.		509.	
Adjustments for items unpaid by seller		**Adjustments for items unpaid by seller**	
210. City/town taxes to		510. City/town taxes to	
211. County taxes to		511. County taxes to	
212. Assessments to		512. Assessments to	
213.		513.	
214.		514.	
215.		515.	
216.		516.	
217.		517.	
218.		518.	
219.		519.	
220. TOTAL PAID BY/FOR BORROWER		**520. TOTAL REDUCTION AMOUNT DUE SELLER**	
300. Cash At Settlement From or To Borrower		**600. Cash At Settlement To or From Seller**	
301. Gross amount due from borrower (line 120)		601. Gross amount due to seller (line 420)	
302. Less amounts paid by/for borrower (line 220)		602. Less reduction amount due seller (line 520)	
303. CASH BORROWER		603. CASH SELLER	

REV. HUD-1 (3/86)

EXHIBIT 16-1   Hud-1 Settlement Statement (continued)

U.S. DEPARTMENT OF HOUSING AND URBAN DEVELOPMENT
SETTLEMENT STATEMENT
PAGE 2

L. SETTLEMENT CHARGES:	PAID FROM BORROWER'S FUNDS AT SETTLEMENT	PAID FROM SELLER'S FUNDS AT SETTLEMENT
700. TOTAL SALES/BROKER'S COMMISSION based on price $ @ =		
Division of commission (line 700) as follows:		
701. $ to		
702. $ to		
703. Commission paid at Settlement		
704.		
800. ITEMS PAYABLE IN CONNECTION WITH LOAN		
801. Loan Origination Fee %		
802. Loan Discount %		
803. Appraisal Fee to		
804. Credit Report to		
805. Lender's Inspection Fee to		
806. Mortgage Application Fee to		
807. Assumption Fee to		
808.		
809.		
810.		
811.		
900. ITEMS REQUIRED BY LENDER TO BE PAID IN ADVANCE		
901. Interest from to @ $ /day		
902. Mortgage Insurance Premium for to		
903. Hazard Insurance Premium for yrs to		
904.		
905.		
1000. RESERVES DEPOSITED WITH LENDER FOR		
1001. Hazard Insurance mo.@$ /mo.		
1002. Mortgage Insurance mo.@$ /mo.		
1003. City Property Taxes mo.@$ /mo.		
1004. County Property Taxes mo.@$ /mo.		
1005. Annual Assessments mo.@$ /mo.		
1006. mo.@$ /mo.		
1007. mo.@$ /mo.		
1008. mo.@$ /mo.		
1100. TITLE CHARGES		
1101. Settlement or closing fee to		
1102. Abstract or title search to		
1103. Title examination to		
1104. Title insurance binder to		
1105. Document Preparation to		
1106. Notary Fees to		
1107. Attorney's fees to		
(includes above items No:)		
1108. Title Insurance to		
(includes above items No:)		
1109. Lender's coverage $ ----		
1110. Owner's coverage $ ----		
1111 TAX REPORT		
1112		
1113		
1200. GOVERNMENT RECORDING AND TRANSFER CHARGES		
1201. Recording Fees: Deed $; Mortgage $; Releases $		
1202. City/county tax/stamps: Deed $; Mortgage $		
1203. State Tax/stamps: Deed $; Mortgage $		
1204		
1205		
1300. ADDITIONAL SETTLEMENT CHARGES		
1301. Survey to		
1302. Pest Inspection to		
1303		
1304		
1305		
1400. TOTAL SETTLEMENT CHARGES (enter on lines 103 and 502, Sections J and K)		

REV. HUD-1 (3/86)

EXHIBIT 16-2
Truth-in-Lending
Disclosure
Statement

CREDITOR:

Form 82-17

FEDERAL TRUTH IN LENDING ACT DISCLOSURE STATEMENT
ADJUSTABLE RATE MORTGAGE

Borrowers name(s) _____

Mailing address of subject property _____

ANNUAL PERCENTAGE RATE	FINANCE CHARGE	Amount Financed	Total of Payments
The cost of your credit as a yearly rate.	The dollar amount the credit will cost you.	The amount of credit provided to you or on your behalf.	The amount you will have paid after you have made all payments as scheduled.
_____ %	$ _____	$ _____	$ _____

Your payment schedule will be:

Number of Payments	Amount of Payments	When Payments Are Due
*		

* Assuming maximum rate change

Insurance: Hazard insurance and flood insurance (if the property lies within a flood plain) is required. You may obtain this insurance from anyone you want that is acceptable to Creditor.

Security: You are giving a security interest in the property being purchased.

Late Charge: If a payment is received more than 15 days after it is due, you will be charged _____ % of the payment.

Prepayment: If you payoff early, you

☐ may   ☐ will not   have to pay a penalty.

☐ may   ☐ will not   be entitled to a refund of part of the Finance Charge.

Assumption: Someone buying your home

☐ may, subject to conditions   be allowed to assume the remainder of the mortgage on the original terms.

☐ cannot   assume the remainder of the mortgage on the original terms.

See your contract documents for any additional information about nonpayment, default, any required repayment in full before the scheduled date, and prepayment refunds and penalties.

_____

"e" means an estimate

Type of Disclosure and Certificate or Acknowledgement (check applicable box)

☐ **Original Disclosure.** The undersigned representative of the Creditor certifies that the Real Estate Settlement Procedures Act (RESPA) Information Booklet, "The RESPA Good Faith Estimate of Settlement Costs," and the above Federal Truth in Lending Act Disclosure Statement appropriately completed so as to reflect the mortgage loan for which Borrower(s) have applied to Creditor were on the date indicated below deposited in the U.S. Mail, first class postage prepaid addressed to the Borrower(s) at the following mailing address:

_____

Date: _____   _____
                                   Signature of Creditor's Representative

☐ **Corrective Redisclosure.** Borrower(s) have applied to Creditor for a mortgage loan the proceeds of which will be used to purchase a dwelling. Shortly after receiving Borrower(s) application the Creditor provided to Borrower(s) a Federal Truth in Lending Act Disclosure Statement (the "Original Disclosure Statement") which contained important information about the mortgage loan for which Borrower(s) have applied. Some of the disclosures contained in the Original Disclosure Statement do not accurately reflect certain details of the actual mortgage loan that Borrower(s) are receiving from Creditor. This is due to the fact that certain disclosures contained in the Original Disclosure Statement were based on estimates or due to the fact that certain details of the requested mortgage loan have changed since the date the Original Disclosure Statement was prepared. The purpose of this Corrective Redisclosure Statement is to provide Borrower(s) with disclosures that accurately reflect the actual mortgage loan that Borrower(s) are receiving from creditor. The undersigned hereby acknowledge receipt of a copy of this Federal Truth in Lending Disclosure Statement this date.

_____   _____
Signature of Borrower   Date

_____   _____   _____
Witness   Signature of Co-Borrower   Date

EXHIBIT 16–3
Notice of Right to
Rescission

NOTICE OF RIGHT TO CANCEL

_____ LOAN NO. _____
(Identification of Transaction)

Your Right to Cancel

You are entering into a transaction that will result in a mortgage, lien, or security interest on your home. You have a legal right under federal law to cancel this transaction, without cost, within three business days from whichever of the following events occurs last:

(1) the date of the transaction, which is _____ ; or
(2) the date you received your Truth in Lending disclosures; or
(3) the date you received this notice of your right to cancel.

If you cancel the transaction, the mortgage, lien, or security interest is also cancelled. Within 20 calendar days after we receive your notice, we must take the steps necessary to reflect the fact that the mortgage, lien, or security interest on your home has been cancelled, and we must return to you any money or property you have given to us or to anyone else in connection with this transaction.

You may keep any money or property we have given you until we have done the things mentioned above, but you must then offer to return the money or property. If it is impractical or unfair for you to return the property, you must offer its reasonable value. You may offer to return the property at your home or at the location of the property. Money must be returned to the address below. If we do not take possession of the money or property within 20 calendar days of your offer, you may keep it without further obligation.

How to Cancel

If you decide to cancel this transaction, you may do so by notifying us in writing, at

You may use any written statement that is signed and dated by you and states your intention to cancel, and/or you may use this notice by dating and signing below. Keep one copy of this notice because it contains important information about your rights.

If you cancel by mail or telegram, you must send the notice no later than midnight of _____
(date)

(or midnight of the third business day following the latest of the three events listed above). If you send or deliver your written notice to cancel some other way, it must be delivered to the above address no later than that time.

I WISH TO CANCEL

_____   _____
Consumer's Signature   Date

I/We Received **Notice of Right to Cancel** in Duplicate this Date_____ , 19_____

_____   _____
(Signature)   (Signature)

EXHIBIT 16–4
Non-Rescind
Statement

With the intention that _____
_____
rely on this statement, the undersigned does hereby certify that (s)he (they) has(ve) not rescinded, attempted to rescind or otherwise attempted to notify
_____
of any intention to rescind the loan transaction involving a security interest in his(er) (their) residence known as:
_____
_____

_____   _____
                                                          Date

_____   _____
                                                          Date

EXHIBIT 16-5
Initial Arm
Disclosure Format

Initial ARM Disclosure Format
H-4(C) Variable-Rate Model Clauses

This disclosure describes the features of the Adjustable Rate Mortgage (ARM) program you are considering. Information on other ARM programs is available upon request.

How Your Interest Rate and Payment are Determined

Your interest rate will be based on [an index plus a margin] [a formula].

Your payment will be based on the interest rate, loan balance, and loan term.

[The interest rate will be based on (identification of index) plus our margin. Ask for our current interest rates and margin.]

[The interest rate will be based on (identification of formula). Ask us for our current interest rate.]

Information about the index [formula for rate adjustments] is published [can be found] _____.

[The initial interest rate is not based on the (index) (formula) used to make later adjustments. Ask us for the amount of current interest rate discounts.]

How Your Interest Rate Can Change

Your interest rate can change (frequency).

[Your interest rate cannot increase or decrease more than _____ percentage points at each adjustment.]

Your interest rate cannot increase [or decrease] more than _____ percentage points over the term of the loan.

How Your Payment Can Change

Your payment can change (frequency) based on changes in the interest rate.

[Your payment cannot increase more than (amount or percentage) at each adjustment.]

You will be notified in writing _____ days before the due date of a payment at a new level. This notice will contain information about your interest rates, payment amount, and loan balance.

[You will be notified once each year during which interest rate adjustments, but no payment adjustments, have been made to your loan. This notice will contain information about your interest rates, payment amount, and loan balance.]

For example, on a $10,000 [term] loan with an initial interest rate of _____ (the rate shown in the interest rate column below for the year 19__), the maximum amount that the interest rate can rise under this program is _____ percentage points, to _____%, and the monthly payment can rise from a first-year payment of $_____ to a maximum of $_____ in the _____ year.

Example

The example below shows how your payments would have changed under this ARM program based on actual changes in the index from 1977 to 1987. This does not necessarily indicate how your index will change in the future.

The example is based on the following assumptions:

**EXHIBIT 16–5
Initial Arm
Disclosure Format
(continued)**

Amount of loan:	$10,000	Caps: [periodic interest rate cap]
Term:	_____	[lifetime interest rate cap]
Change Date:	_____	[payment cap]
		[Interest rate carryover:]
Payment adjustment: (frequency)		[Negative Amortization:]
Interest adjustment: (frequency)		[Interest rate discount:**]
[Margin:*] _____		Index: (Identification of Index or formula)

Year	Index (%)	Margin (percentage points)	Interest Rate (%)	Monthly Payment ($)	Remaining Balance ($)
1979					
1980					
1981					
1982					
1983					
1984					
1985					
1986					
1987					
1988					
1989					
1990					
1991					
1992					
1993					
1994					

*This is a margin we have used recently; your margin may be different.

**This is the amount of a discount we have provided recently; your loan may be discounted by a different amount.

To see what your payments should have been during that period, divide your mortgage amount by $10,000; then multiply the monthly payments by that amount. (For example, in 1987 the monthly payment for a mortgage amount of $60,000 taken out in 1977 would be: $60,000 divided by $10,000 = 6; 6 x ____ = _____ per month.)

EXHIBIT 16–6
Initial Arm
Disclosure Format

Initial Disclosure Example
H–14 Variable-Rate Mortgage Sample

This disclosure describes the features of the Adjustable Rate Mortgage (ARM) program you are considering. Information on other ARM programs is available upon request.

How Your Interest Rate and Payment are Determined

Your interest will be based on an index rate plus a margin

Your payment will be based on the interest rate, loan balance, and loan term.

The interest rate will be based on the weekly average yield on United States Treasury securities adjusted to a constant maturity of 1 year (your index), plus our margin. Ask us for our current interest rate and margin.

Information about the index rate is published weekly in *The Wall Street Journal*.

Your interest rate will equal the index rate plus our margin unless your interest rate "caps" limit the amount of change in the interest rate.

How Your Interest Rate Can Change

Your interest rate can change yearly.

Your interest rate cannot increase or decrease more than 5 percentage points per year.

Your interest rate cannot increase or decrease more than 5 percentage points over the term of the loan.

How Your Monthly Payment Can Change

Your monthly payment can change yearly based on changes in the interest rate.

For example, on a $10,000, 30-year loan with an initial interest rate of 9.71% (the rate shown in the interest rate column below for the year 1987), the maximum amount that the interest rate can rise under this program is 5 percentage points, to 14.71%, and the monthly payment can rise from a first-year payment of $85.62 to a maximum of $123.31 in the fourth year.

You will be notified in writing 25 days before the annual payment adjustment may be made. This notice will contain information about your interest rates, payment amount, and loan balance.

Example

The example below shows how your payments would have changed under this ARM program based on actual changes in the index from 1977 to 1987. This does not necessarily indicate how your index will change in the future. The example is based on the following assumptions:

Amount of loan:	$10,000	Caps:	2 percentage points annual interest rate
Term	30 years		5 percentage points lifetime interest rate
Payment adjustment:	1 year		
Interest adjustment:	1 year	Index:	Weekly average yield on U.S. Treasury securities adjusted to a constant maturity of one year.
Margin*	3 percentage points		

EXHIBIT 16-6
Initial Arm
Disclosure Format
(continued)

Year as of 1st week ending in July	Index (%)	Margin* (percentage points)	Interest Rate (%)	Monthly Payment ($)	Remaining Balance ($)
1977	5.72	3	8.72	78.46	9,927.64
1978	8.34	3	10.72**	92.89	9,874.67
1979	9.44	3	12.44	105.67	9,832.70
1980	8.51	3	11.51	98.79	9,776.04
1981	14.94	3	13.51**	113.51	9,731.98
1982	14.41	3	13.72***	115.07	9,683.39
1983	9.78	3	12.78	108.25	9,618.21
1984	12.17	3	13.72***	114.96	9,554.39
1985	7.66	3	11.72**	101.08	9,456.03
1986	6.36	3	9.72**	88.13	9,311.25
1987	6.71	3	9.71	88.07	9,151.55

*This is a margin we have used recently; your margin may be different.
**This interest rate reflects a 2 percentage points annual interest rate cap.
***This interest rate reflects a 5 percentage points lifetime interest rate cap.

To see what your payments would have been during that period, divide your mortgage amount by $10,000; then multiply the monthly payment by that amount. (For example, in 1987, the monthly payment for a mortgage amount of $60,000 taken out in 1977 would be: $60,000 divided by $10,000 = 6; 6 x $88.07 = $528.42.)

EXHIBIT 16-7
Subsequent Arm
Disclosure

**Subsequent Disclosure/Adjustment Notice Format
H-4 (D) Variable-Rate Model Clauses**

Your new interest rate will be _____%, which is based on an index value of _____%.
    Your previous interest rate was _____%, which was based on an index value of _____%.
        [The new interest rate does not reflect a change of _____ percentage points in the index value which was not added because of _____.]
            [The new payment will be $_____.]
            [Your new loan balance is $_____.]
            [Your (new) (existing) payment will not be sufficient to cover the interest due and the difference will be added to the loan amount. The payment amount needed to pay your loan in full by the end of the term at the new interest rate is $_____.]
            [The following interest rate adjustments have been implemented this year without changing your payment: _____. These interest rates were based on the following index values: _____.]

Real Estate Closing Forms and Examples

Practice is the best of all instructors.

—Pubilius Syrus, Maxim 439

OBJECTIVES

After reading this chapter you will be able to:

- Understand and prepare various kinds of affidavits
- Understand and prepare various real estate closing documents such as deeds, bills of sale, assignment of warranties, assignment of leases, and assignment of contracts
- Understand the importance and particular use of such real estate documents as corporate resolution, agreement regarding survival of loan commitment, indemnity of fees, attorney's opinions, and compliance agreements
- Prepare a HUD–1 Uniform Settlement Statement
- Understand the documentation involved in the closing of a residential sale and loan transaction

GLOSSARY

Affidavit Written statement of fact that is sworn to by the person making the statement under oath as a true statement of facts.

Bill of sale Legal document that transfers ownership to personal property.

At a real estate closing, ownership of real property is transferred from seller to purchaser. At a loan closing, a loan is consummated between the lender and the borrower. The purchaser at a closing expects to receive good title to the real property that he or she has agreed to buy and to obtain whatever warranties and assurances the seller has made in the real estate sale contract. The seller at a closing expects to be paid the contract price for the real property and not obligate himself or herself to perform any duty not required under the contract. In the case of a loan closing, the borrower expects to receive the loan proceeds from the lender, and the lender expects to receive good security for its loan as well as the satisfaction of all the borrower's promises and covenants contained in the loan commitment.

A real estate attorney uses a number of legal documents at the closing to accomplish and satisfy all the expectations of the parties involved. A real estate legal assistant prepares many of the legal documents required. These legal documents are numerous and vary in form from state to state. The legal assistant should become familiar with the various legal forms used in the locality in which he or she works. This information can be obtained from the law firm that employs the legal assistant.

Some of the basic forms that are used in residential and commercial real estate closing transactions are discussed in this chapter. Many forms, such as deeds, notes, and mortgages, have already been discussed. References are made to the chapters in which these forms can be found.

All forms referred to in the sections on affidavits, sale and transfer documents, and miscellaneous closing documents appear at the end of the latter section.

AFFIDAVITS

An affidavit is a written statement of fact that is sworn to by the person making the statement (affiant) under oath as a true statement of facts. The person who administers the oath to the affiant is a notary public. The notary's signature usually appears on the affidavit as well as the notary seal. The penalty for a false affidavit is perjury. Perjury can result in both civil and criminal penalties.

Affidavits are used for many purposes in a real estate closing transaction. Some of the more common affidavits used by the real estate attorney or legal assistant are discussed in this section.

Title Affidavit

New York:
See Appendix for an example of a title affidavit to prove there are no judgments against someone.

Most purchasers of real property require the seller to execute a title affidavit at the time of the sale. In addition, most lenders require the borrower to execute a title affidavit at the time the lender acquires a mortgage on the borrower's real property. The title affidavit is helpful in removing standard exceptions from title insurance policies. A title affidavit is a statement of facts swearing to the following: (a) the affiant owns the real property described in the affidavit; (b) the boundary lines of the real property are certain and not in dispute; (c) the affiant has a right to possession of the real property; (d) there are no liens, encumbrances, easements, or leases affecting the real property unless they are identified in the affidavit; (e) there are no judgments, bankruptcies, or other restrictions against the affiant owner of the real property; and (f) the affidavit is being made by the affiant with knowledge that it will be relied on by purchasers, lenders, and title insurance companies involved with the real property.

Exhibit 17–1 shows a title affidavit. Other title affidavits can be found in Chapter 14.

Hazardous Waste Affidavit

The presence of hazardous waste materials on real property can create serious problems for the property owner. Federal and state laws impose on the owner of real property liability for all damage caused by hazardous waste as well as the cost of the hazardous waste cleanup. Liability is imposed on any owner of real property, regardless of whether that owner was responsible for the creation of the hazardous waste material. Most purchasers and lenders will not purchase or make a loan on real property without having a hazardous waste inspection done by a professional inspection firm. In addition to the independent inspection for hazardous waste, most purchasers and lenders require the seller or borrower to sign a hazardous waste affidavit at the time of the sale or loan closing (see Exhibit 17–2).

Affidavit of No Change

It is not uncommon in loan transactions for several weeks to pass between the time the loan application is made and the time the loan is closed. Many lenders require the borrower, at the time of the loan closing, to sign an affidavit swearing that the borrower's financial condition has not materially changed from the date the loan application was made (see Exhibit 17–3).

Same Name Affidavit

An owner of property may be referred to in the chain of title or in a transaction in a number of ways. For example, a person named William Clyde Smith may be referred to as W.C. Smith in some of the closing documents or the documents within the chain of title. It is important to make certain that W.C. Smith and William Clyde Smith are one and the same person. Often an affidavit to that effect is used (see Exhibit 17–4).

Similar Name Affidavit

It is not unusual for a common name such as William Smith to appear on the judgment index during a title examination. The judgments may be against a person with the name of William Smith other than the borrower or seller of the real property involved in the real estate transaction. To clear up the matter, most title companies will accept an affidavit signed by the real property owner indicating that the real property owner is not the same person mentioned in the judgments (see Exhibit 17–5). On receipt of this affidavit, the title company will insure the real property free and clear of the judgments.

Foreign Person Affidavit

The Internal Revenue Service requires that a purchaser of real property from a foreign person withhold 10 percent of the purchase price and pay it to the Internal Revenue Service. If the purchaser fails to withhold the 10 percent, the purchaser will be responsible for any tax assessed against the foreign person on account of the sale. The purchaser is not excused from this obligation unless the purchaser obtains an affidavit from the seller to the effect that the seller is not a foreign person (see Exhibit 17–6). The foreign person affidavit has become standard on all real estate transactions.

Federal National Mortgage Association Affidavit

This Federal National Mortgage Association is an investor in residential mortgage loans. It buys loans from savings and loan associations, commercial banks, and other originators of loans. The Federal National Mortgage Association requires that all loans purchased be closed on their forms and that an affidavit and agreement be executed by both the real property seller and the borrower. This affidavit and agreement essentially are sworn statements of facts by the borrower and seller indicating that the loan documents truly reflect the terms of the transaction between the seller and the borrower. The affidavit further swears that there are no side agreements or other undisclosed terms involving the sale and the loan. Exhibit 17–7 shows the Federal National Mortgage Association affidavit and agreement.

SALE AND TRANSFER DOCUMENTS

The sale and transfer of real property requires the use of a number of legal documents. The type of real property being transferred often dictates what documents are required. For example, the sale of a home requires less documentation than the sale of a resort hotel. On most real estate transactions, the sale and transfer at least requires the use of a deed, bill of sale, assignment of warranties, and, on commercial contracts, an assignment of leases and assignment of contracts.

Deed

A deed is a legal document that transfers ownership of real property from one person to another. A full discussion of deeds, together with several examples of different types of deeds, can be found in Chapter 9.

Bill of Sale

A deed only transfers ownership to real property. If the real estate transaction involves both real and personal property, which is the case in most residential and commercial transactions, then a separate legal document must be used to transfer ownership of the personal property. The legal document that transfers ownership to personal property is a bill of sale. A bill of sale, similar to a deed, can either contain warranties of title or be a quitclaim bill of sale without warranties. A general warranty bill of sale usually contains warranties that (a) the seller lawfully owns and is possessed of the personal property being sold; (b) the seller has a right to sell, transfer, and convey the personal property to the purchaser; (c) the personal property is free and clear of any and all encumbrances or security interests; and (d) the seller will warrant and forever defend the title of the personal property against the claims of any and all people whomsoever. The bill of sale usually is signed with the same formality as a deed, witnessed, and notarized. A bill of sale usually is not recorded. An example of a general warranty bill of sale appears as Exhibit 17–8.

Assignment of Warranties

A number of warranties may exist in connection with the improvements located on real property. For example, a home may have a twenty-year roof warranty and a ten-year furnace warranty. On commercial properties, there may be warranties that involve the air conditioning system, the furnace, the asphalt sealant on the parking lot, and so on. Most purchasers of the real property require that the right to enforce these warranties be assigned to them as part of the sale. This is done by an assignment of warranties signed by the seller. The assignment of warranties usually is prepared with the same formality as a deed, and the seller's signature is witnessed and notarized. The assignment of warranties usually is not recorded. An example of an assignment of warranties appears as Exhibit 17–9.

Assignment of Leases

The sale of a commercial real property with tenants involves the transfer of the tenant leases from the seller to the purchaser. Most purchasers require that all leases be assigned to them together with all security deposits that must be returned to the tenant on the expiration of the leases. The purchaser also requires that the seller indemnify the purchaser against any claims that the tenants may have against the seller or the purchaser as a result of defaults under the leases that have happened before the date of the sale. Most sellers require that the purchaser indemnify the seller against all claims that may be made by the tenants against the seller because of defaults under the leases that occur after the date of the sale. An assignment of leases usually is signed by both purchaser and seller, and their signatures are witnessed and notarized. The assignment of leases is not recorded unless the leases have been recorded. Exhibit 17–10 is an example of an assignment of leases.

Assignment of Contracts

The sale of commercial property may involve the assignment of certain service contracts that are an integral part of the real property. For example, an apartment project may have a contract with a landscape service to take care of the grounds or a contract with a pool service to take care of the recreational area. The sale of a hotel may have any number of contracts that involve, for example, ice machine, pool maintenance, landscaping, and janitorial services that are to be either terminated at the time of closing or transferred from seller to purchaser. It is not unusual for contracts to be terminated at the time of closing so that the purchaser may enter into its own contractual relations to provide these services. If the contracts are not to be terminated, they are assigned by the seller to the purchaser. The assignment usually contains an indemnity from the seller to the purchaser indemnifying the purchaser against any claims or losses the purchaser may suffer because of defaults under the contracts before the date of the sale. The purchaser likewise indemnifies the seller for any claims or losses incurred by the seller because of defaults under the contracts after the date of the sale. An assignment of contracts is signed by both the seller and the purchaser, and their signatures are witnessed and notarized. The assignment of contracts is not recorded. Exhibit 17–11 is an example of an assignment of contracts.

Loan Documents

A real estate transaction that involves a loan secured by the real estate requires a number of loan documents. The basic loan documents are a note and a mortgage. On commercial properties, the note and mortgage may be supplemented by an assignment of leases and rents, a security agreement, and a Uniform Commercial Code financing statement. If the loan is a construction loan, a construction loan agreement and an assignment of construction and architect's contracts are required. A full explanation of loan documents and several examples of loan document forms are included in Chapter 12.

MISCELLANEOUS REAL ESTATE CLOSING DOCUMENTS —

Corporate Resolution

The sale of real property that involves either a corporate seller or a corporate purchaser requires the corporate entity to provide a corporate resolution. The corporate resolution authorizes the sale or purchase of the real property and empowers certain officers of the company to sign the purchase and sale documents on behalf of the corporation.

Examples of corporate resolutions are shown as Exhibits 17–12, 17–13, and 17–14.

A real estate loan transaction that involves a corporate borrower also requires a corporate resolution. The resolution should authorize the corporation to borrow the money and empower officers to sign the loan documents.

Agreement Regarding Survival of Loan Commitment

A commitment for a loan, in addition to containing many terms and requirements for the loan, often imposes financial reporting obligations and other conditions on a borrower to be performed after the loan closes. It is not unusual for a lender to have a simple agreement prepared that provides that the conditions and terms for the loan commitment that have not been satisfied at closing will survive closing and remain in full force and effect until the loan has been paid in full. An agreement for this purpose is shown in Exhibit 17–15.

Indemnity of Fees

It is not unusual on a real estate sale or loan transaction that brokers and agents representing the seller, purchaser, and borrower are involved. These agents also are entitled to fees usually paid by the person who has hired them—the seller, purchaser, or borrower. The parties to a real estate transaction who have not retained these agents may require indemnities from the other parties concerning the payment of fees to these agents. These indemnities usually take the form of a seller and purchaser each indemnifying the other against brokers' commissions that involve brokers retained by them. Indemnities involved in a loan transaction usually are from the borrower, who indemnifies the lender against any brokers' fees or loan fees that the borrower is responsible for. Examples of a purchaser-seller indemnity and a borrower-lender indemnity appear in Exhibits 17–16 and 17–17, respectively.

Attorney's Opinion

A lender may require on a commercial loan that the borrower's attorney render an opinion involving certain aspects of the loan transaction. A form of opinion is shown as Exhibit 17–18. This borrower's attorney's opinion usually involves an opinion by borrower's counsel that (a) if the borrower is a corporation, it is created and existing in the laws of a certain state; (b) the borrower has the authority to enter into the loan transaction; (c) the loan transaction does not violate or conflict with any provision of the borrower's certificate of incorporation, bylaws, or any other documents to which the borrower is a party or to which it is subject; (d) all loan documents have been validly authorized, executed, and delivered by the borrower and, assuming the due authorization, execution, and delivery thereof by all other parties, constitute binding, enforceable obligations of the borrower; (e) all loan documents are valid and enforceable according to their terms; (f) the interest charged on the loan is not usurious; (g) the property is properly zoned for the use intended; and (h) the attorney knows of no title problems or regulatory matters that would impair the lender's security.

Compliance Agreements

A large number of documents are executed in connection with any residential or commercial sale and loan closing. Even the most careful legal assistant and attorney can make mistakes in the preparation of the documents. Most lenders require the borrower to sign a compliance agreement. This agreement essentially states that if there are typographical errors or other mistakes made in preparing the documents, the borrower agrees to execute corrective documents. An example of a compliance agreement is shown as Exhibit 17–19.

1099–B Report Form

The Internal Revenue Service requires that settlement agents report sales of real estate transactions to the Internal Revenue Service. The settlement agent, in most situations, is the real estate attorney. The failure to provide the informational form subjects the settlement agent to penalties. A 1099–B reporting form is shown as Exhibit 17–20.

Settlement or Closing Statement

A settlement or closing statement sets forth the financial terms of a sale or loan closing. The statement indicates all the money involved and to whom the funds have been disbursed. The settlement and closing statement forms vary, depending on the type of transaction involved. Law firms and even individual lawyers have their own favorite forms they like to use. The Real Estate Settlement Procedures Act of 1974 requires that on all federally related loans, which means residential consumer loans secured by one- to four-family residences, the HUD–1 form be used. Instructions on how to prepare the HUD–1 form follow. These instructions are keyed to the section and line numbers of the HUD–1 form shown as Exhibit 17–21.

Section A—Heading. The heading of the closing statement that appears at the top of page 1 should be completed as follows.

Section A. U.S. Department of Housing and Urban Development Settlement Statement.

Section B. Type of loan, file number, loan number, and mortgage insurance case number. The choices for type of loan are a Federal Housing Administration (FHA)-insured loan, a Veterans Administration (VA)-insured loan, a Farmers' Home Administration–insured loan, a conventional uninsured loan, and a conventional insured loan. In a conventional insured loan, there is no government participation, but the payments of the loan are insured by a private mortgage insurance company.

In a conventional uninsured loan, there is no government participation and the payments of the loan are not insured. The file number is the law firm's internal file number for the loan transaction. The loan number is the lender's loan number for the transaction. Most lenders give a loan number to a particular loan when they issue a commitment. The mortgage insurance case number is the file number for mortgage insurance, if mortgage insurance exists. Mortgage insurance referred to in paragraph B is the private mortgage insurance that insures the payments of the mortgage.

Section C. Explanatory note printed on all HUD–1 statements. This note explains that the form is being furnished to give the borrower a statement of actual settlement costs. The amounts paid to and by the settlement agent are shown. The items marked (p.o.c.) were paid outside the closing. They are shown here for informational purposes and are not included in the total.

Section D. Name and address of the borrower, who also is the purchaser of the property in a sale transaction. If the purchaser is buying the home to live in, the home address may be used as the address of the borrower.

Section E. Name and address of the seller. The forwarding address for the seller should be used.

Section F. Name and address of the lender.

Section G. Description of the property. A street address is acceptable.

Section H. Identification of the settlement agent and the place of settlement. This is the law firm and the law firm's address.

Section I. Settlement date, which is the date of the closing.

Section J. Summary of the borrower's (purchaser's) transaction. It is broken into three separate columns, 100 column, 200 column, and 300 column. The *100 column* is a summary of the gross amount of money due from the borrower (purchaser) in connection with the transaction. The *200 column* is a summary of all moneys previously paid either by the borrower (purchaser) or by other parties in connection with the transaction, or credits that the borrower (purchaser) is entitled to as part of the transaction. *Column 300* is a summary of columns 100 and 200 and determines whether the borrower (purchaser) gets cash from the closing or brings cash to the closing.

Instructions for the various line numbers within each column follow.

Line 101. Contract sales price. This amount is determined from the contract.

Line 102. Any money in addition to the contract sales price that is to be paid by the borrower for any personal property to be used in connection with the real property. If personal property is not being purchased or the personal property is included within the contract sales price, line 102 remains blank.

Line 103. Total of all settlement charges to the borrower. The amount that appears on line 103 is the amount that appears on line 1400. Instructions for arriving at the amount for line 1400 follow.

Lines 104 and 105. Any charges that are unique to the transaction and that are to be paid by the borrower would be itemized on these lines.

Lines 106, 107, and 108. Used to calculate the purchaser's portion of the real estate taxes, assessments, and sanitary taxes for the current year if the taxes have been paid in advance by the seller. These amounts are calculated by obtaining copies of the tax report and calling the sanitary tax office. The real property taxes are prorated by a formula that allocates to the seller the seller's portion of the tax year and to the purchaser the purchaser's portion of the tax year. The amount of the real estate taxes or sanitary taxes is divided by 365, the number of days in a year, to obtain a daily tax rate. The daily tax rate is then multiplied by the number of days in the tax year the purchaser or seller owned the property. These amounts are then entered on lines 106, 107, and 108. Lines 106, 107, and 108 are used only if the seller has already paid the taxes at the time of closing or if the taxes are due and payable at the time of closing and will be paid from the seller's funds at that time. For example, if the sale closes on October 15 of a given year and county taxes in the amount of $1,400 have already been paid by the seller, the purchaser's portion of the county tax bill is $291.84. This amount is entered on line 107 and is arrived at by the following computation: $1,400 ÷ 365 = $3.84 per day; October 16–December 31 = 76 days; $3.84 x 76 = $291.84.

Note that tax prorations are based on the tax year and not the calendar year. For many taxing authorities, the tax year is the calendar year, with the first day of the tax year being January 1 and the last day of the tax year being December 31. In the event the tax year is different, it will be necessary to know what the tax year is to arrive at the proration. For example, assume a tax year of March 1 to February 28. The closing takes place on October 15 and the seller has paid the taxes for the year. The purchaser's share of the taxes would be the number of days from October 16 (sale day usually being a seller's day) through February 28, or 135 days. The 135 days would then be multiplied by the daily tax rate to arrive at the purchaser's share of the tax bill.

Lines 109, 110, 111, and 112. Used to itemize any adjustments other than taxes or assessments that were paid to the seller in advance.

Line 120. Total of lines 101 through 112.

Line 201. Amount of any earnest money or deposit that has already been paid by the purchaser. The real estate contract should indicate this amount.

Line 202. Principal amount of any new loans that the purchaser is obtaining to buy the property. The loan commitment should indicate this amount.

Line 203. Used only if the purchaser is buying the property and assuming an existing loan. An estoppel letter from the existing lender gives the amount needed for line 203.

Lines 204, 205, 206, 207, 208, and 209. Used to itemize any amount unique to the transaction paid by or in behalf of the borrower.

Lines 210, 211, and 212. Tax prorations. These are used if the taxes have not been paid in advance by the seller and are due and payable. The proration is the reverse of the proration used to obtain the numbers for lines 106, 107, and 108. For example, the closing takes place on April 15, and the county taxes are $1,400. The purchaser is entitled to a credit for the seller's portion of the year, January 1 through April 15, or 105 days. The purchaser's credit is $403.20. The computation to arrive at $403.20 is as follows: $1,400 ÷ 365 = $3.84; $3.84 x 105 = $403.20.

Lines 213, 214, 215, 216, 217, 218, and 219. Used to itemize items other than taxes and assessments unpaid by the seller.

Line 220. Total of lines 201 through 219.

Line 301. Repeat of line 120.

Line 302. Repeat of line 220.
　　　Line 301 usually is greater than line 302, and the difference is entered on line 303 as cash required from the borrower at closing. If, for some reason, line 302 is greater than line 303, this indicates that the borrower will receive cash at closing.

Section K. Summary of the seller's transaction. It consists of three columns, column 400, column 500, and column 600. *Column 400* is the gross amount of money due to the seller pursuant to the real estate contract. *Column 500* lists reductions in the amount of money due to the seller at closing. *Column 600* is a summary of columns 400 and 500 and indicates the amount of money the seller will take from the closing or, in some rare cases, the amount of money the seller will need to close. Instructions for the individual lines are as follows.

Line 401. Contract sales price. This amount is taken from the sale contract.

Line 402. Amount of money paid for any personal property in addition to the contract sale price.

Lines 403, 404, and 405. Transfer of any amount that does not appear on lines 104 and 105.

Lines 406, 407, 408, 409, 410, 411, and 412. Transfer of any amounts that appear on lines 106, 107, 108, 109, 110, 111, and 112.

Line 420. Total of lines 401 through 412.

Line 501. Amount of earnest money paid by the purchaser. Same amount as line 201.

Line 502. All settlement charges due from the seller, which is the total that appears on line 1400. Instructions for obtaining this amount follows.

Line 503. Amount of any loans that are being assumed by the purchaser at the time of closing. This line would be used only if the property is being sold subject to an existing loan that is not being paid at the time of closing. This amount is the same as that shown on line 203 and is obtained in the same method.

Line 504. Payoff of any existing first-mortgage loan on the property. This amount is obtained from a satisfaction letter from the mortgage lender.

Line 505. Payoff of any second-mortgage loan on the property. This amount is obtained by a satisfaction letter from the mortgage lender.

Lines 506 through 509. Payment of any other liens or matters that must be paid out of the seller's proceeds at the time of closing.

Lines 510, 511, 512, 513, 514, 515, 516, 517, 518, and 519. Repeat of the tax proration amounts that appear on lines 210, 211, 212, 213, 214, 215, 216, 217, 218, and 219.

Line 520. Total of lines 501 through 519.

Line 601. Amount taken from line 420.

Line 602. Amount taken from line 520.
    Line 601 normally is greater than line 602, and the difference is shown on line 603 as cash to seller. If line 602 is greater than line 601, then line 603 indicates the amount of money needed by the seller to close.

Section L. Breakdown of all settlement charges or closing costs in connection with the sale and loan transaction. The section is divided into two columns, a borrower's column and a seller's column. The responsibility to pay for settlement costs usually is negotiated between the buyer and the seller in the real estate contract. It is not uncommon for a seller to agree to pay the real estate commissions and the loan and closing costs of a purchaser.

Line 700. Amount of the real estate commission. This amount is taken from the real estate contract.

Lines 701 and 702. Division of the real estate commission and the identity of the brokers receiving the money. These lines are used only when more than one broker is involved with the transaction. A listing broker often obtains from the seller the permission to place the property on the market, and a selling broker, a broker who found the purchaser, sells the property. These brokers may split the commission. The real estate contract should provide this information.

Line 703. Total amount of commissions paid at closing. This is a seller-paid item.

800 Items. Items payable in connection with the loan. These items can be obtained from the loan commitment letter or instruction letter from the lender. They consist of loan origination fees, loan discount, appraisal fees, credit reports, lender's inspection fees, mortgage insurance application fees, and any assumption fees or other charges that might be assessed by the lender. These items usually are paid by the borrower, but the contract should be checked to make sure that the seller has not agreed to pay them.

Column 900. List of items required by the lender to be paid in advance at the time of closing.

Line 901. Interest adjustment. The interest on most mortgage loans is paid in arrears. For example, a mortgage payment due on May 1 would pay interest for the month of April. Most lenders require that the payments start on the first day of the second month after the closing. For example, if a closing is on April 15, the first mortgage payment would not be until June 1. The June 1 payment would pay interest from May 1 through May 31 but would not pay the April interest. Therefore, it is necessary at the time of closing to collect interest for the month of closing, April 15 through April 30. A lender may give the per diem interest charge, and it is only necessary to multiply this per diem interest charge by the number of days left in the month, in this case sixteen. If the lender does not give a per diem interest charge, it can be calculated by multiplying the loan amount by the interest rate and dividing by 365 or 360. Some lenders calculate interest based on a 360–day year. The amount from said computation equals the per diem interest, which then can be multiplied by the number of days to be collected. For example, a loan in the amount of $80,000 at 10 percent interest closes on April 15. The amount of money needed to be collected from the borrower at closing for interest for the remaining part of April, April 15 through April 30 (sixteen days), is $355.52 and is calculated as follows: $80,000 x .10 = $8,000; $8,000 ÷ 360 = $22.22; $22.22 x 16 = $355.52.

Line 902. Used only when a private mortgage insurance company is insuring the payments on the loan. The amount to be entered on this line is given in the lender's instruction letter.

Line 903. Name of the insurance company issuing the fire insurance and the amount of the annual premium. If the borrower has already paid for the first year's insurance premium, then the notation p.o.c. (paid outside of closing) is inserted. If the borrower has not paid for the insurance premium, then the amount of the insurance premium must be shown on this line.

Lines 904 and 905. Other items required to be paid by the lender in advance, such as flood insurance premiums that are due. This would be used only if the property is in a flood hazard zone.

Column 1000. Summary of all the insurance and tax reserves required by the lender at closing.

Column 1001. Amount of money necessary to establish an insurance escrow. This amount is arrived at by taking the annual premium for fire insurance and dividing it by 12 to get a monthly amount. Then how many of these monthly amounts are needed before the next due date on the insurance premium is calculated. The number of payments to be received monthly is subtracted from the amount needed and that yields the amount to be collected and entered on line 1001. For example, a closing takes place on April 15, and insurance is paid for one year. The first payment under the loan is not due until June 1; therefore, one-twelfth of the hazard insurance premium will not be received by the lender until June 1. The lender then will receive one-twelfth on the first day of each month thereafter. The lender will receive eleven payments before the next year's April 15 premium due date. It would be necessary to collect at least one payment to have enough money on April 15 of the next year to pay the insurance premium. Lenders usually collect an escrow for insurance premiums for two months.

Line 1002. Computes the private mortgage insurance and is determined by multiplying the loan amount by the factor from a private mortgage insurance factor tables. This number is given in the lender's instruction letter.

Lines 1003, 1004, and 1005. Escrows necessary to pay real estate taxes and assessments. The amounts to be entered on these lines are determined by first looking at the tax report to determine the annual taxes. It also is necessary to know when the tax bill becomes due. Then the tax bill is divided by 12 to arrive at a monthly tax amount. Then how many payments of these monthly tax amounts will be received before the due date of the tax bill is determined and that amount is subtracted from the number of payments needed to pay the tax bill. For example, a loan closes on April 15, and the taxes are due October 1. The lender's first payment is due under the loan on June 1 and on the first day of each month thereafter. The lender receives in the due course of servicing the loan one-twelfth of the taxes of June 1, July 1, August 1, and September 1 before the October 1 due date. The lender will need eight monthly payments collected at closing to have an adequate amount of money in escrow to pay the taxes.

Lines 1006, 1007, and 1008. Used for any reserves other than insurance and taxes required to be escrowed by lender.

Column 1100. Attorneys' fees and title insurance charges in connection with the closing. This column usually is completed by filling in line 1107 and indicating that this line includes lines 1101 through 1106. The attorneys' fees are given by the firm closing the transaction.

Line 1108. Payment for the title insurance premium. This information is obtained from the title company. If the title insurance premium pays for both lender's and owner's coverages, the amount of the coverages should be indicated on lines 1109 and 1110. The lender's coverage is the amount of the loan, and the owner's coverage is the amount of the purchase price.

Column 1200. Summary of all government recording and transfer charges. These charges vary from state to state, and it is necessary to know the local charges in the place where the documents are to be recorded.

Column 1300. Any additional settlement charges that are not covered elsewhere. This column consists of such things as survey bills, pest inspection, and hazardous waste inspection. These amounts can be obtained from the service providers.

Line 1400. Summary of all total settlement charges and the amounts from line 1400 are entered on behalf of the purchaser on line 103, Section J, and on behalf of the seller on line 502, Section K.

EXHIBIT 17-1
Affidavit of Title

STATE OF _____
COUNTY OF _____

    The undersigned, _____,
being duly sworn, states:
    That the undersigned is the fee simple title owner of the real property described on *Exhibit "A"* attached hereto and incorporated herein by reference (the "Property");

**EXHIBIT 17-1
Affidavit of Title
(continued)**

That the lines and corners of the Property are clearly marked and there are no disputes concerning the location of said lines and corners;

That no improvements or repairs have been made or contracted for on the Property during the three (3) months immediately preceding the date of this affidavit, for which there are outstanding bills for labor or services performed or rendered, or for materials supplied or furnished, or incurred in connection with improvements or repairs on the Property, or for the services of architects, surveyors or engineers in connection with improvements or repairs on the Property;

That, except for the matters set forth on Exhibit "B" attached hereto and incorporated herein by reference, the Property is free and clear of all claims, liens and encumbrances, and there is no outstanding indebtedness for or liens against any equipment or fixtures attached to, installed on, incorporated in or located on, or otherwise used in connection with the operation or maintenance of, the Property or the improvements thereon;

That there are no persons or other parties in possession of the Property who have a right or claim to possession extending beyond the date hereof, except for tenants under terms of written leases disclosed on Exhibit "C" attached hereto and incorporated herein by reference;

That there are no suits, proceedings, judgments, bankruptcies, liens, or executions against the undersigned which affect title to the Property, the improvements thereon or the fixtures attached thereto;

That the undersigned is making this affidavit with the knowledge that it will be relied upon by lenders, attorneys, and title insurance companies interested in the title to the Property.

Sworn to and subscribed before
me this _____ day of _____,
19___.

_____   _____ (SEAL)

Notary Public
My Commission Expires:

_____

[NOTARY SEAL]

**EXHIBIT 17-2
Hazardous Waste
Affidavit**

STATE OF _____)
) ss:
COUNTY OF _____)

The undersigned is the fee simple title owner of the real property described in Exhibit "A" attached hereto and incorporated herein by reference (the "Property").

That no pollutants or other toxic or hazardous substances, as defined under the Comprehensive Environmental Response, Compensation, and Liability Act ("CERCLA"), 42 U.S.C. § 9601 *et seq.,* or any other federal or state law, including any solid, liquid, gaseous, or thermal irritant or contaminant, such as smoke, vapor, soot, fumes, acids, alkalis, chemicals or waste (including materials to be recycled, reconditioned or reclaimed) (collectively "Substances") have been or shall be discharged, disbursed, released, stored, treated, gener-

EXHIBIT 17–2
Hazardous Waste
Affidavit
(continued)

ated, disposed of, or allowed to escape (collectively referred to as the "incident") on or from Property.

That no asbestos or asbestos-containing materials have been installed, used, incorporated into, or disposed of on the Property.

That no polychlorinated biphenyls ("PCBs") are located on or in the Property, in the form of electrical transformers, fluorescent light fixtures with ballasts, cooling oils, or any other device or form.

That no underground storage tanks are located on the Property or were located on the Property and subsequently removed or filled.

That no investigation, administrative order, consent order and agreement, litigation, or settlement (collectively referred to as the "action") with respect to substances is proposed, threatened, anticipated or in existence with respect to the Property.

That the Property and undersigned's operations at the Property are in compliance with all applicable federal, state and local statutes, laws and regulations. No notice has been served on undersigned, from any entity, governmental body, or individual claiming any violation of any law, regulation, ordinance or code, or requiring compliance with any law, regulation, ordinance or code, or demanding payment or contribution for environmental damage or injury to natural resources.

That the undersigned are making this affidavit with the knowledge that it will be relied upon by lenders, interested in the title to the Property.

_____ (SEAL)

Sworn to and subscribed before
me this _____ day of _____,
19___.

Notary Public
My Commission Expires:

_____
Notarial Seal

EXHIBIT 17–3
Affidavit of No
Material Change

STATE OF _____)
) ss:
COUNTY OF _____)

The undersigned, being duly sworn, state:

That the undersigned have received from SECOND FEDERAL SAVINGS AND LOAN ASSOCIATION a loan Commitment letter dated August 25, 19___, amended by letter dated December 13, 19__ ("Commitment Letter"), to finance the construction of a 62,128 square foot shopping center located in Gulfport, Mississippi;

That no adverse change has taken place in the undersigneds' business or financial condition or in connection with the property serving as collateral for the loan;

That the undersigned are making this affidavit with the knowledge that it will be relied upon by SECOND FEDERAL SAVINGS AND LOAN ASSOCIATION in making the loan set forth in the commitment letter.

_____ (SEAL)
_____ (SEAL)

Sworn to and subscribed before me this _____ day of _____, 19__.

_____
Notary Public
My Commission Expires:

_____
Notarial Seal

EXHIBIT 17–4
Same Name
Affidavit

STATE OF _____
COUNTY OF _____

Before me came in person William Clyde Smith who, being duly sworn, on oath says:

Deponent states that William Clyde Smith (s)he is one and the same person as W.C. Smith and is the same person as named in Warranty Deed dated November 14, 1988 and recorded at Deed Book 156, page 242, _____ County, State of _____.

_____
William Clyde Smith

Sworn to and subscribed before me this _____ day of _____, 19__.

_____
Notary Public

STATE OF _____
COUNTY OF _____

    Before me, the undersigned attesting officer, came in person _____, who, after having been first duly sworn, deposes and on oath says that deponent is not the _____ referred to in the following:

    That there are no judgments or executions of any kind or nature outstanding against deponent; and

    That this affidavit is made for the purpose of inducing _____ to make a loan secured by a loan deed on or to purchase property known as:

_____

_____

                                     _____

Sworn to and subscribed before me this
_____ day of _____, 19__.

_____
Notary Public

EXHIBIT 17-5
Similar Name Affidavit

STATE OF _____
COUNTY OF _____

    The undersigned, being duly sworn, deposes, certifies and states on oath as follows:

    That the undersigned is not a "foreign person" as such term is defined in the United States Internal Revenue Code of 1954, as amended (the "Code") and regulations promulgated thereunder, and is not otherwise a "foreign person" as defined in Section 1445 of the Code;

    That the undersigned's United States taxpayer identification number is; _____;

    That the undersigned is making this Affidavit pursuant to the provisions of Section 1445 of the Code in connection with the sale of the real property described on Exhibit "A" attached hereto and incorporated herein by reference, from the undersigned to   which sale constitutes the disposition of the undersigned of a United States real property interest, for the purpose of establishing that   is not required to withhold tax pursuant to Section 1445 of the Code in connection with such sale;

    That the undersigned acknowledges that this Affidavit may be disclosed to the Internal Revenue Service by   , that this Affidavit is made under penalty of perjury, that any false statement made herein could be punished by fine, imprisonment, or both.

    Under penalty of perjury, I declare that I have examined the foregoing Affidavit and hereby certify that it is true, correct and complete.

Sworn to and subscribed before
me this _____ day of _____,
19__.

_____   _____
Notary Public

EXHIBIT 17-6
Foreign Person Affidavit

EXHIBIT 17–7
Federal National
Mortgage
Association
Affidavit and
Agreement

◆◆ **FannieMae**

Affidavit and Agreement
(by Borrower and Property Seller)

_____ OF _____)
(Name of State, Dist. or Territ   )

) SS

_____ OF _____)
(Name of County, if applic.)

Before me, _____, a notary public in and for _____ personally appeared
_____ (referred to herein, whether one or more persons, as "Borrower Affiant"); and
_____ (referred to herein, whether one or more persons, as "Seller Affiant"); and each such person,
being of lawful age and being duly sworn according to law, upon oath deposes and makes the applicable statements contained in Section III below; and Borrower Affiant and Seller Affiant also agree as provided in Section II below.

I.   **REPRESENTATIONS:**

Representation No. 1. That Borrower Affiant is the party named in a promissory note (referred to herein as the "Note") and a mortgage, deed of trust, or deed to secure debt (referred to herein as the "Security Instrument"), both bearing date of _____,
19_____, evidencing and securing a loan (referred to herein as the "Loan") constituting a lien on the property located at _____ (Property Address) (referred to herein as the "Property"), the Loan having been made to Borrower Affiant by _____ (referred to herein as the "Lender").

Representation No. 2. That Seller Affiant is the seller of the Property to Borrower Affiant.

Representation No. 3. That the purpose of the Loan is as shown by X in the appropriate space below:

☐ to finance Borrower Affiant's purchase of the Property, at a purchase price of $_____.

☐ to refinance outstanding debt against the Property.

☐ for the following purpose: _____

_____

_____

_____

_____

Representation No. 4. That the financial terms of the transaction constituting or related to the Loan are as follows:

Amount of the First Mortgage on the Property . . . . $_____

Cash Equity (if the Loan is not a refinancing) . . . . $_____

Purchase Price of the Property . . . . $_____

Initial Monthly Payment under the Note . . . . $_____

There is no subordinate financing relating to the Property except as specifically set forth immediately below:

Terms of Subordinate Financing
Amount: $_____
Interest Rate: _____% Term: _____ months
Monthly Payment: $_____
Name and address of the holder of such subordinate financing:

_____

_____

_____

Representation No. 5. That Borrower Affiant has not given, conveyed, permitted, or contracted for, or agreed to give, convey, or permit any lien upon the Property to secure a debt or loan, except for any lien connected with subordinate financing upon the Property, as fully disclosed in Representation No. 4 above, and the lien referred to in Representation No. 1 above.

Representation No. 6. That if the Loan is for the purpose of financing Borrower Affiant's purchase of the Property, no expenses or charges relating to, or in connection with, Borrower Affiant's purchase of the Property, such as interest charges, real estate taxes, hazard insurance premiums, initial mortgage insurance premiums, or of funds to be used for renewal of mortgage insurance relating to the Loan, have been, or will be, paid, funded, or borne by Seller Affiant for or on behalf of Borrower Affiant, except as otherwise specifically stated immediately below.

Representation No. 7. As indicated by X in the appropriate space adjacent to A or B below.

☐ A. That (if indicated by X in the appropriate space adjacent hereto) Borrower Affiant now occupies the Property as Borrower Affiant's principal residence, or in good faith will so occupy the Property, commencing such occupancy not later than: (a) thirty (30) days after this date or (b) thirty (30) days after the Property shall first have become ready for occupancy as a habitable dwelling, whichever is later.

☐ B. That (if indicated by X in the appropriate space adjacent hereto) Borrower Affiant does not occupy the Property as Borrower Affiant's principal residence and does not intend to do so.

Initials of Borrower Affiant: Initials of Seller Affiant:

_____   _____

_____   _____

II.   **AGREEMENT PROVISIONS:**

A. Borrower Covenant. Borrower Affiant agrees that (if an X is placed in the appropriate space adjacent to Representation No. 7A of Section I above): (1) it shall be an additional covenant of the Security Instrument that Borrower/Affiant occupy the property as provided in such Representation No. 7A; and (2) failure to so occupy the property shall constitute a breach of covenant under the Security Instrument that shall entitle the Lender, its successors and assigns, to exercise the remedies for a breach of covenant provided in the Security Instrument.

B. Inducement Agreement. Borrower Affiant and Seller Affiant agree and acknowledge that the foregoing Borrower Covenant (if applicable), the Representations made in Section I above, and the Statements under Oath made in Section III below are made for the purpose of inducing the Lender and its assigns to make or purchase the Loan.

APV-779 2/87

Fannie Mae
Form 1009 Aug. 86

EXHIBIT 17–7
Federal National
Mortgage
Association
Affidavit and
Agreement
(continued)

III.   **STATEMENTS UNDER OATH**

   A. By Borrower Affiant: Borrower Affiant hereby deposes and says upon oath that those Representations referred to and set forth in Section I above as Representations Nos. 1, 3, 4, 5, 6, and (if applicable) Representation No. 7A are true and correct.

   B. By Seller Affiant: Seller Affiant hereby deposes and says upon oath that those Representations referred to and set forth in Section I above as Representations Nos. 2 and 6 are true and correct, and that Representations Nos. 1, 3, 4, 5, and (if applicable) Representation No. 7A, as referred to and set forth in such Section, are true and correct to the best of Seller Affiant's knowledge, information, and belief.

_____   _____
           (Signature)   (Signature)
        (Borrower Affiant)   (Seller Affiant)

_____   _____
           (Signature)   (Signature)
        (Borrower Affiant)   (Seller Affiant)

Sworn to and subscribed before me this _____ day of _____ 19_____.

                                          _____
                                               Notary public in and for

               (SEAL)

My commission expires:

_____
           (Date)

CERTIFICATE AND ACKNOWLEDGEMENT BY LENDER

The Lender hereby represents to, and certifies for the reliance of, any party to which the Loan hereafter is sold or assigned, that all of the applicable representations and statements contained in Sections I and III above are true and correct to the best of the Lender's knowledge, information, and belief. In addition, the Lender hereby acknowledges and accepts the Borrower Covenant (if applicable) and the Inducement Agreement, set forth, respectively, in Paragraphs A and B of Section II above.

_____ by   _____
        (Name of Lender)   (Signature)

_____   _____
           (Date)   (Title)

(This form should be executed by the borrower(s), property seller(s) and lender on the date the Loan is closed.)

ADVISORY NOTICE

If any statement in the foregoing Affidavit and Agreement is made under oath by Borrower Affiant or Seller Affiant with knowledge that such statement is false, the person making such false statement may be subject to civil and criminal penalties under applicable law.

In addition, any breach of the covenant by Borrower Affiant relating to occupancy of the Property (as set forth in Paragraph A of Section II above) will entitle the holder of the Note to exercise its remedies for breach of covenant under the Security Instrument. Such remedies include, without limitation, requiring immediate payment in full of the remaining indebtedness under the Loan together with all other sums secured by the Security Instrument, and exercise of power of sale or other applicable foreclosure remedies, to the extent and in the manner authorized by the Security Instrument.

                                                              Fannie Mae
                                                              Form 1009 Aug. 86

EXHIBIT 17–8
General Warranty
Bill of Sale

STATE OF
COUNTY OF

FOR AND IN CONSIDERATION of the sum of Ten and NO/100 Dollars ($10.00) and other good and valuable consideration in hand paid to _____ (hereinafter referred to as "Seller") by _____ (hereinafter referred to as "Purchaser"), Seller hereby sells and conveys to Purchaser, her successors and assigns, any and all existing fixtures, equipment, furniture, appliances and other personal property owned by Seller and used in connection with and being situated on or within certain improved real estate of Seller located in _____ County, _____, and more particularly described on Exhibit "A" attached hereto and by this reference incorporated herein and made a part hereof.

Seller hereby covenants with and represents and warrants to Purchaser as follows:

1. That Seller is lawfully seized and possessed of said personal property.
2. That Seller has the right to sell, transfer and convey the same;
3. That same is free and clear of any and all encumbrances; and
4. That Seller warrants and will forever defend the title to same against all claims whatsoever.

IN WITNESS WHEREOF, Seller has hereunto caused its hand and seal to be applied this _____ day of _____, 19__.

Signed, sealed and delivered this _____ day of _____, 19__, in the presence of:

(Seal)

_____

_____
Witness

_____
Notary Public
My Commission Expires:

_____

EXHIBIT 17–9
Assignment of
Warranties

For good and valuable consideration, the undersigned, hereby transfers and assigns unto _____

_____ all right, title and interest of the undersigned, in and to any and all equipment, construction, and appliances warranties of any nature whatsoever pertaining to all or part of the real property described in Exhibit "A" attached hereto and incorporated herein by reference and in or pertaining to all or any of the improvements located on such real property.

This Assignment is made without warranty by the undersigned and without recourse, it being the intention of the undersigned and the purpose of this document only to transfer and assign unto _____ whatever right, title and interest that the undersigned may have in such warranties, if any, nothing more.

IN WITNESS WHEREOF, the undersigned, have hereunto set their hands and seals this _____ day of _____, 19__.

Signed, sealed and delivered this _____   _____ (SEAL)
day of _____, 19___.

In the presence of: _____ (SEAL)

_____
Witness

_____
Notary Public
My Commission Expires:

_____
Notarial Seal

EXHIBIT 17-9
Assignment of
Warranties
(continued)

STATE OF _____)
) ss:
COUNTY OF _____)

    THIS INDENTURE, made and entered into this _____ day of _____, 19__, by and between _____
_____ (hereinafter referred to as "Assignor") and _____
_____,
its successors and assigns, (hereinafter referred to as "Assignee").

WITNESSETH:

    WHEREAS, Assignor has on even date herewith conveyed to Assignee certain improved real property located in _____ County, _____ (hereinafter referred to as the "Property"), more particularly described on Exhibit "A" attached hereto and made a part hereof, and in connection therewith Assignor desires to transfer and assign to Assignee the tenant leases and security deposits in existence with regard to the improvements located on the Property;

    NOW, THEREFORE, for and in consideration of the sum of TEN AND NO/100 ($10.00) DOLLARS and other good and valuable consideration, the receipt and sufficiency of which are hereby acknowledged, Assignor and Assignee covenant and agree as follows:

1. Assignment of Leases.

Assignor hereby transfers and assigns to Assignee all of Assignor's right, title and interest as landlord or lessor in and to each of the leases described on Exhibit "B" attached hereto and made a part hereof (hereinafter referred to as the "Leases") affecting all or any part of the Property.

2. Indemnification of Assignee.

Assignor indemnifies, defends and holds Assignee, its successors and assigns, harmless from and against any claim against or liability of Assignee, its successors and assigns, arising out of the covenants and duties of the lessor/landlord under the Leases to be performed before the date hereof by Assignor.

3. Assignment of Security Deposit.

Assignor hereby transfers and conveys to Assignee all of Assignor's right, title and interest in and to all security deposits collected by Assignor under the Leases, said security deposits being more particularly described on Exhibit "B" attached hereto and made a part hereof.

EXHIBIT 17-10
Assignment of
Leases and Security
Deposits

EXHIBIT 17–10
Assignment of
Leases and Security
Deposits
(continued)

4. Indemnification of Assignor.

Assignee indemnifies, defends, and holds Assignor harmless from any and all claims against or liabilities of Assignor arising out of the covenants and duties of Assignor to return the security deposits and fees assigned herein and assumes the obligation of landlord or lessor and agrees to perform under the Leases pursuant to the conditions contained in the Leases.

5. Successors and Assigns.

This Assignment shall be binding upon and inure to the benefit of the Assignor and Assignee and their respective successors and assigns.

6. Governing Law.

This Assignment shall be governed and construed in accordance with the laws of the State of _____.

IN WITNESS WHEREOF, the undersigned parties have hereunto set their hands and seals, as of the day and year first above written.

ASSIGNOR:

Signed, sealed and delivered in the presence of:

_____ (SEAL)

_____
Witness

_____
Notary Public
My Commission Expires:

_____
Notarial Seal

ASSIGNEE:

Signed, sealed and delivered in the presence of:

_____ (SEAL)

_____
Witness

_____
Notary Public
My Commission Expires:

_____
Notarial Seal

EXHIBIT 17–11
Assignment of
Contracts

STATE OF _____)
) ss:
COUNTY OF _____)

THIS INDENTURE, made and entered this _____ day of _____, 19___, by and between _____

_____

(hereinafter referred to as "Assignor") and _____

EXHIBIT 17–11
Assignment of
Contracts
(continued)

_____,
its successors and assigns, (hereinafter referred to as "Assignee").

WITNESSETH:

WHEREAS, Assignor has on even date herewith conveyed to Assignee certain improved real property located in _____ County, _____ (hereinafter referred to as the "Property"), more particularly described on Exhibit "A" attached hereto and made a part hereof, and in connection therewith Assignor desires to transfer and assign to Assignee the service contracts in existence with regard to the improvements located on the Property;

NOW, THEREFORE, for and in consideration of the sum of TEN AND NO/100 ($10.00) DOLLARS and other good and valuable consideration, the receipt and sufficiency of which are hereby acknowledged, Assignor and Assignee covenant and agree as follows:

1. Assignment of Contracts.

Assignor hereby transfers and assigns to Assignee all of Assignor's right, title and interest in and to each of the service contracts described on Exhibit "B" attached hereto and made a part hereof (hereinafter referred to as the "Contracts") affecting all or any part of the Property.

2. Indemnification of Assignee.

Assignor indemnifies, defends and holds Assignee, its successors and assigns, harmless from and against any claims against or liability of Assignee, its successors and assigns, arising out of the covenants and duties of the Assignor under the Contracts to be performed before the date hereof by Assignor.

3. Indemnification of Assignor.

Assignee indemnifies, defends, and holds Assignor harmless from any and all claims against or liabilities of Assignor arising out of the covenants and duties of Assignor and assumes the obligations and agrees to perform under the Contracts pursuant to the conditions contained in the Contracts.

4. Successors and Assigns.

This Assignment shall be binding upon and inure to the benefit of the Assignor and Assignee and their respective successors and assigns.

5. Governing Law.

This Assignment shall be governed and construed in accordance with the laws of the State of _____.

IN WITNESS WHEREOF, the undersigned parties have hereunto set their hands and seals, as of the day and year first above written.

ASSIGNOR:

Signed, sealed and delivered in the presence of:

_____ (SEAL)

_____
Witness

_____
Notary Public

**EXHIBIT 17–11
Assignment of
Contracts
(continued)**

My Commission Expires:

_____

Notarial Seal

ASSIGNEE:

Signed, sealed and delivered in the presence of:

_____ (SEAL)

_____

Witness

_____

Notary Public
My Commission Expires:

_____

Notarial Seal

**EXHIBIT 17–12
Certificate**

I, Zack A. Collins, Secretary of Acme International, Inc. (the "Company"), do hereby certify as follows:

1. Attached hereto as Exhibit "A" is a true and correct copy of resolutions which were duly adopted at a special meeting of the Board of Directors on July 31, 19___, at which a quorum was present and acting throughout and which have not been amended, modified or rescinded in any respect and are in full force and effect on the date hereof.

2. The below named persons have been fully elected and have been qualified and at all times have been and this day are officers of the Company holding the respective offices below set opposite their names and signatures set opposite their names are their genuine signatures.

Mary R. Farris   President   _____
Zack A. Collins   Secretary   _____

Witness my hand and seal of the Company, this _____ day of _____, 19__.

_____
Zack A. Collins, Secretary
[CORPORATE SEAL]

EXHIBIT "A"

RESOLVED, that Acme International, Inc. (hereafter called the "Company") sell the real property described on Exhibit "B" attached hereto and made a part of hereof to Richard Money pursuant to the real estate contract dated May 10, 19__, a copy of which is attached as Exhibit "C" and made a part hereof;

FURTHER RESOLVED, that the President of the Company, Mary R. Farris, is hereby authorized and directed to execute and deliver on behalf of the Company any and all documentation required in connection with the sale of the property.

I, Zack A. Collins, Secretary of Acme International, Inc. (the "Company"), do hereby certify as follows:

1. Attached hereto as Exhibit "A" is a true and correct copy of resolutions which were duly adopted at a special meeting of the Board of Directors on July 31, 19___, at which a quorum was present and acting throughout and which have not been amended, modified or rescinded in any respect and are in full force and effect on the date hereof.

2. The below named persons have been duly elected and have been qualified and at all times have been and this day are officers of the Company holding the respective offices below set opposite their names and signatures set opposite their names are their genuine signatures.

Mary R. Farris	President	_____
Zack A. Collins	Secretary	_____

Witness my hand and seal of the Company, this _____ day of _____, 19___.

_____
Zack A. Collins, Secretary

[CORPORATE SEAL]

EXHIBIT "A"

RESOLVED, that Acme International, Inc. (hereafter called the "Company") purchase the real property described on Exhibit "B" attached hereto and made a part of from Richard Money pursuant to the real estate contract dated May 10, 19--, a copy of which is attached as Exhibit "C" and made a part hereof;

FURTHER RESOLVED, that the President of the Company, Mary R. Farris, is hereby authorized and directed to execute and deliver on behalf of the Company any and all documentation required in connection with the purchase of the property.

EXHIBIT 17-13
Certificate

I, Zack A. Collins, Secretary of Acme International, Inc. (the "Company"), do hereby certify as follows:

1. Attached hereto as Exhibit "A" is a true and correct copy of resolutions which were duly adopted at a special meeting of the Board of Directors on July 31, 19___, at which a quorum was present and acting throughout and which have not been amended, modified or rescinded in any respect and are in full force and effect on the date hereof.

2. The below named persons have been fully elected and have been qualified and at all times have been and this day are officers of the Company holding the respective offices below set opposite their names and signatures set opposite their names are their genuine signatures.

Mary R. Farris	President	_____
Zack A. Collins	Secretary	_____

Witness my hand and seal of the Company, this _____ day of _____, 19___.

_____
Zack A. Collins, Secretary
[CORPORATE SEAL]

EXHIBIT 17-14
Certificate

EXHIBIT 17–14
Certificate
(continued)

EXHIBIT "A"

RESOLVED, that Acme International, Inc. (hereafter called the "Company") borrow money from Second National Bank as outlined by Commitment Letter dated July 31, 19___, a copy of which is attached as Exhibit "B" and made a part hereof;

FURTHER RESOLVED, that the President of the Company, Mary R. Farris, is hereby authorized and directed to execute and deliver on behalf of the Company any and all documentation required in connection with the loan.

EXHIBIT 17–15
Agreement
Regarding Loan
Commitment

FOR VALUABLE CONSIDERATION, the receipt and sufficiency of which are hereby acknowledged, the undersigned hereby agrees that certain Commitment Letter from Second Federal Savings and Loan Association, dated August 25, 19___, amended by letter dated December 13, 19___, a copy of which is attached hereto as Exhibit "A" and made a part hereof, the terms of which have not been satisfied at closing of the loan, shall survive the closing of the loan and shall remain in full force and effect until such time as the loan committed for therein has been paid in full.

IN WITNESS WHEREOF, the undersigned have hereunto set their hands and seals this _____ day of December, 199_.

ACME ASSOCIATES, INC., a Delaware corporation

By: _____
Janice Acme, President

Attest: _____
Aaron Acme, Secretary

[CORPORATE SEAL]

EXHIBIT 17–16
Indemnity
Agreement—
Purchaser–Seller

FOR VALUE RECEIVED, the undersigned Seller and Purchaser of the real property described on Exhibit "A" attached hereto and made a part hereof, (the "Property"), hereby indemnify and agree to hold each other harmless and their successors, assigns, agents, employees, and attorneys, against any and all claims for brokerage fees or commissions claimed by, through or under either of the undersigned and arising from the purchase and sale of the Property.

IN WITNESS WHEREOF, the undersigned have hereunto set their hands and seals this _____ day of _____, 19___.

SELLER:

BY: _____ (SEAL)

PURCHASER:

BY: _____ (SEAL)

FOR VALUE RECEIVED, the undersigned hereby indemnifies and agrees to hold harmless SECOND FEDERAL SAVINGS AND LOAN ASSOCIATION, its successors, assigns, agents, employees, and attorneys, against any and all claims for brokerage fees or commissions claimed by, through or under the undersigned and arising from the issuance of Second Federal Savings and Loan Association's Commitment Letter, dated August 25, 199_, as amended by letter dated December 13, 199_, to the undersigned or in connection with the loan committed for therein.

IN WITNESS WHEREOF, the undersigned has by its duly authorized officers, hereunto set his hand and seal this day of December, 199_.

ACME ASSOCIATES, INC., a Delaware corporation

By: _____

Janice Acme, President

Attest: _____

Aaron Acme, Secretary

[CORPORATE SEAL]

EXHIBIT 17-17
Indemnity Agreement—Borrower-Lender

EXHIBIT 17-18
Attorney's Opinion

To Be Transcribed on Letterhead
for Counsel of Borrower

Date

American Eagle Mortgage Company
Independent Boulevard
U.S.A.

Gentlemen:

We have acted as counsel for Acme, Inc., a Delaware corporation, the "Borrower," in connection with the Loan hereinafter described. The Loan (the "Loan") is secured by a first deed to secure debt in the stated principal sum of One Million and No/Dollars ($1,000,000.00). The Loan has been made by American Eagle Mortgage Company ("Lender") as a loan pursuant to Lender's commitment dated October 18, 199_, as modified by letter dated November 18, 199_. The Loan is evidenced and secured by the following instruments (herein generally called the "Loan Documents"), each dated as of _____,
199_, and each being executed by Borrower.

  A. The Loan is evidenced by the Promissory Note (the "Note") made by Borrower in the stated principal amount of _____
     /100 Dollars ($ _____)
     bearing interest at the rate set out therein, due in regular installments with a final payment due on _____,
     payable to the order of Lender.
  B. The Loan is secured by a Deed to Secure Debt and Security Agreement (with Assignment of Rents) (the "Security Deed") made by Borrower to Lender, as grantee, encumbering certain improved real property, furniture, furnishings, and equipment (all herein generally called the "Premises") owned by Borrower in _____ County, _____.

EXHIBIT 17-18
Attorney's Opinion
(continued)

C. The Loan is also secured by an Assignment of Lessor's Interest in Rents and Leases (the "Assignment") made by Borrower, as assignor, to Lender as assignee, assigning all of the rents, issues, profits, and avails of the Premises, and all of the leases now or hereafter in effect with respect to the Premises.

D. The Loan is also secured by a certain Security Agreement and Financing Statement ("Security Agreement") as evidenced by a certain Financing Statement ("Financing Statement") made by Borrower, as debtor, to Lender, as secured party, creating and perfecting a security interest in personal property, fixtures, and equipment comprising part of the Premises.

In connection with the foregoing, we have examined and reviewed the documents referred to in paragraphs A through D above and such other matters as we determined appropriate and necessary for the formulation and rendition of the opinions hereinafter expressed with the knowledge that Lender is making the loan in reliance on said opinion.

Based on the foregoing, we are of the opinion that:

1. Acme, Inc. is a validly formed corporation under the laws of the State of Delaware and is duly authorized to transact business in the State of _____. Acme, Inc. is in good standing under the laws of Delaware and _____.

2. Each of the Loan Documents constitutes the legal, valid and binding obligation and agreement of the Borrower, properly and validly executed and enforceable in accordance with its terms (except as such enforcement may be affected by bankruptcy, insolvency, or other like laws affecting generally the rights of creditors).

3. The Loan is governed by the laws of the State of _____, and under such laws the Loan, including the interest rate reserved or charged in the Note, and all fees and charges paid or to be paid by or on behalf of Borrower or received or to be received by Lender are wholly lawful and not usurious or violative of any law or regulation of the State of _____ governing the payment or receipt of interest.

4. The Security Deed, Assignment, and Financing Statement when duly recorded and/or filed in such places as are required under the laws of the State of _____ will constitute good and valid liens against the Premises and property covered by said Security Deed, Assignment, Security Agreement and Financing Statement.

5. No further approval, consent, order, or authorization of or designation, resignation, declaration, or filing with any governmental authority is required in connection with the valid execution and delivery of the Note, Security Deed, Assignment, Security Agreement, and Financing Statements, the carrying out of the liens created by the Security Deed, Assignment, Security Agreement and Financing Statements, except the future filing by the secured party thereunder of Continuation Statements with respect to the Financing Statements at the times and in the manner specified in the Uniform Commercial Code of the State of _____.

6. We have examined all of the provisions of the Loan Documents and Lender's commitment with Borrower, and we have no knowledge of any event of default which exists under any of them, and we have no knowledge of any facts that

EXHIBIT 17–18
Attorney's Opinion
(continued)

exist which but for notice and/or passage of time would constitute an event of default under any of them, and we have been advised by Borrower that Borrower intends to borrow the full amount of the loan.

7. The execution and delivery of the Loan Documents, the fulfillment of the respective terms and conditions thereof, and the communication of the respective transactions therein contemplated do not conflict with, or constitute a breach of or default under any agreement, indenture or other instrument to which Borrower is a party and is duly authorized by the requisite partnership or corporate authority governing Borrower.

8. The real property and improvements thereon comprised within the Premises are properly zoned for the uses and purposes to which they are presently devoted; and the use and occupancy of the Premises for the business presently conducted thereon are wholly lawful and not violative of any zoning, use building, or environmental protection laws, ordinances, and regulations applicable thereto.

9. All licenses, permits, and authorizations necessary for the use and occupancy of the Premises by Borrower for its business as presently conducted thereon are in full force and effect.

10. All water, gas, electric, storm and sanitary sewer and other utility necessary for the Premises, and the improvements constructed thereon are available to the Premises, and the utility companies or municipalities providing such service have agreed to make available such services to the Premises and the improvements constructed thereon; and there are no pending, or to the best of our knowledge, threatened proceedings before any governmental agency or moratoria which would interfere with or enjoin the furnishing of any utility service to the Premises and such improvements.

11. To the best of our knowledge, there are not threatened or pending actions against the Borrower at law, equity, or bankruptcy.

Very truly yours,

EXHIBIT 17–19
Compliance Agreement

STATE OF _____
COUNTY OF _____

BORROWER(S):
LENDER:
PROPERTY:

The undersigned borrower(s), in consideration of the lender disbursing funds today for the closing of property located at _____ agrees, if requested by lender or someone acting on behalf of said lender, to fully cooperate and adjust for clerical errors, any and all loan closing documentation deemed necessary or desirable in the reasonable discretion of lender to enable lender to sell, convey, seek guaranty or market said loan to any entity, including but not limited to an investor, Federal National Mortgage Association (FNMA), Government National Mortgage Association (GNMA), Federal Home Loan Mortgage Corporation, Department of Housing and Urban Development, Veterans Administration, or any Municipal Bonding Authority.

EXHIBIT 17-19
Compliance Agreement   (continued)

The undersigned borrower(s) do hereby so agree and covenant in order to assure that the loan documentation executed this date will conform and be acceptable in the market place in the instance of transfer, sale or conveyance by lender of its interest in and to said loan documentation.

Dated effective this _____ day of _____, 19___.

_____
Borrower

_____
Borrower

_____
Notary Public

EXHIBIT 17-20
Information for Real Estate 1099-B Report Filing as Required by the Internal Revenue Service

Section 6045 of the Internal Revenue Code, as amended by the Tax Reform Act of 1986, requires the reporting of certain information on every real estate transaction. From the information you provide below, a Form 1099-B will be produced, and a copy of it will be furnished to the I.R.S. and to you no later than January 31 of the next year. If you fail to furnish adequate information (in particular, a taxpayer ID number), then you will be subject to all I.R.S. Regulations, including the possible withholding of twenty percent (20%) of the current sales price.

FILE NUMBER: _____   FILE NAME: _____
SELLER'S NAME:

_____

_____

SELLER'S MAILING ADDRESS:

_____

_____

SOCIAL SECURITY NO.: _____
OR
FEDERAL TAX ID NO.: _____
CLOSING DATE: _____
PROPERTY ADDRESS: _____

_____

SALES PRICE: _____
WAS THIS YOUR PRINCIPAL RESIDENCE?:   Yes _____   No _____
I (We) certify that the above information is correct and understand that it will appear on a Form 1099 that will be sent to me and to the Internal Revenue Service.

DATE _____   _____
                                              SELLER'S SIGNATURE

                                              _____
                                              SELLER'S SIGNATURE

A. SETTLEMENT STATEMENT   **U.S. Department of Housing and Urban Development**

OMB No. 2502-0265

EXHIBIT 17–21
Settlement
Statement

B. Type of Loan

1. ___ FHA	2. ___ FmHA	3. ___ Conv. Unins.	6. File Number	7. Loan Number	8. Mortgage Insurance Case No.#
4. ___ VA	5. ___ Conv. Ins.				

C. NOTE: This form is furnished to give you a statement of actual settlement costs. Amounts paid to and by the settlement agent are shown. Items marked (P.O.C.) were paid outside the closing; they are shown here for information purposes and are not included in the totals.

D. Name and Address of Borrower	E. Name and Address of Seller	F. Name and Address of Lender

G. Property Location	H. Settlement Agent	
	Place of Settlement	I. Settlement Date

J. SUMMARY OF BORROWER'S TRANSACTION:		**K. SUMMARY OF SELLER'S TRANSACTION:**	
100. Gross Amount Due From Borrower		**400. Gross Amount Due To Seller**	
101. Contract sales price		401. Contract sales price	
102. Personal property		402. Personal property	
103. Settlement charges to borrower (line 1400)		403.	
104.		404.	
105.		405.	
Adjustments for items paid by seller in advance		*Adjustments for items paid by seller in advance*	
106. City/town taxes to		406. City/town taxes to	
107. County taxes to		407. County taxes to	
108. Assessments to		408. Assessments to	
109.		409.	
110.		410.	
111.		411.	
112.		412.	
120. GROSS AMOUNT DUE FROM BORROWER		420. GROSS AMOUNT DUE TO SELLER	
200. Amounts Paid By or In Behalf of Borrower		**500. Reductions In Amount Due To Seller**	
201. Deposit or earnest money		501. Excess Deposit (see instructions)	
202. Principal amount of new loan(s)		502. Settlement charges to seller (line 1400)	
203. Existing loan(s) taken subject to		503. Existing loan(s) taken subject to	
204.		504. Payoff of first mortgage loan	
205.		505. Payoff of second mortgage loan	
206.		506.	
207.		507.	
208.		508.	
209.		509.	
Adjustments for items unpaid by seller		*Adjustments for items unpaid by seller*	
210. City/town taxes to		510. City/town taxes to	
211. County taxes to		511. County taxes to	
212. Assessments to		512. Assessments to	
213.		513.	
214.		514.	
215.		515.	
216.		516.	
217.		517.	
218.		518.	
219.		519.	
220. TOTAL PAID BY/FOR BORROWER		520. TOTAL REDUCTION AMOUNT DUE SELLER	
300. Cash At Settlement From or To Borrower		**600. Cash At Settlement To or From Seller**	
301. Gross amount due from borrower (line 120)		601. Gross amount due to seller (line 420)	
302. Less amounts paid by/for borrower (line 220)		602. Less reduction amount due seller (line 520)	
303. CASH BORROWER		603. CASH SELLER	

REV. HUD-1 (3/86)

EXHIBIT 17-21
Settlement
Statement
(continued)

U.S. DEPARTMENT OF HOUSING AND URBAN DEVELOPMENT
SETTLEMENT STATEMENT
PAGE 2

L. SETTLEMENT CHARGES:		PAID FROM BORROWER'S FUNDS AT SETTLEMENT	PAID FROM SELLER'S FUNDS AT SETTLEMENT
700. TOTAL SALES/BROKER'S COMMISSION based on price $ @ =			
Division of commission (line 700) as follows:			
701. $ to			
702. $ to			
703. Commission paid at Settlement			
704.			
800. ITEMS PAYABLE IN CONNECTION WITH LOAN			
801. Loan Origination Fee %			
802. Loan Discount %			
803. Appraisal Fee to			
804. Credit Report to			
805. Lender's Inspection Fee to			
806. Mortgage Application Fee to			
807. Assumption Fee to			
808.			
809.			
810.			
811.			
900. ITEMS REQUIRED BY LENDER TO BE PAID IN ADVANCE			
901. Interest from to @ $ day			
902. Mortgage Insurance Premium for to			
903. Hazard Insurance Premium for yrs to			
904.			
905.			
1000. RESERVES DEPOSITED WITH LENDER FOR			
1001. Hazard Insurance mo.@$ /mo.			
1002. Mortgage Insurance mo.@$ /mo.			
1003. City Property Taxes mo.@$ /mo.			
1004. County Property Taxes mo.@$ 'mo.			
1005. Annual Assessments mo.@$ /mo.			
1006. mo.@$ /mo.			
1007. mo.@$ /mo.			
1008. mo.@$ /mo.			
1100. TITLE CHARGES			
1101. Settlement or closing fee to			
1102. Abstract or title search to			
1103. Title examination to			
1104. Title insurance binder to			
1105. Document Preparation to			
1106. Notary Fees to			
1107. Attorney's fees to			
(includes above items No:)			
1108. Title Insurance to			
(includes above items No:)			
1109. Lender's coverage $			
1110. Owner's coverage $			
1111 TAX REPORT			
1112			
1113			
1200. GOVERNMENT RECORDING AND TRANSFER CHARGES			
1201. Recording Fees: Deed $; Mortgage $; Releases $			
1202. City/county tax/stamps: Deed $; Mortgage $			
1203. State Tax/stamps: Deed $; Mortgage $			
1204			
1205			
1300. ADDITIONAL SETTLEMENT CHARGES			
1301. Survey to			
1302. Pest Inspection to			
1303			
1304			
1305			
1400. TOTAL SETTLEMENT CHARGES (enter on lines 103 and 502, Sections J and K)			

REV. HUD-1 (3/86)

RESIDENTIAL CLOSING EXAMPLE _____

This closing example involves a sale of a residence by a corporate seller, Markam Industries, Inc., to an individual, Helen Davis. (Exhibits 17–22 through 17–35 appear at the end of this chapter.) Helen Davis is obtaining a loan from the American Eagle Mortgage Company for a portion of the purchase price. A review of the sales contract between Markam Industries, Inc., and Helen Davis (see Exhibit 17–22) and the loan commitment (see Exhibit 17–23) from American Eagle Mortgage Company to Helen Davis produces the following checklist.

IIII➡ C H E C K L I S T

Residential Closing Example

1. Title examination
2. Title commitment and policy
3. Survey
4. Corporate resolution
5. Foreign person affidavit
6. 1099–B form
7. Owner's affidavit
8. Transfer tax certificate
9. Warranty deed

10. Bill of sale
11. Termite letter
12. Truth-in-lending disclosure statement
13. Borrower's affidavit
14. Promissory note
15. Deed to secure debt
16. Hazard and fire insurance
17. Settlement statement

After preparing the checklist, a legal assistant would approach the checklist in the following manner.

Title Examination

The title examination should be ordered the same day the file is opened. The title examiner needs a legal description of the property and the current owner's name. In addition, the title examiner should be informed of the title company that will issue the insurance so that the examination can be certified in favor of the title company. The title examiner should be given a date for the completion of the examination. This date should be at least three to five business days before the closing date. The examiner should be instructed to provide copies of all title exceptions and a copy of any plat involving the property. The seller's name and a description of the property can be taken from the real estate sales contract. The seller in this case is Markam Industries, Inc., and the property is Lot 12, Bassett Hall Subdivision, pursuant to the plat recorded at Plat Book 68, Page 79, lying and being in Land Lot 359 of the 18th District of Fulton County, Georgia. A copy of the title examination report is shown as Exhibit 17–24.

Title Commitment

The title insurance company issuing the title commitment needs to be informed that a title examination is being prepared and will be delivered to it. The title company also needs to know the types of policies to be issued, the owners or lenders, the names of the insureds, and the amount of the insurance. The title company should be provided with the date for the issuance of the title commitment. In this case, assuming that both an owner's and a lender's policy will be issued, the title company should be instructed to issue a commitment for a $38,000 loan policy to American Eagle Mortgage Company and an owner's commitment for $47,500 to Helen Davis.

Survey

The survey should be ordered as soon as possible. The surveyor needs the legal description and the names of the parties to whom the survey should be certified. The survey typically is certified in the names of the purchaser and the lending institution. In this example, these would be Helen Davis and American Eagle Mortgage Company. The surveyor also should indicate on the survey if the property is in a flood zone. The surveyor should provide the title company with a surveyor's inspection report form so that the title company can delete its standard survey exception. The date for completion of the survey, which should be three to five business days before the closing, should be given to the surveyor. The surveyor also should be instructed to provide the legal assistant with a minimum of six prints of the survey.

Corporate Resolution

Markam Industries, Inc., is a corporation, and a corporate seller of property requires a resolution of the board of directors authorizing the sale of the property and the signatures on the various documents. A form of the corporate resolution is shown as Exhibit 17–25.

Foreign Person Affidavit

The Internal Revenue Service requires that the purchaser withhold 10 percent of the sale proceeds if the seller is a foreign corporation. An affidavit is used to indicate that the seller is not a foreign person or foreign corporation so that withholding is not required. The foreign person affidavit is shown as Exhibit 17–26.

Owner's Affidavit

The owner's affidavit is a title affidavit wherein the owner of the property, Markam Industries, Inc., swears that they own the property and that the property is free and clear of all liens and encumbrances except those shown on the exhibit attached. The liens and encumbrances that appear on the exhibit are those that appear from the title examination. The owner's affidavit is shown as Exhibit 17–27.

Transfer Tax Certificate

The transfer tax certificate is unique to Georgia (see Exhibit 17–28). Georgia requires a transfer tax to be assessed on deeds. The tax is 10 cents for each $100 of consideration for the property being transferred. The certificate is filed in duplicate with the deed. Several other states have recording fees and requirements, and it is not unusual for some type of certificate to be provided to the clerk indicating the amount of tax due on the recordation of the deed.

Warranty Deed

The property is transferred by warranty deed, and in this case, the deed is from Markam Industries, Inc., to Helen Davis. The only title exceptions that will appear

New York:
When a deed is transferred, New York State charges a transfer tax for any conveyance of real property (this includes the sale of a home, a cooperative, or a condominium–Article 31 of NY Tax Law). This is discussed in detail earlier in this book.

In addition, New York City, Yonkers, and Mount Vernon also have an additional transfer tax.

If the seller is a foreigner, there is a tax to be paid called the Foreign Investment Real Property Tax (FIRPTA).

on the warranty deed are those title exceptions that survive closing: taxes for the current year and the two easements from the title examination. The warranty deed is shown as Exhibit 17–29.

Bill of Sale

The warranty deed transfers only title to real property. The personal property included in the sale is transferred by bill of sale (see Exhibit 17–30).

Termite Letter

In many states, termites are a problem. This sales contract requires that a termite letter indicating that the property is free and clear of termites or that a termite bond be provided at closing.

Truth-in-Lending Disclosure Statement

Federal law requires on a residential loan that the borrower, Helen Davis, be informed of all the costs of the loan before the closing of the loan. The truth-in-lending disclosure statement is shown as Exhibit 17–31.

Borrower's Affidavit

This title affidavit is similar to the owner's affidavit signed by Markam Industries, Inc. (see Exhibit 17–32). This affidavit is signed by Helen Davis.

Promissory Note

This is the promise to pay money from Helen Davis to American Eagle Mortgage Company. The note should be prepared from the information found in the lender's commitment letter. Typically, payments will begin on the first day of the second month after closing. Only one original note is signed at closing. The promissory note is shown as Exhibit 17–33.

Deed to Secure Debt

This is the security document conveying to American Eagle Mortgage Company the real property as security for the note (see Exhibit 17–34). The grantor of the security deed is Helen Davis and the grantee is American Eagle Mortgage Company. All the necessary information to complete the form can be obtained from the contract for sale and the lender's commitment letter.

Hazard Insurance

The lender requires that the real property be insured and that the lender, American Eagle Mortgage Company, appear as a mortgagee on the policy. The original insurance policy together with an endorsement showing American Eagle Mortgage Company as a mortgagee and a statement that the premium has been paid one year in advance must be made available at closing.

Settlement Statement

The settlement statement form is the HUD–1 required by the Real Estate Settlement Procedures Act. It is an outline and disclosure of all costs involved in the closing of the sale of the loan.

The form of HUD–1 used for the Helen Davis–Markam Industries, Inc., transaction is shown as Exhibit 17–35. The following explanation is a line item-by-line item explanation of how the numbers that appear on the settlement statement were arrived at. The discussion begins with a computation of the settlement costs in Schedule L, which appears on the second page of the settlement statement.

Line 700 is used to compute the sale broker's commissions. These commissions are found in the contract of sale between seller and buyer. The contract provides that the commission will be 7 percent of the sales price of $47,500, or $3,325. The commission is to be split 50/50 between Ajax Realty Company and Northside Realty Co., Inc. Northside has received $1,000 earnest money at closing and will retain the $1,000 as a setoff against the commission owed to it. Therefore, total commissions paid at closing will be $3,325 less the $1,000 earnest money retained by Northside Realty Co., or $2,325. The $2,325 is placed under the seller's column.

Line 800 items are payable in connection with the loan. These items are found in the lender's commitment letter. On this particular transaction, only the items shown on lines 803, 808, and 809 are payable in connection with the loan, and they are payable by the borrower.

Line 900 items are required by the lender to be paid in advance at closing. This loan is closing on April 25, but the first payment is not due until June 1. The June 1 payment will pay interest in arrears from May 1 through May 31. It will, therefore, be necessary to collect, at closing, interest for the remainder of April. Interest will be collected from the date of closing through the end of April, or from April 25 to April 30—six days. A lender may in a commitment letter give a per diem interest charge. This amount has not been shown, and the method for calculating the charges is as follows: loan amount ($38,000) x interest rate (11%) equals $4,180; divide this by 365 (or 360 in some cases) to get $11.45 per day. Multiplying $11.45 by the number of days (six) equals $68.70. The amount of $68.70 should be entered on line 901 under the borrower's column.

Line 1000 items are reserves deposited with the lender for taxes and insurance. To calculate the insurance reserve, take the total insurance bill for the year and divide it by 12 ($185 divided by 12 equals $15.42 per month). Because the premium has been paid for one year in advance of the date of closing, the next premium on the insurance is not due until April 25 of the next year. The lender requires that one-twelfth of the insurance premium be paid each month, with the monthly payments beginning on June 1. Calculate the number of these payments from June 1 until April 25 of next year, and eleven payments will be made. The lender will need to collect at least one month's insurance to have enough to pay the bill. The lender can, under federal law, collect two months' insurance and usually does.

Lines 1003 and 1004 are the tax escrows. Tax bills can be obtained from the title report. Divide this tax bill by 12 to show a monthly amount. You will need to know when the tax bills are due to set up the escrow reserves. Tax bills in the example are due October 1, and the lender is going to receive one-twelfth of the taxes with each monthly payment—June, July, August, and September, or four payments. Therefore, it will be necessary to escrow at least eight payments to have enough money when the bills are due. The computation for this is as follows: city taxes $156.80 divided by 12 equals $13.07 per month times 8 equals $104.56; county taxes $310.56 divided by 12 equals $25.88 per month times 8 equals $207.04.

Line 1100 items are title charges and attorneys' fees. These are invoiced by the providers of the title charges. For this example, the charges are given on the expense sheet (Example 17–1).

Line 1200 items are recording and transfer charges. Recording fees vary from state to state. For this example, the recording fees are given on the expense sheet.

EXAMPLE 17–1 EXPENSE SHEET

FEES

Attorney's Fees	$250.00
Title Insurance	120.00
Survey	75.00
Hazard Insurance Premium	185.00 per year
Recording Fees	$2.00 per page
	$1.00 per instrument
Transfer Tax	.10 per $100.00
Intangibles Tax	1.50 per $500.00
1st Mortgage Payoff	$28,655.00
Jim Baxter is President of Markam Industries, Inc.	
Floyd Knox is Secretary of Markam Industries, Inc.	
Photos	$50.00

Settlement charges are always allocated between borrower and seller and totaled. The contract indicates which charges are assessed to the seller and which to the buyer.

Section J contains a summary of the borrower's transaction. Line 101 is the contract sales price, which can be found in the contract or, in this case, $47,500.

Paragraph 103 contains the settlement charges allocated to the borrower from *line 1400*—$1,284.14.

Paragraph 120 is a total of lines 101 and 103, or $48,784.14.

The *200 columns* are amounts paid by the borrower or on behalf of the borrower. These amounts reduce the borrower's cash requirements at closing.

Line 201 is any earnest money that has been paid. A review of the contract reveals an earnest money check of $1,000. This amount is entered on line 201.

Line 202 is the principal amount of any new loan, which in this case is the loan of $38,000 from American Eagle Mortgage Company. This amount is entered on line 202.

Lines 210 and 211 are prorations of city and county taxes between seller and buyer. The seller is responsible for the current year's taxes for the number of days the seller has owned the property. The computation is made by taking the tax bill for the entire year from the title examination and dividing the bill by 365. The amount received from that computation is then multiplied times the number of days the seller has owned the property to arrive at the appropriate credit amount for the borrower.

All 200 items are totaled and placed on line 220.

Line 300 is the summation of the borrower's transaction and discloses the amount of money needed from the borrower at closing. In this example, the borrower needs $9,636.90. The borrower should be made aware of this as early as possible and informed to bring a cashier's check made payable to the law firm.

Section K is a summary of the seller's transaction. Line 401 is the amount of the sales contract, or $47,500.

Section 500 are reductions from the amount of the sales price due to the seller.

Line 502 is the total of settlement charges due to the seller from *line 1400*, or $2,375.50.

Line 504 is a payoff of the existing first loan of $28,655 on the property. This amount is shown on the expense sheet.

Line 506 is the earnest money deposit of the purchaser.

Lines 510 and 511 are the same prorations under *lines 210 and 211*.

All of the *500 items* are totaled, and the sum is entered on *line 520*.

The *600 column* is the settlement of the seller's transaction and reveals that the seller will leave the closing with $15,322.26.

After a settlement statement is prepared, it is necessary to do a cash reconciliation to make sure that cash in equals cash out. An example of the cash reconciliation for this transaction is shown in Example 17–2.

EXAMPLE 17–2 CASH RECONCILIATION

Cash In:

$38,000.00—American Eagle Mortgage Company
$ 9,636.90—Helen Davis
$47,636.90

Cash Out:

$28,655.00—payment of 1st loan
$15,322.26—payment to seller
$ 2,325.00—real estate commissions
$ 150.00—appraisal fee to American Eagle Mortgage Company
$ 100.00—Commitment fee to American Eagle Mortgage Company
$ 50.00—Photographs
$ 68.70—Prepaid interest to American Eagle Mortgage Company
$ 30.84—Reserves for insurance American Eagle Mortgage Company
$ 104.56—Reserves for city property taxes American Eagle Mortgage Company
$ 207.04—Reserves for county property taxes American Eagle Mortgage Company
$ 250.00—Attorney's fees (law firm)
$ 120.00—Title premium (title company)
$ 17.00—Recording fees
$ 114.00—Intangible tax
$ 47.50—Transfer tax
$ 75.00—Survey
$47,636.90

Closing procedures and document preparation, like other aspects of business life, have been computerized. Software applications exist to assist the legal assistant in preparing a HUD–1 settlement sheet, printing loan documents on residential transactions, and even printing checks for disbursement to the seller, purchaser, and lender. Most law firms that do a reasonable volume of residential work own such software applications. Many of the software applications claim that an entire residential loan package can be completed within thirty minutes, which is far less than the usual three or four hours required without a software package. Software applications also assure accuracy not only in making the computations necessary for the closing statement but also in the repetitive use of data in the various closing documents. Once the correct data is entered into the software, it is accurately and correctly redistributed on the various closing documents.

E T H I C S :   Case Problem

Ann is a real estate legal assistant in a large law firm. Her primary responsibility is to assist two attorneys who represent a bank in the closing of real estate loans. She has developed a good working relationship with the bank's loan officers. In fact, the loan officers send most of their new loans directly to Ann. On receipt from the bank, Ann prepares file opening memorandums for the supervising attorneys' signatures.

It is late Wednesday afternoon, and Ann receives a new loan file from the bank as well as a telephone call from the loan officer. The loan officer indicates that the loan has to close no later than Friday and that it is a super priority matter. A conflicts check on the loan reveals that the borrower had several years ago been represented by one of the lawyers in the firm. It appears that there has been no activity with this client for the past three years. Ann calls the attorney to check out the situation but finds that the attorney is on vacation and will not be back until Monday. The attorney's secretary doesn't know anything about the client. Ann decides that the expedient thing to do is to go ahead and open the file and proceed for a closing.

Thursday morning Ann calls the borrower to go over the closing requirements. Once Ann identifies herself and the firm for which she works, the borrower is relieved to know that she works for the firm that represents him. The borrower is cooperative in providing information for the closing.

After receiving all the necessary information, Ann prepares the closing documents and schedules the closing for 3:00 P.M. on Friday. Ann attempts a number of times to meet with her supervising attorney so that she can review the loan documents but is not successful.

On Friday, Ann receives a call from the borrower, who indicates that he has a surprise business appointment out of town and must leave in an hour. He would like for Ann to come to his office and have him sign the papers. Ann immediately goes to the office. When she arrives, she finds that the borrower has left to pick up airline tickets and will not be back for about forty-five minutes. The borrower's secretary asks that the documents be left with her and she would make sure that the borrower signed them before he left town. She would then courier them back over to Ann. Ann agrees and goes back to the office.

Later that afternoon, the documents arrive in Ann's office and none of them have been notarized. Ann calls the secretary to discuss this fact, and the secretary indicates that she saw the borrower sign the documents. She asks Ann to notarize the documents, everything is O.K. Ann, to close the transaction on time, notarizes the documents.

Later, as Ann is putting the package together for transmittal back to the bank client, her supervising attorney stops by. The attorney would like to review the file before the 3:00 closing. Ann tells her that the closing has already taken place. Ann tells her about the developer's unexpected trip out of town and the trip to his office and the closing at the office. Ann neglects to tell the attorney the part about leaving the documents for signature and her notarization of the documents.

What legal ethics or codes of professional responsibility have been violated in this example?

SUMMARY

Many law firms ask the legal assistant to prepare the documents used in a real estate closing transaction. The legal assistant should be familiar not only with what types of forms must be used but also with the content of these forms. When preparing the forms, the legal assistant must be careful not to make mistakes that will change the transaction or require corrective work. It is important that legal documents be carefully reviewed and proofread to minimize mistakes.

KEY TERMS

Affidavit   Bill of sale

REVIEW QUESTIONS

1. What statement of facts usually is included in a title affidavit?

2. What is the purpose of a hazardous waste affidavit? Why is it important to a purchaser of real property?

3. Why is a foreign person affidavit important to a purchaser?

4. What is the purpose of an assignment of warranties?

An assignment of leases? An assignment of contracts?

5. When is a corporate resolution required in a closing transaction, and why is it important?

6. A lender may require the borrower's attorney to render an opinion as to certain aspects of the loan transaction. What are some of the items that may be covered in an attorney's opinion?

CASE PROBLEMS

1. You are a legal assistant involved in a real estate sale transaction. The seller of the property is Susan T. Clarke. The title examination of the property reveals that there are five judgments against Susan Clarke, S.T. Clarke, and Sue Clarke. You call the seller, Susan T. Clarke, and tell her about the judgments. She informs you on the phone that she is not the Susan Clarke mentioned in the judgments. What do you do to protect the purchaser in the closing?

2. You are a legal assistant representing a purchaser of a home. You have been asked to prepare the sale closing papers. What documents does the Internal Revenue Service require you to prepare in connection with the sale? What information do you need from the various parties to prepare this documentation?

3. You are a legal assistant involved in a real estate sale transaction. The seller is a corporation. You have asked the president of the corporation to bring a corporate resolution authorizing the sale and the execution on behalf of the corporation of the various real estate closing documents. The president of the corporation delivers to you a

corporate resolution signed only by the president and that authorizes only the president to sign all the documents. Is there any additional documentation that you should request from the president to evidence his or her authority to sign the loan closing documents?

4. You are assisting in a real estate sale transaction. The title examination reports that there is an outstanding loan to Second Bank and Trust on the property. The loan is to be satisfied at closing. You believe that the closing will take place on July 10. You obtain from Second Bank and Trust a satisfaction payoff letter indicating how much money is needed to pay the loan as of July 10. The loan closing is delayed and does not take place until July 15. Is there any additional information that you may need from Second Bank and Trust for the July 15 closing?

5. You are preparing a title affidavit for a real estate closing. Exhibit "A" to the affidavit is a legal description of the real property, and Exhibit "B" is a list of title exceptions to the real property. Where would you get the information to complete Exhibits "A" and "B"?

PRACTICAL ASSIGNMENTS

1. You are a legal assistant involved in a real estate sale transaction. The sale is to close on September 10. The title examination reports that county real estate taxes have been paid by the seller for the current year in the amount of $1,640. The tax year for the county begins February 1 and ends January 31. You have been asked to calculate the tax proration between purchaser and seller. What is

the amount of the tax proration, and on which lines of the HUD–1 would the amount appear?

2. You are a legal assistant working on a real estate sale transaction. The title examination reports that real estate taxes for the current year are unpaid in the amount of $1,350 and that they are due November 15 of the year. Your closing is taking place on May 10. The closing also

involves a loan in which the lender wants taxes escrowed. The lender's first payment under the note will be July 1. Calculate the tax proration between seller and purchaser. Calculate the amount of taxes to be escrowed for the lender. Are the amounts the same? If not, should they be?

3. You are a legal assistant involved in a real estate sale transaction. The contract provides that the real estate commission is to be 6 percent of the contract price for the real property. The contract price for the real property is $116,000. The contract also indicates that two brokers are involved, Ajax Realty Company and Beta Realty Company. The commission is to be split 50/50 between these two companies. In addition, Ajax Realty Company has $2,500 earnest money from the purchaser. What information do you need from the parties to prepare lines 700, 701, and 702 of the HUD Uniform Settlement Statement?

4. You are assisting in a real estate closing transaction. The loan is $80,000 at an interest rate of 12 percent per annum. The loan is closing on March 14, and the lender wants the first payment on the loan to begin on May 1. The lender also requires the borrower to pay in advance all interest accruing during March. How much interest would you collect from the borrower at closing?

5. You are assisting in the closing of the sale of a home. The contract price for the home is $86,500. The seller owes a real estate broker a commission of 6 percent of the sales price and other closing costs of $600. In addition, there is an outstanding loan on the property that is to be paid at closing in the amount of $28,400. In addition, real property taxes for the current year in the amount of $2,150 are unpaid. The tax year is the calendar year, and the closing is taking place on August 15. In preparing the Uniform Settlement Statement, how much net money would the seller take home from the closing?

6. You are assisting in the purchase of a home. The contract purchase price is $115,000. The settlement costs allocated to the purchaser are $3,230. Taxes for the current year in the amount of $1,650 have been paid by the seller. The calendar tax year is the calendar year, and the closing takes place on September 25. The purchaser has paid an earnest money deposit of $5,000 for the property and has obtained a loan to purchase the property for $90,000. You are preparing the Uniform Settlement Statement. How much money, if any, does the purchaser need to bring to closing to consummate the sale?

EXHIBIT 17-22
Sales Contract

January 15, _____ , 19 ____

As a result of the efforts of_____ Northside Realty Co., Inc. _____ ,

a licensed Broker, the undersigned Purchaser agrees to buy, and the undersigned Seller agrees to sell, all that tract or parcel of land, with such improvements as are located thereon, described as follows: all that tract or parcel of land lying and being in Land Lot 359 of the 18th District of Fulton County, Georgia, being Lot 12 of Bassett Hall Subdivision, as per plat recorded in Plat Book 68, Page 79, Fulton County, Georgia, being improved property with a house located thereon known as 5167 Tilly Mill Road, Atlanta, Georgia 30302.

together with all electrical, mechanical, plumbing, air-conditioning, and any other systems or fixtures as are attached thereto and all plants, trees, and shrubbery now on the premises.

The purchase price of said property shall be:

_____ Forty Seven Thousand, Five Hundred and No/100 _____ DOLLARS, $ 47,500.00 _____ ,

to be paid as follows:
    All cash at closing

Purchaser has paid to the undersigned, __ One Thousand Dollars ------------------------------- , as Broker,

$ 1,000.00 _____ ( ) cash (X) check, receipt whereof is hereby acknowledged by Broker, as earnest money, which earnest money is to be promptly deposited in Broker's escrow account and is to be applied as part payment of purchase price of said property at the time sale is consummated.

Seller warrants that he presently has title to said property, and at the time the sale is consummated, he agrees to convey good and marketable title to said property to Purchaser by general warranty deed subject only to (1) zoning ordinances affecting said property, (2) general utility easements of record serving said property, (3) subdivision restrictions of record, and (4) leases, other easements, other restrictions and encumbrances specified in this contract. In the event leases are specified in this contract, the Purchaser agrees to assume the Seller's responsibilities thereunder to the tenant and to the Broker who negotiated such leases.

The Purchaser shall move promptly and in good faith after acceptance of this contract to examine title and to furnish Seller with a written statement of objections affecting the marketability of said title. Seller shall have reasonable time after receipt of such objections to satisfy all valid objections and if Seller fails to satisfy such valid objections within a reasonable time, then at the option of the Purchaser, evidenced by written notice to Seller, this contract shall be null and void. Marketable title as used herein shall mean title which a title insurance company licensed to do business in the State of Georgia will insure at its regular rates, subject only to standard exceptions unless otherwise specified herein.

Seller and Purchaser agree that such papers as may be necessary to carry out the terms of this contract shall be executed and delivered by such parties at time the sale is consummated.

Purchaser, its agents, or representatives, at Purchaser's expense and at reasonable times during normal business hours, shall have the right to enter upon the property for the purpose of inspecting, examining (including soil boring), testing, and surveying the property. Purchaser assumes all responsibility for the acts of itself, its agents, or representatives in exercising its rights under this paragraph and agrees to hold Seller harmless for any damages resulting therefrom.

Seller warrants that when the sale is consummated the improvements on the property will be in the same condition as they are on the date this contract is signed by the Seller, natural wear and tear excepted. However, should the premises be destroyed or substantially damaged before the contract is consummated, then at the election of the Purchaser: (a) the contract may be cancelled, or (b) Purchaser may consummate the contract and receive such insurance as is paid on the claim of loss. This election is to be exercised within ten (10) days after the Purchaser has been notified in writing by Seller of the amount of the insurance proceeds, if any, Seller will receive on the claim of loss; if Purchaser has not been notified within forty-five (45) days subsequent to the occurrence of such damage or destruction, Purchaser may, at its option, cancel the contract.

In negotiating this contract, Broker has rendered a valuable service for which reason Broker is made a party to enable Broker to enforce his commission rights hereunder against the parties hereto on the following basis: Seller agrees to pay Broker the full commission when the sale is consummated and in the event the sale is not consummated because of Seller's inability, failure or refusal to perform any of the Seller's covenants herein, then the Seller shall pay the full commission to Broker, and Broker, at the option of Purchaser, shall return the earnest money to Purchaser. Purchaser agrees that if Purchaser fails or refuses to perform any of Purchaser's covenants herein, Purchaser shall forthwith pay Broker the full commission; provided that Broker may first apply one-half of the earnest money toward payment of, but not to exceed, the full commission and may pay the balance thereof to Seller as liquidated damages of Seller, if Seller claims balance as Seller's liquidated damages in full settlement of any claim for damages, whereupon Broker shall be released from any and all liability for return of earnest money to Purchaser. If this transaction involves exchange of real estate, the full commission shall be paid in respect to the property conveyed by each party to the other and notice of the dual agency is hereby given and accepted by Seller and Purchaser. The commission on an exchange shall be calculated on the amount on the basis of which each property is taken in such exchange, according to the contract between the parties, and if no value is placed on any property exchange, then according to the reasonable value thereof. In the event of an exchange, each party shall be regarded as Seller as to the property conveyed by each party.

Commission to be paid in connection with this transaction has been negotiated between Seller and Broker and shall be _____

_____ 7% of the purchase price. _____ .

Time is of essence of this contract.

This contract shall inure to the benefit of, and be binding upon, the parties hereto, their heirs, successors, administrators, executors and assigns.

The interest of the Purchaser in this contract shall not be transferred or assigned without the written consent of Seller.

This contract constitutes the sole and entire agreement between the parties hereto and no modification of this contract shall be binding unless attached hereto and signed by all parties to this agreement. No representation, promise, or inducement not included in this contract shall be binding upon any party hereto.

The following stipulations shall, if conflicting with printed matter, control:

EXHIBIT 17–22
Sales Contract
(continued)

SPECIAL STIPULATIONS

1. Real Estate taxes on said property shall be prorated as of the date of closing.
2. Seller shall pay State of Georgia property transfer tax.
3. Sale shall be closed on or before ___April 25, 19_____.
4. Possession of premises shall be granted by Seller to Purchaser no later than ___April 25, 19_____
5. Seller warrants that all appliances remaining with the dwelling and the heating and air conditioning systems will be in normal operating condition at time of closing. Purchaser shall have the privileges and responsibility of making inspections of said equipment and systems prior to closing of sale.
6. Seller shall provide at time of closing of the transaction a clearance letter from a licensed pest control operator, certified in wood destroying organisms, certifying the property is free from termites and other wood destroying organisms and from structural damage caused thereby and carrying a guarantee that the property will be treated for a period of one year from the date of issuance of said letter.

* continued

    This instrument shall be regarded as an offer by the Purchaser or Seller who first signs to the other and is open for acceptance by the other until _____O'clock ___M., on the ____ day of _____,19___ ; by which time written acceptance of such offer must have been actually received by Broker, who shall promptly notify other party, in writing of such acceptance.

The above proposition is hereby accepted
this _____ day of _____ , 19 ____.

     (Purchaser)   Helen Davis

     (Purchaser)

     (Seller)   Markam Industries, Inc.

     (Seller)

By: Northside Realty Co., Inc.
        (Broker)

* continued

7. All kitchen appliances are included in the sales price.
8. This contract is in cooperation with Ajax Realty Co. and the commission is to be divided 50/50.
9. This contract is subject to the Purchaser obtaining a loan in the principal amount of not less than $38,000.00, shall bear interest at a rate not to exceed 11% per annum and a term of not less than 25 years.

OR IN LIEU OF SAID LETTER

Seller shall provide a Termite Contract that is in full force with a licensed pest control company that may be transferred to the Purchaser, providing said contract covers both ADDITIONAL TREATMENT and REPAIR OF DAMAGE.

FORM 203

IVAN ALLEN CO., ATLANTA

To

From

Commercial Sales Contract

ATLANTA REAL ESTATE BOARD
September, 1972

EXHIBIT 17–23
Loan Commitment

AMERICAN EAGLE MORTGAGE COMPANY

March 7, 19___

Ms. Helen Davis
849 Mentelle Drive, N.E.
Atlanta, Georgia 30308

      Re: Mortgage Loan Commitment—$38,000.00 at 11% for thirty (30) years

Dear Ms. Davis:

    American Eagle Mortgage Company (the "Company") is pleased to inform you that it has acted upon your application and has approved a loan to you, subject to all terms and conditions of this letter. The loan will be in the principal sum of $38,000.00 at an annual rate of 11%, to be repaid as follows:

    In equal consecutive monthly installments of $361.89 per month for thirty (30) years. Each installment, when paid, shall be applied first to the payment of accrued interest and then to the unpaid principal balance.

    The holder may collect a "late charge" not to exceed an amount equal to four percent (4%) of any installment which is not paid within fifteen (15) days of the due date thereof, to cover the extra expenses involved in handling delinquent payments.

    The loan proceeds shall be used for the acquisition of improved real estate (the "Property") located at 5167 Tilly Mill Road, Atlanta, Georgia.

    The loan shall be secured by a first priority lien on the Property and on all improvements now or hereafter existing thereon. The Company's agreement to make the loan to you is subject to satisfaction of the following conditions, all at your sole cost and expense and in a manner acceptable to the Company.

1. The Company shall procure a standard form ALTA mortgagee's policy of title insurance insuring the loan as a first priority lien against the Property, showing there is to be no other encumbrances against the Property which render it unmarketable.

2. You shall provide the Company prior to closing with a recent plat of survey of the Property, together with a surveyor's certificate in form satisfactory to the Company's title insuror, depicting and certifying all improvements on the Property to be completely within the boundary lines of the Property and to be in compliance with all applicable building or set-back line restrictions.

3. You shall provide the Company prior to closing with fire, lightning and extended coverage insurance issued by a company or companies and upon terms acceptable to the Company in at least the sum of $38,000.00. Premiums for such insurance shall be paid by you for not less than one year in advance. All policies shall be issued with a mortgagee clause in favor of and acceptable to the Company and shall be non-cancellable without at least ten (10) days prior written notice to the Company.

4. The Company shall select an attorney to close the loan and to prepare all documents deemed necessary or appropriate by the Company to evidence the loan and to establish the Company's first priority lien against the Property and the Policy. All such loan documents will be in form and substance satisfactory to the Company's closing attorney.

5. All actual fees or expenses (including, without limitation, such closing attorney's fees, title insurance premiums, cost of title examination, abstract of title fee, document preparation fee, cost of survey, appraisal fee, recording fees and intangibles or other taxes) incurred in connection with reviewing your loan application, or with closing, servicing, collecting or cancelling the loan, shall be paid by you.

6. The loan may be assumed by a transferee of the Property, provided the Company gives prior written consent thereto; but any transfer of title to all or any part of the Property whatsoever, or any further encumbrance or other lien imposed against the Property without the Company's prior written consent, will authorize the Company to declare the loan immediately due and payable. Any such assumption, transfer or encumbrance to which the Company shall consent shall be upon such terms and conditions as the Company shall determine and approve.

7. You shall pay a non-refundable commitment fee of $100.00 to the Company upon your acceptance of this commitment letter.

8. You shall provide the Company with photographs of all buildings or other structural improvements on the Property prior to closing.

9. You shall pay an appraisal fee to the Company in the amount of $150.00.

10. The loan is to be escrowed for taxes and insurance premiums.

Very truly yours,
AMERICAN EAGLE MORTGAGE COMPANY

By: _____

     J. Perry Drake
     Treasurer

EXHIBIT 17-23
Loan Commitment (continued)

RE: 5167 Tilly Mill Road, Atlanta, Georgia

A search of the above referenced property as of April 20, 19__ at 5:00 P.M., reveals title to be vested in Markam Industries, Inc., subject to the following objections:

     1. Easement between Sam Turner and Georgia Power Company dated August 6, 1929 recorded at Deed Book 898, page 25, Fulton County Records.

     2. Easement between Markam Industries, Inc. and Georgia Power Company dated February 11, 1988 and recorded in Deed Book 5106, page 810 aforesaid records.

     3. Deed to Secure Debt from Markam Industries, Inc. to The Southern National Bank dated March 3, 1992, recorded in Deed Book 5108, page 83, aforesaid recording securing the original principal amount of $32,000.00.

     4. County taxes have been paid through 19__ but are unpaid for 19__, in the amount of $310.56—due on October 1, 19__.

     5. City of Atlanta taxes paid through 19__; 19__ due in the amount of $156.80 and due on October 1, 19__.

EXHIBIT 17-24
Title Examination

EXHIBIT 17–25
Corporate
Resolution

CERTIFICATE

I, FLOYD KNOX, Secretary of MARKAM INDUSTRIES, INC., a Georgia Corporation (the "Company") do hereby certify as follows:

1. Attached hereto as Exhibit "A" is a true and correct copy of resolutions which were duly adopted at a special meeting of the Board of Directors on _____, 19__, at which a quorum was present and acting throughout and which have not been amended, modified or rescinded in any respect and are in full force and effect from the date hereof.

2. The below-named persons have been duly elected and are qualified and at all times have been and this day are officers of the Company, holding the respective offices below set opposite their names, and signatures set opposite their names are their genuine signatures.

JIM BAXTER
President   _____

FLOYD KNOX
Secretary   _____

WITNESS my hand and seal of the Company this _____ day of _____, 19__.

_____ (SEAL)
FLOYD KNOX
Secretary
[CORPORATE SEAL]

EXHIBIT "A"

RESOLVED, that MARKAM INDUSTRIES, INC., a Georgia Corporation (hereinafter called the "Company"), sell that certain real property more particularly described on Exhibit "B" attached hereto and made a part hereof to HELEN DAVIS pursuant to Contract for Sale dated January 15, 19__;

FURTHER RESOLVED, that the President of the Company, JIM BAXTER, is hereby authorized and directed to execute and deliver on behalf of Company any and all documentation required to sell the property to HELEN DAVIS, including but not limited to, any and all warranty deeds, affidavits, bills of sale and closing statements.

EXHIBIT "B"

All that tract or parcel of land lying and being in Land Lot 359 of the 18th District of Fulton County, Georgia being Lot 12 of Bassett Hall Subdivision as per plat recorded of Plat Book 68, page 79, Fulton County, Georgia Records.

EXHIBIT 17-26
Foreign Person
Affidavit

STATE OF GEORGIA   )
) ss:
COUNTY OF FULTON   )

CERTIFICATE AND AFFIDAVIT
OF NON-FOREIGN STATUS

The undersigned is the President of MARKAM INDUSTRIES, INC., a Georgia corporation (the "Transferor"), and is duly authorized to execute this Certificate and Affidavit in his representative capacity on behalf of the Transferor, as well as in his individual capacity;

That the principal place of business, principal office and chief executive office of the Transferor is located at 210 Corporate Square, Atlanta, Fulton County, Georgia 30303;

That the Transferor is a corporation duly organized and validly existing under the laws of the State of Georgia;

That the Transferor is not a "foreign corporation", as such term is defined in the United States Internal Revenue Code of 1954, as amended (the "Code") and Regulations promulgated thereunder, and is not otherwise a "foreign person", as defined in § 1445 of the Code;

That the Transferor's United States taxpayer identifying number is 58-1004212;

That the undersigned is making this Certificate and Affidavit pursuant to the provisions of § 1445 of the Code in connection with the sale of the real property described on Exhibit "A", attached hereto and incorporated herein by reference, by the Transferor to HELEN DAVIS (the "Transferee"), which sale constitutes the disposition by the Transferor of a United States real property interest, for the purpose of establishing that the Transferee is not required to withhold tax pursuant to § 1445 of the Code in connection with such disposition; and

That the undersigned acknowledges that this Certificate and Affidavit may be disclosed to the Internal Revenue Service by the Transferee, that this Certificate and Affidavit is made under penalty of perjury, and that any false statements made herein could be punished by fine, imprisonment, or both.

Under penalty of perjury, I declare that I have examined the foregoing Certificate and Affidavit and hereby certify that it is true, correct and complete.

                                _____ (SEAL)
                                JIM BAXTER

Certified, sworn to and subscribed before me
this _____ day of _____, 19__.

_____
Notary Public

My Commission Expires:

_____
      [Notarial Seal]

EXHIBIT "A"

All that tract or parcel of land lying and being in Land Lot 359 of the 18th District of Fulton County, Georgia being Lot 12 of Bassett Hall Subdivision as per plat recorded of Plat Book 68, page 79, Fulton County, Georgia Records.

EXHIBIT 17-27
Owner's Affidavit

STATE OF GEORGIA   )
) ss:
COUNTY OF FULTON)

The undersigned, being duly sworn, states:

That the undersigned is the President of MARKAM INDUSTRIES, INC., a Georgia corporation (the "Company"), and is duly authorized to execute this affidavit in his capacity on behalf of the Company as well as in his individual capacity;

That the principal place of business, principal office and chief executive office of the Company is located in Fulton County, Georgia and has been located in said County at all times since the formation of the Company;

That the Company is the fee simple title owner of the real property described on Exhibit "A" attached hereto and incorporated herein by reference (the "Property").

That the lines and corners of the Property are clearly marked and there are no disputes concerning the location of said lines and corners;

That no improvements or repairs have been made or contracted for by the Company on the Property during the three (3) months immediately preceding the date of this affidavit, for which there are outstanding bills for labor or services performed or rendered, or for materials supplied or furnished, or incurred in connection with improvements or repairs on the Property, or for the services of architects, surveyors or engineers in connection with improvements or repairs on the Property;

That, except for the matters set forth on Exhibit "B" attached hereto and incorporated herein by reference, the Property is free and clear of all claims, liens and encumbrances, and there is no outstanding indebtedness for or liens against any equipment or fixtures attached to, installed on, incorporated in or located on, or otherwise used in connection with the operation or maintenance of, the Property or the improvements thereon;

That there are no persons or other parties in possession of the Property who have a right or claim to possession extending beyond the date hereof;

That there are no suits, proceedings, judgments, bankruptcies, liens, or executions against the Company which affect title to the Property, the improvements thereon or the fixtures attached thereto;

That the undersigned is making this affidavit with the knowledge that it will be relied upon by lenders, attorneys, and title insurance companies interested in the title to the Property.

Sworn to and subscribed before me this _____ day of _____, 19___.

_____   _____
Notary Public   JIM BAXTER

My Commission Expires:

_____
[Notarial Seal]

EXHIBIT "A"

All that tract or parcel of land lying and being in Land Lot 359 of the 18th District of Fulton County, Georgia being Lot 12 of Bassett Hall Subdivision as per plat recorded of Plat Book 68, page 79, Fulton County, Georgia Records.

EXHIBIT "B"

1. All taxes for the current year.
2. Easement between Sam Turner and Georgia Power Company dated August 6, 1929, recorded at Deed Book 898, page 25, Fulton County, Georgia Records.
3. Easement between Markam Industries, Inc., and Georgia Power Company dated February 11, 1988 and recorded at Deed Book 5106, page 810, aforesaid records.
4. Deed to Secure Debt from Markam Industries, Inc., to The Southern National Bank dated March 3, 1992, recorded at Deed Book 5108, page 83, aforesaid records securing the original principal amount of $32,000.00.

EXHIBIT 17–27
Owner's Affidavit
(continued)

EXHIBIT 17–28
Transfer Tax
Certificate

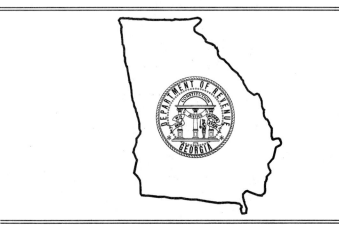

PT-61 (Rev. 8/89) — REAL ESTATE TRANSFER TAX DECLARATION — (Please Type or Print)

SECTION A-SELLER NAME: Markam Industries, Inc.
MAILING ADDRESS (Street and number): 210 Corporate Square
CITY, STATE and ZIP CODE: Atlanta, Georgia 30324

SECTION B-BUYER NAME: Helen Davis
MAILING ADDRESS (Street and number): 5167 Tilly Mill Road
CITY, STATE AND ZIP CODE: Atlanta, Georgia 30302

SECTION C-PROPERTY IDENTIFICATION
1. LOCATION (Street, Route, Hwy. etc.): 5167 Tilly Mill Road
2. COUNTY: Fulton   3. IF WITHIN CITY LIMITS GIVE CITY NAME: Atlanta
4. ACRES   5. DISTRICT: 18   6. LAND LOT: 359   7. SUB LOT AND BLOCK
8. LAST LISTED ON AD VALOREM TAX DIGEST UNDER THE NAME OF
9. YEAR   BILL NUMBER   10. MAP AND PARCEL NUMBER

SECTION D-SALE INFORMATION
1. DATE   2. SALE CONDITIONS   3. CHECK INTENDED USE [ ] R [ ] A [ ] C [ ] I

SECTION E-RECORDING INFORMATION
1. DATE   2. DEED BOOK   PAGE   3. PLAT BOOK   PAGE

SECTION F-TAX COMPUTATION
1. Actual value of consideration received by seller (Fill out 1a below only when value is not known) $47,500.00
1a. Estimated fair market value of Real and Personal property conveyed
2. Fair market value of Personal property only conveyed.
3. Amount of Liens and Encumbrances not removed by transfer.
4. Net Taxable Value (1 minus 2 minus 3) $47,500.00
5. TAX DUE at 10¢ per $100 or fraction thereof. (Minimum $1.00)   47.50

SECTION G-SELLER CERTIFICATION
I hereby certify that all the items of information entered on this transfer form PT-61 are true and correct to the best of my knowledge and belief.
Signature _____ (Seller or Authorized Agent)   (Date)

SECTION H-CLERK OF COURT CERTIFICATION
I hereby certify that the recording information in Section E is correct and that the tax due in Section F5 is computed correctly based upon the information supplied in Section F by the seller or his authorized agent.
Signature _____ (Clerk of Superior Court)   (Date)

REVENUE COPY

STATE OF GEORGIA
REAL ESTATE TRANSFER TAX DECLARATION

(See Instructions Next Page)

(NEW FORM - READ INSTRUCTIONS CAREFULLY BEFORE COMPLETING)

EXHIBIT 17–29
Warranty Deed

WARRANTY DEED

STATE OF   GEORGIA   COUNTY OF   FULTON

THIS INDENTURE, Made the   25th   day of   April   , in the year
one thousand nine hundred   , between

MARKAM INDUSTRIES, INC., a Georgia corporation

of the County of   Fulton   , and State of Georgia, as party or parties of the
first part, hereinafter called Grantor, and

HELEN DAVIS

as party or parties of the second part, hereinafter called Grantee (the words "Grantor" and
"Grantee" to include their respective heirs, successors and assigns where the context requires or
permits).

WITNESSETH that: Grantor, for and in consideration of the sum of   TEN AND NO/100 and
other good and valuable consideration--------------------($10.00   ) DOLLARS
in hand paid at and before the sealing and delivery of these presents, the receipt whereof is hereby
acknowledged, has granted, bargained, sold, aliened, conveyed and confirmed, and by these presents
does grant, bargain, sell, alien, convey and confirm unto the said Grantee,   all that tract or
parcel of land lying and being in Land Lot 359 of the 18th District of Fulton
County, Georgia, being Lot 12 of Bassett Hall Subdivision, as per plat recorded
at Plat Book 68, page 79, Fulton County, Georgia Records.

SUBJECT TO:

Ad valorem taxes for the year 199 and subsequent years.

Easement between Sam Turner and Georgia Power Company dated August 6, 1929,
recorded at Deed Book 898, page 25, Fulton County, Georgia Records.

Easement between Markam Industries, Inc., and Georgia Power Company dated
February 11, 1978 and recorded at Deed Book 5106, page 810, aforesaid records.

TO HAVE AND TO HOLD the said tract or parcel of land, with all and singular the rights,
members and appurtenances thereof, to the same being, belonging, or in anywise appertaining, to the
only proper use, benefit and behoof of the said Grantee forever in FEE SIMPLE.

AND THE SAID Grantor will warrant and forever defend the right and title to the above
described property unto the said Grantee against the claims of all persons whomsoever.

IN WITNESS WHEREOF, the Grantor has signed and sealed this deed, the day and year above
written.

Signed, sealed and delivered in presence of: MARKAM INDUSTRIES, INC.
this ____ day of _____, 19___.

_____ By: _____ (Seal)
Unofficial Witness   JIM BAXTER, President
                        Attest:
_____   _____ (Seal)
Notary Public   FLOYD KNOX, Secretary
                                               [CORPORATE SEAL](Seal)
_____
My Commission Expires   [Notary Seal]

EXHIBIT 17–30
General Warranty
Bill of Sale

STATE OF GEORGIA)

) ss:

COUNTY OF FULTON)

In consideration of the sum of Ten and No/100 ($10.00) Dollars, and other good and valuable consideration in hand paid to MARKAM INDUSTRIES, INC., a Georgia corporation (hereinafter referred to as "Seller") by HELEN DAVIS (hereinafter referred to as "Purchaser"), Seller hereby sells and conveys to Purchaser, its successors and assigns, all personal property, appliances and fixtures located on or used in connection with the property described on Exhibit "A" attached hereto and made a part hereof.

Seller hereby covenants with and represents and warrants to Purchaser as follows:

1. That Seller is lawfully seized and possessed of said personal property;

2. That Seller has a right to sell, transfer and convey the same;

3. That the same is free and clear of any and all encumbrances or security interests;

4. That Seller warrants and forever will defend the title to same against any and all claims whatsoever.

IN WITNESS WHEREOF, Seller, by its duly authorized officers, has hereunto its hand and seal this the _____ day of _____, 19___.

                             MARKAM INDUSTRIES, INC.,

                             a Georgia corporation

                             By: _____ (SEAL)

                                   JIM BAXTER

                                   President

                           Attest: _____ (SEAL)

                                   FLOYD KNOX

                                   Secretary

Signed, sealed and delivered in the presence of this _____ day of _____, 19___.

_____

Unofficial Witness

_____

Notary Pubic

My Commission Expires:

_____

[Notarial Seal]

EXHIBIT "A"

All that tract or parcel of land lying and being in Land Lot 359 of the 18th District of Fulton County, Georgia being Lot 12 of Bassett Hall Subdivision as per plat recorded of Plat Book 68, page 79, Fulton County, Georgia Records.

EXHIBIT 17-31
Truth-in-Lending
Disclosure
Statement

Form 82-17

CREDITOR: AMERICAN EAGLE MORTGAGE COMPANY

FEDERAL TRUTH IN LENDING ACT DISCLOSURE STATEMENT
FIXED RATE MORTGAGE

Borrowers name(s) Helen Davis

Mailing address of subject property 5167 Tilly Mill Road, Atlanta, Georgia 30302

ANNUAL PERCENTAGE RATE	FINANCE CHARGE	Amount Financed	Total of Payments
The cost of your credit as a yearly rate.	The dollar amount the credit will cost you.	The amount of credit provided to you or on your behalf.	The amount you will have paid after you have made all payments as scheduled.
11.125 %	$ 92,380.40	$ 37,900.00	$ 130,280.40

Your payment schedule will be:

Number of Payments	Amount of Payments	When Payments Are Due
360	$361.89	First day of each month commencing on June 1, 19__.

Insurance: Hazard insurance and flood insurance (if the property lies within a flood plain) is required. You may obtain this insurance from anyone you want that is acceptable to Creditor.

Security: You are giving a security interest in the property being purchased.

Late Charge: If a payment is received more than 15 days after it is due, you will be charged 4 % of the payment.

Prepayment: If you payoff early, you
- ☐ may ☒ will not have to pay a penalty.
- ☒ may ☐ will not be entitled to a refund of part of the Finance Charge.

Assumption: Someone buying your home
- ☐ may, subject to conditions be allowed to assume the remainder of the mortgage on the original terms.
- ☐ cannot assume the remainder of the mortgage on the original terms.

See your contract documents for any additional information about nonpayment, default, any required repayment in full before the scheduled date, and prepayment refunds and penalties.

"e" means an estimate

Type of Disclosure and Certificate or Acknowledgement (check applicable box)

☐ **Original Disclosure.** The undersigned representative of the Creditor certifies that the Real Estate Settlement Procedures Act (RESPA) Information Booklet, "The RESPA Good Faith Estimate of Settlement Costs," and the above Federal Truth in Lending Act Disclosure Statement appropriately completed so as to reflect the mortgage loan for which Borrower(s) have applied to Creditor were on the date indicated below deposited in the U.S. Mail, first class postage prepaid addressed to the Borrower(s) at the following mailing address:

_____

Date: _____   _____
                                Signature of Creditor's Representative

☐ **Corrective Redisclosure.** Borrower(s) have applied to Creditor for a mortgage loan the proceeds of which will be used to purchase a dwelling. Shortly after receiving Borrower(s) application the Creditor provided to Borrower(s) a Federal Truth in Lending Act Disclosure Statement (the "Original Disclosure Statement") which contained important information about the mortgage loan for which Borrower(s) have applied. Some of the disclosures contained in the Original Disclosure Statement do not accurately reflect certain details of the actual mortgage loan that Borrower(s) are receiving from Creditor. This is due to the fact that certain disclosures contained in the Original Disclosure Statement were based on estimates or due to the fact that certain details of the requested mortgage loan have changed since the date the Original Disclosure Statement was prepared. The purpose of this Corrective Redisclosure Statement is to provide Borrower(s) with disclosures that accurately reflect the actual mortgage loan that Borrower(s) are receiving from creditor. The undersigned hereby acknowledge receipt of a copy of this Federal Truth in Lending Disclosure Statement this date.

_____   _____
Signature of Borrower HELEN DAVIS   Date

_____   _____   _____
Witness   Signature of Co-Borrower   Date

EXHIBIT 17-32
Owner's Affidavit

STATE OF GEORGIA)
) ss:
COUNTY OF FULTON)

The undersigned, being duly sworn, states:

That the undersigned is the fee simple title owner of the real property described on Exhibit "A" attached hereto and incorporated herein by reference (the "Property").

That the lines and corners of the Property are clearly marked and there are no disputes concerning the location of said lines and corners;

That no improvements or repairs have been made or contracted for by the undersigned on the Property during the three (3) months immediately preceding the date of this affidavit, for which there are outstanding bills for labor or services performed or rendered, or for materials supplied or furnished, or incurred in connection with improvements or repairs on the Property, or for the services of architects, surveyors or engineers in connection with improvements or repairs on the Property;

That, except for the matters set forth on Exhibit "B" attached hereto and incorporated herein by reference, the Property is free and clear of all claims, liens and encumbrances, and there is no outstanding indebtedness for or liens against any equipment or fixtures attached to, installed on, incorporated in or located on, or otherwise used in connection with the operation or maintenance of, the Property or the improvements thereon;

That there are no persons or other parties in possession of the Property who have a right or claim to possession extending beyond the date hereof;

That there are no suits, proceedings, judgments, bankruptcies, liens, or executions against the undersigned which affect title to the Property, the improvements thereon or the fixtures attached thereto;

That the undersigned is making this affidavit with the knowledge that it will be relied upon by lenders, attorneys, and title insurance companies interested in the title to the Property.

Sworn to and subscribed before me this
day of _____, 19___.

_____   _____
Notary Public   HELEN DAVIS
My Commission Expires:

_____

[Notarial Seal]

EXHIBIT "A"

All that tract or parcel of land lying and being in Land Lot 359 of the 18th District of Fulton County, Georgia being Lot 12 of Bassett Hall Subdivision as per plat recorded of Plat Book 68, page 79, Fulton County, Georgia Records.

EXHIBIT "B"

1. All taxes for the current year.
2. Easement between Sam Turner and Georgia Power Company dated August 6, 1929, recorded at Deed Book 898, page 25, Fulton County, Georgia Records.
3. Easement between Markam Industries, Inc., and Georgia Power Company dated February 11, 1988 and recorded at Deed Book 5106, page 810, aforesaid records.

EXHIBIT 17-33
Promissory Note

NOTE

............April 25........................., 19.........   ....Atlanta...................., ...Georgia......
                                                               [City]   [State]

.....5167 Tilly Mill Road, Atlanta, Georgia 30302...
                                       [Property Address]

1. BORROWER'S PROMISE TO PAY

In return for a loan that I have received, I promise to pay U.S. $....38,000.00................ (this amount is called "principal"), plus interest, to the order of the Lender. The Lender is ....AMERICAN EAGLE MORTGAGE COMPANY.. I understand that the Lender may transfer this Note. The Lender or anyone who takes this Note by transfer and who is entitled to receive payments under this Note is called the "Note Holder."

2. INTEREST

Interest will be charged on unpaid principal until the full amount of principal has been paid. I will pay interest at a yearly rate of ....eleven (11)....%.

The interest rate required by this Section 2 is the rate I will pay both before and after any default described in Section 6(B) of this Note.

3. PAYMENTS

(A) Time and Place of Payments

I will pay principal and interest by making payments every month.

I will make my monthly payments on the ....1st..... day of each month beginning on ......June 1........................, 19.......... I will make these payments every month until I have paid all of the principal and interest and any other charges described below that I may owe under this Note. My monthly payments will be applied to interest before principal. If, on ...., ..., I still owe amounts under this Note, I will pay those amounts in full on that date, which is called the "maturity date."

I will make my monthly payments at ....ADDRESS OF AMERICAN EAGLE MORTGAGE COMPANY......... .... or at a different place if required by the Note Holder.

(B) Amount of Monthly Payments

My monthly payment will be in the amount of U.S. $....361.89.........................

4. BORROWER'S RIGHT TO PREPAY

I have the right to make payments of principal at any time before they are due. A payment of principal only is known as a "prepayment." When I make a prepayment, I will tell the Note Holder in writing that I am doing so.

I may make a full prepayment or partial prepayments without paying any prepayment charge. The Note Holder will use all of my prepayments to reduce the amount of principal that I owe under this Note. If I make a partial prepayment, there will be no changes in the due date or in the amount of my monthly payment unless the Note Holder agrees in writing to those changes.

5. LOAN CHARGES

If a law, which applies to this loan and which sets maximum loan charges, is finally interpreted so that the interest or other loan charges collected or to be collected in connection with this loan exceed the permitted limits, then: (i) any such loan charge shall be reduced by the amount necessary to reduce the charge to the permitted limit; and (ii) any sums already collected from me which exceeded permitted limits will be refunded to me. The Note Holder may choose to make this refund by reducing the principal I owe under this Note or by making a direct payment to me. If a refund reduces principal, the reduction will be treated as a partial prepayment.

6. BORROWER'S FAILURE TO PAY AS REQUIRED

(A) Late Charge for Overdue Payments

If the Note Holder has not received the full amount of any monthly payment by the end of ......15........ calendar days after the date it is due, I will pay a late charge to the Note Holder. The amount of the charge will be ....4.........% of my overdue payment of principal and interest. I will pay this late charge promptly but only once on each late payment.

(B) Default

If I do not pay the full amount of each monthly payment on the date it is due, I will be in default.

(C) Notice of Default

If I am in default, the Note Holder may send me a written notice telling me that if I do not pay the overdue amount by a certain date, the Note Holder may require me to pay immediately the full amount of principal which has not been paid and all the interest that I owe on that amount. That date must be at least 30 days after the date on which the notice is delivered or mailed to me.

(D) No Waiver By Note Holder

Even if, at a time when I am in default, the Note Holder does not require me to pay immediately in full as described above, the Note Holder will still have the right to do so if I am in default at a later time.

(E) Payment of Note Holder's Costs and Expenses

If the Note Holder has required me to pay immediately in full as described above, the Note Holder will have the right to be paid back by me for all of its costs and expenses in enforcing this Note to the extent not prohibited by applicable law. Those expenses include, for example, reasonable attorneys' fees.

7. GIVING OF NOTICES

Unless applicable law requires a different method, any notice that must be given to me under this Note will be given by delivering it or by mailing it by first class mail to me at the Property Address above or at a different address if I give the Note Holder a notice of my different address.

Any notice that must be given to the Note Holder under this Note will be given by mailing it by first class mail to the Note Holder at the address stated in Section 3(A) above or at a different address if I am given a notice of that different address.

MULTISTATE FIXED RATE NOTE—Single Family—**FNMA/FHLMC UNIFORM INSTRUMENT**   Form 3200 12/83

EXHIBIT 17–33
Promissory Note
(continued)

8. OBLIGATIONS OF PERSONS UNDER THIS NOTE

If more than one person signs this Note, each person is fully and personally obligated to keep all of the promises made in this Note, including the promise to pay the full amount owed. Any person who is a guarantor, surety or endorser of this Note is also obligated to do these things. Any person who takes over these obligations, including the obligations of a guarantor, surety or endorser of this Note, is also obligated to keep all of the promises made in this Note. The Note Holder may enforce its rights under this Note against each person individually or against all of us together. This means that any one of us may be required to pay all of the amounts owed under this Note.

9. WAIVERS

I and any other person who has obligations under this Note waive the rights of presentment and notice of dishonor. "Presentment" means the right to require the Note Holder to demand payment of amounts due. "Notice of dishonor" means the right to require the Note Holder to give notice to other persons that amounts due have not been paid.

10. UNIFORM SECURED NOTE

This Note is a uniform instrument with limited variations in some jurisdictions. In addition to the protections given to the Note Holder under this Note, a Mortgage, Deed of Trust or Security Deed (the "Security Instrument"), dated the same date as this Note, protects the Note Holder from possible losses which might result if I do not keep the promises which I make in this Note. That Security Instrument describes how and under what conditions I may be required to make immediate payment in full of all amounts I owe under this Note. Some of those conditions are described as follows:

Transfer of the Property or a Beneficial Interest in Borrower. If all or any part of the Property or any interest in it is sold or transferred (or if a beneficial interest in Borrower is sold or transferred and Borrower is not a natural person) without Lender's prior written consent, Lender may, at its option, require immediate payment in full of all sums secured by this Security Instrument. However, this option shall not be exercised by Lender if exercise is prohibited by federal law as of the date of this Security Instrument.

If Lender exercises this option, Lender shall give Borrower notice of acceleration. The notice shall provide a period of not less than 30 days from the date the notice is delivered or mailed within which Borrower must pay all sums secured by this Security Instrument. If Borrower fails to pay these sums prior to the expiration of this period, Lender may invoke any remedies permitted by this Security Instrument without further notice or demand on Borrower.

WITNESS THE HAND(S) AND SEAL(S) OF THE UNDERSIGNED.

....(Seal)
HELEN DAVIS   -Borrower

....(Seal)
                                                          -Borrower

....(Seal)
                                                          -Borrower

[Sign Original Only]

EXHIBIT 17-34
Security Deed

——————————————————— [Space Above This Line For Recording Data] ———————————————————

SECURITY DEED

THIS SECURITY DEED ("Security Instrument") is given on ....April 25,.................................,
19........... The grantor is ....HELEN DAVIS..
.... ("Borrower"). This Security Instrument is given to ...AMERICAN EAGLE
MORTGAGE COMPANY..., which is organized and existing
under the laws of ...., and whose address is 10 Piedmont Center
Atlanta, Georgia 30017.. ("Lender").
Borrower owes Lender the principal sum of ....THIRTY EIGHT THOUSAND AND NO/100——————————————
——————————————————————————Dollars (U.S. $.38,000.00...........). This debt is evidenced by Borrower's note
dated the same date as this Security Instrument ("Note"), which provides for monthly payments, with the full debt, if not
paid earlier, due and payable on ..May 1, 20.....,.. This Security Instrument
secures to Lender: (a) the repayment of the debt evidenced by the Note, with interest, and all renewals, extensions and
modifications; (b) the payment of all other sums, with interest, advanced under paragraph 7 to protect the security of this
Security Instrument; and (c) the performance of Borrower's covenants and agreements under this Security Instrument and
the Note. For this purpose, Borrower does hereby grant and convey to Lender and Lender's successors and assigns, with
power of sale, the following described property located in ....Fulton.. County, Georgia:

     ALL THAT TRACT or parcel of land lying and being in Land Lot 359
of the 18th District of Fulton County, Georgia, being Lot 12 of Bassett Hall
Subdivision, as per plat recorded in Plat Book 68, page 79, Fulton County,
Georgia Records, being improved property with a house located thereon known as
5167 Tilly Mill Road, Atlanta, Georgia 30302.

which has the address of ....5167 Tilly Mill Road.., ...Atlanta................................,
                                     [Street]   [City]
Georgia ....30302.. ("Property Address");
               [Zip Code]

    TO HAVE AND TO HOLD this property unto Lender and Lender's successors and assigns, forever, together with all
the improvements now or hereafter erected on the property, and all easements, rights, appurtenances, rents, royalties,
mineral, oil and gas rights and profits, water rights and stock and all fixtures now or hereafter a part of the property. All
replacements and additions shall also be covered by this Security Instrument. All of the foregoing is referred to in this
Security Instrument as the "Property."

    BORROWER COVENANTS that Borrower is lawfully seised of the estate hereby conveyed and has the right to grant
and convey the Property and that the Property is unencumbered, except for encumbrances of record. Borrower warrants
and will defend generally the title to the Property against all claims and demands, subject to any encumbrances of record.

    THIS SECURITY INSTRUMENT combines uniform covenants for national use and non-uniform covenants with
limited variations by jurisdiction to constitute a uniform security instrument covering real property.

GEORGIA—Single Family—FNMA/FHLMC UNIFORM INSTRUMENT   Form 3011 12/83

EXHIBIT 17–34
Security Deed
(continued)

UNIFORM COVENANTS. Borrower and Lender covenant and agree as follows:

1. Payment of Principal and Interest; Prepayment and Late Charges. Borrower shall promptly pay when due the principal of and interest on the debt evidenced by the Note and any prepayment and late charges due under the Note.

2. Funds for Taxes and Insurance. Subject to applicable law or to a written waiver by Lender, Borrower shall pay to Lender on the day monthly payments are due under the Note, until the Note is paid in full, a sum ("Funds") equal to one-twelfth of: (a) yearly taxes and assessments which may attain priority over this Security Instrument; (b) yearly leasehold payments or ground rents on the Property, if any; (c) yearly hazard insurance premiums; and (d) yearly mortgage insurance premiums, if any. These items are called "escrow items." Lender may estimate the Funds due on the basis of current data and reasonable estimates of future escrow items.

The Funds shall be held in an institution the deposits or accounts of which are insured or guaranteed by a federal or state agency (including Lender if Lender is such an institution). Lender shall apply the Funds to pay the escrow items. Lender may not charge for holding and applying the Funds, analyzing the account or verifying the escrow items, unless Lender pays Borrower interest on the Funds and applicable law permits Lender to make such a charge. Borrower and Lender may agree in writing that interest shall be paid on the Funds. Unless an agreement is made or applicable law requires interest to be paid, Lender shall not be required to pay Borrower any interest or earnings on the Funds. Lender shall give to Borrower, without charge, an annual accounting of the Funds showing credits and debits to the Funds and the purpose for which each debit to the Funds was made. The Funds are pledged as additional security for the sums secured by this Security Instrument.

If the amount of the Funds held by Lender, together with the future monthly payments of Funds payable prior to the due dates of the escrow items, shall exceed the amount required to pay the escrow items when due, the excess shall be, at Borrower's option, either promptly repaid to Borrower or credited to Borrower on monthly payments of Funds. If the amount of the Funds held by Lender is not sufficient to pay the escrow items when due, Borrower shall pay to Lender any amount necessary to make up the deficiency in one or more payments as required by Lender.

Upon payment in full of all sums secured by this Security Instrument, Lender shall promptly refund to Borrower any Funds held by Lender. If under paragraph 19 the Property is sold or acquired by Lender, Lender shall apply, no later than immediately prior to the sale of the Property or its acquisition by Lender, any Funds held by Lender at the time of application as a credit against the sums secured by this Security Instrument.

3. Application of Payments. Unless applicable law provides otherwise, all payments received by Lender under paragraphs 1 and 2 shall be applied: first, to late charges due under the Note; second, to prepayment charges due under the Note; third, to amounts payable under paragraph 2; fourth, to interest due; and last, to principal due.

4. Charges; Liens. Borrower shall pay all taxes, assessments, charges, fines and impositions attributable to the Property which may attain priority over this Security Instrument, and leasehold payments or ground rents, if any. Borrower shall pay these obligations in the manner provided in paragraph 2, or if not paid in that manner, Borrower shall pay them on time directly to the person owed payment. Borrower shall promptly furnish to Lender all notices of amounts to be paid under this paragraph. If Borrower makes these payments directly, Borrower shall promptly furnish to Lender receipts evidencing the payments.

Borrower shall promptly discharge any lien which has priority over this Security Instrument unless Borrower: (a) agrees in writing to the payment of the obligation secured by the lien in a manner acceptable to Lender; (b) contests in good faith the lien by, or defends against enforcement of the lien in, legal proceedings which in the Lender's opinion operate to prevent the enforcement of the lien or forfeiture of any part of the Property; or (c) secures from the holder of the lien an agreement satisfactory to Lender subordinating the lien to this Security Instrument. If Lender determines that any part of the Property is subject to a lien which may attain priority over this Security Instrument, Lender may give Borrower a notice identifying the lien. Borrower shall satisfy the lien or take one or more of the actions set forth above within 10 days of the giving of notice.

5. Hazard Insurance. Borrower shall keep the improvements now existing or hereafter erected on the Property insured against loss by fire, hazards included within the term "extended coverage" and any other hazards for which Lender requires insurance. This insurance shall be maintained in the amounts and for the periods that Lender requires. The insurance carrier providing the insurance shall be chosen by Borrower subject to Lender's approval which shall not be unreasonably withheld.

All insurance policies and renewals shall be acceptable to Lender and shall include a standard mortgage clause. Lender shall have the right to hold the policies and renewals. If Lender requires, Borrower shall promptly give to Lender all receipts of paid premiums and renewal notices. In the event of loss, Borrower shall give prompt notice to the insurance carrier and Lender. Lender may make proof of loss if not made promptly by Borrower.

Unless Lender and Borrower otherwise agree in writing, insurance proceeds shall be applied to restoration or repair of the Property damaged, if the restoration or repair is economically feasible and Lender's security is not lessened. If the restoration or repair is not economically feasible or Lender's security would be lessened, the insurance proceeds shall be applied to the sums secured by this Security Instrument, whether or not then due, with any excess paid to Borrower. If Borrower abandons the Property, or does not answer within 30 days a notice from Lender that the insurance carrier has offered to settle a claim, then Lender may collect the insurance proceeds. Lender may use the proceeds to repair or restore the Property or to pay sums secured by this Security Instrument, whether or not then due. The 30-day period will begin when the notice is given.

Unless Lender and Borrower otherwise agree in writing, any application of proceeds to principal shall not extend or postpone the due date of the monthly payments referred to in paragraphs 1 and 2 or change the amount of the payments. If under paragraph 19 the Property is acquired by Lender, Borrower's right to any insurance policies and proceeds resulting from damage to the Property prior to the acquisition shall pass to Lender to the extent of the sums secured by this Security Instrument immediately prior to the acquisition.

6. Preservation and Maintenance of Property; Leaseholds. Borrower shall not destroy, damage or substantially change the Property, allow the Property to deteriorate or commit waste. If this Security Instrument is on a leasehold, Borrower shall comply with the provisions of the lease, and if Borrower acquires fee title to the Property, the leasehold and fee title shall not merge unless Lender agrees to the merger in writing.

7. Protection of Lender's Rights in the Property; Mortgage Insurance. If Borrower fails to perform the covenants and agreements contained in this Security Instrument, or there is a legal proceeding that may significantly affect Lender's rights in the Property (such as a proceeding in bankruptcy, probate, for condemnation or to enforce laws or regulations), then Lender may do and pay for whatever is necessary to protect the value of the Property and Lender's rights in the Property. Lender's actions may include paying any sums secured by a lien which has priority over this Security Instrument, appearing in court, paying reasonable attorneys' fees and entering on the Property to make repairs. Although Lender may take action under this paragraph 7, Lender does not have to do so.

Any amounts disbursed by Lender under this paragraph 7 shall become additional debt of Borrower secured by this Security Instrument. Unless Borrower and Lender agree to other terms of payment, these amounts shall bear interest from the date of disbursement at the Note rate and shall be payable, with interest, upon notice from Lender to Borrower requesting payment.

EXHIBIT 17-34
Security Deed
(continued)

If Lender required mortgage insurance as a condition of making the loan secured by this Security Instrument, Borrower shall pay the premiums required to maintain the insurance in effect until such time as the requirement for the insurance terminates in accordance with Borrower's and Lender's written agreement or applicable law.

8. Inspection. Lender or its agent may make reasonable entries upon and inspections of the Property. Lender shall give Borrower notice at the time of or prior to an inspection specifying reasonable cause for the inspection.

9. Condemnation. The proceeds of any award or claim for damages, direct or consequential, in connection with any condemnation or other taking of any part of the Property, or for conveyance in lieu of condemnation, are hereby assigned and shall be paid to Lender.

In the event of a total taking of the Property, the proceeds shall be applied to the sums secured by this Security Instrument, whether or not then due, with any excess paid to Borrower. In the event of a partial taking of the Property, unless Borrower and Lender otherwise agree in writing, the sums secured by this Security Instrument shall be reduced by the amount of the proceeds multiplied by the following fraction: (a) the total amount of the sums secured immediately before the taking, divided by (b) the fair market value of the Property immediately before the taking. Any balance shall be paid to Borrower.

If the Property is abandoned by Borrower, or if, after notice by Lender to Borrower that the condemnor offers to make an award or settle a claim for damages, Borrower fails to respond to Lender within 30 days after the date the notice is given, Lender is authorized to collect and apply the proceeds, at its option, either to restoration or repair of the Property or to the sums secured by this Security Instrument, whether or not then due.

Unless Lender and Borrower otherwise agree in writing, any application of proceeds to principal shall not extend or postpone the due date of the monthly payments referred to in paragraphs 1 and 2 or change the amount of such payments.

10. Borrower Not Released; Forbearance By Lender Not a Waiver. Extension of the time for payment or modification of amortization of the sums secured by this Security Instrument granted by Lender to any successor in interest of Borrower shall not operate to release the liability of the original Borrower or Borrower's successors in interest. Lender shall not be required to commence proceedings against any successor in interest or refuse to extend time for payment or otherwise modify amortization of the sums secured by this Security Instrument by reason of any demand made by the original Borrower or Borrower's successors in interest. Any forbearance by Lender in exercising any right or remedy shall not be a waiver of or preclude the exercise of any right or remedy.

11. Successors and Assigns Bound; Joint and Several Liability; Co-signers. The covenants and agreements of this Security Instrument shall bind and benefit the successors and assigns of Lender and Borrower, subject to the provisions of paragraph 17. Borrower's covenants and agreements shall be joint and several. Any Borrower who co-signs this Security Instrument but does not execute the Note: (a) is co-signing this Security Instrument only to mortgage, grant and convey that Borrower's interest in the Property under the terms of this Security Instrument; (b) is not personally obligated to pay the sums secured by this Security Instrument; and (c) agrees that Lender and any other Borrower may agree to extend, modify, forbear or make any accommodations with regard to the terms of this Security Instrument or the Note without that Borrower's consent.

12. Loan Charges. If the loan secured by this Security Instrument is subject to a law which sets maximum loan charges, and that law is finally interpreted so that the interest or other loan charges collected or to be collected in connection with the loan exceed the permitted limits, then: (a) any such loan charge shall be reduced by the amount necessary to reduce the charge to the permitted limit; and (b) any sums already collected from Borrower which exceeded permitted limits will be refunded to Borrower. Lender may choose to make this refund by reducing the principal owed under the Note or by making a direct payment to Borrower. If a refund reduces principal, the reduction will be treated as a partial prepayment without any prepayment charge under the Note.

13. Legislation Affecting Lender's Rights. If enactment or expiration of applicable laws has the effect of rendering any provision of the Note or this Security Instrument unenforceable according to its terms, Lender, at its option, may require immediate payment in full of all sums secured by this Security Instrument and may invoke any remedies permitted by paragraph 19. If Lender exercises this option, Lender shall take the steps specified in the second paragraph of paragraph 17.

14. Notices. Any notice to Borrower provided for in this Security Instrument shall be given by delivering it or by mailing it by first class mail unless applicable law requires use of another method. The notice shall be directed to the Property Address or any other address Borrower designates by notice to Lender. Any notice to Lender shall be given by first class mail to Lender's address stated herein or any other address Lender designates by notice to Borrower. Any notice provided for in this Security Instrument shall be deemed to have been given to Borrower or Lender when given as provided in this paragraph.

15. Governing Law; Severability. This Security Instrument shall be governed by federal law and the law of the jurisdiction in which the Property is located. In the event that any provision or clause of this Security Instrument or the Note conflicts with applicable law, such conflict shall not affect other provisions of this Security Instrument or the Note which can be given effect without the conflicting provision. To this end the provisions of this Security Instrument and the Note are declared to be severable.

16. Borrower's Copy. Borrower shall be given one conformed copy of the Note and of this Security Instrument.

17. Transfer of the Property or a Beneficial Interest in Borrower. If all or any part of the Property or any interest in it is sold or transferred (or if a beneficial interest in Borrower is sold or transferred and Borrower is not a natural person) without Lender's prior written consent, Lender may, at its option, require immediate payment in full of all sums secured by this Security Instrument. However, this option shall not be exercised by Lender if exercise is prohibited by federal law as of the date of this Security Instrument.

If Lender exercises this option, Lender shall give Borrower notice of acceleration. The notice shall provide a period of not less than 30 days from the date the notice is delivered or mailed within which Borrower must pay all sums secured by this Security Instrument. If Borrower fails to pay these sums prior to the expiration of this period, Lender may invoke any remedies permitted by this Security Instrument without further notice or demand on Borrower.

18. Borrower's Right to Reinstate. If Borrower meets certain conditions, Borrower shall have the right to have enforcement of this Security Instrument discontinued at any time prior to the earlier of: (a) 5 days (or such other period as applicable law may specify for reinstatement) before sale of the Property pursuant to any power of sale contained in this Security Instrument; or (b) entry of a judgment enforcing this Security Instrument. Those conditions are that Borrower: (a) pays Lender all sums which then would be due under this Security Instrument and the Note had no acceleration occurred; (b) cures any default of any other covenants or agreements; (c) pays all expenses incurred in enforcing this Security Instrument, including, but not limited to, reasonable attorneys' fees; and (d) takes such action as Lender may reasonably require to assure that the lien of this Security Instrument, Lender's rights in the Property and Borrower's obligation to pay the sums secured by this Security Instrument shall continue unchanged. Upon reinstatement by Borrower, this Security Instrument and the obligations secured hereby shall remain fully effective as if no acceleration had occurred. However, this right to reinstate shall not apply in the case of acceleration under paragraphs 13 or 17.

EXHIBIT 17–34
Security Deed
(continued)

NON-UNIFORM COVENANTS. Borrower and Lender further covenant and agree as follows:

19. Acceleration; Remedies. Lender shall give notice to Borrower prior to acceleration following Borrower's breach of any covenant or agreement in this Security Instrument (but not prior to acceleration under paragraphs 13 and 17 unless applicable law provides otherwise). The notice shall specify: (a) the default; (b) the action required to cure the default; (c) a date, not less than 30 days from the date the notice is given to Borrower, by which the default must be cured; and (d) that failure to cure the default on or before the date specified in the notice may result in acceleration of the sums secured by this Security Instrument and sale of the Property. The notice shall further inform Borrower of the right to reinstate after acceleration and the right to bring a court action to assert the non-existence of a default or any other defense of Borrower to acceleration and sale. If the default is not cured on or before the date specified in the notice, Lender at its option may require immediate payment in full of all sums secured by this Security Instrument without further demand and may invoke the power of sale granted by Borrower and any other remedies permitted by applicable law. Borrower appoints Lender the agent and attorney-in-fact for Borrower to exercise the power of sale. Lender shall be entitled to collect all expenses incurred in pursuing the remedies provided in this paragraph 19, including, but not limited to, reasonable attorneys' fees and costs of title evidence.

If Lender invokes the power of sale, Lender shall give a copy of a notice of sale to Borrower in the manner provided in paragraph 14 and shall give notice of sale by public advertisement for the time and in the manner prescribed by applicable law. Lender, without further demand on Borrower, shall sell the Property at public auction to the highest bidder at the time and place and under the terms designated in the notice of sale in one or more parcels and in any order Lender determines. Lender or its designee may purchase the Property at any sale.

Lender shall convey to the purchaser indefeasible title to the Property, and Borrower hereby appoints Lender Borrower's agent and attorney-in-fact to make such conveyance. The recitals in the Lender's deed shall be prima facie evidence of the truth of the statements made therein. Borrower covenants and agrees that Lender shall apply the proceeds of the sale in the following order: (a) to all expenses of the sale, including, but not limited to, reasonable attorneys' fees; (b) to all sums secured by this Security Instrument; and (c) any excess to the person or persons legally entitled to it. The power and agency granted are coupled with an interest, are irrevocable by death or otherwise and are cumulative to the remedies for collection of debt as provided by law.

If the Property is sold pursuant to this paragraph 19, Borrower, or any person holding possession of the Property through Borrower, shall immediately surrender possession of the Property to the purchaser at the sale. If possession is not surrendered, Borrower or such person shall be a tenant holding over and may be dispossessed in accordance with applicable law.

20. Lender in Possession. Upon acceleration under paragraph 19 or abandonment of the Property, Lender (in person, by agent or by judicially appointed receiver) shall be entitled to enter upon, take possession of and manage the Property and to collect the rents of the Property including those past due. Any rents collected by Lender or the receiver shall be applied first to payment of the costs of management of the Property and collection of rents, including, but not limited to, receiver's fees, premiums on receiver's bonds and reasonable attorneys' fees, and then to the sums secured by this Security Instrument.

21. Release. Upon payment of all sums secured by this Security Instrument, Lender shall cancel this Security Instrument without charge to Borrower. Borrower shall pay any recordation costs.

22. Waiver of Homestead. Borrower waives all rights of homestead exemption in the Property.

23. Assumption not a Novation. Lender's acceptance of an assumption of the obligations of this Security Instrument and the Note, and any release of Borrower in connection therewith, shall not constitute a novation.

24. Security Deed. This conveyance is to be construed under the existing laws of the State of Georgia as a deed passing title, and not as a mortgage, and is intended to secure the payment of all sums secured hereby.

25. Riders to this Security Instrument. If one or more riders are executed by Borrower and recorded together with this Security Instrument, the covenants and agreements of each such rider shall be incorporated into and shall amend and supplement the covenants and agreements of this Security Instrument as if the rider(s) were a part of this Security Instrument. [Check applicable box(es)]

☐ Adjustable Rate Rider   ☐ Condominium Rider   ☐ 2–4 Family Rider

☐ Graduated Payment Rider   ☐ Planned Unit Development Rider

☐ Other(s) [specify]

BORROWER ACCEPTS AND AGREES to the terms and covenants contained in this Security Instrument and in any rider(s) executed by Borrower and recorded with it. IN WITNESS WHEREOF, Borrower has signed and sealed this Security Instrument.

Signed, sealed and delivered in the presence of:
this _____ day of _____, 19___ .

....HELEN DAVIS...(Seal)
Unofficial Witness   —Borrower

....(Seal)
Notary Public, ... **County**   —Borrower

EXHIBIT 17-35
Settlement
Statement

A. SETTLEMENT STATEMENT   U.S. Department of Housing and Urban Development

OMB No. 2502-0265

B. Type of Loan

1. ___ FHA 2. ___ FmHA 3. ___ Conv. Unins. 4. ___ VA 5. ___ Conv. Ins.	6. File Number	7. Loan Number	8. Mortgage Insurance Case No.#

C. NOTE: This form is furnished to give you a statement of actual settlement costs. Amounts paid to and by the settlement agent are shown. Items marked (P.O.C.) were paid outside the closing; they are shown here for information purposes and are not included in the totals.

D. Name and Address of Borrower	E. Name and Address of Seller	F. Name and Address of Lender
HELEN DAVIS 5167 Tilly Mill Road Atlanta, Georgia 30302	MARKAM INDUSTRIES, INC. 210 Corporate Square Atlanta, Georgia 30303	AMERICAN EAGLE MORTGAGE COMPANY 10 Piedmont Center Atlanta, Georgia 30317

G. Property Location	H. Settlement Agent	
5167 Tilly Mill Road Atlanta, Georgia 30302	Place of Settlement	I. Settlement Date 4/25/19

J. SUMMARY OF BORROWER'S TRANSACTION:		K. SUMMARY OF SELLER'S TRANSACTION:	
100. Gross Amount Due From Borrower		**400. Gross Amount Due To Seller**	
101. Contract sales price	$47,500.00	401. Contract sales price	$47,500.00
102. Personal property		402. Personal property	
103. Settlement charges to borrower (line 1400)	1,284.14	403.	
104.		404.	
105.		405.	
Adjustments for items paid by seller in advance		**Adjustments for items paid by seller in advance**	
106. City/town taxes to		406. City/town taxes to	
107. County taxes to		407. County taxes to	
108. Assessments to		408. Assessments to	
109.		409.	
110.		410.	
111.		411.	
112.		412.	
120. GROSS AMOUNT DUE FROM BORROWER	$48,784.14	**420. GROSS AMOUNT DUE TO SELLER**	$47,500.00
200. Amounts Paid By or In Behalf of Borrower		**500. Reductions In Amount Due To Seller**	
201. Deposit or earnest money	1,000.00	501. Excess Deposit (see instructions)	
202. Principal amount of new loan(s)	38,000.00	502. Settlement charges to seller (line 1400)	2,375.50
203. Existing loan(s) taken subject to		503. Existing loan(s) taken subject to	28,655.00
204.		504. Payoff of first mortgage loan	
205.		505. Payoff of second mortgage loan	
206.		506. Earnest Money	1,000.00
207.		507.	
208.		508.	
209.		509.	
Adjustments for items unpaid by seller		**Adjustments for items unpaid by seller**	
210. City/town taxes 1/1 to 4/25(115)	49.40	510. City/town taxes 1/1 to 4/25	49.40
211. County taxes 1/1 to 4/25(115)	97.84	511. County taxes 1/1 to 4/25	97.84
212. Assessments to		512. Assessments to	
213.		513.	
214.		514.	
215.		515.	
216.		516.	
217.		517.	
218.		518.	
219.		519.	
220. TOTAL PAID BY/FOR BORROWER	39,147.24	**520. TOTAL REDUCTION AMOUNT DUE SELLER**	32,177.74
300. Cash At Settlement From or To Borrower		**600. Cash At Settlement To or From Seller**	
301. Gross amount due from borrower (line 120)	48,784.14	601. Gross amount due to seller (line 420)	47,500.00
302. Less amounts paid by/for borrower (line 220)	(39,147.24)	602. Less reduction amount due seller (line 520)	(32,177.74)
303. CASH From BORROWER	9,636.90	603. CASH To SELLER	15,322.26

EXHIBIT 17-35
Settlement
Statement
(continued)

U.S. DEPARTMENT OF HOUSING AND URBAN DEVELOPMENT
SETTLEMENT STATEMENT
PAGE 2

L. SETTLEMENT CHARGES:	PAID FROM BORROWER'S FUNDS AT SETTLEMENT	PAID FROM SELLER'S FUNDS AT SETTLEMENT
700. TOTAL SALES/BROKER'S COMMISSION based on price $47,500.00 @ 7% = 3,325.00		
Division of commission (line 700) as follows:		
701. $ 1,662.50 to Ajax Realty Co.		
702. $ 1,662.50 to Northside Realty Co., Inc.		
703. Commission paid at Settlement $1,000.00 retained by Northside Realty Co., Inc.		$ 2,325.00
704.		
800. ITEMS PAYABLE IN CONNECTION WITH LOAN		
801. Loan Origination Fee %		
802. Loan Discount %		
803. Appraisal Fee to American Eagle Mortgage Company	150.00	
804. Credit Report to		
805. Lender's Inspection Fee to		
806. Mortgage Application Fee to		
807. Assumption Fee to		
808. Commitment Fee to American Eagle Mortgage Company	100.00	
809. Photographs - Acme Photos	50.00	
810.		
811.		
900. ITEMS REQUIRED BY LENDER TO BE PAID IN ADVANCE		
901. Interest from 4/25 to 4/30 @ $11.45 /day	68.70	
902. Mortgage Insurance Premium for to		
903. Hazard Insurance Premium for yrs to		
904.		
905.		
1000. RESERVES DEPOSITED WITH LENDER FOR		
1001. Hazard Insurance 2 mo.@$ 15.42 /mo.	30.84	
1002. Mortgage Insurance mo.@$ /mo.		
1003. City Property Taxes 8 mo.@$ 13.07 /mo.	104.56	
1004. County Property Taxes 8 mo.@$ 25.88 /mo.	207.04	
1005. Annual Assessments mo.@$ /mo.		
1006. mo.@$ /mo.		
1007. mo.@$ /mo.		
1008. mo.@$ /mo.		
1100. TITLE CHARGES		
1101. Settlement or closing fee to		
1102. Abstract or title search to		
1103. Title examination to		
1104. Title insurance binder to		
1105. Document Preparation to		
1106. Notary Fees to		
1107. Attorney's fees to Law Firm		
(includes above items No: 1101, 1102, 1003, 1104, 1105 & 1106	250.00	
1108. Title Insurance to Title Company		
(includes above items No:)	120.00	
1109. Lender's coverage $ 38,000.00		
1110. Owner's coverage $ 47,500.00		
1111 TAX REPORT		
1112		
1113		
1200. GOVERNMENT RECORDING AND TRANSFER CHARGES		
1201. Recording Fees: Deed $ 3.00 ; Mortgage $11.00 ; Releases $ 3.00	14.00	3.00
1202. City/county tax/stamps: Deed $; Mortgage $		
1203. State Tax/stamps: Deed $ 47.50 ; Mortgage $114.00	114.00	47.50
1204.		
1205.		
1300. ADDITIONAL SETTLEMENT CHARGES		
1301. Survey to Survey Company	75.00	
1302. Pest Inspection to		
1303		
1304		
1305		
1400. TOTAL SETTLEMENT CHARGES (enter on lines 103 and 502, Sections J and K)	1,284.14	2,375.00

REV. HUD-1 (3/86)

Leases

And Summer's lease hath all too short a date.

—*William Shakespeare,* Sonnet 18

OBJECTIVES

After reading this chapter you will be able to:

- Review a commercial lease and understand its key provisions
- Define the various methods to compute rent under a lease
- Understand the legal differences between an assignment of lease and a sublease
- Recognize a landlord's remedies for a tenant's default under a lease
- Recognize a tenant's remedies for a landlord's default under lease

GLOSSARY

Assignment With regard to a lease, it is when the tenant transfers all his or her interest under the lease and retains nothing.

Estoppel certificate Written statement signed by either a landlord or a tenant swearing to certain facts concerning a lease.

Gross lease Lease wherein the tenant pays rent only; the operating expenses of the leased premises, such as taxes, utility costs, and insurance, are paid by the landlord.

Landlord, or lessor Generally the owner of real property who transfers possession and use of the real property under a lease to a tenant or lessee.

Lease Legal document that transfers possession of real property from one party to another. The lease also may contain numerous terms and conditions involving the use and possession of the property.

Net lease Lease in which the tenant is responsible for all expenses of the leased premises, such as utilities, taxes, and insurance.

Percentage breakpoint Level of gross sales made during a year at which time a percentage rent obligation will commence.

Percentage rent Rent based on a percentage of sales from a specific location. Percentage rent often is found in retail store leases.

Premises Land and the buildings located on the land. The term often is used to describe real property covered by a lease.

Radius clause Clause contained in a lease that prohibits a tenant from operating another retail store or business within a certain geographical radius of the leased premises.

Rent Money paid by a tenant to a landlord for the use and possession of property pursuant to a lease.

Sublet In regard to a lease, it is when the tenant transfers only a portion of his or her interest under the lease and the tenant retains some interest.

Subrogation Right to be substituted to the rights of another person. For example, an insurance carrier who pays a claim to the insured is given the rights of

GLOSSARY (cont'd)

the insured to proceed against any party who caused the damage resulting in the claim.

Tenant, or lessee   Person who receives possession and use of property pursuant to a lease.

L egal assistants often are involved in the preparation and review of **leases**. Although in many instances a legal assistant is furnished with either a preprinted form or a form prepared by a law firm to review or to use as a guide in the preparation of the new lease, it is important that the legal assistant understand the legal theories and concepts of leases as well as be aware of the general provisions found in most leases.

A lease may be used in a residential situation for the possession and use of an apartment or a house or in a commercial setting such as for a retail store or an office. Because of the legal expense involved, most legal assistants are involved in the preparation and review of commercial leases. For this reason, most of the discussion in this chapter pertains to commercial leases. Many of the issues discussed, however, have equal application to a residential apartment or home lease. Examples of residential and commercial lease forms are included at the end of this chapter.

COMMON LAW AND LEASES

The English common law treated a lease as a combination of property and contract law. Because a lease transfers possession and, in some cases, is an estate for years, it is deemed to be a conveyance of real property. In addition, leases contain numerous terms and conditions that involve the use and possession of the property. In this respect, the lease is a contract and enforceable according to the general terms of contract law.

The common law of leases made a major departure from contract law in holding that lease covenants were independent. This meant that the landlord's promises were independent from the tenant's, and the failure of one party (such as a landlord) to perform its obligations was not an excuse for the other party, the tenant, not to perform. For example, a lease may require the landlord to provide basic utility services to the premises and the tenant to pay rent.

The landlord refuses or fails to provide utility services. Does this excuse the tenant from its obligation to pay rent? The common law theory of independent covenants said no. The tenant must continue to pay rent even though the landlord refuses to perform its obligations. The tenant is left with the remedy of suing the landlord to perform or to compensate the tenant for damages caused by nonperformance. Historically, the common law theory of independent lease covenants has worked to the disadvantage of the tenant. Many states, especially in the area of residential leases, have radically modified the independent theory of lease covenants. For example, many states impose in residential leases a warranty of habitability on the landlord. This means that the landlord warrants to the tenant that the premises are capable of human habitation. This usually means that the landlord must provide basic utility services, such as water, sewer, and heat. In the event the premises prove not to be habitable, this excuses the tenant from payment of rent. Nevertheless, the common law theory of independent covenants is the law in most states as it pertains to commercial leases.

New York:
See Appendix for discussion of leases in New York.

COMMERCIAL LEASE PROVISIONS

New York:
All residential leases in New York must be in plain English, i.e., have large, easy to read print and use words with everyday meaning (General Obligations Law 5–702 and Civil Procedure Law and Rules 4544). See Appendix, Exhibit 18.1, for example of an apartment lease in plain English format.

A legal assistant who is involved in the preparation and review of a commercial lease must be familiar with the various terms commonly found in commercial leases.

Parties to Lease

The parties to a lease are **landlord** and **tenant**, or **lessor** and **lessee**. The landlord usually is the fee owner of the property. In making the lease, the landlord is transferring the possession and use of the property to the tenant. The landlord must have title to the property to grant the lease, and the title must be sufficient to cover the lease term. For example, a landlord who had only a life estate in the property could not necessarily grant a lease for twenty years. If the landlord died during the twenty years, the lease would terminate when the landlord's title terminated.

A lease also is subject to all the landlord's title defects. It is prudent in many cases, when representing a tenant, to examine the landlord's title before entering into the lease. A tenant should pay particular attention to any zoning or restrictive covenants that may affect the use of the leased property. Another area of concern for the tenant is any prior mortgages that may exist on the property. A mortgage that is in existence at the time the lease is entered into is senior to the lease. If the loan payments are not made and the mortgage is foreclosed, the lease will terminate. This could place a tenant at a great disadvantage, not to mention tremendous expense, in moving or renegotiating the terms of the lease with the purchaser at the foreclosure sale.

The tenant under the lease is the party to whom possession and use of the property are being transferred. Particular attention is paid to the financial ability of a tenant. It is crucial that the tenant have the ability to perform all the lease covenants. In many cases, it may be necessary that corporate tenants obtain a personal guaranty from the principal shareholders of the corporation, or a subsidiary corporation obtain a guaranty from the parent corporation, to assure financial ability.

Premises

A lease must describe the property that is being rented. The property being rented in a lease often is referred to as the **premises**. Legal assistants should pay careful attention when preparing or reviewing a lease to make sure that the premises described are exactly those that are being transferred to the tenant and that the landlord intends to transfer. Important questions in a premises clause are (a) where is the premises located? (b) what is the size of the premises? and (c) how is the size of the premises to be determined or confirmed? If the lease covers other premises, such as hallways, streets, bathrooms, or parking privileges, all this should be described and covered in the lease. Many times a lease of real property includes the use of certain personal property; if so, the personal property should be described and listed within the lease.

The location of the premises within a building or project should already be the subject of the parties negotiated understanding by the time the legal assistant starts to prepare or review the lease. The only real concern should be to review the lease to make sure that the lease accurately documents that understanding. A comparable degree of specificity and precision should be used in leases in describing the premises as is used in conveyancing documents such as a deed. The lease should, at a minimum, provide a method whereby the precise size and location of the premises can be (or will be) determined and verified. Legal descriptions, plats of survey, plans and specifications, street addresses, and suite members are all used under different circumstances (and in different combinations) to accomplish this task.

In many situations, the premises will be space that is to be built in a proposed office building or shopping center. When the space is to be built, the tenant should be provided a reasonable means and opportunity to review and confirm the landlord's stated square footage. Many leases contain a provision that the landlord's architect will measure the premises when they are completed, and the determination of the landlord's architect will be binding on both parties. The lease may provide the tenant with a procedure for objecting or contesting the landlord's architect's measurement.

Use

The use the tenant intends to make of the premises should be specified in the lease. The tenant wants a specific use identified in the lease and permission to use the premises for any lawful purpose. A landlord, on the other hand, probably wants to be more restrictive and require that the tenant's use of the premises be only that use set forth in the lease and no other use without prior written consent of landlord.

Term

With respect to the term of a lease, the better practice is to set out the exact commencement and termination dates, rather than merely state a term of years. To the extent renewal options are part of the transaction, this clause also should describe with specificity the term and type of notice required to exercise the renewal option. The length of the term of the lease usually is the subject of the parties' negotiated understanding, and in reviewing a lease, this point should only have to be verified by the legal assistant.

Possession and Commencement of the Rent

A lease should provide for a precise beginning and ending date. The lease may provide that possession will begin in the future. Many developers, when constructing new shopping centers or office buildings, prelease the property before the time of completion. A lease that provides for future possession should clearly state that the lease becomes effective when signed, but possession will be delayed until a date in the future. The exact time of possession should be carefully described within the lease. As a practical note, a date of possession can be crucial to a tenant. Most tenants are at some other location and will have to go to the expense of closing that location and moving to the new premises. If, for some reason, possession is delayed, this can cause a disruption of business and considerable expense. A tenant may try to negotiate a provision that requires the landlord to pay an amount of money for each day possession is late.

Rent

Rent is the sum of money the tenant pays to the landlord for the use and possession of the premises. It usually is payable in advance and in installments. Rent can be paid at any interval (e.g., annually, semiannually, daily, weekly, monthly). In most commercial and residential properties, the landlord's mortgage on the leased premises has payment due monthly, and because the landlord uses the rent to make the payments, rent is due monthly.

New York: Leases are contracts between the landlord and tenant. Most residential leases are uniform and landlords use preprinted forms and add riders if necessary. See Appendix for further discussion of lease use, term, possession and commencement, and rent.

A tenant has a contractual obligation to pay rent. This obligation continues even if the tenant has transferred its interest to the premises or has vacated the premises. The obligation to pay rent, as earlier discussed, usually is independent of the landlord's promises and covenants under the lease. Even though the landlord may be in default under the lease, a tenant must still pay the rent.

Percentage Rent

Rent typically is paid in a fixed amount of dollars and is due and payable on a certain day of the month. Rent, however, may be based on a percentage of sales; this type of rental provision commonly is found in retail store leases. A **percentage rent** clause provides that a percentage of the gross sales sold from the premises will be the amount of the rent. Many leases provide for a minimum rent, or base rent, to be paid plus a percentage of sales over a certain amount. These leases are percentage sales leases with a minimum base of sales guaranteed. For example, if the landlord believes that the tenant will sell $1 million in merchandise from the location in a given year and the landlord wants a 3 percent percentage rent, the landlord will ask that $30,000 of rent (3 percent of $1 million) be payable in twelve equal installments of $2,500 per month. The rent figure is expressed in the lease as a fixed $2,500 per month together with 3 percent of all sales in excess of $1 million.

A percentage rent clause permits a landlord to earn additional rental income based on the amount of a retail tenant's gross sales or net sales from the premises. Such clauses usually are drafted to calculate the tenant's percentage rent obligations on an annual basis. The reason percentage rent has traditionally been due on an annual basis is because each lease year or calendar year (depending on which annual period is used in a given lease) must occur and conclude, and the final gross sales figures must be calculated before the actual percentage rent obligation for the year can be determined. It is not uncommon for leases today to provide for quarterly or even monthly payments of percentage rent. Such payments during the year are stated as payments "made against" the tenant's obligation for percentage rent, which is subject to a final determination. If necessary, a payment adjustment of some amount will be made after the close of the annual period.

Some of the key terms in percentage rent clauses are (a) a percentage rent rate; (b) the percentage rent breakpoint; (c) the amount and definition of gross sales; (d) the amount and nature of permitted exclusions or deductions from gross sales; and (e) the procedure or mechanism for verifying and, if necessary, adjusting payments of percentage rent.

Percentage rent rate and percentage breakpoint are concepts that are interrelated with the base rent obligation. A percentage rent rate is a mutually agreed on amount of the tenant's total annual gross sales that the tenant owes as percentage rent. This amount customarily is stated as a percentage. Different segments of the retail industry appeared to have settled on the "appropriate" percentage rate for their kind of store through negotiations over the years, and no attempt is made here to comment on what rate is appropriate for any given tenant.

The **percentage breakpoint** is the level of gross sales made during the year at which the percentage rent obligation commences. Thereafter, the percentage rent rate applies to all additional gross sales above the breakpoint. The two concepts are interrelated to the base rent because a natural percentage rent breakpoint is an amount determined by dividing the base rent by the percentage rent rate expressed as a number instead of a percentage.

Required inclusions in gross sales and permitted exclusions or deductions from gross sales are fundamental to the percentage rent clause. The starting point of most lease forms is that the proceeds received from or attributed to everything and anything sold for cash or on credit (including lay-away sales, credit card sales, and sales paid for by checks that ultimately are no good) should be included in gross sales.

Most retailers and landlords agree that some or most of the following items should be excluded or deducted from gross sales: (a) the amount of any sales of fixtures, equipment, and property that is not carried as inventory; (b) sale price merchandise sold to tenant's employees at a discount; (c) the amount of any finance, insurance, or service charges on credit sales; (d) charges to customers for making deliveries or repairs to merchandise; (e) the amount of any cash or credit refund made on any sale in which the merchandise sold or some part thereof is thereafter returned by the purchaser and accepted by the tenant; and (f) any sums collected and paid out by the tenant for any sale or excise tax based on gross sales to the extent such taxes have been included in the gross sales price.

Regardless of whether the tenant is paying percentage rent on a monthly, quarterly, or annual basis, the tenant is obligated to provide a written statement of its gross sales for such a period within a prescribed number of days after the period closes. Timing requirements for reports should be reviewed with the tenant to be sure that they comport with the tenant's current practice of keeping books. Similarly, many percentage rent clauses delineate the specific kinds of books and records of gross sales (including the kinds of cash registers, cash register tapes, and sales slips required) that must be kept and maintained by the tenant and made available to the landlord so that the accuracy of the tenant's report of gross sales can be verified. These details must be reviewed and accepted by the tenant. Finally, many percentage clauses require the tenant to keep its books and records of gross sales at the premises. This may not be workable with a tenant who has multiple locations. Most landlords will, in such circumstances, permit the tenant to keep its records at a central office but will require the tenant to produce them at the premises after an agreed notice (five or ten days) requesting such production has been given by the landlord to the tenant.

Many leases also require that annual statements of gross sales either be audited by an independent certified public accountant or be certified as true and correct by the chief financial officer of the tenant, at the landlord's option. Because most tenants would not go to the expense of such an audit for their own purpose, a tenant may negotiate to limit the applicability of this requirement to situations in which the tenant's annual statement of gross sales for a prior annual period has been understated by a certain percentage (e.g., 3 percent or 5 percent), which is mutually agreed to be sufficiently indicative of improper or poor record-keeping practices to trigger the audit obligation.

Most percentage lease provisions permit the landlord to inspect or audit the tenant's books and records of gross sales. If the inspection discloses an understatement of percentage rents by a certain percentage (e.g., 3 percent or 5 percent) or more, the tenant bears the cost of the audit. If either the tenant's preparation of its annual statement of gross sales or the landlord's audit of the tenant's records of gross sales reveals that an overpayment has occurred, most leases provide that the tenant will receive a credit against percentage rent thereafter due.

A lease that contains a percentage rent clause may have a covenant that the tenant will operate and actively conduct the business from the premises. Retail leases often establish the hours the store must be open, such as 10 A.M. through 9 P.M. Monday through Saturday. Percentage sales leases may contain restrictions on assignment and subletting. A percentage sales lease may contain a **radius clause**. A radius clause prohibits a tenant from opening another store within a certain geographical radius of the leased premises. This is a way of protecting a market area for the location and ensuring a particular volume of sales. Example 18–1 shows a percentage rent clause.

EXAMPLE 18-1

Percentage Rent

(a) In addition to Minimum Rent, Tenant shall pay to Landlord a sum equal to the amount, if any, by which _____ (____%) percent of Tenant's gross sales for any whole or partial lease year exceeds the Minimum Rent payable for such lease year (hereinafter referred to as "Percentage Rent"). Percentage Rent shall be due and payable on or before the tenth (10th) day of each calendar month during the term hereof and on or before the tenth (10th) day of the first (1st) calendar month following the termination hereof. On or before the tenth (10th) day of each calendar month during the term hereof, Tenant shall furnish Landlord with a written statement certified to be correct by Tenant showing the amount of gross sales in the Premises from the beginning of the lease year to the end of the previous calendar month or portion thereof. If, by the end of any such preceding calendar month, _____ (____%) percent of the gross sales in the Premises shall have exceeded the Minimum Rent payable for such lease year, Tenant shall pay Landlord the Percentage Rent due hereunder on the basis of such sales less the aggregate of Percentage Rent previously paid by Tenant during the lease year.

(b) The term "gross sales" as used herein shall be construed to include the entire sales price, whether for cash or otherwise, of all merchandise sold (including gift and merchandise certificates) and services rendered, and all other receipts whatsoever of all business conducted in or from the Premises whether made by Tenant or any permissible subtenant, concessionaire or licensee. Each sale upon installment or credit shall be treated as a sale for the full price in the month during which such sale was made, and there shall be no deduction from gross sales for uncollected or noncollectable credit accounts. Gross sales shall not include sums collected and paid out for any sales or retail excise tax imposed by any duly constituted governmental authority.

(c) Tenant shall maintain at the Premises and shall cause any permissible subtenants, concessionaires or licensees to keep and maintain accurate books and records which shall disclose separately for each business day of the term all information required to determine gross sales (including but not limited to inventories and receipts of merchandise, telephone and mail order slips, all federal, state and local sales tax returns, records of daily bank deposits of the entire receipts from transactions in, at, or from the Premises, sales slips, daily dated cash register tapes, sales books and bank statements). Such books and records shall be open to inspection and audit at the Premises by Landlord or its duly authorized agents at any time within two years following the close of the lease year in question. If such audit shall disclose a deficiency in rent, Tenant shall promptly pay such deficiency. If such audit shows gross sales to be understated by two (2%) percent or more, Tenant shall pay the cost of such audit in addition to any deficiency and if such audit shows gross sales to be understated by five (5%) percent or more, Landlord shall have the right to terminate this Lease upon five (5) days' written notice to Tenant, in addition to any other remedies provided for Tenant's default hereunder. Tenant shall keep and preserve said records for not less than twenty-five (25) months after the close of each lease year.

(d) Tenant shall submit to Landlord on or before the thirtieth (30th) day following the end of the lease year a complete statement signed by Tenant and either certified under oath by a duly authorized officer of Tenant or certified by a Certified Public Accountant, showing accurately and in reasonable detail the amount of gross sales made by Tenant and any permissible sublessees, concessionaires, or licensees, upon and within the Premises during the preceding lease year.

Use Clauses

(A) Use.

(a) Tenant covenants and agrees to use the Premises only for the Permitted Uses, and for no other purposes; to operate its business in the Premises under the Tenant's Trade Name (or such other trade name as is adopted by a majority of stores operating under the Trade Name); and to conduct its business at all times in a dignified manner and in conformity with the highest standards of practice obtaining among superior type stores, shops or concerns dealing in the same or similar merchandise and in such manner as to produce the maximum volume of Gross Sales and to help establish and maintain a high reputation for the Shopping Center.

(b) Tenant covenants and agrees to continuously and uninterruptedly use, occupy and operate for retail sales purposes all of the Premises other than such minor portions thereof as are reasonably required for storage and office purposes; to use such storage and office space only in connection with the business conducted by Tenant in the Premises; to furnish and install all trade fixtures and permitted signs; to carry a full and complete stock of seasonal merchandise; to maintain an adequate number of trained personnel for efficient service to customers; to open for business and remain open continuously during the entire Term from at least 10:00 A.M. to 9:30 P.M. Mondays through Saturdays and 12:30 P.M. to 5:30 P.M. Sundays, and to light its display windows and signs during those hours and on those days when the covered mall is kept illuminated by Landlord (but Tenant shall not be obligated to keep the same illuminated beyond 11:00 P.M. on any day). Tenant shall, if not in conflict with any governmental requirements, and provided that (i) at least one Department Store is open on such day and (ii) Landlord shall agree to cause the Shopping Center to remain open for such hours, also open for business for additional hours.

(B) Radius Clause.

Except for existing stores, Tenant shall not, nor shall any officer, director, shareholder, affiliate, franchisee or licensee or the like of Tenant, directly or indirectly operate, manage or have any interest in any other store or other facility for the sale at retail of merchandise or services similar to what is permitted under "Permitted Use" within _____ miles of the Shopping Center. Without limiting Landlord's remedies in the event Tenant should violate this covenant, Landlord may, at its option, include the Gross Sales of such other store in the Gross Sales transacted in the Premises for the purpose of computing Percentage Rent due hereunder. In the event Landlord so elects, all of the provisions of Section _____ hereof (relating to Tenant's records) shall be applicable to all records pertaining to such other store.

Gross Versus Net Lease

Lease rent may be gross or net. A **gross lease** is one under which the tenant pays rent only; the ordinary and necessary operating expenses of the premises, such as taxes, utility costs, and insurance, are paid by the landlord.

In a **net rent lease**, the tenant pays a fixed amount of money to the landlord that is net to the landlord, and the tenant is responsible for all expenses of the property, such as utilities, taxes, and insurance.

Some leases may be a hybrid between the pure gross and the pure net lease. These leases may obligate the tenant to pay a fixed amount of rent to the landlord and then to pay certain escalations in the expenses of the property. It is not uncommon for leases of this type to contain tax escalation, insurance escalation, and operating expense escalation provisions. These provisions operate on a theory that the landlord is responsible for the amount of taxes, insurance premiums, and operating expenses during the first year of the lease. All increases in taxes, insurance, and operating expenses that occur during the term of the lease will be paid by the tenant. Sample provisions of a tax, insurance, and operating expense escalation clauses are set forth in Example 18–2.

New York:
In a triple net lease, the tenant pays taxes, insurance, and all expenses but the underlying mortgage.

EXAMPLE 18-2

Tenant shall pay upon demand, as additional rental during the term of this Lease, or any extension or renewal thereof, the amount by which all taxes, insurance premiums insuring the improvements and charges to maintain the common area, exceed the cost of all taxes, insurance premiums and common area charges for the year _____. In the event the Premises are less than the entire property assessed for such taxes, insurance and common area charges for any such year, then the assessment for any such year applicable to the Premises shall be determined by proration on the basis that the rental floor area of the Premises bear to the rental floor area of the entire property assessed. Tenant's pro-rata portion of the increased taxes, insurance premiums or common area charges, as provided herein, shall be payable within fifteen (15) days after receipt of notice from Landlord as to the amount due.

Rent Escalation Clauses

During periods of inflation, a lease may require an adjustment in the tenant's rent by tying rent to an inflation-based index, such as the consumer price index (CPI). The tenant's rent increases as the index increases. The use of an inflator index protects the landlord's purchasing power of the rent dollar.

A CPI clause typically is an annual rental adjustment mechanism that uses some versions of the CPI or some other governmental or independently determined inflation-measuring statistic to determine the amount of each annual increase in the base or minimum rent. When reviewing a CPI clause, one should be careful to determine when the clause first "kicks in" if it is a "one-way or two-way escalator" and if potential adjustments are limited, or "capped."

Many (if not most) CPI clauses are drafted to operate on a calendar basis, and the effect of this fact must be considered.

If a tenant's lease term commences in the middle or latter part of a calendar year, then the first adjustment (with a CPI) usually is drafted to be effective "as of January 1," even if not determined until sometime thereafter. This arguably occurs prematurely because the tenant has not received the benefit of a year (or close to a year) of base rental payments at the original amount. A reasonable compromise that accommodates both landlord and tenant is to leave the adjustment mechanism intact as far as how it operates and what measuring period (e.g., calendar year) it uses but to have the first adjustment be postponed until the first anniversary of the commencement date of the lease instead of January 1. Subsequent adjustments can be treated similarly and be effective as of subsequent anniversary dates of the lease.

A CPI clause should adjust the minimum rate downward if the CPI declines over the relative measuring period. Although the historical trends of the past several decades belie the likelihood of this occurring, there is no conceptual reason why adjustment should not operate in both directions.

Tenants may try to limit the amount of any potential increase for any single measuring period. This usually is accomplished with language that establishes a ceiling, or cap, on any single adjustment by fixing it at no more than an agreed percentage (e.g., 4 percent or 5 percent of the prior year's adjusted base rent). Tenants also may try to limit the total "life-time adjustments" (to some agreed on percentage) of the original scheduled minimum rent. A sample CPI clause is shown in Example 18–3.

EXAMPLE 18-3

The annual rental hereunder shall be increased by an amount equal to the product of a (a) $_____ X (b) the difference expressed as a percentage between the Consumer Price Index, as hereinbelow defined, published for the month of _____ of the year _____.

"Consumer Price Index," as used herein, shall be the "Consumer Price Index for all urban consumers, U.S., City average, all items (1967) equal 100" issued by the U.S. Bureau of Labor

Statistics. If the Consumer Price Index, published by the U.S. Bureau of Labor Statistics is discontinued, then the Consumer Price Index published by the U.S. Department of Commerce shall be used (with proper adjustment); and if the U.S. Department of Commerce Index is discontinued, then Landlord and Tenant shall in good faith agree on a suitable substitute.[1]

Another mechanism used to adjust base rent is a negotiated "set," or "bump," increase. Under this provision, the minimum rent usually is scheduled to increase a predetermined amount effective as of each anniversary date of the commencement date of the lease term.

Maintenance and Alterations of Premises

Most leases prohibit a tenant from conducting any use or making any modification that would in any way (a) violate a certificate of occupancy, (b) make void or voidable any insurance in force with respect to the premises or make it impossible to obtain such insurance, (c) cause structural injury to all or any part of the premises or to any improvements constructed thereon, and (d) constitute a public or private nuisance. Under appropriate circumstances, the landlord may want to consider granting the tenant the right to make nonstructural additions and modifications after receiving prior notice and detail concerning these additions or modifications. Most leases provide that all modifications, additions, or improvements made by the tenant to the premises shall be done in compliance with all applicable building codes and zoning ordinances and that the tenant shall permit no mechanics' liens to be filed against the premises. Example 18–4 shows a maintenance and alteration provision.

New York:
Tenants may make improvements with the landlord's consent. Generally such alterations become the property of the landlord; they become fixtures. However, for tenants who install trade fixtures (as a wash basis in a beauty parlor), it is customary for them to be removed by the tenant prior to the expiration of the lease.

EXAMPLE 18-4

Tenant shall not make or suffer to be made any alterations, additions, or improvements in, on, or to the premises or any part thereof without the prior written consent of Landlord; and any such alterations, additions, or improvements in, on, or to said premises, except to Tenant's movable furniture and equipment, shall immediately become Landlord's property and, at the end of the Term hereof, shall remain on the premises without compensation to Tenant. In the event Landlord consents to the making of any such alterations, additions, or improvements by Tenant, the same shall be made by Tenant, at Tenant's sole cost and expense, in accordance with all applicable laws, ordinances, and regulations and all requirements of Landlord's and Tenant's insurance policies, and in accordance with plans and specifications approved by Landlord, and any contractor or person selected by Tenant to make the same and all subcontracts must first be approved in writing by Landlord, or, at Landlord's option, the alteration, addition or improvement shall be made by Landlord for Tenant's account and Tenant shall reimburse Landlord for the cost thereof upon demand. Upon the expiration or sooner termination of the Term, Tenant shall upon demand by Landlord, at Tenant's sole cost and expense, forthwith and with all due diligence remove any or all alterations, additions, or improvements made by or for the account of Tenant, designated by Landlord to be removed, and Tenant shall forthwith and with due diligence, at its sole cost and expense, repair and restore the premises to their original condition.

---

[1] Philip G. Skinner, *Office and Retail Leases—Representing the Smaller Tenant.* Real Property Law Institute (1988): Institute of Continuing Legal Education in Georgia, pp. 8.1–8.63. Used by permission.

Most leases also identify the party obligated for repairs, maintenance, and general management of the premises. Items such as foundations, roofs, utility systems, and other major structural mechanical components usually are maintained by the landlord. All other items, including any items that benefit only the premises, usually are maintained and repaired by the tenant.

Most leases provide that the tenant will not permit any lien to be filed with respect to the premises or the building, and in the event such lien is filed based on work performed for or materials supplied to the tenant, the tenant will cause the lien to be satisfied, bonded, or discharged immediately.

Insurance

Most leases impose on a tenant the requirement to carry appropriate kinds of insurance coverage in amounts with a carrier specified in the lease. A commercial tenant's insurance obligation should, at a minimum, encompass fire and extended coverage and comprehensive public liability insurance, including property damage. The tenant may be required to insure not only contents but the actual premises as well. This is especially true in a freestanding structure in which the tenant leases the entire premises. Any policies of insurance required to be obtained by the tenant pursuant to the terms of the lease should provide by endorsement that losses are payable to the landlord and tenant as their respective interest appear. In addition, each policy required under the lease should contain an agreement by the insurer that such policy will in no event be canceled without at least thirty days' prior written notice to each party. The lease may permit the landlord to pay any insurance premiums not promptly paid by the tenant and to assess that cost to the tenant.

In addition, most lease provisions release and hold harmless both the landlord and the tenant from each other's actions in regard to the cause of any casualty to the premises that is covered by insurance. This release and hold harmless impairs an insurance company's right of **subrogation**. An insurance company has a right when it pays a claim to be subrogated or substituted to the party paid and obtain any rights this party may have against the party causing the accident to recover damages. For example, a tenant negligently starts a fire on the premises that causes substantial damage. The insurance carrier pays the landlord the cost of the damage. The insurance carrier then is subrogated or substituted in place of the landlord to proceed against the tenant and recover for the tenant's negligence in destruction of the premises.

When a lease holds both parties harmless from any action that may damage the premises covered by insurance, this release and hold harmless impairs the insurance company's right of subrogation. When subrogation is impaired, an insurance company does not have to pay a claim under the policy. It is easy to see how this situation can create a serious problem. If subrogation is impaired under the policy, then the insurance company pays no claim for the damage, and if the landlord and tenant have already waived rights against each other, the landlord or tenant has no right to recover for the damage either. The damage, therefore, is unrecoverable, and the expense of it must be borne totally by the landlord or the tenant. This potentially dangerous problem can be resolved by having the insurance company waive its rights of subrogation. This is routinely done, and waivers of subrogation oftentimes are already built into the "boiler plate" terms and conditions of a commercial insurance policy. The legal assistant, when reviewing a lease that includes hold harmless language, should review all the appropriate insurance policies to make sure that the right of subrogation has been waived by the insurance carrier.

Damage or Destruction to the Premises

Under common law, a lease continued even after the premises had been damaged and destroyed, and the tenant was obligated to continue paying rent. The common law rule has been changed by statute in many states and often is changed within the lease agreement. It is not unusual for a lease to contain a fire damage clause that provides that the lease will terminate or rent will abate if the building or premises are destroyed by fire. Leases do provide, however, that a tenant is obligated for any damage that the tenant causes to the premises by the tenant's negligence or intentional conduct.

It also should be noted that many leases obligate a tenant to return the premises in the same condition as the tenant received it. This affirmative obligation would require the tenant to keep the premises in good repair throughout the term of the lease and to even protect it against casualties caused by fire or other risk.

A lease typically provides that if there is substantial destruction to the premises, either the landlord or the tenant may terminate the lease. The lease also provides that if there is partial or temporary destruction to the premises, the lease will not be terminated and the premises will be restored; the rent, however, will abate (not be due and payable) during the period of restoration or will abate in proportion to the amount of the premises that can't be used. For example, a tenant leases 10,000 square feet of space. A fire causes 1,000 square feet of the space to be unusable, but the remaining 9,000 is usable. Under the restoration and abatement provisions in most leases, a tenant would only be responsible for 90 percent of the rent during the restoration of the 1,000 square feet of damaged space.

Obligation of Repair

Under common law, a landlord was not responsible for repair of the premises. The tenant leased the premises "as is," with full obligations to repair. The common law not only made the landlord not responsible for the repair of the premises, but also the landlord was not responsible for any injuries caused by the condition of the premises or the lack of repair. An exception to the common law rule was that a landlord was responsible for hidden defects that were known to exist. A hidden defect is a defect that the landlord knew about but did not disclose to the tenant and is a defect that the tenant would not discover on reasonable investigation or inspection of the property.

This common law rule is still followed in many states. Under certain types of leases, such as residential leases, state statutes have made the landlord responsible for defective premises. Under these statutes, the tenant does have an obligation to make the landlord aware of defects and to give the landlord a reasonable time to repair defects before the landlord will be responsible for any injuries caused by the defects. A landlord also usually is responsible for injuries and accidents that occur in the common premises under the landlord's possession and control, such as hallways, stairs, and parking lots.

Condemnation and Eminent Domain

A lease ordinarily provides for what happens in the event that a specified amount of the leased premises is taken by condemnation, eminent domain, or other governmental right. If this happens, the landlord or the tenant usually has an option to terminate the lease. In the event an election to terminate is not made, the rent is apportioned in accordance with the proportion of the premises remaining tenable.

Default

Most leases contain provisions that indicate what shall constitute an event of default under the lease. At minimum, a tenant will be in default under the lease if the tenant (a) fails to pay any installment of rent or any other sum payable by the tenant under the lease, within a certain number of days after the due date; (b) fails to perform or observe any covenant, term, or condition under the lease, which failure continues for a certain period of days beyond the period of time necessary to cure if diligently pursued; (c) fails to continue its business as a going concern or tenant vacates or abandons the premises; and (d) fails to maintain certain evidence of financial stability.

Landlord's Remedies for Tenant's Default

New York:

When a tenant breaches any lease provision, the landlord may sue. If the landlord breaches a lease provision, the tenant may similarly sue. For further discussion, see Appendix.

A landlord's basic remedies for a tenant's default are to (a) sue the tenant for performance, (b) terminate the lease and sue for damages, and (c) dispossess the tenant and sue for damages. A landlord may sue a tenant for performance in the event of a default on the lease. For example, a landlord may sue a tenant for the rent, although this may require a suit brought each month, or the landlord may permit the rent to accumulate for a period of time before bringing suit. A landlord may sue a tenant for a nonmonetary default and ask the tenant to perform, or the landlord may cure the default and sue for reimbursement of the expense. For example, a landlord may sue a tenant to remove an unauthorized sign placed on the premises or the landlord may remove the sign and sue the tenant for the cost of removal.

A landlord has the right to terminate the lease and evict a tenant for the tenant's default. Once the lease is terminated, rental under the lease ceases and the landlord may only recover damages. The damage usually is the amount calculated by what the rent for the remainder of the term would have been less a reasonable rent that could be obtained for the remainder of the term by releasing the premises.

Most leases provide that a landlord may evict and remove a tenant from possession of the premises and not terminate the lease. The landlord then may act as the tenant's agent for purposes of reletting or releasing the space. The tenant remains responsible for the rent less any new rent received through reletting.

A lease may provide that the landlord has the right to serve notice of termination on the tenant that will accelerate all rent and other costs and charges reserved to the landlord under the lease.

An accelerated rent remedy is a provision whereby all the future, unearned rent is accelerated and made immediately due and payable at the election of the landlord in the event that an uncured event of default occurs under the lease.

A typical default paragraph may provide that on receipt of a termination notice, the tenant will peacefully quit and surrender the premises.

Landlord's Right to Perform Tenant's Obligations

Most leases grant the landlord the right to perform any duties and obligations required of the tenant pursuant to the lease and to charge the cost of such performance to the tenant. The right to perform includes the ability to make payment of any sums due and payable by the tenant under the lease on default by the tenant, such as obligations of the tenant to pay taxes or insurance. Most leases provide that any performance rendered by the landlord does not constitute a waiver of the tenant's default, thereby depriving the landlord of the right to exercise its other remedies under the lease for tenant's default.[2]

---

[2] Carleton Richard Kemph, "Drafting Commercial Leases," *Real Estate Law Journal* 10 (1981): 99–111. Used by permission of Warren, Gorham & Lamont, Inc.

A lease provision covering the tenant's default and the landlord's remedies appears in Example 18–5.

EXAMPLE 18-5

The following events shall be deemed to be events of default by Tenant under this Lease:

(1) Tenant shall fail to pay when or before due any sum of money, becoming due to be paid to Landlord hereunder, whether such sum be any installment of the rental herein reserved, any other amount treated as additional rental hereunder, or any other payment or reimbursement to Landlord required herein, whether or not treated as additional rental hereunder, and such failure shall continue for a period of five (5) days from the date such payment was due; or

(2) Tenant shall fail to comply with any term, provision or covenant of this Lease other than failing to pay when or before due any sum of money becoming due to be paid to Landlord hereunder, and shall not cure such failure within twenty (20) days (forthwith, if the default involves a hazardous condition) after written notice thereof to Tenant; or

(3) Tenant shall abandon any substantial portion of the leased premises; or

(4) Tenant shall fail to vacate the leased premises immediately upon termination of this Lease, by lapse of time or otherwise, or upon termination of Tenant's right to possession only; or

(5) If, in spite of the provisions hereof, the interest of Tenant shall be levied upon under execution or be attached by process of law or Tenant shall fail to contest diligently the validity of any lien or claimed lien and give sufficient security to landlord to insure payment thereof or shall fail to satisfy any judgment rendered thereon and have the same released, and such default shall continue for ten (10) days after written notice thereof to Tenant.

(b) Upon the occurrence of any such events of default described in this paragraph or elsewhere in this Lease, Landlord shall have the option to pursue any one or more of the following remedies without any notice or demand whatsoever:

(1) Landlord may, at its election, terminate this Lease or terminate Tenant's right to possession only, without terminating the Lease.

(2) Upon any termination of this Lease, whether by lapse of time or otherwise, or upon any termination of Tenant's right to possession without termination of this Lease, Tenant shall surrender possession and vacate the leased premises immediately, and deliver possession thereof to Landlord, and Tenant hereby grants to Landlord full and free license to enter into and upon the leased premises in such event with or without process of law and to repossess Landlord of the leased premises as of Landlord's former estate and to expel or remove Tenant and any others who may be occupying or within the leased premises and to remove any and all property therefrom, without being deemed in any manner guilty of trespass, eviction or forcible entry or detainer, and without incurring any liability for any damage resulting therefrom, Tenant hereby waiving any right to claim damage for such re-entry and expulsion and without relinquishing Landlord's right to rent or any other right given to Landlord hereunder or by operation of law.

(3) Upon termination of this Lease, whether by lapse of time or otherwise, Landlord shall be entitled to recover as damages, all rental, including any money treated as additional rental hereunder, and other sums due and payable by Tenant on the date of termination, plus the sum of (i) an amount equal to the then-present value of the rental, including any amounts treated as additional rental hereunder, and other sums provided herein to be paid by Tenant for the residue of the stated term hereof, less the fair rental value of the leased premises for such residue (taking into account the time and expense necessary to obtain a replacement tenant or tenants, including expenses hereinafter described in subparagraph (b)(4) relating to recovery of the leased premises, preparation for reletting and for reletting itself), and (ii) the cost of performing any other covenants which would have otherwise been performed by Tenant.

(4)(i) Upon any termination of Tenant's right to possession only without termination of the Lease, Landlord may, at Landlord's option, enter into the leased premises, remove Tenant's signs and other evidences of tenancy, and take and hold possession thereof as provided in subparagraph (b)(2) above, without such entry and possession terminating the Lease or releasing Tenant, in whole or in part, from any obligation, including Tenant's obligation to pay the rental, including any amounts treated as additional rental, hereunder for the full Term. In any such case, Tenant shall pay forthwith to Landlord if Landlord so elects, a sum equal to the entire amount of the rental, including any amounts treated as additional rental hereunder, for the residue of the stated Term hereof, plus any other sums provided herein to be paid by Tenant for the remainder of the Lease Term;

(ii) Landlord may, but is not required to relet the leased premises, or any part thereof, for such rent and upon such terms as Landlord in its sole discretion shall determine (including the right to relet the leased premises for a greater or lesser term than that remaining under this Lease, the right to relet the leased premises as a part of a larger area, and the right to change the character and use made of the leased premises) and Landlord shall not be required to accept any substitute tenant offered by Tenant or to observe any instructions given by Tenant about such reletting. In any such case, Landlord may make repairs, alterations and additions in or to the leased premises, and redecorate the same to the extent Landlord deems necessary or desirable, and Tenant shall, upon demand, pay the cost thereof, together with Landlord's expenses for reletting including, without limitation, any broker's commission incurred by Landlord. If the consideration collected by Landlord upon any such reletting plus any sums previously collected from Tenant are not sufficient to pay the full amount of all rental, including any amounts treated as additional rental hereunder and other sums reserved in this Lease for the remaining Term hereof, together with the costs of repairs, alterations, additions, redecorating, and Lessor's expenses of reletting and the collection of the rental accruing therefrom (including attorneys' fees and broker's commissions), Tenant shall pay to Landlord the amount of such deficiency upon demand and Tenant agrees that Landlord may file suit to recover any sums falling due under this section from time to time.

(5) Landlord may, at Landlord's option, enter into and upon the leased premises, with or without process of law, if Landlord determines in its sole discretion that Tenant is not acting within a commercially reasonable time to maintain, repair or replace anything for which Tenant is responsible hereunder and correct the same, without being deemed in any manner guilty of trespass, eviction or forcible entry and detainer and without incurring any liability for any damage resulting therefrom and Tenant agrees to reimburse Landlord, on demand, as additional rental, for any expenses which Landlord may incur in thus effecting compliance with Tenant's obligations under this Lease.

(6) Any and all property which may be removed from the leased premises by Landlord pursuant to the authority of the Lease or of law, to which Tenant is or may be entitled, may be handled, removed and stored, as the case may be, by or at the direction of Landlord at the risk, cost and expense of Tenant, and Landlord shall in no event be responsible for the value, preservation or safekeeping thereof. Tenant shall pay to Landlord, upon demand, any and all expenses incurred in such removal and all storage charges against such property so long as the same shall be in Landlord's possession or under Landlord's control. Any such property of Tenant not retaken by Tenant from storage within thirty (30) days after removal from the leased premises shall, at Landlord's option, be deemed conveyed by Tenant to Landlord under this Lease as by a bill of sale without further payment or credit by Landlord to Tenant.

(c) Pursuit of any of the foregoing remedies shall not preclude pursuit of any of the other remedies herein provided or any other remedies provided by law (all such remedies being cumulative), nor shall pursuit of any remedy herein provided constitute a forfeiture or waiver of any rental due to Landlord hereunder or of any damages accruing to Landlord by reason of the violation of any of the terms, provisions and covenants herein contained. No act or thing done by Landlord or its agents during the Term shall be deemed a termination of this Lease or an acceptance of the surrender of the leased premises, and no agreement to terminate this Lease or accept a surrender of said premises shall be valid unless in writing signed by Landlord. No waiver by Landlord of any violation or breach of any of the terms, provisions and covenants herein contained shall be deemed or construed to constitute a waiver of any other violation or breach of any of the terms, provisions and covenants herein contained. Landlord's acceptance of the payment of rental or other payments hereunder after the occurrence of an event of default shall not be construed as a waiver of such default, unless Landlord so notifies Tenant in writing. Forebearance by Landlord in enforcing one or more of the remedies herein provided upon an event of default shall not be deemed or construed to constitute a waiver of such default or of Landlord's right to enforce any such remedies with respect to such default or any subsequent default. If, on account of any breach or default by Tenant in Tenant's obligations under the terms and conditions of this Lease, it shall become necessary or appropriate for Landlord to employ or consult with an attorney concerning or to defend any of Landlord's rights or remedies hereunder, Tenant agrees to pay reasonable attorneys' fees so incurred.

(d) Without limiting the foregoing, to the extent permitted by law, Tenant hereby: (i) appoints and designates the leased premises as a proper place for service of process upon Tenant, and agrees that service of process upon any person apparently employed by Tenant upon the leased premises or leaving process in a conspicuous place within the leased premises shall constitute personal service of such process upon Tenant (provided, however, Landlord does not hereby waive the right to serve Tenant with process by any other lawful means); (ii) expressly waives any right to trial by jury; and (iii) expressly waives the service of any notice under any existing or future law of the State of Georgia applicable to landlords and tenants.

Landlord's Lien

Some leases provide that a landlord has a lien against the personal effects of a tenant stored on the leased premises to secure the performance of the tenant under the lease. This lien often is created as a security interest and is perfected by the filing of the Uniform Commercial Code financing statement. If the tenant defaults, the landlord has the right to repossess the tenant's personal property and sell it to pay the tenant's obligations under the lease.

Grace Periods

Most landlords are willing to accept a five- to ten-day notice and cure period for monetary defaults such as failure to pay rent, taxes, or other expenses required of the tenant. Many landlords, however, request that such a notice and cure as to monetary defaults be limited to an obligation to provide such a notice an agreed number of times (e.g., two or three times in any twelve consecutive-month period). This provision prevents a repeat offender from taking advantage of the notice requirement by repeatedly paying monetary obligations only after notices of default have been received.

Other defaults under the lease that are nonmonetary often are more difficult to cure because the requirements for cure may not be solely within the control of the tenant. For example, a lease obligates a tenant to operate its business in full compliance of all health, safety, and fire codes. The tenant installs electrical equipment that requires part of the premises to be rewired. The rewiring is not approved by the building inspector. The tenant is in default under the lease and must not only have the wiring replaced but also schedule another inspection. A longer period of notice and cure (usually twenty or thirty days) is commonplace for nonmonetary defaults.

Tenant's Remedies for Landlord's Default

As previously mentioned, the covenants of a commercial lease are independent, so that a tenant does not have the right to offset or not pay the rent due to a landlord's default under the lease. This leaves the tenant with only the remedy of suing the landlord to perform or for damages caused by nonperformance.

New York:
If the landlord breaches any clause in the lease, tenant can sue for damages. If premises are uninhabitable and thus there is an actual or constructive eviction, tenant may sue for damages.

Quiet Enjoyment

Most leases provide that the landlord covenants that the tenant will peacefully and quietly enjoy the premises without hindrance or interference by the landlord for the entire duration of the lease term, subject to each party's performance of the provisions of the lease.[3] A sample of a quiet enjoyment provision is shown in Example 18–6.

EXAMPLE 18–6

Landlord agrees that if Tenant shall perform all the covenants and agreements herein required to be performed by Tenant, Tenant shall, subject to the terms of this Lease, at times during the continuance of this Lease, have the peaceable and quiet enjoyment and possession of the Demised Premises.

Surrender the Premises

Most leases provide that on expiration or termination of the lease, the tenant will peacefully and quietly surrender the premises in the original condition, less ordinary wear and tear. The tenant usually has a right to remove trade fixtures at the termination of the lease. This right to remove trade fixtures, however, often is limited to the following provisions: (a) the tenant can remove trade fixtures before the termination of the lease; (b) the trade fixtures cannot be removed if the tenant is in default; and (c) the tenant must repair all damage to the premises caused by the removal of the trade fixtures. Most leases provide that if trade fixtures remain in the premises on termination of the lease, the landlord has the right to remove the trade fixtures and store them. The landlord has no liability for any damage caused to the trade fixtures during the removal and storage, and the landlord can recover from the tenant the cost of such removal and storage. A sample provision regarding surrender of the premises is shown in Example 18–7.

EXAMPLE 18–7

(a) Tenant shall, at least one hundred eighty (180) days before the last day of the Lease Term, give to Landlord a written notice of intention to surrender the premises on that date, but nothing contained therein or in the failure of Tenant to give such notice shall be construed as an extension of the Term, or as consent of Landlord to any holding over by Tenant.

(b) At the end of the Term, or any renewal thereof, or other sooner termination of this Lease, the Tenant peaceably will deliver to the Landlord possession of the premises, together with all improvements or additions upon or belonging to the same, by whomsoever made, in the same condition as received, or first installed, ordinary wear and tear, damage by fire, earthquake, act of God or the elements alone excepted. Tenant may, upon the termination of this Lease, remove all movable furniture and equipment belonging to Tenant, at Tenant's sole cost, title to which shall be in the name of Tenant until such termination, repairing any damage caused by such removal. Property not so removed shall be deemed abandoned by the Tenant, and title to the same shall thereupon pass to Landlord. Upon request by Landlord, unless otherwise agreed to in writing by Landlord, Tenant shall remove, at Tenant's sole cost, any or all permanent improvements or additions to the premises installed by or at the expense of Tenant and all movable furniture and

[3] Ibid.

equipment belonging to Tenant which may be left by Tenant and repair any damage resulting from such removal.

(c) The voluntary or other surrender of this Lease by Tenant, or a mutual cancellation thereof, shall not work a merger, and shall, at the option of the Landlord, terminate all or any existing subleases or subtenancies or may, at the option of Landlord, operate as an assignment to it of any or all such subleases or subtenancies.

Estoppel Certificate

It is not unusual for a lease to provide that the tenant shall, on request, provide to the landlord or to a person at the landlord's direction a sworn statement of facts concerning the lease, commonly referred to as an **estoppel certificate**. An institutional lender that is making a loan to the landlord and taking the premises as security will request estoppel certificates from the tenants. A purchaser of the premises from the landlord will likewise request estoppel certificates from the tenants. The estoppel certificates normally refer to an annexed true copy of the lease and should include a confirmation that (a) the lease is in full force and effect; (b) the lease has not been supplemented, amended, or modified in any respect; (c) no default under the lease exists and no event has occurred that, with the giving of notice and/or lapse of time, would become a default under the lease; and (d) there are no defenses, setoffs, recoupments, claims, or counterclaims of any nature by or on behalf of such party against the other.[4] An estoppel certificate is shown as Exhibit 18–1 at the end of this chapter.

Memorandum of Lease

Most leases are not recorded. In some instances, to protect the tenant's interest in the lease or if the lease contains certain additional provisions such as options to purchase the premises by the tenant, a memorandum of lease is recorded. A memorandum of lease includes all operative terms of the lease as well as any purchase options, renewals, and first refusals of additional space. Recording a memorandum in the real property records in which the premises are fully located protects the tenant against a landlord who might otherwise release or wrongfully convey the premises to a bona fide purchaser having no notice of the tenant's rights.[5] An example of a short-form memorandum lease provision is set forth in Example 18–8. An example of a short-form memorandum prepared for recordation is shown in Exhibit 18–2 at the end of this chapter.

EXAMPLE 18-8

SHORT FORM LEASE. LESSOR and LESSEE hereby agree to enter into a Short-Form Lease setting out (a) the names of the parties hereto, (b) the description of Demised Premises as the same appears in Exhibit A hereof (c) the dates of this Lease Agreement and of its initial and extension or renewal terms and (d) LESSEE's rights upon termination of this Lease Agreement; such Short-Form Lease shall be in writing, duly executed by all the parties hereto on the date hereof or at any time thereafter as prepared and requested by either party hereof, and shall be properly attested and acknowledged for recording in Ohio.

---

[4] Ibid.

[5] Ibid.

Limitation on the Landlord's Liability

Landlords in commercial leases strive to minimize personal liability. It is not unusual for the lease to provide that the landlord is not responsible for any damage done to the tenant or to the tenant's property or personal effects because of the landlord's failure to perform the landlord's obligations under the lease and that any recovery for any liability of whatever nature under the lease can only be made against the landlord's interest in the premises. This type of provision protects the landlord but does leave the tenant in a precarious situation of not being able to recover for any of the landlord's defaults under the lease.

A limitation of landlord's liability clause may contain an exception for the landlord's intentional misconduct or gross negligence.[6]

ASSIGNMENTS, SUBLETTING, OR MORTGAGING OF THE LEASED PREMISES

New York:
Generally, the lease says the tenant may assign or sublease with the landlord's consent. New York Real Property Law has detailed requirements the tenant must follow to make a written request to sublet or assign. See Appendix for further discussion.

The general rule is that a tenant may assign, sublet, or mortgage his or her interest in the lease. An **assignment**, by definition, is when the tenant transfers all his or her interest under the lease and retains nothing. A **sublet** is when a tenant transfers only a portion of his or her interest under the lease and the tenant retains some interest. For example, if a tenant leased the premises for five years, a sublet may be when he or she transfers possession for only two of those five years. Another example might be a tenant who has leased 10,000 square feet of space and in turn sublets 5,000 square feet of this space to another person.

Restrictions on assignment or subletting of the lease are strictly construed. This means that if the lease prohibits only assignments, then subletting is permissible. If the lease prohibits only subletting, then assignments are permissible. It is not unusual for leases to provide that both assignments and subletting are prohibited or can only take place with the landlord's prior written consent.

An assignment or sublet in violation of a lease restriction could result in the lease being in default. If the landlord accepts rent from an assignee, or subtenant, after a nonauthorized assignment, the landlord may waive its right to declare the lease in default.

The original tenant, after an assignment or sublet, remains responsible on the lease for rent and other lease obligations unless the lease provides otherwise.

An assignee of a lease has the responsibility for rent as long as the assignee is in possession and is responsible for lease covenants that run with the land. Although the definition and interpretation of lease covenants that run with the land vary from state to state, they usually include any type of use restrictions. An assignee, by express agreement, can be required to assume all obligations under the lease. An express assumption of all lease obligations makes the assignee as responsible as the original tenant. The assumption of lease covenants by an assignee, however, does not release the original tenant. The landlord can sue both the original tenant and the assignee in the event of a default.

A subtenant or sublessee has no responsibility to the original landlord under the lease for either rent or any of the lease covenants. A sublessee is responsible only to the tenant and responsible only pursuant to the terms of the sublease. Great care should be taken when drafting subleases to make sure that the sublease does not con-

---

[6] Ibid.

flict with the main lease and that the tenant has full rights to enforce performance of the main lease covenants against the sublessee. This is important because the original tenant is responsible to the landlord for any acts of the subtenant under the sublease. Example 18–9 shows an assignment and subletting provision.

EXAMPLE 18-9

(a) Tenant shall not sell, assign, encumber or otherwise transfer by operation of law or otherwise this Lease, or any interest herein, nor shall Tenant sublet the premises or any portion thereof, or suffer any other person to occupy or use the premises or any portion thereof, without the prior written consent of Landlord as provided herein, nor shall Tenant permit any lien to be placed on the Tenant's interest by operation of law. Tenant shall, by written notice, advise Landlord of its desire from and after a stated date (which shall not be less than thirty (30) days nor more than ninety (90) days after the date of Tenant's notice) to sublet the premises or any portion thereof for any part of the Term ("Subletting Notice"); and supply Landlord with such information, financial statements, verifications and related materials as Landlord may request or desire to evaluate the written request to sublet or assign. In such event, Landlord shall have the right, to be exercised by giving written notice to Tenant (Landlord's "Termination Notice") within ten days after receipt of Tenant's Subletting Notice, to terminate this Lease as to the portion of the premises described in Tenant's Subletting Notice and this Lease shall thereupon be terminated with respect to the portion of the premises therein described as of the date stated in Tenant's Notice. Tenant's Subletting Notice shall state the name and address of the proposed subtenant, and Tenant shall deliver to Landlord a true and complete copy of the proposed sublease with such Notice. If such Subletting Notice shall indicate that Tenant desires to sublet all of the premises and Landlord shall give its Termination Notice with respect thereto, this Lease shall terminate on the date stated in Tenant's Subletting Notice. If, however, this Lease shall terminate pursuant to the foregoing with respect to less than all the premises, the rental, as defined and reserved hereinabove and as adjusted pursuant to Paragraph 2, shall be adjusted on a pro rata basis according to the number of square feet retained by Tenant, and this Lease as so amended shall continue thereafter in full force and effect. If Landlord, upon receiving Tenant's Subletting Notice with respect to any of the premises, shall not exercise its right to terminate, Landlord will not unreasonably withhold its consent to Tenant's subletting the premises as requested in such Subletting Notice. Tenant shall, at Tenant's own cost and expense, discharge in full any outstanding commission obligation on the part of Landlord with respect to this Lease, and any commissions which may be due and owing as a result of any proposed assignment or subletting, whether or not the Lease is terminated pursuant hereto and rented by Landlord to the proposed subtenant or any other tenant.

(b) Any subletting or assignment hereunder by Tenant shall not result in Tenant being released or discharged from any liability under this Lease. As a condition to Landlord's prior written consent as provided for in this paragraph, the assignee or subtenant shall agree in writing to comply with and be bound by all of the terms, covenants, conditions, provisions and agreements of this Lease, and Tenant shall deliver to Landlord promptly after execution, an executed copy of each sublease or assignment and an agreement of said compliance by each sublessee or assignee.

(c) Landlord's consent to any sale, assignment, encumbrance, subletting, occupation, lien or other transfer shall not release Tenant from any of Tenant's obligations hereunder or be deemed to be a consent to any subsequent occurrence. Any sale, assignment, encumbrance, subletting, occupation, lien or other transfer of this Lease which does not comply with the provisions of this Paragraph shall be void.

A tenant may mortgage the leasehold interests or rights under a lease. The mortgage is subject to the terms of the lease and will terminate if the lease terminates. It is not unusual for lenders who take as security a tenant's obligation under a lease to enter into an agreement with the landlord to provide that the landlord will not terminate the lease unless notice is given to the leasehold mortgagee and the leasehold mortgagee has a right to cure all defaults. It also is important in representing leasehold mortgagees to obtain permission from the landlord to foreclose the mortgage and to accept an assignment of the lease and take over possession of the premises. A landlord often will agree and will recognize anyone who forecloses the leasehold mortgage as the new tenant under the lease. These agreements are called attornment and nondisturbance agreements. A form of attornment and nondisturbance agreement can be found at the end of this chapter as Exhibit 18–3.

The landlord also can mortgage its interest in the fee. The landlord's mortgage will be either subordinate or superior to the lease, depending on the time the mortgage was placed on the premises. The mortgage on the premises at the time the lease was entered into will be superior and the mortgage that was placed on the premises after the lease will be subordinate. These rules can change by contract and lease provision. It is not unusual for leases to provide an automatic subordination that states that the lease will be subordinate to any mortgage on the premises, regardless of when it is placed. Example 18–10 shows a subordination clause.

EXAMPLE 18-10

Tenant's rights shall be subject to any bona fide mortgage or deed of trust which is now, or may hereafter be, placed upon the Premises by Landlord. Tenant shall, if requested by Landlord, execute a separate agreement reflecting such subordination.

A superior mortgage on the leased premises creates a problem for the tenant if the mortgage is foreclosed because the lease will terminate. A tenant often will try to obtain attornment agreements from the landlord's mortgagee, asking the mortgagee to agree that if it forecloses and the tenant is not in default under the lease, the lender will honor the lease.

Special Sublease Issues

A valid sublease effects no change in the relation between the landlord and the tenant and creates no new relation between the landlord and the subtenant. The tenant remains liable to the landlord for any breach of the prime lease. The landlord cannot collect rent directly from the subtenant, and the subtenant cannot bring an action to compel the landlord to comply with its obligations on the prime lease with respect to the subleased premises or to collect damages from the landlord resulting from such breach. Any default by the tenant on the prime lease that results in termination of the prime lease by the landlord automatically terminates the sublease.

Because of the lack of privity between landlord and subtenant, the subtenant's rights to remain in the space are at the sufferance first of the tenant and then of the landlord. If the tenant incurs financial problems and defaults on the prime lease, the subtenant's rights terminate with those of the tenant. If the subtenant does not have a covenant of quiet enjoyment from the tenant, the subtenant has no recourse against the tenant.

Provisions Normally Contained in a Sublease

A sublessor should be careful to stipulate that the term of the sublease ends at some period before termination of the prime lease. A sublessor should seek to avoid any liability for a breach by the prime landlord of its obligations under the prime lease and indemnification for any expenses that it incurs in enforcing the landlord's obligations under the prime lease to the benefit of the sublessee. In addition, the sublessor may desire to make more restrictive certain terms of the prime lease as they apply between the sublessor and the sublessee, such as the right to further sublease and to reduce the periods for making rental payments and curing breaches so that such periods will terminate before the time that the tenant is obligated to perform under the prime lease. For example, if under the prime lease the tenant has a ten-day notice and right to cure for failure to make rent payments on time, the tenant may want to provide in a sublease that sublessee has only five days from notice to make rent payments. This provides the tenant with an additional five days after default by the sublessee to pay the rent under the prime lease without causing a default of the prime lease. A sublessor may want to stipulate that insurance required to be maintained by the sublessee name both the sublessor and the prime landlord as insured and contain waiver of subrogation to both. The sublessor will want all covenants and provisions of the prime lease to be carried over into the sublease. The sublessor may seek indemnification for damages incurred by reason of the sublessee's action or inaction that creates a violation of the prime lease.

The sublessee should attempt to include the following provisions in the sublease: (a) a covenant of quiet enjoyment and an indemnification from the sublessor against damages incurred by reason of the sublessor's action or inaction in violation of the prime lease; and (b) a condition precedent to the effectiveness of the sublease that the prime landlord consents to the sublease and that the prime landlord enter into a nondisturbance agreement with the sublessee. This nondisturbance agreement provides that in the event there is a default under the prime lease, the landlord will honor the sublease according to its terms.

A sublessee may want a covenant that the sublessor shall be liable to cure any breach by the prime landlord, or the sublessor shall diligently commence and prosecute a suit against the prime landlord to force the landlord to perform under the prime lease.[7]

Lease Guaranty

It is not unusual for a tenant's obligation under a lease to be guaranteed by some other party. This may happen when the tenant is a corporation with little or no assets or an individual without substantial financial reserve. For example, a landlord may require that the principal shareholders of a corporate tenant guarantee the tenant's performance under the lease. A form of lease guaranty can be found at the end of this chapter as Exhibit 18–4.

A lease guaranty usually is unconditional, and the guarantor agrees to perform all obligations of the tenant under the lease, including but not limited to all monetary obligations of the tenant such as payment of rent, taxes, insurance, utilities, or maintenance charges as well as all other obligations of the tenant, such as maintenance and repair obligations. It is not unusual for a guaranty to be limited in term. The major risks of tenant default normally are in the early years of the lease. It is common for a guaranty of a long-term lease to be applicable only to the first few years of the lease. For example, a subsidiary corporation enters into a ten-year lease with a land-

[7] Jerome Berkman, "Negotiable Issues in Commercial Subleases," *Real Estate Law Journal* 13 (1984) 28–44. Used by permission of Warren, Gorham & Lamont, Inc.

lord. The landlord may negotiate with the parent corporation to guarantee the first three years of the subsidiary's obligations under the lease.

Most guarantors agree to pay all costs of collection or enforcement of the guaranty, including attorney's fees and court costs.

▐▐▐▶ CHECKLIST

Preparation of a Residential Lease

- ❑ I. Parties to Lease
  - ❑ A. Landlord—fee owner of leased premises
  - ❑ B. Tenant—person who intends to take possession and use the leased premises
- ❑ II. Description of Premises
  - ❑ A. Adequate description of leased premises and any associated personal property
  - ❑ B. Common areas
    1. Hallways
    2. Elevators
    3. Parking lots
- ❑ III. Term
- ❑ IV. Rent
  - ❑ A. Fixed amount
  - ❑ B. Rent commencement date
- ❑ V. Utilities
  - ❑ A. What utilities tenant pays
  - ❑ B. What utilities landlord pays
- ❑ VI. Maintenance and Repair Obligations
  - ❑ A. Identify obligations of landlord and tenant to maintain and repair leased premises
  - ❑ B. Identify tenant's rights to alter leased premises
- ❑ VII. Insurance
  - ❑ A. Identify insurance obligations of landlord and tenant
- ❑ VIII. Damage or Destruction of Leased Premises
  - ❑ A. Termination on total destruction
  - ❑ B. Renovate on partial destruction
  - ❑ C. Termination on partial destruction
- ❑ IX. Assignment and Subletting

- ❑ A. Free right to assign and sublet
- ❑ B. Restriction—no right to assign and sublet
- ❑ C. No assignment or subletting without permission of landlord
- ❑ X. Events of Default
  - ❑ A. Failure to pay rent
  - ❑ B. Failure to comply with lease covenants
  - ❑ C. Notice and grace periods
  - ❑ D. Landlord's right to cure tenant's default
- ❑ XI. Landlord's Remedies
  - ❑ A. Sue for performance
  - ❑ B. Cure default and seek reimbursement
  - ❑ C. Terminate lease
  - ❑ D. Evict and repossess tenant and relet leased premises as agent for tenant
- ❑ XII. Tenant's Remedies for Landlord's Default
  - ❑ A. Withhold rent
  - ❑ B. Sue to enforce
  - ❑ C. Sue for money damages
  - ❑ D. Cure default and offset costs against rent
- ❑ XIII. Quiet Enjoyment
- ❑ XIV. Surrender of Leased Premises
  - ❑ A. Tenant must vacate before lease term expires
- ❑ XV. Holding Over
  - ❑ A. Tenant is deemed to be month-to-month tenant
  - ❑ B. Tenant to pay same rent as during rent term
  - ❑ C. Tenant pays additional rent during holdover period

A form of residential lease can be found at the end of the chapter in Exhibit 18–5.

▐▐▐▶ CHECKLIST

Preparation of Commercial Lease

- ❑ I. Purpose of Lease
  - ❑ A. Retail space
  - ❑ B. Office space
  - ❑ C. Retail space—shopping center
- ❑ II. Parties to Lease
  - ❑ A. Landlord—fee owner of lease premises

- ❑ B. Tenant—entity that intends to take possession and use the property
- ❑ C. Broker—party to lease to enforce commission rights
- ❑ III. Description of Property to Be Leased

- ❑ A. Adequate description of leased premises and any associated personal property
- ❑ B. Common area property
  1. Hallways
  2. Elevators
  3. Parking lots
  4. Mall
  5. Restaurants
- ❑ IV. Term
  - ❑ A. Fixed term
  - ❑ B. Option renewals
  - ❑ C. Term to commence in future
    1. Open for business
    2. Fixed future date
    3. Procedure and remedies for unavailability of space at commencement of term
- ❑ V. Use
  - ❑ A. Specified use
  - ❑ B. Any lawful purpose
- ❑ VI. Rent
  - ❑ A. Fixed amount
  - ❑ B. Percentage rent
    1. What is included
    2. Definition of gross sales
    3. Exclusions from gross sales
    4. Record keeping
    5. When is percentage rent payable
    6. Landlord's right to audit and inspect books
    7. Agreement to operate
    8. Radius clause
  - ❑ C. Rent escalation (tax, insurance, expenses)
  - ❑ D. Gross rent
  - ❑ E. Net rent
  - ❑ F. Inflators (CPI Index)
  - ❑ G. When is rent due
- ❑ VII. Maintenance and Alterations
  - ❑ A. Identify obligations of landlord and tenant to maintain and repair premises
  - ❑ B. Identify tenant's rights to alter premises
  - ❑ C. Alterations and maintenance to be lien-free
- ❑ VIII. Insurance
  - ❑ A. Allocate responsibilities for insurance between landlord and tenant
  - ❑ B. Waiver of subrogation in insurance policies
- ❑ IX. Damage or Destruction to Premises
  - ❑ A. Termination on total destruction
  - ❑ B. Rent abatement on partial destruction
  - ❑ C. Termination on partial destruction
- ❑ X. Condemnation—Eminent Domain
  - ❑ A. Termination on total taking
  - ❑ B. Abatement of rent on partial taking
  - ❑ C. Termination on partial taking
  - ❑ D. Allocation of condemnation award between landlord and tenant
- ❑ XI. Assignment and Subletting
  - ❑ A. Free right to assign and sublet
  - ❑ B. Restriction—no right to assign and sublet
  - ❑ C. No assignment or subletting without permission of landlord
- ❑ XII. Subordination and Nondisturbance
  - ❑ A. Lease period
  - ❑ B. Lease subordinate to mortgages
  - ❑ C. Lease subordinate to mortgages but with attornment and subordination agreement
- ❑ XIII. Events of Default
  - ❑ A. Failure to pay rent
  - ❑ B. Failure to comply with lease covenants
  - ❑ C. Notice and grace period
  - ❑ D. Landlord's right to cure tenant's default
  - ❑ E. Tenant's payment of all expenses of enforcement of lease
    1. Attorney's fees
    2. Court costs
    3. Reimbursement to landlord for expenses to cure or remedy default
- ❑ XIV. Landlord's Remedies
  - ❑ A. Sue for performance
  - ❑ B. Cure default and seek reimbursement
  - ❑ C. Terminate lease
  - ❑ D. Evict and repossess tenant and relet premises as agent for tenant
  - ❑ E. Accelerate rent
  - ❑ F. Landlord's lien against tenant's personal property to secure payment of rent
- ❑ XV. Tenant's Remedies for Landlord's Default
  - ❑ A. Sue to enforce
  - ❑ B. Sue for money damages
  - ❑ C. Cure default and offset cost against rent
  - ❑ D. Withhold rent
- ❑ XVI. Quiet Enjoyment
- ❑ XVII. Surrender of Premises
  - ❑ A. Tenant must vacate before lease term expires
  - ❑ B. Tenant may remove trade fixtures
    1. If tenant is not in default
    2. Repair damage to premises caused by removal
    3. Remove before termination of lease
- ❑ XVIII. Holding Over
  - ❑ A. Tenant is deemed to be month-to-month tenant
  - ❑ B. Tenant to pay same rent as during lease term
  - ❑ C. Tenant pays additional rent for holdover period
- ❑ XIX. Estoppel Certificate
  - ❑ A. Tenant obligated to give estoppel certificate on landlord's demand
    1. To purchasers of leased premises
    2. Mortgage lender
- ❑ XX. Short-Form Lease
  - ❑ A. Short-form lease to be prepared
  - ❑ B. Short-form lease to be recorded

 ETHICS: Legal Needs of the Poor

Attorneys have always considered it a professional obligation to volunteer legal services for the poor. The rules of professional responsibility and conduct that govern attorneys in most states require a public service obligation as part of the ethical requirements of being an attorney. This obligation, often called pro bono participation, should not be limited just to attorneys. A paralegal should consider voluntary pro bono participation as a necessary part of his or her professional life.

One of the major problems of the American justice system is the unmet civil legal needs of the poor. The right to legal counsel in civil cases usually is provided by a number of quasi-governmental or voluntary associations that usually depend on full-time paid staff and volunteers to provide the necessary legal services.

Pro bono participation can provide the legal assistant with an opportunity to develop and improve skills in an area in which the legal assistant specializes. Many poor have landlord-tenant problems, and therefore, a knowledge of lease law can be applied by a legal assistant in a pro bono situation. The pro bono experience may also offer the legal assistant an opportunity to work in areas of the law in which he or she would not otherwise have the opportunity.

SUMMARY

Leasing is an important aspect of the real estate business. As the chapter points out, there are many issues to be considered in a lease transaction. Although lease negotiations are not adversarial in nature, it is obvious that a landlord and tenant do not have mutual interests in negotiating the lease. It is not always possible to please all the parties in a lease transaction, and even in the fairest and most reasonable of leases, some provisions favor the landlord and some favor the tenant. When reviewing or preparing a lease, the legal assistant should keep in mind the effect of any lease provision on the client. Knowledge and experience are the essential ingredients to becoming competent in the area of lease transactions.

KEY TERMS

Assignment
Estoppel certificate
Gross lease
Landlord, or lessor
Lease

Net lease
Percentage breakpoint
Percentage rent
Premises
Radius clause

Rent
Sublet
Subrogation
Tenant, or lessee

REVIEW QUESTIONS

1. Explain the theory of independent covenants.

2. What title concerns should a tenant have when entering into a lease with a landlord?

3. Identify the main concerns that a landlord has when entering into a lease with a tenant.

4. What is the value of a CPI escalation rent clause?

5. Identify and briefly discuss the basic remedies of a landlord for a tenant's default under a lease.

6. What is the difference between a gross rent lease and

a net rent lease?

7. What is the difference between an assignment and a sublease?

8. Under what circumstances would a tenant want a subordination-attornment agreement?

9. Identify and briefly discuss the basic remedies of a tenant for a landlord's default under a lease.

10. What is a lease guaranty, and when would it be used by a landlord?

CASE PROBLEMS

1. Ajax Stores, as a tenant, is negotiating a lease with Farris Realty Company. Ajax intends for the leased premises to be its main store location and is negotiating a twenty-year lease. In addition, Ajax is anticipating that it will spend approximately $250,000 in trade fixtures and other improvements to the leased premises. Ajax conducts a title examination of the leased premises and discovers that Farris Realty Company has encumbered the leased premises with a mortgage to First Bank and Trust to secure a debt of $1.5 million. As a legal assistant working for a law firm that represents Ajax, you have been made aware of the mortgage to First Bank and Trust. Should Ajax be concerned about the mortgage to First Bank and Trust? If so, what safeguards can you think of to protect Ajax?

2. As a landlord, is a gross lease or a net lease more favorable to you? Are there any factors to be considered in answering this question?

3. You are a legal assistant with a law firm that represents a chain of retail jewelry stores. All the stores lease space in shopping malls. The jewelry store chain is large enough that it creates its own standard form lease for submission to prospective landlords in each of the shopping malls. The jewelry stores know that the landlords are expecting a percentage rent clause to be contained in the standard form lease. You have been asked to assist in the preparation of the standard form lease. What factors should you take into account when drafting the percentage rent clause?

4. You are a legal assistant in a law firm representing the owner of a shopping center. The shopping center is being refinanced, and the new lender has requested that the owner obtain estoppel certificates from each of the tenants of the shopping center. You have been asked to prepare the estoppel certificate form. Briefly list the items you intend to include in the form.

5. Toni Tenant entered into a lease with Larry Landlord. The lease contains a provision obligating the tenant to keep the premises insured and to pay a rent of $500 each month. In addition, the lease prohibits assignment of the lease by the tenant. Toni Tenant possesses the premises for a couple of months and then decides to leave town. Toni finds Alice Assignee, who is willing to accept an assignment of the premises from Toni. Toni assigns all her right, title, and interest in the premises to Alice Assignee, who accepts the assignment and assumes the obligation of Toni Tenant under the lease. The assignment is made without the landlord's consent. The landlord discovers the assignment when the rent check is received next month from Alice Assignee, and the landlord cashes the rent check and raises no objections to the assignment. Alice Assignee continues in this relation for the next couple of months, paying her rent each month to the landlord. Each month the landlord cashes the check. After a few months, Alice Assignee is approached by Samantha Subtenant, who wants to sublease the entire premises, but only for two months. Alice Assignee, thinking about a Mediterranean vacation, agrees and subleases the premis-

es to Samantha for two months. During the two-month period, Samantha fails to pay rent to the landlord. The building burns down. Landlord discovers that the building is not insured. Landlord sues Toni, Alice, and Samantha for unpaid rent and for the value of the premis-

es because of their breach of the promise to insure the premises. Can the landlord recover against Toni? Can the landlord recover against Alice? Can the landlord recover against Samantha? What are the rights, liabilities, and responsibilities between Alice, Toni and Samantha?

ADDENDUM

EXHIBIT 18–1
Estoppel Certificate

Date: _____

Re: _____

Gentlemen:

It is our understanding that _____ (hereinafter called "Purchaser") intends to purchase the above-captioned premises, and as a condition precedent, such Purchaser requires that this certification be made by the undersigned (hereinafter called "Tenant").

1. Tenant presently leases approximately _____ square feet of retail space located on the above-referenced Property, pursuant to the terms and provisions of that certain Lease Agreement dated _____, by and between _____, as Landlord and Tenant as Lessee, a copy of said Lease being attached hereto and made a part hereof as Exhibit "A" (the "Lease").

2. Said Lease is in full force and effect and Tenant is primarily liable as Lessee thereunder, and the documents attached hereto as Exhibit "A" constitute a full, complete and accurate copy of said Lease, and said Lease has not been modified, supplemented or amended in any way, and there are no other promises, obligations, understandings, agreements, or commitments between Landlord and Tenant with respect to said Property other than as expressly set forth in said Lease.

3. All contingencies and conditions precedent to the commencement, effectiveness, validity and enforceability of said Lease have been satisfied, and Tenant hereby ratifies said Lease. All duties of an inducement nature and all work required under said Lease to be performed by Landlord have been satisfactorily completed in accordance with the provisions of said Lease, and Tenant claims no offsets, rebates, concessions, abatements, recoupments, or defenses against or with respect to rent, additional rent, or other sums payable under the terms of said Lease, and there are no breaches or defaults under the terms of said Lease, and no event has occurred which, with the passage of time or the giving of notice or both, shall constitute a default by Landlord or Tenant under the terms of said Lease.

4. The base monthly rental presently payable by Tenant under the terms of said Lease is ($_____) Dollars per month, which monthly rental installments have been paid

EXHIBIT 18-1
Estoppel Certificate
(continued)

to Landlord through _____ and no other rent has been prepaid to Landlord or any other party, and there has been a security deposit in the amount of ($_____) Dollars paid to and presently held by Landlord with respect to said Lease.

5. The Lease Term pursuant to said Lease commenced on _____, and shall expire on _____.

6. Tenant has no interest, rights or claims with respect to said Property other than the interest, rights, or claims arising out of or with respect to said Lease.

7. Tenant is a corporation and is in good standing with the State of _____, and has full authority to execute the within document.

8. The undersigned officers of Tenant have full authority to execute and deliver this certificate as agents for and on behalf of Tenant.

9. Tenant is presently in actual, full and complete physical occupancy and possession of said Property, and Tenant has accepted said Property as suitable for all uses and purposes contemplated or intended under said Lease.

10. Upon acquisition of said Property by Purchaser, Tenant shall attorn to Purchaser and recognize Purchaser as Tenant's Lessor and Landlord pursuant to said Lease.

Very truly yours,

By: _____

EXHIBIT 18-2
Short-Form
Memorandum

Memorandum of Lease Agreement

THIS MEMORANDUM OF LEASE AGREEMENT ("Memorandum") is entered into as of this 23rd day of March, 19__ by and between HARROLD ROBERTS AND THOMAS CLARK, whose address is 235 East Paces Ferry Road, Stanton, Ohio 60315 (collectively "Lessor"), and ACME CORPORATION, whose address is 6065 Roswell Road, Suite 120, Stanton, Ohio 60305 ("Lessee").

Recitals

By Lease Agreement dated March 23, 19__ ("Lease Agreement"), Lessor has leased to Lessee certain real property located at 5 West Paces Ferry Road, according to the present numbering system in Stanton, Knox County, Ohio, and being more particulariy described on Exhibit A attached hereto and incorporated herein by reference, together with all buildings, structures, driveways, parking areas and all other improvements now or hereafter located thereon ("Demised Premises").

TO HAVE AND TO HOLD the Demised Premises for an initial term of approximately ten (10) years and three (3) months commencing on the date of the Lease Agreement and expiring approximately on July 31, 19__, together with the option to extend the initial term for one (1) additional term of five (5) years commencing immediately upon the expiration of the initial term, all on the terms and conditions contained in the Lease Agreement, which terms and conditions are made a part hereof by reference.

Pursuant to the terms of Paragraph 18 of the Lease Agreement, Lessor has the right, after the fifth (5th) anniversary of the Commencement Date of the Initial Term, to terminate the Lease Agreement under certain circumstances. In the event of any such termination, Lessee has an option, under certain circumstances, to lease space in the new development located on the property of which the Demised Premises are a part, under the terms and conditions set forth in that Paragraph of the Lease Agreement.

EXHIBIT 18-2
Short-Form
Memorandum
(continued)

In addition to the terms referred to above, the Lease Agreement contains numerous other terms, covenants and conditions which affect the Demised Premises, and notice is hereby given that reference should be had to the Lease Agreement directly with respect to the details of such terms, covenants and conditions. Copies of the Lease Agreement are kept at the offices of Lessor and Lessee at the addresses set forth above. This Memorandum does not alter, amend, modify or change the Lease Agreement or the exhibits thereto in any respect. It is executed by the parties solely for the purpose of being recorded in the public records of Knox County, Ohio, and it is the intent of the parties that it shall be so recorded and shall give notice of and confirm the Lease Agreement and exhibits thereto and all of its terms to the same extent as if all of the provisions of the Lease Agreement and exhibits thereto were fully set forth herein. The Lease Agreement and all exhibits thereto are hereby incorporated by reference in this Memorandum and the parties hereby ratify and confirm the Lease Agreement as if said Lease Agreement were being presently re-executed by both parties and being recorded. In the event of any conflict between the provisions of the Memorandum and the Lease Agreement, the provisions of the Lease Agreement shall control.

IN WITNESS WHEREOF, Lessor and Lessee have set their hands and seals herewith and have caused this instrument to be executed in their names and their seals to be affixed hereunto by duly authorized officials thereof, the day and year first above written.

LESSOR:

_____ (SEAL)

HARROLD ROBERTS

_____ (SEAL)

THOMAS CLARK

LESSEE:

ACME CORPORATION, an Ohio Corporation

By: _____

its President

[CORPORATE SEAL]

EXHIBIT 18-3
Subordination,
Attornment, and
Nondisturbance
Agreement

THIS AGREEMENT is made as of _____, 19__, by and among _____, a _____ ("Lessor"), whose address is _____, and _____, a _____ ("Lessee"), whose address is _____, and   a   corporation ("Lender"), whose address is

A. The Property.

The term "Property," as used herein, shall mean the real property situated in the County of   , State of   legally described in Exhibit "A" attached hereto and by this reference made a part hereof, together with all buildings, structures, improvements and fixtures now or hereafter located thereon, and together with all easements and other rights appurtenant thereto.

EXHIBIT 18–3
Subordination,
Attornment, and
Nondisturbance
Agreement
(continued)

B. The Lease.

Pursuant to the terms and provisions of a lease dated _____, between Lessor and Lessee (the "Lease"), for a term of _____, the Property has been leased to Lessee.

C. The Loan; Security Documents; Security Deed.

Lessor proposed to borrow certain sums from Lender to be evidenced by a promissory note. Lessor proposes to encumber the Property as security for payment of its obligations to Lender and, for such purpose, shall enter into various instruments and documents (collectively the "Security Documents"), including without limitation a Deed to Secure Debt and Security Agreement (the "Security Deed") from Lessor to Lender and an Assignment of Leases and Rents (the "Collateral Assignment"), which Security Deed and Collateral Assignment will be recorded in the real property records of _____ County.

D. Purposes.

In connection with the above-mentioned transactions, Lessor and Lessee have agreed to offer certain assurances and representations to the Lender, and all parties agree to provide for (i) the subordination of the Lease to the Security Documents; (ii) the continuation of the Lease notwithstanding any foreclosure of the Security Deed subject to certain conditions; and (iii) Lessee's attornment to the Lender or to such other parties as may acquire title to the Property as a result of any foreclosure or any conveyance of the Property in lieu of foreclosure.

AGREEMENT

NOW, THEREFORE, in consideration of the mutual terms and provisions hereinafter contained and other good and valuable consideration received by any party from any other, the receipt and sufficiency of which are hereby acknowledged, the parties agree as follows:

1. Notices of Default to Lender.

Notwithstanding anything to the contrary in the Lease, Lessee shall personally deliver or mail to Lender, at Lender's address set forth above, written notice of any default under the Lease by Lessor, and if within the time provided in the Lease for curing thereof by Lessor, Lender performs or causes to be performed all such obligations with respect to which Lessor is in default which can be cured by the payment of money, any right of Lessee to terminate the Lease by reason of such default shall cease and be null and void.

2. Subordination of Lease to Security Documents.

Lessee hereby subordinates its leasehold estate in the Property and all of Lessee's right under the Lease to the Security Documents and to all extensions, renewals, modifications, consolidations and replacements thereof, to the full extent of all obligations secured or to be secured thereby including interest thereon and any future advances thereunder.

3. Non-Disturbance of Lessee.

Lender agrees that, for so long as Lessee shall perform and satisfy all obligations of Lessee under the Lease in accordance with its terms, neither the Lease nor Lessee's rights pursuant thereto shall be disturbed or affected by any foreclosure of the Security Deed or conveyance in lieu of foreclosure. Lender's obligations under this Section 3 shall be null and void if Lessee shall, at any time, default in the timely performance of the Lessee's

EXHIBIT 18-3
Subordination,
Attornment, and
Nondisturbance
Agreement
(continued)

obligations under the Lease of this Agreement and not cure such default within the time, if any, allowed in the Lease.

4. Lender as Landlord after Foreclosure.

In the event that the Lender (or any other party) shall acquire title to the Property or shall succeed to Lessor's interest in the Lease, whether through foreclosure of the Security Deed, conveyance in lieu of foreclosure, or otherwise, Lender (or such other party) shall thereupon, and without the necessity of attornment or other act or agreement, be substituted as Lessee's landlord under the Lease, and shall be entitled to the rights and benefits and subject to the obligations thereof; provided that neither Lender nor any other party shall be:

(a) liable for any act or omission of any prior landlord under the Lease (including Lessor); or

(b) subject to any offsets or defenses which Lessee might have against any prior landlord (including Lessor); or

(c) bound by Lessee's payment of any rent or additional rent beyond the then current rent period to any prior landlord under the Lease (including Lessor); or

(d) bound by any amendment, modification, extension or supplement of the Lease made without Lender's prior written consent; or

(e) bound by any representations or warranties made by any prior landlord under the Lease (including Lessor) whether such representations are set forth in the lease or in any other writing or were made orally, regardless of the knowledge of Lender or such other party of the existence and substance of any such representations or warranties;

and Lessee hereby agrees to attorn to and recognize such Lender (or such other party) as Lessee's landlord.

5. Payment of Rent Upon Default.

Lessee has been advised that the Security Documents give Lender the right to collect rent and other sums payable under the Lease directly from Lessee upon the occurrence of a default thereunder, and that upon the receipt from Lender of notice of any such default, Lessee will thereafter pay all rent and other sums payable under the Lease directly to Lender (or as Lender shall direct) as they become due and payable.

6. Application of Insurance and Condemnation Proceeds.

Lessee has been advised that the insurance and condemnation provisions of the Security Documents give Lender certain rights to require that insurance and condemnation proceeds be applied to payment of the indebtedness secured thereby and not to restoration or rebuilding; and Lessee hereby waives any terms of such Lease with respect to the application of insurance and condemnation proceeds which are inconsistent with the terms of the Security Documents.

7. Estoppel.

Lessee hereby certifies to Lender as follows:

(a) Lessee is the lessee under the Lease, a true and correct copy of which, together with any amendments thereto, is attached hereto;

(b) Except as set forth in the amendment(s), if any, attached hereto, the Lease has not been amended, modified or supplemented and the Lease is in full force and effect;

(c) All of the improvements contemplated by the Lease have been entirely completed as required therein, the leased premises and the improvements thereon have been accepted by Lessee with Lessee in occupancy thereof and all sums, if any, payable by Lessor to Lessee in connection with the construction of such improvements have been paid in full and all conditions precedent to Lessee's obligations under the Lease have occurred;

(d) The term of the Lease commenced on _____, 19__, and will end, if not sooner terminated according to the terms of the Lease, on _____, 19__;

(e) Rent commenced to accrue under the Lease on _____, and there are presently no offsets or credits against rents thereunder and no payments are due from Lessor to Lessee under the Lease;

(f) Lessee has not prepaid (and will not prepay) any rent which is not yet due and payable under the Lease and no concessions, rebates, allowances or other considerations for free or reduced rent in the future have been granted;

(g) Lessee acknowledges that the Lease and the rentals thereunder have been (or will be) pledged to Lender and that Lessee has no knowledge of any assignment, hypothecation or pledge of the Lease or of any rentals thereunder, other than to Lender;

(h) Lessee has no knowledge of (a) any present defaults of the Lessor under the Lease or (b) any present condition or state of facts which by notice or the passage of time, or both, would constitute a default by Lessor under the Lease; and

(i) The party executing this agreement on behalf of Lessee is fully authorized and empowered to do so.

8. Binding Effect.

The provisions of this Agreement shall be covenants running with the Property, and shall be binding upon and shall inure to the benefit of the parties hereto and their respective heirs, representatives, successors and assigns.

IN WITNESS WHEREOF, the parties hereto have executed and sealed this Agreement as of the day and year first above written.

LESSOR:
[Individual]

_____ (SEAL)

_____ (SEAL)

Signed, sealed and delivered this
_____ day of _____,
199__, in the presence of:

[corporation or partnership]

_____

_____
Witness

By: _____
Title: _____

_____
Notary Public
My Commission Expires:

[CORPORATE SEAL]

_____
[Notarial Seal]

LESSEE:

[Individual]

_____ (SEAL)
_____ (SEAL)

[corporation or partnership]

Signed, sealed and delivered this _____
day of _____, 199__, in the
presence of:

_____

By: _____

EXHIBIT 18–3
Subordination,
Attornment, and
Nondisturbance
Agreement
(continued)

EXHIBIT 18–3
Subordination,
Attornment, and
Nondisturbance
Agreement
(continued)

_____
Witness

_____
Notary Public
My Commission Expires:

_____
[Notarial Seal]

Signed, sealed and delivered this _____
day of _____, 199___, in the
presence of:

_____
Witness

_____
Notary Public
My Commission Expires:

_____
[Notarial Seal]

Title: _____
[CORPORATE SEAL]

LENDER:
By: _____
Name: _____
Title: _____

Attest: _____
Name: _____
Title: _____
[CORPORATE SEAL]

EXHIBIT 18–4
Guaranty of Lease

For and in consideration of the leasing by
_____ (referred to as "Landlord"), of certain
Premises (hereinafter referred to as the "Premises") to _____
_____ (here-
inafter referred to as "Tenant"), pursuant to the terms and provisions of that certain Lease
Agreement dated _____ by and between Landlord and Tenant (hereinafter collectively referred to as the "Lease"), and in further consideration of the sum of Ten and
No/100 Dollars ($10.00) to the undersigned paid by Landlord, the receipt and sufficiency of
which are hereby acknowledged, the undersigned (hereinafter collectively referred to as
"Guarantor") hereby unconditionally guarantees to Landlord the full and prompt payment
of any and all rents, percentage rent, if any, or additional rental (hereinafter collectively
referred to as "rent") payable by Tenant under the Lease, and hereby further guarantees the
full and timely performance and observance of all of the covenants and terms therein provided to be performed and observed by Tenant; and Guarantor, to the same extent as
Tenant, hereby agrees that if default or breach shall at any time be made by Tenant in the

payment of rent under the Lease, or if Tenant should default in the performance and observance of any of the covenants and terms contained in the Lease, Guarantor shall pay the rent and any arrears thereof, to Landlord, and shall faithfully perform and fulfill all such covenants and terms of the Lease, and shall forthwith pay to Landlord all damages that may arise or are incident to or in consequence of any default or breach by Tenant under the Lease, and/or by the enforcement of this Guaranty, including without limitation, all attorneys' fees, court costs, and other expenses and costs incurred by Landlord.

This Guaranty shall be enforceable by Landlord in a joint action against Guarantor and Tenant or in a separate and independent action against Guarantor without the necessity of any suit, action, or proceeding by Landlord of any kind or nature whatsoever against Tenant because of Tenant's default or breach under the Lease, and without the necessity of any other notice or demand to Guarantor to which Guarantor might otherwise be entitled, all of which notices Guarantor hereby expressly waives; without limiting the generality of the foregoing, Guarantor hereby expressly waives any statutory right pursuant to   to require Landlord to take action against Tenant. Guarantor hereby agrees that the validity of this Guaranty and the obligations of Guarantor hereunder shall not be terminated, affected, diminished, or impaired by reason of the assertion or the failure to assert by Landlord against Tenant any of the rights or remedies reserved to Landlord pursuant to the provisions of the Lease or any other remedy or right which Landlord may have at law or in equity or otherwise, the obligations of Guarantor being independent of the obligations of Tenant under the Lease.

Guarantor hereby further covenants and agrees that this instrument constitutes a continuing guaranty, and the liability of Guarantor hereunder shall in no way be affected, modified, or diminished by reason of any assignment, renewal, modification, or extension of the Lease or any modification or waiver of or change in any of the covenants and terms of the Lease by agreement of Landlord and Tenant, or by any unilateral action or either Landlord or Tenant, or by any extension of time that may be granted by Landlord to Tenant or any indulgence of whatever kind granted to Tenant, or any dealings or transactions or matter or thing occurring between Landlord and Tenant, including without limitation, any adjustment, compromise, settlement, accord and satisfaction, or release, or any bankruptcy, insolvency, reorganization, arrangement, assignment for the benefit of creditors, receivership, or trusteeship affecting Tenant. Guarantor does hereby expressly waive any suretyship defense it may have by virtue of any statute, law, ordinance of any state or other governmental authority, and further waives any and every defense of tenant, including, without limitation, any defense arising by reason of any disability of Tenant or by reason of the cessation from any cause whatsoever of the liability of Tenant.

In the event that other agreements similar to this Guaranty are executed from time to time by other entities or persons with respect to the Lease, this Guaranty shall be cumulative of any such other agreements to the effect that the liabilities and obligations of Guarantor hereunder shall be joint and several with those of each other such guarantor, and the liabilities and obligations of Guarantor hereunder shall in no event be affected or diminished by reason of any such other agreement.

All of Landlord's rights and remedies under the Lease or under this Guaranty are intended to be distinct, separate, and cumulative and no such right and remedy therein or herein is intended to be to the exclusion of or a waiver of any other.

Guarantor hereby expressly waives presentment, demand for performance, notice of non-performance, protest, notice of protest, notice of dishonor, and notice of acceptance.

Landlord may, without notice, assign this Guaranty in whole or in part, and/or may assign all of its interests in and to the Lease, and, in such event, each and every successive

EXHIBIT 18-4
Guaranty of Lease (continued)

EXHIBIT 18–4
Guaranty of Lease
(continued)

assignee of the Lease and/or of this Guaranty shall have the right to enforce this Guaranty, by suit or otherwise, for the benefit of such assignee as fully as if such assignee were named herein.

Guarantor warrants and represents that they have the legal right and capacity to execute this Guaranty. This Guaranty shall be governed by and construed in accordance with the laws of the State of

This Guaranty shall be binding upon Guarantor and the successors, heirs, executors, and administrators of Guarantor, and shall inure to the benefit of Landlord, Landlord's representatives, successors, and assigns. If more than one party shall execute this Guaranty, all such parties shall be jointly and severally obligated hereunder and are herein collectively referred to as "Guarantor."

IN WITNESS WHEREOF, Guarantor have executed, sealed, and delivered this Guaranty, this _____ day of _____, 19--.

_____ (SEAL)

_____ (SEAL)

EXHIBIT 18-5
Home or Apartment
Lease

FORM 207
IVAN ALLEN CO., ATLANTA

APARTMENT LEASE CONTRACT

THIS AGREEMENT, made this   day of   , 19   , among

(hereinafter referred to as "Lessor")
to as "Lessee"), and

(hereinafter referred
(hereinafter referred to as "Agent").

WITNESSETH: That in consideration of the mutual covenants hereinafter set forth, the parties do hereby covenant and agree as follows:

Premises and Term

1.   Lessor does hereby lease to Lessee and Lessee does hereby lease from Lessor Apartment No.   (hereinafter referred to as "Premises") in Lessor's apartment house situated at

in metropolitan Atlanta,   County, Georgia, according to the present system of numbering buildings in metropolitan

Atlanta,   County, Georgia, for a term commencing on the   day of   , 19   , and ending at

midnight on the   day of   , 19

Rental

2.   Lessee shall pay to Lessor, through   at its office in Atlanta, Georgia, promptly on the first day of each month in advance during the term of this Lease, a monthly rental of $ If such rental is not received by the fifth day of each month, Lessee shall pay to Agent a late charge in the amount of 10% of the monthly rental; Lessee shall also pay Agent a charge for any returned checks of Lessee in the amount of $5.00 for each returned check.

Security Deposit

3.   Lessee herewith deposits with Agent the sum of $ (hereinafter referred to as "Security Deposit") as evidence of good faith on the part of Lessee in the fulfillment of all the terms of this Lease, which Security Deposit shall be held by Lessor during the term of this Lease or any renewal thereof and for fifteen days thereafter. Lessor shall have the right to use said Security Deposit to pay, as fully as possible, the expense of any unpaid rentals, of any accumulated late charges or returned check charges, of any unreturned keys, as well as the expense of repairing any damage to Premises, except reasonable wear and tear occurring from normal use of Premises. Lessor's right to recover additional sums from Lessee for damages to Premises shall not be limited by the amount of said Security Deposit. In no event shall Lessee be entitled to apply the Security Deposit to any rental payment due hereunder.

Utilities

4.   Lessor shall furnish Lessee with the utilities checked as follows:☐ cold water;☐ hot and cold water;☐ heat;☐ all utilities for use in Premises. Lessor shall not be responsible for failure to furnish such utilities if the failure to do so is due to any cause beyond Lessor's control. Lessee shall pay all bills for utilities other than those checked hereinabove and used by Lessee in Premises, but all utilities shall be used only for ordinary household purposes. Lessee shall make a written request for any repairs or services to such utilities to Agent or any representative of Lessor at Premises, except in an extreme emergency in which event such notice may initially be given by telephone and later confirmed in writing. Lessor shall not be obligated to furnish any utilities paid for by Lessor to Premises at any time at which Lessee is in default hereunder. Lessor shall not be responsible for stopped-up plumbing, drains or disposals where such stoppage is caused by the introduction of foreign objects not intended for sewer disposal, and Lessee shall pay on demand all charges for repair of such stoppage.

Occupancy

5.   Premises will be occupied only by the following adults and minors:

No persons other than those named above (occasional overnight guests excepted) shall occupy or share Premises with Lessee. In no event shall more persons than the number of persons listed above occupy Premises.

Pets

6.   Pets may be permitted at the discretion of Agent and Lessor; provided that such pets do not constitute a nuisance to other tenants and provided that Lessee deposits with Lessor an additional damage deposit of $. Lessee recognizes that "reasonable wear and damage" as specified in this Lease does not include damage caused by pets and that Lessor's judgment shall be the sole factor in determining such pet damage. Pets must be on leash when outside of Premises and cannot be tied to anything outside of Premises. Lessee shall be limited to one dog or cat weighing not more than twenty-five pounds. Pets must be approved by Agent and Lessor, and such approval is contingent upon Lessee's observance of the foregoing conditions of this Lease and can be withdrawn at any time.

Extension Terms

7.   Unless another Lease is signed by the parties hereto or unless written notice of termination is given by either party at least thirty calendar days before expiration of the term of this Lease, this Lease shall be automatically extended on a year-to-year basis after the expiration of the initial term hereof without the execution of any new Lease or other instrument whatsoever. If Lessor desires to increase the rental payable hereunder for any such upcoming extension term hereof, Lessor shall give Lessee notice of such increased rental at least thirty days prior to the commencement of such extension term and, unless Lessee promptly otherwise notifies Lessor or Agent, then Lessor and Lessee shall enter in a new lease for such extension term at such increased rental. If Lessee does promptly notify Lessor or Agent that Lessee shall not accept such increased rental, then the term of this Lease shall not be extended and shall terminate as set forth herein.

Lessor's Failure to Give Possession

8.   Lessor shall not be liable to Lessee for failure to deliver possession of Premises at the commencement of the term of this Lease, but Lessor shall use Lessor's best efforts to give Lessee timely possession of Premises; if failure to do so is caused by any tenant holding over, Lessor will use all customary means to oust the old tenant. Lessee may secure a transfer of and prosecute in Lessee's name any cause of action which Lessor may have against such tenant holding over, and Lessee shall be entitled to retain all amounts recovered in such action.

Use of Premises; Maintenance; Indemnity

9.   Premises shall be used as Lessee's residence only and for no other purposes whatsoever; nor shall Premises be used in violation of any laws, ordinances, restrictions or regulations of any governmental body, nor so as to create a nuisance, nor to vitiate or increase the rate of insurance thereon. Lessee accepts Premises in its present condition and as suited for residential use by Lessee. Lessor shall not be required to make any repairs or improvements to Premises, except that, after receipt of written notice from Lessee of any damage or defect rendering Premises unsafe or untenantable, Lessor shall remedy such defective condition or, if the damaged or defective Premises is unfit for occupancy and if Lessor decides not to repair Premises, then upon written notice from Lessor to Lessee this Lease shall terminate, with rent prorated and any balance due Lessee refunded. Lessee shall be liable for, indemnify and hold Lessor and Agent harmless for any claim of damage or injury to the person or property of Lessee, Lessor's other tenants and any other party whatsoever, if such damage or injury be due to the act or neglect of Lessee, any guest of Lessee or anyone in Lessee's control or employ or brought into Premises by Lessee or if such damage or injury be due to any failure of Lessee to report in writing to Lessor any such defective condition. Lessee shall maintain Premises in good condition and repair and shall do no damage thereto. If Premises are rendered untenantable by fire, storm, earthquake or other casualty whatsoever, this Lease shall terminate as of the date of such destruction or damage and rental shall be accounted for as of that date.

Assignment and Subletting

10.   Lessee shall not assign this Lease or sublet Premises or any part thereof or secure a replacement for Lessee hereunder without first obtaining the written approval of Lessor or Agent.

Fixtures and Furniture

11.   Lessee may (if not in default hereunder), prior to the termination of this Lease, remove all fixtures, personalty and equipment which Lessee has placed in Premises; provided that Lessee restores Premises to its condition prior to the installation of such fixtures. Lessor shall not be liable for any loss of or damage to any property whatsoever, and Lessee shall at all times cause Lessee's fixtures, personalty and equipment to be insured in amounts satisfactory to Lessee.

Agent's Commission

12.   Agent's commission under this Lease shall be paid by Lessor under the terms of a separate agreement between Lessor and Agent. If any rent owing under this Lease is collected by or through an attorney at law, Lessee agrees to pay fifteen per cent of the total amount so collected as attorney's fees. Lessee hereby waives and assigns to Lessor all homestead rights and exemptions which Lessee may have under any law as against any obligation owing under this Lease.

**EXHIBIT 18–5
Home or Apartment
Lease
(continued)**

*Lessee's
Conduct;
Common Areas;
Inspection*

13. Lessee, Lessee's family and guests shall not act in a disorderly, boisterous nor unlawful manner and shall not disturb the rights, comforts or convenience of other persons in the building or complex in which Premises is located. The swimming pool, if any, and all other common areas will be used only in compliance with present and future written rules and regulations furnished to Lessee or posted in the common areas, and such pool and common areas are to be used wholly at the risk of the persons making use thereof. Lessor reserves the right to control the method, manner, and time of parking in parking spaces and to control and limit the entry to Premises by agents, messengers, delivery men, solicitors and salesmen. If Lessee or any member of Lessee's family or guest is present in Premises, then Lessor, Lessor's representatives or servicemen may enter Premises at all reasonable times for any reasonable business purpose. If such parties are not present in Premises, then Lessor's representatives or servicemen may enter Premises at all reasonable times (so long as written notice of such entry is left in the apartment after such entry) for the following purposes: repairs, extermination, preventive maintenance, failure to return tools or appliances within prescribed time, emergency, safety or fire inspections and building inspection by fire marshals, mortgage lenders, prospective purchasers or residents or insurance agents.

*Lessee's
Transfer*

14. In the event Lessee is transferred or obtains employment outside of the Metropolitan Atlanta area (such Metropolitan Atlanta area being defined for the purposes of this Lease as any point within sixty miles in any direction from the intersection of Marietta and Peachtree Streets in downtown Atlanta, Fulton County, Georgia), then Lessee shall be released from further obligations under this Lease after Lessee completes the following conditions precedent to such release: (a) Lessee shall provide Agent with written notice of Lessee's intention to seek such release hereunder by virtue of such transfer or new employment at least thirty calendar days prior to termination hereof, and (b) such notice shall be valid only if accompanied by an affidavit from Lessee's employer confirming such transfer or new employment and by Lessee's payment of all rentals and charges whatsoever due under this Lease, including without limitation charges for any damage and repairs to Premises which are the obligation of Lessee under this Lease, and (c) Lessee shall release all Lessee's rights to any Security Deposit made under this Lease as liquidated damages for such cancellation of this Lease. This provision is for the benefit of Lessee, and the foregoing conditions hereof must be strictly complied with by Lessee in order to effectuate such release hereunder.

*Premature
Cancellation*

15. This Lease shall be prematurely cancelled by Lessor as of the first day of any month during the term hereof, if (a) Lessee has given Agent written notice of such desired cancellation at least thirty calendar days prior thereto, and (b) if such notice is accompanied by Lessee's payment of all rental and other charges whatsoever hereunder, including without limitation charges for any damage and repairs to Premises which are the obligation of Lessee under this Lease, due up to such proposed date of cancellation of this Lease and by payment of liquidated damages for such premature cancellation in the amount of one additional month's rental hereunder. In such event any Security Deposit posted by Lessee shall be retained by Lessor as additional liquidated damages hereunder.

*Termination
and Reletting
by Lessor
or Agent*

16. If Lessee defaults for three calendar days after written notice from Lessor or Agent of default by Lessee in the payment of rental due or otherwise defaults under any term, condition or provision of this Lease; or if Lessee fails to reimburse Lessor for any damages, repairs or plumbing service costs when due under this Lease; or if Lessee shall abandon Premises; or if Lessee or any other occupant or guest in Premises shall violate or fail to comply with any term, condition or provision of this Lease or any of the Apartment Rules and Regulations hereinafter set forth in this Lease, as such rules may be reasonably changed or additional rules imposed and Lessee notified thereof, then Lessor or Agent shall have the option to either terminate this Lease by written notice to Lessee or, without terminating this Lease, to enter upon and take possession of Premises, removing all persons and property therefrom and, as Lessee's agent, to rerent Premises at the best price obtainable by reasonable effort, without advertisement and by private negotiations and for any term Lessor or Agent deems proper; Lessee shall be liable to Lessor for any deficiency between all rental due hereunder and the price obtained by Lessor on such reletting. Such termination shall not release Lessee from liability for any unpaid rentals under this Lease, past or future.

*Surrender
of Premises*

17. Whenever under the terms hereof Lessor is entitled to possession of Premises, Lessee shall at once surrender Premises to Lessor and shall remove all of Lessee's effects therefrom; and Lessor may forthwith re-enter Premises and repossess itself thereof, removing all persons and effects therefrom and using such force as may be necessary, without being guilty of forcible entry or detainer, trespass or other tort. Lessee shall not remain in possession of Premises after the expiration of the final term of this Lease. Any holding of Premises by Lessee after the expiration of this Lease (except pursuant to a new lease, or the expiration hereof as provided in paragraph #7 hereof) shall not constitute a tenant-at-will interest on behalf of Lessee, but Lessee shall be a tenant at sufferance. Unless this Lease is extended pursuant to provision of paragraph #7, there shall be no renewal or extension of this Lease by operation of law or otherwise.

*Service of
Notices*

18. Lessee hereby appoints as Lessee's agent to receive service of all dispossessory or other legal proceedings and notices thereunder, and all notices required under this Lease, the person occupying Premises at the time such notice is given, and, if no person be occupying the same, then such service or notice may be made by attaching the same on the front entrance to Premises. A copy of all notices under this Lease shall also be sent to Lessee's last known address if different from Premises.

*Signs;
Carding*

19. Lessee shall place no signs, placards, or other advertisements of any character on Premises. Lessor may card Premises "For Rent" at any time within sixty days prior to the expiration of this Lease and during such sixty day period may exhibit Premises to prospective tenants.

*Storage
and Garage*

20. If Lessor makes available to Lessee any storage space or garage outside Premises, anything placed therein by Lessee shall be stored wholly at the risk of Lessee, and Lessor shall have no responsibility in respect thereof. If Lessor makes available to Lessee any space for use as a garage or for parking cars, Lessor shall not be responsible for any damage to or loss of any vehicle stored or parked therein, nor for any part or accessory of such vehicle, nor for any property of any kind stored or left in said garage or vehicle.

Keys

21. All keys issued to Lessee hereunder shall be returned or the replacement cost thereof paid by Lessee when Lessee vacates Premises.

Definitions

22. "Lessor" as used in this Lease shall include Lessor, Lessor's heirs, executors, administrators, legal representatives, assigns and successors in title to Premises; "Lessee" shall include Lessee, Lessee's heirs, executors, administrators, legal representatives and, if this Lease shall be validly assigned or sublet, shall also include Lessee's assignees and sub-lessees. "Agent" shall include Agent, successors and assigns. Lessor, Lessee and Agent include male, female, singular, plural, corporation, partnership or individual, as may fit the particular parties. The captions used herein are merely descriptive of some matters contained therein and do not necessarily describe the contents of each paragraph.

Miscellaneous

23. Except for the commission agreement between Lessor and Agent referred to hereinabove, this Lease contains the entire agreement of the parties and no representation, inducement, promises or agreements, oral or otherwise, between the parties not embodied herein shall be of any force or effect. No failure of Lessor to exercise any power given Lessor hereunder, or to insist upon strict compliance by Lessee of any obligation hereunder, including without limitation any acceptance of partial payments of rental or other amounts due hereunder, and no custom or practice of the parties at variance with the terms hereof, shall constitute a waiver of Lessor's right to any bona fide mortgage or deed to secure debt which is now or may hereafter be placed upon Premises.

*Special
Stipulations*

In so far as the following special stipulations conflict with any of the foregoing provisions of this Lease, the following shall control.

IN WITNESS WHEREOF, the parties have executed or caused this Lease to be executed by authorized officials in duplicate, the day and year first above written.

Individually and as Agent for Lessor

BY: _____   X _____ (SEAL)
                                                                                  Lessee

RULES AND REGULATIONS OF APARTMENTS

Lessee shall:

1. Not obstruct sidewalks, courts, entry passage, halls, and stairways, nor allow children to loiter or play in them, nor use them for any purpose except ingress and egress, nor leave bicycles or other vehicles therein. Children shall confine their playing to area designated by Lessor.

2. Not cover or obstruct skylights and windows that reflect or admit light to public space.

3. Not use water closets, drains or other plumbing apparatus for any other purposes than those for which they were constructed and not throw sweepings, rubbish, rags, ashes or other substances therein.

4. Be responsible for damage to plumbing, cooling, or heating apparatus, and other equipment from misuse by Lessee.

5. Throw nothing out of the windows or doors, or down the passage, or skylight of the building.

6. Close windows when it rains or snows, and be responsible for any injury to premises or other tenants due to failure so to do.

7. Not alter premises nor change any partition, door, or window, nor add locks thereto, nor paint, paper, bore or screw upon or in the walls, ceiling, floors, woodwork or plaster.

8. Keep whole all glass, locks and trimmings in or upon the door and windows, and immediately replace or repair such thereof as may be broken or out of order under the direction and to the satisfaction of the Lessor.

9. Erect no awnings or shades outside or inside the windows unless approved by Lessor or his agent.

10. Confine his use of porches or balconies in that portion thereof directly in front of his apartment if any and shall keep them clean and shall not use them for storage purposes.

11. Discontinue all phonographs, television, pianos, radios and other musical devices at eleven o'clock P.M. and shall not practice on musical instruments at any time, nor give music lessons, vocal or instrumental, at any time.

12. Preserve perfect order at all times and permit no boisterous conduct.

13. Observe such other and reasonable rules as Lessor in his judgment may from time to time promulgate for the safety, care and cleanliness of the premises, the building, and for the preservation of good order therein.

14. Not hang washing, clothing, bed covers or linen from the windows, or porches, or in any yard space, except that, if any, which Lessor may provide for the specific purpose.

15. Not place flower pots, boxes or other receptacles in hallways or in windows, or porch railings or where they may possibly cause injury to any person, nor place any objects in windows, hallways, or porch railings deemed unsightly by Lessor.

16. No water beds shall be allowed in Premises.

17. No two wheel motor vehicles, nor any tearing down or repairing of any motor vehicles whatsoever, nor any storage or abandonment of inoperative motor vehicles shall be allowed in Premises or on any part of Lessor's real property on which Lessee's Apartment is located.

EXHIBIT 18-6
Small Commercial
Retail Space Lease

ATLANTA BOARD OF REALTORS®
COMMERCIAL LEASE CONTRACT
REVISED JUNE, 1980

_____ , 19 ____

THIS LEASE, made this _____ day of _____ , 19 _____ , by and between _____ ,
first party, (hereinafter called "Landlord"); and _____ , second party, (hereinafter
called "Tenant"); and   third party, (hereinafter called "Agent");
WITNESSETH:

Premises

1. The Landlord, for and in consideration of the rents, covenants, agreements and stipulations hereinafter mentioned, provided for and contained, to be paid, kept and performed by the Tenant, has leased and rented, and by these presents leases and rents, unto the said Tenant, and said Tenant hereby leases and takes upon the terms and conditions which hereinafter appear, the following described property (hereinafter called "Premises"), to wit:

and being known as _____
No easement for light or air is included in the Premises.

Term

2. The Tenant shall have and hold the Premises for a term of _____ beginning on the _____ day of
_____ 19 _____ , and ending on the _____ day of _____ .
19 _____ , at midnight, unless sooner terminated as hereinafter provided.

Rental

3. Tenant agrees to pay to Landlord, by payments to   **Agent of Landlord, who negotiated this Lease,** at the office of
Agent in Atlanta, Georgia, an annual rental in the amount of $_____ , which shall be paid promptly on the first day of each
month in advance during the term of this Lease, in equal monthly installments of $_____

Agent's Commission

4. Agent has rendered Landlord and Tenant a valuable service by assisting in the creation of the Landlord-Tenant relationship hereunder. For this reason, Agent is made a party to this Lease and is given a special lien on the interest of the Landlord and the interest of the Tenant in the Premises in order to enable Agent to enforce its commission rights against the Premises as well as against the other parties hereto as herein provided and as otherwise provided by law or equity. The commission to be paid in conjunction with the creation of the aforesaid Landlord-Tenant relationship by this Lease has been negotiated between Landlord and Agent, and Landlord hereby agrees to pay Agent, as compensation for Agent's services in procuring this Lease and creating the aforesaid Landlord-Tenant relationship, as follows:

If the Tenant becomes a tenant at will or at sufferance pursuant to Paragraph 25 hereof, or if the term of this Lease is extended or if this Lease is renewed or if a new lease is entered into between Landlord and Tenant covering either the Premises, or any part thereof, or covering any other premises as an expansion of, addition to, or substitution for, the Premises, regardless of whether such premises are located adjacent to or in the vicinity of the Premises, Landlord, in consideration of Agent's having assisted in the creation of the Landlord-Tenant relationship, agrees to pay Agent Additional Commissions as set forth below; it being the intention of the parties that Agent shall continue to be compensated so long as the parties hereto, their successors and/or assigns continue the relationship of Landlord and Tenant which initially resulted from the efforts of Agent, whether relative to the Premises or any expansion thereof, or addition thereto or substitution therefor, or relative to any other premises leased by Landlord to Tenant from time to time, whether the rental therefore is paid under this Lease or otherwise:

Landlord, with the consent of Tenant, hereby authorizes Agent to deduct its commission from each rental payment it collects from Tenant; but nothing herein shall relieve Landlord from his obligation to pay to Agent his commission if Tenant fails to pay any rental payment.

Agent agrees that, in the event Landlord sells the Premises, and upon Landlord's furnishing Agent with an agreement signed by Purchaser assuming Landlord's obligations to Agent under this Lease, Agent will release original Landlord from any further obligations to Agent hereunder. Tenant agrees that if this Lease is assigned by him he will secure from assignee an agreement in writing recognizing the assignment of the commissions owed to Agent and agreeing to pay rental to Agent during the continuation of the Landlord-Tenant relationship between or among said assignee, its successors and/or assigns, and Landlord, its successors and/or assigns, whether relative to the Premises or any expansion thereof or substitution therefor, or relative to any other property leased by Landlord to Tenant from time to time, whether rental therefor is paid under this Lease or otherwise. Voluntary cancellation of this Lease shall not nullify Agent's right to collect the commission due for the remaining term of this Lease and the provisions contained hereinabove relative to Additional Commissions shall survive any cancellation or termination of this Lease. In the event that the Premises are condemned, or sold under threat of and in lieu of condemnation, Agent shall, on the date of receipt by Landlord of the condemnation award or sale proceeds, be paid Agent's commission, reduced to its present cash value at the then existing legal rate of interest, which would otherwise be due to the end of the term contracted for under paragraph 2 above.

Purchase of Property by Tenant

5. In the event that Tenant acquires title to the Premises or any part thereof, or any other premises as an expansion of, addition to, or substitution for, the Premises, at any time during the term of this Lease, any renewals thereof, or within six months after the expiration of the term hereof or the extended term hereof, then Landlord shall pay Agent a commission on the sale of the Premises in lieu of any further commissions which otherwise would have been due under this Lease.

Such commission, as negotiated between parties, is to be _____

Utility Bills

6. Tenant shall pay all utility bills, including, but not limited to water, sewer, gas, electricity, fuel, light, and heat bills, for the Premises, and Tenant shall pay all charges for garbage collection services or other sanitary services rendered to the Premises or used by Tenant in connection therewith. If Tenant fails to pay any of said utility bills or charges for garbage collection or other sanitary services, Landlord may pay the same, and such payment shall be added to and become part of the next rental payment due under this Lease.

Use of Premises

7. Premises shall be used for _____
purposes and no other. Premises shall not be used for any illegal purposes, nor in any manner to create any nuisance or trespass, nor in any manner to vitiate the insurance or increase the rate of insurance on premises.

Abandonment of the Premises

8. Tenant agrees not to abandon or vacate the Premises during the period of this Lease and agrees to use the Premises for the purposes herein leased until the expiration hereof.

Repairs by Landlord

9. Landlord agrees to keep in good repair the roof, foundations, and exterior walls of the Premises (exclusive of all glass and exclusive of all exterior doors), and underground utility and sewer pipes outside the exterior walls of the building, except repairs rendered necessary by the negligence of Tenant, its agents, employees or invitees. Landlord gives to Tenant exclusive control of the Premises and shall be under no obligation to inspect said Premises. Tenant shall promptly

EXHIBIT 18–6
Small Commercial
Retail Space Lease
(continued)

report in writing to Landlord any defective condition known to it which Landlord is required to repair, and failure so to report such conditions shall make Tenant responsible to Landlord for any liability incurred by Landlord by reason of such conditions.

Repairs by Tenant

10. Tenant accepts the Premises in their present condition and as suited for the uses intended by Tenant. Tenant shall, throughout the initial term of this Lease and any extension or renewal thereof, at its expense, maintain in good order and repair the Premises, including the building, heating and air conditioning equipment (including but not limited to replacement of parts, compressors, air handling units and heating units), and other improvements located thereon, except those repairs expressly required to be made by Landlord hereunder. Tenant further agrees to care for the grounds around the building, including the mowing of grass, paving, care of shrubs and general landscaping. Tenant agrees to return the Premises to Landlord at the expiration, or prior to termination, of this Lease in as good condition and repair as when first received, natural wear and tear, damage by storm, fire, lightning, earthquake or other casualty alone excepted.

Tax Escalation

11. Tenant shall pay upon demand, as additional rental during the term of this Lease and any extension or renewal thereof, the amount by which all taxes (including, but not limited to, ad valorem taxes, special assessments and any other governmental charges) on the Premises for each tax year exceed all taxes on the

Premises for the tax year _____ . In the event the Premises are less than the entire property assessed for such taxes for any such tax year, then the tax for any such year applicable to the Premises shall be determined by proration on the basis that the rentable floor area of the Premises bears to the rentable floor area of the entire property assessed. If the final year of the lease term fails to coincide with the tax year, then any excess for the tax year during which the term ends shall be reduced by the pro rata part of such tax year beyond the lease term. If such taxes for the year in which the Lease terminates are not ascertainable before payment of the last month's rental, then the amount of such taxes assessed against the property for the previous tax year shall be used as a basis of determining the pro rata share, if any, to be paid by Tenant for that portion of the last lease year. Tenant's pro rata portion of increased taxes, as provided herein, shall be payable within fifteen days after receipt of notice from Landlord or Agent as to the amount due. The Agent's commission shall not apply to any such additional rental resulting from the provisions of this paragraph unless billing and collection thereof is handled by Agent at the request of the Landlord.

Destruction of or Damage to Premises

12. If the Premises are totally destroyed by storm, fire, lightning, earthquake or other casualty, this Lease shall terminate as of the date of such destruction, and rental shall be accounted for as between Landlord and Tenant as of that date. If the Premises are damaged but not wholly destroyed by any such casualties, rental shall abate in such proportion as use of the Premises has been destroyed, and Landlord shall restore Premises to substantially the same condition as before damage as speedily as is practicable, whereupon full rental shall recommence.

Indemnity

13. Tenant agrees to, and hereby does, indemnify and save Landlord harmless against all claims for damages to persons or property by reason of Tenant's use or occupancy of Premises, and all expenses incurred by Landlord because thereof, including attorney's fees and court costs. Supplementing the foregoing and in addition thereto, Tenant shall during all terms of this Lease, and any extension or renewal thereof, and at Tenant's expense maintain in full force and effect comprehensive general liability insurance with limits of $500,000.00 per person and $1,000,000.00 per accident, and property damage limits of $100,000.00, which insurance shall contain a special endorsement recognizing and insuring any liability accruing to Tenant under the first sentence of this Paragraph 13; such insurance policy shall contain a clause expressly waiving any right of the insurer of subrogation against Landlord. Prior to the commencement of the term of this Lease, Tenant shall furnish Landlord with a certificate of such insurance which shall show the waiver of subrogation, and the endorsement required hereby. Such certificate shall provide that Landlord will be given ten (10) days written notice prior to cancellation or expiration of the insurance evidenced thereby.

Governmental Orders

14. Tenant agrees, at his own expense, promptly to comply with all requirements of any legally constituted public authority made necessary by reason of Tenant's occupancy of the Premises. Landlord agrees promptly to comply with any such requirements if not made necessary by reason of Tenant's occupancy. It is mutually agreed, however, between Landlord and Tenant, that if in order to comply with such requirements, the cost to Landlord or Tenant, as the case may be, shall exceed a sum equal to one year's rent, then Landlord or Tenant who is obligated to comply with such requirements may terminate this Lease by giving written notice of termination to the other party, by registered mail, which termination shall become effective sixty (60) days after receipt of such notice, and which notice shall eliminate necessity of compliance with such requirement by party giving such notice unless party receiving such notice of termination shall, before termination becomes effective, pay to party giving notice all cost of compliance in excess of one year's rent, or secure payment of said sum in manner satisfactory to party giving notice.

Condemnation

15. If the whole of the Premises, or such portion thereof as will make the Premises unusable for the purposes herein leased, be condemned by any legally constituted authority for any public use or purpose, then in either of said events the term hereby granted shall cease from the date when possession thereof is taken by public authorities, and rental shall be accounted for as between Landlord and Tenant as of said date. Such termination, however, shall be without prejudice to the rights of either Landlord or Tenant to recover compensation and damage caused by condemnation from the condemnor. It is further understood and agreed that neither the Tenant nor Landlord shall have any rights in any award made to the other by any condemnation authority notwithstanding the termination of the Lease as herein provided. Landlord agrees to pay to Agent, from the award made to Landlord under condemnation, the balance of lease commissions, reduced to their present cash value, as provided in paragraph 4 hereof, and Agent may become a party to the condemnation proceeding for the purpose of enforcing its rights under this paragraph.

Assignment and Subletting

16. Tenant may sublease portions of the Premises to others provided such sublessee's operation is a part of the general operation of Tenant and is under the supervision and control of Tenant, and provided such operation is within the purposes for which the Premises shall be used. Except as provided in the preceding sentence, Tenant shall not, without the prior written consent of Landlord endorsed hereon, assign this Lease or any interest hereunder, or sublet the Premises or any part thereof, or permit the use of the Premises by any party other than Tenant. Consent to any assignment or sublease shall not impair this provision, and all later assignments or subleases shall be made likewise only on the prior written consent of Landlord. Assignee of Tenant, at option of Landlord, shall become directly liable to Landlord for all obligations of Tenant hereunder, but no sublease or assignment by Tenant shall relieve Tenant of any liability hereunder.

Removal of Fixtures

17. Tenant may (if not in default hereunder) prior to the expiration of this Lease, or any extension or renewal thereof, remove all fixtures and equipment which he has placed in the Premises, provided Tenant repairs all damage to the Premises caused by such removal.

Events of Default

18. The happening of any one or more of the following events (hereinafter any one of which may be referred to as an "Event of Default") during the term of this Lease, or any renewal or extension thereof, shall constitute a breach of this Lease on the part of the Tenant: (1) Tenant fails to pay the rental as provided for herein; (2) Tenant abandons or vacates the Premises; (3) Tenant fails to comply with or abide by and perform any other obligation imposed upon Tenant under this Lease; (4) Tenant is adjudicated bankrupt; (5) a permanent receiver is appointed for Tenant's property and such receiver is not removed within sixty (60) days after written notice from Landlord to Tenant to obtain such removal; (6) Tenant, either voluntarily or involuntarily, takes advantage of any debtor relief proceedings under any present or future law, whereby the rent or any part thereof is, or is proposed to be, reduced or payment thereof deferred; (7) Tenant makes an assignment for benefit of creditors; or (8) Tenant's effects are levied upon or attached under process against Tenant, which is not satisfied or dissolved within thirty (30) days after written notice from Landlord to Tenant to obtain satisfaction thereof.

Remedies Upon Default

19. Upon the occurrence of any Event of Default, Landlord may pursue any one or more of the following remedies, separately or concurrently, without any notice (except as specifically provided hereafter) and without prejudice to any other remedy herein provided or provided by law; (a) if the Event of Default involves nonpayment of rental, and Tenant fails to cure such default within ten days after receipt of written notice thereof from Landlord, or if the Event of Default involves a default in performing any of the terms or provisions of this Lease other than the payment of rental, and Tenant fails to cure such default within thirty (30) days after the receipt of written notice of such default from Landlord, Landlord may terminate this Lease by giving written notice to Tenant and, upon such termination, shall be entitled to recover from the Tenant damages in an amount equal to all rental which is then due and which would otherwise have become due throughout the remaining term of this Lease, or any renewal or extension thereof (as if this Lease had not been terminated); or (b) if the Event of Default involves any matter other than those set forth in item (a) of this Paragraph 19, the Landlord may terminate this Lease by giving written notice to Tenant, and upon such termination, shall be entitled to recover from the Tenant damages in an amount equal to all rental which is then due and which would otherwise have become due throughout the remaining term of this Lease, or any renewal or extension thereof (as if this Lease had not been terminated); or (c) upon any Event of Default, Landlord may give to Tenant written notice of such default and advise Tenant that unless such default is cured within ten days after receipt of such notice, the entire amount of the rental for the remainder of the term of this Lease, or any renewal or extension thereof, shall immediately become due an payable upon the expiration of the ten day period, and thereafter, unless all the terms and provisions of this Lease are fully complied with by the Tenant within said ten-day period, the entire amount of said rental shall thereupon become immediately due and payable without further notice to Tenant; or (d) upon any Event of Default, Landlord, as Tenant's agent, without terminating this Lease may enter upon and rent the Premises, in whole or in part, at the best price obtainable by reasonable effort, without advertisement and by private negotiations and for any term Landlord deems proper, with Tenant being liable to Landlord for the deficiency, if any, between Tenant's rent hereunder and the price obtained by Landlord on reletting; provided, however, that Landlord shall not be considered to be under any duty by reason of this provision to take any action to mitigate damages by reason of Tenant's default.

Exterior Signs

20. Tenant shall place no signs upon the outside walls or roof of the Premises except with the written consent of the Landlord. Any and all signs placed on the Premises by Tenant shall be maintained in compliance with rules and regulations governing such signs, and the Tenant shall be responsible to Landlord for any damage caused by installation, use, or maintenance of said signs. Tenant, upon the expiration of this Lease, and any extension or renewal thereof, shall remove said signs and agrees upon removal of said signs to repair all damage incident to such removal.

Entry for Carding, etc.

reasonable hours to exhibit same to prospective purchasers or tenants and to make repairs required of Landlord under the terms hereof, or to make repairs to Landlord's adjoining property, if any.

Effect of Termination of Lease

22. No termination of this Lease prior to the normal ending thereof, by lapse of time or otherwise, shall affect Landlord's right to collect rent for the period prior to termination thereof.

Mortgagee's Rights

23. Tenant's rights shall be subject to any bona fide mortgage or deed to secure debt which is now, or may hereafter be, placed upon the Premises by Landlord. Tenant shall, if requested by Landlord, execute a separate agreement reflecting such subordination.

No Estate in Land

24. This Lease shall create the relationship of Landlord and Tenant between the parties hereto; no estate shall pass out of Landlord. Tenant has only a usufruct, not subject to levy and sale, and not assignable by Tenant except by Landlord's consent.

Holding Over

25. If Tenant remains in possession of the Premises after expiration of the term hereof, with Landlord's acquiescence and without any express agreement of parties, Tenant shall be a tenant at will at the rental rate which is in effect at end of Lease; and there shall be no renewal of this Lease by operation of law. If Tenant remains in possession of the Premises after expiration of the term hereof without Landlord's acquiescence, then Tenant shall be a tenant at sufferance and, commencing on the date following the date of such expiration, the monthly rental payable under Paragraph 3 hereof shall, for each month or fraction thereof during which Tenant so remains in possession, be twice the monthly rental otherwise payable under Paragraph 3 hereof.

Attorney's Fees and Homestead

26. If any rent or other sum owing under this Lease is collected by or through an attorney at law, Tenant agrees to pay fifteen percent (15%) thereof as attorneys' fees. Tenant waives all homestead rights and exemptions which he may have under any law as against any obligation owing under this Lease. Tenant hereby assigns to Landlord his homestead exemption.

Rights Cumulative

27. All rights, powers and privileges conferred hereunder upon parties hereto shall be cumulative and not restrictive of those given by law.

Service of Notice

28. Tenant hereby appoints as his agent to receive service of all dispossessory or distraint proceedings and notices hereunder, and all notices required under this Lease, the person in charge of the Premises at the time, or occupying the Premises; and if no person is in charge of, or occupying the Premises, then such service or notice may be made by attaching the same on the main entrance to the Premises. A copy of all notices under this Lease shall also be sent to Tenant's last known address, if different from the Premises.

Waiver of Rights

29. No failure of Landlord to exercise any power given Landlord hereunder, or to insist upon strict compliance by Tenant of his obligations hereunder, and no custom or practice of the parties at variance with the terms hereof shall constitute a waiver of Landlord's right to demand exact compliance with the terms hereof.

Disclosure of Ownership

30. The owner of the Premises is _____ .

whose address is _____

and the person authorized to manage the Premises is _____ , whose address is

_____

Service of process and demands and notices as to the Landlord shall be made on _____ , whose address is

_____

who is authorized to acknowledge the receipt of same.

Limitation on Agent's Services

31. Agent is a party to this Lease solely for the purpose of enforcing his rights under Paragraph 4 of this Lease, and it is understood by all parties hereto that Agent is acting solely in the capacity as agent for Landlord, to whom Tenant must look as regards all covenants, agreements and warranties herein contained, and that Agent shall never be liable to Tenant in regard to any matter which may arise by virtue of this Lease. It is understood and agreed that the commissions payable to Agent under Paragraph 4 of this Lease are compensation solely for Agent's services in assisting in the creation of the Landlord-Tenant relationship hereunder; accordingly, Agent is not obligated hereunder on account of payment of such commissions, to furnish any management services for the Premises.

Time of Essence

32. Time is of the essence of this Lease.

Definitions

33. "Landlord" as used in this Lease shall include first party, his heirs, representatives, assigns and successors in title to the Premises. "Tenant" shall include second party, his heirs and representatives, and if this Lease shall be validly assigned or sublet, shall include also Tenant's assignees or sublessees, as to the Premises covered by such assignment or sublease. "Agent" shall include third party, his successors, assigns, heirs and representatives. "Landlord," "Tenant," and "Agent" include male and female, singular and plural, corporation, partnership or individual, as may fit the particular parties.

Special Stipulations

In so far as the following stipulations conflict with any of the foregoing provisions, the following shall control:

This Lease contains the entire agreement of the parties hereto and no representations, inducements, promises or agreements, oral or otherwise, between the parties, not embodied herein, shall be of any force or effect.

IN WITNESS WHEREOF, the parties herein have hereunto set their hands and seals, in triplicate, the day and year first above written.

Signed, sealed and delivered as
to Landlord, in the presence of:

_____   _____ (SEAL)
                                          (Landlord)

_____   _____ (SEAL)
Notary Public   (Landlord)

Signed, sealed and delivered as
to Tenant, in the presence of:

_____   _____ (SEAL)
                                          (Tenant)

_____   _____ (SEAL)
Notary Public   (Tenant)

Signed, sealed and delivered as
to Agent, in the presence of:

_____   By: _____ (SEAL)

_____
Notary Public

EXHIBIT 18–6
Small Commercial
Retail Space Lease
(continued)

Glossary

Actual notice Title matters that a purchaser has direct knowledge or information about.

Ad valorem taxes Taxes assessed against real property usually measured by the value of the real property being taxed.

Adverse possession Method of acquiring ownership to real property by possession for a statutory time period.

Affidavit Written statement of fact that is sworn to by the person making the statement under oath as a true statement of facts.

Amortization Reduction in a debt by periodic payments covering interest and part of the principal.

Appropriation In regard to water law, doctrine stating that water belongs to the person who first makes beneficial use of it.

Appurtenant easement Easement created to benefit a particular parcel of real property. The easement transfers automatically with a transfer of the ownership of the real property benefited by the easement.

As-built survey Survey that locates all physical improvements on the land in relation to the boundary lines of the land.

Assessment Sum of money owed by a condominium owner for monthly upkeep of the common areas of the condominium.

Assignment With regard to a lease, it is when the tenant transfers all his or her interest under the lease and retains nothing.

Assigns Persons who obtain the rights to a contract or other legal document by transfer from an original party to the contract or document.

Balloon payment Final payment of all unpaid principal and of accrued and unpaid interest on the loan which payment is greater than the periodic payments on the loan.

Base line Imaginary east-west survey line used in the government survey system to establish township lines.

Bill of sale Legal document that transfers ownership to personal property.

Blanket easement Easement that covers real property without a specific location of the easement.

Bona fide purchaser for value Person who purchases real property in good faith for valuable consideration without notice of any claim to or interest in the real property by any other party.

Bridge loan Short-term loan with a maturity of one to two years that provides the borrower necessary financing to purchase real property. A bridge loan usually is refinanced by a long-term loan.

Building codes Public laws that regulate methods and materials to be used in the construction of improvements.

Call Course and distance describing a boundary line of land in a metes-and-bounds land description.

Caption Portion of the deed that indicates the county and state in which the deed was signed by the grantor.

Cashier's check Check issued by a bank, the payment of which is guaranteed by the full faith and credit of the bank.

Certificate of occupancy Permit issued by an appropriate governmental authority granting occupancy to newly constructed improvements. The certificate usually is evidence that the improvements comply with all zoning, building codes, and health and fire regulations.

Certified check Personal check in which the bank certifies that the funds are in the account and that the check will be honored on presentment for payment.

Chain of title Historical sequence of all owners to a particular tract of real property beginning with the original owner and all successive owners who have derived their title from the original owner.

Chord Straight line drawn from the beginning point of an arc to the ending point of an arc.

Closing Consummation of a real estate purchase and sale transaction.

Closing   Date set forth in a real estate contract on which the parties agree to perform all the promises of the contract. The date on which ownership of the real property is transferred from seller to purchaser and the purchaser pays the seller the purchase price for the real property.

Common areas   Common areas or common elements of a condominium is that portion of the condominium property that is owned in common by all the owners of units in the condominium.

Community property law   Rule of law in states following the civil law of Spain and France, which provides that real property acquired during marriage is owned equally by the husband and wife.

Condition precedent   Condition in a contract that must be satisfied in accordance with the terms of the contract before one or both of the parties are required to perform their contractual obligations.

Condominium   Form of property ownership in which the owner owns an individual unit in a multi-unit building and is a tenant in common with other owners of units in the building in certain common areas.

Condominium association   Governing body of a condominium, the members of which are owners of condominium units. The condominium association usually is in the form of a nonprofit corporation.

Condominium declaration   Legal document required by state condominium acts to create a condominium.

Condominium plat   Plat of survey of condominium property required by state condominium acts. The plat must show in sufficient detail the location and dimensions of the real property, as well as all condominium units located on the real property.

Consideration   Something of value given to make the promises of a contract enforceable. Consideration also is something of value given for a deed.

Construction loan   Mortgage loan made for the purpose of providing money to construct improvements on real property.

Constructive notice   A presumption of law that charges a person with notice of all title matters that can be discovered from an inspection of the real property or an examination of public real property records.

Consumer   Term used in the Truth-in-Lending Act to mean a natural person to whom a loan for personal, family, or household purposes is offered.

Consumer credit   Term used in the Truth-in-Lending Act to mean a loan offered or extended primarily for personal, family, or household purposes.

Consummation   Term used in the Truth-in-Lending Act to mean the time a consumer becomes contractually obligated under state law to make payments under a loan.

Contract   Agreement between two or more persons consisting of a promise, or mutual promises that the law will enforce or the performance of which the law recognizes as a duty.

Contribution   Right for a co-owner of real property to receive reimbursement from other co-owners for their share of expenses that are common to the real property.

Conventional loan   Mortgage loan in which the risk of repayment of the debt rests solely on the ability of the borrower to pay and the value of the security provided by the mortgage.

Conversion   Act of taking a person's property without a legal right to do so.

Conveyance   Transfer of title or ownership to real property from one person to another by deed. The terms may be used to include assignment, lease, mortgage, or encumbrance of real property.

Cooperative   Form of ownership of real property in which a corporation owns a multiunit building and leases living space in the building to the shareholders of the corporation.

Course   In a metes-and-bounds legal description, it is the direction of a property boundary line.

Curtesy   Interest in real property of the wife that the law in some states gives to the surviving husband at the time of the wife's death.

Debt service   Payment of principal and interest on a loan.

Deed   Written document that transfers ownership of real property from one person to another.

Deed to secure debt   Legal document that conveys title to real property to a lender to secure a debt.

Deed of trust   Legal document that conveys title to real property to a trustee who holds the title as security for a debt to a lender.

Devise   Conveyance of real property by means of a last will and testament.

Distance   In a metes-and-bounds legal description, it is the length of a property boundary line, usually measured in feet and hundredths of a foot (example: 82.13 feet).

Dominant tenement   Parcel of land benefited by an appurtenant easement.

Dower   Widow's interest in real property of her husband that provides a means of support after the husband's death.

Due on sale clause   Clause found in a mortgage that prohibits the sale of the real property described in the mortgage without the lender's consent. A sale in violation of this provision is a default of the mortgage.

Earnest money Money paid by the purchaser at the time the real estate contract is signed. The money may be used as a down payment on the purchase price or may be retained by the seller for damages in the event the purchaser defaults on the contract.

Easement Right granted to a nonowner of real property to use the real property for a specific purpose. For example, the right given to an electric utility company to locate an electric power line on a private user's real property.

Easement by necessity Easement for access to a public street that is necessary for the use and enjoyment of the property benefited by the easement.

Easement in gross Easement granting the owner of the easement the right to use real property for a particular purpose. The easement does not benefit a parcel of real property owned by the owner of the easement.

Elective share Right given to a widow in many states to elect, at her husband's death, to receive either dower or some ownership (fee simple) share of her husband's real property.

Eminent domain Power of government to take private property for public use.

Encumbrance Claim, lien, charge, or liability attached to and binding real property that may exist in another person to the diminishment of the value of the real property or that interferes with the use of the real property by the owner.

Endorsement Method of transferring ownership of a promissory note.

Escrow Agreement that requires the deposit of a document or money into the possession of a third party to be held by that party until certain conditions are fulfilled

Estate at will Estate of real property the duration of which is for an indefinite period. An estate at will can be terminated at the will of the parties.

Estate for years Estate of real property the duration of which is for a definite period.

Estoppel certificate Written statement signed by either a landlord or a tenant swearing to certain facts concerning a lease.

Estoppel letter Sworn statement of fact.

Exculpation A real estate loan in which the borrower is not personally responsible for the repayment of the loan. If the loan is not repaid, the borrower will lose the real property pledged as security for the loan. The borrower will not be personally sued for payment of the loan.

Execution Signature of a party to a legal document. The act of signing a legal document.

Fannie Mae Federal National Mortgage Association, a quasi-government agency organized for the purpose of investing in FHA and VA loans.

Fee simple absolute Estate of real property with infinite duration and no restrictions on use.

Fee simple determinable Estate of real property with potential infinite duration. The ownership of a fee simple determinable is subject to a condition the breach of which can result in termination of the estate. A fee simple determinable automatically expires on the nonoccurrence or occurrence of a condition.

Fee simple on condition subsequent Estate of real property with a potential infinite duration. The ownership of a fee simple on condition subsequent is subject to a condition the breach of which can result in termination of the estate. A fee simple on condition subsequent continues in existence until an action is brought to recover the property.

Finance charge Term used in the Truth-in-Lending Act to mean any charge or fee payable directly or indirectly by the consumer to obtain a consumer loan.

Financing statement Form that is recorded to give notice that there is a security interest in personal property owned by a debtor.

Fixture Item of personal property that becomes real property because of its attachment to the land or a building.

Foreclosure Sale brought by a holder of a mortgage, deed of trust, or security deed of the real property conveyed in the instrument for the purposes of paying the debt secured by the real property.

Freddie Mac Federal Home Loan Mortgage Corporation, a corporation designed to purchase and invest in mortgages.

Fully amortized loan Loan in which the partial payments of principal and accrued interest if paid for the stated period of time will result in the entire loan being paid at maturity.

General warranty deed Deed containing full warranty of title.

Ginnie Mae Government National Mortgage Association, a government corporation designed to administer special assistance programs and to work with the Federal National Mortgage Association to provide a market for mortgages.

Graduated payment mortgage Mortgage loan that permits the borrower to pay lower monthly payments for the first few years and larger payments for the remainder of the term.

Grantee index   Alphabetical index of the public real property records that lists the last name of all people who are grantees of real property interest during a given year within the county.

Grantee   Person in whom real property has been transferred by deed.

Grantor   Transferor of real property by deed.

Grantor index   Alphabetical index of the public real property records that lists the last name of all people who are grantors of real property interest during a given year within the county.

Gross lease   Lease wherein the tenant pays rent only; the operating expenses of the leased premises, such as taxes, utility costs, and insurance, are paid by the landlord.

Guarantor   Person who signs a guaranty promising to pay the debt of another person.

Guaranty   Legal document that obligates the maker of the document to pay the debt of another person.

Habendum   Clause found in a deed or mortgage that indicates what estate in real property is being transferred by the deed or mortgage.

Holder   Person who is the owner of a promissory note.

Homestead   Property that is exempt from creditors. A homestead cannot be seized by creditors and sold to satisfy debts.

HUD–1   Uniform settlement statement required by the Real Estate Settlement Procedures Act for all real estate transactions that involve a federally related mortgage loan.

Implied easement   Easement created by the conduct of the parties to the easement, not by written agreement.

Improvements   Permanent structures located on real property, such as a house or an office building.

Inheritance   Ability to acquire ownership to real property because of one's kinship to a deceased property owner.

Insured loan   Mortgage loan in which the repayment of the loan is insured or guaranteed by either a government agency or a private insurance company.

Interest   Charge by a lender to a borrower for the use of money.

Interpleader   Judicial proceeding in which money is paid into the court and all parties who claim an interest in the money are allowed to process their claims to the money in the court proceeding.

Joint and several liability   Each borrower is fully responsible for the payment of the entire debt.

Joint tenancy with right of survivorship   Ownership of real property by two or more persons. Joint tenants with the right of survivorship hold equal interest in the real property, and on the death of any owner, the deceased owner's interest in the real property will pass to the surviving owner.

Judgment   Money debt resulting from a lawsuit. Judgments are liens on real property owned by the judgment debtor.

Kickback   Payment of money or something of value to a person for the purpose of obtaining business from that person.

Landlord, or lessor   Generally the owner of real property who transfers possession and use of the real property under a lease to a tenant or lessee.

Lease   Legal document that transfers possession of real property from one party to another. The lease also may contain numerous terms and conditions involving the use and possession of the property.

Legal description   Description of real property by a government survey, metes and bounds, or lot numbers of a recorded plat, which description is complete enough that a particular parcel of land can be located and identified.

License   Authority or permission to do a particular act or series of acts on another person's land.

Lien   Money debt attached to real property. The holder of the lien can sell the real property to pay the debt.

Life estate   Estate of real property the duration of which is measured by the life or lives of one or more persons.

Limited common area   Common area of a condominium that is limited in use to one or more condominium unit owners.

Limited or special warranty deed   Deed wherein the grantor covenants and warrants only against the lawful claims of people claiming by, through, or under the grantor.

Liquidated damages   Amount of money agreed on by the parties to a contract to be the damages in the event of a default of the contract.

Lis pendens   Notice recorded in the real property records that informs that a lawsuit affecting title to real property described in the notice has been filed and is pending.

Listing agreement   Agreement entered into between an owner and a real estate broker retaining the real estate broker to assist the owner in selling real property.

Loan closing   Consummation of a loan secured by real property

Loan commitment   Contract between a borrower and a lender to make and accept a mortgage loan secured by real property. The loan commitment sets forth the terms, requirements, and conditions for the mortgage loan

Loan-to-value ratio   Ratio of the amount of a mortgage loan to the value of the secured real property. For example, the amount of the loan is $80,000 and the market value of the real property pledged as security for the loan is $100,000, the loan-value ratio is 80 percent.

Maker   Party to a promissory note who promises to pay money.

Marketable title   Title to real property that is free from doubt and enables the owner to hold the real property in peace; free from the hazard of litigation or adverse claims.

Mechanics' or materialmen's lien   Lien imposed by law on real property to secure payment for work performed or materials furnished for the construction, repair, or alteration of improvements on the real property.

Mortgage   Legal document that creates an encumbrance on real property to secure a debt.

Mortgage loan   Loan secured by real property.

Mortgagee loss payable clause   Endorsement to a policy of fire and hazard insurance whereby the owner of the insured property and the insurance company agree that any and all proceeds payable under the policy are to be paid directly to the lender who has a mortgage on the insured property

Mortgagee or loan policy   Policy of title insurance that insures the interest of a mortgagee or lender to the title of real property.

Mortgagee   Person who receives a mortgage.

Mortgagor   Person who signs a mortgage pledging real property to secure a debt.

Negative amortization   Loan in which the payments are not sufficient to pay the interest costs of the loan. The unpaid interest is added to the principal of the loan, resulting in an increase in the principal amount of the loan during the term of repayment.

Negotiable note   Written note, signed by the maker and containing an unconditional promise to pay a certain sum of money on demand or at a definite time. A negotiable note may be transferred to a holder in due course.

Net lease   Lease in which the tenant is responsible for all expenses of the leased premises, such as utilities, taxes, and insurance.

Novation   Substitution of parties to a contract to such an extent that the law declares that a new contract has been entered into. For example, A and B enter into a contract. A assigns its rights under the contract to C, who assumes all of A's obligations to perform under the contract. The law may declare that a novation has taken place; therefore, the old contract between A and B no longer exists and a new contract between B and C now exists.

Open-end or dragnet clause   Mortgage provision that provides that the mortgage will secure any and all debt between the mortgagor and the mortgagee, including past debt, present debt, and even future debt incurred after the mortgage is signed.

Option   A contract by which an owner of property, usually called the optionor, agrees with another person, usually called the optionee, that the optionee shall have the right to buy the owner's real property at a fixed price within a certain time on agreed terms and conditions.

Owner policy   Policy of title insurance that insures an owner's title to real property.

Parol evidence rule   Rule of evidence that provides that a written agreement is the best and only evidence of the agreement between the parties and that the parties are not permitted to bring in oral testimony regarding other agreements concerning the transaction.

Partition   Method by which co-owners of real property can divide the common property into separate ownerships. Partition may be by voluntary agreement of the co-owners or by court action.

Payee   Party to a promissory note to whom a promise to pay money has been made.

Pending disbursement clause   Clause found in a construction loan title insurance policy that provides that the insurance coverage under the policy will be in the amount of the loan as it is disbursed to the borrower up to and not to exceed the face amount of the policy.

Percentage breakpoint   Level of gross sales made during a year at which time a percentage rent obligation will commence.

Percentage rent   Rent based on a percentage of sales from a specific location. Percentage rent often is found in retail store leases.

Permanent loan   Long-term loan that finances the acquisition of real property or refinances a construction loan on improvements.

Plat   Survey of real property that often is recorded.

Plat index   Index of all plats that have been recorded within the county within a given year.

Possession   Occupation of land evidenced by visible acts such as an enclosure, cultivation, the construction of improvements, or the occupancy of existing improvements.

Power of attorney   Written document authorizing another person to act as one's agent.

Preamble   Portion of the deed that sets forth the parties to the deed and the date of the deed.

Premises   Land and the buildings located on the land. The term often is used to describe real property covered by a lease.

Prenuptial agreement   Agreement entered into by a married couple that, among other things, outlines an agreement between the couple regarding the division and ownership of property in the event of separation or divorce.

Prescriptive easement   Easement created when a person uses real property for a period of time without the owner's permission.

Primary mortgage lender   Lender who makes mortgage loans directly to a borrower.

Principal meridians   Imaginary north and south lines used in a government survey system. Meridians intersect the base lines to form a starting point for the measurement of land under that system.

Private mortgage insurance   Insurance through private sources that a debtor will pay his or her loan.

Promissory note   Legal document that contains a promise by one party to pay money to another party.

Quiet title action   Judicial proceeding to establish the ownership of real property.

Quitclaim deed   Deed that contains no warranties of title. A quitclaim deed transfers only the interest that the grantor has in the land and not the land itself.

Radius clause   Clause contained in a lease that prohibits a tenant from operating another retail store or business within a certain geographical radius of the leased premises.

Range lines   Division of a state in a government survey system being a six-mile-wide row of townships running north and south.

Receiver   Third party appointed by a court to take possession of mortgaged property in the event of a mortgage default. The receiver's responsibilities are to collect the rents from the property and to maintain the property in good repair.

Record title holder   Owner of real property as shown on the deed records from a title examination of the property.

Recording statutes   State statutes that regulate the recordation of real property documents.

Redemption   Right of a property owner to buy back his property after a foreclosure.

Rent   Money paid by a tenant to a landlord for the use and possession of property pursuant to a lease.

Rescission   Act of repealing or voiding something or some action.

Rescission   Remedy for default of a real estate contract wherein the contract is terminated and the defaulting party must reimburse the injured party for expenses incurred in connection with the contract.

RESPA   Real Estate Settlement Procedures Act, a federal law designed to reform the real estate settlement process and to ensure that consumers receive more information about real estate settlement costs.

Retainage   Portion of the loan proceeds held by a construction lender until the construction is completed. The term also refers to an owner holding back money from a contractor until construction is completed.

Rider   Attachment to a contract or other document that contains additional provisions to be included within the contract or other document.

Riparian rights   Rights of the owners of lands adjoining streams, rivers, and lakes relating to the water and its use.

Secondary mortgage market   Group of investors who purchase mortgage loans from primary mortgage lenders.

Section   Division or parcel of land on a government survey comprising one square mile, or six hundred forty acres.

Security agreement   Legal document that pledges personal property as security for a debt.

Servicing the loan   Collection of payments from the borrower of a mortgage loan.

Servient tenement   Parcel of land on which an appurtenant easement is located.

Settlement costs   All costs involved in the settlement or closing of a real estate transaction. Such items include but are not limited to attorney's fees, surveyor's fees, title insurance premiums, recording fees, and appraisal fees.

Specific performance   Remedy for breach of real estate contract that requires a defaulting party to perform the promises under the contract.

Straight-line amortized loan   Mortgage loan in which the borrower will pay a different amount for each installment, with each payment consisting of a fixed amount credited toward principal and an additional amount for the interest due on the balance of the principal unpaid since the last payment.

Sublet   In regard to a lease, it is when the tenant transfers only a portion of his or her interest under the lease and the tenant retains some interest.

Subrogation   Right to be substituted to the rights of another person. For example, an insurance carrier who pays a claim to the insured is given the rights of the insured to proceed against any party who caused the damage resulting in the claim.

Survey   Visual presentation of the physical boundaries of real property. The survey is used to describe real property.

Tacking   Combination of possession periods by different adverse possessors.

Tenancy by the entirety   Ownership of real property by a husband and wife. The husband and wife are treated as a single owner, and neither the husband nor the wife can transfer the property without the other's consent.

Tenancy in common   Co-ownership of real property by two or more persons. Each owner's interest in the property is capable of inheritance.

Tenant, or lessee   Person who receives possession and use of property pursuant to a lease.

Term loan   Loan in which the borrower makes periodic payments of interest with the principal being paid in one installment at the end of the loan term.

Testimonium   Portion of the deed that the grantor signs and the signature is witnessed or notarized.

Time is of the essence   Provision contained in a contract that requires strict performance of the contract by the date or dates provided therein.

Time-share   Form of ownership of real property in which an owner owns the property for a short period, usually one or two weeks out of each year. Time-share ownership typically is used for vacation or recreational property.

Title endorsement   Amendment to a title insurance policy that generally modifies existing coverage or adds special coverage to the policy.

Title examination   Examination of the real property records to determine the ownership to a particular tract of real property.

Title insurance commitment   Commitment or contract by a title insurance company to issue a title insurance policy.

Title insurance   Contract to indemnify the insured against loss through defects in the title to real property.

Township   In a government survey, it is a square tract of land six miles on each side, containing thirty-six square miles of land.

Township lines   Lines in a government rectangular survey system, that run east and west at six-mile intervals parallel with baselines and that form strips of land or tiers called townships.

Truth-in-Lending Act   Federal Law designed to provide consumers with information for an informed use of credit. The Truth-in-Lending Act requires creditors to disclose to consumers the true costs of a consumer loan.

Usury   Interest rates that are determined to be in excess of the maximum permitted by law.

Warranty or covenant   Promise that a fact is true or that an event will take place.

Waste   Action or nonaction that causes a loss of value to real property.

Will   Legal document by which a person disposes of his property. A will takes effect on the death of the property owner.

Zoning   Legitimate police power of government to regulate the use of real property.

Index

Appendix

CHAPTER 1—INTRODUCTION TO THE LAW OF REAL PROPERTY _____

Intestacy Distribution Chart, page 8

In New York, if an individual dies without a will, the state writes one for him and the property is distributed in accordance with this chart.

EXHIBIT 1.1
New York Intestate Distribution Chart

	OLD LAW	NEW LAW (CHAPTER 595)
DECEASED SURVIVED BY	Persons dying without a will before 9/1/92	Persons dying without a will on or after 9/1/92
SPOUSE & ONE CHILD OR ISSUE OF DECEASED CHILD	$4,000 & 1/2 of residue to spouse; Balance to child or issue of child *per stirpes*	$50,000 & 1/2 of residue to spouse; Balance to child or issue to child *by representation*
SPOUSE & 2 OR MORE CHILDREN	$4,000 & 1/3 of residue to spouse; Balance to children or issue of children *per stirpes*	$50,000 & 1/2 of residue to spouse; Balance to children or their issue *by representation*
PARENTS ONLY, NO SPOUSE OR CHILDREN	All to the parents	All to surviving parent or parents
SPOUSE ONLY, NO PARENTS OR ISSUE	Everything to spouse	Everything to spouse
SPOUSE, BOTH PARENTS, NO ISSUE	$25,000 & 1/2 of residue to spouse; Balance to parents	Everything to spouse
SPOUSE, ONE PARENT, NO ISSUE	$25,000 & 1/2 of residue to spouse; Balance to parent	Everything to spouse
ISSUE, NO SPOUSE	Whole to the issue *per stirpes*	Whole to the issue *by representation*
BROTHERS & SISTERS OR THEIR ISSUE, NO SPOUSE, ISSUE OR PARENT	Whole to brothers & sisters, or their issue *per stirpes*	Whole to the issue of the parents, *by representation*
GRANDPARENTS ONLY (NO SPOUSE, ISSUE, PARENTS, BROTHER OR SISTER)	The whole to the surviving grandparent or to the surviving grandparents in equal shares	1/2 to surviving paternal grandparent(s) or their issue *by representation*; 1/2 to surviving maternal grandparent(s), or their issue, *by representation* limited to first cousins
ISSUE OF GRANDPARENTS (NO ISSUE, SURVIVING SPOUSE, PARENTS, BROTHERS OR SISTERS OR THEIR ISSUE, OR GRANDPARENTS)	The whole to the issue of the grandparents in the nearest degree of kinship to the decedent per capita (Uncles or aunts; First cousins; First cousins once removed, etc.)	See Above
GREAT GRANDPARENTS ONLY (NO ISSUE, SPOUSE, PARENTS, BROTHERS OR SISTERS OR THEIR ISSUE, GRANDPARENTS OR THEIR ISSUE)	The whole to the surviving greatgrandparent(s) in equal shares	No provision for inheritance by great-grandparent(s)

CHAPTER 3—CONDOMINIUMS AND COOPERATIVES _____

Condominiums and Cooperatives in New York, page 46

In New York, in the 1970's many owners of buildings decided to change the ownership of these buildings and convert them to condominiums or cooperatives. To do this the sponsor (generally the property owner) prepared an offering plan which had to follow in detail the regulations prescribed by the New York State Attorney General and the New York General Business Law. The copy of this proposal is called a *red herring* (because of the red writing on the cover) and this is submitted to each tenant and the New York State Attorney General for review. Once the Attorney General decides it is in compliance, the proposal is accepted for filing. The sponsor then issues a *black book* (blacklettering on the cover) and the sponsor can begin to sell apartments. The building can be converted according to an "eviction" or "non-eviction" plan. In an "eviction" plan, 51% of the tenants must purchase their units. Once 51% of the tenants purchase, the other tenants can be evicted after three years (the elderly and disabled are exempt from eviction by statute). If the sponsor decides to offer a "non-eviction" plan (which is the much more prevalent form today), the sponsor must sell only 15% of the apartments for the plan to be effective. No tenants can be evicted and the non-purchasing tenants can remain as tenants. These sales generally must take place within 15 months of the *black book* being issued.

Cooperative Ownership in New York City, page 53

When representing the purchaser of a cooperative apartment you must carefully check for certain information. Certainly if you were buying stock in a publicly traded corporation you would want to find out all you could about the stock and the company's finances. So, too, when you purchase shares in a cooperative corporation you want to know certain information, such as: review the last three years of financial statements; check if the maintenance is stable and average for apartments of that size; is there a substantial reserve fund for major repairs; how much is the mortgage on the building; is it amortized mortgage; when must the mortgage be refinanced; review the minutes of prior meetings—are there any major repairs to be undertaken and are there sufficient resources to pay for the repairs without having an assessment; what is the physical condition of the building—have the boiler, windows and other major repairs been undertaken; what percentage of apartments are still owned by the sponsor, (if it is more than 50% that could indicate future financial problems and you may have trouble getting a mortgage for the unit); and does the building allow sublets? Talk to other owners in the building and find out all you can about the building before you buy shares in the cooperative corporation.

CHAPTER 4—SURVEYS AND LAND DESCRIPTIONS _____

Surveys in New York, page 86

One of the most important elements in the contract of sale or the deed, is an adequate description of the property. Street addresses are not legal descriptions. Not only must the buyer inspect the property he is purchasing, but he must know its exact location and size and be able to identify easements and encroachments. The buyer will want to visually note any structural changes as this could be a "red flag" and one must make sure the proper building permits and final certificate of occupancy were obtained. A survey that states "proposed dwelling" is not acceptable. Any structural changes or improvements to the property that are not shown on the existing survey will result in the buyer having to obtain a new survey. The actual dwelling and any additions must be noted in detail on the survey.

CHAPTER 5—ENCUMBRANCES

Zoning Classifications in New York, page 111

In New York, zoning districts are usually identified by a letter abbreviation as: R (residential); C (commercial); and I (industrial). There are classifications within each of these categories, such as R–1 (single family residential) and C–1 (commercial-retail). Zoning can effect the building height, setback, lot size, type of structure, etc. The zoning classification can have a dramatic effect on the value of property. For example, if a 5 acre building lot is zoned for only one-family dwellings it may have a value of $60,000 but if it were zoned to permit the construction of a high rise multi-family dwelling it may have a value of $300,000. In New York, the various levels of government have planning commissions that prepare master plans and set out zoning districts.

Building Codes in New York, page 114

Many towns have specific building standards and these are called building codes. These codes require certain materials for electrical wiring, etc. Before you can build you must get a building permit and officials verify the building is in compliance with building codes and zoning ordinances. After it is built, the inspector issues a certificate of occupancy (C.O.).

New York State and local governments also have regulations to preserve buildings and historic areas. These are called "landmark preservation districts" and owners of properties in these areas may be restricted in their ability to alter the facade or even which color paints must be used.

New York Environmental Conservation Law, page 114

New York State has an Environmental Conservation Law that defines responsibility for clean-up. There are additional environmental laws that were triggered by the "Love Canal" disaster in which a toxic waste dump started leaking and contaminated a residential area that ultimately had to be vacated. Liens may be attached to the property subject to clean up.

New York also has legislation to protect designated wetlands, and a special permit is needed to build on wetlands.

Taxation (Full Assessment), page 115

Property is periodically revalued and a uniform tax rate is applied. More and more localities are moving to full assessment. The property may be assessed for only a fraction of its value and the tax rate would be based on that fractional share. In full assessment, the property is assessed for its fair market value and the tax rate is based on that full assessed amount. This is supposed to work out to be more equitable, with more valuable properties paying higher taxes. Each year the property owner has a period of time to protest the assessment (file a grievance) and if it is not changed he may begin a lawsuit to reduce it. New York allows a partial exemption from some property taxes for veterans, religious organizations and homeowners over 65 years of age who have limited income.

Additional Liens in New York, page 116

Estate taxes may also be liens. Generally these continue even if the property is transferred to another and may remain a "cloud" on the title until the taxes are paid. New York also has vendor's liens, which may be placed on property if the seller claims he did not get the agreed upon sales price and there are vendee's liens, which are placed on property when the buyer claims the seller failed to deliver title and he wants his money back. The IRS may place tax liens on property held by delinquent taxpayers. In New York City, parking violations, i.e. unpaid parking tickets, may result in liens on property.

Mechanics Liens, page 116

A notice of lien is filed in the office of the clerk of the county in which the property is located. The notice must be filed within four months of completion of the work or supplying the materials for a single family dwelling and eight months on all other properties. The lien attaches immediately upon filing. A copy must be served on the property owner within 30 days. The mechanic's lien is good for one year and may be renewed.

The language used in the New York deed transferring ownership of property usually states that the transfer is "Subject to the trust fund provisions of Section 13 of the Lien Law." This section of the Lien Law provides that during the four month period (and if a lien hasn't been placed on yet) if the property owner conveys or mortgages the property he must covenant (promise) that any monies he receives will be placed in a trust fund to pay the mechanics who created the improvements. If this provision is in the deed, the lienor can not seek recovery from the buyer of the property but must proceed against the seller who is holding the proceeds of sale in trust for this lienor.

If the owner paid his contractor, but the general contractor did not pay his subcontractor or supplier, under the New York State Lien Law the general contractor may be in violation. New York Lien Law allows certain broker's claims for commissions to be filed as mechanic's liens on the theory that this is an "improvement" to property.

CHAPTER 6—EASEMENTS AND LICENSES

Easements in New York, page 141

An easement usually involves two neighboring parcels. An easement is an intangible right; you do not possess or own the other persons property. As the easement usually benefits the holder and restricts the rights of the property owner, it may affect the value of the property, either up or down.

A common easement in attached buildings are party walls. This is a wall shared by two buildings and built on the boundary line of the two buildings and the wall is shared by each owner. Each owns her side of the party wall and each has an easement right in the other half of the support wall of the building. The party wall agreement should always be in writing. Each owner pays 1/2 the expense to maintain the wall. There is a similar right in a common party driveway.

Easement in gross is the right to use another's land, such as the right to run telephone or cable lines across a property. Do not confuse this with a license, which may be withdrawn at any time. An easement may not be withdrawn.

Once appurtenant easements are established, they are permanent, no matter who owns the land, they are said to "run with the land". These always involve two adjoining parcels of land.

CHAPTER 7—CONTRACTS

Contracts, page 160

Almost all real estate transactions begin with an agreement called a contract. Contracts are used to bind the parties and may provide the basis for the purchaser obtaining a mortgage. The contract is the most important document in the real estate transaction, as it dictates the contents of the "deal." When problems arise, the parties go back to see what the contract provided for. New York requires all contracts for the sale of real property to be in writing to be enforceable. New York adopted the "plain language law" for contracts and requires that certain written agreements for the sale or lease of residential property be written in a clear and coherent manner using everyday words.

EXHIBIT 7.1
Power of Attorney, page 163

Blumbergs Law Products   **M 51**—Statutory short form of General Power of Attorney:
with affidavit of attorney, GOL §§ 5-1501: 12 pt. type, 10-94

JULIUS BLUMBERG, INC.
PUBLISHER, NYC 10013

Power of Attorney

Notice: This is an important document. Before signing this document, you should know these important facts. The purpose of this power of attorney is to give the person whom you designate (your "Agent") broad powers to handle your property, which may include powers to pledge, sell, or otherwise dispose of any real or personal property without advance notice to you or approval by you. You may specify that these powers will exist even after you become disabled, incapacitated, or incompetent. The powers that you give your Agent are explained more fully in New York General Obligations Law, Article 5, Title 15, Sections 5-1502A through 5-1503, which expressly permits the use of any other or different form of power of attorney desired by the parties concerned. This document does not authorize anyone to make medical or other health care decisions for you. If there is anything about this form that you do not understand, you should ask a lawyer to explain it to you.

Know Everyone by These Presents, which are intended to constitute a GENERAL POWER OF ATTORNEY pursuant to Article 5, Title 15 of the New York General Obligations Law:

That I   do hereby appoint:
(insert name and address of the principal)

(If 1 person is to be appointed agent, insert the name and address of the agent above)

(If 2 or more persons are to be appointed agents with each agent to be able to act ALONE without requiring the consent of any other agent appointed in order to act, insert the name and address above of each agent SEPARATELY appointed and BE SURE TO insert the word "OR" between EACH designation of an agent to show that EACH agent has COMPLETE power to act alone)

(If 2 or more persons are to be appointed agents to act TOGETHER and requiring the JOINT consent of ALL appointed agents to act with no one agent to be able to act alone, insert the names and addresses above of all agents JOINTLY appointed and BE SURE TO insert the word "AND" between EVERY designation of each agent to indicate that ALL agents listed are required to act together and NONE can act alone)

MY ATTORNEY(S)-IN-FACT TO ACT

(If more than one agent is designated and the principal wants each agent alone to be able to exercise the power conferred, insert in this blank the word "SEPARATELY")

(If more than one agent is designated and the principal wants all of the designated agents together to exercise the power conferred, insert in this blank the word "JOINTLY")

(The failure to make any insertion in this blank will require the agents to act either separately or jointly, in accordance with the principal's use of the word "OR" or the other word "AND" between every respective designation of such agents above. If the principal's wishes cannot be determined because he or she fails to insert the word "OR", "AND", "SEPARATELY", or "JOINTLY" as he or she is asked to do above, the principal will be deemed to require the agents designated above to act jointly)

IN MY NAME, PLACE AND STEAD in any way which I myself could do, if I were personally present, with respect to the following matters as each of them is defined in Title 15 of Article 5 of the New York General Obligations Law to the extent that I am permitted by law to act through an agent:

Forms may be purchased from *Julius Blumberg, Inc.*, NYC 10013, or any of its dealers. Reproduction prohibited. Reprinted with permission.

EXHIBIT 7.1
Power of Attorney   (continued)

Initial in the opposite box any one or more of the subdivisions as to which the principal WANTS to give the agent authority.

(NOTICE: The principal must write his or her initials in the corresponding blank space of a box below with respect to each of the subdivisions (A) through (N) below for which the principal WANTS to give the agent(s) authority. If the blank space within a box for any particular subdivision is NOT initialed, NO AUTHORITY WILL BE GRANTED for matters that are included in that subdivision)

(A) real estate transactions;.............................. [   ]
(B) chattel and goods transactions;................. [   ]
(C) bond, share and commodity transactions; [   ]
(D) banking transactions;............................... [   ]
(E) business operating transactions;.............. [   ]
(F) insurance transactions;............................. [   ]
(G) estate transactions;.................................. [   ]
(H) claims and litigation;............................... [   ]
(I) personal relationships and affairs;............ [   ]
(J) benefits from military service;.................. [   ]
(K) records, reports and statements; .... [   ]

(L) full and unqualified authority to my
     attorney(s)-in-fact to delegate any
     or all of the foregoing powers
     to any person or persons whom my
     attorney(s)-in-fact shall select;................. [   ]
(M) all other matters;.................................... [   ]
**(N) if the blank space in the box to the
     right is initialed by the principal,
     this power of attorney shall not be
     affected by the subsequent disability
     or incompetence of the principal;**............ [   ]

(Special provisions and limitations may be included in the statutory short form power of attorney only if they conform to the requirements of section 5-1503 of the New York General Obligations Law.)

To induce any third party to act hereunder, I hereby agree that any third party receiving a duly executed copy or facsimile of this instrument may act hereunder, and that revocation or termination hereof shall be ineffective as to such third party unless and until actual notice or knowledge of such revocation or termination shall have been received by such third party, and I for myself and for my heirs, executors, legal representatives and assigns, hereby agree to indemnify and hold harmless any such third party from and against any and all claims that may arise against such third party by reason of such third party having relied on the provisions of this instrument.

𝕴𝖓 𝖂𝖎𝖙𝖓𝖊𝖘𝖘 𝖂𝖍𝖊𝖗𝖊𝖔𝖋, I have hereunto signed my name and affixed my seal on
19

_____ (Seal)
(Signature of Principal)

Editors note: If the principal wishes to allow the attorney to make gifts or to continue a pattern of gifts the principal has begun for estate planning, the IRS may require additional language.

EXHIBIT 7.1
Power of Attorney   (continued)

ACKNOWLEDGEMENTS

STATE OF   COUNTY OF   ss.:

On   19   before me personally came
to me known, and known to me to be the individual   described in, and who executed the foregoing instrument,
and   he   acknowledged to me that   he   executed the same.

_____

STATE OF   COUNTY OF   ss.:

On   19   before me personally came
to me known, and known to me to be the individual   described in, and who executed the foregoing instrument,
and   he   acknowledged to me that   he   executed the same.

_____

AFFIDAVIT AS TO POWER OF ATTORNEY BEING IN FULL FORCE

STATE OF   COUNTY OF   ss.:

being duly sworn, deposes and says:
THAT   as principal,
who resides at
did, in writing, under date of   appoint me his true and lawful
attorney, and that annexed thereto, and hereby made a part hereof, is a true copy of said power of attorney.

THAT, as attorney-in-fact of said principal and under and by virtue of the said power of attorney, I have this day
executed the following described instrument

THAT at the time of executing the above described instrument I had no actual knowledge or actual notice
of revocation or termination of the aforesaid power of attorney by death or otherwise, or notice of any facts
indicating the same.

THAT I hereby represent that the said principal is now alive; has not, at any time, revoked or repudiated
the said power of attorney; and the said power of attorney still is in full force and effect.

THAT I make this affidavit for the purpose of inducing

to accept delivery of the above described instrument, as executed by me in my capacity of attorney-in-fact of the
said principal, with the full knowledge that the said

in accepting the execution and delivery of the aforesaid instrument and in paying a good and valuable
consideration therefor, will rely upon this affidavit.

Sworn to before me on

EXHIBIT 7.1
Power of Attorney   (continued)

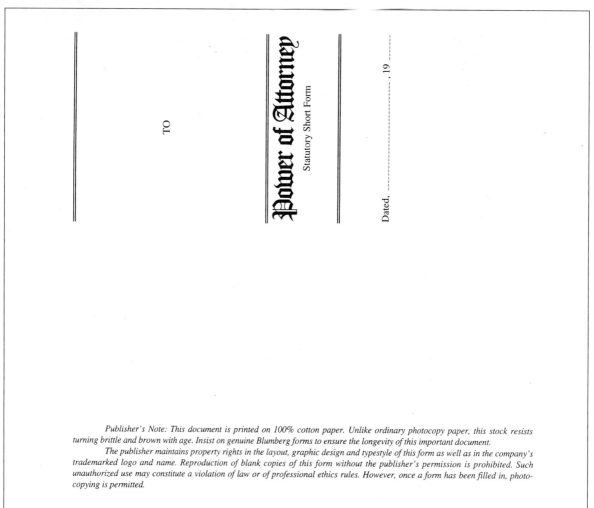

Power of Attorney
Statutory Short Form

TO

Dated, _____, 19 ____

Publisher's Note: This document is printed on 100% cotton paper. Unlike ordinary photocopy paper, this stock resists turning brittle and brown with age. Insist on genuine Blumberg forms to ensure the longevity of this important document.

The publisher maintains property rights in the layout, graphic design and typestyle of this form as well as in the company's trademarked logo and name. Reproduction of blank copies of this form without the publisher's permission is prohibited. Such unauthorized use may constitute a violation of law or of professional ethics rules. However, once a form has been filled in, photocopying is permitted.

Binders in New York, page 171

Most purchases for real estate begin with a binder. Binders are usually prepared by brokers as a means to secure the sale (and guarantee their commission). They are usually signed before the parties have a chance to review them with their attorneys. If the binders are specific enough, the courts may enforce them as a contract. If they are enforceable, the parties may not have thought of everything they wish to include. It is advisable not to sign a binder, but instead to go directly to contract with an attorney to represent you. If you must sign a binder, include the words "subject to my attorney's approval."

An "option" is a written contract for someone to purchase or lease property within a specific time at a set price. If all the elements are included, an option may be a contract. In New York, an option may be recorded.

CHAPTER 8—PREPARATION AND REVIEW OF A REAL ESTATE CONTRACT

New York Sample Contract Forms, page 175

EXHIBIT 8.1
New York Residential Contract of Sale

A 125—Residential contract of sale, 3-92

JULIUS BLUMBERG, INC.
PUBLISHER, NYC 10013

Jointly prepared by the Real Property Section of the New York State Bar Association, the New York State Land Title Association, the Committee on Real Property Law of the Association of the Bar of the City of New York and the Committee on Real Property Law of the New York County Lawyers' Association.

WARNING: NO REPRESENTATION IS MADE THAT THIS FORM OF CONTRACT FOR THE SALE AND PURCHASE OF REAL ESTATE COMPLIES WITH SECTION 5-702 OF THE GENERAL OBLIGATIONS LAW ("PLAIN LANGUAGE").

CONSULT YOUR LAWYER BEFORE SIGNING THIS AGREEMENT

NOTE: FIRE AND CASUALTY LOSSES AND CONDEMNATION.
This contract form does not provide for what happens in the event of fire, or other casualty loss or condemnation before the title closing. Unless different provision is made in this contract, Section 5-1311 of the General Obligations Law will apply. One part of that law makes a Purchaser responsible for fire and casualty loss upon taking possession of the Premises before the title closing.

Residential Contract of Sale

Contract of Sale made as of   19   BETWEEN

Address:
Social Security Number/Fed. I. D. No(s):   hereinafter called "Seller" and

Address:
Social Security Number/Fed. I. D. No(s):   hereinafter called "Purchaser".

The parties hereby agree as follows:

1. Premises. Seller shall sell and convey and Purchaser shall purchase the property, together with all buildings and improvements thereon (collectively the "Premises"), more fully described on a separate page marked "Schedule A", annexed hereto and made a part hereof and also known as:

Street Address:

Tax Map Designation:

Together with Seller's ownership and rights, if any, to land lying in the bed of any street or highway, opened or proposed, adjoining the Premises to the center line thereof, including any right of Seller to any unpaid award by reason of any taking by condemnation and/or for any damage to the Premises by reason of change of grade of any street or highway. Seller shall deliver at no additional cost to Purchaser, at Closing (as hereinafter defined), or thereafter, on demand, any documents that Purchaser may reasonably require for the conveyance of such title and the assignment and collection of such award or damages.

2. Personal Property. This sale also includes all fixtures and articles of personal property now attached or appurtenant to the Premises, unless specifically excluded below. Seller represents and warrants that at Closing they will be paid for and owned by Seller, free and clear of all liens and encumbrances, except any existing mortgage to which this sale may be subject. They include, but are not limited to, plumbing, heating, lighting and cooking fixtures, bathroom and kitchen cabinets, mantels, door mirrors, switch plates and door hardware, venetian blinds, window treatments, shades, screens, awnings, storm windows, storm doors, window boxes, mail box, TV aerials, weather vane, flagpole, pumps, shrubbery, fencing, outdoor statuary, tool shed, dishwasher, washing machine, clothes dryer, garbage disposal unit, range, oven, refrigerator, freezer, air conditioning equipment and installations, wall to wall carpeting and built-ins not excluded below (*strike out inapplicable items*).

Excluded from this sale are furniture and household furnishings and

3. Purchase Price. The purchase price is

$

payable as follows:
(a) on the signing of this contract, by Purchaser's check payable to the Escrowee (as hereinafter defined), subject to collection, the receipt of which is hereby acknowledged, to be held in escrow pursuant to paragraph 6 of this contract (the "Downpayment"):

$

(b) by allowance for the principal amount unpaid on the existing mortgage on the date hereof, payment of which Purchaser shall assume by joinder in the deed: $

(c) by a purchase money note and mortgage from Purchaser to Seller: $

(d) balance at Closing in accordance with paragraph 7:
$

4. Existing Mortgage. (*Delete if inapplicable*) If this sale is subject to an existing mortgage as indicated in paragraph 3(b) above:
(a) The Premises shall be conveyed subject to the continuing lien of the existing mortgage, which is presently payable, with

interest at the rate of   percent per annum, in monthly installments of $ which include principal, interest and escrow amounts, if any, and with any balance of principal being due and payable on

(b) To the extent that any required payments are made on the existing mortgage between the date hereof and Closing which reduce the unpaid principal amount thereof below the amount shown in paragraph 3(b), then the balance of the price payable at Closing under paragraph 3(d) shall be increased by the amount of the payments of principal. Seller represents and warrants that the amount shown in paragraph 3(b) is substantially correct and agrees that only payments required by the existing mortgage will be made between the date hereof and Closing.

(c) If there is a mortgagee escrow account, Seller shall assign it to Purchaser, if it can be assigned, and in that case Purchaser shall pay the amount in the escrow account to Seller at Closing.

(d) Seller shall deliver to Purchaser at Closing a certificate dated not more than 30 days before Closing signed by the holder of the existing mortgage, in form for recording, certifying the amount of the unpaid principal, the date to which interest has been paid and the amounts, if any, claimed to be unpaid for principal and interest, itemizing the same. Seller shall pay the fees for recording such certificate. If the holder of the existing mortgage is a bank or other institution as defined in Section 274-a of the Real Property Law ("Institutional Lender"), it may, instead of the certificate, furnish a letter signed by a duly authorized officer, employee or agent, dated not more then 30 days before Closing, containing the same information.

(e) Seller represents and warrants that (i) Seller has delivered to Purchaser true and complete copies of the existing mortgage, the note secured thereby and any extensions and modificatons thereof, (ii) the existing mortgage is not now, and at the time of Closing will not be, in default, and (iii) the existing mortgage does not contain any provision that permits the holder of the mortgage to require its immediate payment in full or to change any other term thereof by reason of the sale or conveyance of the Premises.

5. Purchase Money Mortgage. (*Delete if inapplicable*) If there is to be a purchase money mortgage as indicated in paragraph 3(c) above:
(a) The purchase money note and mortgage shall be drawn by the attorney for Seller in the form attached or, if not, in the standard form adopted by the New York State Land Title Association. Purchaser shall pay at Closing the mortgage recording tax, recording fees and the attorney's fees in the amount of $
for its preparation.

(b) The purchase money note and mortgage shall also provide that it is subject and subordinate to the lien of the existing mortgage and any extensions, modifications, replacements or consolidations of the existing mortgage, provided that (i) the interest rate thereof shall not be greater than   percent per annum and the total debt service thereunder shall not be greater than
$ per annum, and (ii) if the principal amount thereof shall exceed the amount of principal owing and unpaid on the existing mortgage at the time of placing such new mortgage or consolidated mortgage, the excess be paid to the holder of such purchase money mortgage in reduction of the principal thereof. The purchase money mortgage shall also provide that such payment to the holder thereof shall not alter or affect the regular installments, if any, of principal payable thereunder and that the holder thereof will, on demand and without charge therefor, execute, acknowledge and deliver any agreement or agreements further to effectuate such subordination.

6. Downpayment in Escrow. (a) Seller's attorney ("Escrowee") shall hold the Downpayment for Seller's account in escrow in a segregated bank account at

until Closing or sooner termination of this contract and shall pay over or apply the Downpayment in accordance with the terms of this paragraph. Escrowee shall (*not*) (*Delete if inapplicable*) hold the Downpayment in an interest-bearing account for the benefit of

---

Forms may be purchased from Julius Blumberg, Inc., NYC 10013, or any of its dealers. Reproduction prohibited. Reprinted with permission.

EXHIBIT 8.1
New York Residential Contract of Sale   (continued)

the parties. If interest is held for the benefit of the parties, it shall be paid to the party entitled to the Downpayment and the party receiving the interest shall pay any income taxes thereon. If interest is not held for the benefit of the parties, the Downpayment shall be placed in an IOLA account or as otherwise permitted or required by law. The Social Security or Federal Identification numbers of the parties shall be furnished to Escrowee upon request. At Closing, the Downpayment shall be paid by Escrowee to Seller. If for any reason Closing does not occur and either party gives Notice (as defined in paragraph 25) to Escrowee demanding payment of the Downpayment, Escrowee shall give prompt Notice to the other party of such demand. If Escrowee does not receive Notice of objection from such other party to the proposed payment within 10 business days after the giving of such Notice, Escrowee is hereby authorized and directed to make such payment. If Escrowee does receive such Notice of objection within such 10 day period or if for any other reason Escrowee in good faith shall elect not to make such payment, Escrowee shall continue to hold such amount until otherwise directed by Notice from the parties to this contract or a final, nonappealable judgment, order or decree of a court. However, Escrowee shall have the right at any time to deposit the Downpayment and the interest thereon with the clerk of a court in the county in which the Premises are located and shall give Notice of such deposit to Seller and Purchaser. Upon such deposit or other disbursement in accordance with the terms of this paragraph, Escrowee shall be relieved and discharged of all further obligations and responsibilities hereunder.

(b) The parties acknowledge that, although Escrowee is holding the Downpayment for Seller's account, for all other purposes Escrowee is acting solely as a stakeholder at their request and for their convenience and that Escrowee shall not be liable to either party for any act or omission on its part unless taken or suffered in bad faith or in willful disregard of this contract or involving gross negligence on the part of Escrowee. Seller and Purchaser jointly and severally agree to defend, indemnify and hold Escrowee harmless from and against all costs, claims and expenses (including reasonable attorneys' fees) incurred in connection with the performance of Escrowee's duties hereunder, except with respect to actions or omissions taken or suffered by Escrowee in bad faith or in willful disregard of this contract or involving gross negligence on the part of Escrowee.

(c) Escrowee may act or refrain from acting in respect of any matter referred to herein in full reliance upon and with the advice of counsel which may be selected by it (including any member of its firm) and shall be fully protected in so acting or refraining from action upon the advice of such counsel.

(d) Escrowee acknowledges receipt of the Downpayment by check subject to collection and Escrowee's agreement to the provisions of this paragraph by signing in the place indicated on the signature page of this contract.

(e) Escrowee or any member of its firm shall be permitted to act as counsel for Seller in any dispute as to the disbursement of the Downpayment or any other dispute between the parties whether or not Escrowee is in possession of the Downpayment and continues to act as Escrowee.

7. Acceptable Funds. All money payable under this contract, unless otherwise specified, shall be paid by:

(a) Cash, but not over $1,000.00;

(b) Good certified check of Purchaser drawn on or official check issued by any bank, savings bank, trust company or savings and loan association having a banking office in the State of New York, unendorsed and payable to the order of Seller, or as Seller may otherwise direct upon not less than 3 business days notice (by telephone or otherwise) to Purchaser;

(c) As to money other than the purchase price payable to Seller at Closing, uncertified check of Purchaser up to the amount of $; and

(d) As otherwise agreed to in writing by Seller or Seller's attorney.

8. Mortgage Contingency. (*Delete if inapplicable*) The obligations of Purchaser hereunder are conditioned upon issuance on or before   , 19   , (the "Commitment Date") of a written commitment from any Institutional Lender pursuant to which such Institutional Lender agrees to make a first mortgage loan, other than a VA, FHA or other governmentally insured loan, to Purchaser, at Purchaser's sole cost and expense of $ or such lesser sum as Purchaser shall be willing to accept, at the prevailing fixed rate of interest not to exceed   or initial adjustable rate of interest not to exceed   for a term of at least   years and on other customary commitment terms, whether or not conditional upon any factors other than an appraisal satisfactory to the Institutional Lender. Purchaser shall (a) make prompt application to an Institutional Lender for such mortgage loan, (b) furnish accurate and complete information regarding Purchaser and members of Purchaser's family, as required, (c) pay all fees, points and charges required in connection with such application and loan, (d) pursue such application with diligence, (e) cooperate in good faith with such Institutional Lender to obtain such commitment and (f) promptly give Notice to Seller of the name and address of each Institutional Lender to which Purchaser has made such application. Purchaser shall comply with all requirements of such commitment (or of any other commitment accepted by Purchaser) and shall furnish Seller with a copy thereof promptly after receipt thereof. If such commitment is not issued on or before the Commitment Date, then, unless Purchaser has accepted a commitment that does not comply with the requirements set forth above, Purchaser may cancel this contract by giving Notice to Seller within 5 business days after the Commitment Date, in which case this contract shall be deemed cancelled and thereafter neither

party shall have any further rights against, or obligations or liabilities to, the other by reason of this contract, except that the Downpayment shall be promptly refunded to Purchaser and except as set forth in paragraph 27. If Purchaser fails to give notice of cancellation or if Purchaser shall accept a commitment that does not comply with the terms set forth above, then Purchaser shall be deemed to have waived Purchaser's right to cancel this contract and to receive a refund of the Downpayment by reason of the contingency contained in this paragraph.

9. Permitted Exceptions. The Premises are sold and shall be conveyed subject to:

(a) Zoning and subdivision laws and regulations, and landmark, historic or wetlands designation, provided that they are not violated by the existing buildings and improvements erected on the property or their use;

(b) Consents for the erection of any structures on, under or above any streets on which the Premises abut;

(c) Encroachments of stoops, areas, cellar steps, trim and cornices, if any, upon any street or highway;

(d) Real estate taxes that are a lien, but are not yet due and payable; and

(e) The other matters, if any, including a survey exception, set forth in a Rider attached.

10. Governmental Violations and Orders. (a) Seller shall comply with all notes or notices of violations of law or municipal ordinances, orders or requirements noted or issued as of the date hereof by any governmental department having authority as to lands, housing, buildings, fire, health, environmental and labor conditions affecting the Premises. The Premises shall be conveyed free of them at Closing. Seller shall furnish Purchaser with any authorizations necessary to make the searches that could disclose these matters.

(b) (*Delete if inapplicable*) All obligations affecting the Premises pursuant to the Administrative Code of the City of New York incurred prior to Closing and payable in money shall be discharged by Seller at or prior to Closing.

11. Seller's Representations. (a) Seller represents and warrants to Purchaser that:

(i) The Premises abut or have a right of access to a public road;

(ii) Seller is the sole owner of the Premises and has the full right, power and authority to sell, convey and transfer the same in accordance with the terms of this contract;

(iii) Seller is not a "foreign person", as that term is defined for purposes of the Foreign Investment in Real Property Tax Act, Internal Revenue Code ("IRC") Section 1445, as amended, and the regulations promulgated thereunder (collectively "FIRPTA");

(iv) The Premises are not affected by any exemptions or abatements of taxes; and

(v) Seller has been known by no other name for the past ten years, except

(b) Seller covenants and warrants that all of the representations and warranties set forth in this contract shall be true and correct at Closing.

(c) Except as otherwise expressly set forth in this contract, none of Seller's covenants, representations, warranties or other obligations contained in this contract shall survive Closing.

12. Condition of Property. Purchaser acknowledges and represents that Purchaser is fully aware of the physical condition and state of repair of the Premises and of all other property included in this sale, based on Purchaser's own inspection and investigation thereof, and that Purchaser is entering into this contract based solely upon such inspection and investigation and not upon any information, data, statements or representations, written or oral, as to the physical condition, state of repair, use, cost of operation or any other matter related to the Premises or the other property included in the sale, given or made by Seller or its representatives, and shall accept the same "as is" in their present condition and state of repair, subject to reasonable use, wear, tear and natural deterioration between the date hereof and the date of Closing (except as otherwise set forth in paragraph 16(f)), without any reduction in the purchase price or claim of any kind for any change in such condition by reason thereof subsequent to the date of this contract. Purchaser and its authorized representatives shall have the right, at reasonable times and upon reasonable notice (by telephone or otherwise) to Seller, to inspect the Premises before Closing.

13. Insurable Title. Seller shall give and Purchaser shall accept such title as

shall be willing to approve and insure in accordance with its standard form of title policy approved by the New York State Insurance Department, subject only to the matters provided for in this contract.

14. Closing, Deed and Title. (a) "Closing" means the settlement of the obligations of Seller and Purchaser to each other under this contract, including the payment of the purchase price to Seller, and the delivery to Purchaser of a

deed in proper statutory short form for record, duly executed and acknowledged, so as to convey to Purchaser fee simple title to the Premises, free of all encumbrances, except as otherwise herein stated. The deed shall contain a covenant by Seller as required by subd. 5 of Section 13 of the Lien Law.

EXHIBIT 8.1
New York Residential Contract of Sale (continued)

(b) If Seller is a corporation, it shall deliver to Purchaser at the time of Closing (i) a resolution of its Board of Directors authorizing the sale and delivery of the deed, and (ii) a certificate by the Secretary or Assistant Secretary of the corporation certifying such resolution and setting forth facts showing that the transfer is in conformity with the requirements of Section 909 of the Business Corporation Law. The deed in such case shall contain a recital sufficient to establish compliance with that Section.

15. Closing Date and Place. Closing shall take place at the office of

at   o'clock on   19

or, upon reasonable notice (by telephone or otherwise) by Purchaser, at the office of

16. Conditions to Closing. This contract and Purchaser's obligation to purchase the Premises are also subject to and conditioned upon the fulfillment of the following conditions precedent:

(a) The accuracy, as of the date of Closing, of the representations and warranties of Seller made in this contract.

(b) The delivery by Seller to Purchaser of a valid and subsisting Certificate of Occupancy or other required certificate of compliance, or evidence that none was required, covering the building(s) and all of the other improvements located on the property authorizing their use as a   family dwelling at the date of Closing.

(c) The delivery by Seller to Purchaser of a duly executed and sworn affidavit (in form prescribed by law) claiming exemption of the sale contemplated hereby, if such be the case, under Article 31-B of the Tax Law of the State of New York and the Regulations promulgated thereunder, as the same may be amended from time to time (collectively the "Gains Tax Law"); or if such sale shall not be exempt under the Gains Tax Law, Seller and Purchaser agree to comply in a timely manner with the requirements of the Gains Tax Law and, at Closing, Seller shall deliver to Purchaser (i) an official return showing no tax due, or (ii) an official return accompanied by a certified or official bank check drawn on a New York State banking institution payable to the order of the New York State Department of Taxation and Finance in the amount of the tax shown to be due thereon. Seller shall (x) pay promptly any additional tax that may become due under the Gains Tax Law, together with interest and penalties thereon, if any, which may be assessed or become due after Closing, and/or (y) indemnify, defend and save Purchaser harmless from and against any of the foregoing and any damage, liability, cost or expense (including reasonable attorneys' fees) which may be suffered or incurred by Purchaser by reason of the nonpayment thereof. The provisions of this subparagraph (c) shall survive Closing.

(d) The delivery by Seller to Purchaser of a certification stating that Seller is not a foreign person, which certification shall be in the form then required by FIRPTA. If Seller fails to deliver the aforesaid certification or if Purchaser is not entitled under FIRPTA to rely on such certification, Purchaser shall deduct and withhold from the purchase price a sum equal to 10% thereof (or any lesser amount permitted by law) and shall at Closing remit the withheld amount with the required forms to the Internal Revenue Service.

(e) The delivery of the Premises and all building(s) and improvements comprising a part thereof in broom clean condition, vacant and free of leases or tenancies, together with keys to the Premises.

(f) All plumbing (including water supply and septic systems, if any), heating and air conditioning, if any, electrical and mechanical systems, equipment and machinery in the building(s) located on the property and all appliances which are included in this sale being in working order as of the date of Closing.

(g) If the Premises are a one or two family house, delivery by the parties at Closing of affidavits in compliance with state and local law requirements to the effect that there is installed in the Premises a smoke detecting alarm device or devices.

(h) The delivery by the parties of any other affidavits required as a condition of recording the deed.

17. Deed Transfer and Recording Taxes. At Closing, certified or official bank checks payable to the order of the appropriate State, City or County officer in the amount of any applicable transfer and/or recording tax payable by reason of the delivery or recording of the deed or mortgage, if any, shall be delivered by the party required by law or by this contract to pay such transfer and/or recording tax, together with any required tax returns duly executed and sworn to, and such party shall cause any such checks and returns to be delivered to the appropriate officer promptly after Closing. The obligation to pay any additional tax or deficiency and any interest or penalties thereon shall survive Closing.

18. Apportionments and Other Adjustments; Water Meter and Installment Assessments. (a) To the extent applicable, the following shall be apportioned as of midnight of the day before the day of Closing:

(i) taxes, water charges and sewer rents, on the basis of the fiscal period for which assessed; (ii) fuel; (iii) interest on the existing mortgage; (iv) premiums on existing transferable insurance policies and renewals of those expiring prior to Closing; (v) vault charges; (vi) rents as and when collected.

(b) If Closing shall occur before a new tax rate is fixed, the apportionment of taxes shall be upon the basis of the tax rate for the immediately preceding fiscal period applied to the latest assessed valuation.

(c) If there is a water meter on the Premises, Seller shall furnish a reading to a date not more than 30 days before Closing and the unfixed meter charge and sewer rent, if any, shall be apportioned on the basis of such last reading.

(d) If at the date of Closing the Premises are affected by an assessment which is or may become payable in annual installments, and the first installment is then a lien, or has been paid, then for the purposes of this contract all the unpaid installments shall be considered due and shall be paid by Seller at or prior to Closing.

(e) Any errors or omissions in computing apportionments or other adjustments at Closing shall be corrected within a reasonable time following Closing. This subparagraph shall survive Closing.

19. Allowance for Unpaid Taxes, etc. Seller has the option to credit Purchaser as an adjustment to the purchase price with the amount of any unpaid taxes, assessments, water charges and sewer rents, together with any interest and penalties thereon to a date not less than five business days after Closing, provided that official bills therefor computed to said date are produced at Closing.

20. Use of Purchase Price to Remove Encumbrances. If at Closing there are other liens or encumbrances that Seller is obligated to pay or discharge, Seller may use any portion of the cash balance of the purchase price to pay or discharge them, provided Seller shall simultaneously deliver to Purchaser at Closing instruments in recordable form and sufficient to satisfy such liens or encumbrances of record, together with the cost of recording or filing said instruments. As an alternative Seller may deposit sufficient monies with the title insurance company employed by Purchaser acceptable to and required by it to assure their discharge, but only if the title insurance company will insure Purchaser's title clear of the matters or insure against their enforcement out of the Premises and will insure Purchaser's Institutional Lender clear of such matters. Upon notice (by telephone or otherwise), given not less than 3 business days before Closing, Purchaser shall provide separate certified or official bank checks as requested to assist in clearing up these matters.

21. Title Examination; Seller's Inability to Convey; Limitations of Liability. (a) Purchaser shall order an examination of title in respect of the Premises from a title company licensed or authorized to issue title insurance by the New York State Insurance Department or any agent for such title company promptly after the execution of this contract or, if this contract is subject to the mortgage contingency set forth in paragraph 8, after a mortgage commitment has been accepted by Purchaser. Purchaser shall cause a copy of the title report and of any additions thereto to be delivered to the attorney(s) for Seller promptly after receipt thereof.

(b)(i) If at the date of Closing Seller is unable to transfer title to Purchaser in accordance with this contract, or Purchaser has other valid grounds for refusing to close, whether by reason of liens, encumbrances or other objections to title or otherwise (herein collectively called "Defects"), other than those subject to which Purchaser is obligated to accept title hereunder or which Purchaser may have waived and other than those which Seller has herein expressly agreed to remove, remedy or discharge and if Purchaser shall be unwilling to waive the same and to close title without abatement of the purchase price, then, except as hereinafter set forth, Seller shall have the right, at Seller's sole election, either to take such action as Seller may deem advisable to remove, remedy, discharge or comply with such Defects or to cancel this contract; (ii) if Seller elects to take action to remove, remedy or comply with such Defects, Seller shall be entitled from time to time, upon Notice to Purchaser, to adjourn the date for Closing hereunder for a period or periods not exceeding 60 days in the aggregate (but not extending beyond the date upon which Purchaser's mortgage commitment, if any, shall expire), and the date for Closing shall be adjourned to a date specified by Seller not beyond such period. If for any reason whatsoever, Seller shall not have succeeded in removing, remedying or complying with such Defects at the expiration of such adjournment(s), and if Purchaser shall still be unwilling to waive the same and to close title without abatement of the purchase price, then either party may cancel this contract by Notice to the other given within 10 days after such adjourned date; (iii) notwithstanding the foregoing, the existing mortgage (unless this sale is subject to the same) and any matter created by Seller after the date hereof shall be released, discharged or otherwise cured by Seller at or prior to Closing.

(c) If this contract is cancelled pursuant to its terms, other than as a result of Purchaser's default, this contract shall terminate and come to an end, and neither party shall have any further rights, obligations or liabilities against or to the other hereunder or otherwise, except that: (i) Seller shall promptly refund or cause the Escrowee to refund the Downpayment to Purchaser and, unless cancelled as a result of Purchaser's default or pursuant to paragraph 8, to reimburse Purchaser for the net cost of examination of title, including any appropriate additional charges related thereto, and the net cost, if actually paid or incurred by Purchaser, for updating the existing survey of the Premises or of a new survey, and (ii) the obligations under paragraph 27 shall survive the termination of this contract.

22. Affidavit as to Judgments, Bankruptcies, etc. If a title examination discloses judgments, bankruptcies or other returns against persons having names the same as or similar to that of Seller, Seller shall deliver an affidavit at Closing showing that they are not against Seller.

23. Defaults and Remedies. (a) If Purchaser defaults hereunder, Seller's sole remedy shall be to receive and retain the Downpayment as liquidated damages, it being agreed that Seller's damages in case of Purchaser's default might be impossible to ascertain and that the Downpayment constitutes a fair and reasonable amount of damages under the circumstances and is not a penalty.

EXHIBIT 8.1
New York Residential Contract of Sale   (continued)

(b) If Seller defaults hereunder, Purchaser shall have such remedies as Purchaser shall be entitled to at law or in equity, including, but not limited to, specific performance.

24. Purchaser's Lien. All money paid on account of this contract, and the reasonable expenses of examination of title to the Premises and of any survey and survey inspection charges, are hereby made liens on the Premises, but such liens shall not continue after default by Purchaser under this contract.

25. Notices. Any notice or other communication ("Notice") shall be in writing and either (a) sent by either of the parties hereto or by their respective attorneys who are hereby authorized to do so on their behalf or by the Escrowee, by registered or certified mail, postage prepaid, or

(b) delivered in person or by overnight courier, with receipt acknowledged, to the respective addresses given in this contract for the party and the Escrowee, to whom the Notice is to be given, or to such other address as such party or Escrowee shall hereafter designate by Notice given to the other party or parties and the Escrowee pursuant to this paragraph. Each Notice mailed shall be deemed given on the third business day following the date of mailing the same, except that any notice to Escrowee shall be deemed given only upon receipt by Escrowee and each Notice delivered in person or by overnight courier shall be deemed given when delivered.

26. No Assignment. This contract may not be assigned by Purchaser without the prior written consent of Seller in each instance and any purported assignment(s) made without such consent shall be void.

27. Broker. Seller and Purchaser each represents and warrants to the other that it has not dealt with any broker in connection with this sale other than

("Broker") and Seller shall pay Broker any commission earned pursuant to a separate agreement between Seller and Broker. Seller and Purchaser shall indemnify and defend each other against any costs,

claims and expenses, including reasonable attorneys' fees, arising out of the breach on their respective parts of any representation or agreement contained in this paragraph. The provisions of this paragraph shall survive Closing or, if Closing does not occur, the termination of this contract.

28. Miscellaneous. (a) All prior understandings, agreements, representations and warranties, oral or written, between Seller and Purchaser are merged in this contract; it completely expresses their full agreement and has been entered into after full investigation, neither party relying upon any statement made by anyone else that is not set forth in this contract.

(b) Neither this contract nor any provision thereof may be waived, changed or cancelled except in writing. This contract shall also apply to and bind the heirs, distributees, legal representatives, successors and permitted assigns of the respective parties. The parties hereby authorize their respective attorneys to agree in writing to any changes in dates and time periods provided for in this contract.

(c) Any singular word or term herein shall also be read as in the plural and the neuter shall include the masculine and feminine gender, whenever the sense of this contract may require it.

(d) The captions in this contract are for convenience of reference only and in no way define, limit or describe the scope of this contract and shall not be considered in the interpretation of this contract or any provision hereof.

(e) This contract shall not be binding or effective until duly executed and delivered by Seller and Purchaser.

(f) Seller and Purchaser shall comply with IRC reporting requirements, if applicable. This subparagraph shall survive Closing.

(g) Each party shall, at any time and from time to time, execute, acknowledge where appropriate and deliver such further instruments and documents and take such other action as may be reasonably requested by the other in order to carry out the intent and purpose of this contract. This subparagraph shall survive Closing.

(h) This contract is intended for the exclusive benefit of the parties hereto and, except as otherwise expressly provided herein, shall not be for the benefit of, and shall not create any rights in, or be enforceable by, any other person or entity.

IN WITNESS WHEREOF, this contract has been duly executed by the parties hereto.

_____   _____
            Seller   *Purchaser*

_____   _____
            Seller   *Purchaser*

Attorney for Seller: **Attorney for Purchaser:**

Address: Address:

Tel.:   Fax: Tel.:   Fax:

Receipt of the Downpayment is acknowledged and the undersigned agrees to act in accordance with the provisions of paragraph 6 above.

_____
            Escrowee

𝕮𝖔𝖓𝖙𝖗𝖆𝖈𝖙 𝖔𝖋 𝕾𝖆𝖑𝖊

TITLE No. _____

                                            PREMISES

                                            Section
                                            Block
                                            Lot
                                            County or Town
                                            Street Number Address

        TO

EXHIBIT 8.2
New York Contract of Sale—Condominium Unit

M 146—Contract of sale, condominium unit, 8-91
Prepared by the Committee on Real Property Law of the Association of the Bar of the City of New York.

Distributed by Julius Blumberg, Inc.
NYC 10013

Note: This form is intended to deal with matters common to most transactions involving the sale of a condominium unit. Provisions should be added, altered or deleted to suit the circumstances of a particular transaction. No representation is made that this form of contract complies with Section 5-702 of the General Obligations Law ("Plain Language Law").

CONSULT YOUR LAWYER BEFORE SIGNING THIS AGREEMENT
Contract of Sale — Condominium Unit

Agreement made as of   19   between

residing at

                                                                    ("Seller")

and

residing at

                                                                    ("Purchaser")

1. Unit: Seller agrees to sell and convey, and Purchaser agrees to purchase, Unit No.   ("Unit") in the building ("Building") known as   Condominium ("Condominium") and located at   , New York, together with a   percent undivided interest in the Common Elements (as defined in para. 6) appurtenant thereto, all upon and subject to the terms and conditions set forth herein. The Unit shall be as designated in the Declaration of Condominium Ownership (as the same may be amended from time to time, the "Declaration") of the Condominium, recorded in   County, New York or the By-Laws (as the same may be amended from time to time, the "By-Laws") of the Condominium.

2. Personal Property: (a) The sale includes all of Seller's right, title and interest, if any, in and to:

(i) the refrigerators, freezers, ranges, ovens, dishwashers, washing machines, clothes dryers, cabinets and counters, lighting and plumbing fixtures, air conditioning equipment, venetian blinds, shades, screens, storm windows and other window treatments, wall-to-wall carpeting, bookshelves, switchplates, door hardware, built-ins and articles of property and fixtures attached to or appurtenant to the Unit, except those listed in subpara. 2(b), all of which included property and fixtures are represented to be owned by Seller, free and clear of all liens and encumbrances other than those encumbrances ("Permitted Exceptions") set forth on Schedule A annexed hereto and made a part hereof *(strike out inapplicable items)*; and

(ii)

(b) Excluded from this sale are:
(i) furniture and furnishings (other than as specifically provided in this Contract); and
(ii)

(c) The property referred to in subpara. 2(a)(i) and (ii) may not be purchased if title to the Unit is not conveyed hereunder.

3. Purchase Price: (a) The purchase price ("Purchase Price") is $, payable as follows:
(i) $ ("Downpayment") on the signing of this Contract by check subject to collection, the receipt of which is hereby acknowledged, to be held in escrow pursuant to para. 16; and
(ii) $, constituting the balance of the Purchase Price, by certified check of Purchaser or official bank check (except as otherwise provided in this Contract) on the delivery of the deed as hereinafter provided.

(b) All checks in payment of the Purchase Price shall represent United States currency and be drawn on or issued by a bank or trust company authorized to accept deposits in New York State. All checks in payment of the Downpayment shall be payable to the order of Escrowee (as hereinafter defined). All checks in payment of the balance of the Purchase Price shall be payable to the order of Seller (or as Seller otherwise directs pursuant to subparas. 6(a)(ix) or 19(b)).

(c) Except for the Downpayment and checks aggregating not more than one-half of one percent of the Purchase Price, including payment for closing adjustments, all checks delivered by Purchaser shall be certified or official bank checks as hereinabove provided.

4. Closing of Title: The closing documents referred to in para. 6 shall be delivered, and payment of the balance of the Purchase Price shall be made, at the closing of title ("Closing"), to be held on   19   at   M., at the offices of

or at the office of Purchaser's lending institution or its counsel; provided, however, that such office is located in either the City or County in which either (a) Seller's attorney maintains an office or (b) the Unit is located.

5. Representations, Warranties and Covenants: Seller represents, warrants and covenants that:

(a) Seller is the sole owner of the Unit and the property referred to in subpara. 2(a), and Seller has the full right, power and authority to sell, convey and transfer the same;

(b) The common charges (excluding separately billed utility charges) for the Unit on the date hereof are $ per month;

(c) Seller has not received any written notice of any intended assessment or increase in common charges not reflected in subpara. 5(b). Purchaser acknowledges that it will not have the right to cancel this Contract in the event of the imposition of any assessment or increase in common charges after the date hereof of which Seller has not heretofore received written notice;

(d) The real estate taxes for the Unit for the fiscal year of   through   are $

(e) Seller is not a "sponsor" or a nominee of a "sponsor" under any plan of condominium organization affecting the Unit;

(f) All refrigerators, freezers, ranges, dishwashers, washing machines, clothes dryers and air conditioning equipment included in this sale will be in working order at the time of Closing;

(g) If a copy is attached to this Contract, the copy of the Certificate of Occupancy covering the Unit is a true and correct copy; and

(h) Seller is not a "foreign person" as defined in para. 18. *(If inapplicable, delete and provide for compliance with Code Withholding Section, as defined in para. 18.)*

6. Closing Documents: (a) At the Closing, Seller shall deliver to Purchaser the following:

(i) Bargain and sale deed with   covenant against grantor's acts ("Deed"), complying with RPL § 339-0 and containing the covenant required by LL § 13(5), conveying to Purchaser title to the Unit, together with its undivided interest in the Common Elements (as such term is defined in the Declaration and which term shall be deemed to include Seller's right, title and interest in any limited common elements attributable to or used in connection with the Unit) appurtenant thereto, free and clear of all liens and encumbrances other than Permitted Exceptions. The Deed shall be executed and acknowledged by Seller and, if requested by the Condominium, executed and acknowledged by Purchaser, in proper statutory form for recording;

(ii) If a corporation and if required pursuant to BCL § 909, Seller shall deliver to Purchaser (1) a resolution of its board of directors authorizing the delivery of the Deed and (2) a certificate executed by an officer of such corporation certifying as to the adoption of such resolution and setting forth facts demonstrating that the delivery of the Deed is in conformity with the requirements of BCL § 909. The Deed shall also contain a recital sufficient to establish compliance with such law;

(iii) A waiver of right of first refusal of the board of managers of the Condominium ("Board") if required in accordance with para. 8;

(iv) A statement by the Condominium or its managing agent that the common charges and any assessments then due and payable the Condominium have been paid to the date of the Closing;

(v) All keys to the doors of, and mailbox for, the Unit;

(vi) Such affidavits and/or other evidence as the title company ("Title Company") from which Purchaser has ordered a title insurance report and which is authorized to do business in New York State shall reasonably require in order to omit from its title insurance policy all exceptions for judgments, bankruptcies or other returns against Seller and persons or entities whose names are the same as or are similar to Seller's name;

(vii) Official New York State Real Property Transfer Gains Tax Tentative Assessment and Return (or, if applicable, Official Statement of No Tax Due) duly completed by the New York State Department of Taxation and Finance (or, if applicable, a duly

EXHIBIT 8.2
New York Contract of Sale—Condominium Unit   (continued)

executed and acknowledged affidavit of Seller in form required pursuant to the Gains Tax Law (as hereinafter defined) claiming exemption therefrom;

(viii) New York City Real Property Transfer Tax Return, if applicable, and combined Real Property Transfer Gains Tax Affidavits, prepared, executed and acknowledged by Seller in proper form for submission;

(ix) Checks in payment of all applicable real property transfer taxes except a transfer tax which by law is primarily imposed on the purchaser ("Purchaser Transfer Tax") and any New York State Real Property Transfer Gains Tax ("Gains Tax") due in connection with the sale. In lieu of delivery of such checks, Seller shall have the right, upon not less than 3 business days notice to Purchaser, to cause Purchaser to deliver said checks at the Closing and to credit the amount thereof against the balance of the Purchase Price. Seller shall pay the additional transfer taxes and Gains Taxes, if any, payable after the Closing by reason of the conveyance of the Unit, which obligation shall survive the Closing;

(x) Certification that Seller is not a foreign person pursuant to para.18. *(If inapplicable, delete and provide for compliance with Code Section, as defined in para. 18.)*; and

(xi) Affidavit that a single station smoke detecting alarm device is installed pursuant to New York Executive Law §378(5).

(b) At the Closing, Purchaser shall deliver to Seller the following:

(i) Checks in payment of (y) the balance of the Purchase Price in accordance with subpara. 3(b) and (z) any Purchaser Transfer Tax;

(ii) If required by the Declaration or By-Laws, power of attorney to the Board, prepared by Seller, in the form required by the Condominium. The power of attorney shall be executed and acknowledged by Purchaser and, after being recorded, shall be sent to the Condominium;

(iii) New York City Real Property Transfer Tax Return executed and acknowledged by Purchaser and an Affidavit in Lieu of Registration pursuant to New York Multiple Dwelling Law, each in proper form for submission, if applicable, and combined Real Property Transfer Gains Tax Affidavits; and

(iv) If required, New York State Equalization Return executed and acknowledged by Purchaser in proper form for submission.

(c) It is a condition of Purchaser's obligation to close title hereunder that:

(i) All notes or notices of violations of law or governmental orders, ordinances or requirements affecting the Unit and noted or issued by any governmental department, agency or bureau having jurisdiction which were noted or issued on or prior to the date hereof shall have been cured by Seller;

(ii) Any written notice to Seller from the Condominium (or its duly authorized representive) that the Unit is in violation of the Declaration, By-Laws or rules and regulations of the Condominium shall have been cured; and

(iii) The Condominium is a valid condominium created pursuant to RPL Art. 9-B and the Title Company will so insure.

7. Closing Adjustments: (a) The following adjustments shall be made as of 11:59 P.M. of the day before the Closing:

(i) Real estate taxes and water charges and sewer rents, if separately assessed, on the basis of the fiscal period for which assessed, except that if there is a water meter with respect to the Unit, apportionment shall be based on the last available reading, subject to adjustment after the Closing, promptly after the next reading is available; provided, however, that in the event real estate taxes have not, as of the date of Closing, been separately assessed to the Unit, real estate taxes shall be apportioned on the same basis as provided in the Declaration or By-Laws or, in the absence of such provision, based upon the Unit's percentage interest in the Common Elements;

(ii) Common charges of the Condominium; and

(iii) If fuel is separately stored with respect to the Unit only, the value of fuel stored with respect to the Unit at the price then charged by Seller's supplier (as determined by a letter or certificate to be obtained by Seller from such supplier), including any sales taxes.

(b) If at the time of Closing the Unit is affected by an assessment which is or may become payable in installments, then, for the purposes of this Contract, only the unpaid installments which are then due shall be considered due and are to be paid by Seller at the Closing. All subsequent installments at the time of Closing shall be the obligation of Purchaser.

(c) Any errors or omissions in computing closing adjustments shall be corrected. This subpara. 7(c) shall survive the Closing.

(d) If the Unit is located in the City of New York, the "customs in respect to title closings" recommended by The Real Estate Board of New York, Inc., as amended and in effect on the date of Closing, shall apply to the adjustments and other matters therein mentioned, except as otherwise provided herein.

8. Right of First Refusal: If so provided in the Declaration or By-Laws, this sale is subject to and conditioned upon the waiver of a right of first refusal to purchase the Unit held by the Condominium and exercisable by the Board. Seller agrees to give notice promptly to the Board of the contemplated sale of the Unit to Purchaser, which notice shall be given in accordance with the terms of the Declaration and By-Laws, and Purchaser agrees to provide promptly all applications, information and references reasonably requested by the Board. If the Board shall exercise such right of first refusal, Seller shall promptly refund to Purchaser the Downpayment (which term, for all purposes of this Contract, shall be deemed to include interest, if any, earned thereon) and upon the making of such refund this Contract shall be deemed cancelled and of no further force or effect and neither party shall have any further rights against, or obligations or liabilities to, the other by reason of this Contract. If the Board shall fail to exercise such right of first refusal within the time and in

the manner provided for in the Declaration or By-Laws or shall declare in writing its intention not to exercise such right of first refusal (a copy of which writing shall be delivered to Purchaser promptly following receipt thereof), the parties hereto shall proceed with this sale in accordance with the provisions of this Contract.

9. Processing Fee: Seller shall, at the Closing, pay all fees and charges payable to the Condominium (and/or its managing agent) in connection with this sale, including, without limitation, any processing fee, the legal fees, if any, of the Condominium's attorney in connection with this sale and, unless otherwise agreed to by Seller and Purchaser in writing, all "flip taxes," transfer or entrance fees or similar charges, if any, payable to or for the Condominium or otherwise for the benefit of the Condominium unit owners, which arise by reason of this sale.

10. No Other Representations: Purchaser has examined and is satisfied with the Declaration, By-Laws and rules and regulations of the Condominium, or has waived the examination thereof. Purchaser has inspected the Unit, its fixtures, appliances and equipment and the personal property, if any, included in this sale, as well as the Common Elements of the Condominium, and knows the condition thereof and, subject to subpara. 5(f), agrees to accept the same "as is," i.e., in the condition they are in on the date hereof, subject to normal use, wear and tear between the date hereof and the Closing. Purchaser has examined or waived examination of the last audited financial statements of the Condominium, and has considered or waived consideration of all other matters pertaining to this Contract and to the purchase to be made hereunder, and does not rely on any representations made by any broker or by Seller or anyone acting or purporting to act on behalf of Seller as to any matters which might influence or affect the decision to execute this Contract or to buy the Unit, or said personal property, except those representations and warranties which are specifically set forth in this Contract.

11. Possession: Seller shall, prior to the Closing, remove from the Unit all furniture, furnishings and other personal property not included in this sale, shall repair any damage caused by such removal, and shall deliver exclusive possession of the Unit at the Closing, vacant, broom-clean and free of tenancies or other rights of use or possession.

12. Access: Seller shall permit Purchaser and its architect, decorator or other authorized persons to have the right of access to the Unit between the date of hereof and the Closing for the purpose of inspecting the same and taking measurements, at reasonable times and upon reasonable prior notice to Seller (by telephone or otherwise). Further, Purchaser shall have the right to inspect the Unit at a reasonable time during the 24-hour period immediately preceding the Closing.

13. Defaults and Remedies: (a) If Purchaser defaults hereunder, Seller's sole remedy shall be to retain the Downpayment as liquidated damages, it being agreed that Seller's damages in case of Purchaser's default might be impossible to ascertain and that the Downpayment constitutes a fair and reasonable amount of damages under the circumstances and is not a penalty.

(b) If Seller defaults hereunder, Purchaser shall have such remedies as Purchaser shall be entitled to at law or in equity, including, but not limited to, specific performance.

14. Notices: Any notice, request or other communication ("Notice") given or made hereunder (except for the notice required by para. 12), shall be in writing and either (a) sent by any of the parties hereto or their respective attorneys, by registered or certified mail, return receipt requested, postage prepaid, or (b) delivered in person or by overnight courier, with receipt acknowledged, to the address given at the beginning of this Contract for the party to whom the Notice is to be given, or to such other address for such party as said party shall hereafter designate by Notice given to the other party pursuant to this para. 14. Each Notice mailed shall be deemed given on the third business day following the date of mailing the same and each Notice delivered in person or by overnight courier shall be deemed given when delivered.

15. Purchaser's Lien: The Downpayment and all other sums paid on account of this Contract and the reasonable expenses of the examination of title to, and departmental violation searches in respect of, the Unit are hereby made a lien upon the Unit, but such lien shall not continue after default by Purchaser hereunder.

16. Downpayment in Escrow: (a) Seller's attorney ("Escrowee") shall hold the Downpayment for Seller's account in escrow in a segregated bank account at the depository identified at the end of this Contract until Closing or sooner termination of this Contract and shall pay over or apply the Downpayment in accordance with the terms of this para. 16. Escrowee shall *(not) (Delete if inapplicable)* hold the Downpayment in an interest-bearing account for the benefit of the parties. If interest is held for the benefit of the parties, it shall be paid to the party entitled to the Downpayment and the party receiving the interest shall pay any income taxes thereon. If interest is not held for the benefit of the parities, the Downpayment shall be placed in an IOLA account or as otherwise permitted or required by law. The Social Security or Federal Identification numbers of the parties shall be furnished to Escrowee upon request. At Closing, the Downpayment shall be paid by Escrowee to Seller. If for any reason Closing does not occur and either party gives Notice (as defined in paragraph 14) to Escrowee demanding payment of the Downpayment, Escrowee shall give prompt Notice to the other party of such demand. If Escrowee does not receive Notice of objection from such other party to the proposed payment within 10 business days after the giving of such Notice, Escrowee is hereby authorized and directed to make such payment. If Escrowee does receive such Notice of objection within such 10 day period or if for any other reason Escrowee in good faith shall elect not to make such payment, Escrowee shall continue to hold such amount until otherwise

EXHIBIT 8.2
New York Contract of Sale—Condominium Unit   (continued)

directed by Notice from the parties to this Contract or a final, nonappealable judgment, order or decree of a court. However, Escrowee shall have the right at any time to deposit the Downpayment with the clerk of a court in the county in which the Unit is located and shall give Notice of such deposit to Seller and Purchaser. Upon such deposit or other disbursement in accordance with the terms of this para. 16, Escrowee shall be relieved and discharged of all further obligations and responsibilities hereunder.

(b) The parties acknowledge that, although Escrowee is holding the Downpayment for Seller's account, for all other purposes Escrowee is acting solely as a stakeholder at their request and for their convenience and that Escrowee shall not be liable to either party for any act or omission on its part unless taken or suffered in bad faith or in willful disregard of this Contract or involving gross negligence on the part of Escrowee. Seller and Purchaser jointly and severally agree to defend, indemnify and hold Escrowee harmless from and against all costs, claims and expenses (including reasonable attorneys' fees) incurred in connection with the performance of Escrowee's duties hereunder, except with respect to actions or omissions taken or suffered by Escrowee in bad faith or in willful disregard of this Contract or involving gross negligence on the part of Escrowee.

(c) Escrowee may act or refrain from acting in respect of any matter referred to herein in full reliance upon and with the advice of counsel which may be selected by it (including any member of its firm) and shall be fully protected in so acting or refraining from action upon the advice of such counsel.

(d) Escrowee acknowledges receipt of the Downpayment by check subject to collection and Escrowee's agreement to the provisions of this para. 16 by signing in the place indicated in this Contract.

(e) Escrowee or any member of its firm shall be permitted to act as counsel for Seller in any dispute as to the disbursement of the Downpayment or any other dispute between the parties whether or not Escrowee is in possession of the Downpayment and continues to act as Escrowee.

17. New York State Gains Tax: (a) Seller and Purchaser agree to comply in a timely manner with the requirements of article 31-B of the Tax Law and the regulations applicable thereto, as the same from time to time may be amended (collectively, the "Gains Tax Law"). Purchaser agrees to deliver to Seller a duly executed and acknowledged Transferee Questionnaire simultaneously with the execution of this Contract or within 5 business days after subsequent written request from Seller or Seller's attorney. At the Closing, Seller shall deliver (i) an Official Statement of No Tax Due or (ii) an Official Tentative Assessment and Return accompanied by a certified or official bank check drawn on any banking institution described in subpara. 3(b), payable to the order of the State Tax Commission, in the amount of the tax shown to be due thereon, or (iii) if applicable, a duly executed and acknowledged affidavit in form permitted under the Gains Tax Law claiming exemption therefrom.

(b) Seller agrees (i) to pay promptly any tax due under the Gains Tax Law and any interest and penalties thereon which may be assessed or due after the Closing, (ii) to indemnify and save Purchaser harmless from and against any of the foregoing and any cost, claim and expense (including reasonable attorneys' fees) incurred by Purchaser by reason of the non-payment thereof, and (iii) to make any other payments and execute, acknowledge and deliver such further documents as may be necessary to comply with the Gains Tax Law.

(c) The obligations under this para. 17 shall survive the Closing.

18. FIRPTA: Seller represents and warrants to Purchaser that Seller is not a "foreign person" as defined in IRC § 1445, as amended, and the regulations issued thereunder ("Code Withholding Section"). At the Closing Seller shall deliver to Purchaser a certification stating that Seller is not a foreign person in the form then required by the Code Withholding Section. In the event Seller fails to deliver the aforesaid certification or in the event that Purchaser is not entitled under the Code Withholding Section to rely on such certification, Purchaser shall deduct and withhold from the Purchase Price a sum equal to 10% thereof and shall at Closing remit the withheld amount with the required forms to the Internal Revenue Service.

19. Title Report; Acceptable Title: (a) Purchaser shall, promptly after the date hereof, or after receipt of the mortgage commitment letter, if applicable, order a title insurance report from the Title Company. Promptly after receipt of the title report and thereafter of any continuations thereof and supplements thereto, Purchaser shall forward a copy of each such report, continuation or supplement to the attorney for Seller. Purchaser shall further notify Seller's attorney of any other objections to title not reflected in such title report of which Purchaser becomes aware following the delivery of such report, reasonably promptly after becoming aware of such objections.

(b) Any unpaid taxes, assessments, water charges and sewer rents, together with the interest and penalties thereon to a date not less than two days following the date of Closing, and any other liens and encumbrances which Seller is obligated to pay and discharge or which are against corporations, estates or other persons in the chain of title, together with the cost of recording or filing any instruments necessary to discharge such liens and encumbrances of record, may be paid out of the proceeds of the monies payable at the Closing if Seller delivers to Purchaser at the Closing official bills for such taxes, assessments, water charges, sewer rents, interest and penalties and instruments in recordable form sufficient to discharge any other liens and encumbrances of record. Upon request made not less than 3 business days before the Closing, Purchaser shall provide at the Closing separate checks for the foregoing payable to the order of the holder of any such lien, charge or encumbrance and otherwise complying with subpara. 3(b). If the Title Company is willing to insure Purchaser that such charges, liens and encumbrances will not

be collected out of or enforced against the Unit and is willing to insure the lien of Purchaser's Institutional Lender (as hereinafter defined) free and clear of any such charges, liens and encumbrances, then Seller shall have the right in lieu of payment and discharge to deposit with the Title Company such funds or to give such assurances or to pay such special or additional premiums as the Title Company may require in order to so insure. In such case the charges, liens and encumbrances with respect to which the Title Company has agreed so to insure shall not be considered objections to title.

(c) Seller shall convey and Purchaser shall accept fee simple title to the Unit in accordance with the terms of this Contract, subject only to: (a) the Permitted Exceptions and (b) such other matters as (i) the Title Company or any other title insurer licensed to do business by the State of New York shall be willing, without special or additional premium, to omit as exceptions to coverage or to except with insurance against collection out of or enforcement against the Unit and (ii) shall be accepted by any lender described in RPL § 274-a ("Institutional Lender") which has committed in writing to provide mortgage financing to Purchaser for the purchase of the Unit ("Purchaser's Institutional Lender"), except that if such acceptance by Purchaser's Institutional Lender is unreasonably withheld or delayed, such acceptance shall be deemed to have been given.

(d) Notwithstanding any contrary provisions in this Contract, express or implied, or any contrary rule of law or custom, if Seller shall be unable to convey the Unit in accordance with this Contract (provided that Seller shall release, discharge or otherwise cure at or prior to Closing any matter created by Seller after the date hereof and any existing mortgage, unless this sale is subject to it) and if Purchaser elects not to complete this transaction without abatement of the Purchase Price, the sole obligation and liability of Seller shall be to refund the Downpayment to Purchaser, together with the reasonable cost of the examination of title to, and departmental violation searches in respect of, the Unit, and upon the making of such refund and payment, this Contract shall be deemed cancelled and of no further force or effect and neither party shall have any further rights against, or obligations or liabilities to, the other by reason of this Contract. However, nothing contained in this subpara. 19(d) shall be construed to relieve Seller from liability due to a willful default.

20. Risk of Loss; Casualty: (a) The risk of loss or damage to the Unit or the personal property included in this sale, by fire or other casualty, until the earlier of the Closing or possession of the Unit by Purchaser, is assumed by Seller, but without any obligation of Seller to repair or replace any such loss or damage unless Seller elects to do so as hereinafter provided. Seller shall notify Purchaser of the occurrence of any such loss or damage to the Unit or the personal property included in this sale within 10 days after such occurrence or by the date of Closing, whichever first occurs, and by such notice shall state whether or not Seller elects to repair or restore the Unit and/ or the personal property, as the case may be. If Seller elects to make such repairs and restorations, Seller's notice shall set forth an adjourned date for the Closing, which shall be not more than 60 days after the date of the giving of Seller's notice. If Seller either does not elect to do so or, having elected to make such repairs and restorations, fails to complete the same on or before said adjourned date for the Closing, Purchaser shall have the following options:

(i) To declare this Contract cancelled and of no further force or effect and receive a refund of the Downpayment in which event neither party shall thereafter have any further rights against, or obligations or liabilities to, the other by reason of this Contract; or

(ii) To complete the purchase in accordance with this Contract without reduction in the Purchase Price, except as provided in the next sentence. If Seller carries hazard insurance covering such loss or damage, Seller shall turn over to Purchaser at the Closing the net proceeds actually collected by Seller under the provisions of such hazard insurance policies to the extent that they are attributable to loss of or damage to any property included in this sale, less any sums theretofore expended by Seller in repairing or replacing such loss or damage or in collecting such proceeds; and Seller shall assign (without recourse to Seller) Seller's right to receive any additional insurance proceeds which are attributable to the loss of or damage to any property included in this sale.

(b) If Seller does not elect to make such repairs and restorations, Purchaser may exercise the resulting option under (i) or (ii) of (a) above only by notice given to Seller within 10 days after receipt of Seller's notice. If Seller elects to make such repairs and restorations and fails to complete the same on or before the adjourned closing date, Purchaser may exercise either of the resulting options within 10 days after the adjourned closing date.

(c) In the event of any loss of or damage to the Common Elements which materially and adversely affects access to or use of the Unit, arising after the date of this Contract but prior to the Closing, Seller shall notify Purchaser of the occurrence thereof within 10 days after such occurrence or by the date of Closing, whichever occurs first, in which event Purchaser shall have the following options:

(i) To complete the purchase in accordance with this Contract without reduction in the Purchase Price; or

(ii) To adjourn the Closing until the first to occur of (1) completion of the repair and restoration of the loss or damage to the point that there is no longer a materially adverse effect on the access to or use of the Unit or (2) the 60th day after the date of the giving of Seller's aforesaid notice. In the event Purchaser elects to adjourn the Closing as aforesaid and such loss or damage is not so repaired and restored within 60 days after the date of the giving of Seller's aforesaid notice, then Purchaser shall have the right either to (x) complete the purchase in accordance with this Contract without reduction in the Purchase Price or (y) declare this Contract cancelled and of no further force or effect and receive a refund of the Downpayment, in which latter event neither party shall thereafter have any further rights against, or obligations or liabilities to, the other by reason of this Contract.

EXHIBIT 8.2
New York Contract of Sale—Condominium Unit   (continued)

(d) In the event of any loss of or damage to the Common Elements which does not materially and adversely affect access to or use of the Unit, Purchaser shall accept title to the Unit in accordance with this Contract without abatement of the Purchase Price.

21. Internal Revenue Service Reporting Requirement: Each party shall execute, acknowledge and deliver to the other party such instruments, and take such other actions, as such other party may reasonably request in order to comply with IRC § 6045(e), as amended, or any successor provision or any regulations promulgated pursuant thereto, insofar as the same requires reporting of information in respect of real estate transactions. The provisions of this para. 21 shall survive the Closing. The parties designate

as the attorney responsible for reporting this information as required by law.

22. Broker: Seller and Purchaser represent and warrant to each other that the only broker with whom they have dealt in connection with this Contract and the transaction set forth herein is

and that they know of no other broker who has claimed or may have the right to claim a commission in connection with this transaction. The commission of such broker shall be paid by Seller pursuant to separate agreement. If no broker is specified above, the parties acknowledge that this Contract was brought about by direct negotiation between Seller and Purchaser and each represents to the other that it knows of no broker entitled to a commission in connection with this transaction. Seller and Purchaser shall indemnify and defend each other against any costs, claims or expenses (including reasonable attorneys' fees) arising out of the breach on their respective parts of any representation, warranty or agreement contained in this para. 22. The provisions of this para. 22 shall survive the Closing or, if the Closing does not occur, the termination of this Contract.

23. Mortgage Contingency: *(Delete if inapplicable)* The obligations of Purchaser hereunder are conditioned upon issuance on or before   (the "Commitment Date") of a written commitment from any Institutional Lender pursuant to which such Institutional Lender agrees to make a loan, other than a VA, FHA or other governmentally insured loan to Purchaser, at Purchaser's sole cost and expense, of

$ or such lesser sum as Purchaser shall be willing to accept, at the prevailing fixed rate of interest not to exceed   or initial adjustment rate of interest not to exceed   for a term of at least   years and on other customary commitment terms, whether or not conditioned upon any factors other than an appraisal satisfactory to the Institutional Lender, secured by a first mortgage on the Unit together with its undivided interest in the Common Elements. Purchaser shall (a) make prompt application to an Institutional Lender for such mortgage loan, (b) furnish accurate and complete information on

Purchaser and members of Purchaser's family, as required, (c) pay all fees, points and charges required in connection with such application and loan, (d) pursue such application with diligence, (e) cooperate in good faith with such Institutional Lender to the end of securing such first mortgage loan and (f) promptly give Notice to Seller of the name and address of each Institutional Lender to which Purchaser has made such application. Purchaser shall comply with all requirements of such commitment (or of any commitment accepted by Purchaser) and shall furnish Seller with a copy thereof promptly after receipt thereof. If such commitment is not issued on or before the Commitment Date, then, unless Purchaser has accepted a commitment that does not comply with the requirements set forth above, Purchaser may cancel this Contract by giving Notice to Seller within 5 business days after the Commitment Date, in which case this Contract shall be deemed cancelled and thereafter neither party shall have any further rights against, or obligations or liabilities to, the other by reason of this Contract except that the Downpayment shall be promptly refunded to Purchaser and except as set forth in para. 22. If Purchaser fails to give Notice of cancellation or if Purchaser shall accept a commitment that does not comply with the terms set forth above, then Purchaser shall be deemed to have waived Purchaser's right to cancel this Contract and to receive a refund of the Downpayment by reason of the contingency contained in this para. 23.

24. Gender, Etc.: As used in this Contract, the neuter includes the masculine and feminine, the singular includes the plural and the plural includes the singular, as the context may require.

25. Entire Contract: All prior understandings and agreements between Seller and Purchaser are merged in this Contract and this Contract supersedes any and all understandings and agreements between the parties and constitutes the entire agreement between them with respect to the subject matter hereof.

26. Captions: The captions in this Contract are for convenience and reference only and in no way define, limit or describe the scope of this Contract and shall not be considered in the interpretation of this Contract or any provision hereof.

27. No Assignment by Purchaser: Purchaser may not assign this Contract or any of Purchaser's rights hereunder.

28. Successors and Assigns: Subject to the provisions of para. 27, the provisions of this Contract shall bind and inure to the benefit of both Purchaser and Seller and their respective distributees, executors, administrators, heirs, legal representatives, successors and permitted assigns.

29. No Oral Changes: This Contract cannot be changed or terminated orally. Any changes or additional provisions must be set forth in a rider attached hereto or in a separate written agreement signed by both parties to this Contract.

30. Contract Not Binding Until Signed: This Contract shall not be binding or effective until properly executed and delivered by Seller and Purchaser.

𝕴𝖓 𝖂𝖎𝖙𝖓𝖊𝖘𝖘 𝖂𝖍𝖊𝖗𝖊𝖔𝖋, the parties hereto have duly executed this Contract on the day and year first above written.

Seller   (Soc. Sec. No.   )   Purchaser   (Soc. Sec. No.   )

Seller   (Soc. Sec. No.   )   Purchaser   (Soc. Sec. No.   )

Agreed to as to para. 16:_____   Escrow Depository:_____
                         Escrowee

SCHEDULE A — Permitted Exceptions

1. Zoning laws and regulations and landmark, historic or wetlands designation which are not violated by the Unit and which are not violated by the Common Elements to the extent that access to or use of the Unit would be materially and adversely affected.

2. Consents for the erection of any structure or structures on, under or above any street or streets on which the Building may abut.

3. The terms, burdens, covenants, restrictions, conditions, easements and rules and regulations set forth in the Declaration, By-Laws and rules and regulations of the Condominium, the Power of Attorney from Purchaser to the board of managers of the Condominium and the floor plans of the Condominium, all as may be amended from time to time.

4. Rights of utility companies to lay, maintain, install and repair pipes, lines, poles, conduits, cable boxes and related equipment on, over and under the Building and Common Elements, provided that none of such rights imposes any monetary obligation on the owner of the Unit or materially interferes with the use of or access to the Unit.

5. Encroachments of stoops, areas, cellar steps, trim, cornices, lintels, window sills, awnings, canopies, ledges, fences, hedges, coping and retaining walls projecting from the Building over any street or highway or over any adjoining property and encroachments of similar elements projecting from adjoining property over the Common Elements.

6. Any state of facts which an accurate survey or personal inspection of the Building, Common Elements or Unit would disclose, provided that such facts do not prevent the use of the Unit for dwelling purposes. For the purposes of this Contract, none of the facts shown on the survey, if any, identified below, shall be deemed to prevent the use of the Unit for dwelling purposes, and Purchaser shall accept title subject thereto.

7. The lien of any unpaid common charge, real estate tax, water charge, sewer rent or vault charge, provided the same are paid or apportioned at the Closing as herein provided.

8. The lien of any unpaid assessments to the extent of installments thereof payable after the Closing.

9. Liens, encumbrances and title conditions affecting the Common Elements which do not materially and adversely affect the right of the Unit owner to use and enjoy the Common Elements.

10. Notes or notices of violations of law or governmental orders, ordinances or requirements (a) affecting the Unit and noted or issued subsequent to the date of this Contract by any governmental department, agency or bureau having jurisdiction and (b) any such notes or notices affecting only the Common Elements which were noted or issued prior to or on the date of this Contract or at any time hereafter.

11. Any other matters or encumbrances subject to which Purchaser is required to accept title to the Unit pursuant to this Contract.

The survey referred to in No. 6 above was prepared by
dated   19   and last revised   19

EXHIBIT 8.3
New York Contract of Sale—Cooperative Apartment

M 123—Contract of sale of cooperative apartment, 10-89.   Distributed by Julius Blumberg, Inc.
NYC 10013

Blumbergs Law Products

Prepared by The Committee on Condominiums and Cooperatives of the Real Property Section of the New York State Bar Association.

CONSULT YOUR LAWYER BEFORE SIGNING THIS AGREEMENT

Contract of Sale — Cooperative Apartment

This Contract is made as of   between the **"Seller"** and the **"Purchaser"** identified below.

1. Certain Definitions and Information

1.1 The "Parties" are:

Seller:

Address:

Prior names used by Seller:

Soc. Sec. No.

Purchaser:

Address:

Soc. Sec. No.

1.2. The "Attorneys" are *(name, address and telephone)*:

For Seller:

For Purchaser:

1.3 The "Escrowee" is *(name, address and telephone)*

1.4 The "Managing Agent" is *(name, address and telephone)*

1.5 The name of the cooperative housing corporation ("Corporation") is

1.6 The "Unit" number is

1.7 The Unit is located in "Premises" known as

1.8 The "Shares" are the   shares of the Corporation allocated to the Unit.

1.9 The "Lease" is the proprietary lease for the Unit given by the Corporation.

1.10 The "Broker" (see Par. 12) is

1.11 The "Closing" is the transfer of ownership of the Shares and Lease, which is scheduled to occur on
         19   at   M. (see Pars. 9 and 10)

1.12 The "Purchase Price" is $

1.12.1 the "Contract Deposit" is $

1.12.2 the "Balance" of the Purchase Price due at Closing is $ (see Par. 2)

1.13 The "Maintenance" charge is the rent payable under the Lease which at the date of this Contract is in the monthly amount of $ (see Par. 4)

1.14 The "Assessment" is the additional rent payable under the Lease which at the date of this Contract is $ payable as follows:

1.15 The Party upon whom the Corporation imposes a "Flip Tax" or similar transfer fee, if any, is   (see Par. 11.3)

1.16 If Par. 19 (Financing Contingency) applies:

1.16.1 the "Loan Terms" are:

Amount Financed: $ or any lower amount applied for or acceptable to Purchaser.

Payment Terms and Charges: The customary payment terms (including prevailing fixed or adjustable interest rate, prepayment provisions and maturity) and charges (including points, origination and other fees) then currently being offered to purchasers of cooperative apartments by the Institutional Lender (defined in Par. 19.5.1) to which Purchaser applies.

Security: Pledge of the Shares and Lease.

1.16.2 the period for Purchaser to obtain a Loan Commitment Letter is   business days after a fully executed counterpart of this Contract is given to Purchaser.

1.17 The "Proposed Occupants" of the Unit are the following:

1.17.1 persons and relationship to Purchaser:

1.17.2 pets:

1.18 The Contract Deposit shall be held in a   interest bearing escrow account. Interest shall be payable to the   The escrow account shall be a   type account held at   (See Par. 28)

2. Agreement to Sell and Purchase; Purchase Price; Escrow

2.1 Seller agrees to sell and assign to Purchaser, and Purchaser agrees to purchase and assume from Seller, the Seller's Shares and Lease for the Purchase Price and upon the other terms and conditions stated in this Contract.

2.2 The Purchase Price is payable to Seller by Purchaser as follows:

2.2.1 the Contract Deposit at the time of signing this Contract, by Purchaser's collectible check to the order of Escrowee.

2.2.2 the Balance at Closing, only by cashier's, official bank or certified check of Purchaser made payable to the direct order of Seller. These checks shall be drawn on and payable by a branch of a commercial or savings bank, savings and loan association or trust company located in the same City or County as the Unit. Seller may direct, on not less than 3 business days' Notice (defined in Par. 17) prior to Closing, that all or a portion of the Balance shall be made payable to persons other than Seller.

3. Personal Property

3.1 Subject to any rights of the Corporation or any holder of a mortgage to which the Lease is subordinate, this sale includes all of Seller's ownership, if any, of the following "Property" to the extent existing in the Unit on the date hereof: the refrigerator, freezer, range, oven, microwave oven, dishwasher, cabinets and counters, lighting fixtures, chandeliers, wall-to-wall carpeting, plumbing fixtures, central air-conditioning and/or window or sleeve units, washing machine, dryer, screens and storm windows, window treatments, switch plates, door hardware, built-ins not excluded in Par. 3.2 and

3.2 Specifically excluded from this sale is all personalty not included in Par. 3.1 and

---

EXHIBIT 8.3
New York Contract of Sale—Cooperative Apartment   (continued)

3.3 The Property shall not be purchased if Closing does not occur.

3.4 No consideration is being paid for the Property. Seller makes no representation as to the condition of the Property. Purchaser shall take the Property "as is" on the date of this Contract, except for reasonable wear and tear, and except further, the appliances shall be in working order at Closing.

3.5 At or prior to the time of Closing, Seller shall remove from the Unit all the furniture, furnishings and other personalty not included in this sale, and repair any damage caused by such removal.

4. Representations and Covenants

4.1 Subject to any matter affecting title to the Premises (as to which Seller makes no representations or covenants), Seller represents and covenants that:

4.1.1 Seller is and shall at Closing be the sole owner of the Shares and Lease with the full right and power to sell and assign them;

4.1.2 the Shares and Lease will at Closing be free and clear of liens (other than the Corporation's general lien on the Shares, for which no monies shall be owed), encumbrances and adverse interests ("Liens"); or Seller will deliver to Purchaser at Closing all requisite terminations, releases and/or satisfactions executed in form suitable for filing and/or recording, so as to remove of record, at Seller's expense, any such Liens;

4.1.3 the Shares were duly issued, fully paid for and are non-assessable;

4.1.4 the Lease is, and will at Closing be, in full force and effect and no notice of default under the Lease will be in effect at Closing;

4.1.5 the Maintenance and Assessments payable as of the date hereof are as specified in Pars. 1.13 and 1.14. All sums due to the Corporation will be fully paid by Seller to the end of the payment period immediately preceding the date of Closing;

4.1.6 as of this date, Seller neither has actual knowledge nor has received any written notice of (a) any increase in Maintenance or (b) any proposed Assessment which has been either adopted or is under consideration by the Board of Directors of the Corporation and not reflected in the amounts set forth in Pars. 1.13 and 1.14;

4.1.7 Seller will not at Closing be indebted for labor or material which might result in the filing of a notice of mechanic's lien against the Unit or the Premises;

4.1.8 there are and at closing will be no violations of record which the owner of the Shares and Lease would be obligated to remedy under the terms of the Lease;

4.1.9 Seller has not made any alterations or additions to the Unit, without any required consent of the Corporation;

4.1.10 Seller has not entered and will not enter into, and has no actual knowledge of, any agreement (other than the Lease) affecting the use and/or occupancy of the Unit which would be binding on or adversely affect Purchaser; and

4.1.11 Seller has been known by no other name for the past 10 years except as set forth in Par. 1.1.

4.2 Purchaser represents and covenants that Purchaser is acquiring the Shares and Lease solely for residential occupancy of the Unit by the Proposed Occupants only and will so represent to the Corporation in connection with Purchaser's application to the Corporation for approval of this transaction by the Corporation.

4.3 The representations and covenants contained in Par. 4.1 shall survive Closing, but any action based thereon must be instituted within 1 year from Closing.

5. Corporate Documents

Purchaser has examined and is satisfied with or has waived the examination of the Lease, and the Corporation's certificate of incorporation, bylaws, house rules, most recent audited financial statement and most recent statement of tax deductions available to the Corporation's shareholders under Internal Revenue Code ("IRC") § 216 (or any successor statute).

6. Required Approval and References

6.1 This sale is subject to the approval of the Corporation.

6.2 Purchaser shall in good faith:

6.2.1 submit to the Corporation or its Managing Agent, within 10 business days after the receipt of a fully executed counterpart of this Contract, an application for approval of this sale on the form required by the Corporation containing such data and together with such documents as the Corporation reasonably requires except for the Loan Commitment Letter (defined in Par. 19.5.2), if applicable, which shall be submitted by Purchaser within 3 business days after it is obtained;

6.2.2 attend (and cause any person who will reside in the Unit to attend) one or more personal interviews, as requested by the Corporation; and

6.2.3 promptly submit to the Corporation such further references, data and documents reasonably requested by the Corporation.

6.3 Either Party, after learning of the approval or denial by the Corporation of the application, shall promptly send Notice to the other Party of the Corporation's decision. If approval or denial has not been issued on or before the date set for Closing, the Closing shall be adjourned for 30 business days for the purpose of obtaining such approval unless otherwise agreed to by the Parties. If the approval of this sale is not obtained by said adjourned date, either Party may cancel this Contract on Notice to the other provided that the Corporation's approval is not issued before Notice of cancellation is given. In the event of a denial other than for Purchaser's bad faith

conduct, this contract shall be deemed cancelled. In the event of cancellation pursuant to this Par. 6, the Escrowee shall refund the Contract Deposit to Purchaser. In case of a denial or lack of approval due to Purchaser's bad faith conduct, Purchaser shall be in default and Par. 13.1 shall govern.

7. Condition of Unit and Possession

7.1 Seller makes no representation as to the condition of the Unit. Purchaser has inspected the Unit and shall take the same "as is", on the date of this Contract, reasonable wear and tear excepted.

7.2 Seller shall deliver possession of the Unit at the Closing, vacant, broom-clean and free of all occupants and rights of possession.

8. Risk of Loss

8.1 While Seller has legal title and is in possession of the Unit, Seller assumes all risk of loss or damage ("Loss") to the Unit and Property from fire or other cause not due to the fault of Purchaser or Purchaser's contractors, agents or servants. In the event of a Loss, Seller shall have the option (but not the obligation) to restore the Unit and Property to as near as reasonably possible to the condition immediately prior to the Loss.

8.2 Within 10 calendar days after the Loss occurs, Seller shall give Notice to Purchaser of the Loss and whether or not Seller elects to restore ("Election Notice").

8.3 If Seller elects to restore, Seller must do so within 60 calendar days after sending the Election Notice or by the Closing, whichever is later ("Restoration Period").

8.4 If the Closing is before such 60 calendar day period expires, then the Closing shall be adjourned to a date and time fixed by Seller on not less than 10 calendar days' prior Notice to Purchaser, but in no event shall the Closing be adjourned for more than 70 calendar days after giving of the Election Notice.

8.5 If Seller elects not to restore or fails, in a timely manner, to send the Election Notice or, having sent the Notice, Seller fails to complete the restoration within the Restoration Period, then Purchaser's sole remedy is either to:

8.5.1 cancel this Contract in accordance with Par. 16 and recover all sums theretofore paid on account of the Purchase Price; or

8.5.2 complete the purchase in accordance with this Contract, without reduction in the Purchase Price or claim against Seller, but with the right to receive any "Net Insurance Proceeds" as defined in Par. 8.6 together with an assignment to Purchaser, without recourse to Seller, of any uncollected proceeds, which assignment shall be delivered by Seller at Closing.

8.6 "Net Insurance Proceeds" are proceeds of Seller's insurance covering the Loss which is attributable to the Unit and Property after deducting legal and other collection expenses incurred by Seller and any sums paid or incurred by Seller for restoration.

8.7 If Purchaser fails to exercise one of Purchaser's options pursuant to Par. 8.5 by Notice to Seller within 7 business days after Seller gives the Election Notice or within 7 business days after the Restoration Period expires (in the event Seller fails to complete the restoration within the Restoration Period), then Purchaser will be deemed to have conclusively elected the option to complete the purchase pursuant to Par. 8.5.2.

8.8 If Purchaser is given possession of the Unit prior to Closing:

8.8.1 Purchaser assumes all risk of Loss to the Unit and Property prior to Closing from fire or other cause not the fault of Seller or Seller's contractors, agents, employees or servants; and

8.8.2 Purchaser shall be obligated to complete the purchase in accordance with this Contract, without reduction in the Purchase Price or claim against Seller and without delay.

8.9 Notwithstanding anything to the contrary in Par. 8.1, Purchaser shall have the right to cancel this Contract in accordance with Par. 16 if, prior to Closing and while Seller is in possession, through no fault of Purchaser or Purchaser's contractors, agents, employees and servants, either:

8.9.1 a Loss occurs to the Unit which would cost more than 10% of the Purchase Price to restore; or

8.9.2 more than 10% of the units in the Premises are damaged and rendered uninhabitable by fire or other cause, regardless of whether the Unit is damaged.

8.10 Purchaser shall be deemed to have waived Purchaser's right to cancel under Par. 8.9 if Purchaser fails to elect to cancel by Notice to Seller given within 7 business days after Seller gives Notice to Purchaser of the event which gives rise to Purchaser's right to cancel. In the event Purchaser waives or is deemed to have waived this right to cancel, the provisions of Par. 8.5.2 shall apply.

9. Closing Location

The Closing shall be held at the location designated by the Corporation, or (if none is designated), at the office of Seller's attorney.

10. Closing

10.1 At Closing, Seller shall deliver:

10.1.1 Seller's certificate for the Shares duly endorsed for transfer to Purchaser or accompanied by a separate duly executed stock power to Purchaser, and in either case, with any guarantee of Seller's signature required by the Corporation;

10.1.2 Seller's counterpart original of the Lease and a duly executed assignment thereof to Purchaser in the form required by the Corporation;

10.1.3 a written statement by an officer of the Corporation or its authorized agent consenting to the transfer of the Shares and Lease to Purchaser and setting forth the amounts and payment status of the Maintenance and any Assessments;

EXHIBIT 8.3
New York Contract of Sale—Cooperative Apartment   (continued)

10.1.4 executed FIRPTA document(s) (defined in Par. 26);

10.1.5 keys to the Unit, building entrances, garage, mailbox and any locks in the Unit;

10.1.6 if requested, an assignment to Purchaser of Seller's interest in the Property;

10.1.7 Net Insurance Proceeds and/or assignment of any uncollected Net Insurance Proceeds, if applicable; and

10.1.8 instruments or other documents required under Par. 4.1.2, if any.

10.2 At Closing, Purchaser shall:

10.2.1 pay the Balance in accordance with Par. 2.2.2;

10.2.2 execute and deliver to Seller and the Corporation an agreement assuming the Lease, in the form required by the Corporation; and

10.2.3 if requested by the Corporation, execute and deliver counterparts of a new lease substantially the same as the Lease, for the balance of the Lease term, in which case the Lease shall be cancelled and surrendered to the Corporation together with Seller's assignment thereof to Purchaser.

10.3 At Closing, the Parties shall provide the information necessary for Internal Revenue Service ("IRS") Form 1099-S or other similar form required.

10.4 At Closing, Seller shall provide, and the Parties shall execute, all documents necessary to comply with any applicable transfer and/or gains tax filings.

11. Closing Fees, Taxes and Apportionments

11.1 At Closing, Seller shall pay, if applicable:

11.1.1 the processing fee(s) of the Corporation, its attorneys, and/or agents, except as set forth in Par. 11.2.3;

11.1.2 the cost of stock transfer stamps; and

11.1.3 the transfer tax and transfer gains tax, except a transfer tax which by its terms imposes primary liability on the purchaser.

11.2 At Closing, Purchaser shall pay:

11.2.1 the sales taxes, if any, on this sale, other than the transfer stamps as provided for in Par. 11.1.2;

11.2.2 the cost of any title search;

11.2.3 any fee to the Corporation or its agents and/or attorneys relating to Purchaser's financing; and

11.2.4 a transfer tax which by law is primarily imposed on the purchaser.

11.3 At Closing, the Flip Tax, if any, shall be paid by the Party specified in Par. 1.15.

11.4 At Closing, the Parties shall apportion as of 11:59 P.M. of the day preceding the Closing, the Maintenance and any other periodic charges due the Corporation (other than Assessments).

11.5 Assessments, whether payable in a lump sum or installments, shall not be apportioned, but shall be paid by the Party who is the owner of the Shares on the date specified by the Corporation for payment. Purchaser shall pay any installments payable after Closing provided Seller had the right to and elected to pay the Assessment in installments.

11.6 Each party covenants to the other that it will timely pay any taxes for which it is primarily liable pursuant to law. This Par. 11.6 shall survive Closing.

12. Broker

12.1 Each Party represents to the other that such Party has not dealt with any other person acting as a broker, whether licensed or unlicensed, in connection with this transaction other than the Broker named in Par. 1.10.

12.2 Seller shall pay the Broker's commission pursuant to a separate agreement. The Broker shall not be deemed to be a third-party beneficiary of this provision.

12.3 This Par. 12 shall survive the Closing.

13. Defaults, Remedies and Indemnities

13.1 In the event of a default or misrepresentation by Purchaser, Seller's sole remedy shall be to terminate this Contract and retain the Contract Deposit as liquidated damages, except there shall be no limitation on Seller's remedies for a breach of Par. 12.1. In case of Purchaser's misrepresentation or default, Seller's damages would be impossible to ascertain and the Contract Deposit constitutes a fair and reasonable amount of compensation.

13.2 In the event of a default or misrepresentation by Seller, Purchaser shall have such remedies as Purchaser is entitled to at law or in equity, including specific performance, because the Unit and possession thereof cannot be duplicated.

13.3 Each Party indemnifies and holds harmless the other against and from any claim, judgment, loss, liability, cost or expense resulting from the indemnitor's breach of any of the representations or covenants stated to survive Closing. This indemnity includes, without limitation, reasonable attorneys' fees and disbursements, court costs and litigation expenses. This Par. 13.3 shall survive the Closing.

13.4 Purchaser indemnifies and holds harmless Seller against and from any claim, judgment, loss, cost or expense resulting from the Lease obligations assumed by Purchaser. This indemnity includes, without limitation, reasonable attorneys' fees and disbursements, court costs and litigation expenses. This indemnity does not include or excuse a breach of any representation or covenant by Seller in Par. 4.1. This Par. 13.4 shall survive the Closing.

13.5 In the event any instrument for the payment of the Contract Deposit fails of collection, Seller shall have the right to sue on the uncollected instrument. In addition, such failure of collection shall be a default under this Contract, provided Seller gives Purchaser

Notice of such failure of collection and, within 3 business days after Notice is given, Escrowee does not receive from Purchaser an unendorsed certified check, bank check or immediately available funds in the amount of the uncollected funds. Failure to cure such default shall entitle Seller to the remedy in Par. 13.1 and to retain all sums as may be collected and/or recovered.

14. Entire Agreement; Modification

14.1 All prior oral or written representations, understandings and agreements had between the Parties with respect to the subject matter of this Contract, and with the Escrowee as to Par. 28, are merged in this Contract, which alone fully and completely expresses their agreement.

14.2 A provision of this Contract may be changed or waived only in writing signed by the Party (or Escrowee) to be charged.

14.3 The Attorneys may extend in writing any of the time limitations stated in this Contract.

15. No Assignment by Purchaser

15.1 Purchaser may not assign this Contract or any of Purchaser's rights hereunder and any purported assignment shall be null and void.

15.2 This Contract shall bind and inure to the benefit of the Parties hereto and their respective heirs, personal and legal representatives and successors in interest.

16. Cancellation for Other than Default or Misrepresentation

If Seller shall be unable to transfer the Lease and the Shares in accordance with this Contract for any reason not due to Seller's willful acts or omissions, then the sole obligation of Seller shall be to refund to Purchaser the Contract Deposit and reimburse Purchaser for the actual costs incurred for Purchaser's title or abstract search, except such reimbursement shall not be required if a cancellation is pursuant to Par. 6 or 19. Upon making such refund, this Contract shall be cancelled and neither Party shall have any further claim against the other hereunder.

17. Notices

17.1 Any notice or demand ("Notice") shall be in writing and either delivered by hand or overnight delivery or sent by certified or registered mail to the Party and simultaneously, in like manner, to such Party's Attorney, if any, and to Escrowee at the addresses set forth in Par. 1, or to such other address as shall hereafter be designated by Notice given pursuant to this Par. 17.

17.2 Each Notice shall be deemed given on the same day if delivered by hand or on the following business day if sent by overnight delivery, or the second business day following the date of mailing.

17.3 The Attorneys are authorized to give any Notice specified in this Contract on behalf of their respective clients.

17.4 Failure to accept a Notice does not invalidate the Notice.

18. Margin Headings

The margin headings do not constitute part of the text of this Contract.

19. Financing Contingency *(delete if inapplicable)*

19.1 Purchaser may cancel this Contract and recover the Contract Deposit by following the procedure in Par. 19.4 if after complying with Purchaser's "Financing Obligations" in Par. 19.2 below and Purchaser's other obligations under this Contract:

19.1.1 Purchaser fails through no fault of Purchaser to obtain from an "Institutional Lender" (defined in Par. 19.5.1) a "Loan Commitment Letter" (defined in Par. 19.5.2) for financing on the Loan Terms and within the time period stated in Par. 1.16 (the "Loan"); or

19.1.2 the Institutional Lender and the Corporation cannot agree on the terms of an agreement for the protection of the Institutional Lender (commonly called a recognition agreement), if required by the Institutional Lender.

19.2 Purchaser's right to cancel under Par. 19.1 and recover the Contract Deposit is conditioned upon Purchaser's diligent compliance with all of the following "Financing Obligations":

19.2.1 Purchaser must apply in good faith for the Loan from an Institutional Lender within 7 business days after a fully executed counterpart of this Contract is given to Purchaser;

19.2.2 the Loan application must contain truthful, accurate and complete information as required by the Institutional Lender; and

19.2.3 Purchaser must comply with all requirements of the Institutional Lender to obtain the Loan Commitment Letter and to close the Loan.

19.3 Purchaser may also cancel this Contract and recover the Contract Deposit in accordance with the procedure in Par. 19.4 if:

19.3.1 the Closing is adjourned by Seller or the Corporation for for more than 30 business days from the date set for Closing in Par. 1.11; and

19.3.2 the Loan Commitment Letter expires on a date more than 30 business days after the date set for Closing in Par. 1.11 and before the new date set for Closing pursuant to Par. 19.3.1; or

19.3.3 Purchaser is unable in good faith to obtain from the Institutional Lender an extension or a new Loan Commitment Letter for the Amount Financed stated in Par. 1.16 or the same principal amount stated in the expired Loan Commitment Letter, whichever is lower, without paying any additional fees to the Institutional Lender (unless Seller, within 5 business days after receipt of Notice of such fees, gives Notice that Seller will pay such fees and pays them when due). All other substantive Loan terms may be materially no less favorable than in the expired Loan Commitment Letter.

19.4 In order to cancel pursuant to Par. 19.1 or 19.3, Purchaser shall give Notice of cancellation to Seller within 7 business days after the right to cancel arises. **Purchaser's failure to timely give such Notice of cancellation will be deemed a conclusive waiver of such right to cancel.** In case of cancellation pursuant to Par. 19.1, a copy of any

EXHIBIT 8.3
New York Contract of Sale—Cooperative Apartment   (continued)

loan refusal letter or non-complying Loan Commitment Letter (as the case may be) issued by the Institutional Lender shall accompany the Notice of cancellation, if available, or if not then available, shall be provided promptly after receipt. In case of cancellation pursuant to Par. 19.3, a copy of all written communications between the Institutional Lender and Purchaser concerning the extension or new loan commitment shall accompany the Notice of cancellation (or a copy of any letter refusing to extend the loan commitment or make a new loan commitment received by Purchaser after sending the cancellation Notice shall be sent to Seller promptly after receipt). Purchaser's obligation under this Par. 19.4 shall survive the cancellation of this Contract.

19.5 The definitions for certain terms used in this Par. 19 are:

19.5.1 an "Institutional Lender" is any bank, savings bank, savings and loan association, trust company, credit union of which Purchaser is a member, insurance company or governmental entity which is duly authorized to issue a loan secured by the Shares and Lease in the state where the Unit is located and is then currently extending similarly secured loan commitments; and

19.5.2 a "Loan Commitment Letter" is a written offer to make the Loan with or without recourse, and whether or not conditional upon any factor other than an appraisal satisfactory to the Institutional Lender. An offer to make the Loan which is conditional on obtaining a satisfactory appraisal shall only become a Loan Commitment Letter upon such condition being met.

20. Singular/Plural and Joint/Several

The use of the singular shall be deemed to include the plural, and vice versa, whenever the context so requires. If more than one entity is selling or purchasing the Unit, their obligations shall be joint and several.

21. No Survival

No representation and/or covenant contained herein shall survive Closing except as expressly provided. Computational errors shall survive and be corrected after Closing.

22. Inspections

Purchaser shall have the right to inspect the Unit at reasonable times upon reasonable request to Seller, and within 48 hours prior to Closing.

23. Governing Law

This Contract shall be governed by the laws of the State of New York. Any action or proceeding arising out of this Contract shall be brought in the county where the Unit is located and the Parties hereby consent to said venue.

24. Removal of Liens

24.1 Purchaser shall deliver or cause to be delivered to Seller or Seller's Attorney, not less than 10 calendar days prior to Closing, a list of Liens, if any, which may violate Par. 4.1.

24.2 Seller shall have a reasonable period of time to remove any such Lien.

25. Cooperation of Parties

25.1 The Parties shall each cooperate with the other, the Corporation, Purchaser's Institutional Lender and title company, if any, and obtain, execute and deliver such documents as are reasonably necessary to close.

25.2 The Parties shall timely file or pre-file all required documents in connection with all governmental filings that are required by law. Each Party represents to the other that its statements in such filings will be true and complete. This Par. 25.2 shall survive the Closing.

26. FIRPTA and Gains Tax

26.1 The Parties shall comply with IRC §§ 897, 1445 and related provisions, as amended, and any substitute provisions of any successor statute and the regulations thereunder ("FIRPTA"). The Seller shall furnish to the Purchaser at or prior to Closing a Certification of Nonforeign Status in accordance with FIRPTA. If the Seller fails to deliver such certification by Closing, the Purchaser shall deduct and withhold from the Purchase Price such sum required by law and remit such amount to the IRS. In the event of such withholding by Purchaser, Seller's obligations hereunder, including (but not limited to) the transfer of ownership of the Shares and Lease, shall not be excused or otherwise affected. In the event of any claimed over-withholding, Seller shall be limited solely to an

action against the IRS for a refund. Seller hereby waives any right of action against Purchaser on account of such withholding. This Par. 26.1 shall survive the Closing.

26.2 If a Real Property Transfer Gains Tax pre-filing is required by law, Purchaser shall simultaneously herewith deliver to Seller a completed and executed Transferee Questionnaire or the equivalent thereof.

27. Additional Conditions

27.1 Purchaser shall not be obligated to close unless at the time of the Closing:

27.1.1 the Corporation is duly incorporated and in good standing; and

27.1.2 the Corporation has fee or leasehold title to the Premises, whether or not marketable or insurable; and

27.1.3 there is no pending *in rem* action or foreclosure action of any underlying mortgage affecting the Premises.

27.2 Purchaser shall give Seller Notice of any failure of any of the conditions in Par. 27.1. If any condition in Par. 27.1 is not true and is not cured within a reasonable period of time after giving said Notice, then either Seller or Purchaser shall have the option to cancel this Contract pursuant to Par. 16.

28. Escrow Terms

28.1 Escrowee acknowledges receipt of the check for the Contract Deposit, subject to collection.

28.2 The check for the Contract Deposit shall be deposited by Escrowee in an escrow account as described in Par. 1.18 and the proceeds held and disbursed in accordance with the terms of this Contract. Upon Closing, Escrowee shall deliver the Contract Deposit to Seller. In all other cases, if either Party makes a demand upon Escrowee for delivery of the Contract Deposit, Escrowee shall give Notice to the other Party of such demand. If a Notice of objection to the proposed payment is not received from the other Party within 7 business days after the giving of Notice by Escrowee, time being of the essence, Escrowee is hereby authorized to deliver the Contract Deposit to the Party who made the demand. If Escrowee receives a Notice of objection within said period, or if for any other reason Escrowee in good faith elects not to deliver the Contract Deposit, then Escrowee shall continue to hold the Contract Deposit and thereafter pay it to the Party entitled when Escrowee receives (a) a Notice from the objecting Party withdrawing the objection, or (b) a Notice signed by both Parties directing disposition of the Contract Deposit or (c) a judgment or order of a court of competent jurisdiction.

28.3 In the event of any dispute or doubt as to the genuineness of any document or signature, or uncertainty as to Escrowee's duties, then Escrowee shall have the right either to continue to hold the Contract Deposit in escrow or to pay the Contract Deposit into court pursuant to relevant statute.

28.4 The parties agree jointly to defend (by attorneys selected by Escrowee), indemnify and hold harmless Escrowee against and from any claim, judgment, loss, liability, cost or expense resulting from any dispute or litigation arising out of or concerning Escrowee's duties or services hereunder. This indemnity includes, without limitation, disbursements and reasonable attorneys' fees either paid to retain attorneys or representing the fair value of legal services rendered by Escrowee to itself.

28.5 Escrowee shall not be liable for any error in judgment or for any act done or step taken or omitted in good faith, or for any mistake of fact or law, except for Escrowee's own gross negligence or willful misconduct.

28.6 The Parties acknowledge that Escrowee is merely a stakeholder. Upon payment of the Contract Deposit pursuant to Par. 28.2 or 28.3, Escrowee shall be fully released from all liability and obligations with respect to the Contract Deposit.

28.7 In the event Escrowee is the attorney for either Party, Escrowee shall be entitled to represent such Party in any lawsuit.

28.8 Escrowee shall serve without compensation.

28.9 The signing of this Contract by Escrowee is only to evidence Escrowee's acceptance of the terms and conditions of this Par. 28.

29. Binding Effect

This Contract shall not be binding unless a fully executed counterpart thereof has been delivered to each of the Parties.

In Witness Whereof, the Parties hereto have duly executed this Contract as of the date first above written.

ESCROW TERMS AGREED TO:	SELLER:	PURCHASER:
_____	_____	_____
Escrowee		
	_____	_____

EXHIBIT 8.4
New York Contract of Sale—Commercial

154 Contract of sale for New York office, commercial and multi-family residential premises. 1–86.

Distributed by Julius Blumberg, Inc.
NYC 10013

Prepared by the Real Property Committee of the Association of the Bar of the City of New York.

NOTE: This form is intended to cover matters common to most transactions. Provisions should be added, altered or deleted to suit the circumstances of a particular transaction.

Contract of Sale — Office, Commercial and Multi-Family Residential Premises

Table of Contents

CONTRACT dated   19   between

("Seller") and

("Purchaser").

Seller and Purchaser hereby covenant and agree as follows:

Section 1. Sale of Premises and Acceptable Title

§1.01. Seller shall sell to Purchaser, and Purchaser shall purchase from Seller, at the price and upon the terms and conditions set forth in this contract: (a) the parcel of land more particularly described in Schedule A attached hereto ("Land"); (b) all buildings and improvements situated on the Land (collectively, "Building"); (c) all right, title and interest of Seller, if any, in and to the land lying in the bed of any street or highway in front of or adjoining the Land to the center line thereof and to any unpaid award for any taking by condemnation or any damage to the Land by reason of a change of grade of any street or highway; (d) the appurtenances and all the estate and rights of Seller in and to the Land and Building; and (e) all right, title and interest of Seller, if any, in and to the fixtures, equipment and o ..er personal property attached or appurtenant to the Building (collectively, "Premises"). The Premises are located at or known as

§1.02. Seller shall convey and Purchaser shall accept fee simple title to the Premises in accordance with the terms of this contract, subject only to: (a) the matters set forth in Schedule B attached hereto (collectively, "Permitted Exceptions"); and (b) such other matters as (i) the title insurer specified in Schedule D attached hereto (or if none is so specified, then any title insurer licensed to do business by the State of New York) shall be willing, without special premium, to omit as exceptions to coverage or to except with insurance against collection out of or enforcement against the Premises and (ii) shall be accepted by any lender described in Section 274-a of the Real Property Law ("Institutional Lender") which has committed in writing to provide mortgage financing to Purchaser for the purchase of the Premises ("Purchaser's Institutional Lender"), except that if such acceptance by Purchaser's Institutional Lender is unreasonably withheld or delayed, such acceptance shall be deemed to have been given.

Section 2. Purchase Price, Acceptable Funds, Existing Mortgages, Purchase Money Mortgage, Escrow of Downpayment and Foreign Persons

§2.01. The purchase price ("Purchase Price") to be paid by Purchaser to Seller for the Premises as provided in Schedule C attached hereto is $

§2.02. All monies payable under this contract, unless otherwise specified in this contract, shall be paid by (a) certified checks of Purchaser or any person making a purchase money loan to Purchaser drawn on any bank, savings bank, trust company or savings and loan association having a banking office in the State of New York or (b) official bank checks drawn by any such banking insitution, payable to the order of Seller, except that uncertified checks of Purchaser payable to the order of Seller up to the amount of one-half of one percent of the Purchase Price shall be acceptable for sums payable to Seller at the Closing.

EXHIBIT 8.4
New York Contract of Sale—Commercial   (continued)

§2.03. (a) If Schedule C provides for the acceptance of title by Purchaser subject to one or more existing mortgages (collectively, "Existing Mortgage(s)"), the amounts specified in Schedule C with reference thereto may be approximate. If at the Closing the aggregate principal amount of the Existing Mortgage(s), as reduced by payments required thereunder prior to the Closing, is less than the aggregate amount of the Existing Mortgage(s) as specified in Schedule C, the difference shall be added to the monies payable at the Closing, unless otherwise expressly provided herein.

(b) If any of the documents constituting the Existing Mortgage(s) or the note(s) secured thereby prohibits or restricts the conveyance of the Premises or any part thereof without the prior consent of the holder or holders thereof ("Mortgagee(s)") or confers upon the Mortgagee(s) the right to accelerate payment of the indebtedness or to change the terms of the Existing Mortgage(s) in the event that a conveyance is made without consent of the Mortgagee(s), Seller shall notify such Mortgagee(s) of the proposed conveyance to Purchaser within 10 days after execution and delivery of this contract, requesting the consent of such Mortgagee(s) thereto. Seller and Purchaser shall furnish the Mortgagee(s) with such information as may reasonably be required in connection with such request and shall otherwise cooperate with such Mortgagee(s) and with each other in an effort expeditiously to procure such consent, but neither shall be obligated to make any payment to obtain such consent. If such Mortgagee(s) shall fail or refuse to grant such consent in writing on or before the date set forth in Schedule D or shall require as a condition of the granting of such consent (i) that additional consideration be paid to the Mortgagee(s) and neither Seller nor Purchaser is willing to pay such additional consideration or (ii) that the terms of the Existing Mortgage(s) be changed and Purchaser is unwilling to accept such change, then unless Seller and Purchaser mutually agree to extend such date or otherwise modify the terms of this contract, Purchaser may terminate this contract in the manner provided in §13.02. If Schedule C provides for a Purchase Money Mortgage (as defined in §2.04), Seller may also terminate this contract in the manner provided in §13.02 if any of the foregoing circumstances occur or if Seller is unwilling to accept any such change in the terms of the Existing Mortgage(s).

§2.04. (a) If Schedule C provides for payment of a portion of the Purchase Price by execution and delivery to Seller of a note secured by a purchase money mortgage ("Purchase Money Mortgage"), such note and Purchase Money Mortgage shall be drawn by the attorney for the Seller on the most recent forms of the New York Board of Title Underwriters for notes and for mortgages of like lien, as modified by this contract. At the Closing, Purchaser shall pay the mortgage recording tax and recording fees therefor and the filing fees for any financing statements delivered in connection therewith.

(b) If Schedule C provides for the acceptance of title by Purchaser subject to Existing Mortgage(s) prior in lien to the Purchase Money Mortgage, the Purchase Money Mortgage shall provide that it is subject and subordinate to the lien(s) of the Existing Mortgage(s) and shall be subject and subordinate to any extensions, modifications, renewals, consolidations, substitutions or replacements thereof (collectively, "Refinancing" or "Refinanced Mortgage"), provided that (i) the rate of interest payable under a Refinanced Mortgage shall not be greater than that specified in Schedule D as the Maximum Interest Rate or, if no Maximum Interest Rate is specified in Schedule D, shall not be greater than the rate of interest that was payable on the refinanced indebtedness immediately prior to such Refinancing, and (ii) if the principal amount of the Refinanced Mortgage plus the principal amount of other Existing Mortgage(s), if any, remaining after placement of a Refinanced Mortgage exceeds the amount of principal owing and unpaid on all mortgages on the Premises superior to the Purchase Money Mortgage immediately prior to the Refinancing, an amount equal to the excess shall be paid at the closing of the Refinancing to the holder of the Purchase Money Mortgage in reduction of principal payments due thereunder in inverse order of maturity. The Purchase Money Mortgage shall further provide that the holder thereof shall, on demand and without charge therefor, execute, acknowledge and deliver any agreement or agreements reasonably required by the mortgagor to confirm such subordination.

(c) The Purchase Money Mortgage shall contain the following additional provisions:

(i) "The mortgagor or any owner of the mortgaged premises shall have the right to prepay the entire unpaid indebtedness together with accrued interest, but without penalty, at any time on or after [insert the day following the last day of the fiscal year of the mortgagee in which the Closing occurs or, if a Prepayment Date is specified in Schedule D, the specified Prepayment Date], on not less than 10 days' written notice to the holder hereof."

(ii) "Notwithstanding anything to the contrary contained herein, the obligation of the mortgagor for the payment of the indebtedness and for the performance of the terms, covenants and conditions contained herein and in the note secured hereby is limited solely to recourse against the property secured by this mortgage, and in no event shall the mortgagor or any principal of the mortgagor, disclosed or un-

disclosed, be personally liable for any breach of or default under the note or this mortgage or for any deficiency resulting from or through any proceedings to foreclose this mortgage, nor shall any deficiency judgment, money judgment or other personal judgment be sought or entered against the mortgagor or any principal of the mortgagor, disclosed or undisclosed, but the foregoing shall not adversely affect the lien of this mortgage or the mortgagee's right of foreclosure."

(iii) "In addition to performing its obligations under Section 274–a of the Real Property Law, the mortgagee, if other than one of the institutions listed in Section 274–a, agrees that, within 10 days after written request by the mortgagor, but not more than twice during any period of 12 consecutive months, it will execute, acknowledge and deliver without charge a certificate of reduction in recordable form (a) certifying as to (1) the then unpaid principal balance of the indebtedness secured hereby, (2) the maturity date thereof, (3) the rate of interest, (4) the last date to which interest has been paid and (5) the amount of any escrow deposits then held by the mortgagee, and (b) stating, to the knowledge of the mortgagee, whether there are any alleged defaults hereunder and, if so, specifying the nature thereof."

(iv) "All notices required or desired to be given under this mortgage shall be in writing and shall be delivered personally or shall be sent by prepaid registered or certified mail, addressed to the mortgagor and mortgagee at the addresses specified in this mortgage or to such other parties or at such other addresses, not exceeding two, as may be designated in a notice given to the other party or parties in accordance with the provisions hereof."

(v) The additional provisions, if any, specified in a rider hereto.

§2.05. (a) If the sum paid under paragraph (a) of Schedule C or any other sums paid on account of the Purchase Price prior to the Closing (collectively, "Downpayment") are paid by check or checks drawn to the order of and delivered to Seller's attorney or another escrow agent ("Escrowee"), the Escrowee shall hold the proceeds thereof in escrow in a special bank account (or as otherwise agreed in writing by Seller, Purchaser and Escrowee) until the Closing or sooner termination of this contract and shall pay over or apply such proceeds in accordance with the terms of this section. Escrowee need not hold such proceeds in an interest-bearing account, but if any interest is earned thereon, such interest shall be paid to the same party entitled to the escrowed proceeds, and the party receiving such interest shall pay any income taxes thereon. The tax identification numbers of the parties are either set forth in Schedule D or shall be furnished to Escrowee upon request. At the Closing, such proceeds and the interest thereon, if any, shall be paid by Escrowee to Seller. If for any reason the Closing does not occur and either party makes a written demand upon Escrowee for payment of such amount, Escrowee shall give written notice to the other party of such demand. If Escrowee does not receive a written objection from the other party to the proposed payment within 10 business days after the giving of such notice, Escrowee is hereby authorized to make such payment. If Escrowee does receive such written objection within such 10 day period or if for any other reason Escrowee in good faith shall elect not to make such payment, Escrowee shall continue to hold such amount until otherwise directed by written instructions from the parties to this contract or a final judgment of a court. However, Escrowee shall have the right at any time to deposit the escrowed proceeds and interest thereon, if any, with the clerk of the Supreme Court of the county in which the Land is located. Escrowee shall give written notice of such deposit to Seller and Purchaser. Upon such deposit Escrowee shall be relieved and discharged of all further obligations and responsibilities hereunder.

(b) The parties acknowledge that Escrowee is acting solely as a stakeholder at their request and for their convenience, that Escrowee shall not be deemed to be the agent of either of the parties, and that Escrowee shall not be liable to either of the parties for any act or omission on its part unless taken or suffered in bad faith, in willful disregard of this contract or involving gross negligence. Seller and Purchaser shall jointly and severally indemnify and hold Escrowee harmless from and against all costs, claims and expenses, including reasonable attorneys' fees, incurred in connection with the performance of Escrowee's duties hereunder, except with respect to actions or omissions taken or suffered by Escrowee in bad faith, in willful disregard of this contract or involving gross negligence on the part of Escrowee.

(c) Escrowee has acknowledged agreement to these provisions by signing in the place indicated on the signature page of this contract.

§2.06. In the event that Seller is a "foreign person", as defined in Internal Revenue Code Section 1445 and regulations issued thereunder (collectively, the "Code Withholding Section"), or in the event that Seller fails to deliver the certification of non-foreign status required under §10.12(c), or in the event that Purchaser is not entitled under the Code Withholding Section to rely on such certification, Purchaser shall deduct and withhold from the Purchase Price a sum equal to ten percent (10%) thereof and shall at Closing remit the withheld

EXHIBIT 8.4
New York Contract of Sale—Commercial   (continued)

amount with Forms 8288 and 8288A (or any successors thereto) to the Internal Revenue Service; and if the cash balance of the Purchase Price payable to Seller at the Closing after deduction of net adjustments, apportionments and credits (if any) to be made or allowed in favor of Seller at the Closing as herein provided is less than ten percent (10%) of the Purchase Price, Purchaser shall have the right to terminate this contract, in which event Seller shall refund the Downpayment to Purchaser and shall reimburse Purchaser for title examination and survey costs as if this contract were terminated pursuant to §13.02. The right of termination provided for in this §2.06 shall be in addition to and not in limitation of any other rights or remedies available to Purchaser under applicable law.

Section 3. The Closing

§3.01. Except as otherwise provided in this contract, the closing of title pursuant to this contract ("Closing") shall take place on the scheduled date and time of closing specified in Schedule D (the actual date of the Closing being herein referred to as "Closing Date") at the place specified in Schedule D.

Section 4. Representations and Warranties of Seller

Seller represents and warrants to Purchaser as follows:

§4.01. Unless otherwise provided in this contract, Seller is the sole owner of the Premises.

§4.02. If the Premises are encumbered by an Existing Mortgage(s), no written notice has been received from the Mortgagee(s) asserting that a default or breach exists thereunder which remains uncured and no such notice shall have been received and remain uncured on the Closing Date. If copies of documents constituting the Existing Mortgage(s) and note(s) secured thereby have been exhibited to and initialed by Purchaser or its representative, such copies are true copies of the originals and the Existing Mortgage(s) and note(s) secured thereby have not been modified or amended except as shown in such documents.

§4.03. The information concerning written leases (which together with all amendments and modifications thereof are collectively referred to as "Leases") and any tenancies in the Premises not arising out of the Leases (collectively, "Tenancies") set forth in Schedule E attached hereto ("Rent Schedule") is accurate as of the date set forth therein or, if no date is set forth therein, as of the date hereof, and there are no Leases or Tenancies of any space in the Premises other than those set forth therein and any subleases or subtenancies. Except as otherwise set forth in the Rent Schedule or elsewhere in this contract:

(a) all of the Leases are in full force and effect and none of them has been modified, amended or extended;

(b) no renewal or extension options have been granted to tenants;

(c) no tenant has an option to purchase the Premises;

(d) the rents set forth are being collected on a current basis and there are no arrearages in excess of one month;

(e) no tenant is entitled to rental concessions or abatements for any period subsequent to the scheduled date of closing;

(f) Seller has not sent written notice to any tenant claiming that such tenant is in default, which default remains uncured;

(g) no action or proceeding instituted against Seller by any tenant of the Premises is presently pending in any court, except with respect to claims involving personal injury or property damage which are covered by insurance; and

(h) there are no security deposits other than those set forth in the Rent Schedule.

If any Leases which have been exhibited to and initialed by Purchaser or its representative contain provisions that are inconsistent with the foregoing representations and warranties, such representations and warranties shall be deemed modified to the extent necessary to eliminate such inconsistency and to conform such representations and warranties to the provisions of the Leases.

§4.04. If the Premises or any part thereof are subject to the New York City Rent Stabilization Law, Seller is and on the Closing Date will be a member in good standing of the Real Estate Industry Stabilization Association, and, except as otherwise set forth in the Rent Schedule, there are no proceedings with any tenant presently pending before the Conciliation and Appeals Board in which a tenant has alleged an overcharge of rent or diminution of services or similar grievance, and there are no outstanding orders of the Conciliation and Appeals Board that have not been complied with by Seller.

§4.05. If the Premises or any part thereof are subject to the New York City Emergency Rent and Rehabilitation Law, the rents shown are not in excess of the maximum collectible rents, and, except as otherwise set forth in the Rent Schedule, no tenants are entitled to abatements as senior citizens, there are no proceedings presently pending before the rent commission in which a tenant has alleged an overcharge of rent or diminution of services or similar grievance, and there are no outstanding orders of the rent commission that have not been complied with by Seller.

§4.06. If an insurance schedule is attached hereto, such schedule lists all insurance policies presently affording coverage with respect to the Premises, and the information contained therein is accurate as of the date set forth therein or, if no date is set forth therein, as of the date hereof.

§4.07. If a payroll schedule is attached hereto, such schedule lists all employees presently employed at the Premises, and the information contained therein is accurate as of the date set forth therein or, if no date is set forth therein, as of the date hereof, and, except as otherwise set forth in such schedule, none of such employees is covered by a union contract and there are no retroactive increases or other accrued and unpaid sums owed to any employee.

§4.08. If a schedule of service, maintenance, supply and management contracts ("Service Contracts") is attached hereto, such schedule lists all such contracts affecting the Premises, and the information set forth therein is accurate as of the date set forth therein or, if no date is set forth therein, as of the date hereof.

§4.09. If a copy of a certificate of occupancy for the Premises has been exhibited to and initialed by Purchaser or its representative, such copy is a true copy of the original and such certificate has not been amended, but Seller makes no representation as to compliance with any such certificate.

§4.10. The assessed valuation and real estate taxes set forth in Schedule D, if any, are the assessed valuation of the Premises and the taxes paid or payable with respect thereto for the fiscal year indicated in such schedule. Except as otherwise set forth in Schedule D, there are no tax abatements or exemptions affecting the Premises.

§4.11. Except as otherwise set forth in a schedule attached hereto, if any, if the Premises are used for residential purposes, each apartment contains a range and a refrigerator, and all of the ranges and refrigerators and all of the items of personal property (or replacements thereof) listed in such schedule, if any, are and on the Closing Date will be owned by Seller free of liens and encumbrances other than the lien(s) of the Existing Mortgage(s), if any.

§4.12. Seller has no actual knowledge that any incinerator, boiler or other burning equipment on the Premises is being operated in violation of applicable law. If copies of a certificate or certificates of operation therefor have been exhibited to and initialed by Purchaser or its representative, such copies are true copies of the originals.

§4.13. Except as otherwise set forth in Schedule D, Seller has no actual knowledge of any assessment payable in annual installments, or any part thereof, which has become a lien on the Premises.

§4.14. Seller is not a "foreign person" as defined in the Code Withholding Section.

Section 5. Acknowledgments of Purchaser

Purchaser acknowledges that:

§5.01. Purchaser has inspected the Premises, is fully familiar with the physical condition and state of repair thereof, and, subject to the provisions of §7.01, §8.01, and §9.04, shall accept the Premises "as is" and in their present condition, subject to reasonable use, wear, tear and natural deterioration between now and the Closing Date, without any reduction in the Purchase Price for any change in such condition by reason thereof subsequent to the date of this contract.

§5.02. Before entering into this contract, Purchaser has made such examination of the Premises, the operation, income and expenses thereof and all other matters affecting or relating to this transaction as Purchaser deemed necessary. In entering into this contract, Purchaser has not been induced by and has not relied upon any representations, warranties or statements, whether or implied, made by Seller or any agent, employee or other representative of Seller or by any broker or any other person representing or purporting to represent Seller, which are not expressly set forth in this contract, whether or not any such representations, warranties or statements were made in writing or orally.

Section 6. Seller's Obligations as to Leases

§6.01. Unless otherwise provided in a schedule attached to this contract, between the date of this contract and the Closing, Seller shall not, without Purchaser's prior written consent, which consent shall not be unreasonably withheld: (a) amend, renew or extend any Lease in any respect, unless required by law; (b) grant a written lease to any tenant occupying space pursuant to a Tenancy; or (c) terminate any Lease or Tenancy except by reason of a default by the tenant thereunder.

§6.02. Unless otherwise provided in a schedule attached to this contract, between the date of this contract and the Closing, Seller shall not permit occupancy of, or enter into any new lease for, space in the Building which is presently vacant or which may hereafter become vacant without first giving Purchaser written notice of the identity of the proposed tenant, together with (a) either a copy of the proposed lease or a summary of the terms thereof in reasonable detail and (b) a

EXHIBIT 8.4
New York Contract of Sale—Commercial   (continued)

statement of the amount of the brokerage commission, if any, payable in connection therewith and the terms of payment thereof. If Purchaser objects to such proposed lease, Purchaser shall so notify Seller within 4 business days after receipt of Seller's notice if such notice was personally delivered to Purchaser, or within 7 business days after the mailing of such notice by Seller to Purchaser, in which case Seller shall not enter into the proposed lease. Unless otherwise provided in a schedule attached to this contract, Purchaser shall pay to Seller at the Closing, in the manner specified in §2.02, the rent and additional rent that would have been payable under the proposed lease from the date on which the tenant's obligation to pay rent would have commenced if Purchaser had not so objected until the Closing Date, less the amount of the brokerage commission specified in Seller's notice and the reasonable cost of decoration or other work required to be performed by the landlord under the terms of the proposed lease to suit the premises to the tenant's occupancy ("Reletting Expenses"), prorated in each case over the term of the proposed lease and apportioned as of the Closing Date. If Purchaser does not so notify Seller of its objection, Seller shall have the right to enter into the proposed lease with the tenant identified in Seller's notice and Purchaser shall pay to Seller, in the manner specified in §2.02, the Reletting Expenses, prorated in each case over the term of the lease and apportioned as of the later of the Closing Date or the rent commencement date. Such payment shall be made by Purchaser to Seller at the Closing. In no event shall the amount so payable to Seller exceed the sums actually paid by Seller on account thereof.

§6.03. If any space is vacant on the Closing Date, Purchaser shall accept the Premises subject to such vacancy, provided that the vacancy was not permitted or created by Seller in violation of any restrictions contained in this contract. Seller shall not grant any concessions or rent abatements for any period following the Closing without Purchaser's prior written consent. Seller shall not apply all or any part of the security deposit of any tenant unless such tenant has vacated the Premises.

§6.04. Seller does not warrant that any particular Lease or Tenancy will be in force or effect at the Closing or that the tenants will have performed their obligations thereunder. The termination of any Lease or Tenancy prior to the Closing by reason of the tenant's default shall not affect the obligations of Purchaser under this contract in any manner or entitle Purchaser to an abatement of or credit against the Purchase Price or give rise to any other claim on the part of Purchaser.

§6.05. Seller hereby indemnifies and agrees to defend Purchaser against any claims made pursuant to §7 -107 or §7-108 of the General Obligations Law (the "GOL") by tenants who resided in the Premises on or prior to the Closing Date other than (a) claims with respect to tenants' security deposits paid, credited or assigned to Purchaser pursuant to §10.03, (b) claims made pursuant to §7-107 of the GOL with respect to funds for which Seller was not liable, and (c) claims made pursuant to §7-108 of the GOL to whom Purchaser failed to give the written notice specified in §7-108(c) of the GOL within thirty days after the Closing Date. The foregoing indemnity and agreement shall survive the Closing and shall be in lieu of any escrow permitted by §7-108(d) of the GOL, and Purchaser hereby waives any right it may have to require any such escrow.

Section 7.   Responsibility for Violations

§7.01. Except as provided in §7.02 and §7.03, all notes or notices of violations of law or governmental ordinances, orders or requirements which were noted or issued prior to the date of this contract by any governmental department, agency or bureau having jurisdiction as to conditions affecting the Premises and all liens which have attached to the Premises prior to the Closing pursuant to the Administrative Code of the City of New York, if applicable, shall be removed or complied with by Seller. If such removal or compliance has not been completed prior to the Closing, Seller shall pay to Purchaser at the Closing the reasonably estimated unpaid cost to effect or complete such removal or compliance, and Purchaser shall be required to accept title to the Premises subject thereto, except that Purchaser shall not be required to accept such title and may terminate this contract as provided in §13.02 if (a) Purchaser's Institutional Lender reasonably refuses to provide financing by reason thereof or (b) the Building is a multiple dwelling and either (i) such violation is rent impairing and causes rent to be unrecoverable under Section 302-a of the Multiple Dwelling Law or (ii) a proceeding has been validly commenced by tenants and is pending with respect to such violation for a judgment directing deposit and use of rents under Article 7-A of the Real Property Actions and Proceedings Law. All such notes or notices of violations noted or issued on or after the date of this contract shall be the sole responsibility of Purchaser.

§7.02. If the reasonably estimated aggregate cost to remove or comply with any violations or liens which Seller is required to remove or comply with pursuant to the provisions of §7.01 shall exceed the Maximum Amount specified in Schedule D (or if none is so specified, the Maximum Amount shall be one-half of one percent of the Purchase Price), Seller shall have the right to cancel this contract, in which event the sole

liability of Seller shall be as set forth in §13.02, unless Purchaser elects to accept title to the Premises subject to all such violations or liens, in which event Purchaser shall be entitled to a credit of an amount equal to the Maximum Amount against the monies payable at the Closing.

§7.03. Regardless of whether a violation has been noted or issued prior to the date of this contract, Seller's failure to remove or fully comply with any violations which a tenant is required to remove or comply with pursuant to the terms of its lease by reason of such tenant's use or occupancy shall not be an objection to title. Purchaser shall accept the Premises subject to all such violations without any liability of Seller with respect thereto or any abatement of or credit against the Purchase Price, except that if Purchaser's Institutional Lender reasonably refuses to provide financing by reason of a violation described above, Purchaser shall not be required to accept the Premises subject thereto and Purchaser shall have the right to terminate this contract in the manner provided in §13.02.

§7.04. If required, Seller, upon written request by Purchaser, shall promptly furnish to Purchaser written authorizations to make any necessary searches for the purposes of determining whether notes or notices of violations have been noted or issued with respect to the Premises or liens have attached thereto.

Section 8.   Destruction, Damage or Condemnation

§8.01. The provisions of Section 5-1311 of the General Obligations Law shall apply to the sale and purchase provided for in this contract.

Section 9.   Covenants of Seller

Seller covenants that between the date of this contract and the Closing:

§9.01. The Existing Mortgage(s) shall not be amended or supplemented or prepaid in whole or in part. Seller shall pay or make, as and when due and payable, all payments of principal and interest and all deposits required to be paid or made under the Existing Mortgage(s).

§9.02. Seller shall not modify or amend any Service Contract or enter into any new service contract unless the same is terminable without penalty by the then owner of the Premises upon not more than 30 days' notice.

§9.03. If an insurance schedule is attached hereto, Seller shall maintain in full force and effect until the Closing the insurance policies described in such schedule or renewals thereof for no more than one year of those expiring before the Closing.

§9.04. No fixtures, equipment or personal property included in this sale shall be removed from the Premises unless the same are replaced with similar items of at least equal quality prior to the Closing.

§9.05. Seller shall not withdraw, settle or otherwise compromise any protest or reduction proceeding affecting real estate taxes assessed against the Premises for any fiscal period in which the Closing is to occur or any subsequent fiscal period without the prior written consent of Purchaser, which consent shall not be unreasonably withheld. Real estate tax refunds and credits received after the Closing Date which are attributable to the fiscal tax year during which the Closing Date occurs shall be apportioned between Seller and Purchaser, after deducting the expenses of collection thereof, which obligation shall survive the Closing.

§9.06. Seller shall allow Purchaser or Purchaser's representatives access to the Premises, the Leases and other documents required to be delivered under this contract upon reasonable prior notice at reasonable times.

Section 10.   Seller's Closing Obligations

At the Closing, Seller shall deliver the following to Purchaser:

§10.01. A statutory form of bargain and sale deed without covenant against grantor's acts, containing the covenant required by Section 13 of the Lien Law, and properly executed in proper form for recording so as to convey the title required by this contract.

§10.02. All Leases initialed by Purchaser and all others in Seller's possession.

§10.03. A schedule of all security deposits (and, if the Premises contains six or more family dwelling units, the most recent reports with respect thereto issued by each banking organization in which they are deposited pursuant to GOL §7 -103) and a check or credit to Purchaser in the amount of any cash security deposits, including any interest thereon, held by Seller on the Closing Date or, if held by an Institutional Lender, an assignment to Purchaser and written instructions to the holder of such deposits to transfer the same to Purchaser, and appropriate instruments of transfer or assignment with respect to any security deposits which are other than cash.

§10.04. A schedule updating the Rent Schedule and setting forth all arrears in rents and all prepayments of rents.

§10.05. All Service Contracts initialed by Purchaser and all others in Seller's possession which are in effect on the Closing Date and which are assignable by Seller.

EXHIBIT 8.4
New York Contract of Sale—Commercial   (continued)

§10.06. An assignment to Purchaser, without recourse or warranty, of all of the interest of Seller in those Service Contracts, insurance policies, certificates, permits and other documents to be delivered to Purchaser at the Closing which are then in effect and are assignable by Seller.

§10.07. (a) Written consent(s) of the Mortgagee(s), if required under §2.03(b), and (b) certificate(s) executed by the Mortgagee(s) in proper form for recording and certifying (i) the amount of the unpaid principal balance thereof, (ii) the maturity date thereof, (iii) the interest rate, (iv) the last date to which interest has been paid thereon and (v) the amount of any escrow deposits held by the Mortgagee(s). Seller shall pay the fees for recording such certificate(s). Any Mortgagee which is an Insitutional Lender may furnish a letter complying with Section 274-a of the Real Property Law in lieu of such certificate.

§10.08. An assignment of all Seller's right, title and interest in escrow deposits for real estate taxes, insurance premiums and other amounts, if any, then held by the Mortgagee(s).

§10.09. All original insurance policies with respect to which premiums are to be apportioned or, if unobtainable, true copies or certificates thereof.

§10.10. To the extent they are then in Seller's possession and not posted at the Premises, certificates, licenses, permits, authorizations and approvals issued for or with respect to the Premises by governmental and quasi-governmental authorities having jurisdiction.

§10.11. Such affidavits as Purchaser's title company shall reasonably require in order to omit from its title insurance policy all exceptions for judgments, bankruptcies or other returns against persons or entities whose names are the same as or similar to Seller's name.

§10.12(a) Checks to the order of the appropriate officers in payment of all applicable real property transfer taxes and copies of any required tax returns therefor executed by Seller, which checks shall be certified or official bank checks if required by the taxing authority, unless Seller elects to have Purchaser pay any of such taxes and credit Purchaser with the amount thereof, (b) the Tentative Assessment and Return or Statement of No Tax Due or affidavit (whichever is applicable) and the checks and other items (if any) required under §17.09(a), and (c) a certification of non-foreign status, in form required by the Code Withholding Section, signed under penalty of perjury. Seller understands that such certification will be retained by Purchaser and will be made available to the Internal Revenue Service on request.

§10.13. To the extent they are then in Seller's possession, copies of current painting and payroll records. Seller shall make all other Building and tenant files and records available to Purchaser for copying, which obligation shall survive the Closing.

§10.14. An original letter, executed by Seller or by its agent, advising the tenants of the sale of the Premises to Purchaser and directing that rents and other payments thereafter be sent to Purchaser or as Purchaser may direct.

§10.15. Notice(s) to the Mortgagee(s), executed by Seller or by its agent, advising of the sale of the Premises to Purchaser and directing that future bills and other correspondence should thereafter be sent to Purchaser or as Purchaser may direct.

§10.16. If Seller is a corporation and if required by Section 909 of the Business Corporation Law, a resolution of Seller's board of directors authorizing the sale and delivery of the deed and a certificate executed by the secretary or assistant secretary of Seller certifying as to the adoption of such resolution and setting forth facts showing that the transfer complies with the requirements of such law. The deed referred to in §10.01 shall also contain a recital sufficient to establish compliance with such law.

§10.17. Possession of the Premises in the condition required by this contract, subject to the Leases and Tenancies, and keys therefor.

§10.18. Any other documents required by this contract to be delivered by Seller.

Section 11.   Purchaser's Closing Obligations

At the Closing, Purchaser shall:

§11.01. Deliver to Seller checks in payment of the portion of the Purchase Price payable at the Closing, as adjusted for apportionments under Section 12, plus the amount of escrow deposits, if any, assigned pursuant to §10.08.

§11.02. Deliver to Seller the Purchase Money Mortgage, if any, in proper form for recording, the note secured thereby, financing statements covering personal property, fixtures and equipment included in this sale and replacements thereof, all properly executed, and Purchaser shall pay the mortgage recording tax and recording fees for any Purchase Money Mortgage.

§11.03. Deliver to Seller an agreement indemnifying and agreeing to defend Seller against any claims made by tenants with respect to tenants' security deposits to the extent paid, credited or assigned to Purchaser under §10.03.

§11.04. Cause the deed to be recorded, duly complete all required real property transfer tax returns and cause all such returns and checks in payment of such taxes to be delivered to the appropriate officers promptly after the Closing.

§11.05. Deliver any other documents required by this contract to be delivered by Purchaser.

Section 12.   Apportionments

§12.01. The following apportionments shall be made between the parties at the Closing as of the close of business on the day prior to the Closing Date:

(a) prepaid rents and Additional Rents (as defined in §12.03);

(b) interest on the Existing Mortgage(s);

(c) real estate taxes, water charges, sewer rents and vault charges, if any, on the basis of the fiscal period for which assessed, except that if there is a water meter on the Premises, apportionment at the Closing shall be based on the last available reading, subject to adjustment after the Closing when the next reading is available;

(d) wages, vacation pay, pension and welfare benefits and other fringe benefits of all persons employed at the Premises whose employment was not terminated at or prior to the Closing;

(e) value of fuel stored on the Premises, at the price then charged by Seller's supplier, including any taxes;

(f) charges under transferable Service Contracts or permitted renewals or replacements thereof;

(g) permitted administrative charges, if any, on tenants' security deposits;

(h) dues to rent stabilization associations, if any;

(i) insurance premiums on transferable insurance policies listed on a schedule hereto or permitted renewals thereof;

(j) Reletting Expenses under §6.02, if any; and

(k) any other items listed in Schedule D.

If the Closing shall occur before a new tax rate is fixed, the apportionment of taxes at the Closing shall be upon the basis of the old tax rate for the preceding period applied to latest assessed valuation. Promptly after the new tax rate is fixed, the apportionment of taxes shall be recomputed. Any discrepancy resulting from such recomputation and any errors or omissions in computing apportionments at Closing shall be promptly corrected, which obligations shall survive the Closing.

§12.02. If any tenant is in arrears in the payment of rent on the Closing Date, rents received from such tenant after the Closing shall be applied in the following order of priority: (a) first to the month preceding the month in which the Closing occurred; (b) then to the month in which the Closing occurred; (c) then to any month or months following the month in which the Closing occurred; and (d) then to the period prior to the month preceding the month in which the Closing occurred. If rents or any portion thereof received by Seller or Purchaser after the Closing are payable to the other party by reason of this allocation, the appropriate sum, less a proportionate share of any reasonable attorneys' fees, costs and expenses of collection thereof, shall be promptly paid to the other party, which obligation shall survive the Closing.

§12.03. If any tenants are required to pay percentage rent, escalation charges for real estate taxes, operating expenses, cost-of-living adjustments or other charges of a similar nature ("Additional Rents") and any Additional Rents are collected by Purchaser after the Closing which are attributable in whole or in part to any period prior to the Closing, then Purchaser shall promptly pay to Seller Seller's proportionate share thereof, less a proportionate share of any reasonable attorneys' fees, costs and expenses of collection thereof, if and when the tenant paying the same has made all payments of rent and Additional Rent then due to Purchaser pursuant to the tenant's Lease, which obligation shall survive the Closing.

Section 13.   Objections to Title, Failure of Seller or Purchaser to Perform and Vendee's Lien

§13.01. Purchaser shall promptly order an examination of title and shall cause a copy of the title report to be forwarded to Seller's attorney upon receipt. Seller shall be entitled to a reasonable adjournment or adjournments of the Closing for up to 60 days or until the expiration date of any written commitment of Purchaser's Institutional Lender delivered to Purchaser prior to the scheduled date of Closing, whichever occurs first, to remove any defects in or objections to title noted in such title report and any other defects or objections which may be disclosed on or prior to the Closing Date.

§13.02. If Seller shall be unable to convey title to the Premises at the Closing in accordance with the provisions of this contract or if Purchaser shall have any other grounds under this contract for refusing to consummate the purchase provided for herein, Purchaser, nevertheless, may elect to accept such title as Seller may be able to convey with a credit against the monies payable at the Closing equal to the reasonably estimated cost to cure the same (up to the Maximum Expense described below), but without any other credit or liability on the part of Seller. If Purchaser shall not so elect, Pur-

EXHIBIT 8.4
New York Contract of Sale—Commercial   (continued)

chaser may terminate this contract and the sole liability of Seller shall be to refund the Downpayment to Purchaser and to reimburse Purchaser for the net cost of title examination, but not to exceed the net amount charged by Purchaser's title company therefor without issuance of a policy, and the net cost of updating the existing survey of the Premises or the net cost of a new survey of the Premises if there was no existing survey or the existing survey was not capable of being updated and a new survey was required by Purchaser's Institutional Lender. Upon such refund and reimbursement, this contract shall be null and void and the parties hereto shall be relieved of all further obligations and liability other than any arising under Section 14. Seller shall not be required to bring any action or proceeding or to incur any expense in excess of the Maximum Expense specified in Schedule D (or if none is so specified, the Maximum Expense shall be one-half of one percent of the Purchase Price) to cure any title defect or to enable Seller otherwise to comply with the provisions of this contract, but the foregoing shall not permit Seller to refuse to pay off at the Closing, to the extent of the monies payable at the Closing, mortgages on the Premises, other than Existing Mortgages, of which Seller has actual knowledge.

§13.03. Any unpaid taxes, assessments, water charges and sewer rents, together with the interest and penalties thereon to a date not less than two days following the Closing Date, and any other liens and encumbrances which Seller is obligated to pay and discharge or which are against corporations, estates or other persons in the chain of title, together with the cost of recording or filing any instruments necessary to discharge such liens and encumbrances of record, may be paid out of the proceeds of the monies payable at the Closing if Seller delivers to Purchaser on the Closing Date official bills for such taxes, assessments, water charges, sewer rents, interest and penalties and instruments in recordable form sufficient to discharge any other liens and encumbrances of record. Upon request made a reasonable time before the Closing, Purchaser shall provide at the Closing separate checks for the foregoing payable to the order of the holder of any such lien, charge or encumbrance and otherwise complying with §2.02. If Purchaser's title insurance company is willing to insure both Purchaser and Purchaser's Institutional Lender, if any, that such charges, liens and encumbrances will not be collected out of or enforced against the Premises, then, unless Purchaser's Institutional Lender reasonably refuses to accept such insurance in lieu of actual payment and discharge, Seller shall have the right in lieu of payment and discharge to deposit with the title insurance company such funds or assurances or to pay such special or additional premiums as the title insurance company may require in order to so insure. In such case the charges, liens and encumbrances with respect to which the title insurance company has agreed so to insure shall not be considered objections to title.

§13.04. If Purchaser shall default in the performance of its obligation under this contract to purchase the Premises, the sole remedy of Seller shall be to retain the Downpayment as liquidated damages for all loss, damage and expense suffered by Seller, including without limitation the loss of its bargain.

§13.05. Purchaser shall have a vendee's lien against the Premises for the amount of the Downpayment, but such lien shall not continue after default by Purchaser under this contract.

Section 14.   Broker

§14.01. If a broker is specified in Schedule D, Seller and Purchaser mutually represent and warrant that such broker is the only broker with whom they have dealt in connection with this contract and that neither Seller nor Purchaser knows of any other broker who has claimed or may have the right to claim a commission in connection with this transaction, unless otherwise indicated in Schedule D. The commission of such broker shall be paid pursuant to separate agreement by the party specified in Schedule D. If no broker is specified in Schedule D, the parties acknowledge that this contract was brought about by direct negotiation between Seller and Purchaser and that neither Seller nor Purchaser knows of any broker entitled to a commission in connection with this transaction. Unless otherwise provided in Schedule D, Seller and Purchaser shall indemnify and defend each other against any costs, claims or expenses, including attorneys' fees, arising out of the breach on their respective parts of any representations, warranties or agreements contained in this paragraph. The representations and obligations under this paragraph shall survive the Closing or, if the Closing does not occur, the termination of this contract.

Section 15.   Notices

§15.01. All notices under this contract shall be in writing and shall be delivered personally or shall be sent by prepaid registered or certified mail, addressed as set forth in Schedule D, or as Seller or Purchaser shall otherwise have given notice as herein provided.

Section 16.   Limitations on Survival of Representations, Warranties, Covenants and other Obligations

§16.01. Except as otherwise provided in this contract, no representations, warranties, covenants or other obligations of Seller set forth in this contract shall survive the Closing, and

no action based thereon shall be commenced after the Closing. The representations, warranties, covenants and other obligations of Seller set forth in §4.03, §6.01 and §6.02 shall survive until the Limitation Date specified in Schedule D (or if none is so specified, the Limitation Date shall be the date which is six months after the Closing Date), and no action based thereon shall be commenced after the Limitation Date.

§16.02. The delivery of the deed by Seller, and the acceptance thereof by Purchaser, shall be deemed the full performance and discharge of every obligation on the part of Seller to be performed hereunder, except those obligations of Seller which are expressly stated in this contract to survive the Closing.

Section 17.   Gains Tax and Miscellaneous Provisions

§17.01. If consent of the Existing Mortgagee(s) is required under §2.03(b), Purchaser shall not assign this contract or its rights hereunder without the prior written consent of Seller. No permitted assignment of Purchaser's rights under this contract shall be effective against Seller unless and until an executed counterpart of the instrument of assignment shall have been delivered to Seller and Seller shall have been furnished with the name and address of the assignee. The term "Purchaser" shall be deemed to include the assignee under any such effective assignment.

§17.02. This contract embodies and constitutes the entire understanding between the parties with respect to the transaction contemplated herein, and all prior agreements, understandings, representations and statements, oral or written, are merged into this contract. Neither this contract nor any provision hereof may be waived, modified, amended, discharged or terminated except by an instrument signed by the party against whom the enforcement of such waiver, modification, amendment, discharge or termination is sought, and then only to the extent set forth in such instrument.

§17.03. This contract shall be governed by, and construed in accordance with, the law of the State of New York.

§17.04. The captions in this contract are inserted for convenience of reference only and in no way define, describe or limit the scope or intent of this contract or any of the provisions hereof.

§17.05. This contract shall be binding upon and shall inure to the benefit of the parties hereto and their respective heirs or successors and permitted assigns.

§17.06. This contract shall not be binding or effective until properly executed and delivered by Seller and Purchaser.

§17.07. As used in this contract, the masculine shall include the feminine and neuter, the singular shall include the plural and the plural shall include the singular, as the context may require.

§17.08. If the provisions of any schedule or rider to this contract are inconsistent with the provisions of this contract, the provisions of such schedule or rider shall prevail. Set forth in Schedule D is a list of any and all schedules and riders which are attached hereto but which are not listed in the Table of Contents.

§17.09. (a) Seller and Purchaser agree to comply in a timely manner with the requirements of Article 31-B of the Tax Law of the State of New York and the regulations applicable thereto, as the same from time to time may be amended (collectively, the "Gains Tax Law"). Purchaser agrees to deliver to Seller a duly executed and acknowledged Transferee Questionnaire simultaneously with the execution of this contract or within five (5) business days after subsequent written request from Seller or Seller's attorney. At the Closing, Seller shall deliver (i) an official Statement of No Tax Due or (ii) an official Tentative Assessment and Return accompanied by a certified check or official bank check drawn on any banking institution described in §2.02(a), payable to the order of the State Tax Commission in the amount of the tax shown to be due thereon (it being understood, however, that if Seller has duly elected to pay such tax in installments, the amount so required to be paid shall be the minimum installment of such tax then permitted to be paid), or (iii) if applicable, a duly executed and acknowledged affidavit in form permitted under the Gains Tax Law claiming exemption therefrom.

(b) Seller agrees (i) to pay promptly any installment(s) or additional tax due under the Gains Tax Law, and interest and penalties thereon, if any, which may be assessed or due after the Closing, (ii) to indemnify and save the Purchaser harmless from and against any of the foregoing and any damage, liability, cost or expense (including reasonable attorneys' fees) which may be suffered or incurred by Purchaser by reason of the non-payment thereof, and (iii) to make any other payments and execute, acknowledge and deliver such further documents as may be necessary to comply with the Gains Tax Law.

(c) If this contract is assignable by Purchaser, no assignment of any rights hereunder shall be effective unless every assignor and assignee complies in a timely manner with the requirements of the Gains Tax Law applicable to the assignment transaction and unless an assignor or assignee de-

EXHIBIT 8.4
New York Contract of Sale—Commercial   (continued)

livers to Seller at or before the Closing the applicable items referred to in subparagraph (a) of this Section, all as may be required as a prerequisite to the recording of the deed. In addition to making the payments and delivering the instruments and documents referred to above, Purchaser and any assignor or assignee of this contract shall promptly (i) make any other payments and (ii) execute, acknowledge and deliver such further documents and instruments as may be necessary to comply with the Gains Tax Law.

(d) Purchaser, if request is made within a reasonable time prior to the Closing Date, shall provide at the Closing a separate certified or official bank check drawn on any banking institution described in §2.02(a) in the amount of the tax shown to be due on the official Tentative Assessment and Return, which amount shall be credited against the balance of the Purchase Price payable at the Closing.

(e) The provisions of this §17.09 shall survive the delivery of the deed.

IN WITNESS WHEREOF, the parties hereto have executed this contract as of the date first above written.

Seller:

Purchaser:

Receipt by Escrowee

The undersigned Escrowee hereby acknowledges receipt of $, by check subject to collection, to be held in escrow pursuant to §2.05.

Schedule A

DESCRIPTION OF PREMISES

(to be attached separately and to include tax map designation)

Schedule B

PERMITTED EXCEPTIONS

1. Zoning regulations and ordinances which are not violated by the existing structures or present use thereof and which do not render title uninsurable.

2. Consents by the Seller or any former owner of the Premises for the erection of any structure or structures on, under or above any street or streets on which the Premises may abut.

3. The Existing Mortgage(s) and financing statements, assignments of leases and other collateral assignments ancillary thereto.

4. Leases and Tenancies specified in the Rent Schedule and any new leases or tenancies not prohibited by this contract.

5. Unpaid installments of assessments not due and payable on or before the Closing Date.

6. Financing statements, chattel mortgages and liens on personalty filed more than 5 years prior to the Closing Date and not renewed, or filed against property or equipment no longer located on the Premises or owned by Tenants.

7. (a) Rights of utility companies to lay, maintain, install and repair pipes, lines, poles, conduits, cable boxes and related equipment on, over and under the Premises, provided that none of such rights imposes any monetary obligation on the owner of the Premises.

(b) Encroachments of stoops, areas, cellar steps, trim cornices, lintels, window sills, awnings, canopies, ledges, fences, hedges, coping and retaining walls projecting from the Premises over any street or highway or over any adjoining property and encroachments of similar elements projecting from adjoining property over the Premises.

(c) Revocability or lack of right to maintain vaults, coal chutes, excavations or sub-surface equipment beyond the line of the Premises.

(d) Any state of facts that an accurate survey would disclose, provided that such facts do not render title unmarketable. For the purposes of this contract, none of the facts shown on the survey, if any, identified below shall be deemed to render title unmarketable, and Purchaser shall accept title subject thereto:

EXHIBIT 8.4
New York Contract of Sale—Commercial   (continued)

Schedule C

PURCHASE PRICE

The Purchase Price shall be paid as follows:

(a) By check subject to collection, the receipt of which is hereby acknowledged by Seller: $

(b) By check or checks delivered to Seller at the Closing in accordance with the provisions of §2.02:

(c) By acceptance of title subject to the following Existing Mortgage(s):

(d) By execution and delivery to Seller by Purchaser or its assignee of a note secured by a Purchase Money Mortgage on the Premises, payable as follows:

Purchase Price $ _____

Schedule D

MISCELLANEOUS

1. Title insurer designated by the parties (§1.02):

2. Last date for consent by Existing Mortgagee(s) (§2.03(b)):

3. Maximum Interest Rate of any Refinanced Mortgage (§2.04(b)):

4. Prepayment Date on or after which Purchase Money Mortgage may be prepaid (§2.04(c)):

5. Seller's tax identification number (§2.05):

6. Purchaser's tax identification number (§2.05):

7. Scheduled time and date of Closing (§3.01):

8. Place of Closing (§3.01):

9. Assessed valuation of Premises (§4.10):
   Actual Assessment:
   Transition Assessment:

10. Fiscal year and annual real estate taxes on Premises (§4.10):

11. Tax abatements or exemptions affecting Premises (§4.10):

12. Assessments on Premises (§4.13):

13. Maximum Amount which Seller must spend to cure violations, etc. (§7.02):

14. Maximum Expense of Seller to cure title defects, etc. (§13.02):

15. Broker, if any (§14.01):

16. Party to pay broker's commission (§14.01):

17. Address for notices (§15.01):
    If to Seller:

    with a copy to Seller's attorney:

    If to Purchaser:

    with a copy to Purchaser's attorney:

18. Limitation Date for actions based on Seller's surviving representations and other obligations (§16.01):

19. Additional Schedules or Riders (§17.08):

Schedule E

RENT SCHEDULE

(to be attached separately)

Contract Down Payment in New York, page 187

In New York the contract down payment is called down payment or deposit (it is called earnest money elsewhere). The contract down payment is usually 10% of the contract price (this may be negotiated to be a smaller percentage) and is held by the seller's attorney in a separate escrow account with the bank account named. Outside of New York City the broker may hold the contract down payment. The contract indicates if the down payment shall be placed in an interest bearing account and who will get the interest. Often the contract language says the interest will follow the down payment, so that if the deal closes and the deposit goes to the seller, so will the interest.

In New York, the purchaser of a newly constructed home has the option of requiring the down payment funds to be deposited in an interest bearing escrow account or the seller may post a bond to guarantee the return of the money if the seller defaults.

CHAPTER 9—DEEDS

Deeds in New York, page 246

In the Middle Ages when the seller took the buyer into the field, the seller took up a clod of earth which represented the land and handed it to the buyer. When the buyer took the clod, he became the owner and the property transfer was completed. We still use the word "seized" of property. *Seisin* means ownership and control.

The requirements for a valid deed in New York are:
1) identifiable grantor and grantee with legal capacity
2) recital of consideration
3) granting clause and habendum clause (using words of conveyance, as "I hereby grant, convey and demise"). Parties to whom you are granting should be specified and their rights. If the deed says "to Allen", a fee simple is created, if it says "to David for life" a life estate is created
4) legal description
5) signature of grantor
6) delivery and acceptance

Bargain and Sale Deed with Covenant Against Grantor's Acts, page 247

In the New York City area, the most commonly used deed is the Bargain & Sale with Covenant Against Grantor's Acts. See Exhibit 9.1. The grantor promises he has not done anything to encumber the property while he owned it, i.e. to render title unmarketable. In upstate New York the full warranty deed is more common.

EXHIBIT 9.1
Bargain and Sale Deed

T 691 | Standard N.Y.B.T.U. Form 8002; Bargain & sale deed, with covenant against grantor's acts—Ind. or Corp.: single sheet

JULIUS BLUMBERG, INC., LAW BLANK PUBLISHERS

CONSULT YOUR LAWYER BEFORE SIGNING THIS INSTRUMENT – THIS INSTRUMENT SHOULD BE USED BY LAWYERS ONLY

THIS INDENTURE, made the   day of   , nineteen hundred and

BETWEEN

party of the first part, and

party of the second part,

WITNESSETH, that the party of the first part, in consideration of Ten Dollars and other valuable consideration paid by the party of the second part, does hereby grant and release unto the party of the second part, the heirs or successors and assigns of the party of the second part forever,

ALL that certain plot, piece or parcel of land, with the buildings and improvements thereon erected, situate, lying and being in the

TOGETHER with all right, title and interest, if any, of the party of the first part in and to any streets and roads abutting the above described premises to the center lines thereof; TOGETHER with the appurtenances and all the estate and rights of the party of the first part in and to said premises; TO HAVE AND TO HOLD the premises herein granted unto the party of the second part, the heirs or successors and assigns of the party of the second part forever.

AND the party of the first part covenants that the party of the first part has not done or suffered anything whereby the said premises have been encumbered in any way whatever, except as aforesaid.
AND the party of the first part, in compliance with Section 13 of the Lien Law, covenants that the party of the first part will receive the consideration for this conveyance and will hold the right to receive such consideration as a trust fund to be applied first for the purpose of paying the cost of the improvement and will apply the same first to the payment of the cost of the improvement before using any part of the total of the same for any other purpose. The word "party" shall be construed as if it read "parties" whenever the sense of this indenture so requires.

IN WITNESS WHEREOF, the party of the first part has duly executed this deed the day and year first above written.

IN PRESENCE OF:

EXHIBIT 9.1
Bargain and Sale Deed   (continued)

STATE OF NEW YORK, COUNTY OF   **ss:**

On the   day of   19   , before me
personally came

to me known to be the individual   described in and who
executed the foregoing instrument, and acknowledged that
executed the same.

STATE OF NEW YORK, COUNTY OF   **ss:**

On the   day of   19   , before me
personally came

to me known to be the individual   described in and who
executed the foregoing instrument, and acknowledged that
executed the same.

STATE OF NEW YORK, COUNTY OF   **ss:**

On the   day of   19   , before me
personally came
to me known, who, being by me duly sworn, did depose and
say that   he resides at No.
                                                              ;
that   he is the
of
                                , the corporation described
in and which executed the foregoing instrument; that   he
knows the seal of said corporation; that the seal affixed
to said instrument is such corporate seal; that it was so
affixed by order of the board of directors of said corporation, and that   he signed h   name thereto by like order.

STATE OF NEW YORK, COUNTY OF   **ss:**

On the   day of   19   , before me
personally came
the subscribing witness to the foregoing instrument, with
whom I am personally acquainted, who, being by me duly
sworn, did depose and say that   he resides at No.
                                                              ;
that   he knows

                                              to be the individual
described in and who executed the foregoing instrument;
that   he, said subscribing witness, was present and saw
                execute the same; and that   he, said witness,
at the same time subscribed h   name as witness thereto.

Bargain and Sale Deed
WITH COVENANT AGAINST GRANTOR'S ACTS

TITLE NO.

TO

SECTION

BLOCK

LOT

COUNTY OR TOWN

RETURN BY MAIL TO:

Zip No.

Reserve this space for use of Recording Office.

CHAPTER 11—LEGAL ASPECTS OF REAL ESTATE FINANCE _____

New York Law for Mortgages, page 297

New York Law requires that all mortgages that wish to be recorded must be acknowledged, signed by the borrower and the addresses of the parties must be on the mortgage. New York is a "race notice" state, i.e. the first to record in good faith for valuable consideration and without notice of prior mortgages, has priority.

When you pay off your mortgage, it must be discharged from the records. This is done by filing a "satisfaction" of mortgage with the county clerk where your property is located.

New York is one of the few states which require payment of a tax at the time the mortgage is recorded. The amount of tax varies in each area. In New York City the tax is 2% of the principal amount of the loan (less $25 credit if it is a 1 or 2 family dwelling). One-quarter % of this amount is paid by the lender and the borrower pays 1 3/4%.

There is no mortgage tax due on a home equity loan (this is like a revolving line of credit) or an a cooperative loan (the cooperative shares and proprietary lease are collateral).

New York does not allow the lender to charge a prepaying penalty after the first year of the mortgage. New York has generally enforced the "due on sale" clauses in mortgage. New York does not use a trust deed.

There is no mortgage tax on a cooperative loan. A cooperative is not really real property, but is personal property. When you purchase a cooperative apartment you receive shares and a UCC–1 is issued to give the lender a security interest in these shares. The UCC–1 (Uniform Commercial Code Financing Statement) is evidence of a lien on property (similar to the lien of a mortgage). The UCC–1 is a lien on the personal property, the shares of stock in the cooperative unit being purchased. The UCC–1, a short form, identifies the property being secured and is filed with the county clerk where the property is located and sometimes also with the Secretary of State in Albany. This gives notice to subsequent buyers of the preexisting lien. This financing statement remains in effect until the UCC–3 termination statement is filed and thus eliminates the lien.

New York Mortgage Form, page 299

See Exhibit 11.1, next page.

Foreclosure, page 306

After a default on the payment of the debt the mortgage secures, the mortgagee may foreclose and the most common method of foreclosure is by judicial action and sale. A lawsuit is begun against the defaulting party and other interested parties, e.g., tenants, mechanic lienors, etc. They are served with a summons and complaint and the parties are given an opportunity to raise defenses. The process ends with a judgment of foreclosure and sale and directs that the mortgaged premises be sold to satisfy the debt. Under the New York Real Property Actions & Proceedings Law (RPAPL) sect. 1311, every party whose claim is subordinate to plaintiff's mortgage lien is a necessary party to the suit. The sale extinguishes all subordinate interests.

In New York, a judicial foreclosure requires a *notice of sale* to be published once a week for four successive weeks in a newspaper in the county where the property is located. The defaulting party can always pay up, until the hammer falls at the sale. But his paying up includes the total amount of the mortgage, principal and all interest, court costs, legal fees and expenses. At the sale, the highest bidder wins. The lender may bid in the amount outstanding on his loan. The referee executes a referee's deed.

In a foreclosure action, the mortgagee forecloses the mortgagor's equitable right to redeem the property by tendering payment. Under RPAPL sect. 1341 the mortgagor has the right to redeem up to the moment of sale (this is called the equitable right of redemption). If at the foreclosure sale the debt is not paid off the lender may get a deficiency judgment for the balance, if the sale results in less money than the judgment in foreclosure.

EXHIBIT 11.1
New York Mortgage

682 —Mortgage (First) Statutory Form M.
　　Individual or Corporation.

JULIUS BLUMBERG, INC., LAW BLANK PUBLISHERS

THIS IS A LEGAL INSTRUMENT AND SHOULD BE EXECUTED UNDER SUPERVISION OF AN ATTORNEY.

THIS MORTGAGE, made the　　　　day of　　　　　　　　, nineteen hundred and　　　　　　,

BETWEEN

herein referred to as the mortgagor,

and

herein referred to as the mortgagee,

WITNESSETH, that to secure the payment of an indebtedness in the sum of

dollars,

lawful money of the United States, to be paid on the　　　　day of　　　　　　19

with interest thereon to be computed from　　　　day of　　　　　　, 19　　, at the rate of
　　　　　　per centum per annum, and to be paid

according to a certain bond, note or obligation bearing even date herewith, the mortgagor hereby mortgages to the mortgagee **ALL**

AND the mortgagor covenants with the mortgagee as follows:

1. That the mortgagor will pay the indebtedness as hereinbefore provided.

2. That the mortgagor will keep the buildings on the premises insured against loss by fire for the benefit of the mortgagee; that he will assign and deliver the policies to the mortgagee; and that he will reimburse the mortgagee for any premiums paid for insurance made by the mortgagee on the mortgagor's default in so insuring the buildings or in so assigning and delivering the policies.

3. That no building on the premises shall be removed or demolished without the consent of the mortgagee.

4. That the whole of said principal sum and interest shall become due at the option of the mortgagee: after default in the payment of any instalment of principal or of interest for twenty days; or after default in the payment of any tax, water rate, sewer rent or assessment for thirty days after notice and demand; or after default after notice and demand either in assigning and delivering the policies insuring the buildings against loss by fire or in reimbursing the mortgagee for premiums paid on such insurance, as hereinbefore provided; or after default upon request in furnishing a statement of the amount due on the mortgage and whether any offsets or defenses exist against the mortgage debt, as hereinafter provided.

5. That the holder of this mortgage, in any action to foreclose it, shall be entitled to the appointment of a receiver.

6. That the mortgagor will pay all taxes, assessments, sewer rents or water rates, and in default thereof, the mortgagee may pay the same.

7. That the mortgagor within six days upon request in person or within fifteen days upon request by mail will furnish a written statement duly acknowledged of the amount due on this mortgage and whether any offsets or defenses exist against the mortgage debt.

8. That notice and demand or request may be in writing and may be served in person or by mail.

9. That the mortgagor warrants the title to the premises.

Forms may be purchased from Julius Blumberg, Inc., NYC 10013, or any of its dealers. Reproduction prohibited. Reprinted with permission.

EXHIBIT 11.1
New York Mortgage (continued)

10. That the mortgagor will, in compliance with Section 13 of the Lien Law, receive the advances secured hereby and will hold the right to receive such advances as a trust fund to be applied first for the purpose of paying the cost of the improvement and will apply the same first to the payment of the cost of the improvement before using any part of the total of the same for any other purpose.

This mortgage may not be changed orally.

IN WITNESS WHEREOF, this mortgage has been duly executed by the mortgagor.

IN PRESENCE OF:

STATE OF NEW YORK, COUNTY OF } ss.:	STATE OF NEW YORK, COUNTY OF } ss.:

On the   day of   19   ,
before me came
to me known, who, being by me duly sworn, did depose and say
that   he resides at

                              ; that   he is the
of
the corporation described in and which executed, the foregoing instrument; that   he knows the seal of said corporation; that the seal affixed to said instrument is such corporate seal; that it was so affixed by order of the Board of   of said corporation; and that   he signed h   name thereto by like order.

On the   day of   19   ,
before me came

to me known to be the individual   described in, and who executed
the foregoing instrument, and acknowledged that   he   executed
the same.

TO

Mortgage

Dated, ..., 19.........

Amount, $.........................

Due, ..., 19.........

Int. Payable.........................

The land affected by the within instrument lies in

Record and return to

Reserve this space for use of Recording Office.

CHAPTER 13—TITLE EXAMINATIONS

Recording Statutes in New York, page 380

In New York, in order to give subsequent purchasers constructive notice of a person's interest in real property, mortgages, deeds and other written documents affecting that real estate must be recorded in the county clerk's office in the county in which the real estate is located.

A deed will not be accepted for recording in New York unless it is accompanied by the New York State Board of Equalization and Assessment Real Property Transfer Report (more commonly called the transfer tax return or TP–584, see Exhibit 13.1).

If the property is in New York City, a Real Property Transfer Tax Return (RPT, see Exhibit 13.2) must also be filed with the deed with respect to one and two family dwellings or a cooperative or condominium unit. There is a $25 filing fee for this document. The New York City Administrative Code also requires the seller to file an affidavit concerning the existence of a smoke detector device which affidavit is to be recorded with the RPT. (See Exhibit 13.3).

Along with the filing of the notarized transfer tax affidavits, a transfer tax must be paid. The transfer tax for New York State is $2 per $500 of consideration. There is a "mansion tax" of 1% due if the property sells for one million dollars or more. If the property sold is in New York City, there is an additional transfer tax. The New York City transfer rate is 1% of the consideration on a 1, 2, 3 family house, condominium or cooperative up to $500,000 and 1.425% of the consideration if the consideration for the property is $500,000 or more. New York City also requires a multiple dwelling registration statement to be filed with the deed (see Exhibit 13.4), or an affidavit that the property is not improved by a multiple dwelling. If the seller does not pay the transfer tax the buyer could be responsible.

The recording is in the county where the property is located. Each county in New York has a public recording office that is usually called the County Clerk's office and is administered by a County Clerk. The County Clerk's office has indexes to record the documents. In the four counties in New York City these documents are recorded in the Office of the City Register and in Staten Island the documents are recorded in the County Clerk's office.

The County Clerk photocopies each document that it receives for recording. It is best to use black ink when signing documents for recording. The documents are then filed in the appropriate index and the original document returned to the person who it is recorded for. When the documents are photocopied they are filed in a book (called a *Liber*, the Latin name for book). Each document will be referred to by a *Liber* and page number.

EXHIBIT 13.1
Transfer Tax Return

TP-584 (6/89)

New York State
Department of
Taxation
and Finance

New York State
Combined
Real Property Transfer Gains Tax Affidavit
Real Estate Transfer Tax Return
Credit Line Mortgage Certificate

For department use only

See instructions (TP-584-I) before completing this form. Please print or type.

Schedule A - Information Relating to Conveyance

(Transferor/grantor)

Name *(If individual; last, first, middle initial)* — Social security number

☐ Individual ☐ Corporation ☐ Partnership ☐ Other — Mailing address — ZIP code — Federal employer identification number

(Transferee/grantee)

Name *(If individual; last, first, middle initial)* — Social security number

☐ Individual ☐ Corporation ☐ Partnership ☐ Other — Mailing address — ZIP code — Federal employer identification number

Location and description of property conveyed

Tax map designation	Address	City/Village	Town	County

Type of property conveyed (Check applicable box)

1 ☐ 1 - 3 family house
2 ☐ Residential cooperative
3 ☐ Residential condominium
4 ☐ Vacant land
5 ☐ Commercial/Industrial
6 ☐ Apartment building
7 ☐ Office building
8 ☐ Other _____

Date of conveyance _____ month / day / year

Percentage of real property conveyed which is residential real property _____ %
(see instructions)

Condition of conveyance (Check all that apply)

a. __ Conveyance of fee interest

b. __ Acquisition of a controlling interest (state percentage acquired _____ %)

c. __ Transfer of a controlling interest (state percentage transferred _____ %)

d. __ Conveyance to cooperative housing corporation

e. __ Conveyance pursuant to or in lieu of foreclosure *(Attach Form TP-584.1, Schedule E)*

f. __ Conveyance which consists of a mere change of identity or form of ownership or organization *(Attach Form TP-584.1, Schedule F)*

g. __ Conveyance for which credit for tax previously paid will be claimed *(Attach Form TP-584.1, Schedule G)*

h. __ Conveyance of cooperative apartment(s)

i. __ Syndication

j. __ Conveyance of air rights or development rights

k. __ Contract assignment

l. __ Option assignment or surrender

m. __ Leasehold assignment or surrender

n. __ Leasehold grant

o. __ Conveyance of an easement

p. __ Conveyance for which exemption from transfer tax is claimed. (Complete Schedule C, Part III)

q. __ Conveyance of property partly within and partly without the state

r. __ Other *(Describe)*

Schedule B - Real Property Transfer Gains Tax Affidavit (Article 31-B of the Tax Law)

☐ Check this box if a Tentative Assessment and Return is being filed with respect to your current transfer, and proceed to Schedule C without completing the following affidavit. Also, enter the assessment number shown on the Tentative Assessment: _____

I (we) certify that: *(check appropriate box)*

1 ☐ The transfer of real property consists of the execution of a contract to sell real property without the use or occupancy of such property or the granting of an option to purchase real property without the use or occupancy of such property.

2 ☐ The transfer is a transfer of real property where the consideration is less than $500,000 and which is neither (A) pursuant to a cooperative or condominium plan, nor (B) a partial or successive transfer pursuant to an agreement or plan to effectuate by partial or successive transfers a transfer which would otherwise be included in the coverage of Article 31-B of the Tax Law.

3 ☐ The transfer is a transfer of real property by tenants in common, joint tenants or tenants by the entirety where the aggregate consideration is less than $500,000. (All such transferors must sign this form.)

4 ☐ The conveyance is not a transfer of real property within the meaning of section 1440.7 of Article 31-B of the Tax Law. (Attach documents supporting such claim, and sign on back as required.)

5 ☐ The transfer of real property consists of premises wholly occupied and used by the transferor **exclusively** as his residence, including a cooperative apartment or condominium occupied by the transferor exclusively as a residence. (**This exemption may only be claimed and attested to by a transferor that is an individual, estate or trust.**)

6 ☐ The governmental entity (transferor) is the State of New York, or any of its agencies, instrumentalities, political subdivisions, or public corporations, including a public corporation created pursuant to an agreement or compact with another state or Canada.

7 ☐ The governmental entity (transferor) is the United Nations or any other international organization of which the United States is a member, the United States of America or any of its agencies or instrumentalities.

Schedule C - Real Estate Transfer Tax Return (Article 31 of the Tax Law)

Part I - Computation of Tax Due

1 Enter amount of consideration for conveyance. *(If you are claiming a total exemption from tax, enter consideration and proceed to Part III)* **1**

2 Continuing lien deduction *(See instructions if property is taken subject to mortgage or lien)* .... **2** ( )

3 Taxable consideration *(Subtract line 2 from line 1)* **3**

4 Tax due: $2 for each $500, or fractional part thereof, of consideration on line 3 .... **4**

5 Amount of credit claimed *(See instructions and attach Form TP-584.1, Schedule G)* .... **5** ( )

6 Total tax due* *(Subtract line 5 from line 4)* **6**

Part II - Computation of Additional Tax Due on the Conveyance of Residential Real Property for $1 Million or More

1 Enter amount of consideration for conveyance (same as amount in Part I, line 1) **1**

2 Taxable consideration *(Multiply line 1 by the percentage of the premises which is residential real property) (see instructions)* **2**

3 Total additional transfer tax due* *(1% of line 2)* **3**

*Please make check(s) payable to the county clerk or city register where the recording is to take place or the Department of Taxation and Finance if payment is being made directly to the Tax Department.

For recording officer's use	Amount received ▶	Part I $	Date received	Transaction number
		Part II $		

EXHIBIT 13.1
Transfer Tax Return   (continued)

TP-584 (6/89) (back)

Schedule C - (continued)

Part III - Explanation of Exemption Claimed in Part I, line 1. *(check any boxes that apply)*

The conveyance of real property is exempt from the real estate transfer tax for the following reason:

a. Conveyance is to the United Nations, the United States of America, the State of New York or any of their instrumentalities, agencies or political subdivisions (or any public corporation, including a public corporation created pursuant to agreement or compact with another state or Canada) .... a ☐

b. Conveyance is to secure a debt or other obligation .... b ☐

c. Conveyance is without additional consideration to confirm, correct, modify or supplement a prior conveyance .... c ☐

d. Conveyance of real property without consideration and otherwise than in connection with a sale, including conveyances conveying realty as bona fide gifts .... d ☐

e. Conveyance is given in connection with a tax sale .... e ☐

f. Conveyance is a mere change of identity or form of ownership or organization where there is no change in beneficial ownership. (This exemption cannot be claimed for a conveyance to a cooperative housing corporation of real property comprising the cooperative dwelling or dwellings.) .... f ☐

g. Conveyance consists of deed of partition .... g ☐

h. Conveyance is given pursuant to the federal bankruptcy act .... h ☐

i. Conveyance consists of the execution of a contract to sell real property without the use or occupancy of such property or the granting of an option to purchase real property without the use or occupancy of such property .... i ☐

j. Conveyance of an option or contract to purchase real property with the use or occupancy of such property where the consideration is less than $200,000 and such property was used solely by the grantor as his personal residence and consists of a 1, 2, or 3 family house, a residential individual condominium unit, or the sale of stock in a cooperative housing corporation in connection with the grant or transfer of a proprietary leasehold covering an individual residential cooperative unit .... j ☐

k. Other *(attach explanation)* .... k ☐

Schedule D - Credit Line Mortgage Certificate (Article 11 of the Tax Law)

Complete the following only if the interest being transferred is a fee simple interest.

I (we) certify that: *(Check appropriate box)*

1 ☐ The real property being sold or transferred is not principally improved nor will it be improved by a one-to six-family owner-occupied residence or dwelling.

2 ☐ The real property being sold or transferred is not subject to an outstanding credit line mortgage.

3 ☐ The real property being sold or transferred is subject to an outstanding credit line mortgage. However, an exemption from the tax is claimed for the following reason:

☐ The transfer of real property is a transfer of a fee simple interest to a person or persons who held a fee simple interest in the real property (whether as a joint tenant, a tenant in common or otherwise) immediately prior to the transfer;

☐ The transfer of real property is (A) to a person or persons related by blood, marriage or adoption to the original obligor or to one or more of the original obligors or (B) to a person or entity where a majority of the beneficial interest in such real property after the transfer is held by the transferor or such related person or persons;

☐ The transfer of real property is a transfer to a trustee in bankruptcy, a receiver, assignee or other officer of a court;

☐ Other (attach detailed explanation).

4 ☐ The real property being transferred is presently subject to an outstanding credit line mortgage, however, no tax is due for the following reason:

☐ A certificate of discharge of the credit line mortgage is being offered at the time of recording the deed; or

☐ A check has been drawn payable for transmission to the credit line mortgagee or his agent for the balance due and a satisfaction of such mortgage will be recorded as soon as it is available.

5 ☐ The real property being transferred is subject to an outstanding credit line mortgage on record at _____ (insert liber and page or reel or other identification of the mortgage). The maximum principal amount expressed in the mortgage is _____ . No exemption from tax is claimed and the tax of _____ is being paid herewith. *(Make check payable to county clerk or city register where deed will be recorded.)*

Signature and Affirmation (Both the transferor(s)/grantor(s) and transferee(s)/grantee(s) must sign).

The undersigned, being duly sworn, depose and say under penalty of perjury that the above return, including any affidavit, certification, schedule or attachment, has been examined by the undersigned, and is, to the best of his/her knowledge, true and complete and made in good faith pursuant to Articles 11, 31 and 31-B of the New York State Tax Law.

_____   _____   _____   _____
Transferor/grantor   Title   Transferee/grantee   Title

Subscribed to and sworn before me   Subscribed to and sworn before me

this _____ day of _____ , 19 ___.   this _____ day of _____ , 19 ___.

State of _____   State of _____

County of _____   County of _____

Reminder: Did you complete all of the required information in Schedules A and B? Were you required to complete Schedules C and D? If you checked e, f and g in Schedule A, did you complete TP-584.1? Have you attached your check(s) made payable to the county clerk or city register where recording will take place or the Department of Taxation and Finance if payment is being made directly to the Tax Department?

EXHIBIT 13.2
Real Property Transfer Tax Return

FINANCE
NEW • YORK
THE CITY OF NEW YORK
DEPARTMENT OF FINANCE

REAL PROPERTY TRANSFER TAX RETURN (RPT)

THIS BOOKLET CONTAINS:

❶ Form NYC-RPT - Real Property Transfer Tax Return
❷ General Information for NYC-RPT
❸ Owner's Registration Card
❹ Instructions for Owner's Registration Card

RUDOLPH W. GIULIANI
Mayor

MARC V. SHAW
Commissioner of Finance

THE CITY OF NEW YORK
DEPARTMENT OF FINANCE
REAL PROPERTY TRANSFER TAX GROUP
25 ELM PLACE, 3RD FLOOR
BROOKLYN, NY 11201

EXHIBIT 13.2
Real Property Transfer Tax Return   (continued)

IMPORTANT NOTICE FOR NEW PROPERTY OWNERS

It is very important that new property owners fill out the Owner's Registration Card in the back of this packet. This will insure that bills for real estate tax, water and sewer charges are sent to the party responsible for payment. A moment taken now to register accurately will eliminate errors in the future and protect the owner's interest in the property.

The Owner's Registration Card should be completed by the new owner and forwarded to the Department of Finance with the Real Property Transfer Tax Return.

Questions pertaining to the Owner's Registration Card can be directed to the telephone numbers listed on the card.

EXHIBIT 13.2
Real Property Transfer Tax Return   (continued)

NYC
RPT

FINANCE
NEW • YORK

NEW YORK CITY DEPARTMENT OF FINANCE
REAL PROPERTY TRANSFER TAX RETURN
(Pursuant to Title 11, Chapter 21, NYC Administrative Code)

This return, including all required schedules, must be completely filled out and filed with all necessary attachments before the reported transfer will be recorded. If you are reporting a transfer with a consideration of $25,000 or less, no tax is due; however, you must complete Schedule 1 on page 2 and file a return. This return is applicable for all conveyances made on or after August 1, 1989. Pursuant to Subdivision 3 of Section 333 of the NYS Real Property Law, all RPT forms filed on or after July 1, 1991, must be accompanied by a $25 fee. No forms will be accepted without the fee.

TYPE OR PRINT LEGIBLY
If the transfer involves more than one grantor or grantee or a partnership, the names, addresses and Social Security Numbers or Employer Identification Numbers of all grantors or grantees or partners must be provided on Schedule J on page 9.

▼ **FOR OFFICE USE ONLY** ▼

● RETURN NUMBER

● DEED SERIAL NUMBER

● NYS REAL ESTATE TRANSFER TAX PAID

▶ GRANTOR ▶

● Name

● Grantor is a: (check one)   ☐ Individual   ☐ partnership (must complete Schedule J)   ☐ corporation   ☐ other _____   Telephone Number

● Permanent mailing address after transfer (number and street)

● City and State   Zip Code

● EMPLOYER IDENTIFICATION NUMBER   ☐☐ - ☐☐☐☐☐☐☐   **OR**   ● SOCIAL SECURITY NUMBER   ☐☐☐ - ☐☐ - ☐☐☐☐

▶ GRANTOR'S ATTORNEY ▶

● Name of Attorney

● Address (number and street)   City and State   Zip Code

EMPLOYER IDENTIFICATION NUMBER   ● ☐☐ - ☐☐☐☐☐☐☐   **OR**   SOCIAL SECURITY NUMBER   ● ☐☐☐ - ☐☐ - ☐☐☐☐

▶ GRANTEE ▶

● Name

● Grantee is a: (check one)   ☐ individual   ☐ partnership (must complete Schedule J)   ☐ corporation   ☐ other _____   Telephone Number

● Permanent mailing address after transfer (number and street)   City and State   Zip Code

EMPLOYER IDENTIFICATION NUMBER   ● ☐☐ - ☐☐☐☐☐☐☐   **OR**   SOCIAL SECURITY NUMBER   ● ☐☐☐ - ☐☐ - ☐☐☐☐

▶ GRANTEE'S ATTORNEY ▶

● Name of Attorney

● Address (number and street)   City and State   Zip Code

EMPLOYER IDENTIFICATION NUMBER   ● ☐☐ - ☐☐☐☐☐☐☐   **OR**   SOCIAL SECURITY NUMBER   ● ☐☐☐ - ☐☐ - ☐☐☐☐

▶ PROPERTY LOCATION ▶

LIST EACH LOT SEPARATELY. ATTACH A RIDER IF ADDITIONAL SPACE IS REQUIRED

● Address (number and street)	Borough	Block	Lot	# of Floors	Square Feet	● Assessed Value of Property

● DATE OF TRANSFER TO GRANTEE: _____   ● PERCENTAGE OF INTEREST TRANSFERRED: _____ %

● **TYPE OF PROPERTY TRANSFERRED** (✓)

a. ☐ ...... 1-3 family house
b. ☐ ...... Individual residential condominium unit
c. ☐ ...... Individual cooperative apartment
d. ☐ ...... Commercial condominium unit
e. ☐ ...... Commercial cooperative
f. ☐ ...... Apartment building
g. ☐ ...... Office building
h. ☐ ...... Industrial building
i. ☐ ...... Utility
j. ☐ ...... OTHER (describe): _____

● **TYPE OF INTEREST TRANSFERRED** (✓)

a. ☐ ...... Fee
b. ☐ ...... Leasehold grant
    (attach copy of lease agreement and complete Schedule 1, page 2)
c. ☐ ...... Leasehold assignment or surrender
    (attach copy of agreement or surrender and complete Schedule 1, page 2)
d. ☐ ...... Easement
e. ☐ ...... Development rights
f. ☐ ...... Stock transfer
g. ☐ ...... Partnership interest transfer
h. ☐ ...... OTHER (describe): _____

EXHIBIT 13.2
Real Property Transfer Tax Return   (continued)

Form NYC-RPT

Page 2

● **CONDITION OF TRANSFER**   Check (✓) all of the conditions that apply and fill out the appropriate schedule on pages 4, 5, 6, 7 or 8 of this return. Additionally, Schedule 1 and either Schedule 2 or 3 **must** be completed for all transfers.

a. ☐ ...Arms length transfer

b. ☐ ...Transfer in exercise of option to purchase

c. ☐ ...Transfer from cooperative sponsor to cooperative corporation

d. ☐ ...Transfer by referee or receiver (complete Schedule A, page 4)

e. ☐ ...Transfer pursuant to marital settlement agreement or divorce decree (complete Schedule B, page 4 and attach a copy of agreement or divorce decree)

f. ☐ ...Deed in lieu of foreclosure (complete Schedule C, page 4)

g. ☐ ...Transfer pursuant to partial or complete liquidation of corporation, partnership or other entity (complete Schedule D, page 5)

h. ☐ ...Transfer from principal to agent, dummy, strawman or conduit or vice-versa (complete Schedule E, page 6)

i. ☐ ...Transfer pursuant to trust agreement or will (attach a copy of trust agreement or will)

j. ☐ ...Gift transfer

k. ☐ ...Gift transfer subject to indebtedness

NOTE A conveyance of real property subject to any indebtedness is **not** exempt. The indebtedness is deemed consideration for the transfer. Complete Schedule 1, below.

l. ☐ ...Transfer to a business entity in exchange for an interest in the business entity (complete Schedule F, page 6)

m. ☐ ...Transfer to a governmental body

n. ☐ ...Correction deed

o. ☐ ...Transfer by or to a tax exempt organization (complete Schedule G, page 7). Nonprofit organizations please refer to special note in the instructions for important information on exemption from Real Estate Tax and related charges.

p. ☐ ...Transfer of property partly within and partly without NYC

q. ☐ ...Transfer of controlling economic interest (complete Schedule H, page 7)

r. ☐ ...Transfer of stock in a cooperative housing corporation

s. ☐ ...Transfer of an interest in an entity formed for the purpose of cooperative ownership of real property (other than a cooperative housing corporation)

t. ☐ ...Transfer of successful bid pursuant to foreclosure

u. ☐ ...Transfer by borrower solely as security for a debt or a transfer by lender solely to return such security

v. ☐ ...Other transfer in connection with financing (describe): _____

w. ☐ ...Other (describe): _____

SCHEDULE 1 - Details of consideration

COMPLETE THIS SCHEDULE FOR ALL TRANSFERS. ENTER "ZERO" ON LINE 11 IF THE TRANSFER REPORTED WAS WITHOUT CONSIDERATION.

1. Cash ....● 1.	
2. Purchase money mortgage...............................● 2.	
3. Unpaid principal or pre-existing mortgage(s)* ....● 3.	
4. Accrued interest on pre-existing mortgage(s)...........● 4.	
5. Accrued real estate taxes ....● 5.	
6. Amounts of other liens on property* ....● 6.	
7. Value of shares of stock or of partnership interest received** ...● 7.	
8. Value of real or personal property received in exchange ....● 8.	
9. Amount of Real Property Transfer Tax and/or other taxes or expenses of the grantor which are paid by the grantee ....● 9.	
10. Other (describe):_____ ●10.	
11. **TOTAL CONSIDERATION** (add lines 1 through 10 - must equal amount entered on page 3, line 1 of Schedule 2 or 3) (see instructions) ....●11.	

* In the case of an initial or subsequent transfer of an interest (other than an interest in an individual residential unit) in an entity formed for the purpose of cooperative ownership, a proportionate share of any pre-existing mortgage(s) on the underlying real property must be included in the consideration.

**In the case of a transfer of property or interest therein to a business entity in exchange for an interest in the entity, the value of such interest is equal to the fair market value of the property or interest therein less the amount of mortgages, liens or encumbrances thereon. (see instructions)

EXHIBIT 13.2
Real Property Transfer Tax Return   (continued)

Form NYC-RPT   Page 3

SCHEDULE 2 - Computation of tax for transfers involving certain residential property

USE THIS SCHEDULE FOR THE FOLLOWING TRANSFERS

A. Conveyances where the real property transferred or the real property in which the economic interest is transferred is a one-, two-, or three-family house, an individual cooperative apartment, an individual residential condominium unit, or an individual dwelling unit in a dwelling which is to be occupied or is occupied as the residence or home of four or more families living independently of each other.

B. Grants, assignments or surrenders of leasehold interests in a one-, two-, or three-family house, or an individual dwelling unit in a dwelling which is to be occupied or is occupied as the residence or home of four or more families living independently of each other.

1.   Consideration paid or required to be paid...● 1. |

2.   Tax
     a.   1% of line 1, if the consideration on line 1 is $500,000 or less ....● 2a. |
          OR
     b.   1.425% of line 1, if the consideration on line 1 is greater than $500,000 ....● 2b. |

3.   Penalty *(see instructions)* ....● 3. |

4.   Interest *(see instructions)* ....● 4. |

5.   **TOTAL TAX DUE** (add lines 2a or 2b, 3 and 4) ....● 5. |

SCHEDULE 3 - Computation of tax for all other transfers

USE THIS SCHEDULE FOR ALL TRANSFERS NOT INCLUDED IN SCHEDULE 2 ABOVE

1.   Consideration paid or required to be paid...● 1. |

2.   Tax
     a.   1.425% of line 1, if the consideration on line 1 is $500,000 or less ....● 2a. |
          OR
     b.   2.625% of line 1, if the consideration on line 1 is greater than $500,000 ....● 2b. |

3.   Penalty *(see instructions)* ....● 3. |

4.   Interest *(see instructions)* ....● 4. |

5.   **TOTAL TAX DUE** (add lines 2a or 2b, 3 and 4) ....● 5. |

─ CERTIFICATION ─

I swear or affirm that this return, including any accompanying schedules, affidavits and attachments, has been examined by me and is, to the best of my knowledge, a true and complete return made in good faith, pursuant to Title 11, Chapter 21 of the Administrative Code and the regulations issued thereunder.

GRANTOR

S worn to and subscribed to

before me on this _____ day

of _____, 19____.

EMPLOYER IDENTIFICATION NUMBER OR SOCIAL SECURITY NUMBER
_____

Name of Grantor
_____

Signature of Notary

Signature of Grantor

Notary's stamp or seal

GRANTEE

S worn to and subscribed to

before me on this _____ day

of _____, 19____.

EMPLOYER IDENTIFICATION NUMBER OR SOCIAL SECURITY NUMBER
_____

Name of Grantee
_____

Signature of Notary

Signature of Grantee

Notary's stamp or seal

GRANTEE: To ensure that your property tax bills are sent to the proper address you must complete the Owner's Registration Card which is the last item included in this packet. Owner's Registration Cards can also be obtained by calling the Department of Finance at (718) 935-6153.

IF THERE IS MORE THAN ONE GRANTOR OR GRANTEE, YOU MUST COMPLETE SCHEDULE J, PAGE 9.

EXHIBIT 13.2
Real Property Transfer Tax Return   (continued)

Form NYC-RPT   Page 4

SCHEDULE A - Transfer by referee or receiver

IF CONDITION "d" WAS CHECKED ON PAGE 2, COMPLETE SCHEDULE A BELOW.

NOTE The consideration for a transfer by a referee or receiver under foreclosure or execution is the amount bid for the property and the costs paid by the purchaser, plus the amount of any pre-existing mortgages, liens or other encumbrances remaining on the property after the transfer, whether or not the underlying indebtedness is assumed.

1. Was this transfer the result of a court ordered sale pursuant to foreclosure or execution? (✓) .... ☐ YES   ☐ NO
   If "YES," complete lines 2a through 2g below. If "NO," complete line 3 below.

2a. Status of grantee: (✓)
    ☐ Nominee of plaintiff   ☐ Plaintiff in foreclosure action   ☐ Assignee of plaintiff   ☐ Transferee of successful bidder
    ☐ Other (describe): _____

2b. Priority of mortgage foreclosed upon: ➡ ☐ first   ☐ second   ☐ third or other

2c. Amount of foreclosure judgment ....2c. |$_____|

2d. Price bid by grantee ....2d.

2e. Costs paid by grantee ....2e.

2f. Amount of remaining mortgages, liens or other encumbrances ....2f.

2g. Total consideration (add lines 2d, 2e and 2f) ....2g.

3. If the answer to line 1 above is "NO", state the reason for this transfer:_____
   _____
   _____

SCHEDULE B - Transfer pursuant to marital settlement agreement or divorce decree

IF CONDITION "e" WAS CHECKED ON PAGE 2, ANSWER THE QUESTION BELOW.

NOTE The consideration for a transfer pursuant to a marital settlement agreement or divorce decree includes the value of any marital rights exchanged for the property plus any consideration paid by the grantee for the transfer. The consideration is presumed to equal the fair market value of the property transferred in proportion to the interest transferred, unless otherwise shown.

Does the consideration listed on page 3, line 1 of Schedule 2 or 3 represent the fair market value of the
property in proportion to the interest transferred? (✓) .... ☐ YES   ☐ NO

SCHEDULE C - Deed in lieu of foreclosure

IF CONDITION "f" WAS CHECKED ON PAGE 2, COMPLETE SCHEDULE C BELOW.

NOTE A conveyance by a defaulting mortgagor to the mortgagee (or to a nominee or assignee of the mortgagee) in consideration of the cancellation of the mortgage debt is taxable. The consideration is the amount of the outstanding mortgage debt and unpaid accrued interest, plus the amount of any other mortgages, liens or encumbrances remaining on the property after the transfer, whether or not the underlying indebtedness is assumed and irrespective of whether the cancellation of the mortgage was recorded.

1. Status of grantee: (✓)
   ☐ Mortgagee   ☐ Nominee of mortgagee   ☐ Assignee of mortgagee
   ☐ Other (describe):_____

2. Priority of mortgage in default: ☐ first   ☐ second   ☐ third or other

3. Amount of debt owed by grantor to mortgagee at time of transfer:
   a. Outstanding principal ....3a.

   b. Accrued interest ....3b.

4. Amount of mortgages, liens or other encumbrances remaining on the real property after the transfer....4.

EXHIBIT 13.2
Real Property Transfer Tax Return   (continued)

Form NYC-RPT

Page 5

SCHEDULE D - Transfer pursuant to partial or complete liquidation of corporation, partnership or other entity

IF CONDITION "g" WAS CHECKED ON PAGE 2, COMPLETE SCHEDULE D BELOW.

NOTE A distribution of real property or an economic interest therein within 12 months of liquidation of the distributing entity is presumed to be a distribution in liquidation. *Attach a balance sheet reflecting the grantor's assets and liabilities at the time of the liquidation.*

COMPUTATION OF TAX

1. Present fair market value of real property ....1.

2. Present fair market value of controlling economic interest in real property ....2.

3. Total of line 1 and line 2 ....3.

4. Amount of mortgages or other liens on real property ....4.

5. Amount of encumbrances or other liens on controlling economic interest in real property ....5.

6. Total of line 4 and line 5 ....6.

7. Tax base: line 3 or line 6, whichever is greater ....7.

8. Tax: Certain residential properties *(see Schedule 2, page 3 for description)*
   a. 1% of line 7, if the consideration on line 7 is $500,000 or less ....8a.
      OR
   b. 1.425% of line 7, if the consideration on line 7 is greater than $500,000 ....8b.

   Tax: All other properties
   c. 1.425% of line 7, if the consideration on line 7 is $500,000 or less ....8c.
      OR
   d. 2.625% of line 7, if the consideration on line 7 is greater than $500,000 ....8d.

9. Credit *(see instructions)* ....9.

10. Tax due: line 8a, 8b, 8c, or 8d, whichever is applicable, less line 9 ....10.

11. Penalty *(see instructions)* ....11.

12. Interest *(see instructions)* ....12.

13. **TOTAL TAX DUE.** (add lines 10, 11 and 12 - enter here and on page 3, line 5, Schedule 2 or 3, whichever is applicable) ....13.

IF YOU COMPLETED SCHEDULE D, LIST THE NYC REAL PROPERTY OWNED OR LEASED BY THE CORPORATION, PARTNERSHIP, ASSOCIATION, TRUST OR OTHER ENTITY BEING LIQUIDATED, OR WHICH IS OWNED OR LEASED BY ANY ENTITY WITH RESPECT TO WHICH A CONTROLLING ECONOMIC INTEREST HAS BEEN TRANSFERRED. *(ATTACH A RIDER IF ADDITIONAL SPACE IS NEEDED)*

BOROUGH	BLOCK	LOT	ADDRESS	FAIR MARKET VALUE

EXHIBIT 13.2
Real Property Transfer Tax Return   (continued)

Form NYC-RPT
Page 6

SCHEDULE E - Transfer by or to an agent, dummy, strawman or conduit

IF CONDITION "h" WAS CHECKED ON PAGE 2, COMPLETE SCHEDULE E BELOW.

> **NOTE** A deed from an agent, dummy, strawman or conduit to a principal or from a principal to an agent, dummy, strawman or conduit is exempt from the Real Property Transfer Tax. Complete questions 1 through 8 below to establish the claim of exemption.

1. Name and address of party from whom property was acquired by grantor: _____

2. Date of acquisition: [   ]   Recording date: [   ]
   Reel number: [   ]   Page number: [   ]

3. Is this conveyance either a transfer from an agent to a principal or from a principal to an agent? (✓) .... ☐ YES   ☐ NO
   If "YES," attach a copy of agency agreement or affidavit of explanation.

4. Amount of Real Property Transfer Tax paid upon acquisition by grantor .... [   ]

5. Is this transfer part of a transfer to and from a corporation for the sole purpose of acquiring mortgage financing? (✓) .... ☐ YES   ☐ NO

6. Is this transfer to a dummy, strawman, or conduit from a principal or vice versa? (✓) .... ☐ YES   ☐ NO

7. If this is a transfer to an agent, dummy, strawman, or conduit, is the grantee actively engaged in a business? (✓) .... ☐ YES   ☐ NO

8. If the answers to questions 3, 5, 6 and 7 above are all "NO," describe the relationship of the grantor and the grantee and the purpose of the transfer: _____

SCHEDULE F - Transfer to business entity in return for an interest in the business entity

IF CONDITION "I" WAS CHECKED ON PAGE 2, COMPLETE SCHEDULE F BELOW.

> **NOTE** A transfer of real property or an interest in real property to a corporation in exchange for shares of its capital stock is taxable, even where there is no simultaneous exchange of shares of stock for the real property, so long as the transfer is part of a plan to form a corporation for the purpose of holding title to the property. A transfer to a partnership as a contribution of partnership assets is similarly taxable. The tax is computed on the greater of the fair market value of the real property transferred or the amount of any mortgages, liens or other encumbrances on the property at the time of the transfer, whether or not the underlying indebtedness is assumed.

1. Relationship of grantee to grantor(s) immediately after the transfer: (✓)

   ☐ Corporation wholly owned by grantor(s)   ☐ Partnership consisting wholly of grantor(s)

   ☐ Corporation owned by grantor(s) and other(s)   ☐ Partnership consisting of grantor(s) and other(s)

   ☐ Other (describe): _____

2. If this transfer has more than one grantor, state the percentage of interest transferred by each grantor. (If the grantor is a partnership or limited partnership, state the percentage of interest transferred by each individual partner or limited partner.)

Name	Percentage of interest
	%
	%
	%

3. Date of formation of grantee business .... 3. [   ]

4. Fair market value of real property at time of transfer .... 4. [   ]

5. Amount of basis used for depreciation of the property on federal tax returns by the grantor before this transfer .... 5. [   ]

6. Amount of basis to be used for depreciation of the property on federal tax returns by the grantee after this transfer .... 6. [   ]

7. Amount of mortgages, liens or encumbrances on real property transferred .... 7. [   ]

8. Value of shares of stock or partnership interest received (line 4 less line 7) (see instructions) .... 8. [   ]

EXHIBIT 13.2
Real Property Transfer Tax Return   (continued)

Form NYC-RPT   Page 7

SCHEDULE G - Transfer by or to a tax exempt organization

NONPROFIT ORGANIZATIONS PLEASE REFER TO SPECIAL NOTE IN THE INSTRUCTIONS

IF CONDITION "o" WAS CHECKED ON PAGE 2, COMPLETE SCHEDULE G BELOW.

NOTE A transfer by or to an eligible tax exempt organization is exempt from the Real Property Transfer Tax. To be eligible, an organization must be operated exclusively for religious, charitable or educational purposes and must provide proof of the organization's tax exempt status. If claiming tax exempt status, please answer questions 1 and 2. Additionally, the organization must provide copies of any letters granting IRS or New Yok State sales tax exemption status or New York City exemption status and ATTACH AN AFFIDAVIT stating whether such an exemption remains in effect.

1. Is the grantor or grantee an organization exempt from taxation pursuant to IRS Code Section 501(c)(3)? (✔) .... ☐ YES ☐ NO
   If "YES", attach a copy of of the letter from the U. S. Treasury Department granting tax exemption status.

2. Has the grantor or grantee received an exemption from sales tax from the NYS Department of Taxation and Finance? (✔)... ☐ YES ☐ NO
   If "YES", attach a copy of the letter from the NYS Department of Taxation and Finance granting the exemption.

SCHEDULE H - Transfers of controlling economic interests

IF CONDITION "q" WAS CHECKED ON PAGE 2, COMPLETE SCHEDULE H BELOW.

A. Name, address and Employer Identification Number (EIN) of entity with respect to which a controlling economic interest has been transferred:
   Name :

   Address: Zip Code:

   EIN ☐☐ - ☐☐☐☐☐☐☐

   NOTE If the property that is the subject of this transfer is owned by an entity other than the entity listed above, check (✔) the box and attach a schedule listing the name, address and Employer Identification Number of the entity. ☐

B. Total percentage of economic interest transferred in this transaction .... B. [___] %

C. Total percentage of economic interest transferred by this grantor(s) or others acting in concert or pursuant to plan
   (including this transaction) .... C. [___] %

D. Total percentage of economic interest transferred by this grantor(s) or others within the preceeding three years
   (including this transaction) .... D. [___] %

E. Total percentage of economic interest acquired by this grantee(s) or others acting in concert or pursuant to plan
   (including this transaction) .... E. [___] %

F. Total percentage of economic interest acquired by this grantee(s) or others within the preceeding three years
   (including this transaction) .... F. [___] %

NOTE If any of the above percentages is 50% or more, complete **COMPUTATION OF TAX** section below or attach an explanatory rider.

COMPUTATION OF TAX

1. Total consideration paid or required to be paid for this transfer
   (complete Schedule 1 - enter the result from line 11 here) ....1.

2. Amount apportioned to NYC real property (complete apportionment section below and enter
   amount from item A or B on this line and on line 1, Schedule 2 or 3, whichever is applicable,
   only if the entity has assets in addition to realty) ....2.

APPORTIONMENT COMPLETE EITHER ITEM A OR ITEM B

A. Good Faith Apportionment of Consideration to Real Property - Enter here and on line 2 above
   (attach copy of contract of sale or other documentary basis)..A.
   OR
B. Formula Apportionment
   1. Total consideration of transfer ....B1.
   2. Fair market value of real property...B2.
   3. Fair market value of all assets (including the real property) ....B3.
   4. Divide line B2 by line B3...B4. [___] %
   5. Multiply line B1 by line B4 (enter here and on line 2 above) ....B5.

EXHIBIT 13.2
Real Property Transfer Tax Return   (continued)

Form NYC-RPT   Page 8

SCHEDULE I – Transfer of shares of stock in a cooperative housing corporation

IF CONDITION "r" WAS CHECKED ON PAGE 2, COMPLETE SCHEDULE I BELOW. ▼

A. Name and address of
    cooperative housing corporation: _____

    _____ Zip Code: _____

B. Location of cooperative apartment unit, if different than question A: _____

    _____ Zip Code: _____

C. Borough, block and lot number of building in which cooperative apartment unit is located ▼

    Borough: [   ]   Block: [   ]   Lot: [   ]

D. 1) Is this an initial transfer of shares from either a cooperative housing corporation or a sponsor? (✓) .... ☐ YES   ☐ NO

    2) If "YES," enter the date the NYC Real Property Transfer Tax was paid on the transfer of land
        and/or building to the cooperative housing corporation .... [MONTH] [DAY] [YEAR]

        If this initial transfer is more than 2 years from the above date, enter the date the first of these
        initial transfers was made .... [MONTH] [DAY] [YEAR]

E. Is this a transfer of an individual unit in a housing company organized and operating pursuant to the
    provisions of articles two, four, five, or eleven of the Private Housing Finance Law? (✓) .... ☐ YES   ☐ NO

    If "YES," you are not subject to the Real Property Transfer Tax. However, you must file a return.

COMPUTATION OF TAX

1. Consideration paid or required to be paid for the purchase of shares of stock
    (complete Schedule 1, page 2 - enter the result from line 11 here) ....1. [   ]

2. Tax ▼
    a. 1% of line 1 if the consideration on line 1 is $500,000 or less ....2a. [   ]
        OR
    b. 1.425% of line 1 if the consideration on line 1 is greater than $500,000 ....2b. [   ]

    If you answered "YES" to question D above, you may be entitled to a credit. Complete lines 3 through 6 below.
    If you answered "NO" to question D above, you are not entitled to a credit. Omit lines 3 through 6 and transfer the result from line 2a or 2b,
    whichever is applicable, to line 7 below and complete the remainder of this schedule.

CREDIT CALCULATION

3. Enter the amount of NYC Real Property Transfer Tax paid on
    conveyance of underlying real property to cooperative
    housing corporation ....3. [   ]

4. Enter the number of shares transferred in this transaction ....4. [   ]

5. Enter the total number of outstanding shares of the
    cooperative housing corporation including any shares held
    by the corporation ....5. [   ]

6. Amount of credit (divide line 4 by line 5 and multiply the result by line 3) ....6. [   ]

7. Balance (line 2a or 2b, whichever is applicable, less line 6) (this amount cannot be less than zero) 7. [   ]

8. Penalty (see instructions) ....8. [   ]

9. Interest (see instructions) ....9. [   ]

10. **TOTAL TAX DUE** (add lines 7, 8 and 9 - enter the result here and on line 5, Schedule 2 or 3,
    whichever is applicable) ....10. [   ]

674   APPENDIX

EXHIBIT 13.2
Real Property Transfer Tax Return   (continued)

Form NYC-RPT   Page 9

SCHEDULE J - Transfers involving multiple grantors and/or grantees or a partnership

NOTE | If additional space is needed, attach copies of this schedule or an addendum listing all of the information required below.

GRANTOR(S)/PARTNER(S)

NAME OF GRANTOR OR PARTNER

PERMANENT MAILING ADDRESS AFTER TRANSFER

CITY AND STATE   ZIP CODE

SOCIAL SECURITY NUMBER
OR
EMPLOYER IDENTIFICATION NUMBER

NAME OF GRANTOR OR PARTNER

PERMANENT MAILING ADDRESS AFTER TRANSFER

CITY AND STATE   ZIP CODE

SOCIAL SECURITY NUMBER
OR
EMPLOYER IDENTIFICATION NUMBER

NAME OF GRANTOR OR PARTNER

PERMANENT MAILING ADDRESS AFTER TRANSFER

CITY AND STATE   ZIP CODE

SOCIAL SECURITY NUMBER
OR
EMPLOYER IDENTIFICATION NUMBER

NAME OF GRANTOR OR PARTNER

PERMANENT MAILING ADDRESS AFTER TRANSFER

CITY AND STATE   ZIP CODE

SOCIAL SECURITY NUMBER
OR
EMPLOYER IDENTIFICATION NUMBER

GRANTEE(S)/PARTNER(S)

NAME OF GRANTEE OR PARTNER

PERMANENT MAILING ADDRESS AFTER TRANSFER

CITY AND STATE   ZIP CODE

SOCIAL SECURITY NUMBER
OR
EMPLOYER IDENTIFICATION NUMBER

NAME OF GRANTEE OR PARTNER

PERMANENT MAILING ADDRESS AFTER TRANSFER

CITY AND STATE   ZIP CODE

SOCIAL SECURITY NUMBER
OR
EMPLOYER IDENTIFICATION NUMBER

NAME OF GRANTEE OR PARTNER

PERMANENT MAILING ADDRESS AFTER TRANSFER

CITY AND STATE   ZIP CODE

SOCIAL SECURITY NUMBER
OR
EMPLOYER IDENTIFICATION NUMBER

NAME OF GRANTEE OR PARTNER

PERMANENT MAILING ADDRESS AFTER TRANSFER

CITY AND STATE   ZIP CODE

SOCIAL SECURITY NUMBER
OR
EMPLOYER IDENTIFICATION NUMBER

EXHIBIT 13.2
Real Property Transfer Tax Return   (continued)

General Information for Form NYC-RPT

FINANCE
NEW • YORK
THE CITY OF NEW YORK
DEPARTMENT OF FINANCE

Real Property Transfer Tax Return

IMPOSITION OF TAX

The tax is imposed on conveyances of real property or interests therein, on certain grants, assignments or surrenders of leasehold interests, on transfers of controlling economic interests in real property and on all transfers of shares of stock in a cooperative housing corporation or an entity formed for the purpose of cooperative ownership of real property when the consideration exceeds $25,000.

An *economic interest* in real property means:

a) the ownership of shares of stock in a corporation which owns or leases real property;

b) the ownership of an interest or interests in a partnership, association, or other unincorporated entity which owns or leases real property; and

c) the ownership of a beneficial interest or interests in a trust which owns or leases real property.

A *controlling interest* in the case of a *corporation* means:

● 50% or more of the total combined voting power of all classes of stock of the corporation; or

● 50% or more of the total fair market value of all classes of stock of the corporation.

A *controlling interest* in the case of a *partnership, association, trust or other unincorporated entity* means:

● 50% or more of the capital, profits or beneficial interest in the partnership, association, trust or other unincorporated entity.

DETAILS OF CONSIDERATION

In the case of a transfer of an interest in an individual residential cooperative unit (other than the original transfer of the unit by the cooperative plan sponsor) the consideration does not include any portion of the mortgage on the underlying real property. An individual unit that is used for residential purposes by the occupant shall be presumed to be residential unless such residential use is *de minimis*.

In the case of a liquidation of a corporation, partnership, or other entity, if the fair market value of the property or interest therein distributed exceeds the consideration received, enter such fair market value on Schedule 1, line 11.

TRANSFERS TO BUSINESS ENTITIES

In the case of a transfer to a business entity in exchange for an interest in such entity, total consideration includes the fair market value of the interest in the entity, any mortgages, liens or encumbrances on the property, and any other consideration received from the grantee. The fair market value of the interest in the entity received is deemed to be equal to the fair market value of the real property or the interest therein transferred less the amount of mortgages, liens and encumbrances thereon and less the amount of any other consideration received from the grantee.

RATE OF TAX

Effective for transfers on or after August 1, 1989, the tax rates are as follows:

Certain Residential Property

1% of the consideration where the consideration is $500,000 or less or 1.425% of the consideration where the consideration is greater than $500,000 in the following instances:

● conveyances where the real property transferred or the real property in which the economic interest is transferred is a one-, two-, or three-family house, an individual cooperative apartment, an individual residential condominium unit, or an individual dwelling unit in a dwelling which is to be occupied as the residence or home of four or more families living independently of each other; and

● grants, assignments or surrenders of leasehold interests in a one-, two-, or three-family house, or an individual dwelling unit in a dwelling which is to be occupied or is occupied as the residence or home of four or more families living independently of each other.

An individual condominium that is used for residential purposes by the occupant shall be presumed to be residential, unless such residential use is *de minimis*. *(For illustrations, see RCNY Section 23-03(b) (9) and (10).)*

Other Property

● For all transfers involving property other than the residential property specified above, the rate is 1.425% of the consideration where the consideration is $500,000 or less or 2.625% of the consideration where the consideration is greater than $500,000.

FILING OF RETURN AND PAYMENT OF TAX

A notarized joint return shall be filed by both the grantor and the grantee for each deed, instrument, or transaction, whether or not a tax is due. Thus, a return must be filed although the consideration for the deed, instrument or transaction is $25,000 or less. Where the consideration is $400,000 or more, a copy of the contract of sale or closing statement must be attached to the return. A return need not be filed for the grant of a leasehold interest in a 1-, 2-, or 3-family house or an individual dwelling unit except where tax is owed or the lease is to be recorded.

Returns relating to the transfer of a deed are required to be filed and any tax due paid at the office of the City Register in the county where the deed is recorded within 30 days of the delivery of the deed.

Returns filed on or after February 6, 1990, in connection with a conveyance of a one- or two-family dwelling or a cooperative apartment or condominium unit in a one- or two-family dwelling must be accompanied by an Affidavit of Compliance with Smoke Detector Requirement.

The locations of the City Register's offices are as follows:

MANHATTAN (New York County)
31 Chambers Street, Room 202
New York, New York 10007
(212) 788-8527

BRONX
1932 Arthur Ave, 3rd Floor
Bronx, New York 10457
(212) 579-6820

BROOKLYN (Kings County)
Municipal Building,
210 Joralemon Street, Room 2
Brooklyn, New York 11201
(718) 802-3590

QUEENS
90-27 Sutphin Boulevard, 2nd Fl.
Jamaica, New York 11435
(718) 658-4600

STATEN ISLAND (Richmond County)
Richmond County Clerk
County Court House, Room 103
Staten Island, New York 10301
(718) 390-5386

In the case of transfers of controlling economic interests in real property or transfers of interests in entities formed for cooperative owner-

EXHIBIT 13.2
Real Property Transfer Tax Return   (continued)

ship of real property, returns must be filed within 30 days of the transfer with the:

NYC Department of Finance
Real Property Transfer Tax Group
345 Adams Street, 5th Floor
Brooklyn, NY 11201

The tax may be paid by certified check, or an Attorney's Trust Account check, drawn on U.S. bank, or money order made payable to the order of: **NYC Department of Finance. All returns filed on or after July 1, 1991 must be accompanied by a $25 filing fee whether or not a tax is due.**

Real Property Transfer Tax Returns are available at City Register offices, the offices of the County Clerk of Richmond County, and the Department of Finance, Taxpayer Assistance, 25 Elm Place, 4th Floor, Brooklyn, NY 11201.

INTEREST
If the tax is not paid on or before the due date (determined without regard to any extension of time), interest must be paid on the amount of the underpayment from the due date to the date paid. For information as to the applicable rate of interest call *Taxpayer Assistance* at: *(718) 935-6000*.

PENALTIES
a) If you fail to file a return when due, add to the tax 5% for each month or partial month the form is late up to 25%, unless the failure is due to reasonable cause.

b) If you fail to pay the tax shown on the return by the prescribed filing date, add to the tax (less any payments made) 1/2% for each month or partial month the payment is late up to 25%, unless the failure is due to reasonable cause.

c) The total of the additional charges in a) and b) may not exceed 5% for any one month.

EXEMPTIONS FROM THE TAX
A. The following parties are exempt from the payment of the tax and from filing a return:

1. The State of New York, its agencies, instrumentalities, public corporations (including a public corporation created pursuant to agreement of compact with another state or Canada) or political subdivisions.

2. The United States of America and its agencies and instrumentalities, insofar as they are immune from taxation. The exemption of such governmental bodies does not relieve a grantee from them of liability for the tax or from filing a return.

B. The tax imposed does not apply to any of

the following deeds:

1. A deed, instrument or transaction by or to the United Nations or any other world-wide international organization of which the United States is a member.

2. A deed, instrument or transaction by or to any corporation, association, trust, community chest, fund or foundation, organized and operated exclusively for religious, charitable, or educational purposes, or for the prevention of cruelty to children or animals, and no part of the net earnings of which inures to the benefit of any private shareholder or individual and no substantial part of the activities of which is carrying on propaganda, or otherwise attempting to influence legislation, provided, however, that nothing in this paragraph shall include an organization operated for the primary purpose of carrying on a trade or business for profit, whether or not all of its profits are payable to one or more organizations described in this paragraph.

3. A deed, instrument or transaction to any governmental body listed in "A" above.

4. A deed or instrument given solely as security for a debt, or a deed or instrument given solely for the purpose of returning such security.

5. A deed or instrument or transaction from a mere agent, dummy, strawman or conduit to a principal, or a deed from the principal to an agent, dummy, strawman or conduit.

Where a tax does not apply to any deed, neither the grantor nor the grantee is required to pay the tax. However, a return relating to the deed must be filed.

CREDIT
If a purchaser acquires a controlling economic interest in a corporation, partnership, association, trust or other entity owning real property in a transaction subject to the Real Property Transfer Tax and then within 24 months of such acquisition the entity owning the real property is liquidated and the real property is conveyed to the purchaser of the controlling economic interest, a credit is available against the transfer tax due on the liquidation in the amount of the transfer tax paid with respect to the original acquisition of the controlling economic interest. In no event shall this credit be greater than the tax payable upon the conveyance in liquidation.

In the case of the original transfer of coopera-

tive housing corporation stock by a cooperative corporation or cooperative plan sponsor in connection with the grant or transfer of a proprietary leasehold, a credit is allowed for a proportionate part of the amount of any tax paid upon the conveyance to the cooperative housing corporation of the land and building or buildings comprising the cooperative dwelling or dwellings. This credit applies only for original transfers of stock by the cooperative housing corporation or cooperative plan sponsor. It does not apply to taxable resales of cooperative housing corporation stock.

No credit is allowed for any tax paid more than 24 months prior to the date on which occurs the first in a series of transfers of shares of stock in the offering of cooperative housing corporation shares.

IMPORTANT REAL ESTATE TAX INFORMATION FOR NONPROFIT ORGANIZATIONS
If you are a nonprofit organization you should know:

1. You must apply for an exemption from Real Estate Tax with the Property Division. Exemption forms can be obtained from:

    Exemption Unit, Property Division
    Municipal Building
    1 Centre Street, Room 909
    New York, NY 10007
        or
    any of the Borough Offices of the Property Division.

2. Once you have received an exemption, you must renew it every year with the Property Division.

3. Many groups are exempt from property taxes but still may be required to pay water and sewer charges. You must file separately for an exemption from water and sewer charges with the Bureau of Water and Energy Conservation. Applications can be obtained from any of the Borough Offices of the Bureau of Water and Energy Conservation. Once granted, this exemption need not be renewed annually.

EVEN IF THIS TRANSFER OF REAL PROPERTY IS FROM ANOTHER NONPROFIT ORGANIZATION, YOU MUST STILL COMPLY WITH THE ABOVE REQUIREMENTS.

For additional information and for addresses of the Borough Offices of the Property Division or Bureau of Water and Energy Conservation, please call *Taxpayer Assistance* at (718) 935-6000 or 935-9500.

EXHIBIT 13.2
Real Property Transfer Tax Return   (continued)

FINANCE
NEW · YORK
THE CITY OF NEW YORK
DEPARTMENT OF FINANCE

OWNER'S REGISTRATION CARD

NEW YORK CITY DEPARTMENT OF FINANCE   CENTRAL REGISTRATION   25 ELM PLACE, 3RD FLOOR   BROOKLYN, NY 11201

ONLY ONE (1) PROPERTY (BLOCK AND LOT) MAY BE REGISTERED WITH THIS CARD. MAKE PHOTOCOPIES IF YOU ARE REGISTERING MORE THAN ONE PROPERTY.

FOR OFFICE USE ONLY

Additional instructions appear on the reverse side of this card. Type or print in ink.

PROPERTY OWNER'S INFORMATION (for general correspondence)

1. Borough the property is in: _____   Block: _____   Lot: _____

Owner's name – Fill either 2a or 2b only →

2a. Individual Owner: FIRST   M. I.   LAST

2b. Business Owner:

3. Owner's Residence or Company's Business Address:
City: _____   State: _____   Zip Code: _____

4. Property Address:
City: _____   State: _____   Zip Code: _____

5. If the property has more than one owner, check this box and see instructions → ☐

6. Owner's Tax Identification Number:
SSN (If owner is an individual or trust)   EIN (If owner is a corporation or partnership)

7. Indicate owner's daytime telephone number: ( )

BILLING INFORMATION
REAL ESTATE TAX BILLS ► IF YOUR MORTGAGE PAYMENTS INCLUDE YOUR REAL ESTATE TAXES, FILL IN THE NAME AND ADDRESS OF YOUR BANK/LENDER IN THE SPACE PROVIDED IN 9 BELOW. IF NOT, FILL IN THE NAME AND ADDRESS TO WHICH YOU ARE CHOOSING TO HAVE REAL ESTATE TAX BILLS SENT.

8. Indicate to whom Real Estate Tax bills should be mailed (Check ✓ one):
☐ Agent   ☐ Bank/Lender   ☐ Owner   ☐ Tenant

9. Name of Real Estate Tax Bill Recipient
Address:
City: _____   State: _____   Zip Code: _____

If "TENANT" or "AGENT" is checked provide either Social Security Number or Employer Identification Number, whichever is applicable.
☐ SSN   ☐ EIN

BILLING INFORMATION
WATER/SEWER BILLS ► WATER IS BILLED ON EITHER A FRONTAGE BASIS OR THROUGH THE READING OF A WATER METER ON THE PROPERTY. IF THE PROPERTY IS BILLED ON THE BASIS OF FRONTAGE, FILL IN 10 BELOW. IF THERE IS A WATER METER ON THE PROPERTY FILL IN 11 BELOW.

FRONTAGE   Annual frontage water charges are often included with mortgage payments. In this case water bills are usually sent to the bank/lender. If you are not sure who is responsible for payment, please check with your bank/lender before filling in this section.

10. Name of Frontage Water Bill Recipient
Address:
City: _____   State: _____   Zip Code: _____

METER   Metered water charges are NOT usually included with mortgage payments. Therefore, the owner should register the party to whom they wish to have metered water charge bills sent. If the property has more than two water meters, see instructions.

11. Meter #
Name of Metered Water Bill Recipient
Address:
City: _____   State: _____   Zip Code: _____

Relationship of addressee to property (Check ✓ one):
☐ Agent   ☐ Owner   ☐ Tenant

If "TENANT" or is checked provide either Social Security Number or Employer Identification Number, whichever is applicable.
☐ SSN   ☐ EIN

Meter #
Name of Metered Water Bill Recipient
Address:
City: _____   State: _____   Zip Code: _____

Relationship of addressee to property (Check ✓ one):
☐ Agent   ☐ Owner   ☐ Tenant

If "TENANT" or is checked provide either Social Security Number or Employer Identification Number, whichever is applicable.
☐ SSN   ☐ EIN

Have you recently paid off your mortgage? (✓) _____   ☐ Yes   ☐ No

12. _____
Signature of owner or corporate officer (required by statute)   Date

EXHIBIT 13.2
Real Property Transfer Tax Return   (continued)

- INSTRUCTIONS FOR COMPLETING OWNER'S REGISTRATION CARD -

PLEASE TYPE OR PRINT ALL INFORMATION IN INK

LINE 1. Enter the borough in which the property is located and the block and lot numbers of the property. Only one property (block and lot) may be registered with this card. Make photocopies if you want to register more than one property.

LINE 2A. Enter the full name of the owner if the property is owned by an individual. Please DO NOT abbreviate. If the property has more than one owner, see instructions for line 5.

LINE 2B. Enter the name of the owner if the property is owned by a business entity. If the property has more than one owner, see instructions for line 5.

LINE 3. Enter the address of the owner. (Please note that the address at which the owner lives, or at which the company is located, is not necessarily the property address itself.)

LINE 4. Enter the actual address of the property.

LINE 5. Check the box if the property has more than one owner, and attach an additional sheet with the name, address and EIN/SSN of the other owner(s). Include the property block and lot number on any additional sheet.

LINE 6. Enter the owner's Social Security Number, or if the owner is a corporation or partnership, enter the Employer Identification Number. This will be used for tax compliance purposes. (The same is true of the tenant and agent identification number information requested for real estate and water bills.)

LINE 7. In order that we may provide you with better service, please provide a telephone number at which you can be reached during normal business hours.

> **IMPORTANT ➤ REAL ESTATE BILLS**
> *If your mortgage payments include your real estate taxes, fill in the name and address of your bank/lender in the space provided on line 9. If not, fill in the address to which you are choosing to have real estate tax bills sent.*

LINE 8. Check the box next to the appropriate relationship. For example, if bills are to be sent to your bank/lender, check the box which is marked "Bank/Lender".

LINE 9. Enter the name and address to which you would like Real Estate Tax bills mailed.

> **IMPORTANT ➤ WATER BILLS**
> *Water is billed on either a frontage basis or through the reading of a water meter on the property. If the property is billed on the basis of frontage, fill in "10". If there is a water meter on the property fill in "11". In a few cases a property will be billed both on a frontage basis and through the reading of a meter. In this case with your property fill in "10" and "11". If you are not sure on what basis your property is being billed, contact the Bureau of Water and Energy Conservation. The telephone numbers are listed at the end of these instructions.*

LINE 10. *Annual frontage water/sewer charges* are often included with mortgage payments. In this case water bills are usually sent to the bank/lender. If you are not sure who is responsible for payment, please check with your bank/lender. Enter the name and address to which you would like annual water frontage charge bills sent.

LINE 11. *Metered water/sewer charges* are not usually included with mortgage payments. Therefore, the owner should provide the name and address of the party to receive these bills. Enter the name and address to which metered water charge bills should be sent. Be sure to fill in the water meter number. Copy this number from a recent bill for the metered water charge. If you are not sure what the meter number is, contact the Bureau of Water and Energy Conservation. *If the property has more than two water meters, attach an additional sheet with the meter numbers of the additional meters. Include the property block and lot number on any additional sheet.*

LINE 12. The owner or corporate officer must sign the Registration Card in order for it to be valid. Indicate the date signed.

The law provides that senior citizens and handicapped taxpayers may designate someone to receive duplicate tax bills. If you are interested, contact the Department of Finance and ask for a third party notification form.

DEPARTMENT OF FINANCE

IF YOU NEED FURTHER ASSISTANCE IN COMPLETING THIS FORM, PLEASE CALL (718) 935-6153 OR 935-9500.

SI USTED NECESITA RECIBIR ASISTENCIA EN ESPAÑOL PARA LLENAR ESTO FORMULARIO, LLAME (718) 935-9500.

Si prefiere, usted puede obtener una copia de este formulario (Owner's Registration Card) en Español, comuníquese con la División de Información para el Contribuyente (Taxpayer Assistance Division).

Llame: (718) 935-9500

OFFICES OF THE BUREAU OF WATER AND ENERGY CONSERVATION

BOROUGH	TELEPHONE NUMBER
Manhattan	(212) 643-2111
Bronx	(718) 579-6980
Brooklyn	(718) 780-8000
Queens	(718) 595-4600
Staten Island	(718) 876-6825

EXHIBIT 13.3
Smoke Detecting Alarm (Device) Affidavit

SMOKE DETECTING ALARM (DEVICE) AFFIDAVIT

State of New York)
) ss:
County of   )

_____
The Grantor(s)/Transferor(s) (Please print or type)

_____
The Grantee(s)/Transferee(s) (Please print or type)

Being duly sworn deposes and says we are the grantor(s)/transferor(s) and grantee(s)/transferee(s) of the property located at_____
                                                      Address

_____ (_____County, Tax Block_____, Tax Lot_____)
Unit #/Apt.

Check appropriate box "1" or "2":

1. ___ a. That the Premises is either a one or two-family dwelling or a
          dwelling accommodation located in a building owned as a condominium
          or cooperative used as a dwelling; and,
       b. That installed in the Premises is an approved and operational smoke
          detecting device in compliance with those provisions of Executive
          Law Section 378 subdivision 5 prescribing New York State standards
          for installation of single station smoke detecting alarm devices and
          Article 6 of subchapter 17 of Chapter 1 of the Administrative Code of
          the City of New York prescribing New York City standards for smoke
          detecting devices; and,

2. ___   That the Premises is NOT a one or two-family dwelling or a dwelling
          accommodation located in a building owned as a condominium or cooperative
          used as a dwelling; and therefore, those provisions of Executive Law
          Section 378 Subdivision 5 prescribing New York State standards for in-
          stallation of single station smoke detecting alarm devices do not apply
          to the Premises; and,

3.   That we make this affidavit in compliance with Executive Law Section
          378 subdivision 5 and New York City Administrative Code Section 11-2105(g)
          **(This paragraph numbered "3" is inapplicable if paragraph numbered "2"
          above is checked)**

_____   _____
Grantor/Transferor   Grantee/Transferee

_____   _____
Grantor/Transferor   Grantee/Transferee

Sworn to before me this   Sworn to before me this
___day of _____, 19__.   ___day of _____, 19__.

*The signatures of at least one transferee AND one transferor are required.
This affidavit must accompany the New York City RPT tax return.

EXHIBIT 13.4
Multiple Dwelling Registration Statement

The City of New York · DEPARTMENT OF HOUSING PRESERVATION & DEVELOPMENT · OFFICE OF RENT AND HOUSING MAINTENANCE

Princ. House No.	Street Name	Boro

MULTIPLE DWELLING REGISTRATION APPLICATION

Registration is Due —

FOR DEPARTMENT USE ONLY

RHM FORM 513 (Rev. 12/88)   – DO NOT SEPARATE CARDS – FOLD HERE FOR RETURN –   Card 1A

RHM FORM 513 (Rev. 12/88)   **MULTIPLE DWELLING REGISTRATION APPLICATION** (*Read attached instructions first*)   Card 2A

Princ. House No.	Street Name	Street Code	Boro	SC	Reg. No.	Expiration Date	Amt. Due ▼

Have You Registered This Building Before? YES ☐ NO ☐   This Registration By: OWNER ☐ LESSEE ☐   Redesignation of Managing Agent? YES ☐ NO ☐

OWNER NAME   Type of Ownership? (Check One): Partnership ☐ Corp. ☐ Indiv ☐ Other ☐

BUSINESS ADDRESS (Where you will receive mail — Home address acceptable):

NO. & STREET	APT.	TOWN/COUNTY	STATE	ZIP	Area Code	Telephone No.

HOME ADDRESS

NO. & STREET	APT.	TOWN/COUNTY	STATE	ZIP	Area Code	Telephone No.

MANAGING AGENT (Individual only. Must live or have office within NYC's 5 boroughs) NAME   Age 21 or Over? YES ☐ NO ☐

BUSINESS ADDRESS (where you will receive mail in N.Y.C. — Home address acceptable):

NO. & STREET	APT.	TOWN/COUNTY	STATE	ZIP	Area Code	Telephone No.

HOME ADDRESS

NO. & STREET	APT.	TOWN/COUNTY	STATE	ZIP	Area Code	Telephone No.

I CONSENT TO THE DESIGNATION AS MANAGING AGENT OF THE ABOVE PREMISES

SIGNATURE OF MANAGING AGENT   X   Date   /   /

RHM FORM 513 (Rev. 12/88)   N.Y.C. H.P.D. Office of Rent and Housing Maintenance Division of Code Enforcement   Card 1B

MULTIPLE DWELLING EMERGENCY CONFIDENTIAL 24 HOUR TELEPHONE NUMBER

INSERT 24 Hr. Tel. No. (s) ▶

Area Code: Local Number	Area Code: Local Number

Multiple dwelling owner/managing agent must file with the Department a confidential telephone number where they can reasonably be expected to be reached at all times for emergencies. Phone must be within 50 mile radius of New York City limits.

Failure to produce receipt is prima facie evidence of failure to comply with registration

INSURANCE — Fire/Casualty and/or Liability ☐ YES ☐ NO   (If yes, complete the following)

NAME OF FIRE/CASUALTY INSURANCE CO.				POLICY NO.

ADDRESS OF CO.	NO. & STREET	TOWN/COUNTY STATE	ZIP	EXPIR. DATE / /

NAME OF LIABILITY INSURANCE CO.				POLICY NO.

ADDRESS OF CO.	NO. & STREET	TOWN/COUNTY STATE	ZIP	EXPIR. DATE / /

RHM FORM 513 (Rev. 12/88)   **OFFICERS OF CORPORATION OR PARTNERSHIP FILING APPLICATION**   Card 2B

	NAME	ADDRESS		PHONE NO.
President	Or Partner	Bus.		
		Home		
Vice-President	Or Partner	Bus.		
		Home		
Secretary	Or Partner	Bus.		
		Home		

TO OWNER REGISTERING: If this whole building is leased, give Lessee's Name and Address as indicated on the lease. (Lessee must also file separately).

Lessee — Receiver

BUSINESS ADDRESS:	NO. & STREET	APT.	TOWN/COUNTY	STATE	ZIP	Area Code	Telephone No.

HOME ADDRESS:	NO. & STREET	APT.	TOWN/COUNTY	STATE	ZIP	Area Code	Telephone No.

I CERTIFY THAT ALL STATEMENTS MADE HEREIN ARE TRUE AND CORRECT

SIGNATURE OF BUILDING OWNER, OFFICER OR LESSEE   X   Date   /   /

False statements are punishable under Section 27–2096, Housing Maintenance Code.

CHAPTER 14—TITLE EXAMINATIONS

The Torrens System of Land Registration, page 404

In the Torrens system of land registration, clear title is established and the government issues a certificate of title to the owner. This certificate of title is registered and any subsequent liens or encumbrances are entered on the title (similar to your car title registration). When a new deed is made, the new owner gets a new certificate of title. The owner must be very careful to save this certificate of title as she will need it when it is time to sell. The initial title search to obtain the registration is very expensive and time consuming and may necessitate a quiet title suit and so it has gained limited acceptance throughout the country (only 11 states have land registration acts). In New York, Real Property Law Article 12 allows for Title Registration (it has limited use in this state as well).

Closings in New York, page 475

Roughly 8–10% of the purchase price will be needed for closing costs. It is customary in New York, that the buyer is considered to own the property on the closing date, so that all adjustments are made as of midnight the day before, e.g., if the closing is scheduled for 6/4, the buyer pays for that day and forward.

Checklist of Sellers' charges at closing include:
- attorney
- NYS RPTT
- NYC RP RPT
- capital gains tax
- recording satisfaction
- mortgage payoff
- real estate broker commission

Checklist of Buyers' charges at closing include:
- engineer inspection
- termite inspection
- mortgage title insurance
- owners title insurance
- department search
- survey
- recording fees for deed & mortgage
- mortgage application fees, points, credit check, bank attorney
- appraisal
- NYS mortgage tax
- homeowners insurance
- attorney
- real estate tax adjustments
- water & sewer tax adjustments
- bank escrows

CHAPTER 17—REAL ESTATE CLOSING FORMS AND EXAMPLES

Title Affidavits, page 514

The following Exhibit 17–1 shows an example of a title affidavit to prove there are no judgments against a person.

EXHIBIT 17.1
Title Affidavit

AFFIDAVIT

STATE OF NEW YORK

COUNTY OF   } SS.:   Title No.

each, being duly sworn, says:

I reside at No.

I am about to move to

I am   of the

owner of premises known as

That I have not been known by any other name during the past fifteen years.

That there are no judgments against (me) (it) unsatisfied of record in the courts of this state or of the United States. That no notices of Federal Lien and no Federal Liens have been filed against (me) (it). That no proceedings in bankruptcy have ever been instituted by or against (me) (it) nor (have I) (has it) ever made an assignment of rents of said premises or made an assignment for the benefit of creditors.

That I have read the (judgment) (bankruptcy) (Federal Tax Lien) (Warrant) returns in report of   Title Company numbered above. (I am) (it is) not the party mentioned in said returns, and that none of the said returns is against (me) (it) or affect (me) (it) in any way, and that I have never resided, worked or done business at any of the addresses stated in said report.

This affidavit is made to induce

to accept a (deed) (mortgage) covering said premises, and to induce   Title   Company to issue its policy insuring the same, knowing that they will rely on the statements herein made.

Sworn to before me this

day of   , 19.........   ....

CHAPTER 18—LEASES

Leases in New York, page 575

The theory of independent leases meant that the tenant would have to continue paying rent during the period of the lease, even if the premises burned down.

The trend today is toward greater tenant protection. New York City has rent control and rent stabilization laws which impose guidelines and limits to the amount of rent charged as well as govern the rights and obligations of the tenants and landlords. Not every community in New York is subject to rent control and rent stabilization laws. Commercial leases never fall under rent control and rent stabilization laws.

The rights of tenants in New York State are protected under many different laws. The Multiple Dwelling Law (three or more apartments) applies to New York City and Buffalo. The Multiple Residence Law applies to cities of less than 400,000 people.

Every residential lease in New York contains an implied warranty of habitability, i.e. the tenant is entitled to a safe, and livable apartment (Real Property Law section 235b). The failure to provide heat, hot water or to get rid of insect infestation are examples of violations of the warranty of habitability. If the landlord breaches this warranty, the tenant can sue for a rent reduction. If the tenant responds by not paying rent, the landlord will probably sue for breach of the lease and the tenant will put in a defense of the breach of the warranty of habitability.

Plain English Lease, page 576

Exhibit 18.1, on the next page, shows an example of an apartment lease in plain English format.

EXHIBIT 18.1
Lease Agreement in Plain English

A 55—Apartment lease, comprehensive form, rules, guaranty, plain English format, 6-84   PREPARED BY ARNOLD MANDELL, L.L.B.   © 1984 BY JULIUS BLUMBERG, INC., PUBLISHER, NYC 10013

LEASE AGREEMENT

The Landlord and Tenant agree to lease the Apartment for the Term and at the Rent stated on these terms:

LANDLORD: **TENANT:**

Address for Notices...

Apartment (and terrace, if any)...................at ....
Bank

Lease date:	Term	Yearly Rent	$...............
.... 19.........	beginning .... 19.........	Monthly Rent	$...............
	ending .... 19.........	Security	$...............
Broker*			

Rider   Additional terms on .... page(s) initialed at the end by the parties is attached and made a part of this Lease.

1. Use   The Apartment must be used only as a private Apartment to live in as the primary residence of the Tenant and for no other reason. Only a party signing this Lease may use the Apartment. This is subject to Tenant's rights under the Apartment Sharing Law and to limits on the number of people who may legally occupy an Apartment of this size.

2. Failure to give possession   Landlord shall not be liable for failure to give Tenant possession of the Apartment on the beginning date of the Term. Rent shall be payable as of the beginning of the Term unless Landlord is unable to give possession. Rent shall then be payable as of the date possession is available. Landlord must give possession within a reasonable time, if not, Tenant may cancel and obtain a refund of money deposited. Landlord will notify Tenant as to the date possession is available. The ending date of the Term will not change.

3. Rent, added rent   The rent payment for each month must be paid on the first day of that month at Landlord's address. Landlord need not give notice to pay the rent. Rent must be paid in full without deduction. The first month's rent is to be paid when Tenant signs this Lease. Tenant may be required to pay other charges to Landlord under the terms of this Lease. They are called "added rent." This added rent will be billed and is payable as rent, together with the next monthly rent due. If Tenant fails to pay the added rent on time, Landlord shall have the same rights against Tenant as if Tenant failed to pay rent.

4. Notices   Any bill, statement or notice must be in writing. If to Tenant, it must be delivered or mailed to the Tenant at the Apartment. If to Landlord it must be mailed to Landlord's address. It will be considered delivered on the day mailed or if not mailed, when left at the proper address. A notice must be sent by certified mail. Each party must accept and claim the notice given by the other. Landlord must notify Tenant if Landlord's address is changed.

5. Security   Tenant has given security to Landlord in the amount stated above. The security has been deposited in the Bank named above and delivery of this Lease is notice of the deposit. If the Bank is not named, Landlord will notify Tenant of the Bank's name and address in which the security is deposited.

If Tenant does not pay rent or added rent on time, Landlord may use the security to pay for rent and added rent then due. If Tenant fails to timely perform any other term in this Lease, Landlord may use the security for payment of money Landlord may spend, or damages Landlord suffers because of Tenant's failure. If the Landlord uses the security Tenant, shall, upon notice from Landlord, send to Landlord an amount equal to the sum used by Landlord. That amount is due, when billed, as rent. At all times Landlord is to have the amount of security stated above.

If Tenant fully performs all terms of this Lease, pays rent on time and leaves the Apartment in good condition on the last day of the Term, then Landlord will return the security being held.

If Landlord sells or leases the Building, Landlord may give the security to the buyer or lessee. In that event Tenant will look only to the buyer or lessee for the return of the security and Landlord will be deemed released. The Landlord may use the security as stated in this section. Landlord may put the security in any place permitted by law. Tenant's security will bear interest only if required by law. Landlord will give Tenant the interest when Landlord is required to return the security to Tenant. Any interest returned to Tenant will be less the sum

Landlord is allowed to keep for expenses. Landlord need not give Tenant interest on the security if Tenant is in default.

6. Services   Landlord will supply: (a) heat as required by law, (b) hot and cold water for bathroom and kitchen sink, (c) use of elevator, if any, and (d) cooling if central air conditioning is installed. Landlord is not required to install air-conditioning. Stopping or reducing of service(s) will not be reason for Tenant to stop paying rent, to make a money claim or to claim eviction. Tenant may enforce its rights under the warranty of habitability. Damage to the equipment or appliances supplied by Landlord, caused by Tenant's act or neglect, may be repaired by Landlord at Tenant's expense. The repair cost will be added rent.

Tenant must pay for all electric, gas, telephone and other utility services used in the Apartment and arrange for them with the public utility company. Tenant must not use a dishwasher, washing machine, dryer, freezer, heater, ventilator, air cooling equipment or other appliance unless installed by Landlord or with Landlord's written consent. Tenant must not use more electric than the wiring or feeders to the Building can safely carry.

Landlord may stop service of the plumbing, heating, elevator, air cooling or electrical systems, because of accident, emergency, repairs, or changes until the work is complete.

If Landlord wants to change a person operated elevator to an automatic elevator, Landlord may stop service on 10 days' notice. Landlord will then have a reasonable time to begin installation of an automatic type elevator.

7. Alteration   Tenant must obtain Landlord's prior written consent to install any panelling, flooring, "built in" decorations, partitions, railings, or make alterations or to paint or wallpaper the Apartment. Tenant must not change the plumbing, ventilating, air conditioning, electric or heating systems. If consent is given, the alterations and installations shall become the property of Landlord when completed and paid for. They shall remain with and as part of the Apartment at the end of the Term. Landlord has the right to demand that Tenant remove the alterations and installations before the end of the Term. The demand shall be by notice, given at least 15 days before the end of the Term. Tenant shall comply with the demand at Tenant's own cost. Landlord is not required to do or pay for any work unless stated in this Lease.

If a lien is filed on the Apartment or Building for any reason relating to Tenant's fault, Tenant must immediately pay or bond the amount stated in the Lien. Landlord may pay or bond the lien if Tenant fails to do so within 20 days after Tenant has notice about the Lien. Landlord's costs shall be added rent.

8. Repairs   Tenant must take good care of the Apartment and all equipment and fixtures in it. Landlord will repair the plumbing, heating and electrical systems. Tenant must, at Tenant's cost, make all repairs and replacements whenever the need results from Tenant's act or neglect. If Tenant fails to make a needed repair or replacement, Landlord may do it. Landlord's reasonable expense will be added rent.

9. Fire, accident, defects, damage   Tenant must give Landlord prompt notice of fire, accident, damage or dangerous or defective condition. If the Apartment can not be used because of fire or other casualty, Tenant is not required to pay rent for the time the Apartment is unusable. If part of the Apartment can not be used, Tenant must pay rent for the usable part. Landlord shall have the right to decide which part of the Apartment is usable. Landlord need only repair the damaged

*If no broker, insert "None."

EXHIBIT 18.1
Lease Agreement in Plain English (continued)

part of the Apartment. Landlord is not required to repair or replace any fixtures, furnishings or decorations but only equipment that is originally installed by Landlord. Landlord is not responsible for delays due to settling insurance claims, obtaining estimates, labor and supply problems or any other cause not fully under Landlord's control.

If the apartment can not be used, Landlord has 30 days to decide whether to repair it. Landlord's decision to repair must be given by notice to Tenant within 30 days of the fire or casualty. Landlord shall have a reasonable time to repair. In determining what is a reasonable time, consideration shall be given to any delays in receipt of insurance settlements, labor trouble and causes not within Landlord's control. If Landlord fails to give Tenant notice of its decision within 30 days, Tenant may cancel the lease as of the date of the fire or casualty. The cancellation shall be effective only if it is given before Landlord begins to repair or before Landlord notifies Tenant of its decision to repair. If the fire or other casualty is caused by an act or neglect of Tenant or guest of Tenant all repairs will be made at Tenant's expense and Tenant must pay the full rent with no adjustment. The cost of the repairs will be added rent.

Landlord has the right to demolish, rebuild or renovate the Building if there is substantial damage by fire or other casualty. Even if the Apartment is not damaged, Landlord may cancel this Lease within 30 days after the substantial fire or casualty by giving Tenant notice of Landlord's intention to demolish, rebuild or renovate. The Lease will end 30 days after Landlord's cancellation notice to Tenant. Tenant must deliver the Apartment to Landlord on or before the cancellation date in the notice and pay all rent due to the date of the fire or casualty. If the Lease is cancelled Landlord is not required to repair the Apartment or Building. The cancellation does not release Tenant of liability in connection with the fire or casualty. This Section is intended to replace the terms of New York Real Property Law Section 227.

10. Liability Landlord is not liable for loss, expense, or damage to any person or property, unless due to Landlord's negligence. Landlord is not liable to Tenant for permitting or refusing entry of anyone into the Building.

Tenant must pay for damages suffered and reasonable expenses of Landlord relating to any claim arising from any act or neglect of Tenant. If an action is brought against Landlord arising from Tenant's act or neglect Tenant shall defend Landlord at Tenant's expense with an attorney of Landlord's choice.

Tenant is responsible for all acts or neglect of Tenant's family, employees, guests or invitees.

11. Entry by Landlord Landlord may enter the Apartment at reasonable hours to: repair, inspect, exterminate, install or work on master antennas or other systems or equipment and perform other work that Landlord decides is necessary or desirable. At reasonable hours Landlord may show the Apartment to possible buyers, lenders, or tenants of the entire Building or land. At reasonable hours Landlord may show the Apartment to possible or new tenants during the last 4 months of the Term. Entry by Landlord must be on reasonable notice except in emergency.

12. Assignment and sublease Tenant must not assign all or part of this Lease or sublet all or part of the Apartment or permit any other person to use the Apartment. If Tenant does, Landlord has the right to cancel the Lease as stated in the Tenant's Default section. State law may permit Tenant to sublet under certain conditions. Tenant must get Landlord's written permission each time Tenant wants to assign or sublet. Permission to assign or sublet is good only for that assignment or sublease. Tenant remains bound to the terms of this lease after a assignment or sublet is permitted, even if Landlord accepts money from the assignee or subtenant. The amount accepted will be credited toward money due from Tenant, as Landlord shall determine. The assignee or subtenant does not become Landlord's tenant. Tenant is responsible for acts and neglect of any person in the Apartment.

13. Subordination This Lease and Tenant's rights, are subject and subordinate to all present and future: (a) leases for the Building or the land on which it stands, (b) mortgages on the leases or the Building or land, (c) agreements securing money paid or to be paid by a lender, and (d) terms, conditions, renewals, changes of any kind and extensions of the mortgages, leases or lender agreements. Tenant must promptly execute any certificate(s) that Landlord requests to show that this Lease is so subject and subordinate. Tenant authorizes Landlord to sign these certificate(s) for Tenant.

14. Condemnation If all of the Apartment or Building is taken or condemned by a legal authority, the Term, and Tenant's rights shall end as of the date the authority takes title to the Apartment or Building. If any part of the Apartment or Building is taken, Landlord may cancel this Lease on notice to Tenant. The notice shall set a cancellation date not less than 30 days from the date of the notice. If the Lease is cancelled, Tenant must deliver the Apartment to Landlord on the cancellation date together with all rent due to that date. The entire award for any taking belongs to Landlord. Tenant assigns to Landlord any interest Tenant may have to any part of the award. Tenant shall make no claim for the value of the remaining part of the Term.

15. Construction or demolition Construction or demolition may be performed in or near the Building. Even if it interferes with Tenant's ventilation, view or enjoyment of the Apartment it shall not affect Tenant's obligations in this Lease.

16. Tearing down the building If the Landlord wants to tear down the entire Building, Landlord shall have the right to end this Lease by giving six (6) months notice to Tenant. If Landlord gives Tenant such notice and such notice was given to every residential tenant in the Building, then the Lease will end and Tenant must leave the Apartment at the end of the 6 month period in the notice.

17. Liability for property left with Landlord's employees Landlord's employees are not permitted to drive Tenant's cars or care for Tenant's cars or personal property. Tenant must not leave a car or other personal property with any of Landlord's employees. Landlord is not responsible for (a) loss, theft or damage to the property, and (b) injury caused by the property or its use.

18. Playground, pool, parking and recreation areas If there is a playground, pool, parking or recreation area, Landlord may give Tenant permission to use it. Tenant will use the area at Tenant's own risk and must pay all fees Landlord charges. Landlord's permission may be cancelled at any time.

19. Terraces and balconies The Apartment may have a terrace or balcony. The terms of this Lease apply to the terrace or balcony as if part of the Apartment. The Landlord may make special rules for the terrace and balcony. Landlord will notify Tenant of such rules.

Tenant must keep the terrace or balcony clean and free from snow, ice, leaves and garbage and keep all screens and drains in good repair. No cooking is allowed on the terrace or balcony. Tenant may not keep plants, or install a fence or any addition on the terrace or balcony. If Tenant does, Landlord has the right to remove and store them at Tenant's expense.

Tenant is responsible to make all repairs to the terrace or balcony at its sole expense regardless of the cause and whether or not existing prior to Tenant's occupancy. Tenant shall maintain the terrace and balcony in good repair.

20. Tenant's certificate Upon request by Landlord, Tenant shall sign a certificate stating the following: (1) This Lease is in full force and unchanged (or if changed, how it was changed); and (2) Landlord has fully performed all of the terms of this Lease and Tenant has no claim against Landlord; and (3) Tenant is fully performing all the terms of the Lease and will continue to do so; (4) rent and added rent have been paid to date; and (5) any other reasonable statement required by Landlord. The certificate will be addressed to the party Landlord chooses.

21. Correcting Tenant's defaults If Tenant fails to timely correct a default after notice from Landlord, Landlord may correct it at Tenant's expense. Landlord's costs to correct the default shall be added rent.

22. Tenant's duty to obey laws and regulations Tenant must, at Tenant's expense, promptly comply with all laws, orders, rules, requests, and directions, of all governmental authorities, Landlord's insurers, Board of Fire Underwriters, or similar groups. Notices received by Tenant from any authority or group must be promptly delivered to Landlord. Tenant may not do anything which may increase Landlord's insurance premiums. If Tenant does, Tenant must pay the increase in premium as added rent.

23. Tenant's default A. Landlord must give Tenant written notice of default stating the type of default. The following are defaults and must be cured by Tenant within the time stated:
(1) Failure to pay rent or added rent on time, 3 days.

EXHIBIT 18.1
Lease Agreement in Plain English (continued)

(2) Failure to move into the Apartment within 15 days after the beginning date of the Term, 10 days.

(3) Issuance of a court order under which the Apartment may be taken by another party, 10 days.

(4) Improper conduct by Tenant annoying other tenants, 10 days.

(5) Failure to comply with any other term or Rule in the Lease, 10 days.

If Tenant fails to cure the default in the time stated, Landlord may cancel the Lease by giving Tenant a cancellation notice. The cancellation notice will state the date the Term will end which may be no less than 10 days after the date of the notice. On the cancellation date in the notice the Term of this Lease shall end. Tenant must leave the Apartment and give Landlord the keys on or before the cancellation date. Tenant continues to be responsible as stated in this Lease. If the default can not be cured in the time stated, Tenant must begin to cure within that time and continue diligently until cured.

B. If Tenant's application for the Apartment contains any material misstatement of fact, Landlord may cancel this Lease. Cancellation shall be by cancellation notice as stated in Section 23.A.

C. If (1) the Lease is cancelled; or (2) rent or added rent is not paid on time; or (3) Tenant vacates the Apartment, Landlord may, in addition to other remedies, take any of the following steps: (a) peacefully enter the Apartment and remove Tenant and any person or property, and (b) use eviction or other lawsuit method to take back the Apartment.

D. If this Lease is cancelled, or Landlord takes back the Apartment, the following takes place:

(1) Rent and added rent for the unexpired Term becomes due and payable.

(2) Landlord may relet the Apartment and anything in it. The reletting may be for any term. Landlord may charge any rent or no rent and give allowances to the new tenant. Landlord may, at Tenant's expense, do any work Landlord reasonably feels needed to put the Apartment in good repair and prepare it for renting. Tenant stays liable and is not released except as provided by law.

(3) Any rent received by Landlord for the re-renting shall be used first to pay Landlord's expenses and second to pay any amounts Tenant owes under this Lease. Landlord's expenses include the costs of getting possession and re-renting the Apartment, including, but not only reasonable legal fees, brokers fees, cleaning and repairing costs, decorating costs and advertising costs.

(4) From time to time Landlord may bring actions for damages. Delay or failure to bring an action shall not be a waiver of Landlord's rights. Tenant is not entitled to any excess of rents collected over the rent paid by Tenant to Landlord under this Lease.

(5) If Landlord relets the Apartment combined with other space an adjustment will be made based on square footage. Money received by Landlord from the next tenant other than the monthly rent, shall not be considered as part of the rent paid to Landlord. Landlord is entitled to all of it.

If Landlord relets the Apartment the fact that all or part of the next tenant's rent is not collected does not affect Tenant's liability. Landlord has no duty to collect the next tenant's rent. Tenant must continue to pay rent, damages, losses and expenses without offset.

E. If Landlord takes possession of the Apartment by Court order, or under the Lease, Tenant has no right to return to the Apartment.

24. Jury trial and counterclaims Landlord and Tenant agree not to use their right to a Trial by Jury in any action or proceeding brought by either, against the other, for any matter concerning this Lease or the Apartment. This does not include actions for personal injury or property damage. Tenant gives up any right to bring a counterclaim or set-off in any action or proceeding by Landlord against Tenant on any matter directly or indirectly related to this Lease or Apartment.

25. No waiver, illegality Landlord's acceptance of rent or failure to enforce any term in this Lease is not a waiver of any of Landlord's rights. If a term in this Lease is illegal, the rest of this lease remains in full force.

26. Insolvency If (1) Tenant assigns property for the benefit of creditors, or (2) a non-bankruptcy trustee or receiver of Tenant or Tenant's property is appointed, Landlord may give Tenant 30 days notice of cancellation of the Term of this Lease. If any of the above is not fully dismissed within the 30 days, the

Term shall end as of the date stated in the notice. Tenant must continue to pay rent, damages, losses and expenses without offset. If Tenant files a voluntary petition in bankruptcy or an involuntary petition in bankruptcy is filed against Tenant, Landlord may not terminate this Lease.

27. Rules Tenant must comply with these Rules. Notice of new Rules will be given to Tenant. Landlord need not enforce Rules against other Tenants. Landlord is not liable to Tenant if another tenant violates these Rules. Tenant receives no rights under these Rules:

(1) The comfort or rights of other Tenants must not be interfered with. This means that annoying sounds, smells and lights are not allowed.

(2) No one is allowed on the roof. Nothing may be placed on or attached to fire escapes, sills, windows or exterior walls of the Apartment or in the hallways or public areas.

(3) Tenant may not operate manual elevators. Smoking is not permitted in elevators. Messengers and trade people must only use service elevators and service entrances. Bicycles are not allowed on passenger elevators.

(4) Tenant must give to Landlord keys to all locks. Doors must be locked at all times. Windows must be locked when Tenant is out.

(5) Apartment floors must be covered by carpets or rugs. No waterbeds allowed in Apartments.

(6) Dogs, cats or other animals or pets are not allowed in the Apartment or Building.

(7) Garbage disposal rules must be followed. Wash lines, vents and plumbing fixtures must be used for their intended purpose.

(8) Laundry machines, if any, are used at Tenant's risk and cost. Instructions must be followed.

(9) Moving furniture, fixtures or equipment must be scheduled with Landlord. Tenant must not send Landlord's employees on personal errands.

(10) Improperly parked cars may be removed without notice at Tenant's cost.

(11) Tenant must not allow the cleaning of the windows or other part of the Apartment or Building from the outside.

(12) Tenant shall conserve energy.

28. Representations, changes in Lease Tenant has read this Lease. All promises made by the Landlord are in this Lease. There are no others. This Lease may be changed only by an agreement in writing signed by and delivered to each party.

29. Landlord unable to perform If due to labor trouble, government order, lack of supply, Tenant's act or neglect, or any other cause not fully within Landlord's reasonable control, Landlord is delayed or unable to (a) carry out any of Landlord's promises or agreements, (b) supply any service required to be supplied, (c) make any required repair or change in the Apartment or Building, or (d) supply any equipment or appliances Landlord is required to supply, this Lease shall not be ended or Tenant's obligations affected.

30. End of term At the end of the Term, Tenant must: leave the Apartment clean and in good condition, subject to ordinary wear and tear; remove all of Tenant's property and all Tenant's installations and decorations; repair all damages to the Apartment and Building caused by moving; and restore the Apartment to its condition at the beginning of the Term. If the last day of the Term is on a Saturday, Sunday or State or Federal holiday the Term shall end on the prior business day.

31. Space "as is" Tenant has inspected the Apartment and Building. Tenant states they are in good order and repair and takes the Apartment as is except for latent defects.

32. Landlord's warranty of habitability Landlord states that the Apartment and Building are fit for human living and there is no condition dangerous to health, life or safety.

33. Landlord's consent If Tenant requires Landlord's consent to any act and such consent is not given. Tenant's only right is to ask the Court for a declaratory judgment to force Landlord to give consent. Tenant agrees not to make any claim against Landlord for money or subtract any sum from the rent because such consent was not given.

34. Limit of recovery against Landlord Tenant is limited to Landlord's interest in the Building for payment of a judgment or other court remedy against Landlord.

EXHIBIT 18.1
Lease Agreement in Plain English   (continued)

35. Lease binding on   This Lease is binding on Landlord and Tenant and their heirs, distributees, executors, administrators, successors and lawful assigns.

36. Landlord   Landlord means the owner (Building or Apartment), or the lessee of the Building, or a lender in possession. Landlord's obligations end when Landlord's interest in the (Building or Apartment) is transferred. Any acts Landlord may do may be performed by Landlord's agents or employees.

37. Paragraph headings   The paragraph headings are for convenience only.

38. Furnishings   If the Apartment is furnished, the furniture and other furnishings are accepted as is. If an inventory is supplied each party shall have a signed copy. At the end of the Term Tenant shall return the furniture and other furnishings clean and in good order and repair. Tenant is not responsible for ordinary wear and damage by the elements.

39. Broker   If the name of a Broker appears in the box at the top of the first page of this Lease, Tenant states that this is the only Broker that showed the Apartment to Tenant. If a Broker's name does not appear Tenant states that no agent or broker showed Tenant the Apartment. Tenant will pay Landlord any money Landlord may spend if either statement is incorrect.

Signatures, effective date   Landlord and Tenant have signed this Lease as of the above date. It is effective when Landlord delivers to Tenant a copy signed by all parties.

LANDLORD: TENANT:

....

WITNESS:...   ....

GUARANTY OF PAYMENT   **Date of Guaranty**   ....19.........

Guarantor and address

1.   Reason for guaranty   I know that the Landlord would not rent the Apartment to the Tenant unless I guarantee Tenant's performance. I have also requested the Landlord to enter into the Lease with the Tenant. I have a substantial interest in making sure that the Landlord rents the Premises to the Tenant.

2.   Guaranty   I guaranty the full performance of the Lease by the Tenant. This Guaranty is absolute and without any condition. It includes, but is not limited to, the payment of rent and other money charges.

3.   Changes in Lease have no effect   This Guaranty will not be affected by any change in the Lease, whatsoever. This includes, but is not limited to, any extension of time or renewals. The Guaranty will bind me even if I am not a party to these changes.

4.   Waiver of Notice   I do not have to be informed about any default by Tenant. I waive notice of nonpayment or other default.

5.   Performance   If the Tenant defaults, the Landlord may require me to perform without first demanding that the Tenant perform.

6.   Waiver of jury trial   I give up my right to trial by jury in any claim related to the Lease or this Guaranty.

7.   Changes   This Guaranty can be changed only by written agreement signed by all parties to the Lease and this Guaranty.

Signatures   GUARANTOR:...

WITNESS:...   Guarantor's address:.......................................

STATE OF , COUNTY OF ss.:	STATE OF , COUNTY OF ss.:
On 19 , before me personally	On 19 , before me personally
came to me known, who,	came
being by me duly sworn, did depose and say that deponent resides at	
No.	
deponent is of	
the corporation described in and which executed, the foregoing instrument; deponent knows the seal of said corporation; that the seal affixed to said instrument is such corporate seal; that it was so affixed by order of the Board of Directors of said corporation; deponent signed deponent's name thereto by like order.	to me known to be the individual described in, and who executed the foregoing instrument, and acknowledged that he executed the same.

Lease Use, page 577

Leases are contracts between the landlord and tenant. Most residential leases are uniform and landlords use preprinted forms and add riders if necessary.

In New York State a lease may not restrict occupancy to just the named tenant. In residential buildings use may include the named tenant on the lease and her immediate family and one other person and their family (called the "roommate law"). In 1983 the courts started to recognize non-traditional living arrangements.

Use in a lease may also forbid certain purposes or other proscriptions, such as no pets. If the terms of the lease are lawful, the parties are bound by the terms.

Certain clauses in leases have been held to be unconscionable by the courts. A lease which exempts a landlord from liability for injuries caused by the landlord's negligence on the property have been held to be void as unconstitutional.

Term, page 577

The lease must have a beginning and ending date, and a statement of the total term, e.g., Lease shall begin January 1, 1995 and continue until December 31, 1995 for a period of one year. If the landlord dies the lease does not end, but continues for the period of the lease.

An oral lease for one year or less is enforceable. Leases for more than one year must be in writing to be enforced (General Obligations Law section 5–703(2)).

Tenants who do not have a lease and pay rent monthly or tenants who stay on in the leased property after the lease has expired and the landlord accepts rent after the expiration date, these tenants become month to month tenants. Each time the landlord accepts rent a new tenancy is created for that month. Either party in a month to month tenancy may terminate the agreement by giving notice at least 30 days in advance, e.g., landlord must notify tenant by Aug. 31, before September rent is due that he must vacate by October 1st.

New York City has laws which protect tenants even further. These are Rent Control and Rent Stabilization laws. Rent Regulation is administered by the State Division of Housing and Community Renewal (DHCR). Rent Control was enacted in 1943 as a temporary measure. It arose because of the housing shortage that followed World War II. Rent control laws affect property containing three or more units that were built before 1947 and are continuously occupied by a tenant since 1971. When the apartment is vacated it moves under the Rent Stabilization laws.

Rent Stabilization came into effect in 1969 because of the shortage of affordable rental apartments. The law attempt to balance the needs of the landlord and tenant. In New York City, Rent Stabilization applies to apartments in buildings of six or more units constructed between February 1, 1947 and January 1, 1974. Buildings with three or more units that were constructed or extensively renovated since 1974 may also be subject to rent stabilization while tax benefits continue. Outside New York City, rent stabilization applies to communities that adopted the Emergency Tenant Protection Act (ETPA). Where rent stabilization is in effect, maximum rent increases are set by local rent stabilization boards.

Tenants protected by rent stabilization have a right to either a one or two year lease when they move in and when they renew. Rent stabilization has recently ended for certain high rent apartments (if the rent is over $2000 a month and owner has income of over $250,000 for two years in a row, the apartment will become deregulated and move to the fair market value).

The renewal lease for rent stabilized tenants must be on the same terms and conditions as the prior lease and rent increases are limited by law. Rent stabilization and rent control laws are specialized areas of real estate law and attorneys may not be fully familiar with these laws.

Possession and Commencement of the Rent, page 577

The landlord is obligated to deliver possession of premises at the beginning of lease. If the landlord fails to deliver, the tenant has a right to cancel the lease and obtain a full refund of the deposit (Real Property

Law 223–a). Tenants in a residential lease rarely examine a landlord's title. Some landlords may require guarantors; e.g., if a student seeks to live off campus, landlords may require the parents to guaranty the lease.

Rent, page 577

In a residential lease, rent for the term is set out in full and as a matter of convenience, the tenant is allowed to pay monthly.

Landlord's Remedies for Tenant's Default, page 586

When a tenant breaches any lease provision, the landlord may sue. If the landlord breaches a lease provision, the tenant may similarly sue.

In New York, the grounds for which landlord can sue include nonpayment of rent, illegal use of premises, remaining in possession after the lease ends and bankruptcy of the tenant.

In order to evict a tenant, the landlord must sue in court and win. The landlord can *not* threaten a tenant with violence, change the locks or put the tenant's possessions on the street (RPL section 235).

The law which governs eviction proceedings is found in the Real Property Actions and Proceeding Law. These suits are generally brought in Civil Court in New York City, or County Court or Justice Court. To evict a tenant, in New York City, you sue in housing court (part of the New York City Civil Court).

There are two different lawsuits that can be brought and each requires notice to the tenant prior to commencing the lawsuit: 1) *nonpayment* action is where the landlord seeks to get the rent due and 2) *holdover* proceeding is where the goal is to evict the tenant.

The most common lawsuit by a landlord is for *nonpayment* of rent. Before suing, the landlord must demand the rent from the tenant or serve a three day notice demanding rent. After the three days, the landlord must serve a notice of petition on the tenant, similar to the service of a summons. The tenant has five days to appear in court and file an answer. The courts have form answers for this purpose. After a judgment of eviction is entered only a sheriff or marshall may physically evict the tenant after the expiration of a 72 hour waiting period.

The second form of eviction is a *hold over proceeding*. This is begun after the lease has expired, or where a tenant stays over at the end of a lease. Here the landlord doesn't want rent, but wants the tenant out. Before this action is begun the landlord must serve a thirty-day notice to vacate. After the notice is given, if the landlord accepts rent, then a new thirty-day waiting period must begin.

The tenant may have some defenses to an eviction proceeding, e.g., if there are building code violations (after they have been reported and inspected), failure to provide heat, breach of warranty of habitability, or constructive eviction (if premises are not habitable).

Assignments, Subletting, or Mortgaging of the Leased Premises, page 592

Generally, the lease says the tenant may assign or sublease with the landlord's consent. New York Real Property Law has detailed requirements the tenant must follow to make a written request to sublet or assign.

In a rent stabilized apartment the tenant may only charge 10% more than the regular rent. The property may not be sublet for more than two years as long as the apartment is the tenant primary residence and the tenant intends to return at the end of the sublet. If the landlord consents to the sublet the tenant remains liable to the landlord during the time of the original lease.

In the 1989 landmark case, *Braschi v. Stahl Associates Co.*, 74 NY2d 201, the New York Court of Appeals recognized gay couples as the legal equivalent of a "family". The court held that under certain circumstances the surviving partner could not be evicted under the rent control laws. The court found the lease could be inherited by a "family member" who is someone who has shared the apartment, and the parties had a special relationship characterized by emotional and financial interdependence and were considered a "family." In *Braschi*, family included a life partner who lived with the tenant for ten years in a "family" type setting. DHCR expanded "family" in rent regulated apartments to nontraditional family members. If they lived for at least two years with the person before they died, the surviving person could take over the lease.

New York State laws prohibit discrimination under Executive Law Sect. 290–299. Landlord may not refuse to lease property because of race, creed, color, national origin, age, sex, disability or marital status. Owners of two family homes, who live in one of the units, are exempt. RPL Sect. 236 says you can not discriminate against someone who has children. In New York City, a landlord may not refuse to rent because of a person's lawful occupation, sexual orientation or immigration status (New York Local Law 59, 1986 and NYC Administration Code, Chapter 11 Section 8–107 (1986).)

In New York, *security deposits* are considered trust funds which must be put in an interest bearing account. They can not be commingled with the owner's funds. Landlords in buildings with six or more apartments must put security deposits in a New York City bank account earning interest. The landlord must notify the tenants where the funds are being held and pay over any interest (less 1% administrative handling fee). If the building has less than six apartments, the landlord need not put the money in an interest bearing account. When the owner sells the building, he must turn over the security deposits to the new landlord and notify the tenants. Tenants in rent stabilized apartments are limited to one month's security.

Tenants who live in apartments with four or more tenants have the right to sublet to the landlord's consent and such consent may not be unreasonably withheld. The Real Property Law sets out the requirements to assign and sublet and there is much recent case law on this.

Any questions regarding tenants' rights can be made to the New York State Division of Housing and Community Renewal (DHCR).

Senior Citizens may get a Senior Citizen Rent Increase Exemption (SCRIE) in some rent controlled and rent stabilized apartments if the tenant is 62 or older and their income falls below a set level, and they are not on welfare, they may pay at least 1/3 of their income for rent.